Business Organizations for Paralegals

ASPEN PUBLISHERS

Business Organizations for Paralegals

Fifth Edition

Deborah E. Bouchoux, Esq.

Georgetown University
Member, California (inactive) and District of Columbia bars

Wolters Kluwer
Law & Business

AUSTIN   BOSTON   CHICAGO   NEW YORK   THE NETHERLANDS

To contact Customer Care, e-mail customer.care@aspenpublishers.com, call 1-800-234-
1660, fax 1-800-901-9075, or mail correspondence to:

Aspen Publishers
Attn: Order Department
PO Box 990
Frederick, MD 21705

Printed in the United States of America.

1 2 3 4 5 6 7 8 9 0

ISBN 978-0-7355-7628-5

Library of Congress Cataloging-in-Publication Data

Bouchoux, Deborah E., 1950-
   Business organizations for paralegals / Deborah E. Bouchoux. – 5th ed.
      p. cm.
   Includes bibliographical references and index.
   ISBN 978-0-7355-7628-5 (alk. paper)
 1. Corporation law–United States.   2. Business enterprises–Law and legislation–
United States.   3. Legal assistants–United States–Handbooks, manuals, etc.   I. Title.

   KF1414.3.B68 2009
   346.73′065–dc22   2009021999

About Wolters Kluwer Law & Business

Wolters Kluwer Law & Business is a leading provider of research information and workflow solutions in key specialty areas. The strengths of the individual brands of Aspen Publishers, CCH, Kluwer Law International and Loislaw are aligned within Wolters Kluwer Law & Business to provide comprehensive, in-depth solutions and expert-authored content for the legal, professional and education markets.

CCH was founded in 1913 and has served more than four generations of business professionals and their clients. The CCH products in the Wolters Kluwer Law & Business group are highly regarded electronic and print resources for legal, securities, antitrust and trade regulation, government contracting, banking, pension, payroll, employment and labor, and healthcare reimbursement and compliance professionals.

Aspen Publishers is a leading information provider for attorneys, business professionals and law students. Written by preeminent authorities, Aspen products offer analytical and practical information in a range of specialty practice areas from securities law and intellectual property to mergers and acquisitions and pension/benefits. Aspen's trusted legal education resources provide professors and students with high-quality, up-to-date and effective resources for successful instruction and study in all areas of the law.

Kluwer Law International supplies the global business community with comprehensive English-language international legal information. Legal practitioners, corporate counsel and business executives around the world rely on the Kluwer Law International journals, loose-leafs, books and electronic products for authoritative information in many areas of international legal practice.

Loislaw is a premier provider of digitized legal content to small law firm practitioners of various specializations. Loislaw provides attorneys with the ability to quickly and efficiently find the necessary legal information they need, when and where they need it, by facilitating access to primary law as well as state-specific law, records, forms and treatises.

Wolters Kluwer Law & Business, a unit of Wolters Kluwer, is headquartered in New York and Riverwoods, Illinois. Wolters Kluwer is a leading multinational publisher and information services company.

In memory of my beloved father
Millard C. Eckmann

Summary of Contents

Contents

1

◆ ◆ ◆

Introduction to Business Organizations and Agency Law

2

◆ ◆ ◆

Sole Proprietorships

3

◆ ◆ ◆

General Partnerships

4

◆ ◆ ◆

Limited Partnerships

5
◆ ◆ ◆

Registered Limited Liability Partnerships

7

◆ ◆ ◆

Other Unincorporated Organizations

8

◆ ◆ ◆

Introduction to Corporations

9

◆ ◆ ◆

Formation of Corporations

10

◆ ◆ ◆

Corporate Finances

11

◆ ◆ ◆

Corporate Management

12

◆ ◆ ◆

Corporate Dividends

13

◆ ◆ ◆

Securities Regulation and the Stock Exchanges

14

◆ ◆ ◆

Changes in the Corporate Structure and Corporate Combinations

15

◆ ◆ ◆

Qualification of Foreign Corporations

16

◆ ◆ ◆

Termination of Corporate Existence

17

◆ ◆ ◆

Corporate Variations

18

Employee Compensation and Employment Agreements

19

◆ ◆ ◆

Special Topics in Business Law

Preface

The concepts of business organizations surround us every day. References are made to the stock market during each evening's news broadcasts. Newspapers and television reports often refer to partnerships and other forms of business entities. The ups and downs of major companies such as Microsoft, Coca Cola Company, and Wal-Mart are studied and analyzed in depth. Failures of companies such as Enron Corporation and AIG affect the lives of hundreds of thousands of people and often serve as the impetus for new legislation regarding corporate governance. Mergers and dissolutions of companies are reported as events significantly affecting the economy. Employees eagerly await the granting of stock options. Most newspapers in large cities devote an entire section of each daily issue to business or finance. Nevertheless, many of us have only a vague notion of the import and effect of the news of business organizations that we hear about each day. Some individuals are intimidated by the financial section of the newspaper or weekly news magazines, assuming that only those with degrees in business can appreciate and comprehend the business news.

This text is intended to provide readers with a basic and thorough understanding of the various types of business organizations operating in the United States. Learning about the advantages and disadvantages of different forms of business entities will provide you with the foundation to understand the business concepts that surround us. Equally important, understanding the nature of the various ways in which business is conducted in the United States will enhance your ability to perform competently as a paralegal. According to a 2008 survey by the National Association of Legal Assistants, except for litigation, corporate work represents the largest specialty practice area for paralegals, with 32 percent of paralegals engaged in some corporate work.

Although the study of business organizations is undoubtedly most useful for paralegals intending to participate in the field of corporate law, the concepts discussed in this text cross over to many other practice fields. For example, litigation paralegals will need to know whether partners in a partnership are personally liable for business debts, under which circumstances shareholders in a corporation may be liable for a corporation's obligations, and whether members of a limited liability partnership can be sued. Paralegals engaged in the field of estates and trusts need to understand that the effect of a shareholder's buy-sell agreement requires that shares owned by an individual at the time of death must be transferred to the corporation rather than to the decedent's heirs. Paralegals working with general practitioners will need to know how to form all of the business organizations described in this text, draft resolutions, prepare corporate bylaws, and take minutes of meetings.

Each of the varieties of business organizations will be discussed thoroughly. The nature of the entity, its advantages and disadvantages, the relative ease with which it can be formed, its dissolution, and its tax consequences will be addressed. Each chapter includes an introduction to the material to be covered in that chapter, a complete discussion of the pertinent topic, a section devoted to the possible tasks to be performed by paralegals regarding that business enterprise, a brief summary of a case illustrating a core concept in the chapter, a list of useful Internet resources enabling you to locate additional materials and forms of interest, discussion questions challenging you to apply the concepts discussed in the chapter to fact patterns, Internet questions requiring you to locate and navigate pertinent Web sites to locate information similar to that you will be required to locate "on the job," and a brief summary of the key features covered in that chapter.

The text begins with an introduction to the various business entities, and then progresses from the simplest, the sole proprietorship, through partnerships to the most complex, the business corporation. The newest forms of business organizations, the limited liability partnership and the limited liability company, are also discussed. Chapters include sample forms to illustrate the principles discussed and key terms highlighting concepts discussed. Appendices provide additional forms and model codes or uniform laws from which many state business statutes and concepts are derived. A glossary is included for easy reference to the many and difficult terms used in the law of business organizations.

There are a number of additions and enhancements to this fifth edition of the text, including the following:

- Discussion of the newly revised Uniform Limited Liability Company Act of 2006
- Treatment of the financial crisis of 2008
- Recent amendments to the Model Business Corporations Act
- Discussion of the merger of NASD and the regulatory functions of the New York Stock Exchange into the newly created FINRA (Financial Industry Regulatory Authority)
- Discussion of DRIPs (dividend reinvestment plans)
- Treatment of new amendments to the Model Business Corporations Act providing for householding, shareholder written consent by majority rather than unanimous vote, and other provisions
- Discussion of the practice of backdating and repricing stock options
- Discussion of new and emerging trends in corporate governance, shareholder activism, and corporate reform, including the trend toward electing directors by majority rather than plurality vote
- Enhanced discussion of the key provisions of the Sarbanes-Oxley Act of 2002
- A new Appendix, Appendix K, a full research and resource guide, providing research tips for locating statutes, forms, articles, and other information relating to business organizations

New and updated sample forms have been included and Internet Web site addresses have been updated as online form banks and useful practice tools continue to be posted on Internet sites.

When you begin reading this text, you might be unfamiliar with most, if not all, of the business enterprises and concepts discussed. As you progress in class and through the chapters and discussion questions, you will readily be able to measure your progress. When you complete this text and your class, you will have gained a thorough introduction to business organizations as well as familiarity with the terms and concepts required by paralegals in the business or corporate fields and those that we hear and read about each and every day.

Deborah E. Bouchoux
Spring 2009

Acknowledgments

I would like to express my deep appreciation to the many individuals who contributed greatly to the development of this text. As always, my first thoughts and gratitude go to Susan M. Sullivan, Program Director of the Paralegal Program at the University of San Diego, who gave me my first teaching job and opened a door to an exciting and challenging field. Susan has been a valued friend as well as a competent professional whom I greatly admire.

A special thank you to my family: my husband Don, and my children Meaghan, Elizabeth, Patrick, and Robert for their patience and understanding while I completed this text and its fifth edition.

Many thanks also to the various reviewers who evaluated the manuscript on behalf of the publisher. I have also received continuing evaluation from my students throughout my 20-year career as a paralegal educator. Their comments and insights regarding methods of teaching, productive assignments, and effective class discussion have been a great help.

The author wishes to expressly acknowledge the following states and commonwealths for use of their state forms in this textbook: Alabama, Arizona, California, Delaware, Florida, Illinois, Minnesota, Nebraska, Nevada, New York, North Carolina, Ohio, Tennessee, Virginia, and Washington.

Additionally, the author would like to acknowledge and thank the National Conference of Commissioners on Uniform State Laws, which graciously granted permission to reprint the Uniform Partnership Act (1914), (1994), (1997) and the Uniform Limited Partnership Act (1976) with 1985 amendments. The author wishes to expressly acknowledge and thank the American Bar Association for granting permission to reprint the Model Business Corporation Act. Thomson/Reuters graciously granted permission to reprint from *Uniform Laws Annotated* (Volumes 6 and 6A) the charts provided in Appendices B, C, and E, showing which states have adopted uniform acts and the citations to each state's pertinent statutes.

Finally, a special thank you to the individuals at Aspen Publishers who generously provided guidance and support throughout the development of the fifth edition of this text, including Carol McGeehan, Publisher; Melody Davies, Executive Editorial Director; Betsy Kenny, Developmental Editor; David Herzig, Executive Paralegal Editor; Kaesmene Harrison Banks, Senior Editor; and Teresa Horton, Copyeditor.

Business Organizations for Paralegals

1

◆ ◆ ◆

Introduction to Business Organizations and Agency Law

◆ ◆ ◆

CHAPTER OVERVIEW

There are many different ways in which business is conducted in this country. Selecting the most appropriate form of business enterprise for an individual or a group of individuals involves careful consideration of a variety of factors. These factors must be balanced against each other to ensure the most appropriate form of business enterprise is selected for the client. Businesses often act through designated individuals, called agents, to conduct their operations, and many legal relationships in business are governed by the law of agency. Agency relationships can arise by express agreement or by a course of conduct between the parties. The acts of agents will bind the businesses they serve if the agents have either actual or apparent authority to act.

A. Types of Business Enterprises

This book explores the nine most common ways of doing business in this country. Each type of business structure is described in detail in the following chapters, but a brief overview follows here.

1. Sole Proprietorship

In a **sole proprietorship**, one individual owns all of the business assets and is the sole decision-maker. The sole proprietor has unlimited personal liability for all

Sole proprietorship
Business owned and operated by one person

1

business debts. Due to its ease of formation, this form of enterprise is the most commonly selected form of business for new enterprises. A sole proprietorship does not pay taxes. All profits and losses belong to the owner, who declares them on his or her individual tax return. This concept is called **pass-through** taxation.

Pass-through tax status
The tax status in which all income is passed through to individuals or partners, who pay at their individual rates

2. General Partnership

In a **general partnership**, two or more persons co-own all of the business assets and share decision-making, profits, and losses. General partners suffer unlimited personal liability for all business debts and obligations. The general partnership is easily formed and is managed by mutual agreement. General partnerships are subject to pass-through taxation.

General partnership
Business co-owned by two or more persons

3. Limited Partnership

A **limited partnership** is a type of investment vehicle created so persons can invest in a business enterprise and yet not have unlimited personal liability. A limited partnership is managed by one or more general partners, all of whom have unlimited personal liability for business debts and obligations. The limited partners do not manage or control this enterprise, and their liability is limited to the amount they invested in the business. Limited partnerships are more complex to form than general partnerships and can only be created by strict compliance with pertinent state statutes. Limited partnerships are subject to pass-through taxation.

Limited partnership
Business created under a state statute in which some partners have limited liability

4. Registered Limited Liability Partnership

This new form of business enterprise, also called a *limited liability partnership*, alters a basic principle of partnership law: Partners in this enterprise are not liable for the torts or acts of misconduct of their partners. In nearly all states, the partners are not personally liable either for the torts of their partners or contractual obligations incurred by the entity or other partners. This arrangement is ideally suited to legal, medical, and accounting practices, as partners in one office are not liable for acts of partners in their office or a branch office simply because of the partner relationship. This form of business enterprise, which enjoys pass-through taxation and can be formed only through adherence to state statutes, combines some of the best features of partnerships and corporations.

Registered limited liability partnership
Business entity providing limited liability for its partners

5. Limited Liability Company

Another new form of business organization is the **limited liability company.** This business structure continues the modern trend of combining the best features of a partnership with those of a corporation. Its primary characteristics are that its owners have limited liability (like shareholders in a corporation) and it has the pass-through or flow-through taxation of a partnership, meaning that all income earned by the entity is passed through to the owners, who pay taxes at whatever rate is applicable to them. A limited liability company can be created only by complying

Limited liability company
Business providing pass-through tax status; all members have limited liability

with pertinent state statutes. Almost all states now permit a one-member limited liability company.

6. Business Corporation

A **business** (or *for-profit*) **corporation** is an entity created under state statute. This legal entity may own property, enter into contracts, and sue and be sued. Because it is a "person," it is subject to taxation. Its owners, called *shareholders*, also pay tax on certain distributions made to them, such as cash dividends. This is often referred to as *double taxation*. Shareholders are protected from personal liability, and their loss is limited to the amount of money they invest in the corporation. Although the shareholders own the corporation, the corporation is managed by its board of directors. The directors typically appoint officers to carry out the directors' policies and goals for the corporation. A corporation is subject to regulatory control by the state in which it is formed as well as any other states in which it does business. The sale of its stock may be governed by federal and state law.

Business corporation
Legal entity existing under the authority of the state legislature

7. Professional Corporation

Professionals such as doctors, lawyers, accountants, and engineers may incorporate to obtain certain tax and other benefits available to a business corporation. Nevertheless, these professionals remain personally liable for their own negligence and for the negligence of those working for them, such as nurses or paralegals.

Professional corporation
Corporation formed by professionals

8. S Corporation

Certain small business corporations that adhere to specific requirements of the Internal Revenue Code are provided relief against double taxation, typically common to business corporations. Called an **S corporation** after the original subchapter of the Internal Revenue Code providing such relief, the corporation itself does not pay tax, and all income earned is passed through to the shareholders. All shareholders (who must not number more than 100) must agree to the election of S status, and only eligible corporations may apply for this status. A typical business corporation is referred to as a *C corporation* to distinguish it from an S corporation.

S corporation
Corporation that passes through all income to its shareholders, who pay tax on income received

9. Close Corporation

Close corporations are corporations generally owned by small numbers of family members and friends. Unlike shareholders in a large corporation, such as General Motors Corporation, these shareholders are active in operating the business. Only certain types of corporations can qualify to be treated as close corporations. The shareholders are allowed more flexibility in the operation and management of the corporation and usually function without adhering to all of the formalities required of business corporations.

Close corporation
Small corporation with shareholders who are active in managing the business and that operates informally

Other enterprises, such as joint ventures and nonprofit corporations, are also examined. In many business structures, the more management and control an individual exercises, the greater the liability. For example, the sole proprietor makes all business decisions, and therefore his liability extends beyond what he has invested in the enterprise to personal assets such as his car and art collection. On the other hand, shareholders in a corporation exercise very limited management and control. Their participation in the corporation is typically limited to voting for directors and voting on extraordinary corporate action such as mergers or dissolution. Because they are not managing or controlling the enterprise, shareholder liability is limited: The stock they purchased might fall in value to zero, but they are not personally liable for debts and obligations of the corporation. A newer trend in many business structures is to combine the ability to manage with limited liability, thus affording the best of all worlds to investors. The limited liability partnership and limited liability company are enterprises allowing their owners to manage the enterprise and yet retain limited liability, thus accounting for their enormous popularity.

Key Types
of Business Enterprises

- ◆ Sole Proprietorships
- ◆ General Partnerships
- ◆ Limited Partnerships
- ◆ Registered Limited Liability Partnerships
- ◆ Limited Liability Companies
- ◆ Business Corporations
- ◆ Professional Corporations
- ◆ S Corporations
- ◆ Close Corporations

PRACTICE TIP

It can be difficult to understand the various types of business structures and their features. Consider keeping a "cheat sheet" or index card at your desk that describes the most prominent features of each form of entity. After you refer to this several times, you will likely have no difficulty remembering the differences among a general partnership, a limited partnership, and a limited liability partnership. Alternatively, access the site "My Corporation" at http://mycorporation.intuit.com and select "Comparison Chart" or consult the inside cover of this text for a chart comparing and contrasting business structures.

B.   Considerations in Selection of Business Enterprise

Although a sole proprietorship might be ideal for one client, it might be inappropriate for another. Determining which form of business enterprise is the most advantageous for a client involves careful consideration of a number of factors. The attorney you work with will counsel the client to consider the following factors.

1.   Ease of Formation

The ease with which an enterprise can be formed should be carefully considered. Some enterprises, such as sole proprietorships, are easily formed, whereas others, such as limited partnerships and corporations, require compliance with state statutes and might be more expensive to organize and maintain. Consideration should always be given as to how easy, expeditious, and expensive it is to form the enterprise.

2.   Management

Some individuals prefer to manage their business themselves. For them, a sole proprietorship or general partnership may afford them the greatest ability to manage and control the enterprise. With this management and control, however, could come unlimited personal liability. Other individuals might prefer to invest in a business knowing their maximum potential loss as they enter the enterprise. For these individuals, limited partnerships or corporations could be ideal, so long as they understand that their ability to influence and control the business is limited as well.

3.   Liability and Financial Risk

The financial exposure an individual faces is one of the most critical factors to consider in selecting a form of business enterprise. Some enterprises shield the individual from unlimited personal liability whereas others expose the individual to greater risk. Clients must be fully informed of the potential liability consequences when selecting a particular form of business.

4.   Continuity of Existence

Some business organizations, such as corporations, are capable of existing perpetually. Other forms of business enterprises do not have such continuity of existence. For example, a sole proprietorship generally terminates with the death of the sole proprietor, and limited liability companies are subject to a term of duration in a few states. Consideration should be given to the intended duration of the enterprise.

5.   Transferability

Clients should consider the ease with which they can "get into" and "get out of" the business enterprise. It might be difficult to transfer out of a general partnership because the partnership agreement may severely restrict the ability of partners to transfer their interests. On the other hand, to get out of a corporation, one need only sell his or her stock to another. If clients foresee a need to liquidate their investment in an enterprise for a cash return, they should evaluate how easy or difficult it might be to transfer into and out of the enterprise.

6. Profits and Losses

Although a sole proprietor maintains all profits, he or she is also solely liable for all losses. In a partnership, partners have the ability to bind each other and, thus, although a partner may be able to share a loss with a co-partner, the very reason the partner may have a loss is due to the co-partner's activities. Clients must carefully consider the division of profits and losses when evaluating the form of business enterprise to select.

7. Taxation

Clients should consider applicable tax requirements. For some, the individual tax rates might be best; for others, corporate tax rates could yield the best advantages. Most business entities afford single or pass-through taxation, whereas corporations are burdened by double taxation (see Figure 1-1).

FIGURE 1-1
Checklist for New Businesses

❑ Do I want to be my own boss?

❑ Do I have sufficient expertise to make all business decisions by myself, or do I need the advice and expertise of others to make the business a success?

❑ Do I have sufficient capital to form the business and maintain it, or do I need partners or shareholders to help provide needed capital?

❑ Am I prepared to accept the unlimited personal liability that attaches to sole proprietors and general partners?

❑ Do I have considerable wealth that will be exposed to creditors if I form a sole proprietorship or become a general partner in a general or limited partnership?

❑ Do I want to be actively involved in the business, or do I prefer to be a passive investor?

❑ What are the tax advantages and disadvantages of each form of business structure?

Considerations
in Selecting a Business Enterprise

- ◆ Ease of Formation
- ◆ Management
- ◆ Liability and Financial Risk
- ◆ Continuity of Existence
- ◆ Transferability
- ◆ Profits and Losses
- ◆ Taxation

C.   How Business Is Conducted in This Country

Many individuals perceive that business in the United States is conducted by huge corporations that impact nearly every aspect of financial growth and development. Most would be surprised to find that sole proprietorships (businesses conducted by one person) dominate the business landscape.

According to the *Statistical Abstract of the United States* 483 (128th ed. 2009), more than 70 percent of business in this country is conducted by sole proprietorships. According to returns filed with the Internal Revenue Service in 2004, there were approximately 20.6 million sole proprietorships, 2.5 million partnerships, and 5.6 million business corporations. Nevertheless, business corporations account for a disproportionately high share of revenue. In 2005, business receipts for sole proprietorships were $1.2 trillion, whereas business receipts for partnerships were approximately $3.7 trillion, and business receipts for business corporations were more than $24 trillion (see Figure 1-2). Similarly, although corporations account for a disproportionately high number of business receipts, the number of huge corporations is smaller than expected. For example, more than 90 percent of all workers employed by business firms work in establishments employing fewer than 100 workers. (See Figure 1-3 for a chart showing where individual employees work.)

D.   Agency in Business Organizations

Understanding the basic concepts of agency is necessary to understand the way business enterprises operate. Simply put, an **agent** is one who agrees to act for or represent another, called the **principal.** Because businesses usually act through third parties, it is important to determine whether these third parties have the authority to obligate or bind the business.

Agency relationships arise in a variety of settings. When a client asks a law firm to prepare a will, the law firm acts as the agent for the client, who is the principal.

Agent
One who acts for or represents another

Principal
The person for whom an agent acts

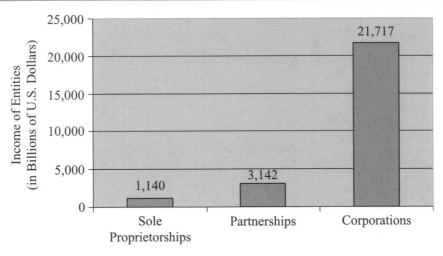

FIGURE 1-2
Business Receipts (2004)

Source: *Statistical Abstract of the United States* 487 (127th ed. 2008)

When an employee of a store sells goods, he does so as the agent of the store owner, the principal. When a partner in a partnership signs a contract, she may bind the partnership under the principles of agency law. When a corporation leases new office space, it acts through its officers, who serve as agents of the corporation. Certain acts and duties, however, cannot be delegated to others. For example, making a statement under oath, testifying, or agreeing to provide certain personal services, such as singing at a concert, cannot be assigned to others to perform.

1. Formation of Agency Relationship

There are two primary ways in which an agency relationship can be created.

Agreement. Most agency relationships are created by mutual consent: One party agrees to act for the other, either orally or in writing. For example, if Candy Ellis decides to sell her house and lists it with a real estate agency, Candy is the principal who has granted permission to the agency to act on her behalf with regard to the sale. In this instance, a written agreement will likely set forth the relationship and duties of the parties. This is an **express agency** agreement. Nevertheless, an agency relationship can be created without a written agreement. An agreement whereby an individual makes an oral agreement with another for child care also creates an express agency relationship.

Express agency
An agency agreement, written or oral

FIGURE 1-3
Companies Indexed by Numbers of Employees (2004) (In thousands)

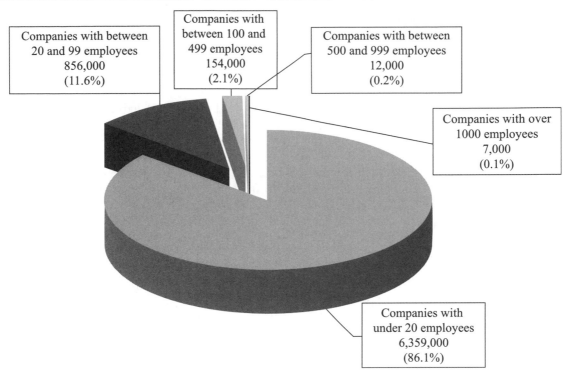

Companies with between 20 and 99 employees
856,000
(11.6%)

Companies with between 100 and 499 employees
154,000
(2.1%)

Companies with between 500 and 999 employees
12,000
(0.2%)

Companies with over 1000 employees
7,000
(0.1%)

Companies with under 20 employees
6,359,000
(86.1%)

Source: *Statistical Abstract of the United States* 496 (127th ed. 2008)

Agency relationships can also be implied. For example, individuals employed by small retail stores or restaurants seldom have formal employment agreements. Yet the acts they perform on behalf of their employers (ordering goods, selling goods, agreeing to give a discount) bind their employers, the principals. These are examples of **implied agency;** there is no formal agreement, yet the parties have agreed to a course of conduct by their actions. In an implied agency relationship, the rights and obligations of the parties have not been expressed (either orally or in writing), yet the parties act as if one of them can bind the other. Their words, conduct, or prior dealings show the existence of their agency relationship.

Estoppel.   Sometimes an agency relationship arises because it would be inequitable to allow the principal to deny the relationship. In such a circumstance, the principal is precluded or "estopped" from denying that an agency relationship existed. For example, suppose that Jean, an interior decorator, visits the home of one of her

> **Implied agency**
> An agency relationship in which there is no express agreement, but the parties' words, conduct, or prior dealings show the existence of their agency relationship

customers. Accompanying her is Linda, a new employee just learning the business. At the customer's house, Jean repeatedly tells the customer that "We can supply all your needs" and "We are the best decorators in the county." If the customer then calls an order in to Linda, Jean is estopped to deny that Linda is her agent inasmuch as she created the reasonable impression that Linda was authorized to act for Jean with regard to the decorating business. In such cases, agency by estoppel arises from acts that lead third parties to believe an agency relationship exists.

Agency by estoppel
An agency arising from acts that lead others to believe an agency relationship exists

2. Authority of Agents

Often a third party seeks to hold a principal liable for acts of the agent. A principal may attempt to avoid liability by distancing herself from the agent's acts by denying that the agent had the authority to perform certain acts on the principal's behalf. The third party will attempt to prove that the agent had the authority to act for the principal and could thus bind the principal.

An agent has the ability to bind the principal in two ways: by being granted actual authority to do an act, whether the authority is express or implied, or by apparent authority. Even when an agent exceeds the scope of his or her authority, the principal may nevertheless ratify the agent's acts and thus become obligated for those acts.

Actual Authority. A person may generally appoint another to perform any act he or she could perform. A principal may grant actual authority to an agent to act for him or her. This actual authority can be express or implied. **Express authority** may be given in writing or orally, and refers to those acts specifically directed or authorized by the principal. For example, if parents go out of town, leaving their children with a neighbor, they may expressly grant the neighbor **power of attorney**, the authority to approve emergency medical care for the children. A **special power of attorney or agency** limits the agent (the neighbor) to performing acts specifically authorized, in this case approving essential medical services. A **general power of attorney or agency**, in contrast, would authorize the agent to transact any kind of activity on behalf of the principal. Theoretically, the neighbor could take the children for a routine dental check-up as easily as to the emergency room under a general power of attorney or general agency. In many cases, a general agent is engaged or employed on a continuing basis for the principal. Most employees are general agents for their employers as they perform acts for their employers in the course of their employment. A special agent, however, is usually assigned specific and limited tasks to perform for the principal.

Express authority
Actual authority granted by one to another, whether in writing or orally

Power of attorney
The authority to act for another

Special power of attorney or agency
Authority to act for another only as to specifically authorized matters

General power of attorney or agency
Authority to act for another as to any matter

Subagent
An agent appointed by another agent

Agents may often appoint others, called **subagents**, to perform certain tasks. For example, if a client engages a law firm to represent her in a case arising out of a car accident, the firm may hire an engineer to testify about the accident. The engineer will be the subagent of the law firm. The relationship between an agent and a subagent closely parallels that between the principal and the original agent.

In some instances, express authority *must* be given in writing. The **equal dignities rule** in most state statutes provides that if an agreement or contract to be entered into must be in writing (such as a contract to sell land or one that cannot be performed within one year), then the agent's authority must be granted in writing also.

Equal dignities rule
Rule that if an agreement must be in writing, then agent's authority to act in regard to the agreement must also be in writing

An agent also has the **implied authority** to perform acts customarily performed by such an agent or those acts reasonably necessary to allow the agent to carry out express authority. For example, a hotel may hire a manager and grant express authority to the manager to operate the hotel. The manager also has the implied authority to perform acts reasonably necessary to operate the hotel (obtaining insurance, hiring and firing employees, ordering supplies, and advertising the hotel's services) or acts customarily performed by hotel managers (giving complimentary meals to unhappy patrons, arranging transportation services to the airport, or arranging to fax documents for a guest). Because it is unlikely that the parties will discuss each and every task the agent is authorized to perform, implied authority allows the agent to accomplish a wide variety of tasks for the principal.

Implied authority
Power to perform acts customarily performed by an agent

Apparent Authority.   Actual authority refers to authority granted by the principal to the agent. **Apparent authority** arises when by his word or conduct, a principal causes a third person reasonably to believe the agent has the authority to act for the principal. Assume that a landlord informs tenants that rent must be delivered by mail to him by the first of every month. One tenant who does not get paid until the last day of each month begins personally delivering the monthly rent check to the on-site manager, who accepts the checks and thereafter delivers them to the landlord. One month, the on-site manager allows the check to fall into the hands of another and the landlord insists that the tenant repay the rent. In this case, the tenant could assert that by the principal's previous conduct of allowing the checks to be hand-delivered rather than mailed, the tenant reasonably believed the on-site manager had the authority to receive the payments. The landlord will be precluded or estopped from asserting that the on-site manager, his agent, lacked authority to accept the rent check and is thus bound by his agent's act of accepting the check. Because the tenant has paid the rent to the agent, it need not be paid again. Thus, apparent authority does not rely on consent but on the appearance of authority to the third party.

Apparent authority
Authority that arises through words or conduct of principal leading others to believe agent has authority to act for principal

Ratified Authority.   Even if an agent has neither express nor implied authority to perform an act, the principal can nevertheless **ratify** or accept the agent's act and thereby become obligated by the agent's actions. Using our example, if Candy's real estate agent has been instructed to present no offer to Candy for her house under $200,000, and yet presents an offer to Candy for $190,000, which Candy accepts, Candy has ratified this unauthorized act by her agent. Ratification thus occurs when the principal accepts the agent's act even though the agent had no authority to do the act, or the act exceeded the scope of the agent's authority.

Ratification
Acceptance of an act; may be express or implied

3. Duties of Agents and Principals

An agency relationship creates **fiduciary duties** between the principal and the agent. The principal places trust and confidence in the agent, and the agent owes the utmost duty of good faith, candor, and fair dealing to the principal. Other duties also arise from the agency relationship.

Fiduciary duties
Duty to act in utmost good faith and fair dealing

Agent's Duties.   Generally, an agent owes four duties to his or her principal.

Performance.   An agent must perform the work or duties required by the principal. These duties may be set forth in the agency agreement or may be implied from the nature of the agency relationship. The agent is required to perform these duties with reasonable diligence and due care. The duty of performance is sometimes called the duty of obedience because the agent has a duty to obey the principal's directions. The level of performance expected of the agent is usually that of an ordinarily prudent person in similar situations. Some agency relationships, however, may impose higher standards of care on the agent. For example, in the attorney–client relationship, the attorney has held himself or herself out as possessing a certain amount of expertise. Thus, agents such as these will be held to a higher standard of care: that possessed by others in the field. Failure to exercise the duty of care required of the agent will render the agent liable to the principal. Even agents acting gratuitously — that is, without compensation — owe a duty of performance to their principals.

Notification.   An agent must disclose all information relating to the agency to his or her principal. Assume a real estate agent has been hired by the Hunters to sell their home. The agent has a duty to notify the Hunters, the principals, of all offers on the house. The agent cannot decide for himself, "This offer is so low I won't bother telling the Hunters about it." In agency law, it is presumed the principal knows all that the agent knows. Failure to provide information and notification to a principal will subject an agent to liability for breach of contract.

Loyalty.   The agent must act solely for the benefit of the principal and cannot engage in any transaction that could be detrimental to the principal. Thus, the agent cannot make a secret profit for his or her own benefit. Similarly, the agent cannot disclose the principal's confidential information or use it for any purpose except that related to the principal's business. Furthermore, the agent cannot represent anyone whose interests conflict with the principal's unless the principal agrees. For example, an attorney cannot represent both the plaintiff and the defendant in a matter unless each party knows of the representation and agrees to it. The agent's loyalty to the principal must be total and undivided.

Accounting.   An agent must account to the principal for all money or property paid out or received on the principal's behalf. Thus, an attorney could not settle a case and keep an extra $10,000 for herself by telling the principal that the settlement was $10,000 less than it actually was. This act is also a violation of the agent's fiduciary duty and of the duties of notification and loyalty. The agent must keep records and maintain separate accounts for the principal's funds and cannot commingle funds. In fact, attorneys who commingle money paid by clients for future legal services (typically called a **retainer**) with money used to pay for office expenses are subject to disciplinary proceedings.

Retainer
Money paid in advance for services to be rendered

Principal's Duties.   Principals typically owe three duties to their agents.

Compensation.   Principals must pay agents for their services. Sometimes the compensation is fixed in a written agreement. An example is the standard real estate

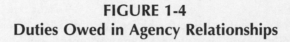

FIGURE 1-4
Duties Owed in Agency Relationships

Duties Owed by Agent	*Duties Owed by Principal*
Performance (using due care and diligence)	Compensation
Notification (duty to inform principal)	Reimbursement and Indemnification
Loyalty	Cooperation
Accounting of Profits	

listing agreement that obligates sellers of a dwelling to pay a 6 percent commission based on the purchase price of the property. If no sum certain is stated, the agent is entitled to compensation in a reasonable and customary amount, unless the agent has agreed to act without pay.

Reimbursement and Indemnification. The principal must reimburse the agent for costs and expenses incurred on the principal's behalf. For example, law firms typically charge clients for long-distance phone calls, postage, and photocopying. Similarly, business brokers are generally reimbursed for travel expenses incurred on behalf of their principals.

In addition to the duty to reimburse agents for costs and expenses reasonably incurred in the course of performance by the agent, the principal is generally required to indemnify or compensate the agent for liability incurred by the agent while performing duties for the principal. Although the agent will not be indemnified or compensated for acts of reckless or willful misconduct, the agent will be indemnified for acts directed or authorized by the principal. Using our example, assume the real estate agent provides an offer to the Hunters for their house. The Hunters accept the offer and agree to vacate the house by the first of the next month. If the Hunters fail to vacate on time, the buyers may be required to incur costs for staying in hotels and eating in restaurants. The Hunters, as principals, are required to indemnify the real estate agent for this liability if the buyers attempt to hold the agent responsible.

Cooperation. The principal must not hinder the agent in the performance of his or her duties. Assume the Hunters have a change of heart and decide not to sell their house. Because they have listed the house with an agent they are required to cooperate with the agent so the agent can perform his duty to sell the house. If the Hunters refuse to show the house, purposefully ruin the appearance of the house, or destroy appliances so that the house will not be attractive to buyers, the agent may sue for breach of contract. Similarly, the Hunters cannot list the house with two agents. Finally, the duty to cooperate encompasses a duty to provide the agent with what he will need to perform duties. This could include a credit card, an office, or equipment. (See Figure 1-4 for chart of duties owed in agency relationships.)

4. *Liability for Agent's Torts*

Tort
A civil wrong

An agent is liable for his or her own **torts** or civil wrongs. Such torts might include assault, battery, false imprisonment, negligence, fraud or misrepresentation, or professional malpractice. The question often arises whether the principal is liable for torts committed by the agent. The answer to this question depends on several variables. The general rule is that a principal is liable for the torts of her agent committed in the course and scope of the agency. Thus, if an employee of a restaurant accidentally spills scalding coffee on a patron, the restaurant may be liable because this act was performed in the routine course of duties by the employee-agent for her employer-principal. On the other hand, if the employee *throws* scalding coffee on a patron, the employer-principal is not likely to be held liable. Employers can be liable for failure to properly supervise an employee and even for improper selection of an employee, as is the case when an employer hires an obviously unqualified person for a position or hires a person with a known history of criminal activity. Similarly, the employer can be liable for wrongful retention of an employee, which occurs when the employee is allowed to remain employed after the employee threatens others or commits violent acts at the workplace.

Courts often examine whether the agent is truly acting in the scope of his assigned duties or whether the employee is on a personal "frolic" or "detour." For example, a trucking company may be liable for accidents caused by its drivers while they are in the process of performing their duties for their employer-principal. On the other hand, if a driver left his designated route to visit a friend and in the course of this act was involved in an accident, the employer-principal would likely not be held liable because the employee-agent was engaged in activity on his own behalf rather than on behalf of the principal.

Respondeat superior
Liability imposed on employers for acts of employees

This liability theory is referred to as *respondeat superior* (literally, "let the master answer") and results in liability being imposed on the employer-principal even though he did not actually commit the wrong. This doctrine imposes **vicarious liability** on the employer-principal, meaning that liability is imposed without regard to actual fault.

Vicarious liability
Liability imposed on one for another's acts, without regard to actual fault

Although a principal is liable for the torts of his agent committed in the course and scope of the agency, a principal is usually not held liable for torts committed by an independent contractor. In general, one is vicariously liable only for the acts of others, such as employees, who he or she can direct and control. Some individuals, however, are **independent contractors** who, rather than being subject to the direction of another as employees are, exercise independent discretion and control of their activities. Generally, employer-principals are not liable for the acts of independent contractors, unless they have directed or authorized the wrongful act. (See Chapter Eighteen for further discussion of independent contractors.)

Independent contractor
Individuals performing services for another who are not employees and who exercise independent discretion and control over their own activities

5. *Liability of Agents*

Disclosed principal
A principal whose existence and identity are known to others

Whether an agent is liable to third parties for acts in the course of an agency relationship often depends on the nature of the principal involved. Generally, there are three types of principals. A **disclosed principal** is one whose existence and identity are known to the third party. Thus, a truck driver who introduces himself by saying, "I'm Sam, the driver for Ace Movers," has disclosed both the principal's existence and identity. Generally, agents are not liable to third parties if disclosed principals do not perform their contractual duties.

A **partially disclosed principal** is one whose existence is known to the third party but whose specific identity is not known. For example, the owner of a house might tell her real estate agent not to disclose her identity to potential buyers to protect her anonymity. The potential buyers of the house would know that a seller-principal exists but would not know her specific identity. Because the third parties do not have an opportunity to conduct any investigation of the unidentified principal and cannot judge her trustworthiness, an agent is usually liable for contracts made on behalf of such a partially disclosed principal.

An **undisclosed principal** is one whose existence and identity are unknown to third parties. For example, a real estate agent might not disclose that he represents a buyer and might appear to be negotiating for the purchase of a home on his own behalf. Because the third party, the seller of the home, has no way of assessing the unknown principal's credibility and indeed believes the agent is acting on his own behalf, the agent will retain liability for contracts made for such undisclosed principals.

In many instances, the parties to an agency agreement will attempt to limit any potential liability by using exculpatory or excusing language in their contract. For example, the contract might state that the agent is not authorized to make certain statements or representations on behalf of the principal and that the agent will be liable if any such representations are made to the third party. Similarly, the parties may agree in writing as to which will be liable for certain acts or obligations.

6. Termination of Agency

On termination of the agency relationship, the agent no longer has the authority to bind the principal. Agency relationships may be terminated when the stated time period expires if the agreement provides a period of duration (such as a six-month listing period for a real estate agent), when the purposes of the agency have been fulfilled, by mutual agreement, by death or bankruptcy of either party, or by either party upon reasonable notice to the other. If the parties have agreed that the agency will exist for some specified time period, a termination by one party prior to this period may constitute a breach of contract and subject the breaching party to damages proximately caused by early termination. If the parties have no agreement specifying a termination date for the agency, it is usually held that the agency relationship will expire after a reasonable time. Agency relationships also terminate if an event occurs that makes it impossible for the agent to perform, such as destruction of property that is the subject of the agency.

7. Agency in Business Relationships

This overview of the relationship, duties, and obligations of agents and principals is fundamental to an understanding of many forms of business enterprise. For example, when sole proprietorships are discussed in Chapter Two, you will see that a sole proprietor is vicariously liable for the acts of her employees. When

Partially disclosed principal
A principal whose existence but not specific identity is known to others

Undisclosed principal
A principal whose existence and identity are unknown to others

general partnerships are discussed in Chapter Three, you will learn that partners are both agents and principals for each other and that any partner in a partnership has the ability to sign contracts, hire employees, and purchase goods for the partnership and that these acts bind the partnership and the other partners as well. Managers of limited liability companies act as agents for their companies. You will learn that directors and officers are agents of a corporation and thus may be reimbursed for expenses incurred on behalf of the corporation, will be indemnified for acts performed on behalf of the corporation, owe fiduciary duties to the corporation, and owe undivided loyalty to the corporation (and thus cannot serve as a director or officer of a competitor corporation).

Agency relationships permeate almost all forms of business enterprise. You will see that even without express agreements, certain individuals in a business have the authority to bind others by their actions. A thorough understanding of some of the basic principles of agency law is thus critical to an understanding of the various forms of business enterprise to be discussed in this book.

Key Features
of Agency Relationships

- ◆ Formation of agency occurs through express agreement, implied agreement, or estoppel.
- ◆ Agents have actual authority (express or implied) or apparent authority to act for their principals. Principals may ratify unauthorized acts of their agents.
- ◆ Agents and principals owe fiduciary duties to each other.
- ◆ Agents are liable for their own torts, and principals are liable for an agent's torts and acts committed in the course and scope of the agency.
- ◆ Agents are liable on contracts made for partially disclosed principals and undisclosed principals but not on contracts made on behalf of disclosed principals.

Case Illustration
Agent's Duty of Disclosure

Case Name: *Sierra Pacific Industries v. Carver*, 163 Cal. Rptr. 764 (Ct. App. 1980)

Facts: An owner of real estate entered into an agreement with a real estate agent to list real estate. The agent sold the real estate to his daughter and son-in-law without informing the seller of the agent's relationship to the buyers. When the seller discovered this fact, it sued the agent for fraud.

Holding: The seller need not pay any commission. An agent has a fiduciary duty to his principal to disclose all material information that is relevant to the subject matter of the agency. An agent must refrain from dual representation in a sales transaction unless both parties consent after full disclosure. In this case, the agent breached his duty of disclosure.

◆   ◆   ◆

WEB RESOURCES

Forming businesses is easier than ever due to the vast number of forms and "how to" guides available on the Internet. Nearly all states have basic business forms available to download. In many cases, one can submit the forms electronically to the appropriate state agency, authorizing payment by credit card. There are a number of Web sites that provide excellent introductory information on business structures. Try the following:

State statutes: www.law.cornell.edu
                         www.findlaw.com
Tax information: www.irs.gov
General information: www.sba.gov (Web site of the U.S. Small Business Administration offers excellent information on starting a business)
                         www.nass.org (Web site of the National Association of Secretaries of State allows direct linking to each state's secretary of state home page for easy access to forms and general information on business entities; select "About NASS," then "Our Members" and then "Contact Roster")
                         www.megalaw.com (Web site of MegaLaw, a general legal site that provides access to a wide array of legal sources, including federal and state statutes, and links to numerous helpful resources)
                         www.hoovers.com (Web site offering addresses, phone numbers, and brief capsules on hundreds of companies doing business in the United States)
Forms: www.allaboutforms.com
                         www.siccode.com/form.php
                         www.megalaw.com

Discussion Questions

1. ABC Inc., the owner of an apartment building, has hired Ava to manage the building. Although the owner wishes to charge $700 per month for rental of each unit, Ava is charging $750 per month and retaining the extra funds. Has Ava breached any duties to her principal? Discuss.

2. Assume the same set of facts as given in Question 1. Assume that although the owner has instructed Ava to investigate the backgrounds of prospective tenants to ensure they can pay the rent and will be good tenants, Ava has begun dispensing with these background checks so that she can rent as many units as possible. Has Ava breached any duties to her principal? Discuss.

3. Assume the same set of facts as given in Question 1. Assume that Ava purchased new lights for the common areas at the premises to ensure that all walkways are well lighted. ABC Inc. and Ava have no agreement as to which party should pay for such items. Will Ava be reimbursed for this expenditure? Discuss.

4. Andrea is an agent for Tess, an actress. Tess has had trouble getting roles recently and has just discovered that Andrea has been steering acting roles to her own niece, who is also an actress. Has Andrea breached any duties to Tess? Discuss.

5. We Will Move You Inc., a corporation, has hired several employees to drive its moving vans. In the course of a move, one of the drivers leaves the designated moving route to buy lunch and causes an accident. Will the corporation be liable for this accident? Discuss. What if one of the movers left the designated moving route to visit an old fraternity friend? Discuss.

Net Worth

1. Access the Web site for Hoover's and locate information about McDonald's Corporation. In how many countries does the corporation operate? What companies are identified as its top three competitors?
2. Access the Web site for the SBA. Access "Start Your Business," "Choose a Structure," and "Forms of Ownership." What is the first advantage given for a sole proprietorship? What is the first disadvantage given for a sole proprietorship?
3. Access the Web site for the National Association of Secretaries of State.
   a. Who is the current Secretary of State for Florida?
   b. Locate the Web site for the Colorado Secretary of State. Select "Business Center" and review the Glossary. What is the definition given for a limited liability company?

2

◆　◆　◆

Sole Proprietorships

◆　◆　◆

CHAPTER OVERVIEW

The sole proprietorship, sometimes called an individual proprietorship, is the most common way of doing business in this country. More than 70 percent of all of the businesses formed in the United States are conducted as sole proprietorships. As its name indicates, the sole proprietorship is carried on by one person. The primary reason that so many businesses are conducted as sole proprietorships is the ease of forming and operating the business. Sole proprietors own and manage their businesses and incur sole liability for any business obligations.

A.　Characteristics of Sole Proprietorships

Many people dream of owning their own business. For most of these entrepreneurs, the sole proprietorship is an ideal way of pursuing this dream. The **sole proprietorship** is an unincorporated business owned and conducted by one person, generally called the **sole proprietor.** Almost any kind of business can be conducted as a sole proprietorship: a law office, a restaurant, a childcare center, or an auto repair service. The key feature of a sole proprietorship is that it is managed and owned by one person. This person may hire managers and employees to assist him or her in running the business, but the business is characterized by a sole decision-maker. There are no limits on how many people may be employed in this type of enterprise; a sole proprietorship can be a large business with numerous employees and great revenue, although it is more likely to be a small business. From 2000 to 2005, the number of sole proprietorships grew from 17,905,000 to 21,468,000. *Statistical Abstract of the United States* 483 (128th ed. 2009).

Sole proprietorship
A business owned and operated by one person

Sole proprietor
Owner of a sole proprietorship

It is often difficult to determine the nature of businesses operated by families. It is common in family-run businesses, for example, for one spouse to work in the shop, the other spouse to do some of the accounting and bill paying, and the children to fill in as employees during summer vacations. To determine the nature of such an enterprise, examine how decisions are made. If one person makes the key business decisions, such as whom to hire and fire, what products and services to offer, and whether additional shops will be opened, it is likely a sole proprietorship. If both spouses, however, share such critical decisions, and either has the ability to enter into contracts, then the business is likely a partnership. It does not matter whether the parties believe the business is a sole proprietorship; a court is not bound by what parties believe, but will examine the actual business structure. If one person manages and controls the business, it is a sole proprietorship; if there is shared decision-making, the business is likely a partnership.

B.   Governing Law

Sole proprietorships are governed exclusively by state and local laws rather than by federal law (except for federal laws relating to taxes, civil rights, and so forth, to which all sole proprietors are subject). Each state regulates businesses that operate within the state through a variety of laws relating to names under which the businesses may operate, licensing considerations, and state tax obligations. Local jurisdictions, such as counties and states, typically require sole proprietorships that will be operating under an assumed or fictitious name (a business name that does not include the sole proprietor's surname or one that implies other owners are involved) to file a statement identifying the true owner of the business. Other than these laws and regulations, sole proprietorships are subject to minimal statutory burdens, and no permission is required from the state to form a sole proprietorship.

C.   Advantages of Sole Proprietorships

One of the reasons the sole proprietorship is such a popular way of doing business is that this enterprise is easily and inexpensively formed and offers great flexibility to the business owner. Sole proprietorships themselves are not created by state or federal statutes, so their formation is readily accomplished. The owner is free to make all decisions regarding the business. The sole proprietor can select the name of the business, establish its location, decide what products and services will be offered by the business, hire and fire employees, and establish the business policies and hours of operation for the business. Vacations can be taken when the sole proprietor desires, and the sole proprietor does not have to secure permission from others to make decisions affecting the business. Furthermore, the sole proprietor retains all of the profits generated by the business and does not have to share them with any co-owner. Finally, the owner is not vulnerable to the incompetence or dishonesty of partners and is free to sell the business without having to secure approval from partners.

D. Disadvantages of Sole Proprietorships

1. Unlimited Personal Liability

The chief disadvantage of doing business as a sole proprietor is that the sole proprietor is personally liable for the debts, obligations, and liabilities of the business. Assume a sole proprietor is operating a restaurant. If rent is owed to the owner of the building or money is owed to the restaurant's chief wine supplier, these creditors are not limited to seizing money only in the restaurant's business accounts. The sole proprietor's liability extends beyond what has been invested in the business to his or her personal assets. In most states, statutes exist to provide that certain property is exempt from attachment, so that the sole proprietor is not stripped of all assets. For example, household furnishings, appliances, and other personal effects may be exempt if they are personally used by the sole proprietor and are reasonably necessary. Similarly, certain heirlooms, jewelry, and artworks may be exempt to the extent they do not exceed some stated statutory value, often $2,500. Moreover, many states have homestead exemptions to protect one's residence from creditors' claims, although the nature and extent of the exemptions vary from state to state. In general, however, view the front door of the sole proprietor's house as wide open and the contents therein as available for picking by any creditors of the business. Thus, the sole proprietorship is so closely affiliated with the sole proprietor that its debts become his or her debts.

Sole proprietors are liable not only for business obligations, but also for the torts or civil wrongs they commit or that are committed by their employees or agents acting in the course and scope of their employment. For example, if one of the restaurant's employees negligently trips a patron or spills scalding coffee on a patron, the sole proprietor will be liable for such acts. On the other hand, if the employee causes a car accident while not on duty, the sole proprietor would not likely have any liability for this act.

Because the risk of a sole proprietor extends to personal assets, the sole proprietorship might not be the best form of business enterprise for a wealthy individual, all of whose assets and wealth are subject to the debts and liabilities of the sole proprietorship.

To protect against the disadvantage of unlimited **personal liability**, the sole proprietor may seek to obtain insurance. General liability insurance, however, is usually costly to secure and might not be available to cover every type of risk. The sole proprietor may also seek to enter into contractual arrangements with creditors whereby, in return for obtaining the proprietor's business, they agree not to look to his or her personal assets to satisfy debts. Additional protection is provided by the fact that the sole proprietor has total control over decision-making and does not have to worry that a partner is obligating the business for unnecessary items. Finally, because all states except Wyoming allow single-person limited liability companies (see Chapter Six), which provide full

Personal liability
Liability extending beyond what is invested in a business to an individual's personal assets (also called *unlimited liability*)

protection against personal liability, some individuals now form limited liability companies rather than sole proprietorships (although formation and maintenance of these LLCs are far more complex processes than formation and maintenance of sole proprietorships).

Generally, when people realize the extent of the liability of a sole proprietor, they often wonder why anyone would select this form of business enterprise. Some businesses, however, such as a typical retail store, often have slight exposure to unknown liabilities. A skating rink, chemical manufacturing plant, construction firm, or a child-care center, however, are far riskier businesses, and thus the sole proprietorship might not be appropriate for such enterprises that have increased exposure to potential liability.

2.   Lack of Continuity

Because the sole proprietorship is merely an extension of the sole proprietor, the sole proprietorship generally terminates with the death of the sole proprietor. Although some state statutes provide for continuity of certain types of businesses, the general rule is that the sole proprietorship cannot survive the death of the sole proprietor. If the business assets descend to an heir who continues to operate the business, a new sole proprietorship has been created. The restaurant might look the same and offer the same products and services, but a new sole proprietorship has been created.

Sole proprietorships can be sold to another. However, because the business is so closely identified with its owner, a change in ownership may dramatically affect the business itself. Moreover, it is difficult to assess the goodwill of the business because it is dependent on the reputation and skills of the original sole proprietor. To provide some continuity, the new owner may employ the previous owner or retain his or her services as an advisor or consultant during a transition period. The new owner, who has created a new sole proprietorship, should obtain a covenant from the previous owner not to compete against the new business for some reasonable period of time. (See Chapter Eighteen for discussion of covenants not to compete.)

3.   Difficulties in Raising Capital

Capital
Money used to form and operate a business or other venture

If a partnership needs to raise additional **capital**, or money, to meet an unforeseen need or to expand the business, there may be several partners who can contribute this needed capital. Corporations can raise money by selling shares. The sole proprietor, on the other hand, is limited in his or her ways of obtaining additional money. The sole proprietor can look only to his or her own funds or can attempt to obtain loans. If banks or other parties do not believe the business has a proven track record, they may refuse to make loans, and the sole proprietorship may collapse just as it is on the verge of becoming a success. This difficulty in obtaining and raising capital is a disadvantage of a sole proprietorship. The Small Business Administration offers a variety of loan programs and loan guaranty programs to small businesses that are unable to secure financing on reasonable terms through normal business channels.

FIGURE 2-1
Sole Proprietorships

Advantages	*Disadvantages*
Easy to form and maintain	Unlimited personal liability
Inexpensive to form	Limited ways of raising capital
Owner is sole decision-maker	Lack of continuity
Management is informal and flexible	Possible lack of expertise in management
All profits are retained by owner	
Pass-through tax status	

---

4. Management Difficulties

The sole proprietor has the flexibility of making all management decisions; however, this can sometimes be a disadvantage. The business may need special assistance or expertise as it grows. A partnership can admit new partners to respond to these needs. A corporation can rely on its board of directors and officers to provide managerial expertise. The sole proprietor, however, is also the sole decision-maker and might lack specific skills to respond to a changing economy, a changing market, or a growing business. Thus, sole proprietors may need to hire experts and advisors.

Sole proprietors tend to work very hard. They often invest their emotion as well as their money into the enterprise. It could be difficult to take a vacation if the sole proprietor cannot find committed employees or managers. The sole proprietor may work in the business all day and then spend evenings doing bookkeeping and marketing. Most sole proprietors find operating the business both exhilarating and exhausting. (See Figure 2-1 for a chart comparing the advantages and disadvantages of sole proprietorships.)

E. Formation of Sole Proprietorships

One of the greatest advantages of a sole proprietorship is the lack of formalities in organizing and forming this enterprise. Most of the requirements for forming the sole proprietorship are common to almost any business and are not imposed on this enterprise simply because it is a sole proprietorship.

1. Licensing Considerations

If the sole proprietor will be engaged in a business that has licensing requirements, he will need to comply with these. For example, attorneys must acquire a license to practice law, real estate and insurance agents must pass a test to become licensed, and restaurants that serve liquor must obtain liquor licenses from the appropriate alcoholic beverage control authority.

To determine whether the business is one that requires a license, review your state's statutes, your state's administrative code (which generally includes all information relating to any testing for the license or prerequisites that must be met), or contact any association that might govern the profession, such as the department of realtors or your state's bar association.

Sole proprietorships can conduct business in other localities or states so long as their licensing and name requirements are followed.

2. Name Considerations

Many sole proprietors choose to operate their businesses under a name other than their own. This is often referred to as an *assumed name, trade name*, or a **fictitious name**. For example, assume Susan Sullivan intends to operate a restaurant. She prefers to call the restaurant The Venetian Garden rather than Susan Sullivan's Restaurant. Because The Venetian Garden is a fictitious name, Susan must generally file a document with her local or state authority informing the public that she intends to "do business as" or "trade as" The Venetian Garden. Sometimes this document is referred to as the **DBA** statement (for "doing business as"). An example of a **fictitious business name statement** is shown in Figure 2-2. This document protects consumers who can then determine the actual owner of the restaurant if a lawsuit must be filed against the sole proprietor. Most jurisdictions provide a form to be completed. The form is generally quite simple to complete and, although a fee might be charged, it is often less than $25.

Although standards vary from state to state, the general rule in determining whether the fictitious business name statement must be filed is as follows: If the business name includes the sole proprietor's last name and does not imply that others are involved (by using terms such as "Associates," "Brothers," and so forth), no statement need be filed. Thus, "Bob's Crafts" is a fictitious business name that must be registered, whereas "Freedman Repairs" is not. Consumers are always entitled to know who may be sued, and signals such as "Associates" or "and Company" imply that other owners may be involved in the business. Thus, names including those terms must be registered.

Because the cost of filing the statement is so low, and because the form is so easy to complete, when in doubt, file the fictitious business name statement. Failure to file the statement could result in a fine or refusal to allow the sole proprietor to institute a legal action, although the sole proprietor can usually cure the defect and file the statement in order to litigate. The statement is usually valid for a few years and can be renewed. Some states, such as California, require that the name be published in a newspaper of general circulation in the area in which the business will be located to afford notice to the public of the sole proprietor's intent to conduct business under an assumed or fictitious name. In some states, the fictitious business name statement must be filed in each county in which the sole proprietor will conduct business. In other states, it is filed only in the county in which the business owner maintains his or her principal place of business. In a few states (for example, Florida and Missouri) the fictitious business name forms may be filed electronically. Similarly, these jurisdictions and others allow online searching of fictitious business names. Registration of a fictitious business

Fictitious name
A name that must be registered with state or local officials because it does not disclose the surname of the business owner

DBA
"Doing business as"; another name for a fictitious business name statement

Fictitious business name statement
Record filed with public officials to identify the owner of a business operating under a name other than the owner's surname

FIGURE 2-2
California Fictitious Business Name Statement

275-321
[Rev. 1/08]

PATRICK O'CONNELL, Alameda County Clerk-Recorder
1106 Madison Street, First Floor
Oakland, CA 94607 Telephone (510) 272-6362

FICTITIOUS BUSINESS NAME STATEMENT
USE BLACK OR DARK BLUE INK ONLY

FILING FEE:
$29.00 FOR FIRST BUSINESS NAME AND FIRST REGISTRANT ON STATEMENT
$ 7.00 FOR EACH ADDITIONAL REGISTRANT AND EACH ADDITIONAL BUSINESS NAME
LISTED ON STATEMENT AND DOING BUSINESS AT THE SAME LOCATION

FILE NUMBER: _____
DO NOT WRITE ABOVE THIS LINE

PLEASE READ INSTRUCTIONS ON BACK OF THIS FORM - TYPE OR PRINT LEGIBLY

A | FICTITIOUS BUSINESS NAME(S) *

B | Street Address of Principal Place of Business (P.O. Box <u>not</u> acceptable) ** | City | County | State | Zip

Mailing Address (Optional) | City | County | State | Zip

C

① Show full name of Registrant. (If Registrant is Corporation, LLC or LLP, show full name of Entity.)***

Residence Street Address (P.O. Box not acceptable)

City | State | Zip

(If a corporation or LLC, show state where registered.)

② Show full name of Registrant. (If Registrant is Corporation, LLC or LLP, show full name of Entity.)***

Residence Street Address (P.O. Box not acceptable)

City | State | Zip

If a corporation or LLC, show state where registered.

③ Show full name of Registrant. (If Registrant is Corporation, LLC or LLP, show full name of Entity.)***

Residence Street Address (P.O. Box not acceptable)

City | State | Zip

If a corporation or LLC, show state where registered.

④ Show full name of Registrant. (If Registrant is Corporation, LLC or LLP, show full name of Entity.)***

Residence Street Address (P.O. Box not acceptable)

City | State | Zip

If a corporation or LLC, show state where registered.

D | BUSINESS CONDUCTED BY: ****
(Check only 1 box)

☐ an Individual ☐ Husband and wife ☐ State or local registered domestic partners ☐ Co-partners
☐ a Joint venture ☐ a General partnership ☐ a Limited liability partnership ☐ a Trust
☐ a Corporation ☐ a Limited partnership ☐ a Limited liability company
☐ an Unincorporated association other than a partnership

E | ☐ The registrant began to transact business under the fictitious business name(s) listed above on _____ *****
(Write "N/A" on the line above if you have not yet begun transacting business using the fictitious business name.) (date)

I DECLARE THAT ALL INFORMATION IN THIS STATEMENT IS TRUE AND CORRECT. (A REGISTRANT WHO DECLARES AS TRUE INFORMATION WHICH HE OR SHE KNOWS TO BE FALSE IS GUILTY OF A CRIME.)
NOTICE: IN ACCORDANCE WITH BUSINESS AND PROFESSIONS CODE SECTION 17920(A), THE FICTITIOUS NAME STATEMENT <u>EXPIRES 5 YEARS</u> FROM THE DATE ON WHICH IT WAS FILED IN THE OFFICE OF THE COUNTY CLERK EXCEPT, AS PROVIDED IN SUBDIVISION (B) OF SECTION 17920, WHEN IT EXPIRES 40 DAYS AFTER ANY CHANGE IN THE FACTS AS SET FORTH IN THE STATEMENT PURSUANT TO SECTION 17913 OTHER THAN A CHANGE IN THE RESIDENCE ADDRESS OF A REGISTERED OWNER. A NEW FICTITIOUS BUSINESS NAME STATEMENT MUST BE FILED BEFORE THE EXPIRATION.
The filing of this statement does not of itself authorize the use in this state of a fictitious business name in violation of the rights of another under federal, state, or common law (see Section 14411 et seq., Business and Professions Code).

SIGNATURE OF REGISTRANT _____

PRINT NAME OF PERSON SIGNING. IF CORPORATION OR LLC, ALSO PRINT TITLE OF SIGNER

THIS STATEMENT WAS FILED WITH THE COUNTY CLERK-RECORDER OF ALAMEDA COUNTY ON THE DATE INDICATED BY THE FILE STAMP ABOVE.

Copy 1— Clerk's Copy

name is typically for public notice only and gives rise to no presumption of the registrant's rights to own or use the name registered; nor does it affect trademark, service mark, or corporate name rights previously acquired by others for the same or similar name.

When selecting a name, the sole proprietor cannot operate under a name likely to cause confusion with another enterprise. The agency with which you file the statement will generally check to see if the name is available in that locality. For a more thorough check, the sole proprietor can have searches conducted of business names throughout the nation. Sole proprietors who intend to conduct business in various localities or jurisdictions should conduct these more thorough searches to avoid trademark infringement. The following are two companies that specialize in such name searches:

CT Corsearch	*Thomson CompuMark*
345 Hudson Street	500 Victory Road
New York, NY 10014	North Quincy, MA 02171
(800) 732-7241	(800) 692-8833
www.ctcorsearch.com	http://compumark.thomson.com

These companies will check trade associations, telephone directories, Internet uses, and other sources to determine if a name is already being used. Alternatively, you can access the trademark database of the U.S. Patent and Trademark Office (www.uspto.gov) to review trademarks applied for or registered with the Patent and Trademark Office. Federal trademark registration, however, is not required and is only available for names or marks used in interstate commerce. Thus, a business name used only in intrastate commerce or on a purely local basis will not be available for searching in the Patent and Trademark Office records.

3.　*Business and Sales Tax Permits*

Many jurisdictions require that the sole proprietor obtain a basic license to do business. For example, New York City requires that an application be completed for most businesses to be conducted in the city, whether they operate as a sole proprietorship, a partnership, or a corporation. In addition to including routine items such as names and addresses, the applicant must indicate whether he or she has been convicted of any offenses or violations of the law and whether any other type of license has previously been denied to the applicant.

If the sole proprietor will be selling goods, arrangements must be made to pay sales tax to the appropriate authority. Contact your state's taxing agency to obtain a sales tax permit.

A sole proprietor who hires employees must apply for an employer identification number to make arrangements to withhold federal income tax. Application for the number is made by obtaining Form SS-4 from the Internal Revenue Service (IRS) and filing it with the IRS. This form (see Figure 2-3) is easily completed. Forms can be obtained by calling the IRS at (800) 829-1040 or accessing the IRS Web site at www.irs.gov.

FIGURE 2-3
IRS Form SS-4

Form **SS-4**	**Application for Employer Identification Number**	OMB No. 1545-0003

Form **SS-4**
(Rev. January 2009)
Department of the Treasury
Internal Revenue Service

Application for Employer Identification Number
(For use by employers, corporations, partnerships, trusts, estates, churches, government agencies, Indian tribal entities, certain individuals, and others.)
► See separate instructions for each line. ► Keep a copy for your records.

OMB No. 1545-0003
EIN

Type or print clearly.

1 Legal name of entity (or individual) for whom the EIN is being requested

2 Trade name of business (if different from name on line 1) | 3 Executor, administrator, trustee, "care of" name

4a Mailing address (room, apt., suite no. and street, or P.O. box) | 5a Street address (if different) (Do not enter a P.O. box.)

4b City, state, and ZIP code (if foreign, see instructions) | 5b City, state, and ZIP code (if foreign, see instructions)

6 County and state where principal business is located

7a Name of principal officer, general partner, grantor, owner, or trustor | 7b SSN, ITIN, or EIN

8a Is this application for a limited liability company (LLC) (or a foreign equivalent)? ☐ Yes ☐ No | 8b If 8a is "Yes," enter the number of LLC members ►

8c If 8a is "Yes," was the LLC organized in the United States? ☐ Yes ☐ No

9a Type of entity (check only one box). Caution. If 8a is "Yes," see the instructions for the correct box to check.
☐ Sole proprietor (SSN) _____ | ☐ Estate (SSN of decedent) _____
☐ Partnership | ☐ Plan administrator (TIN) _____
☐ Corporation (enter form number to be filed) ► _____ | ☐ Trust (TIN of grantor) _____
☐ Personal service corporation | ☐ National Guard ☐ State/local government
☐ Church or church-controlled organization | ☐ Farmers' cooperative ☐ Federal government/military
☐ Other nonprofit organization (specify) ► _____ | ☐ REMIC ☐ Indian tribal governments/enterprises
☐ Other (specify) ► | Group Exemption Number (GEN) if any ►

9b If a corporation, name the state or foreign country (if applicable) where incorporated | State | Foreign country

10 Reason for applying (check only one box)
☐ Started new business (specify type) ► _____ | ☐ Banking purpose (specify purpose) ► _____
☐ Hired employees (Check the box and see line 13.) | ☐ Changed type of organization (specify new type) ► _____
☐ Compliance with IRS withholding regulations | ☐ Purchased going business
☐ Other (specify) ► | ☐ Created a trust (specify type) ► _____
| ☐ Created a pension plan (specify type) ► _____

11 Date business started or acquired (month, day, year). See instructions. | 12 Closing month of accounting year

13 Highest number of employees expected in the next 12 months (enter -0- if none).
Agricultural | Household | Other

14 Do you expect your employment tax liability to be $1,000 or less in a full calendar year? ☐ Yes ☐ No (If you expect to pay $4,000 or less in total wages in a full calendar year, you can mark "Yes.")

15 First date wages or annuities were paid (month, day, year). Note. If applicant is a withholding agent, enter date income will first be paid to nonresident alien (month, day, year) ►

16 Check one box that best describes the principal activity of your business.
☐ Construction ☐ Rental & leasing ☐ Transportation & warehousing ☐ Accommodation & food service | ☐ Health care & social assistance ☐ Wholesale-agent/broker
☐ Real estate ☐ Manufacturing ☐ Finance & insurance ☐ Other (specify) | ☐ Wholesale-other ☐ Retail

17 Indicate principal line of merchandise sold, specific construction work done, products produced, or services provided.

18 Has the applicant entity shown on line 1 ever applied for and received an EIN? ☐ Yes ☐ No
If "Yes," write previous EIN here ►

Third Party Designee | Complete this section only if you want to authorize the named individual to receive the entity's EIN and answer questions about the completion of this form.
Designee's name | Designee's telephone number (include area code) ( )
Address and ZIP code | Designee's fax number (include area code) ( )

Under penalties of perjury, I declare that I have examined this application, and to the best of my knowledge and belief, it is true, correct, and complete. | Applicant's telephone number (include area code) ( )
Name and title (type or print clearly) ►
Signature ► Date ► | Applicant's fax number (include area code) ( )

For Privacy Act and Paperwork Reduction Act Notice, see separate instructions. | Cat. No. 16055N | Form **SS-4** (Rev. 1-2009)

F. Taxation of Sole Proprietorships

Because the sole proprietorship itself is so closely identified with the individual operating it, it is not recognized as a separate taxable entity as is a corporation. Thus, the sole proprietorship itself does not pay any federal income tax. Income derived from the sole proprietorship is simply added to any other income the sole proprietor makes (whether from leasing of a rental unit, game-show winnings, or income earned through receipt of a cash dividend on shares of stock the sole proprietor may own), and the sole proprietor pays tax on this entire amount. The income earned from the business, however, is reported on a separate form called Schedule C (see Figure 2-4), which is attached to the proprietor's individual income tax return (Form 1040). Sole proprietors who meet certain criteria, such as having no employees and claiming less than $5,000 for business expenses, may use a schedule, called Schedule C-EZ, which is simple and easy to complete (see Figure 2-5). The sole proprietor may declare and deduct various business expenses such as advertising, business insurance, and interest paid, and use these to offset income. Taking such deductions may be especially helpful in the first few years of the business when losses may be expected as the business is developing. The sole proprietor pays tax on all net income, even money retained for anticipated business expenditures.

The sole proprietor pays tax at whatever rate or "bracket" is appropriate. (See Figure 2-6 for schedule of tax rates for individuals.) Thus, depending on the individual's income and the income earned from the business, the tax rate might be lower than the corporate tax rate (especially in the first few years of the business when expenses are high and the business might not be an immediate success). If tax circumstances change, the sole proprietor can later incorporate the business to take advantage of corporate tax rates and to take advantage of the limited liability the corporate form provides.

Keogh plan
A retirement plan for sole proprietors

Sole proprietors are entitled to establish qualified retirement plans for themselves and their employees, typically called **Keogh plans** after the Keogh Act, which allows self-employed individuals to make tax-deductible contributions for retirement plans for themselves and their employees. (See Chapter Eighteen for additional information on Keogh plans.)

FIGURE 2-4
IRS Schedule C

SCHEDULE C (Form 1040) Department of the Treasury Internal Revenue Service (99)	**Profit or Loss From Business** (Sole Proprietorship) ▶ Partnerships, joint ventures, etc., generally must file Form 1065 or 1065-B. ▶ Attach to Form 1040, 1040NR, or 1041. ▶ See Instructions for Schedule C (Form 1040).	OMB No. 1545-0074 2008 Attachment Sequence No. 09

Name of proprietor		Social security number (SSN)

A   Principal business or profession, including product or service (see page C-3 of the instructions) | **B** Enter code from pages C-9, 10, & 11 ▶

C   Business name. If no separate business name, leave blank. | **D** Employer ID number (EIN), if any

E   Business address (including suite or room no.) ▶
City, town or post office, state, and ZIP code

F   Accounting method: **(1)** ☐ Cash   **(2)** ☐ Accrual   **(3)** ☐ Other (specify) ▶

G   Did you "materially participate" in the operation of this business during 2008? If "No," see page C-4 for limit on losses   ☐ Yes   ☐ No

H   If you started or acquired this business during 2008, check here   .   .   .   .   ▶ ☐

Part I   Income

1   Gross receipts or sales. **Caution.** See page C-4 and check the box if:

   ● This income was reported to you on Form W-2 and the "Statutory employee" box
   on that form was checked, or

   ● You are a member of a qualified joint venture reporting only rental real estate
   income not subject to self-employment tax. Also see page C-4 for limit on losses.   .   . ▶ ☐ | 1

2   Returns and allowances | 2

3   Subtract line 2 from line 1   .   .   .   . | 3

4   Cost of goods sold (from line 42 on page 2)   .   .   .   . | 4

5   **Gross profit.** Subtract line 4 from line 3.   .   .   .   . | 5

6   Other income, including federal and state gasoline or fuel tax credit or refund (see page C-4).   .   . | 6

7   **Gross income.** Add lines 5 and 6   .   .   .   . ▶ | 7

Part II   Expenses. Enter expenses for business use of your home **only** on line 30.

8 Advertising	8		18 Office expense	18	
9 Car and truck expenses (see page C-5).	9		19 Pension and profit-sharing plans 20 Rent or lease (see page C-6):	19	
10 Commissions and fees . .	10		a Vehicles, machinery, and equipment .	20a	
11 Contract labor (see page C-5)	11		b Other business property. . .	20b	
12 Depletion	12		21 Repairs and maintenance . .	21	
13 Depreciation and section 179 expense deduction (not included in Part III) (see page C-5).	13		22 Supplies (not included in Part III) 23 Taxes and licenses . . . . 24 Travel, meals, and entertainment:	22 23	
			a Travel	24a	
14 Employee benefit programs (other than on line 19) .	14		b Deductible meals and entertainment (see page C-7)	24b	
15 Insurance (other than health) .	15		25 Utilities	25	
16 Interest:			26 Wages (less employment credits) .	26	
a Mortgage (paid to banks, etc.) .	16a		27 Other expenses (from line 48 on page 2)	27	
b Other	16b				
17 Legal and professional services	17				

28   **Total expenses** before expenses for business use of home. Add lines 8 through 27   .   .   .   . ▶ | 28

29   Tentative profit or (loss). Subtract line 28 from line 7   .   .   .   . | 29

30   Expenses for business use of your home. Attach **Form 8829**   .   .   .   . | 30

31   **Net profit or (loss).** Subtract line 30 from line 29.

   ● If a profit, enter on both **Form 1040, line 12,** and **Schedule SE, line 2,** or on **Form 1040NR,
   line 13** (if you checked the box on line 1, see page C-7). Estates and trusts, enter on **Form 1041,
   line 3.** | 31

   ● If a loss, you **must** go to line 32.

32   If you have a loss, check the box that describes your investment in this activity (see page C-8).

   ● If you checked 32a, enter the loss on both **Form 1040, line 12,** and **Schedule SE, line 2,** or on
   Form 1040NR, line 13 (if you checked the box on line 1, see the line 31 instructions on page C-7).
   Estates and trusts, enter on **Form 1041, line 3.** | 32a ☐ All investment is at risk.
32b ☐ Some investment is not
at risk.

   ● If you checked 32b, you **must** attach **Form 6198.** Your loss may be limited.

For Paperwork Reduction Act Notice, see page C-9 of the instructions.   Cat. No. 11334P   Schedule C (Form 1040) 2008

FIGURE 2-5
IRS Schedule C-EZ

SCHEDULE C-EZ
(Form 1040)

Department of the Treasury
Internal Revenue Service (99)

Net Profit From Business
(Sole Proprietorship)

▶ Partnerships, joint ventures, etc., generally must file Form 1065 or 1065-B.
▶ Attach to Form 1040, 1040NR, or 1041. ▶ See instructions on back.

OMB No. 1545-0074

20**08**

Attachment
Sequence No. **09A**

Name of proprietor | Social security number (SSN)

Part I General Information

You May Use Schedule C-EZ Instead of Schedule C Only If You:

- Had business expenses of $5,000 or less.
- Use the cash method of accounting.
- Did not have an inventory at any time during the year.
- Did not have a net loss from your business.
- Had only one business as either a sole proprietor, qualified joint venture, or statutory employee.

And You:

- Had no employees during the year.
- Are not required to file **Form 4562**, Depreciation and Amortization, for this business. See the instructions for Schedule C, line 13, on page C-5 to find out if you must file.
- Do not deduct expenses for business use of your home.
- Do not have prior year unallowed passive activity losses from this business.

A Principal business or profession, including product or service

B Enter code from pages C-9, 10, & 11 ▶

C Business name. If no separate business name, leave blank.

D Employer ID number (EIN), if any

E Business address (including suite or room no.). Address not required if same as on page 1 of your tax return.

City, town or post office, state, and ZIP code

Part II Figure Your Net Profit

1 **Gross receipts. Caution.** See the instructions for Schedule C, line 1, on page C-4 and check the box if:

- This income was reported to you on Form W-2 and the "Statutory employee" box on that form was checked, or
- You are a member of a qualified joint venture reporting only rental real estate income not subject to self-employment tax. } ... ▶ ☐

1

2 **Total expenses** (see instructions on page 2). If more than $5,000, you **must** use Schedule C. | **2**

3 **Net profit.** Subtract line 2 from line 1. If less than zero, you **must** use Schedule C. Enter on both **Form 1040, line 12,** and **Schedule SE, line 2,** or on **Form 1040NR, line 13.** (If you checked the box on line 1, **do not** report the amount from line 3 on Schedule SE, line 2.) Estates and trusts, enter on **Form 1041, line 3** . . . . | **3**

Part III Information on Your Vehicle. Complete this part **only** if you are claiming car or truck expenses on line 2.

4 When did you place your vehicle in service for business purposes? (month, day, year) ▶ ...... / ...... / ....

5 Of the total number of miles you drove your vehicle during 2008, enter the number of miles you used your vehicle for:

a Business .... **b** Commuting (see instructions) .... **c** Other ....

6 Was your vehicle available for personal use during off-duty hours? . . . . ☐ **Yes** ☐ **No**

7 Do you (or your spouse) have another vehicle available for personal use? . . . . ☐ **Yes** ☐ **No**

8a Do you have evidence to support your deduction? . . . . ☐ **Yes** ☐ **No**

b If "Yes," is the evidence written? . . . . ☐ **Yes** ☐ **No**

For Paperwork Reduction Act Notice, see page 2. | Cat. No. 14374D | Schedule C-EZ (Form 1040) 2008

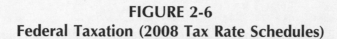

FIGURE 2-6
Federal Taxation (2008 Tax Rate Schedules)

Taxable Income
(Taxpayer Filing Singly)

| Taxable Income | | Tax | Tax | |
Over	But not over	Tax	+%	On amount over
$0	$8,025	$0.00	10	$0
8,025	32,550	802.50	15	8,025
32,550	78,850	4,481.25	25	32,550
78,850	164,550	16,056.25	28	78,850
164,550	357,700	40,052.25	33	164,550
357,700		103,791.75	35	357,700

Taxable Income
(Married Taxpayers Filing Jointly)

| Taxable Income | | Tax | Tax | |
Over	But not over	Tax	+%	On amount over
$0	$16,050	$0.00	10	$0
16,050	65,100	1,605.00	15	16,050
65,100	131,450	8,962.50	25	65,100
131,450	200,300	25,550.00	28	131,450
200,300	357,700	44,828.00	33	200,300
357,700		96,770.00	35	357,700

Key Features
of Sole Proprietorships

◆ Business is owned and managed by one person.
◆ Sole proprietor retains all profits and bears all losses.
◆ Sole proprietor's personal assets can be reached to satisfy business obligations ("personal liability").
◆ Business is easily and inexpensively formed.
◆ All income earned (and loss incurred) is passed through to sole proprietor, who pays tax at appropriate individual tax bracket.

G. Role of Paralegal

Because forming a sole proprietorship is relatively simple, only a few tasks may be required of a paralegal.

1. Paralegals should determine whether the business to be engaged in is one requiring a license, such as the sale of liquor, construction work, or the sale of real estate. Check with your local SBA office or the local governing unit, such as your county or city.
2. Pertinent state statutes should be reviewed to determine whether a fictitious business name statement must be filed. If the name must be filed, retrieve the form (many are now available on the Internet), complete it, and file it. Check to see if the fictitious business name must be published in a newspaper. Maintain accurate files of all documents related to the sole proprietorship.
3. Consider whether a name search should be conducted to ensure the name selected by the sole proprietor does not infringe a name already in use.
4. If the sole proprietorship is engaged in a business subject to local or state sales taxes, a sales tax certificate must be filed with the pertinent authority.
5. If the business employs people, arrangements must be made to withhold taxes and to contribute to Social Security, and a federal employer identification number must be obtained by completing and filing IRS Form SS-4.

Case Illustration
When Fictitious Business Name Statement Must Be Filed

Case: *Williams v. Nuckolls*, 644 S.W.2d 670 (Mo. Ct. App. 1982)

Facts: The plaintiff paid the defendant for an automobile. The bill of sale identified the seller as "Mel Nuckolls Auto Sales" and stated that the sale was "as is." The day after the sale, the plaintiff was involved in an automobile accident when the car's brakes failed. The plaintiff alleged, among other things, that the defendant should have filed a fictitious business name.

Holding: There was no violation of the fictitious business name statement law when the individual, Mel Nuckolls, conducted business under the name "Mel Nuckolls Auto Sales." The inclusion of the sole proprietor's surname in the business name was sufficient such that no fictitious business name needed to be filed.

WEB RESOURCES

Although a few states and jurisdictions have made fictitious business name statements available for searching on the Internet, most have not. Nevertheless, there is a vast array of information available to the small business owner or sole proprietor.

State statutes:	www.law.cornell.edu
Tax forms:	www.irs.gov
Trademark searching:	www.uspto.gov
General information:	www.nass.org
	www.sba.gov
	www.about.com/business ("About" offers numerous business-related resources, including an advice center, descriptions of business enterprises, information on fictitious business name statements, and a glossary of business-related terms.)
	www.nfib.com (The National Federation of Independent Businesses is the largest small-business advocacy group. Its site offers tools, tips, and resources on starting and managing a business and articles on business structures.)
	www.toolkit.cch.com (The "Business Owner's Toolkit" site offers a wealth of information on starting and operating a business.)

Discussion Questions

1. Identify whether the following business names are likely fictitious names such that fictitious business name statements should be filed:

O'Brien Auto Repairs
Pat's Auto Repairs
O'Brien & Sons Auto Repairs
James Sanders: Your Tech Support
Tech Support Services of Richmond
Ellie's Catering Services
Shaw & Associates

2. Janice Woods is a sole proprietor conducting business as an event planner. On many occasions, her husband attends events with her to help transport supplies, run errands, and so forth. Do Janice's husband's activities render the business a partnership? Discuss.

3. Assume the same facts as in Question 2. What if Janice's husband decided to lease new office spaces and placed a security deposit for those premises? Would your answer change? Discuss.

4. Assume the same facts as in Question 2. If Janice's husband causes an automobile accident on his way to one of the events at which he will be helping Janice, which individuals will likely face liability for this accident?

5. Assume the same facts as in Question 2. Janice owes $20,000 to one of her suppliers. Janice has $10,000 in her business accounts. From what sources may the supplier recover the money owed? Is there anything Janice could have done to protect herself? Discuss.

6. A law firm client, William Nichols, has considerable wealth that he has saved over the years. He is now considering forming a sole proprietorship to offer financial consulting services. Discuss the most significant disadvantage to William in operating as a sole proprietorship.

Net Worth

1. Access the SBA Web site. Select "Small Business Planner," then "Start Your Business." Locate information on the disadvantages of operating as a sole proprietorship. Why may a sole proprietorship have a difficult time attracting high-caliber employees?

2. Locate Texas's Business and Commerce Code.
   a. What is the duration of an assumed name certificate in Texas?
   b. What penalty might a defendant incur if a defendant in a civil action failed to file an assumed name certificate?

3. Access the Web site for the Alameda County, California, county clerk and recorder. Locate information about the business "Flowers by Josie." When was the fictitious business name statement filed and when will it expire?

4. Access the Web site for the IRS and locate the individual 1040 tax table. If you are single and earn $48,000, what taxes will you pay?

3

◆ ◆ ◆

General Partnerships

◆ ◆ ◆

CHAPTER OVERVIEW

A partnership is a voluntary agreement between two or more persons to do business together for profit. No particular written document is needed to create a partnership; the agreement may be oral or written. Partnerships range in size from two persons to hundreds of persons. The "persons" in a partnership may be individuals, other partnerships, or even corporations. A partnership is often referred to as a "general partnership" to distinguish it from a "limited partnership." In brief, in general partnerships all partners have rights to manage and control the business and all suffer the disadvantage of unlimited liability. As you will see in Chapter Four, in a limited partnership, some partners (called the limited partners) cannot manage or control the business and their liability is limited to the amount they have invested in the enterprise. General partnerships can be created with very little formality, whereas limited partnerships can be formed only by strict compliance with statutory requirements.

A. Characteristics of General Partnerships

A **general partnership** is a voluntary association of two or more persons who agree to carry on business together for profit. The agreement may be either written or oral, although a written agreement is strongly recommended because it provides certainty in the event of a dispute among partners. General partnerships are easy and inexpensive to form, and there is little state regulation. The partners share decision-making and equally manage the business. In return for their ability to

General Partnership
Voluntary association of two or more persons who agree to carry on a business together for profit

jointly manage the business enterprise and the flexibility in operating the business, partners suffer the disadvantage of **unlimited personal liability**, meaning that their personal assets can be reached by creditors. Because partners are agents of each other and the partnership, one partner can bind the partnership and co-partners by his or her acts, resulting in ruinous personal liability for an act other partners may not have approved or even known about. Partnerships operate with great flexibility, and the partners are generally free to agree to manage the business in almost any way they desire, so long as they do not engage in unlawful acts.

B. Governing Law

Much of the law governing partnerships is located in the **Uniform Partnership Act (UPA)**. This model statute was approved in 1914 by the National Conference of Commissioners on Uniform State Laws (the "Conference"), a group of more than 300 legal scholars, which recommended that each state adopt the Act to govern partnerships so there would be a certain amount of uniformity among the states in their treatment of partnerships.

The UPA acts as a "safety net" for partnerships. Generally, partners can agree to manage and conduct their partnership any way they see fit, so long as they do not engage in some illegal act. Often, however, a dispute may arise between the partners regarding some issue on which the partnership agreement is silent. If partners have not agreed among themselves on how to deal with an issue, the UPA will govern the issue. It therefore acts as a safety net or default statute to provide terms and conditions relating to the partnerships when the partners have failed to reach an understanding.

In 1992, the Conference adopted a **revised Uniform Partnership Act**. Additional changes were incorporated in 1994, 1996, and 1997, and approved by the American Bar Association. The revised act retains most of the basic features of the UPA but does include some significant changes. Although the Conference refers to the revised act as the "Uniform Partnership Act (1997)," for ease of reference, this text refers to the original 1914 act as the UPA and the revised 1997 act as the RUPA. Various states are in the process of adopting the RUPA so that eventually nearly all states will be governed by the RUPA rather than the UPA. At the time of this writing, 36 states and the District of Columbia have adopted the RUPA. The remainder of the states (except for Louisiana) continue to follow the UPA. See Figure 3-1 for designation of which states follow each act. Thus, because the U.S. jurisdictions are divided as to which act is followed, a thorough understanding of the differences between the UPA and RUPA is necessary. Additionally, whereas some states adopt the UPA or RUPA verbatim, other states make changes to the "uniform" acts. Thus, there is a great deal of similarity between the partnership laws in California and Minnesota, both of which have adopted the RUPA, but there can be some differences as well. Louisiana has adopted neither the UPA nor the RUPA. Louisiana partnerships are governed by case law developed in Louisiana and by various statutes relating to partnerships. See Appendix B for selected UPA provisions and Appendix C for selected RUPA provisions. The states that have adopted the UPA and those that have adopted the RUPA, as well as their governing statutes, are also identified in Appendices B and C, respectively.

Unlimited personal liability
Liability for business debt, which extends beyond what is invested in a business to an individual's personal assets

UPA
Uniform Partnership Act, model for partnership legislation in about one-fourth of the states

RUPA
Revised Uniform Partnership Act, model for partnership legislation in about three-fourths of the states

FIGURE 3-1
Table of Jurisdictions Following UPA and RUPA

UPA (1914 Act)	RUPA (1997 Act)
Georgia	Alabama
Indiana	Alaska
Massachusetts	Arizona
Michigan	Arkansas
Missouri	California
New Hampshire	Colorado
New York	Connecticut
North Carolina	Delaware
Pennsylvania	District of Columbia
Rhode Island	Florida
South Carolina	Hawaii
Utah	Idaho
Wisconsin	Illinois
	Iowa
	Kansas
	Kentucky
	Maine
	Maryland
	Minnesota
	Mississippi
	Montana
	Nebraska
	Nevada
	New Jersey
	New Mexico
	North Dakota
	Ohio
	Oklahoma
	Oregon
	South Dakota
	Tennessee
	Texas
	Vermont
	Virginia
	Washington
	West Virginia
	Wyoming

Under the RUPA, a **general partnership** is a distinct entity that operates independently of its member-partners, much like a corporation. Thus the partnership owns property in *its* name, *it* can be a plaintiff or defendant, and *it* is the party that enters into contracts or other obligations. Similarly, there is no need to change

General partnership
A voluntary association of two or more persons to carry on a business for profit

title to property every time a partner leaves the partnership because the property is owned by the partnership entity itself rather than by the individual partners. Under the UPA, a partnership was an entity in some respects but not in others. In general, under the UPA, a partnership is merely an aggregate collection of its members rather than a separate legal entity. Other significant differences between the UPA and RUPA relate to the rules governing breakups of partnerships. Under the UPA, a partnership is dissolved whenever a partner departs, for any reason. The RUPA attempts to provide more stability and continuity to partnerships by providing that only certain departures trigger a dissolution. Most dissociations or departures of partners result merely in a buyout of the withdrawing partner's interest. A chart comparing some of the more significant distinctions between the UPA and RUPA is found in Figure 3-10.

C.   Partnership Defined

According to the UPA and the RUPA a partnership is "an association of two or more persons to carry on as co-owners a business for profit." An examination of each element of this definition is needed to fully understand the nature of a general partnership.

The element of "association" means that the partners have voluntarily agreed to associate or do business together. The agreement may be written, it may be oral, or it may be implied from conduct.

The "two or more persons" element of a partnership excludes sole proprietorships, which are, of course, managed and controlled by one person. The "persons" in the partnership may be individuals, or they may be other business enterprises, such as a partnership (either general or limited) or a corporation.

"Co-ownership" refers to the fact that the partners jointly own partnership property and have rights to participate in management and control of the enterprise and share profits and losses.

The word "business" refers to every trade, occupation, or profession.

By definition, a partnership must be carrying on a business "for profit." Naturally, not all businesses are profitable. Nevertheless, so long as there is the expectation of earning a profit, an enterprise will be deemed a partnership. Nonprofit organizations such as charitable and fraternal groups cannot operate as partnerships.

A partnership can be formed for any purpose so long as it is legal. As seen in Figure 3-2, there are by far more partnerships devoted to finance, insurance, and real estate than any other businesses.

D.   Partnership Property

1.   *Property or Services Contributed by Partners or Acquired by Partnership*

Partners may contribute almost any type of property — cash, real estate, office furniture, a car, a trademark — or services such as legal, accounting, or decorating

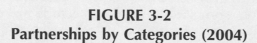

FIGURE 3-2
Partnerships by Categories (2004)

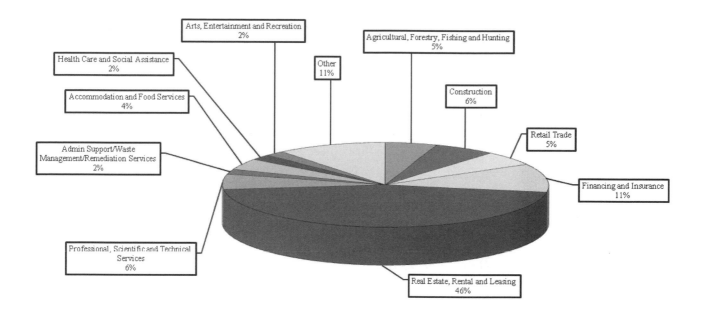

Source: *Statistical Abstract of the United States* 490 (127th ed. 2008)

services, to the partnership. Once contributed, and unless a partner specifies otherwise, the property then becomes the property of the partnership itself. The partner who contributed it cannot change her mind and tell the remaining partners, "Remember that car I provided as my $15,000 contribution? Well, I need it back to give to my husband." The car is no longer owned by that partner; it has become the property of the partnership. If something other than cash is contributed, the value of this contribution should be determined. If the partners cannot agree among themselves as to the value of a contribution, such as land or accounting services, they should retain an expert to value the contribution. If cash is contributed and then used to purchase office supplies and furniture, these items now become property of the partnership as well. The RUPA provides that property acquired by a partnership is partnership property (not property of the individual partners). RUPA § 203.

When it is not clear whether property belongs to the partnership or to some individual partner, a court will look to the parties' intentions. This is another example of why a written partnership agreement clearly setting forth the rights and duties of all partners is important. If a partner intends to retain some right to property contributed, his or her rights should be clearly set forth in the agreement. The money or value of any property contributed by a partner forms the partner's **capital account.** A partner's capital account is increased if a partner makes additional contributions and decreased as distributions are made to the partners.

2. Property Rights of Partners

Partners, as individuals, generally have three property rights: their rights to specific partnership property, their interest in the partnership, and their right to participate in management. UPA § 24.

Specific Partnership Property. Under the UPA, an individual partner has rights in specific partnership property. Thus, a car purchased for the partnership is co-owned by the partners under a theory entitled **tenancy in partnership.** Ownership rights to specific partnership property (cars, inventory, accounts receivable, promissory notes) are very limited: A partner cannot use the specific property for her own benefit without the consent of the other partners; the property cannot be seized by a creditor of the partner; a partner cannot transfer or assign the specific property to another; and upon the death of a partner, the partner's heirs have no rights to such property. Section 203 of the RUPA clarifies the ambiguity in the UPA by eliminating the theory of tenancy in partnership and clearly providing that property acquired by the partnership is owned by the partnership itself, rather than by the individual partners, who therefore cannot assign or transfer that property. This determination avoids the conflict inherent in the UPA which provides in § 24 that a partner has "rights in specific partnership property" and then in § 25 virtually cancels all of the rights one expects to flow from "ownership" (the right to use or transfer property and the right to leave it to one's heirs). Property acquired in the name of an individual partner, without an indication of partnership capacity and without use of partnership funds, is presumed to be owned by the individual partner, even if the property is used by the partnership. RUPA § 204(d). In fact, RUPA § 501 expressly states that an individual partner is not a co-owner of partnership property and thus has no interest in partnership property that can be transferred.

Partnership Profits. A partner has an "interest in the partnership." Simply put, a partner's **interest in the partnership** usually refers to a partner's share of partnership profit (and loss). Under RUPA § 502, the only transferable interest of a partner is that partner's share of the profits and the right to receive distributions from the partnership. Typically, a partnership agreement provides that a partner's share of profits is based on his contribution to the partnership. Thus, if Michael provides 34 percent of the assets or services contributed to the partnership, Michael will usually have the right to 34 percent of the partnership profits, will have to bear 34 percent of the partnership losses, and will have to contribute 34 percent of any additional capital that may be needed. The need to clearly value each partner's original contribution is critical: It typically is "etched in stone" and forms the basis for division of profits and losses.

The right to profit, if any, is a personal property right and a partner may transfer or assign this right to another. For example, if Michael owes spousal

---

Capital account
An account stating the money or value of any property contributed by a partner

Tenancy in partnership
Property co-owned by partners

Interest in partnership
A partner's right to profits

support to his ex-wife, he can have the partnership write a check to his ex-wife each month for his share of the partnership profits rather than writing a check directly to him. Similarly, Michael's share of earned profits can be reached by his individual creditors (such as a landlord or utility company) and will descend to his heirs upon his death. The mere fact that the ex-wife receives Michael's share of the profits does not make her a partner with rights to manage the partnership. A partnership is a voluntary arrangement and the other partners did not agree to do business with Michael's ex-wife, but rather with Michael. In brief, it is of no consequence to the partnership who ultimately receives any partner's share of profits.

Management.   Partners also have the right to participate in management of the partnership. This right to manage and control the affairs of the partnership is typically exercised through voting at partnership meetings. A partner cannot assign or transfer this right to another, even if the partner believes another is more competent to act. Once again, a partnership is a voluntary arrangement; allowing some unknown third party to manage or control the partnership destroys this basic element of the partnership. Unless the partners agree otherwise, each partner has equal rights to manage the partnership. If the partners desire, they can appoint one or more partners to manage the business.

E.   Advantages of General Partnerships

Many of the advantages of doing business as a general partnership are similar to those of doing business as a sole proprietor. A general partnership can be easily formed. Although no written agreement is required (in which case, the UPA or RUPA, as the case may be, will "fill in the gaps"), it is always better to have a written agreement. Hiring an attorney to draft a partnership agreement can be somewhat expensive, but it is still easily accomplished. Often no filings need be made with any state agency, so general partnerships are simple and relatively inexpensive to form.

Another advantage is shared management. A partner will have other partners to rely on to provide expertise in needed areas. Decisions can be made jointly after thorough discussion. Of course, this feature of shared decision-making may also be a disadvantage when a quick decision is needed. Whereas sole proprietors can make all decisions themselves, partners must consult with each other on significant issues. Partnerships, however, have the flexibility of appointing certain partners as managers for the business, and they can be delegated the authority to make certain decisions by themselves.

Other partners can also serve as additional sources for capital. If additional money is needed for the partnership, there is more than one person to help. Other partners may have additional capital to make loans to the partnership or perhaps have strong credit backgrounds and can readily obtain a loan from a bank. The partnership can also consider admitting new partners to provide additional funds for the partnership.

Although partners must share profits with each other, they also share losses, usually in proportion to their contributions or as agreed. Thus, no one partner need bear all of the burden of losses sustained by the partnership.

Finally, as discussed in Section N later in this chapter, partnerships do not pay federal income tax. Income earned is passed through to the individual partners who declare and pay tax on their respective share of partnership profits.

F. Disadvantages of General Partnerships

1. Unlimited Personal Liability

The primary disadvantage of doing business in a general partnership is that each partner has unlimited personal liability for debts and obligations of the partnership. Additionally, because partners, as agents of each other and of the partnership, have the authority to act for and bind each other, one partner may find herself facing unlimited personal liability for an obligation she did not know was incurred by another partner. Thus, personal assets are vulnerable to seizure by partnership creditors, assuming no statutory exemptions exist protecting certain assets.

Not only do partners have unlimited personal liability, but that liability is joint and several for all obligations of the partnership. RUPA § 306. **Joint and several liability** means that a creditor can sue all partners for the wrongful act, can sue the partnership itself for the wrongful act, or may pick and choose among the partners as to which ones may be sued. Thus, a wealthy partner may find he is the sole target in a lawsuit arising because of his partner's misconduct, behavior of which he was not even aware. The theory used by courts to justify this somewhat harsh rule is that outside third parties injured by a partner's misconduct or breach of trust must be protected above all others. If the wealthy partner is "targeted," and he must pay the entire damages sum, he may later seek indemnification or appropriate contribution from his co-partners. In essence, the message is that the innocent third party will be protected first, and it is up to partners to sort out the true allocation of the damages among themselves later on, according to their partnership agreement, the UPA, or the RUPA.

A judgment obtained by a creditor against a partnership is not by itself a judgment against any individual partner. Thus, for the broadest scope of protection, creditors should name both the partnership and all of its members as defendants in any lawsuit. Then the judgment must be satisfied from partnership assets first and thereafter from individual partners' assets on the basis of joint and several liability. In fact, under RUPA § 504, a creditor may obtain an order from a court, called a **charging order**, which directs the partnership to pay to the creditor any distributions that would ordinarily have been paid to the partner until the judgment is fully satisfied.

As in sole proprietorships, partners can attempt to protect themselves against this unlimited personal liability by obtaining insurance or by attempting to secure agreements from third parties so they will not look to a partner's personal assets to satisfy debts. Using a corporation as a general partner will also minimize or eliminate personal liability for this corporate partner because corporations have limited liability. Additional protection is derived from the **marshaling of assets** doctrine (also called the **exhaustion rule**), requiring partnership creditors to first exhaust

Joint and several liability
Principle that each partner and the partnership are liable for all debts and wrongful acts

Charging order
Court order requiring payment of partner's distributions to judgment creditor rather than to partner

Marshaling of assets or exhaustion rule
Partnership theory requiring creditors to first exhaust partnership assets before pursuing partners' individual assets

all partnership assets before they can attack the personal assets of any partner. RUPA § 307(d).

Under 1996 amendments to the UPA, a traditional partnership may choose to operate as a limited liability partnership, the effect of which is to eliminate partners' personal liability for any partnership obligation. Limited liability partnerships are discussed in Chapter Five.

2. Lack of Continuity

Like a sole proprietorship, a partnership under the UPA cannot survive the death or withdrawal of a partner (unless the partners have specified otherwise in their partnership agreement). This lack of continuity is an unattractive feature of a general partnership and provides less stability than does a corporation, which can endure perpetually. If the remaining partners continue doing business together, they have formed a new partnership different from the original partnership inasmuch as its membership is different. The RUPA attempts to reduce the harsh effect of the UPA by providing that partnerships no longer dissolve every time a partner leaves. Sections K and L later in this chapter provide additional discussion of these issues.

3. Difficulty in Transferring Partnership Interest

If a shareholder no longer wishes to own stock in a corporation, the stock can usually be sold freely. A partner, however, may have more difficulty in leaving the partnership or transferring his interest in the partnership to another. As discussed earlier, the only transferable property right a partner has is his share of profits and losses. Because a partnership is a voluntary arrangement, one partner cannot simply sell his partnership interest to another; the other partners have not agreed to do business with the newcomer. Admission of a new partner requires consent from the other partners; when the new partner enters the business, a new partnership is formed.

Withdrawing from a partnership may also be a breach of the partnership agreement. If all partners have signed an agreement stating that the term of the partnership is five years, and one partner withdraws early, she may be liable to the other partners for resulting damages. For example, if the wealthiest partner withdraws, banks may be unwilling to lend money to the partnership inasmuch as there is no longer a wealthy individual to guarantee repayment. Often, partnership agreements make it difficult for partners to withdraw early by providing a term for the existence of the partnership; partners may withdraw earlier than the set term but may be unable to withdraw their contributions to the partnership. Partners are thus faced with the unhappy choice of leaving the partnership, leaving their money behind, and then being unable to control the management of their money because they will no longer be a partner with any right to manage the business. Provisions setting forth a specified term for the partnership or prohibiting a return of contributions to partners who withdraw early are useful for discouraging withdrawal.

G. Formation of General Partnerships

The very definition of a general partnership, namely, that it is an association of two or more persons to operate a business for profit, ensures that there are few formalities involved in creating a general partnership. A partnership can be created by a simple oral agreement to form a catering business or even by a course of conduct in which parties act like partners in that they co-manage the business and share decision-making and profits and losses. There are usually no state filings needed to create a general partnership; the essence of the formation of this entity is the **agreement** to do business together, whether this agreement is memorialized in a document or not.

Nevertheless, certain formalities may apply when creating a general partnership. Similar to a sole proprietorship, the partnership may choose to operate under a fictitious name. The general rule is that if all of the partners' surnames are included in the business name, then it is not fictitious. For example, suppose a partnership of Dave Adams, Susan Baker, Alan Carr, and Geri Dolan is formed. If the partnership operates as Adams, Baker, Carr & Dolan, no fictitious business name filing need be made. If, however, the business operates as Adams & Baker or Adams & Company, then a fictitious business name statement must be filed. The use of signals such as "and Company" or "and Associates" makes the name fictitious in many states, because the signal implies the existence of other partners.

The **fictitious business name statement** is highly similar to, or in some instances, identical to, that required of a sole proprietor. The California fictitious business name statement shown in Figure 2-2 may be used by partnerships as well as sole proprietors. Once again, public policy protects consumers, so they know who is responsible for operating the business and who can be sued for a debt or other obligation. Failure to file the appropriate fictitious business name statement, when required, will result in the same penalties being imposed on a general partnership as are imposed on a sole proprietorship — generally, fines or inability to sue in that jurisdiction until the defect is cured. In no case may a partnership conduct business under a name likely to cause confusion with another business.

Just as with sole proprietorships, if the business is one that is subject to licensing requirements, the partnership must comply with these requirements. Thus, a real estate sales agency, a liquor store, or a general construction business may all have to comply with various statutes relating to the licensing of these businesses. Similarly, if the business will sell goods, it must obtain a sales tax license; and if it will hire employees, it must obtain an employer identification number (see Figure 2-3) and make arrangements to comply with laws relating to Social Security, withholding taxes, and workers' compensation.

In most instances, a partnership can do business in a state other than the one in which it was formed without filing any documents or notices. Thus, a partnership operating in Maryland could expand and offer its services in Virginia and Delaware without any formal requirements (although it must comply with each state's licensing and name requirements). One state, however, New Hampshire, imposes requirements on partnerships that are formed outside New Hampshire and elect to do business therein. New Hampshire requires that the out-of-state partnership (called a **foreign partnership**) qualify to do business within its borders, pay a fee of $50, and appoint an agent who will be available to receive any

Partnership agreement
An agreement by two or more persons to do business together as a partnership; may be written or oral

Fictitious business name statement
Statement filed with public official to indicate names of owners of a business

Foreign partnership
A partnership doing business in a state other than the one in which it was formed

summons and complaint (**service of process**) filed against the partnership. This is clearly a minority approach and could be viewed as a way to raise revenue rather than a scheme of strict state regulation of partnerships.

H. Operation of General Partnerships

1. Duties and Rights of Partners

Fiduciary Duties.   Partners owe each other fiduciary duties. They are required to deal with each other in good faith and to act in good faith for the benefit of the partnership. Partners stand in the same relationship to each other as do principals and agents. Therefore, they cannot engage in any activities that are detrimental to or competitive with the partnership (unless they disclose this conflict and receive consent from the other partners). Although partners can vary or eliminate many UPA or RUPA provisions by their agreement, under RUPA § 103(b), partners cannot eliminate the duties of good faith, loyalty, and fair dealing, or unreasonably reduce the duty of due care each partner owes to the other partners and the partnership. Moreover, the agreement may not unreasonably restrict a partner's right of access to books and records.

Agency.   Each partner is an agent of the partnership for business purposes, and the act of any partner in carrying out the usual business of the partnership will bind the partnership, unless the partner had no authority to so act, and the person with whom the partner was dealing knew or had notice that the partner lacked authority. UPA § 9(1); RUPA § 301(1). This is referred to as **general agency** and, simply put, means that each partner has the authority to sign contracts, execute documents, and make purchases that will bind the partnership. For example, assume Patricia, Allen, and Doug are in a partnership engaged in selling auto supplies and performing automotive services. If Patricia routinely buys supplies for the business at Cars R Us but one day, using a company credit card, buys a CD player, car phone, and spoiler for her own use, the partnership is likely liable to Cars R Us for these purchases. The owners of Cars R Us had no knowledge that Patricia was not acting on behalf of the partnership. In fact, it appeared as if Patricia was acting for the partnership. The partnership must now pay for this debt. Because Patricia has violated her fiduciary duties to the partnership, her partners can then sue her for this breach and recover the money the partnership had to pay on her account. A court, however, will always protect the most innocent party. In this transaction, the most innocent party, Cars R Us, had no way of knowing that the goods sold were for Patricia's personal use rather than for the partnership business. Because Patricia is an agent for the partnership, her acts have bound the partnership. It is obviously important to know fully and trust one's partners because these partners have the authority, under agency principles, to bind the partnership and its partners, whether those partners receive any specific benefit from the transaction or whether they even know about the transaction.

If a partnership is aware that one of its partners is acting irrationally by purchasing unneeded items for the partnership, the partnership should send written notices to as many of its suppliers and creditors as possible, stating that the partner no longer has the authority to bind the partnership and that those creditors who sell items or provide credit to the partnership do so at their own risk and will have to look solely to that partner, rather than the partnership, for payment. In many instances, banks will not loan money to a partner for the partnership business without first reviewing the partnership agreement to ensure that such an act is authorized by the agreement.

Due to the risk inherent in the partnership principle that partners are agents of the partnership and thus their acts bind the partnership (assuming the partner's act is apparently taken for the purpose of carrying out the ordinary business of the partnership), RUPA § 303 allows partnerships to file an optional **Statement of Authority** with state officials to provide public notice of the specific partners who are authorized to execute instruments transferring real estate. For a statement to be effective for real estate transfers, a certified copy of the statement issued must be recorded in the office for recording transfers of real property. The statement may also grant or limit partners' authority to enter into other transactions (see an example in Figure 3-3). Filing the statement thus provides a partnership an opportunity to limit liability that might arise from certain unauthorized acts of its partners. Similarly, the statement assures third parties who deal with partners that those partners have authority to act.

Another new document, allowed by RUPA § 304, is the **Statement of Denial**, typically filed by a partner to deny information given in the Statement of Authority, often filed by a withdrawing partner to provide notice that the partner denies his status as a partner (see Figure 3-4).

Information in the Statement of Authority and Statement of Denial is imputed or charged to members of the public because it is a public record available to all.

2. *Management of the Partnership*

Unless the partners decide otherwise, all partners have equal rights in the management of the partnership business. UPA § 18(e); RUPA § 401(f). Thus, regardless of initial capital contributions, if the partners have not agreed on a formula for voting, each partner has one vote in management matters. Assume that a partnership is composed of Ellen and James. Ellen contributed $60,000 to the partnership and James contributed $40,000. Ellen is likely to assume that because she has contributed more than James her voting and management rights should be greater. This is not the case. Unless Ellen and James agree on how management is to be conducted, the UPA and RUPA supply this missing term and mandate that Ellen and James have equal rights to manage and conduct the partnership's business.

Unless the partners agree otherwise, decision-making in the partnership is by majority vote. Certain extraordinary matters that dramatically affect the partnership usually require unanimous approval. According to UPA § 9, unanimous consent of partners is needed for the following extraordinary activities:

- Assigning the partnership property in trust for creditors
- Disposing of the goodwill of the business
- Performing any act that would make it impossible to carry on the ordinary business of the partnership

Statement of Authority
Document filed with secretary of state providing notice of partners who are authorized to act for partnership

Statement of Denial
Document filed with secretary of state denying information in Statement of Authority or providing notice of withdrawal from partnership

FIGURE 3-3
Tennessee Statement of Partnership Authority

State of Tennessee

Department of State
Corporate Filings
312 Eighth Avenue North
6th Floor, William R. Snodgrass Tower
Nashville, TN 37243

GENERAL PARTNERSHIP
(Statement of Partnership Authority)

For Office Use Only

1. The name of the general partnership (as recorded with the Secretary of State) is:
    _____

2. The *street* address of its chief executive office is:
    _____

3. The *street* address of one of its offices in Tennessee (if any) is:
    _____

4. The names of the partners authorized to execute an instrument transferring real property held in the name of the partnership are:

    _____   _____
    _____   _____
    _____   _____
    _____   _____

5. If applicable, state the authority, or limitations of authority, of some or all partners to enter into other transactions on behalf of the partnership (attach separate sheet if necessary):
    _____
    _____
    _____

The execution of this statement constitutes an affirmation under the penalties of perjury that the undersigned has/have the authority to file this statement and that the contents of the statement are accurate.

Signed and dated this _____ day of _____, _____

_____   _____
Signature   **Printed Name**

_____   _____
Signature   **Printed Name**

Notes:
*   A document filed by a partnership must be executed by at least two partners. Other documents must be executed by a partner or other person authorized by the Revised Uniform Partnership Act.
*   This statement is cancelled by operation of law five years after the date on which the statement, or the most recent amendment, is filed with the Secretary of State.

SS-4514   *Filing Fee: $20*   RDA pending

FIGURE 3-4
Tennessee Statement of Denial

State of Tennessee

Department of State
Corporate Filings
312 Eighth Avenue North
6th Floor, William R. Snodgrass Tower
Nashville, TN 37243

GENERAL PARTNERSHIP
(Statement of Denial)

For Office Use Only

1. The name of the general partnership (as recorded with the Secretary of State) is:
_____

2. The name of the person filing the denial is:
_____

3. State the fact(s) being denied:
_____
_____
_____
_____
_____
_____
_____
_____
_____

The execution of this statement constitutes an affirmation under the penalties of perjury that the undersigned has/have the authority to file this statement and that the contents of the statement are accurate.

Signed and dated this _____ day of _____, _____

_____   _____
Signature   **Printed Name**

_____   _____
Signature   **Printed Name**

Note:
A document filed by a partnership must be executed by at least two partners. Other documents must be executed by a partner or other person authorized by the Revised Uniform Partnership Act.

SS-4515　　　　　　　　　*Filing Fee: $20*　　　　　　　　RDA pending

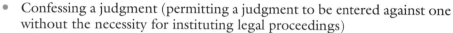
- Confessing a judgment (permitting a judgment to be entered against one without the necessity for instituting legal proceedings)
- Submitting a partnership claim or liability to arbitration

Whereas the UPA includes the foregoing detailed list of extraordinary activities that require unanimous approval of partners, the RUPA includes no equivalent provision, leaving it to the courts to determine which actions are beyond the authority of individual partners. Because, however, the acts identified by the UPA (such as assigning partnership property or submitting a claim to arbitration) are arguably not in the apparent scope of partnership business anyway, such a list may not be necessary, and its omission from the RUPA is thus understandable. Accordingly, the RUPA position is that any act not in the ordinary course of the partnership's business must be authorized by all partners, unless the partners have agreed otherwise. RUPA § 301(2).

In a partnership with a large number of partners, it may be impractical for all partners to manage the business equally. Therefore, some partnerships will appoint a managing partner or a committee of partners for the management of some activities. For example, there may be a compensation committee, a hiring committee, and a marketing committee. These committees may study various proposals and then make reports to the entire membership, which will then vote on these matters. Alternatively, the committees may have some limited authority to act on their own; for example, the hiring committee may be able to hire anyone whose salary will be less than $40,000. Individuals who will be hired at salaries in excess of $40,000 may then need to be approved by a majority vote of all partners.

3. Compensation, Profits, and Accounting

Ordinarily, general partners do not receive a salary for their services to the partnership. It is assumed that they will devote their undivided loyalty to the partnership business and therefore they will be paid from the profits of the business. Both the UPA and RUPA expressly provide that no partner is automatically entitled to remuneration for acting in the partnership business. UPA § 18(f); RUPA § 401(h). Partners often provide otherwise in their partnership agreement so they will be able to anticipate their monthly income. Often, partners will receive a monthly **draw** against the anticipated profits of the partnership, and at the end of the year, the draw is deducted from that partner's percentage of profits. Some partnerships, however, adhere strictly to the rule that partners are paid only from profits. In those partnerships, during a lean time, partners may have to borrow from a bank to pay their personal expenses such as mortgage or rent payments, insurance, and food. When the partnership receives funds, it may then distribute a large profit to its members, who then repay the bank for their short-term loans, retaining the remainder until the next division of profits occurs. A partner having special responsibilities, such as a managing partner, may be paid a stated salary as a partnership expense, one not deducted from her share of the profits.

Draw
An advance payment, usually made against anticipated profits

Because partners do not ordinarily receive compensation merely for performing services for the partnership, they typically expect to receive profits arising from the partnership's business operations. According to UPA § 18(a) and RUPA § 401(b), unless the partners agree otherwise, each partner is entitled to an equal share of the partnership profits (and is chargeable with a share of losses in the same proportion as profits), regardless of capital contributions to the partnership. To avoid these default provisions of the UPA and RUPA, most partnership agreements provide for the sharing of profits and losses in proportion to the amount contributed to the partnership by each partner. Nevertheless, partners are free to devise any arrangement they desire regarding the sharing of profits and losses, and there is no statutory requirement that the division of profits and losses bear some relationship to the contributions made by the partners. For example, one partner may contribute no cash to the partnership but may agree to provide accounting services for the business. The other partners may agree to pay this partner 20 percent of the partnership profits and charge no losses to this partner's account.

Partners who incur or pay for expenses related to the partnership from their own money are entitled to be reimbursed by the partnership. UPA § 18(b); RUPA § 401(c). Thus, if needed inventory is delivered to the business and the partnership accounts are too low to pay for it, a partner advancing this money from her personal checking account is entitled to be reimbursed by the partnership, whether this action has been agreed on or not. Otherwise, partners would be discouraged from taking actions to aid the partnership. Both the UPA and the RUPA treat these advances as loans on which the partnership must pay interest.

To determine whether the distribution of profits is correct, all partners have the right to inspect and copy the partnership's books of account, which must be kept at the principal place of business of the partnership. Partners also have a duty to supply information on matters affecting the partnership to their co-partners. UPA §§ 19, 20; RUPA § 403. In fact, because partners have fiduciary relationships to one another, any knowledge one partner has regarding partnership matters is imputed to all other partners. Finally, under UPA § 22, a partner can demand a formal accounting if he is wrongfully excluded from the partnership affairs or whenever circumstances render such an accounting reasonable and just.

I. The Partnership Agreement

Although partnerships can be formed by oral agreement or even by a course of conduct, it is better practice to have a formal written partnership agreement that fully sets forth the partners' rights, duties, and liabilities. Failure to have a definitive agreement can cause many unanticipated consequences. For example, in our earlier scenario, Ellen and James formed a partnership, with Ellen contributing 60 percent of the capital and James contributing 40 percent of the capital. Because Ellen has contributed more than James she will likely expect to have more power than James in voting issues and to receive a greater portion of the profits. Without an agreement, however, UPA § 18 and RUPA § 401 supply these missing terms and provide that Ellen and James will be equal partners with regard to management, control, and sharing of profits and losses. Thus, if the partnership has net profits of $100,000, Ellen and James will share the profits equally ($50,000 each) without regard to their initial contributions.

Moreover, a partnership agreement will provide guidance in the event of a dispute among partners. If the partnership agreement is oral, it may be difficult to prove what the partners' agreement was with regard to various issues. Finally, investors and bankers prefer the clarity provided by a partnership agreement.

The partnership agreement, sometimes called the articles of partnership, can provide any terms with regard to operation, management, and control of the partnership so long as the terms are not illegal or contrary to statute or public policy. Thus, the parties are free to distribute profits and losses as they like, allowing one partner a greater share of profits because he provides the partnership with expertise and then indemnifying that partner against partnership debts or obligations. To the extent that the partnership agreement does not cover certain matters, the UPA or the RUPA, as the case may be, will govern. The partnership agreement is a contract among the partners and will be enforceable under principles of contract law.

A partnership agreement should be carefully drafted to accomplish the purposes and goals of its partners. Generally, however, a partnership agreement should include provisions relating to the following issues (see Appendix D for a sample partnership agreement).

1. Name of the Partnership

The partnership can operate under the names of its partners or under a fictitious business name, so long as the appropriate filing is made. If all of the partners' last names are included in the name of the partnership, it is likely that the name is not fictitious. In any event, the partnership cannot operate under a name that is likely to cause confusion with another.

2. Names and Addresses of the Partners

The names and addresses of all partners should be set forth. Addresses are provided so that various notices and information can be communicated to the partners.

3. Recitals

A **recital** clause simply states that it is the intent of the parties to the agreement to form a partnership. In the event of any dispute later, a partner will be precluded from alleging that the business arrangement was something other than a partnership.

Recitals
Introductory clauses in agreements setting forth basis for agreement

4. Purpose

The purpose of the partnership should be stated. Be sure that the purpose is not so limited that it restricts the partnership from related activities or discourages growth of the business. It may be a good idea to state a somewhat specific purpose and then broaden it as follows: "The purpose of this partnership is to engage in the purchase and sale of real estate and any other acts incidental thereto or necessary therefor or as may be agreed upon by the partners." Some experts caution against an overly broad purpose clause because it might be viewed as granting partners nearly unlimited power to act on behalf of the partnership.

5. *Address*

The principal place of business of the partnership should be provided so that partners and others can provide communications and notices to the partnership.

6. *Term*

The term or duration of the partnership should be provided. There are several alternatives that the partners can elect.

a. The partners may specify that the partnership shall have a definite term by stating, for instance, "This partnership shall come into existence on May 24, 2006, and shall terminate on December 31, 2009."

b. Because a partnership is a voluntary arrangement, the partners can agree that it will terminate upon their mutual agreement.

c. The partners can state that the partnership will terminate once its purposes have been accomplished; for example, the construction of a certain housing development.

d. The partnership may be terminable at will upon notice by any partner. If such a provision is elected, the partners should consider whether they may wish to continue doing business upon the withdrawal of one member and whether the withdrawing member is entitled to receive a return of his contribution and any profits before the partnership's stated term expires.

Partnership for a term
A partnership with a definite term of duration

Partnership at will
A partnership with no specific term of duration

A partnership that has a specific term or duration is called a **partnership for a term.** A partnership that has no specific duration is called a **partnership at will.**

Under the UPA, partners who continue doing business after the withdrawal of a member will have formed a new partnership, and this new partnership is usually viewed as operating under or having adopted the prior written terms of the agreement.

7. *Financial Provisions*

Various provisions relating to financial items should be set forth, including the following:

a. The initial contributions of the partners and the date for contribution should be specified. If partners contribute money, the exact amount contributed should be set forth. Often, contributions by partners are identified in a separate exhibit or attachment to the partnership agreement. If legal, accounting, management, decorating, or other services are provided, or if property such as real estate is contributed, they should be valued so each partner's initial contribution is clearly set forth.

b. The agreement should indicate under what circumstances additional capital might need to be contributed. For example, if the business sustains a loss or needs additional money to operate, the agreement should state the amount of each partner's expected additional contribution.

I

Typically, calculation of additional contributions is determined by the initial contributions made by each partner. Thus, if Anna contributed 34 percent of the initial capital, Bob contributed 22 percent of the initial capital, and David contributed 44 percent of the initial capital, additional contributions will be made in the same proportion, so that if $100,000 in additional capital is needed, Anna must contribute $34,000, Bob must contribute $22,000, and David must contribute $44,000. If a partner cannot make the required additional contribution, another partner may make it and thereby increase his or her ownership interest in the partnership.

The partners may make alternative arrangements. For example, if one partner is contributing expertise and business acumen to the partnership and is assuming all responsibilities of managing the partnership, he or she may be excused from additional contributions.

This section of the agreement should also specify whether partners may make loans or advances to the partnership, what interest will be paid on such loans, and how they are to be repaid. Under both UPA § 18(c) and RUPA § 401(e), payments or advances made by partners to aid the partnership are viewed as loans to the partnership that automatically carry interest.

The partners may wish to retain some profit in a bank account so that in the event of an emergency (for example, replacement of the roof of the apartment building owned by the partnership) additional contributions are not required.

If the partners wish to withdraw their capital prior to the termination of the partnership, the terms and conditions of such withdrawal should be expressly provided. Many agreements provide that no withdrawal of capital from the partnership is allowed prior to dissolution of the partnership.

8. Profits and Losses

The agreement should clearly specify each partner's share of profits and the losses to be borne by each partner. There are several alternatives:

a. Profits and losses may be shared equally by the partners.
b. Profits are shared and losses may be borne in proportion to the contributions (and any later advances) to the partnerships. Thus, using our example, Anna would be entitled to 34 percent of any profits, Bob would be entitled to 22 percent of any profits, and David would be entitled to 44 percent of any profits. This is the most common scheme.
c. Certain profits may be guaranteed for a partner and he or she may bear no losses or may bear losses in an amount less than the initial contribution. For example, assume Anna is a real estate expert who spent quite a bit of time selecting the apartment building to be purchased by the partnership and manages the partnership business. If she contributed 22 percent of the initial contribution, she may receive 22 percent of the profits and bear only 10 percent of the losses. Bob and David, the remaining partners, will have to make up the difference and bear losses disproportionate to their profits or contributions.
d. The agreement may specify that losses caused by reckless conduct or fraud be borne by the partner committing such acts. Such a provision is common.

   e.   If salaries are to be paid, they should be set forth in this section.

   f.   The agreement may provide that partners will be indemnified by the partnership for obligations and expenses incurred in the ordinary course of partnership business.

9. Management and Control

This section should specify the management policies for the partnership business. If desired, designations of managing partners or committees should be made and each partner's voting power should be set forth. If the partners desire that certain activities, such as selling partnership assets, settling litigation claims, and borrowing, should be subject to a greater than majority vote (for instance, two-thirds voting approval or unanimous approval), the specifications should be set forth.

The partnership may elect to meet at regular intervals to discuss partnership business. The time and place for any such meeting, whether weekly, monthly, or quarterly, should be set forth in the agreement.

There are several alternatives for the management and control of a partnership.

   a.   One partner can be appointed the managing partner with the right to make all decisions in the ordinary course of the partnership business. This partner's rights and duties as well as any limitations on his authority should be clearly specified so that it is clear what activities the managing partner may undertake. For example, the managing partner may be given the authority to run the day-to-day business operations of the partnership but may be precluded from incurring debt or admitting new partners without the other partners' consent.

   b.   There may be various committees established for certain functions. For example, there may be a compensation committee, a recruiting committee, and a business development committee, each with certain specified powers and rights.

   c.   The partners may agree to manage the partnership equally, with each partner having an equal vote.

   d.   The partnership may be managed by all partners who vote in accord with their initial contributions. In our example, Anna would have 34 percent of the votes to cast on any issue, Bob would have 22 percent, and David would have 44 percent. This is the most common approach in smaller partnerships.

   e.   Decisions can be made by majority vote or a greater than majority vote. Certain matters, such as the expulsion of a partner, may require unanimous approval.

10. Admission of New Partners and Withdrawal of Partners

A partnership is a voluntary association and, therefore, there can be no admission of new partners unless all partners agree, or the partners provide otherwise. The partnership agreement may state that the admission of a new member is subject to unanimous approval or subject to the approval of partners holding a certain percentage of the partnership interest. If new members are to be admitted, provisions should be made for their contributions to the partnership. This usually requires reallocating the interests of the existing partners so the new partner has an ownership interest in the partnership.

All matters pertaining to the withdrawal of a partner should be specified. The partners may provide that a withdrawing partner must first offer to sell his or her interest to the partnership or to the remaining partners before offering to sell to an "outsider." Partners who wish to retire or withdraw should provide advance written notice to the partnership. The agreement may specify that a withdrawing partner shall not be repaid his or her contribution until the partnership dissolves or terminates.

If partners may be expelled, the reasons for and methods of expulsion should be clearly provided. For example, a partner may be expelled for willful misconduct detrimental to the partnership, upon conviction of a felony, or for breaching any material duties required by the terms of the partnership agreement.

11. Dissolution

This section of the agreement should not only specify what particular actions may cause a dissolution of the partnership but should also describe the actual process of dissolving the partnership and winding up its affairs.

The partners should identify any acts that may cause a dissolution of the partnership, such as unanimous agreement, completion of the business for which it was formed, or expiration of its term. Similarly, the partners should consider whether the death, disability, retirement, or bankruptcy of a partner will cause a dissolution. Unless the partners agree that the partnership may continue, the death or bankruptcy of a partner will cause a dissolution of the partnership. UPA §§ 31(4), (5). As will be discussed in Section L later in this chapter, the RUPA position is quite different; partnerships no longer dissolve every time a partner leaves. In most cases, a partner's departure merely triggers a buyout of his or her interest. Under the UPA, a partner may petition a court to declare a dissolution when a partner is incapable of performing duties under the partnership or when a partner's conduct prejudicially affects the carrying on of the business. UPA § 32(1)(b), (c).

The partners may wish to designate one partner, or perhaps a committee of partners, who will liquidate or "wind up" the affairs of the partnership. These partners will complete outstanding contracts, collect and dispose of partnership assets, pay creditors, and then distribute the remaining sums to the partners. Third-party creditors must always be fully paid before the partnership can distribute any money to members of the partnership. The UPA sets forth a distribution scheme as follows: Outside creditors must be paid first; partners are repaid money owed to them for advances, loans, or anything other than a return of their capital or any profit; partners then receive a return of their capital; and, finally, partners receive profits. UPA § 40(b). RUPA § 807 also requires that partnership assets must first be applied to discharge any liabilities to creditors (although the RUPA places obligations to partners on an equal footing with outside creditor claims). Thereafter, remaining sums may be distributed to partners. Thus, under both the UPA and RUPA, claims of creditors, including claims for taxes and wages, must always be fully satisfied before any money or assets can be distributed to partners.

12. Miscellaneous Provisions

There are many other provisions that may be included in a partnership agreement. The partners may wish to provide that any withdrawing partner cannot engage in any activity competitive with the partnership business. Known as **non-compete clauses**, these provisions ensure that a withdrawing partner will not take customer lists and knowledge acquired within the partnership and use it for his benefit to the detriment of former partners. Many states specifically regulate the terms of such non-compete clauses because they impose restrictions on a person's ability to earn a living. California forbids their use entirely unless they are bargained for in connection with the sale of a business. Generally, the clause must be reasonable in length of time, scope, and geographic area. Thus, it would be unreasonable to forbid a withdrawing partner to carry on a similar business anywhere in the United States for ten years. (See Chapter Eighteen for additional information on non-compete clauses.)

The agreement also should include provisions for resolving disputes among partners. The partners may elect to resolve disputes by binding arbitration. They may also provide that the prevailing party in any litigation or dispute is entitled to be paid attorney's fees and costs by the losing party. This provision may serve as a disincentive to those partners who might be tempted to litigate minor issues.

Various provisions should be included regarding partnership books and accounting. The agreement may provide that any partner has a right to an accounting upon reasonable advance notice, that reports of the partnership's affairs shall be distributed quarterly, that the partnership books and records are available to any partner for inspection upon reasonable advance notice, that the banking of the partnership shall be done at a specific institution, and that appropriate insurance for the partnership will be obtained. The agreement may specify the manner in which partners are to be reimbursed for incurring expenses, such as travel expenses, on behalf of the partnership. Partners may agree to reimburse or indemnify the partnership and other partners for negligent acts they commit. A tax year for the partnership may be selected.

A **tax year** is an annual accounting period for keeping records and reporting income and expenses. A tax year can be a calendar year (from January 1 through December 31) or a fiscal year (any 12-consecutive month period). A tax year is adopted when the partnership files its first income tax return. Generally, IRS approval is needed to change a tax year.

The partnership should establish the method by which its accounting will be done. Under the **cash method of accounting**, expenses and income are listed in record and ledger books only when paid or received. Most individuals and small businesses use the cash method of accounting. Under the **accrual method of accounting**, income is recorded or "booked" as received at the time it is earned or the customer is billed (which may be several weeks or months before actual receipt), and expenses are recorded or "booked" at the time they are incurred rather than when they are actually paid. The agreement should provide that the partnership will follow generally accepted accounting principles (called **GAAP**).

A variety of other "standard" provisions may be included, such as the following: how notice of any partnership meeting or matter is to be given; that the agreement will be construed under the laws of a certain state; that no

Non-compete clauses
Clauses in agreement restricting signatory from competing with another during and after parties' relationship terminates

Tax year
Annual accounting period for keeping records and reporting income and expenses

Cash method of accounting
Listing expenses and income in business records only when they are paid or received

Accrual method of accounting
Listing expenses and income in business records when they are incurred or billed rather than when they are actually paid or received

GAAP
Generally accepted accounting principles

modifications can be made to the agreement unless in writing and consented to by all partners; that the use of masculine pronouns includes the feminine, and the use of the singular includes the plural; and that if any portion of the agreement is invalid, that provision is severable from the remaining portions of the agreement so that they remain in effect.

13. Signatures and Date

The agreement should be signed and dated by all partners. If a partner is a corporation, it should be signed by the appropriate corporate officer. If a partner is another partnership, it should be signed by the managing partner.

PRACTICE TIP

Make a point of reviewing partnership agreements and collecting sample agreements and sample clauses from agreements you find in your office, in form books, from colleagues, and on the Internet. Make your own form files. Become the "go to" person in your office for partnership agreements. Always be on the lookout for new clauses and provisions, and continually improve the agreements you draft by including these new, improved provisions.

J. Transferability of Partnership Interest

As discussed earlier, partners have various property rights in the partnership. Although they may assign their profits in the partnership to another, they may not, without the consent of the other partners, substitute another partner for themselves. Because a partnership is a voluntary association, one cannot be forced to be a partner with another. In fact, RUPA § 502 expressly states that the only transferable interest of a partner is his or her share of the profits and losses of the partnership. RUPA § 503(d) expressly provides that upon transfer, the transferor retains all rights and duties of a partner (such as the right to participate in management and personal liability for partnership obligations) other than the right to receive the distributions transferred to the transferee. The transferor partner retains partnership rights and duties until he or she is dissociated or withdraws. The transferee does not become a partner of the partnership and thus has no right to inspect books or records or to manage the business. This interest in profits may be attached by a judgment creditor of the partner and thus, for example, may be seized to satisfy a partner's obligations to pay child support or other obligations.

Under the UPA, if there is no definite term of the partnership agreement, the withdrawal by one partner causes a dissolution. UPA § 31(1)(b). Because most partnerships will not wish to dissolve due to the withdrawal of one partner, the agreement should provide a procedure for the withdrawal of partners and the admission of new partners. The agreement can provide that a partner may withdraw upon 30 days' notice and the remaining partners may continue to do business without that partner. The agreement should specify whether and how the withdrawing partner will be paid the value of her interest. The agreement can provide that upon the withdrawal of any partner, she must sell to the partnership her interest in the partnership. The agreement can establish a method to value the partner's interest and a method of payment (for example, installment payments) if there is not enough cash to pay off the withdrawing partner. If the withdrawing partner has breached the partnership agreement (for instance, by withdrawing before the term specified for the partnership), she may be liable for damages caused by this breach. Once the partner leaves, she will not be liable for debts incurred thereafter, although the partner will continue to be liable for debts incurred while she was a partner.

New partners can be admitted upon the consent of all existing partners (or upon less than unanimous consent, if provided by the partnership agreement). They should sign the existing partnership agreement and thereby become bound to its terms. The incoming partner will not be held personally liable for debts or obligations arising before his admission to the partnership; this liability can be satisfied only out of partnership property. The new partner will have personal liability only for debts or obligations incurred after admission. UPA § 17; RUPA § 306(b).

K. Dissolution and Winding Up Under the UPA

Dissolution and **winding up** are not synonymous terms. The UPA specifically provides that dissolution is the change in the relation of the partners caused by any partner's ceasing to be associated in the carrying on of the business. UPA § 29. Thus, under the UPA, whenever a partner leaves the partnership for any reason, the partnership is dissolved. Upon dissolution, partnership relationships end so the fiduciary relationships among partners are terminated. The partnership will continue its existence until its business affairs have been "wound up" by satisfying all obligations and collecting all assets. If the partnership continues its business rather than winding up, it is technically a new partnership.

Dissolution can occur by acts of the partners or by decree of court.

1. Dissolution by Acts of Partners

Under the UPA, dissolution is caused by the following events:

a. By completion of the partnership's term of existence or its purpose;
b. By the will of any partner when no definite term or purpose is specified;
c. By mutual agreement of all of the partners;
d. By the expulsion of a partner according to the terms of the partnership agreement;
e. By the express will of any partner, even if this is in violation of the terms of the partnership agreement;
f. By any event which makes it unlawful for the business of the partnership to be continued, for example, a change in a zoning law that would

---

Dissolution
Change in the relation of partners caused when a partner leaves the business; generally, a termination of a partnership

Winding up
Wrapping up business affairs, terminating business, satisfying obligations, selling assets, and collecting debts

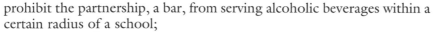

prohibit the partnership, a bar, from serving alcoholic beverages within a certain radius of a school;
g. By the death of any partner;
h. By the bankruptcy of any partner; or
i. By the decree of a court. (UPA § 31).

If the partnership agreement contains terms, however, allowing the partnership to continue doing business after the death, withdrawal, expulsion, or bankruptcy of a partner, the partnership can continue and need not wind up. The partnership that continues is new in the eyes of the law because it does not comprise the same individuals who made up the original membership of the partnership. It is now a partnership at will and can be dissolved upon the withdrawal of any partner. If the partners continue to act according to the terms and conditions of the partnership agreement, they may be viewed as having adopted or ratified its terms by their conduct.

To ensure that the partnership will not have to do business with a deceased partner's estate, the partnership agreement can provide that upon the death of a partner, that partner's interest in the partnership must be sold to the partnership. To fund such a provision, the partnership may purchase life insurance policies, sometimes called **key person policies**, for each partner, naming the partnership as beneficiary. Then upon the death of a partner, the partnership will have sufficient funds to pay to the deceased partner's estate to buy out the decedent's interest in the partnership. (See Chapter Eighteen.)

Key person policies
Insurance policies on the life of key individuals in a business

2. *Dissolution by Decree of Court*

Upon application by a partner, a court may decree a dissolution if any of the following occurs:

a. A partner is shown to be of unsound mind;
b. A partner becomes incapable of performing his or her partnership obligations;
c. A partner has committed an act that prejudicially affects the carrying on of the business;
d. A partner's conduct is such that it is not reasonably practicable to continue doing business with him or her;
e. The partnership business can be carried on only at a loss; or
f. Other circumstances render a dissolution equitable. UPA § 32.

3. *Winding Up*

Winding up is the process of terminating all partnership business, satisfying all obligations, selling assets, collecting debts, and distributing any remaining assets to the business owners. After the assets are collected they must be distributed as specified by UPA § 40, which provides that third-party creditors are to be repaid first, partners are then reimbursed for loans or advances to the partnership, partners are returned their capital, and only then do partners receive profits.

The distribution of profits after winding up is generally in accord with the percentage of initial capital contribution. In our example, Anna would expect to receive 34 percent of all assets remaining after creditors were paid, Bob would expect to receive 22 percent, and David would expect to receive 44 percent. The partners, by agreement, however, may provide otherwise.

If the partnership is unable to satisfy its third-party creditors, the partners must make the appropriate personal contributions to pay these debts.

L.　Dissociation and Dissolution Under the RUPA

The RUPA seeks to avoid the harsh UPA approach that any withdrawal from a partnership for any reason automatically triggers a dissolution by creating a new concept of **dissociation**, thus allowing the partnership to continue although a partner may have departed. The RUPA's position that a partnership is an entity in and of itself justifies the partnership continuing, although a partner has withdrawn from the entity.

Dissociation
A withdrawal of a partner from a partnership; does not necessarily cause a dissolution or termination of partnership

A dissociation is a withdrawal of a partner from a partnership. Under the RUPA, the dissociation of a partner does not necessarily cause a dissolution or termination of the partnership. According to RUPA § 601, a dissociation occurs whenever a partnership receives notice of a partner's express will to leave the partnership, when a partnership agreement provides for events that cause dissociation, upon a partner's expulsion, upon court decree (usually initiated by the partnership because a partner's conduct threatens the partnership business), or upon a partner's death or bankruptcy. Upon a partner's dissociation, the partner's right to participate in the management of the business terminates, as does the duty of loyalty (unless the partner is participating in winding up the partnership's business).

Under the RUPA, partners have the absolute power to dissociate from a partnership at any time, even if the dissociation breaches a provision in the partnership agreement or even if the partner wishes to depart before the term of a partnership expires. Such events are referred to as **wrongful dissociations.** The significance of wrongful dissociation is that it gives rise to damages caused to the partnership by the dissociation.

Wrongful dissociation
A dissociation caused by a breach of partnership agreement

The consequences of dissociation vary and depend largely on whether the partnership is an at-will partnership (one formed for no definite term or undertaking) or whether it is one with a definite term or undertaking. Recall that under the UPA, the withdrawal of a partner for any reason always results in dissolution (usually leading to winding up of the partnership business). To prevent such a technical dissolution, the RUPA provides that only the following departures trigger a dissolution and winding up:

- In a partnership at will, when a partnership receives notice of a partner's will to depart or dissociate (although if none of the partners wants the partnership wound up, and if all partners consent, the partnership may continue); and

- In a partnership for a definite term or undertaking, and within 90 days after a wrongful dissociation occurs or when a dissociation occurs due to judicial expulsion, death, or bankruptcy, and at least half the remaining partners express their will to dissolve and to wind up the partnership business. For example, if a term partnership has eight partners and one dies, the partnership will be dissolved only if four of the remaining partners affirmatively vote in favor of dissolution within 90 days after the death.

Thus, in sum, generally a dissociation from a term partnership does not affect the existence of the partnership, because it continues *unless* a majority affirmatively takes action to dissolve or disband.

In all other instances of dissociation (for example, dissociation due to the bankruptcy of a partner in an at-will partnership), no dissolution is caused, and the effect of the dissociation is only that the departing partner is bought out. RUPA § 701 provides that the partnership must buy out the ownership interest of the dissociated partner, although a partner who wrongfully dissociates by voluntarily departing from a partnership before its term expires (assuming the partnership has decided to continue) is generally not entitled to payment of the buyout price until the partnership term expires. The RUPA provides a method and process for calculating the buyout price. The partnership will then pay the buyout price to the dissociated member, and the partnership itself continues and is not dissolved merely because a member departed. Thus, the RUPA ameliorates the harsh effects of the UPA by allowing partnerships to survive the dissociation of their members in many instances.

In the case of dissociation, a continuing partnership remains bound for two years for the dissociating partner's acts before dissociation if the other party did not have notice of the partner's dissociation or reasonably believed the dissociated partner was still a partner. The dissociating partner has the same liability. The partnership or the dissociating partner may, however, file a voluntary **Statement of Dissociation** with its state agency, identifying the partner who dissociated. Third parties will be bound by this notice 90 days after it is filed, thereby reducing the two-year period of potential liability for the dissociating partner's acts to 90 days (see Figure 3-5).

If the partnership does dissolve and its business must be wound up, creditors must be paid prior to partners. Although the UPA requires third-party creditors' claims to be paid in full prior to claims of partners and requires partners to be repaid their contributions before they receive profits, the RUPA draws no such distinctions and merely requires creditors' claims (including those of partners) to be paid in full before partners receive any assets. RUPA § 807(a). A **Statement of Dissolution** may be filed to cancel an earlier filed Statement of Authority and to provide notice to the public that the partnership has dissolved.

Under RUPA § 802(b), even if the partnership is dissolved, at any time before winding up is completed, all of the partners (including any dissociating partner who is not a wrongfully dissociating partner) can agree to continue doing business,

Statement of Dissociation Document filed with state to identify dissociating partner and filed to limit period for which partnership will be liable for dissociating partner's acts

Statement of Dissolution A formal statement filed with state to notify others of partnership dissolution

FIGURE 3-5
Florida Statement of Dissociation

STATEMENT OF DISSOCIATION FOR PARTNERSHIP

Pursuant to section 620.8704, Florida Statutes, I hereby submit the following statement of dissociation:

FIRST: The name of the partnership is:_____

_____

SECOND: (CHECK ONE)
☐ The partnership was registered with the Florida Department of State on _____

      and assigned registration number _____ .

☐ The partnership has not registered with the Florida Department of State.

THIRD: The purpose of this document is to state that

_____ has dissociated as a partner from
                    (Partner's Name)

_____ .
                    (Partnership Name)

FOURTH: Effective date, if other than the date of filing: _____.
(Effective date cannot be prior to the date of filing nor more than 90 days after the date of filing.)

The execution of this statement in compliance with s. 620.8105(6) constitutes an affirmation under the penalties of perjury that the facts stated herein are true.

Signed this _____ day of _____, _____.

_____
                    (Signature)

_____
(Typed or printed name of person signing above)

Filing Fee:	$25.00
Certified copy:	$52.50 (optional)
Certificate of Status:	$ 8.75 (optional)

Make checks payable to Florida Department of State and mail to:
Division of Corporations P.O. Box 6327 Tallahassee, FL 32314

much the same way the UPA allows the creation of a technically new partnership after the dissolution of a partnership due to the departure of any partner for any reason. Finally, because both the UPA and the RUPA are default statutes, nearly all of their procedures relating to dissociation and dissolution can be varied or limited by the terms of the partners' agreement. Thus, the partnership agreement should be carefully drafted to provide as much continuity as possible and to avoid a forced dissolution and winding up.

In sum, under the UPA, nearly any withdrawal from the partnership for any reason causes a dissolution of the partnership, requiring winding up of the partnership business (although, as discussed earlier, the partners may continue doing business together, thereby creating a new partnership). Under the RUPA, however, most dissociations merely trigger a buyout of the dissociating partner's interest without requiring termination of the partnership business. Even when dissolution is precipitated, the partners may vote to agree to continue the business.

M. Conversions and Mergers

The RUPA adds new provisions (see Article 9) allowing a general partnership to be converted to a limited partnership upon approval of all the partners, although the partnership agreement may provide for a less than unanimous vote. Similarly, a limited partnership may be converted to a general partnership. Such conversions do not affect any property owned by the converting entity or any of its obligations. Moreover, a partnership may be merged with one or more other partnerships or limited partnerships, forming a new entity. Finally, the RUPA allows a partnership to become a limited liability partnership. Limited liability partnerships are discussed in Chapter Five.

N. Taxation of Partnerships

Although a partnership is an entity and can sue and be sued in its own name, it is not a taxpaying entity. All profits or losses earned are "passed through" to the partners, who report their respective income or losses on a separate form called Schedule K-1 (see Figure 3-6) attached to their individual tax returns. Thus, the taxation of partners is much like the taxation of sole proprietors. The partners simply add their share of the partnership income to any income gained from any other sources and pay tax according to the personal income tax rates or "brackets" established by the Internal Revenue Service (see Figure 2-6).

Partners must declare and pay taxes on any income earned, whether or not that income is distributed. Thus, if the partners decide to reserve an emergency account of $10,000 for anticipated repairs to partnership property, each partner must declare and pay tax on his or her respective share of the money reserved, even though the partner has not received that income.

FIGURE 3-6
IRS Schedule K-1

651108

| Final K-1 ☐ | Amended K-1 ☐ | OMB No. 1545-0099 |

Schedule K-1
(Form 1065)

2008

Department of the Treasury
Internal Revenue Service

For calendar year 2008, or tax
year beginning _____ , 2008
ending _____ , 20___

Partner's Share of Income, Deductions,
Credits, etc. ▶ See back of form and separate instructions.

Part I   Information About the Partnership

A   Partnership's employer identification number

B   Partnership's name, address, city, state, and ZIP code

C   IRS Center where partnership filed return

D   ☐ Check if this is a publicly traded partnership (PTP)

Part II   Information About the Partner

E   Partner's identifying number

F   Partner's name, address, city, state, and ZIP code

G   ☐ General partner or LLC member-manager   ☐ Limited partner or other LLC member

H   ☐ Domestic partner   ☐ Foreign partner

I   What type of entity is this partner? _____

J   Partner's share of profit, loss, and capital (see instructions):

	Beginning	Ending
Profit	%	%
Loss	%	%
Capital	%	%

K   Partner's share of liabilities at year end:

Nonrecourse . . . .$_____
Qualified nonrecourse financing . .$_____
Recourse . . . .$_____

L   Partner's capital account analysis:

Beginning capital account . . . .$_____
Capital contributed during the year . .$_____
Current year increase (decrease) . .$_____
Withdrawals & distributions . . .$(_____)
Ending capital account . . . .$_____

☐ Tax basis ☐ GAAP ☐ Section 704(b) book
☐ Other (explain)

Part III   Partner's Share of Current Year Income,
Deductions, Credits, and Other Items

1	Ordinary business income (loss)	15	Credits
2	Net rental real estate income (loss)		
3	Other net rental income (loss)	16	Foreign transactions
4	Guaranteed payments		
5	Interest income		
6a	Ordinary dividends		
6b	Qualified dividends		
7	Royalties		
8	Net short-term capital gain (loss)		
9a	Net long-term capital gain (loss)	17	Alternative minimum tax (AMT) items
9b	Collectibles (28%) gain (loss)		
9c	Unrecaptured section 1250 gain		
10	Net section 1231 gain (loss)	18	Tax-exempt income and nondeductible expenses
11	Other income (loss)		
		19	Distributions
12	Section 179 deduction		
13	Other deductions	20	Other information
14	Self-employment earnings (loss)		

*See attached statement for additional information.

For IRS Use Only

For Paperwork Reduction Act Notice, see Instructions for Form 1065.   Cat. No. 11394R   Schedule K-1 (Form 1065) 2008

Similarly, losses experienced by the partnership can be declared on each partner's individual tax return, thus offsetting other income and lowering tax liability. The income or losses declared will be determined by the partnership agreement. In our example, if the partnership had income of $100,000, whether or not that income is actually distributed to the partners Anna would pay tax on 34 percent of that income, Bob would pay tax on 22 percent of the income, and David would pay tax on the remaining 44 percent of the income earned. If the partners did not agree how income and losses were to be allocated, each partner would declare and pay tax on one-third of the income earned regardless of that partner's initial contribution.

Although the partnership does not pay federal tax, it does file an information return, Form 1065 (see Figure 3-7). This form is used to report the income, deductions, gains, and losses from the operation of the partnership and each partner's distributive share of taxable income. One general partner must sign the form. Information returns and Schedule K-1s can now be filed electronically. Generally, the partnership must file the information tax form by the fifteenth day of the fourth month following the date its tax year ended. The most common tax year for an entity is the calendar year, namely January 1 through December 31, but other tax years may be selected; for example, July 1 through June 30. Extensions can be obtained on request. All partnerships, even those without employees, must apply with the IRS for an employer identification number. (See Form SS-4 at Figure 2-3.)

Corporations are treated quite differently from partnerships regarding taxation. Partnerships do not pay tax although the partners themselves pay tax on income earned, whether distributed or not. Corporations themselves are tax-paying entities and pay at different rates than do individuals (see Chapter Ten). Moreover, when profits are distributed to shareholders as dividends, those shareholders then pay tax on the money they receive. Thus, corporations may retain certain income that will not be taxed to the shareholders (inasmuch as they have not received the distribution).

To afford such opportunities to partnerships, a late 1996 change to the tax code (see 26 C.F.R. § 301.7701-1, et seq.) allows partnerships to **"check the box"** on a designated IRS form (Form 8832) and elect to be taxed as a corporation. Because taxation is a complex issue and election to be taxed as a corporation might not be beneficial to all partners, careful consideration should be given as to whether the partnership wishes to "check the box" and elect to be taxed at corporate rates. Generally, one partner signs on behalf of all partners and states, under penalty of perjury, that she is authorized to do so.

Check the box Method by which businesses elect how they wish to be taxed, namely, whether as partnerships or corporations

According to the regulations, if no election is affirmatively made, the "default" provision is that the entity will automatically be treated as having the typical pass-through status of a partnership rather than the two-tier tax status of a corporation with its different tax rates. Thus, any partnership desiring to elect corporate tax status must file the election (see Figure 3-8 for IRS Form 8832). The election is made by attaching IRS Form 8832 to the partnership's informational return or to a corporate tax return. Generally, once the election is made, it cannot be changed for five years. Additionally, except for certain foreign entities that are always classified as corporations, a foreign entity can also elect whether to be taxed as a partnership or as a corporation.

FIGURE 3-7
IRS Form 1065

Form **1065**	**U.S. Return of Partnership Income**	OMB No. 1545-0099
Department of the Treasury Internal Revenue Service	For calendar year 2008, or tax year beginning ...., 2008, ending ...., 20...... . ▶ **See separate instructions.**	**2008**

		Name of partnership	**D** Employer identification number
A Principal business activity	Use the IRS label. Otherwise, print or type.		
B Principal product or service		Number, street, and room or suite no. If a P.O. box, see the instructions.	**E** Date business started
C Business code number		City or town, state, and ZIP code	**F** Total assets (see the instructions) $

G   Check applicable boxes: **(1)** ☐ Initial return   **(2)** ☐ Final return   **(3)** ☐ Name change   **(4)** ☐ Address change   **(5)** ☐ Amended return
           (6) ☐ Technical termination - also check (1) or (2)

H   Check accounting method: **(1)** ☐ Cash   **(2)** ☐ Accrual   **(3)** ☐ Other (specify) ▶ _____

I   Number of Schedules K-1. Attach one for each person who was a partner at any time during the tax year ▶ _____

J   Check if Schedule M-3 attached . . . . ☐

Caution. *Include* **only** *trade or business income and expenses on lines 1a through 22 below. See the instructions for more information.*

Income	**1a** Gross receipts or sales	**1a**		
	b Less returns and allowances	**1b**	**1c**	
	2 Cost of goods sold (Schedule A, line 8)		**2**	
	3 Gross profit. Subtract line 2 from line 1c		**3**	
	4 Ordinary income (loss) from other partnerships, estates, and trusts *(attach statement)* . .		**4**	
	5 Net farm profit (loss) *(attach Schedule F (Form 1040))*		**5**	
	6 Net gain (loss) from Form 4797, Part II, line 17 *(attach Form 4797)*		**6**	
	7 Other income (loss) *(attach statement)*		**7**	
	8 **Total income (loss).** Combine lines 3 through 7		**8**	
Deductions (see the instructions for limitations)	**9** Salaries and wages (other than to partners) (less employment credits)		**9**	
	10 Guaranteed payments to partners		**10**	
	11 Repairs and maintenance		**11**	
	12 Bad debts		**12**	
	13 Rent		**13**	
	14 Taxes and licenses		**14**	
	15 Interest		**15**	
	16a Depreciation *(if required, attach Form 4562)*	**16a**		
	b Less depreciation reported on Schedule A and elsewhere on return	**16b**	**16c**	
	17 Depletion **(Do not deduct oil and gas depletion.)**		**17**	
	18 Retirement plans, etc.		**18**	
	19 Employee benefit programs		**19**	
	20 Other deductions *(attach statement)*		**20**	
	21 **Total deductions.** Add the amounts shown in the far right column for lines 9 through 20 .		**21**	
	22 **Ordinary business income (loss).** Subtract line 21 from line 8		**22**	

Sign Here	Under penalties of perjury, I declare that I have examined this return, including accompanying schedules and statements, and to the best of my knowledge and belief, it is true, correct, and complete. Declaration of preparer (other than general partner or limited liability company member manager) is based on all information of which preparer has any knowledge.		May the IRS discuss this return with the preparer shown below (see instructions)? ☐ **Yes** ☐ **No**
	▶ Signature of general partner or limited liability company member manager	▶ Date	

Paid Preparer's Use Only	Preparer's signature		Date		Check if self-employed ▶ ☐	Preparer's SSN or PTIN
	Firm's name (or yours if self-employed), address, and ZIP code	▶			EIN ▶	
					Phone no.	( )

For Privacy Act and Paperwork Reduction Act Notice, see separate instructions.   Cat. No. 11390Z   Form **1065** (2008)

FIGURE 3-8
IRS Form 8832

Form **8832**
(Rev. March 2007)
Department of the Treasury
Internal Revenue Service

Entity Classification Election

OMB No. 1545-1516

	Name of eligible entity making election	Employer identification number
Type or Print	Number, street, and room or suite no. If a P.O. box, see instructions.	
	City or town, state, and ZIP code. If a foreign address, enter city, province or state, postal code and country. Follow the country's practice for entering the postal code.	

▶ Check if: ☐ Address change

---

1 Type of election (see instructions):

a ☐ Initial classification by a newly-formed entity. Skip lines 2a and 2b and go to line 3.
b ☐ Change in current classification. Go to line 2a.

2a Has the eligible entity previously filed an entity election that had an effective date within the last 60 months?

☐ **Yes.** Go to line 2b.
☐ **No.** Skip line 2b and go to line 3.

2b Was the eligible entity's prior election for initial classification by a newly formed entity effective on the date of formation?

☐ **Yes.** Go to line 3.
☐ **No.** Stop here. You generally are not currently eligible to make the election (see instructions).

3 Does the eligible entity have more than one owner?

☐ **Yes.** You can elect to be classified as a partnership or an association taxable as a corporation. Skip line 4 and go to line 5.
☐ **No.** You can elect to be classified as an association taxable as a corporation or disregarded as a separate entity. Go to line 4.

4 If the eligible entity has only one owner, provide the following information:
a Name of owner ▶ --
b Identifying number of owner ▶ --

5 If the eligible entity is owned by one or more affiliated corporations that file a consolidated return, provide the name and employer identification number of the parent corporation:
a Name of parent corporation ▶ --
b Employer identification number ▶ --

For Paperwork Reduction Act Notice, see instructions.   Cat. No. 22598R   Form **8832** (Rev. 3-2007)

Key Features
of General Partnerships

◆ Partnerships are formed by agreement, either oral or written.

◆ All partners share rights to manage the partnership.

◆ Partners share profits and losses according to their agreement; if no agreement, profits and losses are shared equally, regardless of capital contribution.

◆ Partners have unlimited personal liability for partnership obligations.

◆ Liability is joint and several, meaning that each partner is completely liable for any debt.

◆ Partnerships are easily and inexpensively formed.

◆ Partners owe each other fiduciary duties.

◆ Partners can transfer their partnership interest (share of profits) but transferee becomes a partner only upon consent of other partners.

◆ Under the UPA, nearly any withdrawal by a partner causes a dissolution of the partnership.

◆ Under the RUPA, withdrawal of a partner may not necessarily cause a dissolution and winding up of the partnership; in many instances the dissociating partner is bought out.

◆ Partnerships file information tax returns but do not pay federal taxes; all income, whether distributed or not, is passed through to the partners who pay tax at their appropriate individual rates.

O. Role of Paralegal

Although the attorney must determine which form of business enterprise is most appropriate for a client, paralegals play an integral role in the formation of a general partnership. The paralegal will likely prepare and file the fictitious business name statement, if needed. He can review the results of searches to determine if a partnership name is available by consulting one of the search firms identified in Chapter Two. The paralegal may also be tasked with obtaining appropriate forms for tax identification numbers and income tax forms. Most important, the paralegal will have an active role in drafting the partnership agreement.

Many law firms have various partnership agreements on file. The various forms should be reviewed to determine which provisions are "standard" (such as partnership name, addresses of the partners, and so forth) and must be included. The paralegal can then discuss these issues with the attorney or client. Preparing a partnership agreement is more than just an exercise in selecting the right form from a database or form file and changing names and addresses; it should be carefully tailored to suit the needs and particular requirements of each partnership client and to comply with the appropriate state statutes.

It may be useful to prepare a form or checklist of questions for the client. These can be asked during a conference or even mailed to the client for completion to assist in drafting the agreement. A sample for such a questionnaire is provided in Figure 3-9.

FIGURE 3-9
Partnership Checklist and Questionnaire

---

1. Proposed Name of Partnership _____
   Alternative Names[s] _____
2. Names and Addresses of all Partners
   a. _____   b. _____
      _____   _____
   c. _____   d. _____
      _____   _____

3. Address of Partnership _____

4. Purpose of Partnership _____

5. Duration of Partnership _____
6. Capital Contributions of Partners
   a. _____   b. _____
   c. _____   d. _____
7. Distribution of Profits and Losses
   a. _____   b. _____
   c. _____   d. _____
8. Management of Partnership/Voting/Decisions That Require Unanimous Approval
   _____
   _____
   _____

9. Designation of Managing Partner _____
10. Rights to Admit New Partners _____
    _____
11. Rights of Partners to Withdraw _____
    _____
12. Events That Will Cause Dissolution and Winding Up _____
    _____
    _____
13. Manner of Resolving Disputes (namely, litigation or arbitration) _____
14. Fiscal Year and Method of Accounting _____
15. Banking Information _____
16. Other _____
    _____
    _____
    _____

FIGURE 3-10
Comparison of UPA and RUPA Provisions

	UPA	*RUPA*
Nature of Partnership	Partnership is an aggregation of individuals	Partnership is an entity for nearly all purposes
Acts Requiring Unanimity	Lists certain acts requiring unanimous consent	No list of acts requiring unanimous consent
Public Filing of Statements of Authority, Denial, Dissociation, Dissolution, Merger, and Conversion	Not provided for	Statements may be filed with state officials
Fiduciary Duties	Generally provides only that partners are accountable as fiduciaries	Provides that partners are subject to the duties of loyalty and due care, which cannot be waived or eliminated; partners must exercise their duties consistent with good faith and fair dealing
Right to Accounting	Partners have a right to formal account of partnership affairs	Partner may bring an action for an accounting
Property Rights	Partner is a co-owner with his partners of specific partnership property (the theory of tenancy in partnership)	Abolishes concept of tenancy in partnership and provides that partnership property is owned by the entity and not by individual partners
Withdrawal by Partner	Withdrawal of a partner for any reason causes a dissolution of the partnership	Provides for dissociation of partner, which causes a dissolution and winding up only in certain situations; otherwise, partnership buys out dissociating partner's interest and continues unaffected by dissociation
Settlement of Accounts upon Dissolution	Outside third-party creditors are paid first, followed by partners' claims, followed by return of partners' capital, and then distribution of profits	Creditors claims are paid first (including claims by partners) and then surplus is paid to partners
Limited Liability Partnerships	Not provided for	Provided for under RUPA
Conversion and Mergers of Partnerships	Not provided for	RUPA allows the merger of two or more partnerships and the conversions of general partnerships to limited partnerships (and the reverse)

Case Illustration
Joint and Several Liability of Partners

Case: *Gildon v. Simon Property Group, Inc.*, 145 P.3d 1196 (Wash. 2006)

Facts: The plaintiff was injured in a slip and fall inside a shopping mall owned by Northgate Mall Partnership, a general partnership. Plaintiff sued Simon Property Group, which was the general partner of the partnership but did not name the partnership itself. The defendant general partner claimed, among other things, that it was a "small" general partner. The trial court dismissed the plaintiff's action and the Court of Appeals reversed.

Holding: The Washington Supreme Court affirmed. Under the RUPA (adopted in Washington), partners are jointly and severally liable for all partnership obligations without regard to whether they are "mere" or small partners. Although partners are allowed to modify many statutory provisions in their partnership agreements, partners are not permitted to modify the principle of joint and several liability. In this case, the plaintiff alleged that the defendant general partner was directly liable to her for its acts. Because a defendant is always liable for its own acts and torts, the plaintiff was not required to name the partnership itself.

◆ ◆ ◆

WEB RESOURCES

A number of sites provide general information about partnerships with clear and concise discussions of the partnership entity, comparing and contrasting it to other forms of business entities. Many of the following sites provide forms for partnership agreements. As with all forms, exercise caution in using the form, inasmuch as it will likely not be suitable for all partnerships. As with any form, you should modify it to suit your needs. Review the Web site Disclaimer or Legal Terms sections to determine if there are any prohibitions on use or reproduction of the forms. In any event, the forms serve as useful starting places.

State forms and information: www.nass.org
Tax information: www.irs.gov

General information:	http://topics.law.cornell.edu/wex/ Partnership www.tannedfeet.com/partnerships.htm www.businessownersideacafe.com www.about.com/business www.megalaw.com
Forms (including partnership agreement forms):	www.allaboutforms.com (Select "Show All Business Topics.") www.findlaw.com www.siccode.com/form.php www.lectlaw.com www.ilrg.com (The Internet Legal Research Group offers a form for a partnership agreement in its "Legal Forms Archive.")

Discussion Questions

Fact Scenario.   Phil, Brian, and Greg have formed a general partnership to provide auto detailing services. Although they have a written partnership agreement, it does not discuss division of profits or losses or how the partnership will be operated. It does provide that the partnership will last for three years. Phil contributed $20,000 to the partnership, Brian contributed $45,000 to the business, and Greg contributed $35,000 to the business.

1. Last year the partnership made a profit of $200,000. How will this be divided among the partners? Why? What if the partnership sustained a loss of $200,000? How would this be allocated? Why?

2. The partnership has decided that it should raise an additional $10,000. What share of this sum must each partner contribute?

3. Without the other partners' knowledge, Greg has purchased a significant amount of supplies for the business. Who is liable to pay for these supplies? Why? Discuss fully.

4. Brian has decided to leave the partnership after only one year. Discuss the effect of his withdrawal from the partnership under both the UPA and the RUPA.

5. The partnership owes $15,000 to its landlord and has $10,000 in its bank accounts. Who is liable for payment of the money owed to the landlord? Discuss.

6. Greg has decided to transfer his partnership interest to Cynthia. What rights, if any, does Cynthia have in the partnership?

7. Assume that at the end of its term, the partnership is dissolving. It owes $5,000 for taxes and $4,000 to Brian for wages Brian paid to certain employees. The partnership has $20,000 in its accounts. Discuss how the debts will be paid and any assets distributed under both the UPA and the RUPA.

8. What is the advantage to the partnership of filing a Statement of Dissociation after a partner leaves the partnership?

Net Worth

1. Access the Web site for the Secretary of State of New Hampshire and review the Application for Certificate of Authority for Foreign Partnership.
   a. What fee is required to file this document?
   b. What information is required in Section 4 of the document?
2. Access the Web site for the Secretary of State of California. What is the fee to file a Statement of Partnership Authority?
3. Access the Web site of the National Conference of Commissioners on Uniform State Laws. Select "Final Acts and Legislation" and then "Partnership Act."
   a. Select "Summary" and review the information relating to dissolution of partnerships. What is the most significant change in the 1994 Act over the 1914 Act?
   b. Select "Illinois" and review Section 101. What is the definition of "partnership at will"?

4

◆ ◆ ◆

Limited Partnerships

◆ ◆ ◆

CHAPTER OVERVIEW

A limited partnership is a unique type of partnership. You will recall from Chapter Three that in a general partnership, all of the partners have the right to manage and control the partnership and they all suffer the risk of unlimited personal liability for business debts, torts, and obligations. In a limited partnership, some of the partners, called *limited partners,* do not have unlimited personal liability. Their liability is limited to what they invested in the enterprise. Although the value of this investment may fall to zero, at the outset of the enterprise limited partners can determine what their maximum risk or exposure will be, namely, the amount they invested in the business. These limited partners also have little ability to manage or govern the partnership. Another critical distinction between general partnerships and limited partnerships relates to the organization of the enterprise. A general partnership may be formed with few formalities; a limited partnership, however, can only be created by strict compliance with pertinent state statutes.

A. Characteristics of Limited Partnerships

Unlike sole proprietorships and general partnerships, which are formed with either no or minimal governmental involvement, limited partnerships are creatures of statute and can only be formed in compliance with state law, by the filing of a certificate of limited partnership with the appropriate state official. A limited partnership includes one or more general partners and one or more limited partners. The primary advantage of a limited partnership is that it affords limited liability to the limited partners, making a limited partner similar to a shareholder in a corporation, so that the maximum potential loss is the investment in the enterprise. In exchange for this protection, limited partners forgo any management of the partnership. Thus, the limited partnership satisfies two goals: the goal of business managers to attract capital to the business without any surrender of their managerial control and the goal of certain investors who wish to invest in an enterprise and yet not expose all of their other assets to personal liability.

Silent partner
An older term for *limited partner*

Years ago, limited partners were sometimes referred to as **silent partners,** in recognition of the fact that they played no role in managing the partnership business. Thus, all management and control of a limited partnership is provided by the general partners, who face the same risks and have the same responsibilities as do general partners in general partnerships, primarily unlimited personal liability. Limited partnerships allow pass-through tax treatment, meaning that the limited partnership does not pay taxes. All taxable income is passed through to the partners, who pay taxes according to their respective tax brackets.

Earlier chapters have discussed that the sole proprietorship and general partnership may not be attractive business enterprises to wealthy individuals because the risks to sole proprietors and general partners extend beyond what has been invested in the business to their personal assets. Thus, an investment of only $10,000 could result in a potential loss of hundreds of thousands of dollars.

The limited partnership originated in continental Europe so that a wealthy individual could invest in a business enterprise and yet not expose all of his or her other assets and funds to unlimited liability. Limited partnerships were first recognized in the United States in the early 1800s.

B.   Governing Law

Limited partnership
Business entity created in accord with state statutes that provides limited liability to some of its members, called *limited partners*

As you will recall from Chapter Three, the National Conference of Commissioners on Uniform State Laws (the "Conference") drafts and proposes specific statutes in areas of law where uniformity is desirable. Most of the law governing **limited partnerships** stems from the **Uniform Limited Partnership Act (ULPA),** approved in 1916, and in the **revised Uniform Limited Partnership Act (RULPA),** approved in the mid-1970s and amended in 1985. All states except Louisiana adopted the RULPA. Louisiana recognizes limited partnerships but has statutes slightly different from the ULPA and the later RULPA.

ULPA
Uniform Limited Partnership Act

RULPA
Revised Uniform Limited Partnership Act; the model for limited partnership legislation in most states

After the Conference proposed the RULPA, most states rapidly adopted it because it provided a much more streamlined approach to creating limited partnerships and reduced the paperwork and administrative burdens of the ULPA. Because various states have modified the RULPA (and not all of them have adopted the 1985 amendments), there are variations from state to state. Because a limited partnership can be created only by complying with pertinent state statutes, a thorough review of those state-specific statutes is necessary for a complete understanding of how limited partnerships operate and are governed in your state. The text of the RULPA is found in Appendix E. The text of the older ULPA (1916) is not included.

Limited partnerships are not nearly as popular now as they once were because two relatively recently recognized entities, limited liability partnerships and limited liability companies, both offer all of their partners or members full protection from personal liability as well as the opportunity to manage the enterprise. These new forms of business structures (discussed in Chapters Five and Six) are part of a recent trend to create new forms of business that afford limited liability coupled with management rights and pass-through taxation. As evidence of the waning popularity of limited partnerships, in 2007, only six limited partnerships were formed in the State of Georgia under the ULPA. In contrast, nearly 60,000 limited liability companies were formed.

Recognizing that these new business entities meet a wide variety of business needs and that limited partnerships needed a more flexible structure, the Conference completely revised the RULPA in 2001 (the 2001 Act). According to the Conference, the **2001 Act** is designed to meet the needs of sophisticated manager-entrenched commercial entities and family limited partnerships. The 2001 Act is significantly more complex and substantially longer than its predecessor, the RULPA. Due to its newness, at the time of the writing of this text, only 14 states had fully adopted it. Thus, it is not reproduced in this text. Its key features are discussed in Section O of this chapter. The full text of the 2001 Act is available for review at the Web site of the Conference at www.nccusl.org. Because the RULPA is at present the dominant law governing limited partnerships, and the one followed by the majority of American jurisdictions, focus in this edition of the text remains on the RULPA.

> **2001 Act**
> Revised version of RULPA, fully adopted in 14 states and providing significant protection from liability for all partners

In sum, limited partnerships are governed by state statutes and by two quite different versions of uniform acts. The majority of states follow the RULPA; only 14 fully follow the 2001 Act. As time progresses, additional states will likely begin to adopt the 2001 Act because it affords significant full shield protection from personal liability for both general and limited partners. Finally, note that the RULPA is linked to general partnership law. Specifically, RULPA § 1105 provides that in any case not governed under the RULPA, the provisions of the Uniform Partnership Act of 1997 govern (which is discussed extensively in Chapter Three).

C. Limited Partnership Defined

A *limited partnership* is a partnership formed by two or more persons pursuant to a statute, having as its members one or more general partners and one or more **limited partners.** RULPA § 101(7). An examination of each element of this definition follows.

> **Limited partner**
> A member of a limited partnership who does not participate in managing the business and whose liability is limited to the amount invested in the business

The "persons" referred to in the definition can be natural persons, general partnerships, limited partnerships, trusts, estates, associations, or corporations. When the members of a business organization are other businesses, it can be extremely complicated to determine who is actually managing and controlling the enterprise. For example, assume that a limited partnership is formed with one general partner. That general partner may be a general partnership consisting of three corporations engaged in business as partners. The controlling stock of the corporations in turn may be held by another partnership or even another corporation. When presented with one of these puzzles, you might need to prepare an organizational tree or flowchart clearly outlining the relationship of each entity to another and identifying the majority owner or decision-maker for each entity.

Perhaps the most critical part of the definition of a limited partnership is the phrase referring to the formation of the entity "under the laws of [a state]," which confirms that the creation of a limited partnership is strictly controlled and regulated by state law. Failure to comply substantially with the appropriate state statutes will result in a failure to create a limited partnership. When presented with an entity not in compliance with the necessary requirements to form a limited partnership, courts often determine that because the entity cannot be a limited partnership it must be a general partnership (in which case, all partners have unlimited personal liability). In most states, and pursuant to RULPA § 201(b), substantial compliance with the pertinent statutes is sufficient to form a limited partnership. Thus, an inadvertent or insignificant error or omission may not result in the entity being forbidden status as a limited partnership.

The general partner in a limited partnership is the same as a general partner in a general partnership, unless otherwise provided in an agreement. RULPA § 403(a). This general partner will manage and control the limited partnership and consequently may face unlimited personal liability.

The "limited partner" in a limited partnership differs from a general partner in two critical respects:

1. Limited partners do not suffer the risk of unlimited liability. Their maximum loss is the amount invested in the business.
2. Limited partners cannot manage or control the partnership business.

A chart comparing some of the more significant distinctions between general and limited partnerships is found in Figure 4-8.

D. Partners' Rights and Duties

1. *General Partners*

General partner
Member in a limited (or general) partnership who manages and controls the business and has unlimited personal liability

Because limited partners cannot participate in the control of the limited partnership, every limited partnership must have at least one **general partner** who will be fully responsible for managing the business. This general partner also has personal liability for the limited partnership's debts and obligations, meaning that his or her personal assets can be taken by creditors.

If a corporation is the general partner, as is often the case, it will manage and control the business through its board of directors. Corporations have limited liability, meaning that the only funds and assets available to creditors are those owned by the corporation itself. Its directors, officers, and shareholders have no personal liability for the corporation's debts and obligations. Thus, if a corporation is the general partner of a limited partnership, no one in the limited partnership has personal liability, and, assuming there has been no fraud, the only assets available to satisfy creditors would be those of the limited partnership itself and those owned by the corporate general partner (and not those of any individual).

The management rights and responsibilities of general partners in a limited partnership are the same as those of general partners in a general partnership. Thus, general partners have fiduciary duties and duties of loyalty and due care to the limited partners and to the limited partnership. They are the agents of the partnership who bind the partnership for contractual and other obligations. They cannot compete with the partnership business. Because the limited partners cannot control the business without losing their limited liability status, the general partner or partners have full responsibility for management of the limited partnership business. If there is more than one general partner, their specific duties and responsibilities will be set forth in the partnership agreement. If the agreement fails to provide specific duties and responsibilities, management and control will be shared equally between general partners, just as in a general partnership.

Under the 1916 ULPA, a general partner had no authority to perform certain acts, such as admitting a new general partner or confessing a judgment against the partnership, without the approval of the limited partners. Under the newer RULPA, there are no such restrictions on general partners; however, admission of a new general partner must be pursuant to the terms of a partnership agreement, and, if the agreement does not so provide, can only be done with the written consent of all of the partners, including the limited partners. RULPA § 401.

Under new statutory provisions, several states allow a limited partnership to file a registration statement with the secretary of state, which results in the general partner(s) having protection from unlimited liability. This attractive variety of limited partnership, called a *limited liability limited partnership,* is discussed in Sections N and O of this chapter.

2. Limited Partners

A limited partner is basically a passive investor in this business enterprise. A limited partner invests his money in the limited partnership and knows that this represents the maximum loss he will face. Because limited partners cannot manage or control the limited partnership business, they have no personal liability for partnership debts and obligations. In general, limited partners can freely assign or transfer their interest in the partnership. This interest, namely, their share of the profits, is viewed as the limited partners' personal property, and it can be transferred in whole or in part. The transferee or assignee may become a limited partner if the agreement so provides or all other partners consent. Many agreements allow the general partner to unilaterally admit new limited partners. Because limited partners do not manage or control the business, the general partner is unlikely to care whether it is *A*'s money that has been contributed or *B*'s money. The partnership agreement might, however, restrict such transfers and assignments.

A limited partner may lose his or her limited liability status by acting as a general partner. Although limited partners have the right to be provided copies of the partnership records and tax returns, the right to be informed of the partnership's business and affairs, and the right to review the corporate books and accounts, they cannot "control" the business. Numerous cases have attempted to interpret what types of activities constitute control of the partnership. Under the RULPA, if a limited partner participates in the control of the business, she is liable only to those persons who transacted business with the limited partnership reasonably believing, based on the limited partner's conduct, that the limited partner was a general partner. RULPA § 303(a). No such limitation existed under the 1916 ULPA.

In an attempt to clarify what activities are permissible for a limited partner, the RULPA specifically provides that a limited partner may engage in the following activities without subjecting himself to personal liability:

1. Being a contractor for or an agent or employee of the limited partnership or an officer, director, or shareholder of a general partner that is a corporation;

2. Consulting with and advising a general partner with respect to the limited partnership business;
3. Acting as a guarantor of partnership obligations;
4. Bringing a derivative action in the name of the limited partnership;
5. Requesting or attending a meeting of partners;
6. Proposing, approving, or disapproving one or more of the following matters:
   - The dissolution and winding up of the limited partnership;
   - The sale, transfer, or mortgage of all or substantially all of the assets of the limited partnership;
   - The incurrence of indebtedness by the limited partnership other than in the ordinary course of its business;
   - A change in the nature of the business;
   - The admission or removal of a general or limited partner;
   - A transaction involving an actual or potential conflict of interest between a general partner and the limited partnership or limited partners;
   - An amendment to the partnership agreement or certificate of limited partnership; or
   - Matters related to the business of the limited partnership not otherwise enumerated that the partnership agreement states may be subject to the approval or disapproval of limited partners;
7. Winding up the limited partnership; or
8. Exercising any right or power permitted to limited partners under the RULPA. (RULPA § 303(b))

Safe harbor
Activities that do not violate a statute

The RULPA also specifies that conduct or activities undertaken by limited partners that are not specifically enumerated in the preceding list, often referred to as the **safe harbor** list, does not necessarily constitute an act of control by a limited partner that would render him subject to personal liability. Thus, a limited partner may perform some act not on this list and it will not necessarily be viewed as an act of control that would subject him to personal liability.

Additionally, a limited partner's last name cannot be used in the name of the limited partnership (unless it is also the name of a general partner or the business operated under that name before that partner's admission). A limited partner who knowingly allows her surname to be used in the partnership name will be liable to creditors who do not know she is a limited partner. RULPA § 303(d).

The general prohibition against a limited partner "controlling" the business or having her last name in the business name seems to be based on what third parties and creditors are likely to perceive. If a third party sees an individual engaged in the management and control of a business or notes that person's last name in the partnership name, he is likely to believe that person is a general partner whose personal assets are available to satisfy obligations of the limited partnership.

The same person can serve as both a general partner and a limited partner. Wearing a hat as a general partner, that individual has full rights to manage the business and has personal liability. Wearing a hat as a limited partner, liability is "capped" at the initial contribution to the limited partnership.

E. Advantages of Limited Partnerships

1. Attracting Capital

A limited partnership is an ideal way of attracting capital for an enterprise. Wealthy individuals who might not prefer to be sole proprietors or general partners with the attendant unlimited personal liability can invest a certain amount of money in an enterprise knowing in advance their maximum exposure is limited to the amount of their contribution. Because new limited partners can easily be admitted to the business, a limited partnership that finds itself in financial difficulties can raise money by admitting new limited partners who will bring an influx of cash with them and will neither have personal liability nor interfere with the enterprise's management. In some instances, investors may prefer to leave the duties of management and control to experienced general partners. Whereas prior laws based on the ULPA allowed limited partners to contribute only cash or property, RULPA § 501 now allows limited partners to contribute cash, property, services, or even a promissory note or other obligation promising to contribute cash, property, or services in the future.

2. Limited Liability

From a wealthy individual's perspective, the limited partnership is an attractive business venture. One of the greatest advantages a limited partnership offers is limited liability to its limited partners. They can invest money in a business and, so long as they do not control the business or knowingly allow their surname to be used in the business name, they will not be liable for any amount beyond their contributions to the limited partnership.

3. Easy Transferability of Partnership Interest

Limited partners can easily transfer their interests, in whole or in part, to another. An assignment will not cause a dissolution of the limited partnership. RULPA § 702. The assignee, however, does not become a new limited partner, but is merely entitled to receive any distribution the original limited partner would receive. The assignee may, however, become a new limited partner if all other partners agree or if such is allowed by limited partnership agreement. General partners have the same rights to assign their partnership interests as limited partners. A partner ceases to be a partner upon the assignment of all of that partner's interest.

Moreover, unless the limited partnership provides a specific term or provides specific events that give rise to a right to withdraw, according to RULPA §§ 603 and 604, a limited partner has the right to withdraw from the limited partnership and demand a return of her contribution upon giving six months' written notice to each general partner. Just as is the case with general partnerships, a judgment creditor of either a general or limited partner may obtain a charging order from a court so that any partner's distributions will be paid to the creditor until the judgment is satisfied. RULPA § 703.

4.   Continuity of Existence

Whereas sole proprietorships and general partnerships governed by the UPA cannot survive the death or withdrawal of the sole proprietor or a partner, the limited partnership will not necessarily dissolve upon the withdrawal of a general partner provided there is at least one other general partner and the limited partnership agreement permits the business to be carried on by the remaining general partner. Additionally, the RULPA provides that if an event of withdrawal occurs that would ordinarily cause dissolution, such as the resignation or removal of a general partner, the limited partnership need not wind up and dissolve if within 90 days after the withdrawal, all partners agree in writing to continue the limited partnership business and appoint one or more general partners. RULPA § 801(4). Additionally, because limited partners do not control the business, their withdrawal, death, or removal generally does not end the existence of the limited partnership, but instead may require only that an amendment to various documents be filed with the state. Thus, limited partnerships can survive events that might ordinarily force a dissolution and winding up of general partnerships.

5.   Pass-Through Taxation

Like general partnerships, limited partnerships do not pay federal income tax. Profits earned by the limited partnership (whether distributed or not) are passed through to the general and limited partners, who then pay according to their appropriate tax brackets. Losses of the limited partnership can be used to offset other income. This treatment may afford tax advantages to both general and limited partners.

F.   Disadvantages of Limited Partnerships

1.   Lack of Control for Limited Partners

Although one of the greatest advantages to being a limited partner is limited liability, it comes at a price. Limited partners cannot control the business or they risk unlimited personal liability. They have a right to be informed about the operation of the business (and can engage in the safe harbor activities described earlier), but they cannot participate in that operation. Thus, for individuals who prefer to manage their own affairs and control decisions relating to their investments, the limited partnership may not be an ideal form of business. Similarly, because the general partner has full responsibility for managing the business, the limited partners must have complete confidence in the general partner and should therefore conduct some investigation, often called **due diligence,** to inquire about the background and trustworthiness of the general partner before contributing their money and then taking their traditional passive roles.

Due diligence
Investigation and research conducted before entering into agreements or transactions

2. *Unlimited Liability for General Partner*

Each limited partnership must have at least one general partner. General partners assume all of the responsibility for management of the limited partnership business. Thus, the disadvantage of being a general partner in a limited partnership is the same as being a general partner in a general partnership: unlimited personal liability for the debts and obligations of the business. If there is more than one general partner, liability will be joint and several, just as it is in general partnerships. If a limited partnership has a corporation as its general partner, the corporation will manage the business through its officers and directors, meaning the corporation will have limited liability. Creditors of the limited partnership could reach only the assets in the limited partnership accounts and those in the corporate general partner's accounts. No individuals would have personal liability. Many limited partnerships thus rely on corporate general partners for such protection from unlimited liability.

3. *Formalities and Expenses of Organization*

A general partnership can be formed with a handshake. No written agreement or statutory formalities are required to form a general partnership. A limited partnership, however, is often said to be a "creature of statute," meaning it cannot be formed without substantial compliance with statutory formalities. Various documents must be filed with the state in which the limited partnership operates. Annual reporting requirements may be imposed. Filing fees must be paid to the appropriate state authority. To do business in another state, the limited partnership is usually required to become formally authorized by the foreign state. This will involve filing documents with that state and paying filing fees.

Because it is necessary to comply with state statutes to create a limited partnership, most limited partnerships will require legal counsel. Thus, legal fees will likely be incurred.

G. Formation of Limited Partnerships

1. *Contents of the Limited Partnership Certificate*

To form a limited partnership, a **limited partnership certificate** must be prepared, signed, and filed with the secretary of state (or an equivalent official) of the state in which the partnership will operate. Under the original 1916 ULPA, the certificate needed to provide 14 items, including the nature of the business, an identification of each limited partner's contribution, how additional contributions were to be made, and each limited partner's share of the profits. ULPA § 2. Under RULPA § 201, the contents of the certificate are streamlined in recognition of the fact that the partnership agreement, not the certificate of limited partnership, is the authoritative document for a limited partnership, and that creditors and others usually refer to that agreement rather than the limited partnership certificate. Thus, only the following must be included:

a. The name of the limited partnership;
b. The address of the office and the name and address of the agent for service of process (namely, litigation summonses and complaints);

Limited partnership certificate
The document filed with the state that creates a limited partnership

c. The name and business address of each general partner;
d. The latest date on which the limited partnership is to dissolve; and
e. Any other matters the general partners determine to include.

As stated earlier, each state may have some modifications and may require additional information. For example, Figure 4-1 shows the form required by the State of Delaware, which requires even fewer than the four items required by the RULPA. Filing fees charged by states can vary from $10 to hundreds of dollars.

The following elements are included in the certificate of limited partnership:

Name.   The rule that sole proprietorships and general partnerships may not select names that are the same as or deceptively similar to that of another business also applies to limited partnerships. To determine name availability, one can contact the secretary of state and inquire whether the client's proposed name is available. See Web Resources at the end of this chapter and Appendix A for a listing of the secretary of state offices for each state. For a more thorough search, contact one of the search companies identified in Chapter Two. In several states you may be able to search online.

According to RULPA § 102(1), the name of a limited partnership must include without abbreviation the words "limited partnership." Many states have modified this requirement slightly and allow a limited partnership name to include either the words "limited partnership" or the abbreviation "L.P." The purpose of these requirements is to afford public notice that the partnership is not a general partnership and that the personal assets of certain partners may not be available to creditors of the business.

The name of the limited partnership may not include the surname of a limited partner unless a general partner shares that surname or unless the limited partnership operated under that name prior to the admission of the limited partner. RULPA § 102(2). As discussed earlier, a limited partner who knowingly permits her name to be used in the name of the limited partnership is liable to creditors who do not know she is a limited partner. These restrictions prevent limited partners from appearing to have authority to act for the business.

PRACTICE TIP

Keep a copy of active clients' certificates of limited partnership in a file folder near your desk. Legal documents (contracts, promissory notes, and so forth) must recite the limited partnership's correct name and be signed by a general partner. Keeping the certificate handy will help you double-check spelling, abbreviations, and punctuation in limited partnership names and the correct presentation of general partners' names without needing to review voluminous files.

Registered Office and Agent.   The limited partnership must designate an office in the state to which documents and notices can be sent. This need not be the limited partnership's principal place of business; however, an address must be provided so that notices and documents can be sent to the limited partnership. RULPA § 105 provides that certain records must be kept at the office, including

FIGURE 4-1
Delaware Certificate of Limited Partnership

STATE OF DELAWARE
CERTIFICATE OF LIMITED PARTNERSHIP

- **The Undersigned,** desiring to form a limited partnership pursuant to the Delaware Revised Uniform Limited Partnership Act, 6 Delaware Code, Chapter 17, do hereby certify as follows:

- **First:** The name of the limited partnership is _____
  _____ .

- **Second:** The address of its registered office in the State of Delaware is _____
  _____ in the city of _____ .
  Zip code _____ . The name of the Registered Agent at such address is
  _____ .

- **Third:** The name and mailing address of each general partner is as follows:

  ┌──┐
  │   │
  │   │
  │   │
  │   │
  └──┘

- **In Witness Whereof,** the undersigned has executed this Certificate of Limited Partnership as of _____ day of _____ , A.D. _____ .

                    By: _____
                           General Partner

                    Name: _____
                              (type or print name)

alphabetical lists of general partners and limited partners, copies of tax records and financial statements for the three most recent years, copies of any partnership agreements, and information relating to the contributions made by each partner and their right to receive distributions. Equally important, an **agent for service of process** must be identified. The agent is either an individual residing in the state or a corporation in the state that is authorized to receive *service of process* for the limited partnership, meaning notices of litigation filed against the limited partnership. In the event any individual wishes to file suit against the limited partnership, the agent has been appointed to receive the summons and complaint. Upon receipt of the appropriate papers by the registered agent, the period for answering the complaint begins, and failure of the limited partnership to respond in a timely fashion may result in a default judgment entered against the partnership. In most states one can determine the name and address of a registered agent by calling the secretary of state. In many states, one can now search online for the name and address of the registered agent.

Names and Addresses of General Partners.   The names and business addresses of the general partner or partners must be identified. Because the limited partners do not participate in the control of the business, they should be able to conduct due diligence to investigate the background of the general partner(s). The identification of the general partner(s) not only provides an official address for correspondence with the limited partnership, but also provides sufficient information that the limited partners, if desired, can conduct some investigation into the general partner(s) to determine whether the general partner has been involved in previous lawsuits, has filed a petition for bankruptcy, or has engaged in other conduct that would influence the decision of a limited partner to invest money in this enterprise.

Dissolution Date.   The latest date for dissolution of the limited partnership is given to provide notice to limited partners so they know when final distributions may be made and when their involvement with the limited partnership ends.

Other Matters.   The general partner may include other items in the limited partnership certificate, including events triggering dissolution, names and addresses of limited partners, information regarding additional contributions that may need to be made by limited partners, and how contributions will be returned to limited partners. Because the certificate of limited partnership is a public document, however, most general partners comply narrowly with the requirements of their state and do not include other matters. The inclusion of additional matters may necessitate amendments to the certificate in the future. Thus, most limited partnerships comply strictly with what their state requires and provide no additional information.

2. *Filing the Certificate of Limited Partnership*

In most states, the form of the certificate of limited partnership is provided by the state. Contact your secretary of state's office (see Appendix A) and request a form for a limited partnership certificate. Alternatively, nearly all states now make

Agent for service of process
One who agrees to accept litigation notices for another

the forms available for downloading from the home page of the secretary of state. Some states may also require that the certificate be filed in the county in which the limited partnership will principally conduct its business. Carefully review your state statutes to ensure compliance with your state's requirements.

The certificate of limited partnership must be signed by all general partners. A limited partnership is formed at the time of the filing of the certificate with the office of the secretary of state. Filing fees are required in all states and many states require that a duplicate certificate be filed as well.

If there is an error in the certificate, it must be determined whether there has been substantial compliance with the pertinent state statute. If substantial compliance has been achieved, the limited partnership certificate will be valid and limited partners will be protected from unlimited liability. If, however, there is no substantial compliance with the appropriate state statutes, all of the members of the enterprise will be treated as if they were members in a general partnership with resulting individual liability. Sometimes, individuals invest in a business enterprise believing they are limited partners but the general partner, through mistake, inadvertence, or willfulness, fails to file the limited partnership certificate. Individuals who erroneously believe they are limited partners are not subject to liability as general partners to creditors of the business if, upon discovering the mistake, they cause the appropriate certificate to be filed or if they renounce their future profit in the enterprise. RULPA § 304(a).

If the certificate contains a false statement, one who suffers loss by reliance on the statement may recover damages from anyone who signed the certificate and knew the statement was false or from any general partner who knew or should have known the statement was false.

3. Amendment of the Limited Partnership Certificate

In the event of significant changes in the limited partnership, a certificate of amendment must be prepared and filed with the secretary of state. RULPA § 202(b) provides that an amendment to the certificate of limited partnership shall be filed within 30 days after any of the following events:

a. Admission of a new general partner;
b. Withdrawal of a general partner; or
c. The continuation of the business after the withdrawal of a general partner.

Amendments may be filed for any other purpose the general partners determine. Moreover, in the event a general partner becomes aware that the certificate of limited partnership contains a false statement, or that any other facts set forth in the original certificate of limited partnership have changed, the general partner must promptly amend the certificate. Amending the original certificate will require preparation of the appropriate form designated for use in that state, signature by a general partner and any new general partner, and payment of a filing fee.

Under the original ULPA, the certificate of limited partnership was required to be amended for a variety of events, including any admission or withdrawal of a limited partner. For a limited partnership with a large number of limited partners, this was an expensive and cumbersome requirement. Thus, the RULPA provides a much narrower list of events that require the filing of an amendment to the certificate of limited partnership. See Figure 4-2 for a sample certificate of amendment.

4. Foreign Limited Partnerships

A limited partnership formed under the laws of one state may decide to expand its operations and conduct business in another state. A limited partnership formed in one state and doing business in another is referred to as a **foreign limited partnership** by the second state, inasmuch as it was not originally created in the second state. In its original state of formation, it is referred to as a **domestic limited partnership.**

To protect its citizens, a state can require that a foreign limited partnership apply to do business within its borders. Many activities, such as bringing or defending a lawsuit, holding meetings, or engaging in an isolated transaction are not considered **"doing business"** such that an application must be filed in the other state. Check state statutes to determine which activities require the foreign limited partnership to apply. In the application, the foreign limited partnership must appoint an agent for service of process so that any citizens injured by acts of the limited partnership in that state will be able to bring claims against the limited partnership. RULPA § 902 sets forth the elements that must be met when a foreign limited partnership wishes to conduct business in a state other than the state of creation. In many respects, the application mimics the requirements of a certificate of limited partnership. Further, a limited partnership conducting business in another state will be required to comply with all of that state's laws, for example, any laws relating to the requirement of the words "limited partnership" or the abbreviation "L.P." in the business name.

Request the appropriate application form from the secretary of state for the state in which the limited partnership wishes to conduct business. Generally, the form must be signed by a general partner and accompanied by a filing fee. Failure to receive permission from a state to transact business may prohibit the limited partnership from maintaining any lawsuit in that state until the defect is cured. A limited partner of a foreign limited partnership is not liable as a general partner, however, merely because the general partner failed to file the appropriate form to become authorized to do business in the state. Figure 4-3 provides a sample application for registration of a foreign limited partnership. Amendment of the application will be required in the event of changes in the foreign limited partnership that make the application inaccurate, and the application should be canceled or withdrawn when the foreign limited partnership ceases to do business in the foreign state.

5. Limited Partnership Agreement

According to RULPA § 101(9), a **limited partnership agreement** is any valid agreement among the partners, whether written or oral, governing the affairs of the limited partnership and the conduct of the business. Although the definition permits an oral agreement, for the sake of certainty a written agreement should always be prepared. The agreement will cover many matters not included in the

Foreign limited partnership
A limited partnership doing business in a state other than the one in which it was formed

Domestic limited partnership
A limited partnership created in the state in which it conducts its business

Doing business
Activities enumerated by a state that require an entity to qualify before entering the state to transact business

Limited partnership agreement
Agreement among partners in a limited partnership, usually written but may be oral

FIGURE 4-2
North Carolina Certificate of Amendment

State of North Carolina
Department of the Secretary of State

Amendment to Certificate of Domestic Limited Partnership

A. Return Acknowledgement to: Name: Mailing Address: <div align="center">City/State/Zip:</div>	Office Use Only

Read Instructions on reverse before beginning. Attach additional pages as needed.   No. pages attached:

B. Name of limited partnership (must contain words "limited partnership"):

C. Date of original filing with Secretary of State: D. File number originally assigned by Secretary of State:

E. Change or amend as follows (complete all applicable sections)

1. Name of limited partnership changed to:

2. Name of registered agent changed to:

3. Address of registered office changed to:
Street/Number: City: **NC**   Zip: County:

4. Address of office where records are kept changed to:
Street/Number: City: **NC**   Zip: County:

5. Address of following general partner(s) changed to:		6. Following general partner(s) added:	
Name		Name	
Street/ Number		Street/ Number	
City/State/Zip		City/State/Zip	
County		County	
Change Date		Add Date	

7. Following general partners withdrawn:		8. ___ CONTINUATION OF BUSINESS. After an event of withdrawal, the limited partnership intends to continue business pursuant to N.C. Gen. Statute §59-801.
Name		
Street/ Number		9 Dissolution date changed to:
City/State/Zip		10. Other information:
County		
Withdrawal Date		

F. The signatures of the following general partners constitute affirmations under the penalties of perjury that the facts herein are true.

Type or print the name of EACH general partner who signs this document.

1. If the general partner is an individual, complete this section.		Date
a. Name	Signature	
b. Name	Signature	
c. Name	Signature	

2. If the general partner is a corporation or other entity, complete this section.		Date
a. Name of corporation or other entity	Name of officer signing	
Title of officer signing	Signature	
b. Name of corporation or other entity	Name of officer signing	
Title of officer signing	Signature	
c. Name of corporation or other entity	Name of officer signing	
Title of officer signing	Signature	

NOTES: Filing fee is $25.00. This document and one exact or conformed copy must be filed with the Secretary of State.
(Revised January 2000)   *Form LP-02*
CORPORATIONS DIVISION   P. O. BOX 29622   RALEIGH, NC 27626-0622

FIGURE 4-3
Nevada Foreign Limited Partnership Application

ROSS MILLER
Secretary of State
206 North Carson Street
Carson City, Nevada 89701-4299
(775) 684 5708
Website: www.nvsos.gov

Application for Registration of Foreign Limited Partnership
(PURSUANT TO NRS CHAPTER 87A)

USE BLACK INK ONLY - DO NOT HIGHLIGHT   ABOVE SPACE IS FOR OFFICE USE ONLY

1. Name of Foreign Limited Partnership:	
2. Name Being Registered with Nevada: (see instructions)	
3. Date and State or Country of Formation:	Date Formed State or Country where Authorized
4. Registered Agent for Service of Process: (check only one box)	☐ Commercial Registered Agent: ____ Name ☐ Noncommercial Registered Agent (name and address below) **OR** ☐ Office or Position with Entity (name and address below) Name of Noncommercial Registered Agent OR Name of Title of Office or Other Position with Entity Street Address City Nevada Zip Code Mailing Address (if different from street address) City Nevada Zip Code This Foreign Limited Partnership hereby undertakes to keep a list of the names and addresses of the limited partners and their capital contributions at this office until its registration in Nevada is canceled or withdrawn. In the event the above-designated Agent for Service of Process resigns and is not replaced or the agent's authority has been revoked or the agent cannot be found or served with exercise of reasonable diligence, then the Secretary of State is hereby appointed as the Agent for Service of Process.
5. Street Address of Principal Office: (see instructions)	Street Address City State Zip Code
6. Name and Business Address of each General Partner: (attach additional page if more than 2)	1) Name Business Address City State Zip Code 2) Name Business Address City State Zip Code
7. Name and Signature of General Partner Making Statement:	I hereby declare and affirm under the penalties of perjury that I am a General Partner in the above-named Foreign Limited Partnership and that the execution of this application for registration is my act and deed and that the facts stated herein are true. Name **X** Authorized Signature
8. Certificate of Acceptance of Appointment of Registered Agent:	*I hereby accept appointment as Registered Agent for the above named Entity.* **X** Authorized Signature of Registered Agent or On Behalf of Registered Agent Entity Date

This form must be accompanied by appropriate fees.

Nevada Secretary of State NRS 87A FLP Registration
Revised on 7-1-08

certificate of limited partnership. The certificate, as a public record, should comply with the state's requirements; to include additional elements not required may only necessitate filing an amendment and paying a filing fee later. Under the prior act, the 1916 ULPA, the agreement could be filed as the certificate in many states so long as it complied with the statutory formalities for the certificate.

Limited partners will obviously desire a comprehensive agreement because their involvement in the business is so strictly curtailed. In many respects, the limited partnership agreement will be similar to a general partnership agreement because the important elements of the two, such as allocation of profits and losses, events causing dissolution, and the general partner's responsibilities, are common. A form of limited partnership agreement is available at www.tannedfeet.com.

The following elements should be included in a limited partnership agreement:

Name of Partnership. Consult the appropriate state statutes to ensure compliance in selecting the name of the limited partnership. After ensuring availability, determine whether the state requires the signal "limited partnership" or "L.P." Recall that a limited partner's surname cannot be used in the business name unless it is also the surname of a general partner or the business was carried on under that name prior to that limited partner's admission. Many states allow limited partnerships to reserve a name so another applicant cannot take it before the formation of the limited partnership.

Names and Addresses of Partners. The names and addresses of all partners should be stated. Additionally, the agreement should designate whether a partner is a general or limited partner. Many limited partnerships that have a large number of limited partners identify the limited partners in an exhibit or attachment to the agreement.

Recitals. The recital clause confirms the intent of the partners to create a limited partnership. This clause clarifies that this is a unique partnership in which individuals who control the enterprise will have unlimited liability, and others are mere passive investors not subject to any risk beyond their contributions.

Purpose. A clause should be included stating the purpose of the limited partnership, for example, real estate development, the maintenance and management of shopping centers, or the operation of a chain of restaurants. The limited partnership can conduct any lawful activity. This clause should not be so restrictive as to limit the limited partnership from carrying on other activities. Thus, after the specific purpose is given, consider including a broader provision, such as "and any other activities reasonably related to the purposes of this partnership or that are lawful in this State."

Address. The principal place of business of the partnership should be provided. Certain documents must be kept by limited partnerships and all partners should be provided with the location of these documents, because, under RULPA § 105(b), the records are subject to inspection by any partner. Furthermore, this address will provide a location for certain notices and communications to be sent to the limited partnership.

Term.   The date for termination of the limited partnership should be stated. Alternatively, this section can set forth any events that will cause a dissolution of the limited partnership. If no time limit is set, under the RULPA, a limited partner may withdraw from the partnership and demand a return of capital on six months' notice.

Certificate of Limited Partnership.   The agreement should mandate that the certificate of limited partnership be recorded in the appropriate state office (or confirm the filing of the certificate). A specific general partner should be designated to be in charge of the original filing of the certificate as well as any needed amendments to it. Under RULPA § 209, a copy of the filed certificate (or any amendment or cancellation) must be delivered to each limited partner unless the agreement provides otherwise.

Financial Provisions.   A variety of provisions relating to finances should be included. First, the initial contributions of all partners should be identified. Originally, limited partners were only allowed to contribute cash or property to a limited partnership and were prohibited from contributing services. This prohibition against contributing services was related to the prohibition against control of the business by limited partners. Under the RULPA, limited partners may contribute money, property, services rendered, a promissory note, or some other obligation to contribute cash or property or to perform services. RULPA § 501. If property or services are contributed, their value should be set forth so that if a limited partner contributes office furniture, for example, and then demands a return of capital, all partners are in agreement as to what this return should be.

   The need for additional contributions also should be addressed so that if the partnership needs additional capital, there is a procedure for effecting this. Typically, as in general partnerships, additional contributions will be required in the same percentage as initial contributions, so that if a limited partner contributed 27 percent of the original capital, she will need to contribute 27 percent of additional capital needed. If desired, limitations can be set so that no limited partner is required to contribute more than a certain percentage of her original contribution. Provisions for reimbursement of expenses incurred for the partnership should be included, as should provisions relating to accounting methods.

Liability.   The agreement should confirm the general principle that the limited partners will have no personal liability for losses or liabilities of the partnership and that the general partners retain personal liability for all partnership losses and obligations.

Profits and Losses.   This section of the agreement should set forth the share of profits to be distributed to each partner and the losses allocated to each partner. As with general partnerships, agreements usually provide that profits and losses be shared in proportion to the contributions to the limited partnerships. If a written agreement fails to provide for allocation of profits and losses, RULPA § 503 provides that profits and losses will be allocated on the basis of the contributions made by partners that have been received and not returned by the partnership. This is quite different from the approach taken by the UPA and the RUPA, which both provide that in the absence of agreement, profits and losses in a general partnership will be shared equally, regardless of contributions. Because general partners have complete responsibility for management and control of the business and face unlimited liability, they are usually provided a salary or perhaps an additional percentage of profit. Any losses caused by the reckless or willful conduct of any partner should be borne by that partner alone. Unless otherwise provided in writing, partners have no right to receive any distribution from a limited partnership in any form other than cash. Thus, if desired, the agreement should set forth any rights of partners to demand property rather than cash as a distribution.

Rights and Duties of General Partner.   Because the general partner has the sole responsibility to conduct partnership business, express authority should be granted to him to conduct such business. Arrangements should be made for the general partner to pay the partnership's obligations, such as rent and insurance, and the general partner should be given the authority to conduct ordinary business on behalf of the partnership, including filing amendments to the certificate of limited partnership. If there are to be any limitations on the general partner's authority, they should be clearly expressed. For example, the partners may wish to limit to a stated dollar amount the general partner's authority to borrow money on behalf of the partnership or to sell partnership assets, to limit the general partner's authority to admit another general partner, or to prohibit the general partner from instituting any litigation or settling any claim without notice to all partners. Unless restrictions are provided, a general partner in a limited partnership has all of the powers and rights of a general partner in a general partnership. RULPA § 403(a). Additionally, if there is more than one general partner, the agreement should provide a formula for their voting. Any compensation and benefits general partners will receive should be described.

Rights and Duties of Limited Partners.   The agreement should incorporate the safe harbor provisions of RULPA § 303(b) setting forth the activities that may be undertaken by limited partners without risk of losing their limited liability status as well as any other permitted acts. Furthermore, the provisions of RULPA § 305 allowing limited partners to inspect and copy partnership records, to obtain information from the general partner regarding the state of affairs and financial conditions of the limited partnership, and to obtain copies of the limited partnership's various tax returns and other reasonable information should be incorporated. Further expansion of the rights of limited partners will jeopardize their limited liability status. Provisions may be included to allow removal of a general partner for certain acts of misconduct.

Admission of New General Partners.   Under RULPA § 401, after the filing of a limited partnership's original certificate of limited partnership, additional general partners may be admitted as provided by the written agreement of the partners or, if the partnership agreement does not provide in writing for the admission of an additional general partner, with the written consent of *all* partners. Thus, if the agreement so provides, a general partner can be admitted upon a less-than-unanimous vote by all partners.

Admission of New Limited Partners.   As to admission of additional limited partners, RULPA § 301(b) provides that after the filing of the original certificate of limited partnership, a person may be admitted as a new limited partner upon compliance with the provisions in the limited partnership agreement, or if the partnership agreement is silent, upon the written consent of *all* partners. Thus, the agreement can provide for the admission of new limited partners solely by the consent of the general partner or a simple majority vote of the partners. Any new partners, whether general or limited, should be required to sign the agreement and agree to be bound by its provisions.

Withdrawal of General Partners.   According to RULPA § 402, unless agreed otherwise by all partners in writing, the following are **events of withdrawal** of a general partner that will cause a dissolution of the partnership:

Events of withdrawal
Events relating to a general partner that cause dissolution of a limited partnership

1. The general partner withdraws by giving written notice to the other partners; however, if this withdrawal violates the terms of the partnership agreement, which might specify a definite date of duration, the limited partnership can recover any damages from the general partner caused by this breach of agreement;
2. The general partner assigns all of her interest to an assignee;
3. The general partner is removed from the partnership in accord with the terms of the partnership agreement (such as removal by a certain percentage of the limited partnership interests);
4. Unless allowed by a written partnership agreement, the general partner:
    a. Makes an assignment for the benefit of creditors;
    b. Is adjudicated bankrupt; or
    c. Files a petition under the Bankruptcy Act or consents to the appointment of a receiver for his or her property; or
5. The general partner dies (if she is a natural person) or is terminated or dissolved (if it is an entity).

The agreement may, of course, provide that the partnership can survive any of these events. Nevertheless, if the general partner withdraws in violation of the terms of the limited partnership agreement, she may be held liable for damages caused by this breach of agreement.

Remember that an event of withdrawal, however, will not cause a dissolution if there is at least one other general partner and the written partnership agreement permits the business to be conducted by the remaining general partner or, if within 90 days after the withdrawal, *all* partners agree in writing to continue the partnership business and a new general partner is appointed, if needed. RULPA § 801.

Withdrawal of Limited Partners.   According to RULPA § 603, a limited partner may withdraw from a limited partnership in accordance with the provisions of the limited partnership agreement, such as those relating to the term of the agreement or the occurrence of certain events. If the agreement does not specify such events, a limited partner may withdraw from the partnership upon giving six months' written notice to each general partner. At the time of withdrawal, a limited partner (or general partner) is entitled to receive any distribution to which he or she may be entitled under the terms of the agreement, or, if not otherwise provided, may receive the fair value of his interest in the limited partnership, so long as partnership assets exceed liabilities (to ensure creditors are fully paid before distributions are paid to a limited partner). Because six months is a fairly lengthy notice period, the agreement may provide for a shorter period. The agreement may provide that a limited partner who wishes to sell his interest must first offer it to other existing partners.

The limited partnership does not dissolve upon the death or withdrawal of a limited partner. Because limited partners are merely passive investors, their membership in the partnership is not critical to the operation of the partnership business, and thus they may freely withdraw from a limited partnership without causing a dissolution.

Transfer of Partnership Interests.   According to RULPA § 702, both general and limited partners may assign, in whole or in part, their **partnership interest,** meaning their share of the profits of the partnership. Such an assignment does not dissolve the partnership or immediately allow the assignee to become a partner. The assignee is entitled to receive only the distribution to which the assignor would be entitled. The assignee may, however, become a limited partner if the assignor so agrees and the partnership agreement provides for such or if all other partners consent. Naturally, any assignee should be required to execute the limited partnership agreement. One ceases to be a partner upon assignment of all of his or her partnership interest.

Partnership interest
A partner's share of partnership profits

Dissolution.   There are two types of dissolution of a limited partnership: nonjudicial and judicial. As the very names indicate, nonjudicial dissolution occurs without the involvement of a court and judicial dissolution involves court action.

As to **nonjudicial dissolution,** under RULPA § 801, a limited partnership is dissolved and its business must be wound up upon the following:

Nonjudicial dissolution
Dissolution of an entity without involvement by a court

1.   The time specified in the certificate of limited partnership;
2.   Upon the occurrence of any events specified in a written partnership agreement;
3.   Written consent of all partners;
4.   An event of withdrawal of a general partner (unless, of course, there is another general partner to carry on the business and the agreement permits the business to be carried on *or* if within 90 days after the withdrawal, all partners agree in writing to continue the partnership business and to the appointment of one or more additional general partners); or
5.   Entry of a decree of judicial dissolution.

As to **judicial dissolution,** any partner may apply to a court to dissolve the limited partnership when it is no longer reasonably practicable to carry on the business in conformity with the partnership agreement. RULPA § 802.

Judicial dissolution
Dissolution of an entity ordered by a court

Liquidation.   Unless a general partner has wrongfully dissolved a limited partnership, the general partner will be responsible for winding up or liquidating the business affairs of the limited partnership. Additionally, upon application by any partner, a court may wind up the partnership's business affairs.

Upon the winding up of a limited partnership, its assets must be distributed as follows:

1.   To creditors, including partners who are creditors (having made loans to the partnership or having incurred expenses on behalf of the partnership);
2.   To partners and former partners who have withdrawn, to satisfy the return of their contributions; and

3. To partners for the return of their contributions, and then to partners
for profits, according to their respective partnership interests (except as
provided in the partnership agreement). RULPA § 804.

Miscellaneous Provisions.   Just as in general partnership agreements, numerous
other provisions may be included in a limited partnership agreement.

1. Non-compete clauses can be provided (in most states) to prohibit withdrawing general partners from competing with the partnership business
for a reasonable period of time within a reasonable geographic area.
2. The partners should provide a method for resolving disputes. They may
elect arbitration or may agree upon a court in which to bring actions.
Attorneys' fees and costs may be allowed to the prevailing party.
3. "Standard" or "boilerplate" provisions may be included, such as how
notice of certain matters is to be given; that the agreement will be inter-
preted according to the laws of a certain state; that if part of the agreement
is invalid, the rest remains valid; that the agreement supersedes and
replaces any prior written or oral agreements; that the agreement can
be modified only in writing upon the consent of all partners; and that
use of masculine and singular terms includes the feminine and plural.

Signatures.   All partners should sign and date the limited partnership agreement.
Any new partners, whether general or limited, should also be required to sign the
agreement. Corporate partners should sign by an authorized officer of the corporation. General partners that are themselves general partnerships should sign by an
authorized general partner.

H.   Transferability of Interest

The transfer or assignment of a limited partner's interest in a limited partnership is
much more easily accomplished than such an assignment by a general partner in a
general partnership.

RULPA § 702 provides that a partner's interest in the partnership, namely,
his right to profits, is assignable in whole or in part. No permission is required from
any partner. The assignment, however, does not automatically entitle the assignee
to become a member of the partnership. Nevertheless, an assignee of either a
general or limited partner may become a limited partner if the assignor gives
that right in accordance with the terms of the limited partnership agreement *or*
all the other partners consent.

The reason for such ready transferability by limited partners is that they are
passive investors who do not participate in the control of the business. Therefore,
business operations and management are not greatly affected by the transfer in and
out of limited partners. In essence, they may be viewed as simply "money men" who
make financial contributions to the partnership and hope that the general partner's
expertise and management skills will enhance the value of their investment.

General partners may also assign their interest in the partnership to another,
unless the agreement provides otherwise. The assignee receives only the distribution

to which the transferring general partner would be entitled. A new general partner may be admitted as provided in the agreement, or if the agreement is silent, upon the written consent of all partners.

Generally, unless the agreement provides otherwise, a partner (whether general or limited) ceases to be a partner upon assignment of all of his or her partnership interest. Such an action by a general partner is an event of withdrawal that triggers dissolution and winding up unless the partnership agreement allows the business to continue or all partners, within 90 days, agree in writing to continue the business and to the appointment of one or more additional general partners.

Any partner's interest in the limited partnership (or right to distributions) may be seized by creditors.

I. Actions by Limited Partners

If a limited partner has been directly injured by the limited partnership, for example, she is refused her statutorily granted right to inspect the books, the limited partner may institute an action for this injury to her. This type of action is called a **direct action** because the limited partner has been directly injured.

Direct action
Action brought by one to redress a wrong done to him or her

In some instances, however, the limited partnership itself is injured and refuses to enforce its own cause of action. For example, assume that a limited partnership loans $50,000 to one of the friends of a general partner. If the loan is not paid, the general partner may be reluctant to enforce a claim against his or her friend. The failure to enforce a claim, however, deprives the limited partnership of capital. In such a case, a limited partner may institute a **derivative suit** to enforce the obligation due to the limited partnership. The action is referred to as derivative because the limited partner is not suing for himself but rather to enforce rights derived from his ownership interest in the limited partnership. The action can be instituted by a limited partner if the general partner has refused to bring the action or if an effort to cause the general partner to bring the action is not likely to be successful. To ensure that individuals do not join partnerships solely to litigate actions, RULPA § 1002 provides that the plaintiff partner must have been a partner at the time of the transaction being complained of. If the derivative action is successful, the recovery will belong to the limited partnership although the limited partner who brought the action may be reimbursed for expenses and attorneys' fees. (See RULPA §§ 1001-1004.) The rules and procedures for derivative actions by limited partners are highly similar to those for derivative actions by stockholders discussed in Chapter Eleven.

Derivative suit
Action brought by one to enforce an obligation owed to another, usually to a business

J. Dissolution and Winding Up of Limited Partnerships

As noted earlier, a limited partnership is dissolved and its business affairs must be wound up when one of the following events occurs:

1. The time specified for the duration of the limited partnership expires;

2. Upon the happening of any events specified in writing in the limited partnership agreement (such as an agreement to dissolve when property is sold, when revenue drops below a certain level, or when a change in tax laws may make it unwise to operate as a limited partnership);
3. Written consent of all partners;
4. An event of withdrawal of the general partner unless there is at least one general partner to conduct the business and the written agreement so provides, or, if within 90 days after the withdrawal, all partners agree in writing to continue the business and to appoint an additional general partner, if necessary; or
5. A decree of judicial dissolution is entered upon application of any partner who shows that it is not reasonably practicable to continue the limited partnership business.

Unless a general partner has wrongfully caused a dissolution (for example, by withdrawing before the term set in the agreement), the general partner may wind up or liquidate the limited partnership by collecting its assets and completing its obligations. Otherwise, a court may oversee the winding up upon the application of any partner.

After creditors are paid (including partners' claims for reimbursement for expenses incurred or loans made on behalf of the partnership), partners and former partners will then receive any outstanding distributions. Then partners will receive a return of their contributions and, finally, their profits. Whereas the original 1916 ULPA preferred limited partners to general partners by requiring distributions to limited partners before distributions to general partners, the RULPA allows for no such distinctions between the two types of partners in the distribution of assets.

K. Cancellation of Limited Partnership Certificate

The creation of a limited partnership is accomplished by the filing of a certificate of limited partnership. When the limited partnership is dissolved and wound up, a certificate of cancellation should be filed with the secretary of state. It will contain basic information about the limited partnership, including the reason for discontinuance of the business. The certificate must be filed and signed by all general partners and must usually be accompanied by a filing fee. (Figure 4-4 provides a certificate of cancellation of limited partnership.) If the partnership is doing business in any other states, it should cancel or withdraw any applications in those foreign states.

L. Taxation of Limited Partnerships

In general, taxation of a limited partnership is highly similar to taxation of a general partnership. Thus, all of the income earned by the partnership is "passed through" to the partners, who declare their share of the profits, whether distributed or not, on their own individual tax returns. Similarly, losses can be used to offset other income of the partners. To ensure that limited partnerships were not used solely as

FIGURE 4-4
Arizona Certificate of Cancellation of Limited Partnership

Please mail Registration to:
Secretary of State Ken Bennett
1700 West Washington 7th Fl. Phoenix, Arizona 85007
Walk-in service: 14 N. 18th Ave., Phoenix, Arizona
Tucson Office: 400 W. Congress, Ste. 252
(602) 542-6187
(800) 458-5842 (within Arizona)
Filing Fee: $10.00
Plus $3.00 per page

SUBMIT IN DUPLICATE with a self-addressed stamped envelope.

PARTNERSHIP CANCELLATION CERTIFICATE
(This form may be used for <u>all</u> types of partnerships)

Partnership Name

Secretary of State File Number: _____

Original Date of Filing:_____

Please State the Reason for Filing the Certificate of Cancellation:
_____
_____
_____
_____

The Effective Date of Cancellation: _____

Please Provide the Name and Signature of All General Partners:
(**Foreign Limited Partnerships only require the signature of <u>one</u> general partner**)

_____   _____
Printed Name   Signature

_____   _____
Printed Name   Signature

_____   _____
Printed Name   Signature

Please Attach Any Additional Sheets, If Necessary.

Tax shelter
A vehicle that focuses on tax savings rather than on profit-making

tax shelters (vehicles that focus on tax savings rather than on profit-making), certain provisions of the Tax Reform Act of 1986 limited the ability of limited partners to take advantage of losses sustained by the limited partnership. Losses of the partnership that are allocated to general partners may be used to offset income from any other source, whereas losses allocated to limited partners can now be used to offset only income received from other similar passive investments and only to the extent that limited partners are at risk, meaning to the extent of their contributions to the limited partnership entity.

Although the limited partnership, itself not a separate taxable entity, does not pay tax (unless it has sufficient characteristics of a corporation that it can be treated and taxed as such by the Internal Revenue Service), it will complete and file an information tax return, just as a general partnership does. In fact, the similarities between general and limited partnerships regarding tax treatment are so great, that the very form used by a general partnership to file its information tax return, Form 1065 (see Figure 3-7), is also used by the limited partnership. Similarly, individual general partners and limited partners in a limited partnership report their respective income or losses on Schedule K-1 and attach it to their individual tax returns. Schedule K-1, shown in Figure 3-6, is used by general partners of general partnerships as well. Although limited partnerships are treated as general partnerships for tax purposes, like general partnerships, a limited partnership can elect to be taxed as a corporation by "checking the box" on the appropriate tax form. (See Chapter Three and Figure 3-8.) Although limited partnerships do not pay federal income taxes, they may be subject to state taxation on income in various states.

Key Features
of Limited Partnerships

- ◆ Limited partnerships must have at least one general partner and one limited partner.
- ◆ The general partner in a limited partnership functions identically to and has the same risks as a general partner in a general partnership.
- ◆ Limited partners do not have personal liability for the limited partnership's obligations (so long as they do not control the business); their liability is limited to the amount invested in the enterprise.
- ◆ Formation of limited partnerships requires filing a Certificate of Limited Partnership with the appropriate state agency.
- ◆ Limited partners can freely enter and exit the partnership.
- ◆ Limited partnership agreements may be oral or written; if there is no written agreement on profits and losses, they are allocated on the basis of contributions made by partners.
- ◆ Limited partnerships offer "pass-through" taxation, meaning that the entity does not pay tax, but, rather, all income is passed through to the partners, who pay at their respective tax rates.

M.   Family Limited Partnerships

A relatively new twist on limited partnerships is the **family limited partnership,** which is not truly a different form of limited partnership, but a vehicle to achieve certain estate and tax planning benefits. In a family limited partnership (sometimes called a "FLiP" or *family limited liability company* if organized as a limited liability company), all partners are family members (or spouses of family members) and income-producing capital assets, such as a family farm, rental property, or securities, are transferred into the family limited partnership. In most cases, parents act as general partners, and children and other family members are limited partners.

Because the first $2 million of income is excluded from one's estate tax (under 2008 law), the parents each initially make a gift of limited partnership interests in this amount to their children/limited partners (for a total of $4 million). Thereafter, because, as of 2007, individuals can annually give away or "gift" up to $12,000 ($24,000 if both parents give) to each child each year, and the giver neither pays gift tax on the amount nor does the recipient pay tax on the amount received, additional fractional interests in the family limited partnership are transferred or gifted from the parents to the children/limited partners each year. In essence, money is shifted out of the parents' estates so the estates will not be subject to taxation upon death of the parents; yet the parents, as general partners, maintain control and management of the limited partnership business itself. In most cases, the parents own far less interest in the family limited partnership than do the children (in many instances, as low as 1 percent each). The children, as limited partners, do not control the business and have no personal liability. The parents, as general partners, often receive a management fee of some type to provide them with a stream of income. The Internal Revenue Service carefully scrutinizes family limited partnerships to ensure that they comply with federal tax regulations. For tax years 2006, 2007, and 2008, the estate tax exclusion was $2 million per person. It will reach $3.5 million in 2009 before it disappears in 2010. The current gift tax exclusion of $12,000 per person is indexed to inflation so it may increase over time.

A family limited partnership is created just like any other limited partnership. However, because of its complexity and because of IRS scrutiny, an attorney will need to be engaged to prepare the appropriate documents. A family limited partnership is essentially a device to minimize or eliminate estate taxes through the transfer of property into the partnership, most of the interest of which is held by the children/limited partners.

Family limited partnership
An investment vehicle entered into by family members to achieve estate and tax planning benefits (sometimes called a *family limited liability company*)

N.   Limited Liability Limited Partnerships

Some states and the 2001 Act, discussed later, provide for limited partnerships to file certain statements with the secretary of state to elect to be classified as **limited liability limited partnerships** (LLLP). The usual procedure is that the Certificate of Limited Partnership requires the filer to state whether the entity is being organized as a "standard" limited partnership or as a limited liability limited partnership. This requirement is intended to force the organizers to affirmatively decide whether the entity is to be a conventional limited partnership or an LLLP, the effect of which is that the general partners then have limited liability

Limited liability limited partnership
A form of limited partnership affording protection from personal liability to its general partners

for partnership debts and obligations, making their liability equivalent to that of limited partners. Alternatively, a limited partnership may convert or change its status to an LLLP.

In this limited partnership, the general partners continue to manage the business but have limited liability. The qualification must generally be approved by all general partners and a majority of limited partners. The name of the limited partnership then must include a signal indicating it has qualified as an LLLP. Thus, the entity's name may be "Colonial Park Associates, L.L.L.P."

Because limited partnerships can convert to limited liability partnerships (discussed in Chapter Five), which provide limited liability to all of their partners, the advantage of a limited partnership qualifying as an LLLP is somewhat academic; thus, at present, only 14 states recognize this form of limited partnership.

In sum, a limited liability limited partnership is a form of limited partnership that, by virtue of electing LLLP status in a form filed with the secretary of state, qualifies to protect all of its partners, both general and limited, from personal liability for the obligations of the business. In all other respects (formation, operation, dissolution, and taxation), it is the same as an ordinary limited partnership.

O.   Uniform Limited Partnership Act of 2001

Introduction.   As discussed earlier, in 2001, the National Conference of Commissioners on Uniform State Laws (the "Conference") completed a full revision of the current uniform acts governing limited partnerships. The Uniform Limited Partnership Act of 2001 ("2001 Act") has been fully adopted in only 14 states as of early 2009 (Arkansas, California, Florida, Hawaii, Idaho, Illinois, Iowa, Kentucky, Maine, Minnesota, Nevada, New Mexico, North Dakota, and Oklahoma).

According to the Conference, the 2001 Act does not change the basic structure of limited partnerships but provides greater flexibility and protection to two types of limited partnerships: sophisticated groups seeking strongly entrenched and centralized management (usually commercial limited partnerships whose participants commit for the long term) and family limited partnerships, formed for estate planning purposes, as discussed in Section M of this chapter. This specific targeting of these two types of businesses is a recognition that the typical limited partnership is waning in interest, having been replaced and superseded by the newer limited liability partnerships and limited liability companies, both of which provide protection from personal liability and yet allow their participants to manage the business. In sum, the 2001 Act is thus designed to target the sophisticated enterprise and the family limited partnership (discussed in the preceding section).

Perhaps the most significant provisions of the 2001 Act relate to liability of the partners in a limited partnership. Under the 2001 Act, limited partners have no liability for any limited partnership obligation even if they manage or control the business. Furthermore, and as discussed previously, at the time of its formation, the limited partnership must state in its certificate of limited partnership whether it will be a limited liability limited partnership. If such an election is made (see Figure 4-5), the general partners are relieved of any personal liability for the partnership's debts or obligations, which can be satisfied solely from the assets of the limited partnership itself. These changes are significant and substantive and clearly ameliorate the harsh effects of current limited partnership laws, which provide that

FIGURE 4-5
Florida Certificate of Limited Partnership or Limited Liability Limited Partnership (Partial)

CERTIFICATE OF LIMITED PARTNERSHIP
FOR
FLORIDA LIMITED PARTNERSHIP
OR
LIMITED LIABILITY LIMITED PARTNERSHIP

1._____.

   (Name of Limited Partnership or Limited Liability Limited Partnership, *which must include suffix*)
Acceptable Limited Partnership suffixes: Limited Partnership, Limited, L.P., LP, or Ltd.
Acceptable Limited Liability Limited Partnership suffixes: Limited Liability Limited Partnership, L.L.L.P.
or LLLP.

2._____
                    (Street address of initial designated office)

_____

3._____
                    (Name of Registered Agent for Service of Process)

4._____
                    (Florida street address for Registered Agent)

_____

5. *I hereby accept the appointment as registered agent and agree to act in this capacity. I further agree to comply with the provisions of all statutes relative to the proper and complete performance of my duties, and I am familiar with and accept the obligations of my position as registered agent.*

            _____
                    Signature of Registered Agent

6._____
                    (Mailing address of initial designated office)

_____

7. If limited partnership elects to be a limited liability limited partnership, check box ☐

Page 1 of 2

general partners have inescapable personal liability for business obligations and that limited partners will lose their protected status if they control the business. The election to be an LLLP recognizes the modern trend of limiting personal liability and places general partners and limited partners on an equal footing with shareholders in a corporation, partners in a limited liability partnership, and members of a limited liability company, all of whom are protected from personal liability.

The Conference also expressly recognized that the rule imposing personal liability on limited partners who "control" partnership affairs was "an anachronism" in a modern world offering new business structures that provide full protection to all members. The 2001 Act thus eliminates the control rule and provides a full shield against limited partner liability for obligations of the entity itself, whether or not the limited partnership is an LLLP or a "standard" limited partnership.

The 2001 Act is a stand-alone act, meaning it is not dependent on either the UPA or the RULPA. Recall from the beginning of this chapter that the RULPA is specifically linked to general partnership statutes (by virtue of RULPA's § 1105, which provides that in any case not provided for, the provisions of the Uniform Partnership Act of 1997 govern). The full text of the 2001 Act is available at the Conference's Web site at www.nccusl.org.

Although only 14 states have fully adopted the 2001 Act, a number of other states (including Delaware, South Dakota, and Virginia) recognize LLLPs. Their statutes allow limited partnerships to elect LLLP status and thereby limit the liability of general partners in a limited partnership.

Significant Provisions of 2001 Act.   Some of the major characteristics of the 2001 Act are as follows:

- *Full liability shield for general partners.* One of the disadvantages for a general partner in a limited partnership under the RULPA is the complete personal liability for any obligations of the limited partnership. The 2001 Act requires a limited partnership to state in its organizing document, the certificate of limited partnership, whether it is a limited liability limited partnership. 2001 Act § 201(a)(4). If such an election is made, the general partners will be shielded from any personal liability, and any obligations of the limited partnership, whether arising in tort or in contract, must be satisfied solely by the limited partnership itself. 2001 Act § 404(c).
- *Full liability shield for limited partners.* Whereas the RULPA position is that a limited partner is shielded from personal liability only if he does not control the limited partnership, the 2001 Act provides that a limited partner is not personally liable for any obligation of the limited partnership even if the limited partner participates in the management and control of the business. 2001 Act § 303. This full shield for limited partners applies whether or not the limited partnership has elected to be a limited liability limited partnership.
- *Perpetual duration.* Under the RULPA, the latest date for dissolution of the limited partnership is required to be set forth in the certificate of limited partnership. Under the 2001 Act, a limited partnership has perpetual duration (although the partnership agreement can vary this by providing for an express term or by specifying events that would cause dissolution). 2001 Act § 104(c).

- *Use of limited partner's name.* The RULPA prohibits the use of a limited partner's surname in the business name except in certain limited circumstances. The 2001 Act, however, allows the use of any partner's name in the limited partnership's name. 2001 Act § 108(a).
- *Annual report.* The 2001 Act requires the limited partnership to file an annual report with the secretary of state providing basic information about the limited partnership. 2001 Act § 210. No such annual report is required under the RULPA.
- *Dissolution by consent.* The RULPA allows a limited partnership to dissolve and wind up at any time upon the written consent of all partners. The 2001 Act provides that the limited partnership may be dissolved and wound up upon consent of all general partners and a majority of the limited partnership interests. 2001 Act § 801(2).
- *Transfers of interests.* The provisions of the RULPA relating to transfers of partnership interests are substantially the same in the 2001 Act; thus, a partner's rights to distributions are fully transferable, although the transferee does not become a partner with rights to manage or control merely by virtue of the transfer. 2001 Act § 702.
- *Dissolutions.* Both the RULPA and the 2001 Act allow a limited partner to dissociate without causing a dissolution and winding up of the entity. Provisions relating to dissociations of general partners are substantially the same in both acts. Under the RULPA, partners must unanimously agree to continue the business after a general partner's dissociation, whereas under the 2001 Act, generally only a majority vote is needed to continue the business after such a dissociation. 2001 Act § 801.
- *Writing requirements.* Generally, under the RULPA, many provisions and agreements need to be in writing to be valid. For example, under the RULPA, to continue a limited partnership after a general partner's dissociation, all partners have to agree to such in writing, whereas the 2001 Act merely requires the majority of the partners to agree to such continuation. Similarly, under the RULPA, a new general partner can be admitted only with the written consent of all partners, whereas the 2001 Act merely provides that a new general partner can be admitted with the consent of all partners. No requirement of a writing is imposed in such circumstances.

Quick Reference: The Alphabet Soup of Partnerships

General Partnerships	Limited Partnerships	Limited Liability Limited Partnerships
Most states follow 1997 Revised Uniform Partnership Act; a few follow 1914 Act	Most states follow Revised Uniform Limited Partnership Act of 1976 (with 1985 Amendments)	Fourteen states follow 2001 Act (called the Uniform Partnership Act). Some other states recognize LLLP form without adopting the 2001 Act.

General Partnerships	*Limited Partnerships*	*Limited Liability Limited Partnerships*
Formed by agreement (written or oral)	Formed by filing Certificate of LP	Formed by filing Certificate of LP
All partners are general partners	Has general and limited partners	Has general and limited partners
All partners may control	Only general partners may control	All partners may control
All partners have unlimited joint and several personal liability	Only general partners have personal liability	No partners have personal liability

See Figure 4-6 for a chart comparing some of the provisions of the RULPA with those of the 2001 Act.

FIGURE 4-6
Comparison of Limited Partnerships Under RULPA and 2001 Act

	RULPA	*2001 Act*
Status of Entity	Entity must be a limited partnership with full liability for general partners.	Entity may elect to be a limited liability limited partnership and thereby eliminate personal liability of general partners and provide full liability shield to limited partners.
Duration	Certificate of limited partnership must provide latest date for dissolution.	A limited partnership has perpetual duration.
Limited Partner's Name	Limited partner's name cannot be used in name of entity except in limited circumstances.	Any partner's name may be used in entity's name.
Annual Report	There is no requirement of filing an annual report.	An annual report must be filed with secretary of state.
Profits and Losses	Unless agreed in writing otherwise, profits and losses will be divided according to contributions of partners.	Unless agreed in writing otherwise, profits and losses will be divided according to contributions of partners.
Liability of General Partners	General partners have full inescapable personal liability for obligations of the limited partnership.	If the entity elects to be a limited liability limited partnership, the general partner will not be personally liable for obligations of the limited partnership.

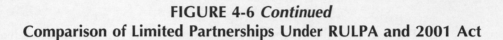

FIGURE 4-6 *Continued*
Comparison of Limited Partnerships Under RULPA and 2001 Act

	RULPA	*2001 Act*
Liability of Limited Partners	Limited partners are protected from personal liability unless they control the business.	Limited partners are protected from personal liability even if they participate in management and control of the business.
Transfer of Interests	Rights to distributions are fully transferable although transferee does not become a partner by virtue of the transfer.	Same. Rights to distributions are fully transferable although transferee does not become a partner by virtue of the transfer.
Dissociation of Limited Partner	Limited partner may withdraw upon six months' notice unless partnership agreement provides a term or provides otherwise.	Limited partner does not have absolute right to dissociate before termination of the limited partnership. Limited partner may give notice of will to withdraw, but such withdrawal is wrongful.
Dissolution	Withdrawal of limited partner does not cause dissolution and winding up. Withdrawal of general partner does not cause dissolution if agreement allows continuation or if all partners agree in writing to continue.	Dissociation of limited partner does not cause dissolution and winding up. Dissociation of general partner does not cause a dissolution if, generally within 90 days, majority agree to continuation of business.

PRACTICE TIP

What is the future of limited partnerships? Will they continue to exist if businesses can adopt new business structures such as LLPs or LLCs or adopt the 2001 Act, which allows limited partners to control without losing their liability and shields general partners from personal liability? Although the trend in forming limited partnerships is declining, many limited partnerships are formed annually, and numerous limited partnerships were formed well before the new business structures developed and thus continue to follow limited partnership statutes. Thus, according to at least one expert, the traditional limited partnership is diminishing, but it hasn't yet disappeared.

P. Role of Paralegal

Because limited partnerships can be formed only by compliance with appropriate state statutes, the organization of limited partnerships offers unique opportunities for paralegals to play an integral role in the creation of limited partnerships.

The paralegal can check the availability of the desired name, determine what signals (such as "limited partnership" or "L.P.," must be included in the name) and ensure that a limited partner's surname is not used improperly in the partnership name of a traditional limited partnership.

The paralegal will likely have an active role in drafting and filing the certificate of limited partnership. Review state statutes carefully to determine what information is required. Changes in the limited partnership should also be monitored to determine when an amendment to the certificate must be filed.

Drafting the limited partnership agreement provides another challenging task. Review your office files to determine if sample forms exist. Prepare a checklist of questions to ask the client so that you can resolve all issues expeditiously rather than continually contacting the client for additional information. Use the checklist and questionnaire provided in Figure 4-7.

Case Illustration
Limited Partners May Not Control Partnership

Case:	*Gonzales v. Chalpin*, 552 N.Y.S.2d 419 (App. Div.), *aff'd*, 565 N.E.2d 1253 (N.Y. 1990)
Facts:	The plaintiff was hired by the defendants as superintendent of their apartment building and to perform extensive repairs. After the plaintiff was fired, he sued the defendant limited partnership and the individual limited partner, Edward Chalpin. The trial court ruled in favor of the plaintiff and the defendants appealed.
Holding:	The judgment against the defendants, including limited partner Chalpin, was affirmed. Chalpin performed an extensive role in running the affairs of the limited partnership (including signing checks for the partnership). If a limited partner plays an active role in partnership affairs, he becomes liable as a general partner.

FIGURE 4-7
Limited Partnership Checklist and Questionnaire

1. Proposed name of partnership _____
    Alternative Names[s] _____
2. Names and Addresses of General Partner[s]
    a. _____   b. _____
       _____   _____
       _____   _____
3. Names and Addresses of Limited Partner[s]
    a. _____   b. _____
       _____   _____
       _____   _____
    c. _____   d. _____
       _____   _____
       _____   _____
4. Address of Limited Partnership _____
    _____
5. Purpose of Limited Partnership _____
6. Duration of Limited Partnership _____
7. Contributions and Profits and Losses of General Partners _____
    Name _____ Profits/Losses _____ Contribution _____
    Name _____ Profits/Losses _____ Contribution _____
8. Contributions and Profits and Losses of Limited Partners
    Name _____ Profits/Losses _____ Contribution _____
    Name _____ Profits/Losses _____ Contribution _____
    Name _____ Profits/Losses _____ Contribution _____
    Name _____ Profits/Losses _____ Contribution _____
9. Conditions Regarding Transferability of Partnership Interests _____
    _____
    _____
    _____
10. Admission of New General and Limited Partners _____
11. Designation of Managing Partner _____
12. Limitations on Rights of General Partners _____
13. Manner of Resolving Disputes _____
14. Events of Dissolution and Responsibility for Winding Up _____
    _____
15. Fiscal Year and Method of Accounting _____
16. Banking Information _____
17. Availability of LLLP Status? _____
18. Other Provisions _____
    _____

FIGURE 4-8
Comparison of General and Limited Partnerships

	General Partnerships Under RUPA	*Limited Partnerships Under RULPA*
Formation	Informal formation, no formal state filings required; agreement may be oral or written.	Must file certificate of limited partnership with secretary of state. Agreement may be oral or written, although it is usually written.
Ownership	Unlimited number of general partners permissible.	Must have at least one general partner and one limited partner.
Management	Unless otherwise agreed, all partners share equal rights to management.	Only general partners manage the business. Limited partners may not manage or control the business or they risk loss of limited liability status.
Profits and Losses	Unless otherwise agreed, profits and losses are divided equally among all partners.	Unless otherwise agreed in writing, profits and losses are divided according to contributions to limited partnership.
Liability	All general partners have unlimited personal liability.	Only general partners have personal liability. Limited partners are liable only to the extent of their contributions to the entity.
Dissolution	Many events of dissociation merely trigger a buyout of the dissociating partner's interest and partnership continues.	Death or assignment of limited partner does not dissolve entity. Entity can survive withdrawal or death of general partner if agreement provides or if all partners agree in writing to continue the entity.
Taxation	Pass-through tax status afforded to all partners.	Pass-through tax status afforded to all partners.

❖   ❖   ❖

WEB RESOURCES

A number of Web sites provide general information about partnerships with clear and concise discussions of limited partnerships, comparing and contrasting them to other forms of business entities. Many of the following sites provide forms for partnership agreements. Only a few provide forms specifically for limited partnership agreements because many professionals use a general partnership agreement as a starting point and then modify it to use for limited partnerships.

Secretaries of state and forms:	www.nass.org
	http://www.premiercorp.com/ _secretariesofstate.asp
State statutes:	www.law.cornell.edu
Text of RULPA and 2001 Act:	www.nccusl.org
Tax forms and instructions:	www.irs.gov
General information:	www.tannedfeet.com/partnerships.htm
	http://topics.law.cornell.edu/wex/ Partnership
	www.megalaw.com
	www.businessownersideacafe.com
Limited partnership agreements:	www.ilrg.com www.lectlaw.com
	www.allaboutforms.com (Select "Show All Business Topics.")
	www.siccode.com/form.php

Discussion Questions

Fact Scenario. Mike Dalton, Tom Peters, and Amy Latham have formed "Dalton & Peters, L.P.," an Alabama limited partnership, under the RULPA. Dalton and Peters are the general partners and Latham is the limited partner. Although the partnership has a written agreement, it does not discuss certain issues, including sharing of profits and losses and withdrawals of general partners. Dalton contributed $40,000 to the partnership, Peters contributed $35,000 to the partnership, and Latham contributed $25,000 to the partnership. Use the RULPA to answer the following questions.

1. The limited partnership certificate was filed but due to a typographical error identified the last date upon which the partnership was to dissolve as June 1, 2110, rather than as June 1, 2010. What is the effect of this error?

2. Which of the following activities are permissible for Latham?

- Contributing a trademark to the partnership rather than cash.
- Decorating the partnership offices (pursuant to a contract between the limited partnership and Latham).

- Guaranteeing a loan made by Bank of America to the limited partnership.
- Suggesting the dissolution of the limited partnership.
- Proposing a meeting to discuss removing Peters as a general partner.
- Inspecting the partnership's tax returns.
- Leasing a new office for the location of the partnership's business.

3. The partnership made $200,000 in profits this year. How will they be divided among the partners? How would these profits be divided if the partnership were a general partnership?

4. Dalton has just withdrawn from the limited partnership. What is the effect on the limited partnership of this withdrawal?

5. The limited partnership has decided to admit Amy Latham's husband, Doug Latham, as a new general partner. May the limited partnership's name be "Peters & Latham, L.P.?" Discuss.

6. The limited partnership has begun doing business in Mississippi without having first registered to do business there. What is the effect of this failure to transact business without registration?

7. The partnership has decided to dissolve and wind up. It has assets of $150,000 and owes $50,000 to the Bank of America. How will its assets be distributed upon winding up?

8. The partnership has decided to convert to a limited liability limited partnership. What effect will this have on the partners' liability for partnership obligations?

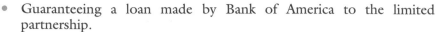

Net Worth

1. Access the Web site of the Secretary of State of Delaware.
   a. What is the filing fee to file a Certificate of Limited Partnership in Delaware?
   b. What is the fee to reserve a name for a limited partnership in Delaware?
2. Access the Web site of the Secretary of State of North Carolina. What is the fee to cancel a Certificate of Limited Partnership?
3. Access the Web site of the Secretary of State of Illinois and review the records for the "LP/LLLP/LLP Database — Certificate of Existence."
   a. Who is the agent for service of process for Alden Gardens L.P.?
   b. When was Franklin Park Associates L.P. originally filed? What is its period of duration?
4. Access the Web site of the Secretary of State of Georgia. How many limited partnerships were formed under the ULPA in Georgia in 2006?
5. Access the Web site of the National Conference of Commissioners on Uniform State Laws. Select "Final Acts & Legislation." Review the Limited Partnership Act ("Final Act 2001") for Arizona. What does Section 404(c) provide?

5

❖ ❖ ❖

Registered Limited
Liability Partnerships

❖ ❖ ❖

CHAPTER OVERVIEW

A registered limited liability partnership is a fairly new form of business organization. Recognized in all states and the District of Columbia, this entity modifies a fundamental principle of partnership law. You will recall that under the RUPA and general partnership law, a partner in a general partnership has unlimited personal liability for the wrongful acts or omissions of his or her partners or of the partnership. In this new form of partnership, the liability of all partners is limited so they are not subject to unlimited personal liability for the negligence and incompetence of their partners and, in nearly all states, for the contractual obligations of the partnership. To protect the public from acts of negligence, some states mandate certain liability insurance requirements. This new form of business organization combines some of the best features of partnership law and corporation law and is ideally suited to partnerships composed of professionals, such as doctors, accountants, and lawyers. The registered limited liability partnership thus continues a trend in modern business law of combining limited liability and pass-through taxation to afford its members a flexible business structure with single taxation.

A.   Characteristics of Registered Limited Liability Partnerships

In the late 1980s, a number of savings and loan institutions failed. Injured investors could not bring effective causes of action against the institutions because those institutions were insolvent. They therefore began commencing malpractice actions for damages against the law firms that had provided legal advice and against the accounting firms that had provided accounting services to the institutions.

Many of those firms were general partnerships. Under general partnership law, partners in one office found themselves subject to unlimited personal liability for advice given by their partners in another office, perhaps thousands of miles away. In many cases, the savings and loan institutions had been represented by only a few attorneys or accountants in a firm and only those individuals had provided any professional services to the financial institutions; yet hundreds of other partners across the country and around the world found themselves facing unlimited personal liability for advice they had not given to clients of whom they had never heard.

The *registered limited liability partnership* (RLLP), sometimes called simply a **limited liability partnership** (LLP), was created in response to this situation. An LLP is highly similar to a general partnership. In fact, an LLP is simply a "standard" general partnership that files a statement electing LLP status with the secretary of state; however, one critical feature of general partnership law is changed: unlimited personal liability. American jurisdictions are divided as to the extent to which personal liability can be avoided in an LLP. There are two approaches:

Limited liability partnership
Partnership providing protection against liability for wrongful conduct of other partners; formed by compliance with statutes

- *Partial shield states.* In these three states, a partner in an LLP will not have personal liability for the wrongful acts or omissions of his or her partners. Partners in partial shield states retain personal liability for other partnership obligations, such as those arising from contract.
- *Full shield states.* In these 48 jurisdictions (and under RUPA § 306(c)), a partner is not personally liable for either the wrongful acts or omissions of his or her partners or for commercial, contractual, or other obligations of the partnership, making the LLP partner much like a shareholder in a corporation with regard to liability. Thus, whether partnership obligations arise in contract or tort, they remain solely the obligations of the partnership. Full shield states are sometimes called **bulletproof states** because the liability of the partners is impenetrable or bulletproof.

Partial shield states
States in which partners in an LLP retain liability for contractual obligations but have no personal liability for obligations arising in tort

Full shield states
States in which partners in an LLP are fully protected from personal liability, whether arising in tort or contract

Bulletproof states
States offering full protection from liability in an LLP, whether arising from tort or from contract (see full shield state)

The initial LLP statutes were all of the partial shield variety, with states later electing or converting to full shield protection beginning in 1994. As each year passes, more and more jurisdictions adopt full shield status. In all jurisdictions, however, partners in an LLP retain liability for their own acts of negligence, those of others in the partnership whom they supervise or direct and, in many states, those of which they know (and fail to prevent or stop). Of course, LLP partners also retain personal liability when they have agreed to do so, for example, if they agree to personally guarantee repayment of a loan made to the LLP itself.

LLPs are governed by state statute. Thus, they cannot be created by a simple oral or written agreement as can a general partnership. An LLP can only be created by compliance with state statutes; in this way, it is similar to a limited partnership. An existing general partnership may convert to an LLP or a business may begin its existence as an LLP. In most states, an existing limited partnership can convert to an LLP. In all states, LLPs are subject to state registration requirements and, in some states, mandatory insurance requirements.

Although the LLP is ideal for professional businesses, such as those practicing law, medicine, or accounting, and was created with those professions in mind, in most states any other partnership or business may also form as an LLP so long as the business it conducts is lawful. A few jurisdictions, however, including California, Nevada, New York, and Oregon, limit LLPs solely to the practice of specified professions, such as law, medicine, and accounting, and the LLP form is not available in those states to other businesses.

B. Governing Law

LLPs are partnerships and are thus governed nearly exclusively by partnership laws and principles, except as specifically modified by state legislation. The LLP originated in Texas in 1991 as a response to lawsuits against lawyers and accountants arising out of the collapse of the real estate and energy markets in Texas in the late 1980s. *See* Conrad S. Ciccotello & C. Terry Grant, *Professions as Commercial Institutions: An Analysis of Evolving Professional Forms*, 7 J. Legal Stud. Bus. 1, 16 (2000). By 2001, all 51 U.S. jurisdictions recognized the LLP form. In 1996, the RUPA (governing general partnerships and discussed in Chapter Three) was expressly amended to add limited liability partnerships. Although many states and the District of Columbia have adopted the RUPA, many have modified its provisions as they relate to LLPs. Some statutes, like those of Texas, preceded the adoption of limited liability provisions in the RUPA. Citation to each state's relevant statutes is provided in Appendices B and C. The text of Article 10 of the RUPA, which governs LLPs, can be found in Appendix C.

Thus, LLPs are governed by state statutes and by the agreement of their partners. In the absence of agreement, the state statutes (many of which are based on the 1997 RUPA) control and serve as default statutes, identical to the way the RUPA serves as a default statute to provide terms and conditions relating to general partnerships when the parties fail to reach agreement on certain terms.

In sum, LLPs are recognized in all states and the District of Columbia, they are governed by state statutes (based largely on the RUPA), the parties are free to modify many of the provisions of those statutes by their agreement, and, in the absence of agreement, the state statutes serve as default laws to fill in the gaps. Particular attention must therefore be paid to the state statutes, especially in cases in which the LLP is formed in one state and will do business in others that may have varying statutory schemes. Like limited partnerships, LLPs can only be formed by compliance with state statutes.

C. Advantages of LLPs

The greatest advantage of an LLP is the one already discussed: In all states, partners in an LLP are protected against unlimited personal liability for the negligent acts and misconduct of their partners or other representatives of the partnership business. Generally, however, this protection will not exist if any of the following occurs:

1. A partner supervised or directed the partner who committed the act of liability at the time the act was committed;

2. The partner was directly involved in the act giving rise to liability; or
3. The partner had knowledge or notice of the act of liability and failed to take reasonable steps to prevent or cure it (in many states).

Partners in LLPs always retain personal liability for their own negligence, incompetence, omissions, misconduct, or wrongful acts.

1. Partial Shield States

In the three partial shield states, the protection against unlimited liability does not apply to all acts of one's partners but only to wrongful acts and omissions, such as negligence. Thus, in those states, a partner in an LLP remains personally liable for other debts and obligations incurred by a partner or partnership, such as money borrowed, contractual commitments, rent, insurance, and other such debts or obligations. Moreover, the partnership itself (as opposed to the individual assets of the LLP members) is fully liable for the negligent acts or omissions of any partner. Therefore, these partnerships, upon collecting assets, will often distribute them to the partners, so as to avoid a "deep pocket" ready and waiting to be reached by a malpractice claim.

For example, assume a law firm has offices in Cleveland, Chicago, and Charleston, South Carolina. The partnership is composed of 100 attorneys employed throughout these offices. Two partners in the Charleston office begin working on a case. As a result of legal malpractice, they miss a statute of limitations deadline and their client therefore cannot bring an action. No one else in the Charleston office is aware of the case and the partners in the other cities have never worked on the case, seen any files relating to this matter, or even heard of the client. Under general partnership law, the partnership itself and all 100 partners in all the offices would have unlimited personal and joint and several liability for this claim of malpractice. If the partnership is an LLP, however, only the partnership itself and the two attorneys who actually committed the act of malpractice would face liability. The individual assets of the other partners in Charleston, Cleveland, and Chicago cannot be reached to satisfy the claim of malpractice. This feature of an LLP makes the partners in an LLP much like shareholders in a corporation who are protected from personal liability for the corporation's acts.

2. Full Shield States

In the 48 American jurisdictions that follow the full shield or bulletproof approach (which is also the approach of RUPA 306(c)), a partner in an LLP is not, solely by reason of being a partner, personally liable for any obligation of the LLP, whether arising in tort, contract, or otherwise, unless the partner knows of the act (and fails to stop it or prevent it), supervised it, or committed it. Even in full shield states, partners in LLPs retain liability for their own wrongful acts and omissions and those of others under their control or supervision.

Full shield statutes have steadily gained in popularity, primarily due to concern in some states that the entire justification for LLP statutes could be eviscerated by clever plaintiffs who can merely construct their pleadings to file malpractice actions as breach of contract actions, rather than as actions sounding in tort, to hold all partners in an LLP liable for an act of malpractice. Only full shield statutes avoid such circumvention.

For example, assume that an accounting company operates as an LLP in New York (a full shield state). Dana, an accountant in the firm, will not be personally liable for acts of malpractice committed by her partners. Moreover, she will not be personally liable for the partnership's obligation to pay its rent, its bank loan, or its car leases. If, however, Dana is employed by the LLP's South Carolina office (South Carolina being a partial shield state), although Dana would not be personally liable for acts of malpractice committed by her partners, she would be personally liable (jointly and severally) for the partnership's rent, bank loan, and car lease obligations. In either jurisdiction, Dana would be personally liable for her own acts of malpractice, negligence, and misconduct (and for those of others under her supervision and control and, in many states, those of which she knew and failed to stop or prevent).

Section 306(c) of the RUPA clearly states that "an obligation of a partnership incurred while the partnership is a limited liability partnership, *whether arising in contract, tort, or otherwise*, is solely the obligation of the partnership. A partner is not personally liable, directly or indirectly, by way of contribution or otherwise, for such an obligation . . . ." (emphasis added). Many states have adopted this exact language, making it clear that partners in an LLP have no personal liability for act of the partnership or their co-partners, whether those acts arise in tort or contract.

Some states, however, have statutory provisions that are less clear. For example, Tennessee's statute provides that a partner in an LLP is not liable for "debts, obligations and liabilities of or chargeable to the partnership or another partner, whether in tort, contract, or otherwise, *arising from omissions, negligence, wrongful acts, misconduct or malpractice* committed while the partnership is a registered limited liability partnership . . . ." Tenn. Code Ann. § 61-1-306 (emphasis added). Thus, although the statute originally states that LLP partners are not liable for obligations in tort or contract, language immediately following suggests that liability is limited only if the obligation arises from negligence, wrongful acts, or misconduct. Language in other states, such as Kentucky, Michigan, New Hampshire, and West Virginia, is similarly ambiguous. Presumably, case law in these states will clarify these issues. In any event, a plaintiff suing an LLP in one of those states may be able to "draft around" the statutory language to allege that the shield does not fully protect the LLP's partners.

See Figure 5-1 for a chart identifying full shield and partial shield states.

Other advantages of a general partnership, such as the sharing of management duties and responsibilities and the ability to raise capital by admitting new partners, exist in the LLP as well. Moreover, at least for many professionals who are accustomed to practicing in a partnership, the LLP is a comfortable and familiar structure. Additionally, if an existing general partnership converts to an LLP, few modifications need to be made to the partnership agreement in use, other than perhaps name changes necessary to comply with state statutes. Finally, LLPs afford the pass-through tax status of partnerships.

FIGURE 5-1
Full Shield and Partial Shield States

Full Shield States		Partial Shield States
Alabama	Missouri	Louisiana
Alaska	Montana	South Carolina*
Arizona	Nebraska	Utah
Arkansas	Nevada	
California*	New Hampshire**	
Colorado	New Jersey	
Connecticut*	New Mexico*	
Delaware	New York	
District of Columbia	North Carolina	
Florida	North Dakota	
Georgia	Ohio	
Hawaii	Oklahoma*	
Idaho	Oregon	
Illinois	Pennsylvania	
Indiana	Rhode Island*	
Iowa	South Dakota	
Kansas	Tennessee**	
Kentucky**	Texas*	
Maine	Vermont	
Maryland	Virginia	
Massachusetts*	Washington*	
Michigan**	West Virginia* **	
Minnesota	Wisconsin	
Mississippi	Wyoming	

*State includes some form of insurance or financial responsibility requirement.
**See note in text regarding extent of liability shield.

D. Disadvantages of LLPs

An LLP can be formed only by strict compliance with statute and, therefore, it may be expensive to form. An attorney will likely have to be engaged. Various forms must be filed with the secretary of state, accompanied by filing fees.

Although the partners in an LLP are protected from personal liability for the wrongful acts and conduct of their partners, they continue to have unlimited personal liability for other acts of their partners in partial shield states. Thus, using our earlier example, if one of the partners in the Charleston office signed a lease to rent new office space for the partnership, the partnership and all of the other partners in Charleston would have unlimited liability for the obligations under that lease. Full shield statutes would protect all "innocent" partners, and in those states, only the partnership would be liable for the obligation. Thus, partial shield states are at a disadvantage over full shield states. Because the LLP does not have to be created in the state in which it will do business, it may thus be wise to select a bulletproof state as the state of organization to attempt to obtain the benefits of the full shield or bulletproof statutes in that state. The LLP can then qualify or register to do business in other states.

Other disadvantages of LLPs include the following:

- *Insurance requirements.* As discussed more fully later, many states require LLPs to have certain liability insurance or cash reserves in place, placing an administrative and perhaps financial burden on LLPs, particularly smaller firms.
- *Restriction to professional firms.* As mentioned earlier, several states allow LLPs to be formed only for the practice of law, medicine, accounting, and so forth. In those states, the LLP structure is then not available for other types of businesses, such as real estate development.
- *Lack of continuity.* In some states, the term of existence of an LLP is one year. At that time, renewal forms or annual reports must be filed and fees paid to the secretary of state to renew the LLP.
- *Filing fees per partner.* Some states base their LLP organization or filing fees on the number of partners in the LLP. For example, in Texas the filing fee to form and renew an LLP is $200 per partner. Thus, a law firm with 100 partners would pay $20,000 to organize as an LLP and to renew the LLP each year, a filing fee that is extraordinarily high. Other states (such as Illinois) place upper limits on the filing fee so that the fee is $100 per partner but not less than $200 or more than $5,000.
- *Annual reports.* The RULPA and many states require that annual reports be filed with the state, necessitating paperwork and additional filing fees.

Finally, because in many states partners who direct or supervise other partners are liable for their acts of negligence or malpractice, LLPs in these states may unwittingly discourage supervision of junior partners. If partners can avoid liability by "turning a blind eye" to junior partners and neglect necessary supervision, the public is not well served, although it is likely a court would nevertheless impose liability for failure to supervise properly. Some LLPs, recognizing that supervisory duties may lead to liability, provide additional compensation to supervisors or agree to indemnify them if they are found liable for a subordinate's negligence.

E. Formation of LLPs

The formation of an LLP is somewhat similar to the formation of a limited partnership. States have application forms of varying extensiveness and choices of names. In Delaware, for example, the Statement of Qualification need contain only the following six elements:

1. Name of the limited liability partnership, which must include a designation of its LLP status, such as "L.L.P.";
2. The address of its principal office in the state and the name and address of the agent for service of process;
3. The number of partners the LLP will have;
4. The effective date of formation;
5. An actual application statement reading as follows: "The partnership elects to be a limited liability partnership"; and
6. The signature of an authorized partner.

See Figure 5-2 for the application form required in Nebraska. Filing fees are always imposed.

Just as a new business may form as an LLP, an existing general or limited partnership may convert into an LLP (upon the vote necessary to amend the partnership agreement). In many instances, law, accounting, and medical practices that have existed as general partnerships have converted or are converting to the LLP form.

The name of the LLP must contain the words "Registered Limited Liability Partnership," "Limited Liability Partnership," the abbreviation "L.L.P.," or "R.L.L.P.," or the designation "LLP" or "RLLP" as the last words or letters of its name. The purpose of this requirement is to afford notice to those dealing with the entity that, at a minimum, the partners are shielded from personal liability for the torts or wrongful acts of their partners. All letterhead, envelopes, business cards, signs, directory listings, brochures, and advertisements must also carry this designation to afford such notice to third parties. Many states require amendment of the application to reflect changes in the LLP.

The LLP should have a written partnership agreement. Because an LLP is a partnership, an agreement used for general partnerships can easily be modified for use in an LLP. (See Appendix D for form of general partnership agreement.)

An LLP formed in one state can operate as an LLP in another. Therefore, a law firm can operate as an LLP in Dover, Delaware; New Orleans, Louisiana; and Washington, D.C. The procedure for operating in another state is much the same as that for a limited partnership: An application must be completed and filed with the new state asking it to recognize the partnership as a foreign limited liability partnership. A certificate of good standing from the jurisdiction in which the LLP was originally formed will also generally be required so that the new state has some assurance that the organization is law-abiding. Filing fees will be required. See Figure 5-3 for the form used in Arizona for registration of a foreign limited liability partnership.

Before filing the application in the foreign jurisdiction, carefully review that state's statutes to ensure the LLP is in fact required to qualify in the foreign state. Many states and the RUPA (see RUPA § 1104) have statutes providing guidance as to what activities constitute "doing business," such as to require businesses formed in other states to qualify to do business therein, and it is possible that the LLP's activities do not constitute "doing business" within the meaning of the statute so as to necessitate a filing. For example, merely holding meetings, maintaining a bank account, or engaging in an isolated transaction in a state are

---

FIGURE 5-2
Nebraska Statement of Qualification as a Limited Liability Partnership

---

STATEMENT OF QUALIFICATION AS A LIMITED LIABILITY PARTNERSHIP

John A. Gale, Secretary of State
Room 1301 State Capitol, P.O. Box 94608
Lincoln, NE 68509
http://www.sos.state.ne.us

Submit in Duplicate

Name of Partnership_____

_____ (Name must end in
the words: registered limited liability partnership; limited liability partnership; R.L.L.P.; RLLP; "L.L.P." or "LLP")

_____ Yes, the above named Limited Liability Partnership will engage in the practice of law (if "Yes" you must attach a current certificate of authority from the Nebraska Supreme Court)

Address of Principal Office_____
          Street Address   City   State   Zip

If the Principal Office is not in Nebraska you must provide a Nebraska Office or agent:

Address of Nebraska Office_____
          Street Address   City   State   Zip

Or

Agent for Service of process_____

Agent Office_____NE_____
          Street Address and post office box number, (if any) City   Zip

Optional: The effective date of this filing is _____ ____, _____
                                        month   day   year
Registration as a: ___ Domestic LLP

          ___ Foreign LLP (originally registered out of state) Name of State _____

Domestic LLPs Only: The above named partnership hereby elects to become a Nebraska Limited Liability Partnership
_____

_____
Neb. Rev. Stat. §67-406 Requires that at least two partners sign the document

_____   _____
Signature of Partner   Signature of Partner

_____   _____
Printed Name   Printed Name

FILING FEE: $205.00 plus $5.00 for each page in addition to this form.
Add $15.00 for the certificate of authority from the Supreme Court if submitted

Revised 7/18/2008   Neb. Rev. Stat. 67-454 & 67-458

FIGURE 5-3
Arizona Foreign LLP Registration Application

Ken Bennett
Secretary of State
Limited Liability Partnerships
1700 W. Washington, 7th Fl.
Phoenix, Arizona 85007

Secretary of State Use:

Make Check Payable to:
Secretary of State

Fee: **$3.00**
Plus $10.00 Authority to Transact Business as an LLP
Plus $3.00 per page

SUBMIT IN DUPLICATE with a self addressed stamped envelope.

All correspondence regarding this filing will be sent to principal office.

STATEMENT OF FOREIGN QUALIFICATION OF A
FOREIGN LIMITED LIABILITY PARTNERSHIP
ARS § 29-1106

_____
Name of Foreign Limited Liability Partnership (end with "Limited Liability Partnership" or "LLP")

_____
The state and date of formation   Authorizing agency (optional)   Registration number (optional)

_____
Name of Agent for Service of Process   Phone Number

_____
Arizona Address of Agent (PO Box and C/O are not acceptable)   City   Arizona   Zip

The address of the chief executive office used by the Limited Liability Partnership in this state (**IF ANY**):

_____
Address (PO Box and C/O are not acceptable)   City   Arizona   Zip

The address of the office to be maintained in the state of organization:

_____
Address   City   State   Zip

A delayed effective date, if any:_____

Signature of General Partners:

_____
Signature   Print Name   Date

_____
Signature   Print Name   Date

**** An affidavit evidencing publication shall be filed with Secretary of State within ninety days after
filing of the statement of qualification. (Filing Fee $3.00)

generally not considered "doing business" such as would require a business to register with a state as a foreign LLP before it commences those activities. (See Chapter Fifteen for a further discussion on "doing business" in other states.)

One question that has arisen is whether the limitations imposed on liability in one jurisdiction will be followed by another jurisdiction in which the LLP does business. For example, if an LLP is formed in a full shield state and begins doing business in a partial shield state in which there is a breach of contract, are all partners jointly and severally liable as they would be in the partial shield state, or is there no liability imposed on the partners for the breach of contract, as would be the case in the home state that is a full shield state? Unfortunately, the answer to this question is not clear. Various state statutes and the cases interpreting them may provide guidance. For example, Cal. Corp. Code § 16958 provides that the laws of the jurisdiction under which a foreign limited liability partnership is organized shall govern its organization and internal affairs and the liability of its partners. At a minimum, LLPs should be scrupulous in inserting "choice of law" provisions in their contracts, providing that the law of a certain jurisdiction (namely, a full shield jurisdiction in which the LLP is organized or doing business) applies in any action relating to the contract, thus affording a credible argument that the full shield law governs so as to bar joint and several personal liability for contractual obligations no matter where the breach of contract occurred or the parties reside. As more and more states adopt full shield or bulletproof status, this issue is becoming moot.

Just as with any business, the LLP may be subject to other requirements such as licensing laws, local tax requirements, and so forth.

PRACTICE TIP

Create your own "form book." Collect all of the LLP forms provided by your state's secretary of state and keep them handy in a file folder. Tape the filing fee schedule on the left side of the folder. Include the citation to your state's LLP statutes. You will then be ready to respond to most questions about LLPs in your state and to prepare most organizational and renewal documents. Also, print the instructions for each form. These instructions often provide valuable information about how and where to file documents, how to calculate filing fees, how to calculate insurance amounts or cash reserves (if required) in your state, and so forth.

F. Operation of LLPs

Because an LLP is a form of partnership, the operation of an LLP is nearly identical to that of a general partnership. The fiduciary duties owed by partners to each other apply. Each partner is an agent of the partnership for business purposes and can bind the partnership by entering into contracts, hiring employees, purchasing office furniture, and so forth. The partners co-manage the business. They will likely have a written partnership agreement highly similar to that of a general partnership. It will include the formula for profits and losses, indicate each partner's contribution to the partnership, set out provisions relating to the admission and withdrawal of partners, and specify the conditions that will cause dissolution of the partnership. (See Appendix D for an example of a written general partnership agreement.)

Similar to the RUPA, on which they are often based, state LLP statutes generally operate as default statutes in that they govern the LLP in the absence of the partners' agreement. The following features are also identical to general partnerships: The LLP agreement may be oral or in writing; LLP partners owe fiduciary duties to each other; in the absence of agreement to the contrary, profits, losses, management, and control will be shared equally regardless of capital contributions; and partners may dissociate without necessarily causing a dissolution and winding up. Similar to a general partnership, to protect creditors, no interim distributions may be made unless the LLP is solvent. Finally, in most states, statements of authority and statements of denial (discussed in Chapter Three) may be filed to provide public notice regarding an LLP partner's authority to act or limitations on that authority.

Probably the most significant difference between the operation of a general partnership and that of the LLP is the requirement imposed on LLPs in several states to maintain liability insurance. This insurance is designed to protect injured parties who previously would have been able to sue numerous partners for acts of negligence or malpractice. Under LLP law, only malfeasing partners have unlimited personal liability for their wrongful acts, so an injured client or patient is limited to the partnership's assets (which may be depleted by distributions to partners) and to the assets of the individual partner or partners who performed the wrongful act. Because these claimants are thus denied a host of other defendants who may have immense resources, the LLP is thus often required to carry a certain amount of insurance. Some states that require insurance alternatively permit the LLP to set aside funds to satisfy any judgments against the partnership or its partners. In Texas, the insurance or reserved capital amount is $100,000; in Connecticut, the amount is at least $250,000.

Similarly, although the California statute is relatively complex, in general, California requires a general liability policy in the amount of at least $100,000, multiplied by the number of licensed persons rendering professional services for the LLP, subject to certain minimum and maximum requirements. Alternatively, in California, LLPs can maintain at least $100,000 (again, multiplied by the number of licensed professionals) in a segregated account such as a bank escrow account. Because professionals practicing in states requiring insurance may be concerned that the partnership might not acquire sufficient insurance, individual partners often purchase their own insurance policies for additional protection. Because of the difficulties of predicting what kind of insurance and how much insurance should be carried for businesses of vastly different sizes and risks, most states do not impose insurance or financial responsibility requirements. Similarly, some states have recently repealed their insurance requirements, reasoning that insurance is not required under the RUPA and that other similar business entities are not required to maintain such insurance. Insurance requirements imposed on domestic LLPs also apply to foreign LLPs that have applied to do business in the state. See Figure 5-1 for identification of states requiring insurance.

If an LLP does not carry and maintain the requisite insurance, it cannot be recognized as an LLP in those states conditioning existence and maintenance of the LLP upon insurance. It will therefore be viewed as a general partnership, in which case all partners have unlimited personal, joint, and several liability for their partners' wrongful acts and misconduct.

Because LLP partners are shielded from some debts, generally they cannot receive distributions unless there are sufficient assets to pay creditors. In sum, the use of insurance requirements and rules prohibiting distributions unless the LLP is solvent serve to protect creditors who can no longer sue numerous LLP partners for certain debts and obligations.

G.   Transferability of Interest and Admission of New Members

Because the LLP is voluntary, just as is a general partnership, the principles relating to transferability of partnership interests in a general partnership apply to LLPs as well. Thus, a partner in an LLP may assign her profits to another but may not substitute another in her place with full rights to participate in the partnership because this would violate the voluntary nature of a partnership.

In most cases, the written partnership agreement will provide that the withdrawal of one partner will not cause a dissolution. Provisions should be made for voluntary withdrawal by partners and return of their contributions and any profit.

New partners are admitted upon the consent of all existing partners or upon less than unanimous consent if so provided by the partnership agreement.

H.   Dissolution and Liquidation of LLPs

Dissolution of LLPs is similar to that of general partnerships. LLPs, however, must generally renew their applications or certificates filed with the state on an annual basis. Failure to renew the application or certificate will result in the would-be LLP being viewed as a general partnership, one subject to that state's version of the RUPA. Many states allow reinstatement of LLPs that have been revoked for failure to file annual reports once the defect is cured.

The partnership agreement will likely provide the events that will cause a dissolution of the LLP. If terms are not provided, the RUPA provides the terms and conditions for dissociation and dissolution. Recall from Chapter Three that under the RUPA not every dissociation of a partner triggers a dissolution and a winding up. If no dissolution is caused, the LLP will buy out the dissociating partner's interest.

Before the LLP dissolves, it must liquidate or wind up by collecting any debts due it, satisfying all obligations, liquidating assets, and distributing the proceeds to third-party creditors and then to the partners. A certificate of withdrawal or cancellation should be filed with the state of formation and in any state in which the LLP is operating.

I. Taxation of LLPs

Only one critical feature of an LLP is different from that of a general partnership: Partners do not have unlimited personal liability for the negligence or misconduct of their partners and, in full shield states, have no personal liability for tort, contractual, or other obligations of the partnership. In nearly all other respects, LLPs are similar to general partnerships, and thus LLPs are treated as general partnerships for purposes of taxation. The tax forms used by general partnerships and general partners (shown in Chapter Three) are also used for LLPs and their partners. Thus, the income earned (whether distributed or not) is passed through to the individual partners, who pay at whatever rate is appropriate to them. The LLP itself does not pay federal income tax but it must file the information tax form required of all partnerships. Like general and limited partnerships, an LLP may elect to be taxed as a corporation by "checking the box" on the appropriate tax form (see Figure 3-8).

J. Growth and Trends in LLPs

LLPs have seen unprecedented growth in the little more than 15 years they have been in existence. Because lawsuits are significant threats for many professionals, the LLP has been of particular interest to professionals. The growth in LLP registrations from 1994-1996 was almost fivefold and far exceeded that for corporations and limited partnerships. Ciccotello & Grant, *supra*, at 19. Professional service firms dominate the types of businesses that register as LLPs. In fact, law firms make up the largest single groups formed as LLPs, followed by medical firms and then accounting firms. *Id*. at 23-24. In fact, all of the "Big Four" accounting firms and most large law firms operate as LLPs. Because most of these firms previously operated as general partnerships and LLPs are nearly identical to general partnerships (except with respect to the all-important feature of liability), it is easy to understand why so many law firms, medical practices, and accountancy firms elected to convert from the general partnership form to the LLP form. As noted in Section A earlier, some states limit LLPs solely to the practice of certain professions, and other types of businesses must operate in some other form (often as a limited liability company, discussed in Chapter Six).

Key Features
of Limited Liability Partnerships

◆ Partners in LLPs have no personal liability in any state for wrongful acts or torts of their co-partners.
◆ In 48 jurisdictions, LLP partners have no personal liability either for wrongful acts of their co-partners or for contractual obligations of the partnership.

- ◆ Partners in LLPs retain personal liability for their own wrongful acts and those they direct or supervise.
- ◆ LLPs may be formed only by complying with state statutes that require the filing of an application with the appropriate state agency.
- ◆ The LLP agreement may be oral or written; in the absence of agreement, profits, losses, management, and control are shared equally regardless of capital contributions.
- ◆ Some states require the LLP to carry insurance or meet financial responsibility standards.
- ◆ Not every dissociation causes a termination and winding up; in many instances a dissociating member's interest will be purchased.
- ◆ LLPs have the pass-through taxation of general partnerships.
- ◆ LLPs continue the modern trend of business structures that allow their members to manage the enterprise and yet be protected from personal liability.

K. Role of Paralegal

The paralegal should check state statutes to determine any particular requirements as to naming an LLP and any designation it must include to notify third parties that the entity is an LLP. The paralegal should contact the secretary of state and request the appropriate forms for application to conduct business as an LLP. The paralegal should also request a federal employer identification number (see Figure 2-3). Research should be conducted to determine whether the state affords full shield or partial shield protection and whether any insurance requirements exist in the state.

Paralegals will also have a role in drafting the partnership agreement. An agreement for an LLP is nearly identical to that for a general partnership, except for a recitation that partners will not have personal liability for acts of misconduct of their partners and, in full shield states, that they will have no personal liability for any obligation of the partnership, whether arising in tort or contract (unless they supervised, directed, participated in, or knew of the acts), a requirement that the application be properly filed and maintained, and that insurance, if required, be obtained. A standard form of general partnership agreement is shown in Appendix D. It can be modified for use by an LLP.

The paralegal should carefully monitor the term of the LLP and ensure that the LLP is renewed at the appropriate time or that annual reports are timely filed. Docketing this date is critical. Many law firms have sophisticated computer programs for docketing dates. Calendar docketing or docketing by index cards known as *tickler* reminder cards is also sufficient. The law firm can then notify its clients of the renewal or reporting requirements a few months before the expiration date of the LLP.

Paralegals can also review the letterhead, business cards, advertisements, brochures, and other items used by the LLP to ensure that the appropriate name designation is provided.

Case Illustration
Limited Liability of LLP Partners

Case: *Verizon Yellow Pages Co. v. Sims & Sims P.C.*, 15 Mass. L.
Rptr. 734 (Super. Ct. 2003)

Facts: In a suit for a business debt, the plaintiff sought to
disqualify an attorney, John Cannavo, from representing
one of the defendants, which was a limited liability
partnership. Cannavo was a partner in the limited liability
partnership and would be a necessary witness at trial.

Holding: The motion to disqualify was granted. Cannavo has no
right to represent the limited liability partnership *pro se*
(on his own behalf). His rights are distinct from those of
the limited liability partnership because only it would be
liable for any judgment rendered in the case. Should the
plaintiff be successful it could collect up to the limit of
the partnership's assets and would never be able to reach
Cannavo's personal assets. Moreover, Cannavo will be a
necessary witness in the trial of this matter and thus
cannot act as counsel under Massachusetts rules of
professional conduct.

◆   ◆   ◆

WEB RESOURCES

A number of sites provide general information about LLPs with clear and
concise discussions of LLPs, comparing and contrasting them to other forms
of business entities. Many of the following sites provide forms for partnership
agreements. Only a few provide forms specifically for limited liability partnership agreements, because many professionals use a general partnership
agreement as a starting point and then modify it to use for limited liability
partnerships. As with all forms, exercise caution in using the form, as it will
likely not be suitable for all LLPs.

State statutes: www.law.cornell.edu
                                    www.findlaw.com
                                    www.megalaw.com
                                    www.nass.org
State forms and   www.premiercorp.com/
  secretaries of state: _secretariesofstate.asp

Text of the limited liability partnership statutes (beginning with Article 10 in the RUPA):	www.nccusl.org
General information:	www.megalaw.com www.businessownersideacafe.com http://topics.law.cornell.edu/wex/ partnership www.toolkit.cch.com
Forms of agreements:	www.ilrg.com www.allaboutforms.com (Select "Show All Business Topics.") www.siccode.com/form.php

Discussion Questions

Fact Scenario.   Young & Diaz, L.L.P., is a law firm with offices in several states. Use the RUPA to answer these questions.

1. The LLP would like to open a new office in Arizona, a state in which it has not conducted business, and would also like to open a bank account in Nevada, a state in which it has not conducted business. What must the LLP do?

2. Cal, one of the LLP partners in Alaska, committed an act of legal malpractice. Discuss the liability for the partnership, Cal, and all other partners for this act.

3. Without authority, Frances, one of the LLP partners in Utah, obligated the partnership to lease new cars for various partners. Discuss the liability for the partnership, Frances, and the partners in Delaware and in Utah for this act.

4. Why would some states require the LLP to obtain liability insurance?

5. Kyle, one of the senior partners in the firm, is the supervisor of Kim, one of the new attorneys in the firm's Chicago office. Kyle has been ill recently and has been unable to meet with Kim. Kim recently committed an act of legal malpractice. Describe the liability of the LLP, Kyle, Kim, and all other LLP partners for this act.

6. The LLP has no specific term. Tim, one of the partners in the California office, has unexpectedly died. What is the effect of Tim's death on the LLP?

7. The partnership has no agreement regarding the division of profits and losses. How will profits be divided this year? Discuss.

8. The LLP neglected to file its annual report this year. What is the effect of this failure? Is there anything the LLP can do to "save" itself?

Net Worth

1. Access the Web site of the Delaware Secretary of State.
   a. What is the fee in Delaware if a partnership with 10 partners wishes to apply to become a Delaware LLP?
   b. What is the fee to file an annual report in Delaware for an LLP?
2. Access the Web site of the Illinois Secretary of State. What is the fee to file a Renewal Statement for an Illinois LLP with 60 partners?
3. Access Rhode Island's statutes. If a law firm has eight partners, what liability insurance must it maintain?
4. Access the Web site of the law firm Mayer Brown. Under what business structure does the firm operate?

6

❖ ❖ ❖

Limited Liability Companies

❖ ❖ ❖

CHAPTER OVERVIEW

Like registered limited liability partnerships, limited liability companies are a fairly new form of business organization recognized in all states and the District of Columbia. Limited liability companies continue the trend seen in registered limited liability partnerships of combining the most attractive features of partnerships and corporations in a new enterprise.

Chapter Eight discusses the characteristics of corporations. In brief, however, two features are notable at this juncture. First, shareholders in a corporation are shielded from liability arising out of the corporation's wrongful acts. Their stock might fall in value to nothing, but assuming no fraud or injustice, they will not be liable to any of the corporate creditors. Second, corporations are often said to be subject to *double taxation*, meaning that income earned by the corporation is taxed at corporate rates and then when this same money is distributed to shareholders as dividends, the shareholders also pay taxes at their individual tax rates on the money or distributions they receive. Thus, the same money is taxed twice.

The limited liability company provides its first benefit from corporation law: Its members are protected from personal liability for the company's acts and the acts of other members whether arising in tort or in contract. Its second benefit comes from partnership law: All money earned by the company is passed through directly to the members who pay tax on the money at their individual rates. The company itself does not pay tax on earnings, thus avoiding the burden imposed on corporations of double taxation.

The limited liability company has become so popular that by 2002, in nearly 30 states, more LLCs were formed than corporations.

A. Characteristics of Limited Liability Companies

Limited liability company
Entity providing full protection for its members from all personal liability, whether arising in tort or contract; must comply with statutes

The **limited liability company** (LLC) was first recognized in 1977 by Wyoming. On occasion, the LLC is referred to as a statutory partnership association, partnership association, or limited partnership association. Limited liability company, however, is the most frequently used name for this form of business organization. After Wyoming drafted its LLC statute from a combination of general partnership laws, limited partnership laws, and corporation laws, few states followed. In 1988, however, the Internal Revenue Service issued a ruling indicating that LLCs would be taxed as partnerships, and, by 1996, all 50 states and the District of Columbia had enacted legislation recognizing LLCs.

Like the limited partnership and the registered limited liability partnership (RLLP or LLP), the LLC is a creature of statute and can be formed only by compliance with state statutes. Its formation is similar to the formation of a corporation and it will be governed by an agreement, commonly known as the *operating agreement*. Unlike corporations, however, the LLC does not always have perpetual existence. In a few states, LLCs exist for a 30-year period (probably because the original Wyoming statute provided for a 30-year term).

Members
Participants in a limited liability company

The LLC can be managed by its participants, called **members**. These members may be either individuals or entities, such as corporations. Some larger LLCs will appoint a manager or a management committee to manage the organization. Thus, LLCs may be either member-managed or manager-managed. There is a presumption that the LLC will be member-managed unless its organizing documents provide otherwise. LLC members may withdraw at will, generally upon giving some period of notice. They may transfer their financial interest in the LLC but cannot transfer their management or voting rights. A dissociation of a member due to death, withdrawal, or bankruptcy will not cause a dissolution. LLC members can bring either direct or derivative actions, just as can limited partners in a limited partnership.

In all states except California, professionals such as lawyers, doctors, and accountants can adopt the LLC form, although the professionals retain liability for their own wrongful acts and those performed under their supervision or control. The professionals, however, are protected from personal liability for the wrongful acts of their colleagues and from all contractual obligations. Many states provide specific statutes for professionals operating as LLCs (see Section L of this chapter).

The most significant features of an LLC are that it protects its members from personal liability (while allowing them to participate fully in the management of the enterprise), and it provides pass-through taxation.

An LLC may transact business in another state. Generally, the LLC must file an application to transact business in the new state and must submit a certificate of its good standing from the state of formation. See Figure 6-1 for a sample application to transact business in another state. Before filing the application for authority to do business in the foreign state, carefully review that state's statutes to ensure that the LLC is in fact required to qualify in the foreign state. Review the state statutes as to what constitutes "transacting business." For example, under ULLCA § 803, the following activities, among others, do not constitute transacting business: maintaining or defending a lawsuit; having LLC meetings; maintaining bank

FIGURE 6-1
Minnesota Foreign LLC Application for Registration

MINNESOTA SECRETARY OF STATE
CERTIFICATE OF AUTHORITY FOR A FOREIGN LIMITED LIABILITY COMPANY
MINNESOTA STATUTES CHAPTER 322B

PLEASE TYPE OR PRINT IN BLACK INK.

READ THE INSTRUCTIONS BEFORE COMPLETING THIS FORM   **FILING FEE $185.00**

1. YOU MUST ATTACH A CERTIFICATE OF GOOD STANDING OR STATUS, DATED WITHIN THE LAST 90 DAYS, ISSUED BY THE FILING OFFICER WHERE THE BUSINESS RECORDS ARE KEPT IN THE STATE OR JURISDICTION IN WHICH THIS ENTITY IS DOMICILED.

2. Name under which LLC will do business in Minnesota:

3. Company name in home state, **if different** from name listed in item 1:

4. State or jurisdiction of formation: _____ 5. Expiration date of company: _____
                                      State   Month   Day   Year

6. Registered office address in Minnesota:

Complete Street Address or Rural Route and Rural Route Box Number   City   MN   State   ZIP Code
      (P.O. Box is Unacceptable)

7. Full name of Registered Agent in Minnesota:

8. Address of the office in the jurisdiction where LLC is organized.

Street Address   City   State   ZIP Code

9. Does this LLC own, lease or have any interest in agricultural land or land capable of being farmed in Minnesota?
                (Check One)   ☐ YES   ☐ NO

10. Name and Telephone Number of Contact Person for this LLC:

Name _____   Daytime Phone ( ) _____

    I certify that I am authorized to execute this application and I further certify that I understand that by signing this application, I am subject to the penalties of perjury as set forth in Minnesota Statutes Section 609.48 as if I had signed this application under oath.

_____
             Signature

accounts; or conducting an isolated transaction that will be completed within 30 days. Thus, engaging in such activities would not require an LLC to file an application in the foreign state.

Failure to obtain the certificate to transact business in another state will preclude the LLC from maintaining a lawsuit in the state, and the state's attorney general could bring an action against the LLC to prevent it from doing business in the state.

In many states, the LLC may register its name even before doing business by filing certain forms with the secretary of state. The name registration holds the proposed name of the LLC in the foreign state for some stated period of time, often several months.

Unlike LLPs, which are a species of partnership, the LLC is an entirely new form of business structure, although it is a hybrid, borrowing from both partnership and corporate law concepts. Because both LLPs and LLCs offer protection from personal liability and the pass-through tax status of a partnership, the two forms are highly similar. Generally, the key distinctions between the two business entities are as follows:

- LLCs can be managed by appointed managers (who need not be members of the LLC), whereas LLPs are generally co-managed by all of their partners.
- Many LLC statutes require a written operating agreement, whereas the partnership agreement for an LLP may be oral or written.
- Only full shield states offer full protection from personal liability for LLP partners for both wrongful acts of co-partners and contractual obligations, whereas a hallmark of LLC statutes is full protection from personal liability for all LLC members whether the liability arises in tort or contract.
- If the parties' agreement fails to address the sharing of profits and losses, in an LLP profits and losses will be shared equally regardless of contributions (i.e., the partnership model), whereas in an LLC, profits and losses are usually allocated in the same ratio as the members' unreturned contributions (i.e., the corporate model), although the Uniform Limited Liability Company Act provides for equal distributions.
- All states but Wyoming allow a one-person LLC, making it attractive for sole proprietors to convert to LLCs and thereby achieve protection from personal liability; LLPs, however, because they are a form of partnership, must always have at least two partners.
- Under the Uniform Limited Liability Company Act, not-for-profit businesses may operate as LLCs, whereas the LLP, as a form of partnership, must be operated with the expectation of making a profit.

Because the LLC is a creative blending of the best features of partnerships and corporations, LLCs have become an increasingly popular vehicle for doing business in the United States. The Illinois Secretary of State noted that the LLC "offers the business community . . . the most modern option available in terms of business structure and function." In fact, due to the tremendous popularity and flexibility of LLCs, and the fact that they offer full protection from liability for their members (who may nevertheless manage the business) as well as offering single pass-through taxation, many experts predict that S corporations and limited partnerships may well become relics of the past and that even general partnerships will be used only for the smallest and least formal businesses that do not wish to incur the costs associated with organizing and maintaining an LLC or corporation.

B.   Governing Law

All 50 states and the District of Columbia have enacted statutes recognizing LLCs. All states provide full protection from personal liability. Because most states so recently passed their LLC laws, little case law exists interpreting the LLC statutes, and the states have differed vastly in their approaches to LLCs. Nevertheless, there has been tremendous acceptance of the LLC form. For example, up until 1990, only two states recognized LLCs, but by 1996 all 50 states had enacted LLC legislation. In fact, it is now rare when a large law firm or accounting firm does not operate as an LLC (or LLP).

Due to the variations among state laws governing LLCs, in 1991 the National Conference of Commissioners on Uniform State Laws ("Conference") recommended that a uniform act be drafted for LLCs. The **Uniform Limited Liability Company Act (ULLCA)** was adopted in 1994 after extensive study of each state's LLC statutes. By the time the ULLCA was finally released in 1996, most states had already adopted their own LLC legislation. Thus, it was adopted in only a few states (Alabama, Hawaii, Illinois, Montana, South Carolina, South Dakota, Vermont, and West Virginia). The ULLCA was amended again in 2006, but as of the writing of this text, this revised 2006 version of the ULLCA (sometimes called the RULLCA) has only been adopted in Idaho and Iowa. The ULLCA borrows heavily both from partnership and corporate laws, reflecting the nature of the LLC as a hybrid entity that combines the best features of partnerships with the best features of corporations. The ULLCA is available at your law library or at the Conference's Web site at www.nccusl.org.

When the Commissioners revised the original ULLCA in 2006, they made several changes, including the following:

- An LLC may be formed with no members. Such an LLC is called a **shelf LLC**, and the organizers must file a second statement once a member is appointed (which must occur within 90 days). This second statement completes the formation of the LLC. *See* ULLCA § 201. As of the time of the writing of this text, no states allow for the creation of a shelf LLC.
- The revised ULLCA does not provide for **series LLCs**, as do some state statutes. Under a series approach, a single LLC can create within itself separate series levels of membership interests, each of which might own its own separate assets, have its own separate group of members, and be responsible for its own obligations. Each series provides limited liability to its series members and each series is an entity separate from other series and also separate from the LLC itself (thus affording limited liability protection for each series in the event another series incurs debts or obligations). The series concept is recognized in a few states (including Delaware and Iowa), but after much debate and discussion, the Conference decided not to allow for the creation of series LLC in the revised 2006 act.

ULLCA
Uniform Limited Liability Company Act, a uniform act to guide operation and management of LLCs

Shelf LLC
A limited liability company originally formed with no members

Series LLC
A separate and distinct group within an LLC, which has its own members and assets; not recognized by revised ULLCA of 2006

The ULLCA is meant to be a "default statute," meaning that LLC members are free to vary its terms to a great extent, and only when they have failed to provide for certain items in their operating agreement will the ULLCA or comparable state provisions control.

In sum, LLCs are governed by state statutes, which vary widely from state to state. It is uncertain whether and to what extent additional states will adopt the 2006 ULLCA. Paralegals are free to create flexible operating agreements for an LLC inasmuch as the ULLCA operates as a default statute the provisions of which generally control only when the parties fail to agree otherwise.

C. Advantages of LLCs

1. Pass-Through Tax Status

An LLC has sufficient characteristics of a partnership so that it is taxed as a partnership. All of the income earned by the LLC, whether distributed or not, is immediately passed through to the members, who then declare their respective portion of the profits on their individual federal tax returns and pay tax at the appropriate rate. This pass-through tax status offers advantages over a corporation, for which income is taxed twice: once when earned by the corporation and again when received by the corporate owners, the shareholders, as dividends. The imposition of two taxes often results in total taxes that are greater than the taxes that would be required if only one tax were imposed, as is the case with partnerships. Thus, the treatment of an LLC as a partnership for taxation purposes can be a significant advantage.

One type of corporation, the S corporation, offers pass-through tax status (see Chapter Seventeen), but it is subject to a number of restrictions. For example, the number of shareholders in an S corporation is limited to 100 individuals. An LLC has no such restrictions and can be composed of hundreds of members, including corporations. Stock in an S corporation can typically be owned only by individuals, estates, or certain trusts — not partnerships or other corporations — and cannot be owned by a nonresident alien. Thus, the S corporation is a poor vehicle for attracting foreign or corporate capital. In sum, the first advantage offered by an LLC is the pass-through tax status or single taxation enjoyed by partnerships.

2. Limited Liability and Full Management

The LLC offers limited liability to its members for obligations of the LLC. Although limited partners have limited liability, that limited liability hinges on their passivity with regard to management of the business enterprise. In the event limited partners are viewed as managing and controlling the limited partnership business, they lose their limited liability status. In an LLC, by contrast, the members can be active in management *and* retain their limited liability, offering tremendous advantages for investors who wish to be active in the management of their money and yet not expose their other assets to liability. The liability of a member of an LLC is limited to the investment contributed by the member. The only exception to this rule is that LLC members are personally obligated to make their promised contributions to the LLC. The LLC itself, of course, has liability for the wrongful acts of its members or managers acting in the ordinary course of the LLC's business, and the LLC members have personal liability for their own wrongful acts (and their judgment creditors can obtain a charging order from court that requires the company to pay over distributions to the creditor rather than to the LLC member).

Although the LLP also shields its partners from personal liability, in a few states, the protection from liability only relates to claims for a co-partner's wrongful acts, leaving LLP partners with personal liability for contractual obligations. By contrast, the LLC affords full protection for its members from all personal liability, whether arising in tort or contract, in all states. In fact, most states have gone further and expressly provided in their LLC statutes that, in general, an LLC member is not a proper party in litigation to enforce such obligations.

3. One-Person LLCs

At present, all jurisdictions except Wyoming allow a one-member LLC. Thus, sole proprietors in those states may form an LLC, allowing them to protect their assets from personal liability. Moreover, if the business grows, the LLC can easily accommodate the admission of new members.

Because the LLC requires filing of articles of organization and perhaps other documents, such as annual reports, its formalities and operation are significantly more expensive and complex than that of a sole proprietorship. Thus, many fledgling businesses operating as sole proprietorships may elect to continue in that form due to the ease and inexpensiveness of formation and maintenance. Nevertheless, for a sole proprietor with significant personal assets, the LLC is an attractive form of business enterprise because it offers full protection against personal liability for obligations of the company.

4. International Recognition

The LLC is similar to many investment vehicles recognized in other countries, primarily Germany, France, Portugal, Saudi Arabia, Switzerland, Japan, and several South American and Central American nations. Due to our increasingly global economy, the LLC is an attractive business organization for foreign investors who may already be familiar with the basic principles of LLCs. Latin American countries recognize a business similar to an LLC that is referred to as a *limitada*. Thus, it is perhaps no surprise that Florida was the second state to recognize LLCs in an effort to attract Latin American investors. Similarly, the *GmbH* business entity recognized in Germany, Austria, and other Central European countries is analogous to American LLCs. On the other hand, an S corporation is limited to 100 individuals who cannot be nonresident aliens. It is thus not an appropriate vehicle for a business desiring to attract foreign investors.

D. Disadvantages of LLCs

Although there are some disadvantages of doing business as an LLC, the advantages far outweigh any disadvantages. The primary disadvantages of LLCs are as follows:

- In many states, although a member of an LLC may transfer his or her financial interest in the LLC to another, the transferee will not become a member of the LLC unless the operating agreement so provides or all other LLC members consent. This limitation may serve to hamper growth within an LLC. (Note that some states, including California and New York, permit the assignee to become a member upon a majority vote.)
- Because the LLC is a relatively new form of business, little case law interpreting LLCs exists. In the event of disputes, therefore, little guidance can be gained from judicial interpretations of LLC laws.
- Because the LLC can only be formed by compliance with state statutes, an attorney must likely be engaged to draft the appropriate forms and documents. Additionally, filing these forms with the secretary of state will necessitate certain fees. Thus, the formation of an LLC can be slightly complex and expensive. Moreover, state LLC statutes vary widely from state to state, making it somewhat complex for a company to do business nationwide as an LLC.
- Finally, to ensure the LLC would have the pass-through tax status of a partnership, a few states limit the LLC to a term, generally 30 years. Thus, in those states, the LLC might not be an appropriate form for a business contemplating activity in perpetuity. Due to the new IRS "check the box" provisions clarifying that LLCs will be treated as partnerships for tax purposes unless they affirmatively elect to be taxed as corporations, many state statutes have begun eliminating any term limit for LLCs and allow them to exist perpetually. Even in those states that do not impose a term on the LLC, the LLC is usually required to file an annual report. Failure to file the annual report may be a ground for administrative dissolution of the LLC (although most states allow reinstatement of the LLC upon compliance with annual report requirements).

E. Formation of LLCs

The formation of an LLC closely parallels the formation of a corporation. The document that creates the LLC, usually called the articles of organization, must be filed with the appropriate state authorities. Additionally, the LLC must be governed by an agreement, usually called the operating agreement. Generally, an LLC may be formed for any lawful purpose (including operating as a nonprofit entity), although most states prohibit insurance and banking companies, with their significant potential liability to consumers, from operating as LLCs. Similarly, as previously discussed, California prohibits professionals from operating as LLCs.

Creation of the LLC results in a new legal entity distinct from its members, who then have no liability for the LLC's debts and obligations.

1. Articles of Organization

An LLC is created by the filing of a document called the **articles of organization** (or the *certificate of organization*, per the ULLCA) with the appropriate state agency, usually the secretary of state. Each state recognizing the LLC has particular statutory requirements for the contents of the articles of organization. Typically, the articles of organization include the following elements:

a. The name of the company (including any required abbreviations or signals);
b. The address of the initial designated office;
c. The name and street address of the initial agent who will receive service of process (which cannot be a post office box);
d. The name and address of each organizer;
e. Whether the company is to have a period of duration; and
f. A statement regarding how the entity is to be managed (for example, whether it will be managed by one person or all members).

Articles of organization
Document filed with the state that creates an LLC

The articles of organization may set forth any provisions that are permitted to be set forth in the operating agreement or any other matters not inconsistent with law. The articles of organization can be amended at any time upon filing an appropriate document with the public official and paying the specified filing fee. Amendments must often be approved by all members unless the operating agreement provides otherwise. See Figure 6-2 for the form of Articles of Organization for California LLCs.

In many states, after review of the articles of organization and acceptance of the required fee, the secretary of state will issue a certificate of organization for the LLC recognizing the existence of the business. Most LLC statutes allow existing general and limited partnerships to convert to the LLC form to achieve protection from liability by making a filing with the secretary of state. In the 50 jurisdictions that allow a one-member LLC, sole proprietors may convert to the LLC form.

2. Operating Agreement

The document containing the provisions for the operation and governance of an LLC is usually called an **operating agreement**. In a few states it must be a written agreement; most states and the ULLCA allow an oral agreement. The operating agreement for an LLC is highly similar to a partnership agreement for a general partnership. It must, however, be tailored to meet the specific requirements of the LLC statute in the state of formation. Due to the novelty of the LLC form and the lack of case law interpreting LLCs, the operating agreement should be carefully drafted. It is a private document and is not filed with any state agency. Moreover, because amending the operating agreement often requires approval of all LLC members (unless the operating agreement provides otherwise), careful drafting is a must. The operating agreement can be flexibly written, and, although it cannot unreasonably restrict a member's right to information or records or restrict certain other rights (such as the right to approve a merger), under the ULLCA it may eliminate the duty of loyalty or duty of due care so long as

Operating agreement
Agreement governing the operation of an LLC; may be oral in most states

FIGURE 6-2
California LLC Articles of Organization

| LLC-1 | File # _____ |

State of California
Secretary of State

LIMITED LIABILITY COMPANY
ARTICLES OF ORGANIZATION

A $70.00 filing fee must accompany this form.

IMPORTANT – Read instructions before completing this form.

This Space For Filing Use Only

ENTITY NAME (End the name with the words "Limited Liability Company," or the abbreviations "LLC" or "L.L.C." The words "Limited" and "Company" may be abbreviated to "Ltd." and "Co.," respectively.)

1. NAME OF LIMITED LIABILITY COMPANY

PURPOSE (The following statement is required by statute and should not be altered.)

2. THE PURPOSE OF THE LIMITED LIABILITY COMPANY IS TO ENGAGE IN ANY LAWFUL ACT OR ACTIVITY FOR WHICH A LIMITED LIABILITY COMPANY MAY BE ORGANIZED UNDER THE BEVERLY-KILLEA LIMITED LIABILITY COMPANY ACT.

INITIAL AGENT FOR SERVICE OF PROCESS (If the agent is an individual, the agent must reside in California and both Items 3 and 4 must be completed. If the agent is a corporation, the agent must have on file with the California Secretary of State a certificate pursuant to Corporations Code section 1505 and Item 3 must be completed (leave Item 4 blank).

3. NAME OF INITIAL AGENT FOR SERVICE OF PROCESS

4. IF AN INDIVIDUAL, ADDRESS OF INITIAL AGENT FOR SERVICE OF PROCESS IN CALIFORNIA   CITY   STATE   ZIP CODE

CA

MANAGEMENT (Check only one)

5. THE LIMITED LIABILITY COMPANY WILL BE MANAGED BY:

☐ ONE MANAGER

☐ MORE THAN ONE MANAGER

☐ ALL LIMITED LIABILITY COMPANY MEMBER(S)

ADDITIONAL INFORMATION

6. ADDITIONAL INFORMATION SET FORTH ON THE ATTACHED PAGES, IF ANY, IS INCORPORATED HEREIN BY THIS REFERENCE AND MADE A PART OF THIS CERTIFICATE.

EXECUTION

7. I DECLARE I AM THE PERSON WHO EXECUTED THIS INSTRUMENT, WHICH EXECUTION IS MY ACT AND DEED.

DATE   SIGNATURE OF ORGANIZER

TYPE OR PRINT NAME OF ORGANIZER

LLC-1 (REV 04/2007)   APPROVED BY SECRETARY OF STATE

eliminating them is not "manifestly unreasonable." Subject to few restrictions, members are free to regulate the affairs of the LLC as they wish. A form of LLC operating agreement is available at www.allaboutforms.com. The operating agreement should include the following minimum provisions:

Name of the LLC. As with any business name, the LLC's name cannot be deceptively similar to that of another business such that there would be a likelihood of confusion in the marketplace. A search should be conducted to ensure the name is available and a check made of the state statutes to determine what signal, such as "L.L.C." or "L.C.," must be used in the business name. The ULLCA provides that the name include "limited liability company," or "limited company," or the abbreviation "L.L.C.," "LLC," "L.C.," or "LC." Most states and the ULLCA allow a new LLC to reserve a name during the formation period by filing an application to reserve the name. The reservation is valid for some period of time, often 90 days, during which another LLC may not file articles of organization using that name. The state will usually impose a fee to reserve the name. See Figure 6-3 for a sample form of the application to reserve a name used in New York. The LLC can also operate under an assumed name, just as a sole proprietor or partnership can. The state simply needs to be informed of the assumed name the LLC has elected. The full name of the LLC, with its signal indicating adoption of the LLC form, should appear on all signage, correspondence, stationery, business cards, and other written documents of the LLC to provide notice to the public that the entity is operating as an LLC.

Names and Addresses of Members. The names and addresses of all members should be provided so that notices and information can be communicated to the members. Corporations and other business entities may be members of LLCs, and they are deemed notified at the addresses provided.

Recitals. A recitation should be made confirming the intent of the members to form an LLC.

Purpose. The purpose of the LLC should be stated. The purpose clause should be broad enough so that the LLC can expand and grow without requiring amendment of the operating agreement. In most states, a general clause stating that the purpose of the LLC is to engage in any business lawful in the state is acceptable.

Address. The principal place of business of the LLC should be provided so that members and others can provide communications to the LLC.

Term. A review of the pertinent state statutes is required to ensure that the LLC complies with any restrictions as to the duration of the LLC. Most states and the ULLCA provide that if no specific term is set forth in the operating agreement, the LLC will have perpetual existence.

LLC Powers. The operating agreement should indicate the powers and activities in which the LLC may engage. Some state LLC statutes provide a model list of powers that LLCs can conduct, including the following powers: to sue and be sued in the LLC name; to purchase, own, use, lease, or sell real or personal property; to make contracts; to lend money; to elect managers and appoint officers; and to

FIGURE 6-3
New York LLC Application for Name Reservation

Application for Reservation of Name
Under §205 of the Limited Liability Company Law

PLEASE TYPE OR PRINT

NYS Department of State
Division of Corporations, State Records and
Uniform Commercial Code
One Commerce Plaza, 99 Washington Avenue
Albany, NY 12231-0001
www.dos.state.ny.us

APPLICANT'S NAME AND STREET ADDRESS

NAME TO BE RESERVED

RESERVATION IS INTENDED FOR (CHECK ONE)

☐ New domestic limited liability company
(The Limited Liability Company Law requires that the name end with "Limited Liability Company," "LLC" or "L.L.C.")

☐ New domestic professional service limited liability company
(The name must end with "Professional Limited Liability Company" or "Limited Liability Company" or an abbreviation in §1212(b) of the Limited Liability Company Law.)

☐ Existing foreign limited liability company intending to apply for authority to do business in New York State

☐ Existing foreign professional service limited liability company intending to apply for authority to do business in New York State

☐ Change of name of an existing domestic or an authorized foreign limited liability company

☐ A person intending to form a foreign limited liability company which will apply for authority to do business in this state

☐ Existing foreign limited liability company intending to apply for authority to do business in New York State whose name is not available for use in New York State and must use a fictitious name

☐ Authorized foreign limited liability company intending to change its fictitious name under which it does business in this state

☐ Authorized foreign limited liability company which has changed its name in its jurisdiction, such new name not being available for use in New York State

X_____
Signature of applicant, applicant's attorney or agent
(If attorney or agent, so specify)

Typed/printed name of signer

INSTRUCTIONS:

1. Upon filing this application, the name will be reserved for 60 days and a certificate of reservation will be issued.
2. The certificate of reservation, which will be in the form of a receipt, must be returned with and attached to the articles of organization, application for authority, certificate of amendment or with a cancellation of the reservation.
3. The name used must be the same as appears in the reservation.
4. A $20 fee payable to the Department of State must accompany this application.

NOTE: In all applications for existing domestic and foreign limited liability companies, the applicant must be the limited liability company.

DOS-1233 (Rev. 5/08)   -1-

establish compensation plans for members and managers. This listing of LLC powers is highly similar to that provided by statutes applying to corporations (see Chapter Eight) and is an example of borrowing of corporate concepts by LLC statutes. The recently revised ULLCA eliminates this list of powers and provides simply that LLCs have the power to do all things necessary or convenient to carry out their activities.

Financial Provisions.   The initial contributions to the LLC should be identified. As with a partnership, these contributions may be present or future cash, services, or property. Typically, profits and losses will be shared according to the respective interests initially contributed by the members. Circumstances that will require additional contributions of capital should be set forth. The general rule is that additional contributions must be made in proportion to the initial capital contributions. This section of the operating agreement should also discuss the distribution of assets, namely, the percentage to be allocated to each member and when distributions will be made. If the agreement is silent, distributions by the LLC before its dissolution must be equal. ULLCA § 404(a). Generally, distributions to members cannot be made if such would preclude the LLC from paying its ongoing obligations.

Operation of the LLC.   One of the distinct advantages of an LLC is that it can be member-managed without subjecting those members to personal liability. The LLC can be managed by all of its members, voting in accord with their respective ownership interests in the LLC. Such LLCs are usually referred to as **member-managed LLCs**. If the operating agreement is silent, each member will have an equal right to manage the LLC business. Member-managed LLCs thus operate similarly to general partnerships in that every member is able to do business on behalf of the LLC. For an LLC with numerous members, it may be cumbersome for the organization to be governed by all members. Therefore, some LLCs elect a managing committee or board of managers, much the same way a corporation is managed by its board of directors rather than its individual shareholders. These LLCs are often referred to as **manager-managed LLCs**. The managers need not be members of the LLC. This feature may be helpful in family businesses when family members prefer to avoid conflict by delegating management duties to a professional.

Member-managed LLC
An LLC managed by its members

Manager-managed LLC
An LLC managed by appointed managers rather than its membership

In a borrowing from general partnership law, the 2006 ULLCA provides that an LLC may file a statement of authority (see Chapter Three) to indicate which members have authority to perform certain acts, such as purchasing real property. Similarly, LLC members can file statements of denial to deny information in statements of authority.

If managers are to be elected, the operating agreement must indicate how often elections will be held and how notice of these election meetings will be given to the members. The members also need to decide the term for each manager, whether it be yearly or some longer term, such as three years.

The duties of the managers should be set forth. In general, managers of an LLC have the same fiduciary duties to the LLC and its members that general partners have, namely, a duty of loyalty and of due care.

If restrictions are to be imposed on managers, they should be clearly stated. For example, the operating agreement may restrict the managers from borrowing money in excess of a certain amount, selling certain assets, or making certain purchases unless a majority of the members approve or unless the managers unanimously agree. If the operating agreement is silent, under the ULLCA, the following activities generally require consent of all members in a manager-managed LLC: amendment of the operating agreement, merger with another entity, and the sale or lease of all or substantially all of the LLC's property. *See* ULLCA § 407(c). Some states, such as California, allow such decisions to be made by majority vote. In any event, routine business decisions are made by majority vote.

Generally, managers of an LLC will not be personally liable for decisions affecting the LLC unless they have breached a certain duty, violated a law, received a personal benefit from a transaction (unless the other managers have been informed of this conflict and agree to the transaction), or acted in bad faith and with conscious disregard of the best interest of the LLC. Thus, managers of an LLC will generally not be liable for some mere error in business judgment. Managers must act with ordinary care (the care that a similar person in a similar position would reasonably exercise). ULLCA § 409. This standard of liability is highly similar to that for a corporation's directors and officers and is another example of the borrowing of corporate concepts by LLCs.

Because no one would agree to be a manager of an LLC if personal liability could be readily imposed, the LLC may agree to indemnify or reimburse the managers for any claims made against them so long as the manager was acting with due care. LLC managers are seldom, if ever, indemnified for acts of recklessness, gross negligence, or acts contrary to law.

Meetings and Voting. Most statutes and the ULLCA do not impose requirements for meetings of the LLC. The operating agreement should thus address this issue and provide for how often regular meetings will be held, where they will be held, the procedure for providing notice of the meetings to the members, and how special meetings can be called to discuss urgent issues, such as an offer by a third party to buy the LLC business.

Most ordinary business decisions are made by majority vote of the members (if the LLC is member-managed) or by majority vote of the managers (if the LLC is managed by a board of managers). Extraordinary matters, such as amending the operating agreement, consenting to dissolve the LLC, or agreeing to sell all of the LLC's assets, often require unanimous approval of all members. Voting is in accord with members' contributions, or if the operating agreement is silent, on an equal basis. Under the ULLCA, members may appoint a proxy to vote or act on their behalf, similar to the proxy process used by shareholders in corporations (see Chapter Eleven).

LLC Members' Rights and Duties. The operating agreement should incorporate state statutory or ULLCA provisions allowing LLC members access to the LLC's records and books. Although the ULLCA does not require the LLC to maintain any specific records (unlike the limited partnership, which is required to maintain specified documents for review), the LLC is required to furnish records and information concerning its business and affairs that would be reasonably needed by a member to exercise rights and perform duties. The member's right to these LLC records may not be unreasonably restricted by the operating agreement. ULLCA § 110(c)(6).

The duty of care owed by members is ordinary care (the care that a person in a similar position would reasonably exercise in similar situations). The operating agreement may alter the duty of care and eliminate the duty of loyalty provided that such is not manifestly unreasonable. ULLCA § 110. Thus, for example, if desired, an LLC operating agreement may allow members to compete with the business of the LLC. Intentional misconduct or knowing violations of law can never be permitted by the operating agreement. Provisions may be included to remove or expel members or managers for certain acts of misconduct.

Admission of New Members and Dissociation of Members.   With regard to the admission of new members of an LLC, the ULLCA approach is that the admission of a new member requires unanimous consent of all members unless the operating agreement provides otherwise. ULLCA § 401(d). This requirement may effectively impose a natural restriction on the size of an LLC. If an LLC has 100 members, it might be extremely difficult for these 100 individuals to agree unanimously on anything.

A member may withdraw or dissociate according to terms specified in the operating agreement or the articles of organization. If no specific provisions are set forth, a member may generally withdraw from the LLC upon giving notice to the LLC. In many states, dissociation from an LLC is similar to dissociation from a general partnership. Thus, in these states, a dissociation does not cause a dissolution of the entity but rather triggers a buyout of the member's interest. Nevertheless, if the withdrawal or resignation is a breach of the operating agreement, or is before the end of a specified term set forth in the operating agreement, the dissociation is wrongful, and the withdrawing member may be liable for any damages caused by such dissociation. Under the revised ULLCA of 2006 there is no longer any obligation to buy out a dissociating member (although the operating agreement can provide for such).

Transferability of Interests.   A member's financial interest in an LLC is personal property. Members, however, have no ownership rights in LLC property. The operating agreement may provide that the financial interest is freely transferable or is transferable only upon certain conditions being met. The ULLCA provides that an LLC member may freely transfer his or her right to distributions but the transferee will become a member of the LLC only if the operating agreement provides or all other members consent. ULLCA § 401. If such consent cannot be obtained, the assignee will have the right to the assignor's financial interest in the LLC and distributions by the LLC but will have no management rights. Once again, this requirement may serve to restrict the size of LLCs, because it can be difficult and cumbersome to obtain the unanimous approval of a large number of people. Under ULLCA § 502(d), a member's interest in the LLC may be evidenced by a written certificate, much the same way a shareholder's interest in a corporation may be represented by a stock certificate.

Dissolution.   The agreement should specify the events that will trigger a dissolution of the LLC. Many operating agreements (and ULLCA § 701) provide that any of the following events will cause a dissolution of the LLC:

1. An event causing dissolution as stated in the operating agreement (for example, the period fixed for duration expires);

2. The consent of all members; or
3. The determination by a court that it is not reasonably practicable to continue the business.

Generally, upon the dissolution of an LLC, the LLC must file articles of termination or dissolution with the state in which it was formed. The articles of termination or dissolution usually recite that all of the debts and obligations of the LLC have been satisfied or provided for. (See Figure 6-4 for a sample form of the articles of dissolution required in Florida.)

Miscellaneous Provisions. Similar to a partnership agreement, the operating agreement for an LLC may contain numerous other provisions. For example, it may provide that members cannot transfer their interest in the LLC without offering it first to existing members of the LLC. It may provide for the purchase of life insurance for each member so that if a member dies, insurance proceeds are available to pay the decedent's estate for purchase of the interest of the decedent. Similarly, provisions should be made for dispute resolution, location and inspection of books and records, accounting rules, reimbursement for expenses, expulsion of managers, amendments to the operating agreement, meetings of the members, whether written ballots are required or voice votes are sufficient, whether members must be present in person or may vote by proxy, and any other matters pertinent to the operation and governance of the LLC.

PRACTICE TIP

If you work closely with several LLC clients, keep their operating agreements handy. Consider drafting a one-page index or table of contents as the first page of the agreement so that you can readily find critical operating agreement provisions relating to distributions, duties, withdrawal, and transfers of LLC interests. Highlight provisions that you find you refer to over and over again, or place notes in the margins next to key provisions. Remember that if the operating agreement does not address a certain issue, your state LLC statute will control.

F. Transferability of Interest

Most state statutes and the ULLCA provide that a member's interest in an LLC, namely the right to profits or distributions, is personal property. Therefore, the interest may be freely transferred or assigned, similar to any item of personal property, such as a car, jewelry, or stock. The assignment typically carries with it only the assignor's right to profits: It does not entitle the new owner to be a member of the LLC with rights to participation unless the operating agreement so provides or *all* other members consent (although some states, including New York and California, require only a majority vote). These restrictions on transferability of interest militate against an LLC with a large number of members because,

FIGURE 6-4
Florida LLC Articles of Dissolution Form

ARTICLES OF DISSOLUTION
FOR
A LIMITED LIABILITY COMPANY

1. The name of a limited liability company is

_____ .

2. The Articles of Organization were filed on _____ and assigned document number

_____ .

3. The date the dissolution was approved: _____ .

4. A description of occurrence that resulted in the limited liability company's dissolution pursuant to section 608.441, Florida Statutes, (copy 608.441 on back cover letter).

_____

_____

_____

_____

5. **CHECK ONE:**

☐ All debts, obligations and liabilities of the limited liability company have been paid or discharged.
-OR-
☐ Adequate provision has been made for the debts, obligations and liabilities pursuant to s. 608.4421.

6. All remaining property and assets have been distributed among its members in accordance with their respective rights and interests.

7. **CHECK ONE:**

☐ There are no suits pending against the company in any court.
-OR-
☐ Adequate provision has been made for the satisfaction of any judgment, order or decree which may be entered against it in any pending suit.

Signatures of the members having the same percentage of membership interests necessary to approve the dissolution:

Signature   Printed Name

_____   _____

_____   _____

_____   _____

_____   _____

_____   _____

FILING FEE: $25.00

as a practical matter, it is extremely difficult to achieve unanimous approval from a large group on even the most noncontroversial item.

G.   Actions by LLC Members

Just as limited partners in a limited partnership may initiate direct or derivative actions, a member of an LLC may also maintain a direct action on his or her own behalf if personally injured by the LLC or may maintain a derivative action to enforce a right of the LLC if the LLC members or managers fail to bring an action. To prevent individuals from joining LLCs to initiate derivative litigation, in many states and under the ULLCA, the LLC member must have been a member at the time of the transaction being complained of. The proceeds of any recovery in a derivative action go the LLC itself, although the LLC member is entitled to be reimbursed for reasonable attorneys' fees and other expenses.

H.   Dissociation and Dissolution of LLCs

Recall that under the RUPA, not every dissociation from a general partnership causes a dissolution of the partnership. In many instances a departing or dissociating partner's interest will be purchased by the partnership. Similarly, under the ULLCA, although many events (such as an individual LLC member's death or bankruptcy) cause a dissociation, fewer events require dissolution and winding up. Naturally, a well-written operating agreement should include a detailed section regarding such matters.

In brief, the following rules apply under ULLCA §§ 601, 602, 603, and 701 (although they may be modified by the LLC's operating agreement):

Events Causing Dissociation.   A member is dissociated from an LLC if any of the following occurs:

- The member provides notice of his or her express will to withdraw;
- An event occurs that has been agreed to in the operating agreement;
- A member transfers all of his or her interest in the LLC;
- A member is expelled;
- A member files for bankruptcy; or
- A member dies.

Remember that unless provided otherwise in the operating agreement, a member has the right to dissociate from an LLC at any time by express will. The dissociation may be wrongful (because it is in breach of a term of the operating agreement, which may give rise to damages), but the member will be able to dissociate nonetheless. The usual effect of a dissociation is that the member no longer has the right to participate in the management of the LLC.

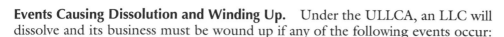

Events Causing Dissolution and Winding Up. Under the ULLCA, an LLC will dissolve and its business must be wound up if any of the following events occur:

- An event occurs that has been specified in the operating agreement;
- All members consent to dissolve (note that some states, including California and New York, provide for dissolution on majority vote and do not require unanimity);
- Ninety days pass with no LLC members; or
- A judicial decree is entered that it is not reasonably practicable to carry on the LLC business or that the managers are acting fraudulently, illegally, or are oppressing the rights of LLC members.

In winding up, assets must first be applied to discharge any obligations to creditors, including members of the LLC who are creditors. Any surplus will then be paid to the LLC members in accordance with their rights to distributions. After distributing its assets, the LLC then terminates its existence by filing articles of termination or dissolution with the secretary of state. The articles of termination or dissolution must contain the name of the LLC, the date of the dissolution, and a statement that the company's business has been wound up and its legal existence has been terminated.

Under the ULLCA and most state statutes, failure to file an annual report or pay any fees or taxes when due will result in an **administrative dissolution** of the LLC. An LLC may be reinstated by the secretary of state (usually within two years) upon compliance with the annual report requirements or payment of appropriate fees or taxes.

Administrative dissolution
Dissolution of a business entity for some technical reason, such as failure to file annual reports or pay taxes

I. Conversions, Mergers, and Domestications

Under Article 10 of the ULLCA, a general partnership or limited partnership or other entity (such as a corporation) may convert to an LLC (or vice versa) either by unanimous vote or by the appropriate vote required by their respective agreements. After the conversion is approved by the entity, it will file its articles of conversion with the secretary of state. The articles must state that the entity was converted from a different type of organization, its former name, and a statement that it was approved by the appropriate vote. As an example of a conversion, in 2006, the corporation America Online Inc. converted to the limited liability company AOL LLC.

Additionally, an LLC may merge with or into nearly any other business entity, including another LLC, a corporation, a general or limited partnership, or other domestic or foreign entity. A plan of merger must address various issues relating to the merger, and the plan must be approved by the membership of all merging entities. After approval of all parties, articles of merger must be filed with the secretary of state.

Finally, a foreign LLC may become a domestic LLC by adopting a plan of domestication and filing articles of domestication, similar to the articles of merger and conversion described earlier.

Conversions, mergers, and domestications do not affect property owned by the converting, merging, or domesticating entity or any of its debts and obligations, and the new or surviving entity will retain liability for any obligations that existed prior to the transaction. Thus, conversions, mergers, and domestications cannot be used to evade liability.

J. Taxation of LLCs

As previously discussed, one of the primary advantages of an LLC is that it offers the pass-through tax status of a partnership. On the other hand, corporate income is taxed twice: once when received by the corporation itself and then again when received by the corporate owners, the shareholders, as dividends.

In an LLC, all income, whether distributed or not, flows through or is "tagged" to the individual members, usually in proportion to their initial contributions and any subsequent contributions to the LLC. LLCs file the same informational tax return used by general partnerships, limited partnerships, and limited liability partnerships (see Figure 3-7). The members then declare their share of the LLC income on their individual federal tax returns and pay tax at whatever rate is appropriate. Similarly, losses sustained by members of LLCs may be used to offset other income and thereby decrease tax liability.

As is the case with general partnerships, limited partnerships, and limited liability partnerships, the LLC (whether a single-member or multiple-member LLC) may elect to be taxed as a corporation at corporate tax rates by "checking the box" on its tax form (see Figure 3-8). This will allow the LLC to retain profits without requiring the LLC members to pay taxes on the retained profits they have not received. If the LLC does not formally declare its election, it will have the pass-through tax status of a partnership. See Figure 6-5 for a chart comparing LLCs with sole proprietorships, general partnerships, limited partnerships, and limited liability partnerships.

FIGURE 6-5
Unincorporated Business Structures

	Sole Proprietorship	General Partnership	Limited Partnership	Limited Liability Partnership	Limited Liability Company
Types of Members	Individuals only	No restrictions	No restrictions	No restrictions	No restrictions
Number of Members Required	One only	At least two	At least two, one general partner and one limited partner	At least two	One member permitted in all states but Wyoming and under ULLCA

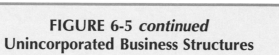

FIGURE 6-5 *continued*
Unincorporated Business Structures

	Sole Proprietorship	*General Partnership*	*Limited Partnership*	*Limited Liability Partnership*	*Limited Liability Company*
Formalities of Organization	None	None	Filing of Certificate of Limited Partnership required	Filing of Application of LLP required	Filing of Articles of Organization required
Management	Managed solely by sole proprietor	Managed jointly by all general partners	Managed solely by general partners	Generally managed jointly by all LLP partners	Can be member-managed or managed by appointed managers
Liability	Unlimited personal liability	Unlimited personal liability	General partners have unlimited personal liability; limited partners liable only to extent of investment	LLP partners are always protected from personal liability for their co-partners' torts; in nearly all states, no personal liability for acts whether arising in tort or contract	Members personally liable only to extent of investment (but professionals retain liability for their own negligence)
Transferability of All Ownership Rights	None; new sole proprietorship created upon transfer	Only partner's share of profits and losses is transferable	Economic interest is assignable; assignee becomes partner if agreement provides or all partners consent	Only partner's share of profits and losses is assignable	Economic interest is transferable; transferee becomes member if agreement provides or all LLC members consent
Ability to Do Business in Other States	Yes	Yes	Yes, if authorized by foreign state	Yes, if authorized by foreign state	Yes, if authorized by foreign state

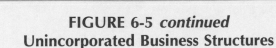

FIGURE 6-5 *continued*
Unincorporated Business Structures

	Sole Proprietorship	General Partnership	Limited Partnership	Limited Liability Partnership	Limited Liability Company
Continuity of Life	No; terminates upon death of sole proprietor	Under RUPA, only certain dissociations cause dissolution and winding up	LP can survive withdrawal of limited partner (and general partner if all consent)	Only certain dissociations cause a dissolution and winding up	Dissolution occurs only if operating agreement requires such, all members consent, 90 days pass with no members, or after judicial order
Taxation	Income taxed directly to sole proprietor	Income taxed directly to all partners*	Income taxed directly to all partners*	Income taxed directly to all partners*	Income taxed directly to all members*
Right to Bring Derivative Action	No	No	Yes	No	Yes

*Under new IRS "check-the-box" regulation, may elect to be taxed as a corporation at corporate tax levels.

Key Features
of Limited Liability Companies

◆ LLCs are neither corporations nor partnerships but a unique hybrid of the two, offering the best advantage of corporations (limited liability) with the best advantages of partnerships (flexible management and pass-through taxation).
◆ LLCs offer their members full protection from personal liability whether it arises in tort or contract. Only the LLC itself is liable for debts and obligations.

◆ LLCs can be managed by their members ("member-managed") or by appointed managers ("manager-managed"). A manager need not be a member.

◆ LLCs can be formed only by compliance with state statutes, which mandate the filing of articles of organization with the state agency.

◆ The LLC is governed by its operating agreement, which is usually written. If the operating agreement is silent on various matters, the pertinent state LLC statute will control.

◆ Unless the operating agreement provides otherwise, admission of a new member usually requires unanimous approval.

◆ In many instances, a member's dissociation does not cause a dissolution of the LLC.

◆ The LLC provides the pass-through taxation of a general partnership.

K. Growth and Trends in LLCs

1. *Growth*

The explosion in growth in LLCs since their first recognition in 1977 is staggering. For example, in 1996 there were nearly 25 times as many LLC registrations as there were in 1992. In 1996, nearly one in every six new business registrations nationwide was an LLC. Conrad S. Ciccotello & Terry Grant, *Professionals as Commercial Institutions: An Analysis of Evolving Organizational Forms*, 7 J. Legal Stud. Bus. 1, 2, 19 (2000). The universally accepted reason for the popularity of the LLC is its unique combination of flexible management, full protection from liability provided to its members, and favorable pass-through tax status. As a measure of the popularity of LLCs, the number of limited liability company filings grew from approximately 119,000 in 1995 to approximately 697,000 in 2002. In fact, in 2002, 40 percent of new businesses in the United States formed as LLCs.

2. *LLPs Versus LLCs*

With the number of organizational structures to choose from (including sole proprietorships, general partnerships, limited partnerships, LLPs, LLCs, and corporations), one might ask why some businesses select one structure over another. The array of business forms is so plentiful that some authors have proposed that states simplify business entity structures and allow only general partnerships, LLCs, and corporations. Warren H. Johnson, *Limited Liability Companies (LLC): Is the LLC Liability Shield Holding Up Under Judicial Scrutiny?*, 35 New Eng. L. Rev. 177, 188 n.77 (2000).

The choice between an LLP and an LLC may seem particularly confusing when one considers that both the LLP and the LLC offer protection from personal liability arising in tort (and liability is fully protected against in the LLC and in the

LLP in the 48 full shield jurisdictions), and both offer pass-through partnership tax status.

According to some experts, the traditional professions, such as law, accounting, and medicine, make up the majority of LLPs, and businesses in the "emerging" professions, such as computer consulting, marketing, and management services, tend to adopt the LLC form. Ciccotello & Grant, *supra* at 2, 8. In fact, evidence suggests that many traditional professions have been leaving the sole proprietorship, partnership, and corporate forms and choosing to become LLPs.

The rationale for the selection of the LLP form may be that professions such as law, medicine, and accounting have traditionally operated as partnerships and thus, because the LLP is simply a variety of partnership (although one offering protection from personal liability), the LLP form is familiar and comfortable to most professionals. On the other hand, the LLC, with its full protection from personal liability, whether arising in tort or contract, may be attractive to emerging professions, where the liability landscape is largely unsettled. *Id.* at 25.

In the broadest sense, there are few significant differences between LLPs and LLCs in terms of personal liability (at least for LLPs in full shield states), management, flexibility, and taxation. There are, however, some significant economic variations from state to state that help to explain why some forms are dominant in some states. For example, although Texas was the first state to recognize LLPs and its laws were specifically designed to protect lawyers from liability, law firms in Texas tend to operate as LLCs rather than LLPs, probably because the state requires an application and imposes an annual fee of $200 for each LLP partner. Thus, a law firm with 200 partners would pay $40,000 annually to be recognized as an LLP in Texas. Accordingly, many Texas firms elect other organizational structures. Robert W. Hamilton, *Professional Partnerships in the United States*, 26 J. Corp. Law 1045, 1053-54 (2001).

In sum, the selection of one entity over another is often based on a complex interplay of considerations of liability, taxation, organizational custom, and fees and taxes.

3. Outstanding Issues

Due to the newness of the LLC and the lack of a fully developed body of case law relating to LLCs, there are a number of issues currently unresolved for LLCs, including the following:

- Jurisdictions vary in their statutes relating to whether a single-person LLC is permissible (with all states but Wyoming allowing such), whether professionals may adopt the LLC form (with nearly all states allowing such), and how an LLC may be dissolved.
- Courts (and statutes) have not fully dealt with the issue whether a member's interest in an LLC is a security such that the offering and sale of which would be subject to federal and state securities laws. Some courts have indicated that the interest is a security if members expect to derive profits solely or primarily from the efforts of others. Thus, to date, usually only interests in manager-managed LLCs with hundreds of nonmanaging

members have been held subject to securities laws (see Chapter Thirteen for discussion of securities laws).

- Courts are considering whether the veil of limited liability afforded to LLC members may be pierced in any circumstances to hold LLC members liable for LLC obligations. To date, courts seem to favor imposing liability on LLC members if necessary to prevent fraud or injustice to a creditor (see Chapter Eleven for a discussion of piercing the veil in corporations).

In sum, due to the lack of case law interpreting LLCs and the variation in statutory treatment from state to state, it is critical that LLCs have detailed operating agreements relating to members' rights and duties and the operation and management of the LLC. A well-drafted operating agreement will lend predictability and stability to the LLC in the face of unsettled case law and lack of uniform treatment in the various states.

L.   Professional Limited Liability Companies

Although the ULLCA and most states allow LLCs to be formed for any lawful purpose (although many states do not allow an LLC to offer insurance or banking services), some states have added provisions into their LLC statutes specifically permitting professional firms (such as those offering legal, medical, and accounting services) to organize as **professional limited liability companies** (PLLCs). Typically, the statutes provide that the professionals retain liability for their own negligence and that of others under their supervision. Nevertheless, the PLLC protects the members' personal assets from obligations of the PLLC itself. Membership in the PLLC is usually restricted to licensed professionals, and the name of the business must indicate by some signal (usually "PLLC") that the entity is a professional limited liability company. In most states, the PLLC is created by a mere statement in the standard form for LLC articles of organization that the entity will operate as a PLLC.

Professional limited liability company
A type of LLC organized by professionals and in which professionals retain liability for their own negligence

M.   Role of Paralegal

The most critical task to be performed by a paralegal with regard to the formation and operation of an LLC is a thorough reading of the state statute authorizing LLCs. The requirements as to naming the LLC should be reviewed to ensure that any particular signal or designation of the adoption of LLC status is properly conveyed to third parties. Paralegals should contact the secretary of state to determine name availability, reserve the name (if the state permits), and request all appropriate forms for formation, operation, amendment, and dissolution of an LLC in that state.

Paralegals may also play a part in drafting the operating agreement. Paralegals should review various general partnership agreements and bylaws for corporations, and then tailor these to meet the needs of the LLC and the requirements of the LLC statute in that jurisdiction.

After forming an LLC, paralegals should prepare a list of procedures to follow in the future and "lessons learned" for the next LLC formation, noting useful phone numbers and the names of helpful state officials.

Paralegals should maintain the LLC's important documents in a binder, including the articles of organization and any amendments to the articles, a copy of the operating agreement, and an identification of the names and business and residence addresses of each member of the LLC.

Paralegals should docket or tickle the date for any required annual renewal or report forms.

Case Illustration
Non-Liability of LLC Member

Case: *Curole v. Ochsner Clinic, LLC*, 811 So. 2d 92 (La. Ct. App. 2002)

Facts: The plaintiff physician sued his former employer, a clinic operating as an LLC, and several of its other member physicians, alleging defamation and other torts. The civil district court granted the defendants' motion to change venue because the action was not brought in the county where the LLC had its principal office. The plaintiff appealed, alleging that venue was appropriate because one of the individual physicians employed by the LLC, Dr. Quinlan, resided in the county.

Holding: The court of appeal affirmed, holding that the plaintiff did not plead sufficient allegations to show that the individual LLC member, Dr. Quinlan, acted outside the scope of his authority as chief executive officer of the entity or contrary to the interests of the LLC. A member of an LLC is not personally liable in his capacity solely as a member for any debts or obligations of the LLC. Thus, venue did not lie where the individual LLC member resided.

◆   ◆   ◆

W E B   R E S O U R C E S

A number of sites provide general information about LLCs with clear and concise discussions of LLCs, comparing and contrasting them to other forms of business entities. Many of the following sites provide forms for LLC operating agreements. As with all forms, exercise caution in using the form, inasmuch as it will likely not be suitable for all LLCs.

State LLC statutes:	www.law.cornell.edu
	www.findlaw.com
	www.megalaw.com
State forms and secretaries of state:	www.nass.org
Text of ULLCA:	www.nccusl.org
General information:	www.tannedfeet.com
	www.llcweb.com (The "Limited Liability Company Website" provides basic information about LLCs and a "Frequently Asked Questions" section.)
	www.llc-reporter.com
	www.megalaw.com
	www.toolkit.com
	www.lectlaw.com
LLC Kit:	www.attorneyscorpservice.com (This attorneys' service company offers an LLC kit with all needed forms for forming and maintaining an LLC.)
Forms:	www.allaboutforms.com (Select "Show All Business Topics" for forms for operating agreements and other LLC forms.)

Discussion Questions

Fact Scenario. Cook & Cole, LLC, is a limited liability company engaged in providing restaurant services in several states. The entity has an operating agreement, but it is silent on several issues. The firm is managed by all of its 10 members. Use the ULLCA to answer the following questions (and identify the controlling ULLCA provision).

1. Doug, one of the LLC members, agreed to personally guarantee a loan for money borrowed from Bank of America. If the LLC fails to pay this loan, who will be liable for it?

2. Pete is a prospective new LLC member. Can Pete contribute a promise to provide accounting services for the LLC next year rather than contributing cash to the LLC?

3. The LLC's operating agreement is silent about distributions of profit. The LLC would like to distribute $200,000 profit to its members. How will this be divided?

4. Mike, an LLC member, owes money on his Visa credit card. The credit card issuer has obtained a judgment against Mike for the $5,000 Mike owes. What rights does the credit card issuer have? Discuss.

5. The LLC would like to ensure that third parties only deal with members Diana and Theresa in any transactions relating to real estate. How might the LLC

go about ensuring that third parties understand that other LLC members have no authority to purchase real estate for the LLC?

6. The LLC failed to file its annual report in two states this year and was dissolved. May the LLC be reinstated? How long does the LLC have to apply for reinstatement?

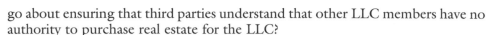

Net Worth

1. Access the Web site for the Georgia Secretary of State. In 2007, how many domestic limited liability companies were formed? How many domestic for-profit corporations were formed that year?
2. What is the fee to reserve a name for an LLC in California? For how long may it be reserved?
3. What is the fee in Texas to file a certificate of conversion of a Texas corporation to a Texas LLC?
4. Access the Web site for the restaurant Five Guys Burgers and Fries (Five Guys Enterprises). What business structure has this company adopted?

7

◆ ◆ ◆

Other Unincorporated Organizations

◆ ◆ ◆

CHAPTER OVERVIEW

With the exception of corporations, we have discussed the primary ways in which business is conducted in this country: sole proprietorships, general partnerships, limited partnerships, registered limited liability partnerships, and limited liability companies. Before turning to corporations, some other ways in which business is conducted in the United States are discussed in this chapter. All of the following organizations (with the exceptions of a real estate investment trust and a cooperative, which may operate as corporations) are "unincorporated associations," meaning that none have applied to a state to be recognized as a corporation. Most of the following business forms are not nearly as well known as the enterprises already discussed or as well known as corporations. Nevertheless, a brief summary of these organizational structures is helpful because they are occasionally desired by clients.

A. Joint Ventures

The most common of the other unincorporated organizations is the joint venture. A **joint venture** (referred to in the past occasionally as a *joint adventure*) is usually viewed as a form or variety of partnership—specifically, a form of general partnership. It is an association of two or more persons or entities who combine their property, skill, or knowledge to carry out *a single enterprise* for profit. Upon completion of the undertaking, the joint venture dissolves. Thus, the primary

Joint venture
A partnership formed to carry out a single enterprise rather than an ongoing business

distinction between a joint venture and a partnership is that a partnership is usually formed to engage in some ongoing business activity, whereas the joint venture is formed to carry out a particular venture.

For example, if an entity intends to engage in real estate development and is formed to construct buildings of any variety, whether commercial or residential, single-family or multifamily units, it may be carried on as a partnership. The partners might reasonably expect that the partnership will last many years, or so long as there is construction to be done. A joint venture, on the other hand, might be formed among three individuals to build a single condominium complex. Upon the completion of that one complex, the joint venture dissolves. A joint venture can best be described as a short-term partnership. Joint ventures are generally governed by state partnership and contract law.

The parties to a joint venture may be individuals, general partnerships, limited partnerships, LLPs, LLCs, or corporations. For example, two utility corporations, one formed in the United States and one formed in China, may enter into a joint venture agreement to construct and operate a nuclear plant in China. In fact, it is becoming increasingly common to see joint ventures formed for the purpose of conducting business activities in some foreign countries, including activities involving agricultural enterprises, construction ventures, and telecommunications businesses, often because many countries restrict the activity of foreign companies to own businesses or remove profit. Moreover, the foreign entity often brings new technologies while the domestic entity in the country has government contacts and insight into its government regulations. For example, in the 1990s, Pepsi-Cola Company entered into a joint venture with an arm of the Sichuan, China, provincial government to establish bottling factories in China. In other instances, joint ventures may be formed when one party, such as a university, does not have sufficient resources to commercially develop an invention or discovery, and thus forms a joint venture with another party, which provides funding and capital to bring the invention to market.

The parties in the joint venture, the *joint venturers,* owe fiduciary duties to each other, just as do partners in a partnership. Other similarities between partnerships and joint ventures include the following:

1. There must be an agreement between the joint venturers to do business together. This agreement may be oral or written. If the agreement is written, it will greatly resemble a general partnership agreement. If the agreement is oral and disputes as to its terms later arise, courts generally rely upon cases dealing with general partnerships or upon general partnership principles in the UPA or the RUPA to resolve the disputed issues.
2. No state formalities are required to form a joint venture.
3. The joint venturers share profits and losses according to their agreement. Typically, as in partnerships, the sharing of profits and losses is determined by the initial contributions to the joint venture. If there is no agreement, profits and losses are usually shared equally, as is the case with general partnerships.
4. Joint venturers have unlimited personal and joint and several liability for the venture's debts and obligations. The ability of joint venturers to bind each other for debts is more limited, however, than in a general partnership, although the joint venturers owe fiduciary duties to each other.

5. The joint venturers share the right to manage and control the business. The amount of voting power or control a joint venturer has is usually determined by his or her initial contribution. In the absence of agreement, control is shared equally.

6. The joint venture is treated as a partnership for tax purposes. In fact, § 761 of the Internal Revenue Code defines the term *partnership* to include joint ventures. Like partnerships, however, joint ventures may elect to be taxed as corporations by checking the box on IRS Form 8832. (See Chapter Three and Figure 3-8.) Usually, however, all of the income is passed through to the joint venturers, who then declare their respective shares of the income (or losses) on their individual tax returns.

A **strategic alliance** differs from a joint venture in that in a strategic alliance the parties remain independent of each other but collaborate for some profit-making purpose. In a joint venture, there is shared ownership of a single entity.

(A form of a joint venture agreement is available at www.ilrg.com.)

Strategic alliance
A form of collaborative business relationship in which the participants remain independent organizations

B. Mining Partnerships

Certain states, such as California, Idaho, Montana, and Nevada, in which mining operations are conducted (including oil and gas exploration) have statutes providing for the organization of mining partnerships. Other states, such as Kentucky, Oklahoma, Texas, and West Virginia, recognize mining partnerships by judicial decision. As the name itself indicates, the **mining partnership** is established for the development of mining property and extracting minerals from the property. Mining partnerships are basically partnerships organized for the specific purpose of mining.

Mining partnerships usually share the following features:

Mining partnership
Partnership organized to develop mining property

1. The partners voluntarily agree to do business together;
2. The agreement need not be express; the partnership arises from the ownership of interests in the mine and working the same;
3. The partners jointly own the partnership property, namely, mineral interests;
4. The partners share profits and losses according to their percentage of ownership interest;
5. Partners may convey their interests without dissolving the partnership, and the purchaser automatically becomes a member of the partnership with full rights of management;
6. No member of the mining partnership can bind the partnership unless there is express authority to do so;
7. Decisions are made by majority rule;
8. The partners owe fiduciary duties to each other; and
9. The mining partnership is taxed as a partnership.

Mining partnerships differ from general partnerships in that interests in the mining partnership are freely transferable, with new purchasers automatically becoming full members, whereas interests in general partnerships are not so freely transferable. Moreover, whereas under the UPA a general partnership dissolves upon the death or bankruptcy of any member, or the transfer of any partner's interest, the mining partnership survives such events and the heirs, bankruptcy trustee, or transferees become partners in the mining partnership with full rights of management and control upon purchase of their interest. Finally, unlike general partnerships, which are characterized by general mutual agency, there is limited ability of one partner to bind another.

C. Joint Stock Companies

Joint stock companies
Unincorporated association combining features of partnerships and corporations; rarely encountered in the United States

Joint stock companies (or associations) are relatively uncommon in the United States. They combine a number of features of partnerships and corporations; unlike the new LLPs and LLCs, however, they combine some of the most unattractive features of these organizations, namely, the personal liability seen in partnerships combined with the double taxation of corporations. In brief, a joint stock company is the polar opposite of LLPs and LLCs, which combine protection from personal liability with single pass-through taxation.

Joint stock companies developed in England. They were formed informally, by agreement, rather than by compliance with statutory formalities. These business organizations were referred to as *joint stock* companies because the interests of the members, called the *stock*, were placed or pooled into one joint account, which was then managed on behalf of the members.

Because English common law and customs were transplanted to America, these joint stock companies also became recognized in the United States. Although originally formed by mere agreement, some American jurisdictions (including Alabama, Minnesota, and New York) subject joint stock companies to compliance with statutes. Many Americans are unfamiliar with this type of organization and therefore joint stock companies are rarely encountered in modern practice. Moreover, due to the popularity of new enterprises, namely, LLPs and LLCs, these joint stock companies likely will become increasingly uncommon.

A joint stock company can be formed with few formalities. In most jurisdictions, no public filings are required. Nevertheless, in those states that govern joint stock companies by statute, certain publicly filed documents may be required. For example, in New York, a written certificate including basic information about the joint stock company, such as its name, its place of business, the number of its members, and the names and addresses of its officers, must be filed with the secretary of state and in the principal county in which the joint stock company will do business. The certificate must be filed within 60 days of transacting business in New York, and annually thereafter.

Articles of association
The agreement governing operation of a joint stock association

The joint stock company is governed by agreement. As in partnerships, there is no requirement for a written agreement. The members of the company, however, generally prefer that a written agreement be prepared. Additionally, many joint stock companies have numerous members, and operation of the business without a written agreement is both foolish and inefficient. This agreement, usually called the **articles of association,** will contain provisions similar to those found in partnership agreements, such as provisions regarding the division of profits and losses, duration of existence, transfer of shares, management of the entity, and causes of dissolution.

1. *Similarities to Corporations*

The following features of the joint stock company make it similar to a corporation:

a. The members of the joint stock company are generally referred to as members or shareholders.

b. The members are issued certificates representing their ownership interest in the entity, referred to as shares.

c. The shares owned by shareholders in a joint stock company are easily transferred, just as shares in a corporation can be easily sold to a third party.

d. The joint stock company is not governed by all of its members, as is the case in general partnerships, but rather is governed by a *board of managers* or *directors* who act on behalf of the shareholders. This form of governance is the classic operation of a corporation: Its shareholders elect individuals to manage the company. In a corporation, these managers are referred to as the board of directors. In the joint stock company, only the board of managers manages the business; the members have no voice in management and operation of the enterprise.

e. Like a corporation, the joint stock company is capable of perpetual existence, and the death of a member of a joint stock company or the transfer of a member's interest does not dissolve the company.

f. There is no mutual agency among the member-shareholders as there is among partners in a partnership. While the managers can act on behalf of the shareholders, the shareholders cannot bind one another by their acts and cannot act for the company.

g. The joint stock company is taxed as a corporation.

2. *Similarities to Partnerships*

The following features of the joint stock company make it similar to a partnership:

a. It is formed by agreement among the member-shareholders and usually does not require any documents to be publicly filed with the state.

b. Profits and losses are shared in proportion to ownership interests of the member-shareholders (which is the usual partnership model, although partners are free to agree otherwise and failure to reach agreement on profits and losses will result in equal sharing).

c. The member-shareholders have unlimited personal liability for the debts and obligations of the joint stock company. Because there is no general agency among the shareholders, however, one shareholder or member may not perform some act that would render other shareholders liable. Thus, the opportunities for unlimited liability are somewhat decreased because only the board of managers may act on behalf of the members and thereby commit them to some debt or obligation.

3. *Modern Application*

One can easily see why the joint stock company is an unattractive form of business enterprise: The member-shareholders have no voice in the management and governance of the enterprise, yet they have unlimited liability for its debts and torts.

Lloyd's (previously called Lloyd's of London), the well-known insurance underwriter in existence for more than 300 years, is operated as a joint stock company. During the late 1980s and early 1990s, Lloyd's suffered record losses due to what it referred to as a "high incidence of catastrophes," such as asbestos and pollution claims and earthquake and hurricane damage for which it had provided insurance. To meet these obligations it had to ask its individual investors, referred to as "Names," for cash. Approximately 3,000 Americans were Names and most were stunned to realize they faced unlimited liability for losses.

In fact, United States Supreme Court Associate Justice Stephen Breyer was a Name, and the issue of his potential liability was a critical issue in his confirmation hearings. Although Breyer had insurance for some of the losses he faced, he was required to resolve the debt fully before being confirmed. In some instances, however, Names were forced to use their savings to cover their liability. Some applied to a special hardship program allowing them to deed over their houses to Lloyd's upon their death. Hundreds were bankrupted by their losses. About 30 Names committed suicide. When some Americans complained they had never been fully informed of the risks, Lloyd's responded that it was never compulsory to join and that people who joined freely had a duty to investigate fully before committing funds. An organization referred to as the American Names Association sued Lloyd's.

Lloyd's offered a Recovery and Renewal Plan to settle the numerous lawsuits against it. Approximately 95 percent of the Names accepted the plan, but a number refused. Lloyd's has generally been successful in the lawsuits it has brought to collect the amounts owed to it by the Names, and the judgments have been upheld by U.S. courts. The Names have also filed suit against Lloyd's U.S. lawyers and bankers. At the time of writing of this text, litigation is still pending by and against Lloyd's.

This modern application of the principles of joint stock companies emphasizes the unfamiliarity American investors generally have with the enterprise as well as some of its most unattractive features, namely unlimited personal liability coupled with the members' lack of management or control of the enterprise.

D.　Business Trusts

Business trust
An unincorporated association governed by the law of trusts in which trustees manage the business for others, called beneficiaries

The **business trust,** sometimes called the "Massachusetts business trust" due to its initial recognition in Massachusetts, is another form of unincorporated business enterprise rarely encountered any longer. A combination or hybrid of a corporation and a partnership, the business trust was developed in an attempt to achieve the limited liability status of corporations while circumventing certain laws and restrictions that earlier applied to corporations regarding acquisition and development of real estate.

The *business trust* is created by a written trust agreement that defines the powers and duties of its managers, called **trustees,** and the interests of its equitable or beneficial owners, called **beneficiaries.** The trustees hold and manage property or carry on business activities for the benefit of the beneficiaries. Generally, the written trust agreement need not be filed with any state authority; however, some states, including Nevada and Wyoming, require certain public filings, treating the business trust somewhat similarly to a corporation. The requirements in New York with regard to public filings for joint stock companies are equally applicable to business trusts. Similarly, in Ohio, before commencing business, the business trust must file a detailed report with the secretary of state, giving specific information about the business trust. When business trusts are governed by statute (as they are in about 30 states, including Delaware, Nevada, New York, Ohio, Virginia, and Wyoming, among other states), they are often referred to as **statutory trusts** to distinguish them from business trusts created pursuant to judicial decision, which are often called **common law trusts.**

Trustee
One to whom property or a business is entrusted to manage it for others

Beneficiary
One for whose benefit property or a business is managed

Statutory trust
A trust governed by state statute

Common law trust
A trust created and governed by case law

1. Similarities to Corporations

The business trust shares the following features with corporations:

a. The equitable owners or investors, called beneficiaries, are issued trust certificates evidencing their ownership rights in the business trust. These are similar to stock certificates issued to the shareholders of a corporation.

b. Just as shares of stock in a corporation are easily transferred to another, ownership interests held by beneficiaries in the business trust can be easily transferred to third parties.

c. A corporation is not managed by its owners, the shareholders, but rather by directors elected by the shareholders. Similarly, the business trust is managed or governed by managers, the trustees. These trustees are solely responsible for the operation of the business.

d. The business trust does not dissolve upon the death of any of its beneficiaries or the transfer of their interests and may exist perpetually. Many business trusts, however, establish periods of duration.

e. There is no mutual general agency among the beneficiaries. They cannot act so as to bind one another or the business trust. The trustees, however, are agents of the beneficiaries and can thus bind the beneficiaries by their actions. The trustees owe fiduciary duties to the trust and to the beneficiaries.

f. The beneficiaries, like shareholders in a corporation, usually enjoy limited liability for the debts and obligations of the business trust. If, however, they participate in management of the business, they may lose their limited liability status. If liability arises due to ordinary activities carried on by the trustees for the business trust, and no negligence or reckless disregard is shown, the trustees may be indemnified or reimbursed by the trust itself or by the beneficiaries. In some states, such as Wyoming, the trustees are held to the same standard of care as directors of a business corporation. Thus, they usually have no liability except for intentional misconduct, fraud, or knowing violations of law.

g. The business trust is usually taxed as a corporation.

2. Similarities to Partnerships

The business trust shares the following features with partnerships:

a. The business trust is formed by agreement and in most states there are relatively few formalities involved in organizing the business trust.
b. Profits and losses are shared in accord with the beneficiaries' respective equitable ownership interests in the business trust (which is the usual partnership model, although failure to agree on profits and losses will result in equal partnership shares).

(See Figure 7-1 for the form of certificate of business trust used in Nevada.)

3. Modern Application

The business trust is unfamiliar to most American investors. For many years it was rarely seen because the reason for its creation, circumvention of certain restrictions on corporations as to acquisition and development of real property, no longer existed. Moreover, there are numerous other ways of doing business, such as the LLP and LLC, that afford more advantages to the owners than does the business trust. In the past few years, the number of business trusts has been increasing. Because of its growth for use by mutual funds, ERISA pension funds, and other types of trusts, in 2008 the National Conference of Commissioners on Uniform State Laws released a draft Uniform Statutory Trust Entity Act to bring about uniformity in the inconsistent state laws governing business trusts and other statutory trusts.

PRACTICE TIP

Determining the difference between some forms of business entities can be very difficult. In particular, informal general partnerships bear a strong resemblance to joint ventures. Focus on whether the enterprise was formed to carry out a single business enterprise (in which case it is a joint venture) or to carry out an ongoing business (in which case it is a partnership). Similarly, joint stock companies bear a strong resemblance to corporations.

Clients can be notoriously inaccurate with regard to the names and structures of their businesses. If they are available, review state filings or tax records to verify correct names and business types. Remember that what parties call their business is not determinative; a court is always free to find that a business is something other than what its principals call it.

E. Real Estate Investment Trusts

Real estate investment trust
Business that invests in real estate on behalf of numerous investors who have limited liability for the business debts

A **real estate investment trust** (REIT, pronounced "reet") is a vehicle for investment in real estate by numerous investors who pool their capital to acquire or provide financing for commercial real estate. After the real estate recession of the 1980s, banks became wary of loaning money to real estate developers and often did

FIGURE 7-1
Nevada Certificate of Business Trust

 ROSS MILLER
Secretary of State
206 North Carson Street
Carson City, Nevada 89701-4299
(775) 684 5708
Website: www.nvsos.gov

Certificate of Business Trust
(PURSUANT TO NRS CHAPTER 88A)

USE BLACK INK ONLY - DO NOT HIGHLIGHT   ABOVE SPACE IS FOR OFFICE USE ONLY

1. Name of Business Trust: (must include the words Business Trust, B.T., or BT)	
2. Registered Agent for Service of Process: (check only one box)	☐ Commercial Registered Agent: _____ Name ☐ Noncommercial Registered Agent (name and address below) **OR** ☐ Office or Position with Entity (name and address below) _____ Name of Noncommercial Registered Agent **OR** Name of Title of Office or Other Position with Entity _____ Nevada ____ Street Address City Zip Code _____ Nevada ____ Mailing Address (if different from street address) City Zip Code
3. Names and Addresses of Trustees: (must include the name and post office box or street address, either residence or business, of at least one trustee; attach an additional page if listing more than 3)	1) _____ Name _____ Address City State Zip Code 2) _____ Name _____ Address City State Zip Code 3) _____ Name _____ Address City State Zip Code
4. Name, Address and Signature of Each Person Forming the Business Trust: (must be signed by each person forming the business trust; attach an additional page if more than 2)	**X** _____ Name Signature _____ Address City State Zip Code **X** _____ Name Signature _____ Address City State Zip Code
5. Certificate of Acceptance of Appointment of Registered Agent:	*I hereby accept appointment as Registered Agent for the above named Entity.* **X** _____ Authorized Signature of Registered Agent or On Behalf of Registered Agent Entity Date

This form must be accompanied by appropriate fees.

Nevada Secretary of State NRS 88A DBT Articles
Revised on 7-1-08

so only on terms unattractive to the developers. To remedy the situation, REITs were created to sell stock to the public, which then provides financing for real estate developers. REITs have become increasingly popular, and there are about 300 REITs in the United States, about two-thirds of which are traded on the major stock exchanges. In brief, a REIT is a company that buys, develops, manages, and sells real estate assets.

REITs are usually formed either as trusts or corporations, although they can be formed as partnerships. REITs formed as trusts are governed by the law of trusts, meaning that they are created by a document called a declaration of trust that provides that the property is managed by a trustee or trustees for the benefit of others, called beneficiaries. The beneficiaries hold transferable certificates representing their ownership interest in the REIT.

REITs are usually managed by an investment advisor, the trustee, selected by the REIT's board of directors and pursuant to a written agreement between the REIT and the advisor. Moreover, there will be a declaration of trust. REITs that are structured as corporations are managed by a board of directors elected by their shareholder-investors. This board of directors usually comprises experienced real estate professionals, who select and manage the REIT's investments. If the REIT offers securities to the public, it must register with the Securities and Exchange Commission and provide a complete prospectus to each prospective investor.

Many states specifically regulate REITs by statute. For example, Ohio requires that REITs transacting business in Ohio file a detailed report with the secretary of state before commencing business (see Figure 7-2). Similarly, in Alabama, REITs must file a declaration of trust giving certain required information about the REIT with the secretary of state. In some states, formation of a REIT is pursuant to common law rather than pursuant to specific statutes.

1. Types of REITs

There are four basic forms of REITs:

- *Equity REITs* own and operate income-producing real estate such as apartment buildings and shopping centers and derive income through rent received. More than 90 percent of all REITs are equity REITs.
- *Mortgage REITs* do not own real estate but rather make loans enabling others to purchase real estate. The loans are secured by mortgages on the real estate, and the REIT derives revenue through interest paid on the mortgage loans.
- *Hybrid REITs* hold and invest in both mortgages and real estate assets.
- *Umbrella partnership REITs* (UPREITS) hold interests in partnerships that themselves own commercial real property. The REIT serves as the general partner in a partnership that owns and operates commercial real estate such as apartment projects.

REITs may also focus on a specific industry and invest solely in targeted fields such as warehouses or shopping centers, or they may focus their investments geographically by state or region.

FIGURE 7-2
Ohio Report by REIT (Partial Form)

 Prescribed by **J. Kenneth Blackwell**

Ohio Secretary of State

Central Ohio: (614) 466-3910

Toll Free: 1-877-SOS-FILE (1-877-767-3453)

e-mail: busserv@sos.state.oh.us

Expedite this Form: (Select One)
Mail Form to one of the Following:
○ Yes PO Box 1390 Columbus, OH 43216 *** Requires an additional fee of $100 ***
○ No PO Box 1329 Columbus, OH 43216

REPORT BY
REAL ESTATE INVESTMENT TRUST
(For Domestic or Foreign)
Filing Fee $125.00
(168-RTO)

TO THE SECRETARY OF STATE, COLUMBUS, OHIO

_____ , a real
(name of trust)

estate investment trust desiring to transact real estate business in Ohio, pursuant to Section 1747.01 et seq., Revised Code of Ohio hereby files the following report:

FIRST Its business name is _____

SECOND It is a real estate investment trust organized in the state of _____ (State)

THIRD The complete address of its principal office is

_____
(street address)   NOTE: P.O. Box Addresses are NOT acceptable.

_____
(city, township, or village)   (state)   (zip code)

FOURTH If this report is being filed by a FOREIGN real estate investment trust, the complete address of its principal office in Ohio, if any, is

_____
(street name and number)

_____ , Ohio _____
(city, village or township)   (zip code)

FIFTH It hereby designates _____ as its agent within Ohio, upon whom process against the trust may be served. The complete address within Ohio of such agent is

_____
(street address)   NOTE: P.O. Box Addresses are NOT acceptable.

_____ , Ohio _____
(city, village or township)   (zip code)

2. Advantages of REITs

REITs provide a number of advantages to their investors:

a. Investors are passive and hold shares in the REITs without assuming personal liability.
b. The REIT is subject to single taxation only. Even REITs formed as corporations are not subject to taxation at the corporate level. Profits earned and distributed to the investors are taxed to the investor shareholders as ordinary income (assuming a variety of tax and regulatory requirements are met, including having a minimum of 100 shareholder investors and distributing at least 90 percent of the taxable income to the investors). REITs use IRS Form 1120-REIT to report their income and elect to be treated as a pass-through entity. This form is used whether the REIT is operated as a corporation, a trust, or some form of unincorporated association. Although profits are distributed to investors, losses suffered by REITs cannot be deducted by the investors.
c. Whereas partners in partnerships and members in limited liability companies often have difficulty selling their interests (inasmuch as there is no ready market for their ownership interests), investors in REITs can readily sell their shares in the REIT and achieve liquidity because the REITs are usually traded on the stock exchanges.
d. REITs are managed by experienced professionals who are accountable to, and elected by, their shareholder-investors.
e. Because REITs are required by law to distribute at least 90 percent of their taxable income, REITs tend to pay high dividends to their investors (however, the recent real estate slump has caused a decline in REIT values, with REIT shares falling nearly 20 percent in 2007).

3. Conclusion

REITs are complex investment vehicles requiring a thorough grounding in accounting principles and tax, corporate, and securities law. Forming the REIT can take up to one year, and registration with the Securities and Exchange Commission is a complex, time-consuming process. Nevertheless, for large real estate transactions, REITs offer several advantages, primarily limited liability for the passive investors coupled with avoidance of double taxation and an often high level of annual distributions.

F. Cooperative Associations

Cooperative association
A business owned and democratically controlled by its members for their mutual benefit

Cooperative associations are businesses owned, controlled, and operated for the mutual benefit of their members. They may be formed as corporations, as LLCs, or as unincorporated associations such as joint ventures and may be formed for nearly any purpose, although many are agricultural co-ops formed by farmers to market their crops, by consumers to obtain credit and financial services, or by consumers to obtain and share utilities. For example, in rural areas, neighbors may form a cooperative to obtain electrical or cable television services. The largest single segment of cooperatives in the United States is credit unions, which offer their members loans, certificates of deposit, and other financial services. Almost all states have statutes permitting the formation of cooperative associations. If they are formed as corporations or LLCs, corporate or LLC statutes, respectively, govern their formation, operation, and termination.

Cooperative associations share the following features:

- They are owned and democratically controlled. Each member receives one vote, regardless of the number of shares or percentage of ownership interest in the cooperative.
- They return profits to their members based on a member's "patronage" or use of the cooperative services rather than on the investment owned in the cooperative. Thus, if a farmer buys 12 percent of his co-op's products, he would receive 12 percent of the benefit (usually called a "patronage refund") regardless of his percentage of ownership in the co-op.
- They are governed by state statute and by their own internal governing documents (often called bylaws, just as is the case with corporations) and are managed by their elected directors.
- They exist solely to serve their members.
- Their capital comes from their members, not from "outside" investors.
- A cooperative's members have no personal liability for the debts or obligations of the cooperative.
- A member's interest in a cooperative is usually freely transferable.
- Cooperatives generally enjoy the single or pass-through federal taxation of partnerships. Patronage dividends or refunds returned to co-op members are passed through to the members, who pay tax on the amount received according to the appropriate tax brackets.

It has been estimated that there are nearly 50,000 cooperative associations in the United States. To advance uniformity for cooperatives, in 2007 the National Conference of Commissioners on Uniform State Laws developed a Uniform Limited Cooperative Association Act, although it has only been adopted in three jurisdictions. The text of the Act is available at the Conference's Web site at www.nccusl.org.

Key Features
of Other Unincorporated Organizations

- ◆ Joint ventures are a form of short-term partnership, usually formed to carry out one single venture; they are governed by partnership law.
- ◆ Mining partnerships are formed to develop mining property and are characterized by joint working of the property and sharing of profits; partners can easily convey their interests, and the transferee automatically becomes a new partner.

- ◆ Joint stock companies are governed by a board of managers rather than their members, the owners have personal liability, and the companies are taxed as corporations, thus combining the most undesirable features of partnerships and corporations.
- ◆ Business trusts are managed by trustees rather than the beneficial owners and are taxed as corporations, combining undesirable features of partnerships and corporations, except that the owners usually have no personal liability.
- ◆ Real estate investment trusts are formed as partnerships, trusts, or corporations to buy, develop, operate, and sell real estate assets; they offer liquidity to their owner investors because the interests are often traded on the major stock exchanges.
- ◆ Cooperative associations can be formed as corporations or LLCs, or they can be unincorporated. They are formed for the mutual benefit of their members and are democratically owned and controlled, with one vote per member. Profits are shared on a "patronage" basis, meaning that one receives a return based on one's use of the cooperative rather than based on ownership interest. They are taxed as partnerships.

G. Role of Paralegal

Because the forms of business enterprises discussed in this chapter are not as familiar to those in the legal profession as other more conventional business enterprises, paralegals assisting in the formation of any of the business enterprises in this chapter will need to conduct research to learn as much as possible about these enterprises. Some are not governed by statute and, therefore, cases might need to be examined and discussed with your attorney to determine how courts have treated these organizations in a particular state.

A good starting point for drafting a joint venture agreement or a mining partnership agreement is a general partnership agreement, which should then be tailored to the laws in your state. The form used in Chapter Three to obtain information from clients (Figure 3-9) can also be used to assist in the drafting of the pertinent documents for formation and operation of these enterprises.

Case Illustration
Similarity of Joint Venture to Partnership

Case:	*Duffy v. Piazza Construction, Inc.*, 815 P.2d 267 (Wash. Ct. App. 1991)
Facts:	The plaintiffs and defendant created a joint venture to bid on a certain construction project. The defendant prepared the bid for the joint venture, but it was rejected because it did not

comply with the proposal requirements. The plaintiffs sued the defendant for negligence. The trial court granted the defendant's motion for summary judgment.

Holding: The court of appeals affirmed. The relationship between joint venturers is like that of partners in a partnership. The associations are so similar that their rights, duties, and liabilities are generally subject to the same rules. Generally, there is no liability of one party to another for negligence in the management of the joint venture. It is only when there is a breach of trust (such as would occur if one party used property belonging to the joint venture for his own use) that an action lies. In the ordinary management and operation of a partnership or joint venture, there is no liability to the other partners or joint venturers for negligence or mere mistakes in business judgment in managing the affairs of the enterprise.

◆ ◆ ◆

WEB RESOURCES

To obtain basic information about the types of business associations described in this chapter, access www.google.com and type in pertinent key words, such as "mining partnerships" or "REIT." You will be directed to a number of sites. As of this date, there is little information on the Internet relating to mining partnerships, joint stock companies, or business trusts, probably because they are either of interest to such a narrow segment of the population or because they are unknown to most investors. More information is provided for REITs. The following sites are of interest, although you should always review a form carefully and modify it to suit a client's specific needs.

State statutes:	www.law.cornell.edu www.megalaw.com
Information about joint ventures:	http://topics.law.cornell.edu/wex/Joint-venture
Forms for joint ventures:	www.ilrg.com www.allaboutforms.com (Select "Show All Business Topics.") www.lectlaw.com/formb.htm
Information about REITs:	www.reit.com (National Association of Real Estate Investment Trusts site) http://invest-faq.com/articles/real-es-reit.html
Information about cooperatives:	www.ncba.coop (National Cooperative Business Association site)

Discussion Questions

1. Last holiday season, Cynthia and Claire decided to offer catering services. After the holiday season they returned to their regular jobs as tutors. Identify the type of business in which Cynthia and Claire were engaged.

2. Without Claire's knowledge, Cynthia purchased an expensive food processor for their use in catering holiday parties. Who is liable to pay for the equipment? Why?

3. Assume that Cynthia and Claire had no agreement regarding how profits were to be divided. They made $10,000 over the holiday season. How will this be divided?

4. George, a partner in a mining partnership, purchased equipment for the partnership that he believed the partnership needed, although no one authorized him to do so. Who is liable to pay for the equipment? Why?

5. After careful consideration, the trustees of a Wyoming business trust purchased some real estate. Real estate values have declined in the area, and the property is now worth far less than it was purchased for. Are the trustees liable for this decision? Discuss.

6. A group of 20 working mothers has decided to create a group that will offer child care services to its members. Each working mother has contributed an initial fee to hire quality employees. The members of the group would like to elect a board of directors. One of the mothers, Pam, contributed quite a bit more to the group than other mothers. What is the nature of this business structure? How many votes will Pam be able to cast in electing the board? Discuss.

Net Worth

1. Access the Web site for the Nevada Secretary of State.
   a. What is the fee to file a Certificate of Business Trust?
   b. Locate the records for Arcanum Business Trust. What type of entity is this? Who is its agent for service of process?
2. Access the Web site for the Iowa Secretary of State. Conduct a business entity search for Cooperative Energy Company. When was this cooperative filed or created?
3. Review the proposed Uniform Statutory Trust Entity Act. Would the following names be acceptable under the Act?
   a. Delaware Investment Club
   b. Investors Syndicate
4. Access the Web site for the National Association of Real Estate Investment Trusts. Review the FAQs. What is a REIT?

8

◆ ◆ ◆

Introduction to Corporations

◆ ◆ ◆

CHAPTER OVERVIEW

Corporations are the first form of business enterprise examined thus far that exist apart from their members, so that the death, withdrawal, or bankruptcy of one of the owners of the corporation never affects the legal existence of the corporation. The next several chapters examine the business corporation, namely a corporation formed for profit-making purposes. Other types of corporations also exist: nonprofit corporations such as charitable and educational corporations, and professional corporations for doctors, lawyers, and accountants. For the most part, these other types of corporations are discussed in Chapter Seventeen.

As discussed in Chapter One, although there are far fewer corporations than sole proprietorships, they account for a disproportionately high share of revenue.

This chapter introduces the business corporation, discusses some of its most notable features, and distinguishes privately held corporations (those whose stock is not sold publicly and is usually held by a small number of friends and relatives) from publicly held corporations (those whose stock is traded publicly).

Because a corporation is truly a "person" in the view of the law, *it* pays taxes. This concept of double taxation has been referred to previously. The corporation itself pays taxes on its earnings; when those earnings are later distributed to the owners of the corporation, the shareholders, they pay taxes on certain distributions or dividends received by them. This chapter also examines some of the ways this double taxation can be avoided or reduced.

Many of the topics introduced in this chapter are discussed in greater detail in later chapters.

A. Characteristics of Corporations

Corporation
A legal entity created by a state to carry out business (if a for-profit entity)

Corporations, like limited partnerships, registered limited liability partnerships, and limited liability companies, are creatures of statute and can only be formed by compliance with various statutory formalities. A corporation exists only when the state declares it to be in existence, and dissolves (or loses its status as a separate entity) only when the state officially terminates its existence. A corporation derives its existence from the state, whereas a partnership derives its existence from the agreement of its members. Corporations can be made up of one shareholder or hundreds of thousands of shareholders.

According to legal theory, the corporation is a *person.* In fact, the root word for *incorporate* is *corpus,* Latin for *body.* Thus, incorporation results in the existence of a new body or person that exists independently from its members, as opposed to sole proprietorships and partnerships, which are merely extensions of their owners. Whereas a sole proprietorship dies with the death of the sole proprietor, all of the shareholders of a corporation could die tomorrow, and the corporation would continue its existence. This new person or entity is also liable for the contracts it signs, the obligations it incurs, and the money it borrows. Because the corporation is not a *natural person* as are living and breathing individuals, but rather is an *artificial person,* it must act through its duly appointed agents: its board of directors and its officers. Although the president of a corporation may actually sign his or her name to a contract, he or she is not bound by the contract. The corporation, the artificial person, the "it," is bound.

B. History and Governing Law

1. History

Beginning in the 1600s, English law allowed the sovereign to grant charters or permission to companies for very limited purposes, often for trading or exploration. Thus, Massachusetts Bay Company, Hudson's Bay Company, and the East India Company, all formed to exploit trade and natural resources, are the predecessors to our modern business corporation. Due to their initial instability, organizations resembling corporations were viewed with skepticism; and most corporations in the early American republic were formed for quasi-public purposes, such as operating canals and turnpikes. Corporate charters were restrictive, and incorporation was viewed as a privilege. Even at the end of the nineteenth century, Andrew Carnegie operated his steel company as a limited partnership so that he, as the managing general partner, would have total control over its operations. As American business grew more complex, larger corporations began to emerge. By the early twentieth century, restrictive provisions disappeared in most state corporation laws, thereby setting the stage for the modern American business corporation.

Corporations have a significant effect on the nation's economy. In 2005, corporations reported approximately $24 trillion in business receipts, compared to $3.7 trillion for partnerships and $1.2 trillion for sole proprietorships. *Statistical Abstract of the United States* 483 (128th ed. 2009). See Figure 8-1 for a chart showing corporate net worth in the United States.

FIGURE 8-1
Corporations: Profits (Before Tax in $ Billions)

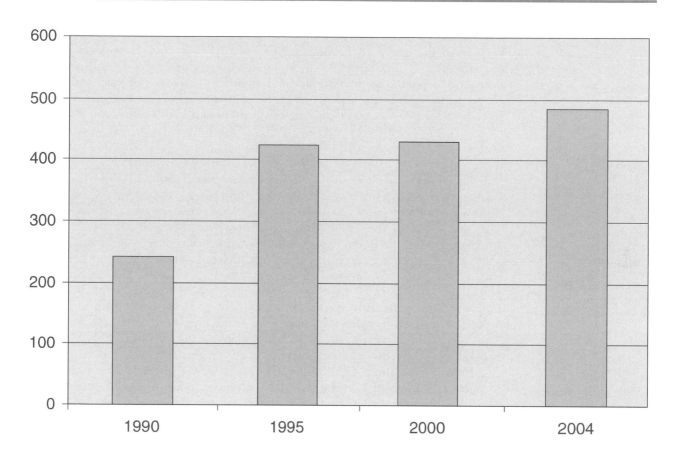

Source: *Statistical Abstract of the United States* 514 (127th ed. 2008)

Corporations also have an important effect on the nation's psyche. Corporate scandals and failures, such as those involving Enron, WorldCom, and AIG, affect people's attitudes about business, government regulation, and ethics, and have given rise to legislation to curb corporate abuse. An examination of these new corporate governance and responsibility issues is found in Chapter Eleven.

2. Governing Law

A corporation is governed by the laws of the state in which it is organized. Similarly, a corporation formed in one state and doing business in another is subject to the laws of both jurisdictions. Corporations operating in every state are often subject to a patchwork quilt of laws. For example, a corporation may be formed in California for restaurant and bar services. If that corporation decides to transact business in Utah, it will be subject to Utah's restrictions regarding the serving of alcoholic beverages. Similarly, some states allow grocery stores to sell hard liquor, wine, and beer; other states allow grocery stores to sell only wine and beer; still others prohibit the stores from selling any alcoholic beverages. For a national food chain, such as Safeway, these conflicts present complex issues of regulation and compliance with a number of laws. Moreover, states can regulate corporations formed outside their jurisdictions differently from their own domestic corporations. Such variation in treatment between domestic and foreign corporations is rarely done in actual practice, however, because to disfavor out-of-state corporations would discourage businesses from coming into the state.

Each of the 50 states and the District of Columbia has its own statutes governing corporations formed in or doing business in that jurisdiction. Nearly all of these state laws are based on the 1950 Model Business Corporation Act, drafted by the Business Law section of the American Bar Association. In 1984 the Model Business Corporation Act was revised (see Appendix F). Other revisions and additions were made in 1969 and 1980, and a complete revision was effected in 1984. This text refers to the 1984 **Model Business Corporation Act** (with its later amendments) as **MBCA.** Each state that has considered and adopted the MBCA has added its own provisions and deleted others. Thus, although the laws relating to corporations are substantially similar across the country, each particular state's statutes must be carefully analyzed to ensure compliance with a state's requirements as to formation, operation, and regulation of business corporations within its borders. See Appendix A for a citation to each state's corporations' statutes. The text of the MBCA is available at the Web site of the American Bar Association (see Web Resources at the end of this chapter).

Delaware's General Corporation Law is also viewed as a model by many states. Moreover, many of the largest publicly traded corporations in this country have been incorporated in Delaware. Delaware statutes are available through www.findlaw.com and www.megalaw.com.

In addition to the statutes governing corporations, some states have a rich and complex body of case law interpreting those statutes. Therefore, to understand fully the requirements of any one state, both its corporation statutes and the cases interpreting those statutes must be consulted.

Various federal statutes, such as the Securities Act of 1933 and the Securities Exchange Act of 1934, also govern corporations whose stock is sold to members of the public at large. A thorough discussion of these federal statutes is found in Chapter Thirteen.

In addition to being governed by various laws, corporations are also governed by two basic documents: the *articles of incorporation,* which provides basic information about and is needed to create the corporation; and the *bylaws* of the corporation, its own internal rules for operation.

MBCA
Model Business Corporation Act; act on which individual state statutes governing corporations are based

C. The Corporation as a Person

Corporations, although artificial persons, enjoy many of the same rights and privileges as natural persons. Thus, many of the rights enjoyed by people under the United States Constitution apply equally to corporations. For example, corporations have certain rights of free speech guaranteed under the First Amendment, including both free commercial speech, such as that found in advertising, and free political speech to express their positions on political issues, although such commercial and political speech receive less protection than noncommercial speech. Corporations have the right under the Fourth Amendment to be protected from unreasonable searches and seizures. However, they do not possess the right against self-incrimination applicable to individuals by the Fifth Amendment. Whereas corporate officers and employees "taking the Fifth" cannot be compelled to testify against themselves, the corporation itself has no such Fifth Amendment privilege. Under the Fourteenth Amendment, corporations, like individuals, cannot be deprived of property without due process. Corporations may be defamed and can bring actions for libel (written defamation) and slander (oral defamation).

In one interesting and recent case, Procter & Gamble Company (P&G) sued Amway for allegedly disseminating a rumor that P&G supported satanic cults. The rumor began in the early 1980s with allegations that P&G's famous 1851 trademark, a bearded "man in the moon," was a symbol of Satanism. The rumor has so plagued P&G that for a long time its own Web site discussed the rumor and strenuously refuted it by describing the origins of the trademark. Although the case filed by P&G against Amway in 1999 was dismissed by the district court, after years of litigation P&G was awarded more than $19 million in damages in 2007 against four ex-distributors of Amway. Thus, this case serves as a potent reminder that corporations can be injured by defamation and can commit defamation or trade disparagement.

A corporation can be held civilly liable for the torts committed by its agents, officers, and employees. For example, a corporation can be liable for defamation of another or can be liable for the act of one of its employees who wrongfully restrains a customer for alleged shoplifting or for acts of wrongful discrimination.

In general, corporations themselves have been found incapable of forming the intent needed to commit certain crimes; however, corporations can be held criminally liable for the illegal acts of their officers, agents, and employees committed in the course of their employment and authorized or acquiesced in by the corporation and can be subjected to fines. The individual corporate wrongdoers can, of course, be found guilty of criminal acts such as bribery, conspiracy, or insider trading and securities fraud, and can be imprisoned or fined.

For the purposes of the confidential communications between attorneys and their clients, the corporation is viewed as a client and, thus, its attorneys must keep privileged information disclosed in confidence (so long as the communication does not involve the commission of fraud or a crime). Advice given by counsel to help a client perpetrate fraud or a crime is neither ethical nor privileged; however, advice given to the corporation after the wrongful act has been completed is privileged.

Other than some exceptions for small-claims court actions, corporations must appear in court through an attorney and cannot represent themselves in court as a natural person may do. Similarly, the corporation does not have certain other rights, such as the power to vote, the ability to adopt a child, or the rights to "life, liberty, and the pursuit of happiness."

When reading statutes that refer to "persons," review the definitions given to determine if a person subject to a certain law includes a corporation (or another association, such as a partnership).

D. Corporate Powers and Purposes

Each state's corporation statute grants certain **powers** to the corporation to enable it to conduct business. MBCA § 3.02 provides a list of corporate powers. Among the powers typically granted to a corporation by state law are the following:

a. To sue and be sued and to defend in the corporation's own name (rather than in the names of the officers, directors, or shareholders);

b. To make and amend bylaws for regulating the business of the corporation;

c. To purchase, acquire, own, hold, improve, sell, lease, or mortgage real or personal property;

d. To enter into contracts, incur liabilities, borrow money, issue bonds, and lend money;

e. To elect directors and appoint officers, employees, and agents;

f. To establish pension and other benefit plans for its directors, officers, agents, and employees;

g. To make donations for the public welfare;

h. To make payments or donations that further the business of the corporation (such as those for political purposes);

i. To purchase and hold shares or other interests in other entities;

j. To be a member or manager of a partnership or other entity;

k. To have and use a corporate seal;

l. To transact any lawful business; and

m. To exist perpetually.

A state's statutes provide the maximum authority for a corporation. A corporation can elect not to engage in all of the activities allowed by the statute, but it cannot engage in any activity that is inconsistent with the statutorily enumerated list of powers. In the event its articles of incorporation or bylaws are inconsistent with the state statutes, the statutes will control.

A corporation's purposes are different from its powers. Its purposes are the goals and objectives it intends to achieve, for example, developing real estate, operating a restaurant, or providing computer services. These specific purposes may be stated in its articles of incorporation. A corporation's purposes are also provided for in the state statute. In the state statutes, however, the purposes are usually stated in general and broad terms, such as the following: "Corporations in this state may be organized for any lawful purpose." A corporation will use its powers to achieve its purposes.

E. Types of Corporations

There are various types of corporations. Most of these will be detailed in Chapter Seventeen, but a brief introduction to the classification of corporations will be helpful to understand thoroughly the modern business corporation, the primary focus of our discussion.

1. *Domestic Corporations*

A corporation is a **domestic corporation** in the state in which it incorporated. For example, See's Candy Shops, Incorporated was incorporated in California. In California, it is referred to as a domestic corporation.

Domestic corporation
A corporation operating in the state of its incorporation

2. *Foreign Corporations*

A corporation formed in one state and doing business in another is referred to in the second state as a **foreign corporation.** Thus, See's Candy Shops, Incorporated, which is authorized to do business in several states, is a domestic corporation in California and a foreign corporation in Nevada and Tennessee. A corporation does not automatically have the right to conduct business in another state; it must be granted authority to do so by the foreign jurisdiction. See Chapter Fifteen for further discussion of foreign corporations. Corporations formed outside of the United States are also sometimes referred to as foreign corporations. The more appropriate term for a corporation formed in another country is **alien corporation.**

Foreign corporation
A corporation operating in a state other than its state of incorporation

Alien corporation
A corporation formed outside the United States

3. *Federal or State Corporations*

Entities formed under the authority of a federal statute, a state constitution, or a state statute may also be corporations. The Tennessee Valley Authority is a federal corporation formed to develop the resources of the Tennessee Valley. The National Railroad Passenger Corporation (Amtrak) is a for-profit government corporation. Many towns and cities are incorporated. These corporations are formed to meet some public or governmental need, and their directors or administrators are usually appointed by government officials. On occasion, they are referred to as "public" corporations. This term is often misconstrued; most people use the term *public corporation* to indicate a corporation whose shares are sold to members of the general public (rather than held by a smaller group, such as a few friends or family members).

Federal or state corporation
An entity formed under the authority of a federal or state statute for some public good

4. *Public Corporations*

Public corporations (also called *publicly held* or *publicly traded* corporations) are corporations whose shares are sold to the public at large. These corporations may be giants in the industry—Nike, Inc., General Motors Corporation, Microsoft Corporation—or simply large corporations whose stock is available for purchase by the public on a public stock exchange. Both purchase and transfer of shares are easily accomplished.

Public corporation
A corporation whose shares are sold to the public at large

5. *Privately Held Corporations*

Many corporations are formed by smaller groups of family members or friends. Ownership of shares is limited to a few people and the shares are not

Privately held corporation
A corporation whose shares are owned by a small group, usually family or friends

sold to the public at large. These **privately held corporations** tend to be smaller enterprises, perhaps a retail store, a computer consulting company, or a landscaping business. Shareholders usually enter into agreements with each other providing that they will not sell their shares to any "outsiders" before offering them to the existing shareholders or to the corporation itself. Although these corporations tend to be smaller, some extremely large corporations are privately owned, including Mars, Incorporated, with annual revenue of more than $25 billion.

6. Nonprofit Corporations

Nonprofit corporation
A corporation formed not to make a profit but for public benefit, religious purposes, or the mutual benefit of its members

A **nonprofit corporation** (or *not-for-profit corporation*) is one that is not formed for the purpose of making a profit, but rather for some charitable, educational, scientific, or religious purpose, or for the mutual benefit of its members. Stock is not issued and these corporations are generally exempt from federal income taxation.

7. Close Corporations

Close corporation
A corporation whose shares are held by a small group of shareholders and that is allowed to act informally

A **close corporation** is one whose shares are held by a few people (usually limited by statute to 50 people or fewer). Under most state laws, a corporation can elect to be a close corporation. A corporation permitted this status is often allowed certain flexibility with regard to corporate formalities that regular business corporations are not. For example, the shareholders in a close corporation are allowed to participate in management of the corporation yet retain their limited liability. They might also be allowed more latitude with regard to holding meetings and elections. The shareholders in a close corporation usually sign agreements restricting the transfer of shares so they cannot offer shares for sale to a third party without first offering them to another member in the close corporation or to the corporation itself. The rapid rise in popularity of the limited liability company, which affords full protection from liability for its members who may manage the company themselves or appoint managers, has caused a decrease in interest in close corporations.

8. Professional Corporations

Professional corporation
A corporation organized by professionals, such as doctors

A **professional corporation** is formed by an individual or group of persons practicing a certain profession, such as law, medicine, accounting, or engineering. The explosion in adoption of limited liability partnerships and limited liability companies by professionals has caused a decrease in interest in professional corporations.

9. S Corporations

S corporation
A corporation that avoids double taxation by passing through all of its income to its 100 or fewer shareholders

S corporations (formerly called *subchapter S corporations* after the Internal Revenue Act subchapter that allowed for their creation) are formed to minimize the drastic effect double taxation has on small business corporations. Corporations that meet certain criteria (those with no more than 100 individual shareholders who cannot be nonresident aliens) may elect to qualify as S corporations. In this event, the corporation does not pay federal tax on income it earns; all of the income is passed through to the shareholders who pay tax on the income at their appropriate rates. In this respect, an S corporation is similar to a partnership; however, it offers the advantages of limited liability for the shareholders. The limited liability company discussed in Chapter Five is thought to provide all of the advantages of an S corporation, without any of its limitations, particularly with regard to number of shareholders. Corporations that are not S corporations are referred to as **C corporations.** An S corporation is not truly a different type of corporation but is merely one that has elected and qualifies for pass-through taxation. All shareholders must consent to the election.

C corporation
A corporation that is not an S corporation and that is subject to double taxation

10.   *Parent and Subsidiary Corporations*

A corporation that creates or forms another corporation is called a **parent corporation.** Typically, the parent will hold all or the vast majority of the stock of the corporation it has formed, the **subsidiary.** Thus, the expression "wholly owned subsidiary" refers to a corporation whose stock is owned entirely by its parent.

Parent corporation
A corporation that creates another corporation (the subsidiary)

Subsidiary corporation
A corporation created by another (the parent)

F.   Advantages and Disadvantages of Incorporation

1.   *Advantages*

Limited Liability.   Probably the greatest advantage of selecting the corporate form for doing business is the limited liability protection the corporation offers to its shareholders, directors, and officers. Because the corporation can enter into contracts and borrow money in its own name (rather than the names of its shareholders, directors, or officers), it is responsible for meeting those obligations and debts.

Shareholders in Ford Motor Company may see their stock fall in value. In a worst case scenario, the stock could become worthless. Nevertheless, except in extraordinary circumstances, the shareholders are not personally liable for the corporation's debts and liabilities. Their risk is limited to their investment: Their stock may decrease in value to nothing, but their personal assets are not at risk to satisfy corporate obligations. Similarly, directors and officers will not be liable for corporate obligations so long as they do not act with gross negligence or breach their duties of due care.

Because personal assets are not available to corporate creditors, these creditors will carefully scrutinize a corporation before extending credit or making loans. The creditors might require the corporation to provide financial statements to ensure the corporation has sufficient assets to meet or repay its obligations. Similarly, a creditor might require a corporation to pledge some asset as security for a loan; in the event the loan is not repaid, the creditor will then seize the asset to satisfy the obligation. In other instances where a corporation is financially weak, or it has no proven track record of financial stability, before lending money a bank or creditor may require that corporate directors, officers, or shareholders personally guarantee a loan so that if the corporation cannot repay the debt, the individual will be liable for it. Thus, in a practical sense, the concept of "limited liability" may be negated by a requirement that the corporate owners guarantee obligations. Nevertheless, the owners will have liability only for those obligations they expressly agree to accept, and they will know in advance their potential risk.

Because limited liability exists for the shareholders of a corporation, it is easy for a corporation to attract capital. Many individuals and businesses are willing to invest in an enterprise when their maximum exposure can be predetermined.

Corporate Deductions. Corporations are taxpaying entities, but they are entitled to a wide range of deductions that can be used to offset corporate income. Items such as rent, insurance, and salaries can be deducted from the corporation's income before determining the amount on which the corporation will pay tax. Other typical deductions include interest expenses, utilities, legal and accounting costs, supplies, and some entertainment and travel expenses, if they are business related.

The corporation may also establish various benefit plans for employees. These not only attract quality workers, but are also used to reduce taxable income. For example, a corporation may provide life insurance for its employees. The corporation is allowed to deduct the expense of the premiums paid to maintain the insurance as a business expense, and the employee is not taxed on the value of this benefit. For some period of time corporations were allowed to exclude from their income the proceeds they received from company-owned life insurance on the lives of their rank-and-file workers (who were sometimes insured by their employers without their knowledge or consent). In 2006, Congress restricted this practice by allowing such advantageous tax treatment only for insurance purchased for highly compensated employees and only when those employees are notified of the policy and consent to such. Company-owned life insurance is discussed further in Chapter Eighteen.

Similarly, a corporation may provide a pension plan or 401(k) for its employees. Employees are allowed to contribute a certain amount of their salary pre-tax. The corporation may match this amount to some percentage. The corporation can deduct the amount it matches as a business expense. The employee does not pay tax on the amount contributed until he receives the money, typically when the employee is older and in a lower tax bracket.

Continuity of Existence. A corporation can endure perpetually. Thus, businesses intending to operate for extended periods should consider the corporate form. The sole proprietorship terminates on the death of the sole proprietor; a general partnership may dissolve upon the death or withdrawal of a partner; and a limited liability company may be limited to an agreed-on term of existence; a corporation, however, survives the death of its shareholders and the transfer of their stock to some third party.

Stock certificate
The document that represents ownership in a corporation

Transferability of Share Ownership. A person's ownership interest in a corporation is shown by a document called a **stock certificate.** The stock certificate is not what is owned; it merely represents ownership in a corporation. Shares (or stock) in a corporation are freely transferable. In many instances, unless there are restrictions on the sale of stock, selling stock to another is no more complex than endorsing a check over to another person. The back of the stock certificate generally contains information for transferring the stock to another. Stock in a publicly traded corporation is also easily acquired. A simple phone call to a broker or an online trade will initiate the purchase of stock. Sales of stock are often made through brokers (or online) as well. This easy transferability is in contrast to sole proprietorships, which cannot be transferred without terminating the sole proprietorship, or other forms of business entities that may dissolve upon a full transfer of an owner's interest. To ensure that stock in a corporation is held by a harmonious group, usually friends or family members, shareholders may voluntarily agree to restrict their sales of stock, but absent such an agreement or a provision in the corporation's articles of incorporation, shares of stock are freely transferable.

Shares can be given as gifts to another person and, similar to other types of property, can be left to one's heirs upon death. The new owner inherits all rights of the deceased shareholder with regard to voting, distribution of dividends, and so forth.

2. Disadvantages

Double Taxation.   The biggest disadvantage of corporations is **double taxation** of the income of the corporation. As a separate person or entity, the corporation's income is subject to taxation at certain rates applicable to corporations. The imposition of tax on the corporate enterprise itself is far different from taxation principles relating to sole proprietorships, general and limited partnerships, registered limited liability partnerships, and limited liability companies, all of which pass through all the income earned by the business to the owners who then pay tax at whatever rate is applicable to them (unless they have elected to be taxed as corporations under the IRS "check the box" provisions).

Double taxation
Concept in corporate law in which money earned by a corporation is taxed; when remainder is distributed to shareholders, they are also taxed

After paying taxes on its income, the corporation may then apportion its profits to shareholders in the form of distributions. Money received by shareholders, even $1, must be declared as income subject to taxation. Thus, the same money is taxed twice: once when the corporation receives it and then again when it is distributed to the shareholders. In mid-2003, however, Congress reduced taxes on dividends to 15 percent (5 percent for the lowest two tax brackets) and agreed to eliminate taxes entirely on dividends in 2008 for the lowest two brackets. These dividend tax reductions will expire in 2010. Corporations may also be subject to various state fees and taxes, including income taxes and **franchise taxes,** which are taxes imposed by states on businesses merely for the privilege of being able to conduct business in the state.

Franchise tax
A fee or tax imposed by a state for the privilege of conducting business in the state

The concept of double taxation is not really so peculiar. In many instances, money is taxed twice. For example, you pay tax on income earned from your employment. When you take a portion of that income and pay your landscaper or piano teacher, or purchase shoes at a retail store, that income must be reported by the recipient, who pays tax on the money received from you. Similarly, in some states, the purchase of a car is subject to sales tax. Assume a car is sold to its first owner for $20,000. Tax will be paid on the sum of $20,000. After five years, the owner might sell the car to another for $15,000. The new owner must now pay sales tax on the sum of $15,000. If the car is sold a third time for $10,000, the final owner must pay sales tax on the sum of $10,000. Thus, the same item has been subject to taxation on several occasions.

For large corporations conducting business on a nationwide basis, double taxation is simply accepted as a necessary evil and a trade-off for the many advantages corporate existence offers.

Avoiding Double Taxation. Various measures can be taken to avoid double taxation. They include the following:

S Corporations. Some corporations avoid the burden of double taxation by electing to be S corporations. There are several restrictions as to the election of S status, and it is not an option for any corporation that has more than 100 individual shareholders. S corporations are discussed in Chapter Seventeen.

Small Corporations Whose Shareholders Are Employees. Small corporations whose stock is held by a few family members or friends all actively employed by the corporation can also reduce the burden of double taxation. Although these corporations pay tax on income received, they do not give distributions to the shareholders. If all of the shareholders are employed in the business, each will receive a merit bonus or Christmas bonus or salary increase rather than a "dividend" as a way of sharing in the corporation's profits. The recipient of the bonus or salary must still pay tax on that money received, but the payment of salaries or bonuses is a deduction for a corporation that can be used to offset income and reduce tax liability. Naturally, this technique is not available to larger or publicly traded corporations whose stock is owned by nonemployees. There would be no justification for General Mills, Inc. giving its shareholders a Christmas bonus and then deducting this as a business expense.

Section 1244 stock
Stock upon the sale of which (at a loss) receives favorable tax treatment and is taxed as an ordinary loss

Section 1244 Stock. "Small business corporations" may automatically qualify under **Section 1244** of the Internal Revenue Code for the individual shareholders to receive certain favorable tax treatment on the sale of their stock at a loss. The definition of a small business corporation for purposes of Section 1244 is different from that used in connection with S corporations. For an S corporation, there is a limit on the number of shareholders who hold stock. For Section 1244 purposes, "small business" relates not to how many people will be in the corporation but to the amount of money the corporation plans to raise by selling stock. The amount of all money and all property received by the corporation for stock cannot exceed $1 million.

Ordinary loss
A loss that can be used to offset ordinary income

Capital loss
A loss that can only be used to offset capital gains rather than ordinary losses

If the requirements of Section 1244 of the Internal Revenue Code are met, stock sold at a loss will automatically receive favorable tax treatment. The corporation does not need to make any special filing or designation for Section 1244 treatment. The loss will be treated as an **ordinary loss,** rather than a "capital" loss, meaning that shareholders can use that loss to offset ordinary income, thus resulting in a lower taxable income. If stock is not qualified as Section 1244 stock, shareholders who sustain losses on the sale of stock must treat those losses as capital losses. **Capital losses** do not offset ordinary income but rather can only be used to offset **capital gains** — gains acquired through the sale of assets that have appreciated in value from the date of their original acquisition. If a shareholder has no capital gains in a year, the shareholder cannot deduct a capital loss sustained that year (although there are some carry-forward provisions that may allow the shareholder some deduction). If the stock is Section 1244 stock, a loss incurred when it is sold can be used to offset ordinary income (such as salaries) up to a maximum of $50,000 per year for individuals and $100,000 in the case of spouses filing joint returns. Any excess losses over these limits are treated as capital losses.

Thus, Section 1244 provides certain tax benefits to shareholders in a small business. Under Section 1244, the corporation's shareholders will receive some favorable tax treatment if they sell their stock at a loss. Qualification of stock as Section 1244 stock presupposes the corporation will suffer losses. Nevertheless, it is a useful device and places shareholders on a more equal footing with sole proprietors and partners who are able to treat losses as ordinary rather than capital losses. Confirmation that the corporation desires the benefits of Section 1244 can be accomplished at a meeting of the corporation's directors. In many cases, confirmation takes place at the corporation's first organizational meeting.

Qualified Small Business Stock. Another way corporations can avoid or minimize the effect of double taxation is through the provisions of Section 1202 of the Internal Revenue Code (26 U.S.C. § 1202), enacted in 1993 to allow individuals who hold **qualified small business stock** for more than five years to exclude one-half of any gain they realize on the sale of such stock (up to certain limits). The remaining one-half of the gain is taxed as a capital gain.

A "qualified small business" must satisfy the following three elements:

- The corporation must be a C corporation (rather than a corporation that has elected S status to achieve pass-through single taxation);
- Its total gross assets must be less than $50 million at the time the stock is issued; and
- At least 80 percent of the value of its assets must be used in the active conduct of qualified trades and businesses (a qualified trade or business is one in which the principal asset is not the reputation or skill of one or more of its employees).

Thus, corporations involving the performance of services in the fields of health, law, accounting, engineering, architecture, and financial services do not qualify for the favored tax treatment, because they are dependent on the skill and reputation of the individuals involved. Additionally, other types of businesses are expressly excluded, such as banking, insurance, farming, and restaurant and hotel businesses. Other businesses, however, will qualify, and their shareholders will be able to exclude from the computation of their taxes one-half of the gain they realize on the sale of stock held for more than five years.

Limited Liability Companies. Limited liability companies, discussed in Chapter Six, avoid double taxation while providing limited liability to the members. All of the income earned by the company is passed through to the members, who then pay taxes on the income received. Limited liability companies have a

Capital gains
Gains acquired through the sale of appreciated assets

Qualified small business stock
Stock issued by a qualified corporation that provides certain tax benefits on the gain realized on sale of the stock

limited period of duration in a few states. Therefore, they might not be suitable for every type of business enterprise and might not be suitable for businesses desiring to do business on a national scale.

Limited Liability Partnerships. Like limited liability companies, limited liability partnerships (discussed in Chapter Five) avoid double taxation by passing through all income earned to the company's partners, who pay tax on the income they earn. Because personal liability in a limited liability partnership is somewhat unresolved (with most states providing full shield protection from liability and a few providing only partial shield protection from negligence and misconduct), the limited liability partnership might not be suitable for a business intending to operate on a nationwide basis.

P R A C T I C E   T I P

Corporations must be accurately named and described in all documents relating to the entity. Thus, note the correct name of a corporation, the state of its incorporation, and whether it has elected S status or C corporation status on the inside of the client's file or on a master list you keep at your desk. Having this critical information handy will save you from having to flip through reams of paper.

Formalities of Organization and Operation. Forming a corporation requires strict compliance with the corporation laws of the state of incorporation. Incorporation fees are charged, and preparing the documents might require the assistance of an attorney, thus necessitating attorneys' fees. Similarly, other documents filed with the state must also be accompanied by fees, such as amendments to the corporation's articles of incorporation, changes to the corporation's name, reports of mergers, or dissolution of the corporation. Corporations that wish to do business in other states must formally apply to do so, which will also result in fees and paperwork.

Moreover, each state imposes annual filing or reporting requirements on corporations either incorporated in or doing business in that state. The documents must be timely filed and accompanied by the appropriate fee. Many states now accept only online filing for annual reports. See Figure 8-2 for California's annual report form. After the corporation is formed, it must continue to comply with various statutory formalities, such as the requirement for an annual meeting of shareholders, elections of directors, and certain financial reporting and disclosure requirements made to shareholders.

The corporation must also file a tax return each year with the Internal Revenue Service and in the various states in which it does business. Publicly traded companies are subject to intensive reporting and disclosure requirements imposed by federal law and by the Securities and Exchange Commission (see Chapter Thirteen).

These reporting and filing requirements make the corporation the most difficult business enterprise to form and maintain. Failure to comply with these

FIGURE 8-2
California Corporation Annual Report Form

State of California
Secretary of State

STATEMENT OF INFORMATION
(Domestic Stock and Agricultural Cooperative Corporations)
FEES (Filing and Disclosure): $25.00. If amendment, see instructions.
IMPORTANT — READ INSTRUCTIONS BEFORE COMPLETING THIS FORM

This Space For Filing Use Only

1. **CORPORATE NAME** (Please do not alter if name is preprinted.)

| S |

DUE DATE: [For forms preprinted by the Secretary of State.]

COMPLETE ADDRESSES FOR THE FOLLOWING (Do not abbreviate the name of the city. Items 2 and 3 cannot be P.O. Boxes.)

		CITY	STATE	ZIP CODE
2.	STREET ADDRESS OF PRINCIPAL EXECUTIVE OFFICE			
3.	STREET ADDRESS OF PRINCIPAL BUSINESS OFFICE IN CALIFORNIA, IF ANY		CA	
4.	MAILING ADDRESS OF THE CORPORATION, IF DIFFERENT THAN ITEM 2			

NAMES AND COMPLETE ADDRESSES OF THE FOLLOWING OFFICERS (The corporation must have these three officers. A comparable title for the specific officer may be added; however, the preprinted titles on this form must not be altered.)

			CITY	STATE	ZIP CODE
5.	CHIEF EXECUTIVE OFFICER/	ADDRESS			
6.	SECRETARY/	ADDRESS			
7.	CHIEF FINANCIAL OFFICER/	ADDRESS			

NAMES AND COMPLETE ADDRESSES OF ALL DIRECTORS, INCLUDING DIRECTORS WHO ARE ALSO OFFICERS (The corporation must have at least one director. Attach additional pages, if necessary.)

			CITY	STATE	ZIP CODE
8.	NAME	ADDRESS			
9.	NAME	ADDRESS			
10.	NAME	ADDRESS			

11. NUMBER OF VACANCIES ON THE BOARD OF DIRECTORS, IF ANY:

AGENT FOR SERVICE OF PROCESS (If the agent is an individual, the agent must reside in California and Item 13 must be completed with a California street address (a P.O. Box address is not acceptable). If the agent is another corporation, the agent must have on file with the California Secretary of State a certificate pursuant to Corporations Code section 1505 and Item 13 must be left blank.)

12. NAME OF AGENT FOR SERVICE OF PROCESS [Note: The person designated as the corporation's agent MUST have agreed to act in that capacity prior to the designation.]

		CITY	STATE	ZIP CODE
13.	STREET ADDRESS OF AGENT FOR SERVICE OF PROCESS IN CALIFORNIA, **IF AN INDIVIDUAL**		CA	

TYPE OF BUSINESS

14. DESCRIBE THE TYPE OF BUSINESS OF THE CORPORATION

15. BY SUBMITTING THIS STATEMENT OF INFORMATION TO THE CALIFORNIA SECRETARY OF STATE, THE CORPORATION CERTIFIES THE INFORMATION CONTAINED HEREIN, INCLUDING ANY ATTACHMENTS, IS TRUE AND CORRECT.

DATE	TYPE/PRINT NAME OF PERSON COMPLETING FORM	TITLE	SIGNATURE

SI-200 C (REV 01/2008)	APPROVED BY SECRETARY OF STATE

various formalities could result in dissolution of the corporation by the state or in the loss of shareholders' limited liability status. (See Chapter Eleven for a discussion of "piercing the corporate veil" to allow creditors to pursue individual shareholders for corporate obligations.)

Centralized Management.   Although shareholders own the corporation, they do not manage it. Shareholders vote for *directors,* who then manage the corporation as a board and appoint individuals called *officers* (president, vice-president, secretary, treasurer, and so forth) to manage the daily activities of the corporation. Individuals who wish to manage and operate a business personally may prefer to operate as sole proprietors, general partners, partners of limited liability partnerships, or members of limited liability companies. Personal liability, however, may result from being a sole proprietor, general partner, or member of an LLP in a partial shield state. Although the shareholders in a corporation have some authority to control the directors (by removing them), this power to affect the corporate business is remote at best.

In a small corporation, however, for example, Mom and Pop Retail, Inc., the shareholders will not only own the corporation, they will elect themselves as directors and appoint themselves as officers, enabling shareholders to manage the business and yet still retain limited liability for the debts or obligations of the corporation. In larger, publicly traded corporations, however, the shareholders' only involvement in corporate affairs takes the form of voting for directors and for extraordinary corporate actions, such as a merger or dissolution of the corporation. In many instances, shareholders perceive this centralized management as an advantage, believing that professional and experienced managers will govern the corporation more expertly than they could.

See Figure 8-3 for a chart summarizing the advantages and disadvantages of corporations.

FIGURE 8-3
Advantages and Disadvantages of Corporations

Advantages	*Disadvantages*
Limited liability for directors, officers, shareholders	Double taxation
Wide range of business deductions	Formalities of organization, expense of organization and maintenance
Easy transferability of shares	Centralized management (rather than management by owner-shareholders)
Continuity of existence	

Key Features
of Corporations

- ◆ Corporations are persons and exist separate and apart from their owner-shareholders.
- ◆ Corporations offer limited liability for their shareholders, officers, and directors, because the corporation itself is liable for its own debts and obligations.
- ◆ Corporations can exist perpetually.
- ◆ Ownership in corporations is easily transferred.
- ◆ Corporations, as persons, are subject to double taxation: The income of a corporation is taxed, and when profits are distributed to shareholders, they also pay tax on the money received.
- ◆ Eligible corporations can attempt to minimize double taxation by electing S status.
- ◆ The issuance of Section 1244 stock or "qualified small business stock" also provides certain tax advantages to corporate shareholders.
- ◆ Corporations can be expensive to form and maintain.
- ◆ Management of corporations is centralized in a board of directors; the owner-shareholders do not manage the typical large business corporation.

G. Role of Paralegal

More paralegals are employed in corporate law than any other field except litigation. The National Association of Legal Assistants reported in 2008 that more than 30 percent of all paralegals are engaged in some corporate work. Paralegals in this practice area engage in a variety of activities including organizing and forming corporations, assisting in maintaining corporations by preparing various resolutions and minutes of meetings, and engaging in corporate transactional work, such as mergers and acquisitions, the sale of stock, or corporate employment issues.

Generally, the attorney involved assists the client in determining which form of business enterprise best suits the client's needs. If it is determined that the corporate form should be selected, the attorney will fully explain the differences between C corporations and S corporations, Section 1244 stock, and the different types of corporations: for-profit, nonprofit, or professional.

The role of the paralegal at this stage is likely limited to fact-gathering and legal research. Inquiries regarding how many shareholders will be involved or how much stock will be issued assist in making determinations such as whether an election for S status should be made or whether stock can be issued pursuant to Section 1244 of the Internal Revenue Code. Information concerning the nature of the activities to be conducted by the enterprise will assist in determining whether the corporation will be for-profit or not-for-profit or perhaps organized as a close corporation or a professional corporation. Research can be conducted to determine any statutory limitations on the powers or purposes of corporations and to prepare to form the corporation. Forms can be gathered and information can be obtained about the costs and procedures of appointing an agent for service of process.

The explanation of these various options is handled by the attorney involved in the matter. Explaining the consequences of double taxation, limited liability, and treatment of losses as ordinary rather than capital is the type of advice only attorneys can give. As discussed in Chapter Nine, paralegals are, however, intimately involved with the formalities of organizing and creating the corporation, once the type of corporation best fitting the client's particular needs is determined.

Case Illustration
Protection of Shareholders from Liability for Corporate Obligations

Case: *First Realvest Inc. v. Avery Builders Inc.*, 600 A.2d 601 (Pa. Super. 1991)

Facts: The plaintiff sued the defendant corporation and its two shareholders for breach of contract. The trial court held that the individual defendants had no personal liability for the contract.

Holding: The court affirmed. When a party enters into a contract with a corporation, no action will lie against the shareholders of that corporation for breach of the contract. Although the plaintiff had alleged that the individual shareholders should be liable because they drew out profits from the corporation, the court noted that shareholders routinely draw out corporate profits. To impose liability on shareholders for corporate promises merely because the corporation is formed for their benefit and they draw out profits would render the corporate form useless.

◆ ◆ ◆

WEB RESOURCES

To obtain basic information about the types of corporations described in this chapter, access www.google.com and type in key words such as "S corporations" or "close corporations" in the box provided. You will be directed to a number of sites. The following sites are of interest and provide a wide variety of general information, forms, and links to other sites.

State statutes:	www.law.cornell.edu www.findlaw.com
Text of MBCA:	www.abanet.org/buslaw/ committees/CL270000pub/ nosearch/mbca/home.shtml
Tax forms and information:	www.irs.gov
General information:	www.nass.org (for links to each state's secretary of state and general information and forms) www.ilrg.com (for links to each state's statutes, forms, and corporate filing information) www.lectlaw.com (for information on businesses in general and corporations in particular) www.findlaw.com www.tannedfeet.com www.megalaw.com www.hg.org (The site HG.org is a broad-based legal research center. Select "Corporate.")
Glossary of financial terms:	www.investordictionary.com

Discussion Questions

Fact Scenario. ABC Inc. is a small corporation, incorporated in Oregon, with four shareholders, all of whom are also employees. The corporation operates a restaurant. Use the MBCA to determine your answers.

1. The corporation would like to reduce its tax liability. What might the corporation do?

2. The corporation owes $12,000 to Bank of America. Who is liable to pay this debt? Why?

3. The corporation is owed $30,000 arising out of a breach of contract signed for ABC Inc. by Ray, the president of the corporation. Who will be the plaintiff in an action arising out of this breach of contract? Why?

4. The corporation would like to expand and do business in the State of Washington. What should it do? What is the corporation called in Oregon? What is it called in Washington?

5. The corporation would like to contribute money to a political action committee that advocates for restaurateurs. May it do so?

6. The corporation would like to sponsor a 5K race to raise money for the local library. May it do so?

Net Worth

1. Access www.investordictionary.com. What is the definition of "shareholder"?
2. Access www.corporateinformation.com. Locate information about Starbucks Corporation. What is its ticker symbol? When does its fiscal year end? What type of shares does it offer?
3. Locate the MBCA through the American Bar Association Web site. What is the definition of "shares" provided in § 1.40?

9

♦ ♦ ♦

Formation of Corporations

♦ ♦ ♦

CHAPTER OVERVIEW

Forming a corporation requires a certain amount of preparation and planning. Thought must be given to selecting the jurisdiction in which to incorporate, selecting the corporate name and ensuring it is available for the corporation, attracting capital for the enterprise, and drafting the various documents to complete the incorporation process.

This chapter discusses the activities taken prior to incorporation and those required to effect and complete the incorporation process. The people involved in the effort of organizing the corporation, promoters, may enter into contracts on behalf of the proposed corporation. They may also assist the attorney and paralegal in preparing the certificate or articles of incorporation, the document that creates a corporation. After a corporation is formed, certain formalities, such as ordering corporate supplies, must be accomplished. Finally, the new corporation needs to adopt bylaws for its governance and hold an organizational meeting to begin its business.

A. Preincorporation Activities by Promoters

1. Duties of Promoters

The people involved in forming a corporation and organizing its structure are referred to as **promoters.** Although that term may have a slightly unsavory connotation in other contexts, in the context of preincorporation activities, it refers solely to the persons who plan and organize the corporation.

During the process of planning and forming the corporation, the promoters are viewed as joint venturers—specifically, partners who have undertaken one particular activity, that of forming a corporation. As joint venturers, the promoters

Promoter
One involved in organizing a corporation

owe duties of good faith and fiduciary duties to each other and to the proposed corporation. The promoters may have a written agreement defining their rights and responsibilities, but because a joint venture can be created without a written agreement, one is not required. If, however, the parties contemplate making substantial contributions to the corporation or will be engaging in extensive activities on behalf of the corporation, the promoters should have a formal written agreement defining their rights and obligations to each other and to the proposed corporation. A form of joint venture agreement is available at www.lectlaw.com.

Even without a written agreement, however, the fiduciary relationship promoters share requires them to deal in good faith. Thus, they may be liable for failing to disclose pertinent information or for secret profits obtained. For example, one promoter may be charged with the responsibility of finding a lot on which to build the corporate offices. If a promoter owns real estate and wishes to sell this to the proposed corporation, he must disclose all material information about the property. Failure to disclose that the property is subject to certain zoning and building restrictions imposing limitations on the size of the building that may be constructed or failure to disclose defects about the lot, such as drainage or access problems, would be a violation of the fiduciary duties owed by a promoter. Disclosure should be made to the other promoters and to any prospective shareholders or others who may be interested in the corporation. Similarly, full disclosure must be made if a promoter might stand to gain by a transaction (such as owning the lot next to the one he proposes the corporation buy and build on when construction would enhance the value of his lot).

In general, promoters are used only by larger businesses that require a great deal of activity and planning before actual incorporation. Smaller businesses that will not require substantial investment do not generally require promoters. Moreover, because incorporation under modern statutes is so easy to accomplish, most smaller businesses complete their incorporation process before engaging in contractual activities, thus avoiding any issues of preincorporation liability.

2. Agreements by Promoters

Preincorporation contracts
Agreements entered into by promoters on behalf of a yet-to-be formed corporation

During the course of planning the corporation and organizing it, promoters frequently enter into agreements, called **preincorporation contracts**, with third parties. For example, assume Carlos, Ellen, and Amanda are the promoters for a proposed corporation that will engage in making and selling gift baskets. Carlos may be assigned the task of finding office space for the corporation, Ellen may be in charge of hiring a receptionist and a secretary, and Amanda may be responsible for ordering stationery and advertising and promotional brochures and contracting for development of a Web site for the new business. Carlos might therefore approach a landlord and offer to lease space. The landlord might engage in remodeling of the space pursuant to Carlos's instructions and may take the property off the market. Ellen might advertise for employees and hire two individuals who leave their present jobs in reliance on getting jobs at the new business. Amanda might order the stationery and brochures printed by a local company at great expense and engage a Web site developer who begins working on the project.

Problems will arise if for some reason, such as a falling-out among the promoters, the corporation is never formed. The landlord is left with a remodeled space that has not been on the market for several weeks; the would-be employees have quit their former jobs; the printer has prepared materials never to be used by anyone; and the Web site developer has created Web content for a site that will never be launched. The landlord, the would-be employees, the printer, and the Web site developer will want compensation for their damages. The corporation cannot be liable because it does not exist. If the promoter had obtained a promise from the third party that it would hold only the corporation liable and not the promoter, the promoter would have no liability in the event of any breach of agreement. More complex issues arise when the parties do not clearly indicate their intentions.

Courts have used a variety of theories to hold the promoters liable for their preincorporation agreements and thereby protect innocent third parties with whom the promoters have been dealing. If the promoter has signed a written agreement (such as Carlos signing a lease), the promoter is clearly bound by the terms of the agreement. If there is no signed agreement, courts generally hold the promoter has impliedly agreed to be bound. Only when there is an express intention to release the promoter from liability will the promoter be able to avoid liability for agreements he or she has entered into before the corporation is formed. In sum, in ambiguous cases, the trend is to hold promoters personally and jointly and severally liable on contracts entered into before the corporation is formed.

In essence, this makes promoters no different from the organizers of other forms of business, who will always be liable to others who act in reliance on their actions. Promoters are thus liable, just as a sole proprietor or partners would be liable, if they enter into some agreement that causes a third party to take some action, even if the business enterprise never really gets off the ground. Some states deal with promoter liability by statute. For example, in Georgia, all persons purporting to act on behalf of a corporation with actual knowledge that there is no incorporation are jointly and severally liable for all liabilities created while so acting. Ga. Code Ann. § 14-2-204. Similarly, the approach of MBCA § 2.04 is to provide that all persons purporting to act on behalf of a corporation knowing there was no incorporation are jointly and severally liable for liabilities created while so acting.

When the corporation is formed, the joint venturer relationship among the promoters dissolves. The promoters may then occupy other relationships. They may be shareholders, directors, or officers of the corporation, or all three. After formation, the promoters will wish to be released from any personal obligations they may have incurred while promoters. Similarly, the corporation will wish to be the party "on the contract," so that it can complain if the roof in the leased spaces leaks, the employees are bunglers, or the stationery, brochures, and Web site contain misspellings of the corporation's name.

States use a variety of legal theories and names so the promoters and the now-formed corporation can accomplish their mutual goals. The corporation may **ratify** a contract, either by express ratification at a meeting of the board of directors, or by implied action; for example, moving into the leased spaces, accepting the employees' work, or using the stationery, brochures, and Web site. Ratification **"relates back"** to the date the contract was entered into, so it is as if the promoter never signed the contract, and the corporation was a party from the very date on which the contract was signed. Similarly, the contract may be *assigned* from the promoter to the corporation. The **assignment** can be made effective as of the date the contract was entered into so that, once again, it is as if the promoter never

Ratification
Approval of a transaction

Relation back
Doctrine that certain actions are viewed as having occurred on an earlier date

Assignment
Transfer of one's interest in some asset or right

Nunc pro tunc
Literally "now for then," a reference to an act or document having an effective date earlier than the date of its execution

Novation
A substitution of one party or document for another

signed the contract and the corporation was always a party to it. Such an assignment is called a **nunc pro tunc** (literally "now for then") assignment, meaning that although the assignment document is executed on one date, it is effective as of a prior date. Some jurisdictions use the concept of **novation**, a term meaning substitution. In novation, the corporation is substituted in place of the promoter as a party to the contract in all respects.

Unless the promoter is released from contractual obligations, she may remain liable under the terms of the contracts she signed. In agreements between promoters and third parties, the parties can always agree that incorporation of the business or adoption of the contract will automatically release the promoter or that the third party will look only to the corporation for performance. Unless misrepresentation or breach of promise by a promoter has occurred, the promoter may usually seek indemnification (or reimbursement) from the corporation for any liability incurred under the terms of a preincorporation agreement signed by a promoter on behalf of the corporation.

3. Preincorporation Share Subscriptions

Promoters may also undertake activities to raise capital for the corporation. Historically, some states required that a corporation have a certain amount of capital before it could begin operating. Others required that each of the promoters subscribe for (or agree to purchase) at least one share of stock. Finally, from a practical standpoint, it is useful that the corporation be assured it will have a certain amount of capital at its disposal upon its formation.

Preincorporation share subscriptions
Offers to purchase shares in a corporation before its formation

Preincorporation share subscriptions, or offers to purchase stock when the corporation is later formed, are used to accomplish these goals. The preincorporation stock subscription is viewed as an offer from a potential investor to purchase stock in a corporation upon its formation. The subscription may be set forth in very simple terms, as follows:

> **I, the undersigned, hereby offer to purchase 100 shares of the common stock of Gift Baskets, Inc. at a purchase price of $25 per share, upon the incorporation of Gift Baskets, Inc. or within thirty days thereafter. The purchase price for said shares shall be payable to Gift Baskets, Inc. upon demand by its board of directors.**
>
> **Dated: January 25, 2009**   **Amanda A. Carlson**

Thus, Amanda has offered to purchase 100 shares of the corporation when it is later formed. More complex share subscriptions may contain certain conditions that must be satisfied before Amanda will be required to purchase the stock; for example, a requirement that the corporation be formed on or before a certain date.

Years ago, subscriptions were revocable. Revocation led to the canny practice of presenting the subscriptions (often signed by friends and family members of the promoters) to the secretary of state as evidence the corporation could satisfy the requirement that it have a certain amount of capital before beginning business.

The subscribers would then revoke their offers, leaving the corporation without the requisite capital. To eliminate this practice of having friends submit phony offers or subscriptions, many states' statutes make the share subscriptions irrevocable for a certain period of time (three months, for example, in New York, and six months according to MBCA § 6.20) unless the parties provide otherwise. During this period of time, the subscriber cannot revoke or retract the offer to purchase stock. The offer may, however, be assigned from one person to another. Thus, Amanda Carlson could assign the offer to her sister Jane, in which case Jane would be obligated under the terms of the offer. If the corporation is formed during the period of irrevocability and accepts the offer to purchase, the subscriber or assignee is bound to pay for the stock in full. Failure to pay for the stock as agreed will leave the subscriber liable to the corporation for breach of contract or may result in a forfeiture of the subscriber's rights. The corporation typically accepts the offers or subscriptions at its first meeting.

B. Selection of Jurisdiction in Which to Incorporate

A business may elect to incorporate in any of the 50 states or in the District of Columbia. Some state corporation laws are considerably more flexible than others. Some jurisdictions favor corporations formed within their boundaries by having a moderately priced and expeditious incorporation process for domestic corporations, but disfavor corporations formed outside their boundaries (foreign corporations) by subjecting them to intense regulation and high taxes and annual fees. Jurisdictions may compete with one another for the purpose of attracting corporations.

Because each jurisdiction has its own corporations code, a review and comparison of all 50 states' codes would be time-consuming and costly. Thus, the first inquiry should always be "Where does the proposed corporation intend to operate its business?" If the client intends to conduct business solely in New Jersey, that state should be the first choice for incorporation. To incorporate in New York when the corporation intends to do business solely in New Jersey would subject the corporation to regulation and taxation in both states. Thus, unless there is something particularly onerous in the New Jersey laws pertaining to corporations, the corporation should select New Jersey as the state of incorporation. If, however, the business will open in New Jersey but plans immediate expansion into other Northeast states within 18 months, and into the Midwest within two years, then perhaps other jurisdictions should be considered. Because the corporation will soon be subject to regulation and taxation in all of the states in which it conducts business, it might as well select the jurisdiction for incorporation with the most permissive and flexible corporations statutes.

As discussed in more detail in Chapter Ten, a newer trend among some American corporations has been to reincorporate in Bermuda, primarily to avoid taxation in the United States. Congress and public opinion were so strongly against such reincorporations that at least one company abandoned its reincorporation plans after activists protested the plan and Congress closed this tax loophole in 2004.

1. *Delaware Incorporation*

Delaware is well known for having liberal and permissive corporations stat-utes. For example, Delaware provides significant protection to corporations against hostile takeovers. This is no accident but rather the result of a carefully planned strategy to attract business and capital to the state of Delaware. In fact, Delaware takes great pride in referring to itself as being the "Incorporating Capital of the World." Delaware collects between 20 and 30 percent of its annual revenue in taxes and fees from corporations. Approximately 60 percent of the Fortune 500 companies are incorporated in Delaware. More than half of the corporations whose stock is publicly traded are incorporated there, including McDonald's Corporation and Google Inc. Why? Because Delaware specifically designed its corporation laws (the Delaware General Corporation Law) to be the most advanced and flexible in the United States. For example, at a time when most states required corporations to have three directors, Delaware allowed corpora-tions to exist with a single director. When most states required that corporations conduct business in the state of incorporation, Delaware allowed corporations to form in Delaware even if no business was to be conducted there. The state also allowed corporations to incorporate in Delaware yet hold their meetings anywhere they desired. Moreover, Delaware has no sales tax and does not impose state income tax on corporations that do not conduct business in Delaware. Addition-ally, jurisdiction over questions arising under Delaware's corporation laws is vested in the Delaware Court of Chancery, which has more than 200 years of legal prec-edent in business entity law. Thus, Delaware's rich body of corporate law is attrac-tive because it lends some predictability to businesses. In fact, a 2008 study released by the United States Chamber of Commerce Institute for Legal Reform ranked Delaware (for the seventh year in a row) as having the most favorable legal system and litigation environment, meaning one that is favorable to business.

After Delaware liberalized its corporations laws, many states followed suit. Thus, there may be no true advantage to incorporating in Delaware over some of the other more permissive states, such as California and New York. Nevertheless, Delaware continues to set the standard with a modern imaging system and customer-oriented service staff. For example, Delaware offers a variety of priority filings. One can be assured of incorporation within 24 hours for up to $100, same-day incorporation for up to $200, and incorporation within one hour for $1,000. Moreover, Delaware accepts documents via facsimile transmission and operates until midnight. Delaware also offers a live chat service, providing online access to a corporate specialist who can answer filing, fee, and tax questions. Thus, Delaware keeps one step ahead of most jurisdictions and succeeds in continuing to attract corporations to the state. All of these corporations, of course, must then pay certain fees and taxes in Delaware. These fees and taxes, however, are relatively moderate and can even be paid by credit card. Delaware bases its annual **franchise tax** (a fee imposed for the privilege of operating in a state) on the number of shares and value of shares. The fee may range from $75 to $165,000. For example, a corporation with 7,000 authorized shares pays $150.00 and a corporation with 100,000 authorized shares pays $825.

In an effort to emulate Delaware, other jurisdictions have modernized their corporations codes. For example, the District of Columbia for years had a cumbersome incorporation process, requiring three individuals to form the

Franchise tax
Fee paid for maintaining a business registration in a state

corporation, three individuals to serve as directors, and four persons to serve as officers. Although the District of Columbia revised its law to be more permissive, an article in *The Washington Post* flatly stated that the District was still no "Delaware on the Potomac." Similarly, Nevada has been attempting to attract business by liberalizing its corporations statutes to make them highly similar to those of Delaware and eliminating state income tax. In fact, in the last few years, incorporations in Nevada have increased 25 to 30 percent. Because California is a costly state in which to incorporate, attorneys in California have been the target of an advertising campaign to encourage them to incorporate their clients in Nevada. Some experts have questioned whether the competition among states to attract corporations is in the best interest of shareholders or is a "race to the bottom."

2. *Factors in Selecting a Jurisdiction*

There are several factors to consider in determining where to incorporate:

a. If a corporation intends to do business in one state only, at least for the time being, that state should be the first choice for incorporation. Incorporating in one state and doing business in another will require the corporation to pay fees and taxes and file reports in both jurisdictions. For example, in California, corporations pay a minimum annual tax rate of the greater of 8.84 percent of their net income or $800 just for the privilege of being incorporated or qualified in California, whether or not they are active or actually doing any business in the state.

b. Determine whether the state disfavors foreign corporations. For example, some states prefer to award public works contracts for construction of buildings, roads, and so forth to domestic corporations. If a client intends to engage in construction work and incorporates elsewhere, this could be a serious obstacle to obtaining public works contracts.

c. States that have attracted corporations often have substantial case law to serve as a guideline as to what corporate activities are permissible. For example, Delaware prides itself on offering over 200 years of legal precedents to assure corporations that their business decisions stand on solid legal foundations.

d. The laws of the jurisdiction of incorporation usually apply to a corporation's internal affairs. Thus, if a lawsuit is brought in California relating to interpreting a Delaware corporation's bylaw provision, the law of Delaware will govern.

e. Consider the costs of formation, the annual reporting requirements, fees and taxes imposed by the state, and the comparative ease of forming and maintaining the corporation in a state.

C. The Corporate Name

The name to be used by the corporation must be given careful consideration. The name must comply with all state statutes, must not be identical or deceptively similar to another's name, and must be available for use in that state (and in any other states in which the corporation anticipates operating). Once it is determined the name is available, it should be reserved during the incorporation process.

1. Selection

The promoters must select a name for the new legal "person" or entity they are creating. Most state statutes require that the name of the corporation include some signal to the public that the business is a corporation and therefore personal assets may not be available to creditors. Generally, most states require that the name include the word "corporation," "company," "incorporated," or "limited," or an abbreviation of one of these words. This is also the position taken by MBCA § 4.01. A few states prohibit the use of "limited" in a corporate name on the basis that it signals a limited partnership or a limited liability company. Delaware allows a wide variety of signals, including "association," "club," or "society."

Other guidelines might be set forth in state statutes. For example, most states prohibit the corporation from selecting a name implying the corporation is organized for a purpose other than that stated in its articles of incorporation. Similarly, most states prohibit the corporation from using certain words in the corporate name that would imply some association with a state or federal agency. Thus, a private corporation could not use the name "Federal Mortgage Lending, Inc." as it implies some affiliation with the U.S. government.

Similarly, many corporation codes prohibit certain selected words such as "bank," "trust," "bond," or "insurance," without prior approval from the state commissioners of banking or insurance. Finally, various federal statutes prohibit the use of certain words such as "Olympic," or "Red Cross," as they suggest an affiliation with the well-known organizations using those names.

As is always the rule, the corporation may not select a name that is the same as or confusingly similar to that used either by another domestic corporation or that used by a foreign corporation qualified to do business in that state. In this regard, a corporation that intends to offer its goods or services nationwide at some point should give careful and deliberate thought to the corporate name. A highly descriptive name such as "Medical Supplies, Inc." is subject to two weaknesses. It is so common that it is likely already taken in at least some jurisdictions, and thus the corporation will not be able to do business under this name in all jurisdictions; and it is so descriptive that it will be given a very narrow scope of protection by courts, thus hindering the corporation in attempts to stop infringers from using the same or a highly similar name. In fact, the "best" names are those that are fanciful, such as "Xerox" or "Kodak." Because these names are made up, they are not only likely available worldwide but are strong names capable of being protected. Unfortunately, however, these names do not say anything about the nature of the goods or services offered under the names and require their owners to expend a great deal of money in establishing recognition of the name.

Thus, the corporation must strike a balance. With an eye toward growth, it should select a name sufficiently distinctive that it will likely be available in other states; and consideration should be given to the fact that the name must not be so unique that it conveys no information about the corporation's products and services. Corporations that anticipate operating in more than one state should check the availability of the name on a nationwide basis by consulting Thomson CompuMark at (800) 692-8833 or CT Corsearch at (800) 732-7241. Imagine if McDonald's could not operate as McDonald's in two or three states and had to operate its fast-food restaurants as Burgers To Go, Inc. in those states. It is much more cost-effective to determine name availability early in the incorporation process, rather than to devote substantial sums to developing consumer recognition of a name, only to be precluded from using the very name consumers have been trained to use when asking for the corporation's products or services.

Equally important, conducting a name availability search may help ensure the corporation does not infringe the name or trademark of another. Approval of a name by a secretary of state is no defense to a claim of trademark infringement.

Trademarks registered with the U.S. Patent and Trademark Office have nationwide protection. It is possible that the owner of a registered trademark may not conduct business in some states. In those states, the name will not appear on the records of the secretary of state. Thus, even if a corporation is allowed to use a confusingly similar name by the secretary of state in that state, such permission cannot supersede federal trademark law.

2. Availability

After reviewing the appropriate state statutes to assure the name complies with all pertinent laws, it must be determined if the name is available in the state of incorporation.

Incorporation matters are handled in almost all states by the secretary of state. Some states, however, designate a particular department for incorporations. For example, in Maryland, incorporations are handled by the Department of Assessments and Taxation. For ease, this text refers to "secretary of state" when discussing the public agency responsible for corporate activity. The secretary of state in each state has the responsibility for determining whether a corporate name is available. Most states now allow online checking for name availability. Alternatively, you can telephone the secretary of state's office to determine availability. Many attorneys' service companies will check name availability and then file the forms necessary to reserve the name to the corporation. Phone numbers, addresses, and Web sites for the secretaries of state are given in Appendix A.

When contacting the secretary of state (either by telephone or online) to determine whether a corporate name is available, be sure to have at least one alternative so that if the secretary of state refuses the corporation's first choice, its second choice can be immediately checked. If a name is identical or confusingly similar to another (either a domestic corporation or a foreign corporation qualified to do business in the state), the secretary of state will refuse to allow incorporation of the corporation under that name. Thus, unless a corporate name is highly unusual or distinctive, always ensure the availability of a name before preparing and applying to file the articles of incorporation. In nearly 40 states, if the secretary of state rejects the name as being too similar to that of another, it is possible to obtain the name if the other party consents in writing and the consent is delivered to the secretary of state.

3. Reservation

If the name is available, it should be reserved for the prospective corporation during the period of time the articles of incorporation are being prepared. Some states allow the proposed corporation to reserve the name by phone call and will charge a modest fee to a credit card or to the telephone bill. The more common approach, however, is to require that the **name reservation** be made in writing and accompanied by a fee. The fee will vary from state to state, with Arizona charging $10 to reserve a name to an average of approximately $25. Many states offer online name reservation. (See Figure 9-1 for a sample name reservation form.)

The reservation will be limited in its duration. MBCA § 4.02 allows for a nonrenewable 120-day period. Some states, such as Georgia, afford only a 30-day reservation period. Other states, such as Michigan and Washington, allow reservations for six months. Still others might allow reservations for a period of one year. The most common reservation period is 120 days.

During the period the reservation is in existence, the name may not be used or taken by any other corporation seeking to incorporate in that state or to qualify to do business in that state. In some states, the reservation might be renewable. Other jurisdictions have a nonrenewable reservation period, aiming to spur businesses to incorporate promptly and to clear the state's corporate rolls of unused names so they can be made available for use by others. You must be sure to docket the date the reservation expires to ensure timely filing of the incorporation papers during the period of the reservation (or to renew the reservation, if possible).

4. Registration

A procedure somewhat similar to reservation of a name is **registration** of a name. Registration is used by foreign corporations to preserve the corporate name in a state in which the corporation plans to do business. For example, assume a corporation is formed in New Jersey to operate a restaurant. After a period of time, the restaurant might become well known and the corporation might consider opening branches in the neighboring states of Pennsylvania and New York. During the period in which the corporation is planning its expansion, conducting market surveys, and so forth, it should register its name in Pennsylvania and New York. A name registration keeps a corporate name available for a substantial length of time, often one year. During this period, no other corporation can be formed in or qualify to do business in those states using an identical or deceptively similar name.

Name registrations are thus used by corporations considering expansion into other jurisdictions and serve to save the name during the process of planning and development. Otherwise, the corporation might establish its reputation under one name, and then be "beat out" in another state by another company operating under that name and thus be unable to capitalize on consumer recognition of the original name. Most states provide specified forms for name registration and impose filing fees therefor. (See Figure 9-2 for a sample registration of corporate name form.)

FIGURE 9-1
New York Application for Reservation of Name

Application for Reservation of Name
Under §303 of the Business Corporation Law

NYS Department of State
Division of Corporations, State Records and Uniform Commercial Code
One Commerce Plaza, 99 Washington Avenue
Albany, NY 12231-0001
http://www.dos.state.ny.us

PLEASE TYPE OR PRINT

APPLICANT'S NAME AND ADDRESS

NAME TO BE RESERVED

RESERVATION IS INTENDED FOR (CHECK ONE)

New domestic corporation (The name must contain "Incorporated" or "Inc." or one of the other words or abbreviations in §301 of the Business Corporation Law.)

New domestic professional service corporation (The name must end with "Professional Corporation" or "P.C.")

Foreign corporation intending to apply for authority to do business in New York State*

Proposed foreign corporation, not yet incorporated, intending to apply for authority to conduct business in New York State

Change of name of an existing domestic or an authorized foreign corporation*

Foreign corporation intending to apply for authority to do business in New York State whose corporate name is not available for use in New York State*

Authorized foreign corporation intending to change its fictitious name under which it does business in this state*

Authorized foreign corporation which has changed its corporate name in its jurisdiction, such new corporate name not being available for use in New York State*

X _____   _____
Signature of applicant, applicant's attorney or agent   *Typed/printed name of signer*
(If attorney or agent, so specify)

INSTRUCTIONS:

1. Upon filing this application, the name will be reserved for 60 days and a certificate of reservation will be issued.

2. The certificate of reservation must be returned with and attached to the certificate of incorporation or application for authority, amendment or with a cancellation of the reservation.

3. The name used must be the same as appears in the reservation.

4. A $20 fee payable to the Department of State must accompany this application.

5. Only names for business, transportation, cooperative and railroad corporations may be reserved under §303 of the Business Corporation Law.

*If the reservation is for an existing corporation, domestic or foreign, the corporation must be the applicant.

DOS-234 (Rev. 5/08)

FIGURE 9-2
Illinois Application for Registration of Foreign Corporate Name

Form **BCA-4.25** (Rev. Jan. 2003)	APPLICATION FOR REGISTRATION, RENEWAL OR CANCELLATION OF FOREIGN CORPORATION NAME	File #

Jesse White
Secretary of State
Department of Business Services
Springfield, IL 62756
Telephone (217) 782-9520
http://www.cyberdriveillinois.com

Payment must be made by certified check, cashier's check or a money order, payable to "Secretary of State."

SUBMIT IN DUPLICATE

This space for use by Secretary of State

Date

Filing Fee $

Approved:

1. CORPORATE NAME: _____

2. STATE OR COUNTRY OF INCORPORATION: _____

3. Date of incorporation: _____

4. Business in which the corporation is engaged: _____

5. Post office address of the corporation to which the Secretary of State may mail notices:

6. The corporation desires to register its corporate name pursuant to Section 4.25, and it is not transacting business in the State of Illinois at this time.

7. Attached to this application is a certificate setting forth that the corporation is in good standing under the laws of the state or country wherein it is organized, executed by the proper officer of the state or country wherein it is organized, which certificate shall not be more than ninety (90) days old.

8. Check the appropriate box:
   ☐ The fee for registration is $50.
   ☐ The fee for renewal is $50.
   ☐ The fee for cancellation is $25.

9. Such registration or renewal of registration shall be effective from the date of filing by the Secretary of State until the first day of the twelfth month following such date.

10. The cancellation shall be effective upon filing with the Secretary of State.

11. The undersigned corporation has caused this statement to be signed by a duly authorized officer, who affirms, under penalties of perjury, that the facts stated herein are true.

Dated _____ , _____
      (Month & Day)   *(Year)*

_____
(Exact Name of Corporation)

by _____
    (Any Authorized Officer's Signature)

_____
(Type or Print Name and Title)

C-197.7

The name registration is generally effective for 12 months or until the end of the calendar year in which the application for registration is filed. In some states, a registration filed late in the calendar year (say after September 30) will be effective until the end of the following calendar year. Name registrations are often renewable.

Not all states permit name registration. In those states that do not, in order to preserve a name for future use, a corporation might have to incorporate another corporation (a subsidiary corporation) solely for the purpose of holding the corporate name. Name reservation is not effective for this purpose because reservations are often for such short periods of time (30-120 days). The subsidiary will have few assets and will conduct no business. Nevertheless, it will be subject to regulation and taxation in the state of formation. Thus, this is a far more expensive and cumbersome route than name registration. It might be necessary, however, if the corporation plans to expand into other jurisdictions. Subsidiaries formed for these purposes are sometimes called **name-savers** or *nameholders*. Because corporations exist perpetually, there is no need to renew any forms when a name-saver is formed (although annual reports are required in all jurisdictions and annual taxes and fees may be imposed on the name-saver corporation). When the parent is ready to conduct business in the state, the subsidiary can be merged into the parent.

Name-saver
Corporation formed by another for purpose of reserving a corporate name in a foreign jurisdiction

In sum, a corporation planning to operate nationally must determine name availability at an early stage, reserve the name in the state in which it will incorporate, and file the papers necessary to effect incorporation during the reservation period. Thereafter, if planning national expansion, the corporation should register its name in all states that permit registration and then form a name-saver corporation in those states that do not, to preserve the name in other states for future use.

5. *Assumed Names*

Just as sole proprietors and general partnerships often operate under an **assumed name** (or *fictitious name*), corporations can also be formed under one name and then elect to operate under another. A corporation might wish each of its separate divisions to operate under its own name. Alternatively, there could be certain marketing and consumer-related issues that necessitate operation under an assumed name. For example, the corporation Desert Palace, Inc. does business as Caesar's Palace Hotel & Casino.

Assumed name
A name under which a business operates that is not the name under which it was formed

Most states provide forms for corporations to adopt an assumed name and will charge a filing fee therefor. (See Figure 9-3 for an application to adopt an assumed corporate name.) In some states, the form used by sole proprietors and partnerships for fictitious names can also be used by corporations (see Figure 2-2). Additionally, the corporation service companies identified in Appendix K can assist with filing, recording, and publication in each state or county that permits assumed names.

D. Articles of Incorporation

The document prepared and filed with the secretary of state creating the corporation is generally called the **articles of incorporation.** Some states, including

Articles of incorporation
The document that creates a corporation; also called *certificate of incorporation* or *charter*

FIGURE 9-3
Illinois Assumed Corporate Name Application

Form **BCA-4.15/4.20**
(Rev. Jan. 2003)

Jesse White
Secretary of State
Department of Business Services
Springfield, IL 62756
Telephone (217) 782-9520
www.cyberdriveillinois.com

Remit payment in check or money
order, payable to "Secretary of State".

**APPLICATION TO ADOPT,
CHANGE OR CANCEL,
AN ASSUMED CORPORATE NAME**

File #

SUBMIT IN DUPLICATE

This space for use by
Secretary of State

Date

Filing Fee
(See Note Below)
Approved:

1.　CORPORATE NAME: _____

2.　State or Country of Incorporation: _____

3.　Date incorporated *(if an Illinois corporation)* or date authorized to transact business in Illinois *(if a foreign corporation)*: _____, _____.
　　(Month & Day)　　　　　　(Year)

(Complete No. 4 and No. 5 if adopting or changing an assumed corporate name.)

4.　The corporation intends to adopt and to transact business under the assumed corporate name of:

　　_____

5.　The right to use the assumed corporate name shall be effective from the date this application is filed by the Secretary of State until_____, _____ , the first day of the corporation's anniversary
　　(Month & Day)　　(Year)
　　month in the next year which is evenly divisible by five.

(Complete No. 6 if changing or cancelling an assumed corporate name.)

6.　The corporation intends to cease transacting business under the assumed corporate name of:

　　_____

7.　The undersigned corporation has caused this statement to be signed by a duly authorized officer who affirms, under penalties of perjury, that the facts stated herein are true.

Dated _____, _____
　　(Month & Day)　　(Year)

_____
(Exact Name of Corporation)

_____
(Any Authorized Officer's Signature)

_____
(Type or Print Name and Title)

NOTE:　The filing fee to adopt an assumed corporate name is $150 if the current year ends with either 0 or 5, $120 if the current year ends with either 1 or 6, $90 if the current year ends with either 2 or 7, $60 if the current year ends with either 3 or 8, $30 if the current year ends with either 4 or 9.
　　The fee for cancelling an assumed corporate name is $5.00.
　　The fee to change an assumed name is $25.00.

C-148.15

Delaware, use the term *certificate of incorporation*, and others use the term *charter*, but most states and the MBCA use *articles of incorporation*. The articles of incorporation serve as the corporation's constitution.

All states provide forms for the articles of incorporation. These allow for easy incorporation and can be simply completed and sent to the secretary of state with the appropriate filing fee. Use of the forms is not mandatory. Other states might provide you with a list of what should be included in the articles of incorporation. Each state's corporations statutes will specify the provisions that must be included in the articles. The statutes also typically provide that other provisions can be included in the articles. As a general rule, however, you should prepare the articles of incorporation to comply with the state requirements and include no optional provisions. The articles are more difficult and costly to amend than the corporation's bylaws because amendment usually requires shareholder approval and then filing with the secretary of state. The articles are also a public document, and the corporation should be sensitive to what provisions are included in the articles. Because optional provisions can also be set forth in the bylaws, it is generally recommended that the articles comply strictly with what the state statute requires and that other optional provisions be included in the bylaws because they are comparatively easy to amend and are not open for public inspection.

1. Elements of Articles of Incorporation

Although there is some variation from state to state, the provisions generally required to be included in the articles of incorporation are as follows:

Name. The corporation's name must be set forth in the articles. If it has been reserved, the articles of incorporation should be filed during the reservation period so that the name is "locked up" for the corporation. Review your state statute to ensure the corporate name complies with any requirements that the name include a designation of corporate status such as "Company," "Inc.," or "Corp."

Address. The corporation must set forth its registered address in the state of incorporation so there will be a public record showing how and where the corporation can be reached. Nearly all states require a street address rather than a mere post office box. If the corporation does not intend to do business in that state and has incorporated there only for the purpose of incorporating under a permissive and flexible corporate code, it can make arrangements with various corporate service companies to maintain a registered office in the state. For example, the following companies will, for a fee, agree to serve as the registered office or address in the state of incorporation: CT Corporation and Corporation Service Company. These companies provide numerous other services as well, such as assistance in reserving the corporate name, filing the articles of incorporation, serving as agent for service of process, and so forth.

Additionally, the California and Delaware Web sites (www.ss.ca.gov/business/bpd_service_companies.htm and http://corp.delaware.gov/agents/agts.shtml) identify numerous corporate service companies.

Agent for Service of Process.   In nearly all states, the corporation must designate an individual residing in the state of incorporation or a domestic corporation or qualified foreign corporation to receive service of legal process (the summons and complaint that initiate legal action). Once again, if the corporation is not actually doing business in the state of incorporation, and no individual residing in the state will agree to accept service of process, the corporation may enter into an agreement with one of the corporation service companies. For an annual fee, they will agree to accept service of process and immediately notify the corporation thereof so it can respond to the complaint and a default is not entered against the corporation. In most states, the secretary of state is also authorized to accept service of process on behalf of the corporation. In New York, the articles must designate the secretary of state as the agent and need not appoint any other. In Minnesota, the articles must identify a registered address, and process will be sent to that address. A list of attorneys' service companies is provided in Appendix K. Generally, changing the registered office or agent for service of process is fairly easy and does not require the complex process required for amending the articles. (See Figure 9-4 for a sample form for changing the registered agent or registered office address.) Many states require that the agent for service of process be located at the registered office.

Under MBCA § 14.20, failure to have a registered agent or registered office for 60 days is grounds for administrative dissolution of a corporation. The Web sites of most of the secretaries of state provide identification of agents for service of process for corporations incorporated in or doing business in the state. Enter a company's name and you will be informed of its date of incorporation, status (active, suspended, or dissolved), and the identity of its agent who will accept service of process.

Purposes.   Many states require the corporation to set forth its purposes in the articles. Most, however, also allow the corporation to use a **broad purpose clause** rather than setting forth in detail its actual purposes. A broad purpose clause typically provides that "the purpose of the corporation is to engage in any lawful act or activity for which a corporation may be organized under the laws of this state." The advantage of using such a clause is that it does not limit the corporation to any specific activity and the corporation thus has room to grow and develop into other endeavors in the years ahead without requiring an amendment of its articles. Moreover, because the articles are open to public inspection, the corporation might not wish to set forth a detailed description of its business purposes. If a state does require that the purposes be specifically set forth, the drafter of the articles should allow room for expansion by setting forth the specific purposes and then adding a clause such as "and may transact any business or perform any act reasonably necessary to accomplish such purposes." The MBCA and many states do not require a purpose clause.

Years ago, when corporations were required to state their specific purposes, corporations would occasionally exceed or act beyond their stated purposes. Such acts were said to be *ultra vires,* literally acts "beyond the powers" of a corporation. The early view was that corporations had no capacity to act beyond their powers and purposes; any act that exceeded such purposes was therefore null and void, and either party to a contract (either the corporation or a third party) could disaffirm the contract, even if the other party had already performed its duties under the

---

Broad purpose clause
Clause in corporate articles that states the corporation is formed to conduct any legal activity; also called *full purpose clause*

Ultra vires doctrine
Seldom-used legal theory that certain acts are invalid as being beyond a corporation's powers

FIGURE 9-4
Florida Statement of Change of Registered Office and/or Registered Agent

STATEMENT OF CHANGE OF REGISTERED OFFICE OR REGISTERED AGENT OR BOTH FOR CORPORATIONS

Pursuant to the provisions of sections 607.0502, 617.0502, 607.1508, or 617.1508, Florida Statutes, this statement of change is submitted for a corporation organized under the laws of the State of _____ _____ in order to change its registered office or registered agent, or both, in the State of Florida.

1. The name of the corporation:_____

2. The principal office address:_____
   _____

3. The mailing address (if different):_____
   _____

4. Date of incorporation/qualification: _____ Document number: _____

5. The name and street address of the current registered agent and registered office on file with the Florida Department of State:

   _____

   _____

   _____

6. The name and street address of the new registered agent (if changed) and /or registered office (if changed):

   _____

   _____
   (P.O. Box NOT acceptable)

   _____

The street address of its registered office and the street address of the business office of its registered agent, as changed will be identical.

Such change was authorized by resolution duly adopted by its board of directors or by an officer so authorized by the board, or the corporation has been notified in writing of the change.

_____   _____
(Signature of an officer or director)   (Printed or typed name and title)

I hereby accept the appointment as registered agent and agree to act in this capacity. I further agree to comply with the provisions of all statutes relative to the proper and complete performance of my duties, and I am familiar with and accept the obligation of my position as registered agent. Or, if this document is being filed merely to reflect a change in the registered office address, I hereby confirm that the corporation has been notified in writing of this change.

_____   _____
(Signature of Registered Agent)   (Date)

If signing on behalf of an entity:

_____
(Typed or Printed Name)

* * * FILING FEE: $35.00 * * *

MAKE CHECKS PAYABLE TO FLORIDA DEPARTMENT OF STATE
MAIL TO: DIVISION OF CORPORATIONS, P.O. BOX 6327, TALLAHASSEE, FL 32314

CR2E045 (8/05)

contract. Thus, the *ultra vires* doctrine allowed disappointed parties to avoid their contractual obligations.

Starting in approximately 1900, courts began recognizing the unfairness of the application of the *ultra vires* doctrine and began to refuse to apply it when one of the parties had substantially performed its duties. Later, as state statutes began allowing full purpose clauses, the ultra vires doctrine became subject to erosion. If a corporation has the power to perform any lawful act, then few acts can be challenged on the basis that they are *ultra vires*, or beyond the power of the corporation.

The MBCA reflects the modern approach to the *ultra vires* doctrine: Neither the corporation nor any third party doing business with the corporation can escape its respective duties on the theory that the corporation lacked authority to enter into the contract or power to act. There are, however, three actions that can be taken with regard to a transaction exceeding the corporation's powers and purposes: the shareholders can sue to enjoin the transaction, the corporation can sue the directors and officers for taking the unauthorized action, and the attorney general can seek dissolution of the corporation. MBCA § 3.04.

Although the *ultra vires* doctrine is largely of historical rather than any practical interest, many contracts entered into by corporations include a clause reciting and warranting that the corporation has the power and authority to enter into the transaction.

Description of Stock.   The corporation's shares must be described. If the corporation will issue more than one class or type of shares, all of the provisions relating to each must be set forth. The number of shares the corporation will issue must be provided. This number forms an upper limit on the number of shares the corporation can issue. If the corporation wishes to issue stock in an amount greater than this number, the articles will need to be amended. Thus, to eliminate this potential difficulty, the articles should provide for a large enough number to accommodate any anticipated growth. The number set forth in the articles is called the corporation's **authorized shares.** The corporation has the authority to issue only this number of shares and no more.

In some states, filing fees are based on the number of shares the corporation will issue. For example, in Delaware, a filing fee tax is based on the number of shares the corporation will issue. For stock with no par value, the filing fee tax is one cent on the first 20,000 shares of stock issued ($200), and a half-cent for the next 1,980,000 shares to be issued ($9,900). Thus, a corporation will pay a filing fee tax of $200 for shares authorized up to 20,000, making it reasonable for all corporations, even Mom and Pop-type operations, to state in their articles that they have the authority to issue up to 20,000 shares of stock.

This section of the articles must also describe any privileges, preferences, or restrictions imposed on any class of stock. If there is only one class of stock, that stock is usually called the "common" stock of the corporation. Common and preferred stock will be fully discussed in Chapter Ten, but at this point it is sufficient to know that **common stock** is stock of a corporation having no special features or privileges, whereas **preferred stock** generally has some feature(s) that often make it more desirable than common stock.

In some states, this section must state the par value of the stock, if any, or include a statement that the stock has no par value. **Par value** is the nominal or face

Authorized shares
The number of shares set forth in a corporation's articles that the corporation has authority to issue

Common stock
Stock of a corporation having no special privileges

Preferred stock
Stock of a corporation issued with desirable privileges

Par value
The minimum amount for which a corporation's stock can be sold

value of each share of stock, which is generally quite low, often ten cents or $1 per share. Par value is the minimum amount for which a share of stock may be issued. Stock that has no par value may be issued for any amount per share that the directors of the corporation deem appropriate. The MBCA approach and that of most states is to eliminate any requirement of referring to par value in the articles.

Although these provisions might seem complex, the statement in the articles describing the stock of the corporation can be quite simple: "The corporation has the authority to issue 20,000 shares of common stock with a par value of $1 per share."

Incorporators.   The name (and usually the address) of each incorporator (those preparing the articles) must be provided. The incorporators must also sign the articles of incorporation. In many instances, the attorney or paralegal preparing the articles will sign as the incorporator. Some states require the incorporator to formally acknowledge the truth of the contents of the articles. (See Figure 9-5 for sample forms for articles of incorporation.)

Although the elements required in each state may vary, MBCA § 2.02 requires the following elements to be included in the articles of incorporation:

- The corporate name (which includes a signal showing corporate status);
- The number of shares the corporation is authorized to issue;
- The street address of the corporation's initial registered office and the name of its registered agent at that office; and
- The name and address of each incorporator.

2. Optional Provisions in Articles of Incorporation

There may be other elements required for the articles of incorporation in certain states. For example, in New Jersey, the certificate of incorporation must set forth the names and addresses of the initial directors of the corporation. N.J. Rev. Stat. § 14A:2-7(1)(h).

Most states and the MBCA allow the inclusion of optional provisions. It must be remembered, however, that any additional provision included in the articles may simply create a reason for amending the articles later, a complex, time-consuming, and somewhat expensive procedure.

Among the more common optional provisions often found in articles of incorporation are the following:

a. Number, names, and addresses of the initial board of directors and a statement as to how directors are to be elected or appointed;
b. The period of duration of the corporation (the articles often provide that the corporation is to exist perpetually, although there is no reason a specific date of termination cannot be set);
c. Provisions requiring greater than majority vote for certain corporate action, such as requiring two-thirds approval by shareholders for a merger;
d. Provisions regarding managing the business of the corporation;
e. Provisions imposing personal liability on shareholders, if desired;

FIGURE 9-5
Articles of Incorporation Forms (California and Delaware)

SAMPLE

ARTICLES OF INCORPORATION

I

The name of this corporation is _____ *(NAME OF CORPORATION)* _____ .

II

The purpose of the corporation is to engage in any lawful act or activity for which a corporation may be organized under the **General Corporation Law** of California other than the banking business, the trust company business or the practice of a profession permitted to be incorporated by the California Corporations Code.

III

The name and address in the State of California of this corporation's initial agent for service of process is:

Name _____

Address _____

City _____ State **CALIFORNIA** Zip _____

IV

This corporation is authorized to issue only one class of shares of stock; and the total number of shares which this corporation is authorized to issue is _____ .

_____
(Signature of Incorporator)
(Typed Name of Incorporator), Incorporator

If an individual is designated as the initial agent for service of process, include the agent's business or residential street address in California (a P.O. Box address is not acceptable). If another corporation is designated as the initial agent for service of process, do not include the address of the designated corporation.

This sample is provided to be used as a guideline ONLY in the preparation of the original document for filing with the Secretary of State.

Secretary of State **Sample**
ARTS-GENERAL (REV 01/2008)

STATE *of* DELAWARE
CERTIFICATE *of* INCORPORATION
A STOCK CORPORATION

- **First:** The name of this Corporation is _____
_____.

- **Second:** Its registered office in the State of Delaware is to be located at _____
_____ Street, in the City of _____
County of _____ Zip Code _____. The registered agent in
charge thereof is _____
_____.

  Third: The purpose of the corporation is to engage in any lawful act or activity for
  which corporations may be organized under the General Corporation Law of
  Delaware.

- **Fourth:** The amount of the total stock of this corporation is authorized to issue is
_____shares (number of authorized shares) with a par value of
_____ per share.

- **Fifth:** The name and mailing address of the incorporator are as follows:
Name _____
Mailing Address_____
_____Zip Code_____

- **I, The Undersigned,** for the purpose of forming a corporation under the laws of the
State of Delaware, do make, file and record this Certificate, and do certify that the
facts herein stated are true, and I have accordingly hereunto set my hand this
_____day of _____, A.D. 20_____.

BY:_____
(Incorporator)

NAME:_____
(type or print)

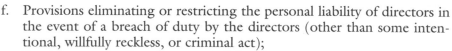

f. Provisions eliminating or restricting the personal liability of directors in the event of a breach of duty by the directors (other than some intentional, willfully reckless, or criminal act);
g. Provisions staggering the terms of the directors;
h. Provisions permitting the corporation to indemnify directors or officers if they incur liability (such provisions usually require that these corporate managers have acted in good faith); or
i. Any provisions that may be set forth in the corporation's bylaws.

In fact, according to the MBCA and many states, certain provisions must be addressed in the articles of incorporation if they are to vary from the norm. For example, under MBCA § 7.25, unless the articles of incorporation provide otherwise, a majority of votes constitute a quorum, and § 8.08 provides that shareholders may remove directors with or without cause unless the articles provide that directors may be removed only for cause (meaning for a reason, such as fraud or dishonesty). In the absence of such special provisions in the articles of incorporation, the state's statutory provisions will apply to the corporation.

3. Preemptive Rights

Preemptive right
Right of shareholders to buy pro rata share of newly issued stock before it is offered to nonshareholders

The articles of incorporation may include a provision allowing preemptive rights for the shareholders. A **preemptive right** is the right of a shareholder, when new shares are being issued, to purchase as much of the newly issued stock as is needed to maintain his or her then-current ownership interest in the corporation. In essence, a preemptive right is a kind of right of first refusal. Before the corporation can sell stock to any outsiders, the current shareholders must be given the opportunity to purchase stock in an amount equal to their present percentage of ownership in the corporation.

Assume that when a corporation is formed, Chris, Sean, and Kevin purchase 37 percent, 42 percent, and 21 percent, respectively, of the stock of the corporation. The corporation has the authority to issue additional shares and wishes to do so to raise capital. If the shareholders have preemptive rights, Chris would have the opportunity to purchase 37 percent of any later stock to be issued, Sean would have the opportunity to purchase 42 percent of any later stock to be issued, and Kevin would have the right to purchase 21 percent of any newly issued stock. Only when the shareholders elect not to exercise their rights to make such purchases can the corporation offer the stock to third parties.

Thus, preemptive rights allow shareholders to maintain their proportionate interest and control in a corporation. Chris will have the right to purchase 37 percent of any stock to be issued so that he can maintain his 37 percent interest in the corporation. The corporation cannot flood the market with shares and thereby reduce Chris's power and control.

In most states, if preemptive rights are to be given, they must be included in the articles of incorporation. A common preemptive provision is as follows: "Shareholders shall have the right to purchase their pro rata interest in shares of any new stock that may be issued by the corporation." Failure to specify that preemptive rights exist typically means that they do not exist. This is the approach in Delaware and of the MBCA. The general trend is that preemptive rights are not highly favored because they tend to restrict the flexibility of a corporation that might need to issue stock quickly to raise capital. Other states have contrary statutory provisions. Such provisions are often referred to as **opt out provisions**, whereas statutes that provide that preemptive rights exist only if the corporation elects them in its articles of incorporation are referred to as **opt in provisions.** Shareholders who have preemptive rights must be given notice and an opportunity to purchase newly issued stock. This notice and waiting period may delay the corporation in raising money. Preemptive rights generally exist for shareholders only when new stock is issued for cash and not when stock is issued under employee stock option plans or other similar plans. Preemptive rights are generally seen only in smaller corporations in which maintaining ownership and control is important to a small group of shareholders. In a larger, publicly traded corporation, shareholders can simply purchase additional shares on the open market.

> **Opt out provisions**
> State laws providing that preemptive rights exist unless specifically denied by the articles
>
> **Opt in provisions**
> State laws providing that unless preemptive rights are provided for in the articles, they do not exist

4. *Filing of Articles of Incorporation*

The articles of incorporation must be filed with the appropriate state agency, usually the secretary of state, in the state of incorporation. Each state's filing requirements vary slightly, and failure to comply with the state's requirements will likely result in refusal of the articles of incorporation.

In most states, the incorporator simply mails the articles of incorporation to the office of the secretary of state with an appropriate cover letter and the required filing fee. Some states, such as Florida, provide a sample cover letter. Many states now permit online filing of the articles of incorporation with payment of fees by credit card. The secretary of state will then review the articles to ensure they comply with the state's requirements. The secretary of state might then return a copy of the articles to the incorporator stamped "Approved" or "Filed" along with a date or might issue a formal certificate of incorporation confirming the date of incorporation. Some states require that additional copies of the articles be provided; one copy is retained for the state's files and another is file-stamped and returned to the incorporators to verify incorporation.

Some states require that other formalities be observed. For example, in Illinois a copy of the articles of incorporation must be recorded in the county in which the corporation's registered office of incorporation is located. Florida requires that the registered agent sign the articles, accepting the appointment as registered agent for the corporation and confirming that the agent understands her duties in connection with acting as the corporation's agent (see Figure 9-6). Pennsylvania requires that the incorporators advertise their intention to file the articles or advertise the actual filing of the articles. Proofs of publication of such advertising must be kept with the minutes of the corporation. A careful reading of the pertinent state statutes is required to ensure that any other miscellaneous formalities are completed.

In most states, and according to the MBCA, corporate existence begins upon filing of the articles of incorporation. Some states, however, provide that corporate existence begins upon issuance of a certificate of incorporation by the secretary of state. Many states and the MBCA permit the articles to provide that they will not become effective until some date after the filing date, but the delayed effective date cannot be later than 90 days after the filing date. It might be necessary to determine the date the corporation comes into existence for tax reasons or for determining

FIGURE 9-6
Florida Articles of Incorporation and Registered Agent Acceptance Statement

ARTICLES OF INCORPORATION
In compliance with Chapter 607 and/or Chapter 621, F.S. (Profit)

ARTICLE I   NAME
The name of the corporation shall be:

ARTICLE II   PRINCIPAL OFFICE
The principal **street** address and mailing address, if different is:

ARTICLE III   PURPOSE
The purpose for which the corporation is organized is:

ARTICLE IV   SHARES
The number of shares of stock is:

ARTICLE V   INITIAL OFFICERS AND/OR DIRECTORS
List name(s), address(es) and specific title(s):

ARTICLE VI   REGISTERED AGENT
The **name and Florida street address** (P.O. Box **NOT** acceptable) of the registered agent is:

ARTICLE VII   INCORPORATOR
The **name and address** of the Incorporator is:

****

Having been named as registered agent to accept service of process for the above stated corporation at the place designated in this certificate, I am familiar with and accept the appointment as registered agent and agree to act in this capacity

_____   _____
Signature/Registered Agent   Date

_____   _____
Signature/Incorporator   Date

when promoters' obligations for preincorporation obligations end and corporate responsibility begins.

PRACTICE TIP

If you work in an active corporate practice, you need to create a working corporate binder with all forms, filing fee schedules, and secretary of state Web site addresses. Download extra copies of the forms and fee schedules from the secretary of state's Web site. When projects arise and you are asked to check name availability, reserve or register a corporate name, draft articles of incorporation, or prepare a client's annual corporate report, you will have everything you need at your fingertips. Make notes as to which forms can be submitted online, telephone numbers of helpful people at the secretary of state's office, whether duplicate copies are required, and so forth. Aim for efficiency so that every project is more streamlined and efficient than the one before.

E. Postincorporation Activities

Once the corporation has been formed by the filing or the acceptance of the articles of incorporation, a few basic activities must be undertaken to organize the corporation. Bylaws must be drafted, corporate supplies must be ordered, and an initial organizational meeting must be held.

1. Bylaws

Bylaws are rules governing the operation and management of a corporation. The bylaws are prepared by the paralegal or attorney and are then presented for adoption at the first organizational meeting of the corporation. According to MBCA § 2.06(b), the bylaws of a corporation may contain any provision for managing the business and regulating the affairs of the corporation that is not inconsistent with law or the articles of incorporation. Bylaws are adopted by either the incorporators or the initial board of directors. They are easily amended. They are not filed with any state or county office but are rather maintained by the corporation in a looseleaf binder also containing minutes of corporate meetings (called the *minute book*). They are not available for public inspection as are the articles. Bylaws can be very thorough or they can be fairly simple. Most attorneys engaged in corporate law have spent some time perfecting their bylaws and have sample forms for bylaws on word processors. These bylaws can then be readily adapted for other corporate clients. Drafting bylaws, however, requires more than merely changing the name of a corporation on a predetermined set of forms. The bylaws should be carefully drafted to ensure they provide a working blueprint for the directors and officers on how to manage the corporation, and for the shareholders, with regard to their rights as owners of the corporation. In general, bylaws are more easily amended than articles inasmuch as bylaws are usually amended by the directors of the corporation, without the necessity of a meeting of the

Bylaws
Internal rules governing corporate procedures and operation

shareholders or any public filings. Thus, any provisions that might be subject to change (the date of the annual meeting, the number of days' notice before an election, a change in the fiscal year) are best set forth in the bylaws due to the relative ease of amending the bylaws.

The following are typical items usually provided in corporate bylaws:

Introductory Information.   The first few sections of the bylaws will set forth the name of the corporation and the address of its principal office and any other office locations. The bylaws may designate one office as the address to which notices and communications must be provided.

Information About Directors.   The bylaws should contain various provisions relating to the managers of the corporation, called the board of directors. Any specific requirements that must be met by directors (such as being residents of the state of incorporation or being shareholders in the corporation) should be set forth. Similarly, the bylaws should provide how many directors the corporation will have and when and how they will be elected, replaced, or removed from office. The bylaws should provide the directors with the authority to manage the corporation. If any limitations are desired (for example, limitations on any one director's ability to incur indebtedness), they should be specified. Authority to declare and pay distributions to shareholders should be granted to the directors. If the board will have any committees, such as compensation committees, executive committees, or audit committees, their membership and duties should be described in full. The bylaws should provide when regular meetings of the directors will be held (weekly, monthly, quarterly, and so forth), where those meetings will be held, and any minimum advance notice required to be given to the directors. Provisions should be made for calling **special meetings** of the directors (any meeting between regularly scheduled meetings) and the appropriate notice therefor. The bylaws should establish how many directors constitute a **quorum** (the minimum number of directors required to transact business), how meetings will be adjourned, how directors may resign, how directors may be removed, how vacancies may be filled, and any liability the directors may have. Because few individuals would agree to serve as directors if they believed they could be held liable for any mere error in business judgment, bylaws often contain provisions indemnifying the directors for any costs or expenses incurred in defending any lawsuit arising out of their ordinary business activities. Directors are not ordinarily indemnified against criminal acts or intentional acts of recklessness. Compensation of directors and reimbursement of their expenses should be addressed. The authority of the directors to take action without a formal meeting (that is, by unanimous written consent or by conference call) should be provided.

Information About Officers.   The bylaws should identify the corporate officers. The most typical offices are president, vice-president, secretary, and treasurer. Nevertheless, a corporation may opt to have additional officers and can create additional titles and positions. The bylaws should confirm that the officers are to be appointed by the directors to carry out whatever management functions are delegated to them by the directors, and, similarly, are removable by the directors. The manner of filling officers' vacancies should be discussed. Specific duties

Special meeting
A meeting held between regularly scheduled meetings

Quorum
Minimum number of persons required to transact business

for each officer can be set forth as should information pertaining to their salaries and reimbursement of expenses incurred by them on behalf of the corporation.

Information About Shareholders.   Just as the bylaws should contain all information pertaining to directors and officers of the corporation, so should they also include information relating to the owners of the corporation, the shareholders. Provisions regarding the holding and location of regular annual meetings as well as the manner for calling special meetings should be set forth. The method of voting and the authority of shareholders to vote in person or by proxy should also be detailed. The manner in which notice of meetings is to be provided should be specified, as well as information as to how many shareholders constitute a quorum to conduct business (typically, a quorum is a majority of shares outstanding), how elections of directors will be held, any particular provisions regarding voting, and any items that will require a **supermajority** (a vote typically of two-thirds) rather than a simple majority. Any restrictions or limitations on voting rights of any classes of stock should be set forth. If the shareholders have the authority to act outside of a meeting, for example, by written consent, this should be indicated. Shareholders should be given the authority to inspect the shareholders' list and other corporate records.

Supermajority
A vote greater than a simple majority, often two-thirds

Miscellaneous Information.   The bylaws should also approve a form of stock certificate (typically attached to the bylaws) as well as the form for the corporate seal (often impressed upon the bylaws). Information regarding reports of the corporation and location of its records can be provided. Provisions relating to inspection of corporate records, how amendment of the bylaws will be effected, and the **tax year** of the corporation, which may be the **calendar year** (January 1 through December 31) or a **fiscal year** (a 12-consecutive-month period), should be set forth. A tax year is an annual accounting period for keeping records and reporting income and expenses. A tax year is adopted when the corporation files its first income tax return and generally requires IRS permission to change. The bylaws should also include any information relating to banking or the issuance or transfer of shares. (A form for bylaws for a nonpublic corporation is provided in Appendix G.)

Tax year
An annual accounting period for keeping records and reporting income and expenses

Calendar year
The period between January 1 and December 31

Fiscal year
Any 12-consecutive-month period

2. Corporate Supplies

As soon as the corporation is formed, the necessary supplies for the corporation should be ordered. It is the responsibility of the law firm to order the various supplies needed to ensure the corporation has the items necessary to transact its business. The corporate supplies are usually ordered from one of the various companies the law firm generally does business with, and consist of three items: the corporate seal, the minute book (which includes a stock transfer ledger to record issuance and transfer of the corporation's stock), and the stock certificate book. These supplies should be ordered only after formation of the corporation has been assured, because the seal (and often the stock certificates) might display the date of incorporation.

The **seal** is a device used to impress the corporation's name on certain documents. Just as kings of England used a specific seal to attest to the validity of

Seal
Device used to impress documents to verify authenticity

documents, corporations are often required to impress their seal upon certain documents to verify their authenticity. Use of a seal is somewhat uncommon now, although it might be required on bids for government contract work, requests to open bank accounts, and various other official documents.

Minute book
Binder or book used to maintain minutes of corporate meetings and other information

The **minute book** is usually a three-ring binder divided or tabbed into different sections. In one section, the corporation may place its articles, and in another its bylaws. The minute book is best known for containing the minutes of meetings of directors and shareholders. The minutes are seldom a verbatim transcript of meetings, but are typically a summary or overview of meetings.

Stock certificate book
Book containing stock certificates to be issued to shareholders

The **stock certificate book** resembles a large checkbook. Rather than checks, however, it contains certificates that are completed and provided to purchasers of the corporation's stock. Each certificate is required to include certain information (the name of the corporation, the type of stock being issued, the number of shares being issued, restrictions on transfer of the shares, if any) and must be signed by the corporate officers, typically, the president and secretary of the corporation. A rosette, or place for impressing the corporate seal, is usually found on the certificate. When the appropriate consideration for the stock has been received, the corporation will issue the certificate to the owner of the shares. A tear-off slip attached to the certificate is to be completed and maintained by the corporation to provide a ledger or accounting of those to whom stock has been issued, the date of issuance, and the number of shares issued. The reverse side of the certificate typically includes endorsement information so that an owner of the stock can transfer it to another person by merely endorsing the certificate over to the new owner. (See Figure 9-7 for a sample stock certificate.)

The supplies are easily ordered from the law firm's usual supplier and will often be received within 48 hours of ordering. The cost of the supplies is generally quite reasonable, often in the range of $50 to $75. Often the law firm will have a pre-established account with the supplier, and ordering the corporate supplies will take only a few minutes via telephone or e-mail. In some instances, the corporate kit includes a form of bylaws for the corporation to use or modify to suit its purposes as well as other forms, such as forms for meeting minutes.

3. *Organizational Meeting*

Although a corporation is legally formed upon the filing or acceptance of its articles of incorporation, some basic organizational activities must be undertaken to complete the process and start the corporation on its way. Accomplishing these goals occurs at the corporation's first meeting, usually referred to as the **organizational meeting** and held at the attorney's office.

Organizational meeting
First corporate meeting held to launch corporation

Most states require that a corporation hold an organizational meeting. MBCA § 2.05(a)(1) provides that if initial directors are named in the articles of incorporation they shall call and hold an organizational meeting to complete the organization of the corporation by appointing officers, adopting bylaws, and carrying on any other business. If initial directors are not named in the articles of incorporation, the MBCA requires that the incorporators hold the organizational meeting to elect directors and complete the organization of the corporation.

Carefully review the statutes in the state of incorporation to determine if there are any requirements for the organizational meeting. For example, must the organizational meeting be held in the state of incorporation or can it be held elsewhere? Must written notice of the organizational meeting be given? Can individuals waive their right to receive notice of the organizational meeting? If so, must the waiver be in writing?

Most attorneys prefer to hold the organizational meeting at their offices to ensure the corporation, its directors, officers, and shareholders are aware of various requirements imposed on them by the state and to emphasize the need to act in compliance with all statutory requirements relating to corporations in that state. The organizational meeting is usually attended by the incorporators, the initial board of directors, the initial officers, and any anticipated shareholders. For small corporations, the meeting may therefore be attended by a mere handful of people.

FIGURE 9-7
Sample Stock Certificate

FIGURE 9-7
Sample Stock Certificate *Continued*

For Value Received, _____ hereby sell, assign and transfer unto _____ Shares represented by the within Certificate, and do hereby irrevocably constitute and appoint _____ Attorney to transfer the said Shares on the books of the within named Corporation, with full power of substitution in the premises. Dated _____ 19___

In presence of

NOTICE: THE SIGNATURE OF THIS ASSIGNMENT MUST CORRESPOND WITH THE NAME AS WRITTEN UPON THE FACE OF THE CERTIFICATE, IN EVERY PARTICULAR, WITHOUT ALTERATION OR ENLARGEMENT OR ANY CHANGE WHATEVER.

If the organizational meeting is to be held at the law firm, the attorney or paralegal may prepare an agenda for the meeting. Following are items typically discussed at the organizational meeting:

Election of Directors. If directors have not already been named in the articles of incorporation, they will be elected by the incorporators. If a "dummy" board was identified in the articles (such as the attorney, paralegal, and legal secretary), these **"dummy directors"** will resign one at a time and be replaced with the actual initial directors. The directors will "take over" and run the meeting. The role of the incorporator is now complete. The initial board of directors will serve until the first meeting of shareholders, at which time their successors will be elected.

Appointment of Officers. The directors of the corporation will appoint the officers of the corporation. The most typical offices are those of president, vice-president, secretary, and treasurer, but large corporations might have numerous other officers.

Adoption of Bylaws. The bylaws drafted by the attorney or paralegal will be presented and adopted.

Acceptance of Preincorporation Stock Subscriptions. If parties have made offers to purchase stock upon the formation of the corporation, these offers or preincorporation share subscriptions should be accepted. The officers will be directed to issue stock certificates upon receipt of the amount offered in the subscription.

Dummy directors
Nominee directors, often a legal team, named in original articles, not intended to be permanent directors

Acceptance of Preincorporation Contracts.   The directors should formally consider and ratify or adopt action taken by the promoters or contracts, if any, entered into by the promoters prior to incorporation. The promoters should be expressly relieved of their liability under those contracts. The corporation will then be a party to the various contracts with the right to enforce the terms and conditions of those contracts. For example, ratification or adoption of a lease for corporate offices entered into by a promoter will allow the corporation to demand that the premises be repaired or maintained. Ratification will also allow for reimbursement of the costs, including legal fees, incurred by the incorporators in preparing and filing the articles of incorporation and drafting the bylaws.

Approval of Corporate Seal and Form of Stock Certificate.   The directors should approve the form of stock certificate and the seal obtained from the corporation's supplier. A sample or specimen of the stock certificate is often attached to the minutes of the meeting. Similarly, the seal is often impressed upon the minutes of the organizational meeting to demonstrate its form.

Banking and Accounting Information.   The directors should discuss where the corporation's accounts will be held and the types of accounts to be opened, as well as any restrictions on banking. For example, the directors can require that for any expenditure in excess of $10,000, two officers must sign the check rather than merely one. The accountants to be used by the corporation may be designated. The directors can establish a fiscal year for the corporation (assuming it is not set forth in the bylaws). The most common fiscal year is the calendar year (January 1 through December 31), but other possibilities may be desired for particular businesses. For example, a corporation operating a resort with its peak season in the summer may elect a fiscal year of September 1 through August 31.

S Election.   The directors should discuss whether it is desirable, when feasible, for the corporation to elect to become an S corporation, meaning that the corporation itself will not pay tax; all income earned by the corporation will be passed through to the shareholders, who will pay tax on their income from the corporation. Because all shareholders must agree with the election, the directors' recommendation on this issue should be discussed with the shareholders if they are all present at the meeting or should be voted on at the first meeting of shareholders (sometimes held immediately following the organizational meeting). To obtain S status for a corporation, the filing must generally be made with the Internal Revenue Service within certain time limits to be effective for that tax year. Thus, election of S status is commonly discussed at the organizational meeting held shortly after incorporation. Subchapter S corporations are discussed further in Chapter Seventeen.

Confirmation of Section 1244 Stock.   As discussed in Chapter Eight, a "small business corporation" is automatically eligible for the benefits of Section 1244 of the Internal Revenue Code, so that losses sustained on the sale of stock will be treated as ordinary losses rather than capital losses (up to certain dollar limits). Although qualified corporations are not statutorily required to take affirmative action to achieve the tax benefits of Section 1244, directors or incorporators often specifically confirm at organizational meetings that it is the corporation's intent that its stock qualify under Section 1244 for the favorable tax treatment provided by that provision.

Issuance of Stock.   The directors should authorize the officers to begin issuing stock and should fix the consideration to be paid per share.

Other Actions Taken at Organizational Meetings.   Other actions taken at organizational meetings include the following:

- Presenting the filed articles of incorporation to the attendees and placement of the articles in the corporation's minute book;
- Adopting employee benefit plans, including health and insurance plans, retirement plans, or other similar benefits;
- Discussing whether the corporation will commence doing business in other states, and, if so, making plans to qualify as a foreign corporation in those other states; and
- Instructing the officers to apply for an Employee Identification Number (required by all corporations).

If the shareholders are present at the organizational meeting, they will likely vote on only two issues: the election of directors and approval of the S corporation election. If the shareholders' initial meeting immediately follows, the shareholders will likely approve the election of the directors by the incorporators and will also vote on S corporation election.

In instances involving small corporations, the incorporators, directors, officers, and shareholders might all be the same few family members or friends. In such cases, the election of directors and appointment of officers is often a mere formality requiring little or no discussion because the parties have agreed long before the meeting as to how the corporation will be managed.

After the organizational meeting, the attorney or paralegal prepares minutes of the meeting reflecting the various actions taken at the meeting. These are signed by the secretary of the corporation and placed in the minute book. Alternatively, for smaller corporations, or when it is known in advance who the directors and officers will be, the attorney or paralegal can prepare minutes prior to the meeting reflecting the standard items to be considered and then use these minutes as an agenda. The secretary of the corporation then has a form to follow in preparing future minutes of corporate meetings.

Some states do not require that an actual formal organizational meeting be held. In those states, all of the activities that would be undertaken at an actual meeting can be done by unanimous written agreement. MBCA § 2.05(b) allows for action by unanimous written consent of the incorporators in place of an organizational meeting. The incorporators waive their right to notice and attendance at a formal meeting and unanimously agree in writing to all of the matters that would ordinarily be discussed at the organizational meeting. The **written consent** sets forth the names of the directors to be elected, the appointment of certain individuals as officers, approval of the preincorporation share subscriptions, and the like. Each director or shareholder will sign his or her name and date the document. The consent is placed in the minute book. (See Appendix H for a form of written consent in lieu of organizational meeting.)

Written consent
Document reflecting action taken by agreement in writing rather than action taken in person at a meeting

Although acting by written consent may be easier than getting all of the principals of the corporation together for a meeting, it precludes the attorney from giving advice to the principals regarding their duties and obligations to the corporation and responding to questions regarding notice of meetings, preparing minutes of meetings, and the like. Thus, even though a state statute might allow for action to be taken by unanimous written consent rather than by a formal in-person organizational meeting, many attorneys prefer that the organizational meeting be held as an opportunity to emphasize corporate responsibilities and to respond to questions.

See Figure 9-8 for an Incorporation Checklist, which can be used as a step-by-step approach for organizing corporations.

4. Annual Report

Although it is not due immediately after incorporation, most state statutes and MBCA § 16.21 require a corporation (both domestic and foreign corporations authorized to do business in the state) to submit an **annual report** providing basic information about the corporation. The MBCA requires the following information:

- Name of the corporation and state of incorporation
- Address of the corporation's registered office and name of the registered agent at that office in the state
- Address of the corporation's principal office
- Names and business addresses of the corporation's directors and principal officers
- Brief description of the nature of the business
- Total number of authorized shares
- Total number of issued and outstanding shares

Annual report
Form required to be filed annually by domestic and foreign corporations in most states providing information about the corporation

A form of annual report is found at Figure 8-2. Although the secretary of state will usually automatically mail the report form to the corporation to be completed, it is a good idea to docket the due dates for annual reports for any law firm corporate clients. For a large corporation that does business in numerous jurisdictions, calendaring, completing, and filing the annual reports is often a full-time job. The annual report is usually accompanied by a filing fee and various state tax payments. Most states now allow electronic filing of annual reports.

F. Defects in Incorporation Process

On occasion, a defect in the incorporation process becomes important. For example, assume that a creditor is owed $50,000 by a corporation having three individuals as the directors, officers, and shareholders. If the corporate assets are limited to $25,000, the creditor might suffer a loss of $25,000 because the corporation protects the shareholders from personal liability for corporate debts and obligations. In such a case, the creditor might begin investigating various

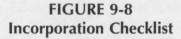

FIGURE 9-8
Incorporation Checklist

1. Select jurisdiction in which to incorporate. Consider whether business will be local in nature or whether extraterritorial expansion is planned.
2. Identify corporate name (and possible alternatives). Research required "signals" in state of incorporation.
3. Determine name availability by checking with secretary of state.
4. If business will be conducted nationally or expansion is planned, consider a full-scope nationwide name search.
5. If name is available, reserve name, and docket period of name reservation.
6. Gather the following information so articles of incorporation can be prepared:
   Determine identity of incorporators
   Determine principal address of corporation within the state of incorporation
   Identify registered agent (or make arrangement with attorneys' service company to serve as registered agent) Identify initial shareholders
   Identify initial directors
   Identify stock of company:
   ◆ Common or preferred stock (if preferred, identify preferences and special rights)
   ◆ Number of authorized shares
   ◆ Par value or no par value
7. Gather incorporation forms and schedule of filing fees from secretary of state.
8. Prepare articles of incorporation, have them signed and filed.
9. Order corporate kit and supplies.
10. Prepare bylaws and provide them to proposed directors for review and comment.
11. Confirm incorporation to client, and schedule first organizational meeting. Prepare notice of meeting or waivers of notice.
12. Prepare agenda for first organizational meeting. Items should include:
    Election of directors
    Appointment of officers
    Approval of bylaws
    Ratification or adoption of preincorporation contracts or actions, including legal and incorporation fees
    Acceptance of preincorporation stock subscriptions
    Discussion of applying for status as S corporation
    Confirmation of Section 1244 stock
    Review of articles, seal, and form of stock certificate
    Authorization of issuance of shares
    Authorization of application for employer identification number
    Review of miscellaneous matters, if not in bylaws (selection of fiscal year, selection of bankers and accountants, and discussion of qualifying in foreign jurisdictions)
13. Prepare minutes of first organizational meeting, and send to client for signature by secretary of corporation and placement in minute book.
14. Docket date for next meeting.
15. Docket date for submission of annual report to secretary of state.

corporate documents in an effort to defeat the shareholders' limited liability and hold them personally liable for the remaining $25,000 owed to the creditor.

Assume that the creditor obtains a copy of the articles of incorporation from the secretary of state and notices that, due to an error, the address given for the corporation's registered office in the state is incorrect. The creditor might attempt to argue that because the state statutes relating to incorporation were not complied with, the corporation has been defectively formed and the shareholders are not entitled to protection from corporate debts. Other "defects" can include failure to have the requisite number of directors, failure to publish articles in newspapers or record them after filing (if required), failure to adopt bylaws, or failure to hold an organizational meeting. In such cases, courts typically examine the nature of the defect and then classify the corporation as *de jure* or *de facto*.

A **de jure corporation** (literally, one "of right") is a corporation that has substantially or strictly complied with the appropriate state statutes. For example, a mere typographical error in an address in the articles would likely be viewed as so minor that substantial compliance with the statutes is acknowledged. The corporation would be classified as de jure. The significance of achieving de jure status is that the corporation's existence and validity cannot be attacked or challenged by any party, including the state in which it was incorporated.

A corporation that fails to achieve de jure status can be classified as a **de facto corporation** (literally, one "in fact"). The significance of being classified as de facto is that the corporation cannot be attacked by any third party, such as a creditor. It can, however, be challenged by its creator, the state, which may bring an action to declare the corporation invalid. To achieve de facto status, there must be some good faith attempt by the corporation to comply with the laws of the state of incorporation and some good faith conduct of business as if a corporation existed. Some courts have held that failure to file the articles in the county in which the corporation does business (although they have been filed with the secretary of state) results in a de facto corporation.

If a corporation is neither de jure nor de facto, it can be attacked by a third party who may then recover from individual shareholders. There are, however, situations in which courts hold that the attacking party or creditor is *estopped* (or precluded) from challenging the validity of the corporation. In such cases, the corporation is said to be a **corporation by estoppel.** If creditors have dealt with the entity believing it was a corporation, they will generally be estopped from later claiming that it is not a valid corporation. Similarly, if an entity has held itself out as being a corporation *it* will later be estopped from claiming that it is not liable for debts and obligations because it is not a validly formed entity.

Various modern statutes dealing with the formation of corporations have eliminated or lessened the use of the de jure and de facto doctrines. For example, MBCA § 2.03(b) provides that the secretary of state's filing of the articles of incorporation is "conclusive proof" that the incorporators satisfied all conditions required for incorporation (except that the state can challenge the validity of the corporation). Many states have similar statutes. These statutes preclude a third party from attacking the corporation based on defects in the formation process. Thus, even if the articles included an error, once the articles are filed, a valid corporation exists, and it cannot be attacked by anyone but the state of incorporation. Consequently, there are far fewer cases today alleging that the shareholders

De jure corporation
A corporation that substantially or strictly complied with statutory requirements and is unassailable

De facto corporation
A corporation that attempted in good faith to comply with statutory requirements and can only be challenged by the state

Corporation by estoppel
Corporation that cannot be attacked by third parties because they have dealt with corporation as if it was validly organized

should be liable for corporate debts due to defects in incorporation than there were years ago, and the de jure/de facto doctrine is of more historical interest than practical interest. If articles of incorporation have not been filed, the MBCA generally imposes joint and several liability on all those who act on behalf of the entity knowing articles were not filed. In sum, the secretary of state's filing of the articles is the demarcation point. Before this, the promoters have personal liability; after this, the corporation is viewed as validly formed (and can be attacked only by the state).

Key Features
in Forming Corporations

◆ Those who plan the corporation are promoters who owe fiduciary duties to each other. Agreements made by them bind them personally until the corporation ratifies or adopts their actions or contracts and releases them from liability.

◆ Interested investors often offer or subscribe to purchase stock when the corporation is later formed. The offer is irrevocable for some period of time. The corporation usually accepts the offer at its first organizational meeting.

◆ Consideration should be given as to the jurisdiction in which to incorporate. The state in which the corporation will conduct business should be the favored candidate unless its statutes are inflexible and costs are high.

◆ The corporate name must usually include a signal showing the entity is a corporation. The name can be reserved prior to the time of incorporation.

◆ The document that creates a corporation is called the articles of incorporation. Its contents are dictated by state statute.

◆ Bylaws must be prepared for the corporation. Bylaws are the internal rules for the corporation's operation and governance.

◆ Corporations must hold a first meeting, called the organizational meeting, to commence the corporation's business.

◆ Defects in the incorporation process no longer permit third parties to attack the corporation, because corporations are conclusively presumed to be validly formed upon filing of the articles.

G. Role of Paralegal

The role of the paralegal in the incorporation process is full and varied. In some instances, paralegals have nearly complete responsibility for forming the corporation. Paralegals are routinely involved in the following activities:

1. Drafting agreements to be entered into by promoters, defining their rights and obligations to each other and to the proposed corporation.

2. Preparing preincorporation share subscriptions and assignments of those subscriptions.
3. Preparing a survey of corporate statutes in various jurisdictions to ensure the corporation is incorporated in a jurisdiction beneficial to the corporation. (The survey will compare costs of incorporation, taxes, fees, requirements imposed on directors, and so forth.)
4. Assisting in selection of the name of the corporation to ensure it includes the appropriate corporate designation, if required, and then determining availability of the name.
5. Reserving the name so it is available for the corporation and docketing the date the reservation expires to ensure that the incorporation process is completed before the reservation expires.
6. Researching registration of the name in foreign jurisdictions if the corporation intends to operate in other states.
7. Preparing the pertinent documents if the corporation will be operating under an assumed name.
8. Preparing the articles of incorporation and reviewing the state statutes to ensure the articles comply with the state's requirements.
9. Filing the articles with the secretary of state and with any county in which they must be recorded.
10. Drafting bylaws for the internal governance of the corporation.
11. Ordering the corporate supplies, namely, the stock certificates, minute book, and seal.
12. Preparing for the organizational meeting by sending out any required notices and preparing an agenda for the meeting.
13. Attending the organizational meeting and taking and preparing minutes of the meeting (or preparing the written consent action if no organizational meeting is actually held).
14. Preparing the appropriate forms for election of S corporation status (where applicable).
15. Applying to the Internal Revenue Service for an employer identification number (see Figure 2-3 for IRS Form SS-4), a nine-digit number assigned to sole proprietorships that will pay wages to one or more employees and to all partnerships and corporations. (See Chapter Two, "Role of Paralegal" section.)
16. Docketing the dates for required corporate meetings and annual report forms.

Case Illustration
Corporate Ratification Eliminates Liability of Promoters

Case: *Tin Cup Pass Ltd. Partnership v. Daniels*, 553 N.E.2d 82 (Ill. App. Ct. 1990)

Facts: Promoters signed a lease for the benefit of a proposed corporation that was named on the lease. Due to a problem with the initially planned corporate name, the corporation was ultimately formed under a different name. When the corporation failed to pay rent for the premises, the plaintiff lessor sued the promoters. The trial court held that the promoters were not individually liable for the lease obligations.

Holding: The appellate court affirmed. The court determined that the parties' intent should control. In this case, the parties intended that the ultimate lessee would be a corporation. The fact that the corporation was created under a different name is not significant, particularly where, as here, the corporation ratified the lease by recognizing it and treating it as valid. In such a case, the promoters will not be personally liable.

◆   ◆   ◆

WEB RESOURCES

Because nearly all states have posted their forms relating to incorporations on their Web sites, the most important Web resources are the home pages of the various secretaries of state. See Appendix A for the specific Web address for each of the state's secretaries of state. Other alternatives follow. Remember that forms provided are anonymous and should serve as a model only. Revise forms to suit the client's needs.

State corporation statutes:	www.law.cornell.edu www.findlaw.com
Secretaries of state:	www.nass.org or http://www.premiercorp.com/_secretariesofstate.asp (with direct links to each state's secretary of state for access to forms, and in many states, preliminary name searching and online determination of agents for service of process)
California agents for service:	www.ss.ca.gov/business/bpd_service_companies.htm
Delaware agents for service:	http://corp.delaware.gov/agents/agts.shtml
Tax information and forms:	www.irs.gov
Company information:	www.hoovers.com (providing addresses and basic information about many U.S. companies)
General information:	www.findlaw.com www.megalaw.com
Forms:	www.lectlaw.com (forms for assignments, articles of incorporation, bylaws, and minutes of organizational meeting)

> www.siccode.com/forms.php (forms for assignment of contract, form for minutes confirming election of Section 1244 benefits, and various forms for minutes and waivers of notice of meetings)

Discussion Questions

Fact Scenario. Peter and Rachel, promoters for a corporation to be formed, have entered into agreements to purchase various textbooks for the corporation. The corporation will engage in tutoring and educational services in Indiana.

1. The corporation is never formed. Who is liable to pay for the textbooks?

2. Assume that the corporation is formed. How can Peter and Rachel ensure that they have no further liability for any contracts made prior to incorporation?

3. In which state should the business be incorporated? Why?

4. Discuss whether the following names would be acceptable for the corporation.

- Exclusive Tutoring
- Teach Your Tots, Inc.
- U.S. Tutoring
- Teach & Tutor Co.

5. Discuss the advisability of placing the following items in the articles of incorporation or in the bylaws:

- Identification of the corporation's stock as common or preferred
- Information about the location of the regular meetings of the board of directors
- Information about where the corporation intends to maintain its bank accounts
- Information about the duties of the corporation's secretary
- A provision allowing the shareholders to exercise preemptive rights

6. Assume that one of the corporation's clients has not paid a bill and recently discovered that when the articles of incorporation were filed, the corporation's street address was identified as Ellwood rather than Elmwood. Under the MBCA, will the client be able to avoid paying the bill on the basis of this error? Discuss.

7. The corporation wishes to expand into Michigan and Ohio. What steps should the corporation take?

8. Prior to incorporation, and on February 1, Rachel's sister Hope agreed to purchase 50 shares of stock in the corporation when it was later formed. May Hope revoke this subscription? Under the MBCA, by what date should the corporation be formed so that it can accept this subscription?

Net Worth

1. In Delaware, are the following corporate names acceptable?
   - Rebecca's Design & Décor Syndicate
   - Rebecca's Design & Décor Club
2. Access the Web site for the California Secretary of State and determine whether the following names are available.
   - Ralph's Electric Inc.
   - Daisy's Florist Inc.
   - Mountain Scribe, Inc.
3. Access the Web site for the Florida Secretary of State. Who is the agent for service of process for Burger King Corporation?
4. Access the Web site for the Indiana Secretary of State. What is the fee to reserve a corporate name in Indiana? How long will the reservation last?
5. Access the Web site for the Wisconsin Secretary of State. What is the fee to file articles of incorporation for a for-profit corporation? What is the fee for expedited service?

10

♦ ♦ ♦
_____

Corporate Finances

_____
♦ ♦ ♦

CHAPTER OVERVIEW

At the beginning of a corporation's existence, it obtains capital from investors who give money to the corporation in return for part ownership of the corporation, in the form of shares of the corporation, or stock. After the corporation is established, it may engage in a variety of methods to obtain additional infusions of capital. The corporation can issue bonds, documents evidencing the corporation's debt, to an investor (the bondholder) who has loaned money to the corporation. Stocks and bonds, collectively referred to as securities, are vehicles used by corporations desiring to raise capital. Capital is also derived from the operation of the corporation's business.

Corporations are often said to be subject to double taxation, meaning the corporation pays tax on the income it earns and then the shareholders pay taxes when corporate profit is distributed to them in the form of dividends.

This chapter explores the various types of securities issued by corporations, and the rights and privileges thereof, as well as aspects of taxation of corporations.

A. Introduction to Securities

All corporations need money to operate and expand their business activities. Generally, to raise money, corporations either sell stock to investors or borrow money from various lenders. The stock sold to investor-shareholders and the evidence of the corporation's obligation to repay borrowed money are referred to as **securities.**

According to the Uniform Commercial Code, which promotes uniformity in various commercial and contractual relationships, a security is a share, participation, or other interest in property of or an enterprise of the issuer or an obligation

Security
A share, participation, or other interest in property or an enterprise of the issuer or an obligation of the issuer

235

of the issuer. U.C.C. § 8-102(1). Thus, viewing the corporation as the issuer, securities fall into two classes: those that show a person's ownership interest in the corporation and those that show an obligation of the corporation. The term **equity securities** refers to shares of a corporation that are sold to investors called shareholders or stockholders (the terms are synonymous). The capital received by a corporation in return for issuance of equity securities is called **equity capital.** The term **debt securities** refers to documents issued by a corporation, usually called *bonds,* representing the corporation's debt to an investor, who is typically called a **bondholder.** The capital received by a corporation in return for issuance of a debt security is known as **debt capital.**

Although the terms *stocks* and *bonds* are often referred to in the same breath, these two types of securities are vastly different from each other. A shareholder who owns equity securities (shares) in a corporation is an insider, an owner of the corporation who will likely be entitled to vote on various corporate issues, might receive distributions of corporate profits (called **dividends**), and might receive assets of the corporation upon its liquidation and dissolution. A lender or bondholder, on the other hand, is an outsider, not a corporate owner, and is thus not entitled to vote, receive dividends, or share in the distribution of net assets upon liquidation and dissolution. The bondholder is, however, entitled to be repaid the amount borrowed by the corporation at the agreed-on time and under the agreed-on terms.

Issuance of each type of security by a corporation offers certain advantages and disadvantages. The issuance of shares offers a corporation the advantage of receiving needed capital that need not be repaid because the shareholder expects to make money either by receiving dividends or from increasing value of the stock. Each new share of stock issued, however, dilutes the power of the current shareholders. Additionally, stockholders, as corporate owners, vote in elections for directors, and a change in stock ownership could result in a change in management, with previous directors being tossed off the board. The issuance of bonds offers the advantage of receiving needed capital without any loss of power to current shareholders. Moreover, the corporation can deduct interest paid to the bondholder as a corporate expense, whereas the payment of dividends to shareholders is not tax-deductible. Nevertheless, the bond must be repaid at some time as must interest on it, whether the corporation is having a profitable year or not.

According to statistics, the number of bonds issued has been decreasing in the past 20 years as the number of stocks listed has been dramatically increasing, reflecting a trend of corporations to raise money through the issuance of stock rather than bonds. The following statistics reflect securities listed on the New York Stock Exchange. See *Statistical Abstract of the United States* 743 (127th ed. 2008).

	1990	1995	2000	2006
Shares Listed (in billions)	90.7	154.7	313.9	411.4
Bonds (number of issues)	2,912	2,097	1,627	850

Similarly, the percentage of American families owning stock continues to increase, from 37 percent in 1992 to 50.3 percent in 2005. *Id.* at 744. The majority of stock sold on the national exchanges, however, is not held by

Equity security
A security representing ownership interest in an enterprise (often called a *share*)

Equity capital
Capital received by a corporation in return for issuance of stock

Debt security
A security representing an obligation of the corporate issuer (often called a *bond*)

Bondholder
One to whom a debt is owed by a corporation

Debt capital
Money received by a corporation in return for issuing debt securities

Dividend
A distribution of corporate profits

individual investors but by institutional investors. For example, institutions such as TIAA-CREF, Barclays, the California Public Employees' Retirement System, and mutual funds now hold nearly 60 percent of all listed corporate stock in the United States.

Most experts believe that stocks have a greater potential for return than bonds; however, stocks also carry a greater risk of loss and can fluctuate wildly in value. Bonds, on the other hand, are far more stable because the investor can predict in advance the expected return. Thus, many investors attempt to diversify their portfolios by allocating their assets into a mix of both stocks and bonds.

Shareholders of **common stock** (the ordinary stock of the corporation) expect reasonable growth. Common stock is not particularly safe, however, as it can plunge in value with little or no warning and because the corporation has no obligation to return the amount invested to the shareholder. Shareholders of **preferred stock** (stock that has some right, privilege, or preference over another type of stock) expect steady income and a reasonably safe investment. Bondholders expect no growth (because the bond amount is fixed) but will receive steady income in the form of regular payments of interest and principal. A bond is the safest form of investment in a corporation (assuming the corporation is stable).

Common stock
Ordinary stock of a corporation having no special privileges

Preferred stock
Stock in a corporation that carries certain rights and privileges

Corporations will issue a mix of equity and debt securities depending on market conditions and risk evaluation. Investors might be unwilling to lend money to a corporation engaged in a high-risk venture. Such a corporation may rely nearly exclusively on equity financing, or the sale of shares, to raise needed capital.

The public sale of corporate securities, whether stock or bonds, is subject to regulation by applicable state laws, as well as the federal Securities Act of 1933 and Securities Exchange Act of 1934 (see Chapter Thirteen). All of these laws are designed to protect the public from fraud and unfair business practices. Many small issuances of stock, such as those in which the total amount of the offering does not exceed $1 million or those offered to a limited number of persons, are exempt from such regulation.

B. Equity Securities

1. Introduction

The corporation's equity securities are identified in the articles of incorporation, which set forth the number of shares the corporation is authorized to issue. This number should be determined after giving careful consideration to the corporation's anticipated needs for capital (and investigating whether the state assesses different fees depending on the number of shares authorized by the articles). The number of shares authorized to be sold should be large enough to accommodate growth because once the corporation has issued the number specified, no further shares can be issued until the articles of incorporation are amended. Because amendment usually requires shareholder approval and always requires state approval and filing fees, failure to allow a sufficient number of authorized shares will delay the corporation from obtaining needed capital until it can hold a shareholders' meeting and file the appropriate documents to amend the articles.

Authorized shares
The number of shares the corporation has the authority to issue according to its articles

The shares identified in the articles are referred to as **authorized shares** of the corporation. Those who wish to purchase shares will give the appropriate consideration for the shares (cash, property, services already performed, contracts for services to be performed, or other securities of the corporation) and the corporation will issue or deliver the shares to the investor. Shares that have been issued are referred to as **outstanding shares.** Thus, shareholders of a corporation hold authorized, issued, and outstanding shares. Large corporations can have significant numbers of outstanding shares. For example, as of 2008, General Mills, Inc., had 336 million shares of common stock issued and outstanding, and Chevron Corporation had more than 2 billion shares issued and outstanding.

Outstanding shares
Shares issued by a corporation and held by investors

The differences in the terms *authorized, issued*, and *outstanding* are important because corporations only pay dividends on outstanding shares, meaning the shares currently held by shareholders. Similarly, only outstanding shares vote at shareholder meetings.

Shares are issued and outstanding unless they are reacquired, redeemed, converted, or canceled by the corporation. Stock reacquired by the corporation (often because the shareholder exercised a right to compel the corporation to repurchase or redeem the stock) is called **treasury stock.** Treasury shares are viewed as issued but are not considered outstanding because they are not held by investors but rather by the corporation itself. Thus, they are not entitled to voting rights or to share in dividends and they are not included in computing a corporation's number of outstanding shares. Moreover, they are not entitled to receive any distribution of the corporation's net assets upon liquidation.

Treasury stock
Stock reacquired by a corporation and which is not outstanding

The decision to issue shares is made by the board of directors acting in the best interest of the corporation. Not only does the number of shares authorized by the articles act as a ceiling on the number of shares that can be issued, but the directors must also observe any preemptive rights given to shareholders by the articles that allow the existing shareholders to purchase their respective ownership proportion of newly issued stock before it can be issued to others.

The articles may authorize more than one type or class of shares. For example, shares can be issued having certain rights or preferences over other types of stock. This stock is usually referred to as *preferred stock*. Although it no longer uses the term *preferred stock*, the MBCA specifically allows corporations to issue various classes of stock, some of which have rights and privileges that other stock will not. This text uses the generally accepted terms *common* and *preferred* stock. Generally, the most typical approach is for a corporation to have only one class of stock, with the holders of that class having identical rights. Again, however, other classes of stock can be created, whatever they might be labeled.

The articles of incorporation *must* authorize one or more classes of shares that together have unlimited voting rights and one or more classes of shares that together are entitled to receive the net assets of the corporation upon dissolution under MBCA § 6.01(b). Most state statutes are similar. This provision ensures that the corporation will have shareholders who can vote on corporate action and receive the net assets of the corporation in the event it liquidates.

An equity security holder or shareholder has three ownership interests in a corporation: the right to vote (usually one vote per share); the right to receive distributions, if declared by the board in its discretion and if the corporation is solvent; and the right to receive net assets on liquidation of the corporation once creditors have been satisfied.

2. *Par Value and No Par Value Stock*

The initial issuance of stock is dependent on the initial capital needs of the corporation. For example, if the business requires $100,000 and ten initial investors wish to invest equally, they can each be issued $10,000 worth of stock. The directors commonly establish the price for the shares. They will be guided by the best interest of the corporation and by market conditions. If the price per share is too high, for example, $10,000 per share, few investors will be able to pay this amount. Thus, in the present example, it might be better to issue each investor 200 shares at a price of $50 per share rather than to issue one share for $10,000 because the division into more shares enhances the ability to sell the stock at a later date. A stockholder might be unable to locate a buyer who wishes to invest $10,000, but could readily find several buyers willing to invest $50 per share. If the price per share is too low, it will dilute the interest of the then-existing shareholders by reducing the value of their shares.

In addition to the directors' duty to establish the value of the stock while acting in the corporation's best interest, there is another limitation relating to the amount for which stock can be issued. The **par value** of the stock as set forth in the articles of incorporation is the nominal or face value set for each share. It is the minimum amount for which stock can be issued. Thus, if the par value is $10, a share of stock can be issued for $10 or any amount in excess of this, but cannot be issued for an amount less than $10. This explains why par value is traditionally set at such a low amount (often $1 or even ten cents): It gives directors the flexibility to issue shares for a small amount of money if they need to raise capital but there is little market for the shares. Par value is not equivalent to market value. In fact, because par value is usually so low, corporations hope that market value is far in excess of par value. The par value of the common stock of General Mills, Inc., is ten cents, while the par value of the common stock of Chevron Corporation is 75 cents.

Par value
The lowest price for which stock can be sold

Some states, however, allow directors to issue stock for less than the par value if the directors determine this is in the best interest of the corporation. In general, shares issued for less than the par value are referred to as **watered stock** (or sometimes *discount* or *bonus stock*). Shares without a par value set forth in the articles, referred to as **no par value shares**, can be sold for whatever price the directors fix so long as this price is reasonable. Thus, no par value stock is merely assigned a stated value by the board of directors.

Watered stock
Stock sold for less than its par value (also called *discount* or *bonus* stock)

The term *watered stock* derives from an unscrupulous practice of cattle drovers who, before the sale of their cattle stock, would feed the cattle large amounts of salt. The salt, in turn, caused the cattle to drink gallons of water, thereby increasing their weight and consequent market price. Thus, the watered cattle stock wasn't worth its sale price. In the corporate context, watered stock also is not worth its sales price.

No par value shares
Stock with no stated par value that can be sold according to the directors' discretion

In most states, corporations now have the option of stating a par value for the stock in the articles of incorporation or stating that there will be no par value. The MBCA typifies the modern trend in not requiring any par value to be stated. In those states that do not require that a par value be specified in the articles, statutes often provide that par value is deemed to be a certain amount, for example, $1; this is solely for the purpose of determining filing fees, annual fees, and taxes. As discussed in Chapter Nine, Delaware bases its annual franchise tax on the number and value of shares. California imposes a statutory par value of $1 per share solely for the purpose of determining taxes and fees.

Historically, par value was used to ensure that shareholders fairly contributed to a corporation; it served as a guarantee that other investors would not be able to buy stock on more advantageous terms. At the present time, because directors are required to use their business judgment in determining adequacy of consideration for shares sold and because many corporations, when required to establish a par value, establish a low and arbitrary amount, the concept of par value has become somewhat meaningless and thus there is a trend in most states to follow the MBCA and eliminate any requirement to state a par value for stock.

Because of the elimination of the concept of par value, under the MBCA there is no minimum price at which shares must be issued. The shares will be issued for whatever consideration is determined adequate by the board of directors, and thus there can be no liability for issuing watered stock. The only limitation on the directors' discretion is that shares issued at approximately the same time must be issued for approximately the same consideration unless there is a valid business reason for the price differential. MBCA § 6.21(c) provides that before the corporation issues shares, the board must determine that the consideration is adequate.

Some general corporate accounting principles are also affected by issuance of par value shares and no par value shares. If shares with a par value of $15 are in fact sold for $15 each, all of the amount received by the corporation is placed in an account referred to as **stated capital.** Any amount received for shares over and above the par value amount is called **capital surplus** and is placed in a capital surplus account. If the stock has no par value, the directors can sell the stock at any price they determine and then in their discretion allocate the proceeds received to the stated capital account and to the capital surplus account. For example, if no par value stock is issued for $25 per share, the directors can allocate $5 to stated capital and $20 to capital surplus. The advantage of a large capital surplus account is that most state statutes permit corporations to repurchase their own shares only if there is sufficient money in the capital surplus account to make the purchase. The existence of no par value stock gives the directors the flexibility to create a large capital surplus account for this purpose (and also for the distribution of dividends in some instances). Because the MBCA has eliminated the concept of par value, the concept of stated capital is likewise eradicated and the corporation can allocate the consideration received as the directors deem appropriate.

Stated capital
Amount received by a corporation when stock is sold at its par value

Capital surplus
Amount received by a corporation in excess of a stock's par value

3. Consideration for Shares

To ensure that corporations were adequately capitalized, the older view required that the consideration given for shares generally be in cash.

Promissory notes (agreements promising to pay a certain sum in the future) and agreements to provide services in the future were generally unacceptable. According to MBCA § 6.21(b) and most modern statutes, shares may be issued for consideration consisting of any tangible or intangible property or benefit to the corporation, including cash, promissory notes, services performed, contracts for services to be performed, or other securities of the corporation. This very flexible standard allows for almost anything to be exchanged for shares so long as there is some benefit to the corporation. Thus, a corporation can issue stock in exchange for a patent or a promise by the corporation's president to work for the corporation for two years, or even the release of a claim against the corporation. Naturally, a corporation cannot issue all of its stock for future services or promissory notes inasmuch as the corporation needs a certain amount of cash to meet its needs. To ensure the individual will pay the note or perform the services, the corporation mayplace the shares in an escrow account or otherwise restrict their transfer until the investor has complied. If tangible or intangible property or services are given as consideration, the board will appraise or determine the value of such contributions and issue stock accordingly. Some states continue to require that the consideration be in the form of cash, property, or already performed services.

Promissory note
An agreement to pay or repay money in the future

Just as stock can be watered by issuance for less cash than par value, it can also be watered if the corporation does not receive adequate property or services in return for stock issued. Some jurisdictions have determined that the holder of watered stock enjoys no rights with respect to the watered stock and can be subject to liability for the difference between what was paid and par value, but most jurisdictions are adopting the modern approach found in the MBCA. Once the board determines what consideration should be paid for the stock, that determination is deemed conclusive as far as adequacy is concerned. MBCA § 6.21(c). Moreover, when the corporation receives the consideration for which the board of directors authorized the issuance of shares, the shares are "fully paid and nonassessable." MBCA § 6.21(d). Thus, under the modern view, the recipient of watered stock has simply gotten a good deal on the stock and can participate in voting and other issues just as other shareholders can without being liable to the corporation for any additional sums (assuming no fraud or misrepresentation by the purchaser of the stock exists).

4. Stock Certificates

Corporations can issue stock without physically delivering a certificate to the shareholder. Shares issued without the formality of stock certificates are called **uncertificated shares.** The ownership of such shares is recorded in the corporate books and is called a "book entry." Owners of uncertificated stock have the same rights as owners of stock evidenced by paper certificates. The issuance of uncertificated stock simply reduces the paperwork burden on a corporation engaged in rapid trading of its stock. The move away from physical certificates to electronic book entry is generally called **dematerialization**. In fact, in today's volatile and modern stock market, many investors never possess actual stock certificates. For today's modern corporations, with their rapid trading of stock, use of actual stock certificates is uncommon. In some instances, purchasers request actual paper

Uncertificated shares
Stock issued without actual stock certificates

Dematerialization
Issuance of stock by electronic book entry rather than paper certificate

certificates when stock is bought as a gift, for example, for a graduation or birthday present. Some corporations charge a modest fee for issuance of a paper stock certificate.

Neither Congress nor the securities industry favors paper certificates. To reduce public interest, many corporations no longer offer beautiful engraved certificates, but rather issue plain paper certificates. Today, only 1 in 98 new stock purchases results in an actual certificate, as compared with 1 in 27 in 1994. In some cases, stock certificates such as that of Playboy Enterprises, Inc. (originally featuring a naked woman), have become collectors' items. Many are actively auctioned on eBay. The SEC recently asked for public comment on whether the agency should mandate destruction of old certificates. Historians and collectors were adamantly opposed. The collecting of historic stocks and bonds is known as scripophily, and the Web site www.scripophily.com offers old stock and bond certificates. Certificate No. 3 of Buffalo Bill's Wild West and Pawnee Bill's Great Far East Show recently sold for $15,000, and stock certificates signed by Enron's late CEO Kenneth Lay fetch more than $300, demonstrating the high level of public interest in historical and collectible stock certificates. Similarly, the Walt Disney Company has stated that it will never eliminate paper certificates, which are decorated with the company's famous cartoon characters.

When actual certificates are used, their content and form is controlled by state statute. MBCA § 6.25 provides that share certificates must provide the following information:

a. The name of the issuing organization and the state law under which it is organized;
b. The name of the person to whom the share is issued; and
c. The number and class of shares (and the designation of the series, if any).

If uncertificated shares are issued, within a reasonable amount of time after issuance, the corporation must send the shareholder a written statement including the information required to be set forth on certificates.

The share certificate must be signed (either manually or by facsimile signature or autopen) by two officers of the corporation, generally the president and the secretary. The seal may be impressed on the face of the certificate, although this is not required. Issuance of new certificates in a small corporation is typically performed by the corporate secretary or treasurer. In large corporations, however, this task would be daunting and is therefore often performed by a **transfer agent**, usually a bank or trust company that has a supply of blank certificates with facsimile signatures of the officers. The transfer agent also records transfer of shares and may act as the corporate **registrar**, and maintain the list of shareholders (as required by MBCA § 16.01(c)). Some transfer agents are professional companies dedicated to handling all transactions with regard to stock ownership, recordkeeping, and dividend payments. For example, American Stock Transfer & Trust Company of New York City has been serving as a transfer agent and registrar for more than 30 years and represents such companies as Revlon, EDS, and Reebok. The company also designs and prints proxy cards for corporate elections.

Transfer agent
An individual or entity that processes and issues a corporation's stock certificates

Registrar
An individual or entity that maintains a corporation's list of shareholders

If corporations issue only one class of stock, the content of the certificate will be as already described. If more than one class of stock is authorized by the articles of incorporation, the preferences, limitations, and rights of each class must be summarized on the certificate. Alternatively, and as is more common, the certificate may state that the corporation will furnish this information without charge to any shareholder upon written request.

Because the certificate is not what is owned but merely represents ownership of an interest in a corporation, the loss, theft, or destruction of a stock certificate is not critical. When the shareholder provides an affidavit to the corporation stating that the certificate is lost and cannot be found, or has been stolen or destroyed, the corporation or its transfer agent will cancel the original certificate and issue a duplicate.

On occasion, shareholders own fractions of shares. This generally occurs when the corporation declares a share dividend. For example, if the corporation declares a dividend of 1 share for every 100 owned, the owner of 150 shares would be entitled to receive 1.5 shares. If the state corporations code allows fractional shares, the corporation may issue a certificate for a fraction of a share. The owner of this fractional share will be entitled to fractional voting right, dividends, and to participate in the assets of the corporation upon liquidation. The MBCA authorizes the payment of cash to a shareholder for the value of fractional shares. MBCA § 6.04(a).

Alternatively, and at the discretion of the board of directors, the corporation can issue scrip rather than a stock certificate for the fractional share. **Scrip** is a document or certificate evidencing ownership of a partial share. The certificate must be conspicuously labeled "scrip." When the shareholder has accumulated sufficient scrip to total one share, the scrip may be surrendered to the corporation for a certificate evidencing one full share. Scrip is transferable but generally does not carry voting, dividend, or liquidation rights. MBCA § 6.04(c). Thus, the difference between fractional shares and scrip is that the holder of scrip is not entitled to exercise any shareholder rights. Scrip is often issued with the requirement that it be exchanged for a full share within some specified period of time or it will be void.

> Scrip
> A document or certificate showing ownership of a partial share

5. *Classes of Stock*

Most corporations issue only one type of stock, generally referred to as common stock. A corporation can, however, if its articles so provide, authorize the issuance of more than one class of stock. These additional classes generally have some benefit or preference over the common stock and are therefore called preferred stock. The preferences might be in the form of cumulative dividends or the right to convert the preferred stock to common stock. Although the MBCA provides various ways in which one class of stock will have privileges or preferences over others, the following enumeration of these preferences is not meant to be exclusive and the directors are free to create other benefits or preferences. Thus, corporations have great flexibility in their financial structuring.

The holders of preferred stock have generally elected a more conservative approach to investing. Because dividends are almost always paid on preferred stock, this type of security provides a reasonably certain cash flow.

Common Stock. If the corporation does not specify in its articles of incorporation the type of stock to be issued and only one class of stock is authorized, it will be common stock. The common shareholders are owners of the corporation. Their interests, however, are often referred to as **residual interests**, meaning that they are entitled to the remains of the corporation after other senior groups have been satisfied, namely, creditors, bondholders, and preferred shareholders. MBCA § 6.22 provides that an individual who purchases shares from a corporation is not liable to the corporation or to its creditors except to pay the consideration required for issuance of the shares.

The holders of common stock usually enjoy the following rights:

Voting Rights. Each outstanding share of common stock is typically entitled to one vote on each matter voted upon, and fractional shares are entitled to corresponding fractional votes. MBCA §§ 7.21(a) and 6.04(c). It is possible to have different classes of common stock, each having different voting rights. For example, Common A shareholders may be entitled to two votes per share, Common B shareholders to one vote per share, and Common C shareholders may have nonvoting stock (nonvoting stock is useful in obtaining capital for the corporation without a corresponding loss of power or control by existing shareholders). Although classes A, B, and C may have different rights from one another, every shareholder within the Common A class must be treated the same, every shareholder within the Common B class must be treated the same, and so forth. Some corporations issue **supervoting stock.** For example, Marriott International once had a class of a stock with ten votes per share.

Distribution Rights. There is no requirement that a corporation ever pay distributions or dividends to its common shareholders. Dividends, whether in the form of cash, property, or other shares of the corporation, are paid within the discretion of the board, assuming profits permit. If an individual owns 18 percent of the Common A stock, she will be entitled to 18 percent of whatever distribution is declared by the board of directors for Common A shareholders. Thus, common shareholders receive distributions in the same proportion that their share ownership bears to the total number of common shares issued and outstanding.

Common shareholders *might* receive distributions, but there is no guarantee that they will. Furthermore, they will receive distributions only if the corporation is solvent (able to pay its debts as they come due or if assets exceed liabilities) and only after the preferred shareholders have received their distributions. Corporate distributions are discussed in Chapter Twelve.

Liquidation Rights. Upon **liquidation** of the corporation (the winding up of its affairs and business), the corporation must satisfy its creditors and bondholders. The shareholders are then entitled to their proportionate share of the corporation's

Residual interests
The interests of common stockholders, who are entitled to assets remaining after others have been satisfied

Supervoting stock
Stock that carries more than one vote per share

Liquidation
The wrapping up of a business and its affairs

net assets. Once again, however, the common shareholders are "junior," in that they receive net assets only after the preferred shareholders have been satisfied.

Other Rights. In addition to the typical rights of common shareholders already described, common shareholders might also have preemptive rights (usually only when provided by the articles of incorporation), which allow them the first opportunity to purchase their pro rata share of newly issued shares before they are offered to others. Common shareholders might also have cumulative voting rights (see Chapter Eleven), which allow them, in an election for directors, to multiply the number of shares owned by the number of directors being elected and to cast these votes as they like. These preemptive rights or cumulative voting rights are usually mandated by statute or provided for in the articles of incorporation.

Preferred Stock. A class of stock that has some sort of right or preference over another class is preferred stock. The preference could be in receipt of dividends, receipt of net assets upon liquidation, or some other preference devised by the board of directors. In many instances, shareholders pay more initially for preferred stock than for common stock because of the preferences attached to it. The creation of preferred stock must be authorized by the articles of incorporation. Preferred stock can be used by a corporation to attract investors with a more conservative approach who desire steady and predictable returns on investments.

In other instances, preferences may be given to certain shareholders to even the playing field. For example, assume that Jessica and Patti intend to operate a golf course. Patti might have minimal funds to contribute, for example, $20,000, but might have experience in the business and agrees to manage the course. Jessica has no experience but is able to invest $80,000. If each is issued common stock according to her investment, Jessica, as the controlling shareholder, will always be able to make the business decisions. To provide some comfort to each investor, the corporation may issue 20,000 common shares to each woman so they have equal voting rights. To compensate Jessica for her added investment, the corporation can issue her $60,000 worth of nonvoting preferred stock with a fixed dividend and the right to receive net assets before Patti in the event of a liquidation of the business. All of the terms, limitations, preferences, and rights of each class of shares must be set forth in the articles and on the share certificate (unless the corporation agrees to furnish this information without charge upon written request).

The MBCA does not use the terms *common* or *preferred* but merely states that the articles of incorporation may authorize one or more classes of stock that have special or preferential rights over other classes as to voting, distributions, or other matters. Although the MBCA does not expressly use the terms *common* or *preferred* to describe stock, those terms are typically used in common parlance and in many state filing forms.

Preferred stock generally has the following features:

Voting Rights. Preferred stock might or might not have voting rights. The articles of incorporation will set forth any limitations or restrictions on the preferred shareholders' rights to vote. So long as there is one class of shares that has unlimited voting rights, other classes may have special, limited, or no voting rights.

When Google Inc. went public in August 2004, its holders of Class A shares received one vote each, whereas its coyly named Class B shares (owned by the company's two founders and chief executives) received ten votes each. *Los Angeles Times* editor Michael Kinsey commented that this meant that "the company can raise money, and the founders can get fabulously rich, by selling stock to the public, but even with a tiny minority of the shares, the founders will control the company. And the public shareholders can't do anything about it." Similarly, approximately 90 percent of the votes in Polo Ralph Lauren and Martha Stewart Living Omnimedia are controlled by Class B shares. Preferred stock might also have contingent or conditional voting rights, meaning that the owners of preferred stock can vote upon the occurrence of certain events, such as failure of the directors to declare a dividend for some period of time. One reason that preferred shareholders often have no voting rights is that they can rely on their contractual rights guaranteed by their preferred stock. Therefore, they do not need to participate in corporate governance.

Distribution Rights.   A common feature of preferred stock designed to attract investors is a preference in distributions. In many cases, these are **cumulative distributions**, meaning that if the distribution is not paid during any given year, it simply adds up, and the corporation is required to pay these cumulative distributions to the preferred stockholders before distributions are paid to common stockholders. This cumulative dividend is generally built into the stock itself. For example, the articles (as well as the certificate itself) might provide that each share of preferred stock is entitled to a $5 annual cumulative dividend. Assume a preferred stockholder owns 100 shares of stock. Each year the stockholder is entitled to a distribution of $500. If the corporation does not have sufficient profits to pay this dividend for three years, the distribution continues to accumulate. In year four, the corporation must pay the preferred stockholder $2,000 ($500 for four years) before any distributions can be made to common shareholders.

> **Cumulative distributions**
> Distributions that add up and must be paid once a corporation has funds to do so

A **noncumulative distribution** means that the distribution does not accumulate. If the corporation has insufficient profits to pay a distribution to our shareholder for three years, the shareholder simply loses his right to the distribution. In year four, the corporation must pay the preferred stockholder $500 (one year's worth of distributions) before distributions are made to other shareholders.

> **Noncumulative distribution**
> A distribution that does not accumulate and is lost if it cannot be paid

These distributions, especially the cumulative distributions, allow preferred shareholders to predict their income from their stock holdings with some amount of certainty. Nevertheless, although these provisions lend certainty, they can also be viewed as restrictive. If the corporation has a record year and the directors declare significant distributions to the common shareholders, the preferred shareholders might actually receive less than the common shareholders inasmuch as their rights are limited to the agreed-on and stated distribution fixed by the articles and the stock certificate.

The distribution preference can be expressed in terms of dollars ("each share of preferred stock is entitled to receive $10 per share each year before any distributions can be made to any other shareholders") or in terms of ownership interest ("each share of preferred stock is entitled to receive 10 percent of the preferred stock's par value [or stated value] each year before any distributions can be made to any other shareholders"). For example, in late 2005, Blockbuster announced it planned to issue 150,000 shares of preferred stock for $1,000 a share, which would pay a dividend of 7.5 percent a year. Similarly, in late 2008, Warren Buffett's company Berkshire Hathaway, Inc. agreed to purchase $3 billion of General Electric's preferred shares, which carried a guaranteed dividend of 10 percent. This was nearly identical to the deal struck by Buffett with failing Goldman Sachs just days before. Both companies needed an infusion of cash, and Buffett believed that in the wake of the collapse of the financial markets in September 2008, the stock in these companies was undervalued, offering Berkshire Hathaway the chance to buy the stock "on sale." These cash infusions signaled Buffett's confidence in the companies, giving them his "seal of approval."

Preferred stock can also be **participating preferred stock**, meaning that the preferred shareholder also has the right to participate in other distributions, if any, declared by the board of directors in addition to the preference. Participating preferred dividends thus allow the preferred shareholders to share with the common shareholders when the corporation has had an exceptional year and large distributions of the corporation's profits are made. Preferred shareholders would receive their cumulative or noncumulative distribution and would then share in the other distribution made by the corporation. Participating preferred dividends are somewhat rare and are usually paid to the preferred shareholders after the common shareholders have received their distribution of the corporation's earnings.

Participating preferred stock
Stock that has the right to participate in other distributions as well as those "built into" the stock

Liquidation Rights. The holders of preferred stock may be entitled to a stated distribution upon liquidation of the corporation. For example, the articles may provide that upon liquidation, the preferred stockholders are entitled to be paid $85 per share for each share of preferred stock together with interest thereon at 5 percent per year, before any other shareholders may receive assets in liquidation (but after creditors are paid). Similarly, the articles may provide that the liquidation preference is some percentage of par value, for example, "full par value plus 10 percent." After the preferred shareholders have been fully satisfied in the agreed-on amount, they may also share with the common shareholders in receiving net assets upon liquidation.

Conversion Rights. Preferred shareholders may be given the **right to convert** their preferred shares into cash, indebtedness, or shares of some other class or series, usually common shares, either at an agreed-on price or an agreed-on ratio. For example, the articles and share certificates might provide that preferred shares with a par value of $50 can be convertible into common stock shares with a par value of $50. Each of the Blockbuster preferred shares previously described could be converted into a little more than 194 shares of common stock. If the preferred shareholders elect to exercise this right, the preferred shares are surrendered to the transfer agent of the corporation and are canceled, and new common shares are issued. Naturally, the articles of incorporation must authorize a sufficient number of shares to accommodate this right of conversion, and the corporation must have an adequate number of authorized but unissued shares to allow the preferred shareholders to exercise their conversion rights. The articles of incorporation will contain all terms and conditions relating to the conversion process, including the conversion formula and the procedures for conversion.

Conversion right
Right to convert preferred stock into some other form of equity security, usually common stock

Conversion rights may be subject to some contingency. For example, they might be exercisable only after some specified period of time or only in the event the corporation has not paid a dividend for two or more consecutive years.

Conversion rights that are noncontingent offer tremendous advantages to preferred shareholders. They can safely and accurately predict their income and have the advantage of this more conservative investment, and yet they might be able to convert their preferred shares to common shares if the common shares are doing extraordinarily well.

Redemption Rights. Preferred stock may be issued with **redemption rights** (sometimes referred to as a **call** or callable shares) by which the corporation has the power to reacquire the shares from the shareholders or to call them back. The right of redemption may be exercised by the board of directors at its option when the distributions required to be given to shareholders of cumulative preferred stock become too much of a financial burden on the corporation, and the corporation desires to stem the flow of cash paid each year to the preferred stockholders. The amount to be paid when the corporation redeems the shares (typically, a percentage of the par value of the stock together with any accrued and unpaid distributions) is governed by the articles of incorporation. The articles should contain all other terms relating to the redemption, such as when it may be exercised, the period of notice required to be given to the shareholder, and whether the redemption will be partial (and relate only to some of the stock owned by the preferred shareholder) or will be total, in which case all of the stock owned by the preferred shareholder can be called back by the corporation.

To ensure sufficient funds to repurchase the redeemable preferred stock, the corporation will usually establish a separate account, called the **sinking fund**, into which the corporation, over time, deposits funds for redemption purposes, for "retiring the stock." The sinking fund cannot be used for other purposes such as the payment of expenses or distributions.

Rights of redemption may also be given to the preferred shareholder. In this case, the shareholder has the right, exercisable at her option, to compel the corporation to redeem or buy back the shares, if it has sufficient funds in the sinking fund to do so, upon the terms and conditions provided in the articles of incorporation. This particular right of redemption is referred to as a **put** and offers a preferred shareholder the advantage of having a ready buyer if the shareholder cannot sell the stock on the market.

When a corporation reacquires shares through redemption (either through the corporation's call for the stock or the shareholder's put), it will usually retire the shares and restore them to the status of authorized but unissued shares. The effect is as if the original issuance of stock to the shareholder had never taken place. This is the MBCA approach. MBCA § 6.31(a). These shares can thereafter be reissued. The transfer agent is responsible for recording the cancellation of the shares.

MBCA § 6.31(b) provides that if the articles of incorporation prohibit the reissue of such reacquired shares, the number of authorized shares is reduced by the number of shares reacquired. In such a case, the directors must file a statement with the secretary of state setting forth the name of the corporation, the reduction in the number of authorized shares (itemized by class and series), and the total number of authorized shares (itemized by class and series) remaining after reduction. The statement is treated as an amendment to the articles of incorporation without the necessity of shareholder approval. (See Figure 10-1 for a statement of cancellation of non-reissuable shares.)

Redemption rights
Right to compel a stockholder or a corporation to sell or buy stock back

Call
Right by a corporation to reacquire its stock from a shareholder

Sinking fund
An account kept for redemption of stock (or for retiring debt/bonds)

Put
Right of shareholder to require corporation to redeem or repurchase shares

FIGURE 10-1
Illinois Statement of Cancellation of Non-Reissuable Shares

FORM **BCA 9.05** (rev. Dec. 2003)
**STATEMENT OF CANCELLATION
OF NON-REISSUABLE SHARES**
Business Corporation Act

Jesse White, Secretary of State
Department of Business Services
Springfield, IL 62756
Telephone (217) 782-6961
www.cyberdriveillinois.com

Remit payment in the form of a
check or money order payable
to the Secretary of State.

_____ File #_____ Filing Fee: $ 5.00   Approved:

——————————Submit in duplicate ——————————Type or Print clearly in black ink——————————Do not write above this line——————————

1.   CORPORATE NAME: _____

2.   **The corporation has acquired and cancelled its own shares, and the articles of incorporation prohibit the re-issuance of such shares.**

3.   Number of shares cancelled and redemption or purchase price:

Class	Series	Par Value	Number of Shares Cancelled	Redemption or Purchase Price	Date of Cancellation
_____	_____	_____			
_____	_____	_____	_____	_____	_____
_____	_____	_____	_____	_____	_____
_____	_____	_____	_____	_____	_____

	BEFORE CANCELLATION				AFTER CANCELLATION			
	Class	Series	Par	Number	Class	Series	Par	Number
4. Number of authorized shares:	____	____	___	_____	____	____	___	_____
	____	____	___	_____	____	____	___	_____
	____	____	___	_____	____	____	___	_____
5. Number of issued shares:	____	____	___	_____	____	____	___	_____
	____	____	___	_____	____	____	___	_____
	____	____	___	_____	____	____	___	_____

6.   Paid-in capital: $_____ $_____

7.   The undersigned corporation has caused this statement to be signed by a duly authorized officer who affirms, under penalties of perjury, that the facts stated herein are true. (All signatures must be in **BLACK INK**.)

Dated _____ , _____   _____
          (Month & Day)   *(Year)*   *(Exact Name of Corporation)*

          _____
          (Any Authorized Officer's Signature)

          _____
          (Type or Print Name and Title)

In brief, the MBCA approach is that shares reacquired by a corporation automatically "bump up" the number of shares the corporation can thereafter issue unless the articles prohibit such reissue, in which case the reacquired shares are canceled by reducing the number of shares that the corporation's articles authorize it to issue.

As an alternative either to cancelling the shares and reissuing them or cancelling the shares and not reissuing them, in some states, the corporation can place the reacquired shares in its treasury. These treasury shares are viewed as authorized and issued but not outstanding. Thus, they do not carry any rights to voting or distributions but they do count in determining how close the corporation is to issuing its limit of authorized shares, and they can be sold for less than par value. The MBCA has eliminated the concept of treasury shares and merely provides that a corporation can acquire its own shares, which then automatically constitute authorized but unissued shares. MBCA § 6.31(a). Many states have similar provisions.

Other Rights.   Just as common shareholders may have preemptive rights (rights of first refusal to newly issued stock) or cumulative voting rights in elections for directors, so also may the preferred shareholders have these rights. (See Figure 10-2 for an Equity Securities Glossary and Figure 10-3 for a chart comparing common and preferred stock.)

PRACTICE TIP

For each active corporate file on which you work, create a Client Data Sheet. The sheet can be maintained in paper form and attached to the inside of the client's general file or can be maintained electronically in your computer files. The Client Data Sheet should provide all of the critical information relating to the client, including accurate corporate name, date and state of incorporation, and a full description of its stock. The number of authorized shares should be noted as well as identification of the classes of stock. If preferred stock has been issued, list its rights (for example, whether dividends are cumulative, whether the stock carries conversion rights, and so forth). The Client Data Sheet will be an invaluable resource. Nearly all contracts and transactions to which the corporate client is a party must give this information. Thus, maintaining it in one specific file will allow you to retrieve this critical data efficiently.

Series of Stock.   Stock of a corporation can be issued in various classes, for example, common and preferred. If more than one class of stock is issued, the terms, preferences, limitations, and rights of each class must be stated in the articles of incorporation and summarized on the stock certificates (or the certificates must indicate that the terms, preferences, limitations, and rights will be provided by the corporation without charge upon written request).

If only one class of stock is authorized, that class will be common stock and no description of the shares is required, it being understood that these common shares have full voting rights and full rights to share the net assets upon liquidation. If, after incorporation, the corporation wishes to create another class of stock, it

FIGURE 10-2
Equity Securities Glossary

Authorized Shares   Shares authorized for issuance in the corporation's articles of incorporation

Common Stock   Shares of a corporation that have rights to vote, receive distributions (if declared by directors of a solvent corporation), and receive a proportionate share of net assets upon liquidation of the corporation

Convertible Preferred Stock   Preferred stock that can be converted or changed into other stock of the corporation, usually common stock

Cumulative Preferred Stock   Preferred stock of the corporation that has a built-in dividend that, if not paid due to the corporation's financial status, will cumulate until it can be paid and that will be paid prior to distributions to common shareholders

Equity Securities   Ownership interests in a corporation

Issued Shares   Shares sold to shareholders

No Par Value Shares   Shares without a stated minimum face value that can be issued for a price set by the board of directors

Outstanding Shares   Shares held by shareholders that are authorized and issued

Participating Preferred Stock   Preferred stock whose owners are entitled to receive dividends for preferred shareholders and then also share or participate in dividends after their distribution to common shareholders

Par Value   The lowest amount for which a share of stock can be sold; the nominal or face value assigned to a security

Par Value Shares   Shares that cannot be sold for less than the minimum amount set forth in the articles of incorporation

Preferred Stock   Shares of a corporation that have some right, privilege, limitation, or preference over other shares of the corporation, usually as to dividends or receipt of net assets upon liquidation

Redeemable Preferred Stock   Preferred stock that can be required to be resold to the corporation, either upon the corporation's call for such, or upon the shareholder's demand (or put)

Sinking Fund   A reserve account dedicated to redemption of stock (or retiring of bonds)

Stock/Shares   Units into which the proprietary interests in the corporation are divided

Treasury Shares   Shares reacquired by the corporation, usually by redemption, which are viewed as authorized and issued, but not outstanding

Watered Stock   Shares issued for less than par value

must amend its articles, an expensive and time-consuming process that requires shareholder approval and public filings and hinders and delays a corporation needing to raise capital promptly.

To avoid the necessity of amending the articles, the board of directors can create a new class or series of shares if the authority to do so is provided in the articles of incorporation. MBCA § 6.02 allows the board of directors to issue

FIGURE 10-3
Comparison of Common and Preferred Stock

	Common Stock	*Preferred Stock*
Voting Rights	Usually one vote per share	Voting rights may or may not exist; articles will specify.
Distribution Rights	No right to distributions; distributions declared in discretion of board and corporation must be solvent	Distributions are usually "guaranteed" and may be cumulative, meaning that if profits do not permit a distribution or corporation is insolvent, the right to distribution carries over until the corporation can pay it. Shareholders may have participating preferred stock, meaning that they receive regularly declared dividends in addition to their cumulative or noncumulative distribution.
Liquidation Rights	Shareholders receive assets after distribution to creditors and then to preferred shareholders	Shareholders receive assets after creditors and before common shareholders; distribution may be guaranteed or specified in articles.
Conversion Rights	No conversion rights	Shareholders may have right to convert their preferred shares into some other type of shares (usually common).
Redemption Rights	No redemption rights	Shareholders may be forced to sell their stock back to corporation or to compel corporation to purchase their stock at agreed-on price.

shares that vary from other shares *within the same class* if the board determines the rights, preferences, and limitations on such stock prior to actual issuance. This approach also allows the directors to tailor stock to suit then-prevailing market conditions quickly without requiring shareholder approval. Thus, corporations might have more than one class of shares, and, in turn, each class can be further divided into one or more series.

Each group of stock within a series will have rights and preferences different from each other group in the series. Similarly, each class of stock will have rights and preferences different from other classes. There is little substantive difference between shares issued in classes (common and preferred) and shares issued in series (Series A, Series B, and Series C) except that the rights of the classes must be set forth in the articles (or the articles must be amended to set forth the specific rights and preferences of each class), whereas stock can be issued in a series within a class without the necessity of amending the articles or obtaining shareholder approval, so long as the articles preauthorize the issuance of the series stock. For this reason, the allowance of **series stock** by the articles of incorporation is sometimes referred to as a "blank check" given to the directors permitting them to establish a series and to fix its rights and preferences. The stock is then referred to as *blank check stock*. Although the articles need not be amended to allow the creation of a series, prior to actual issuance of the stock the directors must file a statement with the secretary of state containing basic information about the new series, such as its rights, limitations, and preferences. No shareholder approval is needed for the statement, which becomes an amendment to the articles of incorporation. Some states, including Pennsylvania, provide forms on their Web sites for notifying the secretary of state of the establishment of the new class and series. Once the directors determine the relative rights of the series stock and file the statement, they may then issue the stock.

Thus, corporations may have several different classes of stock — Common A, Common B, and Common C, as well as Preferred A and Preferred B — and may create series of stock within a class — Common A, Series A and Series B — with each group having certain rights, limitations, and preferences that make it different from any other type.

In reality, the distinction between, for example, common and preferred stock and Series A and Series B stock is artificial. The use of various labels does not affect the fundamental principle that some types of stock might have rights and preferences that others do not, no matter what they are called. The key element to understanding series stock is that if the articles of incorporation preauthorize such, a corporation can, without shareholder approval, create new classes of shares or divide existing classes into one or more series to respond to current market conditions.

Share Subscriptions and Options. A **share subscription** is simply an agreement whereby a party offers to purchase stock in a corporation. These subscriptions can be entered into prior to the corporation's existence (preincorporation share subscriptions, discussed in Chapter Nine) or after incorporation. Similarly, one can become a shareholder in a corporation by acquiring stock from another.

MBCA § 6.24 provides that a corporation may issue options, rights, or warrants for the purchase of its shares (or other securities). An **option** is an agreement whereby the corporation gives a party the right to purchase a specified number of shares from the corporation at a specified price during a specified time period. Options are often given to key employees of the corporation. If the option price is fixed at $30 per share and the corporation's stock is being traded on the market for $50 per share, an option would allow its holder to purchase a specified number of the shares at $20 per share, thus giving the option holder a tremendous savings. The option holder, of course, may allow the option to expire without exercising it. A **right** is a short-term option granted to an existing shareholder, allowing the shareholder the opportunity to purchase additional shares in the future at a price set lower than the stock's current market value. A **warrant** is a long-term option, usually with an option period longer than one year. Warrants are often issued when the corporation borrows money to make the transaction more attractive to the lender. For example, when Berkshire Hathaway infused General Electric with billions of dollars of cash in late 2008, Berkshire Hathaway not only received GE preferred stock with a 10 percent dividend, but warrants to buy $3 billion in GE common stock at $22.50 per share at any time within the next five years. Just one year before the transaction, GE's stock was trading at more than $40 per share. Options and warrants are usually transferable, but they do not have

Series stock
Stock issued within one class including rights different from others and that can be issued without requiring amendment of a corporation's articles; often called *blank check stock*

Share subscription
Agreement to purchase stock

Option
Agreement by corporation granting a right to purchase shares at a specified price at a specified time

Right
A short-term option granted to an existing shareholder

Warrant
A long-term option, often longer than one year, usually granted when a corporation borrows money

voting rights or distribution rights. Some corporations publicly trade warrants on the national exchanges.

In one interesting transaction in early 2000, a start-up communications corporation bought 14.5 acres from the city of Oakland, California, for the company's new headquarters, paying $6 million in cash and awarding the city warrants for 100 shares of its stock. If the company goes public and the city exercises its warrants, the city could make a great deal of money. Stock options are more fully discussed in Chapter Eighteen.

C.   Debt Securities

1.   Introduction

In addition to issuing stock to raise capital, corporations are also empowered to borrow money. Money may be borrowed from banks or other financial institutions or from members of the public. This type of financing through borrowing is called **debt financing.** A *debt security* is the instrument that evidences the corporation's debt to another. The party who has loaned money to the corporation is called the **debt security holder.** The debt security holder is not an owner of the corporation, as is the case with a shareholder (or equity security holder), and therefore enjoys no rights of ownership such as voting rights or rights to distributions. The debt security holder is a creditor of the corporation and is entitled to be repaid the principal amount of the debt at the appropriate time and with the stated interest. Debt security holders, moreover, enjoy greater security than shareholders, inasmuch as they are entitled to be repaid the debt before any distribution of net assets can be made to any shareholders, whether preferred or common.

A corporation usually raises capital through a mix of equity financing (issuing shares) and debt financing (borrowing money). One consideration is tax consequences. Interest paid by a corporation on money it has borrowed is tax deductible, whereas dividend distributions made to its shareholders are not deductible as a corporate expense.

There are a variety of debt securities, ranging from simple unsecured promissory notes to more complex secured bonds that include a number of features to attract lenders. Corporate debt can be unsecured or secured. If a debt is **unsecured,** the creditor has no right to any corporate asset upon default by the corporation, and will simply have to sue the corporation to receive repayment of the debt. Such an unsecured obligation is often called a **debenture.** Debentures are typically long-term obligations, often with a term in excess of ten years. If debt is **secured,** the creditor will have rights to some specified corporate property (trademarks, real estate, accounts receivable) in the event of a default in payment by the corporation. Thus, the creditor enjoys the security of knowing that if the corporation does not pay its debt as promised, the creditor will be able to reach some corporate asset pledged as collateral for its promise to repay money borrowed. Such a secured obligation is often called a *bond.* Many people use the term *bond* loosely to refer to any debt owed by a corporation, whether or not secured. Bonds are often used by corporations in connection with long-term loans that are secured by corporate property.

Debt financing
Obtaining capital for corporate operations through borrowing

Debt security holder
One to whom a corporate obligation or debt is owed

Unsecured debt
Debt for which no collateral is pledged

Debenture
An unsecured debt

Secured debt
Money borrowed by a corporation backed by collateral that can be seized in the event of nonpayment (often called a *bond*)

According to dicta in one case, the terms *bond*, *debentures*, and *notes* are generally used interchangeably. *Metro. Life Ins. Co. v. RJR Nabisco*, 716 F. Supp. 1504 (S.D.N.Y. 1989). The federal government and states and cities also issue bonds to raise money.

Creditors, of course, much prefer that a debt be secured. They might, however, be willing to lend money on an unsecured basis if the interest to be paid to them is higher than the standard rate. Higher interest will compensate them for the risk of making a loan unsecured by any real estate or personal property. The terms and conditions on which money is borrowed by a private corporation can vary greatly and may be fiercely negotiated by both parties. The issuance of bonds by a public company, however, is on stated, published terms, and investors either accept the terms or decide against the investment inasmuch as no negotiation is possible.

Corporations often secure money through loans from banks. The loans can be secured or unsecured. If unsecured, the bank might insist that corporate managers personally guarantee repayment of the loan. In the event the corporation does not repay the loan, the corporate managers' personal funds may be seized. If the bank loan is secured, the corporation's real estate, personal property, intellectual property (such as trademarks, copyrights, or patents), or accounts receivable (money owed to the corporation) may serve as security or collateral for the loan. In the event of a default, the collateral pledged can be seized by the lender. One type of bank loan is a **line of credit**, which is a form of preauthorized loan, up to a certain maximum amount, which the corporation can draw from on a variable basis, as its monthly capital needs fluctuate.

Line of credit
A type of preauthorized loan that a business draws against as needed

2. Unsecured Debt

Corporations can borrow money without pledging any property as collateral or security for the debt. Often, the corporation's obligation is set forth in a simple document called a promissory note, by which the corporation merely promises to repay money borrowed at a specified time and with specified interest. Figure 10-4 shows a form of unsecured promissory note.

The promissory note may be modified to include a variety of other terms, such as providing for installment payments of principal, interest, or both, or providing that in the event the debtor misses any payment, the creditor can declare the entire balance to be immediately payable. The note can also be a **demand note**, meaning that no specific time is stated for repayment and the creditor has the right to demand repayment by the corporation at any time. Some notes contain a provision referred to as a **confession of judgment**, which allows the creditor to obtain an immediate judgment in court against the debtor in the event of a default. In this case, the corporation agrees that an immediate judgment may be taken against it in the event of its default, without the necessity of a trial. Because such a provision does not allow the debtor corporation to assert any defenses as to why it has not repaid the debt, some states prohibit confessions of judgment.

Demand note
A type of promissory note, payment of which can be demanded at any time

Confession of judgment
Clause within a promissory note authorizing immediate court judgment in the event of nonpayment

In the event of a default by the corporation, the creditor will sue the corporation. The creditor will not be entitled to seize any specific corporate property upon default. If the sum remains unpaid, and the corporation liquidates, the

---

FIGURE 10-4
Unsecured Promissory Note

$20,000   January 1, 2009

For value received, the undersigned, Simmons Corp., a corporation organized and existing under the laws of the State of California, promises to pay to Paul J. Higgins at 2725 Delaney Circle, Los Angeles, California, the sum of Twenty Thousand Dollars ($20,000) with interest from January 1, 2009 until paid, at the rate of six percent (6%) per annum, all due and payable on December 31, 2012. Should suit be commenced or an attorney employed to enforce the terms of this note, Simmons Corp. agrees to pay such additional sum as the court might order reasonable as attorneys' fees. Principal and interest payable in lawful money of the United States. This note may be paid in full without any penalty charges. The undersigned hereby waives demand, presentment, and protest, and notices thereof and agrees to remain bound hereunder notwithstanding any extension, modification, or waiver by the holder of this note.

Simmons Corp.

By:_____
Title: _____

---

unsecured creditors will be paid before net assets are distributed to any shareholders but after payment of secured creditors.

3.   Secured Debt

When the corporation's obligation to repay money is secured, upon corporate default in repayment the creditor can seize some specific corporate asset that has been pledged as collateral to ensure the corporation will repay its loan. The property may be sold and the proceeds used to repay the lender or bondholder.

The document evidencing the corporation's obligation to repay is called a *bond*. It will specify the principal amount due (sometimes called the **face value**), the interest required, the date of repayment (often called the **maturity date**), and the property pledged to secure repayment of the loan. Some bonds are represented by coupons that are clipped or cut and sent by the creditor to the corporation for payment. Thus, the expression "clipping coupons" you might have heard refers to a creditor making demand on a corporation to make its periodic payments of its debt.

In some instances, the property pledged by the corporation is real estate, for example, a parcel of land. In the event of a default, the creditor has the

Face value
Principal amount owed by a debtor to a creditor as shown on debt instrument

Maturity date
The date repayment of a debt is due

right to sell the property to satisfy the debt. The document evidencing the corporation's obligations and identifying the real estate as the collateral is called a **mortgage note** or *mortgage bond*. This mortgage does not differ significantly from any other type of mortgage. For example, if an individual purchases a house for $150,000 and pays $30,000 down, the remainder of the purchase price, $120,000, must be borrowed from a bank. The bank will lend this money only on the condition that if the home buyer does not make the required monthly payments, the bank can take back, or foreclose on, the house to ensure repayment of the $120,000 borrowed by the home buyer. In a corporate scenario, the corporation will usually be obligated to keep the property in good condition, to insure it, to pay the taxes due thereon, and to keep it free and clear of other encumbrances.

Real property pledged must not be oversecured by the corporation. For example, if the corporation borrows $100,000 from Bank of America and executes a mortgage pledging a parcel of property with a value of $110,000, the corporation might be able thereafter to pledge the same real estate parcel for another loan in the amount of $10,000. Thereafter, the property cannot be subject to any other mortgages because there is not enough value in the property to satisfy any other creditor. To ensure the corporation does not oversecure or overcollateralize its property, the mortgage will be recorded with the county recorder where the real estate is located. This recordation provides potential creditors notice of previous mortgages placed on the property.

Rather than pledging real estate as collateral for repayment of a debt, the corporation can pledge personal property such as machinery, equipment, inventory, or accounts receivable. Trademarks, patents, and copyrights can also be pledged as security for a loan. As an example of such borrowing, in late 2006 Ford Motor Company pledged a variety of assets (including its manufacturing plants and certain trademarks and patents) as collateral when it borrowed $18 billion from banks, which was the first time the company had used its assets as collateral. Analysts noted that Ford had to seek some secured financing because deep losses had made other borrowing alternatives nearly impossible. When personal property forms the security for the loan, a document called a **security agreement** will be executed by the corporation. The creditor will then file a **financing statement** with the secretary of state or county recorder to provide notice of the security interest claimed in the property. (See Figure 19-2 for a copy of the Uniform Commercial Code National Financing Statement, Form UCC-1.) The financing statement will specify and itemize the specific personal property pledged by the corporation. Banks and other lenders usually conduct "UCC searches" before extending credit to ensure the borrower has not already pledged security interests in its personal property. Obtaining information about financing statements on file with the secretary of state is easily accomplished by filing a simple request for information (see Figure 10-5). In some states, the information is available online, at no cost, at the home page of the state's secretary of state. Records can usually be searched either by the debtor's or creditor's name. The corporation service companies identified in Chapter Nine also conduct nationwide UCC searches for a fee.

Mortgage note
Document by which real estate is pledged as collateral to secure payment of a debt (also called *mortgage bond*)

Security agreement
Document by which personal property is pledged as collateral to secure payment of a debt

Financing statement
Document filed with a secretary of state to provide notice of a security interest

FIGURE 10-5
UCC-11 National Information Request

INFORMATION REQUEST
FOLLOW INSTRUCTIONS (front and back) CAREFULLY

A. NAME & PHONE OF CONTACT	FILING OFFICE ACCT #

B.   RETURN TO: (Name and Address)

[   ]

[   ]

THIS SPACE FOR FILING OFFICER USE ONLY

1. DEBTOR NAME to which this request relates – insert only one debtor name (1a or 1b) – do not abbreviate or combine names

1a. ORGANIZATION NAME

1b. INDIVIDUAL LAST NAME	FIRST NAME	MIDDLE NAME	SUFFIX

2. INFORMATION OPTIONS RELATING TO UCC FILINGS AND OTHER NOTICES FILED IN FILING OFFICE THAT INCLUDE AS A DEBTOR THE NAME IDENTIFIED IN ITEM 1

☐ For 2a and 2b, **mark this box** to request a Search that is **COMPLETE** to include **lapsed and unlapsed** filings. UNLESS MARKED, SEARCH MAY BE INCOMPLETE.

2a. ☐ SEARCH RESPONSE with copies of ALL records found. ☐ Please CERTIFY all copies **(additional $5.00 fee per record)**.

2b. ☐ SEARCH RESPONSE only.

2c. ☐ COPIES ONLY. Please complete the information below, as appropriate. For UCC3 records, include the type of UCC3 and corresponding filing date.

File Number	# of copies	# of Certified copies (add'l fee applies)	File Date (use for UCC3 only)	Filing Type – Financing Statement, Cont., Term., Assign., Amend.

3. CALIFORNIA SECRETARY OF STATE'S OFFICE OFFERS THESE ADDITIONAL SEARCHING OPTIONS - (Please see instructions):

3a. ☐ SEARCH TO REFLECT – Please run the search after the filing document accompanying this request has been filed.

3b. ☐ SEARCH LIMITED TO THE FOLLOWING ADDRESS: _____

3c. ☐ SEARCH LIMITED FROM THIS DATE: _____

4. DELIVERY INSTRUCTIONS
4a. ☐ Pick Up (Only if request was originally delivered to our Public Counter)

4b. ☐ Other: _____
Specify desired method; Completed **prepaid** airbill and packaging must accompany this request, if applicable.

FILING OFFICER COPY – NATIONAL INFORMATION REQUEST (FORM UCC 11)) (Rev5/09/01)   CA Secretary of State (REV. 9/1/02)

4. Trust Indentures

If a corporation issues numerous bonds to the public at once (rather than simply executing bonds sporadically), the corporation may appoint a trustee to act on behalf of the various creditors. The trustee is usually an institutional lender or commercial bank. In the event of a default by the corporation, the trustee will represent the interests of all of the creditors in seizing the property securing the corporation's debt. The trustee's rights and responsibilities and the terms of the securities, the obligations of the corporate issuer, and the rights of creditors are set forth in an agreement called a **trust indenture.** The use of a trustee is an advantage to both the corporation and the creditor. In the event of a default, the corporation will have the advantage of dealing with only one party, the trustee, rather than with numerous creditors, and the creditors have the advantage of having a representative act for them, rather than having to pursue their claims individually. In many cases the trustee is the trust department of a bank or other financial institution.

Trust indenture
Agreement entered into when numerous bonds are issued at once, specifying corporation's and lenders' rights

In 1939, Congress passed the Trust Indenture Act (15 U.S.C. § 77aaa, et seq.) to regulate the public offering of notes, bonds, and debentures in excess of $10 million. The Act requires a corporate issuer to prepare and file a registration statement with the Securities and Exchange Commission to provide information about the proposed issuance. Additionally, trustees must be qualified and file a separate statement signifying the trustee's compliance with various eligibility and standard of conduct rules.

5. Common Features of Debt Securities

Because investors can always place their money in banks and receive interest thereon, the corporation might introduce various features or provisions in its debt securities to induce investors to loan money to the corporation rather than simply placing it in a bank account. Higher rates of interest may be offered than those paid by banks, but other features can also be offered to make the debt security attractive to an investor.

Redemption Terms. Most creditors do not want a debtor to pay off a debt prior to the stated maturity date. The profit made by a creditor is in the interest paid rather than in the repayment of the principal amount borrowed. Therefore, the corporation might include favorable **redemption terms** in the debt security and might agree not to redeem the debt security before its stated maturity date, not to redeem the debt during some specified period, or to pay a penalty or premium to the creditor if the debt is redeemed prior to its date of maturity. Generally, this prepayment penalty will decline as the loan matures. Prepayment penalties assure the lender or debt security holder that it will receive the bargained-for interest. Otherwise, if the debt was negotiated at a 5 percent rate of interest, and the interest rate later fell to 3 percent, the corporation would redeem the debt and renegotiate another loan at the then-prevailing rate of 3 percent, thereby depriving the first creditor of the interest it planned on receiving over the life of the loan. The corporation may create a sinking fund to use for purposes of redeeming or retiring debt.

Redemption terms
Terms relating to a borrower's right to pay off or redeem a debt prior to its maturity date

Conversion terms
Right of a lender to convert a debt security to an equity

Conversion Terms. Debt securities may be convertible into equity securities, or shares of the corporation. Such a feature would allow the creditor to trade in debt for shares evidencing ownership in the corporation. It might be that the corporation is doing extremely well and the debtor would love to buy stock but does not have sufficient liquid assets (cash) to do so. A right of conversion thus allows the creditor to purchase stock without using actual cash; the purchase price is funded by turning in the debenture (unsecured debt) or bond (secured debt). On the other hand, a company may want to eliminate debt to make itself stronger. For example, in March 2009, Ford Motor Company announced that bondholders could convert their bonds for a combination of both cash and stock. Ford's purpose was not only to weather weak auto sales but also to put it in a better position to seek federal aid, if needed. To induce bondholders to convert, Ford offered a cash premium as well as its previously agreed-upon conversion rate for common stock. If conversion rights are to be allowed, the bond must set forth the number of shares into which it can be converted, the procedure for conversion, and any other terms, limitations, or conditions relating to the conversion. See Figure 10-6 for a glossary detailing the types of debt securities.

Priority
Process of making one obligation senior to others

Priority and Subordination Rights. A corporation may borrow money over a period of time and the debtors will know their place in the payment line in the event the corporation defaults in repaying its debts. They may receive payment

FIGURE 10-6
Debt Securities Glossary

Bonds Debts secured by some type of collateral that can be reached by a creditor in the event a corporation defaults in repayment of its debt

Convertible Debt Security Debt security that can be converted or changed into equity security (shares) of the corporation

Debentures Debts (usually, long-term) unsecured by any collateral, which in the event of a default, must be recovered through a lawsuit by the creditor

Debt Securities Documents that evidence a corporation's debt to a party who is a creditor of the corporation and who therefore has no voting rights or rights to participate in distributions

Junk Bond Bond issued by a company that has a higher risk of default and provides higher yield

Mortgage Bonds/Notes Documents executed by a corporation pledging corporate real estate as collateral or security for repayment of a debt

Redeemable Debt Security Debt security that can be paid off or redeemed prior to its stated date of maturity

Security Agreement Document executed by a corporation pledging corporate personal property as collateral or security for repayment of a debt

Subordinated Debt Security Debt junior in order of payment to another debt having priority over it

before (or have priority over) some creditors, and may be paid after (or be **subordinate** to) others. A corporation can entice a creditor to loan it money by inserting a clause into the debenture or bond stating that the debt cannot be subordinated to any other debt. The debt security holder thus knows its debt must be paid first. Alternatively, the debenture or bond might state that the debt is subordinate to any future borrowing by the corporation. Typically, a creditor would agree to accept such a disadvantageous position only in return for favorable interest rates, redemption terms, or conversion terms.

In some instances, a creditor might be willing to lend money to a corporation only if its debt has priority over all others. This will pose problems if various debt security holders already occupy first, second, and third places in the payment line. The corporation might need to approach these debt security holders and ask them to agree to occupy second, third, and fourth places, by subordinating their debt so the corporation can secure needed financing. The debt security holders might agree to do this if it appears the corporation is struggling financially and this influx of new capital is crucial for the corporation's continued existence. The existing debt security holders might also bargain for more favorable interest rates, redemption terms, or conversion terms in return for subordinating their debts to that of the new creditor.

Note that priority and subordination only become critical to lenders when the corporation defaults in paying back its loans. So long as the corporation is current in making its loan payments, lenders are not concerned with which one of them is most senior. If the corporation defaults in making its payments, however, and lawsuits are filed or the corporation dissolves, the various priority and subordination terms in the loan agreements and bonds will determine which lenders have seniority over others.

Subordination
Process of making one obligation junior to others

Voting Rights. Some jurisdictions, including Delaware and New York, authorize the articles of incorporation to allow debt security holders to vote on certain issues, such as election of directors, amendment of the articles of incorporation, and mergers, although this is not a common approach. In Delaware, if bondholders are to vote, such must be provided for in the certificate of incorporation. If the certificate so provides, the bondholders are deemed to be stockholders for purposes of voting and inspection of records. Del. Code. Ann. tit. 8, § 221. (See Figure 10-7 for comparison of equity securities and debt securities.)

6. Junk Bonds

The term **junk bond** is used for high-yield bonds issued by companies with a high credit risk. Bonds are generally rated by various credit agencies, such as Moody's or Standard & Poor's, which assess the credit quality of bond issuers. The highest quality bonds are typically AAA, and the lowest are C. Bonds in default are classified as D. Bonds that are classified BBB or higher are referred to as investment grade and are viewed as having a low risk of default. Bonds that are rated lower than BBB have a higher rate of default and are called junk bonds.

Prior to the 1980s, few people were interested in junk bonds. In the 1980s, however, many investors realized that these bonds yielded significant returns (because their issuers were compensating investors for taking the higher risk of default with the reward of higher returns). Interest in junk bonds then surfaced among investment dealers and individuals who determined that the higher yield more than compensated for the risk of default.

Junk bonds
Bonds issued by companies having poor credit ratings

FIGURE 10-7
Comparison of Equity and Debt Securities

Equity Securities ("Stock")	*Debt Securities ("Bonds")*
Shareholder is an owner of the corporation and is entitled to vote and receive distributions, if earnings permit	Bondholder is an outside creditor of the corporation and is entitled to timely repayment of the debt
Issuance of shares produces cash for the corporation	Issuance of bonds produces cash for the corporation
Issuance of shares dilutes power of existing shareholders but costs the corporation nothing	Issuance of bonds does not dilute power of existing shareholders but bonds must be repaid
If corporation is insolvent, no distributions paid to any shareholder	Bondholder will be entitled to periodic payments of interest and principal or repayment of debt
Corporation cannot deduct distributions to shareholders (and distributions are taxed to the shareholder recipients)	Corporation can deduct interest paid to bondholders and reduce taxable income
In event of liquidation, shareholders receive assets after outside creditors/bondholders	In event of liquidation, bondholders receive assets before shareholders

---

7. A New Security: SQUARZ

SQUARZ
A novel security with a negative coupon rate

In spring 2002, Berkshire Hathaway Inc. (see Figure 10-8) introduced an entirely new type of security, called **SQUARZ.** The security had two parts. First, Berkshire issued bonds paying only 3 percent interest, due in 2007. Second, the bonds were accompanied by a warrant, which gave investors the right to buy Berkshire stock in 2007 for 15 percent more than the price in May 2002; however, investors were required to pay Berkshire 3.75 percent interest each year for the warrant. Thus, the effective interest rate for the bonds was a minus 0.75 percent. The warrants were really the same as stock options, in which investors are given a privilege to buy stock in the future at a predetermined price. In sum, Berkshire persuaded investors to pay it for the privilege of lending it money. SQUARZ were thus the first bonds where investors pay money to the issuer rather than the other way around. All outstanding SQUARZ notes were repaid in late 2007.

D. Taxation of Corporations

1. Introduction

Because a corporation is viewed as a separate person or entity created under the authority of the state, it must pay taxes just as other persons do. Corporations

FIGURE 10-8
Corporate Profile: Berkshire Hathaway Inc.

One of the more interesting corporate stories of the last generation is that of Berkshire Hathaway Inc. and its Chief Executive Officer and Chairman of the Board of Directors, Warren Buffett. Berkshire is a holding company that owns subsidiaries in a wide variety of business activities, including GEICO Corporation (the sixth largest auto insurer in the United States), Benjamin Moore Paint, International Dairy Queen, and See's Candies. Berkshire also owns significant portions of stock in Coca-Cola Company (8 percent), American Express Company (13 percent), and Carmax Inc. (10 percent).

When Buffett took over the helm of Berkshire in 1964, its stock was selling at $19 per share. Its price as of mid-2008 was approximately $128,000 per share, and Berkshire Hathaway has had an annual growth rate of about 20 percent. A $10,000 investment in Berkshire Hathaway on the day Buffett took control was valued at about $50 million in early 2005. Buffett's share in the company is worth more than $60 billion, making him the richest man in the world. In 2006, Buffett announced he would begin giving away 85 percent of his Berkshire holdings to various charitable foundations.

Berkshire has two classes of common stock designated Class A Common Stock and Class B Common Stock. Each share of Class A Common Stock is convertible (at the election or option of its holder) into 30 shares of Class B Common Stock. Berkshire had approximately 4,600 record holders of its Class A Common Stock and 13,900 holders of its Class B Common Stock as of early 2008.

At its annual meetings in Omaha, Nebraska (referred to as the Woodstock of Capitalism), about 10,000 shareholders show up (a record percentage of attendance for a shareholders' meeting). The weekend typically begins with a movie and includes shopping for products of many of Berkshire's companies and several hours of instruction and teaching by the 77-year-old Buffett. Berkshire has not declared a cash dividend since 1967, and Buffett wouldn't consider splitting the stock. In fact, his birthday greetings to friends state, "May you live until Berkshire splits." Buffett has further stated that he has never sold a share of Berkshire stock and has no intention of doing so. The company's annual report to shareholders is personally written by Buffett and is in sharp contrast to the annual reports of many publicly traded companies in that it is highly readable and provides a wealth of easy-to-understand and candid information about the company. Buffett stated frankly in the 2008 annual letter to shareholders that they should be prepared for lower insurance earnings in the next few years because the "party was over." In reviewing both successes and failures, Buffett candidly stated that the purchase of Dexter (a shoe business) was "the worst deal" that he'd ever made, and noted, "but I'll make more mistakes in the future—you can bet on that."

It is hard to imagine any other corporate CEO making such statements. Berkshire's annual reports are posted on its Web site at www.berkshirehathaway.com and provide a lively and entertaining look at a highly unusual publicly traded company.

are subject to federal taxation and may be subject to state and local taxation as well. The taxation of a corporation is accomplished by corporate tax rates different from those for natural persons. The taxation of a corporation is a significant feature of corporate existence and distinguishes the corporation from other forms of business enterprise (sole proprietorships, general partnerships, limited partnerships, limited liability partnerships, limited liability companies, and joint ventures) in which enterprises money earned is simply passed through to the individuals involved, who pay tax at the rate established by the Internal Revenue Code for individuals (unless they elect to be taxed as corporations under the Internal Revenue Code "check the box" approach).

When a corporation files its first federal tax return, it selects its method of accounting. If the corporation later wishes to change its method of accounting, it must obtain IRS approval. As discussed briefly in Chapter Three, under the *cash method* of accounting, one includes all items of income received during the year in calculating gross income for that year, and one deducts expenses in the year in which the expenses are actually paid. Most individuals and many small businesses with no inventory use the cash method of accounting. Under the *accrual method* of accounting, income is reported in the year that it is earned (regardless of when it is actually received), and expenses are deducted in the year they are incurred (regardless of when they are actually paid).

Until 2004, some corporations avoided U.S. taxes by "repatriating" or reincorporating overseas, especially in Bermuda or the Cayman Islands. Congress finally closed this tax loophole with the American Jobs Creation Act of 2004, signed into law in late 2004.

2. *Double Taxation*

Double taxation
Taxation of corporate income at two levels, once when received by corporation and then again when distributed to shareholders

As described in Chapter Eight, corporations are subject to **double taxation.** Corporations pay tax at specified corporate tax rates on income; then when net profits are distributed to shareholders, the shareholders pay income tax on distributions received at their applicable individual tax rates. In mid-2003, however, Congress reduced taxes on dividends to 15 percent (5 percent for the lowest two tax brackets) and agreed to eliminate taxes entirely on dividends in 2008 for the lowest two brackets. These dividend tax reductions will expire in 2010. Figure 10-9 displays the most current available tax rates for individuals and corporations. Figure 10-10 shows Internal Revenue Service Form 1120, the U.S. Corporation Income Tax Return, which must be filed by all corporations. S corporations file Form 1120S.

Subsidiary corporations (those formed by other corporations, called parents) are subject to triple taxation: The subsidiary pays tax on the income it earns; it then distributes that income to its parent as a distribution. The parent pays tax on the distribution it has received, then distributes dividends to its shareholders, who pay taxes on the distributions they received from the parent.

Statistics show that corporate profits subject to tax have steadily risen in the past years, as have dividends paid on common stock. See *Statistical Abstract of the United States* 506 (128th ed. 2009). The following table shows corporate profits and dividends in billions of dollars. Clearly, increased corporate revenue leads to increased revenue for federal and state governments. When the profits are passed

FIGURE 10-9
Federal Taxation (2008)

Taxable Income
(Taxpayer Filing Singly)

Taxable Income		Tax		
Over	*But not over*	*Tax*	*+%*	*On amount over*
$ 0	$ 8,025	$ 0.00	10	$ 0
8,025	32,550	802.50	15	8,025
32,550	78,850	4,481.25	25	32,550
78,850	164,550	16,056.25	28	78,850
164,550	357,700	40,052.25	33	164,550
357,700		103,791.75	35	357,700

Taxable Income
(Married Taxpayers Filing Jointly)

Taxable income				
Over	*But not over*	*Tax*	*+%*	*On amount over*
$ 0	$ 16,050	$ 0.00	10	$ 0
16,050	65,100	1,605.00	15	16,050
65,100	131,450	8,962.50	25	65,100
131,450	200,300	25,550.00	28	131,450
200,300	357,700	44,828.00	33	200,300
357,700		96,770.00	35	357,700

Taxable Income for Corporations

Taxable income			
Over	*But not over*	*Tax is*	*Of the amount over*
$0	$50,000	15%	$0
$50,000	$75,000	$7,500 + 25%	$50,000
$75,000	$100,000	$13,750 + 34%	$75,000
$100,000	$335,000	$22,250 + 39%	$100,000
$335,000	$10,000,000	$113,900 + 34%	$335,000
$10,000,000	$15,000,000	$3,400,000 + 35%	$10,000,000
$15,000,000	$18,333,333	$5,150,000 + 38%	$15,000,000
$18,333,333	—	35%	$0

FIGURE 10-10
IRS Form 1120

Form 1120 — U.S. Corporation Income Tax Return (2008)

OMB No. 1545-0123

Department of the Treasury, Internal Revenue Service. For calendar year 2008 or tax year beginning _____, 2008, ending _____, 20 ____ ► See separate instructions.

A Check if:
- 1a Consolidated return (attach Form 851)
- b Life/nonlife consolidated return
- 2 Personal holding co. (attach Sch. PH)
- 3 Personal service corp. (see instructions)
- 4 Schedule M-3 attached

Use IRS label. Otherwise, print or type.

Name
Number, street, and room or suite no. If a P.O. box, see instructions.
City or town, state, and ZIP code

B Employer identification number
C Date incorporated
D Total assets (see instructions) $

E Check if: (1) Initial return (2) Final return (3) Name change (4) Address change

Income
#	Description		Amount
1a	Gross receipts or sales	b Less returns and allowances	c Bal ► 1c
2	Cost of goods sold (Schedule A, line 8)		2
3	Gross profit. Subtract line 2 from line 1c		3
4	Dividends (Schedule C, line 19)		4
5	Interest		5
6	Gross rents		6
7	Gross royalties		7
8	Capital gain net income (attach Schedule D (Form 1120))		8
9	Net gain or (loss) from Form 4797, Part II, line 17 (attach Form 4797)		9
10	Other income (see instructions—attach schedule)		10
11	**Total income.** Add lines 3 through 10	►	11

Deductions (See instructions for limitations on deductions.)
#	Description	Amount
12	Compensation of officers (Schedule E, line 4) ►	12
13	Salaries and wages (less employment credits)	13
14	Repairs and maintenance	14
15	Bad debts	15
16	Rents	16
17	Taxes and licenses	17
18	Interest	18
19	Charitable contributions	19
20	Depreciation from Form 4562 not claimed on Schedule A or elsewhere on return (attach Form 4562)	20
21	Depletion	21
22	Advertising	22
23	Pension, profit-sharing, etc., plans	23
24	Employee benefit programs	24
25	Domestic production activities deduction (attach Form 8903)	25
26	Other deductions (attach schedule)	26
27	**Total deductions.** Add lines 12 through 26 ►	27
28	Taxable income before net operating loss deduction and special deductions. Subtract line 27 from line 11	28
29	**Less:** a Net operating loss deduction (see instructions) 29a	
	b Special deductions (Schedule C, line 20) 29b	29c

Tax, Refundable Credits, and Payments
#	Description	Amount
30	**Taxable income.** Subtract line 29c from line 28 (see instructions)	30
31	**Total tax** (Schedule J, line 10)	31
32a	2007 overpayment credited to 2008 32a	
b	2008 estimated tax payments 32b	
c	2008 refund applied for on Form 4466 32c ( ) d Bal ► 32d	
e	Tax deposited with Form 7004 32e	
f	Credits: (1) Form 2439 (2) Form 4136 32f	
g	Refundable credits from Form 3800, line 19c, and Form 8827, line 8c 32g	32h
33	Estimated tax penalty (see instructions). Check if Form 2220 is attached ►	33
34	**Amount owed.** If line 32h is smaller than the total of lines 31 and 33, enter amount owed	34
35	**Overpayment.** If line 32h is larger than the total of lines 31 and 33, enter amount overpaid	35
36	Enter amount from line 35 you want: **Credited to 2009 estimated tax ►** Refunded ►	36

Sign Here Under penalties of perjury, I declare that I have examined this return, including accompanying schedules and statements, and to the best of my knowledge and belief, it is true, correct, and complete. Declaration of preparer (other than taxpayer) is based on all information of which preparer has any knowledge.

Signature of officer / Date / Title

May the IRS discuss this return with the preparer shown below (see instructions)? Yes No

Paid Preparer's Use Only
Preparer's signature / Date / Check if self-employed / Preparer's SSN or PTIN
Firm's name (or yours if self-employed), address, and ZIP code / EIN / Phone no.

For Privacy Act and Paperwork Reduction Act Notice, see separate instructions. Cat. No. 11450Q Form **1120** (2008)

along to the shareholders in the form of cash dividends, which they also pay tax on, federal and state government revenues increase again.

	1990	2000	2007
Corporate Profits	$438	$818	$1,595
Net Dividends	$169	$378	$795

Until the late 1980s, some relief against double taxation was provided for dividends received by small-time corporate shareholders: The first $100 received by a shareholder (or $200 if married shareholders filed jointly), was excluded from taxation. The current tax scheme, however, requires individuals to report dividends even if only 51 cents are received in any tax year. Corporations are, however, entitled to deductions for various expenses, such as rent, salaries, interest, contributions to employee benefit plans, group life insurance, and other employee benefits. Corporations are also free to elect their own tax year, which need not be a calendar year but may rather be responsive to the particular seasonal needs of a corporation. Moreover, some relief is provided by the fact that shareholders pay taxes only on distributions actually received by them. If shareholders receive share dividends rather than cash or property as a form of distribution, they need not pay tax on the shares upon receipt but rather when the share is later sold. (See discussion in Chapter Twelve.)

Just as the tax rate for individuals is graduated, the tax rate for corporations is graduated as well. This means that the corporation does not simply calculate its income and plug this entire number into a chart. Rather, the first $50,000 is subject to tax at the rate of 15 percent, the next $25,000 is subject to tax at the rate of 25 percent plus a certain dollar amount, and so forth.

Large publicly held corporations simply accept double taxation as a cost of doing business. Smaller corporations, however, may minimize double taxation through the use of various means, such as S corporation status (in which all income earned by the corporation is passed through to the fewer than 100 shareholders who pay at their individual rates) or small or close corporations (in which the shareholders receive bonuses or salary increases that, although they may be taxable to the shareholder, are deductible to the corporation as expenses). Additional ways by which corporations avoid or reduce the effects of double taxation are discussed in Chapter Eight.

Similarly, the corporation can elect to obtain funds through debt financing rather than equity financing because interest paid to creditors is a deductible corporate expense. To ensure the corporation does not encumber itself by issuing only debt securities, the Internal Revenue Service has devised the theory of **thin incorporation.** This doctrine discourages the corporation from issuing too many debt securities. If debt is deemed excessive by the Internal Revenue Service, meaning the corporation has a high "debt to equity ratio," the Internal Revenue Service may characterize interest payments on debts as dividends on equity securities, which are then nondeductible to the corporation and subject to taxes, which must be paid by the recipient. A number of authorities and cases suggest that the debt to equity ratio not exceed 4:1 or perhaps even 3:1.

As discussed briefly in Chapter Eight and more thoroughly in Chapter Seventeen, a corporation can elect status as an S corporation to alleviate the burdens of

Thin incorporation
A corporation whose debts are disproportionately high to its equity

double taxation. S corporation status, however, is restricted to corporations with 100 or fewer individual shareholders, who cannot be nonresident aliens. Due to the increasingly global nature of our economy, S corporation election may be replaced by adoption of the new limited liability company business structure, which has no maximum number of members (and who may be foreign nationals) and retains limited liability for those members, yet has the pass-through tax status of a partnership (see Chapter Six).

3.   Accumulated Earnings Tax

To discourage corporations from simply holding on to profits and not distributing them (thereby reducing the impact of double taxation), the Internal Revenue Service has also devised certain penalties that give corporations a strong incentive to distribute profits to shareholders rather than hoarding them. The Internal Revenue Service, of course, wishes to see corporate profits distributed to shareholders so that the shareholders will pay taxes on distributions received. According to Internal Revenue Code §§ 531-535 (26 U.S.C. §§ 531-535), C corporations that accumulate earnings beyond the reasonable needs of the business to avoid having shareholders pay income taxes on earnings that should have been distributed to the shareholders are subject to an **accumulated earnings tax** in the current amount of 15 percent of the accumulated taxable amount in excess of $250,000, although certain credits and adjustments are allowed. By imposing this penalty on corporations that retain earnings, the IRS provides incentives to corporations to distribute income. A corporation can accumulate earnings beyond the limit of $250,000 (without paying the tax penalty) if it can prove that it has a valid business reason to do so, such as a need to retain money to expand its business operations or facilities.

Accumulated earnings tax
Tax penalty imposed on corporations that retain earnings beyond reasonable business needs

4.   Alternative Minimum Tax

A corporation might also be subject to the **alternative minimum tax**, an extra tax required in addition to the "regular" income tax the corporation will be required to pay. In essence, the alternative minimum tax rules set a minimum threshold amount for taxes. If the corporation is paying this minimum amount of taxes, it need not pay the alternative minimum tax. If the regular tax liability is less than the minimum threshold amount, then the corporation must make up the difference by paying the alternative minimum tax. See IRS Form 4626 and its instructions on calculating the alternative minimum tax.

Alternative minimum tax
Tax penalty imposed on corporations to ensure that a certain minimum threshold amount of tax is paid

The alternative minimum tax does not apply to small corporations. A corporation is treated as a small corporation for its first tax year (regardless of gross receipts for the year). Additionally, a corporation is exempt from the alternative minimum tax if its average annual gross receipts for the three-year period before 2007 do not exceed $7.5 million (or $5 million, if the corporation had only one tax year). A corporation will continue to be exempt from the alternative minimum tax so long as its average annual gross receipts for the prior three years do not exceed $7.5 million.

The alternative minimum tax also applies to individuals. In fact, according to the IRS, fewer than 20,000 individuals paid the alternative minimum tax in 1970, but more than 2 million were subject to it in 2003. Some experts predict that if not overhauled, the alternative minimum tax will penalize 30 percent of all taxpayers by 2010. On several occasions since 2001 Congress has attempted to remedy the problem by enacting fixes to the alternative minimum tax, including the most recent patch included in President Obama's stimulus package passed in early 2009.

Although corporations are subject to several taxes and tax penalties, the U.S. Government Accountability Office has estimated that about two-thirds of corporations operating in the United States did not pay any taxes between 1998 and 2005. The most common reasons given for the absence of taxable revenue were the costs of salaries and interest payments and the cost of producing their goods.

5. *State and Other Taxes*

With regard to state income taxes, the general rule is that corporations transacting business within any state are subject to that state's income tax, if any. Corporations may also be subject to local taxes or franchise taxes imposed by the state merely as a condition for being permitted to do business there. Some states assess tax based on the revenue generated in the state or on the value of the corporation's assets located in the state. Several states impose a flat tax rate — such as Oklahoma, which imposes a tax rate of 6 percent on corporate income. All states except Nevada, South Dakota, Washington, and Wyoming impose a tax on corporate net income. Delaware does not impose state income tax on corporations unless they are engaged in business in Delaware.

Additionally, many states impose a special tax on corporations merely for the privilege of being incorporated or authorized to do business in the state. Usually called a **franchise tax**, the tax may be a flat fee for all corporations or may be based on annual income.

A variety of other taxes are imposed by federal law. For example, corporations that have employees must withhold federal income tax from their employees' wages. Moreover, the Federal Insurance Contributions Act (FICA, usually referred to as *Social Security*) requires both employers and employees to contribute a stated percentage of wages paid to fund social security, disability, and other benefits for workers. The employee's portion must be withheld by the employer. Additionally, if a corporation employs individuals in states with state income tax, the employer must withhold from employees' wages an appropriate amount to satisfy such state income taxes.

Corporations may also be subject to property and sales taxes. Corporations are required to pay property taxes on real property owned by them and might be required to pay taxes on various items of personal property, such as vehicles. If the corporation sells goods, consumers will actually pay the sales tax but the corporation must collect and remit it to the taxing authorities. Thus, corporations are subject to a dizzying array of taxes.

Franchise tax
Tax paid by corporation for privilege of being a corporate entity

---

Key Features
of Corporate Finances

◆ To raise money, corporations will issue stock (equity securities), which shows ownership interest in the corporation, or bonds (debt securities), which are loans to the corporation.

◆ Shares issued by a corporation must be authorized by the articles.

◆ The par value of a share is the nominal face value of the share and is the lowest price for which it can be sold.

◆ If stock has no par value, it can be sold for whatever amount the directors determine is in the best interest of the corporation.

◆ Corporations may have more than one class of stock.

◆ Common stock is ordinary stock of the corporation and usually has voting rights, distribution rights, and liquidation rights (distribution and liquidation rights are exercised after preferred stockholders exercise their rights).

◆ Preferred stock has some sort of right or preference other classes do not have, often as to cumulating dividends, conversion (changing preferred stock to common stock), or redemption (acquisition of the stock by the corporation, either at the corporation's demand (a "call") or the shareholder's demand (a "put").

◆ Debt securities may be unsecured, in which case, in the event of a default, the creditor simply sues to recover the amount lent to the corporation.

◆ Debt securities may be secured by real estate (a "mortgage bond" or "note") or personal property (a "security agreement"); in the event of a default the creditor can recover the property pledged as security or collateral.

◆ Debt securities may have favorable redemption terms (so the corporation does not pay off the debt early) or conversion terms (so they can be converted into equity securities or shares).

◆ Corporations are said to be subject to "double taxation": The corporation pays tax on money it receives, and shareholders then pay tax on distributions made to them. Interest paid on bonds is a deductible expense for a corporation.

E. Role of Paralegal

Although advice given to corporations regarding the relative advantages and disadvantages of issuing equity securities and debt securities (and the taxation thereof) is the purview of the attorney advising the client, there are a number of activities in which the paralegal will be involved.

Any issuance of stock (including conversion of preferred stock for common stock or conversion of debt securities to equity securities) must be authorized by the articles of incorporation. The paralegal will monitor the issuance of stock to ensure an appropriate number of shares are authorized to accommodate any such transaction. If the authorized number of shares is not sufficient to permit such conversion, the paralegal will need to prepare the appropriate documents to call a shareholders' meeting and amend the articles of incorporation accordingly.

The paralegal will prepare notices of the shareholders' meeting to permit the corporation to amend its articles to allow for the issuance of different classes of shares. Articles of amendment must also be prepared and filed with the secretary of state.

If different series of shares are authorized by the articles, the paralegal will prepare the requisite statement to be submitted to the secretary of state.

The paralegal can assist the corporation in its bookkeeping activities to ensure interest payments are timely made, funds are accumulated for the sinking fund, and share certificates contain the appropriate information regarding preferences and limitations of different classes of stock.

The paralegal can assist the corporation in preparing notices of redemption of stock and notices of redemption of bonds.

Case Illustration
Rights of Preferred Shareholders Are Subordinate to Creditors

Case:	*Warren v. King*, 108 U.S. 389 (1883)
Facts:	Preferred shareholders claimed that they were entitled to have their shares of stock declared to be a lien on the property of the company.
Holding:	Holders of preferred stock occupy a position inferior to all creditors. They have no claim on the property of the company superior to that of creditors who became creditors subsequent to issuance of the preferred stock. They are not preferred as to any but the holders of common stock, and their rights must be determined by the language of the stock certificate.

WEB RESOURCES

The most important Web resources are state and federal statutes relating to issuance of stock and taxation of corporations.

State statutes:	www.law.cornell.edu www.findlaw.com
State forms and information:	www.nass.org (access to forms, fees, and online UCC searching in many states)
Securities and Exchange Commission:	www.sec.gov (The SEC provides access to documents filed by public companies. Select "Search for Company Filings" and then "Companies & Other Filers." Enter a company's name into the search box. Annual reports, called 10-Ks, provide a wealth of information about a company.)
Tax forms, rates, and publications:	www.irs.gov
Company information:	www.hoovers.com
General information:	www.megalaw.com www.money.com
Forms:	www.ilrg.com (form for promissory note) www.siccode.com/forms.php (forms for promissory notes, guarantees, and a security agreement)
Glossary of financial terms:	www.investorwords.com www.investopedia.com (Site also offers information on stocks and bonds and tutorials on financial issues.)

Discussion Questions

Fact Scenario. H & A Inc. is a California corporation authorized to issue 500,000 shares of common stock and 20,000 shares of preferred stock, which preferred shares have the right to cumulative dividends. The articles of incorporation authorize the creation of series stock.

1. The corporation has not issued any dividends for three years. This year the corporation will issue a dividend. Describe the rights of Peter, a preferred shareholder, and the rights of Carrie, a common shareholder.

2. Identify one advantage and one disadvantage to corporations of issuing stock and of issuing bonds.

3. Discuss three features that the corporation could introduce into its bonds to induce investors to purchase the bonds.

4. The corporation is holding its annual meeting to elect its directors. What are the rights of Peter, Carrie, and Bill (a bondholder)?

5. Peter has conversion rights. What advantage does this afford him?

6. Why would Bill prefer that the corporation not redeem his bond prior to its maturity date?

7. The corporation has not distributed any dividends in three years because it has been setting aside $400,000 that it plans to use to expand its business operations in the Western states. Is there any risk to the corporation in adopting this strategy?

Net Worth

1. Access the Web site for the SEC and review the Form 10-K for the Washington Post filed on February 28, 2008. Review the cover sheet.
   a. How many shares of Class A common stock were outstanding?
   b. How many shares of Class B common stock were outstanding?
2. Access the Web site for Berkshire Hathaway, Inc. and locate the proxy statement for the 2008 annual shareholders' meeting.
   a. Where was the meeting held?
   b. How many votes do shares of Class A stock carry?
   c. How may votes do shares of Class B stock carry?
3. Access the Web site for Investorwords. What is the definition of a debenture?
4. Access the UCC search database for New York. Conduct a UCC search on Orville Blythe. When was the UCC statement filed? When will it expire or lapse? Who is the secured party?

11

♦ ♦ ♦

Corporate Management

♦ ♦ ♦

CHAPTER OVERVIEW

A corporation is owned by its shareholders. Although they own the corporation, however, shareholders play little, if any, role in the day-to-day operation of a large corporation. Shareholders' activities are generally limited to electing and removing directors and to taking part in extraordinary corporate actions, such as amendment of the articles of incorporation and other fundamental changes to the corporate structure, including approval of mergers and dissolutions. These limited activities take the form of voting at shareholders' meetings.

Additionally, shareholders have limited liability. Although their stock might decline in value, they are not liable for debts and obligations of the corporation. One exception to this rule of limited liability exists when shareholders do not respect the corporate entity and commingle its funds with theirs or fail to follow corporate formalities, such as failing to hold elections, meetings, and so forth. In such cases, it is said that the veil of limited liability will be "pierced" to prevent fraud and injustice by holding shareholders liable for corporate debts and obligations.

A corporation is governed by its directors functioning as a board. The directors have

responsibility for all policymaking decisions required for operation of the corporation. The board of directors is elected by the shareholders. The directors have fiduciary duties to the shareholders and to the corporation. The directors are not guarantors of a corporation's success, however, and are usually required to act with reasonable diligence as a similar person would exercise in similar circumstances. They can be personally liable if injury to the corporation is a result of their breach of duty. Directors also have a duty of loyalty to the corporation. They cannot engage in competitive activities or, without full disclosure, personally gain from a corporate transaction.

A corporation's officers are appointed and removed by the board. The most commonly seen officers are president, vice president, secretary, and treasurer. The board of directors delegates power and authority to the officers to execute the policies determined by the board. Like directors, officers are also fiduciaries and are subject to the same standard of conduct as directors.

This chapter addresses the three groups of people involved in corporate management and governance: shareholders, directors, and officers.

A. Shareholders' Rights and Responsibilities

1. Introduction

Shareholder
An owner of a corporation; also called *stockholder*

The owners of a corporation are called **shareholders** (or *stockholders*, a synonymous term). Not all shareholders are individuals. In fact, it is becoming increasingly common for ownership in major corporations to be held by institutions such as banks, trusts, mutual funds, and insurance companies. For example, as discussed in Chapter Ten, 8 percent of the stock of Coca-Cola Company is held by Berkshire Hathaway, Inc.

Although they own the corporation, shareholders do not own any specific corporate assets such as cars, real estate, or trademarks. Moreover, these owners do not manage the enterprise they own. The business of a corporation is managed by the officers acting on the board's instructions and subject to its oversight. Shareholder participation in management is somewhat indirect and generally takes the form of voting. Shareholders do not vote on day-to-day activities but rather are restricted to voting to elect directors and on fundamental changes to the corporation, including amendment of the articles of incorporation, mergers, dissolutions, and other similar structural changes to the corporation. These rights to vote take place at two types of meetings: annual and special. Alternatively, in most states, shareholders are allowed to take action without a meeting if they unanimously consent in writing to the action to be taken. Such unanimous written consent is impracticable for all but the smallest corporations. Shareholders' rights, responsibilities, liabilities, and duties are governed by state statutes, the articles of incorporation, and the bylaws.

In small corporations, such as family-owned businesses, in which the shareholders are also directors and officers of the corporation, shareholders play a more active role in corporate management, acting in their capacities as directors and officers. In larger corporations, which are generally the focus of this chapter, shareholder involvement is indirect and is often limited exclusively to voting.

2. Rights to Information

Shareholders have the right to be informed of the affairs of the corporation. At common law, their right to inspect records and books, including the list of shareholders, bylaws, minutes of meetings, and so forth, was qualified by the requirement that the inspection be in good faith. Examples of bad faith or improper purposes were examination of the list of shareholders for personal business reasons (such as to solicit customers for the shareholder's own business), appropriation of trade secrets to sell to competitors, or pursuing political goals. Most states have enacted statutes specifically authorizing inspection of books and records by shareholders (or their agents or attorneys). Some of these statutes (including the MBCA) provide an absolute right to inspect most records, such as articles, bylaws, and minutes of shareholders' meetings. Inspection of other records (such as minutes of directors' meetings) must be for a "proper purpose." MBCA § 16.02. Nevertheless, if a shareholder secures information and uses it to injure the corporation, the corporation may be entitled to damages. Many statutes provide that a shareholder may inspect corporate books and records so long as the inspection is for a purpose "reasonably related" to one's interest as a shareholder. Other states allow inspection of the list of shareholders for any reason whatsoever, while inspection of accounting records and minutes of directors' meetings is subject to the requirement that it be done in good faith. Still other states impose a waiting period on the shareholders. Inspection may not be permitted unless the shareholder owns a specified number of shares (often 5 percent) or has owned shares for a specified period of time. These limitations ensure corporations are not overburdened with demands from shareholders who may only own a few shares. Generally, a proper purpose includes a desire to determine if the corporation is being managed properly or to communicate with other shareholders; an improper purpose would be one designed to harm the corporation or intended for the shareholder's personal benefit.

Although the corporation is usually free to require that the inspection be done upon prior notice and during reasonable business hours and that the shareholder pay the reasonable costs for copies of documents, the articles of incorporation cannot contravene the state statutes. If the corporation wrongfully refuses inspection, it can be subjected to monetary penalties, and a court may grant a request by a shareholder for an injunction requiring inspection.

3. Voting Rights

Shareholders exercise their limited role in the conduct and operation of the corporation primarily through voting, either for election or removal of directors or relating to some structural change in the corporation. The articles of incorporation can grant, deny, or limit voting rights. For example, one class of shares may have nonvoting stock. There are different types of voting: straight voting, cumulative voting, class voting, contingent voting, and disproportionate voting.

Straight Voting. Generally, and unless the articles of incorporation provide otherwise, each share of record is entitled to one vote for each director's position to be filled or for each issue being considered. Thus, if Andrews owns 100 shares of stock and five directors are being elected, Andrews may cast 100 votes either for or against each of the nominees. This is referred to as **straight** (or *statutory*) **voting** and is the most common type of voting exercised by shareholders. Some jurisdictions and MBCA § 6.04(c) allow fractional shares to exercise fractional voting rights. For example, due to a share dividend, a shareholder may have 100.5 shares of stock. Under straight voting, the shareholder would be entitled to 100.5 votes.

Straight voting
Voting in which each share of record has one vote (also called *statutory voting*)

Cumulative Voting. **Cumulative voting** may be provided in the articles of incorporation or mandated by a state's statutes. Cumulative voting applies *only* to the election of directors and not to any other corporate issues, such as voting for mergers, dissolutions, or amendments to the articles of incorporation. Cumulative voting is a particular type of voting designed to allow some representation of minority shareholders on the board of directors. If cumulative voting rights exist, each share is multiplied by the number of vacancies to be filled. The votes may then be cast in any manner desired by the shareholder. For example, if Andrews owns 100 shares of OmniWorld, Inc. and five directors are being elected,

Cumulative voting
Method of voting in election for directors in which each share carries as many votes as there are directors being elected

cumulative voting would allow Andrews 500 votes to cast however he likes, whereas straight voting would allow him only 100 votes for each director. Thus, under both straight and cumulative voting, Andrews has a total of 500 votes to cast. In cumulative voting, however, Andrews can cast all 500 votes for one candidate, 250 votes for each of two candidates, or any other combination. In cumulative voting, all directors stand for election at the same moment, whereas in straight voting, each director is elected one at a time. The result of cumulative voting is to give minority shareholders a chance to elect at least one director who may be responsive to their needs.

To maximize the advantage of cumulative voting, minority shareholders tend to concentrate or "dump" all their votes on one candidate rather than spread the votes among the board and thereby dilute the impact of cumulative voting. For example, assume OmniWorld, Inc. has 1,000 shares outstanding. Its articles provide for cumulative voting. Further assume that the minority shareholders, Andrews and Baker, together own 400 shares, and the majority shareholders, Carter, Dowell, and Edwards together own 600 shares. Three directors are being elected. The candidates are Taylor, Tyler, and Tuttle (candidates the majority shareholders would like to see elected), and O'Brien, whom the minority shareholders would like to elect. If straight voting exists, the majority shareholders will always be able to elect the directors. Under cumulative voting, the minority shareholders, Andrews and Baker, can elect one person to the board who they hope will represent their interests. If voting cumulatively, Andrews and Baker will have 1,200 shares to vote (400 shares multiplied by three vacancies to be filled). The majority shareholders will have 1,800 shares to vote (600 shares multiplied by three vacancies to be filled). If Andrews and Baker dump all 1,200 of their votes on their candidate, O'Brien will be elected. Although the majority shareholders have 1,800 votes, these votes must be divided somehow between their three choices for candidates. No matter which way the majority shareholders divide up their votes, they will elect two directors and the minority shareholders will be able to elect O'Brien if they cast all their votes for O'Brien (see Figure 11-1). Cumulative voting generally requires cohesion and agreement among minority shareholders in order to take advantage of the benefits of cumulative voting.

In a few states, such as Arizona, cumulative voting is mandatory and cannot be denied by the articles of incorporation, the bylaws, or any other corporate

FIGURE 11-1
Cumulative Voting

Ballot	Majority Shareholders			Minority Shareholders	
	Taylor	Tyler	Tuttle	O'Brien	
1	1,300	400	100	1,200	Elected: Taylor, Tyler, & O'Brien
2	601	600	599	1,200	Elected: Taylor, Tyler, & O'Brien
3	1,500	200	100	1,200	Elected: Taylor, Tyler, & O'Brien

document, except that corporations listed on the national exchanges can eliminate cumulative voting. In most states, and according to MBCA § 7.28(b), it is permissive, meaning that the articles of incorporation may provide for cumulative voting; if not provided for in the articles of incorporation, cumulative voting does not exist. In many instances, shareholders wishing to assure election of a representative to the board will examine the shareholder voting list (often kept at the office of the registrar) to identify and locate shareholders with whom they can band together to exercise their voting power.

The impact of cumulative voting can be diluted by decreasing the number of directorships (if only one director is being elected, Andrews and Baker have a total of 400 votes rather than the 1,200 votes they would have if three directors are being elected) or by staggering the board so that not all directors are elected at the same time. The U.S. Senate is a prototypical stagger system: All senators have a term of six years yet only one-third of the group stands for election every two years. If a nine-member board is staggered or classified into three groups of three directors, rather than having 3,600 votes (400 × 9) to cast were all nine directors elected at one time, Andrews and Baker would have a total of 1,200 votes (400 × 3) because only three directors are elected every two years. Because a stagger system so severely dilutes the impact of cumulative voting, a stagger system is sometimes not permitted in states where cumulative voting is mandated by statute.

MBCA § 8.06 provides that the terms of directors may be classified or staggered by dividing the total number of directors into two or three groups, so that one-half or one-third are elected at each annual meeting. To some extent, this approach preserves cumulative voting because at least more than one director will be elected each year, affording minority shareholders the right to ensure some representation on the board.

To ensure that majority shareholders do not defeat the effect of cumulative voting by immediately removing a director elected by minority shareholders, states and corporations mandating cumulative voting usually permit removal of a director only upon cumulative voting as well. Thus, the director cannot be removed if the number of votes sufficient to elect him under cumulative voting is voted against his removal. MBCA § 8.08(c).

Class Voting.   If one or more classes or series of shares exist, classes may vote as a separate unit or block. For example, Common A and Common B shareholders may be one group or class for purposes of voting on amendment of the articles of incorporation and Common C and Common D shareholders are a group or class for voting on other issues, such as election of some or all of the directors.

Class voting
Voting by a class of stock as a separate unit

Contingent Voting.   Some shares vote only upon occurrence of a certain contingency or event. For example, the articles of incorporation might provide that Preferred A shareholders can vote for directors only in those years in which dividends are not distributed.

Contingent voting
Voting rights that exist only upon the occurrence of some event

Disproportionate Voting.   Disproportionate voting exists when one class has voting power disproportionate to that of another. For example, if Common A shareholders had two votes per share and Common B shareholders had one vote per share, disproportionate voting would exist.

Disproportionate voting
Voting rights held by a class that is disproportionate to voting rights of other classes

Nonvoting Stock. **Nonvoting stock** may be authorized and issued so long as full voting rights reside in at least one class of shares.

4. Shareholder Meetings

Shareholders have a limited right to participate in the management and operation of the corporation. Typically, this right takes the form of voting. Voting occurs at two types of shareholder meetings: annual and special.

Annual Meetings. Most state statutes require that corporations hold **annual meetings** of shareholders. MBCA § 7.01 provides that a corporation shall hold a meeting of shareholders annually. Shareholders may apply to a court to order a meeting if one has not been held within six months of the end of the corporation's fiscal year or 15 months after the last annual meeting. MBCA § 7.03. These statutes reflect the legislative policy that because shareholders are not involved in the day-to-day operation of the corporation, they must be provided with some minimum of information about the corporation.

The time and date of annual meetings is usually provided in the corporate bylaws. For example, a typical bylaw provision might specify that "annual meetings of shareholders shall be held the first Monday of May of each calendar year." The key action taken at the annual meeting is the election of directors. Other action also may be taken, such as reports of management, amendment of the articles of incorporation, or appointment of the corporation's accountants. Shareholders may submit proposals for consideration at annual meetings and may formally nominate candidates for election.

Most corporations hold their annual meetings in the spring (April, May, or June) because this allows sufficient time for corporate accounting and payment of taxes to be accomplished. In fact, so many meetings are held at this time of year that it is referred to as "proxy season." Financial reports then discussed at the meeting are current and complete. Failure to hold an annual meeting does not affect the validity of any corporate action.

Special Meetings. **Special meetings** are shareholder meetings held between annual meetings. Shareholders must have some mechanism to call meetings between the annual meetings to investigate fraud, abuse, or mismanagement. For example, if a corporation's annual meeting is in April, and the shareholders discover embezzlement in June, they should not have to wait until the next annual meeting in April to discuss this critical matter. A special meeting allows the shareholders to meet between the annual meetings to discuss and consider matters of interest. Similarly, corporate management might need to call a special meeting to discuss and vote on unanticipated matters, such as an offer to merge with another corporation.

Most state statutes provide the terms and conditions on which special meetings may be called. MBCA § 7.02 is typical of most statutes. It provides that the board of directors of a corporation may call a special meeting or that shareholders owning 10 percent or more of the outstanding stock entitled to vote at the meeting may demand in writing that the corporation call a special meeting. Additionally, any person authorized to do so in the corporation's articles of incorporation or its bylaws may call a special meeting. The demand is made upon the secretary of the corporation. In general, only such transactions as are described in the notice of the special meeting may be considered.

Place of Meetings. The bylaws may designate the location of annual or special meetings. Alternatively, and as is more common, the bylaws may provide that the directors can determine the location of meetings. If no location is specified in the bylaws, the meetings will take place at the corporation's principal office.

Some larger corporations rotate their meetings to allow shareholders across the country to attend. Thus, one year's meeting may be held in Atlanta, and the next year's meeting is held in Dallas. Older statutes required that all meetings be held in the state of incorporation. Modern statutes usually permit meetings to be held in any location, provided proper notice is given.

Notice of Meetings. All jurisdictions require that shareholders receive notice of all meetings. The pertinent state statutes must be reviewed to ensure the notice requirements are followed. Notice requirements can be very detailed and should be scrutinized carefully to avoid having a meeting declared invalid. In general, small corporations tend to act informally and will often provide notice by telephone or e-mail, if permitted by statute and the corporate bylaws. Larger corporations act in a more formal manner and provide written notices to all shareholders entitled to receive notice. Generally, either the corporate secretary or the registrar prepares and sends notices.

Shareholders Entitled to Notice. Generally, unless the articles of incorporation require otherwise, the corporation is only required to give notice to shareholders entitled to vote at a meeting. Thus, if the holders of Preferred A stock have nonvoting shares, they will not be entitled to notice of a meeting to elect directors. Generally, only issued and outstanding shares vote.

To determine the particular shareholders who will receive notice, the corporate bylaws will usually provide a **record date** (some date selected in advance of a meeting) and any persons owning shares on that record date will be entitled to notice of the meeting. Many bylaws provide that the record date will be 30 days before the meeting; any shareholders whose names are "on the books" on that date will be entitled to receive notice. These shareholders are sometimes called the *holders of record* or **record holders.** If the bylaws do not fix or provide for fixing a record date, MBCA § 7.05 states that the record date will be the day before the first notice is delivered to shareholders.

Because the record date is set in advance of the meeting, a shareholder might be entitled to receive notice and to vote even though she no longer owns any shares in the corporation at the time of the meeting. For example, assume the bylaws of Hunter Development Corp. fix the date of the annual meeting as May 1 of each year. The bylaws also provide that any person who owns shares 30 days prior to any meeting is entitled to notice of and to vote at the meeting. If Francie Hoffman owns 100 shares on April 1, she will be entitled to receive notice and to vote. If Francie sells her shares to her sister on April 4, Francie will still receive notice of the meeting and be eligible to vote at the meeting.

To determine the shareholders entitled to receive notice, it is as if the corporation takes a snapshot of its list of shareholders *on that given date.*

Record date
A date selected in advance of a meeting or event

Record holder
The owner of stock as of a specified date

Those individuals whose names are on the list receive notice and they may vote. Shareholders who buy stock in the corporation after the record date and before the meeting date, in this case between April 1 and May 1, are simply out of luck.

This notice prerequisite is similar to that underlying voter registration. One must be "on the books" by a certain date before an election to vote. An individual who moves to a new county may simply miss the cut-off date for registration and be unable to vote in the next election. The rules relating to record dates likewise exist for the orderly administration of corporate matters.

Contents and Timing of Notice. Shareholders are entitled to receive notice of annual and special meetings. MBCA § 7.05(a) provides that the notice shall specify the date, time, and place of each meeting. The notice must be given no fewer than 10 nor more than 60 days before the meeting date. These time limits provide protection to shareholders by ensuring that they get adequate advance notice so they can make arrangements to attend but not so much advance notice that they forget about the meeting.

Notice of a special meeting must describe the purpose for which the meeting is called. Some jurisdictions require that all notices for all meetings describe the purpose for which the meeting is called, but the MBCA rule is similar to that in most jurisdictions in providing that only notices for special meetings must specify the purpose (unless extraordinary matters, such as amendment to the articles of incorporation or dissolution will be voted on, in which case the notice of an annual meeting must describe its purposes). Erring on the side of caution, most corporations specify the purposes of all meetings, whether annual or special.

PRACTICE TIPS

- Make sure your Corporate Data Sheet for each corporate client identifies the corporation's annual meeting date, notice requirements, quorum requirements, and the like.
- To calculate the timing of notices and record dates, use the calculator at wwww.timeanddate.com.

Delivery of Notice. According to MBCA § 1.41(c), written notice by a corporation to its shareholders is effective when mailed (if mailed prepaid and correctly addressed) or when transmitted electronically to the shareholder in a manner authorized by the shareholder. Alternatively, notice may be delivered in person, or by telephone or voice mail, in which case it is effective when communicated.

Defective Notice. If the corporation fails to meet its obligations with regard to sending appropriate notice to the appropriate shareholders within the specified period, the meeting is invalid and can be attacked by any shareholder who failed to receive proper notice. Because rescheduling the meeting, preparing new notices, and transporting the directors and officers to another meeting can be expensive, there are two alternatives corporations can use to save an otherwise invalid meeting. First, a shareholder may sign a written waiver of notice, expressly waiving the right to receive notice. This waiver is effective whether signed before or after the meeting. Second, a shareholder may consent in writing to action taken at the meeting. A shareholder's attendance at a meeting is deemed a waiver of notice unless the shareholder objects to the holding of the meeting as it commences. MBCA § 7.06. See Figure 11-2 for a typical notice of an annual shareholders' meeting.

   As a precautionary matter, many corporations instruct the corporate secretary to prepare an affidavit or certificate of mailing to verify that all notices were properly and timely delivered. Such a certificate is similar in effect to the document signed by process servers who verify in writing that a summons and complaint were properly served upon a defendant and which protects against defendants' claims that they never received the documents. In nearly all cases, a corporation's certificate of mailing will be presumptive evidence that notices were properly prepared and delivered.

   Annual Reports.   When the corporation sends out the notice of the annual shareholders' meeting, it usually includes a formal **annual report**, often a professional and glossy magazine-style presentation explaining the company's performance. Typical sections include a letter from the board's chair, financial reviews (summarizing sales, profit, income, cash flow, liabilities, and shareholders' equity), charts showing stock performance, brief biographies and pictures of the board

Annual report
Report describing corporate performance during the preceding year

---

FIGURE 11-2
Notice of Annual Meeting of Shareholders

Notice is hereby given that the Annual Meeting of Shareholders of FTB, Inc. will be held in Room Three, Fifth Floor, 5 Park Avenue East, New York, New York 10048, on May 16, 2009, at 9:00 A.M., Eastern Standard Time, for the following purposes:

1. To elect five (5) directors to serve until the next annual meeting or until their successors shall have been elected and qualified;
2. To ratify the appointment of PricewaterhouseCoopers as the Company's independent registered public accountants for the next fiscal year;
3. To act upon a shareholder proposal with respect to the distribution of quarterly reports; and
4. To transact such other business as may properly come before the meeting or any adjournment thereof.

   Only shareholders of record at the close of business on April 15, 2009, are entitled to notice of and to vote at the meeting or any adjournments thereof.

April 15, 2009   By order of the Board of Directors
New York, New York   William V. Curtis,
                                       Secretary

---

members, and other information of interest to the shareholders. As part of the continuing trend utilizing technology, many companies now post these reports on their Web sites and provide CDs with audio messages from the board of directors.

Shareholder Lists. After the record date has been determined, the corporation will prepare an alphabetical list of shareholders entitled to receive notice. The list must be arranged by voting groups and provide the address of each shareholder as well as the number of shares held by each shareholder. The list must be made available for inspection by any shareholder beginning two business days after notice of the meeting is given and must remain open for inspection during any meeting. The list will be available at the corporation's principal office or at a place identified in the meeting notice (for larger corporations, possibly the office of the registrar). Shareholders (or their agents or attorneys) have the right to inspect and copy the list upon written demand. MBCA § 7.20.

The rationale for making the list available to all shareholders is to encourage discussion among shareholders. Additionally, shareholders may wish to band together and agree to vote as a group to achieve certain goals.

Quorum

The minimum number of shareholders or directors required to be present before action can be taken

Quorum. No action can be taken at any shareholder meeting unless a certain minimum number of shareholders, a **quorum**, is present. MBCA § 7.25 provides that unless the articles specify otherwise, a quorum is a majority of votes entitled to be cast on a given matter. Thus, if 100 shares are entitled to vote on amending the articles of incorporation, holders representing at least 51 of those shares (a majority of 100) must be present for the meeting to be held. If fewer than 51 shares are present at the meeting, the meeting cannot be held and will have to be rescheduled. This will cause great expense to the corporation because it will be required to provide new notices to all shareholders, reserve a location for another meeting, make arrangements for management to attend the new meeting, and so forth.

Many states allow corporations to modify the requirements for a quorum by providing such in the articles of incorporation, so long as the quorum is not so low as to be unfair. Most states allow such modification so long as a quorum is not less than one-third of the shares entitled to vote. In such a case, if 100 shares were outstanding and entitled to vote on an issue, 34 shares (one-third of 100) must be present for the meeting to go forward.

Quorum requirements prevent small factions of shareholders from controlling all shareholder action. For example, if a corporation had 100 outstanding shares entitled to vote, and the quorum was one-eighth, a shareholder owning only 13 shares could control a meeting and its outcome. The typical provision that a majority of outstanding shares constitute a quorum ensures that action is not taken unless some reasonable and fair number of shareholders have the opportunity to consider the matter.

Once a quorum is established, it cannot be destroyed by a group of shareholders who walk out of a meeting (perhaps for the purpose of preventing action being taken on a certain matter). Once a share is represented at a meeting, it is deemed present for quorum purposes for the remainder of the meeting and any adjournment thereof. MBCA § 7.25(b).

Proxy

Written authorization from one directing another to vote his shares

Proxies. Most states and the MBCA allow shareholders to vote by proxy if they are unable or do not wish to attend a meeting. A **proxy** is a written authorization instructing another person to vote one's shares on one's behalf. The word *proxy* is also used to refer to the person who will act in place of the shareholder. The closest analogy to a proxy form is an absentee ballot: Voters who are unable to be present for voting on election day may vote by absentee ballot. Similarly, shareholders who cannot attend shareholder meetings may vote by proxy.

The proxy creates an agent-principal relationship between the parties. The shareholder, as the principal, authorizes another, the agent, to vote his or her shares. The proxy may be specific and authorize the agent (or **proxy holder**) to vote a certain way on specific issues. If such specific instructions are given, the proxy holder must so vote. This type of proxy is referred to as a **limited proxy.** Alternatively, the proxy may authorize the proxy holder to cast the shareholder's votes in the proxy holder's discretion on any issue properly arising at the meeting. This type of proxy is referred to as a **general proxy.** See Figure 11-3 for an example of a general proxy.

The Securities Exchange Act of 1934 regulates the form and content of proxies for corporations whose stock is traded on an exchange or "over the counter" if the company has at least 500 shareholders and assets of at least $5 million. Among other requirements, SEC regulations ensure that the name of each nominee is listed on the proxy form. The proxy form is accompanied by a proxy statement issued by the corporation. The proxy statement includes certain required information about the matters being voted on at the meeting.

Proxies may generally be revoked by the shareholder at any time before they are voted. If the proxy does not state its duration, it will automatically expire 11 months after it is received by the corporation. MBCA § 7.22(c). This provision ensures that shareholders grant new proxies for each annual shareholders' meeting. One type of proxy that is irrevocable is that granted to an individual who has purchased the shareholder's shares or has agreed to do so. Thus, in the event a shareholder sells shares after the record date and grants the new owner a proxy, this proxy cannot be revoked. Proxies are revoked by delivering a written revocation of

Proxy holder
The person who exercises the rights of a shareholder who has granted a proxy

Limited proxy
A proxy given with specific instructions

General proxy
Proxy given in which proxy holder can exercise discretion in voting

---

FIGURE 11-3
General Proxy

I hereby appoint Edward L. Goodman or Virginia Nelson Andrews my agent with full power to vote and act for me at their discretion upon any business, including the election of directors at any meeting of the shareholders of FTB, Inc. or any adjournment thereof, held during the term of this proxy at which I am not present in person.

This proxy shall be valid for one year unless sooner revoked by me by delivering to the secretary of the corporation a written revocation of this proxy.

All previous proxies are hereby revoked.

_____   _____
       Date   Signature

proxy to the secretary of the corporation or by attending the meeting and voting in person.

Proxies are most often used and needed for large corporations with numerous shareholders. For example, General Electric Company had more than 600,000 shareholder accounts of record as of early 2008. There is no stadium or facility that can accommodate such a large group. Thus, most shareholders vote by proxy rather than voting in person at the meeting.

Proxies may be solicited by corporate management to elect management's slate of directors. In some cases, insurgent or dissident shareholders will also solicit shareholders for proxies to elect candidates favored by the insurgents or for changes in corporate policy desired by them. Each side will set forth its views in its proxy statement which is distributed to all shareholders. This fight for control of the company is a *proxy fight* or **proxy contest.** The costs of a proxy contest can be significant, and the question often arises as to who should pay for the expenses. Generally, if management has acted in good faith and is successful in the proxy contest, the corporation will pay the costs and expenses associated with the proxy contest, at least if it involves policy issues rather than director-personnel issues. Some cases have allowed reimbursement to insurgents of reasonable expenses if they succeed with regard to proxy contests on policy issues. In one recent proxy solicitation, TIAA-CREF, a large institutional investor in Furr's/Bishop's, Inc., a struggling cafeteria company, argued to other shareholders that the then-present board had not provided tangible growth and convinced 80 percent of the company's shareholders to replace the entire nine-member board with a seven-member board proposed by TIAA-CREF. A newer trend is to use the Internet as part of proxy contest strategies. Each side in the hotly contested Hewlett-Packard-Compaq Computer merger in 2002 established Web sites to promote their views and used interactive message boards to communicate with their supporters.

The proxy form or card is generally distributed with the notice of the meeting. Many corporations distribute additional notices with the proxy card that stress the importance of voting by proxy. See Figure 11-4 for a sample notice.

Proxy contest
A fight for control of a company (also called *proxy fight*)

FIGURE 11-4
Important Notice

No matter how many shares you own, please sign, date, and mail your proxy now, especially if you do not plan to attend the meeting. A majority is required by law. Therefore, it is important that you vote so that your corporation will not have to bear the expense of another solicitation of proxies. You may revoke your proxy at any time prior to its exercise by delivering to the secretary of the corporation a written revocation of proxy or by attending the meeting and voting in person.

FTB, Inc.

Conducting the Meeting. At the meeting, items on the agenda are presented in the form of resolutions, which the shareholders then vote on. Most states provide that approval by a majority vote is required to take action. (Some matters, however, such as amending the articles of incorporation or mergers, might require the affirmative vote of a supermajority, perhaps two-thirds approval.)

For example, assume FTB, Inc. has 100,000 voting shares outstanding. For any business to be conducted, a quorum, or majority of shares, must be present (either in person or by proxy). In this case, a quorum would be 50,001. If fewer than 50,001 shares are present, a quorum does not exist, and the meeting must be rescheduled and renoticed. In many corporations, sufficient proxies are received before the actual meeting so that results are known in advance and the meeting is a formality.

Under MBCA § 7.25(c), a measure (other than election of directors) passes when the votes for it exceed the votes against it, regardless of abstentions. This allows a measure to pass without receiving a majority vote. For example, if 100 voting shares are outstanding, at least 51 must be present for a quorum to exist. If 51 shares are present and corporate statutes require a majority vote to take action, at least 26 of those shares must approve a certain action. Under the MBCA approach, however, the measure could pass with fewer than 26 votes if 20 shares voted in favor, 18 shares voted against the action, and 13 shares abstained. The MBCA approach, providing that a measure is approved if the votes cast in favor of it exceed the votes cast in opposition, is not followed in some states, which require that for a measure to be approved, it must receive a majority vote.

In Delaware and most states, as well as under MBCA § 7.28, directors are elected by a **plurality** of votes (unless the corporation's articles provide otherwise). For elections, the distinction between majority votes and plurality votes is as follows: In an election in which two candidates are running for director, he who receives the greatest number of votes is said to have a majority. If, however, there are more than two candidates, the person who receives the greatest number of votes has a plurality, but that person does not have a majority unless he receives more than one-half of all votes cast. For example, if Amanda and Ted are vying for a director's position (100 shares are voting) and Amanda gets 60 votes and Ted gets 40, Amanda received a majority of the votes. If, however, Mike is also running, and Amanda receives 45 votes, Ted receives 30 votes, and Mike receives 25 votes, Amanda has won by a plurality. She cannot win by majority vote unless she receives at least 51 votes. Generally, "plurality voting" means that more "for" votes are cast in favor of a nominee than for other nominees, without counting the number of votes "against" or withheld. As discussed in Section C later in the chapter, the issue of electing directors by a plurality rather than by a majority vote is a controversial matter, and a number of shareholder proposals have been recently passed requiring majority rather than plurality vote in elections for directors.

Most statutes do not address the actual method of voting. For a small corporation with few shareholders, a voice vote or a show of hands may be acceptable, assuming the shareholders own equal shares. If shareholders own differing numbers of shares, a written ballot will lend certainty. Some corporations use election judges or inspectors to tally the ballots, to determine that a quorum is present, and that proxies have been counted and measures have been approved. MBCA § 7.29 provides that if a corporation's shares are publicly traded, it must use election inspectors or judges. In many instances, the **election judges** are employees of

Plurality
The number of votes received by one in an election when the candidate does not have a majority of votes; counting only votes "for" a nominee and not counting votes "against" or withheld

Election judge
Neutral party who oversees election and voting processes

the corporation's registrar or transfer agent. In other instances, they are officers or employees of the corporation. See Figure 11-5 for a sample ballot.

Meetings for Publicly Traded Companies.   In most instances, the conduct of a shareholders' meeting in a publicly traded company is substantially similar to the conduct of any shareholders' meeting; however, a great deal more planning and paperwork is involved. Dissident shareholders may make proposals (within the corporation's stated deadlines), which must be set forth in the company's proxy statement. Many publicly traded companies use the services of a professional share-holder communications company, such as Broadridge Financial Solutions, Inc. or Shareholder.com, whose services include distributing shareholder materials and tallying proxy voting by conventional print form, by telephone, and by Internet proxy voting.

Meetings of publicly traded companies are usually held in hotel meeting rooms or convention facilities, which are able to accommodate a large group of shareholders. Corporate management usually works with the legal team in preparing a "script" for the chairperson to ensure that appropriate announcements are made, resolutions are voted on, and remarks about the company's performance are included.

Shareholder Voting Agreements.   As discussed earlier, there are several types of voting. Straight voting (one vote per share) is the most common. Cumulative voting may exist in elections for directors. Similarly, shareholders may enter into voting agreements or form voting trusts to maximize or concentrate their voting power.

Pooling agreement
An agreement among shareholders specifying how they will vote (also called a *voting agreement*)

A *voting agreement*, sometimes called a **pooling agreement**, is an agreement among shareholders that specifies the manner in which they will vote. Shareholders may agree to cast their votes in a certain way on various matters or to pool their shares and cast them as they agree by majority agreement on a case-by-case basis. Such an agreement allows shareholders to band together to seek control. There is

---

FIGURE 11-5
Sample Ballot

FTB, Inc.

The Board of Directors recommends a vote FOR Items 1, 2, and 3.

1. Election of directors   For all _____ Withheld from all _____

2. Ratification of independent auditors For _____ Against _____ Abstain _____

3. Policy on board diversity   For _____ Against _____ Abstain _____

The Board of Directors recommends a vote AGAINST Item 4.

4. Executive compensation factors   For _____ Against _____ Abstain _____

Signature _____   Date _____

little, if any, state regulation of voting agreements. MBCA § 7.31 simply provides that two or more shareholders may agree on the manner in which they will vote their shares by signing an agreement for that purpose. The MBCA also states that the agreement is specifically enforceable, meaning that a court can order a shareholder to act as previously agreed on in their voting agreement.

A **voting trust** is a written agreement by which shareholders transfer their rights to vote to a trustee who is instructed to vote their shares on their behalf according to the terms of a written trust agreement. The shareholders surrender their shares to the trustee who then becomes the record holder of the shares for purposes of receiving notice and voting. Most states regulate the formation and operation of voting trusts. MBCA § 7.30 specifies the manner of creating a voting trust. Failure to follow the statutory requirements usually voids the trust. The terms of the trust may allow the trustee to exercise his or her independent judgment when voting, or may require the trustee to obtain a consensus of a certain percentage of the beneficial owners of the shares, or may require the trustee to vote in a certain manner.

Under MBCA § 7.30(a), a voting trust agreement must be delivered to the corporation. Thus, the corporation may know in advance how the shares subject to the trust will be voted. On the other hand, a pooling agreement is a private agreement between its parties, and the corporation will generally have no knowledge of its existence or terms. Moreover, whereas voting trusts are generally limited to some specified period of duration, often ten years, pooling agreements can last indefinitely.

When the shareholders relinquish their stock certificates in a voting trust situation, they will receive **voting trust certificates**, which are freely transferable, although the new owner will be bound by the terms of the trust agreement. The shareholders retain their rights to dividends and other rights, and the trustee is substituted for the shareholders only for the purposes of receiving notices of meetings and voting at those meetings. In the pooling agreement situation, new purchasers may or may not take shares subject to the terms of the agreement; the agreement itself will address this matter.

Shares that are subject to any type of voting agreement must generally be marked with a **legend** on the certificate indicating that they are subject to the terms of a restrictive agreement. Typically, the legend provides either the terms of the agreement or states that the agreement will be provided upon request. The legend usually warns that any transaction whereby shares are attempted to be transferred in violation of the agreement is not sufficient to transfer ownership, and the purported new owner will not be recognized for any purpose.

A trustee appointed under a voting trust agreement is subject to fiduciary duties and is usually compensated a fee for services rendered. Typically, the trust agreement provides that the trustee is not liable for errors in business judgment and will be indemnified for acts of ordinary negligence but will be liable for acts of gross negligence or recklessness. There maybe more than one trustee appointed. If so, a mechanism should be established to resolve disputes that could arise among trustees.

Although a voting trust agreement is more expensive and complex than a pooling agreement and will usually involve payment of a fee to the trustee, it lends more certainty in that the shareholders will not have any power to "go back on their word" and vote contrary to terms of the trust inasmuch as they

---

Voting trust
Agreement by which shareholders transfer their rights to a trustee to vote their shares

Voting trust certificate
Document showing ownership in a corporation, which evidences that the shares are subject to a voting trust

Legend
A notation marked on a stock certificate indicating the stock is subject to some restriction or limitation

no longer have any power to vote their shares. With a pooling agreement, a rogue shareholder could decide to breach the agreement and vote contrary to its terms. Although other shareholders can sue for breach of contract and apply to a court to compel the shareholder to vote according to the agreement, a voting trust eliminates the possibility of such events even occurring.

Minutes of Meeting. The corporation's secretary usually has the responsibility for taking **minutes** of the shareholders' meetings. There is no one statutorily required format for minutes. Some law firms provide their smaller corporate clients with "canned" or prepared minutes, allowing the secretary to merely fill in the blanks and indicate action taken at a meeting. Larger corporations tend to keep more detailed minutes. Similarly, statutes seldom address the actual manner of conducting the meeting. Many larger corporations follow *Robert's Rules of Order*, although following parliamentary procedure is not required, and many experts believe *Robert's Rules of Order* is overly complicated. Cases and statutes rarely address how meetings are to be conducted, and no uniform set of rules exists today regarding the conduct of meetings. As a result, a subcommittee of the Business Law Section of the American Bar Association has prepared a handbook of guidelines for the conduct of shareholder meetings. It can be ordered from the ABA at www.abanet.org. MBCA § 7.08(c) provides merely that the rules adopted for and the conduct of the meeting must be fair to shareholders.

To provide protection against later challenges, the minutes should include a variety of recitals: that notice was properly given to all shareholders entitled to receive notice or that the shareholders properly waived notice, that a quorum was present, that a measure passed by sufficient vote, and so forth. The minutes reflect action taken at the meeting and provide an overview rather than a verbatim transcript of what was uttered at the meeting. See Figure 11-6 for sample minutes of an annual shareholders' meeting.

Minutes
Written record of events occurring at a meeting

5. Shareholder Action Without a Meeting

MBCA § 7.04(a) and most state statutes allow shareholders to take action without formally meeting if all shareholders consent in writing. This allows business to be conducted without the expense of holding meetings. Action can be taken without a meeting if all shareholders entitled to vote on the issue consent to the proposed action in writing. The corporate secretary prepares a document called a **written consent action** or a "unanimous consent by shareholders in lieu of meeting" and distributes it to the shareholders for signature. Alternatively, rather than being required to obtain all signatures on one document, the secretary can prepare separate documents and send one to each shareholder. Once signed by the last shareholder, the measure is effective. Shareholders can also consent to action electronically by e-mail. Action by written consent is primarily designed to simplify corporate formalities for smaller corporations when it might be difficult for shareholders to get together for meetings.

Written consent action
Action taken without the necessity of a meeting; generally, must be unanimous

Although the majority of states and the MBCA approach require that the consent be unanimous, a growing number of states, including Delaware and New York, allow for written consent by the minimum number of shares that would be required to take such action at a meeting (usually a majority). In fact, a recent amendment to the MBCA allows a corporation to permit shareholder

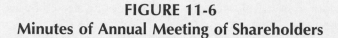

FIGURE 11-6
Minutes of Annual Meeting of Shareholders

An annual meeting of the shareholders of Tech Management Team, Inc., a Delaware corporation, was held on May 1, 2009, at 10:00 A.M., in the Spanish Ballroom of the Four Seasons Olympic Hotel, 411 University Street, Seattle, Washington, for the purpose of electing directors of the corporation, voting on the approval of PricewaterhouseCoopers as independent registered public accountants of the corporation, and to transact such other business properly before the meeting.

Daniel J. Sullivan, Chief Executive Officer, acted as Chairman and Diana Hendrix acted as Secretary.

At 10:00 A.M. the Chairman called the meeting to order.

The Secretary announced that the meeting was called pursuant to Del. Code Ann. tit. 8, § 211(b) and Article VII of the bylaws of the corporation.

The Secretary announced that the meeting was held pursuant to notice properly given as required under the laws of the State of Delaware and the bylaws of the corporation, or that notice had been waived by those entitled to receive notice under the bylaws. Copies of any written waivers executed by those persons entitled to receive notice will be attached to the minutes of this meeting by the Secretary.

The Secretary read the minutes of the last annual meeting of shareholders. The minutes were approved and placed in the minute book.

The Secretary announced that an alphabetical list of the names of shareholders and the number of shares held by each was available for inspection by any person in attendance at the meeting.

The Secretary announced that a quorum was present at the meeting.

All of the directors of the corporation were present at the meeting. The following other persons were present: James K. Eckmann, Chief Financial Officer of the corporation, Susan M. Baker, representative of the corporation's registrar and transfer agent, American Stock Transfer & Trust Company, and Harry S. Hunter, election judge appointed by the corporation's registrar and transfer agent, American Stock Transfer & Trust Company.

The reports of the President and Chief Financial Officer were presented to the shareholders and were placed in the corporate minute book.

The Chairman then called for the election of directors of the corporation.

Upon motion duly made, seconded, and carried, the following persons were elected to the board of directors of the corporation, to serve as directors until their successors are elected at the next annual meeting of shareholders of the corporation and qualify:

Lisa Black
Christopher Wagner
Kenneth Lyons
William Brady
Patricia E. Moore

The Chairman then called for the approval of PricewaterhouseCoopers as independent registered public accountants of the corporation.

Upon motion duly made, seconded, and carried, PricewaterhouseCoopers was appointed as independent registered public accountants of the corporation upon the terms and conditions set forth in the Notice of this Annual Meeting of Shareholders and placed in the minute book.

There being no further business before the meeting, on motion duly made, seconded, and unanimously carried, it was adjourned.

Date: _____   _____
                                                          Diana Hendrix, Secretary

action by written consent by a majority vote (rather than unanimous vote) if the articles of incorporation so provide. MBCA § 7.04(b). Such a provision allows larger and publicly traded corporations to take actions more expeditiously and without the necessity of a meeting. When action is taken by less than unanimous written consent, the MBCA requires that notice of the action be given to nonconsenting shareholders. If a corporation elects its directors by cumulative voting, however, such directors may not be elected by less than unanimous written consent.

The rationale for the preference in most states for unanimous consent is that in the absence of a meeting, there is no opportunity for open discussion. Thus, without such discussion, most states insist that *all* shareholders be in agreement with the action proposed to be taken. See Figure 11-7 illustrating a form of written consent action.

6. Modern Trends

Modern technology is having a significant effect on shareholder meetings and action. Effective January 1, 2009, all publicly traded companies are required to post their proxy materials (namely, the proxy statement and the annual report) on the Internet and then provide their shareholders with notice of the availability of these proxy materials 40 days before the meeting. Companies can also mail their proxy materials and if shareholders request materials by mail, they must be provided at no charge. Shareholders can also now vote by telephone (by calling

---

FIGURE 11-7
Written Consent in Lieu of Shareholders' Meeting

The undersigned, constituting a majority of the shareholders of FTB, Inc., a Delaware corporation, and acting pursuant to Del. Code Ann. tit. 8, § 228(a) and Article VIII of the bylaws of the corporation, hereby take the following action as if present at a meeting duly called pursuant to proper notice.

RESOLVED, that Article I of the Certificate of Incorporation shall be amended to read as follows: The name of the corporation is FTB Access Link, Co.

RESOLVED, that Article III of the Certificate of Incorporation be amended to read as follows: The aggregate number of shares that the corporation shall have authority to issue is 100,000 shares of common stock.

The officers and directors of the corporation are authorized to take all appropriate action to effect these Resolutions.

Date:_____

_____
Signature

Date: _____

_____
Signature

Date: _____

_____
Signature

Date: _____

_____
Signature

a toll-free number, identifying themselves by entering a control number located on a voting instruction card sent to them, and then following recorded instructions) or by accessing a Web site and voting. The method of voting electronically via the Internet is often called **e-proxy voting**. In fact, the SEC has reported that by the 2006 proxy season, nearly 90 percent of shareholders of publicly traded companies voted electronically or by telephone.

E-proxy voting
Method of voting
electronically

The statutes of some states, including California, Delaware, and New York, specifically permit shareholders of companies incorporated in those states to authorize others to act as proxies by transmission of a telegram, cablegram, or other means of electronic transmission, thus explicitly recognizing e-proxies. One site in particular, ProxyVote.com (www.proxyvote.com), a service of Broadridge Financial Solutions, Inc., is active in serving as a monitor for e-proxies cast in various shareholder matters.

These advances not only help the corporation reduce printing and postage costs (which have been estimated to total more than $1 billion each year), but due to their ease, greatly enhance shareholder participation in corporate governance. Moreover, shareholders are increasingly using the Internet to discuss the merits of various corporate activities. For example, when USA Networks, Inc. was considering a merger with Lycos, Inc., USA executives routinely reviewed chat room conversations. When those conversations revealed a high level of shareholder concern over the proposed merger, USA killed the deal. The Internet is thus able to unite investors who once met only at annual meetings, if then. Whereas previously individual investors often threw away their notices of meetings and proxy cards, or forgot to vote, the ease of voting by telephone or through the use of e-proxies promotes shareholder involvement and activism. Companies have discovered that shareholders who receive electronic communications are more likely to vote than those who receive paper notices.

Additionally, experts predict that corporations will eventually hold "cyber-meetings," with shareholders all over the country and around the world participating via the Internet. Holding meetings online would clearly save companies and shareholders time and money and further expand shareholder involvement inasmuch as shareholders could ask pertinent questions and then cast their votes electronically. Delaware has amended its statutes to expressly allow cybermeetings and requires that the shareholder list be available electronically. In April 2001, the first company took advantage of Delaware's new laws and held an all-electronic stockholders' meeting, although no votes were cast at the annual e-meeting.

Legally, the barrier to holding shareholder meetings online is the question whether online involvement constitutes "attendance." Most state statutes impose requirements that shareholders can attend meetings either in person or by proxy. Thus, there is a question of whether viewing the meeting on a screen constitutes attendance. Some modifications to state statutes and corporate bylaws might be necessary before cybermeetings can be effective. Confidentiality and security of meeting proceedings are also issues, and corporations will have to find a way to ensure that outside "hackers" do not access an online meeting and cast phony votes.

At present, several companies, including Xerox Corporation and Target Corporation, broadcast their annual shareholder meetings in live webcasts. They also videotape those meetings to permit later viewing via the Internet. Some allow their shareholders to participate in the meeting by submitting questions by e-mail.

Another new trend, which has been adopted by MBCA § 1.44 and SEC rule, is to allow the delivery of a single annual report and proxy statement to shareholders who share the same last name and address, unless contrary instructions are received from a shareholder. This practice, known as **householding**, is designed to reduce printing and postage costs.

All of these efforts, from posting reports online, to allowing voting telephonically and via the Internet, to the eventual holding of virtual meetings, serve to promote the laudable goal of shareholder participation in matters of corporate governance, and result in increased efficiency and cost savings to corporations.

Householding
Practice of sending only one report and proxy statement to shareholders with same surname at same address

7. Preemptive Rights

A shareholder may have preemptive rights. As discussed in Chapter Nine, a preemptive right gives a shareholder the right to purchase as many newly issued shares as will maintain the shareholder's proportionate ownership interest in the corporation. Shareholders with preemptive rights are given this opportunity before newly issued shares can be offered to others for purchase. Because preemptive rights can delay the corporation from obtaining needed funds by issuing shares under any terms and conditions the board desires, preemptive rights generally do not exist unless specifically provided for in the articles of incorporation.

8. Dividends

Shareholders may have the right to receive dividends. As discussed in Chapter Twelve, directors are usually under no obligation to pay dividends to common shareholders. Dividends may be declared in the discretion of the board of directors from time to time. If preferred shareholders have cumulative dividends, dividends must be paid to them first for the current year and any previous years' arrearages before they can be distributed to other shareholders. Only a solvent corporation may distribute dividends. Thus, shareholders generally have no absolute right to receive dividends.

9. Right to Transfer Shares and Shareholder Agreements

Because shareholders own an interest in the corporation, they can transfer this property to others upon the terms they negotiate. Some shareholders, however, usually those in smaller corporations, enter into agreements with other shareholders or the corporation restricting the transfer of their shares and generally requiring that shareholders who wish to sell their stock must first offer it to the corporation or to the other shareholders, or both. If the corporation and the other shareholders decline to purchase the shares, they may then be sold to an "outsider." Such a provision not only restricts the intrusion of outsiders but also provides a ready market for a shareholder who wishes to sell his or her shares. Such restrictions are permitted by MBCA § 6.27. Such provisions might also be necessary to preserve the status of an S corporation, which may not have more than 100 shareholders. If a shareholder in an S corporation could sell his or her shares without restriction, sales might result in more than 100 shareholders, in which case S status would automatically terminate.

These shareholder agreements, often called **buy-sell agreements**, preserve present ownership interests and prevent the admission of new shareholders who might disturb the relationships among small groups of shareholders, who are frequently family or friends. Agreements cannot absolutely restrict or prohibit shareholders from transferring their shares because one of the key attributes of owning property is the ability to sell it. Nevertheless, some restrictions on transferring stock are acceptable.

The least restrictive agreements generally offer the corporation or its shareholders the right to purchase another shareholder's stock before it can be sold to an outsider. Such a provision does not obligate the corporation or its shareholders to purchase the stock but merely gives them a right of first refusal to do so. The right of first refusal is usually triggered by the receipt of a valid offer made by a third party to a shareholder to purchase her shares. The shareholder then notifies the corporation and the shareholders of the terms of the offer, and the corporation and the shareholders have the right to purchase the stock on the same terms as offered by the offeror. The agreement may provide that the corporation has the right of first refusal to purchase the shares and, if it declines to do so, then the existing shareholders have the right to purchase the stock. If numerous shareholders exist, they may purchase the selling shareholder's stock according to their proportionate ownership interests. Thus, a shareholder who owns 24 percent of the outstanding stock may purchase 24 percent of the stock to be sold.

The agreement may be drafted to allow for either partial or complete purchase of the selling shareholder's stock. For example, if the existing shareholders are allowed to purchase some of the offered stock, each may purchase a few shares. The shareholder can then sell the remaining shares to the offeror (who may not wish to purchase a small block). Other agreements require the corporation or its shareholders to buy all of the stock. If they do not agree to purchase all of the stock, it can be sold to the outsider.

Other provisions might require the corporation to purchase the stock of a shareholder who dies. This ensures that the shareholder's heirs do not try to come in and begin running the corporation. Typically, the purchase is funded by life insurance policies. The corporation will purchase life insurance policies on its few shareholders and upon the death of a shareholder use the proceeds of the policy to purchase the stock from the deceased shareholder's estate. The estate must sell upon the terms agreed on by the shareholder. Many buy-sell agreements include formulas or procedures for determining the value of stock. The agreement can also provide for installment payments. Some agreements are funded by cross-purchase insurance policies. In this case, each shareholder purchases life insurance on the life of every other shareholder. In the event of that shareholder's death, each shareholder receives a fund of money that can be used to purchase the decedent's shares. These insurance policies are also discussed in Chapters Seventeen and Eighteen.

Other events that might trigger a forced sale of shares include a shareholder's retirement, bankruptcy, or disability.

To ensure that shareholders do not violate the terms of a shareholder agreement and sell their shares without complying with the agreement, their share certificates must be conspicuously marked with a notice stating that the transfer of the shares represented by the certificate is subject to restriction. MBCA § 6.27.

Buy-sell agreement
Agreement among shareholders regarding their rights to purchase and sell stock in a corporation and usually imposing some restrictions on those rights

This notation is called a *legend condition*. The terms of the restriction may be set forth on the certificate or the certificate may simply indicate where the agreement containing the restriction can be inspected. Agreements entered into by shareholders will require that the shareholders surrender their certificates so the legend condition can be marked thereon. See Appendix I for a sample buy-sell agreement.

When shares are transferred, the appropriate entry indicating the name, address, and number of shares owned by the new shareholder is made in the stock ledger book. Until the corporation is notified, the record owner of the shares will continue to receive notice of meetings and will be entitled to vote and receive dividends, if declared.

Although the agreement might require the corporation or other shareholders to acquire the restricted shares in the event a shareholder desires to sell his shares, such a provision is somewhat rare; the right of first refusal described earlier is far more common. In any event, any restriction on the transfer of shares must be reasonable.

Shareholder buy-sell agreements are further discussed in Chapter Seventeen.

10. Shareholder Actions

Among the other rights shareholders of a corporation possess is the right to institute litigation either against the corporation or on its behalf. There are two principal types of actions instituted by shareholders of a corporation: direct actions, for injury caused directly to the shareholder by the corporation, and derivative actions, for injury sustained by the corporation that the corporation fails to redress. You might recall from Chapters Four and Six that limited partners and LLC members can also institute direct and derivative actions.

Direct action
Action initiated to address direct harm done to the complainant (sometimes called an *individual action*)

Direct Actions.   A **direct action** is one brought by a shareholder who has been injured by some act of the corporation. In such instances, shareholders bring suit against the corporation in much the same way they would bring suit against any party causing them injury. The shareholder is the plaintiff who asserts his grievance, or *cause of action*, in a complaint filed against the corporation. Reasons for shareholders instituting direct action might be a refusal to distribute a dividend to a shareholder when every other member of the shareholder's class received a dividend, denial of voting rights to a particular shareholder, or refusal to allow inspection of the shareholder list by a shareholder.

If numerous shareholders are similarly situated (for example, if an entire class of shareholders, those 1,000 individuals owning Common B stock, are wrongfully denied their voting rights), one or more of the shareholders can institute a **class action** on behalf of the other shareholders. *Class actions*, sometimes called *representative actions*, promote judicial economy in that similar claims are adjudicated at the same time rather than having the 1,000 shareholders institute 1,000 separate lawsuits.

Class action
Action brought on behalf of a large group of people who are similarly situated (often called *representative action*)

Derivative action
Action initiated to enforce a right owned by another

Derivative Actions.   A derivative suit is brought by one or more shareholders to enforce a right or cause of action owned by the corporation but that it will not enforce. In brief, the shareholder sues the corporation to compel it to enforce corporate rights. The shareholder is the plaintiff (acting for the benefit of the corporation) and both the corporation and any wrongdoer are the defendants. The shareholder is not suing for injury done to herself; the action "derives" from the shareholder's ownership interest in the corporation, which will not sue the wrongdoer. The corporation is the injured party in a derivative suit.

For example, assume that FTB, Inc. has loaned $100,000 to the wife of its director, Dan Donoghue. The time to repay the loan has expired but FTB, Inc. will not sue Mrs. Donoghue, due to Dan's powerful presence on the board. A shareholder could institute a derivative suit on behalf of the corporation to recover the $100,000 from Mrs. Donoghue. If the shareholder prevails, the shareholder does not receive the $100,000 because that sum is properly owned by the corporation. The shareholder will, however, be entitled to reimbursement for the costs and expenses of bringing the action. Presumably, the shareholder will receive some indirect or ultimate benefit by the corporation having an additional $100,000 in assets. In fact, the corporation might then be able to pay a dividend to the shareholders.

Derivative actions involve various procedural complexities, such as requiring that the shareholder make a formal written demand on the corporation (demanding that the corporation bring action) before instituting the derivative action and requiring that the shareholder held stock at the time the wrong occurred (or acquired the stock from one who was a shareholder when the wrong occurred). This latter requirement helps assure that the shareholder is genuinely aggrieved and has not purchased stock for the sole purpose of suing the corporation in hopes of a generous settlement. Under MBCA § 7.46, a court can order a plaintiff to pay any defendant's reasonable expenses (including counsel fees) if the proceeding was commenced for an improper purpose or without reasonable cause. Additionally, a court must dismiss the derivative proceeding if a majority of independent directors determines in good faith that maintaining the derivative suit is not in the corporation's best interests. MBCA § 7.44. Although this might seem like a drastic remedy, remember that a derivative suit is one brought on behalf of the corporation; thus, it should be controlled by those directors who exercise independent business judgment regarding its continuance.

When presented with a shareholder's demand that the corporation initiate action, the board of directors may refuse, presumably based on its business judgment that such an action would not be appropriate. To insulate themselves from having to make such difficult decisions, many corporations have created a special committee of the board of directors, called either the **shareholder litigation committee** or the special litigation committee, whose purpose is to determine whether litigation is appropriate. The litigation committee will not include any directors who might be defendants in the proposed litigation and is usually advised by independent legal counsel. Generally, courts give great deference to the committee's decisions.

Shareholder litigation committee
Committee established by board of directors to determine if litigation is appropriate (also called *special litigation committee*)

If the board refuses the shareholder's demand or fails to respond within the appropriate period (90 days under MBCA § 7.42), the shareholder may proceed with the action. In some states the requirement for a demand is excused if the shareholder can show that making a demand would be futile, such as in cases when the board has directly engaged in wrongful conduct and thus would never agree to initiate a lawsuit. If the corporation agrees to the demand, the shareholder has no right to proceed derivatively.

Modern Shareholder Suits. Shareholder lawsuits showed a dramatic increase in the 1990s. In many instances, shareholders sued on the basis that their company overstated profits, with shareholders viewing quarterly earnings statements and forecasts as to expected performance as representations on which they could rely. When earnings did not meet such projections, shareholders sued. For example, in 1998, the day after a company announced it was restating its revenues downward from $8.3 million to $1.4 million, 23 class actions alleging securities fraud were filed. According to National Economic Research Associates, a New York economic consulting and analysis firm, the likelihood that a company will be sued by its shareholders is nearly 60 percent. Moreover, the cost of settlements has risen from an average of $54.7 million through 2006 to $62.7 million in 2007 (although these figures might be slightly distorted because 2007 saw approval of the settlement of the case involving Tyco International for $3.2 billion, which was the third largest securities settlement in history).

In an effort to reduce such suits, Congress enacted the Private Securities Litigation Reform Act (15 U.S.C. § 78u-4, et seq.) in late 1995 to make it harder for such shareholder suits to succeed. Its advocates had convincingly argued that the law was necessary to combat the increasingly familiar practice of initiating shareholder suits (sometimes called **strike suits**) the moment stock losses occurred.

Although the number of lawsuits declined for several years, the number rose sharply in early 2008, primarily due to a surge in cases related to the collapse of the subprime mortgage market. The median loss alleged in the subprime cases is $4.5 billion. It can be difficult, however, to recover damages from a troubled company, as shown by the fact that the median recovery in settled cases in early 2008 was less than 3 percent of claimed losses. It remains to be seen what the fallout will be from the spectacular financial collapses of 2008 and the government bailout of the banking sector and Wall Street approved in October 2008. The 2008 financial collapse is discussed later.

The 1995 Reform Act requires plaintiffs to state in specific detail any allegations of misrepresentation rather than merely generally alleging misconduct and then using discovery to obtain specificity and perhaps uncover claims. The Act also eliminated joint and several liability for various securities violations. This rule had previously resulted in peripheral defendants with "deep pockets," often attorneys, auditors, and underwriters, being liable for an entire judgment. Under the Act, liability is apportioned such that each party is liable only for the portion of the judgment that corresponds to its actual assigned allocation of fault. Only those who knowingly commit violations remain jointly and severally liable. Finally, the Reform Act provided a "safe harbor" by allowing companies to make certain predictions about future earnings, called **forward-looking statements**, without fear of a lawsuit if actual results differed. Generally, companies must explain the reasons that actual results might differ from the projections, such as the fact that increased competition or government regulation might cause actual earnings to be less than predicted.

The Reform Act allows control of litigation to be assumed by the largest investor, the **lead plaintiff**, who is most capable of adequately representing the interests of the class. There is a rebuttable presumption that the party with the largest financial interest in the relief sought by the class is the most adequate

Strike suit
Lawsuit filed by disgruntled shareholders after a stock drop

Forward-looking statement
Prediction made by corporations about future earnings

Lead plaintiff
The largest investor in a class action alleging corporate misconduct

plaintiff. To eliminate "professional plaintiffs," a person may be a lead plaintiff in no more than five securities class actions during any three-year period.

On average, securities litigation cases tend to settle about three years after they are initiated. According to the Clearinghouse, the top three total settlements in recent years are as follows:

- Enron $7.2 billion
- WorldCom $6.2 billion
- Tyco $3.2 billion

11. Miscellaneous Rights of Shareholders

In addition to the foregoing, shareholders enjoy other rights. Most of these take the form of voting. Although the primary activity engaged in by shareholders is electing directors, shareholders can also vote on removing directors and on certain extraordinary corporate activities such as mergers, amending the articles of incorporation, and voluntary dissolution of the corporation. Additionally, in specific cases, shareholders have the right to have their shares appraised and purchased from them if they disagree with certain extraordinary matters such as mergers.

Shareholders also have the right to submit proposals and raise items of business for consideration at meetings and to formally nominate directors for election, although they must provide adequate written notice to the corporation. See Figure 11-8 for a profile of an activist shareholder.

12. Shareholders' Responsibilities

Generally, shareholders have only one responsibility: to pay for the stock issued to them. MBCA § 6.22(a). Once the stock is paid for, shareholders are not liable to the corporation or to its creditors for debts and obligations. Because the corporation is viewed as a separate person under the law, *it* is responsible for its own debts. Although the shareholder's stock may plummet in value to zero, a shareholder generally has no liability for corporate obligations. In fact, this limited liability is often viewed as the principal purpose for incorporating.

13. Piercing the Corporate Veil

Although the general rule is that shareholders are not personally liable for a corporation's debts and obligations, there are exceptions to this rule. Shareholders can certainly agree to accept personal responsibility for corporate obligations. For example, a newly formed small corporation operating a restaurant will not have a proven track record on which food, equipment, and beverage suppliers can rely. Therefore, before extending credit to the corporation, the suppliers may require that individual shareholders personally guarantee the corporation's obligation to pay for provisions supplied to it. Similarly, banks and other lenders may require

FIGURE 11-8
Profile of a Shareholder Activist

In late 2007, at the annual shareholders' meeting of Fannie Mae (well in advance of the federal government placing Fannie Mae in conservatorship in September 2008), shareholder Evelyn Y. Davis seized the microphone to berate Fannie Mae's leadership, urging nearly all the directors to resign, and stated she was dressed in black "to mourn the demise of Fannie Mae." She also once asked the chairman of U.S. Airways, "Are you going to stay, or jump out and leave us [shareholders] holding the bag?" For more than 40 years, corporate executives have been trying to placate Davis. She has made a career out of attending corporate meetings (about 40 each year) and grilling executives on their pay and on why profits aren't higher. Davis owns stock in about 80 companies and owns anywhere from 100 to 500 shares, enough to place about 50 proposals each year on various corporate agendas. Some of the proposals have been aimed at forcing corporations to end staggered terms for directors, to set term limits for directors, to change procedures to make it easier for dissident investors to secure representation on corporate boards, and to move annual meetings to more convenient locations. She compares proxy season to "opera season."

Davis's questions can be highly critical and personal. At a Goldman Sachs Group, Inc. meeting, she once asked "which idiot" had hired a worker who was later charged with insider trading. She once admonished the chairman of WGL Holdings, "Now, don't play games like that with me." Over the years Davis has confronted a variety of corporate executives. On occasion, other shareholders boo or jeer her but she also wins compliments for her boldness in asking tough questions no one else has the nerve to ask. The SEC itself has posted a biography of her on its Web site.

Among the biggest achievements credited to her are getting Bristol-Myers Squibb to agree to end its staggered system for its board of directors (a reform for which she had fought for 18 years) and getting General Motors to adopt an anti-greenmail policy she'd been advocating for six years (after GM paid Ross Perot $700 million to induce him to leave its board of directors).

Davis belongs to a tradition of shareholder activists dating back to John and Lewis Gilbert, brothers who became interested in shareholders' rights in the 1930s and monitored a variety of corporate issues, including awards of stock options. Called "gadflies," shareholder activists are predicted to increase due to the Internet allowing shareholders to band together and confront corporate management from their living room computers rather than being required to travel the country to attend meetings.

Piercing the veil
Holding individual shareholders liable for corporate obligations

personal guarantees from shareholders of smaller corporations who are active in managing the business.

Because the corporation typically shields its shareholders from liability, it is said that there is a "veil" between it and the shareholders such that creditors cannot **"pierce the veil"** to hold individual shareholders liable for corporate obligations. Nevertheless, courts will pierce the veil whenever it is necessary "to prevent fraud or injustice." Although this standard gives courts great flexibility in determining the circumstances under which liability can be imposed on shareholders, in actual practice, piercing-the-veil cases tend to share a common element: The shareholders have not acted as if the corporation is a separate entity; rather they view the corporation as their mere **alter ego** or business conduit. The most frequent examples seen in piercing cases involve commingling of assets, lack of corporate formalities, and undercapitalization.

Alter ego
Doctrine alleging separate corporate existence has been ignored by shareholders

Commingling of Assets. The corporation is a separate person. Therefore, it has its own bank accounts, funds, and books. In some small corporations, cash flow might be tight or unpredictable. When bills arrive, the corporation's bank account might be low on funds. In this situation, shareholders may be likely to "loan" money to the corporation to help it meet its obligations. Similarly, when shareholders need funds, they may "borrow" from the corporation's accounts. This transferring of money back and forth is called **commingling of funds.** It does not matter whether each party dutifully repays the money, either with or without interest. Just as an individual cannot legally dip into another person's wallet when he is short of funds, the shareholders and corporation cannot dip into each other's accounts. These situations differ from permissible arm's-length loans made by a shareholder to the corporation or by the corporation to the shareholder (which should be formally documented). If the shareholders disregard the fact that the corporation is a separate entity, a court may do so as well. This lack of respect for the separateness of the corporate entity may result in liability being imposed on the shareholders.

Commingling of funds
Combining funds owned by different individuals or entities

Lack of Formalities. Sometimes all of the energy and time of those involved in a corporation is focused on making a success of the business. The individuals involved may devote themselves to making the business work and neglect the fact that corporations are subject to various requirements, such as annual shareholders' meetings, regular action by the board of directors, and so forth. In some instances, individuals have formed corporations, and then never held a meeting, never elected directors, and never issued stock. When corporate owners do not treat the corporation as a separate entity, there is little reason why courts should. Thus, clients should be adequately counseled to observe corporate formalities. The first counseling session should occur at the corporation's organizational meeting. "Canned" or prepared forms for notices, waivers, and minutes can be provided to clients, and the dates for annual meetings can be docketed, all to help ensure that clients observe required corporate formalities.

Inadequate Capitalization. Another situation in which courts may pierce the veil of limited liability to hold individual shareholders responsible for corporate obligations exists when the corporation is so inadequately or thinly capitalized or routinely drains its funds to pay distributions to its shareholders that it could not expect to meet its responsibilities. Failure to ensure that the corporation has sufficient funds to meet its needs works an injustice on creditors and others dealing with the corporation.

Creditors can readily determine if commingling of assets, lack of formalities, or undercapitalization has occurred. Once the creditor has sued the corporation and discovered that it does not have sufficient assets to pay its debt, the creditor will begin scrutinizing the corporate structure to determine if other persons may be available to assist in repaying the debt. Through the discovery process, the creditor may examine various corporate records. Requesting the books of account from the corporation, its minute books, stock transfer ledger, and other records will reveal whether funds have been transferred back and forth or corporate finances depleted, whether meetings and elections have been held, and whether the corporation was operating on a sound fiscal footing. If it is believed that the corporate form has been disregarded by the shareholders, the creditor will amend its complaint to add the individual shareholders as defendants.

Most jurisdictions allow one-person corporations. Even these one-person corporations, however, must be established on a sound fiscal foundation and must operate on a corporate basis rather than a personal basis. They too must observe corporate formalities.

Piercing-the-veil cases tend to be brought more frequently against smaller corporations than larger ones. Larger corporations rely on advice of counsel and accountants to ensure they do not disregard the corporate entity. Smaller corporations have few shareholders, all of whom may be active in managing the business and are often so busy that they ignore corporate formalities and the separateness of the corporate books and accounts. If the corporation has adequate assets, of course, the veil will never need to be pierced. It is only when a creditor cannot obtain full payment of a debt from the corporation that the creditor will ask a court to pierce the corporate veil and impose personal liability on individual shareholders.

B. Directors' Rights and Responsibilities

1. Introduction

Directors
Those who manage a corporation

Corporations are managed or governed by individuals called **directors**, and a corporation must have a board of directors. MBCA § 8.01(a). These directors function as a body rather than as individuals. Their duties and powers derive from state statutes, the articles of incorporation, and the corporate bylaws. Directors have full authority and responsibility for determining corporate policy. Directors exercise this authority in their regular and special meetings. Directors each have one vote, and generally a simple majority is required to take action. All states allow directors to take action without a meeting if they act by unanimous written consent. Directors owe duties of due care and good faith to the corporation. Generally, directors are not liable for a mere error in judgment unless their action (or lack thereof) is clearly and grossly negligent.

2. Number and Qualifications of Directors

Although a few states continue to require at least three directors, the more modern approach, and that of most states and the MBCA, is to require only one director. Corporations having more than one director typically have an odd number (five, seven, or nine) to minimize the possibility of a deadlock. Some bylaws provide that the corporation could have a variable range board — for example, no fewer than three and no more than nine directors. Whereas the older statutes required that directors be residents of the state of incorporation, the modern view is that directors need not be residents of the state of incorporation or shareholders of the corporation, unless the articles or bylaws so require. MBCA § 8.02. The articles or bylaws can set minimum and maximum age standards and residency requirements, but the trend is to avoid such limitations.

To ensure that directors have the legal capacity to enter into contracts, they should have attained the age of majority, namely 18 years of age. Statutes do not set a maximum age. They also set no maximum number of directors. Having an unusually large board, however, makes management difficult and cumbersome. Directors can usually increase or decrease the size of the board by amending the bylaws (or articles, if provisions establishing the size of the board are contained therein), but the corporation can never have fewer directors than required by state statute.

Typically, directors cannot sit on the boards of competing corporations. Because directors owe fiduciary duties and duties of loyalty to the corporation, a director cannot fulfill those duties if he or she is also on the board of directors of a competitor.

Directors who are also employees or officers of the corporation are sometimes called **inside directors**, and those who have no other relationship with the corporation are often called **outside directors** or **independent directors.**

Inside director
A director who is also an employee or officer of the corporation

Outside director
A director who is not an employee or officer of the corporation, also called an *independent director*

Independent director
A director with no family or business ties to a corporation other than board membership

3. *Functions of Directors*

Although directors are elected and removable by shareholders, directors are not puppets of the shareholders. Once elected, their duties are owed to the corporation to promote its welfare. Under MBCA § 8.01, directors are charged with exercising all corporate powers and managing the entire business affairs of a corporation. Although directors may delegate some of their duties to officers or committees, certain duties, such as authorizing dividends, filling vacancies on the board, and amending bylaws, cannot be so delegated.

Directors are generally responsible for taking the following actions:

a. Authorizing distributions;
b. Adopting, amending, and repealing bylaws;
c. Appointing, supervising, and removing officers;
d. Determining financial matters, such as issuing stock, reacquiring stock, obtaining loans, and issuing bonds;
e. Determining products and services to be offered and the prices for them;
f. Determining wages and employee benefits and compensation, including their own benefits and compensation;
g. Initiating extraordinary matters such as mergers or the purchase or sale of corporate assets; and
h. Exercising responsibility for corporate operations.

4. *Election, Term, Vacancies, and Removal of Directors*

Election.   The initial directors may be named in the articles of incorporation. If not, the initial board will be elected at the corporation's first organizational meeting. Those directors will serve until the corporation's first annual shareholders' meeting. The directors will then be elected at the first annual meeting and at every annual meeting thereafter, unless their terms are staggered.

Directors are typically elected by a plurality of votes. For example, assume OmniWorld, Inc., a corporation, has 1,000 shares outstanding, 600 of which are represented at a meeting called to elect a director. Three individuals are running for one vacancy on the board of directors. If Candidate A receives 290 votes, Candidate B receives 220 votes, and Candidate C receives 90 votes, Candidate A will be the winner by a plurality of votes, even though Candidate A did not receive a vote of the majority (in this case, a majority vote would be 301, or one-half of the number of outstanding shares present plus one). A number of recent shareholder proposals have been made to require that directors be elected by majority (rather than plurality) vote. See Section C for further discussion.

Term.   The articles or bylaws may provide that not all of the directors are to be elected each year. This arrangement is referred to as a **staggered system** because the directors do not all face election at the same time; their terms are divided into groupings or are staggered. A common staggered system for boards of directors is a total of nine directors, divided into three groups, with the members of a group standing for election each year. Each director will have a three-year term; however, those terms will not all be served concurrently. In essence, the U.S. Senate is a staggered system, with all senators having a six-year term but only one-third standing for election every two years. Staggered or classified boards provide some continuity of expertise for corporations inasmuch as the entire board of directors will not be replaced at one time. Additionally, a staggered board makes a hostile takeover more difficult because it will take the acquiror some amount of time to replace all directors with her own hand-picked selections. Because a staggered system will reduce the impact of cumulative voting, it might not be allowed when cumulative voting exists. For example, if a shareholder has 100 votes and nine directors are being elected, under cumulative voting, the shareholder will have 900 votes to cast; if the board is staggered, however, and only three directors will be elected each time, the shareholder has only 300 votes to cast. As discussed later, at the insistence of their shareholders, many public corporations are eliminating their staggered or classified boards and moving toward annual elections of all board members.

If the articles authorize dividing the shares into classes, the articles may also authorize the election of all or some directors by one or more classes. Thus, if there are three classes of stock, Common A shareholders might elect three directors, Common B shareholders might elect three directors, and Common C shareholders might elect three directors. Such an arrangement may well promote minority representation on the board because Common A shareholders might own only a small percentage of the corporation's stock (the articles having specified that the corporation can issue only a certain number of shares of Common A stock), but will be guaranteed they can elect one-third of the board.

Staggered system
Method of corporate governance in which not all directors are elected at the same time or election

Vacancies.   If a vacancy occurs in the board of directors due to resignation, retirement, or death, or if a new position is created pursuant to amendment of the corporate articles or bylaws, the vacancy will be filled either by the shareholders or the remaining directors. Most bylaws provide that the remaining directors may fill such a vacancy. If numerous vacancies exist, perhaps due to the simultaneous deaths of directors in an accident, if the remaining directors do not constitute a quorum, they may nevertheless fill vacancies by a majority vote of all directors remaining in office. MBCA § 8.10(a)(3). The new director elected to fill the vacancy usually "steps into the shoes" of his or her predecessor and serves for the remainder of the predecessor's term. Directors may resign at any time, by providing written notice to the corporation.

Removal.   At common law, directors, once elected by the shareholders, could be removed from their positions only "for cause." The "cause" was typically fraud or dishonesty. The modern approach provided by the MBCA and by most state statutes now allows shareholders to remove directors either with or without cause (unless the articles provide that directors can be removed only for cause). "Cause" not only includes fraud or dishonesty but generally encompasses breach of duty and incompetence. The theory underlying the modern policy is that the shareholders own the corporation and they thus have the right at any time to determine who should manage it. This allows the shareholders greater flexibility because it is often difficult to prove fraud or dishonesty. Thus, if the shareholders elect directors in April, they can remove some or even all of those directors at any time thereafter without waiting for the next annual meeting.

Shareholders representing 10 percent of the ownership of the corporation can require that a meeting be held by demanding that the corporation call a special meeting. The notice of the meeting must state its purpose — namely, to consider removal of a director. Generally, a director can be removed only by vote of the shareholders who were entitled to elect him. Thus, if director Smith is elected by Common A shareholders, only Common A shareholders can remove Smith. When cumulative voting is authorized, a director cannot be removed if the number of votes sufficient to elect him under cumulative voting is voted against removal. Thus, if 100 shares would have been sufficient to elect a director under cumulative voting, then the director cannot be removed if 100 shares vote against removal. This ensures that the interests of minority shareholders who cumulatively vote are not circumvented by removal of a director by majority vote immediately after election.

In the event that shareholders cannot muster sufficient votes to remove a director who is also a majority shareholder (because the director has sufficient votes to block his own removal), shareholders (or the board of directors) can apply to court for removal. In this case, removal by the court is dependent on proof of the director's fraudulent or dishonest conduct, gross abuse of authority, and a showing that removal is in the best interest of the corporation. MBCA § 8.09. Generally, directors cannot remove other directors, although some states allow directors to remove directors who have been convicted of a felony or have been adjudged to be of unsound mind.

5. *Directors' Meetings*

The management of the corporation is accomplished by the directors acting at meetings (or by unanimous written consent). Few statutes give guidance regarding the notice and conduct of directors' meetings. Thus, most directors' meetings are governed by the bylaws of the corporation. Just as there are two types of shareholder meetings (annual and special), there are two types of directors' meetings, regular and special.

Regular Meetings.   Most boards meet at regularly scheduled intervals, whether once a week, a month, or once a quarter. These scheduled meetings are called regular meetings and the board conducts its business and manages the corporation at these meetings. Although there is no requirement to do so, many corporations also hold annual board of directors' meetings immediately following the shareholders' annual meeting. New officers are often appointed at this annual directors' meeting.

Special Meetings.   A special meeting is any meeting held between regular meetings. Special meetings are typically called to discuss matters that cannot wait until the next regular meeting. Provisions relating to who is authorized to call a special meeting (generally, the chair of the board) will be found in the bylaws.

Place of Meetings.   The place of the meeting, whether regular or special, may be specified in the bylaws or may be determined by the directors. Meetings need not be held in the state of incorporation and generally can be held anywhere. If no specific location is provided in the bylaws, at the end of each regular meeting, the board should specify the location of the next regular meeting.

Notice of Meetings.   Generally, directors are not entitled to notice of regular meetings. Because it is their duty to manage the corporation, they are expected to know when the board regularly meets. Thus, providing notice of a regular meeting is as unneeded as a phone call from an employer to an employee each morning reminding the employee to come to work.

MBCA § 8.22(b) provides that unless the articles or bylaws provide otherwise, special meetings require two days' advance notice of the date, time, and place of the meeting. Other statutes merely require that reasonable advance notice be given of special meetings. The notice typically need not state the purpose of the directors' special meeting.

Waiver of Notice.   Directors can give up or waive their right to receive notice of any meeting either before or after the meeting. The waiver must be in writing, signed, and filed with the minutes or other corporate records. See Figure 11-9 for a sample waiver of notice by a director. A director's attendance at a meeting constitutes a waiver, unless the director attends the meeting for the purpose of objecting to the meeting. Such an objection must be made at the beginning of any meeting.

The stringent and detailed provisions relating to notice for shareholders are somewhat relaxed with regard to notice for directors. The rationale is generally that because the directors manage the corporation, they have access to information relating to the corporation's affairs and need little protection. Shareholders, on the

---

FIGURE 11-9
Waiver of Notice of Meeting by Director

The undersigned, a director of FTB, Inc., a Delaware corporation, hereby waives notice of and consents to the holding of a special meeting of the board of directors of FTB, Inc., held on May 28, 2009, at 1024 Fifteenth Street, N.W., Washington, D.C. 20005 at 10:00 A.M. for the purpose of selecting officers for FTB, Inc.

Date: _____   _____
                                                 Signature

---

other hand, participate in corporate affairs only by voting, and are therefore entitled to greater protection to ensure their limited rights of participation are safeguarded.

Quorum.   Directors cannot take action at any meeting unless a quorum is present. Generally, a quorum consists of a majority of the number of directors as fixed in the articles or bylaws. Although the articles or bylaws may provide that a greater number than a majority is needed for a quorum, they may not provide that a quorum consists of fewer than one-third of the prescribed number of directors. MBCA § 8.24.

Assume the bylaws of a corporation prescribe that there shall be nine directors. Unless other provisions exist, a quorum will be five directors (regardless of board vacancies). Once five board members are present, action may be taken.

These quorum requirements are typically relaxed with regard to filling vacancies. If the number of directors remaining in office is insufficient to constitute a quorum, the directors may fill a vacancy by the affirmative vote of those directors remaining.

Proxies.   Generally, directors cannot act or vote by proxy. Directors have a fiduciary duty to the corporation and must make a fully informed decision using their personal judgment. Thus, they cannot delegate these duties to a proxy.

Conducting the Meeting.   Action is taken by directors at meetings by majority vote, unless the articles or bylaws require approval by a greater number of directors. Assuming a nine-member board, once a quorum is established, in this case five members, action may be taken by a majority of those present (in this case three). Each director is entitled to one vote on each issue presented at the meeting. Because the number of directors is manageable, a showing of hands or a voice vote is usually acceptable. Action taken at meetings is by resolutions passed by the board of directors. According to MBCA § 8.24(d), a director who is present at a meeting when action is taken is presumed to have agreed with the action unless his dissent is entered in the minutes. Thus, if the vote is not unanimous, each director's respective vote should be reflected in the minutes of the meeting so that if liability arises with respect to action taken by the board, it can be readily determined which directors, if any, violated their duties to the corporation.

The modern statutes recognize the difficulty of gathering a quorum for a meeting, and, therefore, most states (and the MBCA) permit directors to be present at meetings through conference calls or any other means of communication by which the parties may simultaneously hear each other. These statutes would therefore likely permit directors' meetings via the Internet. Many corporations use videoconferencing to conduct directors' meetings.

Minutes. Minutes of directors' meetings are usually taken and signed by the corporate secretary. There is no required format for minutes but they should reflect the action taken on each matter or resolution presented and should recite that notice was properly given, or that directors have signed appropriate waivers of notice (which are then placed in the minute book), that a quorum was present, and that certain actions were taken. Detail any other pertinent matters. See Figure 11-10 for typical minutes of directors' meetings.

6. Directors' Action Without a Meeting

Recognizing the difficulty of getting directors together for a meeting, all states (and MBCA § 8.21) permit directors to take action without a meeting if they unanimously consent in writing. Written consents are popular both for large corporations whose directors may reside in different places and for small corporations that might not take the time to have formal meetings for each action taken. This is a now a very common method of taking board action. The procedure and format of the written consent action for directors is nearly identical to that for shareholders. A document expressing the action to be taken is circulated to all directors for signature. Alternatively, the directors can sign counterparts or separate documents that are then compiled and placed in the minute book. Delaware allows its directors to act by electronic transmission, thus allowing written consents to be effected through e-mail. See Figure 11-11 for a sample action by written consent of directors.

7. Compensation of Directors

The older view was that directors were not required to be compensated merely for serving as directors. Directors were typically shareholders who, having a substantial financial stake in the corporation's affairs, would be amply rewarded through dividends and growth of the corporation. Most statutes now allow for compensation of directors pursuant to the articles or bylaws, or pursuant to action by shareholders or even by the board itself. The MBCA and most states provide that directors may fix their own compensation unless the articles or bylaws provide otherwise. MBCA § 8.11. The safeguard against directors establishing inappropriately high compensation for themselves is provided by the fiduciary duties owed by directors, the directors' liability for self-dealing, and the shareholders' ability to remove directors. Most modern large corporations fix a substantial annual sum to be paid to directors as compensation, as well as a significant stipend, often $1,000,

FIGURE 11-10
Minutes of Regular Meeting of Board of Directors

A regular meeting of the Board of Directors of FTB, Inc., a Delaware Corporation (the "Corporation"), was held on Tuesday, June 2, 2009, at 9:00 A.M. at the principal offices of the Corporation located at 1024 Fifteenth Street, N.W., Washington D.C. 20005.

The following persons, constituting all of the Directors of the Corporation were present at the meeting: Lisa Black, Christopher Wagner, Kenneth Lyons, William Brady, and Patricia E. Moore.

The Chairman of the Board of the Corporation, Frederick G. Tellam, presided as Chairman of the meeting, and Diana Hendrix acted as its Secretary.

The Chairman called the meeting to order and stated that a quorum of directors was present for the meeting.

The Secretary announced that the meeting was called pursuant to Article IX of the Bylaws.

The Secretary read the minutes of the last regular meeting of the Board of Directors. The minutes were approved and placed in the corporate minute book.

A discussion was had on the proposed lease for the Corporation's offices in Maryland, the Corporation's financial status, including the need for additional sums for operating expenses, and dividends to be paid on the outstanding common shares of the Corporation.

After motions duly made, seconded, and carried, the following resolutions were unanimously adopted by the Board of Directors:

> RESOLVED, that the proposed lease between the Corporation and Josephine LaPointe for the premises located at 511 State Street, Baltimore, Maryland, is commercially reasonable and in the best interests of the Corporation and the lease is approved.
>
> RESOLVED, that the Treasurer of the Corporation is authorized to borrow on behalf of the Corporation from one or more banks or other lending institutions such amount as the Treasurer determines necessary to meet the operating needs of the Corporation, and on such terms as the Treasurer may determine, but in no event may the Treasurer borrow more than the sum of $300,000 in total.
>
> RESOLVED, the Corporation shall pay a cash dividend from its capital surplus to those persons identified as owners of its common shares on its books as of June 2, 2009, in the amount of $1.50 per share. The payment date for said dividend shall be July 1, 2009.

The officers were instructed to take appropriate action to effect the purposes of these resolutions.

There being no further business before the meeting, on motion duly made, seconded, and unanimously carried, it was adjourned.

Date: _____

_____
Diana Hendrix, Secretary

per meeting. Courts are reluctant to interfere with director compensation, and a complaining shareholder must generally prove that the compensation is excessive when compared to that paid to others in similar businesses. Publicly traded corporations must disclose the compensation paid to their top five executives over the past three years. Compensation might include not only cash, but also grants of

FIGURE 11-11
Action by Written Consent of Directors

The undersigned, constituting all of the Directors of FTB, Inc. (the "Corporation"), hereby take the following actions by written consent pursuant to Del. Code Ann. tit. 8, § 141(f) and Article IV of the bylaws of the Corporation as if present at a meeting duly called pursuant to notice.

RESOLVED, the Directors approve the hiring of Celia G. Spencer as General Counsel for the Corporation, effective March 9, 2009, to perform such duties and at a salary as determined by the President of the Corporation.

RESOLVED, the Certificate of Incorporation shall be amended to change the name of the Corporation to FTB Access Link, Co. and to increase the aggregate number of common shares which may be issued by the Corporation to 100,000, said actions to be voted on by the shareholders of the Corporation pursuant to a special meeting to be called therefor by the President of the Corporation.

The officers of the Corporation are hereby authorized to take appropriate action to effect the purposes of these resolutions.

Date: _____

Date: _____   Lisa Black

Date: _____   Christopher Wagner

Date: _____   Kenneth Lyons

Date: _____   William Brady

                                                       Patricia E. Moore

stock, stock options, enhanced benefits, and bonuses. Recent scandals involving excessive compensation are discussed later.

8. Rights of Directors to Information

To fulfill their duties to the corporation, directors have the right to inspect corporate records and books. The right of inspection extends to having copies made of various documents, and to having the reasonable assistance of experts, such as accountants and attorneys. If directors use these rights of inspection for an improper purpose, such as obtaining the list of corporate clients and customers to sell to a competitor, they may be liable for breach of their fiduciary duties to the corporation.

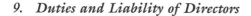

9.   Duties and Liability of Directors

The general standard of conduct for directors is set forth in MBCA § 8.30, which provides that a director must discharge his or her duties:

a.   In good faith; and
b.   In a manner reasonably believed to be in the best interests of the corporation.

Directors owe fiduciary duties, duties of the utmost good faith, to the corporation. This fiduciary responsibility includes a duty of loyalty to the corporation. Directors must exercise the care that a person in similar circumstances would reasonably believe appropriate. Directors can be liable not only for affirmative actions causing injury to the corporation, but also for failure to take appropriate action when required.

Conflicts of Interest.   A director of a corporation might have other business involvements that lead to a conflict of interest. For example, a director might own stock in another corporation desiring to transact business with the corporation of which he is a director. Similarly, a director might own certain property (real estate, inventory, trademarks) that the corporation wishes to acquire. Such situations pose an inherent conflict; the director is bound to exercise due care for the corporation of which he is a director and yet will want to gain personally from the transaction.

The older approach took a dim view of such transactions between the corporation and a director and generally made the transaction voidable at the option of the corporation. This older approach has been substantially relaxed by modern statutes. Delaware law provides that a transaction in which a director is interested is acceptable if any of the following are true:

- The material facts of the transaction and the director's interest were disclosed to or known by the board and the board of directors approves or ratifies the transaction by majority vote (without the interested director's participation in the vote); or
- The material facts of the transaction and the director's interest were disclosed to or known by shareholders entitled to vote on the transaction and they approve or ratify the transaction; or
- The transaction was fair to the corporation. Del. Code Ann. tit. 8, § 144.

Interested directors may be counted in determining the presence of a quorum at a meeting considering the transaction. The MBCA approach is similar and generally allows transactions in which a director might have a conflict if the director discloses his interest and a majority of noninterested directors approve it. MBCA §§ 8.61, 8.62.

Business Judgment Rule.   Courts are somewhat reluctant to impose liability too readily on directors for fear no one would agree to serve as a director if such a specter was likely and because courts recognize that they should not use the advantage of hindsight to second-guess decisions made by directors. Thus,

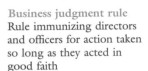

Business judgment rule
Rule immunizing directors and officers for action taken so long as they acted in good faith

most jurisdictions recognize the **business judgment rule,** which immunizes directors from liability for decisions made by the board so long as the board had a reasonable basis for its decision and acted in good faith, even if the corporation sustains harm as a result of the decision. Directors are therefore not placed in the untenable position of being guarantors of the corporation's success. Thus, if mistakes are made or errors in judgment occur, directors are generally not liable unless they failed to act with reasonable care. In essence, a presumption exists that the board acted with sound business judgment, and so long as some rational business purpose can be found for board action or inaction, the directors will be protected from liability. Delaware has taken this approach a step further by providing that the corporation can state in its certificate of incorporation that directors will only be liable for conduct that involves illegality, a breach of the duty of loyalty, personal financial benefit, intentional misconduct, or payment of an unlawful dividend. Del. Code Ann. tit. 8, § 102(b)(7). The MBCA approach is similar (MBCA § 2.02).

The collapse of Enron Corp. and other spectacular corporate crashes in 2001 and 2002 resulted in increased debate about the conduct and responsibilities of boards of directors. Although the board of directors of Enron was named as one of the nation's five best boards in 2000, the investigative report issued in 2002, after Enron's failure, faulted the board for failing to demand more information. Board members of Enron received $70,000 annually merely for serving on the board.

Generally, due to the business judgment rule, although many lawsuits against directors may be filed by furious shareholders, few may succeed absent provable, direct fraud. Lawsuits against accountants, attorneys, and others have often proven more successful.

In one particularly compelling case illustrating the strong presumption of the validity of board action and the business judgment rule, *In re Walt Disney Co. Derivative Litigation*, No. Civ. A. 15452, 2005 WL 2056651 (Del. Ch. Aug. 9, 2005), *aff'd*, 906 A.2d 27 (Del. 2006), Disney's stockholders brought an action against the corporation's directors and officers for breach of fiduciary duty and waste in connection with the hiring and firing of Michael Ovitz, who received $140 million in termination benefits although he had been with the company only 14 months. While noting that the severance package was "breathtaking" and that the directors did a poor job of handling the situation, it was not so poor that they were grossly negligent. In sum, although the court concluded that Disney's board had not breached its fiduciary duties, it was highly critical of the board's conduct and deference to its chief executive, Michael Eisner.

In sum, there is a delicate balance between the need for protecting directors' decisions from endless second-guessing and the need for shareholder and investor protection.

One interesting result of the recent corporate scandals is an evolving reluctance by many individuals to serve on corporate boards. Serving on multiple boards and their committees was previously thought to be an honor for executives and a sign of their business expertise. For example, one director of an American company holds three board seats and observes meetings at one other company, resulting in 48 meetings per year. There is some evidence that multiple board positions are declining. In 2007, the Business Roundtable (an association of the CEOs of leading U.S. companies) reported that 75 percent of CEOs serve on no more than one other public company board and nearly 30 percent do not serve on any other public company boards.

Given the climate of increasing shareholder litigation, many board members are now reconsidering their decisions to serve on corporate boards or are requiring additional compensation due to the increased time commitments required of directors to keep informed of company business in post-Enron corporate America.

Reliance on Others.   Because directors cannot be expected to have knowledge of all matters relating to the corporation, in discharging their duties and making decisions, directors are entitled to rely on information, opinions, reports, and advice of corporate officers, employees, attorneys, accountants, or other professionals, including financial statements and data prepared by committees. Generally, this reliance must be reasonable, and directors cannot bury their heads in the sand when they have actual knowledge or should make inquiries that would make reliance unreasonable. Moreover, directors have a duty of reasonable inquiry and a duty to become informed to ensure reliance is reasonable. Thus, directors may likely rely on appraisals of property performed by competent and professional appraisers; reliance, however, on advice from a neighbor's son taking a real estate class would not be "reasonable."

Extent of Liability and Defenses.   If directors violate their duties, they may be personally liable for the injury caused to the corporation by their breach. For example, directors may be personally liable for the payment of distributions to shareholders in violation of the articles of incorporation or state statutes. Directors may also be liable for acts of corporate officers or other agents of the corporation if the officers or agents were improperly supervised or were obviously incapable of fulfilling their functions.

In one case in mid-1999, a corporation was found liable for the deaths of three employees when a former employee went on a workplace rampage. The jury found that the company's vice president and the company were negligent in failing to prevent the assault because they had actual knowledge of the employee's previous acts of violence and threats. In view of such knowledge, the corporation had a duty to provide adequate security for its employees. The judgment was nearly $8 million.

It is generally not a defense to liability that a director was a "marquee" director, elected only to lend prestige to the board of directors. Once a person accepts the position of director, he or she is subject to the duty of due care. Similarly, directors cannot generally assert that they are not liable because they did not attend board meetings and were not informed of the board's activities. Board members have a duty to be informed of corporate activities. Particularly with the advent of technology enabling meetings to be held by conference call or videoconference, failure to attend meetings will not protect directors from liability. Advanced age, poor health, and inexperience are typically not defenses to liability. Once directors realize they cannot perform their duties because of age, infirmity, or inexperience, they should act in the best interests of the corporation by resigning.

Modern Practice: Insurance, Statutory Limitations, and Indemnification. Fearing litigation, many prospective directors and officers refuse to serve unless the corporation procures **director and officer liability insurance** to insure against claims of breach of duty by directors and officers. In most instances, such insurance provides for attorneys' fees and costs incurred in defending directors and officers

D & O insurance
Insurance procured to protect directors and officers from claims and lawsuits

against claims made for breaches of duty. Moreover, most policies will pay the amount of a judgment rendered against the directors or officer if the director or officer acted in good faith. Willful, reckless, illegal acts are rarely insured. The cost of D & O insurance is very high and for some matters, such as patent infringement protection, is nearly prohibitively expensive. According to industry and insurance experts, the premiums for D & O insurance rose about 33 percent in 2003, and experts predict that industries such as real estate and financial services may face premium increases of 15 percent to 400 percent in 2008 and following years.

Due to rising insurance costs and the increased litigation against directors and officers, many states have enacted statutes allowing corporations to limit the exposure of directors. California and Delaware statutes are typical of many. They state that the certificate of incorporation may include a provision eliminating or limiting the personal liability of a director to the corporation or to its shareholders (but not to third parties). The limitation is not available for breach of the director's duty of loyalty, for unlawful distribution of dividends, for acts or omissions not in good faith or that involve intentional misconduct or a knowing violation of the law, for any transaction from which the director derived an improper benefit, or, in California, for acts or omissions that constitute an unexcused pattern of inattention that amounts to abdication of the director's duty to the corporation or its shareholders. Cal. Corp. Code § 204(10); Del. Code Ann. tit. 8, § 102(b)(7). Other states have adopted different approaches, such as imposing a ceiling for damages against directors.

Indemnify
Reimbursing another for injury sustained by the other; "holding one harmless" from allegations against the person

Corporations may agree to **indemnify** or reimburse directors or officers from liability and expenses incurred in defending a lawsuit brought against them. Generally, corporations will indemnify corporate management only if the directors and officers acted in good faith and in a manner reasonably believed to be in the corporation's best interests. MBCA § 8.52 provides that a corporation must indemnify reasonable expenses incurred by a director who was successful in defending an action brought against her due to alleged acts or omissions as a director. On the other hand, MBCA § 8.51(d) prohibits a corporation from indemnifying a director if she is adjudged liable to the corporation in a derivative action that results in a judgment against the director or in a proceeding in which a director is adjudged liable for receiving an improper financial benefit.

10.   Delegation of Authority

The board of directors has the authority to delegate some of its functions to officers or to various committees. A majority of all directors must approve the creation of a committee. Any such committee will often have at least one member of the board serving on it. These committees assist the board by carrying out ordinary corporate activities. MBCA § 8.25 ensures that committees exercise only limited authority by prohibiting them from taking the following actions, which are nondelegable because they substantially affect shareholders: authorizing distributions, amending the bylaws, filling vacancies on the board, or approving certain matters that only shareholders may approve, such as mergers or dissolutions. The delegation of certain duties to officers or committees does not relieve directors of their responsibilities and duties inasmuch as they are expected to select and supervise carefully those to whom duties have been delegated.

Due to the complexity of managing a large corporation in today's global economy, many corporations have established a variety of committees to deal more efficiently with specific concerns of the corporation. Some of the more common committees are as follows:

- Executive committee: Acts on board matters when board cannot and acts on matters specifically delegated to committee by entire board;
- Audit committee: Reviews financial matters, selects corporate auditors, and supervises audits of corporate accounts;
- Nominating committee: Selects management's slate of candidates for elections of directors;
- Compensation committee: Reviews and approves compensation for senior executives (both cash and noncash, such as stock options); and
- Shareholder litigation committee: Determines whether corporation should initiate litigation.

C. Corporate Scandals, Reform and the Sarbanes-Oxley Act, and Governance

1. Introduction

On October 16, 2001, Enron announced the disappearance of approximately $1 billion of net worth from its balance sheet. The Enron scandal was the first of many that staggered financial markets. Following Enron, WorldCom admitted to improper accounting procedures that caused its stock to plunge nearly 100 percent, and Tyco International also acknowledged questionable accounting methods, causing its stock to drop approximately 60 percent. Coupled with the shattering of reputations of accounting firm Arthur Andersen and wealthy investor Martha Stewart, the parading of corporate wrongdoers in handcuffs, and the bursting of the investment bubble in the stock market in 2001 triggering an economic recession, investor confidence in corporate America and the financial markets was severely shaken.

2. Some Suspected Causes of the Scandals

What caused the boom and the bust and these corporate scandals? A variety of theories have been advanced, including the following:

- *Excessive compensation.* In the late 1990s, cash salaries and bonuses significantly decreased for senior executives at major companies. The total value of pay packages increased, however, with most compensation coming in the form of stock options. To ensure that the options remained valuable, companies inflated earnings so that the stock price would remain high. Some experts believe that executive stock options gave managers a strong inducement to mislead investors about the true financial condition of their companies. Because a plunge in stock price would cause the options to become worthless, companies disguised their losses and focused more on short-term growth than long-term corporate stability.

- *Expensing of stock options.* Under generally accepted accounting principles, stock options (unlike salaries and bonuses) have not been counted as corporate expenses. Thus, a company might issue as many options as it desired and would not have to deduct any money from the earnings reported to shareholders. Once again, this led to granting of mega-options to senior executives and thus to the practice described earlier of disguising losses to ensure that the options would remain valuable. In early 2006, a new accounting rule by the Financial Accounting Standards Board took effect, requiring that stock options be counted as an expense against earnings. As discussed in Chapter Eighteen, a number of companies have thus stopped issuing stock options.

- *Board conflicts of interest.* As executives often looted the corporate treasury, members of boards of directors often looked the other way due to familial and business relationships with corporate wrongdoers.

- *Lack of accounting oversight.* Auditors such as Arthur Andersen not only provided accounting services to corporations but also provided significant consulting services. These auditing firms were thus less likely to challenge a company's financial practices for fear they would lose lucrative consulting contracts. These conflicts of interest thus caused many auditors to look the other way in the face of questionable accounting practices.

- *Euphoria and hype.* As the obsession with the stock market grew in the 1990s, business and financial reporters and stock analysts became cheerleaders for questionable stocks. Analysts, in particular, were encouraged to "hype" a stock and rate it as a "buy" to please prospective banking clients. Investment bankers pressured analysts in their firms to endorse questionable stocks so the firm could then generate increased banking revenue, despite the fact that the analysts were supposed to be neutral and removed from the investment banking business of their firms. Individual investors then bought stock based on these hyped recommendations, which the analysts often acknowledged as phony.

- *Lack of regulatory oversight.* NASDAQ itself encouraged companies to go public and sell stock, enabling thousands of risky companies without solid earnings to list their shares on the market and sell to unsuspecting investors.

- *Greed.* In a money culture in which Jeffrey Skilling, Enron's CEO, told his employees, "All that matters is money," the stage was set for the collapse of the bubble. Kenneth Lay of Enron exercised stock options worth more than $200 million shortly before Enron's collapse. In many other companies as well, stock prices were maintained by accounting devices just long enough to allow senior managers to cash in hundreds of millions of dollars of stock options. Another Enron executive struck deals that cumulatively cost investors $2 billion while she took home $100 million during her tenure with the company. Investors must also take some responsibility, as they were also caught up in the cycle of greed, demanding steady earnings. So long as the market kept rising, the investors were also content to look the other way. As one expert stated, a confluence of all of these factors worked together to create the "perfect storm" of fraud, corruption, boom, and bust.

3. The Fallout

The total cost to investors and the economy is not yet known. What is known is that thousands of employees lost their jobs, thousands of workers who owned shares in their company in retirement plans lost their savings, numerous executives have gone to prison, Enron and WorldCom agreed to settlements of $7.2 and $6.2 million, respectively, and investor confidence in the economy was severely shaken. One report has estimated that U.S. citizens lost more than $200 billion in savings, jobs, and retirement funds.

As to the fallout to corporations and their executives:

- Arthur Andersen has collapsed.
- L. Dennis Kozlowski of Tyco was found guilty of fraud, larceny, and conspiracy and was sentenced from 8 to 25 years in prison and is now serving time.
- In early 2004, Andrew Fastow of Enron pleaded guilty and agreed to serve a 10-year sentence and to cooperate with the authorities and return $23.8 million to investors.
- WorldCom founder Bernard J. Ebbers is serving 25 years in prison for fraud and conspiracy.
- In late 2004, Franklin Brown, former vice chairman and chief counsel for Rite Aid, was sentenced to 10 years in prison for his role in Rite Aid's massive accounting scandal.
- John Rigas of Adelphia was sentenced to 15 years for fraud (and his son to 20 years) in 2005.
- In May 2006, former Enron executives Kenneth Lay and Jeffrey Skilling were found guilty of multiple counts of conspiracy and fraud. Skilling is serving a 24-year sentence. Lay died shortly after his trial, and his convictions were vacated. In all, 16 Enron executives pleaded guilty to crimes.
- Since the collapse of Enron and WorldCom, the federal government has obtained convictions of more than 200 chief executives and presidents, 53 finance chiefs, and more than 20 corporate attorneys.
- In June 2003, Sam Waksal of ImClone Systems was fined more than $4 million and sentenced to seven years for insider trading.
- Martha Stewart, lifestyle maven and close friend of Sam Waksal, was found guilty of obstructing justice and lying to investigators. She served five months in prison and was released in early 2005.
- Between March 2001 and mid-2003 more than 800 companies were delisted from NASDAQ, many for reasons related to the bursting of the stock bubble.
- Ten Wall Street firms agreed to pay $1.4 billion in fines and penalties and agreed to purchase and distribute at least three sources of independent research to their clients.
- Conseco, Inc., WorldCom, Global Crossing, Enron, Tyco, Rite Aid, and Adelphia all filed petitions under the U.S. Bankruptcy Act.

4. *Reform and the Sarbanes-Oxley Act*

To prevent another series of corporate scandals and recession, a number of proposals have been implemented and advanced. The most important reform is the corporate and accounting law, the Sarbanes-Oxley Act of 2002 (15 U.S.C. § 7201 et seq.). "SOX" was signed into law in mid-2002 and constitutes the most far-reaching legislation relating to securities since the 1930s. Following are some of its more important provisions:

- *Oversight board.* The Act creates the Public Company Accounting Oversight Board, a nonprofit corporation rather than a government agency, to establish auditing, quality control, and ethics standards, and to conduct investigations and take disciplinary actions against accountants.
- *Auditor independence.* The Act limits the scope of consulting services that accounting firms can provide to their public company audit clients. This provision prevents auditors from controlling the entire financial reporting system at a company.
- *Conflicts of interest.* The Act requires company insiders to notify the SEC of company stock transactions promptly, prohibits stock transfers by management during certain periods, and forbids personal loans by companies to certain senior managers. The Act also deals with conflicts of interest by analysts by forbidding investment banking staff from supervising the research of analysts.
- *Audit committees.* The Act provides for strong audit committees, all of whose members must be independent from company management.
- *Certification and accountability.* To improve corporate accountability, CEOs and CFOs must certify that company financial statements fairly present their companies' financial condition. Issuers must also publish information in their annual reports assessing the effectiveness of their internal financial reporting control structure and procedures. Smaller public companies, those with market values of less than $75 million, need not document the safeguards they have in place until after 2009. Smaller companies have consistently complained about the high costs of compliance and some have gone private to avoid the expense.
- *Expanded SEC review.* SOX requires the SEC to review public filings of publicly traded companies at least once every three years.
- *Broader sanctions.* SOX imposes tough jail sentences for securities fraud and extends the statute of limitations for securities fraud, allows the SEC to bar directors and officers from serving on public company boards if they are found to be "unfit" for service in a public company, and provides that debts of individuals that arise from civil and criminal penalties imposed as a result of securities fraud violations may not be discharged in bankruptcy.

In the wake of Enron and SOX, a number of companies and entities have voluntarily imposed even more far-reaching reforms, including the following:

- Although SOX requires the SEC to review public filings at least once every three years, the SEC has committed to annually monitoring various public filings of Fortune 500 companies.

- Partly to comply with new SOX requirements, in mid-2002, the New York Stock Exchange and NASDAQ adopted stricter standards for companies listed on their exchanges, including a requirement that boards of directors consist of a majority of independent directors; that independent directors oversee director nominations, corporate governance, and compensation; an expansion of duties and responsibilities for audit committees; and a requirement that the companies adopt a code of conduct.
- Many publicly traded companies have exceeded the NYSE and NASDAQ reforms. For example, a recent survey by the Business Roundtable (an association of CEOs of leading corporations) reported that nine out of ten companies have boards that are at least 80 percent independent, although the exchange requirements call only for a majority of independent directors.

Although there is still great public enthusiasm about the reforms engendered by SOX, there is some pressure to scale back some of its provisions. Many companies are incurring extremely high audit feesand increased turnover among their financial executives. Many critics allege that parts of the law require executives to spend too much time on reporting requirements rather than on leading their companies. Other critics contend that the SOX's strict reporting requirements have caused a reduction in the number of foreign companies that trade on the New York Stock Exchange. The SEC continues to study the issue to lighten the regulatory burden on smaller businesses.

5. *Governance Guidelines*

Perhaps in response to increased shareholder activism and lawsuits, the past several years have witnessed a trend in the adoption by public companies of formal written guidelines dealing with corporate governance. General Motors Company took the lead in 1994, and most large companies are following. In many instances, the guidelines are drafted by institutional investors who have issued statements, called **governance guidelines,** on how they want their investees to operate.

Governance guidelines
Formal written policies relating to management of corporations

Both TIAA-CREF and the California Public Employees' Retirement System have issued such statements to the corporations in which they invest heavily. Although the investors cannot force the corporations to implement the guidelines, the guidelines have spurred many companies to enact guidelines of their own. A recent survey of corporate board practices by the Society of Corporate Secretaries and Governance Professionals found that nearly half of the survey respondents reported they had either adopted guidelines or were seriously considering doing so.

Some guidelines suggested by institutional investors call for the following:

- Clear definitions of director relationships to determine when directors are independent rather than subject to a conflict of interest involving other companies or family members;
- Diversity in boards of directors;
- Periodic reviews by corporations of their processes and structures to provide a "check up" as to how well the corporation is operating;

- Establishment of standards for director attendance at meetings so that failure to attend a certain percentage of meetings will render a director ineligible for further renomination to the board;
- Performance reviews of individual board members and of the boards themselves;
- Mandatory retirement age for directors; and
- Mandatory stock ownership by directors to ensure directors' interests are closely aligned with those of shareholders (with some guidelines setting actual targets, for example, requiring directors to own stock worth five times their annual compensation).

Microsoft Corp. has adopted a number of these guidelines in its formal Corporate Governance Guidelines, including a requirement that at least a majority of its board be independent; that outside directors should retire at age 75; that independent directors should conduct an annual review of the CEO's performance; and that the audit, compensation, governance, nominating, and antitrust committees consist entirely of independent directors.

Although definitions vary, an *independent director* is generally one who has no relationship with the company other than board membership and thus has no business or family ties with the company.

Both GM's and Microsoft's governance guidelines are available on their Web sites, at www.gm.com and www.microsoft.com, respectively.

The adoption of governance guidelines is a direct result of investor pressure to improve board functioning and another sign of the continuing shift of increasing power to shareholders.

6. Trends in Governance

There is no doubt that shareholders have become increasingly activist, resulting in a number of additional reforms and trends in corporate governance practice. Among the trends seen in the past few years are the following:

- A number of corporations have adopted stock ownership guidelines for top managers, often requiring the director or executive officer to hold stock valued at a certain percentage of his or her base salary.
- Numerous shareholder proposals have been made recommending that directors be elected by majority rather than plurality vote. In an extreme situation, in a plurality-vote case, a director could be elected with one vote, because the only two options available to shareholders of most publicly traded companies are to either vote "for" or "withhold" for a director. For example, in an election for one board position, Nominee X could be elected if he received only one vote "for" and 500 votes were withheld if Nominee Y received no votes "for." Moreover, in many companies, there are often only as many candidates for the board as there are empty slots, making it nearly impossible to block the board's desired candidates in these uncontested elections. Several companies, including Intel, General Electric, and FedEx, have voluntarily adopted majority voting in director elections. In fact, nearly 60 percent of Fortune 500 companies

implemented some form of majority voting in director elections prior to the 2008 proxy season. PROXY Governance, Inc., a proxy advisory service, has noted that majority voting is thus on its way to becoming an industry standard.

- Closely related to the trend of electing directors in public corporations by majority rather than plurality vote, 2006 amendments to the MBCA provide that public corporations may adopt alternative voting systems for director elections in their articles of incorporation. (If the articles do not so provide, plurality voting remains the standard or "default" rule.) These new amendments also provide that a nominee who receives more votes against election than in favor of election is still elected. The term of that director, however, is shortened to a period of 90 days after the election results. The remaining board members will fill the office, and the director has no right to hold over. MBCA § 10.22.

- Also related to the move toward electing directors by majority vote rather than a mere plurality are proposals that would make it easier for shareholders to oust directors. For example, in 2006, Lockheed Martin Corp. adopted a rule allowing shareholders to remove a member of its board by majority vote; previously, the corporation had required an 80 percent vote by shareholders to remove a director.

- Another clear trend in corporate governance is a move away from using a staggered or classified board of directors toward electing all directors at the same time. Shareholders have successfully argued that electing directors annually rather than every two or three years makes board members more responsive to them and more accountable for financial missteps.

- A number of shareholder proposals focus on reining in executive pay and requiring more complete disclosures of executive compensation. Called "say on pay" or "pay for performance" proposals, these resolutions reflect growing anger on the part of shareholders about excessive executive compensation (especially for executives whose companies have underperformed) and their desire to link executive compensation directly to company performance. In 1982 the average CEO of a large U.S. company earned 42 times what his or her average employee did; by 2007, the average CEO made 431 times what the average employee did. Generally, say on pay proposals are aimed at giving shareholders only an advisory vote on executive pay. Nevertheless, they provide a way for shareholders to make their views known. Support for such proposals is steadily growing, with 60 proposals filed by shareholders in 2007 and more than 90 in 2008. In early 2009, the new SEC chairman endorsed giving shareholders a nonbinding vote on executive pay. Related to say on pay proposals are "clawbacks," which allow companies to seek recovery of compensation paid to executives when their companies have to restate their financials.

- New disclosure rules by the SEC require executives to explain their compensation in more detail. Marking the biggest changes in disclosure on executive compensation in 25 years, publicly traded companies must now provide more information in their proxy statements about the value of options and stock granted to their top five executives as well as a total compensation figure that includes all forms of cash and noncash pay (which would allow shareholders to compare pay from one company to another).

- Many shareholder proposals focus on "social issues." As examples, one shareholder proposal asked Exxon to publish data on climate change, and shareholders proposed 57 resolutions relating to global warming during the 2008 proxy season, nearly half of which were withdrawn after companies made commitments on setting targets for reducing greenhouse gas emissions and reaching other environmentally related goals.

- The SEC continues to consider the means by which shareholders can gain access to the company's proxy statement for the purpose of proposing their own slate of directors. Although SEC Rule 14a-8 allows shareholders to submit proposals (if they own at least 1 percent of the company's voting stock), companies often refuse these proposals because they do not comply with certain technical requirements. This is a decades-long debate, and 22 SEC chairmen have worked on this problem. As of the writing of this text, the SEC has again delayed taking action on this issue.

- Shareholder activism has accelerated with the use of the Internet, which allows shareholders to communicate with each other. Activists have created blogs, used MySpace, and even launched campaigns on YouTube to promote their agendas.

7. The 2008 Financial Crisis

Public confidence in the financial markets was further shaken in 2008 with the collapse of the Bear Stearns Companies, insurance giant American International Group, Inc. (AIG), Lehman Brothers, and Washington Mutual Bank; the placing of Fannie Mae and Freddie Mac under federal conservatorship; and the government bailout plan or rescue of these troubled financial institutions in the amount of $700 billion, which was approved in October 2008. Experts have cited numerous causes for these failures, including lack of government oversight, reckless speculation, greed, and the housing and credit crises. In particular, experts have focused on the fact that during the housing boom of the early 2000s, lenders relaxed standards for homebuyers and made subprime loans to these buyers. These risky loans were then packaged into pools and purchased by Wall Street. When the housing market slowed and their interest rates moved upward, homeowners were unable to make their mortgage payments and defaulted on their loans. Lenders and banks then became the "owners" of real estate worth less than what was owed for it. As losses mounted, loans became more difficult to obtain, causing a credit crunch. Without loans, spending slows, causing a further slowdown in the economy.

At the time of the writing of this text, the FBI had begun investigating whether fraud played a role in the problems at Fannie Mae, Freddie Mac, Lehman Brothers, and AIG. The SEC has also opened numerous investigations.

Some of the provisions in the American Recovery and Reinvestment Act of 2009 (the Obama administration's "stimulus bill") include the following measures, aimed at promoting the long-term health of American companies:

- Pay caps on senior officers of companies that receive massive government assistance.

- Compensation provisions that restrict additional compensation to executives to the form of stock that can only be redeemed by the executives after federal bailout money is repaid.
- Provisions allowing shareholders whose companies have received federal bailout funds to provide advisory votes on executive compensation, namely, "say on pay" votes.
- Provisions allowing the government to review bonuses and compensation paid to senior executives at companies who received federal bailout money to determine whether such payments should be recaptured or clawed back.

D. Rights and Duties of Officers

1. Introduction

The traditional **officers** of a corporation are president, vice president, secretary, and treasurer. A corporation may have more or fewer officers, if needed. The officers carry out day-to-day corporate activities and are selected, supervised, and removed by the board of directors. Officers are usually subject to the same standards of care as directors and, like directors, are fiduciaries of the corporation.

Officers
Individuals appointed by directors to carry out various corporate activities

2. Qualifications, Appointment, and Tenure

Some statutes require that the president or chief executive officer be a director. Most statutes, however, impose no qualifications or restrictions on those who can serve as officers.

Officers are typically selected or appointed by the board of directors, although some jurisdictions allow the shareholders to elect officers. See Figure 11-12

FIGURE 11-12
Resolution Appointing Officers

RESOLVED, effective immediately, the following persons are appointed to serve in the following corporate offices, at the pleasure of the Board of Directors, at the annual salary set forth next to their names.

President: Francis Fisher	$100,000
Vice President: Timothy J. Mislock	$85,000
Secretary: Nicola Pellegrini	$75,000
Treasurer: James Crittenden	$75,000

Each officer shall have the duties specified in the bylaws and as may be designated by the Board of Directors of the Corporation.

for a sample resolution appointing officers. It is often said that officers serve "at the pleasure of the board," meaning the directors have the authority to remove officers at any time, either with or without cause. MBCA § 8.43(b). Some officers, however, serve pursuant to an employment contract. In such case, removal of an officer contrary to the terms of the contract subjects the corporation to damages caused by the breach. In most instances, boards who remove officers must continue to pay them their contractually stipulated salary, much the same way some coaches of professional teams are "bought out of" their contracts. In fact, MBCA § 8.44 expressly states that an officer's removal does not affect the officer's contract with the corporation. An officer may generally resign at any time by simply delivering notice of the resignation to the board of directors. Directors fill vacancies in offices. Some senior officers may be allowed by the board of directors to appoint other inferior officers or assistant officers.

3. Officers' Functions

The range of functions performed by the officers is extremely broad. In general, officers perform whatever functions are delegated to them by the directors. In large corporations, the board of directors may establish a policy or goal and then charge the officers with achieving the objective. For example, the board of a large corporation engaged in the manufacture of cars may determine that the corporation should introduce a new sports car into the market. The officers may be told, in effect, "Make it happen." The officers would then engage engineers, commission market studies, approve advertising, and perform all other tasks so that the board's goal is met.

MBCA § 8.41 provides that officers have the authority and shall perform the duties set forth in the bylaws or the duties prescribed by the directors. See the bylaws in Appendix H defining the duties and responsibilities of corporate officers. Typically, the only functions statutorily imposed on officers are that one of the officers shall have the responsibility for preparing minutes of the meetings of directors' and shareholders' meetings and maintaining and authenticating records for the corporation (for example, maintaining the articles and bylaws of the corporation).

One common duty performed by various officers, especially by corporate secretaries, is to certify that certain facts are true or documents are correct. These certificates are often provided in connection with a corporate transaction such as a sale of assets or a merger. The officer will certify that copies of articles and bylaws are true and correct, that the president's signature is valid, and that various resolutions were passed to approve the transaction. If time elapses between the date of the certificate and the date of the closing of the transaction, the officer may be asked to provide a **bringdown certificate** verifying that no changes have occurred since the date of the original certificate, so as to assure the other party or a state agency that there have been no material changes in the corporation's status or documents since the original certificate was issued.

Bringdown certificate
Certificate of corporate officer verifying continuing accuracy of facts or documents

4. Titles of Officers

The MBCA does not require any specific officers. The corporation's bylaws may describe the officers desired, or the board of directors may appoint officers as needed. The most common officers are president, vice president, secretary, and treasurer. A corporation is not limited by these titles, however, and is free to create other officer positions with other titles. For example, a large corporation may have a treasurer, a chief financial officer, and a comptroller, each with specific duties relating to the financial affairs of the corporation. Many corporations create officer positions by adding to the title "assistant" or "executive," such as assistant secretary, executive vice president, and so forth. Under the modern approach, and that taken by the MBCA, one person may simultaneously hold more than one corporate office. Some states, however, prohibit the same person from acting as president and secretary, generally because those are the two officers whose signatures are usually required when stock certificates are issued.

President.   The president of a corporation generally presides at directors' and shareholders' meetings and performs all duties assigned by the board of directors. Often, the president acts as general manager of the corporation.

Vice President.   The vice president acts in the place of the president in his absence and assists the president. Some large corporations will have numerous vice presidents, with various titles such as senior vice president, vice president of marketing, vice president of human resources, administrative vice president, and the like.

Secretary.   The corporation's secretary usually has the responsibility for taking minutes of meetings of directors and shareholders and ensuring the minute book is kept in proper condition. The corporate secretary may retain custody of the corporate seal, maintain the list of shareholders, authenticate documents, and prepare and furnish other reports, correspondence, and notices, such as notices of shareholders' meetings.

Treasurer.   The treasurer is the fiscal officer of the corporation and has responsibility for receiving, maintaining, and disbursing corporate funds, paying taxes, and maintaining financial records.

Other Officers.   Many corporations appoint a **chief executive officer** (CEO) who will supervise all of the other officers, preside over meetings of directors and shareholders, and have primary responsibility for managing the corporation. A **chair** of the board, if appointed, is a board member who presides at directors' meetings and performs such duties as may be assigned by the board. A **chief financial officer** (CFO) keeps all financial records and has responsibility for receiving money on behalf of the corporation, depositing money as directed by the board, disbursing money as directed, paying taxes, and preparing various reports relating to the financial affairs of the corporation.

Chief executive officer
Individual who supervises other officers

Chair
Individual who presides at corporate meetings

Chief financial officer
Individual with primary responsibility for all financial matters

5.　*Authority of Officers*

Because the authority given officers comes from the board of directors, officers are agents of the corporation. Thus, the general agency principles discussed in Chapter One apply to them. As agents, officers may have authority to bind the corporation. This authority can be actual, apparent, or inherent. In many instances, however, either the corporation or a third party might try to avoid various obligations by asserting that the corporate officer did not have the authority to bind the corporation when he purported to act on behalf of the corporation.

Actual authority
Express authority or direction given by one to another

Actual Authority. **Actual** (or *express*) **authority** arises from statutes, the articles of incorporation, or the bylaws, all of which may specify the activities to be undertaken by the officers. Additionally, specific direction given to an officer by the board of directors (acting in a meeting or by unanimous written consent), such as an instruction given to the treasurer to pay certain bills, is a form of actual authority. Officers also have the authority to take any actions needed to accomplish these specific instructions. Moreover, a course of conduct acquiesced in by the board is generally sufficient to show that a transaction is authorized. Thus, even a particular transaction not expressly approved by the board yet typical of those performed on numerous prior occasions will bind the corporation for the act of the officer.

Apparent authority
Authority that one believes another to possess due to the other's conduct or position

Apparent Authority. If an agent acts beyond the scope of her authority but the impression created in the mind of a third party is that the agent does have authority to bind the corporation, the corporation may be bound by the agent's (officer's) actions. In such cases, the corporation has manifested to third parties that the agent may act on its behalf and will therefore be bound by the action taken. For example, if the corporation's president informs a job applicant that his annual salary will be $50,000, and yet the board does not approve the salary, the corporation may be bound to pay the new employee $50,000 inasmuch as the employee reasonably relied on an officer of the corporation who had the apparent authority to speak for and bind the corporation. It was reasonable for the candidate to assume the president had the authority to make this decision. On the other hand, it would be unreasonable to assume that an assistant secretary has the sole authority to approve some extraordinary action, such as a merger or a sale of all of the corporation's assets.

Inherent authority
Authority that naturally flows from one's position

Inherent Authority. Officers also have the **inherent authority** to carry out their duties. For example, the president has the inherent authority to bind the corporation for matters in the usual course of day-to-day business. In any event, a corporation may ratify any acts beyond an officer's authority. Ratification "relates back" to the date of the original transaction so that the corporation is bound from the day the transaction was entered into. Ratification may be express (provided by a resolution of the board) or implied (by the corporation's acceptance of the benefits of the transaction).

6.　*Officers' Standard of Conduct, Liability, and Indemnification*

Officers are usually subject to the same duties of care and fiduciary duties imposed on directors. Like directors, they are protected by the business judgment rule and, therefore, liability is usually founded on acts (or omissions) of clear and gross abuse or negligence. Thus, courts will not second-guess officers' decisions so long as there was some reasonable basis for the decision. Like directors, officers are entitled to rely on advice and reports given by others, so long as that reliance is reasonable.

The standard of conduct required of directors and of officers under the MBCA is highly similar. Officers are required to discharge their duties in good faith, with the care that a person would exercise under similar circumstances, and in a manner reasonably believed to be in the best interest of the corporation. So long as directors and officers perform their duties in compliance with these requirements, they will not be liable for any action taken by them as a director or an officer. MBCA §§ 8.30 and 8.42.

The various provisions relating to indemnification of directors for liability and litigation costs and expenses apply equally to officers. Similarly, the corporation may purchase and maintain insurance on behalf of any officer or other agent to insure against liability asserted against or incurred by the officer or other agent.

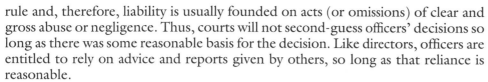

Key Features
of Corporate Management

◆ Corporations involve three groups of people: shareholders (the owners of the corporation), directors (the managers of the corporation), and officers (appointees of the directors).

◆ Although shareholders own the corporation, they do not manage it, and their participation primarily takes the form of voting to elect (or remove) directors and extraordinary actions. In small corporations, shareholders play a far more active role because they wear several "hats" in that they not only own the corporation but also manage it.

◆ There are two types of shareholder meetings: annual meetings (at which directors are elected), and special meetings (those held between annual meetings).

◆ Shareholders often vote by proxy (written instruction to another).

◆ Shareholders may enter into agreements to pool their votes or otherwise concentrate their voting power.

◆ Shareholders may initiate action against the corporation; direct actions allege direct harm to a shareholder while derivative actions allege the corporation has sustained harm and has failed to enforce its own cause of action.

◆ Although shareholders ordinarily have no liability for corporate obligations, they may be liable if they disregard the corporate entity by commingling assets, failing to observe corporate formalities, or undercapitalizing the corporation. These "piercing of the veil" cases are typically brought against smaller corporations.

◆ Directors manage the corporation and are elected by shareholders; they meet in regular meetings or special meetings.

◆ Directors and shareholders may act without a formal meeting if they unanimously consent in writing to take action.

◆ Directors have fiduciary duties to their corporation but will usually be protected from liability under the business judgment rule so long as there is some reasonable business purpose for their actions, and they did not act illegally or with gross negligence.
◆ Directors may rely on others if such reliance is reasonable.
◆ Officers are appointed by directors to carry out whatever functions are assigned to them by the directors.
◆ Unless they have valid employment contracts, officers serve at the discretion of the board of directors.
◆ Officers are subject to the same fiduciary duties as directors.

E. Role of Paralegal

Paralegals are extensively involved in all phases of maintaining the corporation. There are a number of reasons to ensure that all corporate paperwork is up to date and accurate:

1. The documentation of corporate action provides directors and shareholders with notice of corporate decisions. Shareholders and directors may later be precluded from complaining about certain action if they are viewed as having acquiesced to it.
2. Corporate records demonstrate that the corporation is in compliance with state statutes, its articles of incorporation, and its bylaws.
3. Records reflecting basic formalities will help protect against piercing of the corporate veil, which would render shareholders personally liable for corporate obligations.
4. Various banks, creditors, or vendors might require that the corporation provide resolutions and minutes to demonstrate that it has the authority to take certain action, such as borrowing money or entering into contracts.

In some instances, paralegals have nearly complete responsibility for preparing notices, minutes, resolutions, and written consents. Paralegals are routinely involved in the following activities:

1. Maintaining a tickler system for annual meetings for all corporate clients and sending reminders to directors or officers of annual meeting requirements.
2. Preparing and sending out notices for annual and special shareholders' meetings and special meetings of the board of directors.
3. Preparing affidavits verifying the mailing of notices of shareholders' meetings.
4. Assisting in preparation of annual reports and proxy statements.
5. Preparing agendas and scripts for meetings of shareholders and directors.
6. Preparing minutes for meetings of shareholders and directors.
7. Preparing waivers of notice of meetings of shareholders and directors.

8. Preparing and ensuring execution of written consent actions by share-holders or directors when acting by written consent in lieu of meeting.
9. Maintaining the corporate minute book. For easy reference, the first sheet in the minute book should identify all the particulars of the corporation: its state and date of incorporation, tax identification number, date of annual meeting, number of directors required, and whether action may be taken by written consent. Minutes should be carefully organized and kept chronologically with the minutes of the most recent meeting on top.

Case Illustration
Extent of Protection of Business Judgment Rule

Case:	*Hall v. Staha*, 800 S.W.2d 396 (Ark. 1990)
Facts:	Shareholders brought a derivative suit alleging, among other things, breaches of fiduciary duty by directors. A third party had offered to purchase the corporation's stock. The directors did not disclose this offer to the shareholders, in part because these directors would not have been employed at their same salaries if the offer were accepted.
Holding:	Although the business judgment rule protects directors from liability for their decisions, it does not protect the actions of directors who have a conflict of interest. In this case, the directors could not claim the protection of the business judgment rule because of their conflicting interest. Moreover, there was little evidence that the directors investigated the effect of the offer on the corporation or the shareholders (who were never in-formed of the offer). In such a case, the business judgment rule will not protect the directors.

◆　◆　◆

WEB RESOURCES

The most important Web resources are state statutes relating to shareholders' and directors' meetings, voting, notice of meetings, proxies, record dates, directors' and officers' duties to their corporations, and indemnification of directors and officers. Other valuable Web resources are the various forms posted on several Web sites. As always, exercise discretion in using forms. Check the site's "Disclaimer" and "Legal Terms" sections to determine if there are any restrictions on your use of the forms.

Federal and state statutes:	www.law.cornell.edu www.findlaw.com
MBCA:	www.abanet.org/buslaw/committees/ CL270000pub/nosearch/mbca/ home.shtml
Governance issues:	www.governanceprofessionals.org (Site of Society of Corporate Secretaries & Governance Professionals offers publications on corporate management issues, proxy-voting matters, and access to newsletters.) www.corpgov.net/links/links.html (This site provides links to numerous other resources relating to corporate governance.) www.sarbanes-oxley.com (This site offers a wide variety of resources and publications relating to compliance with the Sarbanes-Oxley Act.) www.riskmetrics.com (The site of Risk-Metrics Group offers publications on many shareholder issues, including trends in corporate governance.) www.thecorporatecounsel.net (The Corporate Counsel Net site offers excellent articles about shareholders, directors, governance, and SOX.)
Forms:	www.siccode.com/forms.php (forms for notices of meetings of shareholders and directors, forms for minutes of all meetings, forms for waivers of notice, forms for resignations of directors and officers, a general proxy, an indemnification agreement, and more) www.allaboutforms.com (forms for a shareholders' agreement, forms for minutes of meetings, a proxy, a wavier of notice of a directors' meeting, and more)

Discussion Questions

Fact Scenario. Café Coffee, Inc. operates numerous upscale coffee shops in the Northeast region of the United States. It has 500,000 shares outstanding and seven directors. Its bylaws state that the annual shareholders' meeting will be held April 5 and that the record date for the meeting is 30 days before the meeting. Use the MBCA to answer the following questions.

1. The directors would like to expand into the Southeastern region of the United States. Discuss the quorum and voting requirements for action on this issue by the directors (both at a meeting and by written consent).

2. The shareholders would like to remove one of the directors although there is no evidence that the director has been anything other than scrupulously honest. How would the shareholders go about accomplishing this removal?

3. The corporation is considering purchasing all of its coffee beans from Beanery Inc. Director Jones owns a significant number of shares in Beanery Inc. May Jones vote on this transaction? Discuss.

4. After considerable discussion, market surveys, and reports by several corporate committees, the directors decided to expand into the Southeastern portion of the United States. Unfortunately, due to a slumping economy, the expansion has been a failure. Are the directors and officers liable for this decision? Discuss.

5. Assume that the articles of incorporation allow for cumulative voting. Susan owns 100 shares of stock.
   a. How many shares constitute a quorum?
   b. What is the record date for the annual shareholders' meeting?
   c. How many votes will Susan have if there is straight voting in an election for directors?
   d. How many votes will Susan have if there is cumulative voting in an election for directors?
   e. How many votes will Susan have if a meeting is held to discuss a merger with another corporation?

6. Assume that Susan did not receive notice of the annual shareholders' meeting. What might Susan do? Is there anything the corporation can do to "save" the meeting?

7. Director Peterson has been ill and has thus resigned from the board. How will this vacancy be filled?

8. If a corporation has only four shareholders, what is the danger to its shareholders if they fail to keep accurate records?

Net Worth

1. Access the Web site of the SEC. Review the Definitive 14A proxy statement for Target Corporation for May 2008. What methods of voting were authorized for shareholders?

2. Access the Web site of the SEC. Review the Definitive 14A proxy statement for Berkshire Hathaway for 2008. What compensation do directors receive for attending each meeting in person or by conference call?

3. Access the Web site of the SEC. Review the first-page cover sheet of the annual 10-K report for General Electric Company filed in February 2008 for the fiscal year ended December 31, 2007. How many outstanding shares of voting common stock were there at the time of the filing of the 10 K report?

4. Locate California's Corporations Code. How many shares must a shareholder own to be entitled to inspect corporate records and copy the list of shareholder names?

5. Who is the current chair of the Public Company Accounting Oversight Board?

6. Access the Web site of General Motors. Review its governance guidelines. What level of stock ownership is required for its directors?

12

◆ ◆ ◆

Corporate Dividends

◆ ◆ ◆

CHAPTER OVERVIEW

Shareholders not only hope and expect that the stock they own will increase in value, they also hope and sometimes expect that the corporation will pay distributions to them based on their proportionate ownership of the corporation. These distributions are generally called dividends, and may be paid in the form of cash, property, or the corporation's own shares or those of a subsidiary. The distribution will be allocated to shareholders in direct proportion to their respective ownership interest or shares in the corporation.

Dividends are generally declared by the board of directors in its discretion from time to time. There is no rule requiring that corporations make distributions to shareholders. Directors who fail to do so, however, when corporate profits permit, may find themselves out of a job at the next election. Large publicly traded corporations tend to declare distributions every calendar quarter. Such regularly paid dividends tend to be cash dividends.

Shareholders may also participate in the growth of the corporation by stock splits (divisions of outstanding shares), which tend to encourage trading and ultimately result in an increase in the value of one's shares.

A. Introduction to Dividends

A **distribution** is a direct or indirect transfer of money or other property (except a corporation's own shares) to or for the benefit of shareholders of a corporation. MBCA § 1.40(6). More traditional terminology has been to use the term **dividend** to refer to a distribution of a corporation's profits to its shareholders, and to use the term *distribution* to refer to other payments to shareholders, such as payments made when the corporation liquidates. Many jurisdictions, however, refer to any type of payment whatsoever to a shareholder as a distribution, whether it is a

Distribution
Used strictly to refer to payments to shareholders that are not a sharing of profits; used loosely to refer to any type of payment to shareholders

Dividend
Used strictly to refer to a distribution of a corporation's profits to its shareholders; used loosely to refer to any kind of payment made to shareholders

distribution of profit or some other type of distribution, such as a distribution of net assets in liquidation. In making their determination whether payment of a dividend is proper, directors may rely on financial statements or any other reasonable reports and valuation methods.

There are three types of dividends: those paid in cash, those paid in property, and those paid in shares. **Cash dividends** (typically sent in the form of a check made payable to the shareholder) are the most common type of dividend and are probably the most welcome. If corporate profits permit, the board of directors will declare a cash dividend and fix a certain amount per share. For example, the directors may declare a dividend to all shareholders of the corporation in the amount of $1 per share. An individual owning 100 shares would receive $100, and an individual owning 50 shares would receive $50. All shareholders within a given class or series must be treated uniformly. Thus, all shareholders owning Common A stock must be treated the same, although they may be treated differently from shareholders owning Common B stock.

Some companies allow shareholders to use their cash dividends to immediately purchase additional shares of stock. Under these **dividend reinvestment plans** (commonly called DRIPs), these dividends are immediately reinvested at no fee to the shareholder. Some companies also allow individuals to buy additional shares directly from them on a regular, routine basis, much the way a 401(k) plan allows employees to contribute earnings into a fund to be used in retirement.

Property dividends, distributions that do not consist of cash or other shares of the corporation, are the least common dividend declared. The property may consist of a sample of products of the corporation, such as shampoos, cleaning supplies, or condiments, or may consist of discount coupons to be used at retail stores or restaurants owned by the corporation. Although some corporations distribute property dividends, these are not particularly desirable to shareholders, who might not wish to receive an assortment of the corporation's products. Distribution of such products causes unique problems. If the directors determine that for each 100 shares of stock owned, shareholders will receive $10 worth of products, it could be difficult and burdensome to calculate properly and deliver appropriate amounts of a product to a large number of shareholders, each of whom owns varying amounts of stock. Thus, property dividends are impractical for all but the smallest corporations. A property dividend might also consist of shares in another or subsidiary corporation.

Share dividends are distributions of the corporation's own shares (rather than those of another or subsidiary corporation) made in proportion to the shareholders' respective ownership interests in the corporation. For example, the directors may declare a share dividend in the amount of one share of common stock for every ten shares outstanding. Shareholder Smith, who owns ten shares, would receive one share. Shareholder Jones, who owns 20 shares, would receive two shares, and so forth. Thus, although the raw number of shares owned by a shareholder will increase, the shareholder's proportionate ownership or control is not affected inasmuch as every other shareholder within the class or series will be treated the same. Using our example, it is readily seen that before the share dividend, Jones had twice as much power and control as Smith. After the dividend, Jones still has twice as much power and control as Smith.

Share dividends often result in fractional shares. If Shareholder Daley owns 25 shares, Daley will be entitled to receive 2.5 shares of the corporation's shares as

Cash dividend
Cash distribution made by corporation

Dividend reinvestment plan
Plan allowing shareholders to immediately use cash dividends to purchase more stock; usually called DRIPs

Property dividend
Distribution of some form of property by a corporation

Share dividend
Distribution by a corporation of its own shares

her dividend. As discussed in Chapter Ten, the corporation may issue a stock certificate representing the fractional share or may issue scrip (which may be repurchased by the corporation or must be surrendered to the corporation for a complete share within some time period or it will become void). Rather than issuing fractional shares, large corporations often pay the cash value of the fractional share to the shareholder.

The distributions made to shareholders when the corporation is liquidated are often referred to as **liquidation dividends** or *dissolution dividends*. These one-time distributions are discussed in Chapter Sixteen.

Liquidation dividend
Distributions made to shareholders when corporation liquidates (also called *dissolution dividends*)

B. Restrictions Relating to Dividends

Each state's corporations code will specify the manner by which a corporation distributes dividends as well as the sources from which dividends may be paid. Because the end result of a cash or property dividend is that assets of the corporation are transferred to others, the shareholders, certain restrictions exist governing the distribution of dividends. In general, these restrictions operate to protect creditors and ensure that a financially unhealthy corporation does not take its few profits and distribute them to its owners rather than paying the claims of creditors. Additionally, these restrictions ensure the continued operations of the corporation and provide management with sufficient funds to conduct and expand the business.

1. Solvency and Excess Assets Tests

MBCA § 6.40 provides two alternative tests to determine whether a corporation can legally pay a dividend. The equity insolvency test states that a corporation cannot pay a dividend if to do so would render the corporation unable to pay its debts as they come due in the ordinary course of business. Alternatively, under the excess assets test (sometimes called the balance sheet test), a dividend can be made only if, after giving it effect, the corporation's assets will exceed its liabilities and the amount that would be required to be paid to satisfy the rights of preferred shareholders (whose rights are superior to those receiving the dividend) in the event of a liquidation. For example, assume ABC, Inc. has total assets of $200,000 and total liabilities of $150,000. If preferred shareholders would receive $20,000 in the event the corporation were to liquidate, ABC has $30,000 available for dividends to be paid ($200,000 minus $150,000 minus $20,000).

Solvency
State of being able to pay debts as they come due

The primary purpose of these limitations is to protect the rights of third-party creditors. Some states, such as California, permit the corporation to estimate its expected earnings and expenses for the next year to determine if payment of a dividend is allowable. Cal. Corp. Code § 500(b)(2). The requirement that a corporation be solvent to distribute a dividend does not restrict a share dividend because stock dividends do not involve the transfer of cash or property and are mere paper transactions. Thus, in most states, even an insolvent corporation may distribute share dividends because they do not harm creditors.

2. Legally Available Funds

Most state statutes mandate that dividends can be made only from certain sources or corporate accounts. In general, dividends can usually only be paid from retained earnings and surplus.

Retained Earnings. All states allow corporations to pay dividends out of **retained earnings**, the undistributed net profits accumulated by the corporation.

Surplus. Some states allow dividends to be paid out of any kind of **surplus** account, whether earned surplus or unearned surplus. Other jurisdictions limit the payment of dividends to earned surplus accounts only. *Surplus* is the value of the amount of the corporation's net assets greater than the corporation's stated capital. **Earned surplus** is total corporate profits earned during preceding accounting periods, including net profits, income, and gains. **Unearned surplus** is surplus other than earned surplus, usually capital surplus. **Capital surplus** is the amount received by the corporation for stock in excess of its par value, together with the consideration received by the corporation from the issuance of shares without par value. The MBCA approach is that dividends can be paid from any source, so long as the corporation is able to pay its debts as they come due or its assets exceed its liabilities (plus amounts payable as preferences in the event of a liquidation). MBCA § 6.40(c). Thus, the MBCA has eliminated the concepts of earned surplus and stated capital.

3. Tests for Distribution

In addition to regulation of the sources of funds that can be used for the payment of dividends, several tests have been formulated to determine whether payment of a dividend is proper.

Balance Sheet Test. As mentioned earlier, under the **balance sheet test** (sometimes called the excess assets test), dividends may be paid only when, *after* giving effect to the distribution of the dividend, the corporation's assets exceed its liabilities and the stated capital of the corporation. The corporation's balance sheet shows its assets in one column or on one side of a ledger. On the other side is a listing of the corporation's liabilities and the shareholders' equity. **Shareholders' equity** is the net worth of the corporation, the amount by which assets exceed liabilities. (Some jurisdictions define shareholders' equity as the sum of stated capital and any surplus accounts.) Thus, assets are equal to the sum of liabilities and shareholders' equity.

When an amount is entered on one side of the ledger, an amount must be entered on the other side as well so that there is always a "balance." For example, if a dividend is paid in cash in the amount of $100,000, both the cash account and the surplus account will be reduced by the sum of $100,000. If the corporation borrows $50,000, the sum of $50,000 will be entered on one side of the balance sheet as an "asset" and will also be entered on the other side of the balance sheet as a "liability."

Retained earnings
Undistributed net profits

Surplus
Value of assets greater than stated capital

Earned surplus
Total corporate profits

Unearned surplus
Surplus other than earned surplus, usually capital surplus

Capital surplus
Amount received by corporation for stock in excess of its par value plus amount received for stock with no par value

Balance sheet test
Test to determine if dividends can be paid in which equity exceeds liabilities (also called *excess assets test*)

Shareholders' equity
Net worth of corporation; amount by which assets exceed liabilities

Equity Insolvency Test. As previously discussed, all jurisdictions preclude the payment of a cash or property dividend that would render the corporation insolvent, meaning that it is unable to pay its debts as they become due in the ordinary course of business. The test, often referred to as the **equity insolvency test**, protects creditors who need to be assured that the corporation can pay its obligations to the creditors as the obligations become due and owing. The distribution of share dividends is not subject to the equity insolvency test because it does not involve the transfer of cash or property to shareholders. Thus, even an insolvent corporation may make a dividend of its own shares.

Equity insolvency test
Test to determine if dividends can be paid in which corporation must be able to pay debts as they become due

Modern Tests. The MBCA and a number of jurisdictions have eliminated the concepts of stated capital, capital surplus, and earned surplus. The test set forth in MBCA § 6.40(c) requires that after distribution of the dividend, either the corporation must be able to pay its debts as they become due or assets must exceed liabilities. In this latter event the corporation must have available the total amount that would have to be paid if the corporation were to be dissolved at the time of distribution to satisfy the preferential rights of shareholders whose rights are superior to the shares receiving a distribution. In effect, this latter condition treats the preferential distribution rights of senior shareholders as a liability for determining the amount available for dividend distributions. This test protects not only creditors but also preferred shareholders because the corporation cannot pay a dividend if such would impair the rights of preferred shareholders to receive their liquidation rights.

Still other jurisdictions use the **nimble dividends test**, which permits a corporation to pay dividends if it has current profits.

Nimble dividends test
Test to determine if dividends can be paid in which corporation must have current profits

4. Contractual Limitations

To induce bankers or bondholders to lend it money, the corporation may contractually agree to limit the payment of dividends or may agree to retain a certain level of funds in a specific account, such as earned surplus. This helps assure creditors that the corporate debtor will have sufficient funds from which to repay the debt. If such a restriction exists, the amount held in reserve cannot be used in determining the amount available for dividend distributions. Thus, bankers and other lenders are assured that the corporation will not take money that should be used to repay debt and distribute it to its shareholders. Because these contractual limitations are designed to protect creditors, they usually apply only to cash or property dividends, and the corporation is free to make a distribution of its own shares to its shareholders.

5. Preferences

Articles of incorporation for corporations with complex financial structures may create preferences with regard to dividends (which are often in the form of some minimum dividend amount). These must be honored. Nevertheless, even preferred dividends are payable only when the corporation is solvent and only out of legally available funds. If the corporation decides to issue a total of $1 million as cash dividends, preferred shareholders are entitled to receive their dividends first. If the dividends are cumulative, the corporation must pay the current dividend as well as any arrearages to the preferred shareholders before any distribution can be made to other shareholders.

6. *Classes of Shares*

To ensure that one class of stock does not subsume another, shares of one class cannot generally be used as dividends for another class unless the articles of incorporation permit or if the shareholders of the class from which the distribution is to be made approve the transaction. Thus, share dividends are typically paid to shareholders in shares of the same class as are already owned.

C.   Effect of Illegal Dividends

Illegal dividends
Distributions paid when corporation is insolvent or from unauthorized accounts

If directors pay dividends while the corporation is insolvent, or from unauthorized accounts, the distribution is referred to as an **illegal dividend.** The effect of an illegal dividend on a shareholder often depends on whether the dividend was made when the corporation was insolvent or whether it was made from an improper source or fund. Shareholders who receive dividends while the corporation is insolvent must generally return the dividend, on the basis that the transfer of the corporation's assets to the shareholder is a fraud on creditors, and these shareholders can be sued for the return of the dividend. Shareholders who receive dividends from unauthorized accounts must, however, generally return them only if it can be proven they knew the dividend was illegal when received. In that event, they are liable for the amount received illegally, with interest, or the fair market value of any property received, with interest.

Directors who vote for or assent to a dividend contrary to any restrictions are generally personally liable, jointly and severally, for the amount of the dividend in excess of that which was legally permissible together with interest thereon. Cal. Corp. Code § 316; Del. Code Ann. tit. 8, § 174. If shareholders knowingly receive unlawful dividends, directors are often entitled to reimbursement from the shareholders. MBCA § 8.33(b). As a defense, directors are generally permitted to rely on the corporation's books of account and financial statements, reports of officers, accountants, counsel, or other experts, so long as they are reasonable.

D.   Procedure for Declaring and Paying Dividends

The decision to declare a dividend is made by the board of directors, either by majority vote at a meeting or by unanimous written consent action taken without a meeting. The decision is recorded in the minutes or the written consent as a resolution. (See Figure 12-1 for resolution authorizing dividend.)

FIGURE 12-1
Resolution Authorizing Dividend

The Board of Directors of the Corporation next considered the issue of declaring and distributing a cash dividend to the common shareholders of the Corporation. After reviewing the report furnished to the Corporation by its independent registered public accountants and after receiving reports from the Chief Financial Officer on the financial condition of the Corporation and its anticipated business needs and revenue for the next 12 months, and on motion duly made, seconded, and unanimously carried:

RESOLVED, that a dividend of One Dollar ($1.00) per share be and hereby is declared payable to the holders of record of the common stock of the Corporation shown by the records of the Corporation on December 10, 2008, and said dividend shall be distributed to said shareholders on or about January 1, 2009. The Treasurer of the Corporation is hereby directed and authorized to take appropriate action to effect the purpose of this Resolution.

For cash and property dividends, the directors will establish a record date for determining shareholders' eligibility to receive dividends. In most instances, the rules relating to establishing a record date for a dividend distribution are the same as those for establishing a record date for meetings. Those shareholders who own stock on the record date fixed by the board of directors will be entitled to dividends. If no record date is set, those individuals who were shareholders on the date the directors declared the dividend will be entitled to receive the dividend.

For share dividends, the directors will also typically establish a record date and those individuals who owned shares on the record date are entitled to the share dividend. A payment date will also be established. On this date, the corporation will issue stock certificates reflecting the dividend to be distributed.

For all dividends, the dividend will be paid to the individual who was the shareholder of record on the record date, even if the shareholder sells his or her stock before the time the actual payment or distribution is made. A shareholder or share without the right to receive a declared dividend is called **ex-dividend.** Once the dividend is declared, newspaper financial sections will note the stock is ex-dividend, a situation that often causes the price per share to drop slightly. The ex-dividend date is two business days before the record date.

Ex-dividend
Status of a shareholder without the right to receive a declared dividend

The corporation must accurately account for share dividends. For example, assume that a corporation declares a one share per 100 common stock dividend and the stock has a par value of $1. Ten shareholders each own 100 shares. Thus, the corporation will be issuing each shareholder one new share. If the corporation had simply sold the shares to others, it would have received the fair market value for the shares, which we will assume is $40 per share. Thus, the corporation would have received $400. It would have then placed $10 (the total par value of the stock) in stated capital and $390 in capital surplus (see Chapter Ten). When the corporation distributes the shares as dividends rather than selling them outright to others, the corporation must likewise make the proper allocation and deduct

$400 from surplus and then transfer $10 to stated capital and $390 to capital surplus. Because the MBCA has eliminated the concept of par value, the concept of stated capital is likewise eradicated, and the corporation may allocate the amounts as it deems appropriate.

To distribute share dividends, the corporation must have sufficient authorized and unissued stock to distribute. If the articles of incorporation do not authorize a sufficient number of shares they must be amended to increase the number of shares the corporation is authorized to issue. Under MBCA § 10.05(4)(b), if the corporation has only one class of stock, the directors, acting alone and without shareholder approval, may adopt an amendment to increase the number of authorized shares to permit the issuance of share dividends. Alternatively, the corporation can use treasury stock as the source for share dividends.

If shareholders cannot be located, their dividends will *escheat* (or revert) to the state of their last known residence.

E. Right to Dividends

The general rule is that shareholders receive dividends when and if declared by the board of directors acting in its discretion. Thus, the determination to distribute dividends is a discretionary decision subject to the business judgment of the directors. The directors may properly decide that dividends should not be paid so the corporation can build up a "war chest" to acquire another corporation, for purposes of growth and expansion, or for the purpose of investing its profits. The mere fact that the corporation has sufficient funds from which to pay a dividend does not entitle the shareholders to a dividend. Courts are reluctant to interfere with the management of corporations, and, therefore, unless the shareholders can clearly prove bad faith or an abuse of discretion by the directors, the directors cannot be compelled to pay dividends. This is yet another example of the business judgment rule, which protects directors who make business decisions in good faith. If bad faith or abuse of discretion is shown, a court may issue an order compelling the directors to declare a dividend. As a practical matter, however, directors who fail to declare dividends when profits permit may well find themselves out of a job.

The articles of incorporation may provide for a fixed dividend to one class or series of shares. In such a case, the directors will be required to declare and pay the agreed-on dividend when legally available funds exist. If the dividends are cumulative, any arrearages must be paid for prior years in which the corporation did not pay dividends (often because it did not have the funds to do so) before any dividends can be paid to other, usually common, shareholders.

Although directors are under no obligation to declare dividends, once they have legally declared a cash or property dividend, this decision is irrevocable and the dividend becomes a debt owing from the corporation to the shareholders, who can then enforce the debt just like any other debt. These shareholders are viewed as being on the same footing as other general unsecured creditors of the corporation. MBCA § 6.40(f). If, however, the declaration is illegal in that the corporation intends to pay the dividend out of unauthorized funds, the declaration is likely revocable. The declaration of a stock dividend is revocable until the stock is actually issued.

PRACTICE TIP

It is always important that the minutes of directors' meetings be accurate; however, accuracy is even more critical when meetings discuss and authorize dividends because directors who vote for or assent to unlawful dividends are personally liable for such an act. Thus, it is critical that any votes at any directors' meetings that are not unanimous be accurately reflected in the minutes. For example, if director Ruiz votes against a dividend, the minutes should reflect that fact and identify her by name. The written minutes will then provide a defense for her if it is later alleged that she assented to an illegal dividend. Moreover, any financial reports or expert opinions on which the directors base their decision to issue a dividend should be attached to the minutes. Because directors are entitled to rely on the advice and reports of others (if such reliance is reasonable), these written documents may provide a valid defense if it is later alleged that the directors violated any duties in declaring dividends.

F. Tax Considerations

Because a corporation is a person, it pays taxes on its net profits at the applicable corporate rates. The tax disadvantage referred to as double taxation means that when corporate profits are distributed as dividends, the shareholders receiving those dividends pay tax on the same money or property for which taxes have already been paid by the corporation. As discussed in Chapter Ten, in 2003 Congress reduced taxes on dividends paid to shareholders. Payments made by a corporation as dividends are not deductible by the corporation.

1. Cash Dividends

Shareholders of C corporations must declare and pay taxes on cash dividends received. Until a few years ago, for the purpose of affording some tax relief to small investors, the first $100 of dividends received (or $200 if shareholders filed jointly) was exempt from tax. Now, however, all cash dividends must be declared for tax purposes. Thus, even a cash dividend of $0.89 will be subject to taxation at the individual's appropriate tax rate. Corporations that distribute more than $10 to any shareholder in any year must report the dividend on an informational return (Form 1099-DIV) so the Internal Revenue Service can verify the shareholder declared and paid the appropriate taxes. This is similar to information tax returns filed by general partnerships, limited liability partnerships, and limited liability companies, used by the Internal Revenue Service to verify that partners and members have declared and paid taxes on their share of partnership or company profits. Cash dividends that are immediately reinvested into more shares through DRIPs are also taxable when received.

2. Property Dividends

As to property dividends, for example, the distribution of corporate products such as cosmetics, candy, or tobacco products, shareholders receiving such property dividends must declare and pay tax on the fair market value of the property received. This is another disadvantage of property dividends: A shareholder may receive products she has no use for and yet be required to pay taxes on the unwelcome distribution.

3. Share Dividends

The tax ramifications of stock dividends are quite different from those of cash or property dividends. Tax is not paid when the stock dividend is received but rather when it is later sold. The reason taxes are not paid when a share dividend is issued is that such a dividend is not viewed as a true distribution of value because each shareholder in a class will be treated uniformly and each will have the same proportion of ownership interest after the distribution as before. Moreover, the corporation still has the same assets after distribution of the share dividend as it did before.

Computation of the taxes due at the time of eventual sale of the shares can be confusing. For example, assume a shareholder originally purchased 1,000 shares of stock at $10 per share, for a total original investment of $10,000. If a one-for-50 share dividend is received, the shareholder will now own 1,020 shares for an investment of $10,000, or will have a cost or *basis* per share for these 20 new shares of $9.80 ($10,000 divided by 1,020). This is the figure that will be used to compute capital gains taxes when the shares are ultimately sold. The situation becomes even more complicated over time because the shareholder may purchase additional shares in the future at varying prices each time and thus the basis will continually adjust.

4. Encouraging Dividends

To encourage corporations to pay dividends (which eventually provides the federal government with tax revenue), a "federal accumulated earnings tax" of 15 percent will be imposed on a C corporation's accumulated taxable income in excess of that reasonably needed for the business (which is presumed to be no more than $250,000). 26 U.S.C. § 531-535. (See discussion in Chapter Ten, Section D.) Corporations are thus penalized for having accumulated earnings and given an incentive to declare and pay dividends. In some cases, shareholders have sued directors for negligence in allowing the corporation to be subjected to the federal accumulated earnings tax; personal liability has been imposed on directors for the loss.

5. Avoiding Double Taxation

Small corporations whose shareholders are employed by or are actively involved in the business can reduce the burden of double taxation by distributing corporate profits to the shareholder-employees as bonuses, salaries, or consulting fees rather than dividends. In such a case, the bonus, salary, or fee received by the shareholder-employee is still taxable to the recipient, but the corporation's payment is a deductible business expense, thus reducing taxation of the money at the corporate level. Although this is feasible for smaller corporations, a corporation whose stock is publicly owned cannot justify a "salary" for its hundreds of thousands of shareholders. Thus, double taxation is simply a feature of the corporate landscape for such corporations.

6.   Modern Trends in Dividend Payments

During the 1990s, when investors made money by ever-escalating stock prices, paying dividends became somewhat unfashionable. Investors became accustomed to companies using their money for growth and for often flashy acquisitions rather than for the payment of dividends. Thus, the payment of a dividend was viewed by many as an admission that the company had no vision for growth or that it was financially unsophisticated. In fact, of the stocks traded on all the major indexes, 72 percent paid dividends in 1977, and only 39 percent paid dividends in 2003.

Shortly after 2003, however, dividends became more fashionable. In fact, a number of studies have shown that over the long run, companies paying dividends have outperformed those that do not. For example, one study found that over the past 30 years, the average dividend-paying company offered investors twice the returns of non-dividend-paying companies. Experts attributed the resurgence of dividends to two primary reasons: the lowering of the maximum tax rate for qualified dividends to 15 percent (rather than its previous possible 35 percent) and interest among shareholders who desired tangible evidence that companies are doing well. Microsoft probably started the trend when it began paying dividends in 2003. In mid-2004, Microsoft distributed about $32 billion to its shareholders (about $3 per share), the largest one-time dividend payout in Wall Street history. Following are some statistics showing the upward trend in dividends (in billions of dollars, from *Statistical Abstract of the United States* 506 (128th ed. 2009):

1990	2000	2007
$169	$378	$795

After this upswing in dividends, the financial and housing crisis of 2008 caused many dividends to be eliminated or suspended. For example, Citigroup (which recorded billions in dollars of losses on mortgage securities) reduced its dividend in 2008 by 41 percent. Other institutions either likewise reduced their dividends or cut them entirely. Similarly, Dana Holding Corporation, which had paid more than 250 consecutive cash dividends since 1936 has not paid a dividend since 2006, and Dow Chemical cut its dividend in early 2009, the first time in nearly 100 years that it had done so. In 2009, Standard & Poor's projected that dividends for the S & P 500 companies would fall nearly 14 percent in 2009, the worst decline since 1942. More than half of the companies making dividend cuts in early 2009 were in the financial sector. These decreases engender much public comment in that experts believe that dividends are usually the last thing corporations want to cut because reductions are tantamount to announcing that the company has a cash flow problem.

G. Stock Splits

Stock split
Division of outstanding shares (also called a *share split*)

A **stock split** (or *share split*) occurs when an outstanding share is divided into a larger number of shares. The result is to decrease the price per share. Stock splits resemble share dividends in that each involves the issuance to shareholders of a certain number of shares based on the shares presently held. The tax treatment for stock splits is also the same as that for stock dividends in that taxes are not paid until the shares are later sold. The most common scenario involves a two-for-one split, in which case a shareholder owning 100 shares would own 200 shares after declaration of the split.

A doubling of the shares is accompanied by halving the trading price of each share in a two-for-one split. For example, assume shareholder Robert Martinez owns 100 shares of stock with a price of $1, for a total value of $100. If the directors declare a two-for-one split, shareholder Martinez now owns 200 shares of stock, which are now trading at 50 cents each, for a total value of $100. After the split, twice as many shares will be outstanding. Thus, an amendment to the articles of incorporation might be required to increase the number of shares authorized to be issued to accommodate the split. Although the most common stock split is two-for-one, three-for-one, four-for-one, and other splits are also valid.

A stock split is accomplished by directors' resolution, either by majority vote at a meeting or by unanimous written consent action. If an amendment to the articles will be required as a result of the split, shareholder approval may be required, and shareholders may be entitled to appraisal rights, meaning rights to have their shares purchased from them at their fair value (see Chapter Fourteen). MBCA § 10.05(4), however, allows the directors acting alone to amend the articles to increase the number of issued and unissued authorized shares without shareholder approval if the corporation only has one class of shares. New certificates will be issued to shareholders reflecting the additional shares created by the split. Moreover, because the MBCA has eliminated the concept of par value, there is no distinction between a share dividend and a stock split, and both transactions are referred to simply as "share dividends," which may be authorized by the board.

Because the trading price of each share is decreased, the shares might be more attractive to investors. If enough investors buy stock at this new reduced and "on sale" price, the value of the stock may creep up and achieve its pre-split price. Shareholders may then realize a doubling in profits. For example, stock might traditionally trade at approximately $50 per share. If the price reaches $80 per share, trading might level off as investors fear buying stock at the top of its peak only to see it perhaps decline to its historic trading price. Moreover, many investors buying stock in **round lots** of hundreds might be reluctant to purchase such expensive stock. Thus, to stimulate trading, a corporation may declare a two-for-one stock split whereby the stock is now $40 per share. Assuming the corporation is stable, investors will view the reduced trading price as a bargain and may invest heavily. If the stock reaches its pre-split price of $80 per share, shareholder Martinez will have doubled his money: Before the split, he owned 100 shares at a value of $80 per share, for a total of $8,000; after the split, if the price increases, Martinez will own 200 shares at $80 per share, for a total of $16,000. A stock split, however, is no guarantee that the stock will rise in price after the split.

Round lot
Group of 100 shares

Walmart's stock splits reveal the potential value in stock splits. Walmart has split its stock on a two-for-one basis 11 times since 1970. If you purchased

100 shares of Walmart stock when it went public in 1970 at a total price of $1,650, on October 1, 2008, you would have owned 204,800 shares for a total value of $12,288,000.

Additionally, at the time of the split, there is no true significance to the shareholder. This is analogous to a shareholder who is given one piece of pie by a hostess who then cuts the piece in two. The amount of pie given to the shareholder is the same but it is now in two pieces rather than one.

The opposite of a stock split is a **reverse stock split**, sometimes called a *split down*, in which the corporation reduces rather than increases the number of outstanding shares. For example, a ten-for-one reverse split would have the effect of requiring that each group of ten shares be exchanged or surrendered to the corporation in return for the issuance of one new share. Thus, the result of any reverse stock split is fewer outstanding shares in a corporation and an increase in individual share price.

Reverse stock splits are often used by a corporation to eliminate smaller shareholders. If a corporation is allowed by state law to require that fractional shares be sold to the corporation, the board may declare a reverse stock split in the amount of 1,000 to one, requiring that each 1,000 shares of stock be exchanged for one share. In many cases, this results in fractional shares, which the corporation then repurchases as a means to eliminate shareholders. Reverse stock splits can begin with an amendment of the articles of incorporation to set forth a much lower number of authorized shares than was originally authorized. This reduction in authorized shares then compels the directors to repurchase outstanding shares to be in compliance with the articles. Because shareholders are generally opposed to owning fewer shares of stock (even though their proportionate ownership interest remains the same), they might vote against the amendment, and, therefore, reverse stock splits are somewhat rare. Some companies reverse split their stock in the hope that the higher trading price per share will lend prestige to the company.

A more modern and somewhat unfortunate reason to seek a reverse stock split is to ensure that a corporation's stock can remain listed on one of the national stock exchanges. For example, MicroStrategy, Inc., whose share price once traded at more than $300 per share at the peak of the tech boom and was trading at just over $1 in mid-2002, considered a reverse stock split to keep from being delisted from the NASDAQ Stock Market, which has a minimum requirement of $1 per share. Shares that trade below that level face delisting. Similarly, in September 2008, ExpressJet announced it would seek shareholder approval for a reverse stock split (of one share for every ten shares outstanding) aimed at saving the company from delisting by the New York Stock Exchange.

Reverse stock split Reduction of outstanding shares (also called a *split down*)

H.   Purchase by a Corporation of Its Own Shares

A corporation may acquire all or some of its own outstanding shares from shareholders if state corporations statutes and the articles of incorporation so permit and if the corporation is solvent or would not be rendered insolvent by the transaction. The corporation may wish to redeem or reacquire its shares for a variety of reasons, including a desire to decrease supply of the stock and thereby increase price, a desire to thwart shareholders from selling the shares to outside parties, a desire to improve its equity-debt ratio, or a desire to increase earnings per share by reducing the total number of outstanding shares. Such "buybacks" make the remaining shares more valuable because there are fewer of them. Additionally, the corporation might be required to repurchase the shares pursuant to an agreement with a shareholder.

The repurchase need not be all of a class and may be part of a class (a partial redemption). In such cases, the shares selected for redemption by the corporation are typically chosen on a lottery basis to prevent discrimination against shareholders. For example, if the board elects only to reacquire shares held by the directors and immediately thereafter the stock falls dramatically in price, the directors may be liable for fraud or breach of fiduciary duty.

Exchange
Exchange of cash for shares

A repurchase of stock is sometimes referred to as an **exchange** because the corporation is exchanging cash for shares. This first type of exchange is to be distinguished from a *share exchange* in which a target corporation's shareholders exchange their shares for shares in the acquiring corporation. (See Chapter Fourteen for further discussion of share exchanges.) The repurchase is generally treated as a distribution to shareholders. Assume there are ten shareholders of the corporation, each owning 100 shares of stock. If the corporation redeems ten shares from each of them, and pays $20 per share, when the transaction is completed the shareholders will each own 90 shares of stock and the corporation will have transferred or distributed the sum of $200 to each shareholder. The corporation is poorer, having exchanged its hard-earned cash for shares, and the shareholders are richer. Thus, it can readily be seen that a distribution has occurred even though it was not as immediate and direct as a distribution of cash or property. Because a repurchase of stock by the corporation is a distribution, the same limitations that apply to the distribution of dividends apply equally to the repurchase by a corporation of its own shares, namely, limitations as to solvency or requiring assets to exceed liabilities after the purchase. MBCA §§ 6.31 and 6.40.

In the previous example, the shareholders' proportionate interest in the corporation remained the same: Both before and after the transaction each owned one-tenth of the corporation's outstanding shares. If the repurchase relates only to part of a class, however, and is done on a random basis, the proportionate interests of the remaining shareholders will be changed after the redemption inasmuch as some shareholders will own less stock than before and others will own the same amount of shares as before the transaction. Those whose shares were not purchased will own a greater proportionate interest in the corporation because other shareholders now own fewer shares.

The acquisition by a corporation of its shares is to be distinguished from the situation in which shareholders (usually preferred shareholders) are issued shares with a right of redemption (the right to compel the corporation to repurchase the shares). In such a case, the various limitations applicable to the distribution of dividends do not apply.

When the corporation reacquires the previously outstanding shares, it can cancel them and thereby return them to the status of authorized but unissued shares (the MBCA approach) or it can hold them as treasury shares. If shares are canceled, the corporation must usually file a statement of cancellation with the secretary of state providing information about the number of authorized shares and the number of issued shares before and then after cancellation (see Figure 10-1).

Key Features
of Corporate Dividends

◆ A dividend is a distribution of a corporation's profits to its shareholders.

◆ Dividends may be in the form of cash (the most common form of dividend), property (the least common form of dividend), or shares of the corporation. A share dividend does not increase a shareholder's power or control because every shareholder in a class will be treated uniformly.

◆ To distribute a dividend, a corporation must be solvent, meaning that it is able to pay its debts as they come due or its assets must exceed its liabilities.

◆ Most state statutes mandate that dividends can be paid only from certain funds, usually retained earnings and surplus.

◆ Dividends must be uniform within a class but can vary from class to class.

◆ The decision to declare a dividend is made by the board of directors, who will set a record date for determining the shareholders entitled to a dividend.

◆ Generally, shareholders have no absolute right to receive dividends, and dividends are declared in the discretion of the board.

◆ Shareholders who receive cash must pay taxes on the amount received.

◆ Shareholders who receive a property dividend must pay tax on the fair market value of the property received.

◆ Shareholders who receive share dividends do not pay tax at the time the dividend is received but at the time the share is sold.

I. Role of Paralegal

The decision to distribute dividends originates with the board of directors of a corporation. Usually, this decision is made by the board after consultation with its financial advisors. Thus, the attorney and paralegal do not generally come into play until after this decision has been made. There are, however, many activities the paralegal will be involved in to assist the corporation. These include the following:

1. Corporate Records

The paralegal may need to assist the corporation in preparing minutes of the board meeting authorizing the distribution. This authorization will be in the form of a resolution. It should state a record date to determine the shareholders who will be entitled to the dividend. Alternatively, the decision of the board may be reflected by a resolution adopted by unanimous written consent, the drafting of which may be done by the paralegal. To enhance protection for the board of directors, the resolution may recite that the board is acting in the best interest of the corporation and has based its decision on reasonable reports and recommendations from the corporate officers and its accountants and independent auditors, which reports are then attached.

2. Amending Articles

If the dividend is to be paid in the form of shares, the paralegal must ensure that the articles of incorporation authorize a sufficient number of shares to accommodate the distribution. If the authorized number of shares is not sufficiently large, the paralegal might need to work with the corporation in calling a meeting of shareholders to amend the articles and then prepare the necessary articles of amendment before the dividend can be declared. If the amendment is one that does not require shareholder approval, namely, an amendment to accommodate a share dividend or stock split, no shareholder meeting need be held, although articles of amendment must still be prepared and filed.

3. Honoring of Preferences

The paralegal should carefully scrutinize the articles of incorporation and the pertinent state statutes to ensure that the corporation's distribution complies with any provisions in its articles or any statutes permitting distributions only when the corporation's assets exceed its liabilities plus the dissolution preferences of senior or preferred shareholders.

4. Statement of Cancellation

If the corporation repurchases (and then cancels) its own shares from shareholders, a statement of cancellation must usually be prepared and filed with the secretary of state. (See Figure 10-1 for a sample statement of cancellation.) This statement will inform the secretary of state of the number of authorized and issued shares before cancellation and the changes in the number of authorized shares and issued shares after the cancellation.

5. Authorization of Bonuses

If the corporation is small and the shareholders are all active in managing the business, dividends per se will not be declared. The corporation will rather distribute salaries and bonuses to the employees. The employees thus share in the profits of the enterprise, and the corporation is able to deduct the payments as a business expense. In such cases, the paralegal will prepare minutes of meetings or unanimous written consent actions with the appropriate resolutions authorizing payment of the various bonuses.

Case Illustration
Directors' Discretion in Declaring Dividends and Authorizing Stock Repurchase

---

Case: *Kohn v. Birmingham Realty Co.*, 352 So. 2d 834
            (Ala. 1977)

Facts: Plaintiff, a minority shareholder, brought an action to compel a
            corporation to declare a dividend and to enjoin the
            corporation from buying back some of its common shares.
            The trial court dismissed the action.

Holding: The Alabama Supreme Court affirmed. An Alabama
            corporation can purchase its own shares if the purchase is
            made from earned surplus and such a transaction won't
            render the corporation insolvent. These conditions were
            satisfied here. Moreover, directors have the authority to
            declare dividends out of earnings, and courts won't
            interfere with this management function unless there
            is fraud, abuse of discretion, or misappropriation of
            corporate funds. In this case, most of the earned income
            from which a dividend could have been paid was
            used to repurchase stock. Because there was no fraud
            or illegality in the stock repurchase, there was no duty to
            declare a dividend.

◆   ◆   ◆

WEB RESOURCES

The most important Web resources are state statutes relating to the proce-dure for declaring dividends and the funds from which they may legally be paid. The only forms needed will be forms for the minutes of the meeting of the board of directors declaring the dividend (or a unanimous written consent by the directors if they act without a meeting). For sites posting such minutes, see the Web Resources section for Chapter Eleven. To locate your state's statutes on the Web, try www.law.cornell.edu, www.findlaw.com, or www.megalaw.com. To review the text of the MBCA, access www.abanet.org/buslaw/committees/CL270000pub/nosearch/mbca/home.shtml.

Discussion Questions

Fact Scenario. Kitchen & Bath Renovations Inc. has seven members on its board of directors and 200,000 outstanding shares, 150,000 of which are held by Common A shareholders, and 50,000 of which are held by Common B shareholders. The articles of incorporation authorize 250,000 shares of Common A stock and 80,000 shares of Common B stock. Use the MBCA to answer these questions.

1. The corporation would like to issue a stock dividend to its Common B shareholders. May it use Common A stock to do this?

2. The corporation has decided to issue cash dividends to half of its Common A shareholders and stock dividends to the other half of its Common A shareholders. May it do this?

3. At a board of directors' meeting, the directors authorized a cash dividend of $1 per share for every share of Common A stock outstanding and set the record date as May 1 and the payment date as June 1. Jacob sold all of his 500 shares of Common A stock to Ed on May 15. Who will receive the dividend? Discuss. What is the amount of the dividend?

4. Assume the corporation is having difficulty paying its bills and making payroll. May the corporation declare and pay a cash dividend? May the corporation declare and pay a stock dividend? Assume that at a directors' meeting voting on this issue, the directors authorized the cash dividend. Director Blair vigorously opposed this dividend. Describe any liability the directors may have for declaring the cash dividend.

5. Assume that the corporation has declared a stock dividend for its Common B shareholders, declaring that for every 100 shares of Common B stock outstanding, the holder will receive an additional share of Common B stock. Ava owns 100 shares of Common B stock. Bob owns 150 shares of Common B stock. Caroline owns 1,000 shares of Common B stock. What dividend will each of these shareholders receive?

6. Assume that the corporation has a significant amount of cash on hand and has not paid a dividend for five years. Is there anything that a shareholder can do to remedy this situation? What danger does the corporation run in not paying a dividend?

7. The corporation would like to declare a two-for-one stock split for both the Common A stock and for the Common B stock. Describe any procedures the corporation should follow to accomplish this goal.

Net Worth

1. Access the SEC Web site. Locate the section for investors called "Fast Answers" and review the information about stock splits. According to the SEC, when do companies often do a stock split?

2. Access the SEC Web site and locate the 10-K form filed by Dana Holding Corporation for the fiscal year ended December 31, 2007.

Review page 4. What dividends are payable on the company's preferred stock? What will happen if the company fails to pay the equivalent of six quarterly dividends on the preferred stock?

3. Access the SEC Web site and locate Middleton Doll Company's definitive proxy statement DEF 14A filed on September 29, 2008, or its form 8-K filed on September 29, 2008. Review Section 8.01. What was the purpose of the company's reverse stock split?

4. Access the SEC Web site and locate McDonald's form 8-K (use McDonald's ticker symbol of MCD) filed on September 25, 2008, and its accompanying press release. What quarterly dividend was announced? How many times has McDonald's raised its dividends?

5. Access the Web site of Hormel Foods. Access its Newsroom and review its press release dated September 23, 2008. What dividend was announced? How many quarterly dividends had Hormel Foods paid as of that date?

6. Access the Web site for Standard & Poor's.
   a. Review the information factsheet relating to its index called "S & P Dividend Aristocrats." What is the eligibility requirement for a company to be labeled as a Dividend Aristocrat?
   b. Review the "Constituent List" of the Dividend Aristocrats. What is the first company identified?

13

◆ ◆ ◆

Securities Regulation and the Stock Exchanges

◆ ◆ ◆

CHAPTER OVERVIEW

Investors in corporations are protected not only by state statutes relating to the formation, operation, and management of corporations, but also by various federal and state laws mandating disclosure requirements for the issuance of corporate securities.

The Securities Act of 1933 imposes requirements on corporations issuing stocks and bonds to the public. These requirements relate to disclosure of certain matters through registration of documents with the Securities and Exchange Commission. The 1933 Act focuses on the original issuance of securities to the public.

The Securities Exchange Act of 1934 is concerned primarily with the trading of stock, specifically the buying and selling of securities subsequent to their original issuance. Each state also regulates the issuance and sale of securities within its borders through laws called blue sky laws.

In addition to examining the various federal and state statutes designed for investor protection, this chapter also reviews the process by which stocks are publicly traded on the national exchanges and the effect of the Internet on stock trading.

A. Introduction to Investor Protection

Although public corporations represent a small percentage of all businesses in the United States, their economic impact on the country is significant. Approximately 50 percent of all households in the United States own stock in a public corporation. Many nightly news broadcasts open with a report on the day's stock market activities. Newspapers devote special sections to financial and business news, carefully noting rising and falling stocks and commenting on the stock market in general.

For many years, corporations desiring to sell stock to the public simply distributed securities by having agents sell stock on commission. The stock market crash of October 29, 1929, and the subsequent Great Depression provided the impetus for a public examination of the practices of selling securities. After reports of speculative and unscrupulous trading practices, the public clamored for action. Congress responded in 1931 by examining and investigating trade practices and by passing the Securities Act of 1933, also referred to as the "truth in securities" law. The following year, Congress enacted the Securities Exchange Act of 1934, which created the **Securities and Exchange Commission (SEC)**, an independent federal agency charged with regulation of securities and the administration of the 1933 and 1934 Acts. The SEC is composed of five commissioners appointed by the president for five-year terms, with no more than three from any one political party. It was initially chaired by Joseph P. Kennedy, Sr. Over time, the SEC has expanded its role, promoting harsher penalties for insider trading and addressing corporate governance and the issue of increasing numbers of corporate takeovers. The SEC does not actually approve the securities being issued by a corporation; it rather requires disclosure of material information for consumer protection. The 1933 Act focuses on the initial sale of securities whereas the 1934 Act deals mostly with the resale of securities.

SEC
Securities and Exchange Commission; federal agency charged with regulation of securities

B. Going Public

Going public
Sale of shares to the public at large

Initial public offering
The first offering of stock to the public (an *IPO*)

When a corporation decides to sell its shares to members of the public at large, the decision is referred to as **going public.** This decision is made by the directors acting in the best interest of the corporation. The first offering of the corporation's stock to the public is referred to as the **initial public offering** (IPO). Going public will raise capital for the corporation and will result in prominent exposure for the corporation and its business. Such exposure could allow the corporation to attract and hire highly qualified executives to manage the corporation. The downside of going public is that the influx of new shareholders will result in a loss of control and power by the then-current shareholders. The costs of going public and complying with the various regulations imposed on corporations selling their stock publicly are significant. Additionally, the corporation's financial history and that of its managers will be open for inspection and discussion by the public. Many of the largest companies in the country are still privately held, including Mars, Inc., the candy maker, which has annual revenues of more than $21 billion and 40,000 employees. In fact, in 2008, Mars acquired chewing gum giant Wm. Wrigley Jr. Company, and Wrigley ceased trading its stock publicly.

Underwriting
Process of issuing stock to the public

Underwriter
A securities firm that assists a corporation in offering stock to the public

A corporation selling securities to the public for the first time does not usually offer the securities through any of the stock markets. The process of issuing securities from the corporation to the ultimate shareholder is called an **underwriting.** Once the corporation has made the decision to go public it will enter into an agreement with an investment bank or securities firm, called the **underwriter.**

Some underwriters specialize in certain industries. Nationally known underwriters, such as The Goldman Sachs Group, generally do not display interest in a company unless its sales or value exceed a certain amount, often as high as

$50 million. The underwriters act as middle men between the corporation and future investors.

There are different types of agreements the corporation and the underwriter may enter into:

- *Firm commitment agreement.* With a **firm commitment agreement**, which is the most common type of underwriting agreement, the underwriter agrees to purchase the entire issue from the corporation and then reoffers to sell the stock to others. If the underwriter cannot sell the stock to others, it will pay the agreed-on issue price to the corporation. In a firm commitment, the underwriter has guaranteed the sale of the stock and has assumed all risk for it. To spread the risk, the underwriter may form a **syndicate**, a group of investment banks that will participate in selling the issue, with each agreeing to purchase a stated amount of the stock being sold. Alternatively, the underwriter may enter into agreements with other securities firms (referred to as **dealers**) by which the dealers buy the securities for resale to their customers. For example, assume the directors of Pearson Corp. enter into arrangements with Goldman Sachs to underwrite 2 million of its shares at $20 per share. Goldman Sachs may buy the stock and enter into arrangements for the dealers to purchase portions of the shares for resale to customers of the dealers at a profit, perhaps for $22 per share. In this way, the underwriter makes $2 per share. On the other hand, if Goldman Sachs cannot enter into such arrangements with dealers, it is simply stuck and must buy all the stock from Pearson Corp.
- *Best efforts agreement.* Under a **best efforts agreement**, the underwriter agrees to use its best efforts to sell the securities but does not guarantee the amount of capital that will be raised by the offering.
- *Standby agreement.* With a **standby agreement**, the underwriter agrees to purchase all or a portion of the new securities that remain unsold after the IPO.
- *All-or-nothing agreement.* Under an **all-or-nothing agreement**, which is relatively rare, the underwriter agrees to use its best efforts to sell the entire issue by a certain date. All proceeds from sales are placed in an escrow account. If the entire issue is not sold by the agreed-on date, the money received from buyers is returned to them and the offering is canceled.

C. Securities Act of 1933

1. Introduction

The securities to be issued by the corporation are usually in the form of **equity securities** (*stock* representing ownership interest in the corporation) or **debt securities** (*bonds* representing money owed by a corporation to a creditor). Securities may take other forms, however, such as specific property items, ranging from orange trees to liquor, cosmetics to investment contracts in condominiums. The generally accepted test used to determine if a "security" is being issued is whether the person is investing money in a common enterprise and is reasonably led to expect profits primarily from the managerial or entrepreneurial efforts of

---

Firm commitment agreement
Agreement by underwriter to purchase all stock from corporation at a set price and resell it to others

Syndicate
Group of investors, usually banks, that participate in selling an issue of stock

Dealers
Securities firms that buy stock for resale to their customers

Best efforts agreement
Agreement by underwriter to use its best efforts to sell a corporation's securities

Standby agreement
Agreement by underwriter to purchase all or a portion of a corporation's securities not sold through the IPO

All-or-nothing agreement
Agreement by underwriter to use best efforts to sell all of a corporation's securities by a fixed date; if issue is not sold by date, offering is canceled

Equity security
Stock representing ownership interest in corporation

Debt security
Bond representing money owed by corporation to creditor

others. *SEC v. W.J. Howey Co.*, 328 U.S. 293, 299 (1946). If so, a security is being offered and, unless exemptions exist, the issuer must comply with the **1933 Act.** Although it is easy to understand why stocks and bonds offered by corporations are *securities* subject to the 1933 Act, it should be remembered that limited partnership and LLC interests can also constitute securities, which must comply with the registration requirements of the 1933 Act even though the issuer is not a corporation. The 1933 Act imposes registration requirements and antifraud provisions on the initial or primary distribution of securities.

2. Registration Requirements

The 1933 Act (15 U.S.C. § 77a et seq.) provides that no security may be offered or sold through the mails or any instrumentalities of interstate commerce (telephone, facsimile, Internet, and so forth) without compliance with certain registration requirements unless either the security or the transaction is exempt. The SEC does not evaluate the merits of offerings but rather merely declares registration statements "effective" if companies satisfy SEC disclosure rules.

The form of **registration statement** provided by the SEC is Form S-1. The SEC has adopted regulations requiring the use of "plain English" in the registration form so that it is clear and understandable to the average investor. Since 1993, registration forms must be filed electronically with the SEC through its EDGAR (Electronic Data Gathering and Retrieval) database. The main part (or Part I) of the registration statement is called the **prospectus.** It is this document that must be provided to any investors. The prospectus describes the securities being sold, provides background information about the issuing corporation and its directors and officers, and describes the investment so that all investors can fully evaluate the potential risks involved in purchasing the security. Part II of the registration statement includes "additional information" about the company and the offering and remains on file with the SEC for public inspection.

The registration statement must include the following information:

a. A description of the security offered for sale;
b. A description of the issuer's business, its competitors, and risk factors that might affect the offering;
c. A description of the management of the issuer;
d. A financial statement audited by an independent certified public accountant; and
e. A description of any pending material litigation involving the issuer.

The registration statement is filed electronically in triplicate with the SEC and becomes a matter of public record. It is subject to a 20-day waiting period, sometimes called the "cooling off period," "quiet period," or "waiting period," before it becomes effective, although the SEC might accelerate this period if requested. The SEC may also delay the effective date if the statement is incomplete or inaccurate and often requests additional information or clarifications. In most cases, the SEC will comment on the registration statement and request additional information and disclosures. A filing fee must accompany the registration statement. "Small business issuers" can use a simplified registration form. A small business issuer is one that has had less than $25 million in revenues during its last fiscal year and whose outstanding publicly held stock is worth no more than $25 million.

During the 20-day waiting period, certain activities may occur. For example, oral offers between interested investors and the issuer corporation may take place although actual sales cannot occur. Limited advertising can also take place in the form of **tombstone ads,** called such because of the black border surrounding the advertisement. Tombstone ads (often published electronically) generally merely announce that securities are being issued by a corporation; they are not considered prospectuses and thus need not comply with the 1933 Act's registration requirements, but they must include certain basic information about the issuer. (See Figure 13-1 for a sample tombstone ad.) The issuer corporation might also distribute a form of preliminary prospectus called the **red herring prospectus,** so named for the notation (or *legend*) printed in red ink informing investors that the registration statement has been filed but has not yet become effective. The primary purpose of the red herring is to stimulate interest in the company. No price is noted in the red herring. Exceeding the SEC's permissible forms of solicitation, called "gun jumping," is prohibited. After the effective date of the registration statement, the corporation can commence full-scale sales and promotional efforts and will issue a final prospectus to interested parties. The underwriters and dealers are paid from the proceeds of the issue.

Tombstone ad
Announcement that securities are being issued by a corporation

Red herring prospectus
Preliminary form of prospectus describing stock to be sold

FIGURE 13-1
Sample Tombstone Advertisement

New Issue   *The offering is made only by the Prospectus.*   January 28, 1996

1,500,000 Shares

OPTICAL CABLE
C O R P O R A T I O N

COMMON STOCK
Offered at $10 Per Share

Optical Cable Corporation announced today that it will offer up to 1,500,000 shares of Common Stock for sale to the public at a price of $10.00 per share. Optical Cable Corporation manufactures and markets a broad range of fiber optic cables for "high bandwidth" transmission of data, video and audio communications over moderate distances. OCC's cables can be used both indoors and outdoors, and utilize a tight-buffered coating that protects the optical fiber.

Copies of the Prospectus may be obtained from: Optical Cable Corporation
P.O. Box 11967
5290 Concourse Drive
Roanoke, VA 24022-1967 U.S.A.

Phone No. 1-800-622-7711 or 1-540-265-0690   FAX: 1-540-265-0724 or 1-540-265-0725
****
A registration statement relating to these securities has been filed with the Securities and Exchange Commission but has not become effective. These securities may not be sold nor may offers to buy be accepted prior to the time the registration statement becomes effective. This communication shall not constitute an offer to sell or the solicitation of any offer to buy, nor shall there be any sale of these securities in any State in which such offer, solicitation or sale would be unlawful prior to registration or qualification under the securities laws of any such state.

3. Exemptions from Registration

The exhaustive coverage of the 1933 Act's requirements are moderated by a number of exemptions to the Act. Certain securities, small issues offerings, intrastate offerings, and private offerings are exempt from the complex disclosure and registration requirements of the Act. These exemptions generally make it easier for small businesses to raise money. All offerings, however, are subject to the antifraud provisions of the Act.

Exempt securities
Securities that are exempt from registration requirements of 1933 Act

Securities Exemptions. The Act provides that certain classes of **securities are exempt** from the registration requirements of the Act. Among them are securities issued by the United States or state governments and banks, securities of charitable organizations, securities issued by savings and loan associations and farmers' cooperative associations, insurance policies and annuities, securities issued only to persons residing within a single state, and certain short-term commercial paper financing. These exemptions are found in § 3 and § 4 of the 1933 Act.

Small issues exemptions
Issuances exempt from registration requirements of 1933 Act due to small size of issuance or sophistication of investors, or both

Small Issues Exemptions. Section 3(b) of the 1933 Act exempts certain "small issues" from registration requirements when the total amount of the offering does not exceed $5 million. There is no limit on the number of investors or any requirement that they be financially sophisticated. The SEC has adopted Regulation A detailing the requirements for qualifying for this exemption.

Under Regulation A, the securities offered in any 12-month period must not exceed $5 million. There is no limit on the number of investors or any requirement that they be financially sophisticated. The issuer must file both notice of the issue and an offering circular with the SEC. The documents are filed with the SEC's regional office and are less complex than full registration. For example, the financial statements provided under Regulation A need not be audited. Purchasers must be provided with an offering circular that is similar to a prospectus. Regulation A allows companies to "test the waters" to determine the level of interest in their securities before going through the extensive requirements associated with full registration.

Under the SEC's Regulation D, three offerings are exempt from the SEC registration requirements. The exemptions are either for offerings involving smaller amounts of money or those made in a limited manner.

Under Regulation D, three separate rules provide exemptions:

1. Rule 504 permits an issuer to sell securities in any 12-month period for a total price up to $1 million without registration. General advertising (such as television, radio, or newspaper ads) may not be used to sell the securities.
2. Rule 505 exempts from registration offerings of less than $5 million in any 12-month period to an unlimited number of accredited investors and up to 35 other persons who do not need to satisfy the sophistication or wealth standards associated with accredited investors. General advertising may not be used to sell the securities and purchasers may not resell the securities for one year. Thus, these purchasers are buying for investment purposes and not for resale.

An **accredited investor** is an individual with a net worth in excess of $1 million or yearly income in excess of $200,000 ($300,000 jointly with a spouse), banks, insurance companies, principals of the issuers, and other similarly sophisticated investors. Accredited investors are presumed to be sufficiently knowledgeable that they require less protection than the typical investor.

3. Rule 506 exempts offers and sales in an unlimited amount in any 12-month period to an unlimited number of accredited investors and up to 35 other purchasers (nonaccredited investors); however, the non-accredited investors must be "sophisticated," meaning that they have a certain level of knowledge and experience in financial and business matters such that they are capable of evaluating the risks and merits of the transaction. General advertising may not be used to sell the securities, and purchasers may not freely trade the securities. Usually, purchasers must hold the securities for at least one year.

Under Rules 504, 505, and 506, a Form D notice must be filed with the SEC within 15 days after the first sale of any securities. Form D is a brief notice that includes the names and addresses of the company's owners and stock promoters but contains little other information about the company.

Intrastate Offerings.   To facilitate the financing of local business operations, intrastate offerings (offerings only within one state) are also exempt from the registration and disclosure requirements of the 1933 Act. This exemption applies only if the following conditions are met:

1. The issuer corporation must be incorporated in the state in which it is making the offering;
2. The offering must be made only to residents of the state of incorporation (and no resale to an out-of-state resident may take place during the nine months after the sale); and
3. The issuer corporation must conduct a significant amount of its business in the state (typically, 80 percent of the issuer's assets must be located in the state and 80 percent of its gross revenue must be generated in the state).

There is no limit on the size of the offering or the number of purchasers. Although an intrastate offering is exempt from the registration requirements of the 1933 Act, it might be subject to state securities laws.

Private Placement Offerings.   Nonpublic offerings can be made in an unlimited amount so long as the offering is not generally advertised and the investors are believed to have sufficient knowledge of financial matters that they are capable of evaluating the risks in the transaction. This exemption is often referred to as the "private placement" exemption and the securities are offered through a **private placement offering** (PPO) or *private placement memorandum* (PPM).

This exemption is often viewed as the most important one for corporations wishing to raise capital and yet avoid the rigorous disclosure and registration requirements of the 1933 Act. There is no specific fixed limit either on the amount of money that can be raised through the private placement offering or on the number of people who can be involved, so long as the investors meet the requirement of being sufficiently sophisticated that they understand the risks inherent in the investment, and they agree not to resell the securities to the public.

Exemption for Accredited Investors.   Section 4(6) of the Securities Act exempts from registration offers and sales of securities to accredited investors when the total offering price is less than $5 million.

The definition of accredited investors is the same as that used in Regulation D. Like the exemptions in Rules 505 and 506, this exemption does not permit any form of advertising or public solicitation. There are no document delivery requirements. Of course, all transactions are subject to the antifraud provisions of the securities laws.

Exemption for Nonissuers.   The registration requirements of the 1933 Act apply to every sale of securities unless there is an exemption from registration. What about small investors who ask their brokers to sell their shares of stock in a company such as Ford Motor Company? The 1933 Act provides an exemption for transactions by any person who is not an issuer, underwriter, or dealer. Because individual investors are not issuers (such as Ford), underwriters (those who assist Ford in selling its shares to the public), or dealers (those engaged in the business of selling securities), they may freely resell their shares without any registration.

Shelf registration
A registration of new stock prepared up to three years in advance of sales; registration is automatically effective for well-known seasoned issuers

Shelf Registrations.   A **shelf registration** permits an issuer to file a registration statement for a new issue, which is prepared up to three years in advance of any sale of the securities. A shelf registration is then "ready to go" when a company needs funds or when market conditions are more favorable. Under SEC rules adopted in late 2005, the shelf registration process has been significantly streamlined. Companies that are defined as "well-known seasoned issuers" (which typically means a company that routinely files timely reports with the SEC and has at least $700 million in market value) may use new "automatic" registration and become effective without SEC review. About one-third of companies that offer their stock publicly fall into the category of "well-known seasoned issuers." Thus, these issuers with proven track records may offer securities immediately after filing the shelf registration statement without waiting for SEC review. These shelf registrations must be renewed every three years.

4. Antifraud Provisions of 1933 Act

Although a security or transaction may be exempt from the registration requirements of the 1933 Act, the antifraud provisions of the Act apply to *any* offer or sale of securities, whether public or private, regardless of its size. These provisions apply if the mails or interstate commerce instrumentalities are used in the offer or sale of securities and protect investors from fraud, deceit, material misrepresentations and omissions, half-truths, and so forth.

5. Penalties for Violations of 1933 Act

The SEC has the power to investigate and bring actions against violators of the 1933 Act and may also impose fines. Criminal violations are referred to the

Department of Justice for prosecution. Aggrieved investors or shareholders may also bring actions. In fact, any person damaged by inaccurate or misleading material statements in a registration statement has a cause of action against any person who signed the registration statement, any director of the corporate issuer, accountants and experts involved in the preparation of the statement, and underwriters.

Because a host of individuals will be involved in the preparation of the registration statement, and not all of them will have access to all pertinent information, individuals are not liable if they can prove they conducted **due diligence** in preparing the statement; that is, they conducted a reasonable investigation and had reasonable grounds to believe the statement was true and accurate. Thus, attorneys, paralegals, and accountants who assist in preparing the registration statement have a duty to make a reasonable investigation of the issuer's records, contracts, and so forth. This investigation is often referred to as due diligence work, and it is a time-consuming and expensive process for the issuer corporation. If a violation of the Act is proven, the plaintiff may recover damages for the loss in value of the investment. Alternatively, the purchaser can rescind the transaction and receive a return of the money invested (with interest).

Due diligence
Investigation of records and data

D.   Securities Exchange Act of 1934

1.   Introduction

Whereas the 1933 Act is concerned with the initial offering of securities, the focus of the **Securities Exchange Act of 1934** (15 U.S.C. § 78a et seq.) is on the resale of securities after their original issuance and on various reporting requirements imposed on issuers. The 1934 Act provides for the regulation and registration of those involved in the sale of securities such as brokers, dealers, and exchanges. The Act also created the SEC and authorizes it to investigate fraud, manipulation, and other undesirable trading practices in the market. The 1934 Act requires registration with the SEC of any security to be traded on a national exchange, requires periodic reporting by issuers, and regulates the use of proxies.

1934 Act
Act governing resale of securities after their initial issuance

Under § 12 of the 1934 Act, only certain companies are required to register their securities with the SEC. These companies are those whose securities are listed on a national securities exchange, such as the New York Stock Exchange, or those companies having assets of $10 million or more and 500 or more shareholders. These companies are often called **Section 12 companies**, *registered companies*, or *reporting companies*. Companies such as McDonald's, Coca-Cola Company, General Electric, and FedEx are Section 12 companies subject to compliance with the 1934 Act, which primarily involves periodic reporting to the SEC.

Section 12 companies
Companies that trade on national exchanges or those with significant assets that are required to register securities and file other reports with SEC (also called *reporting companies*)

2.   Registration Requirements

The registration statement required of Section 12 companies under the 1934 Act is substantially similar to that required under the 1933 Act. The statement, called an application, is filed with the appropriate exchange and with the SEC.

It includes information about the corporation, the securities offered, the financial structure of the business, material contracts, profit-and-loss statements, and so forth. Registration is generally effective 30 days after filing the application. The registration under the 1933 Act is done prior to offering securities for sale. The registration under the 1934 Act is primarily for reporting purposes.

3. *Periodic Reporting Requirements*

Section 12 companies must file a variety of reports with the SEC. These include periodic reports of any changes to the original application statements, annual reports, and quarterly reports. Falsification of reports can result in the imposition of criminal penalties.

The SEC furnishes the forms necessary to comply with the periodic reporting requirements. The periodic reports required by the SEC are Form 8-K, Form 10-Q, and Form 10-K.

Form 8-K
Form filed with SEC to report major events in a Section 12 company (also called a *current report*)

Form 10-Q
Quarterly report filed with SEC by Section 12 company

Form 10-K
Annual report filed with SEC by Section 12 company

- **Form 8-K**, often called a *current report*, is used to report the occurrence of any material events or corporate changes that are of importance to investors or security holders and that have previously not been reported by the registrant. Thus, a merger, bankruptcy, or resignation of a director would be reported on Form 8-K, which must generally be filed within four business days after the event.
- **Form 10-Q** is a quarterly report. It includes unaudited financial statements and provides a continuing view of the company's financial position during the year. The report must be filed for each of the three fiscal quarters of the company's fiscal year and is due within 40 days of the close of the quarter for large accelerated filers (companies with a public float of $700 million or more) and accelerated filers (companies that have at least $75 million but less than $700 million in public float) or 45 days of the close of the quarter for all other filers. The fourth quarterly report is subsumed into the annual report on Form 10-K. Smaller reporting companies (those with less than $75 million in float) use a more simplified disclosure. More than 40 percent of reporting companies are eligible for these scaled disclosure reports.
- **Form 10-K** is the annual report filed with the SEC. It must include audited financial reports and current information about the company, its management, and securities, as well as disclosure of the identity and compensation for directors and highly compensated executives and a complete management discussion and analysis of the company's financial condition. This annual report must be filed within 60 days after the end of the company's fiscal year for large accelerated filers, 75 days for accelerated filers, and 90 days for all other filers. Smaller reporting companies use a simplified disclosure.

Note that the SEC typically allows smaller companies to use simplified reports and to have additional time to file various reports. Larger companies are subject to stricter reporting requirements. All reports are available through the SEC's EDGAR database at www.sec.gov.

---

4. Insider Trading: Rule 10b-5

Section 10(b) of the 1934 Act makes it unlawful for any person to use any manipulative or deceptive device in connection with the purchase or sale of any security. To implement this section, the SEC adopted **Rule 10b-5**, often referred to as the antifraud rule, which provides:

> It shall be unlawful for any person, directly or indirectly, by the use of any means or instrumentality of interstate commerce, or of the mails, or of any facility of any national securities exchange,
> (1) to employ any device, scheme, or artifice to defraud,
> (2) to make any untrue statement of a material fact or to omit to state a material fact necessary in order to make the statements made, in the light of the circumstances under which they were made, not misleading, or
> (3) to engage in any act, practice, or course of business which operates or would operate as a fraud or deceit upon any person, in connection with the purchase or sale of any security.

This rule has been used by the SEC and courts to prevent a variety of unscrupulous practices, most notably, **insider trading.** The prohibitions against insider trading are meant to ensure that all investors are on an equal footing. Corporate **insiders**, such as directors and officers, are in a position to know critical matters affecting the corporation and the value of its stock, such as plans to merge, technological advances and discoveries, and adverse financial conditions. If these insiders purchase stock, knowing the stock is about to soar in value due to a recent discovery, they receive a benefit from their position not available to other investors. Similarly, if the insiders sell their stock, knowing that a future public announcement of a lawsuit against the company will cause the stock to fall, they abuse their position to the detriment of others. Insider trading allegations are common in shareholder lawsuits. Because insider trading undermines investor confidence in the fairness and integrity of the securities markets, the SEC has treated the detection and prosecution of insider trading violations as one of its enforcement priorities. Insiders include not only directors and officers but anyone entrusted with corporate information for the corporation's purposes, such as attorneys, accountants, and public relations consultants.

Rule 10b-5 applies to purchases and sales, applies to nearly all securities, and applies whether or not those securities have been registered under either the 1933 Act or the 1934 Act. Thus, the prohibitions against insider trading apply in virtually every instance of the trading of securities, whether those securities are traded on one of the national exchanges, such as the New York Stock Exchange, or whether they are traded over the counter, or traded privately. Liability may result from affirmative misrepresentations of a material fact, nondisclosure of a material fact, or misappropriation of such information.

A **material fact** is one that would have influenced the injured party's conduct. Some examples of facts held to be material are a significant drop in corporate profits, management's decision to pay a dividend, an agreement for the sale of corporate assets, and critical discoveries. In one well-known case, *SEC v. Texas Gulf Sulphur Co.*, 401 F.2d 833 (8th Cir. 1968), a company discovered significant mineral deposits. The news was leaked to the media and the company then downplayed the discovery with a misleading press release. During this period, various

Rule 10b-5 SEC rule prohibiting insider trading

Insider trading Trading in stock by corporate insiders with information unknown by public at large

Insiders Corporate officers and directors and others with knowledge of corporate matters

Material fact A fact that influences conduct

officers, directors, and employees of the company purchased stock. When the announcement of the mineral deposit was eventually made public, the value of the stock increased, and the insiders who had previously purchased stock received a windfall in the increased value of their stock. The company was sued by the SEC as well as by individuals who sold their stock after reading the press release, believing the corporation had not made a significant discovery. The court held that all of the transactions by the corporate insiders were in violation of Rule 10b-5.

In a modern case eerily similar to *Texas Gulf Sulfur*, in early 2008, the SEC obtained a civil settlement with an oceanographic consultant for insider trading. The consultant had discovered a shipwreck with valuable silver coins, and two weeks before the public announcement of the discovery, the consultant bought 42,000 shares of stock in the exploration company. When the discovery was announced, the stock soared nearly 81 percent, and the individual then sold the stock at a huge profit.

Tippee
One who receives a tip from a corporate insider

Tipper
Corporate insider who gives a tip to another

To discourage fraud and manipulative devices, Rule 10b-5 applies not only to corporate insiders but also to individuals who acquire inside information as a result of an insider's breach of fiduciary or good-faith duty. Thus, **tippees** (those who receive tips from insiders) as well as **tippers** (those insiders giving tips) can be held liable. Consequently, corporate insiders cannot avoid liability by having a relative or friend purchase or sell stock for them. Both the insider tipper and the relative and friend tippees have violated Rule 10b-5. Even subtippees of tippees have been held liable.

Rule 10b-5 applies only to actual purchases or sales of securities. For example, if the corporation releases an untrue and pessimistic annual report when the financial situation is actually quite strong, a current shareholder may decide to "hold firm" and not purchase any additional stock until the corporation's financial picture has improved. Although the damage seems clear, the U.S. Supreme Court has held that nonpurchasers and nonsellers do not have standing to bring an action under Rule 10b-5. Despite criticism of this rule, many scholars believe that allowing individuals to claim "I would have purchased [or sold] stock but for the company's misconduct" would open the floodgate to litigation and enormous liability that might be speculative at best.

Effective October 2000, the SEC issued Rule 10b5-2, clarifying that misappropriation can occur when a duty of trust or confidentiality has been breached even when it occurs in a nonbusiness, family, or social setting.

5. Remedies and Penalties for Violation of 1934 Act

Rescission
Cancellation of a transaction

Purchasers or sellers of stock traded in violation of Rule 10b-5 have a wide array of remedies available to them. One remedy is **rescission:** Defrauded purchasers can cancel the transaction and defrauded sellers can get their stock back. Another remedy is to compel those who benefited from the transaction to disgorge their profits, and, in some cases, pay three times the amount of the profit gained or loss avoided as a result of the violation of Rule 10b-5. The most common remedy is to allow the defrauded party to recover "out-of-pocket" damages, namely, the difference between what the victim purchased or sold the stock for and its actual worth at the time of the deception. Additionally, the SEC itself may institute action against the insiders, tippees, or tippers.

Recently enacted federal statutes also provide the SEC with authority to award **bounty payments** to a person who provides information leading to the recovery of a civil penalty from an insider trader. Stricter criminal penalties for violations have also been enacted. Jail terms have been increased to ten years from five years and fines have increased to $1 million for individuals and $2.5 million for firms. Many of these remedies and penalties were prompted by the insider-trading scandals of the 1980s, involving well-known Wall Street traders such as Michael Milken and Ivan Boesky. These penalties do not affect any other actions that can be taken by the SEC or by private investors.

In 2007 NASD (formerly the National Association of Securities Dealers) merged with the regulatory operations of the NYSE to form the Financial Regulatory Authority (FINRA), which is responsible for the oversight of all public securities firms doing business in the United States. This merger will produce one set of regulatory rules and one enforcement staff, thus eliminating redundancies in regulation. FINRA also regulates the industry, enacts and enforces its own rules as well as federal securities laws, educates investors, and provides dispute resolution services. In 2007, FINRA resolved more than 1,000 formal actions and collected nearly $50 million in fines. FINRA can not only impose monetary fines, but it can expel firms from the securities industry. It also engages in electronic surveillance of trading. The NYSE also engages in surveillance. For example, to determine whether insider trading is occurring, the NYSE monitors unusual stock activity and transactions, using a computer system called "Stock Watch," designed to search for odd trading patterns. The computer then alerts NYSE regulatory personnel so an investigation can be conducted. If a trade or transaction raises a red flag, investigation of the owner of the stock is begun by cross-referencing his or her name with employees of the corporation, the underwriter, or the law firm assisting in the issuance to determine if a match has occurred, in that the trader is a relative of an insider, went to the same college, lives in the same neighborhood, and so forth. In this way, the NYSE attempts to keep its own house in order and monitor for insider trading. The NYSE then refers the matter to the SEC for further investigation and possible fines and jail terms.

Because insider trading is so serious and causes lack of public confidence in the stock market, most large companies now appoint their own compliance officers to clear or approve trades by inside company executives who might have access to nonpublic information. Similarly, to ensure fairness and integrity in the securities markets, the SEC has made detection and prosecution of insider trading one of its top priorities.

Insider trading cases brought by the SEC have remained steady at about 7 percent of all of its enforcement cases. About 30 percent of the cases initiated by the SEC relate to financial disclosure issues. Whereas the insider trading scandal of the 1980s involved high-level insiders, many current cases mainly involve young brokerage firm professionals. Some recent cases have involved **front running**, a practice in which floor brokers trade for themselves before trading on behalf of their clients.

Bounty payment
Payment by SEC for information relating to securities fraud

Financial Industry Regulatory Authority (FINRA):
The non-governmental regulator for all securities firms doing business in the United States

Front running
Trading by floor brokers for their own account before trading on behalf of clients

6. *Short Swing Profits: Section 16(b)*

Section 16(b) of the 1934 Act requires all officers, all directors, and shareholders owning 10 percent or more of the beneficial stock of any class of stock of a Section 12 company to report their ownership and trading in their corporation's stock to the SEC. These individuals must report their ownership interest to the SEC and file additional reports within two business days after a change in their stock ownership. Thus, the SEC is provided with detailed records regarding purchases and sales of stock and grants of stock options to corporate insiders. This information must also be posted on the company's Web site, thus allowing shareholders to know when those "in the know" have bought or sold company stock. To ensure that insiders do not obtain any benefit from their intimate knowledge of corporate affairs, Section 16 provides that any profits realized from the purchase or sale of any stock in a company by these officers, directors, or 10-percent shareholders in any six-month period shall be recaptured by the corporation. It is irrelevant whether the insider has actually used insider information; any such profits made in such a short time frame (the **"short-swing" profit** must be disgorged) must be returned to the corporation. Thus, Section 16(b) imposes liability without regard to fraud or intent. The profits obtained through this *short-swing trading* must be disgorged to the corporation even if innocently obtained.

Short-swing profits
Profits made by certain corporate insiders within six months that must be disgorged

In the wake of Enron, Congress appropriated millions of dollars to the SEC for investigations and enforcement. Between 2002 and 2004, the SEC hired more than 1,000 new employees, its largest staffing increase. In fiscal year 2008, the SEC initiated the second-highest number of enforcement actions in its history and the highest number of insider trading cases since its inception. The SEC's 2008 annual report disclosed that the SEC will return up to $55 billion to investors injured by securities law violators — by far the largest settlements in SEC history.

7. *Proxy Regulation*

Section 14 of the Securities Exchange Act of 1934 also regulates the solicitation of proxies (documents by which shareholders direct others to vote their shares) from shareholders of Section 12 companies. The intent of § 14 is to protect shareholders from abuse by corporate management, which might mislead shareholders. The 1934 Act thus requires that any solicitation of proxies must be accompanied by a written proxy statement containing specified information such as information about the management of the corporation, compensation of managers, the background of nominees, stock option grants, and any other matters being voted on. Thus, shareholders are given sufficient information from which to make an informed decision. The form and content of proxy statements are strictly regulated.

To ensure that shareholders do not issue a blank check to management, the form of the proxy card itself is regulated. It must indicate whether the proxy is being solicited on behalf of management and must clearly and impartially identify each matter to be acted on. A form of proxy that provides for the election of directors must set forth the names of all nominees and provide authority for the shareholder to withhold a vote for any nominee.

Definitive copies of the proxy statement and form of proxy must be provided to the SEC at the same time they are sent to shareholders. If proxies are being solicited for an annual meeting, the proxy statement must include comparative financial statements for the corporation so that shareholders can assess management's performance. Generally, shareholders are also allowed to present their proposals in the company's proxy statement. To be eligible to submit a proposal, the shareholder must have at least $2,000 in stock ownership, and the proposal may not exceed 500 words. In general, anyone who solicits a proxy must fully and truthfully disclose any matters pertinent to the proxy or to the matters to be voted on. Remedies for violation include injunctions preventing solicitation or voting of the proxies as well as the imposition of monetary fines. Effective January 1, 2009, all publicly traded companies are required to post their proxy materials (namely, the proxy statement and the annual report) on an Internet Web site and then provide their shareholders with notice of the availability of these proxy materials 40 days before any meeting. Companies may also mail their proxy materials and if shareholders request materials by mail, they must be provided at no charge.

E.   EDGAR

The SEC's **EDGAR** system performs automated collection, indexing, and acceptance of submissions by companies that are required by law to file various forms with the SEC. Companies that must submit documents to the SEC must submit them electronically to the EDGAR system in a specialized format. The process is generally called "Edgarizing" a document. Thus, registration statements, periodic report Forms 8-K, 10-Q, and 10-K, and other forms are all available on EDGAR for public review for both domestic and foreign companies.

> **EDGAR**
> SEC's electronic filing system

Generally, documents are available for public review within minutes after they are filed on EDGAR. To access a company's filings, one may use the company's name or a unique identifier assigned to companies by the SEC, called Central Index Key Number (CIK). It is possible to limit search results by date to request documents filed after a certain date, or to limit results by types of filings, so as to access only a Form 10-K, for example.

F.   State Securities Regulation

A company selling securities must comply with federal and state securities laws. Each state has its own statutes regulating the issuance of securities within its jurisdictional borders. Many of these state statutes predate the federal securities laws. According to *Hall v. Geiger-Jones Co.*, 242 U.S. 539, 550 (1917), these regulations were intended to prevent "speculative schemes which have no more basis than so many feet of 'blue sky.'" As a result, state laws regulating the issuance of securities are referred to as **blue sky laws.** The best-known loose-leaf service containing each state's laws, recent topics, and digests of cases

> **Blue sky laws**
> State laws regulating issuance of securities within a state

relating thereto is the *Blue Sky Law Reporter*, published by CCH, Incorporated. The state blue sky laws exist concurrently with the federal statutes relating to issuance and sale of securities. Therefore, a corporation wishing to go public must comply not only with the federal securities laws but also with a variety of state laws. Under the intrastate offering exemption discussed earlier, securities that are offered and sold only to persons residing in one state are exempt from federal registration, 15 U.S.C. § 77c(a)(11), and need only comply with the pertinent state's regulations.

Provisions of state blue sky laws differ widely among states. Generally, however, there are three common elements:

- *Prohibition of fraud.* Most state blue sky laws contain antifraud provisions highly similar to or patterned after the antifraud provisions of Rule 10b-5. These provisions prohibit fraud in the sale of securities.
- *Broker and dealer registration.* Many states regulate securities by regulating the persons involved in the offer and sale of securities, namely, brokers, dealers, salespersons, and so forth.
- *Registration requirements.* Most states combine securities registration requirements with other provisions to require disclosure of pertinent information by registration. Unless a valid exemption applies, the issuer must register or qualify the securities with the state corporations commissioner before sales to investors. Some states require that certain information be provided in an application to register the securities before the securities may be sold in the state.

Registration by coordination
Allowance of sale of stock within state because issuance has been federally registered

Registration by qualification
Requirement by state that issuer file information statement with state prior to issuance of stock

Registration by notice filing
Notice provided to state that issuer has filed federal registration statement and will be offering securities within state

The actual process of registering securities in the states varies greatly. Some states follow a **registration by coordination** scheme: If the securities have been registered under federal law, they can be issued in the state without further requirements. A copy of the prospectus filed with the SEC is provided to the state. Some states have adopted a **registration by qualification** scheme: The issuer must provide comprehensive information to the state, similar to the registration statement required under the 1933 Act. The state corporations commissioner will carefully review the statement and securities being offered, generally because there has been no federal registration of the securities. Still other states allow **registration by notice filing:** If a registration statement had been filed under the 1933 Act and the issuer has been engaged in business in the United States for some period of time, the issuer provides a simple notification to the state that it will be offering securities in the state. Attached to this is a copy of the latest prospectus filed with the SEC. Generally, if an issuer has filed a registration statement with the SEC, the process of state registration is somewhat simpler than if the issuer is selling securities in the state for the first time without having filed a federal registration statement.

The National Conference of Commissioners on Uniform State Laws has approved a Uniform Securities Act (2000), which replaces earlier versions of the Uniform Securities Act and has been adopted in 13 states. The text of the Uniform Securities Act is available at www.nccusl.org.

As is true of federal registration requirements, there are numerous exemptions from state blue sky laws. Some of the exemptions relate to the type of security being offered and others relate to smaller issues, exempting them from the state registration requirements.

PRACTICE TIP

Make a point of regularly monitoring the EDGAR filings, press releases, and stock quotes of publicly traded clients. Congratulate the company representatives of the client when it announces its expansion, when it has a record trading day, or when new officers are selected. Even clients that are not publicly traded usually issue press releases for significant company events. Remember to mention these events when you speak with company representatives. Clients are both impressed and appreciative when you show your interest in their business activities.

G. The Securities Markets

1. *Introduction*

A **stock exchange** is a marketplace where securities, principally stocks and bonds, are traded. There are two types of markets: primary and secondary. The **primary market** is the underwriting process described earlier, used when a corporation makes its initial issue of securities to the public. The new issuer rarely places its securities for sale on a market. Rather, it reaches an agreement with a securities firm, the underwriter, which either buys the stock itself for resale to customers or enters into arrangements with others, dealers, for the dealers to sell the stock to customers. The **secondary markets** are composed of the principal stock markets, namely NYSE Euronext (formed in 2007 by the combination of NYSE Group, Inc. and Euronext N.V., and referred to in this text as NYSE), regional exchanges such as the Boston Stock Exchange, the over-the-counter market, and The Nasdaq Stock Market, LLC. (NASDAQ), formerly known as the National Association of Securities Dealers Automated Quotations. (Note that the American Stock Exchange was acquired by NYSE Euronext in October 2008). These secondary markets effect the trading of securities of established companies.

Corporations engaged in new issues principally use the primary market and stockholders and investors trade anonymously on the secondary markets, typically called the stock exchanges.

Not all stocks are **listed** or available for purchase on the stock markets. Only those corporations that have met various criteria of the exchange and are well-established list their stock for sale through the exchanges. For example, the NYSE requires that a stock already be widely held before it can be listed. Generally, there must be at least 1.1 million shares held by members of the public with a total market value of $100 million and there must be at least 2,200 shareholders. The NYSE also requires that the company have earned, pretax, at least $2 million during each of the previous two years. These requirements are intended to promote continuous trading and orderly price movements. By their very nature, these

Stock exchange
Marketplace where securities are traded

Primary market
Marketplace for initial trading of securities through the underwriting process

Secondary market
Marketplace for trading of securities to the public through the nationally known exchanges

Listing
Process of qualifying to sell stocks at a marketplace or exchange

requirements exclude start-up companies from listing on the NYSE. Moreover, there are significant initial and annual fees imposed by the NYSE. Initial fees are $37,500 plus an additional fee based on the number of shares issued, with a minimum fee of $150,000. Annual fees are also calculated based on the number of shares issued, subject to a minimum annual fee of $38,000. Fees may range as high as $500,000, depending on the size of the company. Companies that no longer meet the stringent requirements of the NYSE may have their trading suspended by the exchange, or the exchange may impose additional criteria for continued trading, or if the average stock price is below $1 per share for 30 days the stock may be delisted. Delisting is a serious setback to a company not only because it causes a lack of investor confidence, but also because some mutual funds cannot own companies that are not listed on a major exchange. A stock that is delisted may trade over the counter. In January 2009, in response to the 2008-2009 financial crisis, the NYSE eased its listing rules, lowering the minimum market value a company must maintain to keep from being delisted. Similarly, in October 2008, NASDAQ also temporarily waived its requirements that companies maintain a share price of more than $1 for a 30-day average and its minimum market value rule.

In New York City, 24 brokers originally met under a buttonwood tree on Wall Street. In 1792, they organized the New York Stock Exchange. NYSE Euronext (NYSE) is the oldest and most prestigious exchange in the country. It is often referred to as the **big board.** About 4,600 companies with a global capitalization of more than $26 trillion are listed on the NYSE. A listing on the NYSE is a signal that the corporation has joined the elite corporations in this country, that it has become nationally known, and that its earnings are stable. These corporations are often said to offer **blue-chip** stock and they are nationally known — Wal-Mart Stores, Inc., Coca-Cola Company, IBM, and so forth. Many companies send out announcements or clearly state in their advertising "now trading on the New York Stock Exchange." For example, the transfer of Krispy Kreme Doughnuts, Inc., to the NYSE in May 2001 was greeted with great fanfare and the serving of 40,000 doughnuts on the trading floor.

Some companies may prefer to list on NASDAQ, which is the largest electronic stock market in the United States. Approximately 3,200 companies trade on NASDAQ, which also has strict listing requirements. Because NASDAQ is an electronic market rather than a true auction market with a physical location as is the NYSE, many tech-oriented companies trade on NASDAQ. Fees may play a part as well when a company decides on which market to offer its securities. For example, the annual minimum fee imposed by the NYSE for a company selling its stock is $150,000; NASDAQ's annual minimum fee is $30,000.

There are also a number of regional exchanges, such as NYSE Arca (formerly known as the Pacific Exchange). The stocks traded on these exchanges are often of smaller companies of primarily local rather than national interest, although most of the regional exchanges list both local and national stocks. Exchanges also operate in Boston, Chicago, and Philadelphia. A complex computer network routes orders for stock with the exchange then offering the most favorable price.

The New York Stock Exchange is located in the heart of the financial district at the corner of Wall Street and Broad Street in New York City. All share transactions occur in five rooms totaling more than 20,000 square feet of contiguous space in the NYSE building, called the **trading floor,** the *floor,* or *the floor of the Exchange.* Not just anyone may simply walk in and purchase or sell stock. To be able to trade

---

Big board
Reference to the New York Stock Exchange

Blue-chip company
Reference to nationally known and well-established company

Trading floor
Location of NYSE where trading of securities occurs

securities on the trading floor, one must obtain a **trading license** from the Exchange. A trading license entitles its member holder to physical and electronic access to the NYSE trading facilities. The license fee is approximately $40,000 annually, and the NYSE limits trading licenses to 1,366. The sale of these trading licenses to approved member organizations replaced the purchase of "seats" on the Exchange; member seat sales (which reached a high of $4 million paid for one seat in December 2005) ended when the Exchange became a publicly traded company.

Non-U.S. issuers are playing an increasingly significant role in the NYSE. As of 2008, about 420 non-U.S. companies were listed on the NYSE.

2. Trading on the New York Stock Exchange

A Typical Transaction.   The floor of the NYSE consists of a series of 20 horseshoe-shaped desks, called **posts**, at which about 100 specific securities are traded. Members interested in the securities being traded at a certain post collect around the post. All buying and selling takes place around these posts. The posts function as "stores" where individual stocks are bought and sold. Numerous computer screens display information about the stocks traded at the post and a stock ticker operates. The ticker is a teletype machine printing nearly 900 characters each minute on a one-inch-wide paper tape called the ticker tape. The ticker records and prints stock transactions by identifying the issuing corporation, the number of shares involved, and the purchase or sale price of the stock. Most of this information is now displayed on computer screens and there are far fewer actual tickers in operation, perhaps only a few hundred, compared to the thousands that were in operation prior to the advent of the computer in the Exchange in the 1960s. The NYSE uses a high-speed electronic system called the consolidated tape. The terms *ticker* and *consolidated tape* are used interchangeably.

Assume you wish to purchase 100 shares in AT&T Corp. on March 10. On that date, AT&T stock is selling for $110 per share. Thus, to buy 100 shares you will need $11,000 in cash plus commissions. If you have this amount on deposit with your stockbroker, you simply call the broker and place your order by instructing the broker to buy 100 shares of AT&T **"at the market,"** meaning that you will pay the price in effect at the time your order reaches the floor. Alternatively, you can give your broker a **limit order**, instructing the broker that the purchase is to be effected only at $110 per share or less.

An order for 100 shares is referred to as a **round lot**, and this is the standard trading unit. Any purchase or sale involving less than 100 shares is called an **odd lot.** The stock quotations printed in the newspaper are for round lots.

Thus, a buyer who wishes to buy stock and a seller who wishes to sell stock will each contact their brokers (who are members of the NYSE). The brokers then transmit their clients' orders electronically to the floor of the Exchange where a floor broker receives the order and walks to the AT&T post (or accesses it electronically, often by handheld computer). There are more than 400 floor brokers. Near the AT&T post is a **specialist** handling AT&T transactions who generally acts like an auctioneer. Other brokers may also surround the AT&T post, with instructions from their customers to either buy or sell AT&T stock.

Trading license
Membership on an exchange allowing privilege of trading

Posts
Locations on trading floor of NYSE where trading occurs

At market
Expression meaning one will buy stock at whatever price is in effect when purchase occurs

Limit order
Instructions to broker to buy or sell at a certain price

Round lot
Group of 100 shares

Odd lot
Group of less than 100 shares

Specialist
A person assigned to handling securities for one company

Quote
The highest bid to buy and the lowest offer to sell a stock

Bid price
Highest price at which specialist will buy stock

Asked price
Lowest price at which specialist will sell stock

Closing
Settlement of transaction

Street name
Registration of stock on the books of a broker and held for safekeeping

Direct registration
Registration of ownership of stock in buyer's name on the issuer's books in which case it is registered in the owner's name on AT&T's books (or those of its transfer agent)

The current bid-and-asked prices are displayed for view. Known collectively as the **quote**, the **bid price** is the highest price at which the specialist (or buyer) will buy the stock and the **asked price** is the lowest price at which the specialist (or seller) will sell the stock. The asked price is almost always higher than the bid price. Assume the quotations are "110 bid, 111 asked." The broker may indicate that she wishes to buy 100 shares of AT&T at the market. One of the other brokers surrounding the AT&T post may have an instruction to sell 100 shares of AT&T at the market. Your broker and the other broker may consummate the transaction immediately, either at the bid price, the asked price, or some other negotiated price. The transaction is reported by computer and appears within a few seconds on the consolidated tape displays around the country and the world. The transaction is then processed electronically, and both buyer and seller receive a trade confirmation from their respective brokers.

If your broker does not meet another broker at the post who can match your order, the specialist will complete the transaction, usually at the asked price. The specialist's stock will come from one of two sources: The specialist either has his own inventory of stock from which to complete orders or the order will be filled by the specialist matching your order to a limit order on the specialist's books. All of this takes some time and the price of the stock may fluctuate slightly during this period. Specialists are required to ensure all trades are executed fairly and orderly. Although the NYSE is typically referred to as an "auction market" (with the specialist acting as the auctioneer), the NYSE calls itself a "hybrid market," meaning that it believes it integrates the best aspects of a true auction market with automated trading.

Upon completion of the transaction you are the owner of 100 shares of AT&T. The actual **closing** (or *settlement*) of the transaction must be completed in three business days, per NYSE rules. The three-day settlement requirement is known as T + 3. At that time, the broker pays for the shares from your account and you become entitled to a certificate for your 100 AT&T shares. If you do not have an account with a broker, you must pay on the third business day after the purchase. The broker will sell the stock if you do not pay. Rather than providing you with a physical stock certificate, your broker might simply record your ownership in the broker's books and give you periodic statements relating to the value of the stock. Securities registered in the name of the broker and held by it for safekeeping (or because the securities have been bought on margin) rather than in the customer's name are said to be registered in **street name**. This practice facilitates easy trading for the owner, who merely instructs the broker to later sell the stock. In street name registration, the security is registered in the name of the brokerage company on AT&T's books, and the brokerage company's records indicate the actual owner. Finally, stock may be held by **direct registration**, and either AT&T or its transfer agent holds the security for the actual owner in book-entry form; the investor's name appears on the books of AT&T or its transfer agent. The direct registration system allows direct communication to shareholders from the company.

The NYSE now uses a computerized system called Super Designated Order Turnaround (SuperDOT) to expedite and route orders. Many experts believe that SuperDOT is responsible for the tremendous growth in trading over the years. For example, in the 1960s a typical day involved trading of approximately 10 million shares. By 2006 this volume had increased to an average daily trading volume of 1.8 billion shares, a volume that could not have been accomplished before computerization.

SuperDOT allows brokers to transmit orders electronically to the posts (without the need for a floor broker). Your purchase order is simply matched against someone else's selling order or against the specialist's own inventory. SuperDOT accounts for roughly 95 percent of all orders executed on the trading floor of the NYSE (and the NYSE can handle daily volume exceeding 10 billion shares). Thus, only about 5 percent of all orders involve face-to-face negotiations between brokers and specialists. Typically, only larger orders are handled manually by the specialist.

To protect against market plunges, in 1988 the NYSE initiated a series of curbs on trading, often called **collars**, which limit or halt trading when the market moves up or down by more than a certain amount in a trading day. Intended to prevent panic in the marketplace, these mechanisms are also known as *circuit breakers* because they cut off automated trading when certain triggers are met. For example, generally, trading is suspended for one hour if prices drop 10 percent, two hours if prices drop 20 percent, and the remainder of the day if there is a 30 percent drop. The percentage drops reflect current decreases in the Dow Jones Industrial Average, which measures the performance of 30 blue-chip U.S. stocks. Trading begins each day with no curbs in place. These pauses in trading allow buyers and sellers time to assimilate incoming information. NASDAQ does not use circuit breakers; however, all exchanges impose short trading halts to allow a company to announce important news; these trading halts allow the public to assess the effect of this news.

Collars
Automatic halts to trading (also called *curbs* or *circuit breakers*)

Limit Orders.   When you give an order to your broker to purchase or sell shares, you may limit the broker's authority by specifying that the purchase price be "$110 or lower" or the sales price be "$112 or higher." These instructions are called **limit orders.** Assume you have instructed your broker to buy 100 shares of AT&T at "110 or lower." If the market price for AT&T is 113 (namely, three **points** — or dollars — higher than you specified), the broker knows that the seller will not sell at 110 when the market price is 113. The broker cannot wait idly by the post all day hoping the market price will decrease three points. The broker thus gives the limit order to the specialist who records it electronically. If AT&T stock falls three points to 110, the specialist will execute, in order received, all transactions for AT&T at 110. Because the orders are handled in the priority in which they are received, it is possible that the stock price may rise before your order is filled, leaving you without the stock you wished to purchase.

Limit order
Instruction given to a broker specifying purchase or sales price

Points
Dollars

Some limit orders may be **day orders**, meaning that the broker is to buy 100 shares of AT&T at 110 or lower, but in any event the transaction must be completed by the close of that trading day. If the order cannot be filled by the end of the day, it expires. Alternatively, the order can be **good till canceled**, meaning that the order remains open until it is fulfilled or it is specifically canceled. Another variety of limit order is the **stop order.** For example, assume you purchased your 100 shares of AT&T stock for $110 per share. You might be fearful of a decline and thus instruct your broker to sell all of the stock if it hits $107. This enables you to cut your losses at a known figure. On other occasions, you might believe that once a stock increases to a certain point or breaks through its traditional trading price, it is likely to continue to increase. In that event, you give your broker a stop order to buy 100 additional shares of AT&T stock as soon as it reaches $114.

Day order
Order that must be filled within a day

Good till canceled order
Order that stays open until it is specifically canceled or fulfilled

Stop order
Automatic order to sell or buy when stock reaches a stated price, which is an automatic order to sell or buy when the stock reaches a certain price

Margin Rules.   A broker or bank is permitted to lend a customer up to one-half of the cost of the securities being traded. The customer opens a margin account with a broker authorizing purchases of stock and pledges the securities themselves for repayment of the debt. In the event of a default, the broker thus owns sufficient securities for repayment.

Ever since the stock market crash in 1929, there has been concern about **trading on margin**, namely, trading speculatively, without paying the actual cash amount of the purchase because extending the time for payment is another form of extending credit.

The margin and credit rules exist to provide some stability to the market. For example, assume you purchase $1,000 worth of AT&T stock by paying $500 cash and borrowing the remainder on margin from your broker. If the stock declines in value to $600, the broker will become concerned that soon the stock will not be worth enough to cover the $500 debt owed. The broker then makes a **margin call**, meaning that the broker demands additional money or collateral. If the money or collateral is not given, the broker will sell the shares to ensure she is repaid the $500 advanced to you. NYSE rules actually compel margin calls when the value of the collateral drops to a level that does not exceed more than 25 percent. In this case, 25 percent of the loan amount of $500 is $125, or a total of $625. Once the stock drops below $625, the broker *must* make a margin call.

Before the stock market crash of 1929, customers were often allowed to purchase stock by paying only 10 percent of the price in cash, and the remainder on margin. When the market began to decline, few investors had sufficient resources to meet the margin calls. Many people believe this turned a decline into a crash. Margin rules exist to prevent such occurrences in the future.

Block Trades.　**Block trades** involve a trade of at least 10,000 shares of stock or a transaction with a value of at least $200,000. They have become increasingly common over the years. In the mid-1960s, there were only approximately 2,000 block trades per year. By 2007, there were approximately 145,000 block trades each month. Although there is some indication that the number of block trades is decreasing, their dollar value is increasing. Because block trades can be so complex, they are generally put together "upstairs" from the floor by large institutional firms, often called **block positioners.** The block positioners attempt to assemble a group of institutional investors to purchase the block and might purchase part of the block themselves. Technological advances enable the block positioners to solicit nearly instantaneously hundreds of investors to determine if they wish to participate in acquiring the block.

The Specialist's Function.　The six firms designated as specialists by the NYSE are far more than mere functionaries assisting in the purchase and sale of stock. One of their primary duties is to even out fluctuations in the market. By federal law, they are charged with maintaining a fair and orderly market, as far as possible. For example, there might be times when there are no buyers for AT&T stock. If the only people interested in AT&T stock are sellers, the price of the stock would be expected to decline. When such a fluctuation occurs, the specialists are expected to buy AT&T stock to ensure orderly trading. Similarly, if a stock continues rising, the specialist is expected to sell some of his inventory. Specialists typically have large inventories of stock, often acquired in the past at advantageous prices. Similarly, if specialists buy stock when it declines and then resell at a higher price when

---

Trading on margin
Purchasing stock without paying purchase price in full

Margin call
Demand for additional collateral by broker for purchase of stock in which stock was not paid for in full

Block trade
Trade involving at least 10,000 shares of stock

Block positioners
Institutional firms that assemble groups of investors to purchase blocks of stock

the stock later rises, they may realize significant profits. Specialists also earn commissions on the execution of each limit order placed with them by brokers.

Although there are six firms functioning as specialists, more than 200 individuals actually perform as specialists. Each individual specialist (or "spec") handles between five and ten stocks. Very big companies often have a spec devoted solely to them. Specialists are sometimes called **downstairs brokers** because they deal only with members having licenses with the NYSE rather than members of the general public. The brokerage firms dealing with the general public are often called **upstairs brokers** because their location was originally physically above the floor, although now the brokers are arranged in 1,400 trading booths or workspaces along the perimeter of the trading floor.

Downstairs broker
Specialists dealing with NYSE members

Upstairs broker
Brokerage firms dealing with general public

3. Other Trading Systems

Within the last 20 years, alternatives to auction trading on the NYSE have arisen. The best known alternatives are the over-the-counter market and NASDAQ.

The Over-the-Counter Market. There is no physical place or location for the **over-the-counter (OTC) market**, as it is essentially a computerized trading network. There is no floor where stocks are traded. Rather, brokers and dealers communicate via computer or telephone to buy and sell securities for their customers. A stock or bond traded "over the counter" is simply one that is not traded on a national securities exchange, generally because it does not meet the listing requirements for the major exchanges (such as NYSE and NASDAQ). Thus, the OTC market primarily offers penny stocks.

OTC market
Sale of stock "over the counter" and through computerized trading systems, rather than through a securities exchange

A **broker** is an individual or firm acting on instructions from a customer and who usually charges a commission. The broker is thus the agent for the customer, who is the principal, much the same way that a real estate broker acts as an agent to assist a customer in buying or selling a house. The broker is simply an intermediary between a buyer and a seller. A **dealer** is an individual or an institutional securities firm that trades on its own behalf. Some securities firms act as both brokers and dealers. Brokerage firms and dealers are regulated by FINRA.

Broker
Securities firm or individuals that act on behalf of a customer

Dealer
An institutional securities firm trading on its own behalf rather than for a customer

NASDAQ. NASDAQ originally stood for National Association of Securities Dealers Automated Quotations; it is a computerized trading system. Established in 1971, NASDAQ was the world's first electronic exchange, trading securities through computers rather than at a specific location. Thus, in a sense, all stock traded through NASDAQ is over the counter. The NASDAQ system allows users to obtain current price quotations from all dealers for all securities traded in the system.

In 1990, NASDAQ formally changed its name to The NASDAQ Stock Market. NASDAQ trading information is broadcast to more than 500 computers worldwide, allowing NASDAQ participants equal access to the market through simultaneous access to quotes and orders. NASDAQ itself went public in 2005 and publicly offer its common stock.

The NASDAQ Stock Market has three tiers, each with its own listing requirements. To trade on NASDAQ's Global Select Market, a company must have had pretax earnings in the amount of $2.2 million in each of the two most recent fiscal years. To trade on NASDAQ's Global Market, a company must have $1.1 million in income in the most recent fiscal year, a market value of publicly held shares in the amount of $8 million, and it must have at least 400 round lot shareholders. NASDAQ's third tier, known as the Capital Market, requires a market value of publicly held shares in the amount of $15 million and 300 round lot shareholders.

About 3,200 companies trade their stocks on NASDAQ, and it is considered "tech heavy," in that it has attracted many of the emerging e-commerce, Internet-based, and computer consulting companies, such as Google Inc., eBay Inc., and Microsoft Corporation. Although NASDAQ has a larger dollar volume and trades more shares than any other U.S. market, the companies listed on the NYSE have a higher market capitalization. In 2008, NASDAQ's daily share volume was approximately 2 billion. In its heaviest day of trading in 2001, more than 3.2 billion shares were traded. In fact, by 1995, the volume of trading on NASDAQ exceeded that on the NYSE.

Based in New York City, NASDAQ is the largest stock market in the United States and lists more companies and IPOs than any other exchange. The member firms that trade on the NASDAQ market are called **market makers.**

Market maker
Member firms trading on NASDAQ

Stocks listed on the NYSE and NASDAQ are not required to be traded there. For example, the NASDAQ system engages in trading of stocks listed on the NYSE, such as General Motors.

Pink Sheet and Penny Stocks.   Companies that do not meet the criteria required to list their stock on the national securities exchanges such as NYSE or NASDAQ are traded on the **pink sheets**, a reference to the fact that quotes for these stocks historically were shown on pink paper. The more formal name for this market is the Pink OTC Market but the term *pink sheets* is still commonly used. Many companies list in the pink sheets as a primary step to listing on NASDAQ. Similarly, in 1998, when a company was delisted from NASDAQ due to its failure to remain in compliance with NASDAQ's net tangible assets requirement, it sought approval to have its stock traded in the pink sheets. Enron Corp. was delisted from the New York Stock Exchange in January 2002 and then traded over the counter. At the time of its delisting, Enron stock was trading at 67 cents per share, down from its all-time high of $90 per share just over a year earlier.

Pink sheet stocks
Stocks of companies that are not traded on a national securities exchange

Stocks sold "over the counter" are those not traded on the national securities exchanges (generally because they cannot meet the listing requirements of the exchanges). Brokers and dealers negotiate directly with each other over computer networks and by phone. The Over-the-Counter Bulletin Board is an electronic quotation system that displays quotes, last-sale prices, and volume information for many over-the-counter stocks that are not listed on the exchanges. According to the SEC, companies whose stock trades over the counter tend to be closely held and very small. They do not file periodic reports or any financial statements with the SEC, which views them as "among the most risky investments."

Penny stocks are those with a price of $5 per share or less. Although penny stocks generally trade over the counter, such as on the Over-the-Counter Bulletin Board or in the pink sheets, they may also trade on securities exchanges, including foreign securities exchanges. FINRA regulates and operates the over-the-counter securities markets.

Electronic Communications Networks and Their Effect on the NYSE and NASDAQ. Electronic communications networks (ECNs) are private, fully electronic trading systems maintained separately from the public markets such as the NYSE and NASDAQ. ECNs bring buyers and sellers directly together for electronic execution of trades. The first ECN was Instinet, created by Reuters for trading by institutions that desired to buy and sell large blocks of stock. ECNs are powerful communications networks, allowing quick and inexpensive trading 24 hours each day. By promoting fast matching of buyers and sellers, investors are protected from market fluctuations.

As evidence of the major exchanges' concerns about the ECNs or their desires to be ECN "players," in spring 2005, the NYSE announced it was merging with Archipelago Holdings, Inc., a Chicago-based ECN, and in December 2005, NASDAQ acquired INET ECN (Instinet's electronic platform). In fact, these two transactions signaled a historic shift for both exchanges. As a result of the NYSE's merger with Archipelago, in March 2006 the NYSE became a publicly traded, for-profit company for the first time in its more than 200-year history, trading under the ticker symbol NYX. As a result of the merger, each of the NYSE 1,366 members or seat holders became shareholders in the newly formed public corporation, NYSE Group, Inc. Floor trading continues but the NYSE's increased reliance on electronic trading systems will likely reduce the role of the specialists who match buyers with sellers. Most experts concur that these recent developments will benefit investors by improving pricing, increasing information, and speeding trading.

Just as the NYSE is "public" as a result of its merger with Archipelago, since 2005, NASDAQ has also been a publicly traded company.

4. Understanding the Newspaper and Internet Reports of Stock Trading

The financial section of major daily newspapers provides detailed information about stocks traded on the exchanges such as NYSE and NASDAQ. To the uninitiated, however, the numerous symbols, fractions, and figures are nearly incomprehensible. Most newspapers publish either a daily or weekly guide describing the meaning of various abbreviations and symbols. Trading information is also readily available on the Internet. As newspaper circulations decline and more people turn to the Internet to obtain information on stock trading, many newspapers have reduced their coverage of market reporting.

The trading section of the newspaper will likely be divided into different categories: Market Indicators, reporting the Dow Jones Industrial Average, Standard & Poor's Averages, New York Stock Exchange Index, and the NASDAQ Index; information relating to the most actively traded NYSE and NASDAQ stocks; prices of selected bonds offered on the NYSE; averages for various foreign exchanges; the trading of mutual funds and exchange-traded funds; and dividends declared that day. "Up-Down Volume" is also given, showing how many shares advanced and how many shares declined on the NYSE and the NASDAQ.

A typical listing would show the following:

52 Week High	Low	Stock	Div	Yld	PE	Sales 100s	High	Lo	Last	Chg.
39.74	20.69	BarnesNob	1.00	4.2	11	57,226	28.29	20.56	23.96	−2.68

The interpretation of such an entry is as follows:

High-Low: High-Low numbers are the highest and lowest prices paid for the stock during the last 52 weeks.

Stock: Stocks are listed alphabetically, by the company's name. The entry above is for the retailer Barnes & Noble.

Div: The "Div" figure represents the current annual dividend rate paid on the stock, based on the latest quarterly or semiannual dividend declaration.

Yld: The yield figure represents the rate of return on a stockholder's investment. It is calculated by dividing the annual dividend by the current price of the stock, expressed as a percentage.

PE: The price/earnings ratio represents the closing price of the stock divided by the company's earnings per share for the latest 12-month period reported.

Sales 100s: Previous day's volume, in hundreds of shares.

High-Lo: Highest and lowest prices of the stock during the previous day.

Last: The price at which the stock was trading when the exchange closed for the previous day.

Chg.: The loss or gain for the day, compared with the previous session's closing price.

Additionally, a variety of footnote abbreviations may be used. For example, "a" indicates an extra dividend paid in addition to a regular dividend; "d" indicates a new 52-week low; "n" indicates stock newly issued within the past 52 weeks; "pf" indicates preferred stock; "r" indicates a cash dividend declared or paid within the preceding 12 months; and "s" indicates a stock split or stock dividend. When a company is involved in bankruptcy proceedings, the letter "Q" is added to the end of its stock ticker symbol.

Until recently, stock was traded in fractions of eighths and sixteenths. For example, stock would be sold at $26\frac{1}{8}$. In mid-2000, the SEC began requiring exchanges to convert to decimal quoting to make it easier for investors to compare prices and harmonize U.S. policy with that of foreign markets, which trade in decimals. Full conversion was completed by April 2001, and now all U.S. securities are quoted in dollars and cents, such as $10.14.

Under the previous decimal system, the smaller the fractional unit, the more active trading was expected to be. For example, if a $30 stock was rising, the next bid must be 30\frac{1}{8}$ ($30.125). If the stock is priced in sixteenths, the next highest bid could be $30 1/16 ($30.0625). If the stock could increase by a nickel, the next highest bid could be $30.05, allowing you to buy at a more advantageous price. The smallest amount by which stock prices normally change is called a **tick.** The SEC has estimated that trading in decimals saves investors between $1 million and $3 million each day.

Every stock traded on any stock exchange is identified by a short symbol, called the ticker symbol. The NYSE uses some one-letter symbols, such as F for Ford Motor Company, K for Kellogg, and T for AT&T. The chairman of the NYSE once announced publicly that he was reserving the symbols M for Microsoft and I for Intel in hopes of convincing them to move from NASDAQ to the NYSE, but M has since been assigned to Macy's.

Tick
The smallest amount by which stock prices change

H.   Trading in Cyberspace

As in nearly every aspect of modern life, the advent of the Internet and electronic communications is playing a part in the trading of stocks. Some of the more interesting developments of the past few years are as follows:

- In October 1999, the SEC worked jointly with eBay, the online auction service, to stop consumers from auctioning stock on the eBay Web site. Because the Securities Act of 1933 requires that if securities are to be offered to the public, they must be registered with the SEC or must be exempt from registration, an offer on the Web violates the Act.
- As discussed previously, ECNs are changing the face of trading in that they promote nearly instantaneous trading 24 hours per day. In view of the threat of increased trading via ECNs, the NYSE merged with the Archipelago ECN, and NASDAQ has acquired the Instinet/INET ECN.
- The phenomenon of **day trading** emerged in the late 1990s. Day trading involves numerous trades in the course of a day with the intent of profiting from very small increases in stock prices. A day trader usually completes all transactions in a day and ends the day owning no stock whatsoever. Estimates of the number of day traders range widely from 10,000 to 50,000, with the actual number nearly impossible to determine because they come and go so frequently. The SEC estimates the number of full-time day traders to be fewer than 7,000. Day traders execute roughly 35 trades each day and typically operate from one of 70 or 80 day-trading firms, registered broker-dealers, which maintain offices and powerful computers for the day traders to use upon payment of a fee. The SEC's official view is that day trading is highly risky. The SEC offers a publication entitled "Day Trading: Your Dollars at Risk," and warns investors, "Be prepared to suffer severe financial losses." Under the rules of FINRA, customers who are deemed to be "pattern" day traders must have at least $25,000 in their accounts.
- **Online trading** is distinguishable from day trading in that an online trader usually trades a few times each day or a few times each month, from home (rather than a professional office), using an online trading brokerage company, such as Charles Schwab or E*Trade, which charge a small fee per trade. Experts believe that about 25 percent of all U.S. retail stock trades are made by online investors.

Day trading
Trading involving numerous electronic trades in the course of a day

Online trading
Trading from home computers a few times each day or month

After-hours trading
Trading after the normal business hours of the stock exchanges

Suitability rule
Rule requiring that in recommending purchase or sale of stock a broker must have reason for believing transaction is suitable for customer

Spoofing
Scam used to lure investors to buy stock

Pump and dump
Hyping a stock to increase its price and then selling it

- **After-hours trading** (trading before and after the normal business hours of the NYSE and NASDAQ) has occurred for some time and is engaged in primarily by institutional investors. The rise of ECNs has allowed individual investors to gain access to the after-hours market.

- A hotly debated issue has been whether FINRA Rule 2310(a), called the **suitability rule**, applies to day-trading firms that maintain the offices and computers used by professional day traders. The suitability rule requires that in recommending a purchase or sale of stock to a customer, a broker must have reasonable grounds for believing the recommendation is suitable for the customer. Typically, a broker satisfies this duty by obtaining information from his or her customers about their financial status, tolerance for risk, and investment goals. In March 2001, the SEC confirmed that the suitability rule applies to all recommendations, including those made by electronic means.

- The proliferation of false and misleading information disseminated in chat rooms also concerns the SEC. Many experts believe, however, that the SEC will be unable to enact rules relating to chat room discussions about company rumors and news unless fraud is being committed, likening chat room discussions to informal discussions one has with one's hair stylist or neighbor about stock prices. Internet fraud is one of the biggest issues for the SEC, which is concerned about possible stock manipulation and fraud through spam e-mail messages, phony Web sites, and deceptive message board postings. Some of the more recent variations of fraud are **spoofing** and **pump and dump** schemes. In spoofing, traders place large orders to buy stocks online on electronic trading systems and then withdraw the order shortly after posting it. The posting of a large order, sometimes called a *phantom quote*, lures other investors, usually generating a buying stampede. The SEC has instituted a surveillance program to detect spoofing. *Pump and dump* scams involve messages posted online urging readers to buy or sell a stock, usually based on the writer's supposed inside information about the company. This additional interest causes other investors to buy the stock, pumping up the price. The promoters then sell or dump their shares to make a profit on the artificially inflated price. Two twists on pump and dump schemes involve voice mail messages left as secret stock tips or e-mail tips made to appear as though they were sent to the recipient in error. For example, one recent scheme involved e-mails that began similarly to the following message: "I hope this is your e-mail. I was pleased to meet you the other day. The deal I was speaking about involves a company whose stock is heading up, and the big news isn't out yet." The most recent pump and dump schemes involve hacking as well. For example, in 2007, an Eastern European ring hacked into four online trading accounts of unsuspecting investors. The hackers then sold the victims' existing stocks and used the proceeds to purchase penny stocks. The big purchases created the appearance of active trading in the penny stocks and pumped up the stock prices. At the height of the pump, the hackers dumped the stock and turned a profit. These particular schemes are often called "incursions." Fraudsters usually target small, thinly traded companies, such as those offering penny stocks, because there's little known information about these companies. Another famous case involved a 15-year-old New Jersey youth who sent out hundreds of phony postings on the Internet hyping various stocks he owned. The SEC recovered nearly $300,000 in disgorged profits. To combat such schemes and scams, the SEC investigates allegations of Internet investment fraud and works with federal and state criminal authorities.

- Although the first IPO conducted over the Internet occurred in 1998 (pursuant to a small issuance exemption under Regulation A), since that time, only a few companies have raised capital exclusively over the Internet, likely because any Internet offering is viewed as a nationwide dissemination of an offer, thus triggering compliance requirements with each state's blue sky laws.

- The SEC is becoming increasingly concerned about the practice of **cybersmearing**, a form of electronic stock market manipulation in which false information about a company is published on the Internet in an attempt to manipulate the market price of stock. In an early-2000 case, a California judge entered a temporary restraining order to halt the practice and required a full and complete retraction of false statements.

Cybersmearing
Disseminating false information about a company in an attempt to manipulate stock prices

- In some cases, innocent (but false) remarks about a company or its principals can gain traction on the Internet and influence trading. For example, in September 2008, United Airlines stock plummeted more than 70 percent in a single day after a false rumor was circulated about the company declaring bankruptcy. The story was mistaken in its date and referred to the company's earlier 2002 bankruptcy. Similarly, in October 2008, a false Internet report that Apple's Steve Jobs had suffered a heart attack caused Apple stock to hit a 17-month low. Both stocks later recovered, but investors who had sold stock at the low prices were simply "out of luck."

I. New Topics in Securities

A number of new developments relating to securities and trading have occurred in the past few years, including the following:

- *Selective disclosure.* To level the investor playing field, in late 2000, the SEC enacted rules (Regulation FD (for "fair disclosure")) requiring companies to issue a press release, file a notice with the SEC, or open up conference calls to the public at the same time they discuss any "material" company information with analysts or institutional investors. Previously, company managers routinely had private telephone calls with analysts, discussing company performance issues. The analysts then related this information about the company to their institutional investors, providing them with information not made available to the public at large. Allowing the public in on the calls or broadcasts now places individual investors on the same footing as institutional investors who have been a party to what is called **selective disclosure** by the company. SEC enforcement of full and fair disclosure will assist small investors. Thus, any potentially useful information such as advance warnings about earnings results, potential mergers, management changes, product developments, and so forth must be

Selective disclosure
Practice of disclosure of company information only to analysts rather than to public at large

disseminated to the world at large and not selectively disclosed to securities analysts and large institutional investors.

- *Exchange-traded funds.* One of the most innovative new products offered in the stock market is **exchange-traded funds (ETFs)**, which own a "basket" of stocks that tracks the performance of a market index, such as the Dow Jones Industrial Average. For example, one type of ETF, known as spiders (SPDR), invests in all of the stocks contained in the Standard & Poor's Composite Stock Price Index. The purpose of an ETF is to simply match a particular index; thus, they are often said to be passively managed, meaning that the ETF manager makes only small adjustments to keep the ETF tied to its index. This leads to lower administrative costs. This low cost is part of their appeal. An investor purchases (and sells) ETF shares just like common stock in that they are bought not from a fund company but rather from a stock exchange (with the help of a broker who chares a commission). An investor can purchase one share or as many as desired and can trade them whenever desired.

- *Hedge funds.* A **hedge fund** is like a mutual fund in that investors' money is pooled together and then invested in a broad range of investments, including shares, debt, and commodities. The investors are typically wealthy individuals because the minimum required investment is very high. The fund is aggressively managed with the goal of producing high returns. Due to the speculative nature of the investment practices, risk can be high. Moreover, hedge funds are generally not registered with the SEC because they cater to sophisticated investors in private offerings.

- *Stock option backdating.* Generally, stock options granted to employees or high-level executives allow these individuals to buy their company's stock at a certain fixed price at some date in the future. For example, on June 1, 2008, ABC Inc. might grant its CEO the right to purchase shares of ABC for $50 per share on June 1, 2012. If the stock is trading at more than $50 per share on June 1, 2012, the CEO will execute the option and make money on each share purchased. **Stock option backdating** occurs when the grant dates are altered to a date prior to the date the company actually granted the option (namely, at a time the stock price was lower), making the stock options immediately valuable. By 2006, more than 100 companies were enmeshed in stock option backdating scandals, sparking numerous criminal indictments. Stock option backdating is not per se illegal; what is illegal is the failure to disclose to shareholders the practice.

- *Program trading.* **Program trading** involves trading 15 or more securities worth more than $1 million as a portfolio rather than as individual investments. This is effected by computer programs that use algorithms to compare prices and determine when and at what price the trade should be accomplished (rather than making trading decisions based on the quality or achievement of particular companies). Program trading is usually used in the trading of large amounts of stock, which can produce volatility in the market. About one-third of all trading activity is program trading.

- *Short selling.* A **short sale** is generally the sale of a stock that one does not own. Investors who short-sell believe that the price of the stock will fall and they can then buy the stock back at a lower price and make a profit. If the price of the stock rises, and it is bought back at the higher price, the

---

Exchange-traded funds
An investment vehicle traded on a securities exchange that is tied to an index

Hedge fund
A portfolio of aggressively managed investments that caters to sophisticated investors

Stock option backdating
The practice of altering the date of a stock option grant to make it more valuable

Program trading
Large computer-assisted trades of stock based on algorithms

Short sale
The sale of a stock one does not yet own in the belief that the stock price will fall

investor has lost money. For example, assume ABC Inc.'s stock is trading at $60 per share. Tim borrows 100 shares of ABC stock from his broker and immediately sells them (the short-sale). If the stock price declines to $40 per share, Tim will buy the stock on the open market to replace the shares he borrowed earlier, making $20 profit per share. If the price had gone above $60 per share, Tim would have lost money. Generally, the stock is borrowed from a brokerage firm, and it often comes from the firm's own inventory. Although short sales have been around for a long time and are legal, they cannot be used to manipulate the price of a stock. The SEC carefully regulates short sales and has been particularly concerned about the new practice called "naked short-sales," in which the investor sells shares that haven't yet been borrowed or that they don't intend to borrow.

J.   Stock Market Indexes

Nearly every news report during the course of a day will report the Dow Jones Industrial Average or the Standard & Poor's 500 Index. These indexes attempt to show the trend of prices of stocks and bonds by reporting on certain selected stocks traded on the NYSE or other exchanges, enabling investors to determine if the market is a **bull** (rising) or a **bear** (declining) market. If you have difficulty remembering which is a rising market and which is a declining market, remember the way in which these animals attack their victims: A bull uses its horns to toss a victim *up* into the air and a bear typically knocks its victim *down* to the ground. Indexes do not predict what the market will do in the future; they reflect where the market has been.

Indexes
Averages that track movements of stock

Bull market
Rising market

Bear market
Declining market

1.   Dow Jones Averages

Dow Jones & Company is a publishing firm. Its premier publication is *The Wall Street Journal*. It computes averages every hour of every day of trading.

The Dow Jones Industrial Average (DJIA) is the one most often relied on by investors because it is the oldest and the best known of all stock market indexes. The DJIA reports only the averages of the 30 selected (mainly blue-chip) stocks. The average is computed by adding the prices of the stocks in the average and then dividing by a constant called the "divisor" (which is presently less than one). Its advances and declines are given in points, meaning dollars. For example, assume that the industrial average on the close of trading one day is 850.42. If, at the close of trading the next day, the industrial average is 853.55, the average has risen 3.13 points, or $3.13. The DJIA measures market performance of a wide variety of companies across the United States, including stocks in the retail, technology, entertainment, financial services, and consumer goods sectors, such as Bank of America, Intel, Coca-Cola, and Wal-Mart.

On October 13, 2008, the DJIA was 9,119. This number has no true meaning except as a comparison to previous trading. For example, if the month thereafter, the DJIA is at 10,000, you know that the market's basic trend is upward.

The Dow Jones Composite Average reviews 65 different stocks (including Boeing, Citigroup, and E. I. DuPont) in a variety of industries. The theory is that a view of certain selected industrial, energy, retail, finance, transportation, and utility companies will provide information about trends in the market in general. The snapshot of the market revealed by the average may be somewhat limited, however, inasmuch as the companies selected for review tend to be the blue-chip companies.

Companies may be dropped from the Dow Jones averages and other companies can be added, although composition changes are rare and cause great comment. For example, on April 1, 2004, American International Group, Inc., Pfizer, Inc., and Verizon Communications Inc. replaced AT&T Corp., Eastman Kodak Co., and International Paper Co. in the Dow Jones Industrial Average. In 1999, Intel and Microsoft were added. Intel and Microsoft were the first NASDAQ stocks included in the more than 100-year-old average. In September 2008, in the wake of its spectacular financial collapse, American International Group (AIG) was replaced by Kraft Foods. AT & T has since rejoined the DJIA.

In a highly unusual event, in February 2000, a tech equipment maker called Aeroflex Inc. became the first company to leave the NYSE voluntarily since 1939 and list its shares on NASDAQ (although companies that no longer meet NYSE requirements may move to NASDAQ). On the other hand, after tech stocks began dropping in early 2001, the big board, occasionally derided as Old Economy, became more attractive to some companies. As a group executive vice president at NYSE put it, "You go out with the flashier guys, but you marry stable men."

Dow Jones began to publish an industrial average in the late 1800s. It used the stock of 12 companies, totaled their trading prices, and divided by 12. This "average" was announced to the public as an indicator of market trends as a whole.

The Dow is one of the few market indicators that is price-weighted, meaning that high-priced stocks such as IBM have more of an effect on the average than lower priced ones.

Dogs of the Dow
Investment strategy involving investing in certain DJIA stocks

One investment strategy is called investing in **"Dogs of the Dow."** Investors select the ten (or five or one) Dow Jones Industrial stocks with the lowest price-earnings ratio and the highest dividend yield and buy equal amounts of stock in each. These stocks are referred to as "dogs" only because they are the least expensive Dow Jones stocks relative to others. At the end of the year, the investor adjusts the portfolio to select the current "dogs" of the Dow. According to experts, in the last 20 years, this strategy has lost in only three years.

2. Other Indexes

There are a variety of other indexes used to report trends in the market. Among them are Standard & Poor's Index (the S & P 500) and the NYSE Composite Index.

Standard & Poor's Corporation is an investment advisory and research firm. It publishes the *Standard & Poor's 500 Index*, a report reflecting stock prices for 500 leading companies. Most of these companies are listed on the NYSE. Because the S & P 500 considers a wider array of companies, some experts believe it is more reliable than the narrow DJIA of merely 30 companies.

Whereas the Dow average is price weighted, the S & P 500 is weighted by market capitalization, meaning it is influenced most strongly by companies whose total value is the greatest.

The NYSE Composite functions nearly identically to that of Standard & Poor's. It is based on all of the common stocks trading on the NYSE and thus closely reflects the broader market.

The NASDAQ Composite indexes or averages all of the more than 3,000 stocks traded on NASDAQ.

Stock Market Trivia

- The average price of a share traded on the NYSE in 2006 was about $41, and the average daily volume of trading was 1.8 billion shares.
- The tradition of pricing stocks in fractions with 8 or 16 as the denominator derived from Spanish trading in the 1500s when Spanish silver could be cut into "pieces of eight" and gold doubloons could be cut into 16 pieces.
- Originally, a Chinese gong was used to signal the beginning and ending of the trading each day on the floor of the NYSE. It is considered an honor to be invited to ring the opening or closing bell of the exchange, and many companies signal new product launches with a bell ringing.
- The longest listed company on any U.S. exchange is ConEdison, listed on the NYSE in 1824.
- The NYSE began trading in decimals in January 2001, ending the practice of trading in fractions used for more than 200 years.
- Not all large companies are publicly traded. Cargill, Mars, and Bechtel are all privately owned, and all have annual revenues of at least $20 billion.
- In 2004, the NYSE and NASDAQ fiercely competed to list Google, Inc., on their exchanges, with NASDAQ prevailing. Listings provide significant revenues. For example, the NYSE earned about 9 percent of its revenues in 2007 from listing fees.
- The NYSE has the capacity to trade 10 billion shares per day and handle 2,000 messages per second.
- How do you decode a ticker symbol? Companies with one- to three-letter ticker symbols always trade on the NYSE. Ticker symbols of four or five letters indicate that the company trades on NASDAQ. If a company that has a three-letter symbol moves its listing from NASDAQ to the NYSE, it may maintain its three-letter symbol.
- Anheuser-Busch uses BUD as its ticker symbol, showcasing its premier product.
- General Electric Company is the only stock currently on the Dow that was also included in the original 12 Dow stocks in 1896.
- Trades on both NYSE and NASDAQ are executed in less than a second.
- The SEC and some experts estimate that day traders might account for as much as 15 percent of NASDAQ's daily volume.

◆ The largest volume of trading on the NYSE involved 8.7 billion shares in October 2008 during the financial crisis.

◆ The largest volume of trading on NASDAQ (as of the publication of this text) also occurred during the financial crisis, when more than 3.5 billion shares changed hands in October 2008.

K. Glossary of Financial Terms

This section provides a brief description of various other terms often encountered in the financial section of the newspaper.

Arbitrageur: One who buys different stocks and bonds in different markets at the same time, taking advantage of price differences.

Derivative: A financial instrument whose performance is derived from the performance of an underlying asset, security, or index. For example, a stock option is a form of derivative because its value changes in relation to the price movement of the underlying stock. Similarly, futures, discussed below) are another example of a derivative.

Futures Contract: An agreement to buy or sell a specified quantity of an asset (often an agricultural commodity such as wheat, corn, coffee beans, orange juice, and so forth) at a specified price at some designated future date. For example, a buyer may agree to pay $3.10 per bushel for 500 bushels of corn next November 18. The buyer must put up a certain sum of money at the time the agreement is entered into, often 10 percent. The buyer hopes the actual price on November 18 is higher than $3.10 per bushel so that a profit will be realized. Futures and options are traded on exchanges, such as the Chicago Board Options Exchange.

Junk Bonds: Bonds below investment grade as established by various investment rating services. These bonds often produce high yields because they are high-risk.

Money Market Funds: A money market fund is a mutual fund investing only in short-term and nearly risk-free investments. The funds invest in commercial paper, short-term certificates of deposit, and so forth. Depositors are usually allowed to write checks on the amount they have deposited into the fund. The arrangement is highly similar to a bank account, although it may be uninsured.

Mutual Fund: An open-end investment company that invests, reinvests, holds, and trades in the securities of other issuers for an unlimited number of persons wishing to invest in the fund. Basically, a mutual fund is a pool of money from numerous investors invested in various companies and managed by an investment professional. The money may be invested in stocks or bonds, and the fund will charge fees to manage the money invested.

The investors buy shares in the mutual fund rather than in the individual stocks and bonds in the fund's portfolio. The term "open end" refers to the fact that there is no fixed capitalization of the investment company. As it grows in size, it will hold increasingly larger numbers of shares. A *load* (or *front-end load*) is an additional charge imposed on an investor in a mutual fund. A *no-load fund* is a fund usually sold without a broker; the investor must locate the investment herself and will not pay the extra charge associated with a load.

Options: Publicly traded securities, of two types.

   Call Options: The right to buy a certain stock or a certain commodity at a fixed price for a limited period, perhaps several months.

   Put Options: The right to sell certain stock or a certain commodity at a fixed price for a limited period, perhaps several months.

Like futures, options are traded on various exchanges, including the Chicago Board Options Exchange. If the options are not exercised prior to their stated expiration date, the options expire and are worthless.

Key Features
in Securities Regulation and Trading

◆ Securities (stocks and bonds) may not be offered for sale using any means of interstate commerce unless they are either registered with the SEC or exempt from registration.

◆ Two key federal statutes govern the issuance of securities: the Securities Act of 1933, governing initial issuance, and the Securities Exchange Act of 1934, governing resale of securities and reporting by public companies.

◆ Registration with the SEC is accomplished by electronically filing a statement with the SEC providing information about the issuer and the issue.

◆ Certain securities need not be registered, and small issue offerings and private offerings need not be registered.

◆ The 1934 Act imposes periodic reporting requirements on any company whose stock is listed on an exchange or that has assets exceeding a certain amount. The reports are intended to provide information to the public about the company.

◆ The 1934 Act prohibits inside trading, namely the trading of stock by a company insider who has access to information not available to the public, and requires insiders to disgorge short-swing profits, those profits made by certain insiders on the purchase or sale of stock within a six-month period.

- ◆ The individual states regulate the sale of securities through their state laws, called blue sky laws.
- ◆ Stock can be traded on an exchange, such as the NYSE, which involves auction bidding (now enhanced through computer-assisted trading) and selling at a physical location or through entirely automated systems, such as that of NASDAQ.
- ◆ The movement of stocks is tracked by various measures and indexes, including the Dow Jones Industrial Average and Standard & Poor's 500 index. These averages and indexes are viewed as providing a snapshot as to market trends.

L. Role of Paralegal

Paralegals in the securities arena are often experts who have gained tremendous information and experience in a very complex field of law. Some of these paralegals are called "blue sky specialists" and others are called "securities paralegals." Because this area of the law is so technical and because exposure is increased (attorneys practicing in this field typically pay higher premiums for malpractice insurance), a highly skilled securities paralegal can make more than $100,000 per year in cities such as Washington, D.C., or New York.

Due to the ramifications of leaks, any staff having access to information relating to the trading of corporate clients will be expected to maintain the highest level of confidentiality. Most law firms not only have strict policies prohibiting divulging any privileged information but also require attorneys, paralegals, and staff members to sign confidentiality agreements and agreements promising not to trade in any client's securities.

The decision to "go public" will be made by the board of directors of a corporation acting in concert with the officers, accountants, attorneys, and other advisors. Once the decision has been made, there are a number of activities calling for the paralegal's involvement. For companies that are already traded publicly, there is a great deal of "34 Act work," including drafting press releases, proxy statements, and various periodically filed documents. Paralegals also engage in the following tasks:

1. Drafting minutes of meetings and resolutions confirming the decision to offer securities publicly.
2. Assisting in drafting registration statements.
3. Assisting in due diligence work such as verifying information provided by the corporate issuer, preparing and compiling results of questionnaires for officers, directors, and principal shareholders.
4. Researching exemptions from requirements of the 1933 Act.
5. Researching provisions of state blue sky laws and exemptions thereto; obtaining state registration and notification forms.
6. Coordinating exhibits to registration statements, including financial statements, profit-and-loss statements, and so forth.
7. Drafting and filing dealer and/or broker registration forms with FINRA, the SEC, and state corporations commissions.

8. Assisting in the preparation of private placement offerings/memoranda.
9. Reviewing copy for press releases.
10. Proofreading the registration statement, prospectus, and so forth.
11. Docketing dates for and helping prepare and Edgarize periodic filings (annual, quarterly, and periodic reports of changes in issuer's statement) for Section 12 companies and preparing such reports as well as proxy statements for shareholders' meetings.

Case Illustration
Insider Trading

Case: *SEC v. Rocklage*, 470 F.3d 1 (1st Cir. 2006)

Facts: The wife of a company's chief executive officer convinced him to tell her confidential negative information about the company (namely, that a certain drug trial had failed), which she then disclosed to her brother and his friend. The brother and the friend then sold their stock, each avoiding losses of about $100,000.

Held: Although the spouse was not an "insider," liability rested on her misappropriation of the material and nonpublic information. The spouse had a preexisting agreement with her brother that she would tip him off if she had information about the company. When she induced her husband to reveal material negative information to her, she knew that in obtaining that information she would enable her brother to execute a securities transaction. She then actively facilitated this transaction by tipping her brother. These events showed that her deceptive acquisition of material inside information was in connection with a securities transaction and thus violated Rule 10b-5.

❖   ❖   ❖

WEB RESOURCES

The most important Web resources are federal and state statutes relating to registration of securities and fraud in the trading and sale of securities.

Federal and state statutes: www.law.cornell.edu
     www.findlaw.com

Text of Uniform
   Securities Act: www.nccusl.org

Securities regulations:	www.sec.gov (The SEC provides excellent information on securities laws and regulations as well as forms, SEC rules, enforcement actions, and EDGAR, the database of registration statements and periodic reports. Most filings after 1996 are available by company name, type of document, or date of filing.)
	www.law.uc.edu/CCL (The University of Cincinnati College of Law offers "The Securities Lawyer's Deskbook," including the full text of federal securities laws and regulations as well as forms.)
State securities regulations/forms:	www.nass.org
General information:	www.megalaw.com
	www.realcorporatelawyer.com
	www.thecorporatelibrary.com
	http://beginnersinvest.about.com
	http://invest-faq.com
	www.fool.com (Web site of "The Motley Fool" provides investing and trading information and a list of the current "Dogs of the Dow.")
Company information:	www.hoovers.com
Securities markets:	www.nyse.com (New York Stock Exchange)
	www.nasdaq.com (NASDAQ)
FINRA:	www.finra.org
Dow Jones Indexes:	www.djindexes.com

Discussion Questions

Fact Scenario. EnergyTech Inc. is a corporation with 1,000 shareholders and annual pretax income of $2.5 million. The company is considering offering its stock to the public.

1. Identify a few advantages to the company of going public.

2. If the company goes public, what exchange will its shares likely be listed on?

3. Assume that an underwriter has offered to sell the company's securities pursuant to a "best efforts agreement." What does this mean?

4. Assume that the company intends to offer its stock only in Illinois. Must it register with the SEC? Discuss.

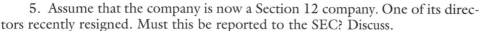

5. Assume that the company is now a Section 12 company. One of its directors recently resigned. Must this be reported to the SEC? Discuss.

6. The board of directors has recently received a letter informing it that it will be sued for patent infringement. If successful, such a lawsuit would cripple the company. After the board meeting held to discuss this issue, Director Reynolds decided to sell a significant amount of his stock in the company. Have any securities laws been violated? If so, discuss.

7. Assume that Director O'Malley purchased stock in his publicly traded company on March 1 of this year for $50 per share. Two months later, O'Malley sold the stock for $70 per share to obtain money to put his twins through college. On October 1, O'Malley sold more stock for $80 per share. Have any securities laws been violated? Discuss fully.

8. The vice president of the corporation has decided to purchase additional stock in the corporation. Must this be reported to the SEC? Why or why not?

9. You have decided to purchase stock in EnergyTech Inc. and you have told your broker to buy 100 shares at $90 per share or lower. What is the name for this specific direction given to your broker?

10. Before working with you, your broker has asked you to complete a form giving details about your financial situation and asking about your tolerance for risk. Why has your broker asked for this information from you?

Net Worth

1. Access the Web site of the SEC. Locate Form S-1, used to register securities. Review the first page. What is the estimated average burden hours per response?

2. Access the Web site of the SEC. Access "Fast Answers."
   a. Identify the national securities exchanges registered with the SEC.
   b. What is the definition of a pump and dump scheme?

3. Use either the Web site of the NYSE or NASDAQ. Identify whether the following companies are listed on NYSE or NASDAQ: Dell Incorporated, Intel Corporation, Gannett Co., Inc., and General Motors Corp.

4. Use the Web site of NYSE and determine what companies trade under the ticker symbols C and V.

5. Access the Web site for Forbes. Select "Lists" and review the list of America's largest private companies. What are the first three companies listed and what are their annual revenues?

6. Access the Web site for Dow Jones and locate the components of the Dow Jones Industrial Average. What are the first three companies listed?

14

◆ ◆ ◆

Changes in the Corporate Structure and Corporate Combinations

◆ ◆ ◆

CHAPTER OVERVIEW

Perhaps the most fundamental feature of corporate operation is that although the shareholders own the corporation, they do not manage it. Their participation in the corporation primarily takes the form of voting, chiefly voting on the election of the directors who will manage the corporation. There are, however, some matters that are viewed as effecting such significant change to the structure of the corporation that shareholder approval is required. These matters are often referred to as extraordinary matters and consist of the amending of the articles of incorporation, mergers, consolidations, share exchanges, sales of corporate assets, and dissolution of the corporation.

Corporations can amend their articles of incorporation to add or delete provisions or to modify existing provisions. Because the articles created the corporation and are available for public inspection by any potential shareholder, amending the articles requires shareholder approval. A procedure somewhat similar to amending the articles is restating the articles of

incorporation. A restatement is a clean-up of previous amendments to articles so there is one easily readable complete document. Because no changes are made to the articles, restating the articles can be done without shareholder approval. Amending the corporate bylaws is typically accomplished by the directors, without shareholder participation.

Corporations can gain control of other corporations through a variety of means: mergers, consolidations, share exchanges, purchase of assets, or purchase of stock.

Mergers and consolidations are combinations of corporations that result in one corporate entity. The new entity, the survivor, takes over all assets and liabilities of any corporations merged or consolidated into it. A share exchange occurs when an acquiring corporation compels a target corporation to exchange all of its shares for cash or for shares of the acquiring corporation. Mergers, consolidations, and share exchanges must be approved by the boards of directors and the shareholders of each corporation involved. Shareholders who dissent from the transaction are usually given appraisal rights, namely, the right to have their stock appraised and bought from them for cash.

One corporation can acquire all or substantially all of another's tangible and intangible assets. The acquiring corporation need not obtain shareholder approval inasmuch as the acquisition is viewed as within the board's ordinary powers. The selling corporation, however, must have approval of its board of directors and its shareholders. Dissenting shareholders will be afforded appraisal rights. As an alternative to acquiring a corporation's assets, a corporation can acquire another corporation's stock. Although most stock acquisitions are negotiated arrangements, some are not. These nonconsensual takeovers are "hostile" and call into play a wide variety of defensive strategies used by the target to avoid takeover by the aggressor. Finally, corporations can change their state of incorporation or convert to a different type of entity.

A. Amending the Articles of Incorporation

1. Reasons for Amending Articles

According to most state statutes and MBCA § 10.01, a corporation may amend its articles at any time to add or change a provision that was permitted or required in the original articles or to delete any provision not required to be included in the articles of incorporation. Thus, amendments can be used to add preemptive rights for shareholders, create new classes of shares, change the par value of the stock, and so forth. The most common reasons for amending the articles are changing the corporation's name and increasing the number of shares the corporation is authorized to issue. Some statutes identify a list of acceptable amendments, but the more modern practice is that followed by the MBCA: If a provision could have been stated in the original articles, it can be included in the amended articles.

Although the articles set forth the basic structure of the corporation, no shareholder has a vested right in the articles, such that his or her individual approval is required before an amendment can be accomplished. In general, majority vote rules. The original articles may, however, set forth certain restrictions on future amendments by requiring approval in excess of that mandated by the state statute, for example, a provision requiring 80 percent shareholder approval to create a new class of stock.

If the corporation has included provisions in its articles that were not required — for example, a provision setting the date for the annual shareholders' meeting — any desired change will require amending the articles. Thus, the better practice is to draft articles that strictly comply with the pertinent state statutes and desired corporate structure, but go no further, because each additional provision may require amendment in the future.

2. Procedure for Amending Articles

The most common procedure for amending the articles (or "charter" or "certificate," if so called by the state) is discussion of the proposed amendment by the board of directors and then adoption by the board of a resolution setting forth the text of the proposed amendment and directing that it be submitted for shareholder approval. The board must also make a recommendation that the amendment be approved. The board may act at a meeting by majority vote, or may act by written consent, which most states require to be unanimous.

Some states and the MBCA allow the directors to make certain amendments to the articles without shareholder approval. In general, these amendments are for routine matters that do not affect the basic rights of shareholders. For example, MBCA § 10.05 provides that the board, acting alone, can adopt the following amendments: extending the duration of the corporation; deleting the names and addresses of the initial directors; deleting the name and address of the initial agent for service of process if a statement of change has been filed with the secretary of state; changing each issued and unissued authorized share of an outstanding class into a greater number of whole shares, if the corporation has only shares of that class outstanding (in other words, increasing the number of authorized shares to accommodate a stock split); increasing the number of authorized shares to accommodate the issuance of share dividends (if the corporation has only one class of shares); or changing the corporate name by substituting the words "corporation," "incorporated," "company," or "limited" or the abbreviations "inc.," "co.," "ltd.," or "corp.," for a similar word or abbreviation or by adding, deleting, or changing a geographic attribute for the name.

A few states permit a specified percentage of shareholders to propose an amendment to the articles. If no shares have yet been issued, the directors or incorporators can amend the articles by themselves. The more typical procedure, however, is that described: The board of directors will adopt a resolution setting forth the amendment and a meeting of shareholders will be held to vote on the amendment. (See Figure 14-1 for a sample resolution.) An amendment merely changing the corporation's agent for service of process can usually be effected by the directors without shareholder approval by filing a simple form with the secretary of state.

FIGURE 14-1
Resolution to Amend Articles

RESOLVED, that Article 1 of the Articles of Incorporation for the Company be amended to read as follows: The name of the corporation is Taylor Visions, Inc.

RESOLVED, that Article 4 of the Articles of Incorporation be deleted in its entirety.

RESOLVED, that Article 6 of the Articles of Incorporation for the Company be added as follows: The holders of shares of the Company shall have preemptive rights to purchase shares issued by the Company from time to time in the respective ratio which the number of shares held by each holder at the time of any issue bears to the total number of shares outstanding at the time of any issue.

The amendment may be voted on by the shareholders at their annual meeting or at a special meeting. The notice of any meeting that will consider an amendment to the articles of incorporation must state the purpose of the meeting and must set forth the text of the proposed amendment. Appropriate notice of any meeting must be given to all shareholders, even those not entitled to vote. If a class of shareholders has nonvoting stock, and a proposed amendment would affect their rights (for example, by cancelling their preemptive rights), those shareholders must also be allowed to vote on the amendment. The board of directors must inform the shareholders that the board recommends the amendment.

Previous versions of the Model Act required first a two-thirds approval and then a majority approval by shareholders. MBCA §§ 7.25 and 10.03(e) now provide only that the amendment will be approved if more votes are cast in favor of it than against it. Most states require a simple majority vote. A few states, however, still require two-thirds approval by shareholders. The original articles, of course, may have provided that amendments to the articles can only be accomplished by a certain percentage, for example, 75 percent; in such a case, these greater than majority requirements must be met. If shareholders are allowed to act by written consent, this procedure may also be used to effect an amendment to the articles of incorporation.

3.   *Articles of Amendment*

Articles of amendment
Document filed with state that amends articles of incorporation

After the amendment has been approved by the shareholders, the corporation must prepare and file **articles of amendment** (or a certificate of amendment) with the secretary of state. Almost all states provide forms for articles of amendment. Most states and MBCA § 10.06(5) also require that the amendment recite that the original articles were amended pursuant to state statute and that the requisite shareholder vote was received, or that shareholder approval was not needed. (See Figure 14-2 for sample articles of amendment.)

Rather than require that the entire articles be redrafted, most states allow corporations to simply set forth the text of the new amendment. The articles are then filed with the secretary of state together with the requisite filing fee. After examination of the articles of amendment, the secretary of state will issue a certificate of amendment, or return a copy of the articles of amendment stamped "approved." Any requirements relating to the original articles must also be complied with when amending articles. For example, if the original articles were required to be published or filed with a county clerk, the amended articles must be also. If the amendment changes the corporation's name or authorized number of shares, new stock certificates and a new corporate seal should be obtained.

In some instances, a minority of states allow shareholders who dissented from amending the articles to have their shares bought by the corporation at the fair market value. This right to dissent and have one's shares appraised and bought out is generally triggered only by an amendment that seriously impairs or adversely affects one's shares, such as an amendment abolishing some preferential right, preemptive rights, or a right to vote. The MBCA approach is to allow appraisal rights only when an amendment reduces the number of shares of a shareholder to a fraction of a share, and the corporation will have the obligation or right to repurchase the fractional share from the shareholder, such as is the case when a reverse stock split is accomplished. MBCA § 13.02(a)(4).

FIGURE 14-2
Washington Articles of Amendment

Page 1 of 1

 STATE OF WASHINGTON SECRETARY OF STATE

 APD

This Box For Office Use Only

Washington Profit Corporation
See attached detailed instructions

☐ **Filing Fee $30.00**

☐ **Filing Fee with Expedited Service $50.00**

UBI Number:

ARTICLES OF AMENDMENT
Chapter 23B.10 RCW

SECTION 1
NAME OF CORPORATION: *(as currently recorded with the Office of the Secretary of State)*

_____

SECTION 2
AMENDMENTS were adopted on this DATE: _____

SECTION 3
ARTICLES OF AMENDMENT WERE ADOPTED BY: *(please check one of the following)*

☐ Board of Directors *(shareholder action was not required)*

☐ Duly approved by shareholders in accordance with 23B.10.030 and 23B.10.040 RCW

☐ Incorporators *(shareholder action was not required)*

SECTION 4
AMENDMENTS TO ARTICLES ON FILE: *(if necessary, attach additional information)*

_____

SECTION 5
EFFECTIVE DATE OF ARTICLES OF AMENDMENT: *(please check one of the following)*

☐ Upon filing by the Secretary of State

☐ Specific Date: _____ *(Specified effective date must be within 90 days AFTER the Articles of Amendment have been filed by the Office of the Secretary of State)*

SECTION 6
SIGNATURE *(see instructions page)*
This document is hereby executed under penalties of perjury, and is, to the best of my knowledge, true and correct.

X _____

Signature	Printed Name/Title	Date	Phone Number

If the only change to the articles is a change of corporate name, consider whether the same result can be accomplished by allowing the corporation to do business under a fictitious business name. The cumbersome and somewhat expensive amendment procedure can be avoided by simply filing a fictitious business name statement with the secretary of state or local county clerk. The fictitious business name will allow the corporation to use a name different from the one it was incorporated under without necessitating a formal amendment to the articles of incorporation. Additionally, corporate name changes should be undertaken with all of the precautions used when selecting the original corporate name: A trade name search should be conducted to ensure the name is not confusingly similar to another, a check with the secretary of state should be conducted to ensure the name is available, and, if available, the name should be reserved during the amendment process.

An amendment to a corporation's articles does not affect the rights of any third parties. For example, the fact that a corporation changes its name does not release the corporation from a debt owed to a creditor who originally contracted with the differently named corporation. The corporate debtor remains the same — only its name has changed.

Finally, if the corporation is doing business in any other jurisdictions, their state statutes should be reviewed to determine whether an amendment to the articles triggers any filing requirements in the other jurisdictions.

B.   Restating the Articles of Incorporation

Over a period of time, a corporation may amend its articles several times. If each document filed with the secretary of state contains only the amending language rather than setting forth all of the articles, the articles may become difficult to read. For example, if a corporation filed its original articles in 1990 and thereafter amended them three times, anyone attempting to review the articles would need to compare all four documents. Therefore, almost all states allow a corporation to restate its articles by combining the original articles with any later amendments into one clean document that supersedes all of the previous documents.

Restated articles
Articles compiled into one readable form with no changes made

Because the **restated articles** of incorporation do not include any changes, but are rather a composite of previously approved amendments, shareholder approval is not necessary to restate articles of incorporation (unless a change to the articles is being made at the same time, in which case, the required procedure for amendments must be followed). The directors will approve a restatement either by majority vote at a meeting or by written consent, and then the entire text of the articles, including any changes, additions, or deletions made since filing of the original articles, will be prepared and filed with the secretary of state accompanied by a filing fee.

C.   Amending the Bylaws of the Corporation

Changes in the corporation's bylaws are easily accomplished. Generally, unless state statute, the articles, or the bylaws themselves require shareholder participation, the bylaws may be amended solely by the directors. If shareholder approval is required, a simple majority vote is generally sufficient. The bylaws may be amended to change the date of the annual meeting of shareholders, to change the duties of the corporate treasurer, to add an officer, and so forth.

In most states, amendment of the bylaws is performed by the directors acting at a meeting or acting by written consent. The minutes of the meeting or written consent action setting forth the change should be placed in the minute book. The section of the minute book containing the bylaws should also reflect the change. Either an entire new set of bylaws should be prepared and marked "Bylaws—Amended as of_____" or the new bylaw provision should be prepared on a separate piece of paper marked "Amendment to Bylaw No. _____, amended as of_____" and inserted at the end of the bylaws.

Because the original bylaws did not require filing with the secretary of state, the amended bylaws need not be filed with the secretary of state.

D. Corporate Combinations

Corporations may take control of other corporations or increase their size by a variety of means. One corporation might be merged into another, with all of the merged corporation's assets and property transferred to the survivor corporation. A corporation may purchase the assets of another corporation. One corporation may acquire sufficient stock in another corporation that it can assume control. The corporations involved in these transactions are usually called **constituents.**

Constituent
Party involved in a merger or other similar transaction

The reasons why such combinations take place are as varied as the means to accomplish the combination. A corporation may wish to acquire some special process or technology owned by another corporation; to diversify and expand its product line; or to rid itself of a competitor. These goals can be accomplished by merger, consolidation, a share exchange, acquisition of assets, or acquisition of stock. Because all of these combinations affect significant rights of shareholders, all are subject, to varying degrees, to the requirement of shareholder approval.

In tax terminology, mergers, consolidations, and share exchanges are called **reorganizations.** The various types of reorganizations have different names and different tax consequences. For example, the IRS calls mergers and consolidations *Type A Reorganizations.* An exchange of shares is referred to as a *Type B Reorganization*, and an acquisition of substantially all of the assets of another corporation in exchange for shares of the acquiror is called a *Type C Reorganization.* The Internal Revenue Code provides varying tax treatment for these different types of reorganizations.

Reorganization
Terminology used by IRS to classify various corporate combinations

1. Mergers and Consolidations

Mergers. State statutes permit the combination of two or more corporations into one corporate entity. This combination is called a **merger.** Because the merger process is controlled by statute, mergers are often referred to as *statutory mergers.* In the classic merger scenario, Corporation A combines with Corporation B. At the conclusion of the combination, one of the corporations (assume Corporation A)

Merger
Combination of two or more corporations into one corporate entity

will cease to exist. The survivor, Corporation B, will acquire everything previously owned by Corporation A: its assets, its contracts, its rights, its debts, its obligations, and usually its shareholders. In the example given, Corporation A is referred to as the *merged corporation* or the **extinguished corporation.** Corporation B is called the **survivor.** Mergers can take place between two or more domestic corporations or between domestic and foreign corporations, so long as the laws of each corporation's state of incorporation are followed. Many state statutes prohibit mergers between corporations and other business entities, such as partnerships and limited liability companies. A merger between such different business entities is called a **cross-species merger** (or *interspecies merger*). MBCA § 11.02 recognizes such cross-species mergers.

Varieties of Mergers.   There are several variations on the classic merger: the upstream merger, the downstream merger, the triangular merger, and the reverse triangular merger. Upstream and downstream mergers involve mergers between parent corporations and their subsidiaries. A corporation owned or formed by another corporation is called a **subsidiary.** The creator corporation is called the *parent.* On occasion, the parent may wish to merge the subsidiary back into itself, perhaps to eliminate the costs and paperwork involved in maintaining two corporations. If the parent owns at least 90 percent of the stock of the subsidiary, the MBCA and most states allow the merger to take place without approval of the shareholders of either the parent or the subsidiary. Approval of the subsidiary's shareholders (or their directors) is not needed because they do not have sufficient voting power to block the merger, and approval of the parent's shareholders is not required because the decision is viewed as an ordinary business decision within the province of the board. This type of merger is called a **short-form merger.** When the subsidiary merges into the parent and the parent is the survivor, it is called an **upstream merger.** When the parent merges into the subsidiary and the subsidiary is the survivor, it is called a **downstream merger.**

A **triangular merger** (sometimes called a *forward triangular merger*) involves three parties or constituent corporations: a parent-buyer, its subsidiary, and a target corporation. The subsidiary (often created for this transaction) merges with the target corporation and is the survivor, although the parent still owns that new entity. Rather than directly acquiring the target itself, the parent may wish to keep the subsidiary separate from it for diversification purposes or to protect itself from either the subsidiary's or the newly acquired target's liabilities. In a classic merger, the parent would be liable for the extinguished corporation's debts. In a triangular merger, the subsidiary remains liable for its own and the target's debts. In many instances, a parent creates a subsidiary for the sole purpose of accomplishing a triangular merger. The subsidiary is thus formed for the target to merge into it. The target is then extinguished, and the subsidiary survives separate and apart from its parent.

A **reverse triangular merger** is substantially similar to a triangular merger, except that rather than the target being merged into the subsidiary, the subsidiary is merged into the target (and ceases to exist). The target then becomes the new subsidiary of the parent. This transaction may be used when the target's leases and other contracts cannot be assigned or transferred to another party; the target remains a party to the leases or other contracts and yet the parent reaps their benefits.

Extinguished corporation
Corporation that does not survive a merger

Survivor
Corporation that survives a merger

Cross-species merger
Merger between corporation and some other business entity (also called an *interspecies merger*)

Subsidiary
Corporation formed by another, called the *parent*

Short-form merger
Merger of a subsidiary into a parent not requiring shareholder approval

Upstream merger
Merger between parent and subsidiary in which parent is survivor

Downstream merger
Merger between parent and subsidiary in which subsidiary is survivor

Triangular merger
Merger involving three parties in which target merges into parent's subsidiary and target is extinguished; also called forward triangular merger

Reverse triangular merger
Merger involving three parties in which subsidiary merges into target and is extinguished and target become new subsidiary

Consolidations.   A **consolidation** is closely similar to a merger. In this transaction, however, two or more corporations combine and form an entirely new corporation, a different legal entity from either of the two constituent corporations involved. At the end of the consolidation, all of the combining constituent corporations cease to exist. The newly formed corporation acquires everything previously owned by the constituents: their assets, contracts, rights, liabilities, and shareholders. In a classic consolidation scenario, Corporation A combines with Corporation B to form Corporation X.

The result of a consolidation can be effected by merger. For example, a parent may create a subsidiary corporation. The parent, subsidiary, and target enter into an agreement to merge, whereby they agree that the parent and the target will merge into the newly formed subsidiary, which was created for the express purpose of surviving the transaction. Because it is nearly always advantageous for one of the constituent corporations in a transaction to survive and because the effect of a consolidation can be achieved through such a merger, the MBCA and some states no longer recognize consolidations. See Figure 14-3 for diagrams showing varieties of mergers and a consolidation.

Consolidation
Combination of two or more corporations into one new entity

P R A C T I C E   T I P S

- When a new corporation is formed to participate in a merger or other transaction, it is often referred to as NEWCO or NEWCORP in all of the pertinent documents. Watch for this entity name; it is a signal that an entirely new corporation is being created solely for the purpose of the transaction.
- Almost all law firms engaged in "M & A" (mergers and acquisitions) work use detailed timetables that provide a blueprint as to when and what documents are to be prepared and filed. Maintain all your timetables for use in future transactions along with your "contact" list of useful contacts at the SEC, helpful Web sites, and so forth.

Procedures for Effecting Mergers and Consolidations.   Mergers and consolidations may be completed in various ways. The following issues may arise.

Director and Shareholder Approval.   The procedures for accomplishing mergers and consolidations are the same. Any references in this section to mergers also include consolidations. The first step in the merger process is negotiation between or among the constituent corporations involved. These preliminary negotiations usually lead to a **letter of intent,** a letter-form document setting forth the basic understanding and intent of the parties. The letter of intent will eventually be replaced with a formal, definitive agreement; however, the letter is sufficiently detailed to outline the key terms of the transaction. (See Appendix J for a form of a letter of intent.) The negotiation process itself can be complex and take several months.

Letter of intent
Initial document setting forth basic understanding of parties to a transaction

---

FIGURE 14-3
Merger and Consolidation

Merger

Upstream Merger

Parent

Subsidiary

Parent + Subsidiary = Parent

Downstream Merger

Parent

Subsidiary

Parent + Subsidiary = Subsidiary

Triangular Merger

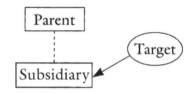

Target merges into parent's subsidiary and target is extinguished

Reverse Triangular Merger

Parent

Subsidiary

Target

Subsidiary merges into target and subsidiary is extinguished and target becomes new subsidiary of parent

CONSOLIDATION

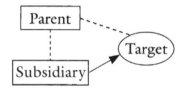

The constituent corporations must then prepare a **plan of merger.** The content of the plan of merger is generally regulated by statute. For example, MBCA § 11.02(c) provides that the plan of merger must set forth the following:

1. The name of each corporation planning to merge and the name of the surviving corporation;
2. The terms and conditions of the merger;
3. The manner and basis of converting the shares of each corporation into shares or other securities of the survivor (or, if desired, the manner of converting the shares of the extinguished corporation into cash, thereby allowing shareholders to be cashed out); and
4. Any amendments that will be required to be made to the survivor's articles of incorporation such as a name change or creation of a new class of stock.

The plan of merger will likely include other provisions as well, such as a description of authorized capital of the constituent corporations, provisions relating to assets being transferred, and a description of any litigation in which the constituents are involved.

The plan of merger is then submitted to the board of directors of each constituent corporation for its approval. After adopting the plan of merger, the boards of the constituent corporations must submit the plan for shareholder approval. The boards of directors must recommend the plan of merger (unless, because of conflict of interest or other circumstances, the board determines it should make no recommendation), and the shareholders entitled to vote must then approve the plan. Unless this activity takes place at or near the time of the annual meeting, the corporations will likely call special meetings of shareholders for approval. The notice of any meeting must specify that the purpose of the meeting is to consider the plan of merger. The notice must include a copy or summary of the plan of merger. The more modern approach is to require a simple majority approval by the shareholders; many states, however, require two-thirds approval. The MBCA approach is similar to its approach on amendments to the articles of incorporation: The merger will be approved if more votes are cast in favor of it than against it. MBCA §§ 11.04(e), 7.25. Some states permit nonvoting shares of stock to vote on the merger. All shareholders, however, must receive notice of the meeting, whether or not they are entitled to vote. MBCA § 11.03(d). Furthermore, the notice must state whether the shareholders will have appraisal rights (discussed later). If so, shareholders must be provided copies of the statutes relating to appraisal rights.

Approval by shareholders of all constituent corporations is required due to the dramatic impact a merger (or consolidation) has on the shareholders. The corporation owned by the shareholders of the merging corporation will be extinguished; such an extraordinary matter should be approved by the owners of that corporation. The corporation owned by the shareholders of the survivor corporation will likely be taking on debts, liabilities, and other obligations of the extinguished corporation. Additionally, share ownership in the survivor will be affected because the survivor must absorb shareholders of the extinguished corporation and issue them shares of the survivor. This issuance of shares to the newcomers might cause a shift in power and control among the shareholders of the survivor. If the shareholders of the extinguished corporation receive cash rather than shares in the

Plan of merger
Document setting forth particulars as to planned merger

survivor, the survivor's shareholders will be affected by what will likely be a large outlay of cash. Thus, in either scenario, their approval is required.

Exceptions to Requirement of Shareholder Approval.   There are generally two exceptions to the requirement that shareholders of all constituent corporations must approve a merger. First, a merger between a parent and subsidiary need not be approved by the shareholders of *either* corporation (or by the directors of the subsidiary) if the parent owns at least 90 percent of the outstanding stock of its subsidiary. MBCA § 11.05. This is the short-form merger discussed earlier. Shareholder approval is simply not needed; if the parent owns 90 percent or more of the subsidiary's stock and it desires that the subsidiary be extinguished, the parent has the necessary votes to make that happen. Voting by the subsidiary's shareholders would be a superfluous exercise. Similarly, voting by the parent's shareholders is not needed because the recapture of the subsidiary by the parent does not materially affect their share ownership.

The second exception provides that a merger need not be approved by the shareholders of the *survivor* corporation if:

- The survivor's articles of incorporation will not be changed;
- Each of the survivor's shareholders will hold the same number of shares with identical rights after the merger; and
- The voting power of shares outstanding after the merger (plus the number issued as a result of the merger) will not exceed by more than 20 percent the total number of the survivor's voting shares outstanding before the merger.

Small-scale merger
Merger involving little transfer of survivor's stock to incoming shareholders

This type of merger, often called a **small-scale merger,** does not dramatically affect the power and control of the shareholders of the survivor. Very little of the survivor's outstanding stock will be issued to any incoming shareholders; therefore, the survivor's shareholders need not approve the transaction. See MBCA § 6.21(f) and 11.04(g).

These exceptions to the requirement of shareholder approval rest on the same premise: Shareholder approval of a merger is not needed when either the merger cannot be prevented or when the transaction has little impact on the survivor's shareholders.

Dissenting shareholders
Shareholders who vote against merger or some other transaction

Appraisal right
Right of dissenting shareholder to have shares purchased at their fair market value

Rights of Dissenting Shareholders.   It is possible that some shareholders are adamantly opposed to a merger; they might have philosophic or moral objections to one or more of the constituents involved. Therefore, all states allow these **dissenting shareholders** the right to have their shares appraised and to receive the fair value of their shares as of the date of the merger in cash. This right is called the **appraisal right,** and, generally, it is a dissenting shareholder's exclusive remedy if she is opposed to a merger.

Dissenting shareholders must follow a fairly complex procedure to be entitled to appraisal rights. Generally, in the meeting notice the corporation must state whether shareholders are or are not entitled to assert appraisal rights and must include a copy of the relevant statutes. If a shareholder wishes to assert appraisal rights, the shareholder must deliver a written notice of intent to demand payment for his or her shares. This notice must be delivered to the corporation before the vote on the merger is held and the shareholder must not vote in favor of the merger. Within ten days after the shareholders' meeting authorizing the merger, the corporation must deliver a written appraisal notice to any shareholder who previously provided written notice of an intent to demand payment. The corporation must include a form for the dissenter to use to demand payment. The shareholder must return the form by a certain date; however, the shareholder must be given not less than 40 and not more than 60 days, per MBCA § 13.22. The corporation must estimate the fair value of the shares. The ultimate payment made to the shareholder must equal or exceed this estimate. Shareholders then surrender their certificates. Assuming compliance with these elaborate requirements have been met, the corporation will pay each dissenter the fair value of her shares, as of the time immediately before effectuation of the merger transaction, together with accrued interest. The payment will be accompanied by financial statements of the corporation. Any appreciation or depreciation of the stock in anticipation of the transaction will be excluded. If the dissenting shareholder objects to the corporation's valuation of the shares, and the parties cannot reach agreement, the corporation will institute a judicial proceeding to determine the fair value of the shares. Unless the dissenting shareholder strictly and timely complies with the various statutory requirements, the corporation has no duty to pay the value of the shares. A shareholder may withdraw from the appraisal process and thereby decline to exercise any appraisal rights.

In a short-form merger in which a parent regains its subsidiary, although the subsidiary's shareholders are not entitled to vote on the transaction, within ten days after the transaction becomes effective, the parent must notify the subsidiary's shareholders that they are entitled to assert appraisal rights. The parent's shareholders are not entitled to appraisal rights.

Some states allow partial appraisal rights so that a shareholder may dissent regarding some shares owned and be cashed out with respect to those shares, and remain a shareholder as to the remainder of the shares. Generally, a shareholder must demand appraisal for all of the shares of a class or series that the shareholder owns. Appraisal rights are not provided to the survivor's shareholders in a small-scale merger (because they do not vote on the transaction).

Most states, including Delaware, do not allow dissent and appraisal rights if the shares are listed on a national exchange or if there are at least 2,000 shareholders of a class of shares. The basis for this market exception is that if the shares are listed on a national exchange or if there are at least 2,000 shareholders, there should be ready and available buyers for the dissenter's shares. Similarly, MBCA § 13.02(b) generally provides that appraisal rights are not available if the shareholders' stock is traded on a national exchange or if there are at least 2,000 shareholders, and the outstanding shares have a market value of at least $20 million. The market itself will provide fair value for the shares, thus making appraisal rights unnecessary.

Articles of Merger. After the merger has been approved by the requisite shareholder vote, **articles of merger** must be prepared and filed with the secretary of state. The articles usually set forth or attach the plan of merger and a statement regarding the approval of the plan of merger by the shareholders, often including the number of votes for and against the merger. If shareholder approval was not required, the articles of merger must so state. See Figure 14-4 for a form for articles of merger. Some states require that the plan of merger be certified as approved and then filed with the secretary of state. A filing fee is required. Additionally, just as the original articles of incorporation and amended articles of incorporation might need to be published or filed with a county recorder, so may the articles of merger. New stock certificates and a new seal might need to be ordered.

Articles of merger
Document filed with state to effect merger

FIGURE 14-4
California Certificate of Merger

State of California
Secretary of State

OBE MERG

CERTIFICATE OF MERGER

(California Corporations Code sections
1113(g), 6019.1, 8019.1, 9640, 12540.1, 15678.4, 15911.14, 16915(b) and 17552)

IMPORTANT — Read all instructions before completing this form.   This Space For Filing Use Only

1. NAME OF SURVIVING ENTITY	2. TYPE OF ENTITY	3. CA SECRETARY OF STATE FILE NUMBER	4. JURISDICTION
5. NAME OF DISAPPEARING ENTITY	6. TYPE OF ENTITY	7. CA SECRETARY OF STATE FILE NUMBER	8. JURISDICTION

9. THE PRINCIPAL TERMS OF THE AGREEMENT OF MERGER WERE APPROVED BY A VOTE OF THE NUMBER OF INTERESTS OR SHARES OF EACH CLASS THAT EQUALED OR EXCEEDED THE VOTE REQUIRED. IF A VOTE WAS REQUIRED, SPECIFY THE CLASS AND THE NUMBER OF OUTSTANDING INTERESTS OF <u>EACH CLASS</u> ENTITLED TO VOTE ON THE MERGER AND THE PERCENTAGE VOTE REQUIRED OF <u>EACH CLASS</u>. ATTACH ADDITIONAL PAGES, IF NECESSARY.

SURVIVING ENTITY			DISAPPEARING ENTITY		
<u>CLASS AND NUMBER</u>	**AND**	<u>PERCENTAGE VOTE REQUIRED</u>	<u>CLASS AND NUMBER</u>	**AND**	<u>PERCENTAGE VOTE REQUIRED</u>

10. IF EQUITY SECURITIES OF A PARENT PARTY ARE TO BE ISSUED IN THE MERGER, CHECK THE APPLICABLE STATEMENT.

☐ No vote of the shareholders of the parent party was required.   ☐ The required vote of the shareholders of the parent party was obtained.

11. IF THE SURVIVING ENTITY IS A DOMESTIC LIMITED LIABLITY COMPANY, LIMITED PARTNERSHIP, OR PARTNERSHIP, PROVIDE THE REQUISITE CHANGES (IF ANY) TO THE INFORMATION SET FORTH IN THE SURVIVING ENTITY'S ARTICLES OF ORGANIZATION, CERTIFICATE OF LIMITED PARTNERSHIP OR STATEMENT OF PARTNERSHIP AUTHORITY RESULTING FROM THE MERGER. ATTACH ADDITIONAL PAGES, IF NECESSARY.

12. IF A DISAPPEARING ENTITY IS A DOMESTIC LIMITED LIABLITY COMPANY, LIMITED PARTNERSHIP, OR PARTNERSHIP, AND THE SURVIVING ENTITY IS NOT A DOMESTIC ENTITY OF THE SAME TYPE, ENTER THE PRINCIPAL ADDRESS OF THE SURVIVING ENTITY.

PRINCIPAL ADDRESS OF SURVIVING ENTITY	CITY AND STATE	ZIP CODE

13. OTHER INFORMATION REQUIRED TO BE STATED IN THE CERTIFICATE OF MERGER BY THE LAWS UNDER WHICH EACH CONSTITUENT OTHER BUSINESS ENTITY IS ORGANIZED. ATTACH ADDITIONAL PAGES, IF NECESSARY.

14. STATUTORY OR OTHER BASIS UNDER WHICH A FOREIGN OTHER BUSINESS ENTITY IS AUTHORIZED TO EFFECT THE MERGER.	15. FUTURE EFFECTIVE DATE, IF ANY ____ - ____ - ____ (Month) (Day) (Year)

16. ADDITIONAL INFORMATION SET FORTH ON ATTACHED PAGES, IF ANY, IS INCORPORATED HEREIN BY THIS REFERENCE AND MADE PART OF THIS CERTIFICATE.

17. I CERTIFY UNDER PENALTY OF PERJURY UNDER THE LAWS OF THE STATE OF CALIFORNIA THAT THE FOREGOING IS TRUE AND CORRECT OF MY OWN KNOWLEDGE. I DECLARE I AM THE PERSON WHO EXECUTED THIS INSTRUMENT, WHICH EXECUTION IS MY ACT AND DEED.

SIGNATURE OF AUTHORIZED PERSON FOR THE SURVIVING ENTITY	DATE	TYPE OR PRINT NAME AND TITLE OF AUTHORIZED PERSON
SIGNATURE OF AUTHORIZED PERSON FOR THE SURVIVING ENTITY	DATE	TYPE OR PRINT NAME AND TITLE OF AUTHORIZED PERSON
SIGNATURE OF AUTHORIZED PERSON FOR THE DISAPPEARING ENTITY	DATE	TYPE OR PRINT NAME AND TITLE OF AUTHORIZED PERSON
SIGNATURE OF AUTHORIZED PERSON FOR THE DISAPPEARING ENTITY	DATE	TYPE OR PRINT NAME AND TITLE OF AUTHORIZED PERSON

For an entity that is a business trust, real estate investment trust or an unincorporated association, set forth the provision of law or other basis for the authority of the person signing: _____

OBE MERGER-1 (REV 01/2008)   APPROVED BY SECRETARY OF STATE

The articles of incorporation of the survivor are deemed amended in accordance with the plan of merger; thus, there is often no requirement for the survivor to file a separate amendment of its articles of incorporation although most corporations do so to ensure their articles are current and can be read without reference to other documents. The secretary of state will examine the articles of merger, ensure that all taxes and fees have been paid, and then issue a certificate of merger. Many states allow a corporation to specify a later effective date for the merger so that simultaneous transactions may be completed in other states.

Upon the effective date of the merger, the merged corporation ceases to exist and the survivor takes over all of the extinguished corporation's assets, properties, personnel, shareholders, debts, obligations, and liabilities. The shareholders of the extinguished corporation, unless they have dissented and exercised their appraisal rights, will be issued shares of the survivor in return for their shares in the extinguished corporation according to the plan of merger, or, as discussed earlier, they may be cashed out.

Modern Trends in Mergers and Consolidations.   One of the more modern twists on mergers and consolidations is the **roll-up,** a combination of several companies. Roll-ups became very popular in the 1990s. In a roll-up, an entrepreneur buys various companies in an industry, combines them, takes the resulting entity public, and then goes on a buying binge of other companies. In theory, the resulting economies of scale of the combined companies would increase earnings, enhancing the roll-up's stock price, thus enabling additional acquisitions. For example, in 1994, one entrepreneur combined four office supply businesses to create U.S. Office Products Company. He then took the company public the next year and thereafter acquired more than 260 companies over the following three years. Unfortunately, what many entrepreneurs discover is that buying companies is relatively easy but integrating them into one smooth operating unit with reliable financial controls is much harder.

At present, most roll-ups have disappeared or are struggling to survive. Nearly 90 percent of the more than 100 roll-ups created in the mid-1990s have lost money for their investors, and half are in bankruptcy or trade for less than $1 per share. U.S. Office Products Company filed for bankruptcy in 2001. The projected economies of scale seldom materialized, and the roll-ups were often marked by redundancies and infighting. Since late 1999, Wall Street has been skeptical of roll-ups, and most companies have adopted a more traditional strategy for growth: A larger public company buys a small public or private company in its industry, integrates it completely, and then pursues another.

Another feature of the merger landscape today is the fairness opinion. In almost all mergers, to satisfy its fiduciary duties, the target will obtain a **fairness opinion** from investment bankers or other experts. The fairness opinion verifies that the consideration offered by the bidder is within the appropriate fair market value range for the target and is fair to the public shareholders. These fairness opinions are often used to demonstrate that the target's board has met its fiduciary duties. Due to FINRA's concern that sometimes the parties issuing the fairness opinions were also acting as advisors in the transaction (and thus might be tempted to determine the transaction was "fair" regardless of its merits), in late 2007, the SEC adopted new regulations requiring those issuing fairness opinions to make certain disclosures to shareholders if there are or could be conflicts of interest by those issuing the fairness opinion.

Roll-up
Combination of several companies in the same industry

Fairness opinion
Expert opinion on the valuation of a target requested by the target's directors to demonstrate they have met their fiduciary duties

Finally, in 2004 the National Conference of Commissioners on Uniform State Laws together with the American Bar Association promulgated a Model Entity Transactions Act to provide a comprehensive framework for changing entity forms, from mergers to share exchanges to conversions and domestications (discussed in Section E later in this chapter). At the time of the writing of this text, it has only been adopted in Idaho. The text of the Act is available at www.nccusl.org.

Merger Trivia

◆ Mergers and acquisitions activity is usually seen as a sign of economic health because companies usually will not transact significant deals if they anticipate an economic slowdown.

◆ United States companies are 20 percent more likely to acquire a foreign company than foreign companies are to acquire U.S. companies.

◆ After a decade of exceptional growth in the number of mergers and the dollar value of merger transactions, merger activity reached its height in 2000, and began to slow down in 2001 and 2002, and then began to increase again in 2003. Merger volume at the Federal Trade Commission increased more than 50 percent between 2004 and 2007.

◆ Merger volume totaled more than $1.3 in the United States in 2006.

◆ Corporations providing business services are the most likely to be involved in mergers, followed by those engaged in providing prepackaged software, those involved in banking, and then those engaged in radio and television broadcasting. Pharmaceutical and telecommunications industries are increasingly engaged in mergers.

◆ The merger of Time Warner Inc. and America Online Inc., announced in early 2000, involved $165 billion and was the largest merger in history.

◆ After a period of decline, foreign acquisitions of U.S. companies have been increasing; nearly 25 percent of all merger activity in 2007 involved non-U.S. acquirers.

---

2. *Share Exchanges*

Share exchange
Exchange of all of target's shares for shares in acquiring corporation

Another way in which a corporation can gain control of another corporation is through a share exchange. In a **share exchange,** one corporation acquires all of the shares of one or more classes of another corporation (the target). The acquiring corporation receives all of the target's shares, and the target receives shares of the acquiror (or cash). Both corporations may continue to exist; the target's shareholders exchange all of their shares for shares in the acquiring corporation (in which case the target becomes the subsidiary of the acquiring corporation), for cash, or for shares in some other corporation. The acquiring corporation is in an identical position to that of the survivor of a merger. Because a share exchange is so similar in its effect to a merger, all of the procedural formalities of a merger must be complied with, namely, approval of a plan of exchange by directors and shareholders of both the acquiring and the target corporations, provision of appraisal rights to dissenting shareholders, and filing of articles or a certificate of share exchange with the secretary of state.

3. Purchase of Assets

A corporation may gain control of another or combine with another by purchasing all or substantially all of its assets, both tangible and intangible. The selling corporation may be paid for its assets in cash or in stock of the acquiring corporation. At the end of the transaction, the acquiring corporation owns additional assets, and the selling corporation may be a mere shell, owning nothing other than the cash or shares it has recently received. After it has paid its liabilities and distributed the proceeds of the sale to its shareholders, it may dissolve.

An asset purchase also affords a corporation the opportunity to buy assets of an unincorporated entity, such as a partnership or a limited liability company. Because state statutes relating to mergers, consolidations, and share exchanges often refer to constituent *corporations*, a corporation cannot merge with a partnership or other noncorporate entity in those states. A corporation can, however, purchase the assets of a partnership or other noncorporate entity.

Because there is no change in the status of the legal entity of the acquiring corporation and it is simply buying additional assets, it need not secure the approval of its shareholders. The transaction is viewed as within the purview of the directors, who have the sole authority to manage the business affairs of the corporation. The selling corporation, however, may be undergoing significant change and disposing of all or substantially all of its assets, thereby impairing its ability to carry out its business. Therefore, the selling corporation must have approval by its board of directors and its shareholders and, in most states, must offer appraisal rights to its dissenting shareholders. MBCA § 12.02 no longer uses the phrase "all or substantially all of its assets"; instead § 12.02 requires shareholder approval if a disposition or sale of assets would leave the corporation without a significant continuing business activity. Under the MBCA, generally, a significant business activity exists if the continuing activity represents at least 25 percent of the seller's assets and either 25 percent of income before taxes or revenue from continuing operations. If so, the selling corporation is conclusively presumed to have retained a significant continuing business activity, and it need not obtain its shareholders' approval.

A purchase of assets may be more advantageous than a merger to an acquiring corporation; the purchase of another corporation's assets may not require shareholder approval, and, in most cases, the seller retains liabilities, having sold only its assets. Moreover, generally, no public filings or amendments to articles are necessitated by the asset transaction.

A mere mortgage or pledge by a corporation of its assets as security to ensure or guarantee repayment of a loan is not viewed as a sale of assets. Thus, there is no need for shareholder approval. When the borrowing corporation repays the loan, the mortgage or pledge of the assets will be released and the corporation may continue its ordinary business.

Asset purchase
Purchase of assets of an entity, terms of which are found in *asset purchase agreement*

A sale of assets in the ordinary course of a corporation's business also does not require shareholder approval. For example, a real estate company can sell all of its inventory of properties without requiring shareholder approval because this is exactly the type of business activity the corporation should be conducting. Shareholder approval is required, however, if there is a sale, lease, exchange, or disposition of all or substantially all of a corporation's assets *not* within the ordinary course of business such that the corporation is left without a significant continuing business activity. Additionally, shareholder approval is not required if the assets of a subsidiary are being transferred to the parent corporation when the parent owns all of the shares of the subsidiary. Because the subsidiary cannot stop the sale, seeking approval would be futile and superfluous.

The procedure for effecting the purchase and sale of assets closely parallels the procedure for effecting mergers and consolidations because the result for the selling corporation is similar to that for an extinguished corporation in a merger—namely, discontinuation of its business operations. After a period of initial negotiation and a letter of intent setting forth the basic terms of the transaction (see Appendix J), the board of directors of the selling corporation recommends the transaction and then directs that it be voted on by the shareholders, either at an annual meeting or a special meeting. All shareholders, even nonvoting shareholders, are entitled to notice of the meeting, which must state that the purpose of the meeting is to consider the sale of the corporation's assets. The board must recommend that the shareholders approve the sale of the corporate assets. A description of the transaction must accompany the notice. The approval requirement is a simple majority in most states and a two-thirds approval in some states. The MBCA approach is similar to its approach on amendments to the articles of incorporation and mergers: The sale of assets will be approved if more votes are cast in favor of it than against it. MBCA § 11:04(e). Most states and the MBCA require appraisal rights for dissenting shareholders. An *asset purchase agreement* will be prepared and signed by both parties. This agreement will identify the parties, list the assets being sold, disclose any pending claims or litigation involving the seller, provide for the method and terms of payment, specify a date and place for closing, and include provisions in the event of either party's default. A complete form of an asset purchase agreement is available from your instructor. Unless the articles of incorporation of either corporation will be amended (perhaps to reflect a corporate name change), generally there are no state filings necessary. If either corporation is a Section 12 company, it must report this material event to the SEC.

In an asset purchase, the acquiring corporation, in effect, "goes shopping," picking and choosing the assets it desires. It seldom, if ever, agrees to assume any liability of the target corporation, which continues its existence and retains responsibility for its obligations and liabilities.

4. Limitation of Shareholder Remedies

Shareholders have very limited remedies to oppose a merger, share exchange, or purchase of assets once it has been approved. Under newly adopted MBCA

§ 13.40, shareholders cannot attempt to enjoin or set aside one of these transactions once it has been approved unless there was some fundamental flaw in the process by which the transaction was approved, if was procured by fraud, or involved a conflict of interest.

The sale of all or substantially all of a corporation's assets may trigger certain requirements of Article 6 of the Uniform Commercial Code relating to **bulk sales,** the sale or transfer of the major portion of a company's business outside the scope of its ordinary course of business. To protect creditors of the selling corporation, the bulk sales provisions require that creditors of the selling corporation be given notice of the intended transfer. Failure to comply with the bulk sales requirements may invalidate the transfer as to creditors who did not receive proper notice. The pertinent state statutes should be consulted to determine if the selling corporation must comply with its state's bulk sales requirements.

Bulk sale
Sale of all or substantially all of one's assets, often triggering various notices

5. De Facto Merger Doctrine and Freeze-Outs

As noted, there are a variety of ways in which one corporation can gain control over another: It can merge another corporation into it; it can create a subsidiary to acquire a target; it can consolidate with another corporation and create a new legal entity; it can negotiate with a target corporation to exchange its shares for cash or other shares; or it can purchase all or substantially all of the assets of another corporation. The determination as to which particular transaction should be selected depends on a variety of factors, including liability, shareholder approval issues, and taxation. For example, the net effect of an asset acquisition is strikingly similar to that of a merger, yet whereas a merger requires shareholder approval of both corporations involved, a corporation acquiring another's assets need not obtain its own shareholders' approval.

To ensure that shareholders are fully protected, the courts have developed what is called the **de facto merger doctrine.** The doctrine requires that corporations comply with all of the formalities of a merger — board approval, shareholder approval, and appraisal rights for dissenters — if a transaction has the effect of a merger, no matter what the parties involved choose to call it. Thus, courts will carefully scrutinize transactions (particularly purchases of assets) to ensure that shareholders have the ability to vote on matters that dramatically affect their share ownership or could result in the assumption of liabilities. In brief, the doctrine allows courts to treat an acquisition as a merger if it is a merger "in fact," although it might not be a merger in name.

De facto merger doctrine
Legal principle that if a transaction has the effect of a merger, it must follow procedural requirements of a merger

Moreover, as discussed in Chapter Sixteen, a merger undertaken for the purpose of "**freezing out**" minority shareholders may be enjoined if there is no legitimate purpose for the transaction other than to oppress minority shareholders. Such a freeze-out (or "squeeze-out") often occurs when a corporation is profitable and directors who are also holders of a majority of the corporation's stock wish to eliminate other shareholders. They thus form a new corporation owned solely by them and merge the old corporation into the new one. Under the plan of merger, shareholders of the old corporation will receive cash only but will not continue as shareholders in the new corporation, thus being frozen out of their corporation.

Freeze-out
Transaction to eliminate minority shareholders (also called *squeeze-out*)

6. *Purchase of Stock*

Stock purchase
Purchase of shares of a corporation, terms of which are found in *stock purchase agreement*

A **stock purchase** is highly similar to an asset acquisition; however, in this transaction, the acquiring corporation (or acquiring individual) purchases all or substantially all of another corporation's stock rather than its assets. The target corporation usually becomes a subsidiary of the acquiring corporation or may merge into it and the acquiring corporation will then be responsible for the debts and liabilities of the corporation whose stock is being acquired.

Many stock acquisition transactions involve negotiations between the management of the constituent corporations. The board of directors of the acquiring corporation seldom needs approval of its shareholders because the board is acting in the ordinary scope of business activities in determining that purchasing the stock is in the acquiring corporation's best interest. The management of the corporation whose stock is being acquired will pass a resolution recommending that the shareholders sell their stock to the acquiring corporation. Of course, the shareholders are free to decide whether or not to sell their stock. Stock acquisitions can be difficult to effect when there are numerous shareholders in the target corporation. The procedures in a consensual stock purchase closely parallel those in mergers, consolidations, and asset purchases. Negotiations will be followed by a letter of intent, which is then followed by a definitive stock purchase agreement that each party signs. At the date of closing, stock in the seller will be assigned to the acquiror and the acquiror will pay the appropriate purchase price to the seller.

Ultimately, a stock purchase agreement will be negotiated and executed, at which time the acquiring corporation will become the owner of the outstanding shares of the other corporation. Because it owns the outstanding shares, it now controls the destiny of the target and may decide to dissolve the target, allow the target to function as a subsidiary, or merge with the target.

Tender offer
Public offer made by bidder to acquire shares in a target corporation

Rather than dealing with management of the corporation whose stock is being purchased, the acquiring corporation may deal directly with the shareholders of the target corporation in seeking to acquire their shares. Once the acquiror possesses a majority of the stock of the target, the acquiror will have the power to remove existing directors and elect its own slate of directors and thereby control the target. A public offer made by the acquiring corporation to the shareholders of the target corporation to purchase a substantial percentage of the company's shares is referred to as a **tender offer,** so called because the acquiring corporation is asking the shareholders to surrender, or tender, their shares to it. The price the acquiring corporation or individual will pay is higher than the stock's current market value. This increased price induces the shareholders to sell. If the target's stock is currently selling at $36 per share, and the acquiring corporation states it will pay $45 per share, it might be very difficult for shareholders to resist this inducement. The tender offer can be made contingent on the acquisition of a specified number of shares by a specified date. For example, the acquiring corporation's tender offer can provide that it is willing to purchase 350,000 shares of the common stock of ABC, Inc., at $45 per share, if the purchases can be effected by December 15. If the requisite 350,000 shares are not tendered by December 15, the acquiring corporation has no obligation to purchase any of the shares. If the tender offer is successful, the end result is that the shareholders have made money by selling their stock, and the acquiror has gained control of the corporation.

The management of the target corporation might or might not know of the aggressor's plans. If it does, the transaction is usually consensual and the corporations will prepare and execute a stock acquisition agreement providing the terms and conditions of the transaction. If the target's management is unaware of the tender offer until it is made public, the acquisition is likely a *hostile* one, and the target may elect to defend itself aggressively from acquisition.

Federal securities laws strictly regulate tender offers. The Securities Exchange Act of 1934 provides that a form be filed with the SEC at the time an offer is made to shareholders, if acceptance of the offer would give the bidder more than 5 percent ownership in the company. In addition, any person who acquires stock in a Section 12 company, and thereby owns more than 5 percent of a class of stock, must file an information statement with the SEC within ten days of the acquisition. The SEC's tender offer rules generally do not apply to tender offers that, if consummated, will result in ownership of 5 percent or less of the target's outstanding shares, which are called "mini-tender offers."

7. Hostile Takeovers

Introduction. Not all combinations of corporations are consensual. Although many transactions involve months and perhaps even years of planning and negotiating by the constituents, some combinations occur without the consent of the acquired, or target, corporation. Because these combinations are not consensual, they are usually referred to as **hostile takeovers.**

Despite the media attention given to hostile takeovers, they still remain the exception rather than the rule. In most proposed combinations, after a period of negotiations the management of the constituent companies either ultimately disagree on the transaction, in which case, it usually dies, or they eventually come to mutually agreeable terms. The boards of directors of the corporations involved then recommend the combination to the shareholders. In the hostile takeover, however, the aggressor or bidder goes over the head of the target's management and courts the shareholders directly. Often, such large amounts of cash are offered to the shareholders for their stock that they simply cannot resist the offer.

One corporation might wish to acquire another to expand its business operations, to acquire new technology and operations, or to eliminate competition. In some instances, the aggressor may set its sights on a target that should be operating more profitably but is not, perhaps due to poor management. The aggressor may believe that a takeover of the company and a replacement of management will result in increased profits. In those instances, management of the target naturally feels threatened and may develop a variety of defenses to ward off the takeover.

Not all takeovers involve large aggressors pitted against weak targets. In many instances, contests involve bids by smaller corporations or even individuals to take over corporations whose assets exceed their own.

Regulation of takeovers is accomplished through § 13(d) of the Securities Exchange Act of 1934 regulating the reporting of acquisitions of stock that result in ownership of more than 5 percent of a class of stock, § 14(d) of the 1934 Act regulating the making of tender offers, and the **Williams Act,** passed in 1968, which is basically a series of refinements to § 13 and § 14 of the 1934 Act that apply to Section 12 companies. The intent of the Williams Act is to impose some

Hostile takeover
Transaction pursued by bidder without support of target's management

Williams Act
Statute regulating tender offers and takeovers

structure and rules for tender offers and eliminate fraud by requiring certain disclosures by both aggressors and targets. It protects shareholders from their own management as well as from the other corporation. Additionally, many states have enacted legislation regulating takeovers of their domestic corporations, generally to attempt to limit takeovers of locally based corporations that contribute significantly to the state's economy.

Preparing for the Takeover.   Assume that both the aggressor and the target are publicly traded corporations. The aggressor's first step might be to build up a war chest of cash to finance the acquisition. It may borrow money or even sell some of its assets to acquire cash. The aggressor may collect information about the target, its management, and its operations to confirm that a takeover of the target is a sound decision. Some of this information is publicly available and on file with the SEC. Additional information can be acquired through private investigators or other sources, perhaps even rumor "on the street," the "street" being Wall Street.

The aggressor must then evaluate whether it wishes to attempt a consensual acquisition and deal with the target's management or whether it should appeal directly to the target's shareholders. Each technique has advantages and disadvantages. An approach to the target's management could yield significant accurate information about the target so that the aggressor does not pay too much for acquiring the target. On the other hand, if the target's management believes it is threatened, it might take immediate steps to thwart the transaction. An approach directly to the shareholders could result in overpaying for their stock, yet it has the distinct advantage of surprise, which may preclude the target's management from taking action to defend itself.

Assume the aggressor decides to proceed by surprise. It will usually begin purchasing the target's stock on the open market. To conceal its intent, the aggressor may place orders for the target's stock with different brokers in different cities using different names. Because a purchase of more than 5 percent of a class of stock requires disclosure and filings with the SEC, the aggressor often purchases up to 4.9 percent of the target's outstanding shares. This is called the **foothold,** *toehold*, or *creeping tender offer*. An acute target will notice that its stock is being actively traded and that the increased trading is causing its stock to rise in value. The target might thus suspect an aggressor is planning a takeover, but it might not know the identity of the aggressor at this time. The target could begin adopting defensive strategies to ward off the anticipated aggressor.

Foothold
Acquisition of up to 4.9 percent of a target's stock (also called a *toehold* or *creeping tender offer*)

The Tender Offer.   Rather than continuing to purchase shares anonymously on the open market, after it obtains its toehold, the aggressor may publicly announce a cash offer for as much of the target's stock as it needs to acquire all or majority control, in this case, 45.2 percent of the target's stock (45.2 percent + 4.9 percent = 50.1 percent). This is a tender offer. Because consummation of the offer would result in the aggressor owning more than 5 percent of a class of stock, the aggressor must comply with reporting and disclosure requirements of § 14(d) of the 1934 Act. The aggressor must file the appropriate statement with the SEC, entitled Schedule TO (for "tender offer"), identifying itself, the source of the money being used to purchase the target's stock, how much of the target's stock it owns, and any plans it has for the target (such as liquidating it, selling its assets, merging it with another corporation, and so forth) in the event the tender offer is successful. Schedule TO is filed with the SEC on the date of the commencement of the tender offer. A copy must be delivered to the target and to any exchange (such as NYSE) on which the target's stock is traded. Tender offer materials must also be delivered to the target's stockholders at the time the bidder provides them with detailed instructions on how to tender their shares. The company that is the subject of the takeover must file its response to the takeover with the SEC and provide a copy of the response to its shareholders within ten business days.

The aggressor may continue to purchase stock during the tender offer period. Announcement of the tender offer is often done by advertisement or press release and is said to put the target "into play." According to the SEC, "a tender offer is a broad solicitation by a company or a third party to purchase a substantial percentage of a company's . . . shares or units for a limited period of time. The offer is at a fixed price, usually at a premium over the current market price, and is customarily contingent on shareholders tendering a fixed number of their shares or units."

The tender offer itself is a public announcement made directly to the target's shareholders, specifying the identity of the bidder, the price at which the aggressor will purchase the stock, the amount of stock it wishes to purchase, the date by which the shares must be tendered by the target's shareholders, and the identification of the place where the shares are to be tendered. For example, the aggressor may offer to buy 45.2 percent of the target's stock, at $43 per share, the offer to expire in 45 business days. The federal statute governing takeovers, the Williams Act, requires that the tender offer remain open for at least 20 business days. Shareholders must be given a right to withdraw their tenders, and all shareholders must be treated equally.

If the aggressor acquires 45.2 percent of the stock, it will have sufficient power to replace the majority of the target's board of directors and thereby effectively control the target corporation. If insufficient shares are tendered to give the aggressor 45.2 percent of the target's stock, the aggressor will return all the tendered shares and might decide not to proceed. At this point, the aggressor has invested only the amount of its toehold and some costs in attempting the takeover.

During the tender offer period, another aggressor corporation might enter the fray and offer to buy the toehold from the first aggressor. The first aggressor may sell this to the second at a substantial profit. The second aggressor will then proceed with the takeover.

Setting the price for the tender offer is highly complex. The aggressor needs to make the offer high enough to induce shareholders to tender their shares yet not so high as to be excessive and wasteful. Many tender offers range from 30 percent to 50 percent above the market price of the stock.

Tender offers can be partial in nature, in which case the bidder attempts to acquire only a majority interest in the corporation, or they can be full, in which case the bidder offers to buy all of the outstanding shares of the corporation. The bidder may offer cash only or a combination of cash and its own shares.

If the shares tendered exceed the amount specified in the tender offer, the offer is **oversubscribed.** To avoid a stampede by shareholders to sell their stock without adequate time for reflection, the Williams Act requires that an oversubscribed tender offer must be effected on a pro rata basis rather than a "first come, first served" basis. Thus, the aggressor cannot simply elect to purchase the first shares tendered to it. For example, if the aggressor needs to purchase 10 million shares, and 12 million shares are actually tendered, it cannot buy the first 10 million

Oversubscription
Situation in which bidder acquires more stock than it offered to buy in its tender offer

tendered; it must purchase 10,000,000/12,000,000 (or ⅚) of each tender. Alternatively, the aggressor can elect to purchase all 12 million shares tendered.

During the period the tender offer is open, the aggressor cannot negotiate with individual shareholders or make purchases other than according to the tender offer. Once the tender offer period expires, however, it can negotiate privately with shareholders in attempts to acquire more shares.

Risk arbitrage
Speculation in target's stock

When a tender offer is made and the target is put into play, other investors may begin trading in the target's shares. For example, as soon as the tender offer is announced, speculators might begin buying the target's stock so that they can then tender the stock to the aggressor and make an immediate profit. This behavior is called **risk arbitrage,** and although it is hugely speculative, it can also be hugely lucrative. The danger to the risk arbitrageurs (the *arbs*), of course, is that insufficient shares will be tendered or some other force might make the aggressor's bid unsuccessful, leaving the risk arbitrageur holding stock that it paid dearly for in a target that is still weak and poorly managed.

Post-Tender Offer Transactions.   If the aggressor abandons its takeover bid, much of the stock of the target might be in the hands of the risk arbitrageurs or other speculators who recently bought stock in the target only to make a profit and not for any desire to control the target, improve its management, or make it more profitable. Thus, if the tender offer is unsuccessful, either the aggressor or some other third party may deal directly with the risk arbitrageurs and other speculators to purchase the target's stock from them. This practice is called a **street sweep,** once again, the reference being to Wall Street.

Street sweep
Purchase of stock from speculators after an unsuccessful tender offer

If the tender offer is successful and the aggressor acquires a controlling interest in the target, the aggressor usually thereafter attempts to gain even more stock, with the ideal being ownership of 100 percent of the target's outstanding stock. No matter how attractive the offer is, however, some individual shareholders will refuse to sell their shares. To obtain 100 percent ownership, the aggressor will proceed with a **mop up** or *back end* **transaction,** essentially a merger, to obtain total ownership of the target's stock. Because there are so few shareholders left, they are powerless to stop a merger initiated by the target with its controlling shares of stock. Although these holdouts might have appraisal rights as dissenters, often the appraisal right is not as attractive as the tender offer, thus encouraging shareholders to accept promptly the terms of the tender offer rather than being forced to sell their shares at a less attractive price later.

Mop up transaction
Attempt by bidder to secure 100 percent ownership in target after tender offer is complete (also called a *back end transaction*)

Ideally, bidders would like to obtain at least 90 percent of the target's shares in the tender offer so that they can quickly gain the remaining 10 percent through a short-form merger. SEC rules allow bidders to give a "subsequent offering period" (after expiration of the initial 20-day tender offer period) to the target's shareholders to give them a second opportunity to tender their shares now that they understand that the takeover is inevitable. So long as the bidder's original tender offer materials disclose that there may be a subsequent offering period and explain its procedures, bidders can then use the procedure to gain additional shares and perhaps effect a short-form merger.

Proxy Fights.   As an alternative to a hostile takeover, an aggressor corporation might solicit the target's shareholders with a proposal that they vote for the aggressor's management team. This is the **proxy fight;** both management and the aggressor will be attempting to obtain proxies from shareholders for election of their own directors. If the aggressor is successful, it effectively obtains control of the target through controlling the majority of the board. Once it has control of the board, it may negotiate a consensual merger. In general, it is more difficult to obtain control of a corporation through a proxy fight than through a tender offer, primarily because it is difficult to induce shareholders to vote out management. Shareholders would much rather be induced with the profit they can make by tendering their shares at above-market prices to the aggressor. See Chapter Eleven for additional information on proxy fights or contests.

Proxy fight
Competition between corporate management and an aggressor to take over board of directors

Defensive Strategies.   Corporations have developed a number of strategies to avoid being taken over. These **takeover defenses** may be developed even before a tender offer is made, to discourage a takeover bid in the first place, or may be adopted after a tender offer has been made, in an attempt by the target to defeat the aggressor. In general, the response of the target's management to the takeover bid is subject to the duty of due care. Directors of the target often set up takeover committees to evaluate the relative merits of the takeover to ensure that the board fulfills its duties. Thus, actions by the target's directors that are directed only to perpetuating their own status, rewarding themselves, and entrenching their positions, rather than promoting the best interests of the corporation and its shareholders, might be breaches of fiduciary duty.

Takeover defenses
Strategies implemented by target to thwart a takeover

Many state statutes also operate to discourage takeovers. For example, Del. Code Ann. tit. 8, § 203 imposes a moratorium for three years on combinations or mergers between the target and anyone who acquires 15 percent or more of the corporation's stock, unless the board of directors of the target had approved the transaction or the bidder owns more than 85 percent of the target's stock. Thus, once a bidder acquires 15 percent of a target's stock, it generally cannot engage in any back-end merger for three years.

Pre-Tender Offer Defenses.   Provisions instituted before a takeover bid are generally designed to make the target less attractive to would-be aggressors. These provisions are usually called **shark repellents** or *porcupine provisions.* Among them are the following:

Shark repellents
Anti-takeover measures implemented before a takeover bid (also called *porcupine provisions*)

- A staggered board of directors might, be introduced together with a provision that directors can only be removed "for cause." This approach means that it could take the aggressor several years to acquire control of the target's board. Of course, if the bidder acquires all or nearly all of the outstanding shares, it can amend the articles to "unstagger" the board.
- The corporation may grant directors, officers, and key employees **golden parachutes** requiring that these individuals, if ousted, must be compensated in some extraordinary amount. The golden parachutes might make the takeover too expensive for the aggressor, as these contractual requirements must be satisfied by the aggressor before installing its own key people. Severance contracts for lower level employees are sometimes called **tin parachutes** (or even *lead parachutes*).
- The target can make itself unattractive by selling off certain assets or divisions, or distributing a huge cash dividend to its shareholders. Thus, the

Golden parachute
Highly favorable financial packages awarded to senior managers in event of a takeover or their retirement

Tin parachute
Financial packages awarded to junior managers in event of a takcover or their retirement; less favorable than golden parachutes

Poison pill
An anti-takeover measure triggered by a tender offer at which time the target's shareholders are given additional rights (also called *shareholder rights plan*)

Dead-hand poison pill
Poison pill that can only be deactivated by the directors who established it (also called a *continuing director plan*)

Slow-hand poison pill
Poison pill that bars newly elected directors from deactivating it for some period of time

No-hand poison pill
Poison pill that cannot be removed by any director if control of the board changes hands

Chewable poison pill
Poison pill that is of short duration and is triggered only when a bidder buys significant numbers of shares

aggressor will be forced to acquire a cash-poor target with few desirable assets.

- The target might adopt a **poison pill** defense, also known as a *shareholder rights plan*. This defense is extremely popular and has been adopted by about 60 percent of S & P 500 companies. The poison pill defense is implemented as part of an anti-takeover program and is triggered by a tender offer made by a bidder. Once the tender offer is announced or an acquisition reaches certain limits (usually 15 percent), the target's shareholders are automatically given additional rights, including increased voting rights, the right to acquire additional shares or bonds of the target at bargain prices (often 50 percent below market value), or the right to turn in shares for cash if the takeover is successful. These rights granted to the shareholders make acquisition of control by a bidder far more difficult and nearly prohibitively expensive.

  Historically, poison pills have been adopted by boards of directors without shareholder approval. They usually include both "flip-in" and "flip-out" components. A flip-in clause allows shareholders to purchase stock in their own company (at a discount) once the bidder acquires a certain percentage of the company's shares; a flip-out clause (also called a *flip-over* clause) allows shareholders to purchase stock (at a discount) in the bidder if a takeover occurs.

  Because aggressors might seize control of a board of directors and then deactivate the poison pill to avoid the shareholders' rights, targets have adopted the following variations or refinements to poison pill defenses.

- A **dead-hand poison pill** is one that can only be deactivated by the directors who established it (or their designated successors). The dead-hand pill is also called a *continuing director plan*. In many instances directors eliminate the dead-hand by redeeming the purchase rights from shareholders by paying them a small fee. The dead-hand pill protects the target's current board because it can only be deactivated by those who continue after a takeover. Some states, notably Delaware, have held that dead-hand pills are invalid because they result in two different classes of directors: those who can deactivate the dead-hand and those who cannot. Moreover, dead-hand pills wrest too much control from shareholders.

- A **slow-hand poison pill** is one that bars newly elected directors from deactivating or redeeming the pill for some limited period of time, often six months. Some states, including Delaware, have also held slow-hand pills invalid on the basis that they impermissibly interfere with directors' abilities to manage the corporation.

- A **no-hand poison** pill provides that no director can remove the pill if control of the board changes hands.

- A **chewable poison pill** is one that is more palatable to shareholders and is one of short duration (often five years rather than the usual ten-year term of a standard poison pill), is triggered only when a significant number of shares are purchased by a bidder (often 20 percent rather than the trigger threshold of 10 percent or 15 percent for most poison pills), and allows a takeover to proceed if it is fully financed and all cash, even if the incumbent board opposes it. Chewable poison pills are a recent innovation that appeal to shareholders.

In sum, poison pills are devices favored by management that are used to fend off takeovers, but there is some concern that they are used by an incumbent board to preserve its own power rather than for the best interests of the shareholders and the corporation. Thus, the enforceability of dead-hand, slow-hand, and no-hand poison pills is subject to much debate and uncertainty. In general, if poison pills and other defensive measures are adopted in good faith and are reasonable in relation to the threat by the bidder, they are acceptable and do not constitute breaches of the directors' fiduciary duties.

Shareholders often dislike poison pills because they might in fact thwart a takeover that the shareholders desire because the acquiring corporation could be offering a premium price for the shares. In recent years, activist shareholders have been successful in getting corporate management to give them a voice in decisions relating to poison pills. For example, any poison pill adopted by General Electric Co. must be ratified by its shareholders within 12 months. Other companies have obtained shareholder approval before adopting a poison pill plan.

Post-Tender Offer Defenses.   Once the tender offer has been made, the target can implement a variety of defenses in an attempt to thwart the aggressor. Some of these defenses are as follows:

- The target might attempt to find another more compatible corporation with which to merge. The third party is called the *white knight* because its function is to save the target from the enemy aggressor, often called the *black knight.*
- The target might turn the tables and make a tender offer to acquire the aggressor. This is the *Pac-Man* defense, because its effect is to eat up the opposition.
- The target could begin selling off some of its most valuable assets to make itself less attractive to the aggressor. This is the *crown jewel* defense.
- The target could engage in a *scorched earth* battle by selling off its crown jewels, loading the target up with debt, or through an immediate and sudden departure of all of the target's management, in an effort to avoid capture.
- The target might use the *Jonestown* defense and effectively commit suicide by going into bankruptcy to avoid a takeover.
- The target could quickly purchase another corporation engaged in a business competitive to the aggressor's business, thereby creating antitrust problems for the aggressor.
- The management of the target might enter into a so-called *suicide pact* or *people pill*, whereby managers agree that if any one of them is fired or demoted after a takeover, they will all resign. Such an en masse walkout leaves the aggressor without any stability or continuity in management.
- The target could attempt a *self-tender*, a purchase of its own shares on the open market or from its own shareholders, to prevent the aggressor from acquiring control. Such a self-tender is subject to various SEC rules imposing disclosure requirements on the target much the same way that disclosure is required of an aggressor.

Most experts advise that companies keep a watchful eye on potential adversaries to avoid being taken over. Some measures recommended include early warning programs to detect stock purchases made in a company, working with corporate counsel to implement anti-takeover measures, and identification and monitoring of companies that might target a company. Although such measures might not absolutely prevent a takeover, they could discourage a bidder from bypassing the board of directors and appealing directly to the shareholders through a tender offer.

Takeover Terminology. You might already have noticed that much of the terminology used in describing hostile takeovers and the defenses thereto has war-like connotations. First, the aggressor builds up a war chest to acquire the target. The target institutes a number of defensive strategies to avoid being captured, including adopting poison pill defenses, suicide pacts, and scorched earth tactics. A number of other colorful terms are also used in the jargon of hostile takeovers. Among them are the following:

Bear hug: An approach by the aggressor to the target after the aggressor has acquired its toehold. The aggressor meets with the target's management and makes clear that if the target does not cooperate in the transaction, the aggressor will pursue a hostile takeover. The target is often offered a generous price per share to induce it to cooperate.

Blitz: A "lightning," no-notice strike against a target sufficiently forceful that the target is so overwhelmed it cannot adopt any defenses. Blitzes and Saturday night specials (discussed later) are less common due to Williams Act requirements that a tender offer be open for at least 20 days.

Greenmail: A kind of legal corporate blackmail in which an aggressor threatens to take over a target, and then sells the toehold back to the target at an inflated price. The target thus "buys" peace from the aggressor who has made money at *not* being successful at its takeover attempt. To discourage greenmail, high taxes are imposed on greenmail money. Moreover, overpaying a troublesome investor for his shares might raise questions about the corporation's use of its financial resources. Under some state laws, greenmail is illegal.

Killer bees: Attorneys, advisors, and public relations teams retained by the target to fight off the takeover.

Midnight raid: A raid by an aggressor after the afternoon closing of the New York Stock Exchange and concluded before the resumption of trading in the morning by securing firm commitments from large institutional shareholders of the target to sell sufficient stock so that the aggressor can obtain control of the target before the target is even aware a raid has begun.

Nuclear war: A hostile takeover involving numerous large publicly traded companies.

Preemptive strike: An extremely attractive offer made by an aggressor with the intent of obtaining immediate control of a target.

Saturday night special: A raid by an aggressor made over a weekend so that the target has difficulty marshaling its management forces. Some experts recommend that companies identify and establish a permanent takeover team, even before a tender offer is made, specifically to ward off and respond to a Saturday night special.

Standstill agreement: An agreement by an aggressor not to purchase any more shares of the target for some specified period of time, perhaps several years. The standstill agreement is usually part of the peace pact entered into between an aggressor and the target when the aggressor accepts greenmail to stay away from the target.

Stock watch: An early warning system employed by corporations to detect fluctuations in the market that might warn them of action by aggressors.

Strike team: The aggressor's legal counsel, investment advisors, public relations teams, and so forth.

Although many of these defensive strategies seem extreme, courts have generally viewed them in light of the business judgment rule, meaning that if directors in good faith believe that a takeover is detrimental to the company or its shareholders, they may take any step that is not illegal to counter the takeover, and in the absence of bad faith or fraud, their business judgment will not be second-guessed by courts.

8. Leveraged Buy-Outs and Share Repurchases

A corporation may decide to "go private" through a transaction called the **leveraged buy-out** (LBO). To avoid a takeover by an aggressor, management of a target might offer to purchase all of its publicly held shares from its own shareholders. Because of the enormous amount of cash required to buy out all of the existing shareholders, the money used is borrowed, with management pledging various corporate assets as security or collateral for repayment of the debts. In some instances, a new entity may be created by management and investors. This new entity borrows the money needed for the buy-out and uses the funds to purchase all of the outstanding shares.

Leveraged buy-out
Purchase of a corporation's stock by its managers using borrowed money

In some transactions, after the buy-out is complete and management (and perhaps other investors) owns all of the stock of the corporation, unneeded assets are sold to reduce the corporation's debt. Then the corporation will "go public" by offering shares at a price higher than management paid for the shares when it went private. If successful, this technique results in great profits for management as well as reduction of the corporation's debt. In other instances, the debt taken on by the corporation to finance the buy-out of all shareholders is so crippling the corporation does not survive.

Some companies buy back their own stock on the open market, primarily to increase demand for the shares to push the stock price up. Simultaneously, a stock buyback strategy increases earnings per share because it reduces the number of shares outstanding in the marketplace. These buybacks are usually referred to as **share repurchases.** See Chapter Twelve for further discussion of share repurchases.

Share repurchase
The buying of its own shares on the open market by a corporation; such buybacks often elevate the market value of the remaining shares

9. Governmental Regulation

The federal government has the authority to review mergers and acquisitions under the Clayton Act (15 U.S.C. § 12) to ensure that such transactions do not

Hart-Scott-Rodino Act
Federal statute requiring notification to government before mergers involving certain amounts or parties

impair competition and result in monopolies. Specifically, the **Hart-Scott-Rodino Antitrust Improvements Act** of 1976 (HSR; 15 U.S.C. § 18a) requires that parties to certain merger transactions file premerger notification with the government and wait for a certain period before closing a transaction. The waiting period, generally 30 days, allows the government to review the transaction and take action, if needed, to protect competition. The waiting period can be shortened on request.

Generally, although there are several exceptions, at present, if either party to the proposed transaction has total annual net sales or total assets of at least $130.3 million and the other party has annual net sales or total assets of at least $13 million and, as a result of the transaction, the acquiring party will hold more than $65.2 million of the acquired party's stock or assets, each party must complete a premerger notification form providing certain information about the parties and the transaction and file it with the Federal Trade Commission (FTC) and the Department of Justice. Generally, the FTC reviews mergers in energy, health care, chemicals, computer hardware, biotech, and other industries. The Department of Justice reviews mergers in media and entertainment, financial services and insurance, telecommunications, and travel. Small acquisitions, acquisitions involving small parties, and other types of acquisitions that are less likely to affect competition are excluded from the coverage of HSR and need not be reported. The filing fee ranges from $45,000 for transactions of less than $130.3 million to $280,000 for transactions of $651.7 million or more. If the government does not object to the transaction or does not request additional information, the parties may proceed once the waiting period expires.

In its Annual Report to Congress for 2007, the FTC reported 2,201 transactions. Despite the number of mergers, government challenges remain few. For example, in 2007, the FTC and the Department of Justice together challenged only 34 transactions. When a transaction is challenged, the parties often enter into consent agreements, agreeing to divest certain assets, or they may restructure the transaction or even abandon it. For example, the FTC challenged the $2.8 billion merger of Nestlé and Dreyer's Grand Ice Cream because the proposed acquisition would have substantially lessened competition in the market for premium ice cream. The parties entered into a consent agreement and agreed to divest certain ice cream brands. The FTC may also challenge a consummated merger; in 2003, it ordered a party to unwind a completed acquisition. Fines for HSR violations can run up to $16,000 per day.

E. Domestication and Entity Conversion

Chapter 9 of the MBCA provides a series of procedures allowing corporations to change their state of incorporation and also allowing corporations to become different business structures. For example, a corporation may change its structure and become a limited liability company, as AOL did in 2006, changing from America Online Inc. to AOL LLC.

1. Domestication

Domestication allows a corporation to change its state of incorporation and be governed by the laws of another state. For example, a corporation formed in Pennsylvania may decide to "go public" and prefer to be a Delaware corporation because of the state's flexible and permissive statutes. Similarly, tax savings might justify a change in the state of incorporation. This transaction previously could have been accomplished by a merger whereby the Pennsylvania corporation would create a new corporation in Delaware and then merge the Pennsylvania corporation into it. The MBCA now allows corporations to achieve this result more directly.

As with the other changes in corporate structure discussed in this chapter, the process begins with the board of directors, who adopt a **plan of domestication** that contains the terms and conditions of the transaction, indicates whether any amendments to the articles are necessitated, and specifies the manner and basis of reclassifying shares based on the laws of the new state of domestication. The plan of domestication is then submitted to the shareholders for their approval (with the directors' recommendation that the shareholders approve the plan). The corporation must notify all shareholders (whether or not they are entitled to vote) of the meeting, at which the plan will be submitted for approval, and the notice of the meeting must state its purpose and must include a summary of the plan. Under the MBCA, if a quorum is present, the plan will be approved if more votes are cast in favor of it than against it. Many states, however, require majority approval.

The corporation will then prepare **articles of domestication** (sometimes called a certificate of domestication) and file them with the secretary of state in the new jurisdiction in which the corporation is to be domesticated. Some states require that articles of incorporation be filed as well. The corporation must also surrender its original charter or articles of incorporation in the state in which it had been originally formed.

On completion of the transaction, the corporation will simply have changed its state of incorporation. In nearly every other respect (and except for any amendments it might have been required to adopt by the new state), the corporation remains the same as it was before the domestication.

2. Entity Conversion

MBCA § 9.50 permits corporations to change their structures to unincorporated associations. For example, an Arizona corporation could become a limited liability partnership (LLP) or limited liability company (LLC). Similarly, the reverse could occur: An LLP or LLC may become a corporation. A business corporation may convert to a nonprofit corporation. Such changes are called **entity conversions.**

The process of effecting an entity conversion is nearly identical to that for effecting a domestication. The converting entity must adopt a **plan of entity conversion,** which sets forth the terms and conditions of the conversion, identifies the type of entity the new business will be, and sets forth the manner and basis of

---

Domestication
The changing of a corporation's state of incorporation

Plan of domestication
The plan that provides the terms and conditions of a corporation's change of its state of incorporation

Articles of domestication
The document filed with the state to effect a change of a corporation's state of incorporation

Entity conversion
A business's change of its structure, for example, converting from a corporation to an LLC

Plan of entity conversion
The plan that provides the terms and conditions of a business's change in its structure

converting shares into other interests (or vice versa). For the purposes of this discussion, we will assume that a California corporation is converting to a California LLC. After adoption by the board, the board must submit the plan to the shareholders for their approval (together with the board's recommendation that the shareholders approve the plan). All shareholders must be notified of the meeting at which the plan is to be submitted for approval. The notice must state that the purpose is to consider the plan of entity conversion and must include a copy or summary of the plan. Although most states require approval by a majority of shareholders, the MBCA provides that the plan is approved if more shareholders vote for it than against it. Because some former shareholders might now face personal liability (for example, if a corporation converts to a general partnership), each person who would become subject to such personal liability must sign a separate written consent. Shareholders of a business corporation that is converting to a noncorporate form have appraisal rights. After the conversion has been adopted and approved, **articles of entity conversion** will be prepared and filed with the state. The articles must provide that the plan was duly approved by the shareholders. A corporation that converts to an unincorporated form must then surrender its articles or charter.

> **Articles of entity conversion**
> The document filed with the state to effect a change in a business's structure

As is the case with domestication, entity conversion does not affect the company's contracts, liabilities, and so forth.

Key Features
of Corporate Changes and Combinations

◆ Significant changes to a corporation typically require shareholder approval.

◆ A corporation can amend its articles at any time by resolution by the directors followed by shareholder approval (either by majority or two-thirds vote). Articles of amendment must be filed with the state agency.

◆ A corporation may restate its articles to create one composite document superseding prior amendments; shareholder approval is unnecessary because nothing new is being added to the articles.

◆ Amending corporate bylaws is typically handled by directors without shareholder approval inasmuch as the bylaws regulate only the internal affairs of the corporation.

◆ A merger is the combination of two or more corporations into one corporate entity. The survivor succeeds to all of the business, debts, liabilities, and assets of the extinguished corporation. Shareholders of both corporations must approve the transaction.

◆ A consolidation is the combination of two or more corporations and the formation of an entirely new entity that succeeds to all of the business, debts, liabilities, and assets of the consolidating corporations. Shareholders of both corporations must approve the transaction.

◆ Shareholders who dissent from a merger or consolidation have the right to have their shares appraised and purchased from them at fair value.

- In a share exchange, the target's shareholders exchange their shares for cash or shares in the acquiring corporation.
- As an alternative to a merger, one corporation can purchase all or substantially all of another's assets. Liabilities are generally not purchased.
- One corporation can purchase a majority or all of another corporation's stock as a means of gaining control of a corporation. If the acquisition is consensual, all directors and the seller's shareholders will vote. In a hostile acquisition or takeover, the bidder bypasses the target's management and appeals directly to the shareholders.
- Some takeovers are regulated by the Securities Exchange Act of 1934. Once a bidder or aggressor acquires 5 percent of another corporation's stock, it must file a § 13(d) statement with the SEC providing information about the proposed takeover.
- If a bidder makes a public offer offering to purchase more than 5 percent of a corporation's stock, a § 14(d) statement must be filed with the SEC providing information about the offer and offeror. Such a public offer is called a tender offer.
- Corporations may enact a variety of defenses to ward off a takeover. Some are put into place even before the attempted takeover. One of the most popular defenses is a poison pill or shareholder rights plan, by which shareholders are given extra voting rights or rights to purchase more shares at fire sale prices once a tender offer is announced. Other defenses are implemented after a tender offer has been made.
- Corporations may change their state of incorporation (domestication) and may convert to another business structure, such as converting to an LLC.

F.   Role of Paralegal

There are numerous tasks for paralegals engaged in changes to corporations or working in the field of mergers and acquisitions. The work is fast-paced, stressful, challenging, and document-intensive. Much of the work is referred to as **due diligence** review, meaning careful review of documents and transactions to ensure a transaction is appropriate, that parties have fulfilled all of their commitments, and that the transaction is in compliance with all applicable federal and state laws. Due diligence work involves investigation of the parties to transactions, review of all documents involved, and evaluation of risks and benefits of the transaction. Paralegals are routinely involved in significant due diligence work. Some of the typical tasks paralegals are involved in include the following:

Due diligence
Careful review of documents and transactions to ensure they are appropriate for a party and in compliance with all pertinent laws

1. Drafting minutes of directors' meetings or written consent actions authorizing amendment of the articles of incorporation, restatement of the articles of incorporation, or amendment of the bylaws.
2. Drafting notices of shareholders' meetings called to consider and vote on amendments of the articles of incorporation; preparing the minutes of shareholders' meetings.
3. Preparing and filing articles of amendment and restated articles.

4. Preparing amended bylaws.
5. Drafting the minutes of directors' meetings or written consent actions authorizing and recommending mergers, consolidations, share exchanges, sales of assets, acquisitions of stock domestications, and entity conversions; researching exceptions to the requirement of shareholder approval for such structural changes; preparing notices for shareholders' meetings called to consider and vote on such transactions; preparing minutes of meetings at which shareholders voted on structural changes.
6. Reviewing and analyzing the plan of merger, plan of consolidation, plan of share exchange, or agreement for asset or stock purchase. Preparing a list of "to do" items and collecting various documents and records needed for the closing of the transaction, for example, reviewing pleadings for any litigation involving the acquired corporation, its directors, officers, or key employees.
7. Preparing and filing articles of merger, consolidation, share exchange, domestication, or entity conversion.
8. Preparing various documents needed to complete transactions, including assignments of various assets, trademarks, and copyrights; deeds for the transfer of real estate; notices for the SEC; premerger HSR notices to the FTC and the Department of Justice; new stock certificates to be issued to shareholders of extinguished corporations; notices relating to appraisal rights, and so forth.
9. Assembling documents for execution by the appropriate parties.
10. Arranging for the closing transaction, ensuring staff is available to assist in photocopying or faxing, and ensuring a notary public is available to notarize signatures, if needed.
11. Preparing and compiling the closing binders so they contain all documents pertinent to the transaction, including the letter of intent, corporate authorizations, the plan or agreement, and all exhibits to such documents.
12. Conducting postclosing checks to ensure all documents have been signed by all appropriate parties, necessary filings have been effected with the secretary of state, recording of assignments or deeds has been accomplished with the appropriate local or federal agencies, and all documents required to be delivered by the other parties have been received.
13. Ordering new corporate supplies such as stock certificates and the corporate seal.

Case Illustration
Business Judgment Rule Applies to Directors' Actions in Opposing a Takeover

Case: *Panter v. Marshall Field & Co.*, 646 F.2d 271 (7th Cir. 1981)

Facts: Shareholders sued their corporation, alleging that it harmed them by fending off a hostile takeover that would have been profitable for them. Among other complaints, the share-holders alleged that their directors acquired other stores to make the corporation less attractive to the bidder. The district court granted the corporation's motion for a directed verdict.

Holding: The court of appeals affirmed. Not every effort to thwart a takeover can be condemned. The test is whether the board fairly and reasonably exercises its business judgment to protect the corporation and its shareholders. The shareholders' contention that their corporation purchased five other stores to make itself less attractive to the bidder is the type of "Monday-morning quarterbacking" that the business judgment rule is intended to prevent. The shareholders showed no evidence that the defendant directors engaged in manipulative conduct, self-dealing, bad faith, or fraud. Thus, even if the desire to fend off the bidder was among the motives of the board in entering the transactions, because the shareholders did not prove that such a motive was a sole or primary purpose, the business judgment rule will protect the directors' decision.

◆   ◆   ◆

WEB RESOURCES

The most important Web resources are the state and federal statutes relating to amending and restating articles and corporate changes, such as mergers and consolidations.

Because many states have posted their forms relating to amending and restating articles and forms for articles of merger, consolidation, and share exchange on their Web sites, important Web resources are the home pages of the various secretaries of state. See Appendix A for the specific Web address for each of the state's secretaries of state. Other alternatives follow.

Federal and state statutes:	www.law.cornell.edu (The Securities Exchange Act of 1934 and the Hart-Scott-Rodino Act are located in Title 15 of the United States Code.)
Secretaries of state:	www.nass.org
Securities information:	www.sec.gov (The SEC's site offers current SEC rules, enforcement actions, and EDGAR, the database of registration statements, periodic reports, and § 13(d) and § 14(d)

	statements. Forms can be accessed by company name, type of document, or date of filing.) www.law.uc.edu/CCL(The Securities Lawyer's Deskbook provides the full text of federal securities laws and regulations as well as forms.)
Hart-Scott-Rodino information:	www.ftc.gov
Company information:	www.hoovers.com
Forms:	www.megalaw.com
	www.siccode.com/forms.php
	(These sites provide forms for resolutions and minutes of meetings authorizing amending articles and bylaws, restating articles, and forms for mergers, consolidations, articles of domestication and conversion, and so forth.)

Discussion Questions

Fact Scenario. TelCom Inc. is a telecommunications company incorporated in Delaware in 2000. Its stock is traded on NYSE and it has 20,000 shareholders and 100,000 shares outstanding. H & A Corp. is a Delaware corporation that has 50,000 shares outstanding. Its stock is not publicly traded. Use the MBCA to answer the following questions.

1. TelCom has decided to change its agent for service of process and to change its name to VisiCom Corp. How will the corporation go about making these changes? Discuss any shareholder approval that may be required.

2. H & A has amended its certificate of incorporation several times, and it is difficult to read. What should H & A do to ensure its certificate is easily readable? Discuss any shareholder approval that may be required.

3. VisiCom has decided to change its fiscal year. How will the corporation go about making this change?

4. VisiCom has decided to acquire H & A. At the conclusion of the transaction, VisiCom will continue to exist but H & A will not. What is this transaction called? Who will vote on it? What will happen to shareholders who disapprove of the transaction? What will happen to a debt that H & A owes to Bank of America?

5. Assume that VisiCom decided to acquire certain assets owned by H & A rather than acquiring the company. What is this transaction called? Who will vote on it? What will happen to shareholders who oppose the transaction?

6. Assume that VisiCom has made a public offer that, if consummated, will result in it owning 8 percent of H & A's stock. What is this called and what requirements, if any, are imposed on VisiCom by making this offer?

7. H & A's contracts with its officers grant them significant amounts of cash and various benefits if they lose their positions as a result of a takeover. What are these provisions called and how do they thwart a takeover?

8. Why might shareholders of H & A dislike a poison pill provision?

9. What government regulations exist to ensure that VisiCom's transaction with H & A does not hinder competition in the communications sector?

10. VisiCom has decided to change its state of incorporation to New York. What is this called and how will VisiCom effect this?

Net Worth

1. What is the fee in Florida for a profit corporation to file articles of amendment?
2. What is the fee in Ohio if a corporation amends its articles by shareholder vote?
3. What is the fee in California if a corporation restates its articles of incorporation?
4. A Florida corporation has decided to change its status to a limited liability company. What fee must be paid to the secretary of state?
5. Access the Web site for the SEC and select "Fast Answers." What is a merger?
6. Access the FTC Web site and locate information about the Hart-Scott-Rodino Act.
   a. May an HSR filing be submitted electronically?
   b. Assume that the size of a merger is valued at $300 million. What filing fee must be paid?

15

◆ ◆ ◆

Qualification of Foreign Corporations

◆ ◆ ◆

CHAPTER OVERVIEW

Corporations may be formed in one state and yet do business in others. You have seen that many large corporations have elected to incorporate in Delaware due to its moderate fees and taxes, extensive case law, and permissive statutes. Most of these corporations transact business in several other states.

For a foreign corporation to lawfully conduct business in a state other than its state of incorporation, it must "qualify" or become authorized to do business there. In general, most states require that the foreign corporation file an application to transact business, appoint an agent for service of process, and pay the appropriate filing fees and taxes. The corporation will then receive permission from the secretary of state to conduct business. Failure to qualify may result in fines being imposed on the corporation or a refusal to allow the corporation to maintain an action in that state. When the corporation ceases to conduct business in a state, it should formally withdraw from doing business as a foreign corporation.

A. Basis for Qualification

A corporation incorporated in a state is a **domestic corporation** in that state. Because recognition of corporate status is granted only by each state's secretary of state, the corporation has no legal existence beyond the borders of the state in which it was incorporated. To conduct intrastate business (business conducted wholly within the borders of a single state) in other states, the corporation must be granted authority; it must qualify to do business in those states. A corporation

Domestic corporation
Corporation doing business in the state in which it was formed

431

doing business in states other than its state of incorporation is a **foreign corporation** to those states.

The qualification requirement imposed on foreign corporations provides a way for states to protect their citizens. Requiring qualification ensures that citizens have some basic information about the corporation (by reviewing its articles of incorporation filed in its state of incorporation) and are able to sue the corporation and serve its registered agent in the state.

The decision to conduct business in other states begins with the board of directors. Upon seeing the need for expansion into other states, the board will pass a resolution (or act by written consent) authorizing the officers to take any needed action so the corporation can transact business in another state or states. The decision to expand into other jurisdictions should be carefully thought out, and the corporation's name should have been registered in the foreign state so it is available to the corporation for use (see Figure 15-1) or the corporation may have incorporated a subsidiary to serve as a "name-saver" for the same purpose.

Just as corporations must qualify to do business in states other than their state of incorporation, so also must limited partnerships, limited liability partnerships, and limited liability companies. (See discussion in Chapters Four, Five, and Six.) Most states provide the pertinent forms for qualifications for these entities.

Remember also, as discussed in Chapter Fourteen, that a corporation can change its state of incorporation by a process called domestication.

B.　Transacting Business

Generally, most state statutes provide that a foreign corporation cannot **"transact business"** within the state until it obtains a certificate of authority from the secretary of state. The critical question, and one that has resulted in much litigation, is what particular activities are considered transacting business such that qualification is required? What if a Minnesota corporation has its annual shareholders' meeting in California? Is that transacting business? What if the Minnesota corporation wishes to sue an individual who has moved from Minnesota to Wisconsin? Must the corporation qualify to do business to institute the litigation in Wisconsin?

To reduce litigation over this issue, many states have enacted statutes enumerating certain activities that may be engaged in by a foreign corporation without having to qualify in the state. MBCA § 15.01(b) states that the following activities do not constitute transacting business:

1. Maintaining, defending, or settling any proceeding;
2. Holding meetings of the board of directors or shareholders or carrying on other activities concerning internal corporate affairs;
3. Maintaining bank accounts;
4. Maintaining offices or agencies for the transfer, exchange, and registration of the corporation's own securities or maintaining trustees or depositories with respect to those securities;
5. Selling through independent contractors;

Foreign corporation
Corporation doing business in a state other than the state in which it was formed

Transacting business
Generally, statutory list of activities in which a corporation can engage in a foreign state without being required to qualify to do business therein

---

FIGURE 15-1
Alabama Foreign Corporation Name Application

STATE OF ALABAMA

**APPLICATION FOR REGISTRATION
OF FOREIGN CORPORATE NAME**

TO THE SECRETARY OF STATE OF THE STATE OF ALABAMA,

PURSUANT TO THE PROVISIONS OF THE ALABAMA BUSINESS CORPORATION ACT, THE UNDERSIGNED HEREBY APPLIES FOR THE REGISTRATION OF ITS CORPORATE NAME THROUGH DECEMBER 31, 20_____ AND SUBMITS THE FOLLOWING STATEMENT.

1. The exact name of the Corporation (Alabama law requires the corporate name to include "Corporation," "Corp," "Incorporated" or "Inc."):

   _____

2. The Corporation is incorporated under the laws of the state of _____.

3. The date of its incorporation is _____.

4. The business in which it is engaged is:

   _____

   _____

   _____

5. This application is accompanied by: (1) a certificate of existence executed by the official having custody of the records pertaining to corporations; and (2) a registration fee of $ _____. *

* **There is a fee of one dollar for each month, or a fraction thereof between the date of filing such application and December 31 of the calendar year in which such application is filed, but not less than five dollars.**

I understand that the Office of the Secretary of State does not assume any responsibility for the availability of the corporate name requested or for any duplication which may occur.

Date: _____

_____
Type or Print Corporate Officer's Name and Title

_____
Signature of Officer

MAIL APPLICATION WITH THE APPROPRIATE FILING FEE TO:
SECRETARY OF STATE, CORPORATIONS DIVISION, POST OFFICE BOX 5616, MONTGOMERY, ALABAMA 36103-5616
(334)242-5324

Rev. 4/2000

6. Soliciting or obtaining orders, whether by mail or through employees or agents or otherwise, if the orders require acceptance outside the state before they become contracts;
7. Creating or acquiring indebtedness, mortgages, and security interests in real or personal property;
8. Securing or collecting debts or enforcing mortgages and security interests in property securing the debts;
9. Owning, without more, real or personal property;
10. Conducting an isolated transaction that is completed within 30 days and that is not one in the course of repeated transactions of a like nature; and
11. Transacting business in interstate commerce.

This list is not exhaustive, and other activities might also not constitute "transacting business" such that qualification would not be necessary.

Some states have similar lists, but others provide little statutory guidance as to what activities constitute "transacting business." In such instances, case law from the state will need to be analyzed to determine what sorts of activities have been considered in the past to be "transacting business." Because qualifying is a rather straightforward procedure, any doubts regarding the issue should be resolved in favor of qualification. Qualification will, however, subject the corporation to service of process in that state as well as to various reporting requirements, fees, and taxes.

C. Procedures in Qualification

Qualifying to transact business
Process of seeking permission from foreign jurisdiction to do business therein

All states have statutes setting forth the requirements for **qualification** of foreign corporations. Most states have forms available from the secretary of state's office. The requirements vary slightly from state to state; however, most states require that detailed information be contained in an application by a foreign corporation for authority to transact business. MBCA § 15.03 requires the following information in the application:

- *Name.* The name of the foreign corporation must comply with the statutes of the state in which it seeks authority to transact business. Thus, it might need to include a corporate signal such as "Inc." or "Corp." Moreover, the name cannot be the same as or confusingly similar to that of a domestic corporation of the state or another foreign corporation already authorized to do business in the state. If the name is not available, the corporation may have to operate under an assumed or fictitious name. To reduce the chances of such an unwelcome possibility, the corporation should register its name in any states in which it intends to do business in the future or set up a name-saver subsidiary in those states so its name will be available for future use. (See Chapter Nine for discussion of name registration and name-savers.) Alternatively, the corporation might be able to secure approval from the other corporation to use a similar name.

- *State of incorporation.* Identification of the state under whose law the foreign corporation is incorporated is also necessary. This information is required so potential investors can conduct investigation of the foreign corporation.
- *Date of incorporation and duration.* The application must include the date of incorporation and the period of duration for the corporation.
- *Address and registered agent.* The application must provide the street addresses of the foreign corporation's principal office. Its registered office in the state in which it is qualifying and the name of the registered agent at that office are also required. A qualified foreign corporation must maintain a registered office in each state in which it transacts business. The registered agent may be an individual who resides in the state or a domestic corporation or another qualified foreign corporation. The function of the registered agent is to receive service of process and other notices or documents. Most statutes provide that if there is no registered agent or no registered agent can be readily found, the secretary of state of the foreign state will receive service of process on behalf of the foreign corporation. Many corporation service companies provide their services to corporations to act as registered agents for foreign corporations. CT Corporation acts as the registered agent for more than 200,000 corporations. A list of service companies is provided at the end of Chapter Nine.
- *Identities of directors and officers.* The names and usual business addresses of the corporation's current officers and directors must be provided. This information can be used by potential investors to investigate the backgrounds of the principals of the corporation before investing in the corporation.

Other states may impose additional requirements, such as requiring a description of the business the foreign corporation proposes doing in the state, an identification of the value of the assets of the corporation and its liabilities, or description of its stock.

The application must usually be accompanied by a **certificate of good standing** (sometimes called a *certificate of existence*) issued by the secretary of state of the state of incorporation. This is obtained from the state of incorporation upon request and payment of a fee. The secretary of state will check various state records to ensure the corporation is in *good standing*, meaning that it has paid its taxes and complied with any reporting or other requirements. This certificate will be presented to the foreign state as a method of assuring it that the foreign corporation will comply with the foreign state's tax, reporting, and other requirements. (See Figure 15-2 for the application for certificate of authority to transact business in Nevada.) Some states require that the qualifying corporation provide a certified copy of its articles of incorporation from its state of incorporation.

Upon its filing with the secretary of state, the application will be examined to ensure it complies with the statutory requirements and that the requisite filing fee has been paid. The secretary of state will then issue a certificate of authority. The foreign corporation may then transact business so long as it adheres to the requirements of the foreign state.

Certificate of good standing
Document issued by state of incorporation verifying corporation is in compliance with state requirements (also called *certificate of existence*)

FIGURE 15-2
Nevada Foreign Corporation Application

ROSS MILLER
Secretary of State
206 North Carson Street
Carson City, Nevada 89701-4299
(775) 684 5708
Website: www.nvsos.gov

Qualification to do Business in Nevada
(PURSUANT TO NRS CHAPTER 80)

USE BLACK INK ONLY - DO NOT HIGHLIGHT   ABOVE SPACE IS FOR OFFICE USE ONLY

1. Name of Corporation: (must be the same as shown on the certificate of existence)	
2. State of Incorporation:	
3. Registered Agent for Service of Process: (check only one box)	☐ Commercial Registered Agent: _____ Name ☐ Noncommercial Registered Agent (name and address below) **OR** ☐ Office or Position with Entity (name and address below) Name of Noncommercial Registered Agent **OR** Name of Title of Office or Other Position with Entity _____ _____ Nevada ___ Street Address City Zip Code _____ _____ Nevada ___ Mailing Address (if different from street address) City Zip Code
4. Authorized Stock: (set forth the total authorized stock indicating number of par shares, par value per share and/or number of no par shares; mark appropriate box if entity is a nonprofit corporation with or without stock; submit required documentation to support statement; stock statement must match documentation exactly)	Total Authorized Stock: _____ (a) Number of shares *with* par value: _____ (b) Par value per share: $ _____ (c) Number of shares *without* par value: _____ If a Nonprofit Entity: ☐ This is a nonprofit entity *with* authorized stock, as listed above. ☐ This entity is a nonprofit, non-stock corporation.
5. Purpose: (required; continue on additional page if necessary)	*The purpose of the corporation shall be:*
6. Name, Title and Signature of Officer Making Statement:	Name _____ _____ **X** _____ Title of Officer Officer Signature
7. Certificate of Acceptance of Appointment of Registered Agent:	*I hereby accept appointment as Registered Agent for the above named Entity.* **X** _____ _____ Authorized Signature of Registered Agent or On Behalf of Registered Agent Entity Date

This form must be accompanied by appropriate fees.

Nevada Secretary of State NRS 80 Qualification
Revised on 7-1-08

> ### PRACTICE TIP
>
> For each corporate client, maintain a master list indicating its state of incorporation and then each of the states in which it is qualified to transact business. The list should specify the agent for service of process in each state and each state's requirements and due date for annual reports. Send reminders to clients about 45 to 60 days before each annual report is due. Periodically revisit the list with the client to make sure that the client withdraws its qualification from any state in which it has ceased to do business.

D. Effects of Qualifying

There are four primary effects on foreign corporations that have qualified to do business in another state.

1. The foreign corporation will be subject to any restrictions imposed on domestic corporations. For example, a corporation formed in New Jersey and operating a gambling casino there will be precluded from operating casinos in Nebraska if Nebraska does not permit its own domestic corporations to operate for gambling purposes. The corporation is now subject to various restrictions in its state of incorporation as well as any foreign state in which it has qualified to do business. Its internal affairs, however, such as amending its bylaws, giving notice of meetings, and other similar matters, are governed by the state of incorporation. MBCA § 15.05(b) specifically provides that a qualified foreign corporation has the same but no greater privileges as a domestic corporation in the state and is subject to the same duties and restrictions as a domestic corporation formed in the state.

2. The foreign corporation will be subject to service of process in the new state. Service of process upon the registered agent in the foreign state is as effective as service of process upon the corporation's agent in its own state of incorporation. Note that a corporation may be subject to the jurisdiction of the courts in another state even if it is not engaged in the types of activities that might require it to qualify as a foreign corporation there.

3. The corporation must pay various taxes to the state that has permitted it to transact business within its borders. Some states assess an annual license or franchise fee for the privilege of doing business. These fees vary from state to state. Similarly, foreign corporations will be required to pay any other taxes imposed on domestic corporations in that state, such as income taxes.

4. The corporation must file annual reports with the state. The annual report is generally a fairly simple form sent to the corporation by the secretary of state and usually requires basic information about the corporation. To determine the amount of taxes or fees the corporation will pay, the annual report in some states requires information about the specific amount of business conducted by the corporation in that state. Other states impose a flat fee. The reporting requirements are usually identical for domestic and foreign corporations. Most states now require that annual reports be filed electronically with the state.

E.   Effects of Failure to Qualify

Although they vary from state to state, sanctions are imposed on corporations that have transacted business without first having qualified to do so. MBCA § 15.02 provides the following penalties for transacting business in a foreign jurisdiction without authority:

1. The foreign corporation may not maintain a proceeding in any court in the foreign state until it obtains a certificate of authority; and
2. Monetary penalties will be imposed for each day the corporation was not properly qualified (not to exceed a stated amount).

Some states, adopting a harsher approach, provide that any acts performed by the unqualified corporation are void, that its contracts are unenforceable, that it cannot bring a lawsuit, that fines may be imposed directly on corporate directors and officers as well as fines for each day the corporation was in violation of the state statutes, and that the attorney general of the state can enjoin the corporation from conducting any further business. For example, Alabama provides that the contracts of unauthorized corporations are void, and Indiana imposes a fine of up to $10,000 on unauthorized corporations. Moreover, the corporation will be liable for any back taxes or fees it should have paid during the period in which it was transacting business in the state as well as penalties thereon.

The more permissive approach and that adopted by the MBCA is to refuse an unqualified corporation to maintain legal action. It may, however, defend itself in any legal action, and its failure to qualify will not impair the validity of its acts or the contracts it entered into during the period of nonqualification. Most states allow a corporation that has failed to qualify to cure the defect by subsequent qualification, even during a lawsuit. Nevertheless, various penalties may still be imposed on the corporation.

Thus, whenever there is a doubt regarding whether a corporation should qualify to do business in another state, it might be wise to resolve the doubt in favor of qualification, particularly if not qualifying subjects the corporation to the risk of excessive fines or having its contracts declared invalid.

F.   Effect of Changes to Domestic Corporation

Just as domestic corporations must inform the secretary of state of a change of corporate name, a merger, or a change in purposes, so also must a corporation qualified to transact business in a state inform that state of such changes.

Generally, when a corporation amends its articles of incorporation in its state of incorporation it must also file a certified copy of the amended articles in any state in which it transacts business as a foreign corporation. MBCA § 15.04 requires that a foreign corporation obtain an amended certificate of authority if it changes its name, its period of duration, or the state in which it is incorporated. A corporation that wishes merely to change its registered agent and/or registered office address usually files a separate and less complex form. Filing fees will be imposed for either of these forms.

If the foreign corporation merges with another and is the surviving entity, it must generally file a copy of the articles of merger with the secretary of state of the foreign jurisdiction.

G. Withdrawal of Foreign Qualification

When a corporation ceases doing business in a state in which it has qualified as a foreign corporation, it should file an application for **withdrawal.** This will ensure that the corporation is no longer subject to service of process, taxes, or annual reporting requirements in the state.

Withdrawal
Process of cancelling authority to do business in a foreign state

The application for withdrawal form is usually provided by the secretary of state. It generally includes the corporation's name and state of incorporation and specifies that the corporation surrenders authority to transact business in the state and revokes the authority of its registered agent to receive service of process. (See Figure 15-3 for a sample form for application for certificate of withdrawal.) The secretary of state is then authorized to receive any later process. The corporation must provide an address so that the secretary of state can forward any process for any action filed against the corporation. Many states and the MBCA also require a commitment to notify the secretary of state of any later change in the mailing address.

Upon receipt of the application for withdrawal and the filing fee therefor, the secretary of state will check to make sure all taxes and fees have been paid and will then issue a certificate of withdrawal. The corporation is then no longer authorized to transact business in the state and no longer subject to any of its laws or requirements.

H. Revocation of Qualification by State

In some instances, a state in which a foreign corporation has qualified to transact business may revoke that authority or qualification. Typically, revocation of the certificate of authority of a foreign corporation is triggered by some unlawful act by the corporation or failure to comply with the state's laws and requirements. The most common reasons for revocation are failure to file annual reports, failure to pay taxes, failure to have a registered agent or to inform the secretary of state of a change in the registered agent, filing a document with the secretary of state that is false, or dissolution or disappearance of the corporation as a result of merger. Some states, such as Illinois, will revoke the certificate of authority if the foreign corporation has not conducted business in the state for one year and has no tangible property there.

Most states provide a delinquency notice to the corporation before revoking the authority of the corporation to transact business in the state. The corporation is usually given some stated period (typically 30 to 90 days) to correct its default. If the default is not corrected, the secretary of state will issue a certificate of revocation that recites the grounds for revocation, and the corporation will no longer have any authority to conduct business in the state.

FIGURE 15-3
Virginia Application for Withdrawal of a Foreign Corporation

SCC767/929
(07/07)

COMMONWEALTH OF VIRGINIA
STATE CORPORATION COMMISSION

APPLICATION FOR A CERTIFICATE OF WITHDRAWAL
OF A FOREIGN CORPORATION AUTHORIZED TO TRANSACT BUSINESS IN VIRGINIA

The undersigned, on behalf of the foreign corporation set forth below, pursuant to § 13.1-767 or § 13.1-929 of the Code of Virginia, hereby makes this application for a certificate of withdrawal and states as follows:

1. The name of the corporation is

    _____

2. The name of the state or country under whose law the corporation is incorporated is

    _____

3. The corporation is not transacting business in Virginia and surrenders its authority to transact business in Virginia.

4. The corporation revokes the authority of its registered agent to accept service on its behalf and appoints the Clerk of the Commission as its agent for service of process in any proceeding based on a cause of action arising during the time it was authorized to transact business in Virginia.

5. The mailing address to which the Commission may mail a copy of any process served on the Clerk of the Commission as agent for the corporation is

    _____

6. The corporation makes a commitment to notify the Clerk of the Commission in the future of any change in its mailing address.

7. The corporation certifies that **[mark appropriate box]:**

    ☐ It has filed returns and has paid all state taxes to the time of this application; **or**
       (APPROPRIATE FOR STOCK AND NONSTOCK CORPORATIONS)

    ☐ It is not required to file any return or pay any state taxes.
       (APPROPRIATE FOR NONSTOCK CORPORATIONS ONLY)

Executed in the name of the corporation by:

_____   _____
            (signature)   (corporate title)

_____   _____
          (printed name)   (date)

_____   _____
      (corporation's SCC ID No.)   (telephone number (optional))

(The execution must be by the chairman or any vice-chairman of the board of directors, the president, or any other of its officers authorized to act on behalf of the corporation.)

PRIVACY ADVISORY: Information such as social security number, date of birth, maiden name, or financial institution account numbers is NOT required to be included in business entity documents filed with the Office of the Clerk of the Commission. Any information provided on these documents is subject to public viewing.

SEE INSTRUCTIONS ON THE REVERSE

Provide a name and mailing address for sending correspondence regarding the filing of this document (if left blank, correspondence will be sent to the address given in paragraph 5, above):

_____
                                  (name)

_____
                            (mailing address)

In many states, a corporation may seek to be reinstated, especially if authority to transact business in the foreign jurisdiction was revoked due to failure to file an annual report, pay taxes, or some other similar administrative reason. Reinstatement is an easier process than seeking to requalify to transact business in the foreign jurisdiction.

Key Features
of Foreign Qualification

- ◆ Corporations that intend to transact business in other states must "qualify" or be authorized by the foreign jurisdiction prior to commencing business in those states.
- ◆ Not all activities are considered to be "transacting business" such that a corporation must qualify in the foreign state. Some activities are considered relatively peripheral or isolated and thus do not require corporate qualification.
- ◆ To qualify, the corporation must complete the foreign state's form and pay a filing fee. The corporation must have an agent for service of process in the foreign jurisdiction. Qualification will result in the corporation being amenable to service of process in the foreign state and will require the corporation to file annual reports and pay various taxes and fees to the foreign jurisdiction.
- ◆ If a corporation transacts business without qualifying, it is usually forbidden from maintaining an action in that state's courts and is usually subject to monetary fines and penalties. A few states take a harsher approach and provide that acts engaged in while the corporation was not qualified are void.
- ◆ When a corporation makes changes in its state of incorporation (such as amending its articles), it should conduct research to determine if foreign jurisdictions in which it operates must be notified of those changes.
- ◆ Once a corporation ceases doing business in the foreign jurisdiction, it should withdraw its qualification.

I. Role of Paralegal

Once the determination has been made by corporate management to expand into other states, the paralegal's involvement will begin. Paralegals are engaged in the following activities:

1. Locating and maintaining all forms and lists of filing fees for foreign qualifications.

2. Applying for name registrations to preserve the corporation's name in the foreign jurisdiction (the expiration date for which should be calendared).
3. Conducting research regarding what activities constitute "transacting business" in the foreign state.
4. Conducting research regarding the process of qualification.
5. Making arrangements for an agent who will accept service on behalf of the foreign corporation.
6. Obtaining a certificate of good standing and certified copies of the articles of incorporation from the secretary of state in the state of incorporation.
7. Preparing and filing the application for authority to transact business.
8. Calendaring dates for payment of taxes and annual reporting in the foreign jurisdiction.
9. Maintaining clients' master lists, identifying all states in which they are qualified.
10. Amending the foreign application, if necessary.
11. Preparing and filing the application for withdrawal of qualification, if necessary.

Case Illustration
Effect of Failure to Qualify

Case:	*Horton v. Richards*, 594 P.2d 891 (Utah 1979)
Facts:	The plaintiff, a Washington corporation, brought suit against a defendant for breach of contract in Utah, although it had not qualified in Utah as a foreign corporation. The trial court dismissed the complaint.
Holding:	The court affirmed the lower court. There was ample evidence that the plaintiff was transacting business in Utah. It maintained telephone directory listings, bank accounts, and its president held himself out to be the president of the company's Utah operations. In such a case, the corporation was required to qualify in Utah before transacting business. Because it did not, it was barred from seeking affirmative relief in Utah's courts.

WEB RESOURCES

The most important resources relating to qualification of foreign corporations are the various state statutes, especially the statutes that enumerate the activities that constitute "transacting business" such that a foreign corporation must qualify in that state.

State statutes: www.law.cornell.edu
                                      www.findlaw.com

Secretaries of state: www.nass.org (for links to secretaries of
                                      state and downloadable forms for ap-
                                      plications to qualify to transact busi-
                                      ness)

California agents for service: www.ss.ca.gov/business/bpd_service_
                                      companies.htm

Delaware agents for service: http://corp.delaware.gov/agents/
                                      agts.shtml

General information: www.megalaw.com
Forms: www.allaboutforms.com
                                      www.siccode.com/forms.php

Discussion Questions

Fact Scenario. Your Fitness, Inc., is an Oregon corporation engaged in providing fitness classes and related products in Oregon. Use the MBCA to answer the following questions.

1. The corporation would like to sell exercise DVDs over the Internet to locations all around the country. Must the corporation qualify in other states to engage in this activity? Discuss.

2. The corporation has decided to expand into Washington and build several fitness centers there, would like to open various bank accounts in Idaho, and would like to offer one training session to Ted Turner while he is at his ranch in Montana next week. The corporation is also selling various vitamin supplements by obtaining telephone orders for them and then shipping the vitamins to other states. Must the corporation qualify in these states to engage in these activities? Discuss.

3. Assume that the corporation has qualified to transact business in California. The corporation has amended its articles to change its name to Your

Fitness Guru, Corp. What effect does this amendment have, if any, with regard to the corporation's activities in California?

4. If a consumer wishes to sue the corporation in California, who should be served with the summons and complaint? How would the consumer know who should receive service of process?

5. Because its California operations are not profitable, the corporation intends to close its fitness centers in California. What should the corporation do?

6. The corporation has opened a large fitness center in Arizona but has not qualified to transact business there. It has sued its landlord for breach of contract, and he has alleged that he need not pay any damages because the corporation was not properly qualified to transact business in Arizona. Is this a valid defense? What are other possible consequences to the corporation of not qualifying?

Net Worth

1. Access the Web site for Florida's secretary of state. Review the form and cover letter for filing an application to transact business for a for-profit corporation in Florida.
   a. What is the fee to file this form?
   b. Is a photocopy of the certificate of existence acceptable?
   c. How long is the certificate of existence valid?
2. Access the Web site for Delaware's secretary of state.
   a. What is the filing fee in Delaware for a foreign corporation to apply to conduct business in Delaware?
   b. Review the information relating to obtaining a corporate certificate of good standing. What is the filing fee to obtain a short-form certificate?
   c. Review the Corporate Certificate Cover Memo. What fee must be paid if one wishes to receive the certificate in one hour?
3. What is the fee in Ohio if a foreign corporation wishes to file a surrender of its application to transact business?

16

◆ ◆ ◆

Termination of Corporate Existence

◆ ◆ ◆

CHAPTER OVERVIEW

Just as a corporation can only be created by strict compliance with state statutes, it can only be terminated or dissolved in accordance with state statutes. There are three types of dissolution: voluntary dissolution, initiated by the directors, or occasionally, the shareholders; administrative dissolution, initiated by the secretary of state for technical defaults (such as failure to pay taxes); and involuntary dissolution, initiated by the state, shareholders, or creditors. Dissolution ends the corporation's life as a legal "person."

Before allowing a corporation to dissolve, a state must usually be assured that all of the business of the corporation has been completed, that creditors have been paid, and that shareholders have received any assets remaining after payment of creditors. This process of wrapping up the business affairs of the corporation is called liquidation. When dissolution is voluntary, corporate management will oversee the liquidation process; when dissolution is involuntary, a court will oversee the liquidation process.

Generally, the corporation's existence is formally ended with the filing and acceptance of articles of dissolution with the state of incorporation.

A. Dissolution

1. Introduction

Corporations may dissolve for any number of reasons. It is possible that the term of duration specified in the articles of incorporation has expired. Absent a specified period of duration, however, a corporation will continue in existence until it is expressly dissolved. Merely ceasing to conduct business will not terminate a corporation's status as a legal entity. Termination of the corporation's existence as a legal entity is referred to as **dissolution.** Dissolution may be caused for a variety of business reasons: The corporation might be unprofitable or even insolvent; its business activities might have ended; it might have merged into another corporation; or its assets might have been acquired by another corporation.

Dissolution can be initiated by the decision of the corporation itself — namely, its directors or shareholders — in which case the dissolution is **voluntary**, or it may be dissolved against its will, by the state, its shareholders, or creditors, in which case the dissolution is referred to as **involuntary.** An **administrative** dissolution can also be initiated by the secretary of state for technical defaults by the corporation, such as failure to pay taxes, file reports, or maintain an agent for service of process.

In some states, the corporation is dissolved upon receipt of the requisite vote by the directors and shareholders or upon entry of a judgment by a court, if the dissolution is judicial. In other states, such as California, and under Chapter 14 of the MBCA, the corporation is not deemed dissolved until the secretary of state accepts and approves articles of dissolution.

2. *Voluntary Dissolution*

A corporation may be dissolved at any time after it is formed, even before shares have been issued to any shareholders or before it has commenced business. In this case, if no directors have been named, the incorporators who formed the corporation will dissolve it. Otherwise, the initial directors will dissolve the corporation. In most cases, however, a corporation dissolves after it has named directors, appointed officers, issued shares, and conducted business. Once shares have been issued, shareholders must approve the decision to dissolve because shareholders are the actual owners of the corporation. A voluntary decision to dissolve the corporation may originate with the directors or with the shareholders.

Typically, the decision to dissolve is initiated by the directors. As the ultimate managers of the corporation, they are in the best position to know whether dissolution is called for or whether the corporation should continue its operations. The directors will propose dissolution and this will be approved at a directors' meeting, by majority vote, or by written consent, which usually must be unanimous. The directors will usually prepare a plan of dissolution.

The directors will recommend dissolution to the shareholders and must call a special meeting of shareholders to vote on the proposed dissolution (unless the matter can be considered at an annual meeting). Notice of the special meeting must generally be given to all shareholders, whether or not they ordinarily have voting rights. The notice must state that the purpose of the meeting is to consider dissolution.

The more modern approach, followed in Delaware, is to require a simple majority vote of shareholders to approve dissolution (unless the corporation's articles require a greater vote). The MBCA approach is similar to its approach on amendments to the articles of incorporation and mergers: The dissolution will be approved if more votes are cast in favor of it than against it. MBCA § 14.02 and § 7.25. Some states, however, require two-thirds approval by shareholders. Some states allow all shareholders to vote; others allow only shareholders holding voting stock to vote on the dissolution. Shareholders are seldom given any right to dissent and have their shares appraised; they will share in any assets remaining after creditors have been satisfied.

In some states, the next step in the dissolution process is for the corporation to file a notice with the secretary of state indicating its intent to dissolve. The MBCA does not require this public notice but simply provides that after dissolution is authorized, the corporation may proceed to dissolve by filing articles of dissolution with the secretary of state. Some states require that all creditors of the corporation also receive a notice stating the corporation's intent to dissolve. Alternatively, many jurisdictions allow the **notice of intent to dissolve** to be published in a legal newspaper in the county in which the corporation's principal office is located. The purpose of these notices is to inform the public and the corporation's creditors that the corporation is dissolving; this allows corporate creditors and other claimants to submit claims for debts owed to them.

Some states, such as Delaware, allow shareholders to initiate a voluntary dissolution. In most instances, when dissolution originates with the shareholders, unanimous approval is required. The shareholders can act by unanimous written consent. The requirement for unanimous consent is based on the fact that because shareholders do not manage the corporation, they are not likely to be in the best position to evaluate whether dissolution is wise. On the other hand, if *all* of the owners of the corporation agree that it should be dissolved, there is no logical reason it should not be.

Articles of Dissolution.   After dissolution has been approved by both the directors and the shareholders, articles of dissolution are prepared and filed with the secretary of state in the state of incorporation. Most states provide forms for the articles of dissolution. (See Figure 16-1 for sample articles of dissolution.) The articles must generally set forth the following items:

1. The name of the corporation;
2. The date dissolution was authorized; and
3. That the dissolution was approved by the requisite shareholder vote (or that the corporation has not issued shares and therefore it is being dissolved by the incorporators).

In some states, the corporation must also state that all of its known debts and liabilities have been paid and that its known assets have been distributed to the persons entitled thereto.

The articles of dissolution are filed in the office of the secretary of state with the appropriate filing fee. The secretary of state will usually require that the corporation submit appropriate documentation showing it does not owe any outstanding taxes to the state. Most states supply forms for tax clearance. Failure to provide the tax clearance form will result in rejection of the articles of dissolution. Additionally, the corporation must notify the Internal Revenue Service (using Form 966) within 30 days that it is dissolving and make arrangements to pay federal taxes. The corporation should also withdraw its authority to transact business in any states in which it has qualified to do business (see Figure 15-3). Once the secretary of state reviews and approves the articles, the corporation ceases to

Notice of intent to dissolve
Document filed with state indicating corporation's intent to dissolve

Articles of dissolution
Final document filed with state effecting termination of an entity (also called *certificate of dissolution*)

FIGURE 16-1
Sample Articles of Dissolution

State of California
Secretary of State

DISS STK

DOMESTIC STOCK CORPORATION
CERTIFICATE OF DISSOLUTION

There is no fee for filing a Certificate of Dissolution.

IMPORTANT – Read instructions before completing this form.

This Space For Filing Use Only

CORPORATE NAME (Enter the name of the domestic stock corporation exactly as it is of record with the California Secretary of State.)

1. Name of corporation

REQUIRED STATEMENTS (The following statements are required by statute and should not be altered.)

2. a) A final franchise tax return, as described by Section 23332 of the Revenue and Taxation Code, has been or will be filed with the Franchise Tax Board, as required under Part 10.2 (commencing with Section 18401) of Division 2 of the Revenue and Taxation Code.

   b) The corporation has completely wound up.

   c) The corporation is dissolved.

DEBTS & LIABILITIES (Check the applicable statement. Note: Only one box may be checked.)

3. ☐ The corporation's known debts and liabilities have been actually paid.

   ☐ The corporation's known debts and liabilities have been paid as far as its assets permitted.

   ☐ The corporation's known debts and liabilities have been adequately provided for by their assumption and the name and address of the assumer is _____

   ☐ The corporation's known debts and liabilities have been adequately provided for as far as its assets permitted.
   (Specify in an attachment to this certificate (incorporated herein by this reference) the provision made and the address of the corporation, person or governmental agency that has assumed or guaranteed the payment, or the name and address of the depositary with which deposit has been made or other information necessary to enable creditors or others to whom payment is to be made to appear and claim payment.)

   ☐ The corporation never incurred any known debts or liabilities.

ASSETS (Check the applicable statement. Note: Only one box may be checked.)

4. ☐ The known assets have been distributed to the persons entitled thereto.

   ☐ The corporation never acquired any known assets.

ELECTION (Check the "YES" or "NO" box, as applicable. Note: If the "NO" box is checked, a Certificate of Election to Wind Up and Dissolve pursuant to Corporations Code section 1901 must be filed prior to or together with this Certificate of Dissolution.)

5. The election to dissolve was made by the vote of all the outstanding shares. ☐ YES ☐ NO

VERIFICATION & EXECUTION (If additional signature space is necessary, the dated signature(s) with verification(s) may be made on an attachment to this certificate. Any attachments to this certificate are incorporated herein by this reference.)

6. The undersigned constitute(s) the sole director or a majority of the directors now in office. I declare under penalty of perjury under the laws of the State of California that the matters set forth in this certificate are true and correct of my own knowledge.

_____
Date

_____   _____
Signature of Director   Type or Print Name of Director

_____   _____
Signature of Director   Type or Print Name of Director

_____   _____
Signature of Director   Type or Print Name of Director

DISS STK (REV 03/2007)   APPROVED BY SECRETARY OF STATE

exist. If the corporation has been authorized to transact business in other states, it should withdraw its certificate of authority in those states.

Revocation of Dissolution. Almost all states allow corporations to revoke the decision to dissolve. Generally, the revocation of dissolution must be authorized in the same manner as was the dissolution. Typically, approval by the board and then the requisite vote of shareholders is needed. The corporation then files articles of revocation of dissolution, usually within some specific time period after the dissolution. MBCA § 14.04 provides that a corporation may revoke its decision to dissolve within 120 days of the effective date of the dissolution. The MBCA also provides that the revocation relates back to the date of dissolution so that it is as if the dissolution had never occurred. Many states permit a revocation only if the corporation has not begun to distribute its assets or only before articles of dissolution are filed.

MBCA Approach. The MBCA and many states require only one publicly filed document to effect dissolution, the articles of dissolution, and the corporation is dissolved on the effective date of the articles of dissolution. After the articles of dissolution are filed, the corporation is referred to as a "dissolved corporation," but it continues its existence only for the purpose of winding up and liquidating its business and affairs. The corporation then proceeds to liquidate by disposing of its known claims and unknown claims and distributing the balance of its assets to its shareholders (see Section B.4 in this chapter). Thus, in this approach, dissolution precedes liquidation. There is no statutorily required period within which liquidation must be completed, although it is obviously in the corporation's interest to proceed with liquidation in an expeditious manner.

In other states, such as California, dissolution is initiated by a notice of the corporation's intent or election to dissolve and then to complete the dissolution process, articles or a certificate of dissolution must be filed, which must recite that all known debts and liabilities have been paid and that assets have been distributed to shareholders. In states following this approach, liquidation precedes formal dissolution. This approach would seem to provide more comfort to creditors and claimants because the corporation is not allowed to dissolve unless its directors state under penalty of perjury that debts and liabilities have been taken care of and assets have been distributed to those entitled to them.

3. *Administrative Dissolution*

Grounds and Procedure for Administrative Dissolution. Nearly all states and the MBCA recognize a type of dissolution that is less serious than involuntary dissolution. In these states, the secretary of state commences a proceeding to administratively dissolve a corporation for one of the following reasons: its failure to pay taxes or file annual reports; failure to have a registered agent for some period of time (often 60 days) or to notify the secretary of state that its registered agent or office have changed; or for continuing to operate after the corporation's period of duration expires. Grounds of this nature are often called *technical* — or *administrative* — *defaults*.

Many states provide written notice to the corporation of technical defaults and give the corporation an opportunity to cure the defaults. If it does not do so, it will be administratively dissolved, and it cannot carry on any routine business except that necessary to wind up and liquidate its affairs.

Reinstatement Process of reviving a corporation dissolved for administrative reasons

Reinstatement.   Most states and MBCA § 14.22 allow a corporation to apply for **reinstatement** or revival within a certain period of time after it has been dissolved on technical grounds. The corporation must cure the default. Reinstatement is retroactive so that after reinstatement, the corporation may continue doing business as if the administrative dissolution had never occurred. Not all states allow reinstatement. If the prior name of the corporation is no longer available, it must select a new name and file an amendment to its original articles of incorporation. (See Figure 16-2 for an application for reinstatement.) A decision by the secretary of state to deny an application for reinstatement may be appealed to the courts. Generally, if the grounds for dissolution were not technical, a corporation may not be reinstated.

PRACTICE TIP

Because a corporation can be dissolved by the state for failure to file annual reports and pay taxes, you should maintain an accurate docket or calendar for all corporate clients. Although many states provide reminder notices to corporations that annual reports are due, clients are often so busy they neglect to file the report on time. Use your docket to remind clients of the critical deadline for filing the annual report.

4. Involuntary Dissolution

State statutes allow for the dissolution of corporations even when dissolution is not desired by the board of directors. This is referred to as an involuntary dissolution or, because the dissolution proceeding is brought before a court, an involuntary dissolution is also called a **judicial dissolution.** A corporation can be forced to dissolve against its will by the state, its shareholders, or unsatisfied creditors.

Judicial dissolution Dissolution brought before a court (also called *involuntary dissolution*)

Actions by the State.   Corporations exist only by virtue of the authority of the state of incorporation. Because a state always has the power and authority to ensure compliance with its laws, a corporation can be dissolved by its creator, the state of incorporation. An action for involuntary dissolution is usually brought in the name of the state attorney general, the individual in each state charged with enforcing the laws of the state.

Generally, the grounds for dissolution by the state include the following:

1. Procuring the articles of incorporation through fraud; or
2. Exceeding or abusing the authority given to the corporation by the state.

Generally, reinstatement is not available after a judicial dissolution.

Action by the Shareholders.   If directors act fraudulently or waste corporate assets, it might be nearly impossible for a voluntary dissolution to occur.

FIGURE 16-2
Illinois Application for Reinstatement

FORM **BCA 12.45/13.60** (rev. Dec. 2003)
APPLICATION FOR REINSTATEMENT
DOMESTIC/FOREIGN CORPORATIONS
BUSINESS CORPORATION ACT

Jesse White, Secretary of State
Department of Business Services
Springfield, IL 62756
217-782-1837 (Foreign)
217-785-5782 or 217-782-5797 (Domestic)
www.cyberdriveillinois.com

Remit payment in the form of a cashier's
check, certified check, money order
or an Illinois attorney's or CPA's check,
payable to Secretary of State.

_____File #_____ Filing Fee: $200 Approved:

_____Submit in duplicate_____Type or Print clearly in black ink_____Do not write above this line_____

1. (a) Corporate name as of date of issuance of Certificate of Dissolution or Revocation:

    _____

    (b) Corporate name if changed *(note 2)*: _____

    _____

    (c) If a foreign corporation having authority under an assumed corporate name restriction, the assumed
         corporate name *(note 3)*: _____

    _____

2. State of incorporation: _____

3. Date Certificate of Dissolution or Revocation issued: _____

4. Name and address of the Illinois registered agent and the Illinois registered office, upon reinstatement:
    NOTICE! Completion of item #4 does not constitute a registered agent or office change *(note 4)*.

    Registered Agent _____
                       First Name   *Middle Name*   *Last Name*

    Registered Office _____
                       Number   *Street*   *Suite #*   *(P.O. BOX ALONE IS NOT ACCEPTABLE.)*

                       _____**IL**_____
                           City   *ZIP Code*   *County*

5. This application is accompanied by all delinquent report forms together with the filing fees, franchise taxes,
    license fee and penalties required *(note 1)*.

6. The undersigned corporation has caused this application to be signed by a duly authorized officer who affirms,
    under penalties of perjury, that the facts stated herein are true. (All signatures must be in **BLACK INK**.)

    Dated _____   _____
                (Month, Day & Year)   *(Exact Name of Corporation)*

    By _____
            (Any Authorized Officer's Signature)

    _____
            (Print name and title)   C-89.22 9/04

The negligent directors will not pass a resolution to dissolve a corporation they are in the process of looting, and, if the directors own stock in the corporation, unanimous shareholder consent is impossible, because acting in their capacity as shareholders, the directors will not vote for dissolution.

In situations such as these, a shareholder can institute a legal action and request that a court dissolve the corporation. To prevail, the shareholder must generally establish:

1. The directors are deadlocked in managing the business affairs of the corporation and irreparable injury is being suffered or threatened to the corporation to the detriment of the shareholders;
2. Corporate management has acted in an illegal, oppressive, or fraudulent manner;
3. The shareholders are deadlocked and have failed to elect directors at two successive annual meetings;
4. The corporate assets are being wasted or misapplied; or
5. The corporation has failed to conduct business for some statutorily specified period of time.

Because dissolution is such a drastic remedy, MBCA § 14.34 and many state statutes provide that if a shareholder petitions to dissolve the corporation for one of the grounds just specified, as an alternative to dissolution, the corporation or another shareholder(s) may elect to purchase all of the shares owned by the complaining shareholder at their fair market value. Such a remedy (and the ability of a shareholder to bring an action for involuntary dissolution) is available only if the corporation's stock is not publicly traded. Shareholders of corporations whose stock is publicly traded are adequately protected, because they can always sell their shares on the open market.

A new provision of the MBCA allows a shareholder to obtain involuntary dissolution in the event the corporation has abandoned its business, but those in control of the corporation have unreasonably delayed in liquidating it and distributing its assets (which may occur if the directors in power wish to continue receiving their salaries). In such an event, a delayed liquidation prejudices creditors and shareholders. MBCA § 14.30(5).

Although the election to purchase a complaining shareholder's shares in lieu of dissolution requires a fairly elaborate procedure, it affords a method of protecting a disputing shareholder and yet continuing the corporation for those who wish to see it continue in existence.

Action by a Creditor. A creditor of the corporation may institute a proceeding for judicial dissolution of a corporation. Typically, the creditor must establish that the corporation is insolvent and that the creditor has either received a judgment against the corporation for the claim or the corporation has acknowledged in writing that the claim is owed. Because creditors' claims must be paid before assets are distributed to shareholders upon dissolution, the creditor may believe it is in his best interest to force a dissolution and thereby collect some amount of the claim rather than no amount at all if the corporation is refusing to satisfy the debt. As discussed later, in many cases, a creditor might simply initiate a bankruptcy petition against the corporation rather than petitioning to dissolve the corporation.

If a court determines that there are grounds for dissolution shown by the state, the shareholders, or the creditors, it will enter a decree of dissolution specifying the effective date of the dissolution. The decree will be provided to the secretary of state by the clerk of the court, and the secretary of state will then file the decree in its records. The court will then order winding up and liquidation of the corporation's business and affairs and notification of its creditors and claimants.

B. Liquidation

1. Introduction

Before a corporation can terminate its legal existence in most states, it must conduct the process of liquidation, sometimes called *winding up*. **Liquidation** involves the following activities:

a. Collecting assets;
b. Disposing of properties that will not be distributed to shareholders;
c. Discharging liabilities or making provisions for discharging liabilities; and
d. Distributing the remaining property to the shareholders according to their respective interests. (MBCA § 14.05)

> **Liquidation**
> Process of collecting assets, paying debts, and distributing remains to business owners (also called *winding up*)

Once a corporation has filed its notice of intent to dissolve (or, in many states, its articles of dissolution), it continues business only for the purpose of liquidating and cannot conduct ordinary or additional business. Many states will not allow a corporation to end its legal existence unless liquidation has been accomplished. Thus, the corporation must wind up its business affairs before a certificate of dissolution will be issued. Under MBCA § 14.09, directors have a duty to discharge any claims against the corporation and may only distribute assets to shareholders after payment of creditors' claims.

2. Nonjudicial Liquidation

> **Nonjudicial liquidation**
> Process of winding up by corporate managers

When dissolution is voluntary (initiated by the directors with shareholder approval or unanimously agreed to by the shareholders) or administrative, the officers and directors will liquidate the corporation. Contracts will be completed, creditors will be notified to submit their claims, and assets will be collected. State statutes do not generally impose any specific time limit within which the liquidation must be completed (although Delaware sets a time limit of three years). Even in a voluntary dissolution, the corporation may request judicial supervision of liquidation if it believes such is appropriate or desirable.

3. Judicial Liquidation

> **Judicial liquidation**
> Process of winding up by court appointee

A dissolution initiated by the state, shareholders, or creditors is often caused by the directors' failure to manage the corporation properly, fraud, or waste of the corporate assets. Because a court therefore cannot place confidence in corporate management to conduct liquidation properly, the court generally appoints a **receiver** whose function is to receive the assets of the corporation and distribute them to the creditors and shareholders. Some jurisdictions refer to the individual or company appointed to oversee the winding up process as the *court-appointed liquidator*. The receiver will be compensated for services rendered in effecting an orderly liquidation. The court may also appoint a separate custodian to manage the business and affairs of the corporation during this time.

Receiver
One appointed by a court to oversee liquidation (also called *liquidator*)

4. Claims Against the Corporation

There are two types of claims that must be discharged or resolved by a dissolving corporation: **known claims** (those claims, debts, and obligations the corporation knows about) and **unknown claims** (claims that have not yet matured or been made against the corporation, for example, claims for injuries that may be sustained in the future due to a defective product the corporation has made).

Known claim
A claim known by an entity

Unknown claim
Claim that has not yet been made against an entity

Corporations cannot use dissolutions to avoid contractual obligations. For example, if the corporation is a party to a long-term employment contract, it must satisfy the obligations thereunder, at least as to money to be paid to the employee, unless the terms of the contract contemplate dissolution and excuse performance by the corporation in the event of a dissolution.

The MBCA provides an orderly process for disposing of claims against the corporation. As to known claims, the corporation may notify the claimants in writing of the dissolution, inform the creditor or claimant where to submit the claim, provide at least 120 days for the creditor to make the claim, and inform the creditor the claim will be barred if not timely submitted to the corporation. If the creditor does not submit the claim in a timely fashion, the claim will be barred. If a claim is submitted and the corporation rejects it, the claimant must institute legal action within 90 days of rejection of the claim to enforce the claim or it will be barred. MBCA § 14.06.

To ensure that unknown claims are also discharged, MBCA § 14.07 provides that the corporation may place in a newspaper of general circulation a notice of dissolution stating that the claim will be barred unless an action to enforce the claim is brought within three years of publication of the notice. If the corporation's assets have been distributed before the claim is made, shareholders may be liable, but only to the extent of assets distributed to them. A shareholder's liability cannot exceed the amount distributed to him or her or the pro rata share of the claim, whichever is less. If the corporation was dissolved because of a merger or consolidation, a creditor is usually able to enforce a claim against the surviving corporation. In many states, the articles of dissolution must recite that no debt remains unpaid or that the corporation's debts and liabilities have been adequately provided for by their assumption by certain individuals or companies whose addresses are provided. Corporations may provide for such unknown claims by purchasing insurance or setting aside a portion of assets. Alternatively, under MBCA § 14.08, a corporation may initiate a court proceeding to establish an amount that should be set aside for unknown claims.

C. Distributions to Shareholders

After all debts have been discharged and any expenses of liquidation have been paid, and assuming any assets remain, the shareholders are entitled to receive a distribution, generally called a **liquidation distribution.** Corporate assets are typically converted to "liquid" form, namely cash, and the shareholders will receive cash payments. Alternatively, they may receive assets. If preferences exist, those must be honored. Shareholders participate in the distribution in accordance with their ownership interests; if a shareholder owns 23 percent of the common stock of a corporation, the shareholder will be entitled to receive 23 percent of any liquidation distribution made to common shareholders. Shareholders must report these distributions to the Internal Revenue Service.

Liquidation distribution Distribution to shareholders in liquidation process

Shareholders are not entitled to appraisal rights arising out of a dissolution inasmuch as all shareholders are equally affected by a dissolution. Their sole right is to receive a distribution, if sufficient assets remain after payment of liquidation costs and creditors' claims.

D. Directors' Duties to Minority Shareholders

In corporations in which directors hold large amounts of stock, it may be possible for the directors to force a dissolution over the wishes of minority shareholders. For example, assume a corporation has five directors, three of whom own stock in the corporation in a total amount of 52 percent. The remaining 48 percent of the stock is held by 100 individuals. The three powerful directors could compel a dissolution: Because they constitute a majority of the board, they can pass a directors' resolution recommending dissolution; because they own more than a majority of the outstanding stock, as shareholders their affirmative vote is sufficient to approve a dissolution. If the corporation's business is extremely profitable, these three directors-shareholders may decide to force a voluntary dissolution, pay off the 100 individual shareholders, and reform a corporation by themselves to do the same business and thereby keep all of the profits. Alternatively, as discussed in Chapter Fourteen, the director-shareholders could form a new corporation owned solely by them and merge the old corporation into the new one. Under the plan of merger, shareholders of the old corporation will receive cash only; they do not continue as shareholders in the new survivor corporation. This type of oppression is called a *freeze-out* or *squeeze-out.*

Because a freeze-out is patently inequitable to the minority shareholders, courts will prevent or enjoin dissolutions or mergers that have the effect of oppressing minority shareholders and have no legitimate business purpose.

E. Corporate Bankruptcy

Although corporations dissolve for a number of reasons, one common reason for a corporation to dissolve is that it is financially insolvent. For the 12 months ending June 30, 2008, the total number of business bankruptcy filings was 33,822, representing a more than 40 percent increase over the previous year's figures.

Although insolvency does not always lead to dissolution (because the corporation may be able to secure new funding), many corporations do file for relief under the United States Bankruptcy Act, a federal law designed to protect both debtors and creditors.

All bankruptcy proceedings are held in federal court and are governed exclusively by federal law (11 U.S.C. §§ 101 et seq.). The Bankruptcy Act is divided into different chapters, each designed to provide certain relief. In any case, the filing of a bankruptcy petition operates as an automatic stay of proceedings against a debtor so that any legal action threatened or pending against the debtor is automatically suspended by the filing of a bankruptcy petition.

On April 20, 2005, President George W. Bush signed into law the Bankruptcy Abuse Prevention and Consumer Protection Act of 2005 (**BAPCPA**). BAPCPA made substantial changes to the Bankruptcy Code, most of which apply only to cases filed on or after October 17, 2005. The new law generally makes it more difficult for consumers to discharge payment of all their debts and requires credit counseling. BAPCPA is discussed in Chapter Nineteen.

All bankruptcy proceedings are initiated by the filing of a petition. If the corporation initiates bankruptcy, the petition is a **voluntary petition;** however, creditors can force a corporation into bankruptcy by filing an **involuntary petition.** Involuntary petitions are filed by three creditors with claims totaling at least $13,475. If there are fewer than 12 creditors, one or more may file the petition so long as a creditor has a claim in the amount of $13,475.

Following are the most common types of bankruptcy proceedings applicable to corporations:

- *Chapter 7.* Petitions for relief under **Chapter 7** (called "Liquidation") of the Bankruptcy Act are the most common type of bankruptcy proceedings. A Chapter 7 proceeding is a liquidation proceeding selected by a debtor (an individual, partnership, or corporation) that has no hope of being solvent and that cannot restructure its debts. A trustee is appointed to collect any nonexempt assets (for example, certain life insurance policies are exempt and the value of a car to a certain limit is exempt). The nonexempt assets are then distributed to creditors according to the priorities provided by the Bankruptcy Act. In a Chapter 7 proceeding, often called a "no asset" matter, the corporation will fully liquidate and will cease doing business.

- *Chapter 11.* Petitions for relief under **Chapter 11** (called "Reorganizations") are filed by individuals, corporations, or partnerships that are in debt but believe they can reorganize and remain in business. The corporation will remain in possession of its assets and will continue to operate its business under court supervision and for the benefit of its creditors. The corporation will submit a **plan of reorganization**, which is its proposal to solve its financial problems, to the court. The creditors must agree to the plan and the court must confirm it. In most cases, the debtor pays a portion of its debts and is relieved of responsibility for the remainder. After Chapter 11 proceedings are completed, the corporation will emerge from bankruptcy and continue its now reorganized business.

Bankruptcy proceedings are further discussed in Chapter Nineteen.

BAPCPA
Bankruptcy Abuse Prevention and Consumer Protection Act of 2005; new bankruptcy legislation that makes it more difficult for consumers to discharge payment of debts

Voluntary petition
Bankruptcy initiated by debtor

Involuntary petition
Bankruptcy initiated by creditors

Chapter 7
Bankruptcy proceedings in which debtor's business is terminated

Chapter 11
Bankruptcy proceedings in which debts are reorganized and debtor emerges from bankruptcy

Plan of reorganization
Proposal submitted by entity in bankruptcy to solve its financial problems

---

Key Features
of Corporate Dissolution and Liquidation

- ◆ Corporations can dissolve voluntarily (usually by action of the directors, which is then approved by shareholders), administratively (for technical defaults such as failure to pay taxes), or involuntarily (by action by the state, shareholders, or creditors).

- ◆ Dissolution usually refers to termination of the corporate entity, whereas liquidation refers to termination of the corporation's business and affairs.

- ◆ If dissolution is voluntary, articles of dissolution will be filed with the state. If dissolution is involuntary, a court will enter a decree of dissolution.

- ◆ An administrative dissolution may be initiated by the state for technical reasons (such as failure to file annual reports or pay taxes). A corporation that is dissolved for such reasons can generally apply to be reinstated.

- ◆ Shareholders may initiate a dissolution, often because of director or shareholder deadlock, waste of assets, or fraud by directors. In lieu of ordering a dissolution, in some states a court can allow the complaining shareholder's shares to be purchased.

- ◆ Creditors can initiate a dissolution if the corporation is insolvent and their claim is undisputed. The court will order winding up and liquidation so the creditor may be paid the money owed to it.

- ◆ If dissolution is voluntary, corporate management will oversee liquidation; if dissolution is involuntary, the court will supervise liquidation.

- ◆ Corporations must generally notify known claimants and instruct them to submit their claims against the corporation within a certain period of time or be barred thereafter. As to unknown claims, corporations generally publish a notice in a newspaper, and claimants can enforce the claim within three years thereafter.

- ◆ Corporations must dispose of known claims and make provision for unknown claims.

- ◆ During liquidation, the expenses of liquidation will be paid, creditors will be paid, and then remaining assets will be distributed to shareholders on a pro rata basis in accordance with any preferences.

F. Role of Paralegal

The decision to dissolve is generally made by corporate management with the advice of attorneys and accountants. The effective date of the dissolution may trigger various tax consequences. Therefore, the corporation's accountants are often directly involved in the dissolution process.

Paralegals play a direct role in dissolutions and may be involved in the following:

1. Drafting resolutions contained in the minutes of board of directors' meetings (or written consent actions) recommending dissolution.
2. Preparing notice of the shareholders' meeting to vote on dissolution.
3. Preparing minutes of the meeting of shareholders approving dissolution.
4. Preparing and filing the notice of intent to dissolve with the secretary of state, if required by the state.
5. Reviewing corporate documents to prepare a list of known claims.
6. Preparing notices to be sent to individual creditors notifying them of the corporation's intended dissolution and the process for submitting claims against the corporation.
7. Arranging for publication of notices of dissolution in newspapers so creditors can raise unknown claims against the corporation.
8. Obtaining the tax clearance certificate.
9. Preparing and filing the articles of dissolution.
10. Assisting in the distribution of assets by preparing deeds, assignments, and other instruments to transfer title from the corporation to the shareholders.
11. Preparing petitions for bankruptcy relief, preparing lists of creditors and their claims, and working with the bankruptcy trustee and creditors.

Case Illustration
Dissolution Cannot Be Used to Accomplish a Freeze-Out

Case: *Callier v. Callier*, 378 N.E.2d 405 (Ill. App. Ct. 1978)

Facts: A shareholder brought a suit to liquidate the assets and business of the corporation, and the court ordered such liquidation, based on allegations that the management was deadlocked and irreparable injury was being threatened. The other shareholder (who held an equal interest) was opposed to liquidation.

Holding: The appellate court reversed. There was no evidence of any management deadlock. In fact, the evidence showed that the director-shareholder who petitioned for liquidation was in the process of forming another company to carry on the same kind of business with many of the corporation's employees and customers. Such siphoning off the value of the corporation is a breach of fiduciary duty and would deprive the other shareholder of his value in the corporation.

WEB RESOURCES

The most important resources relating to dissolution of corporations are the various state statutes. Following is a site allowing access to state statutes.

State statutes:	www.law.cornell.edu
	www.findlaw.com
Secretaries of state:	www.nass.org (for links to secretaries
	of state and downloadable forms
	relating to dissolution of
	corporations)
General information:	www.megalaw.com
Forms:	www.allaboutforms.com
	www.siccode.com/forms.php
	www.lectlaw.com
	www.megalaw.com

Discussion Questions

Fact Scenario.   KidVid, Inc., a California corporation, was incorporated several years ago but has recently experienced a slowdown, and several creditors are demanding payment for their debts. The corporation has two classes of stock, one of which is nonvoting stock. Use the MBCA to answer these questions.

1. The board of directors has proposed dissolving the corporation and will now submit this proposal for dissolution to the shareholders. Which shareholders are entitled to notice of a meeting to vote on dissolution?

2. The corporation filed its articles of dissolution on March 1 of this year and began to liquidate. On May 1, it received a significant contract that will allow the corporation to make a profit. Is there anything the corporation can do with respect to its dissolution?

3. The corporation sent a notice to one of its creditors, Thad, and stated that Thad's claim would be barred if not received in six months. Thad submitted his claim to the corporation seven months after the corporation sent him notice. Will Thad's claim be paid? Discuss. What result would occur if the corporation's notice stated that the claim would be barred if not received in three months?

4. May Thad initiate an action to dissolve the corporation? Discuss.

5. Assume that the corporation's six directors have not been able to make any decisions regarding the corporation's business and have not been able to make a decision whether the corporation should be dissolved. What might Shareholder A do to resolve such a dilemma? Is there anything Shareholder B can do if Shareholder B is opposed to Shareholder A's action?

6. Assume that the secretary of state dissolved a corporation on June 1 of this year because it did not timely file its annual report. May the corporation be revived? If so, when must the corporation apply for reinstatement? Assume that the corporation entered into a contract after the time it was administratively dissolved and before it was revived. Is the contract valid? Discuss.

7. Assume that a corporation distributed all of its assets in liquidation, and its three shareholders received 50 percent, 40 percent, and 10 percent of the corporation's net assets of $100,000, respectively. If a valid claim is made against the dissolved corporation in the amount of $50,000, how will this be paid?

Net Worth

1. Access the Web site of the South Carolina Secretary of State. What is the fee to file articles of dissolution?
2. Access the Web site of the California Secretary of State and review the Certificate of Election to Wind Up and Dissolve. What "Note" is provided at the top of the form?
3. Access the Web site of the Pennsylvania Secretary of State. What is the fee to file a Statement of Revival for a domestic corporation?
4. Access the Web site of the Ohio Secretary of State and review the form for reinstatement of a corporation. If a corporation has been administratively dissolved, and applies for reinstatement 18 months later, what will happen if its name was taken by another entity last month?
5. Review IRS form 966. Who must file this form?

17

❖ ❖ ❖

Corporate Variations

❖ ❖ ❖

CHAPTER OVERVIEW

The major portion of this text has been devoted to the business corporation, the most common corporation in the United States. Its distinguishing characteristics are its status as a legal person, which gives rise to double taxation, and the protection of its owners from personal liability. Formed for a profit-making purpose, the business corporation is well suited to the needs of many entrepreneurs. However, other forms of corporations respond to specialized purposes, goals, and groups. This chapter examines those other types of corporations.

The close corporation is a corporation whose stock is not publicly traded and is generally held by a small group of family or friends. In most instances, these shareholders are involved in the management of the business of the corporation. Failure to adhere strictly to some corporate formalities, such as holding meetings and elections, will generally not result in piercing the corporate veil to hold individual shareholders liable for corporate liabilities.

A nonprofit or not-for-profit corporation is one formed for a purpose other than to earn a profit. It may be formed for educational, scientific,

charitable, or even social reasons. The selection of the corporate form provides protection from liability for the nonprofit's members as well as significant tax benefits to the corporation itself.

A subsidiary corporation is one formed by another corporation, called the parent. The parent may create subsidiaries to operate different business divisions, to hold certain assets, and so forth. The parent usually owns all or the majority of the stock of the subsidiary. Nevertheless, the parent will not be liable for the subsidiary's debts unless the parent controls and directs the subsidiary.

For many years, individuals were not allowed to incorporate their professional practices. The authority now given to most professionals to incorporate provides them with significant corporate benefits and tax advantages.

Finally, to avoid double taxation, qualified corporations may elect to be S corporations. If a corporation meets the statutory requirements for S status, none of the income earned by the corporation itself is taxable; all of the taxable income is passed through to the individual shareholders in the corporation who then declare and pay taxes on this income.

A. Close Corporations

1. Introduction to Close Corporations

In a large or publicly held corporation, the rationale for the separation of ownership and management is readily apparent. The corporation is best managed by a dedicated core of professional managers, the board of directors, because it cannot readily be managed by thousands of shareholders who have little or no interest in the corporation other than their wish that it make money.

In smaller corporations, this division of ownership and management is a dilemma. A small group of family members or friends who have formed a corporation naturally want to manage it themselves. The very limited participation available to shareholders through voting will not be acceptable to a small group of investors who desire hands-on exposure to the business operations of a corporation in which they have invested their capital and themselves. Recognizing the need for some relaxation of the general corporate rules restricting shareholder participation in the management of the corporation, many states (including Delaware, California, Illinois, Maryland, and Wisconsin) and the MBCA have adopted special statutes to address the needs of these smaller owner-managed corporations, typically called *closely held* (or *close*) *corporations,* or **statutory close corporations** if they have elected to be governed by special statutes in the state of incorporation. In other states, there are no statutes designed solely for close corporations; in those states, close corporations are required to adhere to all of the statutes relating to corporations in general, except when judicial decisions have liberalized those statutes. The American Bar Association has approved a Model Statutory Close Corporation Supplement (MSCCS) to the MBCA designed to be adopted in states to govern the formation and operation of close corporations.

In brief, participants in a close corporation act as general partners yet they have selected the corporate form of business enterprise for protection from personal liability and for certain tax advantages.

The increasing acceptance of limited liability partnerships and limited liability companies, now recognized in all states, will undoubtedly result in fewer close corporations being formed than in the past. The limited liability company, discussed in Chapter Six, can be managed by its members, who are protected from personal liability as are shareholders in a close corporation. A limited liability company, moreover, has no restrictions on the number of people who may be involved in the enterprise, as does a close corporation. Additionally, a limited liability company offers the "pass through" tax status of a partnership and thereby avoids the burden of double taxation. Finally, in a limited liability company, members can be allocated profits and losses in an amount disproportionate to their contributions, whereas in a close corporation, shareholders will receive profit in accordance with their investment. Thus, limited liability companies (and limited liability partnerships) offer all of the advantages of close corporations and none of the disadvantages.

2. Characteristics of Close Corporations

Close corporations share a number of features in common, whether or not they are incorporated under statutes that expressly recognize this

Close corporation
Corporation whose shares are held by a small group that is active in managing the corporation (also called *statutory close corporation*)

corporate form. The most common characteristics of a close corporation are as follows:

a. There is a limitation on the number of shareholders in a close corporation. Some states and the MSCCS permit up to 50 shareholders, whereas other states restrict the number of shareholders to 25 or 30.
b. The shareholders typically enter into agreements restricting the transfer of shares. Thus, there is no readily available outside market for the shares of a close corporation. Moreover, its stock is not publicly traded.
c. All or most of the shareholders participate in the management of the corporation (and the corporation typically functions informally).

Because there are typically agreements restricting the free transfer of shares in a close corporation, the possibility of attracting outside investors is reduced. Few investors, other than family members or friends, wish to be involved in a corporation whose stock is subject to restrictions on its sale.

3. Formation of Close Corporations

A corporation may initially incorporate as a close corporation. Alternatively, a corporation that has been in existence may amend its articles of incorporation to elect close corporation status.

A close corporation is formed in the same way as any corporation: by filing of articles of incorporation. The articles of incorporation for a close corporation must generally recite that the corporation is being formed as a close corporation. Additionally, some states require a recitation of the various restrictions to which close corporations are generally subject. For example, the articles of incorporation form provided in Delaware (see Figure 17-1) contains four elements not found in the form used for incorporation of other entities:

a. The title of the document provides public notice of the type of corporation being incorporated by specifying "State of Delaware — Certificate of Incorporation — A Close Corporation";
b. The articles confirm that all of the corporation's issued stock, exclusive of treasury stock, will be held by less than 30 shareholders of record (stock held jointly by a husband and wife is treated as being held by one shareholder);
c. The articles recite that all of the issued stock of all classes will be subject to restrictions on their transfer; and
d. The articles confirm that there will be no "public offering" of any class of stock within the meaning of the Securities Act of 1933.

When the articles of incorporation are filed with the secretary of state, they will be reviewed for compliance with the pertinent state statutes and will be approved. Any other requirement imposed for the formation of corporations, such as publication of the articles in newspapers or recording of the articles with county clerks, must generally be followed. Additionally, the MSCCS and most states require that the close corporation's stock certificates contain a conspicuous legend alerting

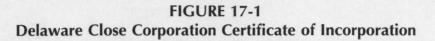

FIGURE 17-1
Delaware Close Corporation Certificate of Incorporation

STATE *of* **DELAWARE**
CERTIFICATE *of* **INCORPORATION**
A **CLOSE CORPORATION**
Of

_____

(name of corporation)

- **First:** The name of this Corporation is _____
  _____.

- **Second:** Its Registered Office in the State of Delaware is to be located at _____
  _____(street), in the City of _____
  _____County of _____Zip Code_____. The name of the
  registered agent is _____
  _____.

- **Third:** The nature of business and the objects and purposes proposed to be
  transacted, promoted and carried on, are to engage in any lawful act or activity for
  which corporations may be organized under the General Corporation Law of
  Delaware.

- **Fourth:** The amount of the total stock of this corporation is authorized to issue is
  _____shares (number of authorized shares) with a par value
  of _____ per share.

- **Fifth:** The name and mailing address of the incorporator are as follows:
  Name _____
  Mailing Address _____
  _____Zip Code_____

- **Sixth:** All of the corporation's issued stock, exclusive of treasury shares, shall be held
  of record by not more than thirty (30) persons.

- **Seventh:** All of the issued stock of all classes shall be subject to one or more of the
  restrictions on transfer permitted by Section 202 of the General Corporation Law.

- **Eighth:** The corporation shall make no offering of any of its stock of any class which
  would constitute a "public offering" within the meaning of the United States
  Securities Act of 1933, as it may be amended from time to time.

- **I, The Undersigned,** for the purpose of forming a corporation under the laws of the
  State of Delaware, do make, file and record this Certificate, and do certify that the
  facts herein stated are true, and I have accordingly hereunto set my hand this
  _____day of _____, A.D. 20_____.

BY:_____

(Incorporator)

NAME:_____

(type or print)

potential purchasers that the corporation is a close corporation and that the rights of shareholders in a close corporation may differ materially from those of shareholders in other corporations.

A close corporation may be terminated by an amendment to its articles of incorporation, approved by a two-thirds shareholders' vote, ending its status as a close corporation. Status as a close corporation will automatically terminate if any of the conditions required of a close corporation are breached, for example, if the corporation "goes public." Alternatively, the close corporation may terminate as would any other corporation: by voluntary or involuntary dissolution.

4.   Restrictions on Transfer of Shares

Perhaps the most significant characteristic of a close corporation is an agreement among shareholders to restrict or limit their ability to transfer (or **alienate**) their ownership interests in the corporation.

Alienation
Transfer of property

Because the close corporation almost always involves a group of individuals well known to each other either through family ties or friendship, the group will be reluctant to allow "outsiders" in who might change the dynamics of the organization. Therefore, shareholders in close corporations typically enter into agreements whereby they agree to certain restrictions placed on their ability to sell their shares. In states with separate statutes for close corporations and under the MSCCS, restrictions on transfer are imposed by statute. Generally, transfers to the corporation, other shareholders, family members, in a merger, or to an executor upon the death of a shareholder are permissible and are subject to no restrictions. Transfers to "outsiders," however, are restricted and can only be effected after the corporation has been offered the shares and the offer is rejected by a majority vote of the shareholders. MSCCS § 12. These restrictions may be a disadvantage for an individual requiring certain and ready liquidity of her investments, and, therefore, in such a case, the close corporation might not be a suitable investment vehicle. If the shareholders approve the offer, the corporation may allocate the purchased shares among shareholders. An attempted share transfer in violation of these prohibitions is ineffective.

There are several reasons why restrictions on the transfer of shares in close corporations exist. The shareholders, who are almost always friends or relatives, might desire continuity in management and might not wish to answer to outsiders. The restrictions also help ensure that a corporation maintains its S status so that it is not subject to double taxation (see Section E later in this chapter). Finally, restrictions on transfer prohibit a "palace coup" by a faction of shareholders who combine together to oust other shareholders.

Restrictions on the transfer of shares may be placed in the articles of incorporation, the bylaws, or in a private agreement among the shareholders or between the shareholders and the corporation. The private agreements are generally called **buy-sell agreements.** See Appendix I for a sample buy-sell agreement.

Buy-sell agreement
Agreement among
shareholders regarding
transfer of shares

The restrictions placed on the transferability or alienability of shares can vary. Although some courts have upheld absolute prohibitions against the transfer of shares, this is a minority view inasmuch as one of the characteristics of property ownership is the right to transfer it. Therefore, absolute bars to transfer are often invalidated on the basis that they are inherently at odds with the rights of a property owner.

The most common restriction on the transfer of shares is a **right of first refusal.** The shareholders enter into an agreement, either with each other or with the corporation, whereby they agree that before they can sell their shares to any outsider, either the corporation or the shareholders, or both, shall have the right to purchase the shares on the same terms as any third party who has made an offer for the shares. Only if the corporation and other shareholders decline to purchase the shares may they then be sold to the outsider. Any transfer of the shares in violation of such an agreement is ineffective.

Right of first refusal
Agreement to allow another to purchase something before it is sold to a third party

If the corporation or other shareholders elect not to purchase the shares within some time period specified in the agreement, the shareholder may then sell them to the third party. Many agreements anticipate the possibility of phony or rigged offers by requiring that any offer be bona fide and that it be submitted for review by the corporation or other shareholders.

Many close corporations also take great care in providing for the disposition of the shares of a deceased shareholder. Agreements often provide that upon the death of a shareholder the decedent's shares will be immediately transferred to the corporation, which is then obligated to pay the fair value of the shares to the shareholder's estate. Placing a value on shares that do not have a public market can be difficult. Therefore, appraisers are often used. Alternatively, a pre-established formula can be used.

Cross-purchase agreement
Agreement under which each shareholder insures the life of each other shareholder

There are two types of agreements for the sale of a shareholder's interest upon the death or disability of the shareholder. A **cross-purchase agreement** provides for the purchase of the shareholder's interest from him or his estate by the remaining shareholders. Under a cross-purchase agreement, each shareholder takes out a life/disability policy on the life of each of the other shareholders. Upon a shareholder's death or disability, each other shareholder then has funds from the insurance policy to purchase a portion of the deceased or disabled shareholder's shares.

Entity purchase agreement
Agreement under which entity purchases insurance on life of each member or shareholder (also called *stock redemption agreement*)

The other type of agreement is generally referred to as an **entity purchase agreement,** or *stock redemption agreement.* In this case, the corporate entity itself is the beneficiary under the terms of an insurance policy, and in the event of the death or disability of a shareholder, the entity receives the insurance proceeds and then purchases the deceased or disabled shareholder's interest. Such an agreement is often preferable when there are more than two or three shareholders, because the number of policies required to fund such an agreement will be fewer than the number required to fund a cross-purchase agreement. Under an entity purchase or stock redemption agreement, the corporation simply pays the premiums for and owns a single policy on the life of each shareholder.

Some corporations employ mandatory buy-sell provisions that flatly require the corporation to purchase the shares of a shareholder who dies or wishes to withdraw. Such provisions provide certainty for both parties: The individual shareholders know that the shares can be disposed of and the corporation knows that it need never worry about outsiders. Many agreements allow the corporation to pay the purchase price for the shares in installments, with appropriate interest.

Under MSCCS § 14, if the articles of incorporation provide such, the estate of a deceased shareholder may require a close corporation to purchase all of the deceased shareholder's shares. Life insurance is usually used to fund the compulsory purchase obligation. Such statutory provisions provide basic protection to shareholders if they have failed to enter into an appropriate private agreement.

5. Operation of Close Corporations

Management Flexibility.   Shareholders are almost always active in managing the close corporation and are often employees of the corporation as well. Management and governance tend to be less formal than in larger or nonclose corporations. In fact, many statutes expressly allow the shareholders to enter into an agreement to regulate the management and business affairs of the corporation. Under MSCCS § 20, such an agreement is effective even if it eliminates a board of directors, restricts the discretion or powers of the board, or its effect is to treat the corporation as a partnership. Bylaws are not required if sufficient provisions are provided in the articles of incorporation or an agreement among shareholders. Annual meetings need not be held unless one or more shareholders request a meeting in writing. Delaware's statutes governing close corporations are similar to the MSCCS.

If the shareholders agree to eliminate the board, this decision must generally be unanimous. The management and control of the corporation are then conducted by the shareholders. The shareholders may appoint one or more shareholders as **designated directors** to sign documents on behalf of the corporation. If shareholders act like directors in managing the corporation, they will be subject to the liabilities and fiduciary duties of directors. MSCCS § 20(c).

> **Designated director**
> Shareholder appointed in a close corporation to operate its affairs when there is no board of directors

Piercing the Veil.   Dissatisfied creditors of close corporations often try to pierce the corporate veil to hold shareholders liable for corporate obligations. Because piercing the veil can occur when a corporation fails to follow statutory formalities required of corporations, it would seem that the close corporation (which might not have directors, bylaws, or annual meetings) is particularly vulnerable to attack on this ground. Most statutes anticipate this potential problem by providing that the failure of a close corporation to observe the usual corporate formalities is not a ground for imposing personal liability on the shareholders for liabilities of the corporation. Although a court can pierce the veil of a close corporation if circumstances warrant, a court cannot pierce the veil merely on the basis that the corporation is a close one, functioning like a partnership and not observing the usual corporate formalities.

Judicial Supervision.   Because close corporations typically involve small groups of individuals familiar to one another, and because almost all of the individuals are actively involved in managing the business, the close corporation provides many opportunities for dissension and in-fighting. For example, majority shareholders might reduce the compensation of minority shareholders, remove them from positions of authority, and so forth. The minority shareholders could petition for judicial relief from oppressive conduct and breach of fiduciary duties. The most dramatic remedy is for a shareholder to initiate an action for involuntary dissolution, based on waste of corporate assets, fraud, or oppression.

Another common scenario in close corporations is deadlock among directors or shareholders that results in corporate paralysis. Dissatisfied shareholders may initiate court action to seek relief. Courts may fashion several alternatives to remedy a deadlock or a dispute. A court might appoint a custodian or provisional director until deadlocked issues are resolved and the corporation's business can again be conducted for the advantage of the shareholders. A court might appoint a custodian to manage corporate business to protect the interests of shareholders or might order a forced buy-out of shares of oppressed minority shareholders. The most drastic remedy is a court-ordered involuntary dissolution; it is a last resort appropriate only after other approaches to resolving the dispute have failed.

Fundamental Changes. Close corporations may engage in mergers, share exchanges, and asset sales, although these transactions must be approved by a two-thirds vote under the MSCCS.

Shareholder Dissolution. Under MSCCS § 33, if authorized by the articles of incorporation, a shareholder in a close corporation may dissolve the corporation at will. This provision places shareholders in a close corporation on an equal footing with partners in a general partnership controlled by the UPA, who generally have the right to dissolve a partnership at will.

B. Nonprofit Corporations

1. Introduction

Nonprofit corporation
Corporation formed for a purpose other than to earn profit (also called *not-for-profit corporation*)

Nonprofit (or *not-for-profit*) **corporations** are not formed to earn a profit and do not distribute any part of their income or profit to their members, directors, or officers. These corporations are often formed for some charitable, scientific, religious, or educational purpose, or for the mutual benefit of the members of the corporation. Most states have specific statutes governing formation, operation, and termination of nonprofit corporations in their jurisdictions. Many of these statutes are based on the Model Nonprofit Corporation Act. Merely incorporating in a state as a nonprofit corporation does not automatically qualify the corporation for exemption from federal taxes. The corporation must file a separate application with the Internal Revenue Service for tax-exempt status.

Some states, such as Florida, provide a laundry list of all of the purposes for which nonprofit corporations may be organized. Fla. Stat. Ann. § 617.0301 provides in pertinent part as follows:

> Corporations may be organized under this act for any lawful purpose or purposes not for pecuniary profit and not specifically prohibited to corporations under other laws of this state. Such purposes include, without limitation, charitable, benevolent, eleemosynary, educational, historical, civic, patriotic, political, religious, social, fraternal, literary, cultural, athletic, scientific, agricultural, horticultural, animal husbandry, and professional, commercial, industrial, or trade association purposes.

Other states classify their nonprofit corporations into separate categories based on the purpose of the corporation. For example, California and many other states recognize three types of nonprofit corporations: those formed primarily for **religious** purposes; those organized primarily for charitable purposes, such as those promoting science, health, education, or the arts (called **public benefit corporations**); and those organized for other than religious, charitable, civic, or social welfare purposes, such as country clubs, homeowners' associations, and professional associations (called **mutual benefit corporations**).

2. Formation of Nonprofit Corporations

Nonprofit corporations are formed in the same manner as other corporations: by the filing of articles of incorporation. The contents of the articles will be specified in the pertinent state statutes and most states provide forms for articles of incorporation for nonprofit corporations. (See Figure 17-2 for sample articles of incorporation for a nonprofit corporation.)

The name of the corporation may be subject to various requirements. Some states do not permit a nonprofit corporation's name to contain a corporate designation such as "incorporated," "company," or "limited." Other states, such as Florida, prohibit "company" or "co." but allow "corporation" or "incorporated" or their abbreviations. Some statutes specify that designations such as "association," "club," "group," and so forth be used.

Many states prohibit the use of general purpose clauses and require that the purposes of the nonprofit corporation be expressly stated in the articles. A registered agent must be designated and a registered address must be given. Some states require that the corporation provide how its assets will be distributed upon dissolution. Other states, such as California, require a recitation by public benefit and religious corporations that "no substantial part of the activities of this corporation shall consist of carrying on propaganda, or otherwise attempting to influence legislation, and the corporation shall not participate or intervene in any political campaign (including the publishing or distribution of statements) on behalf of any candidate for public office." Mutual benefit corporations formed for political purposes are, of course, not subject to such restrictions.

The articles are submitted to the secretary of state with the appropriate filing fee. Other formalities required in the state, such as publishing the articles in a newspaper, must be followed as well. The corporation is formed upon filing of the articles.

3. Operation and Governance of Nonprofit Corporations

In many ways, nonprofit corporations function similarly to business corporations. A board of directors will be elected, bylaws will be adopted, the directors will manage and control the affairs of the corporation at regular meetings or by unanimous written consent, and the directors must perform their duties in good faith and with the care of ordinarily prudent and diligent persons. In most states, the state attorney general has the authority to take a public benefit corporation to court to ensure it is being operated in the public interest, whereas disputes regarding mutual benefit corporations are typically resolved by their members.

FIGURE 17-2
Tennessee Articles of Incorporation for Nonprofit Corporation

State of Tennessee

Department of State
Corporate Filings
312 Eighth Avenue North
6th Floor, William R. Snodgrass Tower
Nashville, TN 37243

CHARTER
(Nonprofit Corporation)

For Office Use Only

The undersigned acting as incorporator(s) of a nonprofit corporation under the Tennessee Nonprofit Corporation Act adopts the following Articles of Incorporation.

1. The name of the corporation is: _____

2. Please complete all of the following sentences by checking one of the two boxes in each sentence:
   This corporation is a ☐ public benefit corporation / ☐ mutual benefit corporation.
   This corporation is ☐ a religious corporation / ☐ not a religious corporation.
   This corporation will ☐ have members / ☐ not have members.

3. The name and complete address of the corporation's initial registered agent and office in Tennessee is:
   TN
   Name   Street Address   City   State, Zip Code   County

4. List the name and complete address of each incorporator:
   Name   (Include Street Address, City, State, and Zip Code)
   Name   (Include Street Address, City, State, and Zip Code)
   Name   (Include Street Address, City, State, and Zip Code)

5. The complete address of the corporation's principal office is:
   Street Address   City   State/Country   Zip Code

6. The corporation is not for profit.

7. If the document is not to be effective upon filing by the Secretary of State, the delayed effective date and time are:
   Date _____, _____, Time _____ (Not to exceed 90 days.)

8. Insert here the provisions regarding the distribution of assets upon dissolution:

9. Other provisions:

Signature Date

Incorporator's Signature

Incorporator's Name (typed or printed)

SS-4418 (Rev. 9/04)   Filing Fee: $100   RDA 1678

In some important respects, however, the nonprofit corporation is far different from a business corporation. For example, **membership** in the nonprofit corporation is what is offered, if anything. Stock is not sold. Generally, an individual or business is entitled to only one membership. Thus, there are no issues of majority shareholders oppressing minority shareholders. Members of public benefit or religious corporations do not usually vote unless the articles or bylaws so provide.

A nonprofit corporation may have no members, one class of members, or more than one class of members. For example, you might refer to yourself as a member of a church but it is unlikely that the church has issued a formal membership to you. On the other hand, you might be a registered "parishioner," entitling you to vote on limited church issues. You might also be a member of a homeowners' association. Generally, one membership accompanies each parcel of real estate sold. As a member of a homeowners' association, you might have specific rights to written notice of meetings, to vote either personally or by proxy at those meetings, and to inspect the books of the association. Membership or registration in a church or other religious organization seldom confers such rights.

There may be different classes of members. For example, in a nonprofit country club, there may be "A" memberships, which are expensive and carry certain rights and privileges, and there may be "B" memberships, offered at lower prices and which may carry certain restrictions on use of the club facilities and on voting. The rights and privileges of each class must be set forth in the articles or bylaws. If memberships are issued, the corporation may issue a certificate of membership. Members may be liable for dues, assessments, or fees, but are not liable for any liability or obligation of the corporation.

Although the nonprofit corporation is formed for some purpose other than making a profit, it is possible that the corporation may invest and manage wisely and thereby earn a profit. The earning of profit will not affect the corporation's nonprofit status. The corporation, however, cannot pay any dividend or take any part of its income or profit and distribute it to its members, directors, or officers. Generally, any profits made should be devoted to the purposes of the corporation: providing medical assistance to the needy, scholarships for underprivileged students, grants for scientific research, and so forth. Alternatively, the corporation may improve its offices, hire more skilled employees, and purchase new equipment. Although the nonprofit corporation is allowed to compensate its directors, officers, and employees, one that extravagantly compensates its personnel and provides plush accommodations and yet expends little, if any, of its income accomplishing its proclaimed purposes may be dissolved by the state or may lose its federal tax-exempt status.

Upon dissolution, and after payment to its creditors, a nonprofit mutual benefit corporation may make a payment or distribution to its members. Whereas this one-time distribution is commonly seen when mutual benefit or civic corporations (homeowners' associations, country clubs, and so forth) are involved, upon dissolution of a public benefit or religious organization, any distribution usually must be made to a like-minded group or association rather than to the members.

Nonprofit corporations may generally be dissolved in the same manner as business corporations: voluntarily by the directors or members, or involuntarily by the state, the members, or creditors. Nonprofit corporations formed in one state may transact business in others so long as they properly qualify to do so (see Chapter Fifteen).

Membership
What is offered by nonprofit corporations to their "owners" rather than stock

4. *Exemption from Taxation for Nonprofit Corporations*

After the nonprofit corporation is formed, it should apply for federal tax-exempt status. Because the provisions of the Internal Revenue Code relating to most nonprofit corporations are set forth in § 501(c)(3) of Title 26, nonprofit corporations that have tax-exempt status are often referred to as **501(c)(3) corporations** although other provisions within § 501(c) cover other nonprofit organizations. Section 501(c) specifies the purposes that qualify a corporation for an exemption from paying federal taxes.

Tax-exempt status is a privilege that must be applied for rather than an automatic right conferred on a nonprofit corporation. The IRS identifies more than 30 types of tax-exempt organizations in its publication IRS No. 557, *Tax-Exempt Status for Your Organization*. After the application is filed, the IRS will issue a ruling or determination letter recognizing the organization's tax-exempt status. Typically, a nonprofit corporation will be granted tax-exempt status if it is organized and operated exclusively for charitable, religious, literary, scientific, educational, or other similar purposes. Generally, churches need not file the IRS application.

Contributions made to a public benefit corporation (the American Heart Association, Inc., The Sudden Infant Death Research Foundation, and the like) are usually tax deductible. Similarly, contributions made to religious organizations generally result in a tax deduction for the donor. On the other hand, memberships in mutual benefit associations are typically not deductible unless they qualify as valid business expenses. Thus, membership dues paid to Riverbend Country Club or Oak View Homeowners' Association may not be deductible, whereas membership in the National Capital Area Paralegal Association could well be tax deductible.

Nonprofit corporations generally pay no state income or any real property taxes. Certain annual fees and reports, however, are usually required by the state of incorporation.

C.   Parent and Subsidiary Corporations

1. *Introduction*

One corporation may form another. The creator corporation is called the **parent,** and the corporation it creates is called a **subsidiary.** A corporation may create subsidiaries for a variety of reasons: It might wish each of its different business activities to be carried out by a separate corporation; it might wish certain subsidiaries to hold title to certain assets and then license their use to the parent or to others; it might form subsidiaries to do business in other jurisdictions; or it might form a subsidiary to conduct more risky ventures and not subject the parent's assets to possible liability for these activities.

2. *Formation and Characteristics of Subsidiary Corporations*

A subsidiary corporation is formed like any other corporation: by filing articles of incorporation that comply with the state of incorporation. No special provisions

501(c)(3) corporation
Term used to refer to tax-exempt nonprofit corporations, after § 501(c)(3) of the Internal Revenue Code

Parent
A corporation that forms another

Subsidiary
A corporation formed by another

are required in the articles and the articles need not recite that the corporation being formed is a subsidiary of another. A close review of the signature block on the articles of incorporation may reveal, however, that rather than an individual signing as an incorporator, an individual has signed as president or vice president of a corporate incorporator. In general, however, the creation of a subsidiary corporation does not differ in any significant respect from the creation of any other corporation; the only difference is that the incorporator may be another corporation.

If a parent (P) creates several different subsidiaries (*A, B, C,* and *D*), the subsidiaries *A, B, C,* and *D* are sometimes referred to as brother-sister corporations (because they share the same parent) or as **affiliates** with respect to their relationships to each other.

Affiliates
Corporations with common parents (also called *brother-sister* corporations)

The distinguishing characteristic of a parent-subsidiary relationship is that the parent will either own all of the subsidiary's stock or will own the majority of it, such that it can elect the directors of the subsidiary and thereby control its business activities. A subsidiary whose stock is issued only to the parent is called a **wholly owned subsidiary.**

Wholly owned subsidiary
A corporation the stock of which is entirely owned by the parent

In general, all of the rules and policies governing other business corporations also apply to parents and subsidiaries. They are each managed by elected directors who owe fiduciary duties to the respective shareholders, their operation parallels that of other business corporations, and dissolution may be either voluntary or involuntary. When the parent owns all of the stock of the subsidiary, however, decisions such as whether to merge or sell assets will not be subject to approval by the subsidiary's shareholder(s) because the parent is the only shareholder of the subsidiary. Once the parent has made certain decisions with respect to the subsidiary, the subsidiary might be powerless to stop them.

The existence of a subsidiary may subject the parent to additional taxation. For example, the subsidiary will pay taxes on the income it earns. When the income is then distributed as a dividend to its sole shareholder, the parent has received additional corporate income on which it pays taxes. If the parent distributes cash dividends to its shareholders, they will pay taxes on the distribution they have received. Rather than double taxation, this is triple taxation. The same money has been subject to taxation three times: when received by the subsidiary, when received by the parent, and when received by the parent's shareholders.

3. *Liability of Parent for Subsidiary's Debts*

In general, the primary issue giving rise to litigation involving parents and subsidiaries is whether, and under what circumstances, the parent may be liable for a subsidiary's debt. For example, assume P Corp. has incorporated Sub Corp. and is its sole shareholder. If Sub Corp. enters into a contract to purchase certain items from a creditor and then cannot pay for those items, the creditor may allege that the parent is liable for the subsidiary's debts. Absent some condition calling for "piercing the corporate veil," shareholders are not liable for their corporation's debts. Should a corporate parent nonetheless be liable for a subsidiary's debts solely on the basis that it is the only shareholder of the subsidiary?

The parent and subsidiary are typically viewed as separate legal entities, and each remains liable for its own debts. Just because the parent is the sole or majority shareholder of the subsidiary does not mean the parent will be liable for the subsidiary's debts. According to the United States Supreme Court, "it is a general principle of corporate law deeply 'ingrained in our economic and legal systems' that a parent corporation (so-called because of control through ownership of another corporation's stock) is not liable for the acts of its subsidiaries. . . . Limited liability is the rule, not the exception." *United States v. Bestfoods,* 524 U.S. 51, 61 (1998) (citations omitted). There are, however, a number of instances in which courts have pierced the veil between a parent and subsidiary to impose liability upon the parent for the subsidiary's obligations. The factors that result in the veil being pierced between a parent and subsidiary are closely parallel to those that result in the veil being pierced between a corporation and its individual shareholders. Generally, the parent will not be liable for its subsidiary's debts if:

a. The respective bank accounts, records, financial information, and business transactions are kept separate from each other;
b. The corporations have separate employees, directors, officers, and meetings;
c. The subsidiary has been sufficiently capitalized so that it can meet the normal business obligations that would be expected to arise;
d. The respective corporations are held out to the public as separate enterprises (thus, the common announcement by a parent that another corporation is a wholly owned subsidiary provides public notice of the separate nature of the entities); and/or
e. The policies of the subsidiary are directed to its own interests rather than solely to the interests of the parent.

In determining whether to impose liability on a parent for its subsidiary's debts, all of these factors are considered. The court will conduct a balancing test to determine if sufficient separateness of the two entities has been maintained. If the parent treats the subsidiary's accounts as its own, commingles funds, shares personnel or business departments, files consolidated financial statements or tax returns with the subsidiary, pays the subsidiary's salaries and expenses, and controls and dominates the subsidiary to the extent that it is a mere instrumentality, agent, or puppet of the parent, courts will reason that if the parent does not respect the separate nature of the subsidiary, there is no need for a creditor to do so. Similarly, looting of the subsidiary's profits by distributing dividends to the sole shareholder, the parent, such that the subsidiary has insufficient assets to meet its obligations, is viewed as an injustice to or fraud on creditors, in which case the parent may be liable for the subsidiary's obligations.

For example, in one 1998 case, in holding that the court could exercise jurisdiction over a parent due to its control over its subsidiaries, the U.S. District Court for the Eastern District of Pennsylvania noted the following factors: many of the material functions of all three companies were performed in a central office; the three companies shared common directors and officers; the corporations shared a common payroll department; the companies used their employees interchangeably; and the corporations projected a unified marketing image by using the same corporate logo and by holding themselves out as a single entity. The court remarked that taken separately, none of these factors would require a finding of jurisdiction, but that taken together they portrayed a picture of virtually total interrelationships and inordinate parental control over the subsidiaries.

D. Professional Corporations

1. Introduction

Until relatively recently, professionals, including doctors, lawyers, accountants, and architects, were not permitted to incorporate their professional practices. Because a distinctive characteristic of a corporation is that it protects its owners from liability, a fear existed that professionals would use the corporate form to shield themselves from claims, leaving victims of professional negligence without sufficient redress. The absolute bar against incorporation of the professions also resulted in professionals being unable to take advantage of other benefits of incorporation, such as possible tax advantages and benefit plans available to other individuals or businesses wishing to incorporate.

Approximately 30 years ago, in response to demands by professionals that they be allowed to incorporate their practices, many states began enacting statutes permitting professional practices to operate as corporations. In the late 1970s, the Model Professional Corporation Act was adopted to serve as a model for states enacting statutes dealing with professionals.

All states now allow the incorporation of professional practices, primarily by separate statutes or acts enacted for **professional corporations** (or *professional associations,* as they are called in some states). The definition of a "professional" differs greatly from state to state. Many states identify specific professions that may incorporate, with the more modern approach including an ever-increasing variety of professionals, such as physical and occupational therapists, marriage counselors, registered nurses, and acupuncturists. Other states, following the Model Professional Corporation Act, do not enumerate the particular professions that may incorporate but rather limit the formation of professional corporations to those individuals who must be licensed by the state to provide a certain service.

An individual who incorporates his professional practice becomes an employee of the corporation. The corporation may then establish certain benefit plans for its employee.

The distinguishing characteristics of a professional corporation are that share ownership is limited to the licensed professionals and that professionals retain liability for their own acts of malpractice and the acts of others under their authority and control. Thus, although perhaps the most important feature of corporate existence, limited liability, is unavailable to the professional, other advantages of the corporate form, namely fringe benefit plans available to employees, may make the selection of the corporate form attractive to a professional. Moreover, for professionals who practice in a group, incorporation may shield each against the negligence of their colleagues. Professional corporations are subject to the same tax treatment as business corporations and they may have perpetual existence.

The emergence of the new business entity, the limited liability partnership (sometimes called the registered limited liability partnership), might result in a decrease in the number of professional corporations. The LLP, discussed in Chapter Five, is an ideal business enterprise for professionals because it protects its members from personal liability for acts of negligence of their co-partners. The LLP is taxed as a partnership and all taxable income earned by the

Professional corporation The incorporation of the practice of a professional, including a doctor or lawyer (also called *professional association*)

partnership is passed through to the individual partners who pay tax thereon at their appropriate rates. Similarly, as discussed in Chapter Six, limited liability companies, recognized in all jurisdictions, can be formed by professionals in most states, although the professionals retain personal liability for their own wrongful acts and those performed under their supervision or control. LLCs are also taxed as partnerships, namely, with pass-through taxation. In all of these entities (the professional corporation, the LLP, and the LLC), professionals remain liable for their own improper acts and the improper acts of those they supervise.

2. *Formation, Operation, and Liability of Professional Corporations*

A professional corporation is formed by filing articles of incorporation. A professional corporation may be formed by an individual professional or by a group composed of professionals. For example, if Gail Wagner is an attorney practicing in the firm of Reed, Markey, and Maguire, Gail may incorporate herself. Alternatively, the law firm itself may incorporate and then issue shares in the professional corporation of Reed, Markey, and Maguire to its attorneys, including Gail.

The articles must usually specify the particular service to be rendered by the corporation (medical services, accounting services, and so forth) and typically recite that the corporation is organized for the sole and specific purpose of rendering those services. Most states also require that the name of the corporation include some signal to provide notice to the public that the professional has adopted the corporate form. The most typical signals required are "professional corporation," "professional association," or "service corporation," or their initials, "P. C.," "P. A.," or "S. C." The appropriate signal must usually be displayed on all letterhead and business stationery of the professional, as well as on any signs, literature, or nameplates. Because the name of the corporation is often the name of the individual professional, for example, "Howard A. Ross, P. C.," individuals may use a name similar or identical to that of another professional if it is their personal name. Thus, although states prohibit a corporation from using a name likely to cause confusion with another, the names of professional corporations may duplicate each other because some professionals share the same names.

The articles of incorporation must specify the number of shares the corporation is authorized to issue. Share ownership is generally restricted to the licensed professionals. In the example given earlier, the law firm Reed, Markey, and Maguire could issue shares only to its licensed attorneys, not to their spouses, the office administrator, or office support staff. Most statutes typically require that the directors and officers of the corporation be licensed as well so that management of the corporation is not conducted by lay persons. Other states require that a certain percentage of directors and officers (usually at least one-half) be licensed professionals. If nonlicensed professionals may serve as directors or officers, they are usually prohibited from making decisions on professional matters. Most statutes impose express restrictions on the transfer of shares in the professional corporation. The shares of a professional who dies, or who loses a license to practice the profession, or who wishes to leave the group must be transferred to another qualified shareholder or to the corporation itself. Thus, professional corporations should be sure to use shareholders' agreements (or buy-sell agreements) for that purpose. The share certificates must also include a notice that the corporation is a professional corporation and that its shares are subject to restrictions on their transfer. The articles of incorporation must identify a registered office and an agent for service of process. Most states will supply forms for articles of incorporation for a professional corporation (see Figure 17-3).

The licensed professional retains liability for her own wrongful acts or those performed under her supervision and control. Thus, attorneys are generally liable for mistakes made by their secretaries and paralegals. The attorney is liable for acts of malpractice, such as failing to file a document on time, even if the filing was the responsibility of the secretary or clerk. In most states, and under the Model Professional Corporation Act, the professional is liable only for her own acts of negligence and not for those of other professionals in the group. In such cases, of course, the corporation itself is liable for the negligent act. Using our example, Gail Wagner would therefore be liable for missing a statute of limitations, but in most states she would not share any liability if Thomas Barnes, another attorney in the office, committed an act of negligence. In these states, a professional corporation is similar to an LLP or LLC with regard to liability. In other states, however, liability is imposed jointly and severally so that liability may be imposed on Gail Wagner for Thomas Barnes's negligence. An LLP and LLC, however, provide protection from the negligent acts or omissions of one's colleagues. Still, in actual practice a claim is usually made against the law firm employing the attorney, the group employing the doctor, and so forth, as these entities generally have more extensive assets than the individuals and often maintain significant professional liability insurance.

The Model Professional Corporation Act approach is similar to that of the LLP and LLC: Any individual who renders professional services as an employee of a professional corporation is liable for a negligent or wrongful act or omission in which he personally participates to the same extent as if he rendered the services as a sole practitioner; however, the individual is not liable for the conduct of other employees of the corporation, unless he is at fault in appointing, supervising, or cooperating with them.

Professional corporations engage in many of the same activities as business corporations: They may amend their articles, merge with another corporation, and dissolve, either voluntarily or involuntarily. A professional corporation may usually operate in another state upon filing the appropriate documents to qualify to conduct business in the other state.

E. S Corporations

1. Introduction

An **S corporation** is not truly a different form of corporation but is rather an existing small business corporation qualifying for special tax treatment. Any business corporation that is not an S corporation is typically referred to as a "C" corporation. Small corporations will nearly always give serious consideration to electing status as an S corporation. According to subchapter S of the Internal Revenue Code (26 U.S.C. §§ 1361-1364), a "small business

S corporation
Corporation whose income is not taxed at corporate level but is passed through to its shareholders who pay tax at their rates

FIGURE 17-3
Nevada Professional Corporation Articles of Incorporation

ROSS MILLER
Secretary of State
206 North Carson Street
Carson City, Nevada 89701-4299
(775) 684 5708
Website: www.nvsos.gov

Articles of Incorporation
Professional Corporation
(PURSUANT TO NRS CHAPTER 89)

USE BLACK INK ONLY - DO NOT HIGHLIGHT   ABOVE SPACE IS FOR OFFICE USE ONLY

1. Name of Corporation: (see instructions)	
2. Registered Agent for Service of Process: (check only one box)	☐ Commercial Registered Agent: _____ Name ☐ Noncommercial Registered Agent (name and address below) *OR* ☐ Office or Position with Entity (name and address below) _____ Name of Noncommercial Registered Agent OR Name of Title of Office or Other Position with Entity _____ Nevada ____ Street Address City Zip Code _____ Nevada ____ Mailing Address (if different from street address) City Zip Code
3. Authorized Stock: (number of shares corporation is authorized to issue)	Number of shares *with par value:* _____ Par value per share: $ _____ Number of shares *without par value:* _____
4. Names and Addresses of the Directors/Trustees and Stockholders: **IMPORTANT:** **a)** A certificate from the regulatory board showing that each individual is licensed at the time of filing with this office must be presented with this form. **b)** Each Director/Trustee, Stockholder and Incorporator must be a licensed professional.	1) _____ Name _____ Street Address City State Zip Code 2) _____ Name _____ Street Address City State Zip Code 3) _____ Name _____ Street Address City State Zip Code
5. Purpose: (see instructions)	The purpose of this corporation shall be:
6. Name, Address and Signature of Incorporator: (attach additional page if more than one incorporator)	_____ X _____ Name Incorporator Signature _____ Address City State Zip Code
7. Certificate of Acceptance of Appointment of Registered Agent:	I hereby accept appointment as Registered Agent for the above named Entity. X _____ _____ Authorized Signature of Registered Agent or On Behalf of Registered Agent Entity Date

This form must be accompanied by appropriate fees.   Nevada Secretary of State NRS 89 Articles
Revised on 7-1-08

corporation" may elect not to have its income taxed at the corporate level, but to have the income passed through to the shareholders who then pay tax at their appropriate rates. Tax must be paid on income whether or not it is distributed. Thus, if the corporation decides to retain $50,000 in an emergency account, the individual shareholders must declare and pay tax on their pro rata share of this sum as if they had received it personally. Losses sustained by the corporation can be used by the shareholders to offset other income and thereby decrease taxes. Deductions for losses, however, are limited to the adjusted basis of the stock and any debt owed to the shareholder by the corporation. Any loss or deduction not allowed because of this limit is carried over and treated as a loss for the next tax year. Additionally, rules apply that limit losses from passive activities.

The requirement that the corporation be "small" refers to the number of its shareholders, not the size of the business or its amount of revenue. Thus, a corporation with a handful of shareholders could elect S status, even if revenue is in the millions of dollars. Electing S status avoids double taxation (taxation of the corporate income and then taxation of individual shareholders when income is distributed to them) by eliminating payment of federal taxes by the corporation. In brief, tax-wise, the S corporation is treated like a sole proprietorship, partnership, limited liability partnership, or limited liability company. "S corps" are now the most common form of corporation.

2.   *Formation, Operation, and Termination of S Corporations*

To elect to be treated and exist as an S corporation, a corporation must file Forms 2553 and 1120S with the Internal Revenue Service. The election permits the income of the S corporation to be taxed to the shareholders of the corporation, whether or not that income is distributed.

A corporation may make the election to be treated as an S corporation only if it meets all of the following tests:

a.   It is a domestic corporation rather than one formed in a foreign country;
b.   It has no more than 100 shareholders (a husband and wife are treated as one shareholder, and all members of a family are treated as one shareholder);
c.   It has only individuals, estates, or certain trusts (rather than other corporations or partnerships) as shareholders;
d.   It has no nonresident alien shareholders;
e.   It generally has a calendar year as its tax year;
f.   It has only one class of stock;
g.   It is not a bank, insurance company, or domestic international sales corporation; and
h.   All shareholders consent to the election.

The S corporation election is not mentioned or addressed in the corporation's articles of incorporation, and the state of incorporation has no interest in whether its domestic corporations elect S status. The S election is made with the Internal Revenue Service after incorporation. Individual shareholders will sign consent statements to make the election. These will be filed with Form 2553. Within approximately 60 days after submission of Form 2553 to the Internal Revenue Service, the corporation will be informed of the acceptance or rejection of the S election.

The S election must be made within a specified time period: S status must be elected on or before the fifteenth day of the third month of the corporation's tax year for which the S status is to be effective. For example, a corporation with a calendar tax year could elect S status until March 15, 2009, and its 2009 income would be passed through to the shareholders rather than being taxed at the corporate level.

Because the number of shareholders involved in an S corporation is relatively small, these shareholders are nearly always active in managing the business. Additionally, to ensure that stock is not transferred to others (which could jeopardize the corporation's S status), shareholders in most S corporations enter into agreements restricting the transfer of their shares so that shares are not transferred to a one hundred first shareholder, a nonresident alien, or a corporation, LLP, or LLC — any of which transfers would result in automatic termination of S status. S election may be made by a close corporation, assuming the requirements for S status are met.

S status may be particularly helpful during the first few years of a corporation's existence, when it may sustain losses. These losses may be passed through to the shareholders who may then use them to offset other income, thereby decreasing their tax liability. S status might also be desirable when individual shareholders' tax rates are lower than the applicable corporate tax rates.

Although S corporations do not pay federal income tax, they must report their annual income to the Internal Revenue Service using Form 1120S. Attached to Form 1120S is Schedule K-1, which discloses each shareholder's portion of corporate income and losses. The individual shareholders report their income (whether distributed or not) or losses on Schedule E, a form attached to their individual 1040 tax forms. Thus, a shareholder owning 14 percent of the stock of an S corporation declares and pays tax on 14 percent of the income earned and declares 14 percent of any losses sustained.

S corporation status remains in effect until formally revoked by a majority of the shareholders. Additionally, S status will automatically terminate if the corporation no longer meets the requirements for small business corporations, for example, a transfer occurs that results in a one hundred first shareholder, or it issues a second class of stock.

The emergence and popularity of the limited liability company (see Chapter Six) — which also protects its members from personal liability, is member-managed, has no limitations on the number of members (who need not be individuals and can be nonresident aliens), all while allowing pass-through of income — could make the S corporation a relic of the past. The LLC avoids the restrictions imposed on S corporations while maintaining pass-through tax status. Therefore, it is an increasingly popular investment vehicle.

Because the corporations discussed in this chapter are subject to special requirements, develop checklists for each type of corporation. For example, for S corporations, questions could include the following:

- How many shareholders will the corporation have?
- Are all shareholders individuals?
- How many classes of stock will the corporation issue?

Such checklists will streamline the process of determining whether clients qualify to be treated as close corporations, professional corporations, and so forth. Additionally, the checklists can be easily modified to use as annual audit forms to ensure clients remain in compliance with all statutory requirements.

Key Features of Other Forms of Corporations

- A close corporation is a smaller corporation owned and operated by a group of family and/or friends. There is usually a limit of 50 or fewer shareholders who enter into agreements restricting the transfer of shares. Close corporations are generally allowed less formality in operation than other business corporations.
- A nonprofit (or not-for-profit) corporation is one formed not to earn a profit but for some charitable or religious purpose or for the mutual benefit of its members. Stock is not sold. Memberships are often granted to the members of the nonprofit corporation. If nonprofits apply for and are granted tax-exempt status, they need not pay federal taxes. Contributions made to charitable or religious nonprofits are generally tax deductible, whereas contributions made to a mutual benefit nonprofit are deductible only if they are valid business expenses.
- A subsidiary corporation is one formed by another, the parent. The parent either owns all of the stock of the subsidiary or the vast majority of it. A parent will be liable for a subsidiary's debts only if it dominates and controls the subsidiary such that they do not operate as two separate corporations.
- A professional corporation is formed by a group of professionals, such as doctors or lawyers. The professionals retain liability for their own acts of negligence and for those performed under their supervision and authority. The corporate form has been selected for certain tax advantages and benefit plans available to corporations.
- An S corporation is not a different type of corporation but is a corporation that has qualified for special tax treatment such that none of its income is taxed at the corporate level but is passed through to the shareholders who pay tax at their appropriate brackets. An S corporation is limited to 100 shareholders who must all be individuals.

F. Role of Paralegal

Paralegals are involved in a variety of activities when both forming and maintaining the status of close corporations, nonprofit corporations, parent and subsidiary corporations, professional corporations, and S corporations. Typical tasks conducted by paralegals include the following:

1. Preparing and filing the articles of incorporation to create close corporations, nonprofit corporations, subsidiary corporations, or professional corporations.
2. Researching state statutes to determine special requirements for the names of nonprofit and professional corporations and special provisions required for the articles of close corporations, nonprofit, and professional corporations.
3. Preparing shareholders' statements of consent to election of S corporation status.
4. Drafting agreements among shareholders of a close corporation, professional corporation, or S corporation imposing restrictions on transfer of stock and ensuring that stock certificates include a legend condition stating that the transfer of shares is subject to restriction.
5. Preparing Internal Revenue Service Form 2553 to elect S corporation status.
6. Applying for tax-exempt status for nonprofit corporations.
7. Preparing notices of meetings and minutes of the meetings of board of directors and of shareholders for all varieties of corporations.
8. Conducting annual reviews, often called legal audits, of close corporations, professional corporations, and S corporations to ensure compliance with statutory requirements, including reviewing stationery, share certificates, signs, literature, and other materials to ensure that the corporate name is correctly displayed, that share certificates bear proper legends, that the number of shareholders in close and S corporations does not exceed the statutory maximum, and ensuring that shareholders, directors, and officers in professional corporations are duly licensed.

Case Illustration
Piercing the Veil Between a Parent and Subsidiary

Case: *Ocala Breeders' Sales Co. v. Hialeah, Inc.*, 735 So. 2d 542 (Fla. Dist. Ct. App. 1999)

Facts: A tenant received a judgment against a subsidiary for breach of a lease. When the tenant learned the subsidiary had no assets, it brought proceedings against the parent to hold it liable for its subsidiary's debts.

Holding: The parent is liable in this case for the act of the subsidiary. To pierce the veil under Florida law, the subsidiary must be a mere instrumentality of the parent and must have been used by the parent to mislead creditors. In this case, the subsidiary had never been capitalized and any funds earned by it went directly to the parent. The two corporations were controlled by the same person and operated out of the same facilities. In such a case, the subsidiary was a mere instrumentality of the parent and was used to mislead creditors. Thus, the tenant may pierce the subsidiary's corporate veil to hold the parent liable.

◆   ◆   ◆

WEB RESOURCES

The most important resources relating to other forms of corporations and S corporations are the various state and federal statutes. The following is a site allowing access to statutes.

Federal and state statutes: www.law.cornell.edu
                                Cornell University Law School's Web site offers a wide array of legal materials. Select "Constitutions & Codes" to be linked to federal and state statutes. Select "Law About" and then "All Topics" to locate articles and materials relating to business enterprises. Statutes relating to S corporations and tax treatment of nonprofit corporations are located in Title 26 of the United States Code.

Secretaries of state: www.nass.org
Tax forms and publications: www.irs.gov
Forms: www.allaboutforms.com (forms for share-holders' agreements used in close corporations or in S corporations)
                                www.washlaw.edu
                                www.megalaw.com

Discussion Questions

1. ABC, Inc. is a close corporation with 25 shareholders. The corporation has no board of directors and no bylaws. A creditor of the corporation is owed money,

and the corporation cannot pay all of the debt. Discuss whether the creditor would be successful in attempting to pierce the veil to hold the individual shareholders liable because the corporation is not observing formalities.

2. Why do close corporations usually have agreements among the shareholders restricting their transfer of stock?

3. Discuss whether your contributions to the following organizations would be tax-deductible to you: American Red Cross, United Methodist Church, and River Oaks Country Club.

4. P Corp. has formed a subsidiary, Sub Corp. P owns all of Sub's outstanding shares. The two corporations use separate offices, have different bank accounts, and have different boards and officers. Discuss whether a creditor would be able to pierce the veil between the two corporations to hold P liable for Sub's debt to the creditor.

5. Dana Powers, M.D., has incorporated her medical practice. Is Dr. Powers liable for malpractice committed by her nurse? May Dr. Powers issue stock to her insurance clerk? Discuss.

6. XYZ Corp. is a corporation with 90 shareholders. What advantage does electing S status afford the corporation or its shareholders? What if one of the shareholders objects to the proposal to elect S status and will not consent to the election? Assume the corporation elects S status. What is the result if one of its shareholders transfers his shares to 12 of his book group members? How could such a transfer be prevented?

Net Worth

1. Access the Web site for the Delaware Secretary of State. What is the basic fee to form a close corporation?
2. Access the Web site for the California Secretary of State and review the articles of incorporation for a professional association. What does Article II provide?
3. Access the New York Secretary of State Web site. Search the New York Corporations and Business Database. What "type" of corporation is each of the following?
   a. Cancer Action, Inc.
   b. Alpha Delta Gamma, Inc.
   c. Medical Associates of Manhattan, P.C.
4. Access www.hoovers.com. What type of corporation is The Iams Company?

18

◆ ◆ ◆

Employee Compensation and Employment Agreements

◆ ◆ ◆

CHAPTER OVERVIEW

To attract and retain quality employees, employers need to be creative in compensating employees. A fixed salary is the most common form of compensation, but numerous other benefits can be offered to employees to motivate them to remain with the company. These additional benefits may take the form of commissions, bonuses, stock options, insurance, retirement plans, and other fringe benefits. Some retirement plans provide tax advantages to both employers and employees. Plans may be qualified or nonqualified. Qualified plans are those complying with various Internal Revenue Code provisions. Contributions to the plan made by employers may be deductible as business expenses; similarly, the money contributed to the plan is not taxed to the employees at the time of contribution. Nonqualified plans do not provide the same tax advantages to the employer as do qualified plans.

Unless an employment agreement exists, employment is deemed to be "at will," meaning that it can be terminated by either the employer or employee at any time for any reason. To recruit skilled personnel, an employer may offer an employee an employment contract. The contract not only provides job security for the employee, but usually protects valuable proprietary information of the company as well. Employment agreements are formal contracts, typically in writing, specifying the terms and conditions of employment. They can be used for employees with special skills and talents as well as for senior executives. Most employment contracts include a variety of restrictive covenants or contractual prohibitions designed to prevent uniquely skilled employees from working for competitors, misappropriating proprietary information, or misusing valuable trade secrets.

A. Employee Compensation

1. Introduction

In addition to paying fixed salaries or hourly wages, corporations and other businesses can provide a variety of additional forms of compensation to their employees. Generally, these noncash forms of compensation are referred to as **fringe benefits.** In recognition of the increasing importance of these forms of compensation, they are more commonly referred to as *benefits* today. The benefits might include insurance, stock options, and various profit-sharing and retirement plans. The employee compensation plans may provide tax advantages for the employer as well as play a primary role in attracting and retaining skilled employees. Moreover, the benefits provided are generally not taxed as "income" to the employees.

Fringe benefits
Benefits provided to employees in addition to salary (often called *benefits*)

A few general principles apply to any form of fringe benefit provided to employees. The benefits:

a. Should be reasonable in amount;
b. Should be based on services rendered to the employer;
c. Should not be subject to any claim of *self-dealing* on the part of corporate management, for example, extraordinary benefits awarded by corporate managers to themselves; and
d. Must be provided fairly and evenly without discrimination in favor of highly compensated employees.

Although employers may elect to provide a variety of benefits, three are mandated by law: unemployment insurance, workers' compensation insurance, and Social Security disability insurance, all of which are government programs designed to provide an employee with income when the employee cannot work.

2. Insurance Benefits

Welfare benefit plans
Insurance and other similar plans offered to employees

All forms of health care, life insurance, disability insurance, death benefits, and other similar benefits provided by companies for their employees are generally referred to as **welfare benefit plans.** Welfare benefit plans may take a variety of forms, including the following:

Premium
Amount paid to insurer to provide coverage

Health Insurance. Health insurance is of ever-increasing importance to employees. Health insurance covers costs and expenses incurred by an employee resulting from sickness or physical injury. Although many (if not most) employers offer health insurance, they are not required by federal law to do so. The corporate employer will pay the insurance **premium,** the amount paid to the insurance company to provide the insurance. Employees typically pay part of the premium as well in the form of some amount deducted from their paychecks. Employees might also be required to make a small co-payment at the time of treatment. There might be some restrictions on coverage, for example, a requirement that the employee be employed for a certain period of time before insurance is provided, a provision that health insurance is available only to full-time employees, or a provision refusing coverage for illnesses or conditions that existed before the commencement of the employee's employment. Note, however, that the Health Insurance Portability and Accountability Act of 1996 limits the exclusions for preexisting conditions and prohibits discrimination on the basis of health status.

Premiums paid by the corporation are deductible business expenses. Employees are not taxed on the premiums paid by the corporation to the insurance company for this employee benefit.

Under the 1986 federal Consolidated Omnibus Budget Reconciliation Act (**COBRA**), employers are required to offer former employees the option to continue group health insurance (at group rates) for 18 months after termination of employment. The former employee pays all costs but is provided with insurance for this period of time until, presumably, other employment offering insurance is found.

Accident and Disability Insurance. **Accident insurance** covers the insured for expenses arising out of an accident that causes physical injury. If the insured is unable to work, **disability insurance** provides a certain income stream to the insured for some stated period of time or for as long as the disability lasts. Although disability insurance exists under Social Security as well, the amount provided is usually less than the employee's income, so disability insurance fills in the income gap.

Premiums paid by the corporation for accident and disability insurance are tax-deductible. Whereas employees need not pay tax on the value of this benefit provided to them, a payment made to the insured to compensate for lost wages is generally taxable income to the employee because it is a mere replacement for taxable wages.

Life Insurance. Corporations may purchase life insurance policies for employees. For key persons in the corporation, an additional policy may be purchased naming the corporation (rather than the employee's heirs) as the beneficiary. This type of policy is called *key person* insurance. Upon the death of the employee, the corporation will receive a lump-sum payment to compensate it for the loss of this critical employee and perhaps to fund the repurchase of the employee's stock from his heirs.

In an interesting twist, many corporations purchased life insurance not only for their key persons but also for their rank-and-file employees, naming the corporate entity as the beneficiary. When the employee died, the corporation received all of the proceeds of the policy, called **corporate-owned life insurance (COLI)**. In the interim, the corporation had taken deductions for the premiums paid for these policies. Known derisively as "dead peasants insurance," COLI was criticized by both the IRS and Congress. Several states now outlaw the practice if the employee is not informed that his or her employer has purchased life insurance on his or her life. In 2006, Congress restricted this practice by allowing such advantageous tax treatment only for insurance purchased for highly compensated employees and only when the employee is notified in writing of the COLI policy and consents to such.

Some policies are split-dollar plans. In **split-dollar insurance,** the corporation and the employee each pay a portion of the premium for insurance on the life

COBRA
Federal law requiring insurance continuation after employee departs employment

Accident insurance
Insurance designed to protect insured who cannot work due to accident

Disability insurance
Insurance designed to protect insured who cannot work due to disability

Corporate-owned life insurance (COLI)
Insurance purchased by companies on the lives of rank-and-file employees, often without their notice

Split-dollar insurance
Insurance for which employer and employee each pay part of premium

of the employee. The corporation is a named beneficiary of the policy to the extent of any premiums it has paid, and the employee's heirs are the beneficiaries of the remainder of the proceeds of the policy. Upon the employee's death, the corporation will be reimbursed the amount it has paid for the premiums over the years, and the employee's heirs receive the major part of the proceeds of the policy. The corporation thus recovers all the money it has paid, the beneficiaries receive most of the proceeds, and the employee's cost of the premiums was shared with the employer. Effective September 2003, new IRS regulations make split-dollar insurance less attractive from a tax perspective. Generally, employees must pay tax on the economic benefit split-dollar insurance provides.

Corporations may purchase group term life insurance for the life of each employee for a policy amount up to $50,000 without causing employees any taxable income. Premiums paid by the employer are tax-deductible and the insurance proceeds ultimately received by the beneficiaries are tax-free. If the corporation purchases a policy that will pay more than $50,000, the premium paid for the amount of insurance in excess of $50,000 will be considered income to the employee upon which tax must be paid.

Death Benefits.   A corporation can agree to make a cash payment to an employee's heirs upon his or her death. This one-time lump-sum payment is deductible to the corporation as a business expense. Proceeds received by the beneficiaries in excess of $5,000 are taxable income.

3. *Retirement Plans*

Introduction.   Employers may establish retirement plans for their employees so that upon retirement, employees will have funds in addition to those provided by Social Security benefits. The most significant legislation regulating these retirement plans is the **Employee Retirement Income Security Act (ERISA)** enacted in 1974. 29 U.S.C. § 1001. There is no requirement imposed on employers to establish a retirement plan. Once a plan exists, however, ERISA governs its management. Certain retirement plans, however, such as those offered by the U.S. government or nonprofit corporations, are exempt from the provisions of ERISA. Although retirement or pension plans need not include all workers, they cannot be structured to benefit only senior executives. ERISA requires plans to provide participants with information about plan features and funding, requires plans to establish a grievance and appeals process for participants to obtain benefits from their plans, and provides regulations for those who manage and control plan assets.

Retirement plans are referred to as qualified or nonqualified. A **qualified plan** is one that meets certain requirements of the Internal Revenue Code and is thus eligible for special tax treatment. Employers typically submit the proposed qualified plan to obtain a determination letter indicating that the plan has been reviewed by the IRS and that it satisfies the requirements imposed on qualified plans. Alternatively, to save time and money, an employer may adopt a **master plan** (or *prototype plan*) that has been prequalified by the IRS and is sold by pension plan specialists to employers desiring qualified plans. A **nonqualified plan** is not subject to the extensive regulation governing a qualified plan; it does not provide the same

ERISA
Federal law governing retirement plans

Qualified plan
Retirement plan meeting IRS requirements that is eligible for favorable tax treatment

Master plan
Retirement plan prequalified by IRS (also called *prototype plan*)

Nonqualified plan
Usually a private agreement between employer and employee that does not meet requirements needed to achieve favorable tax treatment

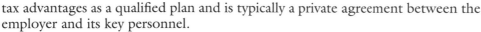

tax advantages as a qualified plan and is typically a private agreement between the employer and its key personnel.

The tax advantages of a qualified plan are as follows:

1. Contributions made by the employer are deductible as business expenses just as wages would be.
2. The interest earned on funds paid into the plan is not taxable. Therefore, the funds grow more quickly than if a portion was being siphoned off for taxes.
3. The employee does not pay any tax on the funds contributed until they are actually received, generally upon retirement, when the employee is in a lower tax bracket.
4. Retirement plan funds do not go through probate and therefore pass free of estate taxes.

Although qualified plans are not subject to taxation, an annual report must be filed with the IRS. ERISA requires that employers providing defined benefit plans (such as IRAs, 401(k)s, profit sharing, stock bonuses, and other plans) complete IRS Form 5500 to provide certain information about the plan, its benefits, participants, and coverage.

Qualified Retirement Plans.   Qualified plans are generally classified as defined benefit plans or defined contribution plans. Both of these types of qualified plans share a variety of features in common. Most important, qualified plans receive the favorable tax treatment previously described. The social justification for depriving the government of tax revenue until some later date is that the plans assist individuals in providing for their retirement, thereby supplementing Social Security.

The plan itself is a written document containing the terms and conditions of the employer's retirement program. The plan is usually described in a booklet or pamphlet given to employees, called a *summary plan description*. The employer providing the plan is referred to as the **sponsor.** The sponsor of a qualified retirement plan may be a corporation, a partnership, or a sole proprietor. The people for whom the plan is designed, namely, employees, are called the **plan participants.** The plan is managed by the **plan administrator,** who owes fiduciary duties to the sponsor and the plan participants and is responsible for accounting for all contributions made to the plan and all distributions made from the plan. The plan administrator is usually entitled to a fee for these services. Contributions to the plan may be made by the plan sponsor, plan participants, or both. Plans in which both the employer and employee contribute are referred to as **contributory plans.** Plans funded solely by the employer are called **noncontributory plans.** Certain limits are imposed on the amounts that may be contributed. A corporate sponsor may contribute either cash or shares of its own stock.

Employees are generally eligible to participate in the plan when they reach age 21 or have completed 1,000 hours of employment, whichever is later. The time at which an employee is entitled to receive the benefits of the plan (referred to as **vesting** of the benefits) is mandated by ERISA. Once the benefits have vested, the employee has an absolute right to them. At this point, the employee's incentive to remain with the employer may decrease. Therefore, employers often prefer to

Sponsor
Party providing a retirement plan

Plan participant
One for whom a retirement plan is designed

Plan administrator
Party who manages retirement plan

Contributory plan
Retirement plan funded by both employer and employee

Noncontributory plan
Retirement plan funded solely by employer

Vesting
The time at which an employee's rights occur or when employee is entitled to benefits of a plan

impose the longest vesting periods they can. The employee's right to the benefits derived from her own contribution is nonforfeitable under any circumstance.

The Internal Revenue Code provides two alternate schemes for vesting. The plan may provide that benefits do not vest until three years of service have been completed. At that time, the benefits are 100 percent vested and nonforfeitable. This type of vesting is often called *cliff vesting*. Alternatively, the plan may provide for two to six years vesting. After two years of service, the employee has a non-forfeitable right to 20 percent of the employer's contribution. This amount increases 20 percent for each year of completed service, until year six, when the nonforfeitable percentage is 100 percent. This type of vesting is often called *graded vesting*. The plan may, of course, allow immediate vesting and then impose a certain waiting requirement, such as requiring employees to complete two years of service before they may participate in the plan. As soon as they participate, however, all benefits derived from their contributions are 100 percent nonforfei-table. Generally, the plan must benefit at least 70 percent of non-highly compen-sated employees to be qualified. A *highly compensated employee* is an employee who is a 5 percent owner of the company or one who receives annual compen-sation of $110,000 or more (for tax year 2009).

Additionally, a plan cannot be **"top heavy"** or "discriminate" by favoring more highly compensated employees over lower paid employees. A plan is top heavy if more than 60 percent of the plan is in the accounts of senior or key employees. Another requirement imposed is that the employer must physically set aside or "fund" the money for the plan. Typically, the employer contributes funds to a trust or other entity that invests the funds for the employees' benefit. The plan may generally be terminated only for circumstances not within the employer's control, such as dissolution of the corporate employer.

Top-heavy plan
A retirement plan that discriminates in favor of senior employees

Defined Benefit Plans. **Defined benefit plans** are those that set a preestab-lished benefit that will be paid to employees, usually monthly, after they leave the company. The amount of the employer's contribution is set in stone. The retirement plan provided by the military is a prototype of a defined benefit plan. Military members know that after 20 years of service, they will receive 50 percent of their base pay. Employee participants in a defined benefit plan can predetermine exactly how much money will be available to them upon retirement. Pension plans are a type of defined benefit plan.

Defined benefit plan
Retirement plan that fixes a preestablished benefit that will be paid to employees

A pension plan provides for the payment of benefits to employees after their retirement. Typically, pension plans contemplate payments for the employee's lifetime, postretirement. The amount required to be contributed by the employer to achieve the desired payment goal is calculated annually by actuaries using math-ematical models based on employees' ages and lengths of service. Thus, establish-ing and maintaining a defined benefit plan can be costly and complex. Because the employer's annual contributions are mandated, a pension plan may impose some hardship on a company going through a difficult financial period in as much as the employer is required to contribute an established amount regardless of its profits. Contributions to the pension plan are held in trust.

The number of companies offering traditional pension plans has been steadily declining. In the past 20 years, the number of pension plans declined by two-thirds. Among the companies that no longer offer guaranteed pensions to their employees are IBM, Lockheed Martin, and Verizon. In most cases benefits earned by workers are preserved, but the employers have stopped further contributions to the plans. Moreover, new hires at those companies are not offered pensions. Most companies have replaced pension plans with 401(k) plans.

Defined Contribution Plans. Rather than guaranteeing a specified total retirement payout to an employee, a **defined contribution plan** simply specifies the amount the employer (or employee, or both) will place into the individual account each year for each participant. If the plan trustee does not invest wisely, less money will be available to the plan participants upon their retirement than if the investments succeeded. For example, the employer could agree to contribute $100 per month (per employee) to the company's pension plan. The size of monthly payments the employee receives after retirement will vary depending on how the sum was invested.

There are many types of defined contribution plans, including profit-sharing plans, money-purchase pension plans, and 401(k) plans, the most popular of all defined contribution plans. Most small businesses adopt defined contribution plans rather than defined benefit plans, and the use of defined benefit plans decreased by one-third from 1993 to 2003. The disadvantage to most defined contribution plans for the employer is that the employer's contribution is fixed, requiring a contribution even in years without profit. As of 2006, 54 percent of all American employees had defined contribution retirement plans.

Typically, defined contribution plans establish a certain percentage amount that the employer is required to contribute. This amount is usually based on the participant's annual compensation. For example, the plan might specify that the employer will contribute 5 percent of each eligible employee's salary per year. Employees generally have some choices as to where the funds are invested. Interest earned on funds invested is credited to the participant's account and is not taxable until received, thus deferring taxes for the employee. Additionally, employees may borrow a portion of the funds in their account to meet certain expenses. The employee may also contribute to the plan, usually up to some specified percentage of annual salary. The employee's contribution is vested as of the date of any contribution; employer's contributions are vested in accordance with the ERISA requirements. The employer's contributions are tax-deductible up to a specified amount. This type of plan is often referred to as a **money-purchase pension plan.** In money-purchase pension plans, the employer's commitment to contribute a specified percentage of an employee's salary is fixed, allowing employees to calculate how much money will be in the plan upon their retirement, assuming some standard rate of return on the investment.

Another common type of defined contribution plan is a **profit-sharing plan.** As the name indicates, money contributed to the plan is funded by the employer's profits, usually a percentage of profits from the previous fiscal year. Amounts contributed by the employer are divided among employee accounts, usually in proportion to employee compensation. The fact that contributions hinge on the company's performance may motivate employees to work hard and may help to establish a team or collegial atmosphere. The percentage to be contributed annually does not have to be established in advance and usually varies from year to year. The board of directors usually has the discretion to fix the annual contribution. In fact, in lean years, the company might not make any contribution at all. This is a significant advantage to a company inasmuch as other plans may require

Defined contribution plan
Retirement plan that specifies the contribution that will be made to it

Money-purchase pension plan
Retirement plan by which employer contributes a certain percentage of employee's salary each year

Profit-sharing plan
Retirement plan funded by employer's profits

yearly contributions, regardless of the employer's profitability. The tax deduction available to the corporate employer in a profit-sharing plan is more limited than for other defined contribution plans. Thus, the amount contributed by an employer in a profit-sharing plan might be somewhat less than that contributed under other defined contribution plans, such as the money-purchase pension plan. The risk under a profit-sharing plan is that the benefit might not be adequate at retirement, because contributions based on profits will undoubtedly vary from year to year.

Stock bonus plans are similar to profit-sharing plans, but the employer's contribution is in the form of stock, allowing participants to become shareholders of the corporation without requiring a substantial cash outlay on the part of the corporate employer. The corporation will have the discretion to establish its annual contribution to the plan. If the stock is not publicly traded, the employee may usually opt for a cash contribution rather than stock. Corporations whose stock is publicly traded often purchase their own stock on the securities market for their employees.

A unique plan entitled the **employee stock ownership plan** (ESOP) is also designed to give ownership rights in a corporation to the employees. In this plan, the employer contributes funds (from its profits or money it has borrowed) to a trust it has established. The money is then used to purchase stock in the corporation. The employer's contributions to the trust are tax-deductible. The stock may be purchased from shareholders wishing to sell stock or may be from the corporation's authorized but unissued shares. Shares in the trust are then allocated to individual employee accounts. Employees must be 100 percent vested after seven years of service. When an employee leaves the company, she receives her stock, which the company must buy back from her at its fair market value. Similar to stock bonus plans, if the company's stock is not publicly traded, the employee may require the company to repurchase the stock she owns at its fair market value.

The ESOP offers a unique advantage to an employer who can borrow money from a bank to fund its contribution rather than using cash on hand. The money is then lent by the corporation to the fund or trust. The corporation has cash in its accounts and the employees own stock in the company. ESOPs have been used in defending hostile takeovers by distributing sufficient amounts of stock to employees such that the aggressor has difficulty in obtaining stock in the target.

Companies can mix and match plans. For example, a company could establish a money-purchase pension plan and then add a somewhat limited profit-sharing plan. Defined contribution plans can be combined with defined benefit plans to create **target benefit plans,** usually to increase the amount of tax-deductible contributions that may be made by the employer.

401(k) Plans. A **401(k) plan,** so called because it is authorized by Internal Revenue Code § 401(k), offers advantages to small and midsized corporations because most contributions are made by the employees rather than the employer. 401(k)s allow employees to save and invest for their own retirement. Employees contribute an annual amount to the 401(k) account, usually a percentage of their annual compensation. Employee contributions are capped at a maximum amount, which may change each year because it is indexed to cost of living adjustments. The maximum contribution for 2009 is $16,500. This is deducted from wages by the employer prior to receipt by the employee without being taxed. The amount might be matched by the employer or the employer might make some lesser

Stock bonus plan
Plan in which employer contributes stock

Employee stock ownership plan
Plan in which employer contributes funds it has borrowed to a trust and which money is then used to buy stock in the corporation for employees

Target benefit plan
Combination of defined contribution and defined benefit plans

401(k) plan
Retirement plan funded by employee's nontaxable contributions

contribution; for example, it might match an employee's contribution dollar for dollar, ten cents on the dollar, or in a fixed amount of X percent of the employee's annual salary, regardless of what the employee contributes. A common matching formula is a 50 percent match up to 6 percent of the amount contributed by the employee. Some companies match employee contributions with company stock, leaving employees' retirement savings vulnerable in the event of a company's collapse, such as those experienced by Enron Corp. and WorldCom, Inc. in 2001. Company stock presently accounts for about 30 percent of all assets in the average employee defined contribution benefit plan. A 401(k) plan provides retirement funds for employees; however, it also reduces their present salaries. Additionally, although it defers federal income tax for employees, the amount contributed is still subject to social security taxes.

The funds contributed are usually invested in various mutual funds or stocks predetermined by the plan sponsor, the employer, but selected by the employee. The money earned in the 401(k) each year is not subject to tax. Taxes are paid when the money is withdrawn, presumably when the employee has reached age $59\frac{1}{2}$ and is in a lower tax bracket. Contributions attributable to the employer may not be withdrawn without penalty by an employee unless the employee retires, leaves the company's service, becomes disabled, reaches age $59\frac{1}{2}$, or suffers some hardship. An employee who leaves one place of employment can usually "roll over" funds in the 401(k) account to the new employer's plan. Thus, 401(k)s are highly portable. Participants must begin taking distributions by age $70\frac{1}{2}$.

Keogh Plans. The significant tax advantages provided by qualified employee benefit plans were not available to the self-employed or to sole proprietors until passage of the Keogh Act, named for New York Congressman Eugene Keogh. Self-employed individuals or sole proprietors may establish accounts for retirement purposes called **Keogh plans.** Contributions made to the Keogh plan are then deducted from the person's taxable income. Maximum contributions (generally, $46,000) and deductions are specified by the Keogh Act. The money is invested with a bank or financial institution. Interest earned on the amount invested is not subject to taxation until withdrawal. Tax penalties are imposed on funds withdrawn before the participant reaches age $59\frac{1}{2}$. Withdrawals must begin before age $70\frac{1}{2}$. Taxes are imposed when the money is distributed.

Keogh plan
Retirement plan for self-employed individuals

Individual Retirement Accounts. Some individuals are employed by companies that have not established any qualified retirement plan. These individuals may plan for their retirement by creating traditional **individual retirement accounts** (IRAs) with banks or other financial institutions. They make periodic contributions to the IRA, which are then deducted from their taxable income. At one point, Congress allowed any individual (even those covered by qualified plans established by their employers) to establish IRAs and make a tax-deductible contribution up to $2,000 per year. Since the mid-1980s, deductions are permitted for IRA contributions only by those persons not covered by other plans, and thus IRAs are less popular than they once were. Moreover, deductibility of contributions decreases the greater one's income is until it is phased out completely once one's gross income is between $53,000 and $63,000 (for a single individual). The maximum contribution for 2009 is $5,000. Money withdrawn from the IRA account before the individual reaches the age of $59\frac{1}{2}$ is subject to tax penalties, and money must

Individual retirement account
Retirement plans funded by employees not covered by company-sponsored retirement plans (*IRAs*)

be withdrawn once the IRA owner reaches age 70$\frac{1}{2}$. The main difference between an IRA and a Keogh plan is the contribution limit.

SEP-IRAs. A **Simplified Employee Pension (SEP)** is a written plan that allows an employer or self-employed individual to make contributions to his or her own retirement (and those of his or her employees if there are employees) without getting involved in the more complex Keogh plan. Under a SEP, contributions are made to an individual retirement account (thus, the name SEP-IRA). Contributions cannot be more than 25 percent of the individual's compensation or $49,000 (for 2009) each year, whichever is less. Contributions made to the SEP-IRA are tax-deductible. Distributions are subject to the same rules as IRAs, discussed earlier.

SIMPLE-IRAs. A **Savings Incentive Match Plan for Employees** (SIMPLE plan) is a written agreement between employers (who must have fewer than 100 employees) and their employees. Both employer and employee must contribute to the plan. A SIMPLE-IRA, considered to be a "starter plan" for small employers, is subject to the same rules as an IRA except for a higher contribution limit. The plan is usually structured as a type of IRA into which employees contribute up to $11,500 (for 2009) of their income annually, compared with $5,000 contributable under ordinary IRAs. There are few administrative burdens or costs, making the plan attractive to smaller employers.

Roth IRAs. The **Roth IRA** (named for its sponsor, Sen. William Roth of Delaware) was created in 1998 to allow taxpayers to save money for use in retirement. Unlike ordinary IRAs, contributions to a Roth IRA are never deductible; however, distributions taken after age 59$\frac{1}{2}$ are free of tax. Withdrawals are not taxed at all at this time, because tax has already been paid on the money before its deposit into the Roth IRA. Moreover, earnings on the money in the Roth IRA are not taxed. Roths are only available to individuals with certain income levels. If an individual's gross income is greater than $114,000 (or $166,000 for married couples filing jointly), a Roth is unavailable. Unlike traditional IRAs, the money need never be withdrawn from a Roth IRA. Thus, the money in the account can be passed on to one's heirs. Traditional IRAs can be converted to Roth IRAs. As of 2009, a person may contribute up to $5,000 per year.

Cash Balance Plans. A new type of benefit plan is a **cash balance plan**, a type of hybrid plan that combines features of a traditional pension and a 401(k) plan. In a cash balance plan, an employer contributes a fixed amount of money (for example, 5 percent of an employee's salary) into an account. The employer is responsible for investing the money. When the employee leaves the job or retires, he or she may take the balance in a lump sum and roll it into an IRA or invest it in an annuity that will provide a guaranteed monthly payment.

Nonqualified Plans. Employers may establish plans that do not comply with all of the regulations imposed on qualified plans. These *nonqualified plans*, however, do not achieve the same tax advantages as do qualified plans. Nonqualified plans may be established by a corporation wishing to reward its top executives yet not include other employees, whereas a qualified plan cannot be top heavy or

---

SEP-IRA
Plan allowing self-employed individual to contribute to his or her retirement

SIMPLE-IRA
Plan in which both employer (a small employer) and employee contribute

Roth IRA
Retirement plan in which contributions are not deductible but distributions (after a certain age) are

Cash benefit plan
A hybrid retirement plan combining features of a traditional pension plan with a 401(k)

discriminate. Alternatively, the employer may wish to reward employees in excess of the limits imposed on qualified plans. Nonqualified plans are often in the form of private agreements between the employer and its key executives. Regulation and paperwork are minimal.

4. Incentive Stock Option Plans

A corporation may also award cash or property bonuses to its employees as incentives for meeting certain production goals or sales quotas. Bonuses consisting of shares of the corporation or of its subsidiary may also be used to compensate employees. Share bonuses do not affect the corporation's cash flow; however, they do dilute the proportionate power and control of existing shareholders. Stock option plans are also utilized by corporations to motivate and reward workers. Under a **stock option** plan, employees are granted the right to purchase the corporation's shares for fixed prices at certain times, regardless of the market price of the stock at the time the option may be exercised. An option would typically be exercised when the option price is lower than the market price of the stock. For example, if Martin Shelby, an employee of ABC, Inc., has an option to buy 100 shares of ABC, Inc. at $20 per share when the market price is $50 per share, Martin would likely exercise his option and realize an immediate benefit of $3,000 (the difference in the option price and market price multiplied by 100, the number of shares purchased). If the option price is higher than the market price, the employee will generally not exercise his or her rights to purchase the stock. Options that would be exercised at a loss are said to be **underwater options.** However, if the employee exercises the option and purchases shares that later increase in value, the employee will profit from this increase. Options that can be exercised at a gain are said to be **in the money.** Stock option plans also enhance employer-employee relations because the employees realize that the better they perform, the more the company's shares will be worth, and they will be direct beneficiaries of any such increases. Employees thus share in the company's growth and success and become owners of the corporation.

Incentive stock option plans are those that are qualified under various Internal Revenue Code provisions and thereby receive advantageous tax treatment. The Internal Revenue Code imposes various requirements on qualified incentive stock option plans, including provisions relating to the terms of the option plan, the option price, the employees covered under the plan, and the amount of stock that may be subject to the option. An employee is not taxed upon receipt of the stock purchased through a qualified incentive option plan. Tax will be paid later, when the stock is ultimately sold, at which time the employee may be in a lower tax bracket. If the employee holds the stock for one year from the date of exercise, appreciation in value is taxed as a long-term capital gain (rather than at the higher rate at which ordinary income is taxed). A **nonqualified stock option** (NSO) does not qualify for such preferential tax treatment. In an NSO, employees pay no tax when the option is granted but rather pay ordinary income tax on the difference (the **spread**) between the grant price and the stock's value at the time the option is exercised by purchase of the stock. Careful consideration should be given to the awarding of stock to ensure that this issuance of securities is in compliance with, or exempt from, the applicable federal and state securities regulations.

Stock option
Right to purchase fixed number of shares at a certain date at a fixed price

Underwater options
Stock options that would be exercised at a loss

In the money options
Stock options that can be exercised at a gain

Incentive stock option plan
Stock option plan that is qualified under IRS regulations, allowing for favorable tax treatment

Nonqualified stock option
Stock option that does not qualify for favorable tax treatment

Spread
Difference between stock price at which option is granted and stock price when option is exercised or purchased

Options usually are granted with a vesting period, meaning that the employee cannot exercise the option for some period of time, often two or three years. Such a vesting period helps the company retain valuable employees. Generally, employees who voluntarily resign or who are terminated for cause lose their unvested options. Once options vest, the employee has a right to exercise the option, even if employment is terminated (although exercise must often occur within some specified time period after termination, and the employee might be required to sell the stock back to the employer at its fair value, if the stock is not traded publicly).

Once options vest, employees can exercise the option, buy the stock at the **strike price** (the price at which the option was granted), and then sell on the open market for more than the strike price (although minimum holding periods must be met to receive favorable tax treatment). Alternatively, they can exercise the option, buy the stock at the strike price, and then hold the stock in the hope it continues to increase in value. Many senior executives are granted **reload options,** in which case the executive may pay the company for stock options he wishes to exercise with stock he has just bought. Usually, one new option is then issued for each share tendered to pay for the purchase price. The practice of using options to pay for options or borrowing money from the company or a broker to buy options is called a **cashless exercise.**

Options were extremely popular in the 1990s, particularly with high-tech companies. Critics of options charged that large option grants were a cause of the Enron, WorldCom, and other corporate scandals because they encouraged executives to focus on boosting share prices in the short term while disguising the company's real financial condition.

Beginning in 2003, options began a steady decline. Many experts believe the trend away from stock options began with Microsoft, which announced in the summer of 2003 that it would no longer give stock options to its employees but would instead give Microsoft stock that would vest over five years. Additionally, new accounting rules that took effect in January 2006 require companies to count options as an expense against earnings. In advance of the new rules, companies began abandoning option grants. In fact, about two-thirds of all companies have eliminated or decreased stock options in recent years. Stock options make up about 30 percent of a typical CEO's compensation, a decline from 69 percent in 2001.

A newer trend is to pay CEOs with actual shares of stock if they meet certain performance standards or to award the CEOs "premium priced" options, meaning that the executives will make money on stock options grants only if the company's stock prices rise a certain amount, a form of compensation that is often referred to as "pay for performance" rather than the stock option model, which is often called "pay for pulse."

In January 2003, Walt Disney Co. awarded its chief executive, Michael Eisner, a bonus of $5 million in **restricted stock** (stock that generally must be held for some fixed period, often two or three years, before it can be sold). Mr. Eisner was awarded no cash bonus and no options. Restricted stock encourages executives to focus on long-term growth rather than managing for the short term to increase the value of their own options. Another trend is the awarding of **performance shares,** popular in Great Britain, in which shares are awarded to executives only when they achieve certain performance goals.

A corporate scandal that has emerged in the past few years is **option back-dating**, which is the practice of altering the date on which options are granted.

Strike price
Price at which option was granted

Reload options
Options purchased with other options, also called a *cashless exercise*

Cashless exercise
Using options or borrowed money to pay for options

Restricted stock
Stock that must be held for some period before it can be sold

Performance shares
Shares awarded only when certain goals are achieved

Stock option backdating
The practice of altering the date of a stock option grant to make it more valuable

Such a practice allows a corporation to cherry pick a date when stock prices are low to grant options to senior executives who are then assured of big payoffs when they exercise their stock options. Although backdating of option grants is not necessarily illegal, companies must obtain board approval and adequately inform investors. In many cases, company executives falsified records to cover up backdating. On investigation, it became apparent that many companies had fortuitously granted options to their executives on dates on which the company's stock was trading at its lowest price (which would then allow the recipients to exercise their options at a higher value). Both the FBI and SEC commenced investigations and shareholder derivative litigation has followed. Some of the corporations allegedly involved in backdating scandals include Apple Computer Inc. and Monster Worldwide, Inc. (the parent of Web site monster.com). In 2008, the SEC announced a settlement with Brocade Communications, in which Brocade paid $12 million to settle SEC charges. Two of Brocade's executives were sentenced to prison, and the company paid $160 million to settle a shareholder derivative lawsuit.

In the wake of the stock market collapse of 2008-2009, the newest practice is for companies whose stock options are underwater to allow their employees (many of them executives) to exchange their severely depreciated or worthless stock options for new awards with more favorable terms. As of late 2008, about 99 percent of Fortune 500 chief executives held options that were underwater. Companies that implement such repricing or exchange programs claim that they need to reprice their options to retain talented employees. Generally, such plans require shareholder approval. Shareholders, however, have been critical of such programs, noting that they have no choice but to hang onto poorly performing stock or to sell it at a loss.

The stock options described herein are different from the option contracts traded on the Chicago Board Options Exchange and the Philadelphia Stock Exchange discussed in Chapter Thirteen.

5. Other Fringe Benefits

In addition to providing insurance and retirement benefits, employers can provide numerous other fringe benefits or perquisites **(perks).** Thus, employers might compensate their employees in the form of licensing fees (for doctors, lawyers, and so forth), country club dues, health club memberships, reimbursement of legal fees or group legal services plans, car leases, cell phones, pagers and BlackBerrys, interest-free loans, discounts on company products or services, tuition plans for employees wishing to return to school, and numerous other benefits. Some corporations have undertaken to pay or reimburse employees for some or all of the taxes imposed on the employee. The tax reimbursement payment itself is taxable income, which the corporation pays taxes on, and so forth, with a continual "pyramiding effect."

Some directors receive payments, called **honoraria,** for attending directors' meetings. These payments may range from $100 per meeting to more than $1,000 per meeting for larger publicly traded corporations. (Enron Corp. paid its directors more than $70,000 annually merely for sitting on the board.)

Perks
Perquisites or fringe benefits provided by employers

Honoraria
Payments given for appearing at an event or meeting

6. Reimbursement of Expenses

Employees are typically reimbursed by the employer for expenses incurred on behalf of the employer. For example, transportation costs and food and lodging expenses incurred on business trips are generally reimbursed by employers. Some employers establish a certain daily allowance for traveling employees. This *per diem* may be as high as $150. If the employee does not use $150 per day in lodging or other expenses, the employee retains the excess tax-free. Most companies have various forms and procedures in place for claiming and receiving expense reimbursement. Other companies issue credit cards to employees for business expenses. The bill may go directly to the employer for payment or to the employee who pays it and then seeks reimbursement from the company.

PRACTICE TIP

Keep your own "summary plan description" of a client's benefits. Note the vesting schedule for any benefits, whether the employer matches any amount contributed by an employee to a 401(k), and, if so, what amount, the price at which any options were granted (so you can readily tell if the options are "underwater" or "in the money," and whether the plans are qualified or nonqualified. Periodically review the IRS definition for "highly compensated employee" and its schedule for the amounts that may be contributed to plans. As items change, provide benefit updates or FAQs (Frequently Asked Questions) for clients.

B. Employment Agreements

1. Introduction

Employment at will
Employment relationship that either party can terminate for any reason or no reason

Most individuals in the United States are **employed at will,** meaning they can be fired at any time at the will of the employer, for a valid reason, such as incompetence, or for no reason at all. Similarly, the employee can terminate the employment at any time, leaving the employer for another opportunity. The employment at will doctrine has been modified by statute in some states and by court decisions to ensure that employees are not terminated for exercising certain rights and privileges, such as their rights to engage in free speech, unionization activities, or to complain about unfair or unsafe working conditions.

Wrongful discharge
Termination of employee for improper reason

Recent years have witnessed an explosion in cases brought by employees whose employment has been terminated. The cases, usually referred to as **wrongful discharge** or *termination* cases, have often resulted in significant damages being imposed on employers for improper termination. Similarly, corporate downsizing has resulted in increased litigation between employers and employees. Under the Worker Adjustment and Retraining Notification Act, effective in 1989, employers with more than 100 employees must provide at least 60 days' advance notice of mass layoffs or plant closings (although such notice is not required if a closing or layoff is a result of an unforeseen business circumstance or natural disaster).

Terminated employees may have several options to pursue: Claims based on age, disability, religious, gender, or racial discrimination may be filed with administrative agencies such as the Equal Employment Opportunity Commission or a similar state agency, or they may be brought in federal district court alleging violation of constitutionally protected rights. Other issues, such as termination in retaliation for an employee's complaints about smoke in the workplace, may be initiated in state court, especially if the state or local jurisdiction has enacted laws requiring smoke-free work environments. These employees may be protected under the **whistle-blower** doctrine, meaning they cannot be punished or terminated for raising valid safety complaints or revealing unlawful conduct by the employer.

Employee handbooks or manuals often include provisions relating to termination of employees or provisions that employees will be terminated only for cause. Some courts have held that such provisions constitute implied contracts and that employees terminated contrary to the terms of the handbook or manual, or perhaps contrary to an unstated office policy or custom, may sue the employer for breach of contract.

Although most employees are hired at will pursuant to a simple oral agreement, certain employees who bring needed skills and expertise to the employer may be subject to a formal written employment contract specifying the terms and conditions of their employment. A written employment contract benefits both parties: The employer can be assured of having the employee's skills for a certain time period (and may afterward bar him from working for competitors), and the employee receives job security and potential advancement in the company. Employment contracts are used not only for top-level and highly compensated employees, but also for other employees who possess special skills, such as researchers or scientists, volume-producing salespeople, or computer wizards.

Generally, an employee may terminate his employment before the term specified in the written agreement without incurring any liability. Courts are reluctant to force people to work in places against their will, classifying such a situation as a type of involuntary servitude. Other provisions in the agreement, however, such as prohibitions against the employee working for a competitor for a certain period of time, or using the employer's trade secrets, will remain binding on the employee. If the employer terminates the employment before the specified time, it might be required to continue paying the employee pursuant to the contract, unless the employer can show the employee breached some term or condition of the employment.

Whistle-blower
One who discloses improper conduct of his or her superior

2.   Terms of Employment Agreements

Introduction.   Most employment agreements or contracts are drafted by the employer's attorney. Some employment agreements are relatively simple and straightforward, containing only the basic elements, whereas others may be fiercely negotiated and contain complex provisions for compensation, benefits, and protection of the employer's proprietary information.

Each agreement should be fashioned to fit the particular needs of the parties, but typical employment agreements contain certain standard provisions, such as those specifying each party's duties and obligations, compensation of the employee, the term of the agreement, termination of the agreement, and various restrictive covenants prohibiting the employee from working for competitors or using the employer's trade secrets. Inherent in every employment agreement is a covenant of good faith and fair dealing imposed on all parties to the agreement.

Recitals.   The employment agreement usually begins with an identification of the parties, their names and addresses, and a recital that it is the intent of the parties to enter into an employment agreement. If the employee has adopted the corporate form, as a lawyer or accountant might, the individual as well as the corporate employee should be a party to the agreement, so that in the event of breach, the employer is not limited to pursuing only the corporation.

Duties of Parties.   Each party's duties and responsibilities should be set forth clearly. This section should be as specific as possible so each party knows what is expected and, in the event of breach of the agreement, a party will be able to prove that the other party failed to perform certain identifiable duties. The hours the employee is expected to work, the location of the workplace, and a description of duties should be included. The employee's title should be specified.

Some employment contracts include specific duties, such as those requiring an employee to achieve certain sales volumes, produce a certain product, or develop a computer program for corporate accounting purposes. In other instances, the duties of the employee might necessarily be general in nature. For example, an individual hired to be the chief executive officer of a company will have myriad duties, most of which cannot be specifically described. Thus, provisions for such an employee might be somewhat vague, imposing a duty of good faith on the employee to act at all times in the employer's best interests, to work full-time, to devote her best efforts and attention to company business, and to perform tasks typically expected of those in such positions. Most employment contracts provide a catch-all provision permitting the employer to specify additional reasonable duties from time to time. This type of provision allows flexibility so that if the nature of the position changes or the parties realize that other tasks should be performed, these needs can be accommodated.

The employer may be required to provide a safe, well-ventilated, private work space for the employee. Additionally, the employer may be required generally to provide such assistance needed by the employee to perform his duties, such as support personnel, supplies, or access to corporate information.

Any restrictions to be placed on the employee should be set forth in this section. For example, the employee may be restricted to soliciting sales in certain territories, may be subject to a dollar limit in spending money for supplies, or may be prohibited from entering into certain contracts without the prior approval of more senior employees or the board of directors.

Compensation of Employee.   The employment agreement should clearly set forth any compensation to which the employee is entitled, whether in terms of salary or benefits. Because the matter of compensation is often the most critical issue for both employer and employee, this section of the agreement should be carefully drafted.

The simplest form of compensation is a fixed annual salary. The times for payment should be specified (biweekly, monthly, and so forth). Annual increases can be based on a fixed percentage, may be tied to annual cost-of-living increases, or may be based on company profits. Incentives may be added so that if the employee achieves certain goals or sales, compensation increases proportionately.

Some executives of large publicly traded corporations receive staggering compensation. Forbes has reported that the heads of the country's 500 largest companies received an aggregate 34 percent pay raise in 2006. Some have received extremely lucrative compensation packages even when their companies have not performed. For example, Richard Fuld, the chief executive of Lehman Holdings Inc., took home more than $70 million in 2007, yet in September 2008, the nearly 160-year-old firm filed for bankruptcy. Fuld will reportedly get to keep $480 million. Forbes reported that one of the worst performers was chief executive J. Willard Marriott, Jr. of Marriott International, whose 2007 pay jumped 22 percent to $44 million annually while his investors suffered a 28 percent stock drop. Forbes rated Amazon.com's Jeff Bezos as the best performer. Bezos was paid a relatively modest $1 million in 2007 and delivered a 32 percent annual return to his shareholders. Early twentieth-century financier J.P. Morgan believed that a corporation's chief executive officer should never make more than 20 times the salary of a company's average employee, but the ratio in major companies is now between 400:1 and 500:1.

Some employees, primarily those in sales, are compensated on a **commission** basis, meaning they receive a fixed percentage based on the amount of goods or services sold by them. Managers might be awarded a certain commission on profits earned by their departments or divisions. The commission may vary and increase as certain sales levels are achieved. Because total sales or profits cannot be determined until the end of an employer's fiscal year, the employee might be entitled to a **draw,** or advance payment, against anticipated compensation. If the employee draws more during the course of the year than that to which she is ultimately entitled, the employee could be required to repay the employer. Alternatively, the overpayment can be credited against the next year's draw. Most employers carefully monitor profits, however, and may periodically reduce draws to ensure employees are not "negative" at the end of the year.

Compensation based on "sales" or "profits" should expressly specify whether these sales or profits are total sales, net sales, net sales adjusted for discounts and bad checks, and so forth. Clear definition of terms will prevent later misunderstandings. In general, however, any ambiguity in an employment agreement is construed against the employer because the employer is viewed as being in a stronger bargaining position than the employee.

The compensation section of the employment agreement should also specify any benefits to be provided to the employee, including bonuses, insurance, vacation, retirement plans and benefits, fringe benefits, stock options, reimbursement of expenses, and any other form of compensation to which the employee is entitled, such as discounts on the company's products or services, right to retain and use frequent-flier mileage earned traveling on behalf of the employer, interest free loans, and so forth.

Commission
Payment based on sales generated

Draw
An advance payment against future salary or commission

Term of the Agreement. The beginning and ending date of the employment agreement should be provided. If renewal of the agreement will be permitted, the terms and conditions for exercising the right to renew should be specified. For example, the right to renew may be granted to either the employer or employee, may be made mutual, or may occur automatically unless one of the parties objects.

If no term of employment is specified, the arrangement between the parties will likely be viewed as one at will, in which case either party can terminate the agreement at any time, with or without cause.

Confidentiality and Nondisclosure Provisions. The employee should be required to agree to maintain and protect the employer's confidential and proprietary information both during and after employment. Figure 18-3 shows a nondisclosure clause that can be used to ensure the confidentiality of the employer's critical information.

Termination of the Agreement. The employment agreement should provide for termination of the agreement prior to the specified term in the event of default, breach, or other stated reasons. Generally, either party may terminate the agreement in the event of breach or default by the other party or "upon cause." Breach of duties will be easier to prove if those duties have been expressly stated in the agreement. Some employers specify that the agreement will terminate if the employee dies, becomes permanently disabled or otherwise unable to perform his duties, is convicted of a crime, fails to achieve certain sales or production goals, the business becomes insolvent or is sold or merged, and so forth.

FIGURE 18-1
Covenant Not to Compete

For one year after termination of Employee's employment with Employer, for any reason or cause whatsoever, other than material breach of this Agreement by Employer, Employee agrees that he will not directly, or indirectly, as owner, shareholder, partner, joint venturer, consultant, agent, principal, licensor, officer, director, or in any capacity whatsoever, engage in, become financially interested in, be employed by, or have any connection with any cable television business or operation in Cook County, Illinois. This limitation will only apply for one year from the date of termination or expiration of the Agreement and will only apply in the County of Cook, Illinois. In addition, for two years after termination of Employee's employment with Employer, for any reason or cause whatsoever, other than material breach of this Agreement by Employer, Employee shall not contact any party who is a customer of Employer during the term of this Agreement in Cook County, Illinois, in any manner which could be detrimental to the interests of Employer or solicit for employment or employ any employee of Employer during the term of this Agreement without the prior written consent of Employer.

Senior executives may be entitled to a severance package, a golden parachute, if the company terminates their employment before the agreed-on date. These severance benefits are often tied to the employee's agreement not to compete with the employer or divulge trade secrets.

Restrictive Covenants and Protection of Intellectual Property.   Although an employer cannot generally force an employee to work for the employer, the employer may be able to enforce certain prohibitions or restrictions, called **restrictive covenants,** even after the employee leaves the company. Most of these restrictions are imposed to protect valuable knowledge, skill, and know-how the employee has accumulated over the years. For example, Coca-Cola Company would lose a distinct competitive advantage if its marketing chief quit and then went to work for PepsiCo Company and disclosed Coca-Cola's future marketing plans and advertising strategies. Therefore, most employers will impose certain restrictions on employees with special skills and knowledge. These restrictions must serve a valid purpose and must be reasonable and fair. Courts dislike covenants unfairly restricting the right of persons to work. Using our example, it would be grossly unfair if Coca-Cola's advertising manager were unable to work in the advertising field at any time after termination of her employment with Coca-Cola. If such a restriction were allowed, the employee would forfeit all of his or her accumulated knowledge and skills and be forced to enter another industry. Thus, a balance must be struck between the rights of employers to protect their valuable and proprietary information and the right of employees to move and work freely.

Restrictive covenants
Agreements imposing certain restrictions or prohibitions on employees on an employee

Employers will also want to own inventions or unique processes discovered by the employee while on company time. Finally, employers will want to protect their trade secrets and customer lists from disclosure to competitors. Such restrictions are generally valid and enforceable by the employer if they serve the legitimate need of the employer for protection, are limited in scope, and do not impose an undue hardship on the employee.

Covenants Not to Compete.   The most common restrictive covenant is an agreement by the employee not to compete against the employer. Under common law principles of good faith and fair dealing, employees cannot compete against their employer while employed by the employer. However, once an employee leaves her employment, she can generally compete against the former employer unless the parties have agreed otherwise. Such a restriction is designed to prevent employees from leaving one company with valuable information and know-how and then going directly to a competitor. Because **covenants not to compete** are disfavored and are viewed as restraints on trade, many states have enacted statutes specifically dealing with such covenants and outlining the circumstances for their validity and enforcement.

Covenant not to compete
Agreement by employee not to compete against employer

In general, covenants not to compete can only be imposed on employees with special skills and talents. A mass restriction imposed by McDonald's Corporation prohibiting all of its food handlers from working for other fast-food franchisors or restaurants after termination of their employment with McDonald's serves no legitimate public purpose and no legitimate business need of McDonald's. On the other hand, if a company has carefully recruited top personnel, trained them, and invested money and time in teaching them the employer's methods and processes, it would be inequitable for a competitor to reap the advantage of this investment of years of training.

Courts have developed several guidelines to assist in balancing the legitimate business needs of the employer with the employee's right to pursue his livelihood. Generally, covenants not to compete must be limited in duration and must be limited in scope. An employer cannot forever prohibit a former employee from working for a competitor; however, a reasonable restriction of one or two years might be enforceable. Similarly, a blanket prohibition forbidding the employee from working anywhere in the world is grossly overbroad. Therefore, the prohibition should be limited in its geographic scope. For example, an employee might be prohibited from working within 50 miles of any of the former employer's plants or within the territorial limits of a certain city or county.

The covenant not to compete should be carefully drafted to ensure the employee does not find a loophole enabling her to circumvent the restriction. For example, if the covenant merely precludes employment with a competitor, the employee could establish her own business or could serve as a consultant for a competitor. The provision should be drafted to afford the employer with the protection it needs. (See Figure 18-1 for a sample noncompetition provision.)

In a 1999 case, the Southern District of New York refused to enforce a covenant that would have prevented a Web site content manager from working for a competitor company for one year. The judge ruled that in the Internet environment, a one-year restriction was "several generations, if not an eternity."

In some states, notably California, covenants not to compete are invalid as constituting a restraint against trade (unless they are procured in the course of the sale of a business). Cal. Bus. & Prof. Code §§ 16600 and 16601. In late 1999, a San Francisco Superior Court ordered Aetna Inc., an insurance company, to pay $1.2 million to an employee who was fired after she refused to sign a noncompete covenant. The court held that Aetna knew the covenant not to compete violated the California statute. Aetna attempted to require all of its employees to agree not to compete against Aetna for six months after leaving.

These new cases demonstrate that the area of noncompete covenants must be carefully researched, and any covenants must be carefully drafted to ensure they comply with state laws.

Finally, courts generally will not enforce a covenant not to compete if the employee has left employment due to the employer's breach of the employment agreement. Otherwise, an employer could hire uniquely talented individuals, have them sign covenants not to compete, refuse to pay them, and still reap the benefits of precluding them for working for others.

In the event of any doubt or ambiguity, the covenant not to compete will be construed against the employer and in favor of the employee. Courts will, however, often use injunctions to enforce covenants not to compete, prohibiting the employee from working for a certain employer or within a certain geographical area. In the event the restriction is overly broad, some courts have revised the covenant to make it fit the parties' intentions rather than strike the entire covenant, a procedure called **blue-penciling.**

Blue-penciling
Procedure of correcting noncompete clauses to make them legal

Inventions, Intellectual Property, and Work Product. Employees might be hired to develop new products or computer programs for the employer. Similarly, the employee might develop a new slogan or a corporate logo for the company.

These types of property are referred to as **intellectual property** because they are property rights capable of being owned, sold, exploited, and transferred, but are neither real property nor tangible personal property.

Generally, under the **work made-for-hire doctrine, copyrightable works** (namely, rights in literary, artistic, musical, sculptural, architectural works, sound recordings, and motion pictures) prepared by an employee within the scope of his employment are owned by the employer, not by the employee. Although copyrightable works developed by an employee during the scope of employment are thus presumptively owned by the employer, the situation is somewhat different for patentable inventions. If the employer and employee do not agree in advance about which party will own inventions conceived by the employee during the course and scope of employment, generally the employee will retain patent ownership rights, subject, however, to a **shop right** in favor of the employer. A shop right allows the employer to make and use the invention royalty-free, on a nonexclusive basis. Nevertheless, if the employee is hired specifically by an employer to develop or invent a product, the resulting invention will be owned by the employer.

Employers hiring inventors, scientists, engineers, artists, and other individuals who might develop or create work products will want to ensure and confirm that the employer owns all of the rights to the intellectual property created by the employee. The employment agreement should therefore provide that any inventions, designs, or other intellectual property developed by the employee while working for the employer are the property of the employer. Additional provisions should specify that the employee will cooperate in signing any applications filed with the U.S. Patent and Trademark Office or U.S. Copyright Office or any other documents to reflect the employer's ownership rights. Most agreements include a provision for extra protection specifying that, if for some reason the intellectual property is not viewed by a court as being owned by the employer, by virtue of the employment contract the employee thereby irrevocably and immediately assigns any interest he might have in the property to the employer. The employer will then have the rights to further exploit the intellectual property, to license it to others and collect royalties thereon, or to sell it to some third party. Most agreements also require the employee to warrant and represent that his work is original and does not infringe on anyone else's rights. This protects the employer from some later claim that the work infringes some other party's interests. (See Figure 18-2 for a model provision relating to an employer's ownership of work product.)

Employers generally attempt to draft provisions relating to ownership of intellectual property sufficiently broadly that the employer owns all rights to copyrights, inventions, designs, or processes, as well as any later enhancements or modifications to those work products. The parties may, of course, negotiate so that although the employer owns the intellectual property, the employee may receive a royalty based on sales of any product incorporating the employee's contributions.

Many disputes have arisen over inventions and processes developed by employees. If employees develop the work on their own time, for example, in the evenings and weekends at home, and do not use any information, skills, or supplies acquired through the employer, they may individually own the rights in any such intellectual property.

Intellectual property
Products of human creative thought and effort

Work made-for-hire doctrine
Legal doctrine that copyrightable work created by employee is owned by employer

Copyright
Right in original literary, artistic, dramatic, and other works

Shop right
Employer's royalty-free license to use an invention developed by an employee

FIGURE 18-2
Ownership of Work

Employee agrees that all inventions, improvements, data, processes, materials, systems, or discoveries (hereinafter called "Proprietary Information") that are conceived of or made by Employee, whether alone or with others, while employed by Employer are the sole property of Employer.

Employee agrees that if any of the Proprietary Information described in this Agreement is protectable by copyright and is deemed in any way to fall within the definition of "work made for hire," as such term is defined in 17 U.S.C. § 101, such work shall be considered a "work made for hire," and by virtue of this Agreement, the copyright of which shall be owned solely, completely, and exclusively by Employer, free and clear from any claims of any nature relating to Employee's contributions and other efforts. Employer shall have the right to copyright the work in its name as author and proprietor thereof.

Employee intends that Employer shall have full ownership of any of the aforesaid items with no rights of ownership in Employee. Employee agrees that in the event any of the items described herein are determined by a court not to be work made for hire under federal copyright laws, this Agreement shall operate as an irrevocable assignment by Employee to Employer of the copyright in the aforementioned items. Under this irrevocable assignment, Employee hereby assigns to Employer the sole and exclusive right, title, interest in and to the aforementioned items, without further consideration, and agrees to assist Employer in registering and enforcing the copyrights and other rights relating to the aforementioned items.

It is Employee's specific intention to assign all right, title, and interest whatsoever in any and all copyright rights in the aforesaid items, in any media, and for any purpose, to Employer. To that end, Employee agrees to execute and deliver all appropriate documents requested by Employer in connection therewith.

The rights of independent contractors can differ from the rights of employees, especially with regard to copyrights. Generally, as discussed, copyrightable works that are developed by employees in the course and scope of their employment are owned by employers under the work made-for-hire doctrine. The work made-for-hire doctrine is found in the United States Copyright Act, at 17 U.S.C. § 101. That section provides that if a party hires an independent contractor to create special types of commissioned or ordered works (such as motion pictures, translations, texts, supplementary works, tests, and atlases) and the parties agree in writing that it is to be a work made for hire, the employer will be the owner of the work. If the work is not a specially commissioned item of the type identified in the statute, and the parties have not agreed in writing that the commissioning party will be the owner, the creator retains ownership rights in the work (assuming the creator is not an employee). The parties are always free to agree in writing that the commissioning party owns the work, and the creator can assign his or her rights in the work to the commissioning party.

Because copyrightable work prepared by an employee within the scope of her employment is a work made for hire belonging to the employer, the creator will often attempt to argue that she was not an employee, but rather an **independent contractor,** and thus retains ownership of the work created. In determining whether an individual is an employee or an independent contractor, courts consider a variety of factors: control by the hiring party over the work itself, for example, control as to how the work is done, whether it is done at the hiring party's location, and whether the hiring party provides equipment or other means to create the work; control by the hiring party over the individual, for example, control over the individual's schedule in creating the work; and the status of the hiring party, for example, whether the hiring party provides the individual with benefits and/or withholds tax from the individual's payment. In general, the more control a hiring party exercises over the work and the individual, the more likely it is that an employer-employee relationship has been created, in which case work created by the employee is presumptively owned by the employer.

Independent contractors are not eligible for benefits provided to employees, and employers need not pay Social Security, withholding, and unemployment taxes for independent contractors. Thus, the IRS and the Department of Labor carefully scrutinize employers' classifications of workers to ensure true employees are not improperly classified as independent contractors.

Trade Secrets. Many companies have invested time, money, and effort in developing new products or systems. Similarly, data about customers, their preferences, credit ratings, and so forth can be extremely valuable to a company. This type of information might qualify as a trade secret. According to Section 1(4) of the Uniform Trade Secrets Act, a **trade secret** is defined as information, including a formula, pattern, compilation, program, device, method, technique, or process that derives independent commercial value from not being generally known or ascertainable and is the subject of reasonable efforts to keep it secret. Trade secrets need not be complex to be protectable, and they can endure forever if properly protected.

Perhaps one of the most famous trade secrets is the recipe and process for Coca-Cola. Maintaining the confidentiality of the recipe allows the Coca-Cola Company a competitive edge in the marketplace. If another company were able to market an identical product, Coca-Cola's unique and identifiable product would be lost. A variety of other information can also qualify as a trade secret, such as sales data, marketing plans, market studies, customer lists, or virtually any concrete information that gives the owner a competitive advantage over others who do not know it or use it. To qualify as a trade secret, the owner must generally have made some effort to protect the information and prevent it from becoming disclosed.

To retain the confidentiality of such trade secrets, employers will include provisions in employment contracts prohibiting employees from disclosing confidential information or trade secrets. The covenant not to disclose the trade secret can bind the employee not only during employment but afterward as well, perhaps indefinitely. Because it can be difficult to prove damages arising out of misappropriation of a trade secret, many agreements provide for fixed, or liquidated, damages upon disclosure of trade secrets.

Independent contractor One who provides work or services for another but is not an employee; one who controls and directs one's own work

Trade secret Information providing a competitive edge to its owner

A matter cannot be a trade secret if it is in the public domain (a matter of public knowledge) or was already known to the employee or independently developed by the employee. (See Figure 18-3 for typical nondisclosure provisions.)

Intellectual property and trade secrets are discussed further in Chapter Nineteen.

Manner of Resolving Disputes. The employment agreement should provide for the resolution of disputes, for example, by arbitration or litigation. A clause may be included that the prevailing party is entitled to recover attorneys' fees and costs from the losing party.

Miscellaneous Provisions. A variety of other provisions should be included in a well-drafted employment agreement, including the following:

- A provision specifying which state's law governs the contract;
- Provisions for amending the agreement;
- A warranty by the employee that entering into the agreement does not violate any other agreement to which he or she may be a party;

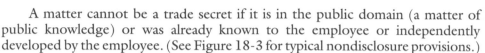

FIGURE 18-3
Covenant of Nondisclosure of Trade Secrets

Employee acknowledges and agrees that Employer's subscriber lists, customer lists, maps, diagrams, computer programs, financial information, terms of contracts with clients and customers, pricing information, marketing information, and sales techniques (hereinafter referred to as the "Confidential Information") are valuable trade secrets of Employer and that any disclosure or unauthorized use thereof will cause irreparable harm to Employer. In consideration of Employer's employment of Employee, Employee agrees to treat the Confidential Information in confidence and to use the Confidential Information for the sole purpose of performing his or her obligations under this Employment Agreement, not to disclose or divulge the Confidential Information outside of Employer, not to copy the Confidential Information or any portion thereof, and to return the Confidential Information and any material relating thereto to Employer upon the expiration or termination of this Agreement for any reason whatsoever.

This Agreement shall not bind Employee to maintain the confidentiality of any Confidential Information which has been widely published, patented, or which has become part of the public domain and no longer constitutes a trade secret of Employer, or any information which Employee can demonstrate was known to him or her prior to the date of disclosure or which was legally acquired from an independent, legitimate source.

The restrictions and obligations of this Section shall survive any expiration, termination, or cancellation of the Agreement and shall bind Employee, his or her successors, heirs, and assignees.

- A provision stating that the agreement supersedes any prior agreements between the parties and constitutes their entire agreement with respect to the employment;
- A provision relating to how notices should be delivered, for example, whether by mail, e-mail, or registered mail;
- A provision making the agreement binding on successors and assignees of the parties; and
- A provision providing that in the event any part of the agreement is held invalid, such invalidity will not affect the remainder of the agreement.

The agreement should then be signed and dated by each party.

Key Features
of Employee Compensation and Employee Agreements

◆ Employers often provide benefits in addition to salary to attract and retain valuable employees. Among these benefits are insurance (health, disability, and life) and retirement plans.

◆ Retirement plans can be qualified (meaning they qualify for favorable tax treatment) or nonqualified (meaning they do not qualify for favorable tax treatment).

◆ Retirement plans can be "defined benefit plans," meaning that a pre-established benefit is set that will be paid to employees when they retire, or they can be "defined contribution plans," meaning that the employer must place a specified amount of money into individual accounts for employees. Profit-sharing plans and 401(k) plans are examples of defined contribution plans.

◆ Employers may grant employees stock options or the right to buy shares in the company at a fixed price at some later time. As a company grows in value, stock options can be extremely profitable.

◆ Employment is generally "at will," meaning that either the employer or employee is free to terminate the relationship at any time for any reason or no reason.

◆ Employment agreements are often used for more senior or key employees.

◆ In most states, an employer may restrict an employee from competing against the employer upon termination of employment if the restriction is limited in scope, duration, and geographical area.

◆ Under the work made-for-hire doctrine, employers own the copyright-able work product created by their employees. To be safe, many employers use agreements confirming such ownership rights. Employers should use such agreements for their independent contractors because copyrightable works created by them are owned by the independent contractor unless the work is a special type, and the parties have agreed in writing that the commissioning party will own the work.

C. Role of Paralegal

The area of employment law is becoming increasingly more complex. A number of law firms and attorneys specialize in advising clients on various retirement, pension, and profit-sharing plans. These law firms and attorneys generally use paralegals to assist in drafting qualified plans, conducting research regarding requirements for the plan, and preparing the explanation of benefits for employees. Similarly, many corporations with in-house legal, personnel, and human resources departments rely on paralegals to assist in drafting various employee compensation plans and additional documents.

Paralegals also conduct research to determine a state's statutory and judicial treatment of restrictive covenants. With increased advances in the technological and communications fields, the validity of covenants not to compete, ownership of intellectual property, and protection of trade secrets has been much litigated. Due to continuing changes and developments both by legislatures and courts, paralegals will need to be alert to recent developments in the field of restrictive covenants.

Paralegals are commonly involved in the following tasks:

1. Conducting research regarding the statutory requirements for various employee compensation plans, both qualified and nonqualified.
2. Drafting qualified plans and supplementary materials.
3. Preparing and submitting determination letters to the IRS for approval of the plan and preparing annual reports for the IRS.
4. Preparing employee handbooks or manuals setting forth the terms and conditions of employment and describing any retirement plans and other fringe benefits.
5. Assisting in legal audits to ensure plans are not top-heavy, do not impose illegal vesting periods, or do not exclude eligible employees.
6. Preparing descriptions of the plans for employees.
7. Drafting minutes of directors' meetings adopting resolutions that approve compensation and benefit plans.
8. Conducting research regarding permissible terms and conditions of employment agreements, especially with regard to restrictive covenants.
9. Collecting information from clients regarding desired terms and conditions in preparation for drafting employment agreements.
10. Preparing worksheets or questionnaires for the employer to complete setting forth employee duties, the term of agreement, whether restrictive covenants are needed, renewal of the agreement, and benefits to which an employee is entitled.
11. Drafting the employment agreement.
12. Preparing resolutions for the board of directors to approve hiring of key personnel and the terms and conditions of employment.
13. Ensuring the employment agreement is signed by all parties.
14. Docketing dates for termination and renewal of employment contracts.
15. Assisting in a legal audit to advise the client as to any need for restrictive covenants for certain employees and for protection of intellectual property.

Case Illustration
Noncompetition Covenants

Case: *Alliant Insurance Services, Inc. v. Gaddy*, 72 Cal. Rptr. 3d 259 (Ct. App. 2008)

Facts: When he sold his company to the plaintiff, the defendant, Gaddy, agreed in writing to refrain from soliciting clients or carrying on any business competitive to that of the plaintiff within the 58 counties of California. When the plaintiff discovered Gaddy was contacting its clients it sought a preliminary injunction to prohibit such conduct. The trial court granted the injunction.

Holding: Affirmed. Although Gaddy argued that the covenant was too broad because the plaintiff buyer was only conducting business in six counties in the state, the court found that the business depended on goodwill in all 58 counties in California. The seller of the business should be prevented from depriving the buyer of the full value of its acquisition, including the sold company's goodwill.

◆ ◆ ◆

WEB RESOURCES

The most important resources relating to compensation for employees, benefit plans, and employment agreements are the various state and federal statutes. The following are sites allowing access to statutes.

Federal and state statutes:
www.law.cornell.edu
www.findlaw.com

Tax information about employee benefits:
www.irs.gov (information about IRAs, Keogh plans, and access to Publication 560, relating to retirement plans)

Employee benefits information:
www.dol.gov (The Department of Labor offers information about health plans, benefits, and ERISA.)
www.dol.gov/ebsa (The Employee Benefits Security Administration, a department within the Department of Labor, is organized to provide assistance for employee benefit plan participants.)

> www.pbgc.gov (The Pension Benefit Guaranty Corporation was created under ERISA to encourage maintenance of and provide protection for defined benefit plans.)
> www.invest-faq.com
> www.benefitnews.com
> www.nceo.org (site of National Center for Employee Ownership, providing information about employee benefits, stock options, and ESOPs)

Intellectual property information:
> www.uspto.gov (trademarks and patents)
> www.copyrights.gov (U.S. Copyright Office)

Employment and independent contractor forms:
> www.siccode.com/forms.php
> www.lectlaw.com/formb.htm
> www.allaboutforms.com

Discussion Questions

Fact Scenario. Woodson & Garcia, Inc. is a large corporation with several thousand employees.

1. Is the corporation obligated to provide health insurance for its employees? Is it obligated to provide workers' compensation insurance for its employees?

2. The corporation is concerned about the health of its chief executive officer and is particularly concerned about the cost of replacing her and recruiting a capable replacement for her in the event of her death. What might the corporation do to ease any financial burdens it might suffer upon her death?

3. May the company implement a plan that is specifically designed to be "top heavy" such that senior executives are favored over the rank-and-file employees?

4. What are some advantages to the company of establishing a profit-sharing plan?

5. Grace, one of the corporation's employees, was granted an option to purchase 1,000 shares of stock in the corporation for $25 per share on October 1 of this year. On that date, the stock was trading at $30 per share. Should Grace exercise the option? Would your answer change if the stock were trading at $20 per share? Discuss.

6. The company would like to lay off 30 of its employees due to a slight dip in the economy. May it terminate these employees without any advance notice?

7. Hal, one of the company's senior computer experts, was hired to develop new accounting software for the company. When Hal develops the software, who will own it?

8. The company required Hal to sign an agreement that upon termination with the company, he will not work for a competitive business anywhere in the United States for five years and that he will maintain the status of any company trade secrets indefinitely. Are these covenants valid? Discuss.

9. The company has valuable trade secret information relating to a new process that will be produce significant returns for the company. The board of directors, senior officers, and the company's attorneys and accountants have recently been informed of the new process. Does such disclosure destroy the trade secret? Discuss.

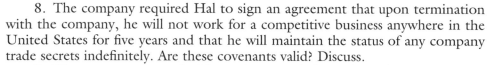

Net Worth

1. Access the Department of Labor Web site for its Employee Benefits Security Administration.
   a. Review "About EBSA." How many Americans are covered by private retirement plans?
   b. Review the FAQs about Pension Plans and ERISA. What is a money purchase plan? Can a pension be attached to satisfy obligations for family or child support?
2. Access the Web site for the Bureau of Labor Statistics. Review information about employee benefits (specifically, employee benefits in private industry). What percentage of workers participate in defined benefit plans and what percentage participate in defined contribution plans?
3. Access IRS Publication 15-B, *Employer's Tax Guide to Fringe Benefits.* If an employer provides athletic facilities for its employees, must the employees pay tax on such? If an employer gives its employees small gifts for the Christmas holiday, must the employees pay tax on such?
4. Access IRS Publication 4222, *401(k) Plans for Small Business.* What is a "catch up" provision, and what is the current amount that an employee over the age of 50 may contribute each year to his or her 401(k) plan as a catch up?

19

◆ ◆ ◆

Special Topics in Business Law

◆ ◆ ◆

CHAPTER OVERVIEW

This chapter discusses some of the ethical dilemmas facing attorneys and paralegals as well as the increased need for attention to ethics in the marketplace. Although there are no perfect answers for every question that might arise, even recognizing that certain ethical concerns must be addressed represents a step forward.

This chapter also discusses the interplay between corporate law and other practice areas, such as the sale of goods, franchising, leasing, intellectual property, antitrust and unfair competition law, and bankruptcy. Corporate law is not practiced in a vacuum. Skilled attorneys and paralegals need to be familiar with a variety of other

principles, including those relating to contracts, torts, real property, and crimes.

Finally, the roles and relationships of outside counsel and the corporation's own inside counsel are discussed. Until relatively recently, in-house legal departments were skeleton crews, working on only the most basic legal issues. In an effort to contain legal costs, many corporations have increased the size and quality of their inside legal departments. They now perform many of the legal tasks formerly conducted exclusively by private practitioners. The types of tasks performed by internal and outside counsel and their delicate relationship to each other is discussed.

A. Ethics

1. Introduction

With the extensive media attention given to the corporate and financial scandals of 2001 and 2008, the jail terms imposed on corporate executives Dennis Kozlowski and Andrew Fastow, the fast-paced world and jargon of hostile takeovers, movies such as *Wall Street* and *Boiler Room* promoting the philosophy of "greed is good," nearly obscene executive compensation, and reported stock disparagement occurring in Internet chat rooms, one might be tempted to think that the world of business is populated by unethical financiers and managers motivated solely by self-interest.

The basic ethical question faced by businesspeople is how to balance the need to act responsibly with the duty to earn profits for the owners of a business. There is no one perfect answer to this question, just as there is no text that will provide guidance for every ethical dilemma that might arise in business situations. Your own ethical convictions will serve as the basis for your decision-making. Be alert to more than just the immediate consequences of business activities. Consider whether the action serves the business owners at the expense of the community and whether there is a win-win situation that benefits both the business owners and society.

2. Business Ethics

Ethics
Study of right and wrong

Ethics is the study of standards of right and wrong. Ethics is not merely some remote philosophical concept existing in a vacuum. Ethical questions arise in your life every day. What if a salesperson undercharges you for an item? Are requests for reimbursement of various expenses padded? Do you tell a client that a document has been prepared and will be sent shortly when you have not yet begun working on the project? Do you use office supplies and equipment for personal purposes? These issues and numerous other issues of basic morality arise each day and constantly challenge us to make ethical decisions.

Business ethics
Study of standards of right and wrong in the business environment

If ethics is the study of standards of right and wrong, **business ethics** is the study of standards of right and wrong in the business environment. Whereas laws are designed to preserve order, ethics deal with the propriety of relationships between people. Laws and ethics are not necessarily synonymous. An action can be both illegal and unethical; for example, insider trading. An act can be legal but not ethical, such as a decision by a board of directors to award themselves bonuses in a lean year. Finally, an act can be illegal but ethical, such as a journalist's refusal to reveal sources even after a court order to do so. Thus, the fact that some action is legal does not necessarily mean that it is ethical, moral, or right. Our laws are limited and cannot be relied on to provide answers to all of our ethical questions. Personal ethical convictions must complement the law.

Additionally, ethics may have a cultural component. In many countries, gifts to officials are customary signs of respect and are an accepted part of business transactions. In the United States, however, a gift given in certain circumstances might be viewed as a bribe or an attempt to exert improper influence. Thus, some questions of ethics may be resolved differently in different cultures.

3. Ethical Approaches

We have all debated whether "the end justifies the means," or whether a good result can be justified by dishonest methods. For example, if a prosecutor knows a defendant is guilty of the crime charged, is the prosecutor justified in withholding evidence from the defense? Was *Les Miserables'* Jean Valjean justified in stealing a single loaf of bread to prevent his nephew's starvation?

Many religions adhere to the philosophy that ethical standards are absolute rather than relative and that a wrongful act can never be justified. This philosophy takes an absolute view of the duties imposed by religious strictures such that there is a reason, for instance, they are called the Ten Commandments rather than the Ten Suggestions.

In addition to setting forth absolute rules and duties, religions also advocate mercy and compassion. There may be a conflict between the absolute duty to do right and the concept of compassion. For example, a corporation might be experiencing severe financial difficulties. Unless the corporation merges with a stronger corporation, the corporation will be forced to lay off 10 percent of its work force. The area in which the corporation is located is economically depressed. If workers are laid off, it is unlikely they will be able to find jobs and many might have to apply for public assistance or move. Would a corporate executive be justified in verbally painting a rosier picture of the corporation to the prospective buyer to make the corporation more attractive? Which precept controls: the absolute duty to avoid wrongful acts, including any form of misrepresentation, or the duty to be compassionate to one's employees and shareholders who will genuinely suffer if the merger does not take place?

Many ethical dilemmas are like this one. There might be no bright line defining and delineating good from bad, but rather only shades of gray delineating good from better and bad from worse.

Under other ethical approaches, an action is judged not by absolute rules and duties, but rather by outcome: If the action benefits the majority of people, it is right, even if a minority is adversely affected. This ethical approach is exemplified by traditional cost-benefit analysis. For example, if survival of the corporation depends on a 10 percent reduction in work force, the benefit to the corporation (survival) outweighs the cost of the action (the misery and unhappiness of 10 percent of the workers). The movie *Class Action* revealed risk analysis conducted by a fictitious company that decided it was cheaper to pay damages in lawsuits for injuries and death rather than to fix a known defect in a car. The drawback to this approach to ethical questions is that it treats human beings as fungibles, items that can be easily substituted for each other, like pennies. Human beings are complex individuals, however, with needs and desires. Simply looking at a group of people as "cost ineffective" denies them their humanity.

Another approach to ethical questions is demonstrated by basic capitalist theory: Left alone, the marketplace will naturally produce social good. This philosophy argues that consumers' needs will dictate the marketplace. Consumers will only buy products that are useful and will only pay a certain price for them. Businesses that provide quality goods at lower prices will thrive and those that do not will fail. The competitive business environment will naturally work for the good of consumers and society by encouraging lower prices. Nevertheless, capitalist theory also has some drawbacks. For example, a product may be useful to consumers and offered at a competitive price. The consumers "win" by possessing a useful product at a lower price. The company "wins" by selling numerous units of its goods and making a profit. But what if a necessary by-product of producing the goods is toxic waste? Society itself bears the burden of this ill. Thus, profit cannot be the sole determinant in whether a product is good for society.

4. *Making Decisions*

Making business decisions requires a constant interplay and balancing of ethical issues, legal concerns, and the need for a company to make a profit to survive and serve the needs of its owners and community. You have seen that just because something is legal, it is not necessarily ethical. Similarly, you have seen that just because profit is made, a result is not always for the good of society. This delicate balance among ethics, law, and profit confronts business owners daily. There might be a need to sacrifice or compromise one of these elements for the good of the others. For example, a company might be willing to accept less profit to achieve some socially useful goal or to ensure that its actions are legal. Similarly, a company might be willing to bend the rules (namely, sacrifice ethics) so long as its actions are legal and produce revenue for the good of the business and its owners.

Decisions made by businesspeople thus involve an evaluation of whether an anticipated action is ethical, whether it is legal, and whether it is profitable. There are no perfect rules or answers for the dilemmas confronting business owners. In each instance, an analysis of these three factors will be combined with the decision-maker's own ethical standards to produce a decision.

Interestingly, a professor at the University of Michigan Business School claims that organizations at which employees perceive higher levels of "virtuousness" (measured by volunteer and compassionate activity, perceptions of respect, and integrity in the workplace, and so forth) result in about a 15 percent increase in shareholder value.

5. *Legal Duties*

In the business arena, a number of court decisions and statutes have combined to create a blueprint for ethical decision-making. These concepts have been discussed throughout the text, but are examined here briefly insofar as they relate to ethical issues.

Fiduciary Duties. Partners owe fiduciary, or good-faith, duties to each other. Similarly, corporate directors and officers owe fiduciary duties to the corporate enterprise. These fiduciary duties require business and corporate managers to act in the best interests of the enterprise and with the highest degree of good faith. Thus, some ethical conflicts may be resolved by determining which course of action is supported by the trust and confidence reposed in management.

Duty of Due Care. Corporate officers and directors are required to act with due care, and with a duty of inquiry, as ordinarily prudent persons would exercise in like circumstances. Thus, corporate managers must inform themselves of all aspects relating to decision-making. Management cannot look solely to the bottom line and ignore the legality of an action. Any reasonably diligent person acting with due care would examine whether certain actions are legal and whether the consequences of those actions will produce harm to society and perhaps harm to the corporation (which may ultimately be held liable for acts of wrongdoing).

Duty of Loyalty and Prohibition Against Self-Dealing. Partners and corporate managers are required to devote their time, skill, and energy to the business enterprise. They cannot engage in activities that are competitive with those of the business and cannot undertake actions that benefit themselves personally at the expense of their partners, the business, or its owners. Instituting unreasonable compensation packages for managers, buying property or stock back from insiders at a price higher than market value, and structuring mergers and benefit plans to benefit senior executives are all examples of breaches of the duty of loyalty. Corporate managers or partners cannot put their own interests above the interests of those to whom they owe fiduciary duties.

Covenants of Good Faith and Fair Dealing. Whether expressed or not, every contract includes an **implied covenant of good faith and fair dealing.** Thus, whether or not an employee has been promised specific benefits, a court would likely determine that an employer who arbitrarily changed the employee's title, belittled him in meetings, refused to provide support staff assistance and supplies to the employee, and moved the employee into a cramped office, would likely have breached the covenant of good faith inherent in an employment agreement, even if these actions did not amount to a technical breach of any specific terms and conditions of a written agreement.

> **Implied covenant of good faith and fair dealing**
> An implied condition in every contract requiring each party to deal fairly with the other

The covenant of good faith and fair dealing applies not only to contracts made between the corporation and its internal staff, but also to agreements between the corporation and third parties. Thus, in a merger, a corporation is required to disclose any matter that would be deemed material or relevant to the other party, even if specific disclosure was not called for by the merger agreement. Each party to a contract must act so as not to deprive the other party of receiving that for which it has bargained.

Fiduciary duties, duties of due care, duties of loyalty, and covenants of good faith assist businesspeople in making ethical decisions. By examining case law, decision-makers can review court interpretations of these duties to arrive at an ethical and legal decision that still produces profit for the business enterprise and its owners. In addition, a recent addition to the MBCA requires that directors of public corporations ensure that there are policies and practices in place to foster the corporation's compliance with law and ethical conduct. MBCA § 8.01(c)(4).

6. Ethical Codes

Some companies set forth their ethical standards in written codes or publications. These codes may specify the mission of the company and may describe the standard of conduct expected in the workplace. (See Figure 19-1 for an ethical code.) The publication may be posted in various prominent places throughout the company offices and provided to each employee upon commencement of employment. These codes provide a solid foundation for employer-employee relations and foster an atmosphere of trust and confidence. Nevertheless, a set of written policies and guidelines can never cover every ethical dilemma that might arise and can never substitute for individual standards of right and wrong. Moreover, the benefits of a formal code will be illusory if managers' actions are in contradiction to

FIGURE 19-1
Ethical Business Code

FIGURE 19-1
Ethical Business Code

ABC Inc.'s customers have played an important role in our continuous growth and success. In order to avoid any conflict of interest between our suppliers and our employees and to maintain all business relationships on a professional basis, ABC has established the following business practices:

◆ ABC expects all of its employees to provide a quality product or service and to act professionally at all times.

◆ All work performed by ABC employees must be of the highest quality possible. All work must be performed competently, professionally, and courteously.

◆ No ABC employee may ask for or receive anything of value from a customer. Gifts from a customer such as tickets to athletic or entertainment events or any type of personal item are not permitted by ABC.

◆ If any ABC employee is offered or accepts any item of value from a customer, the employee is to report it to the appropriate ABC manager.

◆ Occasional meals during visits to a customer's facilities or during business meetings are acceptable, although ABC employees are required to report such activities to the appropriate ABC manager.

◆ Violations of these practices may constitute grounds for ABC to take appropriate disciplinary action against the employee, including a warning, probation, suspension without pay, or termination of employment.

the written policy. Employees are quick to observe that a standard is not truly "Do as the code says" but "Do as we do."

A newly emerging career is that of professional ethics officers who are employed by companies and organizations to ensure their organizations act responsibly. Most are members of the Ethics & Compliance Officer Association (www.theecoa.org).

The American Bar Association has promulgated a code of ethics for attorneys, entitled Model Rules of Professional Conduct. Most states, using the ABA code as a model, have adopted their own codes of ethics for attorneys in their jurisdictions. These codes relate to duties owed to clients, courts, and adversaries. The bar associations of most states have set up ethics "hotlines" to respond to questions dealing with ethics. Although legal advice will not be given, callers are generally referred to provisions in their state's code of ethics and pertinent case law.

Moreover, the two major paralegal associations have each prepared ethical codes. Model Code of Ethics and Professional Responsibility and Guidelines for Enforcement is the product of the National Federation of Paralegal Associations. The National Association of Legal Assistants' code is called Code of Ethics and Professional Responsibility. These ethical codes may provide guidelines for ethical dilemmas.

Many states are considering ethics codes for paralegals that will discipline paralegals for ethical violations. At the present time, most state guidelines are designed to instruct and educate attorneys on how to use paralegals ethically.

The attorneys remain responsible for supervision of paralegals and are disciplined in the event of ethical violations by their paralegals.

Many law firms are drafting their own codes for paralegals. These codes usually include guidelines regarding the disclosure of client confidences and conflict-of-interest clearance checks to ensure that paralegals who switch law firms do not work on matters involving clients of their former firms. In one recent Arizona case, a paralegal switched jobs during litigation and went to work for a law firm representing the plaintiffs in a case in which the paralegal had formerly assisted with the defense. The Arizona appellate court agreed with the trial court that because of the paralegal's former relationship with the defendants, the entire law firm should be disqualified from representing the plaintiffs.

In some states, paralegal associations are establishing codes of ethics and disciplinary committees that can hold hearings and take action against paralegals violating ethical standards. Discipline can range from counseling to revocation of the paralegal's membership in the association.

PRACTICE TIP

To maintain a client's confidences:

- Do not leave client materials where third parties might see them.
- Do not discuss a client's case outside the office or in front of strangers (such as in an elevator or at a restaurant).
- Avoid sensitive discussions on a cell phone or other nonsecure method of communication.
- Do not use client materials as writing samples to show prospective employers.
- Be careful with confidential information stored on easily stolen laptops or BlackBerry-type PDAs.

B. Common Interdisciplinary Issues

1. Introduction

In corporate or business practice, a number of issues commonly arise that are not strictly corporate law matters, but are intertwined with other areas of law, primarily commercial, contractual, real property, intellectual property, and antitrust law. These issues deal with the purchase and sale of goods, franchise relationships, leases, intellectual property, anticompetitive and deceptive practices, and bankruptcy law.

2. Commercial Transactions and the Sale of Goods

Until relatively recently, state statutes regarding sales varied significantly from state to state, hindering interstate transactions. To remedy this problem, the National Conference of Commissioners on Uniform State Laws developed the

UCC
Uniform Commercial
Code, which governs
commercial transactions

Uniform Commercial Code (UCC), which governs contracts of sale. The UCC provides a national framework for commercial transactions governing merchants of goods, whether the merchants are sole proprietors, partnerships, or corporations. Many states have made revisions to the UCC in adopting it.

Although there is some variation among states, the UCC serves as the standard reference for laws governing the sale of goods. The UCC covers more than just an actual sale. It governs payment methods, banking, warranties relating to the goods, leases, the extension of credit for the purchase of goods, and nearly all aspects of commercial transactions.

The best known portion of the UCC is Article 2, entitled Sales, relating to "transactions in goods" (as opposed to transactions relating to real property or intellectual property). Article 2 has been adopted in every state but Louisiana. Common law and statutory principles relating to contracts, such as offer, acceptance, consideration, and so forth, are not superseded by the UCC. If the UCC does not cover a certain issue, general state law will control.

The UCC provides a national approach to the interpretation of contracts for the sale of goods. For example, the UCC provides that if a contract was unfair and overreaching when made, it can be set aside as "unconscionable." In determining unconscionability, courts will consider the express terms of the contract as well as what is ordinary and customary in the relevant trade or industry. For example, some contracts contain clauses of *adhesion,* clauses that dramatically and unfairly prejudice one party's rights, yet must be accepted if the affected party, usually in a weaker bargaining position, wants to make the deal. In general, adhesion contracts or clauses are unenforceable.

The UCC also covers which party to a contract must bear the risk of loss of the goods due to damage in shipment or actual loss of the goods. Parties may mutually determine which one of them will bear the risk of loss, but if they fail to agree the UCC provides specific rules, depending on whether the goods are transported by a common carrier, whether the goods must be delivered to a particular destination, or whether the goods can be "delivered" even without actual movement, as is the case when the buyer picks up the goods.

The UCC provides remedies for both the buyer and seller in the event of the other party's breach of contract. The Code discusses return of the goods, resale of the goods to some third party, or rejection of nonconforming goods.

Perhaps one of the most significant sections of UCC Article 2 relates to warranties on the sale of goods. For centuries, the maxim governing the sale of goods was *caveat emptor,* literally, "Let the buyer beware." Sellers historically had little liability for defective goods. The UCC, however, provides a detailed and consumer-oriented approach in establishing a series of warranties included in nearly every sale. For example, UCC § 2-314 provides that in every sale of goods, there is an implied warranty that the goods are "merchantable," meaning that the goods are reasonably fit for their intended purposes. Thus, consumers have a right to expect that televisions will provide clear pictures and sound, that coffeemakers will brew coffee, and that watches will accurately tell time.

Caveat emptor
Latin expression meaning
"let the buyer beware"

Although sellers may attempt to disclaim warranties — for example, by selling goods "as is" or by expressly stating that no warranties are made with respect to an item sold — courts disfavor such disclaimers. To protect consumers, the UCC requires that certain disclaimers be set forth in clear and conspicuous writing. Thus, a disclaimer "in fine print" is likely ineffective.

Article 9 of the UCC covers **secured transactions,** namely, transactions in which certain property is pledged as collateral to secure the repayment of a debt. For example, you might wish to borrow $100 from a friend. The friend, having some concerns about your ability to repay the debt, might require that you surrender your watch as "collateral" for the loan. When you repay the loan, your watch will be returned to you. If you do not repay the loan, your friend has a watch that can be used or sold to defray the bad debt. In this sense, your friend has "security" for repayment of the debt. She holds a **security interest** in the watch and is referred to as the **secured party.** In most instances, the secured property, the watch, will be retained by the borrower or purchaser and surrendered to the lender or seller only upon default.

The lender will want to be assured that you do not pledge the watch as collateral to numerous other lenders, so that in the event of a default of the loan, there is sufficient collateral to satisfy the debt and creditors are not left fighting among themselves.

Article 9 regulates these secured transactions. Generally, to enforce a security interest, there must be a writing, the **security agreement,** granting a security interest in favor of the lender. To protect, or *perfect,* her rights against some other party, the lender must prepare and file a **financing statement** (usually called a *UCC-1*) with the secretary of state. The financing statement identifies the debtor, the creditor, and the collateral, and provides a public record so that later lenders have a means of assuring that the property has not been "over-collateralized," or pledged to satisfy more debt than it is worth. UCC-1 filings thus establish priority in the event of a debtor's default or bankruptcy. Because these UCC filings are a matter of public record, it is easy to determine whether security interests have been claimed in certain property. Article 9 was amended in 1999 to promote centralized and electronic filing of the UCC forms. To eliminate state variations in the appearance of the forms, national forms were developed and are now in use. (See Figure 19-2 for a UCC-1 form.) Data on outstanding UCC filings and liens can be located on WESTLAW, using the UCC database.

Just as the secretary of state accepts articles of incorporation, he or she will accept UCC-1 forms and requests for information. A filing fee is generally charged. In Delaware, the fee varies depending on how quickly the creditor would like to assure filing of the financing statement. The secured party may pay additional fees to assure same-day filing or even filing within two hours of receipt.

When the debt is paid in full, the secured party will release the security interest in the property by filing an additional form verifying that the debt has been paid and that the creditor therefore releases any interest it might have in the secured property. Paralegals often conduct UCC-1 searches when corporations are merging or acquiring the assets of another entity to ensure that the assets purchased are free and clear of outstanding security interests. In most states, filing and searching can be done online through the home page of the secretary of state.

Article 2 was amended in 2003 to provide, among other things, that electronic records and signatures are the equivalent to their paper counterparts and to create a new category of sales contracts, consumer contracts. A disclaimer of the implied warranty of quality of a consumer contract must be in language that clearly informs the consumer of the nature of the risk being assumed.

In August 1999, the National Conference of Commissioners on Uniform State Laws promulgated a model law, called the Uniform Computer Information

Secured transaction
Transaction in which property is pledged as collateral for a debt

Security interest
The interest the creditor has in collateral pledged for a debt

Secured party
The creditor in a secured transaction

Security agreement
Agreement setting forth parties' rights in a secured transaction

Financing statement
Document filed with state to provide notice of a security interest (also called a *UCC-1*)

FIGURE 19-2
National Financing Statement (UCC-1)

UCC FINANCING STATEMENT
FOLLOW INSTRUCTIONS (front and back) CAREFULLY

A. NAME & PHONE OF CONTACT AT FILER [optional]

B. SEND ACKNOWLEDGEMENT TO: (Name and Address)

Print   Reset

THE ABOVE SPACE IS FOR FILING OFFICE USE ONLY

1. DEBTOR'S EXACT FULL LEGAL NAME – insert only one debtor name (1a or 1b) – do not abbreviate or combine names

1a. ORGANIZATION'S NAME

OR

1b. INDIVIDUAL'S LAST NAME | FIRST NAME | MIDDLE NAME | SUFFIX

1c. MAILING ADDRESS | CITY | STATE | POSTAL CODE | COUNTRY

ADD'L INFO RE ORGANIZATION DEBTOR | 1e. TYPE OF ORGANIZATION | 1f. JURISDICTION OF ORGANIZATION | 1g. ORGANIZATIONAL ID#, if any | ☐ NONE

2. ADDITIONAL DEBTOR'S EXACT FULL LEGAL NAME – insert only one debtor name (2a or 2b) – do not abbreviate or combine names

2a. ORGANIZATION'S NAME

OR

2b. INDIVIDUAL'S LAST NAME | FIRST NAME | MIDDLE NAME | SUFFIX

2c. MAILING ADDRESS | CITY | STATE | POSTAL CODE | COUNTRY

ADD'L INFO RE ORGANIZATION DEBTOR | 2e. TYPE OF ORGANIZATION | 2f. JURISDICTION OF ORGANIZATION | 2g. ORGANIZATIONAL ID#, if any | ☐ NONE

3. SECURED PARTY'S NAME (or Name of TOTAL ASSIGNEE of ASSIGNOR S/P) – insert only one secured party name (3a or 3b)

3a. ORGANIZATION'S NAME

OR

3b. INDIVIDUAL'S LAST NAME | FIRST NAME | MIDDLE NAME | SUFFIX

3c. MAILING ADDRESS | CITY | STATE | POSTAL CODE | COUNTRY

4. This FINANCING STATEMENT covers the following collateral:

5. ALTERNATIVE DESIGNATION [if applicable]: ☐LESSEE/LESSOR ☐CONSIGNEE/CONSIGNOR ☐BAILEE/BAILOR ☐SELLER/BUYER ☐AG. LIEN ☐NON-UCC FILING

6. ☐ This FINANCING STATEMENT is to be filed [for record] (or recorded) in the REAL ESTATE RECORDS. Attach Addendum [if applicable] | 7. Check to REQUEST SEARCH REPORT(S) on Debtor(s) [ADDITIONAL FEE] [optional] ☐All Debtors ☐Debtor 1 ☐Debtor 2

8. OPTIONAL FILER REFERENCE DATA

FILING OFFICE COPY – NATIONAL UCC FINANCING STATEMENT (FORM UCC1) – CALIFORNIA (REV. 01/01/08)

Transaction Act, to regulate electronic commerce, namely the purchase and sale of goods, including software, online. The Act has already been subject to much debate and dissension, and attorneys general from nearly half of the states oppose it, many on the basis that it favors the Internet industry to the detriment of consumers. Due to the vigorous debate over the Act, few experts expect passage in all states. As of 2008, it had only been adopted in Maryland and Virginia.

Effective October 2000, by federal law, electronic signatures on contracts have the same force and effect as their pen-and-ink counterparts. Consumers can elect whether to use an electronic signature (usually consisting of a keystroke on an "I agree" button) or handwritten signature for most documents. Nevertheless, certain documents, such as those canceling basic services such as heat and water, must be provided to consumers in conventional print form.

3. Franchising

A **franchise** is a license granted by one party to another enabling the latter to use the licensor's proprietary system and trademarks in selling goods and services. Arguably, the best known example of franchising in the United States is McDonald's restaurants. An individual or entity wishing to offer McDonald's products will enter into an agreement with McDonald's, called a **franchise agreement,** whereby a certain initial franchise fee will be paid for the privilege of using McDonald's recipes, systems, trademarks, logos, and so forth.

Franchise
License granted by one party to another to use the first party's system and trademarks

Franchise agreement
Agreement setting forth parties' rights in a franchise relationship

The franchisee can operate his own business and yet enjoy the proven track record of McDonald's, the franchisor. Whereas 15 states have separate statutory provisions governing franchises, the remainder of the states follow regulations established by the Federal Trade Commission (FTC). The FTC has promulgated regulations requiring certain disclosures by franchisors to franchisees. For example, the franchisor must disclose the anticipated costs in establishing the franchise, the number of other franchisees in the system, any litigation pending against the franchisor, and the number and circumstances of termination of other franchisees.

A franchise relationship is a contractual relationship. The rights and duties of the parties are governed by their franchise agreement. The FTC, however, requires that certain items and information be disclosed to the potential franchisee. These disclosures are set forth in a document called the **franchise offering circular,** which must be provided to every potential franchisee.

Franchise offering circular
Document provided to prospective franchisee providing information on the franchised business and franchisor

Typically, the franchisee pays a certain initial franchise fee for the privilege of operating the franchise, whether it is a McDonald's, a Dunkin' Donuts shop, or a Midas muffler repair shop. Additionally, franchisees are generally required to pay stated royalties to the franchisor based on their sales. Thus, the better the franchisee does, the better the franchisor does. The franchisor, however, must provide certain support and training to franchisees. Many franchisors collect money from franchisees to fund national advertising campaigns to benefit all franchisees in the system or to promote a new product or service.

Because of the potential for abuse, the law is replete with complex franchise litigation cases. For example, what if you expend a significant amount of money for a McDonald's franchise and then McDonald's itself establishes its own restaurant half a block away from yours and undersells your products? What if you have expended a great deal of money to purchase a Baskin-Robbins franchise and then the franchisor begins offering its ice cream products in ordinary grocery stores, thus competing against you? What if Taco Bell franchisees are required by the terms of their franchise agreement to purchase salsa only from the franchisor and then the franchisor sets the price of the salsa so high that it drives the franchisee out of business?

From the franchisor's perspective, what if the franchisee refuses to follow the recipe for KFC chicken and independently begins offering new products? What if the franchisee refuses to follow the franchisor's requirements as to appearance and sanitation of the business so that the franchisor begins suffering a loss of its reputation as a clean and healthy restaurant?

Just as the general trend in other contracts is away from caveat emptor, and toward a wider recognition of rights of consumers, the general trend in franchising is to ensure that franchisees obtain the benefit of that for which they have paid and bargained. Nevertheless, the needs of franchisees are balanced with the need of franchisors to impose quality controls and standards on their franchisees to ensure that consumers who order a hamburger in Des Moines receive the same product and quality they would if ordering the product in Jacksonville.

4. Leases

Many businesses either rent office space from another party or perhaps rent to others their own excess space. Just as for centuries the guiding principle in contract law was caveat emptor, the general principle in real property law was that only the landlord had rights, not the tenant.

In the past several years, cases and statutes have taken a more aggressive posture in protecting tenants, on the basis that they are in an inferior bargaining position to the landlord. Thus, over the past generation, a number of compelling cases have changed the landscape of landlord-tenant law. In general, whereas the earlier view was that the tenant took the premises as she found them, and accepted any risk or deterioration, modern law has fashioned a number of principles to ensure that tenants are not subject to unconscionable contracts.

Landlord
Owner of premises (also called *lessor*)

The owner of premises is called the **landlord** or *lessor*. The party who uses the real property and pays a sum therefor is called the **tenant** or *lessee*.

Tenant
One who uses or rents a landlord's property (also called *lessee*)

The agreement whereby the tenant agrees to occupy the premises may be oral or written and may be for a specified term or at will, meaning that either party has the right to terminate the lease upon notice to the other. Whether the lease or rental agreement is oral or written, each party must abide by its terms, as is the case with any contract. Moreover, the law may impose additional obligations on the landlord. For example, if a state statute requires that landlords can only institute an eviction action against tenants after providing 30 days' notice, the landlord cannot circumvent that law by requiring otherwise. Similarly, a landlord cannot require the tenant to assume the burden of the landlord's statutory duties. The landlord cannot, therefore, require the tenant to release the landlord from a statutory duty to install a fire detection system; such an **exculpatory clause** is unconscionable and is unenforceable.

Exculpatory clause
A clause attempting to excuse oneself from one's own negligence or fault

The landlord-tenant relationship is subject to a number of rights, duties, and responsibilities. For example, the landlord must deliver physical possession of the premises to the tenant. The landlord cannot allow a former tenant to occupy the space and inform the incoming tenant that it is his responsibility to take possession.

Tenants have a **right of quiet enjoyment,** meaning they have a right to use and enjoy the premises for that purpose for which they are designed. If the landlord permits raucous parties, routinely explodes fireworks in the parking lot, or allows other tenants to destroy the premises, a tenant may have the right to terminate the lease based on the fact that the right to quiet enjoyment of the premises has been breached by the landlord.

Landlords cannot evict tenants without prior notice. Even in the event the tenant has failed to pay rent, the landlord must provide the tenant with notice and an opportunity to cure the default. Similarly, the landlord is generally precluded from **constructive eviction** of the tenant, by turning off heat, water, or other essential services. The tenant should be provided with an opportunity to defend any default in the terms of the lease. It is possible the tenant has withheld rent due to a leak in the roof that has caused the tenant to incur expenses for repair or to cease operating its business. Similarly, landlords are generally prohibited from **retaliatory eviction,** or evicting tenants who have exercised certain statutory rights, such as complaining to the local health department about the condition of the premises.

The tenant may be restricted as to use of the premises. In some commercial leases, business tenants often negotiate for written covenants by the landlord that a similar business will not be allowed to lease premises in the building or space. Thus, for example, if a tenant operates a yogurt shop in a shopping center, she will want to make sure that the landlord does not lease other spaces in the center to some competitive business, such as another yogurt shop or possibly even an ice cream store or deli.

Generally, tenants have a duty to maintain the leased premises in good condition; however, tenants are not required to repair defective plumbing, wiring, and so forth. Additionally, tenants may not alter the premises without the landlord's approval, even if the tenant believes the alteration, such as removal of a wall, is an improvement. A concomitant duty is imposed on the landlord: The landlord is generally required to maintain the premises in good condition, including repairing leaky pipes, replacing broken appliances, and so forth, but has no duty to improve the premises. Landlords must maintain common areas, such as parking lots, hallways, and elevators, in good condition.

A tenant cannot typically be charged with ordinary wear and tear of the premises. In previous years, a common practice of landlords was to retain all or a significant portion of security deposits for such items as cleaning or painting the premises after the tenant vacated. Many modern statutes attempt to control this practice by requiring that the landlord bear the cost of ordinary wear and tear and return the security deposit within a certain time period unless the landlord provides the former tenant with an itemized list of the repairs needed. Cases instituted in small claims courts dealing with disputes over retention of security deposits are plentiful, revealing that this remains an area of much dissension.

A common conflict in landlord-tenant relations relates to the withholding of rent by a tenant due to some alleged breach of the lease or misconduct by the landlord. Many states have enacted laws dealing with this issue because it has given rise to so much litigation. In some states, tenants may withhold rent in an amount equivalent to the sum by which the premises have decreased in value due to any

Right of quiet enjoyment
Provision inherent in all leases allowing tenant to use and enjoy rented premises

Constructive eviction
Impairment of tenant's rights that is so significant the tenant might as well have been physically evicted

Retaliatory eviction
Eviction of tenant by landlord in retaliation for tenant's lawful exercise of rights

defect, such as a leaky roof or faulty plumbing. Rent withholding, sometimes called a **rent strike** (especially if numerous tenants are protesting poor conditions), is a complex and hotly debated matter. Some statutes require and many attorneys advise that rather than merely withholding rent, tenants deposit the rent into a special account to be released to the landlord upon resolution of the dispute. This gesture shows the tenant's good faith and demonstrates that the tenant is not merely avoiding payment obligations.

The amount charged for rent of the premises is subject to agreement of the parties. A landlord who sets the rent excessively high will not be successful in attracting tenants as they will simply shop for better bargains. Thus, courts rarely interfere with the agreement of the parties dealing with the amount of rent to be paid. Rent need not always be paid in cash. The parties are free to work out other arrangements, such as providing space rent-free to the tenant in return for the tenant's agreement to manage the building, providing one year's free rent in exchange for an advantageously long rental term, and so forth. The parties may agree that the rent will increase periodically. The increase can be established in advance or might be based on increases in the consumer price index or other relevant statistics. If there is no written lease agreement and the tenant rents at will, the landlord may increase the rent upon appropriate notice, usually one month.

Generally, the landlord may assign or transfer his interest in the leased premises. A tenant, however, seldom has the right to transfer his rights without prior approval of the landlord. An **assignment** of a lease is a transfer of all of the renter's interest in the space to another. A **sublease,** however, is a transfer of the premises for a period less than the term of the lease agreement. Because landlords have the right to interview and screen candidates to ensure they have a proven track record as reliable tenants, to allow a tenant to transfer the space to another without the approval of the owner of the premises would jeopardize the valuable property rights the owner has in the premises. Although landlords may use valid criteria in screening applicants, such as rent history, employment information, and references, landlords are prohibited from discriminating against tenants due to their religion, race, sex, and so forth.

With regard to liability to third persons, the tenant is liable for reasonably foreseeable injuries proximately caused by her. For example, if a tenant fails to shovel snow at the doorstep of her store premises, or fails to adequately warn customers of the condition, the tenant might be liable. Landlords are liable to third parties on the same basis. Although landlords may not be liable for totally unpredictable events, such as the shooting of a tenant by a deranged individual, the landlord will be liable for acts that reasonably could have been foreseen. To illustrate, if a particular locale has been the scene of a number of rapes, and the landlord has notice of the rapes and has been provided a description of the suspected rapist by the police, the landlord might be liable for damages for a resulting rape of a tenant if the landlord failed to disclose this pertinent and known information to tenants. Similarly, the landlord might be liable for injury to tenants or third parties caused by defective conditions on the premises such as potholes or inadequate lighting. Although not a guarantor of safety and well-being, a landlord is charged with maintaining the premises. Additionally, if the landlord knows information that would be viewed as material to tenants, the landlord has an affirmative duty to disclose that information.

Courts may fashion a variety of remedies for breach of lease agreements. If the tenant is not provided with what it bargained for, the court may allow the tenant to set off rent previously paid or terminate its obligations under the lease. In the event

Rent strike
Withholding of rent

Assignment
A transfer of all of lessee's interest to another

Sublease
Transfer by lessee of less than all of its rights to another

of a breach by the tenant, the landlord must usually initiate an eviction action (called an **unlawful detainer** action) in court. Evidence will be presented and the court will render a decision. If the court determines that eviction is necessary, a certain period of time is generally given to the tenant to remove himself from the premises. If the tenant fails to vacate the premises, after a period of notice, the local sheriff will forcefully evict the tenant by placing the tenant's personal possessions in the street, physically removing the tenant from the premises, and changing the locks on the doors. If a tenant vacates the premises prior to the agreed-on term, the tenant will remain liable for the rent owed under the lease. The landlord, however, has an affirmative duty to mitigate these damages by making a good-faith effort to lease the premises to a third party.

Unlawful detainer
Action brought by landlord to evict a tenant

5. *Intellectual Property*

Introduction.   As discussed in Chapter Eighteen, businesses desire to own all work products produced by their employees. Moreover, some companies own valuable products, including software, which can be licensed to other parties. The products of human creativity are called **intellectual property,** to distinguish them from items of real property (real estate) and personal property (tangible items, such as jewelry and cars). Intellectual property consists of four types of property rights: trademarks, copyrights, patents, and trade secrets.

Intellectual property
Products of human creative thought, including trademarks, copyrights, patents, and trade secrets

Trademarks.   A **trademark** is any word, name, symbol, or device used by a person to identify and distinguish his or her goods and to indicate the source of those goods. 15 U.S.C. § 1127. Technically, the term **trademark** is used to identify one's product (such as the use of NIKE® in connection with shoes), and the term **service mark** is used to identify one's services (such as HILTON® for lodging services). Many companies use both trademarks and service marks, such as the use of STARBUCKS® in connection with products, such as coffee and mugs, and in connection with restaurant services. In common usage, however, the term *trademark* is often used to refer to marks identifying products or services.

Trademark
A logo, symbol, word, or device used to identify and distinguish goods

Service mark
A logo, symbol, word, or device used to identify and distinguish services

Trademarks can consist of slogans (such as YOU DESERVE A BREAK TODAY®), designs (such as the famous GOLDEN ARCHES® used by McDonald's Corporation), sounds (such as NBC's distinctive three-note chime), and even fragrances and colors.

Although the use of the word *device* in the definition of a trademark is broad enough to encompass a variety of items, there are some exclusions from trademark protection, including marks that are merely descriptive, marks that are confusingly similar to others' marks, marks that are scandalous or immoral, and marks that are primarily merely surnames. Moreover, some marks are stronger than others: marks that are coined (such as XEROX®) are the strongest and most protectable, followed by marks that involve the arbitrary use of a word for a product or service (such as APPLE® for computers), and then marks that are suggestive (such as CIRCUIT CITY® for electronic goods). Marks that merely describe a product cannot be registered with the U.S. Patent and Trademark Office (USPTO) unless they have achieved **secondary meaning** such that upon encountering the mark, consumers immediately associate it with the source or offeror of the goods. Secondary meaning can also be achieved through five years of continuous use of a mark. Words that are generic (such as BREAD for bread) cannot function as trademarks.

Secondary meaning
Achieving wide renown

Trademarks provide guarantees of quality and consistency so that a consumer purchasing a latte at a Starbucks in Miami knows it will be of the same quality as one purchased at a Starbucks in San Francisco.

Rights in trademarks arise from use of the mark. Federal registration of a mark is not required to acquire trademark rights; however, registration with the USPTO does afford a number of advantages to an owner, including the right to bring an action for infringement in federal court. Only marks in use in interstate commerce can be registered with the USPTO. If a mark is in use exclusively intrastate, for example, solely in Denver, it might be registered with the state of Colorado, but it may not achieve federal registration. A mark in use in such a local area will have prior rights over any later user who uses a confusingly similar mark in the area of use or a reasonable area of geographic expansion. A federal registration, however, affords nationwide priority so that its owner can preclude a later user from use of a confusingly similar mark anywhere in the United States. Marks used without being subject to federal registration are often called **common law marks.**

Common law mark
A trademark in use without benefit of federal registration

If a mark qualifies for federal registration, an application should be filed with the USPTO. Additionally, if one has a bona fide intent to use a mark in interstate commerce, one can file an application for federal registration. The USPTO registration process is fairly lengthy, and generally takes about one year. The filing fee is presently $375 ($325 if the application is filed electronically). After registration, the owner of the mark will be required to periodically confirm use of the mark to the USPTO and to renew registration of the mark. Once a mark is registered, its owner may use the federal registration symbol ®. Use of the symbol is not required, but is advisable because it affords notice to others of the owner's rights. The statutes governing federal registration and trademark infringement are found at 15 U.S.C. §§ 1051, et seq.

The standard for determining infringement of a mark is whether the two marks are likely to be confused. Courts examine a variety of factors to determine if marks are confusingly similar, including their appearance, connotation, whether consumers have actually been confused, and whether the marks and goods are used in the same channels of trade.

Properly protected, trademarks can last forever and afford their owners significant competitive advantages. With sufficient advertising, marks can become so well known that just a bar or two of music or a combination of colors is sufficient for consumers to identify a mark. It has been estimated that the average person in the United States encounters approximately 1,500 trademarks each day, making trademarks among the most visible items of intellectual property.

Companies must therefore actively protect and monitor their marks to ensure they continue to identify the company's products and services.

Copyrights. Copyright is a form of protection provided to the authors of original works of authorship, including literary, dramatic, musical, artistic, and other works. Like trademarks, copyright requires no federal registration. Copyright rights arise from the time a work is created in fixed form, whether or not registration is sought with the Copyright Office.

The scope of copyright protection is quite broad. The copyrightability of "literary" works affords protection to more than serious works of literature. Even advertising and marketing materials are protectable as literary works. Computer programs are also protectable as literary works, because they are expressed in words and numbers. Copyright is available for original works — no judgment is made as to their artistic merit or quality. Nevertheless, certain works are not protectable under copyright law, including slogans, titles, lists of ingredients, ideas, processes, and methods, although the expression of ideas, processes, and methods is protectable. Thus, having a great idea for a new sitcom is not protectable. Once you write a script, however, that expression of your idea is protected by copyright.

Copyright owners have the exclusive right to reproduce, distribute, display, and perform the copyrighted work, and to create derivative works (such as sequels) based on the work. Only the author of the work can rightfully claim copyright. There is, however, an exception to this rule: In the case of **works made-for-hire,** the employer or commissioning party is viewed as the author of the work. Under 17 U.S.C. § 101, a work made-for-hire is one prepared by an employee in the scope and course of employment or a work specially ordered or commissioned for use as part of a motion picture, a translation, or other types of special works, if the parties agree in writing that the work shall be considered a work made for hire and will be owned by the commissioning party. Thus, the copyright in all work produced by employees in the course of their employment is owned by the employer, whether or not the parties have agreed to or discussed ownership rights.

No publication of a work or registration or other action in the Copyright Office is required to secure copyright. Copyright is secured automatically when the work is created in a fixed form. Thus, typing the sitcom script on paper or into a word processor "fixes" the work. Although registration is not required to secure copyright, it does afford enhanced protection for a work, and registration is required for works of U.S. origin before an infringement suit may be filed in federal court.

Registration with the Copyright Office is a very straightforward and inexpensive process. An application is filed with a $45 filing fee, and unless the work is uncopyrightable, a registration will issue in about four months. Use of the copyright notice (© plus the year of first publication and the owner's name) is not required, although it does afford notice to the public that the work is protected by copyright. Copyright protection endures for the life of the author plus 70 years after the author's death. For works made-for-hire, however, the term of protection is 95 years from publication or 120 years from creation, whichever is shorter. There is no provision for state registration of copyright, and copyright is exclusively governed by federal law (17 U.S.C. §§ 101, et seq.).

Patents. A **patent** is a grant by the federal government to exclude others from making, using, or selling another's invention. There are three types of patents: **Utility patents** protect any new, useful, and nonobvious process, machine, or composition of matter, or improvements thereto (and are broad enough to cover inventions such as the disposable razor, the airplane, and genetically altered mice); **design patents** protect new, original, and ornamental designs for useful articles, such as furniture and containers; and **plant patents** cover new and distinct asexually reproduced plant varieties, such as a new variety of rose or grass.

Patents are governed exclusively by federal law (35 U.S.C. §§ 100, et seq.). There is no such thing as a common law patent, and a patent is only enforceable if it has been issued by the federal government, specifically the USPTO.

Patent law requires that the invention must be novel, useful, and nonobvious. An insignificant improvement to an invention is obvious and would therefore be unpatentable. An invention already in use by another would not be novel and would not qualify for patent protection. Additionally, laws of nature, physical

Work made-for-hire
A work created by an employee, which is presumptively owned by employer (or a specially commissioned work that the parties have agreed in writing will be owned by the commissioning party)

Patent
Grant by the federal government to exclude others from making, selling, or using an invention

Utility patent
Patent for a new and useful process or machine

Design patent
Patent for new, original, and ornamental designs

Plant patent
Patent for new and distinct asexually reproduced plants

phenomena, and abstract ideas are not patentable subject matter, although business methods that produce a useful and tangible result are patentable. Thus, Amazon.com has received a patent for its "one-click" shopping method.

To obtain a patent, the inventor must file an application with the USPTO. The process is expensive and time-consuming. Filing, search, and examination fees are presently $1,090 ($545 for small entities), and the application process can take from one to two years. Protection lasts for 20 years from the date of filing of an application for utility and plant patents and 14 years from the date of issuance of a design patent. Additionally, maintenance fees are due during the term of protection for a utility patent, at $3\frac{1}{2}$, $7\frac{1}{2}$, and $11\frac{1}{2}$ years after the date of grant.

If a patent is infringed (by unauthorized making, using, or selling of the invention), an action may be brought in federal court. The patentee is not required to mark the invention with the word "Patent" and the number of the patent, although marking is highly recommended, inasmuch as a patentee may not recover damages from an infringer unless the infringer was notified of the infringement and continued to infringe thereafter. Marking gives notice of one's patent rights.

Trade Secrets. A **trade secret** is any valuable information that, if known to a competitor, would afford the competitor some benefit or advantage. Trade secrets need not be complex and can consist of customer lists, recipes, financial projections, methods of doing business, and marketing plans. Nearly any type of information can qualify as a trade secret so long as it affords its owner a competitive edge, and the owner has taken reasonable methods to protect the information. Such methods would include limiting access to confidential material, marking materials with legends such as "confidential," and monitoring use of the material.

There is no federal registration of trade secrets, and they are governed nearly exclusively by state statutes and case law. If properly protected, trade secrets can last forever.

Trade secret
Any valuable information that, if known by a competitor, would afford the competitor a benefit

Use of Intellectual Property. Companies need to be aware of the value of their intellectual property assets. Names and slogans can be protected as trademarks; marketing materials and software can be protected under copyright law; inventions can be protected under patent law; and customer lists and valuable information about the business can be protected as trade secrets. Once companies understand the full range of materials that can be protected, they will be in a better position to use those assets to increase revenue, either by licensing or selling the property to others. Intellectual property must be actively monitored to be protected. Courts are reluctant to protect intellectual property assets in cases in which owners have routinely allowed infringing uses. Thus, companies must be vigilant about monitoring and protecting intellectual property assets, particularly in the electronic age, when valuable trade secret information or copyrighted material can be disseminated to thousands with a single keystroke.

6. Antitrust Law

The free enterprise system presumes that competition is healthy: Companies that offer competing products will attempt to attain greater market share by decreasing the price of the product offered or increasing its attractiveness to the consumer, or both. The ultimate winner in such a system is the consumer. Conversely, if one company is allowed to dominate an entire business or industry, such as airline transportation, there would be no incentive to improve the service offered or to decrease the price, because the supplier, the airline carrier, would have a captive audience with no choice to go elsewhere with business patronage. The one airline carrier could then charge whatever prices it wanted, and would fail to remain competitive by developing better systems and products because it would know that consumers have no option but to continue using its services. Such a situation is referred to as a *monopoly* (literally, "single sale") or an exclusive privilege or advantage to offer a product or service.

A number of laws have been enacted to avoid monopoly situations and to encourage suppliers to offer ever-better products and services at even more competitive prices. The body of law regulating competition in the business arena to foster competition is **antitrust law.**

The first efforts to regulate business occurred in the late 1800s when Congress passed the Sherman Act (15 U.S.C. §§ 1, et seq.) to rein in railroad companies that had been organized as trusts and dominated the transportation field. The Sherman Act, sometimes called the Sherman Antitrust Act, was aimed at *trust-busting,* or breaking up monopolistic companies. It prohibits agreements that restrain trade, as well as monopolization or attempts to monopolize. The primary focus of the Sherman Act is to preclude agreements between businesses to fix prices, lower supply of goods, divide the market into specific regions (with each business having complete unrestricted control over its designated territory), or reduce competition in the marketplace. These types of activities undertaken by "equal" rivals are referred to as **horizontal restraints** and are considered the most serious of antitrust violations. Thus, criminal penalties are often imposed for horizontal restraints. Agreements restraining trade between buyers and sellers are **vertical restraints,** and might include, for example, an agreement between Hanes Hosiery and the Nordstrom Company by which Hanes would agree to provide Nordstrom with its products only if Nordstrom agreed not to offer the goods in its stores at a price below that specified by Hanes.

The Sherman Act also prohibits refusals to deal, or group boycotts by which two or more companies refuse to do business with another person or company, generally in an attempt to drive that company out of the marketplace.

The Clayton Act and the Federal Trade Commission Act were passed in the early 1900s to prohibit specific monopolistic acts and practices not covered by the Sherman Act. The Robinson-Patman Act prohibits **price discrimination,** namely, the practice of imposing different prices for the same goods on different purchasers. Also precluded are **exclusive-dealing contracts,** agreements for the sale of goods in which the purchaser is required to agree not to use or deal in competitors' products. Thus, the sellers of Hunt's tomato sauce could not preclude your local grocery from also offering Contadina products, S & W sauces, or even a house brand product. Similarly, tying arrangements are precluded. A **tying arrangement** occurs when a seller conditions the sale of one product on the purchase of another. For example, if McDonald's were allowed to condition its sale of a franchise upon an agreement that franchisees would order all cups and paper products only from McDonald's and no other supplier, McDonald's would have tied the sale of the franchise to the purchase of the paper products. Although McDonald's may lawfully insist that its franchisee use paper goods of a certain quality that clearly display

Antitrust law
Field of law protecting against monopolies

Horizontal restraint
Activities engaged in by equal competitors to restrain trade

Vertical restraint
Activities engaged in between buyers and sellers to restrain trade

Price discrimination
Practice of charging different prices for the same goods

Exclusive-dealing contracts
Agreements requiring a purchaser not to use a competitor's product

Tying arrangement
Linking the sale of one product to another

McDonald's trademarks and logos, there is nothing so inherently special about paper products that they could not be ordered from some other supplier at a lower price. Thus, although McDonald's may offer the paper products to its franchisees, it cannot insist that such products be purchased as a condition of obtaining or retaining the franchise. On the other hand, if the products are special or proprietary, for example, a special recipe that gives a product its unique taste, such as the seasoning for KFC's chicken, the franchisor *may* lawfully require that the franchisee purchase this product only from it.

Mergers between companies will be carefully scrutinized by the Department of Justice and the FTC to ensure that the effect of a merger will not create a monopoly or adversely affect competition in the marketplace. Mergers between rival firms or firms offering similar products or services are called **horizontal mergers.**

Horizontal merger
Mergers between competitors

The Department of Justice and the FTC have jointly issued Horizontal Merger Guidelines to clarify the factors considered in their review of mergers. If the effect of a horizontal merger is an entity that has a disproportionate or concentrated market share, the merger will be prohibited by the Justice Department. For example, a merger between Alcoa, with nearly 30 percent of the market share for aluminum products, and a rival in the aluminum industry, with less than 5 percent market share, was prohibited on the basis that even though Alcoa would have less than 50 percent of the market share for aluminum products after the merger, the effect would decrease competition. Because Alcoa was a leader in the industry, the practice of buying out or merging with its smallest rivals would eventually give Alcoa a monopoly or near monopoly on aluminum goods.

Vertical mergers
Mergers between companies in a buyer-seller relationship

Vertical mergers involve companies in a buyer-seller relationship or between parties that do not operate in the same market. For example, a merger between McDonald's and Kimberly-Clark may be prohibited on the basis that McDonald's control of the paper products giant would impact or "foreclose" Burger King's ability to purchase paper products. In one case, Du Pont was prohibited from purchasing a large block of the stock of General Motors on the basis that this would foreclose producers of other fabrics and finishes from selling their products to General Motors, which presumably would use Du Pont's fabrics and finishes in its car seats and interiors.

Product extension
Expansion of product offerings by a company

Diversification
Offering of new product or service by a company

Some mergers occur because a company wants to diversify or offer a new service or product. Rather than start from scratch, a company might simply acquire a firm already established in the relevant industry. **Product extension** occurs when a company wishes to expand by offering a new product somewhat related to its previous products. For example, if a company engaged in the business of selling cosmetics acquired a company offering bath products, this would be a mere extension of its business. **Diversification** occurs when a company merges with another company whose products and services are totally unrelated to its own. Thus, the acquisition of a publishing company by McDonald's Corporation would be a diversification of McDonald's business. Mergers resulting in diversification are rarely prohibited because they do not greatly affect market concentration; however, a product extension that might lead to decreased competition may be prohibited.

Not every industry is subject to antitrust regulation. A number of industries are exempt from antitrust law, including insurance, labor unions, agricultural cooperatives, and a variety of other businesses and activities, most notably baseball.

Baseball has been exempt from antitrust laws since 1922, when it was classified as an entertainment activity rather than a commercial one and an activity that was intrastate in nature rather than interstate. There has been significant debate about this exemption over the past several years, especially since the baseball strike of 1994-1995, and because other professional sports are subject to antitrust law. Additionally, some industries are subject to oversight and control by administrative agencies having the primary authority to regulate them, such as the authority of the Federal Communications Commission to regulate the communications industry.

The Department of Justice and the Federal Trade Commission are charged with regulating and enforcing antitrust law. They can act prospectively by preventing anticompetitive activities (by enjoining certain practices or mergers), and can act retrospectively by correcting practices (by requiring companies to divest themselves of certain business divisions and by punishing violators). The Justice Department can punish violations of the Sherman Act through either civil or criminal actions. The Justice Department can ask a court for the remedy of **divestiture,** requiring a company to relinquish some of its operations, or the remedy of **dissolution,** which would terminate the existence of the offending company. A private party injured by anticompetitive acts or practices may also sue for treble damages or may seek injunctive relief to prevent antitrust violations that would result in irreparable harm. In one 1999 case, LePage, Inc., a maker of transparent tape, was awarded more than $22 million (which was automatically trebled to more than $68 million) against 3M Company (the maker of Scotch and Highland brand adhesive tapes) in an antitrust suit that had alleged that 3M drove LePage out of the market for transparent tape. LePage proved that retailers offering its tape were forced to dump LePage's to obtain generous rebates from 3M.

Divestiture
Relinquishing certain assets or companies

Dissolution
Termination of a business entity

As discussed herein and in Chapter Fourteen, the federal government has the authority to review mergers and acquisitions to ensure that such transactions do not impair competition in the marketplace. Under the **Hart-Scott-Rodino Antitrust Improvements Act** (15 U.S.C. § 18a), parties to certain merger transactions must notify the federal government and wait for 30 days before closing a transaction. The transaction or the parties in question must involve a certain amount of money before the Act applies. When the government receives the notice, it will review the transaction for its anticompetitive effect. If the government does not object to the transaction, the transaction may proceed. In cases in which the government objects, companies may divest themselves of certain assets, restructure the transaction, or abandon the transaction.

Hart-Scott-Rodino
Federal act requiring premerger notification to the federal government so it can investigate anticompetitive effect of proposed transaction

7. Unfair Competition

The law of **unfair competition** seeks to ensure that individuals are protected against unfair and deceptive commercial practices. In general, the most common types of unfair competition are as follows:

Unfair competition
Legal field attempting to protect consumers from unfair and deceptive commercial practices

- *Passing off (or palming off).* Passing off occurs when one party attempts to sell his goods as those of another, such as placing the REEBOK® trademark on shoes of an inferior quality, leading consumers to believe that REEBOK® is the source of the goods.

- *Misappropriation.* Misappropriation occurs when one party takes or appropriates another's property, for example, the pirating of a news story created by another party at great expense and cost.
- *Right of publicity.* The right of publicity protects a person's identity, voice, likeness, or persona from unauthorized commercial exploitation, such as would occur by using a celebrity look-alike or voice to advertise a product without permission.
- *False advertising.* Making false statements about one's own goods or services is false advertising, unless the statements are vague; are opinions; or are **puffery,** statements no reasonable person would believe (such as "our KEEBLER® cookies are made by elves"). Advertisements that purport to be objectively certifiable or statistical (such as "nine out of ten doctors recommend our product") must be supported by evidence.
- *Product disparagement (or trade libel).* Making false statements about another's goods or services is actionable as product disparagement.
- *Dilution.* Unauthorized acts that tend to blur the distinctiveness of a famous trademark or to tarnish it (by using it in an unsavory manner) are actionable as dilution.
- *Infringement of trade dress.* Adopting the overall image and appearance of another's distinctive product, packaging, or image (such as establishing another restaurant with menus, logos, uniforms, decor, and products confusingly similar to those of Taco Bell) is actionable as trade dress infringement.

Parties found liable for acts of unfair competition can be enjoined from further deceptive practices and can be liable for damages as well.

8. Bankruptcy Law

Introduction. As discussed in Chapter Sixteen, corporations sometimes dissolve due to their bankruptcy. In other instances, corporations reorganize their debts through bankruptcy and emerge to continue doing business, sometimes stronger than ever. In other instances, corporations must pursue their debtors into bankruptcy court to recover assets owed to the corporation. Thus, a brief overview of bankruptcy law is helpful for legal professionals in the business and corporate field.

Bankruptcy proceedings are governed exclusively by federal law, specifically, the United States Bankruptcy Act (11 U.S.C. §§ 101, et seq.). All bankruptcy matters are heard in bankruptcy courts, which are considered to be units of the United States district courts. Thus, there is no such thing as a state bankruptcy. There are two ways by which a bankruptcy proceeding may be initiated: by the filing of a **voluntary petition** or the filing of an **involuntary petition.** Voluntary petitions are used by debtors to initiate their own bankruptcy proceedings. Because some debtors will not pay their debts voluntarily, federal law allows creditors to force a debtor into bankruptcy by filing an involuntary petition under Chapter 7 or Chapter 11 of the Bankruptcy Act. If a debtor has 12 or more creditors, three of those creditors (who have claims totaling $13,475 or more) may file the involuntary petition. If there are fewer than 12 creditors, the

Puffery
Commercial boasting; statements no reasonable person would believe

Voluntary petition
Bankruptcy initiated by a debtor

Involuntary petition
Bankruptcy initiated by creditors

involuntary petition may be filed by any one creditor so long as the claim is $13,475 or more.

The filing of a bankruptcy petition operates as an **automatic stay** of most proceedings threatened or initiated against a debtor. Thus, any pending lawsuits against the debtor are automatically suspended by the filing of a bankruptcy petition. The stay allows the bankruptcy court to handle all matters relating to the debtor in one proceeding.

The Bankruptcy Act prohibits fraudulent transfers, such as those made to defraud creditors. Such transfers made by a debtor can be voided by the bankruptcy trustee. Similarly, to ensure all creditors are treated on an equal footing, the Act prohibits any **preferential payment** to a creditor. A preferential payment is one made to a creditor within 90 days before the filing of the bankruptcy petition that allows the creditor to receive more than it would have in the bankruptcy proceeding. Such a preference can be recovered by the bankruptcy trustee. Finally, some debts cannot be discharged in a Chapter 7 bankruptcy, including payments owed for taxes, for spousal and child support, for some student loans, for willful injury to another, and for those debts arising through the debtor's fraud.

Certain types of property are exempt from bankruptcy. The debtor is allowed to retain items necessary to life and her ability to continue to earn a living. Thus, the debtor's interest in an automobile (not to exceed a certain amount), life insurance, homestead (to a certain value), and certain household furnishings are exempt from the proceeding, and the debtor may retain these items. Additionally, IRAs and 401(k) plans are protected.

Certain types of debts have priority over others under the Bankruptcy Act. Thus, expenses and fees incurred in administering the bankrupt's estate have priority over general unsecured claims, and secured claims also have priority over unsecured claims. Generally, secured creditors do fairly well in bankruptcy proceedings but unsecured creditors often receive very little or nothing.

Nearly 851,000 bankruptcy petitions were filed in 2007. The vast majority were voluntary petitions.

There are four primary types of bankruptcy: those filed under Chapters 7, 11, 12, and 13 of the Bankruptcy Act.

Chapter 7 Liquidations.   An individual, a corporation, a partnership, or any other business entity may initiate a Chapter 7 proceeding when the debtor has no hope of financial recovery. Chapter 7 is often referred to as a liquidation because the trustee collects all of the debtor's assets, liquidates them, and pays any creditors. The debtor files its voluntary petition and prepares a list of all of its creditors and the amounts owing to each for the bankruptcy court. The creditors are notified to submit their claims to the bankruptcy court, using a form called a proof of claim. A meeting of creditors is called and a trustee is appointed. If there are no assets to be distributed, the trustee notifies the creditors that it is a no-asset bankruptcy and that there is no need to submit a claim. (Most Chapter 7 cases involving individual debtors are no asset cases.) The trustee takes possession of the debtor's property and liquidates it for the benefit of the creditors. Priority claims (including costs of administration) are then fully paid. Only then will unsecured creditors be paid. At the end of a Chapter 7 proceeding, the corporation's assets are liquidated and it is no longer in business. In 2007, 61 percent of all bankruptcy filings were brought under Chapter 7.

Chapter 11 Reorganizations.   Chapter 11 proceedings are available to individuals and business entities that believe they can reorganize their debts and emerge from bankruptcy. Once a petition for a Chapter 11 proceeding is filed, either voluntarily or involuntarily, the court usually appoints a committee of creditors and a trustee. The debtor remains in possession of its business and continues business operations under the supervision of the trustee. The debtor develops a reorganization plan for resolving its financial problems and the claims of creditors. The reorganization plan is submitted to the creditors for their approval and then to the court for confirmation. If the plan is confirmed, the debtor proceeds to carry it out. The debtor will emerge from bankruptcy and continue to operate its business.

Chapter 12 Family Farm or Fisherman Bankruptcies.   Chapter 12 is a simplified reorganization for family farmers and fishermen with regular income. The debtor usually remains in business and continues to operate the business. Unnecessary assets are sold by the trustee, and the debtor files a plan to reorganize its debts, which will be confirmed by the court.

Chapter 13 Individual Debt Adjustments.   Chapter 13 allows individuals with regular income and unsecured debts of less than $336,900 and secured debts of less than $1,010,650 to develop a plan to repay their debts. Under Chapter 13 (sometimes called a *wage earner's plan*), individuals pay their debts in installments under the supervision of the bankruptcy court. Once the repayment plan is confirmed by the court, the trustee pays creditors from payments made by the debtor. A Chapter 13 proceeding, which can only be initiated voluntarily, allows the debtor to work out financial difficulties over a period of time (usually between three and five years). Chapter 13 allows financially strapped consumers to avoid the stigma of a Chapter 7 liquidation, to save their homes from foreclosure, and an opportunity to repay creditors.

Bankruptcy Abuse Prevention and Consumer Protection Act of 2005 (BAPCPA). In October 2005, the Bankruptcy Abuse Prevention and Consumer Protection Act took effect. The Act is the most significant overhaul in U.S. bankruptcy law in a generation and generally makes it harder for individuals to file Chapter 7 bankruptcies. Among the Act's provisions, which largely affect consumers rather than businesses, are the following:

- A requirement that debtors receive credit counseling before and after filing for bankruptcy.
- A "means test" to determine whether individual debtors are eligible for a total liquidation under Chapter 7 or must file under Chapter 13 and pay back their debts. (Generally, if the debtor's income exceeds certain benchmarks, he or she might not be eligible for Chapter 7 relief, and the court may dismiss the case or convert it to a Chapter 13 proceeding to require at least partial repayment of debts.) In fact, one of the goals of the legislation is to discourage people from filing Chapter 7 bankruptcies if they do not have to and to enter Chapter 13 so they can pay off as much of their debt as possible.
- A requirement that debtors complete a money management class before receiving a discharge of their debts.
- Stricter homestead exemptions.

Because the new law makes it harder to erase debts in bankruptcy, bankruptcy filings in 2005 hit a record level. In fact, in the one year after the new law took effect, Chapter 7 bankruptcy filings decreased nearly 80 percent.

C. Transactional and Business Law Practice

1. Introduction

In general, the practice of law is divided into two types: criminal law and civil law. Criminal law relates to the defense and prosecution of individuals and companies for alleged violations of federal law or a state's penal code. Civil law is typically any practice of law that is not criminal law, and would thus include family law, securities regulation, taxation, corporate law, wills and estates, torts, and so forth. Even within civil law, there are two primary divisions: litigation and transactional work. Litigation involves civil actions filed in court, whether for medical malpractice, personal injury, or breach of contract. Transactional law is generally viewed as being nonlitigation work relating to business organizations, including the formation of partnerships, corporations, and other business organizations; counseling clients with regard to mergers and acquisitions; and providing general advice to business clients on matters such as establishment of retirement plans or termination of employees, or guiding a client through dissolution of an entity. Thus, advising business organizations is generally referred to as **transactional law.** Because much of the legal work involves corporations, the field is specifically referred to as *corporate law.* Although most corporate attorneys and paralegals work in law firms, called **private practice,** a growing number of them work in the legal departments of corporations or business organizations, and are typically referred to as being **in-house.** This portion of this chapter examines the types of tasks and activities involved in the corporate field, both in private practice and in-house.

> **Transactional law**
> Field of law that is not litigation; generally, advising business entities
>
> **Private practice**
> Working in a law firm
>
> **In-house**
> Working in the legal department of a business or corporation

2. Private Corporate Law Practice

Small Firm Practice. Although some sole practitioners and small law firms may provide general advice and assistance to sole proprietors, partnerships, and corporations, these business clients tend to be smaller and in the emerging development stage. The sole practitioner or small law firm will generally be involved in other practice areas rather than focusing solely on the corporate field. Once a business achieves a certain size, whether in terms of employees or revenues, it will generally require a larger law firm with several legal professionals offering special skills and experience to handle its more complex needs.

Sole practitioners may give general advice to business clients, assist them in obtaining fictitious business names and various business licenses, draft partnership agreements, and form and dissolve corporations. The relationship between a new business and its counsel is intimate and challenging. The client generally needs a wealth of information on topics as diverse as naming the enterprise, making arrangements for contributions to Social Security, calling and conducting meetings, drafting resolutions, terminating employees, entering into contracts, and so forth. The sheer variety of the tasks makes it a challenging field. Similarly, there is satisfaction and excitement in playing a part in a client's growth and success.

Paralegals working for sole practitioners and small law firms typically share in both this challenge and excitement. Because these newly emerging companies are generally cost-conscious, the teaming of an attorney and a paralegal offers great advantages to the client. The attorney provides legal advice and opinions and the paralegal executes that advice by preparing agreements, drafting documents, and performing other tasks such as checking name availability, reserving names, and qualifying the corporation to conduct business in other states.

Paralegals generally have a great amount of client contact in solo or small practices. There will be no "hoarding" of the client by senior attorneys anxious to be the client's sole contact in the firm and no hiding of the paralegal's role by having all of the paralegal's work prepared exclusively for the attorney's signature. Small practices encourage paralegals to get to know the client. It can be tremendously satisfying to accomplish specific tasks and receive sincere appreciation from the client and the attorney.

Large Firm Practice. Larger law firms often have specialized departments devoted solely to the corporate field; the attorneys and paralegals in this department work exclusively on corporate matters. Thus, within a relatively short time, paralegals can become extremely proficient in corporate law. Even within corporate departments, there might be subspecialties, such as specific practice groups focusing on formation of businesses, mergers, takeovers and acquisitions, issuance and regulation of securities, or employee benefit issues. Others in the litigation department might work with the corporate department if a business client is involved in litigation.

Although larger law firms might represent some of the nationally known corporate giants, the paralegal might have little, if any, contact with these clients. Attorneys might jealously safeguard their relationships with their corporate clients and, although paralegals may be intimately involved in the work itself, they might have little direct participation with or exposure to the clients themselves.

The relationship between larger corporate clients and law firms is often facilitated through the attorney employed directly by the corporate client, typically called the *in-house counsel*. Matters may arise for which the in-house corporate counsel might need advice. In that event, the in-house counsel often calls the private "outside" counsel to assist in some specific task. Some law firms with specialized practices may provide specific representation for corporate clients, such as **boutique law firms** that represent corporations exclusively with regard to intellectual property matters or firms representing the client only in connection with labor and employment issues. Thus, the in-house counsel may have relationships with numerous outside counsel at different firms, each of whom handles specific matters on behalf of the corporation.

Boutique law firms
Firms that specialize in a particular practice field

Practice Diversity and Needed Skills. Corporate law practice is diverse and challenging. There are crossovers with many different areas of law: When the corporation leases its office space, real property issues are involved; the purchase and sale of goods and services necessitates familiarity with contract law and the UCC; corporations entering into employment agreements with specially skilled employees require guidance in both contract and intellectual property law. If the corporate client is involved in a particular type of enterprise, the practitioner might need knowledge of specific regulations, such as those imposed by the Federal Trade Commission and state law regulating franchise relationships, the intricate tax treatment and advantages relating to employee benefits, or statutes and regulations relating to unfair competition. Because laws can change so frequently, simply learning legal concepts will not be sufficient. The corporate practitioner will need to stay current in the field by becoming knowledgeable about new laws, cases, and regulations that could affect the corporation.

Additionally, successful corporate practitioners might need experience in nonlegal areas of expertise such as accounting and finance. Strong interpersonal skills are also needed. The practitioner may have contact with numerous other attorneys representing the client as well as the in-house counsel and a variety of corporate officers and directors, each of whom has a different style and approach to problems. A great deal of time can be spent on the phone responding to questions, relaying information, and assisting in negotiations. Successful business entrepreneurs are highly demanding and know that "time is money." They therefore expect the legal team to return phone calls promptly, be available at a moment's notice, and be willing to switch approaches and arrive at creative solutions to ensure a transaction is accomplished. Often, transactions must occur within a certain time period so that particular tax advantages can be secured. These constraints require corporate practitioners to be highly organized and efficient so that time-sensitive deadlines are met.

Increased Competition and Pressure.   The legal field has become highly competitive. Whereas years ago clients formed strong relationships with their attorneys and would change attorneys only in the event of a major mistake or misunderstanding, many corporate clients are now lured away by other law firms offering lower rates, more responsive service, and creative fee arrangements. Moreover, a corporate client may be acquired by another corporation and its legal business is then transferred to the law firm representing the acquiring corporation.

Many law firms have high expectations for "business development," meaning the ability to attract new clients. Attorneys who provide this role as **rainmaker** might be more highly compensated than others who sit at their desks and prepare documents. Thus, there is competition not only between law firms but within law firms. Corporate clients may demand unique fee arrangements. Some clients will negotiate with the law firm on prices for photocopying and faxing. Some corporate clients will put the law firm on an annual retainer, meaning a fixed sum is set for providing legal services for the client. The client will pay a certain sum of money to the law firm per year, in return for which the client may seek unlimited legal advice. Because of the possibility of abuse by both parties, these arrangements are somewhat uncommon and must be carefully structured.

Rainmaker
One who generates business for a law firm

A newer trend in corporate representation is the **success fee.** In this type of arrangement, the corporate client agrees to pay for legal services for a transaction either by the hour or in a fixed amount. If the law firm can achieve certain goals for the client, such as closing the transaction before a certain date, negotiating a monetary savings for the client, or producing a certain result, the client might pay an additional success fee to the law firm. This motivates the law firm to act as efficiently and aggressively as possible; every dollar or day saved for the client also represents dollars for the law firm.

Success fee
Fee paid to legal team based on success or closing of a transaction on specified terms or dates

Thus, corporate practice has become increasingly more stressful. Nevertheless, the fast pace, challenging legal problems, and need for creativity and flexibility

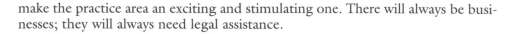

make the practice area an exciting and stimulating one. There will always be businesses; they will always need legal assistance.

3. In-House Corporate Practice

Growth of In-House Legal Departments.   Years ago, corporations generally sent all of their legal work to outside counsel. In-house counsel, if they existed, functioned more as managers or gatekeepers, keeping track of the corporation's legal matters and communicating with the outside counsel. Only the most basic of legal tasks were accomplished by inside counsel, such as preparing minutes of meetings, forming new corporate subsidiaries, and the like. Within the past ten years, however, many corporations came to realize how expensive their outside legal bills had become. In a concerted effort to reduce costs, many corporations began increasing the size of their in-house legal departments. In many instances, these corporations made offers to the attorneys in private practice who had been working with the corporation and had become familiar with the corporation's needs and demands. It has therefore become relatively common for attorneys and paralegals to work with corporate clients for a few years and then go in-house with the corporate client. Such arrangements can be extremely helpful for the corporate client. It continues working with the same legal team, a known commodity having intimate knowledge of the corporation's business needs and structure and, rather than paying $250 or more per hour for advice, the corporation pays annual salaries to the team members and obtains the advantage of having them on-site every day to assist the corporation.

The arrangement can be simultaneously disadvantageous to the law firm. The firm might have invested several years in training the attorney and paralegal; once they become productive, knowledgeable, and efficient, they are spirited away from the firm. Additionally, because more legal work will be done in-house, the corporate client might have a substantially decreased need for the firm's services. Thus, some law firms might attempt to minimize contact between corporate clients and attorneys and paralegals so that relationships cannot be formed that might lead to the luring away of legal talent by the corporate client.

Rather than looting the outside law firm for legal talent, the chief legal counsel in-house might hire additional attorneys. These attorneys work with the outside counsel on a variety of matters until the in-house attorneys have been essentially trained and taught by the outside counsel to handle these matters independently. The corporation then relies nearly exclusively on its inside legal department, consulting the outside counsel only if complex or novel problems arise.

For many years, in-house legal work was considered relatively staid and predictable. As challenging and exciting issues occurred, they were generally turned over to outside counsel. Moreover, pay was significantly lower in-house than in private practice. As a result, in-house positions were generally not the first choice for recent law school graduates who knew that more money could be made in private practice. The changing nature of the legal profession, however, has dramatically changed these facts as well. As corporate clients have become more conscious of their legal budgets, they expect more from their in-house counsel. Corporations began making a priority of upgrading and staffing their legal departments to cut back on the enormous sums spent on outside counsel. Thus, in-house counsel today face the same challenging and demanding tasks as private practitioners. Moreover, rather than billing by the hour, with the attendant pressure to keep one's billable hours high, the in-house legal staff can devote themselves wholeheartedly to an issue without worrying about billing, costs, and so forth. Many attorneys and paralegals find being freed from their time sheets extremely liberating and more conducive to their role as business strategists. Although the salaries at larger law firms typically remain higher than those for in-house counsel, pay has increased for inside counsel to attract and retain quality legal talent. Additionally, the in-house counsel receives some distinct advantages for any reduction in salary: the work day is slightly more predictable; the killer hours expected at the largest law firms are not as frequently encountered; the high stress and competitive atmosphere of the law firm is often reduced; pressure to bring in clients is nonexistent; the atmosphere may be more secure and stable than that of a law firm; and the in-house legal staff often play an integral role in corporate management and policy and may have the opportunity to become part owners of the company through stock options and so forth. All of these factors combine to make in-house positions considerably more attractive than they were several years ago.

A number of studies have confirmed that businesses in the United States have reduced spending on outside counsel and have expanded their in-house legal departments. Nevertheless, according to the Association for Corporate Counsel, controlling and reducing outside legal costs has been either the first or second most pressing issue for in-house counsel for several years.

In-House Legal Departments. Some major corporations have immense legal departments with more than 100 attorneys. These legal departments somewhat resemble large firms in that there may be an intellectual property section, a tax section, a contracts group, an employment and labor practice group, and a litigation team. The most senior attorney is usually called the **general counsel.** His tasks include not only representation of the corporation, his employer, but management of the legal department itself. The general counsel's advice may be sought on many issues other than solely legal ones, such as how to deal with a difficult employee, diversity training for all corporate employees, and negotiating with the company's insurance carrier. Many in-house counsel are also officers of the corporation. Some serve pursuant to formal written employment contracts with specified terms. All are salaried.

> **General counsel**
> The most senior lawyer in-house

In-house counsel generally report directly to the corporation's board of directors or one of its committees. Counsel generally attend directors' meetings to assist in taking minutes and to be available to answer any legal questions that arise in the course of the meeting. Therefore, the in-house counsel is generally conversant with the corporation's most sensitive and private issues and enjoys close contact with the corporation's decision-makers. As a result, some counsel eventually become members of the board of directors or even the chief executive officer of the corporation.

This closeness to the corporation is both a benefit and a burden. The benefit, of course, is having detailed knowledge of the corporation's workings and the confidence of the corporation's management team. The burden flows from this same closeness. For example, although outside counsel never relish being the bearer of bad news — such as telling the corporate client that a certain planned activity is unlawful or subject to substantial risk — giving this advice is what outside counsel are paid for, and they are seldom reticent in expressing their opinions in the strongest terms possible. Inside counsel, however, are often part of the corporate management team, and therefore might be reluctant to have to put the brakes on a transaction that is viewed as highly favored by the corporation and its management. Therefore, in-house counsel often ask for a second opinion from outside counsel on such issues. Similarly, knowing that inside counsel identify so strongly with the corporation, many third parties, such as accountants and insurance companies, often require opinions on sensitive issues from outside counsel rather than inside counsel.

Delegating Work to Outside Counsel.   If inside legal staffs do increasingly more diverse and complex legal tasks, what is left for outside counsel? The assumption of greater legal work by in-house counsel has led to greater specialization in private practice. The in-house legal staff may have neither the experience nor the time to devote to certain tasks. This work can be delegated to outside counsel. Additionally, there are four situations that typically call for direct involvement of outside counsel.

Large-Scale Litigation.   Complex litigation requires the sophistication, personnel, and experience of outside counsel. Large-scale litigation can involve hundreds of thousands of documents (in both paper and electronic form), numerous depositions, and an avalanche of written materials. Most of these written materials must be coded, indexed, and organized for easy retrieval and reference. Many large law firms have litigation teams experienced in the paper war often encountered in complex litigation. Moreover, in-house counsel will seldom have sufficient time to devote to such cases because ordinary corporate tasks, negotiations, and transactions are still occurring. Thus, outside counsel are typically relied on to handle large-scale litigation on behalf of the corporation.

Internal Conflicts.   Conflicts of interest or even the appearance of impropriety could prevent in-house counsel from performing certain legal tasks. For example, involvement in the termination of employment of senior executives might create a conflict. The departure of some senior executive could work in favor of in-house counsel, who might assume some of the departed employee's functions. Thus, outside counsel will become involved to ensure that such sensitive issues are handled fairly and impartially. An outside counsel's ethical duties are owed to the corporation itself rather than to the in-house attorney who referred the issue to her. Similarly, lawsuits or claims by shareholders should be referred to outside counsel. Because in-house counsel are employees of the corporation and often enjoy close relationships with directors and officers, they might not have the confidence of shareholders that they will act on behalf of the corporation's owner-shareholders rather than in a manner benefiting management or that will result in increased value of their own stock. Additionally, management might not wish in-house counsel to be privy to certain matters, such as compensation packages offered to certain executives. Thus, outside counsel may draft and negotiate employment contracts for senior managers.

Efficiency.   Crisis issues typically require the involvement of outside counsel. To be cost-effective, the in-house legal department should staff only as many attorneys, paralegals, and support staff as are needed to handle the corporation's routine business. Thus, when a crisis arises requiring immediate and intense attention, in-house counsel might not have sufficient time to devote to these issues as well as perform ordinary work on behalf of the corporation. In such cases, the matter will be turned over to outside counsel for resolution.

Expertise.   Highly specialized issues that fall outside the ordinary legal work performed by the in-house staff must be referred to outside counsel. Such matters might include complex employment issues, patent infringement cases, proxy fights, and so forth.

More important, outside counsel often act as a sounding board for in-house counsel. Many decisions in-house legal counsel are called on to make are sensitive and complex. In such cases, just as attorneys in private practice will discuss the issue with other attorneys in the firm, in-house counsel will wish to seek the opinion of private practitioners. In many instances, the approach is quite informal. In-house counsel might call the outside counsel, explain the issue, summarize his conclusion, and then simply ask, "Am I missing anything?" Outside counsel is often then asked to prepare a confirming letter to the corporation. This provides the in-house counsel with an objective view and reassurance that his view is appropriate.

Some outside counsel, if asked what tasks they perform at the request of inside counsel, might cynically reply, "I do what in-house counsel doesn't want to do." Although this may be a bit of an oversimplification, in many instances there is some truth to this statement. Additionally, there could be some friction between the two counsel. Typically, attorneys in private practice are not grilled by their business clients as to the wisdom and effectiveness of their legal conclusions. They become accustomed to being unchallenged. Because inside counsel are also skilled attorneys, however, they might propose alternate solutions to a problem, insist on certain tactics or strategy, or refuse to follow outside counsel's recommendations. In such cases, outside counsel often protect themselves by preparing correspondence or memoranda reflecting the dispute and their conclusions.

In sum, although the working relationship between private practitioners and inside counsel can be delicate, there is plenty of work to go around, and there is always a need for talented corporate attorneys and paralegals. The Web site of the Association of Corporate Counsel (www.acc.com) offers information and resources to in-house attorneys.

Key Features
of Special Topics in Business Law

◆ Businesses should be conducted not only in accordance with the law but also in accordance with ethical principles.

◆ Representing businesses involves an interplay with other areas of law, including the following:

1. Contract law, specifically relating to the purchase and sale of goods, governed by the Uniform Commercial Code;

2. Franchise law, in which an owner grants the right to operate a business to another under the owner's marks and using the owner's business methods and procedures;

3. Real estate law, specifically the leasing of property for or by the business;
4. Intellectual property law, by which a company uses its assets to achieve its unique identity, including trademarks (names and logos), copyrights (written materials, including software), patents (inventions), and trade secrets (confidential competitive information);
5. Antitrust law, which plays a part in business combinations and mergers;
6. Unfair competition law, which attempts to ensure that the marketplace is free from deceptive practices; and
7. Bankruptcy law, which attempts to provide relief to companies and individuals by allowing them to liquidate or reorganize their debts.

◆ Business or corporate law is practiced in law firms and in-house in companies.

D. Role of Paralegal

Just as the need to reduce legal costs led corporations to increase the size and quality of their in-house legal staffs, the same consideration has led to increased utilization of paralegals in the corporate field, both in private practice and in the legal departments of corporations and other businesses. Paralegals routinely perform tasks that would have previously been done by associate attorneys in private practice. To remain competitive, law firms must provide corporate clients with the best services at the best price. Paralegals are an integral component in this objective. Similarly, in-house legal departments often believe they can get "more bang for the buck" by hiring two or more paralegals rather than one overpriced and underexperienced attorney. Thus, the corporate field remains an attractive area for paralegals. For example, E.I. du Pont de Nemours and Company (DuPont) has compiled a list of tasks that it will not pay attorneys to do and that it insists paralegals perform, including preparing summaries of depositions, organizing documents for document productions, maintaining documents and files, and drafting subpoenas.

With regard to ethical issues, paralegals should be alert to potential conflicts and ethical concerns. At a minimum, these concerns should be pointed out to the attorney. A better practice might be to set forth your concerns in a written memorandum, provide it to the attorney, place a copy in the file, and then retain a copy in your own files. Almost all state bar associations have ethics hotlines offering information and guidance on ethical issues. Be sure to contact your state bar association if ethical concerns arise during the course of your work.

The role of paralegals is rich and varied in the areas of law that cross over with the corporate field. Paralegals are routinely involved in the following activities:

- Conducting legal research regarding the Uniform Commercial Code; drafting agreements for the purchase and sale of goods; searching UCC records; and preparing and filing UCC-1 forms to perfect security interests and UCC-3 forms to terminate security interests.

- Drafting franchise offering circulars and franchise agreements; preparing state registrations for franchise clients; reviewing franchisees' advertising materials for compliance with the franchisor's requirements; drafting notices of default; and preparing agreements relating to franchise agreements, including assignments of leases, noncompetition agreements, and the like.

- Conducting legal research regarding required lease terms; preparing lease agreements, assignments of leases, and notices of default; docketing dates for termination and renewal of lease agreements; and assisting in the representation of clients in actions to enforce terms of leases.

- Preparing trademark and copyright applications and assisting in preparing patent applications; drafting trade secret policies; and monitoring the use of clients' and competitors' trademarks and advertising materials.

- Conducting research regarding applicability of the Sherman, Clayton, Hart-Scott-Rodino, and Federal Trade Commission Acts; and assisting in the preparation of briefs and memoranda regarding antitrust matters.

- Preparing petitions (both voluntary and involuntary) for relief under the Bankruptcy Act, preparing proofs of claims for creditors, compiling lists of assets and creditors for clients involved in bankruptcy proceedings, and monitoring bankruptcy proceedings.

Case Illustration
Bankruptcy Automatic Stay

Case: *In re Taylor*, 190 B.R. 459 (S.D. Fla. 1995)

Facts: After a debtor filed a petition for relief under Chapter 13 of the Bankruptcy Act, a default judgment was entered against her by a creditor's attorney. The debtor's attorney informed the creditor's attorney of the automatic stay and requested that the attorney vacate the judgment. The creditor's attorney refused to do so. The debtor sought an order finding the attorney in contempt and for an award of her attorney's fees.

Holding: The filing of a bankruptcy petition automatically stays the commencement or continuation of a proceeding against the debtor. The automatic stay is a basic protection afforded debtors and is intended to be broad. Once the creditor's attorney was informed that a petition under the Bankruptcy Act had been filed, he had an affirmative duty to vacate the judgment. Because he willfully refused to do so, the court found him in contempt and ordered him to pay the debtor's attorneys fees.

◆ ◆ ◆

WEB RESOURCES

Ethics information:
www.legalethics.comwww.abanet.org/
cpr/pubs/ethicopinions.html (The
American Bar Association offers summaries of its ethics opinions and a link to
the ABA Model Rules of Professional
Conduct.)

www.nala.org/code.htm (NALA's Code
of Ethics for paralegals)

www.paralegals.org (NFPA's Code of
Ethics for paralegals)

Federal and state statutes:
www.law.cornell.edu
www.findlaw.com

Uniform Commercial Code:
www.nccusl.org
www.law.cornell.edu/uniform/ucc.html

UCC forms and information:
www.nass.org (Each state's secretary of
state provides information and forms
related to creating and terminating UCC
interests. Many states allow online UCC
searching.)

Franchising information:
www.ftc.gov (Federal Trade Commission)

Intellectual property
information:
www.uspto.gov (U.S. Patent and
Trademark Office)
www.copyright.gov (U.S. Copyright Office)

Antitrust information:
www.ftc.gov (Federal Trade Commission)
www.doj.com (Department of Justice)

Bankruptcy information:
www.uscourts.gov (Select "Bankruptcy
Courts" to be directed to explanations
about bankruptcy law, forms, and fee
schedules.)

Forms:
www.lectlaw.com/formb.htm (forms for
assignment of copyright, contracts for
the sale of goods, bills of sale, and leases)

www.siccode.com/forms.php (forms for
assignment of trademarks, forms related
to the sale of goods, and lease forms)

www.megalaw.com (Select "Law Topic
Pages" and then "Antitrust Law,"
"Contracts," "Real Property,"
"Uniform Commercial Code,"
"Intellectual Property," or "Bankruptcy
Law" to be directed to materials and
forms of interest.)

www.allaboutforms.com

Discussion Questions

1. Susan, a senior contracts manager with ABC Inc., was given an expensive gift by one of the company's vendors. What ethical implications arise from accepting such a gift? What if Susan were treated to lunch by the vendor? Would your answer change? Discuss.

2. Luis, a paralegal, works for XZY Inc., a corporation that is purchasing Jacobs Corp. Why should Luis conduct a search for any UCC-1s filed that identify Jacobs Corp.?

3. One of the franchisees of Baskin-Robbins has developed several new flavors of ice cream and has been serving them although they have not been approved by the franchisor. Why might the franchisor object to this practice?

4. Without his landlord's knowledge, Frank, a tenant, has assigned his lease to a college friend, Carl. Why might the landlord object to such an assignment?

5. Discuss whether the following are protectable as trademarks, copyrights, patents, or trade secrets:

- A new recipe for a fudge coating for cookies
- A new type of digital camera
- The song "My Way"
- The slogan "Have It Your Way"
- A company's plans to acquire several other companies
- A newly developed type of drought-resistant corn

6. The franchisor KFC demands that its franchisees purchase the following from it and from no other supplier: the secret herb recipe and spices that coat the chicken products, the paper cups used in the restaurants, and the cole slaw sold in the restaurants. Discuss whether any of these arrangements violate any antitrust laws.

7. A company has begun using one of Bette Midler's songs in its commercials without her permission. Is this a violation of any of Ms. Midler's rights? Discuss.

8. Two weeks before filing a bankruptcy petition, a debtor, Baker Corp., repaid one of its creditors, Sam, the $20,000 he was owed. Sam is the brother of one of the directors of Baker Corp. Is there anything other creditors can do about this payment? Discuss.

9. Gregson Inc. is burdened with debt but believes it has a significant chance of becoming more financially viable in the next year or two. If Gregson considers filing a petition under the Bankruptcy Act, under which chapter should the petition be filed? May a Gregson creditor who is owed $15,000 force the company into bankruptcy? Discuss.

Net Worth

1. In Delaware, what is the fee to expedite a UCC-1 filing for same day filing?
2. Access the Web site of the Utah Secretary of State. Conduct a UCC-1 search for the debtor Brodie Taylor.

a. Who is the secured party?

     b. When was the UCC-1 filed?

     c. Briefly, what collateral was secured?

3. Access the Web site of the U.S. Patent and Trademark Office. What is the fee to file an application for trademark renewal?

4. Access the Web site of the Federal Trade Commission. Identify whether the following states require state franchise filings:

- California
- Georgia
- Hawaii
- Iowa
- Wisconsin

5. Access the Web site for the U.S. Bankruptcy Courts and review Bankruptcy Form B9B and its explanations.

     a. For what type of bankruptcy is this form used?

     b. May a creditor call a debtor by telephone about a debt owed?

     c. May a creditor repossess a debtor's car?

     d. Why are creditors instructed not to file a proof of claim?

A

◆ ◆ ◆

Secretaries of State and State Corporations Statutes

◆ ◆ ◆

The following are the references to each state's business corporations statutes and the addresses of each state's secretary of state. Web sites for each secretary of state are also given. All states have Web sites for their secretaries of state, and all sites offer basic information about corporations. All Web sites provide forms for downloading; all Web sites provide fee schedules; and nearly all states offer searching for corporate and UCC data through their Web sites. An easy way to locate individual state Web sites is to access the home page of the National Association of Secretaries of State at www.nass.org. Go to "About NASS," then "Our Members," and then "Contact Roster" and you will be presented with a link to each state's secretary of state. When you access the Secretary of State's Web site, select "Corporations," "Business Services," and so forth.

ALABAMA

Ala. Code §§ 10-2B-1.01, et seq.

Secretary of State
P.O. Box 5616
Montgomery, AL 36103-5616
(334) 242-5324
www.sos.state.al.us/

ALASKA

Alaska Stat. §§ 10.06.005, et seq.

Division of Corporations, Business, and Professional Licensing
State Office Building, Ninth Floor
P.O. Box 110808
Juneau, AK 99811-0808
(907) 465-2530
www.commerce.state.ak.us/occ/home.htm

ARIZONA

Ariz. Rev. Stat. Ann. §§ 10-120, et seq.

Secretary of State
Corporations Division
1300 West Washington
Phoenix, AZ 85007-2929
(602) 542-3026 or (800) 345-5819
www.azsos.gov/

ARKANSAS

Ark. Code Ann. §§ 4-27-101, et seq.

Secretary of State
State Capitol
Little Rock, AR 72201-1094
(501) 682-3409 or (888) 233-0325
www.sosweb.state.ar.us/

CALIFORNIA

Cal. Corp. Code §§ 1, et seq.

Secretary of State
1500 11th Street, Third Floor
Sacramento, CA 95814-5701
(916) 657-5448
www.ss.ca.gov/

COLORADO

Colo. Rev. Stat. §§ 7-101-101, et seq.

Secretary of State
1700 Broadway, Suite 200
Denver, CO 80290
(303) 894-2200
www.sos.state.co.us/

CONNECTICUT

Conn. Gen. Stat. §§ 33-600, et seq.

Secretary of State
210 Capitol Avenue
Suite 104
Hartford, CT 06106
(860) 509-6200
www.sots.state.ct.us/

DELAWARE

Del. Code Ann. tit. 8, §§ 101, et seq.

Secretary of State
P.O. Box 898
Dover, DE 19903
(302) 739-3073
http://corp.delaware.gov/default.shtml

DISTRICT of COLUMBIA

D.C. Code Ann. §§ 29-101.01, et seq.

Department of Consumer and Regulatory Affairs
    (Corporate Division)
941 N. Capitol Street, N.E.
Washington, DC 20002
(202) 442-4400
http://dcra.dc.gov/dcra/site/default.asp

FLORIDA

Fla. Stat. Ann. §§ 607.0101, et seq.

Department of State
Division of Corporations
P.O. Box 6327
Tallahassee, FL 32314
(850) 245-6000
www.dos.state.fl.us/

GEORGIA

Ga. Code Ann. §§ 14-2-101, et seq.

Secretary of State
315 West Tower
2 Martin Luther King, Jr. Drive
Atlanta, GA 30334-1530
(404) 656-2817
www.sos.state.ga.us/

HAWAII

Haw. Rev. Stat. §§ 414-1, et seq.

Department of Commerce and Consumer Affairs
Business Registration Division
220 South King Street
Suite 2190
Honolulu, HI 96810
(808) 586-2744
www.state.hi.us/

IDAHO

Idaho Code Ann. §§ 30-1-101, et seq.

Secretary of State
700 West Jefferson, Room 203
P.O. Box 83720
Boise, ID 83720-0080
(208) 334-2300
www.idsos.state.id.us/

ILLINOIS

805 Ill. Comp. Stat. 5/1.01, et seq.

Secretary of State
Michael J. Howlett Bldg.
501 S. 2nd Street, Room 328
Springfield, IL 62756
(217) 782-6961
www.sos.state.il.us

INDIANA

Ind. Code §§ 23-1-17-1, et seq.

Secretary of State
Business Services
302 W. Washington
Room E-018
Indianapolis, IN 46204
(317) 232-6531
www.in.gov/sos/

IOWA

Iowa Code §§ 490.101, et seq.

Business Services Division
Office of the Secretary of State

Lucas Building, 1st Floor
321 E. 12th Street
Des Moines, IA 50319
(515) 281-5204
www.sos.state.ia.us/

KANSAS

Kan. Stat. Ann. §§ 17-6001, et seq.

Secretary of State
Corporation Division
First Floor, Memorial Hall
120 S.W. 10th Avenue
Topeka, KS 66612-1594
(785) 296-4564
www.kssos.org/

KENTUCKY

Ky. Rev. Stat. Ann. §§ 271B.1-010, et seq.

Secretary of State
Filings Branch
700 Capitol Avenue
Suite 154
Frankfort, KY 40601-3493
(502) 564-2848
www.sos.state.ky.gov/

LOUISIANA

La. Rev. Stat. Ann. §§ 12:1, et seq.

Secretary of State
Corporations Section
P.O. Box 94125
Baton Rouge, LA 70804-9125
(225) 925-4704
www.sos.louisiana.gov/

MAINE

Me. Rev. Stat. Ann. tit. 13C, §§ 101, et seq.

Secretary of State
Bureau of Corporations, Elections and Commissions
101 State House Station
Augusta, ME 04333-0101
(207) 624-7752
www.state.me.us/

MARYLAND

Md. Code Ann., Corps. & Ass'ns §§ 1-101, et seq.

Assessments and Taxation Department
301 West Preston Street, Room 809
Baltimore, MD 21201-2395
(410) 767-1340
www.dat.state.md.us/

MASSACHUSETTS

Mass. Gen. Laws ch. 155, §§ 1, et seq.

Secretary of the Commonwealth
Corporations Division
One Ashburton Place, 17th Floor
Boston, MA 02108
(617) 727-9640
www.sec.state.ma.us/

MICHIGAN

Mich. Comp. Laws §§ 450.1101, et seq.

Department of Labor and Economic Growth,
  Corporation Division
Bureau of Commercial Services, Corporation Division
P.O. Box 30054
Lansing, MI 48909-7554
(517) 241-6470
www.michigan.gov/sos

MINNESOTA

Minn. Stat. §§ 302A.001, et seq.

Secretary of State
Retirement Systems of Minnesota Building
60 Empire Drive
Suite 100
St. Paul, MN 55103
(651) 296-2803
www.sos.state.mn.us

MISSISSIPPI

Miss. Code Ann. §§ 79-4-1.01, et seq.

Secretary of State
P.O. Box 136
Jackson, MS 39205-0136
(601) 359-1633
www.sos.state.ms.us/

MISSOURI

Mo. Rev. Stat. §§ 351.010, et seq.

Business Services
P.O. Box 778
Jefferson City, MO 65102-0778
(573) 751-4153
www.sos.mo.gov

MONTANA

Mont. Code Ann. §§ 35-1-112, et seq.

Secretary of State
P.O. Box 202801
Helena, MT 59620-2801
(406) 444-2034
www.sos.mt.gov

NEBRASKA

Neb. Rev. Stat. §§ 21-2001, et seq.

Secretary of State
State Capitol, Room 1301
P.O. Box 94608
Lincoln, NE 68509-4608
(402) 471-4079
www.sos.state.ne.us

NEVADA

Nev. Rev. Stat. §§ 78.010, et seq.

Secretary of State
Capitol Complex
202 N. Carson Street
Carson City, NV 89701-4201
(775) 684-5708
http://sos.state.nv.us/

NEW HAMPSHIRE

N.H. Rev. Stat. Ann. §§ 293-A:1.01, et seq.

Secretary of State Corporation Division
107 N. Main Street
Concord, NH 03301
(603) 271-3246
www.state.nh.us/sos

NEW JERSEY

N.J. Stat. Ann. §§ 14A:1-1, et seq.

New Jersey Division of Revenue
Business Services
P.O. Box 308
Trenton, NJ 08646
(609) 292-9292
www.state.nj.us/hjbgs

NEW MEXICO

N.M. Stat. Ann. §§ 53-11-1, et seq.

Office of the New Mexico Secretary of State
Public Regulation Commission
P.O. Box 1269
Santa Fe, NM 87504
(505) 827-4502 or (800) 947-4722
www.nmprc.state.nm.us/cb.htm

NEW YORK

N.Y. Bus. Corp. Law §§ 101, et seq.

Secretary of State
Division of Corporations, State Records and
   Uniform Commercial Code

One Commerce Plaza
99 Washington Avenue
Suite 600
Albany, NY 12231-0001
(518) 473-2492
www.dos.state.ny.us/

NORTH CAROLINA

N.C. Gen. Stat. §§ 55-1-01, et seq.

Secretary of State
P.O. Box 29622
Raleigh, NC 27626-0622
(919) 807-2225
www.secstate.state.nc.us/

NORTH DAKOTA

N.D. Cent. Code §§ 10-19.1-01, et seq.

Secretary of State
State Capitol
600 East Boulevard Avenue, Dept. 108
First Floor
Bismarck, ND 58505-0500
(701) 328-2900
www.nd.gov/sos

OHIO

Ohio Rev. Code Ann. §§ 1701.01, et seq.

Secretary of State
P.O. Box 1390
Columbus, OH 43216
1-877-SOS-FILE
www.sos.state.oh.us/

OKLAHOMA

Okla. Stat. Ann. tit. 18, §§ 1001, et seq.

Secretary of State
2300 North Lincoln Boulevard, Suite 101
Oklahoma City, OK 73105-4897
(405) 521-3912
www.sos.state.ok.us/

OREGON

Or. Rev. Stat. §§ 60.001, et seq.

Secretary of State
Corporations Division
Public Service Building, Suite 151
255 Capitol Street, NE
Salem, OR 97310
(503) 986-2200
www.sos.state.or.us/

PENNSYLVANIA

15 Pa. Stat. Ann., §§ 1101, et seq.

Secretary of State
Corporations Bureau
206 North Office Building
Harrisburg, PA 17120
(717) 787-1057
www.dos.state.pa.us/

RHODE ISLAND

R.I. Gen. Laws §§ 7-1.2-101, et seq.

Secretary of State
Corporations Division
148 W. River Street
Providence, RI 02904-2615
(401) 222-3040
www.sec.state.ri.us

SOUTH CAROLINA

S.C. Code Ann. §§ 33-1-101, et seq.

Secretary of State
P.O. Box 11350
Columbia, SC 29211
(803) 734-2158
www.scsos.com/

SOUTH DAKOTA

S.D. Codified Laws §§ 47-1A, et seq.

Secretary of State
Capitol Building
500 East Capitol Avenue, Suite 204
Pierre, SD 57501-5070
(605) 773-4845
www.sdsos.gov/

TENNESSEE

Tenn. Code Ann. §§ 48-11-101, et seq.

Secretary of State
312 Eighth Avenue North, 6th Floor
William R. Snodgrass Tower
Nashville, TN 37243
(615) 741-2286
www.state.tn.us/sos

TEXAS

Tex. Bus. Orgs. Code Ann. §§ 1.001, et seq.

Secretary of State
Corporations Section
P.O. Box 13697
Austin, TX 78711
(512) 463-5555
www.sos.state.tx.us

UTAH

Utah Code Ann. §§ 16-10a-101, et seq.

Division of Corporations and Commercial Code
160 East 300 South
2nd Floor
Salt Lake City, UT 84111
(801) 530-4849
www.commerce.utah.gov/

VERMONT

Vt. Stat. Ann. tit. 11A, §§ 1.01, et seq.

Secretary of State
81 River Street, Drawer 09
Montpelier, VT 05609
(802) 828-2386
www.sec.state.vt.us/

VIRGINIA

Va. Code Ann. §§ 13.1, et seq.

State Corporation Commission
1111 East Broad Street
4th Floor
Richmond, VA 23219
(804) 786-2441
www.soc.state.va.us/

WASHINGTON

Wash. Rev. Code Ann. §§ 23B.01.010, et seq.

Secretary of State
Corporations Division
801 Capitol Way South
Olympia, WA 98504-0234
(360) 725-0377
www.secstate.wa.gov/

WEST VIRGINIA

W. Va. Code §§ 31D-1-101, et seq.

Secretary of State
1900 Kanawha Boulevard East
Charleston, WV 25305-0770
(304) 558-8000
www.wvsos.com/

WISCONSIN

Wis. Stat. Ann. §§ 180.0101, et seq.

Department of Financial Institutions
Corporations Bureau, 3rd Floor
P.O. Box 7846
Madison, WI 53707-7846
(608) 261-7577
www.wdfi.org

WYOMING

Wyo. Stat. Ann. §§ 17-16-101, et seq.

Secretary of State
214 West 15th Street
Cheyenne, WY 82002
(307) 777-2843
http://soswy.state.wy.us/

B

◆ ◆ ◆

Uniform Partnership Act (1914) (Selected Provisions)

◆ ◆ ◆

UNIFORM PARTNERSHIP ACT (1914)
Table of Jurisdictions Wherein Act Has Been Adopted

Jurisdiction	Laws	Effective Date	Statutory Citation
Georgia	1984, p. 1439	4-1-1985	O.C.G.A. §§ 14-8-1 to 14-8-61.
Indiana	1949, c. 114	1-1-1950	West's A.I.C. 23-4-1-1 to 23-4-1-53.
Massachusetts	1922, c. 486	1-1-1923	M.G.L.A. c. 108A, §§ 1 to 49.
Michigan	1917, No. 72	4-17-1917	M.C.L.A. §§ 449.1 to 449.48.
Missouri	1949, p. 506	8-9-1949	V.A.M.S. §§ 358.010 to 358.520.
New Hampshire	1973, c. 378	8-29-1973	RSA 304-A:1 to 304-A:62.
New York	1919, c. 408	10-1-1919	McKinney's Partnership Law, §§ 1 to 74, 121-1500 to 121-1506.
North Carolina	1941, c. 374	3-15-1941	G.S. §§ 59-31 to 59-73.
Pennsylvania	1915, P.L. 18	7-1-1915	15 Pa. C.S.A. §§ 8301 to 8365.
Rhode Island	1957, c. 74	10-1-1957	Gen. Laws 1956, §§ 7-12-12 to 7-12-59.
South Carolina	1950, p. 1841	2-13-1950	Code 1976, §§ 33-41-10 to 33-41-1220.
Utah	1921, c. 89	5-10-1921	U.C.A. 1953, 48-1-1 to 48-1-48.
Wisconsin	1915, c. 358	7-6-1915	W.S.A. 178.01 to 178.53.

From *Uniform Laws Annotated*, © Thomson Reuters, reprinted by permission.

PART I.   PRELIMINARY PROVISIONS

§ 1.   Name of Act

This act may be cited as Uniform Partnership Act.

§ 2.   Definition of Terms

In this act, "Court" includes every court and judge having jurisdiction in the case.

"Business" includes every trade, occupation, or profession.

"Person" includes individuals, partnerships, corporations, and other associations.

"Bankrupt" includes bankrupt under the Federal Bankruptcy Act or insolvent under any state insolvent act.

"Conveyance" includes every assignment, lease, mortgage, or encumbrance.

"Real property" includes land and any interest or estate in land.

§ 3.   Interpretation of Knowledge and Notice

(1) A person has "knowledge" of a fact within the meaning of this act not only when he has actual knowledge thereof, but also when he has knowledge of such other facts as in the circumstances shows bad faith.

(2) A person has "notice" of a fact within the meaning of this act when the person who claims the benefit of the notice:

(a) States the fact to such person, or

(b) Delivers through the mail, or by other means of communication, a written statement of the fact to such person or to a proper person at his place of business or residence.

PART II.   NATURE OF PARTNERSHIP

§ 6.   Partnership Defined

(1) A partnership is an association of two or more persons to carry on as co-owners a business for profit.

(2) But any association formed under any other statute of this state, or any statute adopted by authority, other than the authority of this state, is not a partnership under this act, unless such association would have been a partnership in this state prior to the adoption of this act; but this act shall apply to limited partnerships except in so far as the statutes relating to such partnerships are inconsistent herewith.

§ 7.   *Rules for Determining the Existence of a Partnership*

In determining whether a partnership exists, these rules shall apply:

(1) Except as provided by section 16 persons who are not partners as to each other are not partners as to third persons.

(2) Joint tenancy, tenancy in common, tenancy by the entireties, joint property, common property, or part ownership does not of itself establish a partnership, whether such co-owners do or do not share any profits made by the use of the property.

(3) The sharing of gross returns does not of itself establish a partnership, whether or not the persons sharing them have a joint or common right or interest in any property from which the returns are derived.

(4) The receipt by a person of a share of the profits of a business is prima facie evidence that he is a partner in the business, but no such inference shall be drawn if such profits were received in payment:

(a) As a debt by installments or otherwise,

(b) As wages of an employee or rent to a landlord,

(c) As an annuity to a widow or representative of a deceased partner,

(d) As interest on a loan, though the amount of payment vary with the profits of the business,

(e) As the consideration for the sale of a good-will of a business or other property by installments or otherwise.

§ 8.   *Partnership Property*

(1) All property originally brought into the partnership stock or subsequently acquired by purchase or otherwise, on account of the partnership, is partnership property.

(2) Unless the contrary intention appears, property acquired with partnership funds is partnership property.

(3) Any estate in real property may be acquired in the partnership name. Title so acquired can be conveyed only in the partnership name.

(4) A conveyance to a partnership in the partnership name, though without words of inheritance, passes the entire estate of the grantor unless a contrary intent appears.

PART III.   RELATIONS OF PARTNERS TO PERSONS DEALING WITH THE PARTNERSHIP

§ 9.   *Partner Agent of Partnership as to Partnership Business*

(1) Every partner is an agent of the partnership for the purpose of its business, and the act of every partner, including the execution in the partnership name of any instrument, for apparently carrying on in the usual way the business of the partnership of which he is a member binds the partnership, unless the partner so acting has in fact no authority to act for the partnership in the particular matter, and the person with whom he is dealing has knowledge of the fact that he has no such authority.

(2) An act of a partner which is not apparently for the carrying on of the business of the partnership in the usual way does not bind the partnership unless authorized by the other partners.

(3) Unless authorized by the other partners or unless they have abandoned the business, one or more but less than all the partners have no authority to:

(a) Assign the partnership property in trust for creditors or on the assignee's promise to pay the debts of the partnership,

(b) Dispose of the good-will of the business,

(c) Do any other act which would make it impossible to carry on the ordinary business of a partnership,

(d) Confess a judgment,

(e) Submit a partnership claim or liability to arbitration or reference.

(4) No act of a partner in contravention of a restriction on authority shall bind the partnership to persons having knowledge of the restriction.

§ 10.   *Conveyance of Real Property of the Partnership*

(1) Where title to real property is in the partnership name, any partner may convey title to such property by a conveyance executed in the partnership name; but the partnership may recover such property unless the partner's act binds the partnership under the provisions of paragraph (1) of section 9, or unless such property has been conveyed by the grantee or a person claiming through such grantee to a holder for value without knowledge that the partner, in making the conveyance, has exceeded his authority. [subsections 2, 3, and 4 omitted]

(5) Where the title to real property is in the names of all the partners a conveyance executed by all the partners passes all their rights in such property.

§ 11.   *Partnership Bound by Admission of Partner*

An admission or representation made by any partner concerning partnership affairs within the scope of his authority as conferred by this act is evidence against the partnership.

§ 12.   *Partnership Charged with Knowledge of or Notice to Partner*

Notice to any partner of any matter relating to partnership affairs, and the knowledge of the partner acting in the particular matter, acquired while a partner or then present to his mind, and the knowledge of any other partner who reasonably could and should have communicated it to the acting partner, operate as notice to or knowledge of the partnership, except in the case of a fraud on the partnership committed by or with the consent of that partner.

§ 13.   *Partnership Bound by Partner's Wrongful Act*

Where, by any wrongful act or omission of any partner acting in the ordinary course of the business of the partnership or with the authority of his co-partners, loss or injury is caused to any person, not being a partner in the partnership, or any penalty is incurred, the partnership is liable therefor to the same extent as the partner so acting or omitting to act.

§ 15.   *Nature of Partner's Liability*

All partners are liable

(a) Jointly and severally for every thing chargeable to the partnership under sections 13 and 14.

(b) Jointly for all other debts and obligations of the partnership; but any partner may enter into a separate obligation to perform a partnership contract.

§ 17. *Liability of Incoming Partner*

A person admitted as a partner into an existing partnership is liable for all the obligations of the partnership arising before his admission as though he had been a partner when such obligations were incurred, except that this liability shall be satisfied only out of partnership property.

PART IV. RELATIONS OF PARTNERS TO ONE ANOTHER

§ 18. *Rules Determining Rights and Duties of Partners*

The rights and duties of the partners in relation to the partnership shall be determined, subject to any agreement between them, by the following rules:

(a) Each partner shall be repaid his contributions, whether by way of capital or advances to the partnership property and share equally in the profits and surplus remaining after all liabilities, including those to partners, are satisfied; and must contribute towards the losses, whether of capital or otherwise, sustained by the partnership according to his share in the profits.

(b) The partnership must indemnify every partner in respect of payments made and personal liabilities reasonably incurred by him in the ordinary and proper conduct of its business, or for the preservation of its business or property.

(c) A partner, who in aid of the partnership makes any payment or advance beyond the amount of capital which he agreed to contribute, shall be paid interest from the date of the payment or advance.

(d) A partner shall receive interest on the capital contributed by him only from the date when repayment should be made.

(e) All partners have equal rights in the management and conduct of the partnership business.

(f) No partner is entitled to remuneration for acting in the partnership business, except that a surviving partner is entitled to reasonable compensation for his services in winding up the partnership affairs.

(g) No person can become a member of a partnership without the consent of all the partners.

(h) Any difference arising as to ordinary matters connected with the partnership business may be decided by a majority of the partners; but no act in contravention of any agreement between the partners may be done rightfully without the consent of all the partners.

§ 19. *Partnership Books*

The partnership books shall be kept, subject to any agreement between the partners, at the principal place of business of the partnership, and every partner shall at all times have access to and may inspect and copy any of them.

§ 20. *Duty of Partners to Render Information*

Partners shall render on demand true and full information of all things affecting the partnership to any partner or the legal representation of any deceased partner or partner under legal disability.

§ 21. *Partner Accountable as a Fiduciary*

(1) Every partner must account to the partnership for any benefit, and hold as trustee for it any profits derived by him without the consent of the other partners from any transaction connected with the formation, conduct, or liquidation of the partnership or from any use by him of its property.

(2) This section applies also to the representatives of a deceased partner engaged in the liquidation of the affairs of the partnership as the personal representatives of the last surviving partner.

§ 22. *Right to an Account*

Any partner shall have the right to a formal account as to partnership affairs:

(a) If he is wrongfully excluded from the partnership business or possession of its property by his co-partners,

(b) If the right exists under the terms of any agreement,

(c) As provided by section 21,

(d) Whenever other circumstances render it just and reasonable.

§ 23. *Continuation of Partnership Beyond Fixed Term*

(1) When a partnership for a fixed term or particular undertaking is continued after the termination of such term or particular undertaking without any express agreement, the rights and duties of the partners remain the same as they were at such termination, so far as is consistent with a partnership at will.

(2) A continuation of the business by the partners or such of them as habitually acted therein during the term, without any settlement or liquidation of the partnership affairs, is prima facie evidence of a continuation of the partnership.

PART V. PROPERTY RIGHTS OF A PARTNER

§ 24. *Extent of Property Rights of a Partner*

The property rights of a partner are (1) his rights in specific partnership property, (2) his interest in the partnership, and (3) his right to participate in the management.

§ 25. *Nature of a Partner's Right in Specific Partnership Property*

(1) A partner is co-owner with his partners of specific partnership property holding as a tenant in partnership.

(2) The incidents of this tenancy are such that:

(a) A partner, subject to the provisions of this act and to any agreement between the partners, has an equal right with his partners to possess specific partnership property for partnership purposes; but he has no right to possess such property for any other purpose without the consent of his partners.

(b) A partner's right in specific partnership property is not assignable except in connection with the assignment of rights of all the partners in the same property.

(c) A partner's right in specific partnership property is not subject to attachment or execution, except on a claim against the partnership. When partnership property is attached for a partnership debt the partners, or any of them, or the representatives of a deceased partner, cannot claim any right under the homestead or exemption laws.

(d) On the death of a partner his right in specific partnership property vests in the surviving partner or partners, except where the deceased was the last surviving partner, when his right in such property vests in his legal representative. Such surviving partner or partners, or the legal representative of the last surviving partner, has no right to possess the partnership property for any but a partnership purpose.

(e) A partner's right in specific partnership property is not subject to dower, curtesy, or allowances to widows, heirs, or next of kin.

§ 26. *Nature of Partner's Interest in the Partnership*

A partner's interest in the partnership is his share of the profits and surplus, and the same is personal property.

§ 27. *Assignment of Partner's Interest*

(1) A conveyance by a partner of his interest in the partnership does not of itself dissolve the partnership, nor, as against the other partners in the absence of agreement, entitle the assignee, during the continuance of the partnership, to interfere in the management or administration of the partnership business or affairs, or to require any information or account of partnership transactions, or to inspect the partnership books; but it merely entitles the assignee to receive in accordance with his contract the profits to which the assigning partner would otherwise be entitled.

(2) In case of a dissolution of the partnership, the assignee is entitled to receive his assignor's interest and may require an account from the date only of the last account agreed to by all the partners.

§ 28. *Partner's Interest Subject to Charging Order*

(1) On due application to a competent court by any judgment creditor of a partner, the court which entered the judgment, order, or decree, or any other court, may charge the interest of the debtor partner with payment of the unsatisfied amount of such judgment debt with interest thereon; and may then or later appoint a receiver of his share of the profits, and of any other money due or to fall due to him in respect of the partnership, and make all other orders, directions, accounts and inquiries which the debtor partner might have made, or which the circumstances of the case may require. [subsections 2 and 3 omitted]

PART VI. DISSOLUTION AND WINDING UP

§ 29. *Dissolution Defined*

The dissolution of a partnership is the change in the relation of the partners caused by any partner ceasing to be associated in the carrying on as distinguished from the winding up of the business.

§ 30. *Partnership Not Terminated by Dissolution*

On dissolution the partnership is not terminated, but continues until the winding up of partnership affairs is completed.

§ 31. *Causes of Dissolution*

Dissolution is caused:

(1) Without violation of the agreement between the partners,

(a) By the termination of the definite term or particular undertaking specified in the agreement,

(b) By the express will of any partner when no definite term or particular undertaking is specified,

(c) By the express will of all the partners who have not assigned their interests or suffered them to be charged for their separate debts, either before or after the termination of any specified term or particular undertaking,

(d) By the expulsion of any partner from the business bona fide in accordance with such a power conferred by the agreement between the partners;

(2) In contravention of the agreement between the partners, where the circumstances do not permit a dissolution under any other provision of this section, by the express will of any partner at any time;

(3) By any event which makes it unlawful for the business of the partnership to be carried on or for the members to carry it on in partnership;

(4) By the death of any partner;

(5) By the bankruptcy of any partner or the partnership;

(6) By decree of court under section 32.

§ 32. *Dissolution by Decree of Court*

(1) On application by or for a partner the court shall decree a dissolution whenever:

(a) A partner has been declared a lunatic in any judicial proceeding or is shown to be of unsound mind,

(b) A partner becomes in any other way incapable of performing his part of the partnership contract,

(c) A partner has been guilty of such conduct as tends to affect prejudicially the carrying on of the business,

(d) A partner willfully or persistently commits a breach of the partnership agreement, or otherwise so conducts himself in matters relating to the partnership business that it is not reasonably practicable to carry on the business in partnership with him,

(e) The business of the partnership can only be carried on at a loss,

(f) Other circumstances render a dissolution equitable.

(2) On the application of the purchaser of a partner's interest under sections 28 or 29 [should read 27 or 28];

(a) After the termination of the specified term or particular undertaking,

(b) At any time if the partnership was a partnership at will when the interest was assigned or when the charging order was issued.

§ 33. General Effect of Dissolution on Authority of Partner

Except so far as may be necessary to wind up partnership affairs or to complete transactions begun but not then finished, dissolution terminates all authority of any partner to act for the partnership,

(1) With respect to the partners,

(a) When the dissolution is not by the act, bankruptcy or death of a partner; or

(b) When the dissolution is by such act, bankruptcy or death of a partner, in cases where section 34 so requires.

(2) With respect to persons not partners, as declared in section 35.

§ 36. Effect of Dissolution on Partner's Existing Liability

(1) The dissolution of the partnership does not of itself discharge the existing liability of any partner.

(2) A partner is discharged from any existing liability upon dissolution of the partnership by an agreement to that effect between himself, the partnership creditor and the person or partnership continuing the business; and such agreement may be inferred from the course of dealing between the creditor having knowledge of the dissolution and the person or partnership continuing the business.

(3) Where a person agrees to assume the existing obligations of a dissolved partnership, the partners whose obligations have been assumed shall be discharged from any liability to any creditor of the partnership who, knowing of the agreement, consents to a material alteration in the nature or time of payment of such obligations.

(4) The individual property of a deceased partner shall be liable for all obligations of the partnership incurred while he was a partner but subject to the prior payment of his separate debts.

§ 37. Right to Wind Up

Unless otherwise agreed the partners who have not wrongfully dissolved the partnership or the legal representative of the last surviving partner, not bankrupt, has the right to wind up the partnership affairs; provided, however, that any partner, his legal representative or his assignee, upon cause shown, may obtain winding up by the court.

§ 38. Rights of Partners to Application of Partnership Property

(1) When dissolution is caused in any way, except in contravention of the partnership agreement, each partner, as against his co-partners and all persons claiming through them in respect of their interests in the partnership, unless otherwise agreed, may have the partnership property applied to discharge its liabilities, and the surplus applied to pay in cash the net amount owing to the respective partners. But if dissolution is caused by expulsion of a partner, bona fide under the partnership agreement and if the expelled partner is discharged from all partnership liabilities, either by payment or agreement under section 36(2), he shall receive in cash only the net amount due him from the partnership.

(2) When dissolution is caused in contravention of the partnership agreement the rights of the partners shall be as follows:

(a) Each partner who has not caused dissolution wrongfully shall have,

I. All the rights specified in paragraph (1) of this section, and

II. The right, as against each partner who has caused the dissolution wrongfully, to damages for breach of the agreement.

(b) The partners who have not caused the dissolution wrongfully, if they all desire to continue the business in the same name, either by themselves or jointly with others, may do so, during the agreed term for the partnership and for that purpose may possess the partnership property, provided they secure the payment by bond approved by the court, or pay to any partner who has caused the dissolution wrongfully, the value of his interest in the partnership at the dissolution, less any damages recoverable under clause (2a II) of this section, and in like manner indemnify him against all present or future partnership liabilities.

(c) A partner who has caused the dissolution wrongfully shall have:

I. If the business is not continued under the provisions of paragraph (2b) all the rights of a partner under paragraph (1), subject to clause (2a II), of this section,

II. If the business is continued under paragraph (2b) of this section the right as against his co-partners and all claiming through them in respect of their interests in the partnership, to have the value of his interest in the partnership, less any damages caused to his co-partners by the dissolution, ascertained and paid to him in cash, or the payment secured by bond approved by the court, and to be released from all existing liabilities of the partnership; but in ascertaining the value of the partner's interest the value of the good-will of the business shall not be considered.

§ 40. Rules for Distribution

In settling accounts between the partners after dissolution, the following rules shall be observed, subject to any agreement to the contrary:

(a) The assets of the partnership are:

I. The partnership property,

II. The contributions of the partners necessary for the payment of all the liabilities specified in clause (b) of this paragraph.

(b) The liabilities of the partnership shall rank in order of payment, as follows:

I. Those owing to creditors other than partners,

II. Those owing to partners other than for capital and profits,

III. Those owing to partners in respect of capital,

IV. Those owing to partners in respect of profits.

(c) The assets shall be applied in the order of their declaration in clause (a) of this paragraph to the satisfaction of the liabilities.

(d) The partners shall contribute, as provided by section 18(a) the amount necessary to satisfy the liabilities; but if any, but not all, of the partners are insolvent, or, not being subject to process, refuse to contribute, the other partners shall contribute their share of the liabilities, and, in the relative proportions in which they share the profits, the additional amount necessary to pay the liabilities.

(e) An assignee for the benefit of creditors or any person appointed by the court shall have the right to enforce the contributions specified in clause (d) of this paragraph.

(f) Any partner or his legal representative shall have the right to enforce the contributions specified in clause (d) of this paragraph, to the extent of the amount which he has paid in excess of his share of the liability.

(g) The individual property of a deceased partner shall be liable for the contributions specified in clause (d) of this paragraph.

(h) When partnership property and the individual properties of the partners are in possession of a court for distribution, partnership creditors shall have priority on partnership property and separate creditors on individual property, saving the rights of lien or secured creditors as heretofore.

(i) Where a partner has become bankrupt or his estate is insolvent the claims against his separate property shall rank in the following order:

I. Those owing to separate creditors,

II. Those owing to partnership creditors,

III. Those owing to partners by way of contribution.

C

◆ ◆ ◆

(Revised) Uniform Partnership Act (1997) (Selected Provisions)

◆ ◆ ◆

(REVISED) UNIFORM PARTNERSHIP ACT (1997)
Table of Jurisdictions Wherein Act Has Been Adopted

Jurisdiction	Laws	Effective Date	Statutory Citation
Alabama	1996, No. 96-528	1-1-1997	Code 1975, §§ 10-8A-101 to 10-8A-1109.
Alaska	2000, c. 115	1-1-2001	AS §§ 32.06.201 to 32.06.997.
Arizona	1996, c. 226	7-20-1996	A.R.S. §§ 29-1001 to 29-1111.
Arkansas	1999, Act 1518	1-1-2000	A.C.A. §§ 4-46-101 to 4-46-1207.
California	1996, c. 1003	1-1-1997	West's Ann. Cal. Corp. Code, §§ 16100 to 16962.
Colorado	1997 H.B. 97-1237	1-1-1998	West's C.R.S.A. §§ 7-64-101 to 7-64-1206.
Connecticut	1995, P.A. 95-341	7-1-1997	C.G.S.A. §§ 34-300 to 34-434.
Delaware	1999, c. 151	1-1-2000	6 Del. C. §§ 15-101 to 15-1210.
District of Columbia	1997, D.C. Law No. 11-234	4-9-1997	D.C. Official Code, 2001 Ed. §§ 33-101.01 to 33-112.04.
Florida	1995, c. 95-242	1-1-1996	West's F.S.A. §§ 620.81001 to 620.9902.
Hawaii	1999, Act 284	7-1-2000	H.R.S. §§ 425-101 to 425-145.
Idaho	1998, c. 65	1-1-2001	I.C. §§ 53-3-101 to 53-3-1205.
Illinois	2002, c. 740	1-1-2003	S.H.A. 805 ILCS 206/100 to 206/1207.
Iowa	1998, S.F. 2311	1-1-1999	I.C.A. §§ 486A.101 to 486A.1302.
Kansas	1998, c. 93	1-1-1999	K.S.A. §§ 56a-101 to 56a-1305.
Kentucky	2006, c. 149	7-12-2006	K.R.S. §§ 362.1-101 to 362.1-1205
Maine	2006, c. 543	7-1-2007	31 M.R.S.A. §§ 1001 to 1105
Maryland	1997, c. 654	7-1-1998	Code, Corporations and Associations, §§ 9A-101 to 9A-1205.
Minnesota	1997, c. 174	1-1-1999	M.S.A. §§ 323A.1-01 to 323A.1203.

Jurisdiction	*Laws*	*Effective Date*	*Statutory Citation*
Mississippi	2004, c. 458	1-1-2005	Code 1972, §§ 79-13-101 to 79-13-1206.
Montana	1993, c. 238	10-1-1993	MCA §§ 35-10-101 to 35-10-710.
Nebraska	1997, L.B. 523	1-1-1998	R.R.S. 1943, §§ 67-401 to 67-467.
Nevada	2005, c. 128	7-1-2006	N.R.S. §§ 87.4301 to 87.4357
New Jersey	2000, c. 161	12-8-2000	N.J.S.A. §§ 42:1A-1 to 42:1A-56.
New Mexico	1996, c. 53	7-1-1997	NMSA 1978 §§ 54-1-47, 54-1A-101 to 54-1A-1206.
North Dakota	1995, c. 430	1-1-1996	NDCC 45-13-01 to 45-21-08.
Ohio	2008, H. 332	8-6-2008	Rev. Code §§ 1776.01 to 1776.96
Oklahoma	1997, c. 399	11-1-1997	54 Okl. St. Ann. §§ 1-100 to 1-1207.
Oregon	1997, c. 775	1-1-1998	ORS 67.005 to 67.815.
South Dakota	2001, No. 249	7-1-2001	SDCL §§ 48-7A-101 to 48-7A-1208.
Tennessee	2001, No. 353	1-1-2002	T.C.A. §§ 61-1-101 to 61-1-1208.
Texas	1993, c. 917	1-1-1994	Vernon's Ann. Civ.St. art. 6132b-1.01 to 6132b-11.05.
Vermont	1998, No. 149	1-1-1999	11 V.S.A. §§ 3201 to 3313.
Virginia	1996, c. 292	5-1-1998	Code 1950, §§ 50-73.79 to 50-73.149.
Washington	1998, c. 103	1-1-1999	West's RCWA 25.05.005 to 25.05.907.
West Virginia	1995, c. 250	90 days from 3-19-1995	Code, 47B-1-1 to 47B-11-5.
Wyoming	1993, c. 194	1-1-1994	Wyo. Stat. Ann. §§ 17-21-101 to 17-21-1003.

From *Uniform Laws Annotated*. © Thomson Reuters, reprinted by permission.

Article 1.   General Provisions

101. Definitions.
102. Knowledge and Notice.
103. Effect of Partnership Agreement; Nonwaivable Pro-visions.
104. Supplemental Principles of Law. [omitted]
105. Execution, Filing, and Recording of Statements.
106. Law Governing Internal Relations.
107. Partnership Subject to Amendment or Repeal of [Act].

Article 2.   Nature of Partnership

201. Partnership as Entity.
202. Formation of Partnership.
203. Partnership Property.
204. When Property Is Partnership Property.

Article 3.   Relations of Partners to Persons Dealing with Partnership

301. Partner Agent of Partnership.
302. Transfer of Partnership Property.
303. Statement of Partnership Authority.
304. Statement of Denial.
305. Partnership Liable for Partner's Actionable Conduct.
306. Partner's Liability.
307. Actions By and Against Partnership and Partners.
308. Liability of Purported Partner.

Article 4.   Relations of Partners to Each Other and to Partnership

401. Partner's Rights and Duties.
402. Distributions in Kind.

403. Partner's Rights and Duties With Respect to Information.
404. General Standards of Partner's Conduct.
405. Actions by Partnership and Partners.
406. Continuation of Partnership Beyond Definite Term of Particular Undertaking.

Article 5.   Transferees and Creditors of Partner

501. Partner Not Co-owner of Partnership Property.
502. Partner's Transferable Interest in Partnership.
503. Transfer of Partner's Transferable Interest.
504. Partner's Transferable Interest Subject to Charging Order.

Article 6.   Partner's Dissociation

601. Events Causing Partner's Dissociation.
602. Partner's Power to Dissociate; Wrongful Dissociation.
603. Effect of Partner's Dissociation.

Article 7.   Partner's Dissociation When Business Not Wound Up

701. Purchase of Dissociated Partner's Interest.
702. Dissociated Partner's Power to Bind and Liability to Partnership.
703. Dissociated Partner's Liability to Other Persons.
704. Statement of Dissociation.
705. Continued Use of Partnership Name. [omitted]

Article 8.   Winding Up Partnership Business

801. Events Causing Dissolution and Winding up of Partnership Business.

ARTICLE 1.   GENERAL PROVISIONS

§ 101.   *Definitions.*

In this [Act]:

(1) "Business" includes every trade, occupation, and profession.

(2) "Debtor in bankruptcy" means a person who is the subject of:

(i) an order for relief under Title 11 of the United States Code or a comparable order under a successor statute of general application; or

(ii) a comparable order under federal, state, or foreign law governing insolvency.

(3) "Distribution" means a transfer of money or other property from a partnership to a partner in the partner's capacity as a partner or to the partner's transferee.

(4) "Foreign limited liability partnership" means a partnership that:

(i) is formed under laws other than the laws of this State; and

(ii) has the status of a limited liability partnership under those laws.

(5) "Limited liability partnership" means a partnership that has filed a statement of qualification under Section 1001 and does not have a similar statement in effect in any other jurisdiction.

(6) "Partnership" means an association of two or more persons to carry on as co-owners a business for profit formed under Section 202, predecessor law, or comparable law of another jurisdiction.

(7) "Partnership agreement" means the agreement, whether written, oral, or implied, among the partners concerning the partnership, including amendments to the partnership agreement.

(8) "Partnership at will" means a partnership in which the partners have not agreed to remain partners until the expiration of a definite term or the completion of a particular undertaking.

(9) "Partnership interest" or "partner's interest in the partnership" means all of a partner's interests in the partnership, including the partner's transferable interest and all management and other rights.

(10) "Person" means an individual, corporation, business trust, estate, trust, partnership, association, joint venture, government, governmental subdivision, agency, or instrumentality, or any other legal or commercial entity.

(11) "Property" means all property, real, personal, or mixed, tangible or intangible, or any interest therein.

(12) "State" means a State of the United States, the District of Columbia, the Commonwealth of Puerto Rico, or any territory or insular possession subject to the jurisdiction of the United States.

(13) "Statement" means a statement of partnership authority under Section 303, a statement of denial under Section 304, a statement of dissociation under Section 704, a statement of dissolution under Section 805, a statement of merger under Section 907, a statement of qualification under Section 1001, a statement of foreign qualification under Section 1102, or an amendment or cancellation of any of the foregoing.

(14) "Transfer" includes an assignment, conveyance, lease, mortgage, deed, and encumbrance.

§ 102.   *Knowledge and Notice.*

(a) A person knows a fact if the person has actual knowledge of it.

(b) A person has notice of a fact if the person:

(1) knows of it;

(2) has received a notification of it; or

(3) has reason to know it exists from all of the facts known to the person at the time in question.

(c) A person notifies or gives a notification to another by taking steps reasonably required to inform the other person in ordinary course, whether or not the other person learns of it.

(d) A person receives a notification when the notification:

(1) comes to the person's attention; or

(2) is duly delivered at the person's place of business or at any other place held out by the person as a place for receiving communications. [subsections (e) and (f) omitted]

§ 103. Effect of Partnership Agreement; Nonwaivable Provisions.

(a) Except as otherwise provided in subsection (b), relations among the partners and between the partners and the partnership are governed by the partnership agreement. To the extent the partnership agreement does not otherwise provide, this [Act] governs relations among the partners and between the partners and the partnership.

(b) The partnership agreement may not:

(1) vary the rights and duties under Section 105 except to eliminate the duty to provide copies of statements to all of the partners;

(2) unreasonably restrict the right of access to books and records under Section 403(b);

(3) eliminate the duty of loyalty under Section 404(b) or 603(b)(3), but:

(i) the partnership agreement may identify specific types or categories of activities that do not violate the duty of loyalty, if not manifestly unreasonable; or

(ii) all of the partners or a number or percentage specified in the partnership agreement may authorize or ratify, after full disclosure of all material facts, a specific act or transaction that otherwise would violate the duty of loyalty;

(4) unreasonably reduce the duty of care under Section 404(c) or 603(b)(3);

(5) eliminate the obligation of good faith and fair dealing under Section 404(d), but the partnership agreement may prescribe the standards by which the performance of the obligation is to be measured, if the standards are not manifestly unreasonable;

(6) vary the power to dissociate as a partner under Section 602(a), except to require the notice under Section 601(1) to be in writing;

(7) vary the right of a court to expel a partner in the events specified in Section 601(5);

(8) vary the requirement to wind up the partnership business in cases specified in Section 801(4), (5), or (6);

(9) vary the law applicable to a limited liability partnership under Section 106(b); or

(10) restrict rights of third parties under this [Act].

§ 105. Execution, Filing, and Recording of Statements.

(a) A statement may be filed in the office of [the Secretary of State]. A certified copy of a statement that is filed in an office in another state may be filed in the office of [the Secretary of State]. Either filing has the effect provided in this [Act] with respect to partnership property located in or transactions that occur in this State. [subsection (b) omitted]

(c) A statement filed by a partnership must be executed by at least two partners. Other statements must be executed by a partner or other person authorized by this [Act]. An individual who executes a statement as, or on behalf of, a partner or other person named as a partner in a statement shall personally declare under penalty of perjury that the contents of the statement are accurate.

(d) A person authorized by this [Act] to file a statement may amend or cancel the statement by filing an amendment or cancellation that names the partnership, identifies the statement, and states the substance of the amendment or cancellation.

(e) A person who files a statement pursuant to this section shall promptly send a copy of the statement to every nonfiling partner and to any other person named as a partner in the statement. Failure to send a copy of a statement to a partner or other person does not limit the effectiveness of the statement as to a person not a partner. [subsection (f) omitted]

§ 106. Law Governing Internal Relations

(a) Except as otherwise provided in subsection (b), the law of the jurisdiction in which a partnership has its chief executive office governs relations among the partners and between the partners and the partnership.

(b) The law of this State governs relations among the partners and between the partners and the partnership and the liability of partners for an obligation of a limited liability partnership.

§ 107. Partnership Subject to Amendment or Repeal of [Act].

A partnership governed by this [Act] is subject to any amendment to or repeal of this [Act].

ARTICLE 2. NATURE OF PARTNERSHIP

§ 201. Partnership as Entity.

(a) A partnership is an entity distinct from its partners.

(b) A limited liability partnership continues to be the same entity that existed before the filing of a statement of qualification under Section 1001.

§ 202. Formation of Partnership.

(a) Except as otherwise provided in subsection (b), the association of two or more persons to carry on as co-owners a business for profit forms a partnership, whether or not the persons intend to form a partnership.

(b) An association formed under a statute other than this [Act], a predecessor statute, or a comparable statute of another jurisdiction is not a partnership under this [Act].

(c) In determining whether a partnership is formed, the following rules apply:

(1) Joint tenancy, tenancy in common, tenancy by the entireties, joint property, common property, or part ownership does not by itself establish a partnership, even if the co-owners share profits made by the use of the property.

(2) The sharing of gross returns does not by itself establish a partnership, even if the persons sharing them have a joint or common right or interest in property from which the returns are derived.

(3) A person who receives a share of the profits of a business is presumed to be a partner in the business, unless the profits were received in payment:

(i) of a debt by installments or otherwise;

(ii) for services as an independent contractor or of wages or other compensation to an employee;

(iii) of rent;

(iv) of an annuity or other retirement benefit to a beneficiary, representative, or designee of a deceased or retired partner;

(v) of interest or other charge on a loan, even if the amount of payment varies with the profits of the business, including a direct or indirect present or future ownership of the collateral, or rights to income, proceeds, or increase in value derived from the collateral; or

(vi) for the sale of the goodwill of a business or other property by installments or otherwise.

§ 203.   *Partnership Property.*

Property acquired by a partnership is property of the partnership and not of the partners individually.

§ 204.   *When Property Is Partnership Property.*

(a) Property is partnership property if acquired in the name of:

(1) the partnership; or

(2) one or more partners with an indication in the instrument transferring title to the property of the person's capacity as a partner or of the existence of a partnership but without an indication of the name of the partnership.

(b) Property is acquired in the name of the partnership by a transfer to:

(1) the partnership in its name; or

(2) one or more partners in their capacity as partners in the partnership, if the name of the partnership is indicated in the instrument transferring title to the property.

(c) Property is presumed to be partnership property if purchased with partnership assets, even if not acquired in the name of the partnership or of one or more partners with an indication in the instrument transferring title to the property of the person's capacity as a partner or of the existence of a partnership.

(d) Property acquired in the name of one or more of the partners, without an indication in the instrument transferring title to the property of the person's capacity as a partner or of the existence of a partnership and without use of partnership assets, is presumed to be separate property, even if used for partnership purposes.

ARTICLE 3.   RELATIONS OF PARTNERS TO PERSONS DEALING WITH PARTNERSHIP

§ 301.   *Partner Agent of Partnership.*

Subject to the effect of a statement of partnership authority under Section 303:

(1) Each partner is an agent of the partnership for the purpose of its business. An act of a partner, including the execution of an instrument in the partnership name, for apparently carrying on in the ordinary course the partnership business or business of the kind carried on by the partnership binds the partnership, unless the partner had no authority to act for the partnership in the particular matter and the person with whom the partner was dealing knew or has received a notification that the partner lacked authority.

(2) An act of a partner which is not apparently for carrying on in the ordinary course the partnership business or business of the kind carried on by the partnership binds the partnership only if the act was authorized by the other partners.

§ 302.   *Transfer of Partnership Property.*

(a) Partnership property may be transferred as follows:

(1) Subject to the effect of a statement of partnership authority under Section 303, partnership property held in the name of the partnership may be transferred by an instrument of transfer executed by a partner in the partnership name.

(2) Partnership property held in the name of one or more partners with an indication in the instrument transferring the property to them of their capacity as partners or of the existence of a partnership, but without an indication of the name of the partnership, may be transferred by an instrument of transfer executed by the persons in whose name the property is held.

(3) Partnership property held in the name of one or more persons other than the partnership, without an indication in the instrument transferring the property to them of their capacity as partners or of the existence of a partnership, may be transferred by an instrument of transfer executed by the persons in whose name the property is held. [subsections (b), (c), and (d) omitted]

§ 303.   *Statement of Partnership Authority.*

(a) A partnership may file a statement of partnership authority, which:

(1) must include:

(i) the name of the partnership;

(ii) the street address of its chief executive office and of one office in this State, if there is one;

(iii) the names and mailing addresses of all of the partners or of an agent appointed and maintained by the partnership for the purpose of subsection (b); and

(iv) the names of the partners authorized to execute an instrument transferring real property held in the name of the partnership; and

(2) may state the authority, or limitations on the authority, of some or all of the partners to enter into other transactions on behalf of the partnership and any other matter.

(b) If a statement of partnership authority names an agent, the agent shall maintain a list of the names and mailing addresses of all of the partners and make it available to any person on request for good cause shown.

(c) If a filed statement of partnership authority is executed pursuant to Section 105(c) and states the name of the partnership but does not contain all of the other information required by subsection (a), the statement nevertheless operates with respect to a person not a partner as provided in subsections (d) and (e).

(d) Except as otherwise provided in subsection (g), a filed statement of partnership authority supplements the authority of a partner to enter into transactions on behalf of the partnership as follows:

(1) Except for transfers of real property, a grant of authority contained in a filed statement of partnership authority is conclusive in favor of a person who gives value without knowledge to the contrary, so long as and to the extent that a limitation on that authority is not then contained in another filed statement. A filed cancellation of a limitation on authority revives the previous grant of authority.

(2) A grant of authority to transfer real property held in the name of the partnership contained in a certified copy of a filed statement of partnership authority recorded in the office for recording transfers of that real property is conclusive in favor of a person who gives value without knowledge to the contrary, so long as and to the extent that a certified copy of a filed statement containing a limitation on that authority is not then of record in the office for recording transfers of that real property. The recording in the office for recording transfers of that real property of a certified copy of a filed cancellation of a limitation on authority revives the previous grant of authority.

(e) A person not a partner is deemed to know of a limitation on the authority of a partner to transfer real property held in the name of the partnership if a certified copy of the filed statement containing the limitation on authority is of record in the office for recording transfers of that real property.

(f) Except as otherwise provided in subsections (d) and (e) and Sections 704 and 805, a person not a partner is not deemed to know of a limitation on the authority of a partner merely because the limitation is contained in a filed statement.

(g) Unless earlier canceled, a filed statement of partnership authority is canceled by operation of law five years after the date on which the statement, or the most recent amendment, was filed with the [Secretary of State].

§ 304. *Statement of Denial.*

A partner or other person named as a partner in a filed statement of partnership authority or in a list maintained by an agent pursuant to Section 303(b) may file a statement of denial stating the name of the partnership and the fact that is being denied, which may include denial of a person's authority or status as a partner. A statement of denial is a limitation on authority as provided in Section 303(d) and (e).

§ 305. *Partnership Liable for Partner's Actionable Conduct.*

(a) A partnership is liable for loss or injury caused to a person, or for a penalty incurred, as a result of a wrongful act or omission, or other actionable conduct, of a partner acting in the ordinary course of business of the partnership or with authority of the partnership.

(b) If, in the course of the partnership's business or while acting with authority of the partnership, a partner receives or causes the partnership to receive money or property of a person not a partner, and the money or property is misapplied by a partner, the partnership is liable for the loss.

§ 306. *Partner's Liability.*

(a) Except as otherwise provided in subsections (b) and (c), all partners are liable jointly and severally for all obligations of the partnership unless otherwise agreed by the claimant or provided by law.

(b) A person admitted as a partner into an existing partnership is not personally liable for any partnership obligation incurred before the person's admission as a partner.

(c) An obligation of a partnership incurred while the partnership is a limited liability partnership, whether arising in contract, tort, or otherwise, is solely the obligation of the partnership. A partner is not personally liable, directly or indirectly, by way of contribution or otherwise, for such an obligation solely by reason of being or so acting as a partner. This subsection applies notwithstanding anything inconsistent in the partnership agreement that existed immediately before the vote required to become a limited liability partnership under Section 1001(b).

§ 307. *Actions By and Against Partnership and Partners.*

(a) A partnership may sue and be sued in the name of the partnership.

(b) An action may be brought against the partnership and, to the extent not inconsistent with Section 306, any or all of the partners in the same action or in separate actions.

(c) A judgment against a partnership is not by itself a judgment against a partner. A judgment against a partnership may not be satisfied from a partner's assets unless there is also a judgment against the partner.

(d) A judgment creditor of a partner may not levy execution against the assets of the partner to satisfy a judgment based on a claim against the partnership unless the partner is personally liable for the claim under Section 306 and:

(1) a judgment based on the same claim has been obtained against the partnership and a writ of execution on the judgment has been returned unsatisfied in whole or in part;

(2) the partnership is a debtor in bankruptcy;

(3) the partner has agreed that the creditor need not exhaust partnership assets;

(4) a court grants permission to the judgment creditor to levy execution against the assets of a partner based on a finding that partnership assets subject to execution are clearly insufficient to satisfy the judgment, that exhaustion of partnership assets is excessively burdensome, or that the grant of permission is an appropriate exercise of the court's equitable powers; or

(5) liability is imposed on the partner by law or contract independent of the existence of the partnership.

(e) This section applies to any partnership liability or obligation resulting from a representation by a partner or purported partner under Section 308.

§ 308. *Liability of Purported Partner.*

(a) If a person, by words or conduct, purports to be a partner, or consents to being represented by another as a partner, in a partnership or with one or more persons not partners, the purported partner is liable to a person to whom the representation is made, if that person, relying on the representation, enters into a transaction with the actual or purported partnership. If the representation, either by the purported partner or by a person with the purported partner's consent, is made in a public manner, the purported partner is liable to a person who relies upon the purported partnership even if the purported partner is not aware of being held out as a partner to the claimant. If partnership liability results, the purported partner is liable with respect to that liability as if the purported partner were a partner. If no partnership liability results, the purported partner is liable with respect to that liability jointly and severally with any other person consenting to the representation. [subsections (b), (c), (d), and (e) omitted]

ARTICLE 4.   RELATIONS OF PARTNERS TO EACH OTHER AND TO PARTNERSHIP

§ 401.   *Partner's Rights and Duties.*

(a) Each partner is deemed to have an account that is:

(1) credited with an amount equal to the money plus the value of any other property, net of the amount of any liabilities, the partner contributes to the partnership and the partner's share of the partnership profits; and

(2) charged with an amount equal to the money plus the value of any other property, net of the amount of any liabilities, distributed by the partnership to the partner and the partner's share of the partnership losses.

(b) Each partner is entitled to an equal share of the partnership profits and is chargeable with a share of the partnership losses in proportion to the partner's share of the profits.

(c) A partnership shall reimburse a partner for payments made and indemnify a partner for liabilities incurred by the partner in the ordinary course of the business of the partnership or for the preservation of its business or property.

(d) A partnership shall reimburse a partner for an advance to the partnership beyond the amount of capital the partner agreed to contribute.

(e) A payment or advance made by a partner which gives rise to a partnership obligation under subsection (c) or (d) constitutes a loan to the partnership which accrues interest from the date of the payment or advance.

(f) Each partner has equal rights in the management and conduct of the partnership business.

(g) A partner may use or possess partnership property only on behalf of the partnership.

(h) A partner is not entitled to remuneration for services performed for the partnership, except for reasonable compensation for services rendered in winding up the business of the partnership.

(i) A person may become a partner only with the consent of all of the partners.

(j) A difference arising as to a matter in the ordinary course of business of a partnership may be decided by a majority of the partners. An act outside the ordinary course of business of a partnership and an amendment to the partnership agreement may be undertaken only with the consent of all of the partners.

(k) This section does not affect the obligations of a partnership to other persons under Section 301.

§ 402.   *Distributions in Kind.*

A partner has no right to receive, and may not be required to accept, a distribution in kind.

§ 403.   *Partner's Rights and Duties With Respect to Information.*

(a) A partnership shall keep its books and records, if any, at its chief executive office.

(b) A partnership shall provide partners and their agents and attorneys access to its books and records. It shall provide former partners and their agents and attorneys access to books and records pertaining to the period during which they were partners. The right of access provides the opportunity to inspect and copy books and records during ordinary business hours. A partnership may impose a reasonable charge, covering the costs of labor and material, for copies of documents furnished.

(c) Each partner and the partnership shall furnish to a partner, and to the legal representative of a deceased partner or partner under legal disability:

(1) without demand, any information concerning the partnership's business and affairs reasonably required for the proper exercise of the partner's rights and duties under the partnership agreement or this [Act]; and

(2) on demand, any other information concerning the partnership's business and affairs, except to the extent the demand or the information demanded is unreasonable or otherwise improper under the circumstances.

§ 404.   *General Standards of Partner's Conduct.*

(a) The only fiduciary duties a partner owes to the partnership and the other partners are the duty of loyalty and the duty of care set forth in subsections (b) and (c).

(b) A partner's duty of loyalty to the partnership and the other partners is limited to the following:

(1) to account to the partnership and hold as trustee for it any property, profit, or benefit derived by the partner in the conduct and winding up of the partnership business or derived from a use by the partner of partnership property, including the appropriation of a partnership opportunity;

(2) to refrain from dealing with the partnership in the conduct or winding up of the partnership business as or on behalf of a party having an interest adverse to the partnership; and

(3) to refrain from competing with the partnership in the conduct of the partnership business before the dissolution of the partnership.

(c) A partner's duty of care to the partnership and the other partners in the conduct and winding up of the partnership business is limited to refraining from engaging in grossly negligent or reckless conduct, intentional misconduct, or a knowing violation of law.

(d) A partner shall discharge the duties to the partnership and the other partners under this [Act] or under the partnership agreement and exercise any rights consistently with the obligation of good faith and fair dealing.

(e) A partner does not violate a duty or obligation under this [Act] or under the partnership agreement merely because the partner's conduct furthers the partner's own interest.

(f) A partner may lend money to and transact other business with the partnership, and as to each loan or transaction, the rights and obligations of a partner are the same as those of a person who is not a partner, subject to other applicable law.

(g) This section applies to a person winding up the partnership business as the personal or legal representative of the last surviving partner as if the person were a partner.

§ 405. *Actions by Partnership and Partners.*

(a) A partnership may maintain an action against a partner for a breach of the partnership agreement, or for the violation of a duty to the partnership, causing harm to the partnership.

(b) A partner may maintain an action against the partnership or another partner for legal or equitable relief, with or without an accounting as to partnership business, to:

(1) enforce the partner's rights under the partnership agreement;

(2) enforce the partner's rights under this [Act], including:

(i) the partner's rights under Sections 401, 403, or 404;

(ii) the partner's right on dissociation to have the partner's interest in the partnership purchased pursuant to Section 701 or enforce any other right under Article 6 or 7; or

(iii) the partner's right to compel a dissolution and winding up of the partnership business under Section 801 or enforce any other right under Article 8; or

(3) enforce the rights and otherwise protect the interests of the partner, including rights and interests arising independently of the partnership relationship.

(c) The accrual of, and any time limitation on, a right of action for a remedy under this section is governed by other law. A right to an accounting upon a dissolution and winding up does not revive a claim barred by law.

§ 406. *Continuation of Partnership Beyond Definite Term or Particular Undertaking.*

(a) If a partnership for a definite term or particular undertaking is continued, without an express agreement, after the expiration of the term or completion of the undertaking, the rights and duties of the partners remain the same as they were at the expiration or completion, so far as is consistent with a partnership at will.

(b) If the partners, or those of them who habitually acted in the business during the term or undertaking, continue the business without any settlement or liquidation of the partnership, they are presumed to have agreed that the partnership will continue.

ARTICLE 5. TRANSFEREES AND CREDITORS OF PARTNER

§ 501. *Partner Not Co-owner of Partnership Property.*

A partner is not a co-owner of partnership property and has no interest in partnership property which can be transferred, either voluntarily or involuntarily.

§ 502. *Partner's Transferable Interest in Partnership.*

The only transferable interest of a partner in the partnership is the partner's share of the profits and losses of the partnership and the partner's right to receive distributions. The interest is personal property.

§ 503. *Transfer of Partner's Transferable Interest.*

(a) A transfer, in whole or in part, of a partner's transferable interest in the partnership:

(1) is permissible;

(2) does not by itself cause the partner's dissociation or a dissolution and winding up of the partnership business; and

(3) does not, as against the other partners or the partnership, entitle the transferee, during the continuance of the partnership, to participate in the management or conduct of the partnership business, to require access to information concerning or an account of partnership transactions, or to inspect or copy the partnership books or records.

(b) A transferee of a partner's transferable interest in the partnership has a right:

(1) to receive, in accordance with the transfer, distributions to which the transferor would otherwise be entitled;

(2) to receive upon the dissolution and winding up of the partnership business, in accordance with the transfer, the net amount otherwise distributable to the transferor; and

(3) to seek under Section 801(6) a judicial determination that it is equitable to wind up the partnership business.

(c) In a dissolution and winding up, a transferee is entitled to an account of partnership transactions only from the date of the latest account agreed to by all of the partners.

(d) Upon transfer, the transferor retains the rights and duties of a partner other than the interest in distributions transferred.

(e) A partnership need not give effect to a transferee's rights under this section until it has notice of the transfer.

(f) A transfer of a partner's transferable interest in the partnership in violation of a restriction on transfer contained in the partnership agreement is ineffective as to a person having notice of the restriction at the time of transfer.

§ 504. *Partner's Transferable Interest Subject to Charging Order.*

(a) On application by a judgment creditor of a partner or of a partner's transferee, a court having jurisdiction may charge the transferrable interest of the judgment debtor to satisfy the judgment. The court may appoint a receiver of the debtor's share of the distributions due or to become due to the debtor in respect of the partnership and make all other orders, directions, accounts, and inquiries the judgment debtor might have made or which the circumstances of the case may require.

(b) A charging order constitutes a lien on the judgment debtor's transferable interest in the partnership. The court may order a foreclosure of the interest subject to the charging order at any time. The purchaser at the foreclosure sale has the rights of a transferee. [subsections (c), (d), and (e) omitted]

ARTICLE 6.   PARTNER'S DISSOCIATION

§ 601.   *Events Causing Partner's Dissociation.*

A partner is dissociated from a partnership upon the occurrence of any of the following events:

(1) the partnership's having notice of the partner's express will to withdraw as a partner or on a later date specified by the partner;

(2) an event agreed to in the partnership agreement as causing the partner's dissociation;

(3) the partner's expulsion pursuant to the partnership agreement;

(4) the partner's expulsion by the unanimous vote of the other partners if:

(i) it is unlawful to carry on the partnership business with that partner;

(ii) there has been a transfer of all or substantially all of that partner's transferable interest in the partnership, other than a transfer for security purposes, or a court order charging the partner's interest, which has not been foreclosed;

(iii) within 90 days after the partnership notifies a corporate partner that it will be expelled because it has filed a certificate of dissolution or the equivalent, its charter has been revoked, or its right to conduct business has been suspended by the jurisdiction of its incorporation, there is no revocation of the certificate of dissolution or no reinstatement of its charter or its right to conduct business; or

(iv) a partnership that is a partner has been dissolved and its business is being wound up;

(5) on application by the partnership or another partner, the partner's expulsion by judicial determination because:

(i) the partner engaged in wrongful conduct that adversely and materially affected the partnership business;

(ii) the partner willfully or persistently committed a material breach of the partnership agreement or of a duty owed to the partnership or the other partners under Section 404; or

(iii) the partner engaged in conduct relating to the partnership business which makes it not reasonably practicable to carry on the business in partnership with the partner;

(6) the partner's:

(i) becoming a debtor in bankruptcy;

(ii) executing an assignment for the benefit of creditors;

(iii) seeking, consenting to, or acquiescing in the appointment of a trustee, receiver, or liquidator of that partner or of all or substantially all of that partner's property; or

(iv) failing, within 90 days after the appointment, to have vacated or stayed the appointment of a trustee, receiver, or liquidator of the partner or of all or substantially all of the partner's property obtained without the partner's consent or acquiescence, or failing within 90 days after the expiration of a stay to have the appointment vacated;

(7) in the case of a partner who is an individual:

(i) the partner's death;

(ii) the appointment of a guardian or general conservator for the partner; or

(iii) a judicial determination that the partner has otherwise become incapable of performing the partner's duties under the partnership agreement;

(8) in the case of a partner that is a trust or is acting as a partner by virtue of being a trustee of a trust, distribution of the trust's entire transferable interest in the partnership, but not merely by reason of the substitution of a successor trustee;

(9) in the case of a partner that is an estate or is acting as a partner by virtue of being a personal representative of an estate, distribution of the estate's entire transferable interest in the partnership, but not merely by reason of the substitution of a successor personal representative; or

(10) termination of a partner who is not an individual, partnership, corporation, trust, or estate.

§ 602.   *Partner's Power to Dissociate; Wrongful Dissociation*

(a) A partner has the power to dissociate at any time, rightfully or wrongfully, by express will pursuant to Section 601(1).

(b) A partner's dissociation is wrongful only if:

(1) it is in breach of an express provision of the partnership agreement; or

(2) in the case of a partnership for a definite term or particular undertaking, before the expiration of the term or the completion of the undertaking:

(i) the partner withdraws by express will, unless the withdrawal follows within 90 days after another partner's dissociation by death or otherwise under Section 601(6) through (10) or wrongful dissociation under this subsection;

(ii) the partner is expelled by judicial determination under Section 601(5); or

(iii) the partner is dissociated by becoming a debtor in bankruptcy; or

(iv) in the case of a partner who is not an individual, trust other than a business trust, or estate, the partner is expelled or otherwise dissociated because it willfully dissolved or terminated.

(c) A partner who wrongfully dissociates is liable to the partnership and to the other partners for damages caused by the dissociation. The liability is in addition to any other obligation of the partner to the partnership or to the other partners.

§ 603.   *Effect of Partner's Dissociation.*

(a) If a partner's dissociation results in a dissolution and winding up of the partnership business, Article 8 applies; otherwise, Article 7 applies.

(b) Upon a partner's dissociation:

(1) the partner's right to participate in the management and conduct of the partnership business terminates, except as otherwise provided in Section 803;

(2) the partner's duty of loyalty under Section 404(b)(3) terminates; and

(3) the partner's duty of loyalty under Section 404(b)(1) and (2) and duty of care under Section 404(c) continue only with regard to matters arising or events occurring

before the partner's dissociation, unless the partner participates in winding up the partnership's business pursuant to Section 803.

ARTICLE 7. PARTNER'S DISSOCIATION WHEN BUSINESS NOT WOUND UP

§ 701. *Purchase of Dissociated Partner's Interest.*

(a) If a partner is dissociated from a partnership without resulting in a dissolution and winding up of the partnership business under Section 801, the partnership shall cause the dissociated partner's interest in the partnership to be purchased for a buyout price determined pursuant to subsection (b).

(b) The buyout price of a dissociated partner's interest is the amount that would have been distributable to the dissociating partner under Section 807(b) if, on the date of dissociation, the assets of the partnership were sold at a price equal to the greater of the liquidation value or the value based on a sale of the entire business as a going concern without the dissociated partner and the partnership were wound up as of that date. Interest must be paid from the date of dissociation to the date of payment.

(c) Damages for wrongful dissociation under Section 602(b), and all other amounts owing, whether or not presently due, from the dissociated partner to the partnership, must be offset against the buyout price. Interest must be paid from the date the amount owed becomes due to the date of payment.

(d) A partnership shall indemnify a dissociated partner whose interest is being purchased against all partnership liabilities, whether incurred before or after the dissociation, except liabilities incurred by an act of the dissociated partner under Section 702.

(e) If no agreement for the purchase of a dissociated partner's interest is reached within 120 days after a written demand for payment, the partnership shall pay, or cause to be paid, in cash to the dissociated partner the amount the partnership estimates to be the buyout price and accrued interest, reduced by any offsets and accrued interest under subsection (c).

(f) If a deferred payment is authorized under subsection (h), the partnership may tender a written offer to pay the amount it estimates to be the buyout price and accrued interest, reduced by any offsets under subsection (c), stating the time of payment, the amount and type of security for payment, and the other terms and conditions of the obligation.

(g) The payment or tender required by subsection (e) or (f) must be accompanied by the following:

(1) a statement of partnership assets and liabilities as of the date of dissociation;

(2) the latest available partnership balance sheet and income statement, if any;

(3) an explanation of how the estimated amount of the payment was calculated; and

(4) written notice that the payment is in full satisfaction of the obligation to purchase unless, within 120 days after the written notice, the dissociated partner commences an action to determine the buyout price, any offsets under subsection (c), or other terms of the obligation to purchase.

(h) A partner who wrongfully dissociates before the expiration of a definite term or the completion of a particular undertaking is not entitled to payment of any portion of the buyout price until the expiration of the term or completion of the undertaking, unless the partner establishes to the satisfaction of the court that earlier payment will not cause undue hardship to the business of the partnership. A deferred payment must be adequately secured and bear interest.

(i) A dissociated partner may maintain an action against the partnership, pursuant to Section 405(b)(2)(ii), to determine the buyout price of that partner's interest, any offsets under subsection (c), or other terms of the obligation to purchase. The action must be commenced within 120 days after the partnership has tendered payment or an offer to pay or within one year after written demand for payment if no payment or offer to pay is tendered. The court shall determine the buyout price of the dissociated partner's interest, any offset due under subsection (c), and accrued interest, and enter judgment for any additional payment or refund. If deferred payment is authorized under subsection (h), the court shall also determine the security for payment and other terms of the obligation to purchase. The court may assess reasonable attorney's fees and the fees and expenses of appraisers or other experts for a party to the action, in amounts the court finds equitable, against a party that the court finds acted arbitrarily, vexatiously, or not in good faith. The finding may be based on the partnership's failure to tender payment or an offer to pay or to comply with subsection (g).

§ 702. *Dissociated Partner's Power to Bind and Liability to Partnership.*

(a) For two years after a partner dissociates without resulting in a dissolution and winding up of the partnership business, the partnership, including a surviving partnership under [Article] 9, is bound by an act of the dissociated partner which would have bound the partnership under Section 301 before dissociation only if at the time of entering into the transaction the other party:

(1) reasonably believed that the dissociated partner was then a partner;

(2) did not have notice of the partner's dissociation; and

(3) is not deemed to have had knowledge under Section 303(e) or notice under Section 704(c).

(b) A dissociated partner is liable to the partnership for any damage caused to the partnership arising from an obligation incurred by the dissociated partner after dissociation for which the partnership is liable under subsection (a).

§ 703. *Dissociated Partner's Liability to Other Persons.*

(a) A partner's dissociation does not of itself discharge the partner's liability for a partnership obligation incurred before dissociation. A dissociated partner is not liable for a partnership obligation incurred after dissociation, except as otherwise provided in subsection (b).

(b) A partner who dissociates without resulting in a dissolution and winding up of the partnership business is liable as a partner to the other party in a transaction entered into by the partnership, or a surviving partnership under Article 9, within two years after the partner's dissociation, only if the partner is liable for the obligation under Section 306 and at the time of entering into the transaction with the other party:

(1) reasonably believed that the dissociated partner was then a partner;

(2) did not have notice of the partner's dissociation; and

(3) is not deemed to have had knowledge under Section 303(e) or notice under Section 704(c).

(c) By agreement with the partnership creditor and the partners continuing the business, a dissociated partner may be released from liability for a partnership obligation.

(d) A dissociated partner is released from liability for a partnership obligation if a partnership creditor, with notice of the partner's dissociation but without the partner's consent, agrees to a material alteration in the nature or time of payment of a partnership obligation.

§ 704. *Statement of Dissociation.*

(a) A dissociated partner or the partnership may file a statement of dissociation stating the name of the partnership and that the partner is dissociated from the partnership.

(b) A statement of dissociation is a limitation on the authority of a dissociated partner for the purposes of Section 303(d) and (e).

(c) For the purposes of Sections 702(a)(3) and 703(b)(3), a person not a partner is deemed to have notice of the dissociation 90 days after the statement of dissociation is filed.

ARTICLE 8. WINDING UP PARTNERSHIP BUSINESS

§ 801. *Events Causing Dissolution and Winding up of Partnership Business.*

A partnership is dissolved, and its business must be wound up, only upon the occurrence of any of the following events:

(1) in a partnership at will, the partnership's having notice from a partner, other than a partner who is dissociated under Section 601(2) through (10), of that partner's express will to withdraw as a partner or on a later date specified by the partner;

(2) in a partnership for a definite term or particular undertaking:

(i) within 90 days after a partner's dissociation by death or otherwise under Section 601(6) through (10) or wrongful dissociation under Section 602(b), the express will of at least half of the remaining partners to wind up the partnership business, for which purpose a partner's rightful dissociation pursuant to Section 602(b)(2)(i) constitutes the expression of that partner's will to wind up the partnership business;

(ii) the express will of all of the partners to wind up the partnership business; or

(iii) the expiration of the term or the completion of the undertaking;

(3) an event agreed to in the partnership agreement resulting in the winding up of the partnership business;

(4) an event that makes it unlawful for all or substantially all of the business of the partnership to be continued, but a cure of illegality within 90 days after notice to the partnership of the event is effective retroactively to the date of the event for purposes of this section;

(5) on application by a partner, a judicial determination that:

(i) the economic purpose of the partnership is likely to be unreasonably frustrated;

(ii) another partner has engaged in conduct relating to the partnership business which makes it not reasonably practicable to carry on the business in partnership with that partner; or

(iii) it is not otherwise reasonably practicable to carry on the partnership business in conformity with the partnership agreement. [subsection (6) omitted]

§ 802. *Partnership Continues After Dissolution.*

(a) Subject to subsection (b), a partnership continues after dissolution only for the purpose of winding up its business. The partnership is terminated when the winding up of its business is completed.

(b) At any time after the dissolution of a partnership and before the winding up of its business is completed, all of the partners, including any dissociating partner other than a wrongfully dissociating partner, may waive the right to have the partnership's business wound up and the partnership terminated. In that event:

(1) the partnership resumes carrying on its business as if dissolution had never occurred, and any liability incurred by the partnership or a partner after the dissolution and before the waiver is determined as if dissolution had never occurred; and

(2) the rights of a third party accruing under Section 804(1) or arising out of conduct in reliance on the dissolution before the third party knew or received a notification of the waiver may not be adversely affected.

§ 803. *Right to Wind up Partnership Business.*

(a) After dissolution, a partner who has not wrongfully dissociated may participate in winding up the partnership's business, but on application of any partner, partner's legal representative, or transferee, the [designate the appropriate court], for good cause shown, may order judicial supervision of the winding up. [subsections (b) and (c) omitted]

§ 804. *Partner's Power to Bind Partnership After Dissolution.*

Subject to Section 805, a partnership is bound by a partner's act after dissolution that:

(1) is appropriate for winding up the partnership business; or

(2) would have bound the partnership under Section 301 before dissolution, if the other party to the transaction did not have notice of the dissolution.

§ 805. *Statement of Dissolution.*

(a) After dissolution, a partner who has not wrongfully dissociated may file a statement of dissolution stating the name of the partnership and that the partnership has dissolved and is winding up its business.

(b) A statement of dissolution cancels a filed statement of partnership authority for the purposes of Section 303(d) and is a limitation on authority for the purposes of Section 303(e).

(c) For the purposes of Sections 301 and 804, a person not a partner is deemed to have notice of the dissolution and the limitation on the partners' authority as a result of the statement of dissolution 90 days after it is filed.

(d) After filing and, if appropriate, recording a statement of dissolution, a dissolved partnership may file and, if appropriate, record a statement of partnership authority which will operate with respect to a person not a partner as provided in Section 303(d) and (e) in any transaction, whether or not the transaction is appropriate for winding up the partnership business.

§ 806. *Partner's Liability to Other Partners After Dissolution.*

(a) Except as otherwise provided in subsection (b) and Section 306, after dissolution a partner is liable to the other partners for the partner's share of any partnership liability incurred under Section 804.

(b) A partner who, with knowledge of the dissolution, incurs a partnership liability under Section 804(2) by an act that is not appropriate for winding up the partnership business is liable to the partnership for any damage caused to the partnership arising from the liability.

§ 807. *Settlement of Accounts and Contributions Among Partners.*

(a) In winding up a partnership's business, the assets of the partnership, including the contributions of the partners required by this section, must be applied to discharge its obligations to creditors, including, to the extent permitted by law, partners who are creditors. Any surplus must be applied to pay in cash the net amount distributable to partners in accordance with their right to distributions under subsection (b).

(b) Each partner is entitled to a settlement of all partnership accounts upon winding up the partnership business. In settling accounts among the partners, the profits and losses that result from the liquidation of the partnership assets must be credited and charged to the partners' accounts. The partnership shall make a distribution to a partner in an amount equal to any excess of the credits over the charges in the partner's account. A partner shall contribute to the partnership an amount equal to any excess of the charges over the credits in the partner's account but excluding from the calculation charges attributable to an obligation for which the partner is not personally liable under Section 306.

(c) If a partner fails to contribute the full amount required under subsection (b), all of the other partners shall contribute, in the proportions in which those partners share partnership losses, the additional amount necessary to satisfy the partnership obligations for which they are personally liable under Section 306. A partner or partner's legal representative may recover from the other partners any contributions the partner makes to the extent the amount contributed exceeds that partner's share of the partnership obligations for which the partner is personally liable under Section 306.

(d) After the settlement of accounts, each partner shall contribute, in the proportion in which the partner shares partnership losses, the amount necessary to satisfy partnership obligations that were not known at the time of the settlement and for which the partner is personally liable under Section 306.

(e) The estate of a deceased partner is liable for the partner's obligation to contribute to the partnership.

(f) An assignee for the benefit of creditors of a partnership or a partner, or a person appointed by a court to represent creditors of a partnership or a partner, may enforce a partner's obligation to contribute to the partnership.

ARTICLE 9. CONVERSIONS AND MERGERS

§ 901. *Definitions.*

In this article:

(1) "General partner" means a partner in a partnership and a general partner in a limited partnership.

(2) "Limited partner" means a limited partner in a limited partnership.

(3) "Limited partnership" means a limited partnership created under the [State Limited Partnership Act], predecessor law, or comparable law of another jurisdiction.

(4) "Partner" includes both a general partner and a limited partner.

§ 902. *Conversion of Partnership to Limited Partnership.*

(a) A partnership may be converted to a limited partnership pursuant to this section.

(b) The terms and conditions of a conversion of a partnership to a limited partnership must be approved by all of the partners or by a number or percentage specified for conversion in the partnership agreement.

(c) After the conversion is approved by the partners, the partnership shall file a certificate of limited partnership in the jurisdiction in which the limited partnership is to be formed. [remainder of section omitted]

§ 903. *Conversion of Limited Partnership to Partnership.*

(a) A limited partnership may be converted to a partnership pursuant to this section.

(b) Notwithstanding a provision to the contrary in a limited partnership agreement, the terms and conditions of a conversion of a limited partnership to a partnership must be approved by all of the partners.

(c) After the conversion is approved by the partners, the limited partnership shall cancel its certificate of limited partnership. [subsections (d) and (e) omitted]

§ 904. *Effect of Conversion; Entity Unchanged.*

(a) A partnership or limited partnership that has been converted pursuant to this article is for all purposes the same entity that existed before the conversion.

(b) When a conversion takes effect:

(1) all property owned by the converting partnership or limited partnership remains vested in the converted entity;

(2) all obligations of the converting partnership or limited partnership continue as obligations of the converted entity; and

(3) an action or proceeding pending against the converting partnership or limited partnership may be continued as if the conversion had not occurred.

§ 905.　Merger of Partnerships.

(a) Pursuant to a plan of merger approved as provided in subsection (c), a partnership may be merged with one or more partnerships or limited partnerships.

(b) The plan of merger must set forth:

(1) the name of each partnership or limited partnership that is a party to the merger;

(2) the name of the surviving entity into which the other partnerships or limited partnerships will merge;

(3) whether the surviving entity is a partnership or a limited partnership and the status of each partner;

(4) the terms and conditions of the merger;

(5) the manner and basis of converting the interests of each party to the merger into interests or obligations of the surviving entity, or into money or other property in whole or part; and

(6) the street address of the surviving entity's chief executive office.

(c) The plan of merger must be approved:

(1) in the case of a partnership that is a party to the merger, by all of the partners, or a number or percentage specified for merger in the partnership agreement; and

(2) in the case of a limited partnership that is a party to the merger, by the vote required for approval of a merger by the law of the State or foreign jurisdiction in which the limited partnership is organized and, in the absence of such a specifically applicable law, by all of the partners, notwithstanding a provision to the contrary in the partnership agreement. [subsections (d) and (e) omitted]

§ 906.　Effect of Merger.

(a) When a merger takes effect:

(1) the separate existence of every partnership or limited partnership that is a party to the merger, other than the surviving entity, ceases;

(2) all property owned by each of the merged partnerships or limited partnerships vests in the surviving entity;

(3) all obligations of every partnership or limited partnership that is a party to the merger become the obligations of the surviving entity; and

(4) an action or proceeding pending against a partnership or limited partnership that is a party to the merger may be continued as if the merger had not occurred, or the surviving entity may be substituted as a party to the action or proceeding. [subsections (b), (c), (d), and (e) omitted]

§ 907.　Statement of Merger.

(a) After a merger, the surviving partnership or limited partnership may file a statement that one or more partnerships or limited partnerships have merged into the surviving entity. [subsections (b), (c), (d), and (e) omitted]

§ 909.　Nonexclusive.

This [article] is not exclusive. Partnerships or limited partnerships may be converted or merged in any other manner provided by law.

ARTICLE 10.　LIMITED LIABILITY PARTNERSHIP

§ 1001.　Statement of Qualification.

(a) A partnership may become a limited liability partnership pursuant to this section.

(b) The term and conditions on which a partnership becomes a limited liability partnership must be approved by the vote necessary to amend the partnership agreement except, in the case of a partnership agreement that expressly considers contribution obligations, the vote necessary to amend those provisions.

(c) After the approval required by subsection (b), a partnership may become a limited liability partnership by filing a statement of qualification. The statement must contain:

(1) the name of the partnership;

(2) the street address of the partnership's chief executive office and, if different, the street address of an office in this State, if any;

(3) if the partnership does not have an office in this State, the name and street address of the partnership's agent for service of process;

(4) a statement that the partnership elects to be a limited liability partnership; and

(5) a deferred effective date, if any.

(d) The agent of a limited liability partnership for service of process must be an individual who is a resident of this State or other person authorized to do business in this State.

(e) The status of a partnership as a limited liability partnership is effective on the later of the filing of the statement or a date specified in the statement. The status remains effective, regardless of changes in the partnership, until it is canceled pursuant to Section 105(d) or revoked pursuant to Section 1003.

(f) The status of a partnership as a limited liability partnership and the liability of its partners is not affected by errors or later changes in the information required to be contained in the statement of qualification under subsection (c).

(g) The filing of a statement of qualification establishes that a partnership has satisfied all conditions precedent to the qualification of the partnership as a limited liability partnership.

(h) An amendment or cancellation of a statement of qualification is effective when it is filed or on a deferred effective date specified in the amendment or cancellation.

§ 1002.　Name.

The name of a limited liability partnership must end with "Registered Limited Liability Partnership," "Limited Liability Partnership," "R.L.L.P.," "L.L.P.," "RLLP," or "LLP."

§ 1003. *Annual Report.*

(a) A limited liability partnership, and a foreign limited liability partnership authorized to transact business in this State, shall file an annual report in the office of the [Secretary of State] which contains:

(1) the name of the limited liability partnership and the State or other jurisdiction under whose laws the foreign limited liability partnership is formed;

(2) the street address of the partnership's chief executive office and, if different, the street address of an office in this State, if any; and

(3) if the partnership does not have an office in this State, the name and street address of the partnership's current agent for service of process.

(b) An annual report must be filed between [January 1 and April 1] of each year following the calendar year in which a partnership files a statement of qualification or a foreign partnership becomes authorized to transact business in this State.

(c) The [Secretary of State] may revoke the statement of qualification of a partnership that fails to file an annual report when due or to pay the required filing fee. To do so, the [Secretary of State] shall provide the partnership at least 60 days' written notice of intent to revoke the statement. The notice must be mailed to the partnership at its chief executive office set forth in the last filed statement of qualification or annual report. The notice must specify the annual report that has not been filed, the fee that has not been paid, and the effective date of the revocation. The revocation is not effective if the annual report is filed and the fee is paid before the effective date of the revocation.

(d) A revocation under subsection (c) only affects a partnership's status as a limited liability partnership and is not an event of dissolution of the partnership.

(e) A partnership whose statement of qualification has been revoked may apply to the [Secretary of State] for reinstatement within two years after the effective date of the revocation. The application must state:

(1) the name of the partnership and the effective date of the revocation; and

(2) that the ground for revocation either did not exist or has been corrected.

(f) A reinstatement under subsection (e) relates back to and takes effect as of the effective date of the revocation, and the partnership's status as a limited liability partnership continues as if the revocation had never occurred.

ARTICLE 11. FOREIGN LIMITED LIABILITY PARTNERSHIP

§ 1101. *Law Governing Foreign Limited Liability Partnership.*

(a) The laws under which a foreign limited liability partnership is formed govern relations among the partners and between the partners and the partnership and the liability of partners for obligations of the partnership.

(b) A foreign limited liability partnership may not be denied a statement of foreign qualification by reason of any difference between the laws under which the partnership was formed and the laws of this State.

(c) A statement of foreign qualification does not authorize a foreign limited liability partnership to engage in any business or exercise any power that a partnership may not engage in or exercise in this State as a limited liability partnership.

§ 1102. *Statement of Foreign Qualification.*

(a) Before transacting business in this State, a foreign limited liability partnership must file a statement of foreign qualification. The statement must contain:

(1) the name of the foreign limited liability partnership which satisfies the requirements of the State or other jurisdiction under whose laws it is formed and ends with "Registered Limited Liability Partnership," "Limited Liability Partnership," "R.L.L.P.," "L.L.P.," "RLLP," or "LLP";

(2) the street address of the partnership's chief executive office and, if different, the street address of an office in this State, if any;

(3) if there is no office of the partnership in this State, the name and street address of the partnership's agent for service of process; and

(4) a deferred effective date, if any.

(b) The agent of a foreign limited liability partnership for service of process must be an individual who is a resident of this State or other person authorized to do business in this State.

(c) The status of a partnership as a foreign limited liability partnership is effective on the later of the filing of the statement of foreign qualification or a date specified in the statement. The status remains effective, regardless of changes in the partnership, until it is canceled pursuant to Section 105(d) or revoked pursuant to Section 1003.

(d) An amendment or cancellation of a statement of foreign qualification is effective when it is filed or on a deferred effective date specified in the amendment or cancellation.

§ 1103. *Effect of Failure to Qualify.*

(a) A foreign limited liability partnership transacting business in this State may not maintain an action or proceeding in this State unless it has in effect a statement of foreign qualification.

(b) The failure of a foreign limited liability partnership to have in effect a statement of foreign qualification does not impair the validity of a contract or act of the foreign limited liability partnership or preclude it from defending an action or proceeding in this State.

(c) A limitation on personal liability of a partner is not waived solely by transacting business in this State without a statement of foreign qualification.

(d) If a foreign limited liability partnership transacts business in this State without a statement of foreign qualification, the [Secretary of State] is its agent for service of process with respect to a right of action arising out of the transaction of business in this State.

§ 1104. *Activities Not Constituting Transacting Business.*

(a) Activities of a foreign limited liability partnership which do not constitute transacting business within the meaning of this [article] include:

(1) maintaining, defending, or settling an action or proceeding;

(2) holding meetings of its partners or carrying on any other activity concerning its internal affairs;

(3) maintaining bank accounts;

(4) maintaining offices or agencies for the transfer, exchange, and registration of the partnership's own securities or maintaining trustees or depositories with respect to those securities;

(5) selling through independent contractors;

(6) soliciting or obtaining orders, whether by mail or through employees or agents or otherwise, if the orders require acceptance outside this State before they become contracts;

(7) creating or acquiring indebtedness with or without a mortgage, or other security interests in property;

(8) collecting debts or foreclosing mortgages or other security interests in property securing the debts, and holding, protecting, and maintaining property so acquired;

(9) conducting an isolated transaction that is completed within 30 days and is not one in the course of similar transactions; and

(10) transacting business in interstate commerce.

(b) For purposes of this [article], the ownership in this State of income-producing real property or tangible personal property, other than property excluded under subsection (a), constitutes transacting business in this State.

(c) This section does not apply in determining the contacts or activities that may subject a foreign limited liability partnership to service of process, taxation, or regulation under any other law of this State.

§ 1105. *Action by [Attorney General].*

The [Attorney General] may maintain an action to restrain a foreign limited liability partnership from transacting business in this State in violation of this [article].

General Partnership Agreement

◆ ◆ ◆

GENERAL PARTNERSHIP AGREEMENT

THIS AGREEMENT is entered into this _____ day of _____, 20_____, by and among Christopher Walter (Walter), an individual residing at _____, Timothy Mislock (Mislock), an individual residing at_____, and Erin Murphy (Murphy), an individual residing at _____. Walter, Mislock, and Murphy are hereinafter sometimes referred to individually as "Partner" and collectively as "Partners."

RECITALS

WHEREAS the Partners desire to form a partnership for the purpose of _____ and have decided that it is in their best commercial interests to do so. NOW, THEREFORE, for good and valuable consideration, the receipt and sufficiency of which are hereby acknowledged, the parties hereto agree as follows:

1. *Formation and Purpose of the Partnership.* The Partners hereby form a general partnership (the Partnership) under the laws of the State of _____ for the purpose of _____, and the carrying on of any and all activities necessary and incident thereto.

2. *Partnership Name and Address.* The name of the Partnership is "WMM Enterprises" and its principal place of business shall be located at _____, in the City of _____, State of _____, and at such other places as may be mutually agreed upon by the Partners.

3. *Term.* The Partnership shall commence on _____ and shall continue until dissolved by mutual agreement of the Partners or as provided in Paragraph 13 below.

4. *Capital Contributions.*

(a) Initial Capital Contributions. Each Partner shall contribute the following amounts:

Name	Amount
Walter	$_____
Mislock	$_____
Murphy	$_____

The contributions shall be made to the Partnership on or before _____, 20_____, or this Agreement shall be void and of no effect.

(b) Additional Capital Contributions. At such time or times as the Partners mutually agree that additional capital is necessary to operate the business of the Partnership, the Partners shall contribute additional capital in accordance with their respective partnership interests at the relevant time and in accordance with the agreed amount of the additional capital contribution and the method of payment thereof determined by the Partners. In the event that a Partner fails to make an additional capital contribution required to be made under this Agreement within the time period prescribed, such Partner shall be deemed to be a "Defaulting Partner" and a non-defaulting Partner shall be entitled to make the contribution on behalf of the Defaulting Partner and such contribution shall be a personal debt due and owing to the non-defaulting Partner from the Defaulting Partner(s) with interest at the rate of _____ percent (_____%) per annum until paid. No money or assets may be distributed by the Partnership to a Defaulting Partner unless and until the Defaulting Partner shall have paid in full the amount owed to the non-defaulting Partner(s), together with interest. Accordingly, all distributions from the Partnership which would have been made to the Defaulting Partner shall instead be made to the non-defaulting Partner(s) until the personal debt of the Defaulting Partner to the non-defaulting Partner(s) is paid in full.

(c) Return of Capital Contribution. No interest shall be paid on any Partner's capital contribution. No Partner has a right to receive a return of all or any part of his or her capital contribution except as expressly provided in this Agreement or in the event of liquidation or dissolution of the Partnership, and then only to the extent of the net assets of the Partnership available for distribution.

5. *Interests of Partners in Partnership.* Each Partner shall own the following percent interest in the Partnership:

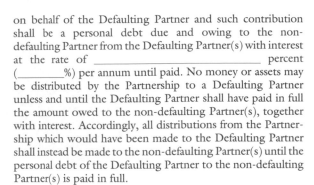

Name	Partnership Interest
Walter	_____ %
Mislock	_____ %
Murphy	_____ %

Any change in the partnership interest of any Partner shall be reflected in writing and signed by all Partners.

6. *Profits and Losses.* Partners shall share in the profits and losses of the Partnership in accordance with his or her respective partnership interest.

7. *Voting.* The Partners shall be vested with voting rights in the Partnership equal to their respective partnership interests. Except as otherwise agreed by the Partners, actions of the Partnership shall require majority action of the outstanding partnership interests.

8. *Management.* The management and operation of the business and affairs of the Partnership shall be conducted by the Partners or by such person or persons as are designated by the Partners to perform such functions on behalf of the Partnership. Walter shall be the Managing Partner and shall be entitled to enter into contracts and agreements on behalf of the Partnership for the conduct of partnership operations in the ordinary course of business. Persons dealing with the Partnership shall be entitled to rely on the power and authority of Walter.

Notwithstanding the foregoing, nothing herein is intended to grant Walter the authority to make all decisions regarding the business of the Partnership. The authority vested in Walter pertains only to the right to bind the Partnership, without the consent or approval of any other Partner, for contracts or obligations in the ordinary course of business which are necessary, appropriate, or incidental to the performance of the Partnership's business.

Walter shall not undertake any of the following business activities without the majority vote of the Partners:

(a) borrow money in excess of _____ Dollars ($_____);

(b) purchase or sell any real estate;

(c) enter into any agreement which requires the Partnership to make any payment of more than $_____ per year;

(d) compromise any claim or institute any litigation or other proceeding on behalf of the Partnership; or

(e) sell all or substantially all of the Partnership's assets.

9. *Duties of Partners.* Each of the Partners shall give his or her undivided time and attention to the business and affairs of the Partnership and shall use his or her best efforts to promote the interests of the Partnership. Partners shall have fiduciary duties to each other and to the Partnership.

10. *Books of Account.* Books of account of the transactions of the Partnership shall be kept at the principal place of business of the Partnership and shall be available at all reasonable times for inspection by any Partner. Financial statements shall be prepared on a quarterly basis and shall include a statement of cash flow. The financial statements shall be prepared by independent certified public accountants selected by the Partners. The tax and accounting year of the partnership shall be the calendar year. Any Partner, at his or her sole expense, may cause the books of the Partnership to be audited at any time. No later than thirty (30) days after the close of the fiscal year, an annual accounting shall be prepared by the Partnership's independent certified public accountants.

11. *Bank Accounts.* The funds of the Partnership shall be kept in such bank accounts or in such manner designated by the Partners. Checks drawn on partnership funds in any account shall be signed by Walter or such person or persons as the Partnership shall designate from time to time.

12. *Withdrawals, Distributions, and Expenses.*

(a) Withdrawal. Each Partner shall be permitted to draw from the funds of the Partnership _____ Dollars ($_____) per _____ for the Partner's living expenses. The sums so drawn shall be charged to the Partner and at the annual accounting shall be charged against that Partner's share of the profits. If the Partner's share of the profits is insufficient to equal the sum drawn, the Partner must pay the amount of the deficiency within ten (10) days notice from the Partnership and said deficiency shall draw interest at the rate of _____ percent (_____%) per year until paid.

(b) Distributions. So far as is practicable, the net cash flow, if any, of the Partnership (after allocation of an amount agreed upon by the Partners for working capital obligations and contingencies) shall be distributed among the Partners in accordance with their respective partnership interests at least annually or on a more frequent basis as decided by the Partners.

(c) Expenses. Partners who have incurred expenses on behalf of the Partnership in the ordinary course of Partnership business shall be reimbursed therefor upon submission to the Partnership of appropriate evidence of such expenses, as determined in the sole discretion of the Partners.

13. *Dissolution.* The Partnership shall be dissolved upon the agreement of all Partners or the sale or other disposition of all or substantially all of its assets. Upon dissolution of the Partnership, the Partners shall proceed with reasonable promptness to liquidate the assets of the Partnership. Thereafter, the assets of the

Partnership shall be used and distributed in the following order: first, to pay or provide for the payment of all Partnership liabilities and liquidating expenses; and second, to distribute to the Partners, in accordance with their respective partnership interests, the remaining assets of the Partnership.

14. *Change of Partners.* Any change of Partners shall be done only in the manner set forth in this Paragraph and any attempt to transfer otherwise shall be null and void.

(a) <u>Withdrawal of Partner.</u> Any Partner may withdraw from the Partnership by giving to each of the other Partners and the Partnership at least thirty (30) days' prior written notice of the Partner's intent to withdraw. On withdrawal of a Partner, that Partner's partnership interest shall be determined by appraisal of the value of the Partnership, and the withdrawing Partner shall be repaid his or her capital contributions within _____ days of the appraisal of the Partnership's value. After deduction for any draw or indebtedness, the withdrawing Partner shall receive cash payments in _____ equal installments, commencing immediately after the end of the fiscal year for the Partner's interest in the Partnership's profits.

(b) <u>Bankruptcy, Death, or Permanent Disability.</u> The bankruptcy, death, or permanent disability of a Partner shall not result in the dissolution of the Partnership unless required by law. The death of a Partner, the filing of any petition by any Partner under the federal Bankruptcy Act, or the permanent disability of a Partner due to sickness or injury shall immediately terminate all right, title, and interest of that Partner in the Partnership. The deceased, bankrupt, or permanently disabled Partner's share of the Partnership shall be established based on the Partner's date of death or permanent disability or date of filing of any petition under the federal Bankruptcy Act, and, after deduction for any draw or any indebtedness of the Partner, the Partner's estate, trustee in bankruptcy, or the permanently disabled Partner shall be paid a cash payment representing the Partner's capital contribution to the Partnership, the Partner's share of the net profits or losses for the current fiscal year to the date of death or permanent disability or of such filing of such petition, and the Partner's share of the current Partnership business as of the date of death or permanent disability or the date of filing of such petition.

(c) <u>New Partner.</u> New partners may be added to the Partnership by invitation from the then-existing Partners or by purchase of a withdrawing, deceased, bankrupt, or permanently disabled Partner's interest.

An invitation to a new Partner may be extended on a vote of existing Partners representing _____ percent (_____%) of the outstanding interests in the Partnership. When a Partner's interest is to be sold to a third party by a Partner leaving the Partnership, a vote on the acceptability of the proposed new partner shall be made by a vote of existing Partners representing _____ percent (_____%) of the outstanding interests of the Partnership. A new partner must execute an Amendment to this Agreement agreeing to the terms and conditions of this Agreement. In the event a proposed new partner is not found acceptable as herein provided, the Partnership shall purchase the departing Partner's interest at the price and upon the terms offered by the third party and the Partnership may resell the interest to a candidate acceptable to the Partners.

15. *Miscellaneous Provisions.*

(a) <u>Valuation.</u> Any valuation or appraisal of the Partnership or any Partner's interest therein shall be conducted by an independent appraiser selected by Partners representing a majority of the outstanding interests of the Partnership.

(b) <u>Notices.</u> All notices required by law or this Agreement shall be in writing and may be delivered to the Partners personally or may be deposited in the United States mail, postage prepaid, addressed to the Partners at their addresses identified in this Agreement.

(c) <u>Disputes.</u> Any dispute arising under the terms of this Agreement that cannot be resolved amicably by the parties shall be submitted to binding arbitration in accordance with the rules of the American Arbitration Association.

(d) <u>Amendments to Agreement.</u> No change or modification of this Agreement shall be valid or binding upon the Partners, nor shall any waiver of any term or provision hereof be deemed a waiver of such term or provision unless such change, modification, or waiver shall be in writing and signed by all of the Partners.

(e) <u>Time of Performance.</u> Whenever performance by a Partner or the Partnership is required under this Agreement, time shall be of the essence.

(f) <u>Counterparts.</u> This Agreement may be executed in one or more counterparts, but all such counterparts shall constitute one and the same Agreement.

(g) <u>Severability.</u> In the event any provision of this Agreement is invalid or unenforceable, then such provision shall be deemed severable from this Agreement.

(h) <u>Applicable law.</u> This Agreement shall be governed under the laws of the State of _____.

IN WITNESS WHEREOF, the Partners have executed this Agreement at _____ as of the day and year given herein.

Name: _____   Address: _____

Name: _____   Address: _____

Name: _____   Address: _____

E

◆ ◆ ◆

Revised Uniform Limited Partnership Act (1976) with 1985 Amendments (Selected Provisions)

◆ ◆ ◆

TABLE OF JURISDICTIONS
Wherein Act Has Been Adopted

Jurisdiction	Laws	Effective Date	Statutory Citation
Alabama	1997, 1st Sp. Sess. 97-921	10-1-1998	Code 1975, §§ 10-9B-101 to 10-9B-1206.
Alaska	1992, c. 128	7-1-1993	AS 32.11.010 to 32.11.990.
Arizona	1982, c. 192	4-22-1982[1]	A.R.S. §§ 29-301 to 29-376.
Colorado[2]	1981, c. 77	11-1-1981	West's C.R.S.A. §§ 7-62-101 to 7-62-1201.
Connecticut	1979, P.A. 440	6-14-1979[1]	C.G.S.A. §§ 34-9 to 34-38u.
Delaware	L.1982, c. 420	7-21-1982[1]	6 Del.C. §§ 17-101 to 17-1111.
Dist. of Columbia	1987, D.C. Law 7-49		D.C. Official Code, 2001 Ed. §§ 33-201.01 to 33-211.07.
Georgia[2]	1988, pp. 1016, 1018		O.C.G.A. §§ 14-9-100 to 14-9-1204.
Indiana	1988, P.L. 147	7-1-1988	West's A.I.C. 23-16-1-1 to 23-16-12-6.
Kansas	1983, c. 88	1-1-1984	K.S.A. 56-1a101 to 56-1a609.
Maryland	1981, c. 801	7-1-1982	Code, Corporations and Associations, §§ 10-101 to 10-1105.
Massachusetts	1982, c. 202	7-1-1982	M.G.L.A. c. 109, §§ 1 to 62.
Michigan	1982, P.A. 213	1-1-1983	M.C.L.A. §§ 449.1101 to 449.2108.
Mississippi	1987, c. 488	1-1-1988	Code 1972, §§ 79-14-101 to 79-14-1107.
Missouri	1985, H.B. 512, 650	1-1-1987	V.A.M.S. §§ 359.011 to 359.691.
Montana	1981, c. 522		MCA §§ 35-12-501 to 35-12-1404.
Nebraska	1981, LB 272	1-1-1982	R.R.S. 1943, §§ 67-233 to 67-296.

Jurisdiction	*Laws*	*Effective Date*	*Statutory Citation*
New Hampshire	1987, c. 349	1-1-1988	RSA 304-B:1 to 304-B:64.
New Jersey	1983, c. 489	1-1-1985	N.J.S.A. 42:2A-1 to 42:2A-73.
New York[2]	1990, c. 950	4-1-1991	McKinney's Partnership Law, §§ 121-101 to 121-1300.
North Carolina	L.1985 (Reg. Sess. 1986), c. 989	10-1-1986	G.S. §§ 59-101 to 59-1107.
Ohio	1984, H.B. 607	4-1-1985	R.C. §§ 1782.01 to 1782.63.
Oregon	1985, c. 677	7-1-1986	ORS 70.005 to 70.625.
Pennsylvania	1988, Act 177	10-1-1989	15 Pa. C.S.A. §§ 8501 to 8594.
Rhode Island	1985, c. 390	1-1-1986	Gen. Laws 1956, §§ 7-13-1 to 7-13-68.
South Carolina	1984, No. 491	6-27-1984	Code 1976, §§ 33-42-10 to 33-42-2040.
South Dakota	SL 1986, c. 391	7-1-1986	SDCL 48-7-101 to 48-7-1106.
Tennessee	1988, c. 922	1-1-1989	T.C.A. §§ 61-2-101 to 61-2-1208.
Texas	1987, c. 49	9-1-1987	Vernon's Ann. Texas Civ. St. art. 6132a-1.
Utah	1990, c. 233	7-1-1990	U.C.A. 1953, 48-2a-101 to 48-2a-1107.
Vermont	1998, no. 149	1-1-1999	11 V.S.A. §§ 3401 to 3503.
Virginia	1985, c. 607	1-1-1987	Code 1950, §§ 50-73.1 to 50-73.78.
Washington	1981, c. 51	1-1-1982	West's RCWA 25.10.010 to 25.10.955.
West Virginia	1981, c. 208	1-1-1982	Code, 47-9-1 to 47-9-63.
Wisconsin	1983-85, Act 173	9-1-1984	W.S.A. 179.01 to 179.94.
Wyoming	1979, c. 153	7-1-1979	Wyo. Stat. Ann. §§ 17-14-201 to 17-14-1104.

From *Uniform Laws Annotated,* © Thomson Reuters, reprinted by permission.
Louisiana limited partnerships are governed by La. Rev. Stat. Ann. § 9:3401 et seq.

---

[1] Date of approval.

[2] Enacted Revised Limited Partnership Act of 1976 without repealing the 1916 Limited Partnership Act.

TABLE OF JURISDICTIONS
Wherein 2001 Act Has Been Adopted

Jurisdiction	*Laws*	*Effective Date*	*Statutory Citation*
Arkansas	2007, No. 15	9-1-2007	A.C.A. §§ 4-47-101 to 4-47-1302.
California[4]	2006, c. 495	1-1-2008	Cal. Corp. Code §§ 15900 to 15912.07.
Florida	2005, c. 2005-267	1-1-2006	West's F.S.A. §§ 620.1101 to 620.2205.
Hawaii	2003, c. 210	7-1-2004	H.R.S. §§ 425E-101 to 425E-1205.
Idaho	2006, c. 144	7-1-2006	I.C. §§ 53-2-101 to 53-2-1205.
Illinois[2]	2004, c. 93-967	1-1-2005	S.H.A. 805 ILCS 215/0.10 to 215/1402.
Iowa	2004, c. 1201	1-1-2005	I.C.A. §§ 488.101 to 488.1207.
Kentucky[3]	2006, c. 149	7-12-2006	KRS 362.2.102 to 362.2.1207.
Maine[3]	2006, c. 543	7-1-2007	31 M.R.S.A. §§ 1301 to 1461.
Minnesota[1]*	2004, c. 199	1-1-2005	M.S.A. §§ 321.0101 to 321.1208.
Nevada	2007, c. 146	5-29-2007	N.R.S. 87A.010 to 87A.700.
New Mexico[5]	2007, c. 129	1-1-2008	NMSA 1978, §§ 54-2A-101 to 54-2A-1206.

Jurisdiction	Laws	Effective Date	Statutory Citation
North Dakota	2005, c. 384	7-1-2005	NDCC 45-10.2-01 to 45-10.2-117.
Oklahoma[6]	2008, c. 382	1-1-2010	54 Okla. St. Ann. §§ 500-101 to 500-1207.

[1] Enacted the Uniform Limited Partnership Act (2001), and repeals the Revised Limited Partnership Act (1976) effective January 1, 2007 without repealing the 1916 Limited Partnership Act.

*Approval date.

[2] Enacted the Uniform Limited Partnership Act (2001), and withdrew a prospective repeal of the Revised Limited Partnership Act (1976).

[3] Enacted the Uniform Limited Partnership Act (2001), and repeals the Revised Limited Partnership Act (1976) effective July 1, 2007.

[4] Enacts the Uniform Limited Partnership Act (2001) operative January 1, 2008, and repeals the Revised Limited Partnership Act (1976) effective January 1, 2010.

[5] Enacted the Uniform Limited Partnership Act (2001) effective January 1, 2008, and repeals the Revised Uniform Limited Partnership Act (1976) effective January 1, 2009.

[6] Enacted Revised Limited Partnership Act of 1976 without repealing the 1916 Limited Partnership Act. Enacts the Uniform Limited Partnership Act (2001), and repeals the Revised Uniform Limited Partnership Act (1976) and the 1916 Limited Partnership Act effective January 1, 2010.

Article I. General Provisions

101. Definitions
102. Name
103. Reservation of Name
104. Specified Office and Agent
105. Records to Be Kept
106. Nature of Business
107. Business Transactions of Partner With Partnership

Article 2. Formation; Certificate of Limited Partnership

201. Certificate of Limited Partnership
202. Amendment to Certificate
203. Cancellation of Certificate
204. Execution of Certificates
205. Execution by Judicial Act [omitted]
206. Filing in Office of Secretary of State
207. Liability for False Statement in Certificate
208. Scope of Notice
209. Delivery of Certificates to Limited Partners

Article 3. Limited Partners

301. Admission of Limited Partners
302. Voting
303. Liability to Third Parties
304. Person Erroneously Believing Himself [or Herself] Limited Partner
305. Information

Article 4. General Partners

401. Admission of Additional General Partners
402. Events of Withdrawal

403. General Powers and Liabilities
404. Contributions by General Partner
405. Voting

Article 5. Finance

501. Form of Contribution
502. Liability for Contribution
503. Sharing of Profits and Losses
504. Sharing of Distributions

Article 6. Distributions and Withdrawal

601. Interim Distributions
602. Withdrawal of General Partner
603. Withdrawal of Limited Partner
604. Distribution Upon Withdrawal
605. Distribution in Kind
606. Right to Distribution
607. Limitations on Distribution
608. Liability Upon Return of Contribution

Article 7. Assignment of Partnership Interests

701. Nature of Partnership Interest
702. Assignment of Partnership Interest
703. Rights of Creditor
704. Right of Assignee to Become Limited Partner
705. Power of Estate of Deceased or Incompetent Partner

Article 8. Dissolution

801. Nonjudicial Dissolution
802. Judicial Dissolution
803. Winding Up
804. Distribution of Assets

ARTICLE 1. GENERAL PROVISIONS

§ 101. Definitions

As used in this [Act], unless the context otherwise requires:

(1) "Certificate of limited partnership" means the certificate referred to in Section 201, and the certificate as amended or restated.

(2) "Contribution" means any cash, property, services rendered, or a promissory note or other binding obligation to contribute cash or property or to perform services, which a partner contributes to a limited partnership in his capacity as a partner.

(3) "Event of withdrawal of a general partner" means an event that causes a person to cease to be a general partner as provided in Section 402.

(4) "Foreign limited partnership" means a partnership formed under the laws of any state other than this State and having as partners one or more general partners and one or more limited partners.

(5) "General partner" means a person who has been admitted to a limited partnership as a general partner in accordance with the partnership agreement and named in the certificate of limited partnership as a general partner.

(6) "Limited partner" means a person who has been admitted to a limited partnership as a limited partner in accordance with the partnership agreement.

(7) "Limited partnership" and "domestic limited partnership" mean a partnership formed by two or more persons under the laws of this State and having one or more general partners and one or more limited partners.

(8) "Partner" means a limited or general partner.

(9) "Partnership agreement" means any valid agreement, written or oral, of the partners as to the affairs of a limited partnership and the conduct of its business.

(10) "Partnership interest" means a partner's share of the profits and losses of a limited partnership and the right to receive distributions of partnership assets.

(11) "Person" means a natural person, partnership, limited partnership (domestic or foreign), trust, estate, association, or corporation.

(12) "State" means a state, territory, or possession of the United States, the District of Columbia, or the Commonwealth of Puerto Rico.

§ 102. Name

The name of each limited partnership as set forth in its certificate of limited partnership:

(1) shall contain without abbreviation the words "limited partnership";

(2) may not contain the name of a limited partner unless (i) it is also the name of a general partner or the corporate name of a corporate general partner, or (ii) the business of the limited partnership had been carried on under that name before the admission of that limited partner;

(3) may not be the same as, or deceptively similar to, the name of any corporation or limited partnership organized under the laws of this State or licensed or registered as a foreign corporation or limited partnership in this State; and

(4) may not contain the following words [here insert prohibited words].

§ 103. Reservation of Name

(a) The exclusive right to the use of a name may be reserved by:

(1) any person intending to organize a limited partnership under this [Act] and to adopt that name;

(2) any domestic limited partnership or any foreign limited partnership registered in this State which, in either case, intends to adopt that name;

(3) any foreign limited partnership intending to register in this State and adopt that name; and

(4) any person intending to organize a foreign limited partnership and intending to have it register in this State and adopt that name.

(b) The reservation shall be made by filing with the Secretary of State an application, executed by the applicant, to reserve a specified name. If the Secretary of State finds that the name is available for use by a domestic or foreign limited partnership, he [or she] shall reserve the name for the exclusive use of the applicant for a period of 120 days. Once having so reserved a name, the same applicant may not again reserve the same name until more than 60 days after the expiration of the last 120-day period for which that applicant reserved that name. The right to the exclusive use of a reserved name may be transferred to any other person by filing in the office of the Secretary of State a notice of the transfer, executed by the applicant for whom the name was reserved and specifying the name and address of the transferee.

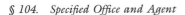

§ 104.   Specified Office and Agent

Each limited partnership shall continuously maintain in this State:

(1) an office, which may but need not be a place of its business in this State, at which shall be kept the records required by Section 105 to be maintained; and

(2) an agent for service of process on the limited partnership, which agent must be an individual resident of this State, a domestic corporation, or a foreign corporation authorized to do business in this State.

§ 105.   Records to Be Kept

(a) Each limited partnership shall keep at the office referred to in Section 104(1) the following:

(1) a current list of the full name and last known business address of each partner, separately identifying the general partners (in alphabetical order) and the limited partners (in alphabetical order);

(2) a copy of the certificate of limited partnership and all certificates of amendment thereto, together with executed copies of any powers of attorney pursuant to which any certificate has been executed;

(3) copies of the limited partnership's federal, state and local income tax returns and reports, if any, for the three most recent years;

(4) copies of any then effective written partnership agreements and of any financial statements of the limited partnership for the three most recent years; and

(5) unless contained in a written partnership agreement, a writing setting out:

(i) the amount of cash and a description and statement of the agreed value of the other property or services contributed by each partner and which each partner has agreed to contribute;

(ii) the times at which or events on the happening of which any additional contributions agreed to be made by each partner are to be made;

(iii) any right of a partner to receive, or of a general partner to make, distributions to a partner which include a return of all or any part of the partner's contribution; and

(iv) any events upon the happening of which the limited partnership is to be dissolved and its affairs wound up.

(b) Records kept under this section are subject to inspection and copying at the reasonable request and at the expense of any partner during ordinary business hours.

§ 106.   Nature of Business

A limited partnership may carry on any business that a partnership without limited partners may carry on except [here designate prohibited activities].

§ 107.   Business Transactions of Partner With Partnership

Except as provided in the partnership agreement, a partner may lend money to and transact other business with the limited partnership and, subject to other applicable law, has the same rights and obligations with respect thereto as a person who is not a partner.

ARTICLE 2.   FORMATION; CERTIFICATE OF LIMITED PARTNERSHIP

§ 201.   Certificate of Limited Partnership

(a) In order to form a limited partnership, a certificate of limited partnership must be executed and filed in the office of the Secretary of State. The certificate shall set forth:

(1) the name of the limited partnership;

(2) the address of the office and the name and address of the agent for service of process required to be maintained by Section 104;

(3) the name and the business address of each general partner;

(4) the latest date upon which the limited partnership is to dissolve; and

(5) any other matters the general partners determine to include therein.

(b) A limited partnership is formed at the time of the filing of the certificate of limited partnership in the office of the Secretary of State or at any later time specified in the certificate of limited partnership if, in either case, there has been substantial compliance with the requirements of this section.

§ 202.   Amendment to Certificate

(a) A certificate of limited partnership is amended by filing a certificate of amendment thereto in the office of the Secretary of State. The certificate shall set forth:

(1) the name of the limited partnership;

(2) the date of filing the certificate; and

(3) the amendment to the certificate.

(b) Within 30 days after the happening of any of the following events, an amendment to a certificate of limited partnership reflecting the occurrence of the event or events shall be filed:

(1) the admission of a new general partner;

(2) the withdrawal of a general partner; or

(3) the continuation of the business under Section 801 after an event of withdrawal of a general partner.

(c) A general partner who becomes aware that any statement in a certificate of limited partnership was false when made or that any arrangements or other facts described have changed, making the certificate inaccurate in any respect, shall promptly amend the certificate.

(d) A certificate of limited partnership may be amended at any time for any other proper purpose the general partners determine.

(e) No person has any liability because an amendment to a certificate of limited partnership has not been filed to reflect the occurrence of any event referred to in subsection (b) of this section if the amendment is filed within the 30-day period specified in subsection (b).

(f) A restated certificate of limited partnership may be executed and filed in the same manner as a certificate of amendment.

§ 203. *Cancellation of Certificate*

A certificate of limited partnership shall be cancelled upon the dissolution and the commencement of winding up of the partnership or at any other time there are no limited partners. A certificate of cancellation shall be filed in the office of the Secretary of State and set forth:

(1) the name of the limited partnership;

(2) the date of filing of its certificate of limited partnership;

(3) the reason for filing the certificate of cancellation;

(4) the effective date (which shall be a date certain) of cancellation if it is not to be effective upon the filing of the certificate; and

(5) any other information the general partners filing the certificate determine.

§ 204. *Execution of Certificates*

(a) Each certificate required by this Article to be filed in the office of the Secretary of State shall be executed in the following manner:

(1) an original certificate of limited partnership must be signed by all general partners;

(2) a certificate of amendment must be signed by at least one general partner and by each other general partner designated in the certificate as a new general partner; and

(3) a certificate of cancellation must be signed by all general partners.

(b) Any person may sign a certificate by an attorney-in-fact, but a power of attorney to sign a certificate relating to the admission of a general partner must specifically describe the admission.

(c) The execution of a certificate by a general partner constitutes an affirmation under the penalties of perjury that the facts stated therein are true.

§ 206. *Filing in Office of Secretary of State*

(a) Two signed copies of the certificate of limited partnership and of any certificates of amendment or cancellation (or of any judicial decree of amendment or cancellation) shall be delivered to the Secretary of State. A person who executes a certificate as an agent or fiduciary need not exhibit evidence of his [or her] authority as a prerequisite to filing. Unless the Secretary of State finds that any certificate does not conform to law, upon receipt of all filing fees required by law he [or she] shall:

(1) endorse on each duplicate original the word "Filed" and the day, month, and year of the filing thereof;

(2) file one duplicate original in his [or her] office; and

(3) return the other duplicate original to the person who filed it or his [or her] representative.

(b) Upon the filing of a certificate of amendment (or judicial decree of amendment) in the office of the Secretary of State, the certificate of limited partnership shall be amended as set forth therein, and upon the effective date of a certificate of cancellation (or a judicial decree thereof), the certificate of limited partnership is cancelled.

§ 207. *Liability for False Statement in Certificate*

If any certificate of limited partnership or certificate of amendment or cancellation contains a false statement, one who suffers loss by reliance on the statement may recover damages for the loss from:

(1) any person who executes the certificate, or causes another to execute it on his behalf, and knew, and any general partner who knew or should have known, the statement to be false at the time the certificate was executed; and

(2) any general partner who thereafter knows or should have known that any agreement or other fact described in the certificate has changed, making the statement inaccurate in any respect within a sufficient time before the statement was relied upon reasonably to have enabled that general partner to cancel or amend the certificate, or to file a petition for its cancellation or amendment under Section 205.

§ 208. *Scope of Notice*

The fact that a certificate of limited partnership is on file in the office of the Secretary of State is notice that the partnership is a limited partnership and the persons designated therein as general partners are general partners, but it is not notice of any other fact.

§ 209. *Delivery of Certificates to Limited Partners*

Upon the return by the Secretary of State pursuant to Section 206 of a certificate marked "Filed," the general partners shall promptly deliver or mail a copy of the certificate of limited partnership and each certificate of amendment or cancellation to each limited partner unless the partnership agreement provides otherwise.

ARTICLE 3. LIMITED PARTNERS

§ 301. *Admission of Limited Partners*

(a) A person becomes a limited partner:

(1) at the time the limited partnership is formed; or

(2) at any later time specified in the records of the limited partnership for becoming a limited partner.

(b) After the filing of a limited partnership's original certificate of limited partnership, a person may be admitted as an additional limited partner:

(1) in the case of a person acquiring a partnership interest directly from the limited partnership, upon compliance with the partnership agreement or, if the partnership agreement does not so provide, upon the written consent of all partners; and

(2) in the case of an assignee of a partnership interest of a partner who has the power, as provided in Section 704, to grant the assignee the right to become a limited partner, upon the exercise of that power and compliance with any conditions limiting the grant or exercise of the power.

§ 302. *Voting*

Subject to Section 303, the partnership agreement may grant to all or a specified group of the limited partners the right to vote (on a per capita or other basis) upon any matter.

§ 303.   Liability to Third Parties

(a) Except as provided in subsection (d), a limited partner is not liable for the obligations of a limited partnership unless he [or she] is also a general partner or, in addition to the exercise of his [or her] rights and powers as a limited partner, he [or she] participates in the control of the business. However, if the limited partner participates in the control of the business, he [or she] is liable only to persons who transact business with the limited partnership reasonably believing, based upon the limited partner's conduct, that the limited partner is a general partner.

(b) A limited partner does not participate in the control of the business within the meaning of subsection (a) solely by doing one or more of the following:

(1) being a contractor for or an agent or employee of the limited partnership or of a general partner or being an officer, director, or shareholder of a general partner that is a corporation;

(2) consulting with and advising a general partner with respect to the business of the limited partnership;

(3) acting as surety for the limited partnership or guaranteeing or assuming one or more specific obligations of the limited partnership;

(4) taking any action required or permitted by law to bring or pursue a derivative action in the right of the limited partnership;

(5) requesting or attending a meeting of partners;

(6) proposing, approving, or disapproving, by voting or otherwise, one or more of the following matters:

(i) the dissolution and winding up of the limited partnership;

(ii) the sale, exchange, lease, mortgage, pledge, or other transfer of all or substantially all of the assets of the limited partnership;

(iii) the incurrence of indebtedness by the limited partnership other than in the ordinary course of its business;

(iv) a change in the nature of the business;

(v) the admission or removal of a general partner;

(vi) the admission or removal of a limited partner;

(vii) a transaction involving an actual or potential conflict of interest between a general partner and the limited partnership or the limited partners;

(viii) an amendment to the partnership agreement or certificate of limited partnership; or

(ix) matters related to the business of the limited partnership not otherwise enumerated in this subsection (b), which the partnership agreement states in writing may be subject to the approval or disapproval of limited partners;

(7) winding up the limited partnership pursuant to Section 803; or

(8) exercising any right or power permitted to limited partners under this [Act] and not specifically enumerated in this subsection (b).

(c) The enumeration in subsection (b) does not mean that the possession or exercise of any other powers by a limited partner constitutes participation by him [or her] in the business of the limited partnership.

(d) A limited partner who knowingly permits his [or her] name to be used in the name of the limited partnership, except under circumstances permitted by Section 102(2), is liable to creditors who extend credit to the limited partnership without actual knowledge that the limited partner is not a general partner.

§ 304.   Person Erroneously Believing Himself [or Herself] Limited Partner

(a) Except as provided in subsection (b), a person who makes a contribution to a business enterprise and erroneously but in good faith believes that he [or she] has become a limited partner in the enterprise is not a general partner in the enterprise and is not bound by its obligations by reason of making the contribution, receiving distributions from the enterprise, or exercising any rights of a limited partner, if, on ascertaining the mistake, he [or she]:

(1) causes an appropriate certificate of limited partnership or a certificate of amendment to be executed and filed; or

(2) withdraws from future equity participation in the enterprise by executing and filing in the office of the Secretary of State a certificate declaring withdrawal under this section.

(b) A person who makes a contribution of the kind described in subsection (a) is liable as a general partner to any third party who transacts business with the enterprise (i) before the person withdraws and an appropriate certificate is filed to show withdrawal, or (ii) before an appropriate certificate is filed to show that he [or she] is not a general partner, but in either case only if the third party actually believed in good faith that the person was a general partner at the time of the transaction.

§ 305.   Information

Each limited partner has the right to:

(1) inspect and copy any of the partnership records required to be maintained by Section 105; and

(2) obtain from the general partners from time to time upon reasonable demand (i) true and full information regarding the state of the business and financial condition of the limited partnership, (ii) promptly after becoming available, a copy of the limited partnership's federal, state, and local income tax returns for each year, and (iii) other information regarding the affairs of the limited partnership as is just and reasonable.

ARTICLE 4.   GENERAL PARTNERS

§ 401.   Admission of Additional General Partners

After the filing of a limited partnership's original certificate of limited partnership, additional general partners may be admitted as provided in writing in the partnership agreement or, if the partnership agreement does not provide in writing for the admission of additional general partners, with the written consent of all partners.

§ 402.   Events of Withdrawal

Except as approved by the specific written consent of all partners at the time, a person ceases to be a general partner of a limited partnership upon the happening of any of the following events:

(1) the general partner withdraws from the limited partnership as provided in Section 602;

(2) the general partner ceases to be a member of the limited partnership as provided in Section 702;

(3) the general partner is removed as a general partner in accordance with the partnership agreement;

(4) unless otherwise provided in writing in the partnership agreement, the general partner: (i) makes an assignment for the benefit of creditors; (ii) files a voluntary petition in bankruptcy; (iii) is adjudicated a bankrupt or insolvent; (iv) files a petition or answer seeking for himself [or herself] any reorganization, arrangement, composition, readjustment, liquidation, dissolution, or similar relief under any statute, law, or regulation; (v) files an answer or other pleading admitting or failing to contest the material allegations of a petition filed against him [or her] in any proceeding of this nature; or (vi) seeks, consents to, or acquiesces in the appointment of a trustee, receiver, or liquidator of the general partner or of all or any substantial part of his [or her] properties;

(5) unless otherwise provided in writing in the partnership agreement, [120] days after the commencement of any proceeding against the general partner seeking reorganization, arrangement, composition, readjustment, liquidation, dissolution, or similar relief under any statute, law, or regulation, the proceeding has not been dismissed, or if within [90] days after the appointment without his [or her] consent or acquiescence of a trustee, receiver, or liquidator of the general partner or of all or any substantial part of his [or her] properties, the appointment is not vacated or stayed or within [90] days after the expiration of any such stay, the appointment is not vacated;

(6) in the case of a general partner who is a natural person,

(i) his [or her] death; or

(ii) the entry of an order by a court of competent jurisdiction adjudicating him [or her] incompetent to manage his [or her] person or his [or her] estate;

(7) in the case of a general partner who is acting as a general partner by virtue of being a trustee of a trust, the termination of the trust (but not merely the substitution of a new trustee);

(8) in the case of a general partner that is a separate partnership, the dissolution and commencement of winding up of the separate partnership;

(9) in the case of a general partner that is a corporation, the filing of a certificate of dissolution, or its equivalent, for the corporation or the revocation of its charter; or

(10) in the case of an estate, the distribution by the fiduciary of the estate's entire interest in the partnership.

§ 403.   *General Powers and Liabilities*

(a) Except as provided in this [Act] or in the partnership agreement, a general partner of a limited partnership has the rights and powers and is subject to the restrictions of a partner in a partnership without limited partners.

(b) Except as provided in this [Act], a general partner of a limited partnership has the liabilities of a partner in a partnership without limited partners to persons other than the partnership and the other partners. Except as provided in this [Act] or in the

partnership agreement, a general partner of a limited partnership has the liabilities of a partner in a partnership without limited partners to the partnership and to the other partners.

§ 404.   *Contributions by General Partner*

A general partner of a limited partnership may make contributions to the partnership and share in the profits and losses of, and in distributions from, the limited partnership as a general partner. A general partner also may make contributions to and share in profits, losses, and distributions as a limited partner. A person who is both a general partner and a limited partner has the rights and powers, and is subject to the restrictions and liabilities, of a general partner and, except as provided in the partnership agreement, also has the powers, and is subject to the restrictions, of a limited partner to the extent of his [or her] participation in the partnership as a limited partner.

§ 405.   *Voting*

The partnership agreement may grant to all or certain identified general partners the right to vote (on a per capita or any other basis), separately or with all or any class of the limited partners, on any matter.

ARTICLE 5.   FINANCE

§ 501.   *Form of Contribution*

The contribution of a partner may be in cash, property, or services rendered, or a promissory note or other obligation to contribute cash or property or to perform services.

§ 502.   *Liability for Contribution*

(a) A promise by a limited partner to contribute to the limited partnership is not enforceable unless set out in a writing signed by the limited partner.

(b) Except as provided in the partnership agreement, a partner is obligated to the limited partnership to perform any enforceable promise to contribute cash or property or to perform services, even if he [or she] is unable to perform because of death, disability, or any other reason. If a partner does not make the required contribution of property or services, he [or she] is obligated at the option of the limited partnership to contribute cash equal to that portion of the value, as stated in the partnership records required to be kept pursuant to Section 105, of the stated contribution which has not been made.

(c) Unless otherwise provided in the partnership agreement, the obligation of a partner to make a contribution or return money or other property paid or distributed in violation of this [Act] may be compromised only by consent of all partners. Notwithstanding the compromise, a creditor of a limited partnership who extends credit, or, otherwise acts in reliance on that obligation after the partner signs a writing which reflects the obligation and before the amendment or cancellation thereof to reflect the compromise may enforce the original obligation.

§ 503.   *Sharing of Profits and Losses*

The profits and losses of a limited partnership shall be allocated among the partners, and among classes of partners, in the manner provided in writing in the partnership agreement. If the partnership agreement does not so provide in writing, profits and losses shall be allocated on the basis of the value, as stated in the partnership records required to be kept pursuant to Section 105, of the contributions made by each partner to the extent they have been received by the partnership and have not been returned.

§ 504. *Sharing of Distributions*

Distributions of cash or other assets of a limited partnership shall be allocated among the partners and among classes of partners in the manner provided in writing in the partnership agreement. If the partnership agreement does not so provide in writing, distributions shall be made on the basis of the value, as stated in the partnership records required to be kept pursuant to Section 105, of the contributions made by each partner to the extent they have been received by the partnership and have not been returned.

ARTICLE 6. DISTRIBUTIONS AND WITHDRAWAL

§ 601. *Interim Distributions*

Except as provided in this Article, a partner is entitled to receive distributions from a limited partnership before his [or her] withdrawal from the limited partnership and before the dissolution and winding up thereof to the extent and at the times or upon the happening of the events specified in the partnership agreement.

§ 602. *Withdrawal of General Partner*

A general partner may withdraw from a limited partnership at any time by giving written notice to the other partners, but if the withdrawal violates the partnership agreement, the limited partnership may recover from the withdrawing general partner damages for breach of the partnership agreement and offset the damages against the amount otherwise distributable to him [or her].

§ 603. *Withdrawal of Limited Partner*

A limited partner may withdraw from a limited partnership at the time or upon the happening of events specified in writing in the partnership agreement. If the agreement does not specify in writing the time or the events upon the happening of which a limited partner may withdraw or a definite time for the dissolution and winding up of the limited partnership, a limited partner may withdraw upon not less than six months' prior written notice to each general partner at his [or her] address on the books of the limited partnership at its office in this State.

§ 604. *Distribution Upon Withdrawal*

Except as provided in this Article, upon withdrawal any withdrawing partner is entitled to receive any distribution to which he [or she] is entitled under the partnership agreement and, if not otherwise provided in the agreement, he [or she] is entitled to receive, within a reasonable time after withdrawal, the fair value of his [or her] interest in the limited partnership as of the date of withdrawal based upon his [or her] right to share in distributions from the limited partnership.

§ 605. *Distribution in Kind*

Except as provided in writing in the partnership agreement, a partner, regardless of the nature of his [or her] contribution, has no right to demand and receive any distribution from a limited partnership in any form other than cash. Except as provided in writing in the partnership agreement, a partner may not be compelled to accept a distribution of any asset in kind from a limited partnership to the extent that the percentage of the asset distributed to him [or her] exceeds a percentage of that asset which is equal to the percentage in which he [or she] shares in distributions from the limited partnership.

§ 606. *Right to Distribution*

At the time a partner becomes entitled to receive a distribution, he [or she] has the status of, and is entitled to all remedies available to, a creditor of the limited partnership with respect to the distribution.

§ 607. *Limitations on Distribution*

A partner may not receive a distribution from a limited partnership to the extent that, after giving effect to the distribution, all liabilities of the limited partnership, other than liabilities to partners on account of their partnership interests, exceed the fair value of the partnership assets.

§ 608. *Liability Upon Return of Contribution*

(a) If a partner has received the return of any part of his [or her] contribution without violation of the partnership agreement or this [Act], he [or she] is liable to the limited partnership for a period of one year thereafter for the amount of the returned contribution, but only to the extent necessary to discharge the limited partnership's liabilities to creditors who extended credit to the limited partnership during the period the contribution was held by the partnership.

(b) If a partner has received the return of any part of his [or her] contribution in violation of the partnership agreement or this [Act], he [or she] is liable to the limited partnership for a period of six years thereafter for the amount of the contribution wrongfully returned.

(c) A partner receives a return of his [or her] contribution to the extent that a distribution to him [or her] reduces his [or her] share of the fair value of the net assets of the limited partnership below the value, as set forth in the partnership records required to be kept pursuant to Section 105, of his contribution which has not been distributed to him [or her].

ARTICLE 7. ASSIGNMENT OF PARTNERSHIP INTERESTS

§ 701. *Nature of Partnership Interest*

A partnership interest is personal property.

§ 702. *Assignment of Partnership Interest*

Except as provided in the partnership agreement, a partnership interest is assignable in whole or in part. An assignment of a partnership interest does not dissolve a limited partnership or entitle the assignee to become or to exercise any rights of a partner. An assignment entitles the assignee to receive, to the extent assigned, only the distribution to which the assignor would be entitled. Except as provided in the partnership agreement, a partner ceases to be a partner upon assignment of all his [or her] partnership interest.

§ 703. Rights of Creditor

On application to a court of competent jurisdiction by any judgment creditor of a partner, the court may charge the partnership interest of the partner with payment of the unsatisfied amount of the judgment with interest. To the extent so charged, the judgment creditor has only the rights of an assignee of the partnership interest. This [Act] does not deprive any partner of the benefit of any exemption laws applicable to his [or her] partnership interest.

§ 704. Right of Assignee to Become Limited Partner

(a) An assignee of a partnership interest, including an assignee of a general partner, may become a limited partner if and to the extent that (i) the assignor gives the assignee that right in accordance with authority described in the partnership agreement, or (ii) all other partners consent.

(b) An assignee who has become a limited partner has, to the extent assigned, the rights and powers, and is subject to the restrictions and liabilities, of a limited partner under the partnership agreement and this [Act]. An assignee who becomes a limited partner also is liable for the obligations of his [or her] assignor to make and return contributions as provided in Articles 5 and 6. However, the assignee is not obligated for liabilities unknown to the assignee at the time he [or she] became a limited partner.

(c) If an assignee of a partnership interest becomes a limited partner, the assignor is not released from his [or her] liability to the limited partnership under Sections 207 and 502.

§ 705. Power of Estate of Deceased or Incompetent Partner

If a partner who is an individual dies or a court of competent jurisdiction adjudges him [or her] to be incompetent to manage his [or her] person or his [or her] property, the partner's executor, administrator, guardian, conservator, or other legal representative may exercise all of the partner's rights for the purpose of settling his [or her] estate or administering his [or her] property, including any power the partner had to give an assignee the right to become a limited partner. If a partner is a corporation, trust, or other entity and is dissolved or terminated, the powers of that partner may be exercised by its legal representative or successor.

ARTICLE 8. DISSOLUTION

§ 801. Nonjudicial Dissolution

A limited partnership is dissolved and its affairs shall be wound up upon the happening of the first to occur of the following:

(1) at the time specified in the certificate of limited partnership;

(2) upon the happening of events specified in writing in the partnership agreement;

(3) written consent of all partners;

(4) an event of withdrawal of a general partner unless at the time there is at least one other general partner and the written provisions of the partnership agreement permit the business of the limited partnership to be carried on by the remaining general partner and that partner does so, but the limited partnership is not dissolved and is not required to be wound up by reason of any event of withdrawal if, within 90 days after the withdrawal, all partners agree in writing to continue the business of the limited partnership and to the appointment of one or more additional general partners if necessary or desired; or

(5) entry of a decree of judicial dissolution under Section 802.

§ 802. Judicial Dissolution

On application by or for a partner the [designate the appropriate court] court may decree dissolution of a limited partnership whenever it is not reasonably practicable to carry on the business in conformity with the partnership agreement.

§ 803. Winding Up

Except as provided in the partnership agreement, the general partners who have not wrongfully dissolved a limited partnership or, if none, the limited partners, may wind up the limited partnership's affairs; but the [designate the appropriate court] court may wind up the limited partnership's affairs upon application of any partner, his [or her] legal representative, or assignee.

§ 804. Distribution of Assets

Upon the winding up of a limited partnership, the assets shall be distributed as follows:

(1) to creditors, including partners who are creditors, to the extent permitted by law, in satisfaction of liabilities of the limited partnership other than liabilities for distributions to partners under Section 601 or 604;

(2) except as provided in the partnership agreement, to partners and former partners in satisfaction of liabilities for distributions under Section 601 or 604; and

(3) except as provided in the partnership agreement, to partners first for the return of their contributions and secondly respecting their partnership interests, in the proportions in which the partners share in distributions.

ARTICLE 9. FOREIGN LIMITED PARTNERSHIPS

§ 901. Law Governing

Subject to the Constitution of this State, (i) the laws of the state under which a foreign limited partnership is organized govern its organization and internal affairs and the liability of its limited partners, and (ii) a foreign limited partnership may not be denied registration by reason of any difference between those laws and the laws of this State.

§ 902. Registration

Before transacting business in this State, a foreign limited partnership shall register with the Secretary of State. In order to register, a foreign limited partnership shall submit to the Secretary of State, in duplicate, an application for registration as a foreign limited partnership, signed and sworn to by a general partner and setting forth:

(1) the name of the foreign limited partnership and, if different, the name under which it proposes to register and transact business in this State;

(2) the State and date of its formation;

(3) the name and address of any agent for service of process on the foreign limited partnership whom the foreign limited partnership elects to appoint; the agent must be an individual resident of this State, a domestic corporation, or a foreign corporation having a place of business in, and authorized to do business in, this State;

(4) a statement that the Secretary of State is appointed the agent of the foreign limited partnership for service of process if no agent has been appointed under paragraph (3) or, if appointed, the agent's authority has been revoked or if the agent cannot be found or served with the exercise of reasonable diligence;

(5) the address of the office required to be maintained in the state of its organization by the laws of that state or, if not so required, of the principal office of the foreign limited partnership;

(6) the name and business address of each general partner; and

(7) the address of the office at which is kept a list of the names and addresses of the limited partners and their capital contributions, together with an undertaking by the foreign limited partnership to keep those records until the foreign limited partnership's registration in this State is cancelled or withdrawn.

§ 903.   Issuance of Registration

(a) If the Secretary of State finds that an application for registration conforms to law and all requisite fees have been paid, he [or she] shall:

(1) endorse on the application the word "Filed," and the month, day, and year of the filing thereof;

(2) file in his [or her] office a duplicate original of the application; and

(3) issue a certificate of registration to transact business in this State.

(b) The certificate of registration, together with a duplicate original of the application, shall be returned to the person who filed the application or his [or her] representative.

§ 904.   Name

A foreign limited partnership may register with the Secretary of State under any name, whether or not it is the name under which it is registered in its state of organization, that includes without abbreviation the words "limited partnership" and that could be registered by a domestic limited partnership.

§ 905.   Changes and Amendments

If any statement in the application for registration of a foreign limited partnership was false when made or any arrangements or other facts described have changed, making the application inaccurate in any respect, the foreign limited partnership shall promptly file in the office of the Secretary of State a certificate, signed and sworn to by a general partner, correcting such statement.

§ 906.   Cancellation of Registration

A foreign limited partnership may cancel its registration by filing with the Secretary of State a certificate of cancellation signed and sworn to by a general partner. A cancellation does not terminate the authority of the Secretary of State to accept service of process on the foreign limited partnership with respect to [claims for relief][causes of action] arising out of the transactions of business in this State.

§ 907.   Transaction of Business Without Registration

(a) A foreign limited partnership transacting business in this State may not maintain any action, suit, or proceeding in any court of this State until it has registered in this State.

(b) The failure of a foreign limited partnership to register in this State does not impair the validity of any contract or act of the foreign limited partnership or prevent the foreign limited partnership from defending any action, suit, or proceeding in any court of this State.

(c) A limited partner of a foreign limited partnership is not liable as a general partner of the foreign limited partnership solely by reason of having transacted business in this State without registration.

(d) A foreign limited partnership, by transacting business in this State without registration, appoints the Secretary of State as its agent for service of process with respect to [claims for relief] [causes of action] arising out of the transaction of business in this State.

§ 908.   Action by [Appropriate Official]

The [designate the appropriate official] may bring an action to restrain a foreign limited partnership from transacting business in this State in violation of this Article.

ARTICLE 10.   DERIVATIVE ACTIONS

§ 1001.   Right of Action

A limited partner may bring an action in the right of a limited partnership to recover a judgment in its favor if general partners with authority to do so have refused to bring the action or if an effort to cause those general partners to bring the action is not likely to succeed.

§ 1002.   Proper Plaintiff

In a derivative action, the plaintiff must be a partner at the time of bringing the action and (i) must have been a partner at the time of the transaction of which he [or she] complains or (ii) his [or her] status as a partner must have devolved upon him [or her] by operation of law or pursuant to the terms of the partnership agreement from a person who was a partner at the time of the transaction.

§ 1003.   Pleading

In a derivative action, the complaint shall set forth with particularity the effort of the plaintiff to secure initiation of the action by a general partner or the reasons for not making the effort.

§ 1004.   Expenses

If a derivative action is successful, in whole or in part, or if anything is received by the plaintiff as a result of a judgment, compromise, or settlement of an action or claim, the court may award the plaintiff reasonable expenses, including reasonable attorney's fees, and shall direct him [or her] to remit to the limited partnership the remainder of those proceeds received by him [or her].

ARTICLE 11. MISCELLANEOUS

§ 1101. *Construction and Application*

This [Act] shall be so applied and construed to effectuate its general purpose to make uniform the law with respect to the subject of this [Act] among states enacting it.

§ 1102. *Short Title*

This [Act] may be cited as the Uniform Limited Partnership Act.

§ 1103. *Severability*

If any provision of this [Act] or its application to any person or circumstances is held invalid, the invalidity does not affect other provisions or applications of the [Act] which can be given effect without the invalid provision or application, and to this end the provisions of this [Act] are severable.

§ 1105. *Rules for Cases Not Provided for in This [Act]*

In any case not provided for in this [Act] the provisions of the Uniform Partnership Act govern.

Model Business Corporation Act (Selected Provisions)

◆ ◆ ◆

CHAPTER 1. GENERAL PROVISIONS

SUBCHAPTER A. SHORT TITLE AND RESERVATION OF POWER

§ 1.01. Short Title

This Act shall be known and may be cited as the "[name of state] Business Corporation Act."

SUBCHAPTER D. DEFINITIONS

§ 1.40. Act Definitions

In this Act:

(1) "Articles of incorporation" means the original articles of incorporation, all amendments thereof, and any other documents filed with the secretary of state with respect to a domestic business corporation under any provision of this Act except section 16.21. If any document filed under this Act restates the articles in their entirety, thenceforth the "articles" shall not include any prior documents.

(2) "Authorized shares" means the shares of all classes a domestic or foreign corporation is authorized to issue.

(3) "Conspicuous" means so written that a reasonable person against whom the writing is to operate should have noticed it. For example, printing in italics or boldface or contrasting color, or typing in capitals or underlined, is conspicuous.

(4) "Corporation" or "domestic corporation" means a corporation for profit, which is not a foreign corporation, incorporated under or subject to the provisions of this Act.

(5) "Deliver" or "delivery" means any method of delivery used in conventional commercial practice, including delivery by hand, mail, commercial delivery, and electronic transmission.

(6) "Distribution" means a direct or indirect transfer of money or other property (except its own shares) or incurrence

of indebtedness by a corporation to or for the benefit of its shareholders in respect of any of its shares. A distribution may be in the form of a declaration or payment of a dividend; a purchase, redemption, or other acquisition of shares; a distribution of indebtedness; or otherwise.

(6A) "Domestic unincorporated entity" means an unincorporated entity whose internal affairs are governed by the laws of this state.

(7) "Effective date of notice" is defined in section 1.41.

(7A) "Electronic transmission" or "electronically transmitted" means any process of communications not directly involving the physical transfer of paper that is suitable for the retention, retrieval, and reproduction of information by the recipient.

(7B) "Eligible entity" means a domestic or foreign unincorporated entity or a domestic or foreign nonprofit corporation.

(7C) "Eligible interests" means interests or memberships.

(8) "Employee" includes an officer but not a director. A director may accept duties that make him also an employee.

(9) "Entity" includes a domestic and foreign business corporation; domestic and foreign nonprofit corporation; estate; trust; domestic and foreign unincorporated entity; and state, United States, and foreign government.

(9A) The phrase "facts objectively ascertainable" outside of a filed document or plan is defined in section 1.20(k).

(9AA) "Expenses" means reasonable expenses of any kind that are incurred in connection with a matter.

(9B) "Filing entity" means an unincorporated entity that is of a type that is created by filing a public organic document.

(10) "Foreign corporation" means a corporation incorporated under a law other than the law of this state, which would be a business corporation if incorporated under the laws of this state.

(10A) "Foreign nonprofit corporation" means a corporation incorporated under a law other than the law of this state, which would be a nonprofit corporation if incorporated under the laws of this state.

(10B) "Foreign unincorporated entity" means an unincorporated entity whose internal affairs are governed by an organic law of a jurisdiction other than this state.

(11) "Governmental subdivision" includes an authority, county, district, and municipality.

(12) "Includes" denotes a partial definition.

(13) "Individual" means a natural person.

(13A) "Interest" means either or both of the following rights under the organic law of an unincorporated entity:

(i) the right to receive distributions from the entity either in the ordinary course or upon liquidation; or

(ii) the right to receive notice or vote on issues involving its internal affairs, other than as agent, assignee, proxy or person responsible for managing its business and affairs.

(13B) "Interest holder" means a person who holds of record an interest.

(14) "Means" denotes an exhaustive definition.

(14A) "Membership" means the rights of a member in a domestic or foreign nonprofit corporation.

(14B) "Nonfiling entity" means an unincorporated entity that is not created by filing a public organic document.

(14C) "Nonprofit corporation" or "domestic nonprofit corporation" means a corporation incorporated under the laws of this state and subject to the provisions of the [*Model Nonprofit Corporation Act*].

(15) "Notice" is defined in section 1.41.

(15A) "Organic document" means a public organic document or a private organic document.

(15B) "Organic law" means the statute governing the internal affairs of a domestic or foreign business or nonprofit corporation or unincorporated entity.

(15C) "Owner liability" means personal liability for a debt, obligation or liability of a domestic or foreign business or nonprofit corporation or unincorporated entity that is imposed on a person:

(i) solely by reason of the person's status as a shareholder, member or interest holder; or

(ii) by the articles of incorporation, bylaws or an organic document under a provision of the organic law of an entity authorizing the articles of incorporation, bylaws or an organic document to make one or more specified shareholders, members or interest holders liable in their capacity as shareholders, members or interest holders for all or specified debts, obligations or liabilities of the entity.

(16) "Person" includes an individual and an entity.

(17) "Principal office" means the office (in or out of this state) so designated in the annual report where the principal executive offices of a domestic or foreign corporation are located.

(17A) "Private organic document" means any document (other than the public organic document, if any) that determines the internal governance of an unincorporated entity. Where a private organic document has been amended or restated, the term means the private organic document as last amended or restated.

(17B) "Public organic document" means the document, if any, that is filed of public record to create an unincorporated entity. Where a public organic document has been amended or restated, the term means the public organic document as last amended or restated.

(18) "Proceeding" includes civil suit and criminal, administrative, and investigatory action.

(18A) "Public corporation" means a corporation that has shares listed on a national securities exchange or regularly traded in a market maintained by one or more members of a national securities association.

(19) "Record date" means the date established under chapter 6 or 7 on which a corporation determines the identity of its shareholders and their shareholdings for purposes of this Act. The determinations shall be made as of the close of business on the record date unless another time for doing so is specified when the record date is fixed.

(20) "Secretary" means the corporate officer to whom the board of directors has delegated responsibility under section 8.40(c) for custody of the minutes of the meetings of the board of directors and of the shareholders and for authenticating records of the corporation.

(21) "Shareholder" means the person in whose name shares are registered in the records of a corporation or the beneficial owner of shares to the extent of the rights granted by a nominee certificate on file with a corporation.

(22) "Shares" means the units into which the proprietary interests in a corporation are divided.

(22A) "Sign" or "signature" includes any manual, facsimile, conformed, or electronic signature.

(23) "State," when referring to a part of the United States, includes a state and commonwealth (and their agencies and governmental subdivisions) and a territory and insular possession (and their agencies and governmental subdivisions) of the United States.

(24) "Subscriber" means a person who subscribes for shares in a corporation, whether before or after incorporation.

(24A) "Unincorporated entity" means an organization or artificial legal person that either has a separate legal existence or has the power to acquire an estate in real property in its own name and that is not any of the following: a domestic or foreign business or nonprofit corporation, an estate, a trust, a state, the United States, or a foreign government. The term includes a general partnership, limited liability company, limited partnership, business trust, joint stock association and unincorporated nonprofit association.

(25) "United States" includes district, authority, bureau, commission, department, and any other agency of the United States.

(26) "Voting group" means all shares of one or more classes or series that under the articles of incorporation or this Act are entitled to vote and be counted together collectively on a matter at a meeting of shareholders. All shares entitled by the articles of incorporation or this Act to vote generally on the matter are for that purpose a single voting group.

(27) "Voting power" means the current power to vote in the election of directors.

§ 1.41. Notice

(a) Notice under this Act must be in writing unless oral notice is reasonable under the circumstances. Notice by electronic transmission is written notice.

(b) Notice may be communicated in person; by mail or other method of delivery; or by telephone, voice mail, or other electronic means. If these forms of personal notice are impracticable, notice may be communicated by a newspaper of general circulation in the area where published; or by radio, television, or other form of public broadcast communication.

(c) Written notice by a domestic or foreign corporation to its shareholder, if in a comprehensible form, is effective (i) upon deposit in the United States mail, if mailed postpaid and correctly addressed to the shareholder's address shown in the corporation's current record of shareholders, or (ii) when electronically transmitted to the shareholder in a manner authorized by the shareholder.

(d) Written notice to a domestic or foreign corporation (authorized to transact business in this state) may be addressed to its registered agent at its registered office or to the secretary of the corporation at its principal office shown in its most recent annual report or, in the case of a foreign corporation that has not

yet delivered an annual report, in its application for a certificate of authority.

(e) Except as provided in subsection (c), written notice, if in a comprehensible form, is effective at the earliest of the following:

(1) when received;

(2) five days after its deposit in the United States Mail, if mailed postpaid and correctly addressed;

(3) on the date shown on the return receipt, if sent by registered or certified mail, return receipt requested, and the receipt is signed by or on behalf of the addressee.

(f) Oral notice is effective when communicated if communicated in a comprehensible manner.

(g) If this Act prescribes notice requirements for particular circumstances, those requirements govern. If articles of incorporation or bylaws prescribe notice requirements, not inconsistent with this section or other provisions of this Act, those requirements govern.

§ 1.42. Number of Shareholders

(a) For purposes of this Act, the following identified as a shareholder in a corporation's current record of shareholders constitutes one shareholder:

(1) three or fewer co-owners;

(2) a corporation, partnership, trust, estate, or other entity;

(3) the trustees, guardians, custodians, or other fiduciaries of a single trust, estate, or account.

(b) For purposes of this Act, shareholdings registered in substantially similar names constitute one shareholder if it is reasonable to believe that the names represent the same person.

§ 1.43. Qualified Director

(a) A "qualified director" is a director who, at the time action is to be taken under:

(1) section 7.33, does not have (i) a material interest in the outcome of the proceeding, or (ii) a material relationship with a person who has such an interest;

(2) section 8.53 or 8.55, (i) is not a party to the proceeding, (ii) is not a director as to whom a transaction is a director's conflicting interest transaction or who sought a disclaimer of the corporation's interest in a business opportunity under section 8.70, which transaction or disclaimer is challenged in to proceeding, and (ii) does not have a material relationship with a director described in either clause (i) or clause (ii) of this subsection (a)(2).

(3) section 8.62, is not a director (i) as to whom the transaction is a director's conflicting interest transaction, or (ii) who has a material relationship with another director as to whom the transaction is a director's conflicting interest transaction; or

(4) section 8.70, would be a qualified director under subsection (a)(3) if the business opportunity were a director's conflicting interest transaction.

(b) For purposes of this section:

(1) "material relationship" means a familial, financial, professional, employment or other relationship that would

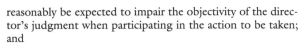

reasonably be expected to impair the objectivity of the director's judgment when participating in the action to be taken; and

(2) "material interest" means an actual or potential benefit or detriment (other than one which would devolve on the corporation or the shareholders generally) that would reasonably be expected to impair the objectivity of the director's judgment when participating in the action to be taken.

(c) The presence of one or more of the following circumstances shall not automatically prevent a director from being a qualified director:

(1) nomination or selection of the director to the current board by any director who is not a qualified director with respect to the matter (or by any person that has a material relationship with that director), acting alone or participating with others

(2) service as a director of another corporation of which a director who is not a qualified director with respect to the matter (or any individual who has a material relationship with that director), is or was also a director; or

(3) with respect to action to be taken under section 7.44, status as a named defendant, as a director against whom action is demanded, or as a director who approved the conduct being challenged.

§ 1.44. *Householding*

(a) A corporation has delivered written notice or any other report or statement under this Act, the articles of incorporation or the bylaws to all shareholders who share a common address if:

(1) The corporation delivers one copy of the notice, report or statement to the common address;

(2) The corporation addresses the notice, report or statement to those shareholders either as a group or to each of those shareholders individually or to the shareholders in a form to which each of those shareholders has consented; and

(3) Each of those shareholders consents to delivery of a single copy of such notice, report or statement to the shareholders' common address. Any such consent shall be revocable by any of such shareholders who deliver written notice of revocation to the corporation. If such written notice of revocation is delivered, the corporation shall begin providing individual notices, reports or other statements to the revoking shareholder no later than 30 days after delivery of the written notice of revocation.

(b) Any shareholder who fails to object by written notice to the corporation, within 60 days of written notice by the corporation of its intention to send single copies of notices, reports or statements to shareholders who share a common address as permitted by subsection (a), shall be deemed to have consented to receiving such single copy at the common address.

CHAPTER 2. INCORPORATION

§ 2.01. *Incorporators*

One or more persons may act as the incorporator or incorporators of a corporation by delivering articles of incorporation to the secretary of state for filing.

§ 2.02. *Articles of Incorporation*

(a) The articles of incorporation must set forth:

(1) a corporate name for the corporation that satisfies the requirements of section 4.01;

(2) the number of shares the corporation is authorized to issue;

(3) the street address of the corporation's initial registered office and the name of its initial registered agent at that office; and

(4) the name and address of each incorporator.

(b) The articles of incorporation may set forth:

(1) the names and addresses of the individuals who are to serve as the initial directors;

(2) provisions not inconsistent with law regarding:

(i) the purpose or purposes for which the corporation is organized;

(ii) managing the business and regulating the affairs of the corporation;

(iii) defining, limiting, and regulating the powers of the corporation, its board of directors, and shareholders;

(iv) a par value for authorized shares or classes of shares;

(v) the imposition of personal liability on shareholders for the debts of the corporation to a specified extent and upon specified conditions;

(3) any provision that under this Act is required or permitted to be set forth in the bylaws; and

(4) a provision eliminating or limiting the liability of a director to the corporation or its shareholders for money damages for any action taken, or any failure to take any action, as a director, except liability for (A) the amount of a financial benefit received by a director to which he is not entitled; (B) an intentional infliction of harm on the corporation or the shareholders; (C) a violation of section 8.33; or (D) an intentional violation of criminal law; and

(5) a provision permitting or making obligatory indemnification of a director for liability (as defined in section 8.50(5)) to any person for any action taken, or any failure to take any action, as a director, except liability for (A) receipt of a financial benefit to which he is not entitled, (B) an intentional infliction of harm on the corporation or its shareholders, (C) a violation of section 8.33, or (D) an intentional violation of criminal law.

(c) The articles of incorporation need not set forth any of the corporate powers enumerated in this Act.

(d) Provisions of the articles of incorporation may be made dependent upon facts objectively ascertainable outside the articles of incorporation in accordance with section 1.20(k).

§ 2.03. *Incorporation*

(a) Unless a delayed effective date is specified, the corporate existence begins when the articles of incorporation are filed.

(b) The secretary of state's filing of the articles of incorporation is conclusive proof that the incorporators satisfied all conditions precedent to incorporation except in a proceeding by the state to cancel or revoke the incorporation or involuntarily dissolve the corporation.

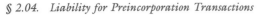

§ 2.04. *Liability for Preincorporation Transactions*

All persons purporting to act as or on behalf of a corporation, knowing there was no incorporation under this Act, are jointly and severally liable for all liabilities created while so acting.

§ 2.05. *Organization of Corporation*

(a) After incorporation:

(1) if initial directors are named in the articles of incorporation, the initial directors shall hold an organizational meeting, at the call of a majority of the directors, to complete the organization of the corporation by appointing officers, adopting bylaws, and carrying on any other business brought before the meeting;

(2) if initial directors are not named in the articles, the incorporator or incorporators shall hold an organizational meeting at the call of a majority of the incorporators:

(i) to elect directors and complete the organization of the corporation; or

(ii) to elect a board of directors who shall complete the organization of the corporation.

(b) Action required or permitted by this Act to be taken by incorporators at an organizational meeting may be taken without a meeting if the action taken is evidenced by one or more written consents describing the action taken and signed by each incorporator.

(c) An organizational meeting may be held in or out of this state.

§ 2.06. *Bylaws*

(a) The incorporators or board of directors of a corporation shall adopt initial bylaws for the corporation.

(b) The bylaws of a corporation may contain any provision for managing the business and regulating the affairs of the corporation that is not inconsistent with law or the articles of incorporation.

CHAPTER 3. PURPOSES AND POWERS

§ 3.01. *Purposes*

(a) Every corporation incorporated under this Act has the purpose of engaging in any lawful business unless a more limited purpose is set forth in the articles of incorporation.

(b) A corporation engaging in a business that is subject to regulation under another statute of this state may incorporate under this Act only if permitted by, and subject to all limitations of, the other statute.

§ 3.02. *General Powers*

Unless its articles of incorporation provide otherwise, every corporation has perpetual duration and succession in its corporate name and has the same powers as an individual to do all things necessary or convenient to carry out its business and affairs, including without limitation power:

(1) to sue and be sued, complain and defend in its corporate name;

(2) to have a corporate seal, which may be altered at will, and to use it, or a facsimile of it, by impressing or affixing it or in any other manner reproducing it;

(3) to make and amend bylaws, not inconsistent with its articles of incorporation or with the laws of this state, for managing the business and regulating the affairs of the corporation;

(4) to purchase, receive, lease, or otherwise acquire, and own, hold, improve, use, and otherwise deal with, real or personal property, or any legal or equitable interest in property, wherever located;

(5) to sell, convey, mortgage, pledge, lease, exchange, and otherwise dispose of all or any part of its property;

(6) to purchase, receive, subscribe for, or otherwise acquire; own, hold, vote, use, sell, mortgage, lend, pledge, or otherwise dispose of; and deal in and with shares or other interests in, or obligations of, any other entity;

(7) to make contracts and guarantees, incur liabilities, borrow money, issue its notes, bonds, and other obligations (which may be convertible into or include the option to purchase other securities of the corporation), and secure any of its obligations by mortgage or pledge of any of its property, franchises, or income;

(8) to lend money, invest and reinvest its funds, and receive and hold real and personal property as security for repayment;

(9) to be a promoter, partner, member, associate, or manager of any partnership, joint venture, trust, or other entity;

(10) to conduct its business, locate offices, and exercise the powers granted by this Act within or without this state;

(11) to elect directors and appoint officers, employees, and agents of the corporation, define their duties, fix their compensation, and lend them money and credit;

(12) to pay pensions and establish pension plans, pension trusts, profit sharing plans, share bonus plans, share option plans, and benefit or incentive plans for any or all of its current or former directors, officers, employees, and agents;

(13) to make donations for the public welfare or for charitable, scientific, or educational purposes;

(14) to transact any lawful business that will aid governmental policy;

(15) to make payments or donations, or do any other act, not inconsistent with law, that furthers the business and affairs of the corporation.

§ 3.04. *Ultra Vires*

(a) Except as provided in subsection (b), the validity of corporate action may not be challenged on the ground that the corporation lacks or lacked power to act.

(b) A corporation's power to act may be challenged:

(1) in a proceeding by a shareholder against the corporation to enjoin the act;

(2) in a proceeding by the corporation, directly, derivatively, or through a receiver, trustee, or other legal representative, against an incumbent or former director, officer, employee, or agent of the corporation; or

(3) in a proceeding by the Attorney General under section 14.30.

(c) In a shareholder's proceeding under subsection (b)(1) to enjoin an unauthorized corporate act, the court may enjoin or set aside the act, if equitable and if all affected persons are parties to the proceeding, and may award damages for loss (other than anticipated profits) suffered by the corporation or another party because of enjoining the unauthorized act.

CHAPTER 4.   NAME

§ 4.01.   Corporate Name

(a) A corporate name:

(1) must contain the word "corporation," "incorporated," "company," or "limited," or the abbreviation "corp.," "inc.," "co.," or "ltd.," or words or abbreviations of like import in another language; and

(2) may not contain language stating or implying that the corporation is organized for a purpose other than that permitted by section 3.01 and its articles of incorporation. . . . [remainder of section omitted]

§ 4.02.   Reserved Name

(a) A person may reserve the exclusive use of a corporate name, including a fictitious name for a foreign corporation whose corporate name is not available, by delivering an application to the secretary of state for filing. The application must set forth the name and address of the applicant and the name proposed to be reserved. If the secretary of state finds that the corporate name applied for is available, he shall reserve the name for the applicant's exclusive use for a nonrenewable 120-day period.

(b) The owner of a reserved corporate name may transfer the reservation to another person by delivering to the secretary of state a signed notice of the transfer that states the name and address of the transferee.

§ 4.03.   Registered Name

(a) A foreign corporation may register its corporate name, or its corporate name with any addition required by section 15.06, if the name is distinguishable upon the records of the secretary of state from the corporate names that are not available under section 4.01(b)(3).

(b) A foreign corporation registers its corporate name, or its corporate name with any addition required by section 15.06, by delivering to the secretary of state for filing an application:

(1) setting forth its corporate name, or its corporate name with any addition required by section 15.06, the state or country and date of its incorporation, and a brief description of the nature of the business in which it is engaged; and

(2) accompanied by a certificate of existence (or a document of similar import) from the state or country of incorporation.

(c) The name is registered for the applicant's exclusive use upon the effective date of the application.

(d) A foreign corporation whose registration is effective may renew it for successive years by delivering to the secretary of state for filing a renewal application, which complies with the requirements of subsection (b), between October 1 and Decem-ber 31 of the preceding year. The renewal application renews the registration for the following calendar year.

(e) A foreign corporation whose registration is effective may thereafter qualify as a foreign corporation under that name or consent in writing to the use of that name by a corporation thereafter incorporated under this Act or by another foreign corporation thereafter authorized to transact business in this state. The registration terminates when the domestic corporation is incorporated or the foreign corporation qualifies or consents to the qualification of another foreign corporation under the registered name.

CHAPTER 5.   OFFICE AND AGENT

§ 5.01.   Registered Office and Registered Agent

Each corporation must continuously maintain in this state:

(1) a registered office that may be the same as any of its places of business; and

(2) a registered agent, who may be:

(i) an individual who resides in this state and whose business office is identical with the registered office;

(ii) a domestic corporation or not-for-profit domestic corporation whose business office is identical with the registered office; or

(iii) a foreign corporation or not-for-profit foreign corporation authorized to transact business in this state whose business office is identical with the registered office.

§ 5.02.   Change of Registered Office or Registered Agent

(a) A corporation may change its registered office or registered agent by delivering to the secretary of state for filing a statement of change that sets forth:

(1) the name of the corporation;

(2) the street address of its current registered office;

(3) if the current registered office is to be changed, the street address of the new registered office;

(4) the name of its current registered agent;

(5) if the current registered agent is to be changed, the name of the new registered agent and the new agent's written consent (either on the statement or attached to it) to the appointment; and

(6) that after the change or changes are made, the street addresses of its registered office and the business office of its registered agent will be identical.

(b) If a registered agent changes the street address of his business office, he may change the street address of the registered office of any corporation for which he is the registered agent by notifying the corporation in writing of the change and signing (either manually or in facsimile) and delivering to the secretary of state for filing a statement that complies with the requirements of subsection (a) and recites that the corporation has been notified of the change.

§ 5.03.   Resignation of Registered Agent

(a) A registered agent may resign his agency appointment by signing and delivering to the secretary of state for filing the signed original and two exact or conformed copies of a statement of resignation. The statement may include a statement that the registered office is also discontinued.

(b) After filing the statement the secretary of state shall mail one copy to the registered office (if not discontinued) and the other copy to the corporation at its principal office.

(c) The agency appointment is terminated, and the registered office discontinued if so provided, on the 31st day after the date on which the statement was filed.

§ 5.04. *Service on Corporation*

(a) A corporation's registered agent is the corporation's agent for service of process, notice, or demand required or permitted by law to be served on the corporation.

(b) If a corporation has no registered agent, or the agent cannot with reasonable diligence be served, the corporation may be served by registered or certified mail, return receipt requested, addressed to the secretary of the corporation at its principal office. Service is perfected under this subsection at the earliest of:

(1) the date the corporation receives the mail;

(2) the date shown on the return receipt, if signed on behalf of the corporation; or

(3) five days after its deposit in the United States Mail, if mailed postpaid and correctly addressed.

(c) This section does not prescribe the only means, or necessarily the required means, of serving a corporation.

Chapter 6. Shares and Distributions

Subchapter A. Shares

§ 6.01. *Authorized Shares*

(a) The articles of incorporation must set forth any classes of shares and series of shares within a class, and the number of shares of each class and series, that the corporation is authorized to issue. If more than one class or series of shares is authorized, the articles of incorporation must prescribe a distinguishing designation for each class or series and must describe, prior to the issuance of shares of a class or series, the terms, including the preferences, rights, and limitations, of that class or series. Except to the extent varied as permitted by this section, all shares of a class or series must have terms, including preferences, rights and limitations, that are identical with those of other shares of the same class or series.

(b) The articles of incorporation must authorize (1) one or more classes or series of shares that together have unlimited voting rights, and (2) one or more classes or series of shares (which may be the same class or classes as those with voting rights) that together are entitled to receive the net assets of the corporation upon dissolution.

(c) The articles of incorporation may authorize one or more classes of shares that:

(1) have special, conditional, or limited voting rights, or no right to vote, except to the extent otherwise provided by this Act;

(2) are redeemable or convertible as specified in the articles of incorporation: (i) at the option of the corporation, the shareholder, or another person or upon the occurrence of a specified event; (ii) for cash, indebtedness, securities, or other property; (iii) at prices and in amounts specified, or determined in accordance with a formula;

(3) entitle the holders to distributions calculated in any manner, including dividends that may be cumulative, noncumulative, or partially cumulative;

(4) have preference over any other class or series of shares with respect to distributions, including distributions upon the dissolution of the corporation.

(d) Terms of shares may be made dependent upon facts objectively ascertainable outside the articles of incorporation in accordance with section 1.20(k).

(e) Any of the terms of shares may vary among holders of the same class or series so long as such variations are expressly set forth in the articles of incorporation.

(f) The description of the preferences, rights and limitations of classes or series of shares in subsection (c) is not exhaustive.

§ 6.02. *Terms of Class or Series Determined by Board of Directors*

(a) If the articles of incorporation so provide, the board of directors is authorized, without shareholder approval, to:

(1) classify any unissued shares into one or more classes or into one or more series within a class,

(2) reclassify any unissued shares of any class into one or more classes or into one or more series within one or more classes, or

(3) reclassify any unissued shares of any series of any class into one or more classes or into one or more series within a class.

(b) If the board of directors acts pursuant to subsection (a), it must determine the terms, including the preferences, rights and limitations, to the same extent permitted under section 6.01, of:

(1) any class of shares before the issuance of any shares of that class, or

(2) any series within a class before the issuance of any shares of that series.

(c) Before issuing any shares of a class or series created under this section, the corporation must deliver to the secretary of state for filing articles of amendment setting forth the terms determined under subsection (a).

§ 6.03. *Issued and Outstanding Shares*

(a) A corporation may issue the number of shares of each class or series authorized by the articles of incorporation. Shares that are issued are outstanding shares until they are reacquired, redeemed, converted, or canceled.

(b) The reacquisition, redemption, or conversion of outstanding shares is subject to the limitations of subsection (c) of this section and to section 6.40.

(c) At all times that shares of the corporation are outstanding, one or more shares that together have unlimited voting rights and one or more shares that together are entitled to receive the net assets of the corporation upon dissolution must be outstanding.

§ 6.04. *Fractional Shares*

(a) A corporation may:

(1) issue fractions of a share or pay in money the value of fractions of a share;

(2) arrange for disposition of fractional shares by the shareholders;

(3) issue scrip in registered or bearer form entitling the holder to receive a full share upon surrendering enough scrip to equal a full share.

(b) Each certificate representing scrip must be conspicuously labeled "scrip" and must contain the information required by section 6.25(b).

(c) The holder of a fractional share is entitled to exercise the rights of a shareholder, including the right to vote, to receive dividends, and to participate in the assets of the corporation upon liquidation. The holder of scrip is not entitled to any of these rights unless the scrip provides for them.

(d) The board of directors may authorize the issuance of scrip subject to any condition considered desirable, including:

(1) that the scrip will become void if not exchanged for full shares before a specified date; and

(2) that the shares for which the scrip is exchangeable may be sold and the proceeds paid to the scripholders.

SUBCHAPTER B.   ISSUANCE OF SHARES

§ 6.20.   *Subscription for Shares Before Incorporation*

(a) A subscription for shares entered into before incorporation is irrevocable for six months unless the subscription agreement provides a longer or shorter period or all the subscribers agree to revocation.

(b) The board of directors may determine the payment terms of subscriptions for shares that were entered into before incorporation, unless the subscription agreement specifies them. A call for payment by the board of directors must be uniform so far as practicable as to all shares of the same class or series, unless the subscription agreement specifies otherwise.

(c) Shares issued pursuant to subscriptions entered into before incorporation are fully paid and nonassessable when the corporation receives the consideration specified in the subscription agreement.

(d) If a subscriber defaults in payment of money or property under a subscription agreement entered into before incorporation, the corporation may collect the amount owed as any other debt. Alternatively, unless the subscription agreement provides otherwise, the corporation may rescind the agreement and may sell the shares if the debt remains unpaid more than 20 days after the corporation sends written demand for payment to the subscriber.

(e) A subscription agreement entered into after incorporation is a contract between the subscriber and the corporation subject to section 6.21.

§ 6.21.   *Issuance of Shares*

(a) The powers granted in this section to the board of directors may be reserved to the shareholders by the articles of incorporation.

(b) The board of directors may authorize shares to be issued for consideration consisting of any tangible or intangible property or benefit to the corporation, including cash, promissory notes, services performed, contracts for services to be performed, or other securities of the corporation.

(c) Before the corporation issues shares, the board of directors must determine that the consideration received or to be received for shares to be issued is adequate. That determination by the board of directors is conclusive insofar as the adequacy of consideration for the issuance of shares relates to whether the shares are validly issued, fully paid, and nonassessable.

(d) When the corporation receives the consideration for which the board of directors authorized the issuance of shares, the shares issued therefor are fully paid and nonassessable.

(e) The corporation may place in escrow shares issued for a contract for future services or benefits or a promissory note, or make other arrangements to restrict the transfer of the shares, and may credit distributions in respect of the shares against their purchase price, until the services are performed, the note is paid, or the benefits received. If the services are not performed, the note is not paid, or the benefits are not received, the shares escrowed or restricted and the distributions credited may be cancelled in whole or part.

(f) (1) An issuance of shares or other securities convertible into or rights exercisable for shares, in a transaction or a series of integrated transactions, requires approval of the shareholders, at a meeting at which a quorum exists consisting of at least a majority of the votes entitled to be cast on the matter, if:

(i) the shares, other securities, or rights are issued for consideration other than cash or cash equivalents, and

(ii) the voting power of shares that are issued and issuable as a result of the transaction or series of integrated transactions will comprise more than 20 percent of the voting power of the shares of the corporation that were outstanding immediately before the transaction.

(2) In this subsection:

(i) For purposes of determining the voting power of shares issued and issuable as a result of a transaction or series of integrated transactions, the voting power of shares shall be the greater of (A) the voting power of the shares to be issued, or (B) the voting power of the shares that would be outstanding after giving effect to the conversion of convertible shares and other securities and the exercise of rights to be issued.

(ii) A series of transactions is integrated if consummation of one transaction is made contingent on consummation of one or more of the other transactions.

§ 6.22.   *Liability of Shareholders*

(a) A purchaser from a corporation of its own shares is not liable to the corporation or its creditors with respect to the shares except to pay the consideration for which the shares were authorized to be issued (section 6.21) or specified in the subscription agreement (section 6.20).

(b) Unless otherwise provided in the articles of incorporation, a shareholder of a corporation is not personally liable for the acts or debts of the corporation except that he may become personally liable by reason of his own acts or conduct.

§ 6.23.   *Share Dividends*

(a) Unless the articles of incorporation provide otherwise, shares may be issued pro rata and without consideration to the corporation's shareholders or to the shareholders of one or more classes or series. An issuance of shares under this subsection is a share dividend.

(b) Shares of one class or series may not be issued as a share dividend in respect of shares of another class or series unless (1) the articles of incorporation so authorize, (2) a majority of the votes entitled to be cast by the class or series to be issued approve the issue, or (3) there are no outstanding shares of the class or series to be issued.

(c) If the board of directors does not fix the record date for determining shareholders entitled to a share dividend, it is the date the board of directors authorizes the share dividend.

§ 6.24. Share Options

(a) A corporation may issue rights, options, or warrants for the purchase of shares or other securities of the corporation. The board of directors shall determine (i) the terms upon which the rights, options, or warrants are issued and (ii) the terms, including the consideration for which the shares or other securities are to be issued. The authorization by the board of directors for the corporation to issue such rights, options, or warrants constitutes authorization of the issuance of the shares or other securities for which the rights, options or warrants are exercisable.

(b) The terms and conditions of such rights, options or warrants, including those outstanding on the effective date of this section, may include, without limitation, restrictions or conditions that:

(1) preclude or limit the exercise, transfer or receipt of such rights, options or warrants by any person or persons owning or offering to acquire a specified number or percentage of the outstanding shares or other securities of the corporation or by any transferee or transferees of any such person or persons, or

(2) invalidate or void such rights, options or warrants held by any such person or persons or any such transferee or transferees.

§ 6.25. Form and Content of Certificates

(a) Shares may but need not be represented by certificates. Unless this Act or another statute expressly provides otherwise, the rights and obligations of shareholders are identical whether or not their shares are represented by certificates.

(b) At a minimum each share certificate must state on its face:

(1) the name of the issuing corporation and that it is organized under the law of this state;

(2) the name of the person to whom issued; and

(3) the number and class of shares and the designation of the series, if any, the certificate represents.

(c) If the issuing corporation is authorized to issue different classes of shares or different series within a class, the designations, relative rights, preferences, and limitations applicable to each class and the variations in rights, preferences, and limitations determined for each series (and the authority of the board of directors to determine variations for future series) must be summarized on the front or back of each certificate. Alternatively, each certificate may state conspicuously on its front or back that the corporation will furnish the shareholder this information on request in writing and without charge.

(d) Each share certificate (1) must be signed (either manually or in facsimile) by two officers designated in the bylaws or by the board of directors and (2) may bear the corporate seal or its facsimile.

(e) If the person who signed (either manually or in facsimile) a share certificate no longer holds office when the certificate is issued, the certificate is nevertheless valid.

§ 6.26. Shares Without Certificates

(a) Unless the articles of incorporation or bylaws provide otherwise, the board of directors of a corporation may authorize the issue of some or all of the shares of any or all of its classes or series without certificates. The authorization does not affect shares already represented by certificates until they are surrendered to the corporation.

(b) Within a reasonable time after the issue or transfer of shares without certificates, the corporation shall send the shareholder a written statement of the information required on certificates by section 6.25(b) and (c), and, if applicable, section 6.27.

§ 6.27. Restriction on Transfer of Shares and Other Securities

(a) The articles of incorporation, bylaws, an agreement among shareholders, or an agreement between shareholders and the corporation may impose restrictions on the transfer or registration of transfer of shares of the corporation. A restriction does not affect shares issued before the restriction was adopted unless the holders of the shares are parties to the restriction agreement or voted in favor of the restriction.

(b) A restriction on the transfer or registration of transfer of shares is valid and enforceable against the holder or a transferee of the holder if the restriction is authorized by this section and its existence is noted conspicuously on the front or back of the certificate or is contained in the information statement required by section 6.26(b). Unless so noted, a restriction is not enforceable against a person without knowledge of the restriction.

(c) A restriction on the transfer or registration of transfer of shares is authorized:

(1) to maintain the corporation's status when it is dependent on the number or identity of its shareholders;

(2) to preserve exemptions under federal or state securities law;

(3) for any other reasonable purpose.

(d) A restriction on the transfer or registration of transfer of shares may:

(1) obligate the shareholder first to offer the corporation or other persons (separately, consecutively, or simultaneously) an opportunity to acquire the restricted shares;

(2) obligate the corporation or other persons (separately, consecutively, or simultaneously) to acquire the restricted shares;

(3) require the corporation, the holders of any class of its shares, or another person to approve the transfer of the restricted shares, if the requirement is not manifestly unreasonable;

(4) prohibit the transfer of the restricted shares to designated persons or classes of persons, if the prohibition is not manifestly unreasonable.

(e) For purposes of this section, "shares" includes a security convertible into or carrying a right to subscribe for or acquire shares.

§ 6.28.   *Expense of Issue*

A corporation may pay the expenses of selling or underwriting its shares, and of organizing or reorganizing the corporation, from the consideration received for shares.

SUBCHAPTER C.   SUBSEQUENT ACQUISITION OF SHARES BY SHAREHOLDERS AND CORPORATION

§ 6.30.   *Shareholders' Preemptive Rights*

(a) The shareholders of a corporation do not have a preemptive right to acquire the corporation's unissued shares except to the extent the articles of incorporation so provide.

(b) A statement included in the articles of incorporation that "the corporation elects to have preemptive rights" (or words of similar import) means that the following principles apply except to the extent the articles of incorporation expressly provide otherwise:

(1) The shareholders of the corporation have a preemptive right, granted on uniform terms and conditions prescribed by the board of directors to provide a fair and reasonable opportunity to exercise the right, to acquire proportional amounts of the corporation's unissued shares upon the decision of the board of directors to issue them.

(2) A shareholder may waive his preemptive right. A waiver evidenced by a writing is irrevocable even though it is not supported by consideration.

(3) There is no preemptive right with respect to:

(i) shares issued as compensation to directors, officers, agents, or employees of the corporation, its subsidiaries or affiliates;

(ii) shares issued to satisfy conversion or option rights created to provide compensation to directors, officers, agents, or employees of the corporation, its subsidiaries or affiliates;

(iii) shares authorized in articles of incorporation that are issued within six months from the effective date of incorporation;

(iv) shares sold otherwise than for money.

(4) Holders of shares of any class without general voting rights but with preferential rights to distributions or assets have no preemptive rights with respect to shares of any class.

(5) Holders of shares of any class with general voting rights but without preferential rights to distributions or assets have no preemptive rights with respect to shares of any class with preferential rights to distributions or assets unless the shares with preferential rights are convertible into or carry a right to subscribe for or acquire shares without preferential rights.

(6) Shares subject to preemptive rights that are not acquired by shareholders may be issued to any person for a period of one year after being offered to shareholders at a consideration set by the board of directors that is not lower than the consideration set for the exercise of preemptive rights. An offer at a lower consideration or after the expiration of one year is subject to the shareholders' preemptive rights.

(c) For purposes of this section, "shares" includes a security convertible into or carrying a right to subscribe for or acquire shares.

§ 6.31.   *Corporation's Acquisition of Its Own Shares*

(a) A corporation may acquire its own shares and shares so acquired constitute authorized but unissued shares.

(b) If the articles of incorporation prohibit the reissue of acquired shares, the number of authorized shares is reduced by the number of shares acquired.

SUBCHAPTER D.   DISTRIBUTIONS

§ 6.40.   *Distributions to Shareholders*

(a) A board of directors may authorize and the corporation may make distributions to its shareholders subject to restriction by the articles of incorporation and the limitation in subsection (c).

(b) If the board of directors does not fix the record date for determining shareholders entitled to a distribution (other than one involving a purchase, redemption, or other acquisition of the corporation's shares), it is the date the board of directors authorizes the distribution.

(c) No distribution may be made if, after giving it effect:

(1) the corporation would not be able to pay its debts as they become due in the usual course of business; or

(2) the corporation's total assets would be less than the sum of its total liabilities plus (unless the articles of incorporation permit otherwise) the amount that would be needed, if the corporation were to be dissolved at the time of the distribution, to satisfy the preferential rights upon dissolution of shareholders whose preferential rights are superior to those receiving the distribution.

(d) The board of directors may base a determination that a distribution is not prohibited under subsection (c) either on financial statements prepared on the basis of accounting practices and principles that are reasonable in the circumstances or on a fair valuation or other method that is reasonable in the circumstances.

(e) Except as provided in subsection (g), the effect of a distribution under subsection (c) is measured:

(1) in the case of distribution by purchase, redemption, or other acquisition of the corporation's shares, as of the earlier of (i) the date money or other property is transferred or debt incurred by the corporation or (ii) the date the shareholder ceases to be a shareholder with respect to the acquired shares;

(2) in the case of any other distribution of indebtedness, as of the date the indebtedness is distributed; and

(3) in all other cases, as of (i) the date the distribution is authorized if the payment occurs within 120 days after the date of authorization or (ii) the date the payment is made if it occurs more than 120 days after the date of authorization.

(f) A corporation's indebtedness to a shareholder incurred by reason of a distribution made in accordance with this section is at parity with the corporation's indebtedness to its general, unsecured creditors except to the extent subordinated by agreement.

(g) Indebtedness of a corporation, including indebtedness issued as a distribution, is not considered a liability for purposes of determinations under subsection (c) if its terms provide that payment of principal and interest are made only if and to the extent that payment of a distribution to shareholders could then be made under this section. If the indebtedness is issued as a distribution, each payment of principal or interest is treated as a distribution, the effect of which is measured on the date the payment is actually made.

(h) This section shall not apply to distributions in liquidation under chapter 14.

CHAPTER 7. SHAREHOLDERS

SUBCHAPTER A. MEETINGS

§ 7.01. Annual Meeting

(a) Unless directors are elected by written consent in lieu of an annual meeting as permitted by section 7.04, a corporation shall hold a meeting of shareholders annually at a time stated in or fixed in accordance with the bylaws; provided, however, that if a corporation's articles of incorporation authorize shareholders to cumulate their votes when electing directors pursuant to section 7.28, directors may not be elected by less than unanimous written consent.

(b) Annual shareholders' meetings may be held in or out of this state at the place stated in or fixed in accordance with the bylaws. If no place is stated in or fixed in accordance with the bylaws, annual meetings shall be held at the corporation's principal office.

(c) The failure to hold an annual meeting at the time stated in or fixed in accordance with a corporation's bylaws does not affect the validity of any corporate action.

§ 7.02. Special Meeting

(a) A corporation shall hold a special meeting of shareholders:

(1) on call of its board of directors or the person or persons authorized to do so by the articles of incorporation or bylaws; or

(2) if shareholders having at least 10 percent of all the votes entitled to be cast on an issue proposed to be considered at the proposed special meeting sign, date, and deliver to the corporation one or more written demands for the meeting describing the purpose or purposes for which it is to be held, provided that the articles of incorporation may fix a lower percentage or a higher percentage not exceeding 25 percent of all the votes entitled to be cast on any issue proposed to be considered. Unless otherwise provided in the articles of incorporation, a written demand for a special meeting may be revoked by a writing to that effect received by the corporation prior to the receipt by the corporation of demands sufficient in number to require the holding of a special meeting.

(b) If not otherwise fixed under section 7.03 or 7.07, the record date for determining shareholders entitled to demand a special meeting is the date the first shareholder signs the demand.

(c) Special shareholders' meetings may be held in or out of this state at the place stated in or fixed in accordance with the bylaws. If no place is stated or fixed in accordance with the bylaws, special meetings shall be held at the corporation's principal office.

(d) Only business within the purpose or purposes described in the meeting notice required by section 7.05(c) may be conducted at a special shareholders' meeting.

§ 7.03. Court-Ordered Meeting

(a) The [name or describe] court of the county where a corporation's principal office (or, if none in this state, its registered office) is located may summarily order a meeting to be held:

(1) on application of any shareholder of the corporation entitled to participate in an annual meeting if an annual meeting was not held or action by written consent in lieu thereof did not become effective within the earlier of six months after the end of the corporation's fiscal year or 15 months after its last annual meeting; or

(2) on application of a shareholder who signed a demand for a special meeting valid under section 7.02, if:

(i) notice of the special meeting was not given within 30 days after the date the demand was delivered to the corporation's secretary; or

(ii) the special meeting was not held in accordance with the notice.

(b) The court may fix the time and place of the meeting, determine the shares entitled to participate in the meeting, specify a record date for determining shareholders entitled to notice of and to vote at the meeting, prescribe the form and content of the meeting notice, fix the quorum required for specific matters to be considered at the meeting (or direct that the votes represented at the meeting constitute a quorum for action on those matters), and enter other orders necessary to accomplish the purpose or purposes of the meeting.

§ 7.04. Action Without Meeting

(a) Action required or permitted by this Act to be taken at a shareholders' meeting may be taken without a meeting if the action is taken by all the shareholders entitled to vote on the action. The action must be evidenced by one or more written consents bearing the date of signature and describing the action taken, signed by all the shareholders entitled to vote on the action, and delivered to the corporation for inclusion in the minutes or filing with the corporate records.

(b) The articles of incorporation may provide that any action required or permitted by this Act to be taken at a shareholders' meeting may be taken without a meeting, and without prior notice, if consents in writing setting forth the action so taken are signed by the holders of outstanding shares having not less than the minimum number of votes that would be required to authorize or take the action at a meeting at which all shares entitled to vote on the action were present and voted.

The written consent shall bear the date of signature of the shareholder who signs the consent and be delivered to the corporation for inclusion in the minutes or filing with the corporate records.

(c) If not otherwise fixed under section 7.07 and if prior board action is not required respecting the action to be taken without a meeting, the record date for determining the shareholders entitled to take action without a meeting shall be the first date on which a signed written consent is delivered to the corporation. If not otherwise fixed under section 7.07 and if prior board action is required respecting the action to be taken without a meeting, the record date shall be the close of business on the day the resolution of the board taking such prior action is adopted. No written consent shall be effective to take the corporate action referred to therein unless, within 60 days of the earliest date on which a consent delivered to the corporation as required by this section was signed, written consents signed by the holders of shares having sufficient votes to take the action have been delivered to the corporation. A written consent may be revoked by a writing to that effect delivered to the corporation before unrevoked written consents sufficient in number to take the corporate action are delivered to the corporation.

(d) A consent signed pursuant to the provisions of this section has the effect of a vote taken at a meeting and may be described as such in any document. Unless the articles of incorporation, bylaws or a resolution of the board of directors provides for a reasonable delay to permit tabulation of written consents, the action taken by written consent shall be effective when written consents signed by the holders of shares having sufficient votes to take the action are delivered to the corporation.

(e) If this Act requires that notice of a proposed action be given to nonvoting shareholders and the action is to be taken by written consent of the voting shareholders, the corporation must give its nonvoting shareholders written notice of the action not more than 10 days after (i) written consents sufficient to take the action have been delivered to the corporation, or (ii) such later date that tabulation of consents is completed pursuant to an authorization under subsection (d). The notice must reasonably describe the action taken and contain or be accompanied by the same material that, under any provision of this Act, would have been required to be sent to nonvoting shareholders in a notice of a meeting at which the proposed action would have been submitted to the shareholders for action.

(f) If action is taken by less than unanimous written consent of the voting shareholders, the corporation must give its nonconsenting voting shareholders written notice of the action not more than 10 days after (i) written consents sufficient to take the action have been delivered to the corporation, or (ii) such later date that tabulation of consents is completed pursuant to an authorization under subsection (d). The notice must reasonably describe the action taken and contain or be accompanied by the same material that, under any provision of this Act, would have been required to be sent to voting shareholders in a notice of a meeting at which the action would have been submitted to the shareholders for action.

(g) The notice requirements in subsections (e) and (f) shall not delay the effectiveness of actions taken by written consent, and a failure to comply with such notice requirements shall not invalidate actions taken by written consent, provided that this subsection shall not be deemed to limit judicial power to fashion any appropriate remedy in favor of a shareholder adversely affected by a failure to give such notice within the required time period.

(h) An electronic transmission may be used to consent to an action, if the electronic transmission contains or is accompanied by information from which the corporation can determine the date on which the electronic transmission was signed and that the electronic transmission was authorized by the shareholder, the shareholder's agent or the shareholder's attorney-in-fact.

(i) Delivery of a written consent to the corporation under this section is delivery to the corporation's registered agent at its registered office or to the secretary of the corporation at its principal office.

§ 7.05. *Notice of Meeting*

(a) A corporation shall notify shareholders of the date, time, and place of each annual and special shareholders' meeting no fewer than 10 nor more than 60 days before the meeting date. Unless this Act or the articles of incorporation require otherwise, the corporation is required to give notice only to shareholders entitled to vote at the meeting.

(b) Unless this Act or the articles of incorporation require otherwise, notice of an annual meeting need not include a description of the purpose or purposes for which the meeting is called.

(c) Notice of a special meeting must include a description of the purpose or purposes for which the meeting is called.

(d) If not otherwise fixed under sections 7.03 or 7.07, the record date for determining shareholders entitled to notice of and to vote at an annual or special shareholders' meeting is the day before the first notice is delivered to shareholders.

(e) Unless the bylaws require otherwise, if an annual or special shareholders' meeting is adjourned to a different date, time, or place, notice need not be given of the new date, time, or place if the new date, time, or place is announced at the meeting before adjournment. If a new record date for the adjourned meeting is or must be fixed under section 7.07, however, notice of the adjourned meeting must be given under this section to persons who are shareholders as of the new record date.

§ 7.06. *Waiver of Notice*

(a) A shareholder may waive any notice required by this Act, the articles of incorporation, or bylaws before or after the date and time stated in the notice. The waiver must be in writing, be signed by the shareholder entitled to the notice, and be delivered to the corporation for inclusion in the minutes or filing with the corporate records.

(b) A shareholder's attendance at a meeting:

(1) waives objection to lack of notice or defective notice of the meeting, unless the shareholder at the beginning of the meeting objects to holding the meeting or transacting business at the meeting;

(2) waives objection to consideration of a particular matter at the meeting that is not within the purpose or purposes described in the meeting notice, unless the shareholder objects to considering the matter when it is presented.

§ 7.07. Record Date

(a) The bylaws may fix or provide the manner of fixing the record date for one or more voting groups in order to determine the shareholders entitled to notice of a shareholders' meeting, to demand a special meeting, to vote, or to take any other action. If the bylaws do not fix or provide for fixing a record date, the board of directors of the corporation may fix a future date as the record date.

(b) A record date fixed under this section may not be more than 70 days before the meeting or action requiring a determination of shareholders.

(c) A determination of shareholders entitled to notice of or to vote at a shareholders' meeting is effective for any adjournment of the meeting unless the board of directors fixes a new record date, which it must do if the meeting is adjourned to a date more than 120 days after the date fixed for the original meeting.

(d) If a court orders a meeting adjourned to a date more than 120 days after the date fixed for the original meeting, it may provide that the original record date continues in effect or it may fix a new record date.

§ 7.08. Conduct of the Meeting

(a) At each meeting of shareholders, a chair shall preside. The chair shall be appointed as provided in the bylaws or, in the absence of such provision, by the board.

(b) The chair, unless the articles of incorporation or bylaws provide otherwise, shall determine the order of business and shall have the authority to establish rules for the conduct of the meeting.

(c) The rules adopted for, and the conduct of, the meeting shall be fair to shareholders.

(d) The chair of the meeting shall announce at the meeting when the polls close for each matter voted upon. If no announcement is made, the polls shall be deemed to have closed upon the final adjournment of the meeting. After the polls close, no ballots, proxies or votes nor any revocations or changes thereto may be accepted.

Subchapter B. Voting

§ 7.20. Shareholders' List for Meeting

(a) After fixing a record date for a meeting, a corporation shall prepare an alphabetical list of the names of all its shareholders who are entitled to notice of a shareholders' meeting. The list must be arranged by voting group (and within each voting group by class or series of shares) and show the address of and number of shares held by each shareholder.

(b) The shareholders' list must be available for inspection by any shareholder, beginning two business days after notice of the meeting is given for which the list was prepared and continuing through the meeting, at the corporation's principal office or at a place identified in the meeting notice in the city where the meeting will be held. A shareholder, his agent, or attorney is entitled on written demand to inspect and, subject to the requirements of section 16.02(c), to copy the list, during regular business hours and at his expense, during the period it is available for inspection.

(c) The corporation shall make the shareholders' list available at the meeting, and any shareholder, his agent, or attorney is entitled to inspect the list at any time during the meeting or any adjournment.

(d) If the corporation refuses to allow a shareholder, his agent, or attorney to inspect the shareholders' list before or at the meeting (or copy the list as permitted by subsection (b)), the [name or describe] court of the county where a corporation's principal office (or, if none in this state, its registered office) is located, on application of the shareholder, may summarily order the inspection or copying at the corporation's expense and may postpone the meeting for which the list was prepared until the inspection or copying is complete.

(e) Refusal or failure to prepare or make available the shareholders' list does not affect the validity of action taken at the meeting.

§ 7.21. Voting Entitlement of Shares

(a) Except as provided in subsections (b) and (c) or unless the articles of incorporation provide otherwise, each outstanding share, regardless of class, is entitled to one vote on each matter voted on at a shareholders' meeting. Only shares are entitled to vote.

(b) Absent special circumstances, the shares of a corporation are not entitled to vote if they are owned, directly or indirectly, by a second corporation, domestic or foreign, and the first corporation owns, directly or indirectly, a majority of the shares entitled to vote for directors of the second corporation.

(c) Subsection (b) does not limit the power of a corporation to vote any shares, including its own shares, held by it in a fiduciary capacity.

(d) Redeemable shares are not entitled to vote after notice of redemption is mailed to the holders and a sum sufficient to redeem the shares has been deposited with a bank, trust company, or other financial institution under an irrevocable obligation to pay the holders the redemption price on surrender of the shares.

§ 7.22. Proxies

(a) A shareholder may vote his shares in person or by proxy.

(b) A shareholder or his agent or attorney-in-fact may appoint a proxy to vote or otherwise act for the shareholder by signing an appointment form, or by an electronic transmission. An electronic transmission must contain or be accompanied by information from which one can determine that the shareholder, the shareholder's agent, or the shareholder's attorney-in-fact authorized the electronic transmission.

(c) An appointment of a proxy is effective when a signed appointment form or an electronic transmission of the appointment is received by the inspector of election or the officer or agent of the corporation authorized to tabulate votes. An appointment is valid for 11 months unless a longer period is expressly provided in the appointment.

(d) An appointment of a proxy is revocable unless the appointment form or electronic transmission conspicuously states that it is irrevocable and the appointment is coupled

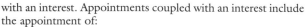

with an interest. Appointments coupled with an interest include the appointment of:

(1) a pledgee;

(2) a person who purchased or agreed to purchase the shares;

(3) a creditor of the corporation who extended it credit under terms requiring the appointment;

(4) an employee of the corporation whose employment contract requires the appointment; or

(5) a party to a voting agreement created under section 7.31.

(e) The death or incapacity of the shareholder appointing a proxy does not affect the right of the corporation to accept the proxy's authority unless notice of the death or incapacity is received by the secretary or other officer or agent authorized to tabulate votes before the proxy exercises his authority under the appointment.

(f) An appointment made irrevocable under subsection (d) is revoked when the interest with which it is coupled is extinguished.

(g) A transferee for value of shares subject to an irrevocable appointment may revoke the appointment if he did not know of its existence when he acquired the shares and the existence of the irrevocable appointment was not noted conspicuously on the certificate representing the shares or on the information state ment for shares without certificates.

(h) Subject to section 7.24 and to any express limitation on the proxy's authority stated in the appointment form or electronic transmission, a corporation is entitled to accept the proxy's vote or other action as that of the shareholder making the appointment.

§ 7.23. Shares Held by Nominees

(a) A corporation may establish a procedure by which the beneficial owner of shares that are registered in the name of a nominee is recognized by the corporation as the shareholder. The extent of this recognition may be determined in the procedure.

(b) The procedure may set forth:

(1) the types of nominees to which it applies;

(2) the rights or privileges that the corporation recognizes in a beneficial owner;

(3) the manner in which the procedure is selected by the nominee;

(4) the information that must be provided when the procedure is selected;

(5) the period for which selection of the procedure is effective; and

(6) other aspects of the rights and duties created.

§ 7.24. Corporation's Acceptance of Votes

(a) If the name signed on a vote, consent, waiver, or proxy appointment corresponds to the name of a shareholder, the corporation if acting in good faith is entitled to accept the vote, consent, waiver, or proxy appointment and give it effect as the act of the shareholder. [Remainder of section omitted.]

§ 7.25. Quorum and Voting Requirements for Voting Groups

(a) Shares entitled to vote as a separate voting group may take action on a matter at a meeting only if a quorum of those shares exists with respect to that matter. Unless the articles of incorporation or this Act provide otherwise, a majority of the votes entitled to be cast on the matter by the voting group constitutes a quorum of that voting group for action on that matter.

(b) Once a share is represented for any purpose at a meeting, it is deemed present for quorum purposes for the remainder of the meeting and for any adjournment of that meeting unless a new record date is or must be set for that adjourned meeting.

(c) If a quorum exists, action on a matter (other than the election of directors) by a voting group is approved if the votes cast within the voting group favoring the action exceed the votes cast opposing the action, unless the articles of incorporation or this Act require a greater number of affirmative votes.

(d) An amendment of articles of incorporation adding, changing, or deleting a quorum or voting requirement for a voting group greater than specified in subsection (a) or (c) is governed by section 7.27.

(e) The election of directors is governed by section 7.28.

§ 7.26. Action by Single and Multiple Voting Groups

(a) If the articles of incorporation or this Act provide for voting by a single voting group on a matter, action on that matter is taken when voted upon by that voting group as provided in section 7.25.

(b) If the articles of incorporation or this Act provide for voting by two or more voting groups on a matter, action on that matter is taken only when voted upon by each of those voting groups counted separately as provided in section 7.25. Action may be taken by one voting group on a matter even though no action is taken by another voting group entitled to vote on the matter.

§ 7.27. Greater Quorum or Voting Requirements

(a) The articles of incorporation may provide for a greater quorum or voting requirement for shareholders (or voting groups of shareholders) than is provided for by this Act.

(b) An amendment to the articles of incorporation that adds, changes, or deletes a greater quorum or voting requirement must meet the same quorum requirement and be adopted by the same vote and voting groups required to take action under the quorum and voting requirements then in effect or proposed to be adopted, whichever is greater.

§ 7.28. Voting for Directors; Cumulative Voting

(a) Unless otherwise provided in the articles of incorporation, directors are elected by a plurality of the votes cast by the shares entitled to vote in the election at a meeting at which a quorum is present.

(b) Shareholders do not have a right to cumulate their votes for directors unless the articles of incorporation so provide.

(c) A statement included in the articles of incorporation that "[all] [a designated voting group of] shareholders are entitled to cumulate their votes for directors" (or words of similar import) means that the shareholders designated are entitled to multiply the number of votes they are entitled to cast by the number of directors for whom they are entitled to vote and cast the product for a single candidate or distribute the product among two or more candidates.

(d) Shares otherwise entitled to vote cumulatively may not be voted cumulatively at a particular meeting unless:

(1) the meeting notice or proxy statement accompanying the notice states conspicuously that cumulative voting is authorized; or

(2) a shareholder who has the right to cumulate his votes gives notice to the corporation not less than 48 hours before the time set for the meeting of the shareholder's intent to cumulate his votes during the meeting, and if one shareholder gives this notice, all other shareholders in the same voting group participating in the election are entitled to cumulate their votes without giving further notice.

§ 7.29. *Inspectors of Election*

(a) A public corporation shall, and any other corporation may, appoint one or more inspectors to act at a meeting of shareholders and make a written report of the inspectors' determinations. Each inspector shall take and sign an oath faithfully to execute the duties of inspector with strict impartiality and according to the best of the inspector's ability.

(b) The inspectors shall

(1) ascertain the number of shares outstanding and the voting power of each;

(2) determine the shares represented at a meeting;

(3) determine the validity of proxies and ballots;

(4) count all votes; and

(5) determine the result.

(c) An inspector may be an officer or employee of the corporation.

Subchapter C. Voting Trusts and Agreements

§ 7.30. *Voting Trusts*

(a) One or more shareholders may create a voting trust, conferring on a trustee the right to vote or otherwise act for them, by signing an agreement setting out the provisions of the trust (which may include anything consistent with its purpose) and transferring their shares to the trustee. When a voting trust agreement is signed, the trustee shall prepare a list of the names and addresses of all owners of beneficial interests in the trust, together with the number and class of shares each transferred to the trust, and deliver copies of the list and agreement to the corporation's principal office.

(b) A voting trust becomes effective on the date the first shares subject to the trust are registered in the trustee's name. A voting trust is valid for not more than 10 years after its effective date unless extended under subsection (c).

(c) All or some of the parties to a voting trust may extend it for additional terms of not more than 10 years each by signing an extension agreement and obtaining the voting trustee's written consent to the extension. An extension is valid for 10 years from the date the first shareholder signs the extension

agreement. The voting trustee must deliver copies of the extension agreement and list of beneficial owners to the corporation's principal office. An extension agreement binds only those parties signing it.

§ 7.31. *Voting Agreements*

(a) Two or more shareholders may provide for the manner in which they will vote their shares by signing an agreement for that purpose. A voting agreement created under this section is not subject to the provisions of section 7.30.

(b) A voting agreement created under this section is specifically enforceable.

§ 7.32. *Shareholder Agreements*

(a) An agreement among the shareholders of a corporation that complies with this section is effective among the shareholders and the corporation even though it is inconsistent with one or more other provisions of this Act in that it:

(1) eliminates the board of directors or restricts the discretion or powers of the board of directors;

(2) governs the authorization or making of distributions whether or not in proportion to ownership of shares, subject to the limitations in section 6.40;

(3) establishes who shall be directors or officers of the corporation, or their terms of office or manner of selection or removal;

(4) governs, in general or in regard to specific matters, the exercise or division of voting power by or between the shareholders and directors or by or among any of them, including use of weighted voting rights or director proxies;

(5) establishes the terms and conditions of any agreement for the transfer or use of property or the provision of services between the corporation and any shareholder, director, officer or employee of the corporation or among any of them;

(6) transfers to one or more shareholders or other persons all or part of the authority to exercise the corporate powers or to manage the business and affairs of the corporation, including the resolution of any issue about which there exists a deadlock among directors or shareholders;

(7) requires dissolution of the corporation at the request of one or more of the shareholders or upon the occurrence of a specified event or contingency; or

(8) otherwise governs the exercise of the corporate powers or the management of the business and affairs of the corporation or the relationship among the shareholders, the directors and the corporation, or among any of them, and is not contrary to public policy.

(b) An agreement authorized by this section shall be:

(1) set forth (A) in the articles of incorporation or bylaws and approved by all persons who are shareholders at the time of the agreement or (B) in a written agreement that is signed by all persons who are shareholders at the time of the agreement and is made known to the corporation;

(2) subject to amendment only by all persons who are shareholders at the time of the amendment, unless the agreement provides otherwise; and

(3) valid for 10 years, unless the agreement provides otherwise.

(c) The existence of an agreement authorized by this section shall be noted conspicuously on the front or back of each certificate for outstanding shares or on the information statement required by section 6.26(b). [Remainder of subsection omitted.]

(d) An agreement authorized by this section shall cease to be effective when the corporation becomes a public corporation. If the agreement ceases to be effective for any reason, the board of directors may, if the agreement is contained or referred to in the corporation's articles of incorporation or bylaws, adopt an amendment to the articles of incorporation or bylaws, without shareholder action, to delete the agreement and any references to it.

(e) An agreement authorized by this section that limits the discretion or powers of the board of directors shall relieve the directors of, and impose upon the person or persons in whom such discretion or powers are vested, liability for acts or omissions imposed by law on directors to the extent that the discretion or powers of the directors are limited by the agreement.

(f) The existence or performance of an agreement authorized by this section shall not be a ground for imposing personal liability on any shareholder for the acts or debts of the corporation even if the agreement or its performance treats the corporation as if it were a partnership or results in failure to observe the corporate formalities otherwise applicable to the matters governed by the agreement.

(g) Incorporators or subscribers for shares may act as shareholders with respect to an agreement authorized by this section if no shares have been issued when the agreement is made.

SUBCHAPTER D. DERIVATIVE PROCEEDINGS

§ 7.40. Subchapter Definitions

In this subchapter:

(1) "Derivative proceeding" means a civil suit in the right of a domestic corporation or, to the extent provided in section 7.47, in the right of a foreign corporation.

(2) "Shareholder" includes a beneficial owner whose shares are held in a voting trust or held by a nominee on the beneficial owner's behalf.

§ 7.41. Standing

A shareholder may not commence or maintain a derivative proceeding unless the shareholder:

(1) was a shareholder of the corporation at the time of the act or omission complained of or became a shareholder through transfer by operation of law from one who was a shareholder at that time; and

(2) fairly and adequately represents the interests of the corporation in enforcing the right of the corporation.

§ 7.42. Demand

No shareholder may commence a derivative proceeding until:

(1) a written demand has been made upon the corporation to take suitable action; and

(2) 90 days have expired from the date the demand was made unless the shareholder has earlier been notified that the demand has been rejected by the corporation or unless irreparable injury to the corporation would result by waiting for the expiration of the 90-day period.

§ 7.43. Stay of Proceedings

If the corporation commences an inquiry into the allegations made in the demand or complaint, the court may stay any derivative proceeding for such period as the court deems appropriate.

§ 7.44. Dismissal

(a) A derivative proceeding shall be dismissed by the court on motion by the corporation if one of the groups specified in subsections (b) or (e) has determined in good faith after conducting a reasonable inquiry upon which its conclusions are based that the maintenance of the derivative proceeding is not in the best interests of the corporation.

(b) Unless a panel is appointed pursuant to subsection (e), the determination in subsection (a) shall be made by:

(1) a majority vote of independent directors present at a meeting of the board of directors if the independent directors constitute a quorum; or

(2) a majority vote of a committee consisting of two or more independent directors appointed by majority vote of independent directors present at a meeting of the board of directors, whether or not such independent directors constituted a quorum.

(c) None of the following shall by itself cause a director to be considered not independent for purposes of this section:

(1) the nomination or election of the director by persons who are defendants in the derivative proceeding or against whom action is demanded;

(2) the naming of the director as a defendant in the derivative proceeding or as a person against whom action is demanded; or

(3) the approval by the director of the act being challenged in the derivative proceeding or demand if the act resulted in no personal benefit to the director.

(d) If a derivative proceeding is commenced after a determination has been made rejecting a demand by a shareholder, the complaint shall allege with particularity facts establishing either (1) that a majority of the board of directors did not consist of independent directors at the time the determination was made or (2) that the requirements of subsection (a) have not been met.

(e) If a majority of the board of directors does not consist of independent directors at the time the determination is made, the corporation shall have the burden of proving that the requirements of subsection (a) have been met. If a majority of the board of directors consists of independent directors at the time the determination is made, the plaintiff shall have the burden of proving that the requirements of subsection (a) have not been met.

(f) The court may appoint a panel of one or more independent persons upon motion by the corporation to make a determination whether the maintenance of the derivative proceeding is in the best interests of the corporation. In such case, the plaintiff shall have the burden of proving that the requirements of subsection (a) have not been met.

§ 7.45. Discontinuance or Settlement

A derivative proceeding may not be discontinued or settled without the court's approval. If the court determines that a proposed discontinuance or settlement will substantially affect the interests of the corporation's shareholders or a class of shareholders, the court shall direct that notice be given to the shareholders affected.

§ 7.46. Payment of Expenses

On termination of the derivative proceeding the court may:

(1) order the corporation to pay the plaintiff's expenses incurred in the proceeding if it finds that the proceeding has resulted in a substantial benefit to the corporation;

(2) order the plaintiff to pay any defendant's expenses incurred in defending the proceeding if it finds that the proceeding was commenced or maintained without reasonable cause or for an improper purpose; or

(3) order a party to pay an opposing party's expenses incurred because of the filing of a pleading, motion or other paper, if it finds that the pleading, motion or other paper was not well grounded in fact, after reasonable inquiry, or warranted by existing law or a good faith argument for the extension, modification or reversal of existing law and was interposed for an improper purpose, such as to harass or to cause unnecessary delay or needless increase in the cost of litigation.

§ 7.47. Applicability to Foreign Corporations

In any derivative proceeding in the right of a foreign corporation, the matters covered by this subchapter shall be governed by the laws of the jurisdiction of incorporation of the foreign corporation except for sections 7.43, 7.45, and 7.46.

SUBCHAPTER E. PROCEEDING TO APPOINT CUSTODIAN OR RECEIVER

§ 7.48. Shareholder Action to Appoint Custodian or Receiver

(a) The [name or describe court or courts] may appoint one or more persons to be custodians, or, if the corporation is insolvent, to be receivers, of and for a corporation in a proceeding by a shareholder where it is established that:

(1) The directors are deadlocked in the management of the corporate affairs, the shareholders are unable to break the deadlock, and irreparable injury to the corporation is threatened or being suffered; or

(2) the directors or those in control of the corporation are acting fraudulently and irreparable injury to the corporation is threatened or being suffered.

(b) The court

(1) may issue injunctions, appoint a temporary custodian or temporary receiver with all the powers and duties the court directs, take other action to preserve the corporate assets wherever located, and carry on the business of the corporation until a full hearing is held;

(2) shall hold a full hearing, after notifying all parties to the proceeding and any interested persons designated by the court, before appointing a custodian or receiver; and

(3) has jurisdiction over the corporation and all of its property, wherever located. [Remainder of section omitted.]

CHAPTER 8. DIRECTORS AND OFFICERS

SUBCHAPTER A. BOARD OF DIRECTORS

§ 8.01. Requirements for and Functions of Board of Directors

(a) Except as provided in section 7.32, each corporation must have a board of directors.

(b) All corporate powers shall be exercised by or under the authority of, and the business and affairs of the corporation managed by or under the direction of, its board of directors, subject to any limitation set forth in the articles of incorporation or in an agreement authorized under section 7.32.

(c) In the case of a public corporation, the board's oversight responsibilities include attention to:

(1) business performance and plans;

(2) major risks to which the corporation is or may be exposed;

(3) the performance and compensation of senior officers;

(4) policies and practices to foster the corporation's compliance with law and ethical conduct;

(5) preparation of the corporation's financial statements;

(6) the effectiveness of the corporation's internal controls;

(7) arrangements for providing adequate and timely information to directors; and

(8) the composition of the board and its committees, taking into account the important role of independent directors.

§ 8.02. Qualifications of Directors

The articles of incorporation or bylaws may prescribe qualifications for directors. A director need not be a resident of this state or a shareholder of the corporation unless the articles of incorporation or bylaws so prescribe.

§ 8.03. Number and Election of Directors

(a) A board of directors must consist of one or more individuals, with the number specified in or fixed in accordance with the articles of incorporation or bylaws.

(b) The number of directors may be increased or decreased from time to time by amendment to, or in the manner provided in, the articles of incorporation or the bylaws.

(c) Directors are elected at the first annual shareholders' meeting and at each annual meeting thereafter unless their terms are staggered under section 8.06.

§ 8.04. Election of Directors by Certain Classes of Shareholders

If the articles of incorporation authorize dividing the shares into classes, the articles may also authorize the election of all or a specified number of directors by the holders of one or more authorized classes of shares. A class (or classes) of shares entitled to elect one or more directors is a separate voting group for purposes of the election of directors.

§ 8.05. *Terms of Directors Generally*

(a) The terms of the initial directors of a corporation expire at the first shareholders' meeting at which directors are elected.

(b) The terms of all other directors expire at the next, or if their terms are staggered in accordance with section 8.06, at the applicable second or third, annual shareholders' meeting following their election, except to the extent (i) provided in section 10.22 if a bylaw electing to be governed by that section is in effect or (ii) a shorter term is specified in the articles of incorporation in the event of a director nominee failing to receive a specified vote for election.

(c) A decrease in the number of directors does not shorten an incumbent director's term.

(d) The term of a director elected to fill a vacancy expires at the next shareholders' meeting at which directors are elected.

(e) Except to the extent otherwise provided in the articles of incorporation or under section 10.22 if a bylaw electing to be governed by that section is in effect, despite the expiration of a director's term, the director continues to serve until the director's successor is elected and qualified or there is a decrease in the number of directors.

§ 8.06. *Staggered Terms for Directors*

The articles of incorporation may provide for staggering the terms of directors by dividing the total number of directors into two or three groups, with each group containing one-half or one-third of the total, as near as may be. In that event, the terms of directors in the first group expire at the first annual shareholders' meeting after their election, the terms of the second group expire at the second annual shareholders' meeting after their election, and the terms of the third group, if any, expire at the third annual shareholders' meeting after their election. At each annual shareholders' meeting held thereafter, directors shall be chosen for a term of two years or three years, as the case may be, to succeed those whose terms expire.

§ 8.07. *Resignation of Directors*

(a) A director may resign at any time by delivering written notice to the board of directors or its chair, or to the secretary of the corporation.

(b) A resignation is effective when the notice is delivered unless the notice specifies a later effective date or an effective date determined upon the happening of an event or event. A resignation that is conditioned upon failing to receive a specified vote for election as a director may provide that it is irrevocable.

§ 8.08. *Removal of Directors by Shareholders*

(a) The shareholders may remove one or more directors with or without cause unless the articles of incorporation provide that directors may be removed only for cause.

(b) If a director is elected by a voting group of shareholders, only the shareholders of that voting group may participate in the vote to remove him.

(c) If cumulative voting is authorized, a director may not be removed if the number of votes sufficient to elect him under cumulative voting is voted against his removal. If cumulative

voting is not authorized, a director may be removed only if the number of votes cast to remove him exceeds the number of votes cast not to remove him.

(d) A director may be removed by the shareholders only at a meeting called for the purpose of removing him and the meeting notice must state that the purpose, or one of the purposes, of the meeting is removal of the director.

§ 8.09. *Removal of Directors by Judicial Proceeding*

(a) The [name or describe] court of the county where a corporation's principal office (or, if none in this state, its registered office) is located may remove a director of the corporation from office in a proceeding commenced by or in the right of the corporation if the court finds that (1) the director engaged in fraudulent conduct, with respect to the corporation or its shareholders, grossly abused the position of director, or intentionally inflicted harm on the corporation; and (2) considering the director's course of conduct and the inadequacy of other remedies, removal would be in the best interest of the corporation.

(b) A shareholder proceeding on behalf of the corporation under subsection (a) shall comply with all of the requirements of subchapter 7D, except section 7.41(1).

(c) The court, in addition to removing the director, may bar the director from reelection for a period prescribed by the court.

(d) Nothing in this section limits the equitable powers of the court to order other relief.

§ 8.10. *Vacancy on Board*

(a) Unless the articles of incorporation provide otherwise, if a vacancy occurs on a board of directors, including a vacancy resulting from an increase in the number of directors:

(1) the shareholders may fill the vacancy;

(2) the board of directors may fill the vacancy; or

(3) if the directors remaining in office constitute fewer than a quorum of the board, they may fill the vacancy by the affirmative vote of a majority of all the directors remaining in office.

(b) If the vacant office was held by a director elected by a voting group of shareholders, only the holders of shares of that voting group are entitled to vote to fill the vacancy if it is filled by the shareholders, and only the directors elected by that voting group are entitled to fill the vacancy if it is filled by the directors.

(c) A vacancy that will occur at a specific later date (by reason of a resignation effective at a later date under section 8.07(b) or otherwise) may be filled before the vacancy occurs but the new director may not take office until the vacancy occurs.

§ 8.11. *Compensation of Directors*

Unless the articles of incorporation or bylaws provide otherwise, the board of directors may fix the compensation of directors.

SUBCHAPTER B. MEETINGS AND ACTION OF THE BOARD

§ 8.20. *Meetings*

(a) The board of directors may hold regular or special meetings in or out of this state.

(b) Unless the articles of incorporation or bylaws provide otherwise, the board of directors may permit any or all directors to participate in a regular or special meeting by, or conduct the meeting through the use of, any means of communication by which all directors participating may simultaneously hear each other during the meeting. A director participating in a meeting by this means is deemed to be present in person at the meeting.

§ 8.21. Action Without Meeting

(a) Except to the extent that the articles of incorporation or bylaws require that action by the board of directors be taken at a meeting, action required or permitted by this Act to be taken by the board of directors may be taken without a meeting if each director signs a consent describing the action to be taken and delivers it to the corporation.

(b) Action taken under this section is the act of the board of directors when one or more consents signed by all the directors are delivered to the corporation. The consent may specify the time at which the action taken thereunder is to be effective. A director's consent may be withdrawn by a revocation signed by the director and delivered to the corporation prior to delivery to the corporation of unrevoked written consents signed by all the directors.

(c) A consent signed under this section has the effect of action taken at a meeting of the board of directors and may be described as such in any document.

§ 8.22. Notice of Meeting

(a) Unless the articles of incorporation or bylaws provide otherwise, regular meetings of the board of directors may be held without notice of the date, time, place, or purpose of the meeting.

(b) Unless the articles of incorporation or bylaws provide for a longer or shorter period, special meetings of the board of directors must be preceded by at least two days' notice of the date, time, and place of the meeting. The notice need not describe the purpose of the special meeting unless required by the articles of incorporation or bylaws.

§ 8.23. Waiver of Notice

(a) A director may waive any notice required by this Act, the articles of incorporation, or bylaws before or after the date and time stated in the notice. Except as provided by subsection (b), the waiver must be in writing, signed by the director entitled to the notice, and filed with the minutes or corporate records.

(b) A director's attendance at or participation in a meeting waives any required notice to him of the meeting unless the director at the beginning of the meeting (or promptly upon his arrival) objects to holding the meeting or transacting business at the meeting and does not thereafter vote for or assent to action taken at the meeting.

§ 8.24. Quorum and Voting

(a) Unless the articles of incorporation or bylaws require a greater number, a quorum of a board of directors consists of:

(1) a majority of the fixed number of directors if the corporation has a fixed board size; or

(2) a majority of the number of directors prescribed, or if no number is prescribed the number in office immediately

before the meeting begins, if the corporation has a variable-range size board.

(b) The articles of incorporation or bylaws may authorize a quorum of a board of directors to consist of no fewer than one-third of the fixed or prescribed number of directors determined under subsection (a).

(c) If a quorum is present when a vote is taken, the affirmative vote of a majority of directors present is the act of the board of directors unless the articles of incorporation or bylaws require the vote of a greater number of directors.

(d) A director who is present at a meeting of the board of directors or a committee of the board of directors when corporate action is taken is deemed to have assented to the action taken unless: (1) he objects at the beginning of the meeting (or promptly upon his arrival) to holding it or transacting business at the meeting; (2) his dissent or abstention from the action taken is entered in the minutes of the meeting; or (3) he delivers written notice of his dissent or abstention to the presiding officer of the meeting before its adjournment or to the corporation immediately after adjournment of the meeting. The right of dissent or abstention is not available to a director who votes in favor of the action taken.

§ 8.25. Committees

(a) Unless this Act, the articles of incorporation or bylaws provide otherwise, a board of directors may create one or more committees and appoint one or more members of the board of directors to serve on any such committee.

(b) Unless this Act otherwise provides, the creation of a committee and appointment of members to it must be approved by the greater of (1) a majority of all the directors in office when the action is taken or (2) the number of directors required by the articles of incorporation or bylaws to take action under section 8.24.

(c) Sections 8.20 through 8.24 apply both to committees of the board and to their members.

(d) To the extent specified by the board of directors or in the articles of incorporation or bylaws, each committee may exercise the powers of the board of directors under section 8.01.

(e) A committee may not, however:

(1) authorize or approve distributions, except according to a formula or method, or within limits, prescribed by the board of directors;

(2) approve or propose to shareholders action that this Act requires be approved by shareholders;

(3) fill vacancies on the board of directors, subject to subsection (g), on any of its committees; or

(4) adopt, amend, or repeal bylaws.

(f) The creation of, delegation of authority to, or action by a committee does not alone constitute compliance by a director with the standards of conduct described in section 8.30.

(g) [omitted]

SUBCHAPTER C. DIRECTORS

§ 8.30. Standards of Conduct for Directors

(a) Each member of the board of directors, when discharging the duties of a director, shall act: (1) in good faith, and (2) in a manner the director reasonably believes to be in the best interests of the corporation.

(b) The members of the board of directors or a committee of the board, when becoming informed in connection with their decision-making function or devoting attention to their oversight function, shall discharge their duties with the care that a person in a like position would reasonably believe appropriate under similar circumstances.

(c) In discharging board or committee duties a director, shall disclose, or cause to be disclosed, to the other board or committee members information not already known by them but known to the directors to be material to the discharge of their decision-making or oversight functions, except that disclosure is not required to the extent that the director reasonably believes that doing so would violate a duty imposed under law, a legally enforceable obligation of confidentiality, or a professional ethics rule.

(d) In discharging board or committee duties a director, who does not have knowledge that makes reliance unwarranted, is entitled to rely on the performance by any of the persons specified in subsection (f)(1) or subsection (f)(3) to whom the board may have delegated, formally or informally by course of conduct, the authority or duty to perform one or more of the board's functions that are delegable under applicable law.

(e) In discharging board or committee duties a director, who does not have knowledge that makes reliance unwarranted, is entitled to rely on information, opinions, reports or statements, including financial statements and other financial data, prepared or presented by any of the persons specified in subsection (f).

(f) A director is entitled to rely, in accordance with subsection (d) or (e), on:

(1) one or more officers or employees of the corporation whom the director reasonably believes to be reliable and competent in the functions performed or the information, opinions, reports or statements provided;

(2) legal counsel, public accountants, or other persons retained by the corporation as to matters, involving skills or expertise the director reasonably believes are matters (i) within the particular person's professional or expert competence or (ii) as to which the particular person merits confidence; or

(3) a committee of the board of directors of which the director is not a member if the director reasonably believes the committee merits confidence.

§ 8.31. *Standards of Liability for Directors*

(a) A director shall not be liable to the corporation or its shareholders for any decision to take or not to take action, or any failure to take any action, as a director, unless the party asserting liability in a proceeding establishes that:

(1) no defense interposed by the director based on (i) any provision in the articles of incorporation authorized by section 2.02(b)(4), (ii) the protection afforded by section 8.61 for action taken in compliance with section 8.62 or section 8.63, or (iii) the protection afforded by section 8.70, precludes liability; and

(2) the challenged conduct consisted or was the result of:
(i) action not in good faith; or
(ii) a decision

(A) which the director did not reasonably believe to be in the best interests of the corporation, or

(B) as to which the director was not informed to an extent the director reasonably believed appropriate in the circumstances; or

(iii) a lack of objectivity due to the director's familial, financial or business relationship with, or a lack of independence due to the director's domination or control by, another person having a material interest in the challenged conduct

(A) which relationship or which domination or control could reasonably be expected to have affected the director's judgment respecting the challenged conduct in a manner adverse to the corporation, and

(B) after a reasonable expectation to such effect has been established, the director shall not have established that the challenged conduct was reasonably believed by the director to be in the best interests of the corporation; or

(iv) a sustained failure of the director to devote attention to ongoing oversight of the business and affairs of the corporation, or a failure to devote timely attention, by making (or causing to be made) appropriate inquiry, when particular facts and circumstances of significant concern materialize that would alert a reasonably attentive director to the need therefor; or

(v) receipt of a financial benefit to which the director was not entitled or other breach of the director's duties to deal fairly with the corporation and its shareholders that is actionable under applicable law.

(b) The party seeking to hold the director liable:

(1) for money damages, shall also have the burden of establishing that:

(i) harm to the corporation or its shareholders has been suffered, and

(ii) the harm suffered was proximately caused by the director's challenged conduct; or

(2) for other money payment under a legal remedy, such as compensation for the unauthorized use of corporate assets, shall also have whatever persuasion burden may be called for to establish that the payment sought is appropriate in the circumstances; or

(3) for other money payment under an equitable remedy, such as profit recovery by or disgorgement to the corporation, shall also have whatever persuasion burden may be called for to establish that the equitable remedy sought is appropriate in the circumstances.

(c) Nothing contained in this section shall (1) in any instance where fairness is at issue, such as consideration of the fairness of a transaction to the corporation under section 8.61(b)(3), alter the burden of proving the fact or lack of fairness otherwise applicable, (2) alter the fact or lack of liability of a director under another section of this Act, such as the provisions governing the consequences of an unlawful distribution under section 8.33 or a transactional interest under section 8.61, or (3) affect any rights to which the corporation or a shareholder may be entitled under another statute of this state or the United States.

§ 8.33.   *Directors' Liability for Unlawful Distributions*

(a) A director who votes for or assents to a distribution in excess of what may be authorized and made pursuant to section 6.40(a) or 14.09(a) is personally liable to the corporation for the amount of the distribution that exceeds what could have been distributed without violating section 6.40(a) or 14.09(a) if the party asserting liability establishes that when taking the action the director did not comply with section 8.30.

(b) A director held liable under subsection (a) for an unlawful distribution is entitled to:

(1) contribution from every other director who could be held liable under subsection (a) for the unlawful distribution; and

(2) recoupment from each shareholder of the prorata portion of the amount of the unlawful distribution the shareholder accepted, knowing the distribution was made in violation of section 6.40(a) or 14.09(a). [remainder of section omitted]

SUBCHAPTER D.   OFFICERS

§ 8.40.   *Officers*

(a) A corporation has the offices described in its bylaws or designated by the board of directors in accordance with the bylaws.

(b) The board of directors may elect individuals to fill one or more offices of the corporation. An officer may appoint one or more officers if authorized by the bylaws or the board of directors.

(c) The bylaws or the board of directors shall assign to one of the officers responsibility for preparing minutes of the directors' and shareholders' meetings and for maintaining and authenticating the records of the corporation required to be kept under sections 16.01(a) and 16.01(e).

(d) The same individual may simultaneously hold more than one office in a corporation.

§ 8.41.   *Functions of Officers*

Each officer has the authority and shall perform the functions set forth in the bylaws or, to the extent consistent with the bylaws, the functions prescribed by the board of directors or by direction of an officer authorized by the board of directors to prescribe the duties of other officers.

§ 8.42.   *Standards of Conduct for Officers*

(a) An officer, when performing in such capacity, shall act:
(1) in good faith;
(2) with the care that a person in a like position would reasonably exercise under similar circumstances; and
(3) in a manner the officer reasonably believes to be in the best interest of the corporation.

(b) [omitted]

(c) In discharging his or her duties, an officer who does not have knowledge that makes reliance unwarranted, is entitled to rely on:

(1) the performance of properly delegated responsibilities by one or more employees of the corporation whom the officer reasonably believes to be reliable and competent in performing the responsibilities delegated; or

(2) information, opinions, reports or statements, including financial statements and other financial data, prepared or presented by one or more employees of the corporation whom the officer reasonably believes to be reliable and competent in the matters presented or by legal counsel, public accountants, or other persons retained by the corporation as to matters involving skills or expertise the officer reasonably believes are matters (i) within the particular person's professional or expert competence or (ii) as to which the particular person merits confidence.

(d) An officer shall not be liable to the corporation or its shareholders for any decision to take or not to take action, or any failure to take any action, as an officer, if the duties of the office are performed in compliance with this section. Whether an officer who does not comply with this section shall have liability will depend in such instance on applicable law, including those principles of § 8.31 that have relevance.

§ 8.43.   *Resignation and Removal of Officers*

(a) An officer may resign at any time by delivering notice to the corporation. A resignation is effective when the notice is delivered unless the notice specifies a later effective date. If a resignation is made effective at a later time and the board or the appointing officer accepts the future effective time, the board or the appointing officer may fill the pending vacancy before the effective time if the board or the appointing officer provides that the successor does not take office until the effective time.

(b) An officer may be removed at any time with or without cause by: (i) the board of directors; or (ii) the officer who appointed such officer, unless the bylaws or the board of directors provide otherwise; or (iii) any other officer if authorized by the bylaws or the board of directors.

(c) In this section, "appointing officer" means the officer (including any successor to that officer) who appointed the officer resigning or being removed.

§ 8.44.   *Contract Rights of Officers*

(a) The appointment of an officer does not itself create contract rights.

(b) An officer's removal does not affect the officer's contract rights, if any, with the corporation. An officer's resignation does not affect the corporation's contract rights, if any, with the officer.

SUBCHAPTER E.   INDEMNIFICATION

§ 8.50.   *Subchapter Definitions*

In this subchapter:

(1) "Corporation" includes any domestic or foreign predecessor entity of a corporation in a merger.

(2) "Director" or "officer" means an individual who is or was a director or officer, respectively, of a corporation or who, while a director or officer of the corporation, is or was serving at the corporation's request as a director, officer, partner,

trustee, employee, or agent of another domestic or foreign corporation, partnership, joint venture, trust, employee benefit plan, or other entity. A director or officer is considered to be serving an employee benefit plan at the corporation's request if his duties to the corporation also impose duties on, or otherwise involve services by, him to the plan or to participants in or beneficiaries of the plan. "Director" or "officer" includes, unless the context requires otherwise, the estate or personal representative of a director or officer.

(3) "Expenses" includes counsel fees.

(4) "Liability" means the obligation to pay a judgment, settlement, penalty, fine (including an excise tax assessed with respect to an employee benefit plan), or reasonable expenses incurred with respect to a proceeding.

(5) "Official capacity" means: (i) when used with respect to a director, the office of director in a corporation; and (ii) when used with respect to an officer, as contemplated in section 8.56, the office in a corporation held by the officer. "Official capacity" does not include service for any other domestic or foreign corporation or any partnership, joint venture, trust, employee benefit plan, or other entity.

(6) "Party" means an individual who was, is, or is threatened to be made, a defendant or respondent in a proceeding.

(7) "Proceeding" means any threatened, pending, or completed action, suit, or proceeding, whether civil, criminal, administrative, arbitrative, or investigative and whether formal or informal.

§ 8.51. *Permissible Indemnification*

(a) Except as otherwise provided in this section, a corporation may indemnify an individual who is a party to a proceeding because he is a director against liability incurred in the proceeding if:

(1)(i) he conducted himself in good faith; and

(ii) he reasonably believed:

(A) in the case of conduct in his official capacity, that his conduct was in the best interests of the corporation; and

(B) in all other cases, that his conduct was at least not opposed to the best interests of the corporation; and

(iii) in the case of any criminal proceeding, he had no reasonable cause to believe his conduct was unlawful; or

(2) he engaged in conduct for which broader indemnification has been made permissible or obligatory under a provision of the articles of incorporation (as authorized by section 2.02(b)(5)).

(b) A director's conduct with respect to an employee benefit plan for a purpose he reasonably believed to be in the interests of the participants in, and the beneficiaries of, the plan is conduct that satisfies the requirement of subsection (a)(1)(ii)(B).

(c) The termination of a proceeding by judgment, order, settlement, or conviction, or upon a plea of nolo contendere or its equivalent, is not, of itself, determinative that the director did not meet the relevant standard of conduct described in this section.

(d) Unless ordered by a court under section 8.54(a)(3), a corporation may not indemnify a director:

(1) in connection with a proceeding by or in the right of the corporation, except for reasonable expenses incurred in connection with the proceeding if it is determined that the director has met the relevant standard of conduct under subsection (a); or

(2) in connection with any proceeding with respect to conduct for which he was adjudged liable on the basis that he received a financial benefit to which he was not entitled, whether or not involving action in his official capacity.

§ 8.52. *Mandatory Indemnification*

A corporation shall indemnify a director who was wholly successful, on the merits or otherwise, in the defense of any proceeding to which he was a party because he was a director of the corporation against reasonable expenses incurred by him in connection with the proceeding.

§ 8.53. *Advance for Expenses*

(a) A corporation may, before final disposition of a proceeding, advance funds to pay for or reimburse the reasonable expenses incurred by a director who is a party to a proceeding because he is a director if he delivers to the corporation:

(1) a written affirmation of his good faith belief that he has met the relevant standard of conduct described in section 8.51 or that the proceeding involves conduct for which liability has been eliminated under a provision of the articles of incorporation as authorized by section 2.02(b)(4); and

(2) his written undertaking to repay any funds advanced if he is not entitled to mandatory indemnification under section 8.52 and it is ultimately determined under section 8.54 or section 8.55 that he has not met the relevant standard of conduct described in section 8.51.

(b) The undertaking required by subsection (a)(2) must be an unlimited general obligation of the director but need not be secured and may be accepted without reference to financial ability of the director to make repayment. [subsection (c) omitted]

§ 8.54. *Court-Ordered Indemnification and Advance for Expenses*

(a) A director who is a party to a proceeding because he is a director may apply for indemnification or an advance for expenses to the court conducting the proceeding or to another court of competent jurisdiction. After receipt of an application and after giving any notice it considers necessary, the court shall:

(1) order indemnification if the court determines that the director is entitled to mandatory indemnification under section 8.52;

(2) order indemnification or advance for expenses if the court determines that the director is entitled to indemnification or advance for expenses pursuant to a provision authorized by section 8.58(a); or

(3) order indemnification or advance for expenses if the court determines, in view of all the relevant circumstances, that it is fair and reasonable

(i) to indemnify the director, or

(ii) to advance expenses to the director, even if he has not met the relevant standard of conduct set forth in section 8.51(a), failed to comply with section 8.53 or was adjudged liable in a proceeding referred to in subsection 8.51(d)(1) or (d)(2), but if he was adjudged so liable his indemnification shall be limited to reasonable expenses incurred in connection with the proceeding. [subsection (b) omitted]

§ 8.55. Determination and Authorization of Indemnification

(a) A corporation may not indemnify a director under section 8.51 unless authorized for a specific proceeding after a determination has been made that indemnification of the director is permissible because he has met the relevant standard of conduct set forth in section 8.51.

(b) The determination shall be made:

(1) If there are two or more qualified directors, by the board of directors by a majority vote of all the qualified directors (a majority of whom shall for such purpose constitute a quorum), or by a majority of the members of a committee of two or more qualified directors appointed by such a vote;

(2) by special legal counsel:

(i) selected in the manner prescribed in subdivision (1); or

(ii) if there are fewer than two qualified directors, selected by the board of directors (in which selection directors who are not qualified directors may participate); or

(3) by the shareholders, but shares owned by or voted under the control of a director who at the time is not a qualified director may not be voted on the determination.

(c) Authorization of indemnification shall be made in the same manner as the determination that indemnification is permissible, except that if there are fewer than two qualified directors or if the determination is made by special legal counsel, authorization of indemnification shall be made by those entitled under subsection (b)(2)(ii) to select special legal counsel.

§ 8.56. Indemnification of Officers

(a) A corporation may indemnify and advance expenses under this subchapter to an officer of the corporation who is a party to a proceeding because he is an officer of the corporation

(1) to the same extent as a director; and

(2) if he is an officer but not a director, to such further extent as may be provided by the articles of incorporation, the bylaws, a resolution of the board of directors, or contract except for (A) liability in connection with a proceeding by or in the right of the corporation other than for reasonable expenses incurred in connection with the proceeding or (B) liability arising out of conduct that constitutes (i) receipt by him of a financial benefit to which he is not entitled, (ii) an intentional infliction of harm on the corporation or the shareholders, or (iii) an intentional violation of criminal law.

(b) The provisions of subsection (a)(2) shall apply to an officer who is also a director if the basis on which he is made a party to the proceeding is an act or omission solely as an officer.

(c) An officer of a corporation who is not a director is entitled to mandatory indemnification under section 8.52, and may apply to a court under section 8.54 for indemnification or an advance for expenses, in each case to the same extent to which a director may be entitled to indemnification or advance for expenses under those provisions.

§ 8.57. Insurance

A corporation may purchase and maintain insurance on behalf of an individual who is a director or officer of the corporation, or who, while a director or officer of the corporation, serves at the corporation's request as a director, officer, partner, trustee, employee, or agent of another domestic or foreign corporation, partnership, joint venture, trust, employee benefit plan, or other entity, against liability asserted against or incurred by him in that capacity or arising from his status as a director or officer, whether or not the corporation would have power to indemnify or advance expenses to him against the same liability under this subchapter.

§ 8.58. Variation by Corporate Action; Application of Subchapter

(a) A corporation may, by a provision in its articles of incorporation or bylaws or in a resolution adopted or a contract approved by its board of directors of shareholders, obligate itself in advance of the act or omission giving rise to a proceeding to provide indemnification in accordance with section 8.51 or advance funds to pay for or reimburse expenses in accordance with section 8.53. Any such obligatory provision shall be deemed to satisfy the requirements for authorization referred to in section 8.53(c) and in section 8.55(c). Any such provision that obligates the corporation to provide indemnification to the fullest extent permitted by law shall be deemed to obligate the corporation to advance funds to pay for or reimburse expenses in accordance with section 8.53 to the fullest extent permitted by law, unless the provision specifically provides otherwise.

(b) Any provision pursuant to subsection (a) shall not obligate the corporation to indemnify or advance expenses to a director of a predecessor of the corporation, pertaining to conduct with respect to the predecessor, unless otherwise specifically provided. Any provision for indemnification or advance for expenses in the articles of incorporation, bylaws, or a resolution of the board of directors or shareholders of a predecessor of the corporation in a merger or in a contract to which the predecessor is a party, existing at the time the merger takes effect, shall be governed by section 11.07(a)(4).

(c) A corporation may, by a provision in its articles of incorporation, limit any of the rights to indemnification or advance for expenses created by or pursuant to this subchapter.

(d) This subchapter does not limit a corporation's power to pay or reimburse expenses incurred by a director or an officer in connection with his appearance as a witness in a proceeding at a time when he is not a party.

(e) This subchapter does not limit a corporation's power to indemnify, advance expenses to or provide or maintain insurance on behalf of an employee or agent.

§ 8.59. Exclusivity of Subchapter

A corporation may provide indemnification or advance expenses to a director or an officer only as permitted by this subchapter.

SUBCHAPTER F. DIRECTORS' CONFLICTING INTEREST TRANSACTIONS

§ 8.60. Subchapter Definitions

In this subchapter:

(1) "Director's conflicting interest transaction" means a transaction effected or proposed to be effected by the corporation (or by an entity controlled by the corporation)

(i) to which, at the relevant time, the director is a party; or

(ii) respecting which, at the relevant time, the director had knowledge and a material financial interest known to the director; or

(iii) respecting which, at the relevant time, the director knew that a related person was a party or had a material financial interest.

(2) "Control" (including the term "controlled by") means (i) having the power, directly or indirectly, to elect or remove a majority of the members of the board of directors or other governing body of an entity, whether through ownership of voting shares or interests, by contract, or otherwise, or (ii) being subject to a majority of the risk of loss from the entity's activities or entitled to receive a majority of the entity's residual returns.

(3) "Relevant time" means (i) the time at which directors' action respecting the transaction is taken in compliance with section 8.62, or (ii) if the transaction is not brought before the board of directors of the corporation (or its committee) for action under section 8.62, at the time the corporation (or an entity controlled by the corporation) becomes legally obligated to consummate the transaction.

(4) "Material financial interest" means a financial interest in a transaction that would reasonably be expected to impair the objectivity of the director's judgment when participating in action on the authorization of the transaction.

(5) "Related person" means:

(i) the director's spouse;

(ii) a child, stepchild, grandchild, parent, step parent, grandparent, sibling, step sibling, half sibling, aunt, uncle, niece or nephew (or spouse of any thereof) of the director or of the director's spouse;

(iii) an individual living in the same home as the director;

(iv) an entity (other than the corporation or an entity controlled by the corporation) controlled by the director or any person specified above in this subdivision (5);

(v) a domestic or foreign (A) business or nonprofit corporation (other than the corporation or an entity controlled by the corporation) of which the director is a director, (B) unincorporated entity of which the director is a general partner or a member of the governing body, or (C) individual, trust or estate for whom or of which the director is a trustee, guardian, personal representative or like fiduciary; or

(vi) a person that is, or an entity that is controlled by, an employer of the director.

(6) "Fair to the corporation" means, for purposes of section 8.61(b)(3), that the transaction as a whole was beneficial to the corporation, taking into appropriate account whether it was (i) fair in terms of the director's dealings with the corporation, and (ii) comparable to what might have been obtainable in an arm's length transaction, given the consideration paid or received by the corporation.

(7) "Required disclosure" means disclosure of (i) the existence and nature of the director's conflicting interest, and (ii) all facts known to the director respecting the subject matter of the transaction that a director free of such conflicting interest would reasonably believe to be material in deciding whether to proceed with the transaction.

§ 8.61. Judicial Action

(a) A transaction effected or proposed to be effected by a corporation (or by an entity controlled by the corporation) may not be the subject of equitable relief or give rise to an award of damages or other sanctions against a director of the corporation, in a proceeding by a shareholder or by or in the right of the corporation, on the ground that the director has an interest respecting the transaction if it is not a directors' conflicting interest transaction.

(b) A director's conflicting interest transaction may not be the subject of equitable relief, or give rise to an award of damages or other sanctions against a director, in a proceeding by a shareholder or by or in the right of the corporation, on the ground that the director has an interest respecting the transaction, if:

(1) directors' action respecting the transaction was taken in compliance with section 8.62 at any time; or

(2) shareholders' action respecting the transaction was taken in compliance with section 8.63 at any time; or

(3) the transaction, judged according to the circumstances at the relevant time, is established to have been fair to the corporation.

§ 8.62. Directors' Action

(a) Directors' action respecting a director's conflicting interest transaction is effective for purposes of section 8.61(b)(1) if the transaction has been authorized by the affirmative vote of a majority (but no fewer than two) of the qualified directors on the board of directors or on a duly empowered committee of the board who voted on the transaction after required disclosure by the conflicted director of information not already known by such qualified directors, or after modified disclosure in compliance with subsection (b), provided that:

(1) the qualified directors have deliberated and voted outside the presence of and without the participation by any other director; and

(2) where the action has been taken by a committee, all members of the committee were qualified directors, and either (i) the committee was composed of all the qualified directors on the board of directors or (ii) the members of the committee were appointed by the affirmative vote of a majority of the qualified directors on the board.

(b) Notwithstanding subsection (a), when a transaction is a director's conflicting interest transaction only because a related person described in clause (v) or clause (vi) of section 8.60(5) is a party to or has a material financial interest in the transaction, the conflicted director is not obligated to make required disclosure to the extent that the director reasonably believes that doing so would violate a duty imposed under law, a legally enforceable obligation of confidentiality, or a professional ethics rule, provided that the conflicted director discloses to the qualified directors voting on the transaction:

> (1) all information required to be disclosed that is not so violative,
>
> (2) the existence and nature of the director's conflicting interest, and
>
> (3) the nature of the conflicted director's duty not to disclose the confidential information.

(c) A majority (but no fewer than two) of all the qualified directors on the board of directors, or on the committee, constitutes a quorum for purposes of action that complies with this section.

(d) Where directors' action under this section does not satisfy a quorum or voting requirement applicable to the authorization of the transaction by reason of the articles of incorporation, the bylaws or a provision of law, independent action to satisfy those authorization requirements must be taken by the board of directors or a committee, in which action directors who are not qualified directors may participate.

§ 8.63. Shareholders' Action

(a) Shareholders' action respecting a transaction is effective for purposes of section 8.61(b)(2) if a majority of the votes entitled to be cast by the holders of all qualified shares are in favor of the transaction after (1) notice to shareholders describing the action to be taken respecting the transaction, (2) provision to the corporation of the information referred to in subsection (b), and (3) communication to the shareholders entitled to vote on the transaction of the information that is the subject of required disclosure, to the extent the information was not known by them.

(b) A director who has a conflicting interest respecting the transaction shall, before the shareholders' vote, inform the secretary or other officer or agent of the corporation authorized to tabulate votes, in writing, of the number of shares that the director knows are not qualified shares under subsection (c), and the identity of the holders of those shares. [subsections (c), (d), (e), and (f) omitted]

CHAPTER 9. DOMESTICATION AND CONVERSION

§ 9.20. Domestication

A foreign business corporation may become a domestic business corporation only if the domestication is permitted by the organic law of the foreign corporation.

(a) A domestic business corporation may become a foreign business corporation if the domestication is permitted by the laws of the foreign jurisdiction. Regardless of whether the laws of the foreign jurisdiction require the adoption of a plan of domestication, the domestication shall be approved by the adoption by the corporation of a plan of domestication in the manner provided in this subchapter. [subsections (c), (d), (e), and (f) omitted]

§ 9.22. Articles of Domestication

(a) After the domestication of a foreign business corporation has been authorized as required by the laws of the foreign jurisdiction, articles of domestication shall be executed by any officer or other duly authorized representative. [remainder of section omitted]

§ 9.24. Effect of Domestication

(a) When a domestication becomes effective:

> (1) the title to all real and personal property, both tangible and intangible, of the corporation remains in the corporation without reversion or impairment;
>
> (2) the liabilities of the corporation remain the liabilities of the corporation;
>
> (3) an action or proceeding pending against the corporation continues against the corporation as if the domestication had not occurred. [remainder of section omitted]

SUBCHAPTER E. ENTITY CONVERSION

§ 9.50. Entity Conversion Authorized; Definitions

(a) A domestic business corporation may become a domestic unincorporated entity pursuant to a plan of entity conversion.

(b) A domestic business corporation may become a foreign unincorporated entity if the entity conversion is permitted by the laws of the foreign jurisdiction.

(c) A domestic unincorporated entity may become a domestic business corporation. [remainder of section omitted]

§ 9.53. Articles of Entity Conversion

(a) After the conversion of a domestic business corporation to a domestic unincorporated entity has been adopted and approved as required by this Act, articles of entity conversion shall be executed on behalf of the corporation by any officer or other duly authorized representative. [remainder of section omitted]

§ 9.55. Effect of Entity Conversion

(a) When a conversion under this subchapter becomes effective:

> (1) the title to all real and personal property, both tangible and intangible, of the converting entity remains in the surviving entity without reversion or impairment;
>
> (2) the liabilities of the converting entity remain the liabilities of the surviving entity;
>
> (3) an action or proceeding pending against the converting entity continues against the surviving entity as if the conversion had not occurred. [remainder of section omitted]

CHAPTER 10. AMENDMENT OF ARTICLES OF INCORPORATION AND BYLAWS

SUBCHAPTER A. AMENDMENT OF ARTICLES OF INCORPORATION

§ 10.01. Authority to Amend

(a) A corporation may amend its articles of incorporation at any time to add or change a provision that is required or

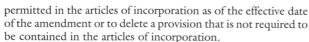
permitted in the articles of incorporation as of the effective date of the amendment or to delete a provision that is not required to be contained in the articles of incorporation.

(b) A shareholder of the corporation does not have a vested property right resulting from any provision in the articles of incorporation, including provisions relating to management, control, capital structure, dividend entitlement, or purpose or duration of the corporation.

§ 10.02. Amendment Before Issuance of Shares

If a corporation has not yet issued shares, its board of directors, or its incorporators if it has no board of directors, may adopt one or more amendments to the corporation's articles of incorporation.

§ 10.03. Amendment by Board of Directors and Shareholders

If a corporation has issued shares, an amendment to the articles of incorporation shall be adopted in the following manner:

(a) The proposed amendment must be adopted by the board of directors.

(b) Except as provided in sections 10.05, 10.07, and 10.08, after adopting the proposed amendment the board of directors must submit the amendment to the shareholders for their approval. The board of directors must also transmit to the shareholders a recommendation that the shareholders approve the amendment, unless the board of directors makes a determination that because of conflicts of interest or other special circumstances it should not make such a recommendation, in which case the board of directors must transmit to the shareholders the basis for that determination.

(c) The board of directors may condition its submission of the amendment to the shareholders on any basis.

(d) If the amendment is required to be approved by the shareholders, and the approval is to be given at a meeting, the corporation must notify each shareholder, whether or not entitled to vote, of the meeting of shareholders at which the amendment is to be submitted for approval. The notice must state that the purpose, or one of the purposes, of the meeting is to consider the amendment and must contain or be accompanied by a copy of the amendment.

(e) Unless the articles of incorporation, or the board of directors acting pursuant to subsection (c), requires a greater vote or a greater number of shares to be present, approval of the amendment requires the approval of the shareholders at a meeting at which a quorum consisting of at least a majority of the votes entitled to be cast on the amendment exists, and, if any class or series of shares is entitled to vote as a separate group on the amendment, except as provided in section 10.04(c), the approval of each such separate voting group at a meeting at which a quorum of the voting group consisting of at least a majority of the votes entitled to be cast on the amendment by that voting group exists.

§ 10.05. Amendment by Board of Directors

Unless the articles of incorporation provide otherwise, a corporation's board of directors may adopt amendments to

the corporation's articles of incorporation without shareholder approval:

(1) to extend the duration of the corporation if it was incorporated at a time when limited duration was required by law;

(2) to delete the names and addresses of the initial directors;

(3) to delete the name and address of the initial registered agent or registered office, if a statement of change is on file with the secretary of state;

(4) if the corporation has only one class of shares outstanding:

(a) to change each issued and unissued authorized share of the class into a greater number of whole shares of that class; or

(b) to increase the number of authorized shares of the class to the extent necessary to permit the issuance of shares as a share dividend.

(5) to change the corporate name by substituting the word "corporation," "incorporated," "company," "limited," or the abbreviation "corp.," "inc.," "co.," or "ltd.," for a similar word or abbreviation in the name, or by adding, deleting, or changing a geographical attribution for the name;

(6) to reflect a reduction in authorized shares, as a result of the operation of section 6.31(b), when the corporation has acquired its own shares and the articles of incorporation prohibit the reissue of the acquired shares;

(7) to delete a class of shares from the articles of incorporation, as a result of the operation of section 6.31(b), when there are no remaining shares of the class because the corporation has acquired all shares of the class and the articles of incorporation prohibit the reissue of the acquired shares; or

(8) to make any change expressly permitted by section 6.02(a) or (b) to be made without shareholder approval.

§ 10.06. Articles of Amendment

After an amendment to the articles of incorporation has been adopted and approved in the manner required by this Act and by the articles of incorporation, the corporation shall deliver to the secretary of state, for filing, articles of amendment, which shall set forth:

(1) the name of the corporation;

(2) the text of each amendment adopted or the information required by section 1.20(k)(5);

(3) if an amendment provides for an exchange, reclassification, or cancellation of issued shares, provisions for implementing the amendment if not contained in the amendment itself, which may be made dependent upon facts objectively ascertainable outside the articles of amendment in accordance with section 1.20(k)(5);

(4) the date of each amendment's adoption; and

(5) if an amendment:

(a) was adopted by the incorporators or board of directors without shareholder approval, a statement that the amendment was duly approved by the incorporators or by the board of directors, as the case may be, and that shareholder approval was not required;

(b) required approval by the shareholders, a statement that the amendment was duly approved by the shareholders in the manner required by this Act and by the articles of incorporation; or

(c) is being filed pursuant to section 1.20(k)(5), a statement to that effect.

§ 10.07.   *Restated Articles of Incorporation*

(a) A corporation's board of directors may restate its articles of incorporation at any time, with or without shareholder approval, to consolidate all amendments into a single document.

(b) If the restated articles include one or more new amendments that require shareholder approval, the amendments must be adopted and approved as provided in section 10.03.

(c) a corporation that restates its articles of incorporation shall deliver to the secretary of state for filing articles of restatement setting forth the name of the corporation and the text of the restated articles of incorporation together with a certificate which states that the restated articles consolidate all amendments into a single document and, if a new amendment is included in the restated articles, which also includes the statements required under section 10.06.

(d) Duly adopted restated articles of incorporation supersede the original articles of incorporation and all amendments thereto.

(e) The secretary of state may certify restated articles of incorporation as the articles of incorporation currently in effect, without including the certificate information required by subsection (c).

§ 10.09.   *Effect of Amendment*

An amendment to articles of incorporation does not affect a cause of action existing against or in favor of the corporation, a proceeding to which the corporation is a party, or the existing rights of persons other than shareholders of the corporation. An amendment changing a corporation's name does not abate a proceeding brought by or against the corporation in its former name.

Subchapter B.   Amendment of Bylaws

§ 10.20.   *Amendment by Board of Directors or Shareholders*

(a) A corporation's shareholders may amend or repeal the corporation's bylaws.

(b) A corporation's board of directors may amend or repeal the corporation's bylaws unless:

(1) the articles of incorporation, section 10.21 or, if applicable, section 10.22 reserve that power exclusively to the shareholders in whole or part; or

(2) the shareholders in amending, repealing, or adopting a bylaw expressly provide that the board of directors may not amend, repeal, or reinstate that bylaw.

§ 10.21.   *Bylaw Increasing Quorum or Voting Requirement for Directors*

(a) A bylaw that increases a quorum or voting requirement for the board of directors may be amended or repealed:

(1) if adopted by the shareholders, only by the shareholders unless the bylaw otherwise provides;

(2) if adopted by the board of directors, either by the shareholders or by the board of directors.

(b) A bylaw adopted or amended by the shareholders that increases a quorum or voting requirement for the board of directors may provide that it may be amended or repealed only by a specified vote of either the shareholders or the board of directors.

(c) Action by the board of directors under subsection (a) to amend or repeal a bylaw that changes the quorum or voting requirement for the board of directors must meet the same quorum requirement and be adopted by the same vote required to take action under the quorum and voting requirement then in effect or proposed to be adopted, whichever is greater.

§ 10.22.   *Bylaw Provisions Relating to the Election of Directors*

(a) Unless the articles of incorporation (i) specifically prohibit the adoption of a bylaw pursuant to this section, (ii) alter the vote specified in section 7.28(a), or (iii) provide for cumulative voting, a public corporation may elect in its bylaws to be governed in the election of directors as follows:

(1) each vote entitled to be cast may be voted for or against up to that number of candidates that is equal to the number of directors to be elected, or a shareholder may indicate an abstention, but without cumulating the votes;

(2) to be elected, a nominee must have received a plurality of the votes cast by holders of shares entitled to vote in the election at a meeting at which a quorum is present, provided that a nominee who is elected but receives more votes against than for election shall serve as a director for a term that shall terminate on the date that is the earlier of (i) 90 days from the date on which the voting results are determined pursuant to section 7.29(b)(5) or (ii) the date on which an individual is selected by the board of directors to fill the office held by such director, which selection shall be deemed to constitute the filling of a vacancy by the board to which section 8.10 applies. Subject to clause (3) of this section, a nominee who is elected but receives more votes against than for election shall not serve as a director beyond the 90-day period referenced above; and

(3) the board of directors may select any qualified individual to fill the office held by a director who received more votes against than for election [subsection (b) omitted]

(c) A bylaw electing to be governed by this section may be repealed:

(1) if originally adopted by the shareholders, only by the shareholders, unless the bylaw otherwise provides;

(2) if adopted by the board of directors, by the board of directors or the shareholders.

Chapter 11.   Mergers and Share Exchanges

§ 11.01.   *Definitions*

As used in this chapter:

(a) "Merger" means a business combination pursuant to section 11.02.

(b) "Party to a merger" or "party to a share exchange" means any domestic or foreign corporation or eligible entity that will either:

(1) merge under a plan of merger;

(2) acquire shares or eligible interests of another corporation or an eligible entity in a share exchange; or

(3) have all of its shares or eligible interests or all of one or more classes or series of its shares or eligible interests acquired in a share exchange.

(c) "Share exchange" means a business combination pursuant to section 11.03.

(d) "Survivor" in a merger means the corporation or eligible entity into which one or more corporations or other entities are merged. A survivor of a merger may preexist the merger or be created by the merger.

§ 11.02. Merger

(a) One or more domestic corporations may merge with one or more domestic or foreign business corporations or other eligible entities pursuant to a plan of merger, or two or more foreign business corporations or domestic or foreign eligible entities may merge into a new domestic business corporation to be created in the merger in the manner provided in this chapter.

(b) A foreign business corporation, or a foreign eligible entity, may be a party to a merger with a domestic business corporation, or may be created by the terms of the plan of merger, only if the merger is permitted by the foreign business corporation or eligible entity.

(b.1) If the organic law of a domestic eligible entity does not provide procedures for the approval of a merger, a plan of merger may be adopted and approved, the merger effectuated, and appraisal rights exercised in accordance with the procedures in this chapter and chapter 13. For the purposes of applying this chapter and chapter 13:

(1) the eligible entity, its members or interest holders, eligible interests and organic documents taken together shall be deemed to be a domestic business corporation, shareholders, shares and articles of incorporation, respectively and vice versa as the context may require; and

(2) if the business and affairs of the eligible entity are managed by a group of persons that is not identical to the members or interest holders, that group shall be deemed to be the board of directors.

(c) The plan of merger must include:

(1) The name of each domestic or foreign business corporation or eligible entity that will merge and the name of the domestic or foreign business corporation or eligible entity that will be the survivor of the merger;

(2) the terms and conditions of the merger;

(3) the manner and basis of converting the shares of each merging domestic or foreign business corporation and eligible interests of each merging domestic or foreign eligible entity into shares or other securities, eligible interests, obligations, rights to acquire shares, other securities or eligible interests, cash, other property, or any combination of the foregoing;

(4) the articles of incorporation of any domestic or foreign business or nonprofit corporation, or the organic documents of any domestic or foreign unincorporated entity, to be created by the merger, or if a new domestic or foreign business or nonprofit corporation or unincorporated entity is not to be created by the merger, any amendments to the survivor's articles of incorporation or organic documents.

(5) any other provisions required by the laws under which any party to the merger is organized or by which it is governed, or by the articles of incorporation or organic document of any such party.

(d) Terms of a plan of merger may be made dependent on facts objectively ascertainable outside the plan in accordance with section 1.20(k).

(e) The plan of merger may also include a provision that the plan may be amended prior to filing articles of merger but if the shareholders of a domestic corporation that is a party to the merger are required or permitted to vote on the plan, the plan must provide that subsequent to approval of the plan by such shareholders the plan may not be amended to change:

(1) the amount or kind of shares or other securities, eligible interests, obligations, rights to acquire shares, other securities or eligible interests, cash, or other property to be received under the plan by the shareholders of or owners of eligible interests in any party to the merger;

(2) the articles of incorporation of any corporation, or the organic documents of any unincorporated entity, that will survive or be created as a result of the merger, except for changes permitted by section 10.05 or by comparable provisions of the organic laws of any such foreign business or nonprofit corporation or domestic or foreign unincorporated entity; or

(3) any of the other terms or conditions of the plan if the change would adversely affect such shareholders in any material respect.

(f) Omitted

§ 11.03. Share Exchange

(a) Through a share exchange:

(1) a domestic business corporation may acquire all of the shares of one or more classes or series of shares of another domestic or foreign business corporation, or all of the eligible interests of one or more classes or series of eligible interests of a domestic or foreign eligible entity, in exchange for shares or other securities, interests, obligations, rights to acquire shares or other securities, cash, other property, or any combination of the foregoing, pursuant to a plan of share exchange, or

(2) all of the shares of one or more classes or series of shares of a domestic business corporation may be acquired by another domestic or foreign business corporation or eligible entity, in exchange for shares or other securities, interests, obligations, rights to acquire shares, other securities or securities, cash, other property, or any combination of the foregoing, pursuant to a plan of share exchange.

(b) A foreign corporation or eligible entity may be a party to a share exchange only if the share exchange is permitted by the organic law of the corporation or eligible entity.

(c) The plan of share exchange must include:

(1) the name of each corporation or other entity whose shares or interests will be acquired and the name of the

corporation or other entity that will acquire those shares or interests;

(2) the terms and conditions of the share exchange;

(3) the manner and basis of exchanging shares of a corporation or interests in an other entity whose shares or interests will be acquired under the share exchange into shares or other securities, interests, obligations, rights to acquire shares, other securities or interests, cash, other property, or any combination of the foregoing.

(d) Omitted

(e) The plan of share exchange may also include a provision that the plan may be amended prior to filing articles of share exchange but if the shareholders of a domestic corporation that is a party to the share exchange are required or permitted to vote on the plan, the plan must provide that subsequent to approval of the plan by such shareholders the plan may not be amended to change:

(1) the amount or kind of shares or other securities, interests, obligations, rights to acquire shares, other securities or interests, cash, or other property to be issued by the corporation or to be received under the plan by the shareholders of or holders of eligible interests in any party to the share exchange; or

(2) any of the other terms or conditions of the plan if the change would adversely affect such shareholders in any material respect.

(f) Section 11.03 does not limit the power of a domestic corporation to acquire shares of another corporation or interests in another entity in a transaction other than a share exchange.

§ 11.04. *Action on a Plan of Merger or Share Exchange*

In the case of a domestic corporation that is a party to a merger or share exchange:

(a) The plan of merger or share exchange must be adopted by the board of directors.

(b) Except as provided in subsection (g) and in section 11.05, after adopting the plan of merger or share exchange the board of directors must submit the plan to the shareholders for their approval. The board of directors must also transmit to the shareholders a recommendation that the shareholders approve the plan, unless the board of directors makes a determination that because of conflicts of interest or other special circumstances it should not make such a recommendation, in which case the board of directors must transmit to the shareholders the basis for that determination.

(c) The board of directors may condition its submission of the plan of merger or share exchange to the shareholders on any basis.

(d) If the plan of merger or share exchange is required to be approved by the shareholders, and if the approval is to be given at a meeting, the corporation must notify each shareholder, whether or not entitled to vote, of the meeting of shareholders at which the plan is to be submitted for approval. The notice must state that the purpose, or one of the purposes, of the meeting is to consider the plan and must contain or be accompanied by a copy or summary of the plan. If the corporation is to be merged into an existing corporation or other entity, the notice shall also include or be accompanied

by a copy or summary of the articles of incorporation or organizational documents of that corporation or other entity. If the corporation is to be merged into a corporation or other entity that is to be created pursuant to the merger, the notice shall include or be accompanied by a copy or a summary of the articles of incorporation or organizational documents of the new corporation or other entity.

(e) Unless the articles of incorporation, or the board of directors acting pursuant to subsection (c), requires a greater vote or a greater number of votes to be present, approval of the plan of merger or share exchange requires the approval of the shareholders at a meeting at which a quorum consisting of at least a majority of the votes entitled to be cast on the plan exists, and, if any class or series of shares is entitled to vote as a separate group on the plan of merger or share exchange, the approval of each such separate voting group at a meeting at which a quorum of the voting group consisting of at least a majority of the votes entitled to be cast on the merger or share exchange by that voting group is present.

(f) [omitted]

(g) Unless the articles of incorporation otherwise provide, approval by the corporation's shareholders of a plan of merger or share exchange is not required if:

(1) the corporation will survive the merger or is the acquiring corporation in a share exchange;

(2) except for amendments permitted by section 10.05, its articles of incorporation will not be changed;

(3) each shareholder of the corporation whose shares were outstanding immediately before the effective date of the merger or share exchange will hold the same number of shares, with identical preferences, limitations, and relative rights, immediately after the effective date of change; and

(4) the issuance in the merger or share exchange of shares or other securities convertible into or rights exercisable for shares does not require a vote under section 6.21(f).

(h) If as a result of a merger or share exchange one or more shareholders of a domestic corporation would become subject to owner liability for the debts, obligations, or liabilities of any other person or entity, approval of the plan of merger shall require the execution, by each such shareholder, of a separate written consent to become subject to such owner liability.

§ 11.05. *Merger Between Parent and Subsidiary or Between Subsidiaries*

(a) A domestic parent corporation that owns shares of a domestic or foreign subsidiary corporation that carry at least 90 percent of the voting power of each class and series of the outstanding shares of the subsidiary that have voting power may merge the subsidiary into itself or into another such subsidiary, or merge itself into the subsidiary, without the approval of the board of directors or shareholders of the subsidiary, unless the articles of incorporation of any of the corporations otherwise provide, and unless, in the case of a foreign subsidiary, approval by the subsidiary's board of directors or shareholders is required by the laws under which the subsidiary is organized.

(b) If under subsection (a) approval of a merger by the subsidiary's shareholders is not required, the parent corporation shall, within 10 days after the effective date of the merger, notify each of the subsidiary's shareholders that the merger has become effective.

(c) Except as provided in subsections (a) and (b), a merger between a parent and a subsidiary shall be governed by the provisions of chapter 11 applicable to mergers generally.

§ 11.06. *Articles of Merger or Share Exchange*

(a) After a plan of merger or share exchange has been adopted and approved as required by this Act, articles of merger or share exchange shall be executed on behalf of each party to the merger or share exchange by any officer or other duly authorized representative. The articles shall set forth:

(1) the names of the parties to the merger or share exchange;

(2) if the articles of incorporation of the survivor of a merger are amended, or if a new corporation is created as a result of a merger, the amendments to the survivor's articles of incorporation or the articles of incorporation of the new corporation;

(3) if the plan of merger or share exchange required approval by the shareholders of a domestic corporation that was a party to the merger or share exchange, a statement that the plan was duly approved by the shareholders and, if voting by any separate voting group was required, by each such separate voting group, in the manner required by this Act and the articles of incorporation;

(4) if the plan of merger or share exchange did not require approval by the shareholders of a domestic corporation that was a party to the merger or share exchange, a statement to that effect; and

(5) as to each foreign corporation or eligible entity that was a party to the merger or share exchange, a statement that the participation of the foreign corporation or eligible entity was duly authorized as required by the organic law of the corporation or eligible entity.

(b) Articles of merger or share exchange shall be delivered to the secretary of state for filing by the survivor of the merger or the acquiring corporation in a share exchange, and shall take effect at the effective time provided in section 1.23. Articles of merger or share exchange filed under this section may be combined with any filing required under the organic law of any domestic eligible entity involved in the transaction if the combined filing satisfies the requirements of both this section and the other organic law.

§ 11.07. *Effect of Merger or Share Exchange*

(a) When a merger becomes effective:

(1) the corporation or eligible entity that is designated in the plan of merger as the survivor continues or comes into existence, as the case may be;

(2) the separate existence of every corporation or eligible entity that is merged into the survivor ceases;

(3) all property owned by, and every contract right possessed by, each corporation or eligible entity that merges into the survivor is vested in the survivor without reversion or impairment;

(4) all liabilities of each corporation or eligible entity that is merged into the survivor are vested in the survivor;

(5) the name of the survivor may, but need not be, substituted in any pending proceeding for the name of any party to the merger whose separate existence ceased in the merger;

(6) the articles of incorporation or organic documents of the survivor are amended to the extent provided in the plan of merger;

(7) the articles of incorporation or organic documents of a survivor that is created by the merger become effective; and

(8) the shares of each corporation that is a party to the merger, and the interests in an eligible entity that is a party to a merger, that are to be converted under the plan of merger into shares, eligible interests, obligations, rights to acquire securities, other securities, eligible interests, cash, other property, or any combination of the foregoing, are converted, and the former holders of such shares or eligible interests are entitled only to the rights provided to them in the plan of merger or to any rights they may have under chapter 13 or the organic law of the eligible entity.

(b) When a share exchange becomes effective, the shares of each domestic corporation that are to be exchanged for shares, other securities, interests, obligations, rights to acquire shares or other securities, cash, other property, or any combination of the foregoing, are entitled only to the rights provided to them in the plan of share exchange or to any rights they may have under chapter 13.

(c) A person who becomes subject to owner liability for some or all of the debts, obligations, or liabilities of any entity as a result of a merger or share exchange shall have owner liability only to the extent provided in the organic law of the entity and only for those debts, obligations, and liabilities that arise after the effective time of the articles of merger or share exchange.

(d) Upon a merger becoming effective, a foreign corporation, or a foreign eligible entity, that is the survivor of the merger is deemed to:

(1) appoint the secretary of state as its agent for service of process in a proceeding to enforce the rights of shareholders of each domestic corporation that is a party to the merger who exercise appraisal rights, and

(2) agree that it will promptly pay the amount, if any, to which such shareholders are entitled under chapter 13.

(e) Omitted

§ 11.08. *Abandonment of a Merger or Share Exchange*

(a) Unless otherwise provided in a plan of merger or share exchange or in the laws under which a foreign business corporation or a domestic or foreign eligible entity that is a party to a merger or share exchange is organized or by which it is governed, after the plan has been adopted and approved as required by this chapter, and at any time before the merger or share exchange has become effective, it may be abandoned by a domestic business corporation that is a party thereto without action by its shareholders in accordance with any procedures set forth in the plan of merger or share exchange or, if no such procedures are set forth in the plan, in the manner determined by the board of directors, subject to any contractual rights of other parties to the merger or share exchange.

(b) [omitted]

CHAPTER 12. DISPOSITION OF ASSETS

§ 12.01. Disposition of Assets Not Requiring Shareholder Approval

No approval of the shareholders of a corporation is required, unless the articles of incorporation otherwise provide:

(1) to sell, lease, exchange, or otherwise dispose of any or all of the corporation's assets in the usual and regular course of business;

(2) to mortgage, pledge, dedicate to the repayment of indebtedness (whether with or without recourse), or otherwise encumber any or all of the corporation's assets, whether or not in the usual and regular course of business;

(3) to transfer any or all of the corporation's assets to one or more corporations or other entities all of the shares or interests of which are owned by the corporation; or

(4) to distribute assets pro rata to the holders of one or more classes or series of the corporation's shares.

§ 12.02. Shareholder Approval of Certain Dispositions

(a) A sale, lease, exchange, or other disposition of assets, other than a disposition described in section 12.01, requires approval of the corporation's shareholders if the disposition would leave the corporation without a significant continuing business activity. If a corporation retains a business activity that represented at least 25 percent of total assets at the end of the most recently completed fiscal year, and 25 percent of either income from continuing operations before taxes or revenues from continuing operations for that fiscal year, in each case of the corporation and its subsidiaries on a consolidated basis, the corporation will conclusively be deemed to have retained a significant continuing business activity.

(b) A disposition that requires approval of the shareholders under subsection (a) shall be initiated by a resolution by the board of directors authorizing the disposition. After adoption of such a resolution, the board of directors shall submit the proposed disposition to the shareholders for their approval. The board of directors shall also transmit to the shareholders a recommendation that the shareholders approve the proposed disposition, unless the board of directors makes a determination that because of conflicts of interest or other special circumstances it should not make such a recommendation, in which case the board of directors shall transmit to the shareholders the basis for that determination.

(c) The board of directors may condition its submission of a disposition to the shareholders under subsection (b) on any basis.

(d) If a disposition is required to be approved by the shareholders under subsection (a), and if the approval is to be given at a meeting, the corporation shall notify each shareholder, whether or not entitled to vote, of the meeting of shareholders at which the disposition is to be submitted for approval. The notice shall state that the purpose, or one of the purposes, of the meeting is to consider the disposition and shall contain a description of the disposition, including the terms and conditions thereof and the consideration to be received by the corporation.

(e) Unless the articles of incorporation or the board of directors acting pursuant to subsection (c) requires a greater vote, or a greater number of votes to be present, the approval of a disposition by the shareholders shall require the approval of the shareholders at a meeting at which a quorum consisting of at least a majority of the votes entitled to be cast on the disposition exists.

(f) After a disposition has been approved by the shareholders under subsection (b), and at any time before the disposition has been consummated, it may be abandoned by the corporation without action by the shareholders, subject to any contractual rights of other parties to the disposition.

(g) A disposition of assets in the course of dissolution under chapter 14 is not governed by this section.

(h) The assets of a direct or indirect consolidated subsidiary shall be deemed the assets of the parent corporation for the purposes of this section.

CHAPTER 13. APPRAISAL RIGHTS

SUBCHAPTER A. RIGHT TO APPRAISAL AND PAYMENT FOR SHARES

§ 13.01. Definitions

In this chapter:

(1) "Affiliate" means a person that directly or indirectly through one or more intermediaries controls, is controlled by, or is under common control with another person or is a senior executive thereof. For purposes of section 13.02(b)(4), a person is deemed to be an affiliate of its senior executives.

(2) "Beneficial shareholder" means a person who is the beneficial owner of shares held in a voting trust or by a nominee on the beneficial owner's behalf.

(3) "Corporation" means the issuer of the shares held by a shareholder demanding appraisal and, for matters covered in sections 13.22-13.31, includes the surviving entity in a merger.

(4) "Fair value" means the value of the corporation's shares determined:

(i) immediately before the effectuation of the corporate action to which the shareholder objects;

(ii) using customary and current valuation concepts and techniques generally employed for similar businesses in the context of the transaction requiring appraisal; and

(iii) without discounting for lack of marketability or minority status except, if appropriate, for amendments to the articles pursuant to section 13.02(a)(5).

(5) "Interest" means interest from the effective date of the corporate action until the date of payment, at the rate of interest on judgments in this state on the effective date of the corporate action.

(5.1) "Interested transaction" means a corporate action described in section 13.02(a), other than a merger pursuant to section 11.05, involving an interested person in which any of the shares or assets of the corporation are being acquired or converted. As used in this definition:

(i) "Interested person" means a person, or an affiliate of a person, who at any time during the one-year period immediately preceding approval by the board of directors of the corporate action:

(A) was the beneficial owner of 20 percent or more of the voting power of the corporation, excluding any shares acquired pursuant to an offer for all shares having voting power if the offer was made within one year prior to the corporate action for consideration of the same kind and of a value equal to or less than that paid in connection with the corporate action;

(B) had the power, contractually or otherwise, to cause the appointment or election of 25 percent or more of the directors to the board of directors of the corporation; or

(C) was a senior executive or director of the corporation or a senior executive of any affiliate thereof, and that senior executive or director will receive, as a result of the corporate action, a financial benefit not generally available to other shareholders as such, other than:

(I) employment, consulting, retirement, or similar benefits established separately and not as part of or in contemplation of the corporate action; or

(II) employment, consulting, retirement, or similar benefits established in contemplation of, or as part of, the corporate action that are not more favorable than those existing before the corporate action or, if more favorable, that have been approved on behalf of the corporation in the same manner as is provided in section 8.62; or

(III) in the case of a director of the corporation who will, in the corporate action, become a director of the acquiring entity in the corporate action or one of its affiliates, rights and benefits as a director that are provided on the same basis as those afforded by the acquiring entity generally to other directors of such entity or such affiliate.

(ii) "Beneficial owner" means any person who, directly or indirectly, through any contract, arrangement, or understanding, other than a revocable proxy, has or shares the power to vote, or to direct the voting of, shares; except that a member of a national securities exchange is not deemed to be a beneficial owner of securities held directly or indirectly by it on behalf of another person solely because the member is the record holder of the securities if the member is precluded by the rules of the exchange from voting without instruction on contested matters or matters that may affect substantially the rights or privileges of the holders of the securities to be voted. When two or more persons agree to act together for the purpose of voting their shares of the corporation, each member of the group formed thereby is deemed to have acquired beneficial ownership, as of the date of the agreement, of all voting shares of the corporation beneficially owned by any member of the group.

(6) "Preferred shares" means a class or series of shares whose holders have preferences over any other class or series with respect to distributions.

(7) "Record shareholder" means the person in whose name shares are registered in the records of the corporation or the beneficial owner of shares to the extent of the rights granted by a nominee certificate on file with the corporation.

(8) "Senior executive" means the chief executive officer, chief operating officer, chief financial officer,

and anyone in charge of a principal business unit or function.

(9) "Shareholder" means both the record shareholder and a beneficial shareholder.

§ 13.02. Right to Appraisal

(a) A shareholder is entitled to appraisal rights, and to obtain payment of the fair value of that shareholder's shares, in the event of any of the following corporate actions:

(1) consummation of a merger to which the corporation is a party (i) if shareholder approval is required for the merger by section 11.04 and the shareholder is entitled to vote on the merger, except that appraisal rights shall not be available to any shareholder of the corporation with respect to shares of any class or series that remain outstanding after consummation of the merger, or (ii) if the corporation is a subsidiary and the merger is governed by section 11.05;

(2) consummation of a share exchange to which the corporation is a party as the corporation whose shares will be acquired if the shareholder is entitled to vote on the exchange, except that appraisal rights shall not be available to any shareholder of the corporation with respect to any class or series of shares of the corporation that is not exchanged;

(3) consummation of a disposition of assets pursuant to section 12.02 if the shareholder is entitled to vote on the disposition;

(4) an amendment of the articles of incorporation with respect to a class or series of shares that reduces the number of shares of a class or series owned by the shareholder to a fraction of a share if the corporation has the obligation or right to repurchase the fractional share so created; or

(5) any other amendment to the articles of incorporation, merger, share exchange or disposition of assets to the extent provided by the articles of incorporation, bylaws or a resolution of the board of directors.

(6) consummation of a domestication if the shareholder does not receive shares in the foreign corporation resulting from the domestication that have terms as favorable to the shareholder in all material respects, and represent at least the same percentage interest of the total voting rights of the outstanding shares of the corporation, as the shares held by the shareholder before the domestication;

(7) consummation of a conversion of the corporation to nonprofit status pursuant to subchapter 9C; or

(8) consummation of a conversion of the corporation to an unincorporated entity pursuant to subchapter 9E.

(b) Notwithstanding subsection (a), the availability of appraisal rights under subsections (a)(1), (2), (3), (4), (6) and (8) shall be limited in accordance with the following provisions:

(1) Appraisal rights shall not be available for the holders of shares of any class or series of shares which is:

(i) a covered security under Section 18(b)(1)(A) or (B) of the Securities Act of 1933, as amended or

(ii) traded in an organized market and has at least 2,000 shareholders and the outstanding shares of such class or series has a market value of at least $20 million (exclusive of the value of such shares held by its subsidiaries, senior executives, directors and beneficial shareholders owning more than 10 percent of such shares).

   (iii) [omitted]

  (2) The applicability of subsection (b)(1) shall be determined as of:

   (i) the record date fixed to determine the shareholders entitled to receive notice of, and to vote at, the meeting of shareholders to act upon the corporate action requiring appraisal rights; or

   (ii) the day before the effective date of such corporate action if there is no meeting of shareholders.

  (3) Subsection (b)(1) shall not be applicable and appraisal rights shall be available pursuant to subsection (a) for the holders of any class or series of shares who are required by the terms of the corporate action requiring appraisal rights to accept for such shares anything other than cash or shares of any class or any series of shares of any corporation, or any other proprietary interest of any other entity, that satisfies the standards set forth in subsection (b)(1) at the time the corporate action becomes effective.

  (4) Subsection (b)(1) shall not be applicable and appraisal rights shall be available pursuant to subsection (a) for the holders of any class or series of shares where the corporate action is an interested transaction.

  (c) [omitted]

§ 13.03. *Assertion of Rights by Nominees and Beneficial Owners*

  (a) A record shareholder may assert appraisal rights as to fewer than all the shares registered in the record shareholder's name but owned by a beneficial shareholder only if the record shareholder objects with respect to all shares of the class or series owned by the beneficial shareholder and notifies the corporation in writing of the name and address of each beneficial shareholder on whose behalf appraisal rights are being asserted. The rights of a record shareholder who asserts appraisal rights for only part of the shares held of record in the record shareholder's name under this subsection shall be determined as if the shares as to which the record shareholder objects and the record shareholder's other shares were registered in the names of different record shareholders.

  (b) A beneficial shareholder may assert appraisal rights as to shares of any class or series held on behalf of the shareholder only if such shareholder:

   (1) submits to the corporation the record shareholder's written consent to the assertion of such rights no later than the date referred to in section 13.22(b)(2)(ii); and

   (2) does so with respect to all shares of the class or series that are beneficially owned by the beneficial shareholder.

SUBCHAPTER B. PROCEDURE FOR EXERCISE OF APPRAISAL RIGHT

§ 13.20. *Notice of Appraisal Rights*

  (a) Where any corporate action specified in section 13.02(a) is to be submitted to a vote at a shareholders' meeting, the meeting notice must state that the corporation has concluded that the shareholders are, are not or may be entitled to assert appraisal rights under this chapter. If the corporation concludes that appraisal rights are or may be available, a copy of this chapter must accompany the meeting notice sent to those record shareholders entitled to exercise appraisal rights.

  (b) In a merger pursuant to section 11.05, the parent corporation must notify in writing all record shareholders of the subsidiary who are entitled to assert appraisal rights that the corporate action became effective. Such notice must be sent within 10 days after the corporate action became effective and include the materials described in section 13.22.

  (c) Where any corporate action specified in section 13.02(a) is to be approved by written consent of the shareholders pursuant to section 7.04:

   (1) written notice that appraisal rights are, are not or may be available must be given to each record shareholder from whom a consent is solicited at the time consent of such shareholder is first solicited and, if the corporation has concluded that appraisal rights are or may be available, must be accompanied by a copy of this chapter. [remainder of section omitted]

§ 13.21. *Notice of Intent to Demand Payment*

  (a) If a corporate action specified in section 13.02(a) is submitted to a vote at a shareholders' meeting, a shareholder who wishes to assert appraisal rights with respect to any class or series of shares:

   (1) must deliver to the corporation before the vote is taken written notice of the shareholder's intent to demand payment if the proposed action is effectuated; and

   (2) must not vote, or cause or permit to be voted, any shares of such class or series in favor of the proposed action.

  (b) If a corporate action specified in section 13.02(a) is to be approved by less than unanimous consent, a shareholder who wishes to assert appraisal rights with respect to any class or series of shares must not execute a consent in favor of the proposed action with respect to that class or series of shares.

  (c) A shareholder who fails to satisfy the requirements of subsection (a) or (b) is not entitled to payment under this chapter.

§ 13.22. *Appraisal Notice and Form*

  (a) If proposed corporate action requiring appraisal rights under section 13.02(a) becomes effective, the corporation must deliver a written appraisal notice and form required by subsection (b)(1) to all shareholders who satisfied the requirements of section 13.21(a) or section 13.21(b). In the case of a merger under section 11.05, the parent must deliver a written appraisal notice and form to all record shareholders who may be entitled to assert appraisal rights.

  (b) The appraisal notice must be sent no earlier than the date the corporate action specified in section 13.02(a) became effective and no later than 10 days after such date and must:

   (1) supply a form that (i) specifies the first date of any announcement to shareholders made prior to the date the corporation action became effective of the principal terms of the proposed corporate action, (ii) if such announcement was

made, and requires the shareholder asserting the appraisal rights to certify whether beneficial ownership of those shares for which appraisal rights are asserted was acquired before that date, and (iii) requires the shareholder asserting appraisal rights to certify that the shareholder did not vote for or consent to the transaction;

(2) state:

(i) where the form must be sent and where certificates for certificated shares must be deposited and the date by which those certificates must be deposited, which date may not be earlier than the date for receiving the required form under subsection (2)(ii);

(ii) a date by which the corporation must receive the form which date may not be fewer than 40 nor more than 60 days after the date the subsection (a) appraisal notice and form are sent, and state that the shareholder shall have waived the right to demand appraisal with respect to the shares unless the form is received by the corporation by such specified date;

(iii) the corporation's estimate of the fair value of the shares;

(iv) that, if requested in writing, the corporation will provide, to the shareholder so requesting, within 10 days after the date specified in subsection (2)(ii) the number of shareholders who return the forms by the specified date and the total number of shares owned by them; and

(v) the date by which the notice to withdraw under section 13.23 must be received, which date must be within 20 days after the date specified in subsection (2)(ii); and

(3) be accompanied by a copy of this chapter.

§ 13.23.   Perfection of Rights; Right to Withdraw

(a) A shareholder who receives notice pursuant to section 13.22 and who wishes to exercise appraisal rights must sign and return the form sent by the corporation and, in the case of certificated shares, deposit the shareholder's certificates in accordance with the terms of the notice by the date referred to in the notice pursuant to section 13.22(b)(2)(ii). In addition, if applicable, the shareholder must certify on the form whether the beneficial owner of such shares acquired beneficial ownership of the shares before the date required to be set forth in the notice pursuant to section 13.22(b)(1). If a shareholder fails to make this certification, the corporation may elect to treat the shareholder's shares as after-acquired shares under section 13.25. In addition, a shareholder who wishes to exercise appraisal rights must execute and return the form and, in the case of certificated shares, deposit the shareholder's certificates in accordance with the terms of the notice by the date referred to in the notice pursuant to section 13.22(b)(2)(ii). Once a shareholder deposits that shareholder's certificates or, in the case of uncertificated shares, returns the signed forms, that shareholder loses all rights as a shareholder, unless the shareholder withdraws pursuant to subsection (b).

(b) A shareholder who has complied with subsection (a) may nevertheless decline to exercise appraisal rights and withdraw from the appraisal process by so notifying the corporation in writing by the date set forth in the appraisal notice pursuant to section 13.22(b)(2)(v). A shareholder who fails to so withdraw

from the appraisal process may not thereafter withdraw without the corporation's written consent.

(c) A shareholder who does not execute and return the form and, in the case of certificated shares, deposit that shareholder's share certificates where required, each by the date set forth in the notice described in section 13.22(b), shall not be entitled to payment under this chapter.

§ 13.24.   Payment

(a) Except as provided in section 13.25, within 30 days after the form required by section 13.22(b)(2)(ii) is due, the corporation shall pay in cash to those shareholders who complied with section 13.23(a) the amount the corporation estimates to be the fair value of the shares, plus interest.

(b) The payment to each shareholder pursuant to subsection (a) must be accompanied by:

(1)(i) the annual financial statements specified in section 16.20(a) of the corporation that issued the shares to be appraised, which shall be as of a date ending not more than 16 months before the date of payment, and shall comply with section 16.20(b); provided that, if such annual financial statements are not reasonable available, the corporation shall provide reasonably equivalent financial information, and (ii) the latest available quarterly financial statements of such corporation, if any;

(2) a statement of the corporation's estimate of the fair value of the shares, which estimate must equal or exceed the corporation's estimate given pursuant to section 13.22(b)(2)(iii);

(3) a statement that shareholders described in subsection (a) have the right to demand further payment under section 13.26 and that if any such shareholder does not do so within the time period specified therein, such shareholder shall be deemed to have accepted such payment in full satisfaction of the corporation's obligations under this chapter.

§ 13.25.   After-Acquired Shares [omitted]

§ 13.26.   Procedure if Shareholder Dissatisfied with Payment or Offer

(a) A shareholder paid pursuant to section 13.24 who is dissatisfied with the amount of the payment must notify the corporation in writing of that shareholder's estimate of the fair value of the shares and demand payment of that estimate plus interest (less any payment under section 13.24). A shareholder offered payment under section 13.25 who is dissatisfied with that offer must reject the offer and demand payment of the shareholder's stated estimate of the fair value of the shares plus interest.

(b) A shareholder who fails to notify the corporation in writing of that shareholder's demand to be paid the shareholder's stated estimate of the fair value plus interest under subsection (a) within 30 days after receiving the corporation's payment or offer of payment under section 13.24 or section 13.25, respectively, waives the right to demand payment under this section and shall be entitled only to the payment made or offered pursuant to those respective sections.

SUBCHAPTER C. JUDICIAL APPRAISAL OF SHARES

§ 13.30. Court Action

(a) If a shareholder makes demand for payment under section 13.26 which remains unsettled, the corporation shall commence a proceeding within 60 days after receiving the payment demand and petition the court to determine the fair value of the shares and accrued interest. If the corporation does not commence the proceeding within the 60-day period, it shall pay in cash to each shareholder the amount the shareholder demanded pursuant to section 13.26 plus interest.

(b) [omitted]

(c) [omitted]

(d) The jurisdiction of the court in which the proceeding is commenced under subsection (b) is plenary and exclusive. The court may appoint one or more persons as appraisers to receive evidence and recommend a decision on the question of fair value. The appraisers shall have the powers described in the order appointing them, or in any amendment to it. The shareholders demanding appraisal rights are entitled to the same discovery rights as parties in other civil proceedings. There shall be no right to a jury trial.

(e) Each shareholder made a party to the proceeding is entitled to judgment (i) for the amount, if any, by which the court finds the fair value of the shareholder's shares, plus interest, exceeds the amount paid by the corporation or (ii) for the fair value, plus interest, of the shareholder's shares for which the corporation elected to withhold payment under section 13.25.

§ 13.31. Court Costs and Counsel Fees

(a) The court in an appraisal proceeding commenced under section 13.30 shall determine all court costs of the proceeding, including the reasonable compensation and expenses of appraisers appointed by the court. The court shall assess the court costs against the corporation, except that the court may assess court costs against all or some of the shareholders demanding appraisal, in amounts the court finds equitable, to the extent the court finds such shareholders acted arbitrarily, vexatiously, or not in good faith with respect to the rights provided by this chapter.

(b) The court in an appraisal proceeding may also assess the fees and expenses of counsel and experts for the respective parties, in amounts the court finds equitable. [subsections (b), (c), and (d) omitted]

SUBCHAPTER D. OTHER REMEDIES

§ 13.40. Other Remedies Limited

(a) The legality of a proposed or completed corporate action described in section 13.02(a) may not be contested, nor may the corporate action be enjoined, set aside or rescinded, in a legal or equitable proceeding by a shareholder after the shareholders have approved the corporate action.

(b) Subsection (a) does not apply to a corporate action that:

(1) was not authorized and approved in accordance with the applicable provisions of:

(i) chapter 9, 10, 11 or 12,

(ii) the articles of incorporation or bylaws, or

(iii) the resolution of the board of directors authorizing the corporate action;

(2) was procured as a result of fraud, a material misrepresentation, or an omission of a material fact necessary to make statements made, in light of the circumstances in which they were made, not misleading;

(3) is an interested transaction [remainder of section omitted].

CHAPTER 14. DISSOLUTION

SUBCHAPTER A. VOLUNTARY DISSOLUTION

§ 14.01. Dissolution by Incorporators or Initial Directors

A majority of the incorporators or initial directors of a corporation that has not issued shares or has not commenced business may dissolve the corporation by delivering to the secretary of state for filing articles of dissolution that set forth:

(1) the name of the corporation;

(2) the date of its incorporation;

(3) either (i) that none of the corporation's shares has been issued or (ii) that the corporation has not commenced business;

(4) that no debt of the corporation remains unpaid;

(5) that the net assets of the corporation remaining after winding up have been distributed to the shareholders, if shares were issued; and

(6) that a majority of the incorporators or initial directors authorized the dissolution.

§ 14.02. Dissolution by Board of Directors and Shareholders

(a) A corporation's board of directors may propose dissolution for submission to the shareholders.

(b) For a proposal to dissolve to be adopted:

(1) the board of directors must recommend dissolution to the shareholders unless the board of directors determines that because of conflict of interest or other special circumstances it should make no recommendation and communicates the basis for its determination to the shareholders; and

(2) the shareholders entitled to vote must approve the proposal to dissolve as provided in subsection (e).

(c) The board of directors may condition its submission of the proposal for dissolution on any basis.

(d) The corporation shall notify each shareholder, whether or not entitled to vote, of the proposed shareholders' meeting. The notice must also state that the purpose, or one of the purposes, of the meeting is to consider dissolving the corporation.

(e) Unless the articles of incorporation or the board of directors acting pursuant to subsection (c) require a greater vote, a greater number of shares to be present, or a vote by voting groups, adoption of the proposal to dissolve shall require the approval of the shareholders at a meeting at which a quorum consisting of at least a majority of the votes entitled to be cast exists.

§ 14.03. Articles of Dissolution

(a) At any time after dissolution is authorized, the corporation may dissolve by delivering to the secretary of state for filing articles of dissolution setting forth:

(1) the name of the corporation;

(2) the date dissolution was authorized; and

(3) if dissolution was approved by the shareholders, a statement that the proposal to dissolve was duly approved by the shareholders in the manner required by this Act and by the articles of incorporation.

(b) A corporation is dissolved upon the effective date of its articles of dissolution.

(c) For purposes of this subchapter, "dissolved corporation" means a corporation whose articles of dissolution have become effective and includes a successor entity to which the remaining assets of the corporation are transferred subject to its liabilities for purposes of liquidation.

§ 14.04. *Revocation of Dissolution*

(a) A corporation may revoke its dissolution within 120 days of its effective date.

(b) Revocation of dissolution must be authorized in the same manner as the dissolution was authorized unless that authorization permitted revocation by action of the board of directors alone, in which event the board of directors may revoke the dissolution without shareholder action.

(c) After the revocation of dissolution is authorized, the corporation may revoke the dissolution by delivering to the secretary of state for filing articles of revocation of dissolution, together with a copy of its articles of dissolution, that set forth:

(1) the name of the corporation;

(2) the effective date of the dissolution that was revoked;

(3) the date that the revocation of dissolution was authorized;

(4) if the corporation's board of directors (or incorporators) revoked the dissolution, a statement to that effect;

(5) if the corporation's board of directors revoked a dissolution authorized by the shareholders, a statement that revocation was permitted by action by the board of directors alone pursuant to that authorization; and

(6) if shareholder action was required to revoke the dissolution, the information required by section 14.03(a)(3).

(d) Revocation of dissolution is effective upon the effective date of the articles of revocation of dissolution.

(e) When the revocation of dissolution is effective, it relates back to and takes effect as of the effective date of the dissolution and the corporation resumes carrying on its business as if dissolution had never occurred.

§ 14.05. *Effect of Dissolution*

(a) A dissolved corporation continues its corporate existence but may not carry on any business except that appropriate to wind up and liquidate its business and affairs, including:

(1) collecting its assets;

(2) disposing of its properties that will not be distributed in kind to its shareholders;

(3) discharging or making provision for discharging its liabilities;

(4) distributing its remaining property among its shareholders according to their interests; and

(5) doing every other act necessary to wind up and liquidate its business and affairs.

(b) Dissolution of a corporation does not:

(1) transfer title to the corporation's property;

(2) prevent transfer of its shares or securities, although the authorization to dissolve may provide for closing the corporation's share transfer records;

(3) subject its directors or officers to standards of conduct different from those prescribed in chapter 8;

(4) change quorum or voting requirements for its board of directors or shareholders; change provisions for selection, resignation, or removal of its directors or officers or both; or change provisions for amending its bylaws;

(5) prevent commencement of a proceeding by or against the corporation in its corporate name;

(6) abate or suspend a proceeding pending by or against the corporation on the effective date of dissolution; or

(7) terminate the authority of the registered agent of the corporation.

§ 14.06. *Known Claims Against Dissolved Corporation*

(a) A dissolved corporation may dispose of the known claims against it by notifying its known claimants in writing of the dissolution at any time after its effective date.

(b) The written notice must:

(1) describe information that must be included in a claim;

(2) provide a mailing address where a claim may be sent;

(3) state the deadline, which may not be fewer than 120 days from the effective date of the written notice, by which the dissolved corporation must receive the claim; and

(4) state that the claim will be barred if not received by the deadline.

(c) A claim against the dissolved corporation is barred:

(1) if a claimant who was given written notice under subsection (b) does not deliver the claim to the dissolved corporation by the deadline;

(2) if a claimant whose claim was rejected by the dissolved corporation does not commence a proceeding to enforce the claim within 90 days from the effective date of the rejection notice.

(d) For purposes of this section, "claim" does not include a contingent liability or a claim based on an event occurring after the effective date of dissolution.

§ 14.07. *Other Claims Against Dissolved Corporation*

(a) A dissolved corporation may also publish notice of its dissolution and request that persons with claims against the dissolved corporation present them in accordance with the notice.

(b) The notice must:

(1) be published one time in a newspaper of general circulation in the county where the dissolved corporation's principal office (or, if none in this state, its registered office) is or was last located;

(2) describe the information that must be included in a claim and provide a mailing address where the claim may be sent; and

(3) state that a claim against the dissolved corporation will be barred unless a proceeding to enforce the claim is commenced within three years after the publication of the notice.

(c) If the dissolved corporation publishes a newspaper notice in accordance with subsection (b), the claim of each of the following claimants is barred unless the claimant commences a proceeding to enforce the claim against the dissolved corporation within three years after the publication date of the newspaper notice:

(1) a claimant who was not given written notice under section 14.06;

(2) a claimant whose claim was timely sent to the dissolved corporation but not acted on;

(3) a claimant whose claim is contingent or based on an event occurring after the effective date of dissolution.

(d) A claim that is not barred by section 14.06(b) or section 14.07(c) may be enforced:

(1) against the dissolved corporation, to the extent of its undistributed assets; or

(2) except as provided in section 14.08(d), if the assets have been distributed in liquidation, against a shareholder of the dissolved corporation to the extent of the shareholder's pro rata share of the claim or the corporate assets distributed to the shareholder in liquidation, whichever is less, but a shareholder's total liability for all claims under this section may not exceed the total amount of assets distributed to the shareholder.

§ 14.08.　Court Proceedings

(a) A dissolved corporation that has published a notice under section 14.07 may file an application with the [name or describe] court of the county where the dissolved corporation's principal office (or, if none in this state, its registered office) is located for a determination of the amount and form of security to be provided for payment of claims that are contingent or have not been made known to the dissolved corporation or that are based on an event occurring after the effective date of dissolution but that, based on the facts known to the dissolved corporation, are reasonably estimated to arise after the effective date of dissolution. Provision need not be made for any claim that is or is reasonably anticipated to be barred under section 14.07(c).

(b) Within 10 days after the filing of the application, notice of the proceeding shall be given by the dissolved corporation to each claimant holding a contingent claim whose contingent claim is shown on the records of the dissolved corporation.

(c) The court may appoint a guardian ad litem to represent all claimants whose identities are unknown in any proceeding brought under this section. The reasonable fees and expenses of such guardian, including all reasonable expert witness fees, shall be paid by the dissolved corporation.

(d) Provision by the dissolved corporation for security in the amount and the form ordered by the court under section 14.08(a) shall satisfy the dissolved corporation's obligations with respect to claims that are contingent, have not been made known to the dissolved corporation or are based on an event occurring after the effective date of dissolution, and such claims may not be enforced against a shareholder who received assets in liquidation.

§ 14.09.　Director Duties

(a) Directors shall cause the dissolved corporation to discharge or make reasonable provision for the payment of claims and make distribution of assets to shareholders after payment or provision for claims.

(b) Directors of a dissolved corporation which has disposed of claims under sections 14.06, 14.07, or 14.08 shall not be liable for breach of section 14.09(a) with respect to claims against the dissolved corporation that are barred or satisfied under sections 14.06, 14.07, or 14.08.

SUBCHAPTER B.　ADMINISTRATIVE DISSOLUTION

§ 14.20.　Grounds for Administrative Dissolution

The secretary of state may commence a proceeding under section 14.21 to administratively dissolve a corporation if:

(1) the corporation does not pay within 60 days after they are due any franchise taxes or penalties imposed by this Act or other law;

(2) the corporation does not deliver its annual report to the secretary of state within 60 days after it is due;

(3) the corporation is without a registered agent or registered office in this state for 60 days or more;

(4) the corporation does not notify the secretary of state within 60 days that its registered agent or registered office has been changed, that its registered agent has resigned, or that its registered office has been discontinued; or

(5) the corporation's period of duration stated in its articles of incorporation expires.

§ 14.21.　Procedure for and Effect of Administrative Dissolution

(a) If the secretary of state determines that one or more grounds exist under section 14.20 for dissolving a corporation, he shall serve the corporation with written notice of his determination under section 5.04.

(b) If the corporation does not correct each ground for dissolution or demonstrate to the reasonable satisfaction of the secretary of state that each ground determined by the secretary of state does not exist within 60 days after service of the notice is perfected under section 5.04, the secretary of state shall administratively dissolve the corporation by signing a certificate of dissolution that recites the ground or grounds for dissolution and its effective date. The secretary of state shall file the original of the certificate and serve a copy on the corporation under section 5.04.

(c) A corporation administratively dissolved continues its corporate existence but may not carry on any business except that necessary to wind up and liquidate its business and affairs under section 14.05 and notify claimants under sections 14.06 and 14.07.

(d) The administrative dissolution of a corporation does not terminate the authority of its registered agent.

§ 14.22.　Reinstatement Following Administrative Dissolution

(a) A corporation administratively dissolved under section 14.21 may apply to the secretary of state for reinstatement within two years after the effective date of dissolution. The application must:

(1) recite the name of the corporation and the effective date of its administrative dissolution;

(2) state that the ground or grounds for dissolution either did not exist or have been eliminated;

(3) state that the corporation's name satisfies the requirements of section 4.01; and

(4) contain a certificate from the [taxing authority] reciting that all taxes owed by the corporation have been paid.

(b) If the secretary of state determines that the application contains the information required by subsection (a) and that the information is correct, he shall cancel the certificate of dissolution and prepare a certificate of reinstatement that recites his determination and the effective date of reinstatement, file the original of the certificate, and serve a copy on the corporation under section 5.04.

(c) When the reinstatement is effective, it relates back to and takes effect as of the effective date of the administrative dissolution and the corporation resumes carrying on its business as if the administrative dissolution had never occurred.

§ 14.23. *Appeal from Denial of Reinstatement*

(a) If the secretary of state denies a corporation's application for reinstatement following administrative dissolution, he shall serve the corporation under section 5.04 with a written notice that explains the reason or reasons for denial.

(b) The corporation may appeal the denial of reinstatement to the [name or describe] court within 30 days after service of the notice of denial is perfected. The corporation appeals by petitioning the court to set aside the dissolution and attaching to the petition copies of the secretary of state's certificate of dissolution, the corporation's application for reinstatement, and the secretary of state's notice of denial.

(c) The court may summarily order the secretary of state to reinstate the dissolved corporation or may take other action the court considers appropriate.

(d) The court's final decision may be appealed as in other civil proceedings.

SUBCHAPTER C. JUDICIAL DISSOLUTION

§ 14.30. *Grounds for Judicial Dissolution*

(a) The [name or describe court or courts] may dissolve a corporation:

(1) in a proceeding by the attorney general if it is established that:

(i) the corporation obtained its articles of incorporation through fraud; or

(ii) the corporation has continued to exceed or abuse the authority conferred upon it by law;

(2) in a proceeding by a shareholder if it is established that:

(i) the directors are deadlocked in the management of the corporate affairs, the shareholders are unable to break the deadlock, and irreparable injury to the corporation is threatened or being suffered, or the business and affairs of the corporation can no longer be conducted to the advantage of the shareholders generally, because of the deadlock;

(ii) the directors or those in control of the corporation have acted, are acting, or will act in a manner that is illegal, oppressive, or fraudulent;

(iii) the shareholders are deadlocked in voting power and have failed, for a period that includes at least two consecutive annual meeting dates, to elect successors to directors whose terms have expired; or

(iv) the corporate assets are being misapplied or wasted;

(3) in a proceeding by a creditor if it is established that:

(i) the creditor's claim has been reduced to judgment, the execution on the judgment returned unsatisfied, and the corporation is insolvent; or

(ii) the corporation has admitted in writing that the creditor's claim is due and owing and the corporation is insolvent; or

(4) in a proceeding by the corporation to have its voluntary dissolution continued under court supervision.

(5) in a proceeding by a shareholder if the corporation has abandoned its business and has failed within a reasonable time to liquidate and distribute its assets and dissolve.

(b) Section 14.30(a)(2) shall not apply in the case of a corporation that, on the date of the filing of the proceeding, has shares that are:

(i) listed on the New York Stock Exchange, the American Stock Exchange or any exchange owned or operated by the NASDAQ Stock Market LLC, or listed or quoted on a system owned or operated by the National Association of Securities Dealers, Inc.; or

(ii) not so listed or quoted, but are held by at least 300 shareholders and the shares outstanding have a market value of at least $20 million (exclusive of the value of such shares held by the corporation's subsidiaries, senior executives, directors and beneficial shareholders owning more than 10 percent of such shares).

(c) In this section, "beneficial shareholder" has the meaning specified in section 13.01(2).

§ 14.31. *Procedure for Judicial Dissolution*

(a) Venue for a proceeding by the attorney general to dissolve a corporation lies in [name the county or counties]. Venue for a proceeding brought by any other party named in section 14.30 lies in the county where a corporation's principal office (or, if none in this state, its registered office) is or was last located.

(b) It is not necessary to make shareholders parties to a proceeding to dissolve a corporation unless relief is sought against them individually.

(c) A court in a proceeding brought to dissolve a corporation may issue injunctions, appoint a receiver or custodian pendente lite with all powers and duties the court directs, take other action required to preserve the corporate assets wherever located, and carry on the business of the corporation until a full hearing can be held.

(d) Within 10 days of the commencement of a proceeding under section 14.30(2) to dissolve a corporation that is not a public corporation, the corporation must send to all shareholders, other than the petitioner, a notice stating that the shareholders are entitled to avoid the dissolution of the corporation by electing to purchase the petitioner's shares under section 14.34 and accompanied by a copy of section 14.34.

§ 14.32. Receivership or Custodianship

(a) Unless an election to purchase has been filed under section 14.34, a court in a judicial proceeding brought to dissolve a corporation may appoint one or more receivers to wind up and liquidate, or one or more custodians to manage, the business and affairs of the corporation. The court shall hold a hearing, after notifying all parties to the proceeding and any interested persons designated by the court, before appointing a receiver or custodian. The court appointing a receiver or custodian has jurisdiction over the corporation and all its property wherever located.

(b) The court may appoint an individual or a domestic or foreign corporation (authorized to transact business in this state) as a receiver or custodian. The court may require the receiver or custodian to post bond, with or without sureties, in an amount the court directs.

(c) The court shall describe the powers and duties of the receiver or custodian in its appointing order, which may be amended from time to time. Among other powers:

(1) the receiver (i) may dispose of all or any part of the assets of the corporation wherever located, at a public or private sale, if authorized by the court; and (ii) may sue and defend in his own name as receiver of the corporation in all courts of this state;

(2) the custodian may exercise all of the powers of the corporation, through or in place of its board of directors or officers, to the extent necessary to manage the affairs of the corporation in the best interests of its shareholders and creditors.

(d) The court during a receivership may redesignate the receiver a custodian, and during a custodianship may redesignate the custodian a receiver, if doing so is in the best interests of the corporation, its shareholders, and creditors.

(e) The court from time to time during the receivership or custodianship may order compensation paid and expenses paid or reimbursed to the receiver or custodian from the assets of the corporation or proceeds from the sale of the assets.

§ 14.33. Decree of Dissolution

(a) If after a hearing the court determines that one or more grounds for judicial dissolution described in section 14.30 exist, it may enter a decree dissolving the corporation and specifying the effective date of the dissolution, and the clerk of the court shall deliver a certified copy of the decree to the secretary of state, who shall file it.

(b) After entering the decree of dissolution, the court shall direct the winding up and liquidation of the corporation's business and affairs in accordance with section 14.05 and the notification of claimants in accordance with sections 14.06 and 14.07.

§ 14.34. Election to Purchase in Lieu of Dissolution

(a) In a proceeding under section 14.30(2) to dissolve a corporation, the corporation may elect or, if it fails to elect, one or more shareholders may elect to purchase all shares owned by the petitioning shareholder at the fair value of the shares. An election

pursuant to this section shall be irrevocable unless the court determines that it is equitable to set aside or modify the election.

(b) An election to purchase pursuant to this section may be filed with the court at any time within 90 days after the filing of the petition under section 14.30(2) or at such later time as the court in its discretion may allow. If the election to purchase is filed by one or more shareholders, the corporation shall, within 10 days thereafter, give written notice to all shareholders, other than the petitioner. The notice must state the name and number of shares owned by the petitioner and the name and number of shares owned by each electing shareholder and must advise the recipients of their right to join in the election to purchase shares in accordance with this section. Shareholders who wish to participate must file notice of their intention to join in the purchase no later than 30 days after the effective date of the notice to them. All shareholders who have filed an election or notice of their intention to participate in the election to purchase thereby become parties to the proceeding and shall participate in the purchase in proportion to their ownership of shares as of the date the first election was filed, unless they otherwise agree or the court otherwise directs. After an election has been filed by the corporation or one or more shareholders, the proceeding under section 14.30(2) may not be discontinued or settled, nor may the petitioning shareholder sell or otherwise dispose of his shares, unless the court determines that it would be equitable to the corporation and the shareholders, other than the petitioner, to permit such discontinuance, settlement, sale, or other disposition.

(c) If, within 60 days of the filing of the first election, the parties reach agreement as to the fair value and terms of purchase of the petitioner's shares, the court shall enter an order directing the purchase of petitioner's shares upon the terms and conditions agreed to by the parties.

(d) If the parties are unable to reach an agreement as provided for in subsection (c), the court, upon application of any party, shall stay the section 14.30(2) proceedings and determine the fair value of the petitioner's shares as of the day before the date on which the petition under section 14.30(2) was filed or as of such other date as the court deems appropriate under the circumstances.

(e) Upon determining the fair value of the shares, the court shall enter an order directing the purchase upon such terms and conditions as the court deems appropriate, which may include payment of the purchase price in installments, where necessary in the interests of equity, provision for security to assure payment of the purchase price and any additional costs, fees, and expenses as may have been awarded, and, if the shares are to be purchased by shareholders, the allocation of shares among them. In allocating petitioner's shares among holders of different classes of shares, the court should attempt to preserve the existing distribution of voting rights among holders of different classes insofar as practicable and may direct that holders of a specific class or classes shall not participate in the purchase. Interest may be allowed at the rate and from the date determined by the court to be equitable, but if the court finds that the refusal of the petitioning shareholder to accept an offer of payment was arbitrary or otherwise not in good faith, no interest shall be allowed. If the court finds that the petitioning shareholder had probable grounds for relief under paragraphs (ii) or (iv) of section

14.30(2), it may award to the petitioning shareholder reasonable fees and expenses of counsel and of any experts employed by him.

(f) Upon entry of an order under subsections (c) or (e), the court shall dismiss the petition to dissolve the corporation under section 14.30, and the petitioning shareholder shall no longer have any rights or status as a shareholder of the corporation, except the right to receive the amounts awarded to him by the order of the court which shall be enforceable in the same manner as any other judgment.

(g) The purchase ordered pursuant to subsection (e), shall be made within 10 days after the date the order becomes final unless before that time the corporation files with the court a notice of its intention to adopt articles of dissolution pursuant to sections 14.02 and 14.03, which articles must then be adopted and filed within 50 days thereafter. Upon filing of such articles of dissolution, the corporation shall be dissolved in accordance with the provisions of sections 14.05 through 07, and the order entered pursuant to subsection (e) shall no longer be of any force or effect, except that the court may award the petitioning shareholder reasonable fees and expenses in accordance with the provisions of the last sentence of subsection (e) and the petitioner may continue to pursue any claims previously asserted on behalf of the corporation.

(h) Any payment by the corporation pursuant to an order under subsection (c) or (e), other than an award of fees and expenses pursuant to subsection (e), subject to the provisions of section 6.40.

SUBCHAPTER D. MISCELLANEOUS

§ 14.40. Deposit with State Treasurer

Assets of a dissolved corporation that should be transferred to a creditor, claimant, or shareholder of the corporation who cannot be found or who is not competent to receive them shall be reduced to cash and deposited with the state treasurer or other appropriate state official for safekeeping. When the creditor, claimant, or shareholder furnishes satisfactory proof of entitlement to the amount deposited, the state treasurer or other appropriate state official shall pay him or his representative that amount.

CHAPTER 15. FOREIGN CORPORATIONS

SUBCHAPTER A. CERTIFICATE OF AUTHORITY

§ 15.01. Authority to Transact Business Required

(a) A foreign corporation may not transact business in this state until it obtains a certificate of authority from the secretary of state.

(b) The following activities, among others, do not constitute transacting business within the meaning of subsection (a):

(1) maintaining, defending, or settling any proceeding;

(2) holding meetings of the board of directors or shareholders or carrying on other activities concerning internal corporate affairs;

(3) maintaining bank accounts;

(4) maintaining offices or agencies for the transfer, exchange, and registration of the corporation's own securities or maintaining trustees or depositaries with respect to those securities;

(5) selling through independent contractors;

(6) soliciting or obtaining orders, whether by mail or through employees or agents or otherwise, if the orders require acceptance outside this state before they become contracts;

(7) creating or acquiring indebtedness, mortgages, and security interests in real or personal property;

(8) securing or collecting debts or enforcing mortgages and security interests in property securing the debts;

(9) owning, without more, real or personal property;

(10) conducting an isolated transaction that is completed within 30 days and that is not one in the course of repeated transactions of a like nature;

(11) transacting business in interstate commerce.

(c) The list of activities in subsection (b) is not exhaustive.

§ 15.02. Consequences of Transacting Business Without Authority

(a) A foreign corporation transacting business in this state without a certificate of authority may not maintain a proceeding in any court in this state until it obtains a certificate of authority.

(b) The successor to a foreign corporation that transacted business in this state without a certificate of authority and the assignee of a cause of action arising out of that business may not maintain a proceeding based on that cause of action in any court in this state until the foreign corporation or its successor obtains a certificate of authority.

(c) A court may stay a proceeding commenced by a foreign corporation, its successor, or assignee until it determines whether the foreign corporation or its successor requires a certificate of authority. If it so determines, the court may further stay the proceeding until the foreign corporation or its successor obtains the certificate.

(d) A foreign corporation is liable for a civil penalty of $_____ for each day, but not to exceed a total of $_____ for each year, it transacts business in this state without a certificate of authority. The attorney general may collect all penalties due under this subsection.

(e) Notwithstanding subsections (a) and (b), the failure of a foreign corporation to obtain a certificate of authority does not impair the validity of its corporate acts or prevent it from defending any proceeding in this state.

§ 15.03. Application for Certificate of Authority

(a) A foreign corporation may apply for a certificate of authority to transact business in this state by delivering an application to the secretary of state for filing. The application must set forth:

(1) the name of the foreign corporation or, if its name is unavailable for use in this state, a corporate name that satisfies the requirements of section 15.06;

(2) the name of the state or country under whose law it is incorporated;

(3) its date of incorporation and period of duration;

(4) the street address of its principal office;

(5) the address of its registered office in this state and the name of its registered agent at that office; and

(6) the names and usual business addresses of its current directors and officers.

(b) The foreign corporation shall deliver with the completed application a certificate of existence (or a document of similar import) duly authenticated by the secretary of state or other official having custody of corporate records in the state or country under whose law it is incorporated.

§ 15.04. *Amended Certificate of Authority*

(a) A foreign corporation authorized to transact business in this state must obtain an amended certificate of authority from the secretary of state if it changes:

(1) its corporate name;

(2) the period of its duration; or

(3) the state or country of its incorporation.

(b) The requirements of section 15.03 for obtaining an original certificate of authority apply to obtaining an amended certificate under this section.

§ 15.05. *Effect of Certificate of Authority*

(a) A certificate of authority authorizes the foreign corporation to which it is issued to transact business in this state subject, however, to the right of the state to revoke the certificate as provided in this Act.

(b) A foreign corporation with a valid certificate of authority has the same but no greater rights and has the same but no greater privileges as, and except as otherwise provided by this Act is subject to the same duties, restrictions, penalties, and liabilities now or later imposed on, a domestic corporation of like character.

(c) This Act does not authorize this state to regulate the organization or internal affairs of a foreign corporation authorized to transact business in this state.

§ 15.06. *Corporate Name of Foreign Corporation*

(a) If the corporate name of a foreign corporation does not satisfy the requirements of section 4.01, the foreign corporation to obtain or maintain a certificate of authority to transact business in this state:

(1) may add the word "corporation," "incorporated," "company," or "limited," or the abbreviation "corp.," "inc.," "co.," or "ltd.," to its corporate name for use in this state; or

(2) may use a fictitious name to transact business in this state if its real name is unavailable and it delivers to the secretary of state for filing a copy of the resolution of its board of directors, certified by its secretary, adopting the fictitious name.

(b) Except as authorized by subsections (c) and (d), the corporate name (including a fictitious name) of a foreign corporation must be distinguishable upon the records of the secretary of state from:

(1) the corporate name of a corporation incorporated or authorized to transact business in this state;

(2) a corporate name reserved or registered under section 4.02 or 4.03;

(3) the fictitious name of another foreign corporation authorized to transact business in this state; and

(4) the corporate name of a not-for-profit corporation incorporated or authorized to transact business in this state.

(c) A foreign corporation may apply to the secretary of state for authorization to use in this state the name of another corporation (incorporated or authorized to transact business in this state) that is not distinguishable upon his records from the name applied for. The secretary of state shall authorize use of the name applied for if:

(1) the other corporation consents to the use in writing and submits an undertaking in form satisfactory to the secretary of state to change its name to a name that is distinguishable upon the records of the secretary of state from the name of the applying corporation; or

(2) the applicant delivers to the secretary of state a certified copy of a final judgment of a court of competent jurisdiction establishing the applicant's right to use the name applied for in this state.

(d) A foreign corporation may use in this state the name (including the fictitious name) of another domestic or foreign corporation that is used in this state if the other corporation is incorporated or authorized to transact business in this state and the foreign corporation:

(1) has merged with the other corporation;

(2) has been formed by reorganization of the other corporation; or

(3) has acquired all or substantially all of the assets, including the corporate name, of the other corporation.

(e) If a foreign corporation authorized to transact business in this state changes its corporate name to one that does not satisfy the requirements of section 4.01, it may not transact business in this state under the changed name until it adopts a name satisfying the requirements of section 4.01 and obtains an amended certificate of authority under section 15.04.

§ 15.07. *Registered Office and Registered Agent of Foreign Corporation*

Each foreign corporation authorized to transact business in this state must continuously maintain in this state:

(1) a registered office that may be the same as any of its places of business; and

(2) a registered agent, who may be:

(i) an individual who resides in this state and whose business office is identical with the registered office;

(ii) a domestic corporation or not-for-profit domestic corporation whose business office is identical with the registered office; or

(iii) a foreign corporation or foreign not-for-profit corporation authorized to transact business in this state whose business office is identical with the registered office.

§ 15.08. Change of Registered Office or Registered Agent of Foreign Corporation

(a) A foreign corporation authorized to transact business in this state may change its registered office or registered agent by delivering to the secretary of state for filing a statement of change that sets forth:

(1) its name;

(2) the street address of its current registered office;

(3) if the current registered office is to be changed, the street address of its new registered office;

(4) the name of its current registered agent;

(5) if the current registered agent is to be changed, the name of its new registered agent and the new agent's written consent (either on the statement or attached to it) to the appointment; and

(6) that after the change or changes are made, the street addresses of its registered office and the business office of its registered agent will be identical.

(b) If a registered agent changes the street address of his business office, he may change the street address of the registered office of any foreign corporation for which he is the registered agent by notifying the corporation in writing of the change and signing (either manually or in facsimile) and delivering to the secretary of state for filing a statement of change that complies with the requirements of subsection (a) and recites that the corporation has been notified of the change.

§ 15.09. Resignation of Registered Agent of Foreign Corporation

(a) The registered agent of a foreign corporation may resign his agency appointment by signing and delivering to the secretary of state for filing the original and two exact or conformed copies of a statement of resignation. The statement of resignation may include a statement that the registered office is also discontinued.

(b) After filing the statement, the secretary of state shall attach the filing receipt to one copy and mail the copy and receipt to the registered office if not discontinued. The secretary of state shall mail the other copy to the foreign corporation at its principal office address shown in its most recent annual report.

(c) The agency appointment is terminated, and the registered office discontinued if so provided, on the 31st day after the date on which the statement was filed.

§ 15.10. Service on Foreign Corporation

(a) The registered agent of a foreign corporation authorized to transact business in this state is the corporation's agent for service of process, notice, or demand required or permitted by law to be served on the foreign corporation.

(b) A foreign corporation may be served by registered or certified mail, return receipt requested, addressed to the secretary of the foreign corporation at its principal office shown in its application for a certificate of authority or in its most recent annual report if the foreign corporation:

(1) has no registered agent or its registered agent cannot with reasonable diligence be served;

(2) has withdrawn from transacting business in this state under section 15.20; or

(3) has had its certificate of authority revoked under section 15.31.

(c) Service is perfected under subsection (b) at the earliest of:

(1) the date the foreign corporation receives the mail;

(2) the date shown on the return receipt, if signed on behalf of the foreign corporation; or

(3) five days after its deposit in the United States mail, as evidenced by the postmark, if mailed postpaid and correctly addressed.

(d) This section does not prescribe the only means, or necessarily the required means, of serving a foreign corporation.

SUBCHAPTER B. WITHDRAWAL OR TRANSFER OF AUTHORITY

§ 15.20. Withdrawal of Foreign Corporation

(a) A foreign corporation authorized to transact business in this state may not withdraw from this state until it obtains a certificate of withdrawal from the secretary of state.

(b) A foreign corporation authorized to transact business in this state may apply for a certificate of withdrawal by delivering an application to the secretary of state for filing. The application must set forth:

(1) the name of the foreign corporation and the name of the state or country under whose law it is incorporated;

(2) that it is not transacting business in this state and that it surrenders its authority to transact business in this state;

(3) that it revokes the authority of its registered agent to accept service on its behalf and appoints the secretary of state as its agent for service of process in any proceeding based on a cause of action arising during the time it was authorized to transact business in this state;

(4) a mailing address to which the secretary of state may mail a copy of any process served on him under subdivision (3); and

(5) a commitment to notify the secretary of state in the future of any change in its mailing address.

(c) After the withdrawal of the corporation is effective, service of process on the secretary of state under this section is service on the foreign corporation. Upon receipt of process, the secretary of state shall mail a copy of the process to the foreign corporation at the mailing address set forth under subsection (b).

§ 15.21. Automatic Withdrawal Upon Certain Conversions

A foreign business corporation authorized to transact business in this state that converts to a domestic nonprofit corporation or any form of domestic filing entity shall be deemed to have withdrawn on the effective date of the conversion.

§ 15.22. Withdrawal Upon Conversion to a Nonfiling Entity

(a) A foreign business corporation authorized to transact business in this state that converts to a domestic or foreign nonfiling entity shall apply for a certificate of withdrawal by delivering an application to the secretary of state for filing. [remainder of section omitted]

§ 15.23. *Transfer of Authority*

(a) A foreign business corporation authorized to transact business in this state that converts to a foreign nonprofit corporation or to any form of foreign unincorporated entity that is required to obtain a certificate of authority or make a similar type of filing with the secretary of state if it transacts business in this state shall file with the secretary of state an application for transfer of authority executed by any officer or other duly authorized representative. [remainder of section omitted]

SUBCHAPTER C. REVOCATION OF CERTIFICATE OF AUTHORITY

§ 15.30. *Grounds for Revocation*

The secretary of state may commence a proceeding under section 15.31 to revoke the certificate of authority of a foreign corporation authorized to transact business in this state if:

(1) the foreign corporation does not deliver its annual report to the secretary of state within 60 days after it is due;

(2) the foreign corporation does not pay within 60 days after they are due any franchise taxes or penalties imposed by this Act or other law;

(3) the foreign corporation is without a registered agent or registered office in this state for 60 days or more;

(4) the foreign corporation does not inform the secretary of state under section 15.08 or 15.09 that its registered agent or registered office has changed, that its registered agent has resigned, or that its registered office has been discontinued within 60 days of the change, resignation, or discontinuance;

(5) an incorporator, director, officer, or agent of the foreign corporation signed a document he knew was false in any material respect with intent that the document be delivered to the secretary of state for filing;

(6) the secretary of state receives a duly authenticated certificate from the secretary of state or other official having custody of corporate records in the state or country under whose law the foreign corporation is incorporated stating that it has been dissolved or disappeared as the result of a merger.

§ 15.31. *Procedure for and Effect of Revocation*

(a) If the secretary of state determines that one or more grounds exist under section 15.30 for revocation of a certificate of authority, he shall serve the foreign corporation with written notice of his determination under section 15.10.

(b) If the foreign corporation does not correct each ground for revocation or demonstrate to the reasonable satisfaction of the secretary of state that each ground determined by the secretary of state does not exist within 60 days after service of the notice is perfected under section 15.10, the secretary of state may revoke the foreign corporation's certificate of authority by signing a certificate of revocation that recites the ground or grounds for revocation and its effective date. The secretary of

state shall file the original of the certificate and serve a copy on the foreign corporation under section 15.10.

(c) The authority of a foreign corporation to transact business in this state ceases on the date shown on the certificate revoking its certificate of authority.

(d) The secretary of state's revocation of a foreign corporation's certificate of authority appoints the secretary of state the foreign corporation's agent for service of process in any proceeding based on a cause of action which arose during the time the foreign corporation was authorized to transact business in this state. Service of process on the secretary of state under this subsection is service on the foreign corporation. Upon receipt of process, the secretary of state shall mail a copy of the process to the secretary of the foreign corporation at its principal office shown in its most recent annual report or in any subsequent communication received from the corporation stating the current mailing address of its principal office or, if none are on file, in its application for a certificate of authority.

(e) Revocation of a foreign corporation's certificate of authority does not terminate the authority of the registered agent of the corporation.

§ 15.32. *Appeal from Revocation*

(a) A foreign corporation may appeal the secretary of state's revocation of its certificate of authority to the [name or describe] court within 30 days after service of the certificate of revocation is perfected under section 15.10. The foreign corporation appeals by petitioning the court to set aside the revocation and attaching to the petition copies of its certificate of authority and the secretary of state's certificate of revocation.

(b) The court may summarily order the secretary of state to reinstate the certificate of authority or may take any other action the court considers appropriate.

(c) The court's final decision may be appealed as in other civil proceedings.

CHAPTER 16. RECORDS AND REPORTS

SUBCHAPTER A. RECORDS

§ 16.01. *Corporate Records*

(a) A corporation shall keep as permanent records minutes of all meetings of its shareholders and board of directors, a record of all actions taken by the shareholders or board of directors without a meeting, and a record of all actions taken by a committee of the board of directors in place of the board of directors on behalf of the corporation.

(b) A corporation shall maintain appropriate accounting records.

(c) A corporation or its agent shall maintain a record of its shareholders, in a form that permits preparation of a list of the names and addresses of all shareholders, in alphabetical order by class of shares showing the number and class of shares held by each.

(d) A corporation shall maintain its records in written form or in another form capable of conversion into written form within a reasonable time.

(e) A corporation shall keep a copy of the following records at its principal office:

(1) its articles or restated articles of incorporation, all amendments to them currently in effect, and any notices to shareholders referred to in section 1.20(k)(5) regarding facts on which a document is dependent;

(2) its bylaws or restated bylaws and all amendments to them currently in effect;

(3) resolutions adopted by its board of directors creating one or more classes or series of shares, and fixing their relative rights, preferences, and limitations, if shares issued pursuant to those resolutions are outstanding;

(4) the minutes of all shareholders' meetings, and records of all action taken by shareholders without a meeting, for the past three years;

(5) all written communications to shareholders generally within the past three years, including the financial statements furnished for the past three years under section 16.20;

(6) a list of the names and business addresses of its current directors and officers; and

(7) its most recent annual report delivered to the secretary of state under section 16.22.

§ 16.02. *Inspection of Records by Shareholders*

(a) A shareholder of a corporation is entitled to inspect and copy, during regular business hours at the corporation's principal office, any of the records of the corporation described in section 16.01(e) if he gives the corporation written notice of his demand at least five business days before the date on which he wishes to inspect and copy.

(b) A shareholder of a corporation is entitled to inspect and copy, during regular business hours at a reasonable location specified by the corporation, any of the following records of the corporation if the shareholder meets the requirements of subsection (c) and gives the corporation written notice of his demand at least five business days before the date on which he wishes to inspect and copy:

(1) excerpts from minutes of any meeting of the board of directors, records of any action of a committee of the board of directors while acting in place of the board of directors on behalf of the corporation, minutes of any meeting of the shareholders, and records of action taken by the shareholders or board of directors without a meeting, to the extent not subject to inspection under section 16.02(a);

(2) accounting records of the corporation; and

(3) the record of shareholders.

(c) A shareholder may inspect and copy the records identified in subsection (b) only if:

(1) his demand is made in good faith and for a proper purpose;

(2) he describes with reasonable particularity his purpose and the records he desires to inspect; and

(3) the records are directly connected with his purpose.

(d) The right of inspection granted by this section may not be abolished or limited by a corporation's articles of incorporation or bylaws.

(e) This section does not affect:

(1) the right of a shareholder to inspect records under section 7.20 or, if the shareholder is in litigation with the corporation, to the same extent as any other litigant;

(2) the power of a court, independently of this Act, to compel the production of corporate records for examination.

(f) For purposes of this section, "shareholder" includes a beneficial owner whose shares are held in a voting trust or by a nominee on his behalf.

§ 16.03. *Scope of Inspection Right*

(a) A shareholder's agent or attorney has the same inspection and copying rights as the shareholder represented.

(b) The right to copy records under section 16.02 includes, if reasonable, the right to receive copies made by xerographic or other means, including copies through an electronic transmission if available and so requested by the shareholder.

(c) The corporation may comply at its expense with a shareholder's demand to inspect the record of shareholders under section 16.02(b)(3) by providing the shareholder with a list of shareholders that was compiled no earlier than the date of the shareholder's demand.

(d) The corporation may impose a reasonable charge, covering the costs of labor and material, for copies of any documents provided to the shareholder. The charge may not exceed the estimated cost of production, reproduction, or transmission of the records.

§ 16.04. *Court-Ordered Inspection*

(a) If a corporation does not allow a shareholder who complies with section 16.02(a) to inspect and copy any records required by that subsection to be available for inspection, the [name or describe court] of the county where the corporation's principal office (or, if none in this state, its registered office) is located may summarily order inspection and copying of the records demanded at the corporation's expense upon application of the shareholder.

(b) If a corporation does not within a reasonable time allow a shareholder to inspect and copy any other record, the shareholder who complies with section 16.02(b) and (c) may apply to the [name or describe court] in the county where the corporation's principal office (or, if none in this state, its registered office) is located for an order to permit inspection and copying of the records demanded. The court shall dispose of an application under this subsection on an expedited basis.

(c) If the court orders inspection and copying of the records demanded, it shall also order the corporation to pay the shareholder's expenses incurred to obtain the order unless the corporation proves that it refused inspection in good faith because it had a reasonable basis for doubt about the right of the shareholder to inspect the records demanded.

(d) If the court orders inspection and copying of the records demanded, it may impose reasonable restrictions on the use or distribution of the records by the demanding shareholder.

§ 16.05. *Inspection of Records by Directors*

(a) A director of a corporation is entitled to inspect and copy the books, records and documents of the corporation at any reasonable time to the extent reasonably related to the performance of the director's duties as a director, including duties as a member of a committee, but not for any other purpose or in any manner that would violate any duty to the corporation.

(b) The [name or describe the court] of the county where the corporation's principal office (or if none in this state, its registered office) is located may order inspection and copying of the books, records and documents at the corporation's expense, upon application of a director who has been refused such inspection rights, unless the corporation establishes that the director is not entitled to such inspection rights. The court shall dispose of an application under this subsection on an expedited basis.

(c) If an order is issued, the court may include provisions protecting the corporation from undue burden or expense, and prohibiting the director from using information obtained upon exercise of the inspection rights in a manner that would violate a duty to the corporation, and may also order the corporation to reimburse the director for the director's expenses incurred in connection with the application.

§ 16.06. Exception to Notice Requirements

(a) Whenever notice is required to be given under any provision of this Act to any shareholder, such notice shall not be required to be given if:

(i) Notice of two consecutive annual meetings, and all notices of meetings during the period between such two consecutive annual meetings, have been sent to such shareholder at such shareholder's address as shown on the records of the corporation and have been returned undeliverable; or

(ii) All, but not less than two, payments of dividends on securities during a twelve-month period, or two consecutive payments of dividends on securities during a period of more than twelve months, have been sent to such shareholder at such shareholder's address as shown on the records of the corporation and have been returned undeliverable.

(b) If any such shareholder shall deliver to the corporation a written notice setting forth such shareholder's then current address, the requirement that notice be given to such shareholder shall be reinstated.

SUBCHAPTER B. REPORTS

§ 16.20. Financial Statements for Shareholders

(a) A corporation shall furnish its shareholders annual financial statements, which may be consolidated or combined statements of the corporation and one or more of its subsidiaries, as appropriate, that include a balance sheet as of the end of the fiscal year, an income statement for that year, and a statement of changes in shareholders' equity for the year unless that information appears elsewhere in the financial statements. If financial statements are prepared for the corporation on the basis of generally accepted accounting principles, the annual financial statements must also be prepared on that basis.

(b) If the annual financial statements are reported upon by a public accountant, his report must accompany them. If not, the statements must be accompanied by a statement of the president

or the person responsible for the corporation's accounting records:

(1) stating his reasonable belief whether the statements were prepared on the basis of generally accepted accounting principles and, if not, describing the basis of preparation; and

(2) describing any respects in which the statements were not prepared on a basis of accounting consistent with the statements prepared for the preceding year.

(c) A corporation shall mail the annual financial statements to each shareholder within 120 days after the close of each fiscal year. Thereafter, on written request from a shareholder who was not mailed the statements, the corporation shall mail him the latest financial statements.

§ 16.21. Annual Report for Secretary of State

(a) Each domestic corporation, and each foreign corporation authorized to transact business in this state, shall deliver to the secretary of state for filing an annual report that sets forth:

(1) the name of the corporation and the state or county under whose law it is incorporated;

(2) the address of its registered office and the name of its registered agent at that office in this state;

(3) the address of its principal office;

(4) the names and business addresses of its directors and principal officers;

(5) a brief description of the nature of its business;

(6) the total number of authorized shares, itemized by class and series, if any, within each class; and

(7) the total number of issued and outstanding shares, itemized by class and series, if any, within each class.

(b) Information in the annual report must be current as of the date the annual report is executed on behalf of the corporation.

(c) The first annual report must be delivered to the secretary of state between January 1 and April 1 of the year following the calendar year in which a domestic corporation was incorporated or a foreign corporation was authorized to transact business. Subsequent annual reports must be delivered to the secretary of state between January 1 and April 1 of the following calendar years.

(d) If an annual report does not contain the information required by this section, the secretary of state shall promptly notify the reporting domestic or foreign corporation in writing and return the report to it for correction. If the report is corrected to contain the information required by this section and delivered to the secretary of state within 30 days after the effective date of notice, it is deemed to be timely filed.

CHAPTER 17. TRANSITION PROVISIONS

§ 17.01. Application to Existing Domestic Corporations

This Act applies to all domestic corporations in existence on its effective date that were incorporated under any general statute of this state providing for incorporation of corporations for profit if power to amend or repeal the statute under which the corporation was incorporated was reserved.

§ 17.02. Application to Qualified Foreign Corporations

A foreign corporation authorized to transact business in this state on the effective date of this Act is subject to this Act but is not required to obtain a new certificate of authority to transact business under this Act.

§ 17.04. Severability

If any provision of this Act or its application to any person or circumstance is held invalid by a court of competent jurisdiction, the invalidity does not affect other provisions or applications of the Act that can be given effect without the invalid provision or application, and to this end the provisions of the Act are severable.

§ 17.05. Repeal

The following laws and parts of laws are repealed: [to be inserted].

§ 17.06. Effective Date

This Act takes effect _____.

G

Corporate Bylaws

BYLAWS OF _____

ARTICLE I — OFFICES

Section 1. *Registered Office:* The registered office of _____
("the Corporation") in the State of _____shall
be _____, County of _____,
_____. The registered agent of the Corporation at such
address shall be _____.

    Section 2. *Other Offices:* The Corporation may also have offices at such other
places, both within and without the State of _____, as the
Board of Directors may from time to time determine or the business of the Corporation may require.

ARTICLE II — MEETINGS OF SHAREHOLDERS

Section 1. *Place of Meetings:* Meetings of shareholders shall be held at the principal
office of the Corporation or at such place as may be determined from time to time by
the Board of Directors.

    Section 2. *Annual Meetings:* The Corporation shall hold annual meetings of
shareholders commencing with the year _____, on such date and at such
time as shall be determined from time to time by the Board of Directors, at which
meeting shareholders shall elect a Board of Directors and transact such other business
as may properly be brought before the meeting.

Section 3. *Special Meetings:* Special meetings of the shareholders, for any purpose or purposes, may be called at any time by the President of the Corporation, or the Board of Directors, or shareholders holding at least _____ percent (_____%) of the issued and outstanding voting stock of the Corporation.

Business transacted at any special meeting shall be confined to the purpose or purposes set forth in the notice of the special meeting.

Section 4. *Notice of Meetings:* Whenever shareholders are required or permitted to take any action at a meeting, a written notice of the meeting shall be provided to each shareholder of record entitled to vote at or entitled to notice of the meeting, which shall state the place, date, and hour of the meeting, and, in the case of a special meeting, the purpose or purposes for which the meeting is called.

Unless otherwise provided by law, written notice of any meeting shall be given not less than ten nor more than sixty days before the date of the meeting to each shareholder entitled to vote at such meeting.

Section 5. *Quorum at Meetings:* Shareholders may take action on a matter at a meeting only if a quorum exists with respect to that matter. Except as otherwise provided by law, a majority of the outstanding shares of the Corporation entitled to vote, represented in person or by proxy, shall constitute a quorum at a meeting of shareholders. Once a share is represented for any purpose at a meeting (other than solely to object to the holding of the meeting), it is deemed present for quorum purposes for the remainder of the meeting and the shareholders present at a duly organized meeting may continue to transact business until adjournment, notwithstanding the withdrawal of sufficient shareholders to leave less than a quorum.

The holders of a majority of the outstanding shares represented at a meeting, whether or not a quorum is present, may adjourn the meeting from time to time.

Section 6. *Proxies:* Each shareholder entitled to vote at a meeting of shareholders or to express consent or dissent to corporate action in writing without a meeting may authorize another person or persons to vote for him or her by proxy, but no such proxy shall be voted or acted upon after one year from its date, unless the proxy provides for a longer period.

A duly executed proxy shall be irrevocable if it states that it is irrevocable and if, and only so long as, it is coupled with an interest sufficient in law to support an irrevocable power.

Except as otherwise provided herein or by law, every proxy is revocable at the pleasure of the shareholder executing it by communicating such revocation, in writing, to the Secretary of the Corporation.

Section 7. *Voting at Meetings:* If a quorum exists, action on a matter (other than the election of directors) is approved if the votes cast favoring the action exceed the votes cast opposing the action. Directors shall be elected by a plurality of the votes cast by the shares entitled to vote in the election (provided a quorum exists).

Unless otherwise provided by law or in the Corporation's Articles of Incorporation, and subject to the other provisions of these Bylaws, each shareholder shall be entitled to one vote on each matter, in person or by proxy, for each share of the Corporation's capital stock that has voting power and that is held by such shareholder. Voting need not be by written ballot.

Section 8. *List of Shareholders:* The officer of the Corporation who has charge of the stock ledger of the Corporation shall prepare and make, at least ten days before any meeting of shareholders, a complete list of the shareholders entitled to vote at the meeting, arranged alphabetically, and showing the address of each shareholder and the number and class of shares held by each shareholder. The list shall be open to the examination of any shareholder for any purpose germane to the meeting, during ordinary business hours, for a period of at least ten days before the meeting, either at a place in the city where the meeting is to be held, which place must be specified in the notice of the meeting, or at the place where the meeting is to be held. The list shall also be produced and kept available at the time and place of the meeting, for the entire duration of the meeting, and may be inspected by any shareholder present at the meeting.

Section 9.   *Consent in Lieu of Meetings:* Any action required to be taken or which may be taken at any meeting of shareholders, whether annual or special, may be taken without a meeting, without prior notice, and without a vote, if a consent in writing, setting forth the action so taken, shall be signed by the holders of all outstanding shares.

The action must be evidenced by one or more written consents, describing the action taken, signed and dated by the shareholders entitled to take action without a meeting, and delivered to the Corporation at its registered office or to the officer having charge of the Corporation's minute book.

No consent shall be effective to take the corporate action referred to in the consent unless the number of consents required to take action are delivered to the Corporation or to the officer having charge of its minute book within sixty days of the delivery of the earliest-dated consent.

Prompt notice of the taking of the corporate action without a meeting by less than unanimous vote shall be given to those shareholders who have not consented in writing.

Section 10.   *Conference Call:* One or more shareholders may participate in a meeting of shareholders by means of conference telephone, videoconferencing, or similar communications equipment by means of which all persons participating in the meeting can hear each other. Participation in this manner shall constitute presence in person at such meeting.

Section 11.   *Annual Statement:* The President and the Board of Directors shall present at each annual meeting a full and complete statement of the business and affairs of the corporation for the preceding year.

ARTICLE III — DIRECTORS

Section 1.   *Powers of Directors:* The business and affairs of the Corporation shall be managed by or under the direction of the Board of Directors, which may exercise all such powers of the Corporation and do all lawful acts and things, subject to any limitations set forth in these Bylaws or the Articles of Incorporation for the Corporation.

Section 2.   *Number, Qualification, and Election:* The number of directors which shall constitute the whole board shall be not fewer than _____ nor more than _____. Each director shall be at least 18 years of age. The directors need not be residents of the state of incorporation. Directors need not be shareholders in the Corporation. The directors shall be elected by the shareholders at the annual meeting of shareholders by the vote of shareholders holding of record in the aggregate at least a plurality of the shares of stock of the Corporation present in person or by proxy and entitled to vote at the annual meeting of shareholders. Each director shall be elected for a term of _____ year[s], and until his or her successor shall be elected and shall qualify or until his or her earlier resignation or removal.

Section 3.   *Nomination of Directors:* The Board of Directors shall nominate candidates to stand for election as directors; and other candidates may also be nominated by any shareholder of the Corporation, provided such nomination[s] is submitted in writing to the Corporation's Secretary no later than _____ days prior to the meeting of shareholders at which such directors are to be elected, together with the identity of the nominator and the number of shares of the stock of the Corporation owned by the nominator.

Section 4.   *Vacancies:* Except as otherwise provided by law, any vacancy in the Board of Directors occurring by reason of an increase in the authorized number of directors or by reason of the death, withdrawal, removal, disqualification, inability to act, or resignation of a director shall be filled by the majority of directors then in office. The successor shall serve the unexpired portion of the term of his or her predecessor. Any director may resign at any time by giving written notice to the Board or the Secretary.

Section 5.   *Meetings:*

a.   <u>Regular Meetings:</u> Regular meetings of the Board of Directors shall be held without notice and at such time and at such place as determined by the Board.

b.   <u>Special Meetings:</u> Special meetings of the Board may be called by the Chairperson or the President on _____ days' notice to each director, either personally or by telephone, express delivery service, telegram, or facsimile or electronic transmission, and on _____ days' notice by mail (effective upon deposit of such notice in the mail). The notice need not specify the purpose of a special meeting.

Section 6.   *Quorum and Voting at Meetings:* A majority of the total number of authorized directors shall constitute a quorum for transaction of business. The act of a majority of directors present at any meeting at which a quorum is present shall be the act of the Board of Directors, except as provided by law, the Articles of Incorporation, or these Bylaws. Each director present shall have one vote, irrespective of the number of shares of stock, if any, he or she may hold.

Section 7.   *Committees of Directors:* The Board of Directors, by resolution, may create one or more committees, each consisting of one or more Directors. Each such committee shall serve at the pleasure of the Board. All provisions of the law of the State of _____ and these Bylaws relating to meetings, action without meetings, notice, and waiver of notice, quorum, and voting requirements of the Board of Directors shall apply to such committees and their members.

Section 8.   *Consent in Lieu of Meetings:* Any action required or permitted to be taken at any meeting of the Board of Directors or of any committee thereof, may be taken without a meeting if all members of the Board or committee, as the case may be, consent thereto in writing, such writing or writings to be filed with the minutes of proceedings of the Board or committee.

Section 9.   *Conference Call:* One or more directors may participate in meetings of the Board or a committee of the Board by any communication, including videoconference, by means of which all participating directors can simultaneously hear each other during the meeting. Participation in this manner shall constitute presence in person at such meeting.

Section 10.   *Compensation:* The Board of Directors shall have the authority to fix the compensation of Directors. A fixed sum and expenses of attendance may be allowed for attendance at each regular or special meeting of the Board. No such payment shall preclude any director from serving the Corporation in any other capacity and receiving compensation therefor.

Section 11. *Removal of Directors:* Any director or the entire Board of Directors may be removed, with or without cause, by the holders of a majority of the shares then entitled to vote at an election of directors.

ARTICLE IV — OFFICERS

Section 1. *Positions:* The officers of the Corporation shall be a Chairperson, a President, a Secretary, and a Treasurer, and such other officers as the Board may from time to time appoint, including one or more Vice Presidents and such other officers as it deems advisable. Any number of offices may be held by the same person, except that the President and the Secretary may not be the same person. Each such officer shall exercise such powers and perform such duties as shall be set forth herein and such other powers and duties as may be specified from time to time by the Board of Directors. The officers of the Corporation shall be elected by the Board of Directors. Each of the Chairperson, President, and/or any Vice Presidents may execute bonds, mortgages, and other documents under the seal of the Corporation, except where required or permitted by law to be otherwise executed and except where execution thereof shall be expressly delegated by the Board to some other officer or agent of the Corporation.

Section 2. *Chairperson:* The Chairperson shall have overall responsibility and authority for management and operations of the Corporation, shall preside at all meetings of the Board of Directors and shareholders, and shall ensure that all orders and resolutions of the Board of Directors and shareholders are effected.

Section 3. *President:* The President shall be the chief operating officer of the Corporation and shall have full responsibility and authority for management of the day-to-day operations of the Corporation. The President shall be an ex-officio member of all committees and shall have the general powers and duties of management and supervision usually vested in the office of president of a corporation.

Section 4. *Secretary:* The Secretary shall attend all meetings of the Board and all meetings of the shareholders and shall act as clerk thereof, and record all the votes of the Corporation and the minutes of all its transactions in a book to be kept for that purpose, and shall perform like duties for all committees of the Board of Directors when required. The Secretary shall give, or cause to be given, notice of all meetings of the shareholders and special meetings of the Board of Directors, and shall perform such other duties as may be prescribed by the Board of Directors or President, and under whose supervision the Secretary shall be. The Secretary shall maintain the records, minutes, and seal of the Corporation and may attest any instruments signed by any other officer of the Corporation.

Section 5. *Treasurer:* The Treasurer shall be the chief financial officer of the Corporation, shall have responsibility for the custody of the corporate funds and securities, shall keep full and accurate records and accounts of receipts and disbursements in books belonging to the Corporation, and shall keep the monies of the Corporation in a separate account in the name of the Corporation. The Treasurer shall provide to the President and directors, at the regular meetings of the Board, or whenever requested by the Board, an account of all financial transactions and of the financial condition of the Corporation.

Section 6. *Term of Office:* The officers of the Corporation shall hold office until their successors are chosen and have qualified or until their earlier resignation or removal. Unless an officer or agent serves subject to a valid written agreement, any officer or agent elected or appointed by the Board may be removed at any time, with or without cause, by the affirmative vote of a majority of the Board of Directors. Any vacancy occurring in any office as a result of death, resignation, removal, or otherwise, shall be filled for the unexpired portion of the term by a majority vote of the Board of Directors.

Section 7. *Compensation:* The compensation of officers of the Corporation shall be fixed by the Board of Directors.

ARTICLE V — CAPITAL STOCK

Section 1. *Stock Certificates:* The shares of the Corporation shall be represented by certificates, provided that the Board of Directors may provide by resolution that some or all of any or all classes or series of the stock of the Corporation shall be uncertificated shares. Notwithstanding the adoption of such a resolution by the Board of Directors, every holder of stock represented by certificates and, upon request, every holder of uncertificated shares, shall be entitled to have a certificate signed in the name of the Corporation, by the Chairperson, President or any Vice President, and by the Treasurer or Secretary. Any or all of the signatures on the certificate may be by facsimile. The stock certificates of the Corporation shall be numbered and registered in the share ledger and transfer books of the Corporation as they are issued and shall bear the corporate seal.

Section 2. *Lost Certificates:* The Corporation may issue a new certificate of stock in place of any certificate previously issued and alleged to have been lost, stolen, or destroyed, and the Corporation may require the owner of the lost, stolen, or destroyed certificate, or his or her legal representative, to make an affidavit of that fact, and the Corporation may require indemnity against any claim that may be made against the Corporation on account of the alleged loss, theft, or destruction of any such certificate or the issuance of such new certificate.

Section 3. *Transfers:* Transfers of shares shall be made on the books of the Corporation upon surrender and cancellation of the certificates therefor, endorsed by the person named in the certificate or by his or her legal representative. No transfer shall be made which is inconsistent with any provision of law, the Articles of Incorporation for the Corporation, or these Bylaws.

Section 4. *Record Date:* In order that the Corporation may determine the shareholders entitled to notice of or to vote at any meeting of shareholders, or any adjournment thereof, or to take action without a meeting, or to receive payment of any dividend or other distribution, or to exercise any rights in respect of any change, conversion, or exchange of stock, or for the purpose of any other lawful action, the Board of Directors may fix a record date, which record date shall not precede the date upon which the resolution fixing the record date is adopted by the Board of Directors and shall not be less than ten nor more than fifty days before the meeting or action requiring a determination of shareholders.

If no record date is fixed by the Board of Directors:

a.   for determining shareholders entitled to notice of or to vote at a meeting, the record date shall be at the close of business on the day next preceding the day on which notice is given, or, if notice is waived, at the close of business on the day next preceding the day on which the meeting is held or other action taken;

b. for determining shareholders entitled to consent to corporate action without a meeting, the record date shall be the day on which the first written consent is delivered to the Corporation in accordance with these Bylaws; and

c. for determining shareholders for any other purpose, the record date shall be at the close of business on the day on which the Board of Directors adopts the resolution relating thereto.

ARTICLE VI — DIVIDENDS

Section 1. *Dividends:* The Board of Directors may declare and pay dividends upon the outstanding shares of the Corporation, from time to time and to such extent as the Board deems advisable, in the manner and upon the terms and conditions provided by law and the Articles of Incorporation of the Corporation.

Section 2. *Reserves:* The Board of Directors may set apart, out of the funds of the Corporation available for dividends, said sum as the directors, from time to time, in their absolute discretion, think proper as a reserve fund for any proper purpose. The Board of Directors may abolish any such reserve in the manner it was created.

ARTICLE VII — GENERAL PROVISIONS

Section 1. *Insurance and Indemnity:* The Corporation shall purchase and maintain insurance in a reasonable amount on behalf of any person who is or was a director, officer, agent, or employee of the Corporation against liability asserted against or incurred by such person in such capacity or arising from such person's status as such.

Subject to applicable statute, any person made or threatened to be made a party to any action, suit, or proceeding, by reason of the fact that he or she, his or her testator or intestate representative, is or was a director, officer, agent, or employee of the Corporation, shall be indemnified by the Corporation against the reasonable expenses, including attorneys' fees, actually and necessarily incurred by him or her in connection with such an action, suit, or proceeding.

Notwithstanding the foregoing, no indemnification shall be made by the Corporation if judgment or other final determination establishes that the potential indemnitee's acts were committed in bad faith or were the result of active or deliberate fraud or dishonesty or clear and gross negligence.

Section 2. *Inspection of Corporate Records:* Any shareholder of record, in person or by attorney or other agent, shall, upon written demand under oath stating the purpose thereof, have the right during the usual hours for business to inspect for any proper purpose the Corporation's stock ledger, a list of its shareholders, and its other books and records, and to make copies or extracts therefrom. A proper purpose shall mean a purpose reasonably related to such person's interest as a shareholder. In every instance in which an attorney or other agent shall be the person seeking the right to inspection, the demand under oath shall be accompanied by a power of attorney or such other writing authorizing the attorney or other agent to so act on behalf of the shareholder. The demand under oath shall be directed to the Corporation at its registered office or its principal place of business.

Section 3.   *Fiscal Year:* The fiscal year of the Corporation shall be the calendar year.

Section 4.   *Seal:* The corporate seal shall be in such form as the Board of Directors shall approve. The seal may be used by causing it or a facsimile thereof to be impressed, affixed, or otherwise reproduced.

Section 5.   *Execution of Instruments:* All contracts, checks, drafts, or demands for money and notes and other instruments or rights of any nature of the Corporation shall be signed by such officer or officers as the Board of Directors may from time to time designate.

Section 6.   *Notice:* Whenever written notice is required to be given to any person, it may be given to such person, either personally or by sending a copy thereof through the United States mail, or by telegram, facsimile, or by electronic transmission, charges prepaid, to his or her address appearing on the books of the Corporation, or supplied by him or her to the Corporation for the purpose of notice. If the notice is sent by mail or by telegraph, it shall be deemed to have been given to the person entitled thereto when deposited in the United States mail or with a telegraph office for transmission to such person. If the notice is sent by facsimile, it shall be deemed to have been given at the date and time shown on a written confirmation of the transmission of such facsimile communication. If the notice is sent by electronic transmission, it shall be deemed to have been given at the close of business on the day transmitted. Such notice shall specify the place, day, and hour of the meeting, and, in the case of a special meeting of shareholders, the purpose of and general nature of the business to be transacted at such special meeting.

Section 7.   *Waiver of Notice:* Whenever any written notice is required by law, or by the Articles of Incorporation or by these Bylaws, a waiver thereof in writing, signed by the person or persons entitled to such notice, whether before or after the time stated therein, shall be deemed equivalent to the giving of such notice. Except in the case of a special meeting of shareholders, neither the business to be conducted at nor the purpose of the meeting need be specified in the waiver of notice of the meeting. Attendance of a person either in person or by proxy, at any meeting, shall constitute a waiver of notice of such meeting, except where a person attends a meeting for the express purpose of objecting to the transaction of any business because the meeting was not lawfully convened or called.

Section 8.   *Amendments:* The Board of Directors shall have the power to make, adopt, alter, amend, and repeal from time to time the Bylaws of the Corporation except that the adoption, amendment, or repeal of any Bylaw regulating the election of directors shall be subject to the vote of shareholders entitled to cast at least a majority of the votes which all shareholders are entitled to cast at any regular or special meeting of the shareholders, duly convened after notice to the shareholders of that purpose.

The foregoing Bylaws were adopted by the Board of Directors on _____.

_____
Secretary

Written Consent in Lieu of the Organizational Meeting

WRITTEN CONSENT IN LIEU OF THE ORGANIZATIONAL MEETING OF THE BOARD OF DIRECTORS OF

(A Delaware Corporation)

Pursuant to Section 108 of the Delaware General Corporation Law, the undersigned, constituting all _____ (_____) of the initial director(s) of _____, a corporation organized and existing under the laws of the State of Delaware (the "Corporation"), do/does hereby consent in writing to the adoption of the following resolutions, such resolutions to have effect as if adopted at a duly held meeting of the directors of the Corporation:

RESOLVED, that the Charter issued to the Corporation by the Division of Corporation of the Delaware Department of State be filed in the minute book of the Corporation.

RESOLVED, that the Bylaws attached to this Consent are hereby adopted as the Bylaws of the Corporation.

RESOLVED, that the corporate seal, an impression of which is affixed in the margin hereof, is adopted as the corporate seal of the Corporation.

RESOLVED, that the form of stock certificate, a copy of which is attached to this Consent, is hereby adopted as the certificate for the common stock of the Corporation.

RESOLVED, that the following persons are hereby elected to the offices set forth after their respective names, to assume the duties and responsibilities fixed by the Bylaws, each such officer to hold office until a successor is chosen and qualifies in that officer's stead, or until that officer's earlier resignation or removal:

Name	*Office*
_____	President
_____	Vice-President
_____	Treasurer
_____	Secretary

RESOLVED, that any officer of the Corporation is hereby authorized to open such bank accounts as may be necessary or appropriate to conduct the business of the Corporation with such banks or financial institutions as that officer deems necessary; and

FURTHER RESOLVED, that the corporate banking resolutions of any such bank or financial institution are hereby incorporated by reference and are adopted as if fully set forth herein.

RESOLVED, that the Corporation elects to be treated as an S corporation for income tax purposes, subject to the receipt of written consent to such election by each shareholder; and

FURTHER RESOLVED, that upon receipt of written consent of said election by each shareholder, the President is hereby authorized and directed to take any and all action necessary or desirable to comply with all of the requirements of the Internal Revenue Service for making said election.

RESOLVED, that the Corporation hereby confirms that all shares of the common stock of the Corporation issued upon acceptance of the following subscription offers shall be treated as Section 1244 stock; and

RESOLVED, that the officers of the Corporation are authorized and directed to perform such actions and execute such documents as they shall deem necessary or appropriate to enable the Corporation to carry out its business in such jurisdictions as its activities make such qualification necessary or appropriate.

WHEREAS, the following person(s) has/have offered the amounts set forth next to his/her/their name(s) below in consideration of the issuance of the number of shares of the common stock, one cent ($0.01) par value per share, of the Corporation set forth below;

RESOLVED, that in consideration of the amounts indicated below, an aggregate of _____ (_____) shares of the common stock of the Corporation be and hereby are issued to the person(s) listed below, and that upon receipt from such person of the amount set forth opposite the person's name, the President and Secretary are hereby authorized and directed to issue to such person a certificate representing the number of shares set forth opposite that person's name, as follows:

Name	*Shares*	*Consideration*
_____	_____	$_____
_____	_____	$_____
_____	_____	$_____

RESOLVED, that the [accrual/cash] method of accounting shall be the basis on which the Corporation computes its income and keeps its books; and

FURTHER RESOLVED, that the fiscal year of the Corporation shall be the twelve-month period ending _____.

RESOLVED, that any officer of the Corporation be and hereby is authorized to pay all expenses incurred in connection with the organization of the Corporation and to reimburse the incorporators or directors for any amounts expended by them on behalf of the Corporation prior to the date hereof; and

FURTHER RESOLVED, that the Secretary of the Corporation be and hereby is authorized and directed to procure all corporate books, including books of account and stock books, required by the statutes of the State of Delaware or necessary or appropriate in connection with the business of the Corporation, and to apply in the name and on behalf of the Corporation on Form SS-4 for a Federal Employer Identification Number.

RESOLVED, that any officer of the Corporation be and hereby is authorized to take such actions and execute such documents as may be necessary, appropriate, or convenient to carry out the foregoing resolutions.

Dated as of _____, 20_____.

_____
Name

_____
Name

_____
Name

CONSENT

I,_____, hereby consent to my election as Director of _____, by_____, the Sole Incorporator of the Corporation.

_____   _____
Date of Execution   Name

WAIVER OF SOLE INCORPORATOR OF _____

I,_____, being the Sole Incorporator named in the Certificate of Incorporation of _____ (the "Corporation"), which Certificate of Incorporation was received and filed with the Delaware Secretary of State on _____, 20_____, hereby waive all right, title, and interest in and to any stock or property of the Corporation and any right in the management thereof.

_____   _____
    Date of Execution   Sole Incorporator

Shareholders' Buy-Sell Agreement

◆ ◆ ◆

SHAREHOLDERS' BUY-SELL AGREEMENT

THIS AGREEMENT is made this _____ day of _____, 20_____, by and among Celia G. Spiritos, James Hays, and Mary Jo Stanton (hereinafter referred to individually as a "Shareholder" and collectively as "the Shareholders") and SHS Corporation (the "Corporation"), a corporation organized under the laws of the State of _____.

RECITALS

WHEREAS, all of the issued and outstanding shares of the stock of the Corporation are owned by the Shareholders in the following percentages as of the date of this Agreement:

Shareholder	Shares Owned
Celia G. Spiritos	_____
James Hays	_____
Mary Jo Stanton	_____

WHEREAS, the parties desire to restrict the transfer, encumbrance, pledge, or assignment of the shares of the Corporation;

WHEREAS, the parties desire to provide for the purchase and sale of shares of the Corporation under specified conditions; and

WHEREAS, the parties desire to provide for continuity and harmony in the management and affairs of the Corporation and for the orderly operation of its business.

NOW, THEREFORE, for good and valuable consideration, the receipt and sufficiency of which are hereby acknowledged, the parties hereto agree as follows:

1.   Stock Subject to This Agreement.

All of the shares of the Corporation, which are owned by the Shareholders and which represent all of the issued and outstanding shares of the Corporation as of the date of this Agreement, shall be subject to the terms of this Agreement. Any additional shares of the Corporation, of whatever class, which from time to time shall be issued by the Corporation, shall automatically and without any further required action become subject to the terms of this Agreement.

2.   Restrictive Legend on Stock Certificates.

The certificates evidencing shares of the Corporation which are or hereafter become subject to the terms of this Agreement shall include the following restrictive legend which shall be displayed prominently on each certificate:

The shares represented by this certificate are issued and held subject to a Shareholders' Buy-Sell Agreement made the _____ day of _____, 20_____, to which this Corporation is subject. A copy of the Agreement is on file at the principal business office of the Corporation. Any assignment or transfer of any nature of any shares represented by this certificate shall be void and without any effect, unless undertaken and effected in compliance with the terms of the Agreement.

3.   Stock Transfer Restrictions.

(a)   No Shareholder shall have the right or power to sell, assign, transfer, pledge, or otherwise dispose of (hereinafter collectively referred to as a "transfer") all or any portion of his or her shares of the Corporation, or any interest therein, except in accordance with the terms and conditions of this Agreement.

(b)   Notwithstanding the foregoing provision, this Agreement shall not apply to a transfer of shares in the Corporation to the Corporation, a transfer to all of the Shareholders on a pro rata basis for equal consideration, or to shares acquired by way of merger.

4.   Permitted Transfers.

(a)   An interest in shares of the Corporation that is not exempt under Paragraph 3(b) above can only be transferred if the Shareholder desiring to make a transfer (the "offering Shareholder") first makes an offer to the remaining Shareholders to sell all of his or her shares to the remaining Shareholders. The offer by the offering Shareholder must be in writing, must state the offeror's name and address and all terms and conditions of the offer, and must be delivered to the remaining Shareholders pursuant to Paragraph 8 of this Agreement.

(b)   Within sixty (60) days of receipt of the offer, the remaining Shareholders shall provide notice to the offering Shareholder of their determination whether to purchase the offered shares. If no written notice shall be given within the sixty

(60) day period, the offer to purchase shall be deemed rejected. The remaining Shareholders may make a counteroffer to the offering Shareholder.

(c)   If an offer to purchase is accepted by more than one of the remaining Shareholders, the shares of the offering Shareholder shall be allocated among the remaining Shareholders according to their pro rata interest in the Corporation.

(d)   If the offer to purchase is rejected by the remaining Shareholders, the offering Shareholder shall be entitled, for a period of sixty (60) days after the rejection of the offer to sell all of his or her shares to a third person in accordance with the terms of the original offer made to the remaining Shareholders. As a prerequisite to ownership rights to shares being transferred to a third person, such third person must execute a counterpart of this Agreement, agreeing to be bound by all of its terms.

(e)   If the remaining Shareholders accept the offer to purchase, certificates for the shares shall be delivered to the purchasing Shareholder(s) and the purchasing Shareholder(s) shall comply with the terms of the offer within thirty (30) days after the notice of acceptance of the offer.

(f)   Any attempt to transfer any interest in shares of the Corporation in violation of this Paragraph 4 shall be ineffective, and the Corporation shall refuse to register the shares in question in the name of the purported transferee.

5. Buy-Out Rights.

(a)   Buy-Out Price. For purposes of this Agreement, the term "Buy-Out Price" shall mean the sum of One Thousand Dollars ($1,000) multiplied by the number of shares sold by the selling Shareholder or his or her successor in interest. The Buy-Out Price may be modified by the Shareholders at any time, by unanimous written consent, and the Shareholders shall reassess the Buy-Out Price on an annual or more frequent basis.

(b)   Death. Upon the death of any individual Shareholder, the personal representative or administrator of his or her estate shall sell and the Corporation shall purchase all of the deceased Shareholder's shares at a price equal to the greater of any insurance proceeds payable to the Corporation by reason of the death of such Shareholder or the Buy-Out Price.

(c)   Disability. In the event an individual Shareholder who is employed by the Corporation in an executive capacity as an officer or director shall become disabled, as defined below, the disabled Shareholder shall sell and the Corporation shall purchase all of the disabled Shareholder's shares at a price equal to the Buy-Out Price. For purposes of this Agreement, a Shareholder is disabled if he or she has been declared legally incompetent by a final court decree, receives disability insurance benefits from any disability income insurance policy, or due to medically determinable disease, injury, or other mental or physical impairment is unable to perform substantially all of his or her regular duties to the Corporation and such disability is reasonably expected to last six (6) months or longer.

(d)   Termination of Employment. In the event that a Shareholder voluntarily terminates employment with the Corporation or the Corporation terminates the employment of a Shareholder for cause, as defined below, the terminated Shareholder shall sell, and the Corporation shall purchase, all of the terminated Shareholder's shares at a price equal to one-half (1/2) of the Buy-Out Price. For purposes of this Agreement, the term "cause" shall mean conviction of a felony, breach of fiduciary duty, proven dishonesty in the course of employment or failure to perform the duties of employment, theft, fraud, or substance abuse. A determination of "cause" may be made only upon the unanimous vote of the remaining Shareholders. The Shareholder sought to be terminated for cause shall have the right to contest the termination in a court of competent jurisdiction during the pendency of which the provisions of this Paragraph 5(d) shall be suspended.

(e)   Transfers by Operation of Law. In the event any Shareholder files a voluntary petition under any bankruptcy or insolvency laws or is subjected involuntarily to such a petition or is subjected to any other legal process, including but not limited to, an assignment or transfer pursuant to a divorce decree, the Shareholder shall sell and the Corporation shall purchase all of the Shareholder's shares at a purchase price equal to the Buy-Out Price.

(f)   Procedural Requirements. Whenever the Corporation is required to purchase the shares of a Shareholder pursuant to one or more of the events causing a Buy-Out as described in this Paragraph 5, the following procedures shall apply:

(i)   The closing upon such purchase shall take place at the offices of the Corporation or at such other place as mutually agreed upon, within sixty (60) days of the event triggering the buy-out.

(ii)   The purchase price of any such shares shall be paid as follows:

1.   At closing, there shall be a cash payment equal to at least fifty percent (50%) of the Buy-Out Price. The balance of the purchase price shall be made by promissory note by the Corporation in a principal amount equal to the unpaid portion of the Buy-Out Price and carrying interest at the prime interest rate and which note shall be paid in equal quarterly installments, until paid in full. The Corporation shall have the right to prepay, without penalty, all or any part of the amount due under the terms of the promissory note.

2.   At closing, the selling Shareholder shall take all steps necessary to legally transfer possession and ownership of the certificate(s) representing all of the shares sold. Delivery of the certificate(s) shall constitute a representation and warranty that good and valid title to the stock is being delivered and that the shares are free and clear or all claims or liens of any kind. Title to and possession of the shares shall pass to the Corporation at the closing, regardless of any balance of the purchase price for such shares which may be payable after the closing.

6.   Specific Performance.

Each Shareholder acknowledges that the restrictions contained in this Agreement are reasonable and necessary in order to protect the interests of the Corporation, and that any violation thereof would result in irreparable and substantial harm to the Corporation. The Shareholders understand and acknowledge that the monetary loss or damage that will be suffered by any party by reason of failure to perform the obligations imposed by this Agreement is impossible to determine. Accordingly, it is agreed that in the event of any dispute concerning the sale or other transfer of shares of the Corporation, an injunction may issue restraining any such sale or other transfer pending the determination of such controversy. Such remedy shall not be exclusive and shall be in addition to any other remedies that the parties may have.

7.   Binding Nature of Agreement.

This Agreement shall be binding upon the parties hereto and their transferees, assignees, heirs, executors, administrators, and other representatives and it is understood and acknowledged that such transferees, assignees, heirs, executors, administrators, and other representatives shall execute any documents necessary to carry out the intent of this Agreement.

8. Miscellaneous.
    (a) This Agreement supersedes all prior agreements and understandings, whether written or oral, relating to the subject matter hereof.
    (b) This Agreement may be modified or amended at any time upon written agreement of all the parties hereto.
    (c) This Agreement shall be governed by the law of the State of _____.
    (d) Any notice required by this Agreement shall be deemed given when sent certified mail, return receipt requested, first class, postage prepaid to the party to whom such notice is required to be given, at such person's last known address.

    IN WITNESS WHEREOF, the parties have executed this Agreement on the date provided herein.

    _____
    Celia G. Spiritos

    _____
    James Hays

    _____
    Mary Jo Stanton

◆ ◆ ◆

Letter of Intent

◆ ◆ ◆

March 19, 2009

Quality Systems, Inc.
Attention: Mr. Francis P. Taylor, President
340-A Fairfax Road
Boston, MA 01887

Dear Mr. Taylor:

This letter confirms our mutual intention to pursue the proposed business arrangement (the "Transaction") outlined below:

1. *Transaction.* Management Technology Consultants, Inc. ("MTC") wishes to acquire all of the assets of Quality Systems, Inc. ("QSI"), a Massachusetts corporation (the "Transaction"). MTC will assume no liabilities of QSI of any kind or nature but will assume QSI's obligations under scheduled agreements with third parties, subject to review during due diligence. It is our understanding that QSI will liquidate as soon as practicable following the closing of the Transaction.

2. *Purchase Price.* The purchase price (the "Purchase Price") will be Thirty Million Dollars ($30,000,000) payable in cash at the time of the Closing, as herein defined. Five Hundred Thousand Dollars ($500,000) will be held in escrow for ninety (90) days after the Closing to allow for any adjustments to the Purchase Price resulting from shortfalls in assets, inventory, or other issues not uncovered in due diligence (through the exercise of reasonable and good faith efforts by the parties).

3. *Employment.* MTC believes that Mr. Taylor's continued involvement in QSI's operations is critical to the long-term success of the Transaction. Therefore, MTC will offer him employment with MTC with a base annual salary of $200,000, payable in accordance with MTC's normal payroll procedures. Mr. Taylor will be eligible for all benefits provided to MTC employees. Historically, MTC has paid bonuses to employees who meet or exceed company goals and expectations. The parties will use their best efforts to reach mutually satisfactory terms relating to specific and quantifiable performance goals to be achieved by Mr. Taylor and providing that as each goal is met or exceeded, he will be paid a bonus for each such goal for a total aggregate potential bonus payment of $200,000.

4. *Non-Competition Agreements.* QSI shareholders who are employees of QSI will execute customary non-competition agreements in favor of MTC providing that during and upon termination of employment with MTC for any reason former QSI employees will be precluded from performing any work or engaging in any activities that would compete directly or indirectly with MTC's business and operations for five years within a 150-mile radius of any then-existing MTC office location. We will work together to draft appropriate non-competition agreements.

5. *Stock Options.* Mr. Taylor will be granted options to purchase 100,000 shares of MTC stock pursuant to the 2006 MTC Stock Option Plan, exercisable in accordance with the normal vesting schedule applicable to MTC employees.

6. *QSI Employees.* We will discuss issues related to the offer of employment by MTC to various QSI employees and the terms and conditions of such employment. Any individuals who are offered employment with MTC will be granted options to purchase 5,500 shares of MTC stock pursuant to the 2006 MTC Stock Option Plan, exercisable in accordance with the normal vesting schedule applicable to MTC employees. Options are granted at the end of each calendar quarter for newly hired employees. The next meeting of the MTC Stock Option Committee is set for June 30, 2009.

7. *Closing.* The parties desire that closing (the "Closing") of the Transaction occur as soon as practicable, preferably on or before May 15, 2009. Prior to Closing, QSI will conduct its business in the ordinary course.

8. *Due Diligence.* Representatives of MTC will have the opportunity to perform a due diligence investigation of the assets, business, contracts, equipment, inventory, and operations of QSI. A Due Diligence Information Request List is attached hereto. The scope of the investigation will include, but not be limited to, a review of QSI's facilities, material contracts, intellectual property, employee benefit plans, corporate documents, financial statements, and tax returns for prior years. In order to enable MTC to perform and complete its investigation, QSI shall provide representatives of MTC with access to its books, clients, vendors, records, personnel, and premises during normal business hours.

9. *Confidentiality of Discussions.* The parties will keep strictly confidential the existence and content of this letter and the fact that these discussions are taking place, except as required by applicable law and except as agreed to in writing by both

parties. MTC and QSI will jointly draft and release a press release announcing the Transaction after this letter of intent has been signed by both parties.

10. *Transaction Fees.* The parties shall bear their own respective costs in connection with the Transaction, including the negotiation and consummation of a definitive agreement.

11. *Definitive Agreement.* During the period prior to Closing, the parties will work in good faith to prepare and execute a definitive agreement for the Transaction contemplated hereby. This letter is intended to serve only as a framework to identify issues and matters that would have to be addressed in such a definitive agreement, which shall contain customary representations, warranties, covenants, and conditions for a transaction of the type contemplated hereby.

12. *Exclusive Dealings.* In consideration of the time, energy, and money that MTC will expend toward consummation of the Transaction, QSI agrees not to solicit other bids for the sale of its stock or assets, accept any bids therefor, whether solicited or unsolicited, or negotiate with any other person or entity with respect to the sale thereof, either in whole or in part, or a similar transaction, through May 15, 2009. Prior to such date, QSI will not dispose of any of its material assets, incur any material indebtedness, issue additional debt or equity securities, declare or pay any dividend or make any other distribution with respect to its capital stock or repurchase any capital stock, agree to any material contract or amend any existing material contract, or agree to any material expenditure out of the ordinary course of business, without the express written consent of MTC. Notwithstanding the foregoing, in the event that either of the parties notifies the other in writing that it wishes to terminate negotiations relating to the Transaction, QSI's obligations hereunder shall terminate ten (10) business days thereafter.

13. *Conditions Precedent.* In order to consummate the Transaction contemplated hereby, and as an express condition precedent to the parties' obligations hereunder, MTC and QSI must each secure approval from their respective boards of directors and lenders for the Transaction. Moreover, QSI must secure the approval of its shareholders to the Transaction. Each party will use its best efforts to secure said approval and will at all times keep the other apprised of the process of obtaining such approval. Moreover, the parties understand and acknowledge that certain government approvals must be secured prior to Closing and the parties will work together and cooperate in making any filings with the government related thereto.

Except as provided in Paragraphs 9, 10, and 12 hereof, which are intended to be and are legally binding agreements between the parties hereto upon QSI's acceptance below, the parties do not intend for this letter to create any enforceable obligations or rights, and no legal and enforceable obligations or rights shall arise unless and until the parties negotiate, execute, and deliver a definitive written agreement setting forth the specific terms and conditions of the Transaction contemplated hereby.

If this letter is an accurate reflection of our mutual understanding of the proposed Transaction, please indicate your concurrence by countersigning and dating the enclosed copy of this letter in the place provided and returning a fully signed copy to me as soon as possible.

We look forward to working with you on the Transaction and in the years to come.

Very truly yours,

Management Technology Consultants, Inc.
By: Timothy Lyden, President

ACCEPTED AND APPROVED:

Quality Systems, Inc.

_____   _____
Francis P. Taylor, President   Date

Research and Resource Guide

Although each chapter provides pertinent Web resources, this Appendix provides a thorough list of conventional or print research and other resources that are helpful in understanding various business organizations.

Statutes

State Statutes

In almost every instance, the initial source to consult to obtain information about the formation, operation, and dissolution of all business organizations is your state's statutes. Locate your state's annotated code. Use the general index to the set and look for "partnerships," "limited liability companies," "corporations," and so forth. You will be directed to the specific sections governing that area of law. Review the statutes as well as the annotations or summaries of cases that follow the statutes. Always check the pocket parts or supplements to ensure there have been no recent modifications or revisions of the statutes.

Federal Statutes

Federal statutes control only matters of federal law, such as matters relating to taxation and securities regulations. Use U.S.C.A. or U.S.C.S. to locate federal statutes and cases interpreting those statutes.

Martindale-Hubbell

Martindale-Hubbell Law Directory includes brief overviews of the laws of all 50 states, allowing you quick and easy information on the partnership, corporate, and other laws of each state. Use the "Law Digest Volumes." Since 2007, the Law Digest Volumes are no longer available in print and are available only on CD-ROM.

Westlaw

Use Westlaw's "50 State Surveys" to link to all states' corporations codes so you can compare and contrast their statutes relating to corporate formation.

Introductory Information

For general background information on sole proprietorships, partnerships, limited liability companies, corporations, and other topics, consult one of the two general legal encyclopedias, C.J.S. or Am. Jur. 2d. If your state has a local set (such as Cal. Jur. 3d or New York Jur. 2d), consult it. Although the treatment of legal topics is somewhat elementary, encyclopedias offer a great place to "get your feet wet." Check the index to any encyclopedia and you will be directed to the appropriate volume and section. Many state-specific sets include a Table of Statutes Construed, allowing you to determine quickly which portion of the encyclopedia discusses specific state statutes.

Specialized Texts and Treatises

There are numerous texts and sets of books that provide thorough and detailed information about business organizations. Check the shelves in your school or firm law library to determine what is available. For example, probably the best known treatise in the corporate law field is *Fletcher's Cyclopedia of the Law of Private Corporations*, a multivolume set containing excellent information about corporations and more than 250,000 citations to relevant cases. This treatise is also available on Westlaw. Similar texts and treatises exist for partnerships and other business entities.

Periodical Articles

To locate articles on various business-related topics, use *The Index to Legal Periodicals* or *Current Law Index*. Both indexes can be accessed by subject. Therefore, look up "partnership," "blue sky laws," or other relevant topics and you will be referred to articles written about these topics.

Form Books

Because paralegals are typically involved in drafting various forms, you need to be acquainted with the form books that will assist you in preparing documents. Some of the better known form books are the following:

- *Current Legal Forms with Tax Analysis* by Jacob Rabkin and Mark H. Johnson. This multivolume set offers numerous business forms, including partnership agreements, LLC operating agreements, corporate bylaws, minutes of corporate meetings, and many others.
- *Am. Jur. Legal Forms 2d.* This set includes more than 60 alphabetically arranged volumes of forms and provides forms for numerous

business-related topics as well as drafting tips, practice comments, and
checklists.

- *West's Legal Forms 3d.* This set includes more than 40 volumes containing
  forms that may be used as models for business drafting needs.
- *Fletcher's Corporate Forms Annotated.* This set is a companion set to
  the Fletcher encyclopedia discussed previously. It includes forms for
  resolutions by directors, forms for minutes of corporate meetings, and
  so forth. The word "annotated" in the title indicates that you will also
  be sent to pertinent cases relating to the specific topic covered in a
  form.
- *Nichols Cyclopedia of Legal Form Annotated.* This set offers a useful variety
  of forms for organizing, maintaining, and dissolving corporations.

In drafting forms, consider the forms, letters, and other documents that may be
available at your law office. Law firms routinely use standard or model sets of
bylaws, operating agreements, and so forth. You can usually retrieve the form
from the office's computer database and then modify it to fit a client's particular
needs.

Other Resources

There are several other resources you can tap into to locate pertinent business-
related information. Consider the following:

- *IRS.* The IRS offers numerous publications that not only explain the use of
  its tax forms, but also provide thorough explanations of certain business
  topics. Access www.irs.gov and search through the list of forms and
  publications.
- *SEC.* The SEC's Web site offers access to all filings for publicly traded
  companies. Searching is done by company name. The site also offers
  straightforward explanations of various financial and securities concepts
  and a glossary of financial terms.
- *Agencies and organizations.* A number of agencies and organizations offer
  a wealth of information.
  - The Small Business Administration maintains a toll-free line to answer
    inquiries at (800) 827-5722. Contact your local SBA office or chamber
    of commerce for information on businesses and start-up assistance.
  - The Web sites of the various Secretaries of State offer a wealth of infor-
    mation on business formation, maintenance, and dissolution. A list of
    all of these offices, together with their addresses, phone numbers, and
    Web sites is found in Appendix A.
  - The text of various uniform acts (including the Revised Uniform Part-
    nership Act and the Uniform Limited Liability Company Act) can be
    located at the Web site of the National Conference of Commissioners
    on Uniform State Laws at www.nccusl.org.
- *Service companies.* The various attorneys' service companies can provide
  information, forms, and fees relating to business formation. Many service
  companies also provide partnership, LLP, LLC, and corporate kits, some

of which include "canned" or prepared bylaws, minutes, and other useful forms. Some of the better known attorneys' service companies are the following:

- Attorneys' Corporation Service, Inc.
  3021 W. Magnolia Blvd.
  Burbank, CA 91505
  phone: (800) 462-5487
  www.attorneyscorpservice.com
- CT Corporation
  111 8th Avenue
  New York, NY 10011
  phone: (800) 624-0909
  www.ctadvantage.com
- Corporation Service Company
  2711 Centerville Road
  Wilmington, DE 19808
  phone: (800) 927-9800
  www.incspot.com
- The Company Corporation
  (a wholly owned subsidiary of Corporation Service Company)
  2711 Centerville Road
  Suite 400
  Wilmington, DE 19808
  phone: (800) 818-0204
  www.incorporate.com
- Corpex Banknote Company, Inc.
  1440 Fifth Avenue
  Bayshore, NY 11706-9807
  phone: (800) 221-8181
  www.corpexnet.biz

Glossary

Accredited investor: A bank, a savings and loan, or an investor with a certain net worth, generally income in excess of $200,000, or otherwise sufficiently sophisticated that they do not require the registration protections afforded by the Securities Act of 1933.

Accrual method of accounting: Accounting method of listing expenses and income in business records when they are incurred or billed rather than when they are actually paid or received.

Accumulated earnings tax: Tax penalty imposed on corporations that retain earnings beyond reasonable business needs.

Actual authority: The grant of authority, either express or implied, by a principal to an agent.

Administrative dissolution: Dissolution of a business entity, often for technical reasons such as failing to pay taxes or file annual reports; most states allow reinstatement of the entity upon cure of defaults.

Affiliates: Subsidiaries formed by a common parent corporation.

After hours trading: Trading after the normal business hours of the stock exchanges.

Agency: Relationship between parties whereby one agrees to act on behalf of another.

Agent: One who acts for or represents another, called a principal.

Agent for service: *See* Registered agent.

Aggressor: Corporation (or individual) attacking or wishing to acquire control over another corporation, typically called the target.

Alienation: The transfer of some property.

Alien corporation: Corporation formed in a country other than the United States.

Alter ego: When corporate shareholders fail to respect the fact that the corporation is an entity separate and apart from them, they are said to view the corporation as their "alter ego," namely, a mere extension of themselves. Shareholders who treat the corporation as their alter ego may have personal liability imposed on them for the corporation's debts.

Amended articles of incorporation: A document filed with the secretary of state of a corporation's state of incorporation to effect a change in the corporation's articles of incorporation.

Annual meeting: Yearly meeting of shareholders of a corporation to elect directors and conduct other business.

Annual report: Yearly form required to be filed by business entities in most states, providing information about the entity.

Antitrust: Area of law regulating business competition to ensure fair business conduct and a competitive economy.

Apparent authority: Conduct of a principal causing a third party to believe an agent had authority to act for the principal.

Appraisal rights: Authority given to dissenting shareholders to have their shares appraised, or valued, and bought out.

Arbitrageurs: Individuals or companies trading in a target's stock after announcement of a tender offer or trading in different stocks and bonds in different markets at the same time. Sometimes called risk arbitrageurs or simply "arbs."

Articles of dissolution: Document filed with the secretary of state to effect a dissolution or termination of a corporation as a legal entity. Sometimes called a *certificate of dissolution*.

Articles of domestication: The document filed with the state to effect a change of a corporation's state of incorporation.

Articles of entity conversion: The document filed with the state to effect a change in a business's structure.

Articles of incorporation: Document that creates a corporation. Sometimes called a *certificate of incorporation*.

Articles of merger: Document filed with the secretary of state to effect a merger or other combination of two or more corporations.

Articles of organization: Document filed with the appropriate state official creating a limited liability company.

Asked price: Lowest price at which a corporation will sell its shares.

Asset purchase: Acquisition by one corporation of another's properties.

Assignment: Transfer of one's interest in certain property.

Assumed name: *See* Fictitious business name.

At-will employment: Employment that may be terminated upon the will of an employer or employee, at any time.

Authorized share: Share identified in the articles of incorporation as being capable of and subject to issuance by a corporation.

Back-end transaction: *See* Mop up.

Bankruptcy: The condition of a person or entity being declared bankrupt under federal law.

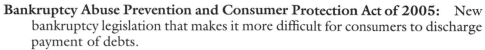

Bankruptcy Abuse Prevention and Consumer Protection Act of 2005: New bankruptcy legislation that makes it more difficult for consumers to discharge payment of debts.

Bear hug: Approach by an aggressor to a target after the aggressor has acquired a toehold in the target.

Bear market: A declining market.

Bid price: Highest price at which a share of stock can be purchased.

Black knight: Aggressor attempting to acquire a target.

Blank check stock: Provision in articles of incorporation authorizing directors to create a new class or series of stock.

Blank stock: *See* Series stock.

Blitz: Lightning and no-notice strike against a target's stock so forceful that the target is sufficiently overwhelmed and cannot adopt any defenses to prevent a takeover.

Block trade: Trade involving at least 10,000 shares of stock.

Blue-chip stock: Stock of the elite and nationally known corporations.

Blue sky law: State law regulating the issuance, purchase, and sale of securities.

Board of directors: *See* Director.

Boilerplate: Standard provisions typically found in contracts or other legal documents.

Bond: Debt security secured by some corporate asset that can be seized by a creditor upon default by the corporation.

Bounty payment: Payment made by the SEC to those who provide information relating to violations of the Securities Exchange Act of 1934.

Bringdown certificate: Certificate of corporate officer verifying continuing accuracy of facts or documents.

Broker: Securities firm that acts on behalf of a customer, rather than trading on its own account, as does a dealer.

Bulk sale: Sale or transfer of the major portion of a company's business outside the scope of its ordinary course of business, usually triggering notices to creditors.

Bulletproof state: A state offering full protection from liability in a limited liability partnership (also called *full shield state*).

Bull market: A rising market.

Business judgment rule: Court-made rule immunizing directors and officers from liability for their decisions so long as the decision was reasonable and made in good faith.

Business trust: Unincorporated business association governed by the law of trusts in which equitable title to property is held by a trustee for the benefit of others; rarely seen in modern times.

Buy-sell agreement: Agreement entered into by shareholders restricting the transfer or sale of their stock.

Bylaws: Rules governing the management and operation of a corporation.

C corporation: Corporation for profit which is subject to double taxation; one other than an S corporation.

Call: Right of a corporation to reacquire stock it has issued to a shareholder (generally, a preferred shareholder).

Cancellation: Elimination of shares reacquired by a corporation.

Capital: Generally, money.

Capital surplus: Amount of consideration in excess of par value of shares that a corporation receives for its shares.

Cash benefit plan: A hybrid retirement plan combining features of a traditional pension plan with a 401(k).

Cash dividend: Distribution of cash by a corporation to its shareholders.

Cashless exercise: Using options to pay for options.

Cash method of accounting: Accounting method of listing expenses and income in business records only when they are paid or received.

Certificate of good standing: Document issued by a secretary of state showing that a corporation is in compliance with that state's laws (also called *certificate of existence*).

Chapter 7 bankruptcy: Bankruptcy proceeding in which debtor's estate is liquidated.

Chapter 11 reorganization: Bankruptcy proceeding in which a debtor's debts are reorganized and debtor continues its business.

Charging order: Order from a court requiring partnership to pay distributions a partner would have received to the partner's creditor until a judgment is fully satisfied.

Charter: Name used by some states to refer to a corporation's articles of incorporation.

Chewable poison pill: An anti-takeover defense; a type of poison pill that is of short duration and is triggered only when a bidder buys significant numbers of shares.

Circuit breaker: *See* Collars.

Class action: Action brought by one or a few shareholders on behalf of numerous other shareholders who are similarly situated.

Class voting: Voting rights given to a class of stock.

Close (closely held) corporation: Corporation whose shares are held by a few people, usually friends or relatives active in managing the business. Some flexibility is permitted with regard to observing corporate formalities.

Collars: Automatic halts to trading at the NYSE that occur when the market declines certain percentages (also called *curbs* or *circuit breakers*).

Commingling: Combining shareholders' personal funds improperly with those of the corporation; liability can be imposed on shareholders who fail to respect the corporate entity by commingling funds.

Common law trust: A business trust governed by judicial decision rather than state statutes.

Common stock: Stock in a corporation that has no special features, as does preferred stock; usually has the right to vote and to share in liquidation dividends.

Comprehensive Omnibus Budget Reconciliation Act (COBRA): Federal law requiring insurance continuation after employee leaves employment.

Confession of judgment: Provision contained in a promissory note entitling a creditor to obtain an immediate judgment against a debtor in default; not valid in all states.

Consolidation: Combination of two or more corporations into a new corporate entity (example: A + B = C).

Constituent corporations: Corporations that are parties to a merger, consolidation, or other combination.

Contingent voting: Voting that is dependent on the occurrence of some event such as default by a corporation in the payment of dividends.

Conversion right: 1. Right of preferred shareholders to convert preferred stock into some other security of the corporation, usually common stock.
2. Right of creditors to convert debt security (bond) into equity security (shares).

Cooperative association: A business owned and democratically controlled by its members for their mutual benefit.

Copyright: Right given in original works of authorship including literary, artistic, dramatic, and other works.

Corporate-owned life insurance: Insurance purchased by companies on the lives of rank-and-file employees, often without their notice.

Corporation: Legal entity existing by authority of state law, owned by its shareholders, and managed by its elected directors and appointed officers.

Corporation by estoppel: Defectively formed corporation that cannot be attacked due to a party's dealing with the corporation as if it were a valid corporation; party is estopped, or precluded, from treating the entity as anything other than a corporation.

Covenant not to compete: Provision in an agreement or an independent agreement prohibiting employees from working in certain industries or in certain geographic areas after termination of employment; to be valid, the clause must be reasonable in scope and duration and can typically be imposed only on employees with special skill and talents.

Cross-purchase insurance: Insurance policies taken out by each shareholder on the life of each other shareholder to provide funds to purchase shares from a deceased shareholder's estate.

Crown jewel defense: Sale by a target of its valuable assets, usually to make itself unattractive to an aggressor.

Cumulative dividend: Distribution that "adds up" over time and must be paid to a preferred shareholder, when the corporation has funds to do so, before any distribution can be made to other shareholders.

Cumulative voting: In an election of directors, a type of voting whereby each share carries as many votes as there are directors' vacancies to be filled; assists minority shareholders in electing representatives to the board of directors.

Curb: *See* Collars.

Day trading: Trading stock electronically numerous times each day, usually from another's business location.

Dead-hand poison pill: An anti-takeover defense; a type of poison pill that can only be deactivated by the directors who established it (also called a *continuing director plan*).

Dealer: Securities firm that buys securities for resale to its customers; the firm trades "on its own account."

Debenture: Debt security that is unsecured, such as a simple promissory note.

Debt financing: Borrowing money to raise capital.

Debt security: Instrument evidencing a corporation's debt to another.

De facto: Literally, "in fact"; a corporation with a defect in its incorporation process such that it cannot have de jure status; cannot be attacked by a third party, although the state can invalidate it.

De facto merger: Transaction that has the effect of a merger and must comply with all statutory formalities pertaining to mergers.

Defined benefit plan: Qualified retirement plan that sets a preestablished benefit that will be paid to employees leaving the company.

Defined contribution plan: Qualified retirement plan specifying the amount the employer will place into the plan account each year on behalf of an employee.

De jure: Literally, "of right"; a corporation formed in substantial compliance with the laws of the state of incorporation, the validity of which cannot be attacked by any party or the state.

Dematerialization: Issuance of stock by electronic book entry rather than paper certificate.

Derivative: Asset with performance derived from the performance of an underlying asset, security, or index, such as a stock option or futures contract.

Derivative action: Action brought by a limited partner or shareholder not to enforce his or her own cause of action but to enforce an obligation due to the business entity; the action "derives" from the claimant's ownership interest in the business entity.

Designated order turnaround (DOT): Computerized trading system used by NYSE.

Direct action: Action brought by a limited partner or shareholder of a corporation for a direct injury sustained by the claimant; for example, being refused the right to examine corporate books and records.

Direct registration: Registration of ownership of stock in the buyer's name on the issuer's books.

Director: One who directs or manages a corporation; when more than one director exists, they function as a board.

Disclosed principal: Principal whose existence and identity are known to others.

Disproportionate voting: Voting rights that differ in one class from those granted to another class.

Dissenter's rights: *See* Appraisal rights.

Dissenting shareholder: Shareholder opposing some corporation action, such as an amendment to the articles of incorporation, merger, or consolidation.

Dissolution: Termination of a business organization as a legal entity, such as a partnership or corporation; may be voluntary or involuntary for a corporation.

Distribution: Direct or indirect transfer by a corporation of money or other property (other than its own shares) to or for the benefit of its shareholders, whether a distribution of corporate profits or a distribution at the time of liquidation. The older view used this term to refer to distributions to shareholders *other than* distributions of a corporation's own profits.

Dividend: Corporation's distribution of its profits to its shareholders by way of cash, property, or shares. The modern approach is to refer to any distribution as a dividend, whether a distribution of corporate profits or a distribution at the time of liquidation.

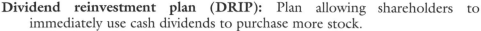

Dividend reinvestment plan (DRIP): Plan allowing shareholders to immediately use cash dividends to purchase more stock.

Domestication: The changing of a corporation's state of incorporation.

Domestic corporation: A corporation created or incorporated in the state in which it is conducting business.

Double taxation: Taxation of corporate income at two levels: once when the corporation earns money and then again when shareholders receive distributions from the corporation.

Dow Jones average: Average of the stock prices of 65 major stocks.

Downstream merger: Merger of a parent and a subsidiary in which the subsidiary survives (example: $P + S = S$).

Draw: Advance payment to an employee against anticipated compensation.

Due diligence: Careful review of documents and transactions to ensure they are appropriate for a party and in compliance with all pertinent laws.

Dummy directors: Nominal directors in the articles of incorporation, often an attorney and staff members named for the convenience of signing documents; dummies will resign at the organizational meeting and be replaced with the corporation's true directors.

Earned surplus: Total corporate profits earned during some particular accounting period.

Election judge: Neutral party who oversees corporate elections to determine whether a quorum is present, that proxies have been counted, and that a measure has received sufficient votes for approval.

Electronic communication network (ECN): A private electronic trading system allowing quick and inexpensive trading 24 hours per day.

Employee: One who performs services for another for some form of compensation and is subject to the other's control and direction.

Employee Retirement Income Security Act (ERISA): Federal statute regulating retirement plans for employees.

Employee stock ownership plan (ESOP): Retirement plan in which the employer contributes funds (that may be borrowed from a bank or other lender) to a trust. The money is then used to purchase stock in the corporation for employees.

Employment contract: Agreement between employer and employee specifying the terms and conditions of employment.

Entity conversion: A business's change of its structure — for example, a conversion from a corporation to an LLC.

E-proxy voting: Method of voting electronically.

Equal dignities rule: Rule that if an agreement must be in writing, then agent's authority to act in regard to that agreement must also be in writing.

Equity financing: Issuance of shares to raise capital.

Equity security: Security demonstrating a person's ownership interest in a corporation.

Estoppel: Prohibition imposed on a party to preclude a challenge to some fact or event because such a challenge would be inequitable based on the party's conduct.

Ethics: Study of standards of right and wrong.

Exchange-traded fund: An investment vehicle traded on a securities exchange that is tied to an index.

Ex-dividend: The status of a shareholder or share with no right to receive a declared dividend.

Exempt security: Security that is exempt from compliance with the Securities Act of 1933.

Exempt transaction: Transaction exempt from compliance with the registration requirements of the Securities Act of 1933, such as a small issue.

Express authority: Acts specifically directed or authorized by a principal.

Extinguished corporation: Corporation that does not survive a merger or other combination. Sometimes called a merged corporation.

Face value: Principal amount owed by a debtor to a creditor as shown on debt instrument.

Fairness opinion: Expert opinion on the valuation of a target requested by the target's directors to demonstrate that they have met their fiduciary duties.

Family limited partnership: A type of partnership composed of family members and designed to achieve estate and tax planning benefits (also called a *family limited liability company*).

Fictitious business name: Name adopted for use by a person, partnership, corporation, or other business that is other than its true or legal name. Sometimes called an assumed name.

Fiduciary relationship: Relationship in which a party owes a duty of good faith to another or to others.

Financial Industry Regulatory Authority (FINRA): The nongovernmental regulator for all securities firms doing business in the United States.

Financing statement: Document recorded with the secretary of state or county recorder to provide notice of a security interest claimed in personal property; also called a *UCC-1 form*.

Fiscal year: Twelve-month reporting period adopted by a business for accounting purposes; it need not be the calendar year.

Floor: Location at NYSE where share transactions occur.

Foothold: *See* Toehold.

Foreign corporation: Corporation conducting business in a state other than the one in which it is incorporated. Occasionally, corporations formed outside the United States are called foreign corporations, although they are more properly termed *alien corporations*.

Foreign partnership: Partnership conducting business in a state other than the one in which it is organized.

Forward-looking statement: Predictions made by corporations about future earnings.

401(k) plan: Retirement plan funded by the pre-tax contributions of employers and nontaxable contributions of employees.

Fractional share: A portion of a share; typically entitled to proportionate voting and distribution rights.

Franchise: License granted by one party to another enabling the latter to use the licensor's proprietary system and trademark in offering goods or services.

Franchise tax: Fee or tax imposed by a state for the privilege of conducting business in the state.

Freeze-out: Impermissible tactic by directors to compel a corporate dissolution or merger to dispose of minority shareholders; sometimes called a *squeeze-out.*

Fringe benefit: Noncash form of compensation for employees.

Front running: An unscrupulous trading practice in which floor brokers trade for themselves before trading on behalf of their clients.

Full shield state: State offering full protection from liability for partners in a limited liability partnership.

Futures contract: Agreement between two parties to exchange a specified quantity of some asset at a specified price on a specified date.

GAAP: Generally accepted accounting principles.

General agency: Act of a partner in carrying out the usual business of the firm that will bind the partnership unless the person with whom the partner is dealing knows the partner has no authority to perform that act.

General partner: Individual or entity managing or controlling a (general) partnership or a limited partnership.

General proxy: A proxy authorizing the proxy holder to vote a shareholder's shares in the proxy holder's discretion.

Going private: *See* Leveraged buy-out.

Going public: Offering securities to members of the public at large. *See* Initial public offering.

Golden parachute: Lucrative compensation package given to key corporate managers who leave or are let go by a corporation.

Good till canceled order: An order to purchase stock that remains open until it is specifically canceled.

Governance guidelines: Formal written policies relating to management of corporations and often sought by shareholders.

Greenmail: Form of legal corporate blackmail in which an aggressor threatens to take over a target and then sells the toehold back to the target at an inflated price in return for an agreement not to take over the target.

Hart-Scott-Rodino Antitrust Improvements Act: A federal statute requiring premerger notification to the government so it can determine if the proposed transaction would have an anticompetitive effect.

Hedge fund: A portfolio of aggressively managed investments that caters to sophisticated investors.

Holder of record: Owner of stock as of a particular date. *See* Record date.

Horizontal restraint: Agreement between business rivals that restrains trade.

Hostile takeover: Acquisition of a corporation against the will of its directors and shareholders.

Householding: Practice of sending only one report and proxy statement to shareholders with same surname at same address.

Hybrid market: Reference to NYSE that combines auction trading with automated trading systems.

Illegal dividend: Dividend paid out of an unauthorized account or made while a corporation is insolvent.

Implied authority: Authority to perform acts customarily performed by agents, even if not expressly so directed by a principal.

Incorporator: Person who prepares and signs the articles of incorporation to form a corporation.

Indemnify: Compensating or reimbursing one who has incurred a debt or obligation on another's behalf.

Independent contractor: One who is not subject to the control and direction of another but exercises independent judgment and discretion while performing duties and activities for that party.

Independent director: Director with no family or business ties to a corporation other than board membership.

Individual retirement account (IRA): Retirement plan funded by an individual not covered under some other retirement plan.

Information returns: Documents filed with the Internal Revenue Service reporting income earned by or distributed to partners or shareholders.

Initial public offering: First offering of securities to the public; usually, the offering by a corporation of its securities to the public as a means of raising capital; often referred to as *going public.*

Inside director: A director who is also an employee or officer of the corporation.

Insider trading: Transaction by corporate insiders, such as directors and officers, to achieve some benefit in the purchase or sale of securities based on inside information, namely information that is not available to the public at large, prohibited by SEC Rule 10b-5.

Insolvency: Inability to pay one's debts as they become due in the usual course of business or excess of liabilities over assets.

In the money options: Stock options that may be exercised at a gain.

Intellectual property: Property rights in intangibles, such as trade secrets, inventions, copyrights, trademarks, and related intangibles, capable of being owned but which are neither real property nor tangible personal property.

Involuntary dissolution: Dissolution forced on an entity, such as a partnership or corporation, through a judicial proceeding initiated by either the state or owners of the entity, or perhaps by creditors. Sometimes called *judicial dissolution.*

Involuntary petition: Bankruptcy initiated by creditors.

Issuance: Process of selling corporate securities.

Joint and several liability: When each member of an association is liable to pay all of a debt or obligation; when a creditor may sue all individuals in an association or pick among them to satisfy a debt.

Joint stock company: Unincorporated association combining features of partnerships and corporations; ownership interests are represented by transferable shares of stock; rarely seen in the United States.

Joint venture: Type of partnership formed to carry out a particular enterprise rather than an ongoing business.

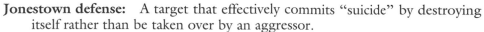

Jonestown defense: A target that effectively commits "suicide" by destroying itself rather than be taken over by an aggressor.

Judicial dissolution: *See* Involuntary dissolution.

Judicial liquidation: Liquidation of a corporation that has been involuntarily dissolved by a court; often performed by a court-appointed receiver or trustee.

Junk bond: Bond below investment grade.

Keogh plan: Retirement plan adopted by a sole proprietor or self-employed individual.

Key person policy: Insurance policy taken out on the life of a senior manager. In the event of the manager's death, the policy proceeds go to the business entity to provide sufficient funds to purchase the decedent's ownership interest in the entity.

Killer bees: Attorneys, advisors, and others retained by a target to fight off a takeover.

Legend: Generally, a notation on a stock certificate stating that it is subject to some restriction, typically as to transfer of stock represented by the certificate; a notation on a corporate document such as a prospectus.

Leveraged buy-out: Offer by a target's management to purchase all of the publicly held shares of a target corporation. Sometimes called *going private.*

Limited liability: Liability that is confined to that amount contributed by an investor to an enterprise; when personal assets of an investor cannot be used to satisfy business debts or obligations.

Limited liability company: New form of business enterprise, recognized in all states, offering the pass-through tax status of a partnership and the limited liability of a corporation.

Limited liability limited partnership: A limited partnership that files with the secretary of state so its general partner has no personal liability for partnership obligations. Recognized fully only in some states.

Limited liability partnership: *See* Registered limited liability partnership.

Limit order: Order given to a broker limiting the broker's authority regarding the price of stock, when to purchase or sell stock, and so forth.

Limited partner: Individual or entity having membership in a limited partnership, but does not manage or control the enterprise, and whose liability is limited to the amount contributed to the limited partnership.

Limited partnership: Partnership formed under statutory requirements that has as members one or more general partners and one or more limited partners.

Limited partnership agreement: Agreement among partners in a limited partnership, usually written, regarding the affairs of the limited partnership, the duties of the general partner, rights of limited partners, and the conduct of the business.

Limited partnership certificate: Document filed with a state agency to create a limited partnership.

Limited proxy: A proxy directing a proxy holder to vote as specified by the shareholder giving the proxy.

Line of credit: A type of preauthorized loan that the borrower draws against as needed.

Liquidation: Process of completing the affairs of a business; for corporations, the process of collecting corporate assets, discharging debts, and distributing any remains to the shareholders; may be judicial or nonjudicial. Sometimes called *winding up.*

Liquidation distribution: Distribution made to business owners after creditors have been paid upon dissolution of a business entity.

Liquidator: *See* Receiver.

Load: Additional charge imposed on an investor in a mutual fund, usually imposed when the individual invests in the fund.

Margin: Practice of using a loan or credit for some of the purchase price of stock.

Margin call: Demand by a broker for additional collateral to secure the purchase price of securities bought on margin or credit.

Market maker: Members who trade on the NASDAQ market.

Marshaling of assets: Requirement that partnership creditors must first exhaust partnership assets before attacking a partner's personal assets to satisfy a debt or obligation.

Member: Owner or investor in a limited liability company; Individual or firm holding a trading license on NYSE.

Membership: What is offered by a nonprofit corporation rather than stock.

Merger: Combinations of two or more corporations into one corporate entity (example: A + B = A).

Midnight raid: Raid by aggressor after the afternoon closing of a stock exchange and concluded before resumption of trading in the morning.

Mining partnership: Partnership formed for the purpose of mining or oil or gas exploration; recognized by statute in some states and by judicial decision in others.

Mini-tender offer: A tender offer to purchase less than 5 percent of a target's outstanding shares; not subject to SEC rules relating to tender offers.

Minutes: Written summary of the proceedings at directors' or shareholders' meetings.

Money market fund: Mutual fund that invests in short-term and nearly risk-free investments.

Monopoly: Exclusive privilege or advantage to offer a product or service generally resulting in an illegal restraint of trade.

Mop up: Attempt by a successful aggressor to acquire 100 percent ownership of a target's stock.

Mortgage bond or note: Debt security in which a corporation pledges real estate as security for its promise to repay money borrowed from a creditor.

Mutual fund: Open-end investment management company that continually trades in other issuers' securities for an unlimited number of persons; an entity engaged primarily in the business of investing or trading in the securities of others.

Name registration: Reservation of a corporate name in foreign states in which the corporation intends to do business in the future.

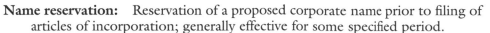

Name reservation: Reservation of a proposed corporate name prior to filing of articles of incorporation; generally effective for some specified period.

Name saver: Subsidiary incorporated in a state expressly to ensure a name is available for corporate parent in that state.

National Association of Securities Dealers Automated Quotation (NAS-DAQ): Computerized trading system of the National Association of Securities Dealers; has no physical location for trading as does NYSE.

Nimble dividends test: Test to determine if dividends can be paid in which a corporation must have current profits.

No-hand poison pill: An anti-takeover device; a poison pill that cannot be removed by any director if control of the board changes hands.

Nonaccredited investor: Investor who is not sophisticated or "accredited"; *see* Accredited investor.

Noncompetition agreements: *See* Covenant not to compete.

Nonjudicial liquidation: Liquidation of an entity that has been voluntarily dissolved; in a corporation, such liquidation is performed by corporate directors and officers.

Nonprofit corporation: Corporation formed for some charitable, religious, educational, or scientific purpose or for the mutual benefit of its members, rather than for the purpose of making a profit.

Nonqualified retirement plan: Retirement plan not subject to the extensive regulation governing a qualified plan; does not provide the same tax advantages as a qualified plan.

No par value stock: Stock having no stated minimum value; the price can be determined by a corporation's board of directors.

Nuclear war: Hostile takeover involving numerous large publicly traded companies.

NYSE Euronext: Largest secondary market for trading of securities; located in New York City and usually referred to as NYSE.

Odd lot: Purchase or sale of less than 100 shares of stock.

Officer: One appointed by a corporation's board of directors to carry out management functions as delegated by the board.

Online trading: The practice of trading electronically from one's home computer a few times each day or month.

Operating agreement: Agreement governing the operation of a limited liability company.

Opt-in provisions: State laws providing that unless preemptive rights are provided for in the articles of incorporation, they do not exist.

Option: Right to purchase stock or commodities at a specified price during a specified time period.

Opt-out provisions: State laws providing that preemptive rights exist unless specifically denied by the articles of incorporation.

Organizational meeting: First meeting of a corporation held after incorporation to finalize the incorporation process by electing directors, appointing officers, adopting bylaws, and so forth.

Outside director: Director who is not an employee or officer of the corporation (also called *independent director*).

Outstanding shares: Shares issued by a corporation and held by a shareholder.

Oversubscription: Shares tendered to an aggressor in excess of the amount requested in the aggressor's tender offer.

Over-the-counter market: Computerized securities trading network with no physical trading location.

Pac-Man defense: Tender offer by a target to acquire an aggressor's stock.

Parent corporation: Corporation that creates another corporation (called a subsidiary) and holds all or a majority of its shares.

Partial shield state: A state offering limited protection from liability to partners in a limited liability partnership for acts arising out of wrongful conduct of co-partners.

Partially disclosed principal: Principal whose existence but not specific identity is known to others.

Participating preferred stock: Stock that enjoys the right to participate in corporate distributions in addition to those "built into" the preferred stock.

Partnership: An association of two or more persons to carry on a business as co-owners for profit; often called a general partnership to distinguish it from a limited partnership.

Partnership at will: Partnership with no specific term of duration.

Partnership for a term: Partnership with a definite term of duration.

Par value: Minimum consideration for which a share of stock can be issued; set forth in a corporation's articles of incorporation.

Patent: A grant by the federal government allowing one to exclude others from making, using, or selling one's new and nonobvious invention or discovery.

Penny stock: A stock selling for less than $5 per share; also called *Over-the-Counter Bulletin Board Stock*.

Performance shares: Shares awarded only when certain goals are achieved.

Person: According to most statutes, a "person" is a natural individual or a business organization, such as a partnership or corporation.

Personal liability: Liability for debts and obligations in excess of that originally invested, namely, liability extending to one's personal assets.

Piercing the veil: Holding individual investors liable for a business's debt to prevent fraud or injustice.

Pink sheets: A listing for the sale of stock of companies that do not meet the listing requirements of other exchanges.

Plan of domestication: The plan that provides the terms and conditions of a corporation's change of its state of incorporation.

Plan of entity conversion: The plan that provides the terms and conditions of a business's change in its structure.

Plan of merger: Blueprint for a merger containing all of the terms and conditions of a merger.

Plurality: The number of votes received by a successful candidate who does not receive a majority of votes cast in an election; counting only votes "for" a nominee and not counting votes "against" or withheld.

Poison pill: Privileges and rights of a target's shareholders triggered by a tender offer that are designed to thwart a takeover; also called *shareholder rights plan*.

Pooling agreement: Agreement between or among shareholders specifying the manner in which they will vote.

Porcupine provision: *See* Shark repellent.

Post: A desk at NYSE where securities are traded.

Preemptive right: Right given to shareholders in articles of incorporation allowing shareholders to purchase newly issued stock in an amount proportionate to their current share ownership.

Preemptive strike: Highly attractive offer made by an aggressor with the intent of obtaining immediate control of a target.

Preference: Voidable prebankruptcy payment made to a creditor.

Preferred stock: Corporate stock that has some right, privilege, or preference over another type of stock.

Preincorporation agreement: Agreement entered into between promoters of a corporation and some third party prior to creation of the corporation; promoter is bound by the agreement.

Preincorporation share subscription: Offer by a party to purchase stock in a corporation made before the corporation is formed.

Primary market: Investment firms, underwriters, and so forth involved in the process of selling an issuer's initial offering of securities.

Principal: One who appoints another, called an agent, to act for or represent him or her.

Priority: Process of making one debt senior, or prior, to another (which is referred to as *subordinate*).

Privately held corporation: Corporation whose shares are not sold to the public but are held by a small group of investors, often family and friends.

Private placement offering: Nonpublic offering of a corporation's stock, generally exempt from the registration requirements of the Securities Act of 1933. Sometimes called a *private placement memorandum.*

Process: Complaint filed in court by a plaintiff and the summons issued thereafter by the court to the party named as defendant requiring an appearance or response.

Professional corporation: Corporation formed by a person or persons practicing a certain profession, such as law, medicine, or accounting, who retain liability for their own misconduct and those acting under their control.

Professional limited liability company: A type of limited liability company organized by professionals who retain liability for their own negligence.

Profit-sharing plan: Retirement plan funded by an employer's profits.

Program trading: Large computer-assisted trades of stock based on algorithms.

Promissory note: Document evidencing one's debt to another.

Promoter: One who plans and organizes a corporation.

Property dividend: Distribution that is not cash or shares in the issuing corporation but is generally some physical or tangible item.

Prospectus: Document that must be provided to any purchaser of securities registered under the Securities Act of 1933; it includes information relating to the corporation, its management, and the securities being issued.

Proxy: Written authorization by a shareholder directing another to vote his or her shares.

Proxy fight: Solicitation of a target's shareholders by management of the aggressor and management of the target to vote for each party's management slate; also called a *proxy contest.*

Public corporation: Corporation whose shares can be purchased and sold by members of the general public.

Public offering: Issuance of securities to the general public that generally must first be registered according to the Securities Act of 1933.

Pump and dump: Hyping a stock to increase its price and then selling it.

Put: Right of a shareholder (usually, a preferred shareholder) to compel a corporation to reacquire stock issued to the shareholder.

Qualification: Process by which a corporation formed in one state is authorized to transact business in another.

Qualified retirement plan: Retirement plan that meets certain Internal Revenue Code requirements and is eligible for special tax treatment.

Qualified small business stock: Stock in certain small businesses (C corporations with less than $50 million) that qualifies for tax advantages by excluding from taxable income one-half of any gain on the sale of the stock.

Quorum: Minimum number of shareholders or directors required to be present at a meeting to conduct business; usually a majority.

Quote: The highest bid to buy and the lowest offer to sell a stock; the bid and asked prices are collectively called the quote.

Ratification: Acceptance or approval of a certain act; may be express or implied from conduct.

Real estate investment trust (REIT): A vehicle usually organized as a trust for investing in real estate by numerous investors who pool their capital to acquire commercial real estate.

Receiver: Individual or firm appointed by a court to oversee a judicial or involuntary dissolution. Sometimes called a *liquidator*.

Recitals: Preliminary clauses in agreements, often identifying the parties to agreement and the intent or purpose of the agreement.

Record date: Date selected in advance of a meeting used to determine who will be entitled to notice of a meeting and who will be entitled to vote at a meeting.

Redemption right: 1. Right given to a corporation to repurchase the stock of preferred shareholders (call) or the right given to a preferred shareholder to compel the corporation to repurchase preferred stock (put).
2. Right of a corporation to pay off, or redeem, debt owed to a creditor before the stated maturity date.

Red herring prospectus: Form of prospectus distributed by an issuer corporation between the filing of a registration statement and its effective date (named for the legend printed in red ink on the prospectus).

Registered agent: Individual or company designated by a business to receive notices, litigation pleadings, documents, and service of process on the business's behalf.

Registered limited liability partnership: Newly recognized form of partnership in which a partner has no personal liability for the misconduct of another partner (and, in some states no personal liability for contractual obligations of the partnership); formed by filing an application with the appropriate state official; also called *limited liability partnership*.

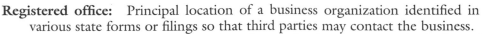

Registered office: Principal location of a business organization identified in various state forms or filings so that third parties may contact the business.

Registrar: Bank or other institution that maintains a corporation's list of shareholders.

Registration: 1. Process of reserving a corporate name in another state.
2. Process of complying with the Securities Act of 1933 for issuance of securities to the public.

Registration statement: Form or document filed with the Securities and Exchange Commission, pursuant to the Securities Act of 1933, when securities are first offered to the public.

Regular meeting: Routinely scheduled meeting of corporate directors.

Regulations A and D: *See* Small issues.

Reinstatement: Process of reviving a corporation after it has been dissolved for a technical violation of state law, such as failure to file an annual report.

Reload options: Options purchased with other options (also called a *cashless exercise*).

Rent strike: Refusal by a tenant to pay rent, usually due to some defect in the leased premises.

Reorganization: Tax term for mergers, consolidations, and share exchanges.

Representative action: Action brought by numerous shareholders or partners against a corporation, directors, or partnership; a class action by shareholders or partners.

Reservation: *See* Name reservation.

Respondeat superior: Latin phrase meaning "let the master answer"; legal theory by which liability is imposed on an employer-principal for an employee-agent's acts committed in the course and scope of the employment or agency.

Restated articles of incorporation: Document filed with the secretary of state to combine previously amended articles into a more comprehensible document.

Restricted stock: Stock that must be held for a fixed period of time.

Restrictive covenant: Clause in an agreement that prohibits or restricts certain activities, such as those prohibiting the disclosure of trade secrets or restricting former employees from working for competitors or in related industries; to be valid, restrictive covenants must be reasonable in scope and duration.

Retained earnings: Undistributed net profits accumulated by a corporation.

Reverse stock split: Reduction by a corporation in the number of its outstanding shares; often done to eliminate smaller shareholders.

Reverse triangular merger: Merger among a parent, its subsidiary, and a target corporation in which the subsidiary merges into the surviving target.

Right: A short-term option, as distinguished from a warrant, a long-term option.

Roll-up: Combination of several companies in the same industry.

Roth IRA: Retirement plan in which contributions are not deductible and withdrawals are not subject to taxation.

Round lot: Order involving 100 shares of stock.

Safe harbor: Activities that a person or entity may engage in that do not violate a statute.

Saturday night special: Raid by an aggressor made over a weekend so the target cannot marshal its management team.

Scorched earth: Extreme and dramatic efforts by a target to ward off a hostile takeover.

S corporation: Corporation in which all income is passed through to shareholders who pay taxes at appropriate individual rates. Certain eligibility requirements must be met to elect S status.

Scrip: Certificate evidencing a fractional share; scrip does not typically possess voting, dividend, or liquidation rights.

Secondary market: Stock exchange where established corporations trade their securities, such as the NYSE.

Section 12 company: Company required to register its securities pursuant to Section 12 of the Securities Exchange Act of 1934 (namely, a company traded on a national securities exchange or one having assets of $10 million or more and 500 or more shareholders).

Section 1224 stock: Stock that, when sold at a loss, provides certain tax advantages; the loss is treated as an ordinary rather than a capital loss. Certain requirements must be met to issue Section 1244 stock.

Secured debt or transaction: Debt secured by some corporate asset that can be seized upon the corporation's default in repayment of its loan obligation.

Securities Act of 1933: Federal law imposing requirements on a company's original issuance of securities to the public.

Securities and Exchange Commission (SEC): Independent federal agency charged with the regulation of securities.

Securities Exchange Act of 1934: Federal law imposing requirements on the trading of stock, primarily the purchase and sale of securities after their original issuance.

Securities Litigation Reform Act: 1995 federal law intended to reduce frivolous shareholder suits for securities fraud.

Security: Share or ownership interest in a corporation (equity security) or obligation of the corporation to an investor (debt security).

Security agreement: Agreement between a debtor and a lender in which the debtor pledges personal property (rather than real estate) as collateral to secure repayment of the debtor's loan to the creditor.

Selective disclosure: The disclosure by a company of relevant information to its analysts before the information is made known to the public at large (now unlawful).

Self-tender: Target's purchase of its own shares to prevent a hostile takeover.

SEP-IRA: A retirement plan allowing self-employed individuals to contribute to their retirement.

Series LLC: A separate and distinct group within an LLC, which has its own members and assets; not recognized by revised Uniform Limited Liability Company Act of 2006.

Series stock: Stock issued within a class including rights and preferences different from those of other series and issued without the necessity of amending the articles of incorporation; sometimes referred to as *blank stock*.

Service mark: A word, symbol, or device used to identify and distinguish one's services.

Service of process: Delivery of a summons and complaint (i.e., process) on a defendant or its agent.

Share: Units in which the proprietary interests of a corporation are divided.

Share dividend: Distribution to shareholders of the corporation's own shares.

Share exchange: Process by which the shareholders of a target exchange their shares for those of another corporation.

Shareholder: One who owns an interest in a corporation; synonymous with stockholder.

Shareholder litigation committee: Committee established by a board of directors to determine if litigation is appropriate (also called *special litigation committee*).

Share repurchase: The buying of its own shares on the open market by a corporation; such buybacks often elevate the market value of the remaining shares.

Share subscription: Agreement whereby a party offers to purchase stock in a corporation.

Shark repellent: Attempts by a target to ward off an aggressor even before a tender offer is made. Sometimes called a *porcupine provision*.

Shelf LLC: An LLC initially formed with no members; recognized under revised Uniform Limited Liability Company Act of 2006.

Shelf registration: A registration of new stock prepared up to three years in advance of sales; registration is automatically effective for well-known seasoned issuers.

Shop right: Employer's royalty-free license to use an invention developed by an employee.

Short-form merger: Merger between a parent and its subsidiary in which the parent owns at least 90 percent of the subsidiary's stock.

Short sale: The sale of a stock one does not yet own in the belief that the stock price will fall.

Short-swing profits: Profits made by a Section 12 company's officers, directors, or principal shareholders within a six-month period which must be disgorged to the corporation, even without a showing of insider trading or bad faith.

SIMPLE IRA: A retirement plan to which both employer (which has less than 100 employees) and employee contribute.

Sinking fund: Fund of money set aside by a corporation to enable it to redeem or reacquire shares from preferred shareholders or to pay off money borrowed by the corporation from a creditor.

Slow-hand poison pill: An anti-takeover device; a poison pill that bars newly elected directors from deactivating it for some period of time.

Small business corporation: Domestic corporation, with no more than 75 shareholders, all of whom are individuals and that meet other requirements, which may elect to be treated as an S corporation and thereby avoid double taxation.

Small issue: Offering of stock that does not exceed $5 million and is exempt from the registration requirements of the Securities Act of 1933.

Small-scale merger: Merger not dramatically affecting the survivor corporation's shareholders that is therefore not subject to approval by the survivor's shareholders.

Sole proprietorship: Business managed and owned by one person who has sole authority for all decision-making and faces unlimited personal liability for business debts and obligations.

Solvency: Ability to pay debts as they come due.

Specialist: Individual who handles the stock of one company traded on the NYSE.

Special meeting: Any meeting held between the annual meetings of shareholders or regular meetings of directors.

Split-dollar insurance: Insurance policy on the life of an employee, the premiums for which are paid by both the employer and employee.

Spoofing: Scam used to lure investors to buy stock.

SQUARZ: New security with a negative coupon rate.

Squeeze-out: *See* Freeze-out.

Stagger system: Process of varying election dates for board members so that they are not all elected at same time; a stagger system defeats cumulative voting.

Standby agreement: Agreement by an underwriter to purchase all or a portion of a corporation's securities not sold through the IPO.

Standstill agreement: Agreement by an aggressor not to purchase more shares of the target for some specified period of time; the target may pay greenmail to the aggressor for this agreement.

Stated capital: Amount equivalent to the par value of issued stock or consideration received for stock issued without par value.

Statutory trust: A business trust governed by state statute.

Stock: *See* Share.

Stock bonus plan: Retirement plan for employees in which the employer's contribution is stock rather than cash.

Stock certificate: Document evidencing an ownership interest in a corporation.

Stock exchange: Marketplace where securities are traded.

Stockholder: *See* Shareholder.

Stock option backdating: The practice of altering the date of a stock option grant to make it more valuable.

Stock option plan: Plan used by a corporation to compensate employees who have the right to buy the corporation's stock at certain times at fixed prices.

Stock purchase: Acquisition of stock in a corporation.

Stock split: Division by a corporation of its outstanding shares, often done to encourage trading.

Stock watch: Early warning system used by a corporation to detect fluctuations in the market price of its shares that might warn off action by aggressors.

Stop order: Order given to a broker to sell stock when it declines to a certain price or to buy stock when it has increased to a certain price.

Straight voting: The right carried by each outstanding share of record to one vote.

Strategic alliance: A form of collaborative business relationship in which the participants remain independent organizations.

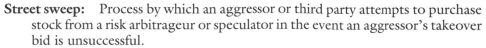

Street sweep: Process by which an aggressor or third party attempts to purchase stock from a risk arbitrageur or speculator in the event an aggressor's takeover bid is unsuccessful.

Strike suit: Lawsuit filed by disgruntled shareholders after a stock drop.

Strike team: Aggressor's legal counsel, advisors, public relations team, and so forth.

Subagent: An agent appointed by another agent.

Sublease: Transfer by a tenant of less than all of the interest in leased premises to another party.

Subordination: Process of making one debt junior, or subordinate, to another (which is said to have priority over it).

Subsidiary: Corporation formed by another corporation, called the parent; all or the majority of the subsidiary's stock is owned by the parent.

Suicide pact: Agreement by a target's management team to resign en masse in the event any one of them is fired or demoted after a hostile takeover (also called *people pill*).

Suitability rule: SEC rule requiring brokers who recommend the purchase or sale of stock to determine the suitability of the investment for the investor.

Surplus: Excess of a corporation's net assets over the corporation's stated capital.

Survivor: Corporation that continues in existence after a merger.

Syndicate: A group of investors, usually banks, that participate in selling an issue of stock.

Takeover: *See* Hostile takeover.

Target: Corporation being attacked or subject to takeover by another corporation or some third party.

Tender offer: Public offer by an aggressor to shareholders of a target corporation seeking to acquire their shares.

The street: Nickname for Wall Street in New York City.

Thin incorporation: Condition of a corporation's debt being disproportionately higher than its equity.

Tick: The smallest amount by which stock prices normally change.

Ticker: Teletype machine that prints and records stock transactions.

Tin parachute: Moderate settlement given to lower level corporate employees who leave a company.

Tippee: One who receives a tip or information from a corporate insider about the corporation.

Tipper: Corporate insider who gives tips or information to others about the corporation's finances or operations.

Toehold: Stock of a target purchased by an aggressor wishing to take over the target, usually less than 5 percent. Sometimes called a *foothold* or *creeping tender offer.*

Tombstone ad: Limited advertising offering securities during the 20-day period between filing of a registration statement with the SEC and its effective date.

Top-heavy plan: Retirement plan that discriminates in favor of more highly compensated employees.

Trademark: A word, symbol, or device used to identify and distinguish one's goods.

Trade secret: Valuable information that gives its owner a competitive advantage, such as a recipe or customer list.

Trading license: Annually granted written permission granted by NYSE allowing approved members to trade securities at the NYSE.

Transacting business: Activities engaged in by a corporation doing business in a state other than its state of incorporation that will require it to formally qualify with that host state to conduct business.

Transfer agent: Bank or other institution that physically issues or cancels stock certificates for large corporations.

Treasury stock: Stock reacquired by a corporation; it is considered issued but not outstanding.

Triangular merger: Merger among a parent, its subsidiary, and a target corporation in which the subsidiary merges with the target, leaving the subsidiary as the survivor; also called *forward triangular merger*.

Triple taxation: Taxation of income when received by a subsidiary, then when received by the parent as a distribution, and finally when received by the parent's shareholders as a distribution.

Trust indenture: Agreement specifying a trustee's rights and responsibilities when a corporation issues numerous bonds at one time.

2001 Act: Revised version of the Uniform Limited Partnership Act, adopted fully in six states, providing significant protection from liability for all partners.

Ultra vires **act:** Act beyond the purposes and powers of a corporation. The doctrine of *ultra vires* is limited by modern statutes that allow a corporation to perform any lawful act and that prohibit the corporation or a third party from disaffirming a contract.

Uncertificated share: Share issued without a formal share certificate.

Underwater options: Stock options that would be exercised at a loss.

Underwriter: Securities firm used by a corporation issuing stock for the first time. The underwriter buys stock itself for resale to the public or enters into arrangements with dealers for the dealers to sell the stock to their customers.

Underwriting: Process of issuing securities from the corporation to the ultimate shareholder.

Undisclosed principal: Principal whose existence and identity are unknown to others.

Unfair competition: Acts that constitute deceptive and unfair commercial practices.

Uniform Commercial Code (UCC): Statute drafted by the National Conference of Commissioners on Uniform State Laws and adopted by every state but Louisiana governing the sale of goods, leases, bulk transfers, secured transactions, and so forth; state variations exist.

Unlimited liability: Liability not limited to a party's investment in an enterprise but rather may be satisfied from the investor's other assets, savings, and property.

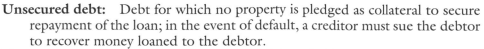

Unsecured debt: Debt for which no property is pledged as collateral to secure repayment of the loan; in the event of default, a creditor must sue the debtor to recover money loaned to the debtor.

Upstream merger: Merger of a parent and its subsidiary in which the parent survives (example: $P + S = P$).

Vertical restraint: Agreement between a buyer and seller restraining trade.

Vesting: Nonforfeitable right of an employee to receive the benefits of a retirement plan.

Vicarious liability: Liability imposed on another for an act that is not his or her fault; typically it is liability imposed on an employer for an employee's torts.

Voluntary dissolution: Dissolution of an entity initiated by the entity itself; with regard to a corporation, a dissolution initiated by corporate directors or shareholders.

Voluntary petition: Bankruptcy initiated by a debtor.

Voting agreement: Agreement among shareholders specifying the manner in which they will vote. Sometimes called a pooling agreement.

Voting trust: Agreement among shareholders by which they transfer their voting rights to a trustee to vote on their behalf.

Waiver of notice: Giving up the right to receive notice of some action or event, usually a meeting of directors or shareholders.

War chest: Funds collected or borrowed by an aggressor to acquire a target.

Warrant: Long-term option enabling its holder to purchase shares at a specified price during a specified time period.

Watered stock: Stock issued for less than its par value or for property or services worth less than its par value. Sometimes called *discount stock* or *bonus stock*.

Welfare benefit plan: Insurance and other similar plans offered to employees.

White knight: Corporation that saves a target from a hostile takeover.

Williams Act: Federal statute relating to tender offers.

Winding up: See Liquidation.

Withdrawal: Request by an entity wishing to cease being qualified in a state in which it has transacted business.

Work made-for-hire: Work prepared by an employee in the course of employment and thus owned by the employer.

Written consent: Action taken by a board of directors or shareholders without the necessity of meeting in person; most states require written consent to be unanimous.

Index